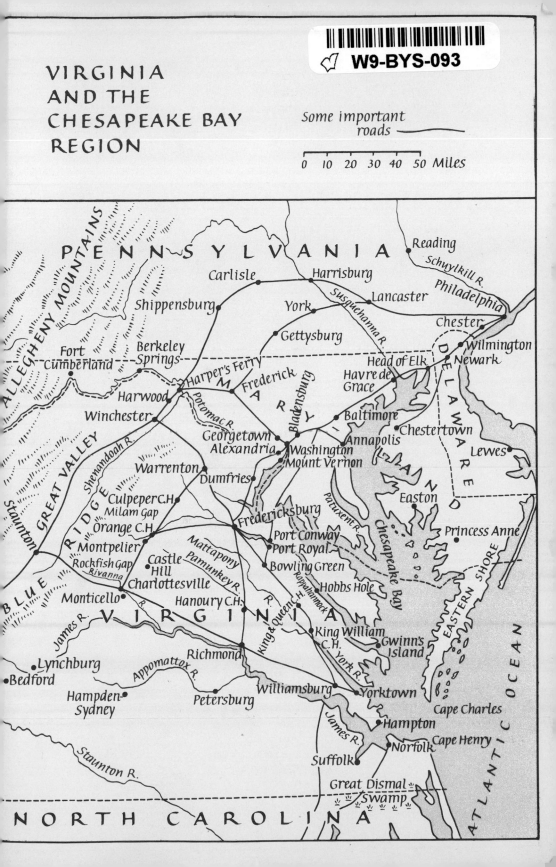

VIRGINIA AND THE CHESAPEAKE BAY REGION

Some important roads

0 10 20 30 40 50 Miles

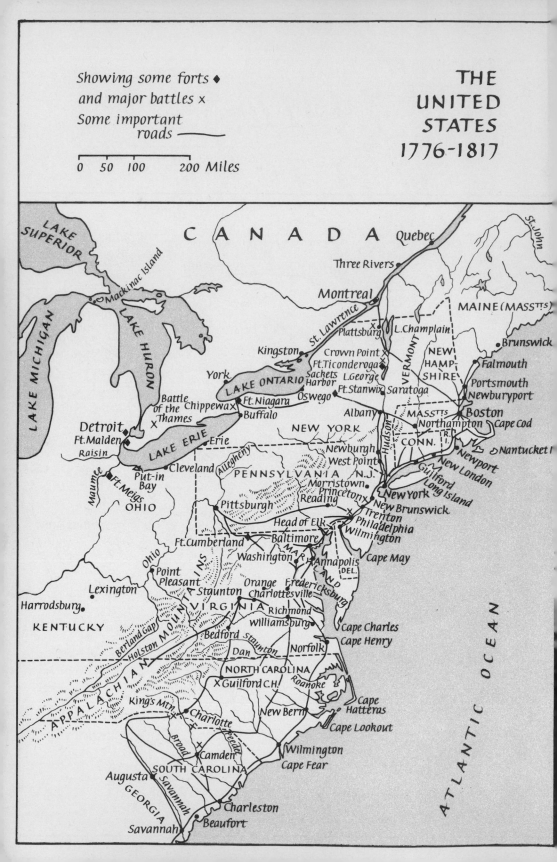

THE
UNITED
STATES
1776-1817

Showing some forts ♦
and major battles ×
Some important
roads ——

0   50   100   200 Miles

LAKE SUPERIOR

CANADA

Quebec

Three Rivers

Montreal

MAINE (MASS^{TTS})

St. John

Mackinac Island

LAKE MICHIGAN

LAKE HURON

Kingston

St. Lawrence

Plattsburg ×   L. Champlain

VERMONT

NEW HAMPSHIRE

Brunswick

Crown Point
Ft. Ticonderoga ×
Sackets
Harbor   L. George

Falmouth

York

LAKE ONTARIO

Ft. Niagara

Oswego

Ft. Stanwix

Saratoga

Portsmouth
Newburyport

Battle
of the   Chippewa×
Thames ×

Buffalo

Albany

MASS^{TTS}

Boston

Cape Cod

Detroit
Ft. Malden

LAKE ERIE

Erie

Cleveland

NEW YORK

Hudson

Northampton

CONN.

R.I.

Newport

Nantucket I.

Raisin

Allegheny

PENNSYLVANIA

Newburgh

West Point

N.J.

New London

Guilford

Long Island

New York

Put-in
Bay
Ft. Meigs

Maumee

OHIO

Pittsburgh

Morristown

Princeton×

Reading

New Brunswick

Ohio

Head of Elk×

Trenton ×
Philadelphia
Wilmington

Ft. Cumberland

Baltimore

MAR
Y
LAND

DEL.

Cape May

Point
Pleasant

Washington

Annapolis

Lexington

Orange
Staunton

Fredericksburg

Harrodsburg

VIRGINIA

Charlottesville

KENTUCKY

APPALACHIAN   MOUNTAINS

Berland Gap

Holston

Bedford
Staunton

Dan

Richmond
Williamsburg

Cape Charles
Cape Henry

Norfolk

NORTH CAROLINA

Roanoke

King's Mtn.
×

Charlotte

Broad

Pedee

Guilford C.H.
×

New Bern

Cape
Hatteras

Camden×

SOUTH CAROLINA
Cape Fear

Wilmington

Cape Lookout

Augusta

Savannah

GEORGIA

Charleston

Savannah

Beaufort

ATLANTIC   OCEAN

JAMES MADISON

A BIOGRAPHY

BY

Ralph Ketcham

UNIVERSITY PRESS OF VIRGINIA

Charlottesville and London

for Julia

THE UNIVERSITY PRESS OF VIRGINIA
Copyright © 1990 by the Rector and Visitors
of the University of Virginia

First paperback edition 1990

Second printing 1992

First published © 1971 by Ralph Ketcham

Library of Congress Cataloging-in-Publication Data

Ketcham, Ralph Louis, 1927–
    James Madison : a biography / by Ralph Ketcham. — 1st pbk. ed.
    p. cm.
    Reprint. Originally published: New York : Macmillan, © 1971.
    Includes bibliographical references.
    ISBN 0-8139-1265-2
    1. Madison, James, 1751–1836. 2. Presidents—United States—
Biography. 3. United States—Politics and government—1783–1789.
4. United States—Politics and government—1789–1815. I. Title.
E342.K46 1990
973.5′1′092—dc20
[B]   89-70418
                                                                   CIP

Printed in the United States of America

CONTENTS

Preface to the Paperback Edition

IN THE first preface to this book written nearly two decades ago, I noted that, with the new material available, information about Madison was "almost oppressively abundant." In the intervening years, the flow has not diminished, nor has the scholarly attention to Madison at all declined. Most notably, the volumes of *The Papers of James Madison* have continued to issue from the University Press of Virginia and number some sixteen volumes (into 1797) in the regular chronological series, with separate series begun on Madison's service as Secretary of State and as President. As one of the first editors of that project, I had had access to much of the material gathered for it, but to have the information in bound volumes provides Madison scholarship with resources unimaginable to Irving Brant and others who began the modern study of Madison a half century ago. All students of Madison and his time must acknowledge this bounty and point those seeking detailed, firsthand information to it. The continuing publication of the papers of the other "Founding Fathers," and of other documentary series, provides further abundant and easily available source material. The study of the transition from government under the Articles of Confederation to the new Constitution, for example, has been transformed by the publication of documentary series on both the ratification contest and the first federal elections. I often marvel at how my task of describing those critical years in Madison's career would have been altered had those volumes been at my elbow.

Important new studies have been published that would have illuminated my biography. To mention just the most important ones, my account of Madison's years in the Continental Congress could have benefited enormously had Jack Rakove's *The Beginning of National Politics: An Interpretive History of the Continental Congress* (Johns Hopkins University Press, 1979) been available. Noble Cunningham's *The Process of Government under Jefferson* (Princeton University Press, 1978) would have been an invaluable guide to how the President and the Secretary of State worked together from 1801 to

1809. Then, perhaps most pathbreaking of all, J. C. A. Stagg's *Mr. Madison's War: Politics, Diplomacy, and Warfare in the Early American Republic, 1783–1830* (Princeton University Press, 1983), which concentrates on the coming and conduct of the War of 1812, would have allowed me to make a more detailed and surefooted assessment of Madison's presidential career. Finally, the completion of Dumas Malone's splendid biography of Jefferson provides exactly the counterpoint needed for any study of the other half of one of the longest, most fruitful, and most like-minded collaborations in American political history. Though access to these works would have improved in detail my Madison biography, none requires major revisions in fact or interpretation.

The most significant change since 1971, at least in emphasis, in my own view of Madison arises from the brilliant scholarship of J. G. A. Pocock, Joyce Appleby, Lance Banning, Drew McCoy, Isaac Kramnick, John Murrin, and others who have assessed the place of classical and "civic republican" political thought in early American political ideas and institutions. Central to this reassessment has been whether the American founders, including Madison, were full "moderns" to the extent that they accepted the burgeoning liberal, commercially oriented, competition-validating, empirical outlook of Francis Bacon, Thomas Hobbes, John Locke, Adam Smith, and the "radical whig" critique of eighteenth-century British government. Reacting against this school of thought, the new scholars take seriously Aristotelian emphasis on the importance and quality (results) of government and republican insistence on public virtue and pursuit by the polity of the common good as the essential posture and goal of politics. This perspective, only dimly on the scholarly horizon in 1971, has profound implications for understanding the thought and career of Madison and the other founders.

Hence, what seemed only occasional puzzlements to me in 1971 in considering Madison's generally Lockean frame by mind are now seen as an important added dimension in his thought. I suggested, for example, that Madison's introduction to the study of government under Witherspoon at Princeton rested on an Aristotelian frame of seeing good or bad government possible whether rule was by one, the few, or the many. Quality of result, not numbers or process of government, was crucial. I now see this as a critically important aspect of Madison's political understanding, which was in a sense coequal with his Lockeanism, just as it was with Jefferson. This view conditioned Madison's part in the drafting and defense of the Constitution of 1787, his attitude toward political parties in the new republic, his conduct as chief executive, and other aspects of his public career. Though my response to Madisonian source materials as I wrote the biography led me fitfully toward that view, I would have been able to articulate it more clearly and consistently had the work of the "civic republican" scholars been available. My more recent book *Presidents above Party: The First American Presidency, 1789–1829* (University of N.C. Press, 1984) reveals the influence of these scholars on my interpretation of Madison's view of executive leadership.

Also, more than ever I dissent from the view that sees Madison, especially in his tenth *Federalist Paper*, as validating modern conflict-of-interest politics. Precisely because Madison was so firmly grounded in classical and Augustan thought, he saw faction (and its eighteenth-century synonym, party) as a malignant opposite to "the permanent and aggregate interests of the community," a concept foreign to modern conflict-of-interest theory. Madison was also a firm believer in the revolutionary (Lockean) ideals of freedom and government by consent, but he always assumed they had to be harmonized with concern for the public good.

Thus, though I would make some shift in emphasis in interpreting Madison's thought, especially in paying more attention to his classical and Augustan orientation, and I would add detail and precision to my account of some events, the Madison I see today is still the same ardent revolutionist, resourceful framer of government, clever political strategist, cautious, sometimes ineffectual leader, devoted husband, loyal Virginian, and sage in retirement described in this volume. At least as much as I would have supposed in 1971, subsequent Madison scholarship makes him one of the major, looming figures in the founding of the American republic. The bicentennial of the Constitution has been *his* bicentennial more than that of any other single figure. For better or worse, as we consider "the framers' intent," we are, preeminently, examining *Madison's* intent. Hence, I hope the reissue of this biography will illuminate and clarify an assessment of large importance to the conduct of American public life as the twentieth century draws to a close.

RALPH KETCHAM

The Maxwell School
Syracuse University

Preface

THIS BOOK SEEKS to record, with reasonable fairness and completeness, the life of James Madison. In the last thirty years or so, an immense amount of new material on Madison has become available, publication of *The Papers of James Madison* has begun, and an excellent six-volume biography has appeared. From a scantily known major figure in American history, Madison has become one about whom information is now almost oppressively abundant. Furthermore, he lived eighty-five years and played a part in virtually every major public event from the Stamp Act protests to the nullification crisis. Thus, in the past five years I have sometimes envied Cy Syrett, who was able to remark while editing *The Papers of Alexander Hamilton*, that he had considered dedicating his volumes "to Aaron Burr who made *completion* of this task possible." Nonetheless, I have tried to use the new resources and at the same time present Madison's long and full life within the covers of one volume, hopefully in a way useful to general readers as well as to scholars.

My own study of Madison began fifteen or more years ago under the guidance of Stuart Gerry Brown and the late T. V. Smith. In making Madison both real and relevant they gave me the incalculable benefits of stimulation and long-lasting intellectual habits one derives only from his "great teachers." A quite different but equally valuable approach to Madison's life and thought came from the editors of *The Papers of James Madison*, Miss Jean Schneider, William M. E. Rachal, Robert L. Scribner, the late Leonard D. White, and especially that perfect combination of teacher and scholar, William T. Hutchinson, with whom I had the pleasure of working for four years while at the University of Chicago. The six volumes of their work thus far in print transforms our understanding of Madison's first thirty-two years and are sure evidence of the unique value of complete publication and thorough editing. I am deeply indebted to these learned, perceptive, and gracious scholars, who while counseling me about Madison, often supplied nuggets of information from their abundant resources.

I owe another very special debt to Irving Brant, author of a six-volume life of Madison published between 1941 and 1961. Mr. Brant's volumes have literally been at my elbow throughout my own work, and beginning long before he completed his work, he has responded helpfully and kindly to my many inquiries. Visits to his study in the Library of Congress were for me pilgrimages to the fount of all useful knowledge. Though I have worked throughout from original sources—some of them pointed out to me by Mr. Brant—and have in places used materials unavailable to Mr. Brant and made interpretations different from his, I have benefited immeasurably from his work. When readers think I have been incomplete or neglectful, they should turn to Mr. Brant's volumes for fuller accounts. I hope no one embarrasses me by counting the number of citations I make to his work—I would then have to admit that even that indecent number does not fully record my dependence!

Of the surprisingly large collections of Madison papers in private hands when I saw them, the most important are the Cutts family papers owned by Mr. and Mrs. George B. Cutts of Brookline, Massachusetts, and by Mr. Charles M. Storey of Boston, and the private letters of Madison to William Pinkney (American minister to Great Britain, 1806–1811), first made available to me by his great-granddaughter, the late Mrs. Laurence R. Carton of Baltimore. Manuscript collections at the Library of Congress and the Historical Society of Pennsylvania have been the most valuable of those consulted at dozens of depositories. The source notes, and the introduction to Volume I of *The Papers of James Madison*, record the hundreds of other persons and institutions owning relevant material. Mrs. Marian Dupont Scott, the present owner of Madison's Montpelier estate, and Mr. Chester Hazard, its manager, kindly allowed me to visit there, and shared with me their feeling for its environs. Mr. R. Carter Pittman of Dalton, Georgia, led me through the maze of the George Mason–Madison dealings in Kentucky lands, and Professor Philip White of the University of Texas unraveled for me some of the complexities of early American economic history. Miss Jane Carson of Colonial Williamsburg was a skillful guide for Virginia gastronomy and social history, while Professor John Reardon of Loyola University (Chicago) shared his great knowledge of the career of Edmund Randolph. I have learned enormously, too, from those peerless editor-scholars Julian P. Boyd, Lyman H. Butterfield, and Leonard W. Labaree, and I am indebted to Professor Daniel J. Boorstin, who arranged for me to write this volume. The staffs of the libraries of the Institute of Early American History and Culture,

Yale University, the University of Texas, the American Studies Institute of Tokyo University, and Syracuse University have been unfailingly generous and helpful.

To my great benefit, many scholars read, criticized, and corrected portions of the manuscript: W. T. Hutchinson, W. M. E. Rachal, and R. L. Scribner of *The Papers of James Madison*, Herbert J. Storing of the University of Chicago, Alfred Young of Northern Illinois University, William Stinchcombe of Syracuse University, Donald O. Dewey of California State College at Los Angeles, and Mrs. Helene H. Fineman of *The Papers of Albert Gallatin*. Professor Harry Ammon of Southern Illinois University permitted me to read and use portions of his forthcoming biography of James Monroe, and Professor Robert D. Meade of Randolph-Macon Woman's College let me read and use a manuscript copy of the second volume of his work on Patrick Henry. Lester J. Cappon, W. W. Abbot, Thad Tate, John Selby, and Edward M. Riley were wisely and congenially helpful during a summer I spent in Williamsburg, Virginia.

Research grants from Colonial Williamsburg, the University of Texas, and The Macmillan Company are gratefully acknowledged. Mrs. Mal Sherman, Mrs. Anne Rath, Stuart Peskin, Mrs. Nancy Dore, Mrs. Connie Good, Mrs. Patricia Reichenbach, and Mrs. Marian Borst helped expertly as typists. I am especially indebted to Mrs. Charlotte Darehshori who performed the considerable miracle of deciphering and typing most of my handwritten draft.

My steadiest reliance, however, is indicated in the dedication.

Syracuse University   RALPH KETCHAM
December, 1970

ABBREVIATIONS AND SHORT TITLES

Adams, *Hist.*: Henry Adams, *History of the United States during the Administrations of Jefferson and Madison,* 10 vols., New York, 1889–1891.

Brant: Irving Brant, *James Madison,* 6 vols., Indianapolis, 1941–1961.

Hopkins *PC*: James F. Hopkins and others, eds., *The Papers of Henry Clay,* 3 vols., Lexington, Kentucky, 1959– .

Cutts, *Memoirs: Memoirs and Letters of Dolly Madison Wife of James Madison, President of the United States. Edited by her Grand-niece* (Lucia B. Cutts), Boston, 1886. Though bowlderized and often inaccurate, nonetheless exceedingly valuable for Dolley Madison because material in it derives from nieces who were her close companions and who had full access to her papers. Where possible, Dolley Madison's letters printed in it have been corrected from originals owned by Mr. and Mrs. George B. Cutts of Brookline, Massachusetts.

AG: Albert Gallatin.

Writings of AG: Henry Adams, ed., *The Writings of Albert Gallatin,* 3 vols., Philadelphia, 1879 (New York, 1960).

HSP: Historical Society of Pennsylvania.

AH: Alexander Hamilton.

Syrett *PH*: Harold C. Syrett and others, eds., *The Papers of Alexander Hamilton,* 13 vols., New York, 1961–1968.

TJ: Thomas Jefferson.

Boyd *PJ*: Julian P. Boyd and others, eds., *The Papers of Thomas Jefferson,* 17 vols., Princeton, 1950–1967.

Writings of TJ: Paul L. Ford, ed., *The Writings of Thomas Jefferson,* 10 vols., New York, 1892–1899.

Fed. ed. Writings: A. A. Lipscomb and A. E. Bergh, eds., *The Writings of Thomas Jefferson,* 20 vols., Washington, D.C., 1903.

LC: Library of Congress.

JM: James Madison.

DPM: Dolley Madison.

MPLC: James Madison Papers, Library of Congress.

Cong. ed.: William C. Rives and Philip R. Fendall, eds., *Letters and Other Writings of James Madison,* 4 vols., Phila., 1865.

Hunt: Gaillard Hunt, ed., *The Writings of James Madison,* 9 vols., New York, 1900–1910.

MP: William T. Hutchinson, W. M. E. Rachal, and others, eds., *The Papers of James Madison,* Vols. I–VI, Chicago, 1962–1969.

Messages: James D. Richardson, compiler, *Messages and Papers of the Presidents,* 20 vols., Washington, D.C., 1897–1917.

Writings of Monroe: Stanislaus M. Hamilton, ed., *The Writings of James Monroe,* 7 vols., New York, 1898–1903.

PMHB: The Pennsylvania Magazine of History and Biography.

Rives, *Life of Madison*: William C. Rives, *History of the Life and Times of James Madison*, 3 vols., Boston, 1859–1868.

VMHB: The Virginia Magazine of History and Biography.

GW: George Washington.

Writings of Washington: John C. Fitzpatrick, ed., *The Writings of George Washington*, 39 vols., Washington, D.C., 1931–1940.

WMQ: The William and Mary Quarterly (third series unless otherwise indicated).

Note: Though spelling, punctuation, and word usage in quotations generally follows that in the source cited, I have deleted some superfluous punctuation, occasionally added marks, and even less occasionally amended spelling for clarity to modern readers. My insertions in quotations are indicated by brackets, and deletions are noted by ellipses.

All material of substance appears on the pages of the narrative itself; the notes are source citations only. *The Annals of Congress* is cited by date only; other documents are described, wherever possible, by character as well. Citations of letters to and from Madison usually omit his name (*e.g.*, "to Monroe, August 20, 1814"); other citations are fuller: e.g., "TJ to Monroe, July 6, 1806."

The bibliography lists only the most important sources; see source notes for works or depositories referred to only occasionally.

Sources for each paragraph are gathered in a note keyed to the end of the paragraph. Occasionally, when a number of paragraphs depend as a whole on a source or several sources, a note for all the paragraphs is keyed to the end of the final paragraph.

Madison's brief autobiography has been quoted in a variety of ways. It is published in full in the *WMQ* source cited in the selected bibliography, but this publication depends on a not always complete and accurate version Madison had copied late in his life. Thus, in some cases I have used an earlier rough draft in Madison's writing now at the Princeton University Library, and at other times I have used quotes in *The Papers of James Madison* depending on more reliable manuscript sources than those used in the *WMQ* publication.

CHAPTER I

A Virginia Family Background

Frances Taylor Madison, daughter of one of the first settlers in the Piedmont county of Orange in the colony of Virginia, died on Wednesday, November 25, 1761. Her first grandson in a male line, James Madison, later father of the Constitution of the United States and its fourth President, was ten years old. Her grandnephew Zachary Taylor, the twelfth President of the United States, would be born twenty-three years after her death. She was buried the following Sunday in the family plot on her plantation, and a month later, for her funeral sermon in nearby Anglican Brick Church, a large group of "connections," as Virginians called those related by ties of blood, marriage, and affection, came to honor her memory, in spite of the prevalance of small-pox in the vicinity. Indeed Frances Madison may herself have been carried off by the disease, which had erupted in Orange County the preceding spring. If the Madison plantation was considered "safe" during the winter, some visiting relatives doubtless stayed at the house Frances Madison had managed so long and which now passed to her only son, James Madison (1723–1801), whose own son, James, was the future President. Thus the young boy may have seen relatives he had not known before, probably shared in the family mourning, and lived through days of excited comings and goings. If he had not sensed it before, he learned at his grandmother's funeral something of the large and respectable family of which he was a part.[1]

Frances Taylor Madison's father, James Taylor II (1674–1729), had established his family in Orange County by patenting 13,500 acres of land there in 1722. He acquired this estate after traveling through the Virginia Piedmont with the "Knights of the Golden Horseshoe" in the late sum-

mer of 1716. Twelve gentlemen, headed by Governor Alexander Spotswood and accompanied by thirty servants, Indian guides, and soldiers,
had left the settlements above Fredericksburg on the Rappahannock and
proceeded into the wilderness up the north fork of the river, going within
six or eight miles of lands which later belonged to President James
Madison. On the night the expedition camped in this region one of its
members recorded in his journal that they had passed "the largest timber,
the finest and deepest mould, and the best grass I ever did see." Then the
party went over Milam's Gap in the Blue Ridge, and looked across the
Shenandoah, or Great, Valley, the first Virginians to record that feat.
Thus, seven years before his father's birth, the rich lands and rolling hills
of James Madison's home, always his haven from public demands and
duties, were a virgin wilderness known only to Indians and perhaps to
some nameless trappers and traders.

Spotswood's party recognized the value of the lands they had surveyed, and soon staked out huge claims to them. As happened over and
over again in the settlement of North America, the vast open lands inspired men to dream of adventure and fortune, and then to settle and
exploit them with a rapidity unimaginable to those who first saw the
bounty. The Virginia Piedmont, where James Madison grew to manhood, was such a region. As a boy he probably heard of the Golden
Horseshoe expedition from some of its members. As Secretary of State,
he helped plan the Lewis and Clark expedition, which carried the American flag to the Pacific, and in 1830, then in his eightieth year, he calculated that the population of the United States would be 192 million by
the middle of the twentieth century. The excitement of exploration and
an experience of incredible development and growth surrounded Madison
throughout his life.

In looking from Milam's Gap across the western wilderness, Spotswood and his companions sought more, however, than open lands awaiting
pioneer settlement. His chief purpose in making the journey, he wrote
later, was "to ascertain whether Lake Erie, occupying as it does a central
position in the French line of communications between Canada and
Louisiana, was accessible from Virginia." After a generation of war with
France, the peace treaty of Utrecht in 1713 had strengthened Britain's
position in North America but left France in possession of vast and
immensely rich lands stretching from the Gulf of Saint Lawrence to the
mouth of the Mississippi. Zealous Englishmen such as Spotswood, who
had fought at Blenheim under the Duke of Marlborough, had no illusion
that the struggle with France for North America was over. The dynastic
duels in Europe and the tense rivalry between the Protestant and Catholic
powers were sure to reverberate in the New World as the ambitions of
France and England clashed in the Mississippi valley. Just beyond the
Shenandoah valley were the upper reaches of the Great Kanawha,

which itself formed part of the Ohio basin claimed by France. The thirst for new lands that carried Madison's great-grandfather, James Taylor II, to the crest of the Blue Ridge in 1716 was part of a quest for possession that lasted until the Louisiana Purchase (1803) and the battle of New Orleans (1815). James Madison lived his life, private and public, in the presence of this vast struggle for world power.[2]

Though James Madison's forebears seem not to have shared the tribulations of Captain John Smith, they had settled in Virginia by the third quarter of the seventeenth century. At least four generations of Madison's family had lived in Virginia for a century before his birth, and he knew nothing of his ancestors before their arrival in America. By rummaging English genealogical records, his collateral descendants have traced the family back to Charlemagne and the barons of Runnymede, but James Madison told friends simply that "in both the paternal and maternal line [my ancestors] were planters and among the respectable though not the most opulent class."

In 1653 John Maddison, a ship's carpenter and great-great-grandfather of President Madison, patented six hundred acres of land he acquired by the "headright" system—that is, he received fifty acres of land for each of twelve immigrants whose passage he paid from England. Though "headrights" could be earned on relatives and friends, they were generally acquired by importing indentured servants, who worked for a term of years as artisans, laborers, clerks, or household servants in exchange for their passage. Before John Maddison died, about 1683, through "headrights" he secured thirteen hundred more acres on the York River and its northern branch, the Mattaponi, in King and Queen and King William counties. His son, John, continued to enlarge the family estates on the Tidewater, and served as sheriff and justice of the peace in King and Queen County, a sign that he was among the substantial gentry of the region.

John's three sons, John, Henry, and Ambrose (grandfather of President Madison), who seem to have used the "Madison" spelling of their last name, provided for growing families by patenting tracts of land farther and farther inland. In 1728 Ambrose owned over five thousand acres of land in the "little mountains" and "the great mountains," clear evidence that though he himself was addressed as a "Merchant, York River, Virginia," his holdings had spread to the Piedmont area, soon to be the principal seat of his family. Fragmentary account books and business letters of Ambrose Madison reveal only that he was a careful manager respected by his associates. In 1721, he married Frances Taylor, eldest daugher of Knight of the Golden Horseshoe James Taylor II, who the next year patented a huge estate in Orange County on the Rapidan River. These rich lands afforded much more dazzling prospects than seemed possible on the thinner and more quickly exhausted soil of the Tidewater, so with other "connections" of James Taylor, Ambrose Madison and his bride turned eventually to the Piedmont.

Frances Taylor's family was prolific and energetic. Her four sisters had between them at least fifteen children, and her four brothers, James III, Zachary, George, and Erasmus, had dozens of male heirs, who spread across Virginia and Kentucky. One grandson of James III served as quartermaster general of the western army during the War of 1812, and another, Hubbard, managed James Madison's own land interests in Kentucky, while one of Zachary Taylor's grandsons became President of the United States. George Taylor, a near neighbor and lifelong friend of the Madisons, had ten sons who served in the Revolutionary War. Many of them later moved to Kentucky, doubtless because opportunities at home seemed usurped by a multitude of relatives. Erasmus Taylor had at least seven children, including Lucy, whose husband, the Reverend Alexander Balmain, married James and Dolley Madison in 1794. Thus, James Madison, Sr.,* grew up with forty or more first cousins on his mother's side, and they, together with their children, furnished a host of influential connections and companions for his son.

Other relatives of Madison's paternal grandmother included Edmund Pendleton (1721–1803), the lawyer, judge, revolutionary leader, and statesman with whom James Madison had close personal and political ties until the elder man's death, and John Taylor of Caroline (1753–1824), a schoolboy friend of James Madison's, and himself a distinguished farmer and states' rights philosopher. Pendleton and Taylor were for seventy-five years the political leaders of Caroline County and often dominated the thought and conduct of all of Virginia. Having such connections and working through them were characteristic and important in politics in Virginia throughout James Madison's life.

When Ambrose and Frances Taylor Madison moved to Orange County, not long after the death of James Taylor II (in 1729), they built a house, probably near the site of the still-extant family graveyard where James Madison is buried. On one side lived Martha Taylor Chew and her husband, Thomas, sheriff of Orange County. One of the Chew children, Joseph, later a merchant in New London, Connecticut, and a loyalist refugee in Montreal, seems to have been James Madison, Sr.'s, closest friend and companion in amorous adventures, while two of his brothers were notable Indian fighters. Two of the Chew girls, Alice and Mildred (Milly), seem not to have married, but went about "doing good" and served as godmothers to children in the neighborhood, including some of the Madisons. Frances Madison's younger brother, James III, lived on

* The father of President James Madison, always so designated in this volume.

the other side of her lands and managed much of the family business. When Ambrose Madison died in 1732 he had a family of three children (his eldest, James, Sr., was nine) and owned twenty-nine Negro slaves, of whom only ten were adult males able to work in the rich fields of tobacco. His will left the management of the family fortunes in his wife's hands until James, Sr., reached his eighteenth birthday. As she arranged for the care of her slaves, negotiated with English merchants for sale of her crops, purchased goods from abroad, and planned the major projects needed to expand a large plantation, she depended heavily on her nearby relatives.[3]

By the early seventeen-forties James Madison, Sr., had begun to manage more and more of the plantation himself. His two sisters came of age, married into prominent families, and left home. At about the same time his cousin John Madison moved across the Blue Ridge into the Great Valley of Virginia, where he became a prominent citizen and began to raise his own family of eight boys and three girls. One was Bishop James Madison (1749–1812),* a lifelong friend of his second cousin's, who became president of the College of William and Mary, and in 1785, first bishop of the Protestant Episcopal Church in Virginia. Another son, Thomas, married Susannah, sister of Patrick Henry, while yet another son, and two daughters as well, married children of Andrew Lewis, kinsman of George Washington and the famed conqueror of the Indians at the battle of Point Pleasant in 1774. Still another son, George, served as governor of Kentucky in 1816.

As James Madison, Sr., managed his Piedmont farm, his attention was not distracted entirely from the "country below," as dwellers in the foothills called the lands on the Tidewater. He probably had to travel frequently to the navigable waters of the Rappahannock to market his tobacco, perhaps stored at the warehouse of his future father-in-law, Francis Conway (1696–1733), nine miles below Fredericksburg. Conway was a substantial merchant and planter of Caroline County who, since he was named an executor of the will of Ambrose Madison, probably had been a friend of the family's from the days when its estate centered on the Tidewater. In 1718 he had married Rebecca Catlett, and in the fifteen years of their marriage they had at least six children, the youngest of whom, born the year before his death, was Nelly Conway (1732–1829), mother of President James Madison. Two of Nelly Conway's sisters married into the Taylor family of Orange County, and her brother Francis II seems to have been a particular friend of James Madison, Sr. Two sons of Francis II, Francis III (1749–1794), and Catlett (1751–1827), were childhood playmates of President Madison's and remained his intimate friends as long as each lived.

* Always designated either the Reverend or Bishop Madison in this volume.

After the early death of the first Francis Conway, his widow Rebecca, a dauntless person whose grandfather had been killed by the Indians in 1670, married John Moore, who lived on the north shore of the Rappahannock at Port Conway, across from Port Royal and about ten miles below the Conway warehouse. The immediate family of President Madison's mother, Nelly Conway, then, consisted of her mother and stepfather, her own brothers and sisters, the children of her mother's second marriage, William and Jane Moore, and her mother's sisters, the Misses Judith and Elizabeth Catlett and Mary Catlett Gibson. These three sisters were President Madison's godmothers, and his godfathers were his grandmother's husband, John Moore, and her brother-in-law, Jonathan Gibson. When Nelly Conway Madison went to her mother's home to bear her first child, she surrounded the infant with a family as large and substantial as those to which he was heir in the Taylor and Madison lines.[4]

The size and significance of this complex of relatives probably meant little to ten-year-old James Madison as he watched many of them gather for his grandmother's funeral sermon in 1761. The expression of family concern and solidarity thus evoked, however, symbolized the fold within which he lived all his life. Moreover, his aversion to travel and his own childlessness left him closer to his collateral connections than he might have been otherwise. In his will he left important shares of his estate to his thirty-odd nieces and nephews. After serving in the Continental Congress in his thirties he seems only once to have been away from Orange County for a full year, and his visits there were the occasions for large family gatherings; during his presidency Dolley Madison once wrote that the house was filled with more than a hundred relatives and friends. During much of his life Madison was "connected" with most of the landowners in Orange County. Since Virginians in Madison's day often married relatives (matches between first cousins were common), he had multiple ties with many of his kinfolk.

Such a network of relatives was of special importance to a man in public life. Madison's family standing assured him of easy access, if he desired it, to the offices where a political career in Virginia nearly always began—those of justices of the peace, sheriffs, county lieutenants, and members of the legislature. Furthermore, when a man from a family such as Madison's went to Williamsburg (or later to Richmond) as a legislator, he was sure to find a few men who were close relatives and many who felt some kindred tie. When James Madison took his seat in the Virginia Convention of 1776 he found his "connections" Edmund Pendleton and Patrick Henry among its leaders. The delegates from Caroline, King and Queen, Spotsylvania, and King George counties knew him and his family. He was of the substantial gentry, of the three or four hundred families that throughout his lifetime dominated Virginia politics and made such a large contribution to the public life of the new United States. Madison's political precepts were founded on the practices of this extraordinary group, from which his colleagues in statecraft —Washington, Jefferson, Marshall, Henry, Pendleton, Mason, and Monroe—likewise came. The career of the father of the Constitution and the fourth President of the United States, then, had its origin in the family to which he was born. Though Madison took a leading role in the sharp political disputes in Virginia, and thus often differed importantly with many of his colleagues and even his "connections," he accepted the family-based system and functioned as a part of it for half a century.[5]

CHAPTER II

Boyhood and Early Education

I N February 1746 James Madison, Sr.'s, cousin and good friend Joseph Chew, then in Annapolis, Maryland, beginning a business career, wrote home of the threat posed to commerce by the rebellion in Scotland of the Young Pretender, Bonnie Prince Charlie, and of the regiment of a thousand men being raised to guard the Virginia frontier against expected attacks by Indian allies of the French. More than three years later the wars were over and Chew wrote of more personal affairs: "the famous Miss Tasker" was to marry Daniel Dulany, thus depriving Chew of his "Mistress"; the much-admired Miss North of Baltimore kept him "at a distance"; and a "Lady at the head of the [Chesapeake] Bay" who engrossed most of his thought was likewise beyond his power to win. He wrote more encouragingly, however, of his cousin's prospects: "I hope before this Miss Nelly has made you happy. If so you have my compliments on the occasion, [and] my earnest and hearty wishes that you may enjoy a Compleat, uninterrupted happiness." The marriage of James Madison, Sr., and Nelly Conway took place on September 15, 1749, nine days after Chew wrote of his own frustrations. Eight months later he complained of his failure to hear from his friend in Orange but remarked understandingly, "I make every allowance in your favor I can. The marrying of a Young, agreeable wife will certainly make moments slide away pleasantly."[1] Ten months after Chew wrote this letter, at midnight on March 16, 1751,* Nelly Conway Madison gave birth to her

---

* Because of his birth just before Great Britain's calendar reform in 1752, Madison has two "birthdates," a Julian, or Old Style, one and a Gregorian, or New Style, one. A calendar on the wall the night of his birth would have read March 5, 1750, reflecting the eleven-day lag accumulated by the inaccu-

first child, a boy, James, at her stepfather's plantation on the Rappahannock River in King George County, Virginia.

The Reverend William Davis, rector of the Hanover Parish Church in
King George County, attended by the Moores, Catletts, and Conways,
baptized the infant James Madison on Sunday, March 31, 1751. Sometime
after that, perhaps in May or June, when the rivers were less swollen
and the spring mud had dried, the mother and baby, probably accompanied by a male member of the family and some servants, traveled the
fifty-five miles to the Madison lands southwest of Orange Court House.
After this early journey James Madison lived on his father's plantation,†
though he may have spent considerable time at his birthplace in the years
before his grandmother Catlett Moore died in 1760. Thus he probably
knew well the sandy yards and fields of the Moore farm, the banks of
the broad, deep Rappahannock, and the low hills which stretched southward across the river to Caroline Court House and northward to the
Potomac. The big event for farmers along the Rappahannock, anxious to
market their tobacco and receive goods from England, was the arrival of
the sailing vessels which drew tidewater Virginia closer in many ways to
Liverpool, Bristol, and London than to Philadelphia or Charleston. The
appearance of the stubby, rather awkward-looking ships, the bustle of
unloading and loading, and the eager opening of the boxes of English
goods must have been times of intense excitement for a young lad.
Despite the advantage of tidewater and the resulting communication with
the Atlantic world, though, it must have been apparent even to a boy
that by mid-eighteenth century the rich, growing part of Virginia was
in the fertile red earth of the Piedmont rather than in the thin, sandy
soil of the lowlands.

Beyond a few old-age recollections, there is no documentation of
particular events in James Madison's youth. The story can be surmised,
however, from farm records, from important events that would have
affected a boy in Madison's situation, and from what is known generally
of Virginia family and plantation life in his day. Though the account thus
obtained is necessarily conjectural in some of its details, something of an
otherwise hidden boyhood assumes sketchy form.

---

rate Julian calendar, and the designation of March 25 rather than January 1
as the first day of the new year. Adoption of the Gregorian calendar added
eleven days to Old Style dates and changed the first of the year date, thus
making Madison's birthdate March 16, 1751, New Style, though like many of
his contemporaries he sometimes used the Old Style date and/or year in
speaking of his birth. Unless written in the form 1745/46 or designated O.S.,
all dates in this volume are New Style.
† Not known to have been called Montpelier until about 1780, but nevertheless
so designated hereafter in this volume.

At James Madison's birth the family holdings in Orange County had been under development for about twenty years. His grandfather Ambrose Madison's first lands had been half of a 4,600-acre tract, which twenty years later had been enlarged to over three thousand acres. By 1757 the plantation consisted of nearly four thousand acres in the hills south and east of the Rapidan River. Judging from the trees named as landmarks in Madison deeds, the woods included red, white, and Spanish oak, hickory, pine, poplar, chestnut, and dogwood, in the eighteenth century still in great virgin stands in places not yet cleared for farming. Much of the land is gently rolling and thus readily cultivated, but portions along the streams (called "runs") are deeply gullied, and in areas reaching up into the Southwest Mountains on the eastern side of the plantation the terrain is rugged and presumably was wooded in 1760 as it is today. The soil is red, and judging from the quick prosperity achieved by the Madisons, as rich as the journal of the Knights of the Golden Horseshoe had reported it to be. It is fertile clay and loam, still capable, after more than two centuries of intensive farming, of holding the minerals necessary for abundant crops of corn, barley, wheat, and hay. The flourishing appearance of the countryside in the Rapidan valley upstream from the junction with the Rappahannock is eloquent testimony that the Taylors, Madisons, Chews, and others who settled there had chosen wisely in staking out their claims.[2]

The site of the early plantation house built by Ambrose Madison about 1730 is not known, though local tradition places it on a knoll near the Madison family graveyard and about three hundred yards southwest of the present mansion. If the old house faced the same direction as its replacement, then the magnificent sweep of the Blue Ridge—nearly thirty miles away—stretched before it. This great range, visible on a clear day from almost every spot on the Madison lands, dominates the scene, an omnipresent part of the consciousness of those growing up beneath it. The fresh, cool air of the foothills, away from lowland swamps and tidewater humidity, was healthy and invigorating in Madison's day, and has been ever since. Madison thought it the finest climate in the world and sought always to spend as much time in it as he possibly could. The impression is inescapable that among James Madison's many blessings there were few more important—certainly there is none he grew to value more highly—than the good fortune of living all his life amid the fertile beauty of the Piedmont country presided over so majestically by the Blue Ridge Mountains.

Like most frontier dwellings, the 1730 Madison house was probably rough and utilitarian, comfortable enough but lacking the refinement usually associated with plantation houses. The contrast between the crude "first house" one may now view at Andrew Jackson's Hermitage and the graceful mansion he built later suggests something of the change wrought by years of labor and planning on a frontier farm. Though it would be inappropriate to picture the Madisons, even in grandfather Ambrose's day, as struggling frontiersmen, they had, within the adult lifetime of Frances Taylor Madison, who died at age sixty-one in 1761, seen their estate grow from a virgin wilderness into a plantation where time and resources were beginning to be available to cultivate beauty, grace, and learning. In James Madison's boyhood, though, the family farm still bustled and grew more in response to practical necessities than anything else. Sheds, barns, and slave cabins came into being helter-skelter around the old house, and as Madison's father and mother produced five children in the first eleven years of their marriage, they may have required a temporary house of their own while the as yet unbuilt mansion was planned.

Details of life on the plantation during James Madison's boyhood emerge from his father's account book, kept between 1755 and 1765. He bought clothing and brandy for "my Negroes," and "white arsenic" to poison troublesome crows. One John Connor seems to have been responsible for the slaves; in five years he received one shilling each for eighteen pairs of "Negro shoes," and his spouse, acting as a midwife, "delivered 15 Negro wenches" at ten shillings each. Payment for "Milliners Work at Williamsburg," receipt of rent on lots owned in Fredericksburg, and payment for an advertisement (presumably in *The Virginia Gazette*) for a lost bull all suggest the spread of family interests beyond Orange County. At age five, on September 17, 1756, James Madison may have heard his father grumble about paying £6 12s. 10d. in quitrents, poll tax, land tax, and miscellaneous public, county, and parish levies. Three years later the senior Madison paid £15 12s. 4d. for "Public Dues" in Spotsylvania County, indicating that the family had interests, probably lands, there. Payments for silver shoe buckles, fancy sewing by female relatives, and mantuas (ladies' robes) signify some attention to the amenities, as do payments to dancing master Francis Christien in 1756 and 1758.

Accounts with "John Bell, Merchant of London," and many transactions with Colonel Fielding Lewis of Fredericksburg show that the Madisons had trading patterns common for Virginia planters in the eighteenth century. The business with Lewis, George Washington's brother-in-law, connects the Madisons with families prominent in Virginia politics, as do payments of legal fees to Joseph Jones and Edmund Pendleton, both later personal friends and important political allies of James Madison. Among doctors' fees are many paid to Dr. Thomas Walker, of nearby Castle Hill in Albemarle County, who was famous in Virginia history as an explorer, Indian agent, and land speculator. These entries are the first record of another family association, culminating in

Madison's friendship with Walker's grandson-in-law, William Cabell Rives, who wrote the first biography of Madison. A 1761 payment to Dr. Walker for a debt owed the Loyal Company suggests that the Madisons, like most Virginia planters, speculated in western lands; those of the Loyal Company grant were in the mountain valleys of Tennessee River tributaries in what is now southwest Virginia. In addition to those famous names, the plantation accounts are full of references to members of nearby families who were to be James Madison's neighbors all his life: Beale, Willis, Taylor, Taliaferro, Battaile, Barbour, Lee, Grymes, Throckmorton, Conway, Chew, Moore, and Maury.[3]

The numerous children born in these families shortly before and after 1750 were James Madison's playmates, and some of them became lifelong friends and associates. His two oldest brothers, Francis born in 1753 and Ambrose in 1755, were doubtless his most constant companions. One of the nearby Taylor plantations produced a steady stream of boys: Francis (1747), Richard (1749), John (1751), William (1753), Charles (1755), Reuben (1757), and Benjamin (1759); while another produced girls almost as regularly: Mildred (1751), Frances (1753), Elizabeth (1755), and Lucy (1758). After a shifting of residences and marriage alliances, probably caused by the smallpox epidemic of 1761 and 1762, Madison's cousins and stepcousins on his mother's side, including Francis and Catlett Conway (born in 1749 and 1751) and the family of William Moore, seem also to have lived in Orange County.

The house nearest the old Madison dwelling was that of Thomas and Martha Taylor Chew, just south of the boundary line between the Madison and Chew properties. The head of this adventurous, sometimes harsh family was Thomas Chew, long sheriff of Orange County, who in 1748 executed a slave, Eve, accused of poisoning her master, by burning her at the stake upon orders of the local court. Another bloody deed is suggested by a court order to exhibit the head of an executed slave on a pole, and by the naming of a brook Negrohead Run. Are the event and the name linked by the grisly sight?

Though such inhumanities reveal the brutality of the slave system as it existed in Virginia, there is no evidence that the Madisons subjected their slaves to anything like the cruel treatment implicit in these executions. In fact, judging from references to them as "of the family" and from James Madison's lifelong abhorrence of the institution of slavery, it seems likely that at Montpelier they received attention in the best rather than the worst tradition of the colonial South. The number of slaves the family owned grew rapidly; by 1782 there were at least 118. More black than white children, then, ran about the yards and fields, and young James Madison, in the custom of the day, doubtless played with them and formed ties which lasted all his life. The presence of many slaves and the restraints and subordinations they bore were part of Madison's daily

environment from the time of his earliest recollections. He was, therefore, burdened with the preconceptions of superiority, and perhaps even
with the psychological hazards of unrestrained power and the latent
sense of guilt often attending the system.[4]

If daily life centered on the farm, the big event of the week was the
trip, six or seven miles long, and therefore taking perhaps two hours
each way, to the Brick Church (Anglican), built during the seventeen-
fifties on the lands of great-uncle James Taylor, whose plantation,
Meadow Farm, stretched along the old road toward Fredericksburg from
Orange Court House. Since in Madison's youth dissenting congregations
were rare in Virginia, the Sunday gathering at church included almost the
whole community of aunts, uncles, cousins, in-laws, friends, and neighbors. Political gossip and exchange of family news competed for attention with the official parish announcements and the religious services.
As a vestryman, James Madison, Sr., took part in the various legal
functions of the parish, including the management of church affairs and
collection of the taxes to support the established Anglican Church. The
vestrymen were also charged with enforcing the social codes of the day:
no one but physicians could ride horseback on Sunday except to go to
church; profane language was forbidden; and drunkards were subject to
arrest on court day, the day the circuit court met at any particular
county seat. The vestrymen were, in short, the conservative symbols of
the community, responsible for restraining disorder and for maintaining
the mores shaping daily life. Since they could hire or fire the rector, in
their hands, not his, were the reins of power in church and community.
Vestrymen carried out such functions of local government as providing
for the poor and censoring morals. Like selectmen and deacons in New
England, vestrymen in Virginia received invaluable training in self-
government, and from their ranks came the sheriffs, county lieutenants,
and burgesses who guided the civil government. The Madison family,
through its participation in this system, knew the meaning of self-government long before 1776.[5]

Of the particular events in Madison's youth of which there is some
documentary evidence, none, perhaps, was of more daily interest to him
than the building of the new mansion. Madison recalled in old age that
as a boy he had helped carry some of the light furniture from the old
house to the new, suggesting that the family moved into the new building
about 1760. James Madison, Sr.'s, account book confirms this date, but it
also indicates that building the new mansion and perhaps adding out-
buildings took ten years or more, a not unusual length of time for such a
project on a Virginia farm. For example, in the seventeen-nineties, Jefferson took nearly that long to enlarge and rebuild Monticello, proceeding

one step at a time as material was gathered and workmen could be hired from neighbors or spared from pressing farm duties. In 1756 the senior Madison paid for having over 3,300 feet of plank sawed and for hiring Negro carpenters George and Peter from his relatives. In 1759, however, payments for materials ceased and the Negro carpenters were hired out for eighteen months at two shillings per day, Sundays excluded. In 1761 building seems to have resumed, and in 1763 bricks were ordered, indicating that by then the mansion was ready for its outer layer.

The dwelling thus constructed, and apparently inhabited by the Madisons by the time James went away to school in 1762, was a simple rectangular building facing west and slightly north, toward the Blue Ridge. In front was a broad porch looking over, if not a lawn, a field, which sloped gently downward, while in back a smaller porch, level with the ground, faced a small lawn or yard, behind which was a steep, wooded gully; behind that were the slopes of the Southwest Mountains. Presumably slave cabins, barns, sheds, storehouses, and kitchens surrounded the main house, though such buildings dating from Madison's day no longer exist. Inside, on the first floor was a spacious center hall flanked by two large rooms, one apparently a dining room including a small serving room, and the other a parlor or drawing room. Each room contained a large fireplace. Bedrooms upstairs, a spacious attic, and a full ground floor afforded no more than adequate living space, one would imagine, for a family with six or eight children. The still-apparent basic design, simple, well-proportioned, and pleasing, attests to the good taste of the builders employed by James Madison, Sr., and makes it easy to understand why his son merely added symmetrical extensions when he enlarged the house about 1809. The graceful house, set magnificently among the rolling fields and woods and facing one of the great vistas in eastern North America, became, understandably, one of the fixed points in James Madison's life. Though the house was greatly enlarged late in the nineteenth century and no longer has about it the hustle and bustle of a plantation, it and its grounds are still one of the most beautiful places in Virginia.

In addition to the peaceful progress of housebuilding, the years from 1754 to 1763 were also marked by the terror and anxiety caused by Indian attacks accompanying the French and Indian War. On August 19, 1755, in the month following Braddock's disastrous defeat near Fort Duquesne (Pittsburgh), John Madison wrote his cousin, James Madison, Sr., of the massacre at Draper's Meadow in the Great Valley: "Could you see dear Friend the women who escaped crying after their murdered husbands with their helpless orphans hanging on them, it could not but wound your very soul." He then thanked his cousin for guns he had sent and for his kind offer to care for the threatened small children, but John Madison declined to send them east, protesting the trouble the large brood would be and observing pathetically that "should I lose my all with my life, I think my children had as well go hence, whilst in a state of innocency." At news of an Indian invasion, a company of men from the counties east of the Blue Ridge, probably including near relatives of the Madisons, marched to Winchester in the spring of 1756.[6]

Two of the Chew clan who lived "next door" to the Madisons and who had enviable reputations as Indian fighters, were casualties in the warfare. Larkin was wounded in Washington's thwarted effort to recapture Fort Duquesne in 1754, and four years later his brother Colby, after being wounded in the successful Forbes expedition against the fort, drowned when he fell into the Monongahela River. News of this tragedy and of other events of the fighting in the mountains, sometimes told by men who had taken part, must have furnished moments of both excitement and terror to a lad of seven years.

With war also came increased taxes, inflation, and impressment of men and horses to guard the frontier. Moreover, a severe drought in 1755 had ruined the grain and even the Indian corn, "the main support of man and beast in this part of the world"—Albemarle, Hanover, and Orange counties. Then the flood of refugees fleeing the Indian attacks and the threat, after Braddock's defeat, of full-scale French invasion, made the colonists all the more anxious. In spite of the fortitude John Madison displayed in his letter to his cousin, it is likely that he too was forced to leave his home and lands to seek relative safety east of the Blue Ridge; Colonel George Washington reported in the fall of 1755 that the roads out of the Great Valley were crowded with people "flying as if every moment was death." The following spring an observer in Orange County wrote that the frontier had been pushed eastward in some places as much as 150 miles and that there was no sign that the retreat would soon end.[7]

In fact, from Braddock's defeat in July 1755 until Forbes recaptured Fort Duquesne in November 1758, the frontiers of Pennsylvania and Virginia were at the mercy of the Indians emboldened by the successes of their French allies. When the remnants of Braddock's army fled to Philadelphia, city-dwellers on the seaboard imagined that savages would soon be in their midst. Though no French troops invaded, and even Indian raids east of the mountains were rare, the early years of defeat and frustration during the French and Indian War were times of fear, apprehension, and hardship in the regions near the frontier. Young James Madison doubtless sensed this atmosphere, and as the tide of war changed in 1758 and 1759, with the great English victories at Louisburg, Duquesne, Quebec, and Niagara, he would have been old enough to share in the exultation. The victorious conclusion of the war, hailed as uniquely glorious all over the British Empire, marked a high point in English pride, probably swollen in the Virginia Piedmont by the renewed prospect of westward expansion. The sense of deliverance from

terror granted by the victories, and the mood of hopefulness that followed, surely helped form Madison's early consciousness of public affairs.

Along with the excitement of watching a new home going up and the
fright of Indian war, the young James Madison lived through what may
have been the severest trauma of his boyhood, an epidemic of the dreaded
smallpox. This scourge literally decimated the population of Great
Britain and her North American colonies during the seventeenth and
eighteenth centuries. The high toll among slaves and indentured servants
caused them at times to be scarcely worth purchasing unless they bore
the pocked scars, the mark of their future immunity. In 1755, 1756, and
1757, as war caused unsanitary conditions and mass movements of men,
the disease broke out severely in Canada, in the English colonies north
of Virginia, and among the Ohio valley Indians. In 1759 it spread to the
southern Indians, and in 1760, 10 per cent of a population of eight
thousand died in Charleston, South Carolina. Up to one half of those who
took the disease naturally died, as did at least 1 per cent and perhaps as
high as 5 per cent of those who underwent the harrowing vaccination
experience. Though the outbreak in Orange in 1761 and 1762, which
apparently spread southward from Frederick County, was probably less
severe than that in Charleston, even one case caused terror in any neighborhood, since the disease was so contagious and its course and effects
were so remorseless—three days or so of high temperature, headache,
vomiting, and body pains, followed so often by death, or at the very
least, by permanent scars from the pox, which spread over the body after
their first appearance on the forehead and in the hair roots.[8]

Three bits of evidence document the epidemic in Orange County. On
April 10, 1761, Joseph Chew wrote from New London, Connecticut,
thanking James Madison, Sr., for "repeated kindnesses" to his mother,
and telling of his sorrow at the "melancholly acct. of the situation of my
Unkle George Taylor's Family with the smallpox and the death of his
son George. I hope that Raging Disorder has made no more breaks in
his Family. . . ." In June 1761 James Madison, Sr., entered payment of
nineteen shillings for a mourning ring, perhaps a sign that the disease continued its ravages, and on April 6, 1762, "paid for a messenger to town in
the time of the smallpox," indicating that at least one outbreak had
passed.[9]

There is no way of knowing how many friends and connections of the
Madisons had the disease or died from it, but there is a marked concen-
tration of death dates in the family in the years 1760, 1761, and 1762.
Frances Taylor Madison died in November 1761, and her sister Mrs.
Martha Chew may also have been dead by then. Mrs. George Taylor
and her infant son died that year, as did her cousin Francis Conway II
(James Madison's uncle). Mrs. Rebecca Catlett Conway Moore (Mad-

ison's maternal grandmother) had died in 1760, and his great-grandmother, Mrs. James Taylor II, died at age eighty-three in 1762. Though some of these deaths may have been coincidental, it is likely that many of them, and doubtless many more unrecorded, were caused by the smallpox occurrences noted unmistakably in the fragmentary surviving records. One suspects that for a year housebuilding, the price of crops, and even Indian attacks were of less interest on the Madison farm than the frantic concern to preserve the white and black population from smallpox. Enough was known of its contagious qualities so that young James Madison and his brothers may have been sent away or otherwise isolated. Anyway, from this experience he learned at an early age of the dreadful scourge smallpox was in the eighteenth century; "ten times more terrible," John Adams wrote in 1776, "than Britons, Canadians and Indians together."[10]

More significant than these random and uncertain glimpses into James Madison's boyhood, though, is the sketchy evidence of the early education of the future chief theorist of the Constitution of the United States. The family farm had from its early days at least some simple means for learning. At grandfather Ambrose Madison's death in 1732 he owned twenty-eight books on religion, practical medicine, and what Daniel Boorstin has called "manuals for plantation living"—handbooks on agriculture, building, horses, hunting, and fishing. Though James Madison, Sr., may have had to curtail his own "book learning" because of his father's early death, he and his friends had a surprisingly sophisticated awareness of the culture of the English-speaking world. He wrote in a clear, well-trained hand, and his letters display none of the crude phonetic spelling and faulty grammar characteristic of the semiliterate farmer of his day. Two years before the birth of his first son he ordered from his English agent a four-volume commentary on the Epistles of Saint Paul, two volumes of *The Guardian*, and most important of all, the popular eight-volume set of *The Spectator*. Though in the middle of the eighteenth century the Madison plantation probably was not notable for its intellectual atmosphere, obviously present were a concern for English literature and learning, and an opportunity to know its brightest ornaments.[11]

We do not know the circumstances of James Madison's education in the fundamentals. His mother and grandmother Madison were probably capable in rudimentary instruction. If the Madisons followed a pattern common in Virginia, the women presided over his earliest exercises. He may for a time have been instructed by the local Anglican clergymen, the Reverend James Marye or the Reverend James Maury. Furthermore, James Madison, Sr., paid one schoolmaster, John Bricky, five shillings in 1754 and another, Kelly Jennings, two pounds six years later. These payments were made through his brother-in-law, Richard Beale, suggesting that Bricky and Jennings taught a number of children in the neighborhood, probably including Beale's stepdaughter, Mary Willis (James Madison's cousin). If schoolmasters Bricky and Jennings followed a routine common in Virginia schools in the eighteenth century, their pupils put in a long day: studies continued from early in the morning until midday, when the pupils might have two or three hours off, and then back to the books and slates until late afternoon. The plantation schools were ordinarily conducted in small, separate buildings (the one at Belvedere, the Daingerfield plantation, was twenty feet by twelve), something like the one-room schools familiar in rural areas of the United States until well into the twentieth century. If the children attending the school came from scattered farms, the building might be in a field at some intermediate point. James Madison, Sr.'s, payments through Richard Beale hint that the school was on his plantation.[12]

The school routine gave way, doubtless much to the delight of the scholars, to holiday visits and to the appearance of such "special instructors" as dancing masters. The "Francis Christien dancing master" paid by James Madison, Sr., was probably the same "Mr. Christian" whose visits at Robert Carter's Nomini Hall plantation in 1773 suspended the usual school activities. Tutor, pupils, and adults all gathered in the "Dancing-Room," where each youngster received individual instruction from Christian in the minuet. If any of the young people performed poorly or acted impudently, Christian reprimanded them before the entire company. Occasionally the fault was so serious that the master struck the offender. The lessons gradually gave way to "Minuets danced with great ease and propriety; after which the whole company Joined in country-dances." After the lessons and formal dancing, the young pupils were dismissed and the remaining company played parlor games. One, called "Button," was a guessing and kissing game, while another, "break the Pope's neck," seems to have been a role-playing affair, perhaps resembling charades. As James Madison grew, he doubtless took part in activities similar to these at Nomini Hall. Plantation life, it seems safe to say, was not all drudgery for young students.[13]

Though James Madison's early schooling probably amounted to little more than instruction in reading, writing, and arithmetic, if he showed early the bookish inclination always evident in his adult life, we may imagine that as he learned to read he devoured almost every scrap of printed matter on the family farm. His earliest surviving writing is the date "Dec. 24, 1759" on the first page of a twenty-four-page notebook, though some of the material in this notebook was certainly written when Madison was much more than eight years old. A poem copied in it from the July 1758 issue of *The American Magazine and Monthly Chronicle for the British Colonies* (printed in Philadelphia by William Bradford) may indicate his family subscribed to this intensely patriotic magazine, which during the war with France extolled the glory and honor of British arms and damned her despotic and papist foes. The poem Madison copied was "Upon the Tropes of Rhetoric," or the uses of figures of speech in achieving clear, forceful expression. The poet referred to Virgil, Cicero, and Alexander Pope, but most of his examples were from the Bible.[14]

We may suppose, then, that by the time of Madison's eleventh birthday, in March 1762, a few months after his grandmother's death, he had acquired the rudiments of learning, and had probably read as well much of the miscellaneous printed matter available in his father's house. Since his parents seem always to have admired their son's intellectual accomplishments, James Madison probably had every opportunity they could furnish him as a youth to develop his mind. We do not need to imagine him struggling against obscurantism or poverty to gain an education. His parents had the means and inclination to provide their children with a sound though simple education, and their eldest son took full advantage of what was available.

On June 14, 1762, Donald Robertson recorded payment of a £1 5s. tuition fee for James Madison, thus marking the beginning of a long and fortunate episode in his education. Robertson was, as Madison remembered and wrote down fifty years later, when he was President of the United States, "a man of great learning, and an eminent teacher in the County of King and Queen." Born in Scotland in 1717, Robertson received his education in Aberdeen and the University of Edinburgh, was licensed to preach, came to Virginia in 1753, lived for five years (on an indenture?) as a tutor in the family of Colonel John Baylor of Caroline County, and in 1758 established a school north of the Mattapony River near the tidewater lands James Madison's ancestors had patented in the seventeenth century. Robertson conducted the school on the plantation of the Reverend Robert Innes, probably in partnership with him, and boarded Madison and the other students with the Innes family, at least until his marriage in 1764 to Rachel Rogers, aunt of one of Madison's schoolmates, George Rogers Clark. Robertson seems to have been one of the best of the many pre-Revolutionary Scots schoolmasters who dispensed "learning with a burr." He maintained both an English and a Latin school, having occasionally as many as forty pupils at one time. Among the many Taylors at the Robertson school during Madison's attendance there was one "Johnny," a ward of Edmund Pendleton's, destined to be known in history as John Taylor of Caroline. There, too, were James and Harry Innes, each to have a distinguished legal career and to be associated in many ways with Madison in public life, and John Tyler, father of President Tyler. The school was, in fact, filled both with connections of the Madison family and with boys Madison would know publicly and privately for the rest of his life.[15]

During Madison's first year at the Robertson school he was listed as in the English course, perhaps indicating there were gaps in the education he had received at home. In the next year, though, then presumably well trained in the fundamentals, Madison, age twelve, began to learn Latin, which was everywhere accorded the central place in schools in the English-speaking world in the eighteenth century. So well did he master the universal language of learning that forty years later he wrote long footnotes correcting the English translations of Latin works by the international law authorities Grotius, Pufendorf, and Vattel. After working through a basic grammar and struggling with its declensions and conjugations, Madison probably turned, as students still do today, to Cicero and Virgil, though apparently not to Caesar. According to Robertson's accounts, Madison also read the history and schoolboy biographies of Cornelius Nepos in his first year of Latin. He learned Nepos so well that a few years later he used a quotation from him in commenting on a later historical work. The teacher's records also indicate that Madison studied Horace, Justinian, Ovid, Terence, and Sallust. Along with Latin, Madison probably studied Greek in his first years at Robertson's school, since an ability to read the New Testament and certain authors, such as Xenophon, Demosthenes, and Homer, in Greek was an admission requirement at many colleges in the eighteenth century.

Though to learn the ancient languages was Madison's basic task in Robertson's school, he also studied arithmetic, algebra, geometry, geography, "Miscellaneous literature," French ("taught to read but not to speak"), Italian, perhaps Spanish, and even less likely, logic. In view of Madison's studious inclination and his grateful recollection of Robertson as a teacher, we may suppose that he relished this introduction to the learning of his own day. Sensing the spirit of the new science as he studied mathematics, and learning the features of the earth as they were being discovered by still-active explorers, must have been especially stimulating. Furthermore, Robertson's accounts show he owned copies of histories of Greece and Rome, Smollett's *History of England*, Robert Dodsley's *The Preceptor: Containing a General Course of Education*, Montaigne's *Essays*, Montesquieu's *The Spirit of Laws*, and the uniquely significant *Essay Concerning Human Understanding* by John Locke. Presumably Madison did not read every book in his teacher's library, but it is apparent that the small collection of "great books" gave Madison an early, propitious opportunity. Many Virginia youths, preparing for college under ignorant, indifferent tutors or rectors who owned only a few Latin grammars and some volumes on divinity, were not nearly so fortunate.[16]

Other than what can be inferred from the scanty records of Robertson's school and what is known generally of preparatory education in

Virginia, we know nothing of the details, the day-to-day round of James Madison's life during the five years he spent at Robertson's school. John C. Payne, Madison's brother-in-law and amanuensis in old age, wrote of the schooling that "the letters from the tutor to the father give favorable evidence of the conduct and progress of the pupil." These now-missing letters might have told of the safe arrival of the pupil from trips home, of money needed to pay bills for room, board, and books, of occasional difficulties with the Innes or Taylor boys, of punishments, and of spells of sickness, but presumably they told most importantly of lessons learned, books borrowed, and tasks completed. The journey of seventy miles or more between Orange County and the school (taking from three days to a week) must have been exciting to the young schoolboy, interrupted at times, probably, with stops at the Taylors or Pendletons in Caroline County, his mother's family near Port Royal, or with the Lewises or Maurys in the little town of Fredericksburg. "Coming home" also meant crisper air, a quickened pace, and a grand vista of the Blue Ridge, visible for ten miles or more before reaching the family plantation. Robertson's school, though, meant principally to Madison extended intellectual horizons: new and perhaps more interesting companions, relief from the isolation of home, and most important, an opportunity to learn from Donald Robertson, of whom Madison reportedly said later, "all that I have been in life I owe largely to that man."[17]

In 1767, though, when Madison was sixteen, near college age, and perhaps in need of more advanced tutoring, he left the Robertson school to study for two years at home under the Reverend Thomas Martin, newly appointed rector of the Brick Church, who lived with the Madisons as a "family teacher." Martin came from a Scotch-Irish family living for a time in New Jersey but later distinguished in North Carolina, where his brother Alexander served as governor, delegate to the Federal Convention in 1787, and United States Senator. Thomas Martin, about twenty-five years old when he came to live with the Madisons, had graduated from the College of New Jersey at Princeton in 1762, then under the zealous guidance of New Light Presbyterians. He was, therefore, little like most of the indolent, parochial Anglican rectors and tutors in Virginia. Instead, he had been touched by the relatively cosmopolitan vigor and earnestness characterizing the College of New Jersey under Samuel Davies and Samuel Finley. At the Madison plantation Martin taught not only James Madison, but his brothers Francis and Ambrose (aged fourteen and twelve), and probably seven-year-old Nelly, five-year-old William, and some neighbor children as well. The family also included by this time two more girls, Sarah born in 1764 and Elizabeth born in 1768, so when James returned home from Robertson's, he was the scholarly eldest brother of a large brood.

Something of the range of Martin's teaching may be gleaned from that

undertaken by another Princetonian, Philip Vickers Fithian, at another
Virginia plantation in 1773. Fithian taught a boy seventeen Sallust and
Greek and Latin grammar; a boy fourteen studied English and arithmetic;
a girl thirteen read *The Spectator*; a girl eleven practiced spelling and
learned to write; a girl nine was learning to spell; and a girl five was just
beginning the alphabet. We may imagine Martin, no doubt bored with
drilling the younger pupils on fundamentals, turning with relief to guide
James Madison in the last phases of his college preparatory work.
Madison's few references to Martin show that he respected the teacher,
and his rapid progress in college testifies to the quality of instruction he
received. A student of Madison's endowments can sometimes overcome
a series of poor teachers; that he was blessed with good ones at almost
every step of his education undoubtedly contributed importantly to the
characteristic discipline, keenness, and polish of his intellect.[18]

As Madison studied under Martin and renewed his acquaintance with
the friends and fields of his boyhood, he probably came as well to a more
mature interest in the momentous current events of the day. Edmund
Pendleton, James Madison, Sr.'s, legal adviser, wrote his client in April
1765 that "the House of Commons have resolved and ordered in a Bill to
establish a stamp duty. . . . Poor America!" Eight months later, shortly
after the Stamp Act took effect, Pendleton wrote again, explaining the
difficulties he faced as a judge: "Our distributor of stamps having resigned, a great part of the business of this Colony must stop and some
Courts decline to sit altogether, but I don't think that prudent. The
appearance of courts may convince the people that there is not a total end
of laws tho' they are disabled to act in some instances." If the Madisons,
junior and senior, showed the same zeal for resistance they were to display ten years later, they may have thought Pendleton's course a bit too
prudent, but they must have approved his earnestness to uphold as best he
could the local enforcement of law and order. Pendleton showed in his
next letter, though, that he had no use for British oppressions and would
resist them stoutly: if the Stamp Act wasn't repealed, "we must resolve
either to admit the stamps or to proceed without them, for to stop all
business must be a greater evil than either. And who is there that will
agree to admit them? Not one in 1000, I believe." At an age when an
interest in current events sometimes becomes deeply absorbing, Madison
heard his father and others talk gravely about the injustice of the Stamp
Act and means of resistance to it.[19]

That the Madisons were vitally concerned with the trade curtailment
used to oppose the Stamp Act and other oppressive measures, and that
they were earnest patriots, is evident in an order James Madison, Sr.,
placed with Clay and Midgly, merchants in Liverpool, the summer his
eldest son left for college (1769). He ordered "German steel, black-
smith's rubbers, crosscut and hand saw files, a 30 gallon copper kettle,

horse shoe nails, a 3 pint brass wash basin . . . 4 Ivory and 12 horn combs, 1 doz. stampt linen handkerchiefs [for young James to take to college?], 1 Common Prayer book in folio and two in octavo." and four other books on religion. He then added, "If the American Revenue Acts should be repealed before your ship comes out, then Please add: 16 pairs assorted dress shoes, 6 pr. Men's worsted hose, 1 Man's fine white Hatt 22½ inches around the crown, and 1 Woman's black silk bonnet, at 8 *s.*" Thus did the Madisons, doubtless familiar by this time with John Dickinson's famous *Letters from a Farmer in Pennsylvania* protesting the Townshend duties, heed the call for "the disuse of foreign superfluties" to which the colonies adhered in resistance to the duties. Since the despised acts were not repealed until April 1770, presumably the Madisons got along without the desired finery. Clay and Midgly, confronted with the economic lesson of the conditional Madison order, may have been among the British merchants who clamored against the American duties.[20]

If James Madison had followed the most common path to higher education in Virginia, he would have gone to the College of William and Mary in Williamsburg. Three circumstances, however, conspired to turn his footsteps northward. Madison tells us in his autobiography that he didn't go to the Virginia school because "the climate at William and Mary [is] regarded as unfavorable to the health of persons from the mountainous region." His lifelong care to avoid the tidewater regions as much as possible during the "sickly season" (July or August through October) supports this recollected reason. Perhaps equally important in ruling out William and Mary was the bad reputation of the college. Jefferson's brilliant and beloved teacher, William Small, had departed in 1764, leaving the college largely in the hands of men like former President Thomas Dawson (Governor Fauquier reported he applied "for consolation to spirituous liquors"), the Reverend William Yates, remembered by John Pope for his arid teaching, and an unnamed group of professors who in 1773 were known to have "played all Night at Cards in publick Houses in the City, and . . . often [were] seen drunken in the Street." Though Jefferson and some of his friends, due largely to Small, received fine educations at the college in the early seventeen-sixties, and another group including Edmund Randolph, John Taylor of Caroline, John Marshall, and James Monroe were fortunate in the seventeen-seventies, when Madison might have gone there, the college was in a dissolute and unenviable state.[21]

James Madison and his father, then, doubtless listened eagerly as tutor Martin, and his brother Alexander, who visited Orange County in the summer of 1769, praised their alma mater, the College of New Jersey at Princeton. Furthermore, the Reverend Samuel Davies, for years the most famous dissenting preacher in Virginia, was a former president, a connection perhaps welcome to a family nominally Anglican but not notably zealous either in its orthodoxy or its support of an established church. Finally in the summer of 1768 John Witherspoon, a learned Scottish clergyman, had accepted the presidency of the College of New Jersey, thus further enhancing its reputation. We may imagine, therefore, that the family turned with a certain relief, in the summer of 1769, to the task of preparing its eldest son for the long journey to Princeton, happy in the conviction that there he would be safe from the unhealthy air and depravity of Williamsburg and at the same time benefit from the vitality of the College of New Jersey. When James Madison left Orange County, he was about four months past his eighteenth birthday, a little older than most beginning college students of his day, serious, bookish, and confident in his family standing and in his good education. In many ways, the mature young man embodied the best qualities of his Virginia heritage.

CHAPTER III

The College of New Jersey at Princeton

I T was late June or early July 1769 when Madison left his father's plantation for Princeton. With him were his tutor, Thomas Martin, Martin's brother Alexander, and at least one servant, a Negro slave called Sawney. The party traveled on horseback, carrying baggage for the journey as well as college clothes and books for the young scholar. Though it is possible they traveled partly by water, down one of the tidewater rivers and up Chesapeake Bay, it is more likely they took the lowland road that ran northward through Annapolis, Newcastle, and Philadelphia and crossed the Potomac, Susquehanna, Delaware, and other rivers by ferry. If they traveled at the usual pace, they went about thirty or forty miles per day, thus taking perhaps ten days to make the journey of more than three hundred miles from Orange to Princeton. The first part of the trip, down the crude road to Fredericksburg, was familiar enough; Madison had traveled it often in going to his mother's family home and to the Robertson school. Never, though, had he seen the countryside so parched from drought. Tobacco shriveled in the fields, and temperatures rose to levels "not . . . known these many years," when the party crossed the Rappahannock River and began the dusty trip northward.[1]

The road wound through woods much of the way, crossed the Acquia, Quantico, and Occoquan rivers by ferry, passed Stafford Court House, Payton's Tavern, and the trading town of Dumfries, to Colchester, about a day's journey (thirty-three miles) from Fredericksburg. The party then passed the lands of George Mason and George Washington, Pohick Church, and the old town of Alexandria. The road next went along the Potomac River for about seven miles (past where the Pentagon now stands) to a ferry which crossed to Georgetown, Maryland, in what is now the District of Columbia. Riding along the river, Madison may have observed, as other travelers had, the sport of fishing hawks and bald eagles. A hawk would dive into the water and catch a fish in its talons, but then often lose its prey to an eagle that would soar down from above, frighten the hawk into dropping the fish, and then swoop below to catch the fish before it reached the water. Leaving the Potomac, the party went carefully through the gorge of Rock Creek and across the rolling lands where forty years later Madison would live in the White House and watch the slow rise of the other buildings in the "Federal City." The travelers may have spent the night in Bladensburg where, in 1814, President Madison endured the humiliation of seeing American militia flee from British regulars intent on burning Washington.[2]

In 1769, though, seven years before independence, there was no hint of the future national capital on the Potomac. Madison and his companions were doubtless anxious to press on through Annapolis and across the lower reaches of the Patapsco, Gunpowder, and Bush rivers, which emptied into Chesapeake Bay, before the party reached the Susquehanna River, two or three days' journey from Annapolis. In traveling through Maryland, Madison may have been impressed as John Adams was eight years later: "We saw excellent Farms all along the Road, and what was very striking to me, I saw more sheep and more flax in Maryland than I ever saw in riding a like Distance in any other State. We scarce passed a Farm without seeing a fine flock of sheep, and scarce an House without seeing Men and Women, dressing Flax. Several Times We saw Women, breaking and swingling this necessary article." After ferrying the Susquehanna, the Virginians passed through Charlestown and crossed the head of the Elk River shortly before entering Delaware. Near Newark they met the road to the eastern shore of the Chesapeake and from there traveled through Newport and past the Admiral Boscawen Tavern to Newcastle, a long day's journey from the Susquehanna ferry. From there the road soon crossed into Pennsylvania and passed through countryside that probably pleased Madison just as it had another traveler from Virginia, who ten years before had described the trip to Philadelphia: "The country all the way bore a different aspect from any thing I had hitherto seen in America. It was much better cultivated, and beautifully laid out into fields of clover, grain, and flax. I passed by a very pretty village called Wilmington; and rode through two others, viz. Chester and Derby. The Delaware river is in sight great part of the way, and is three miles broad. Upon the whole nothing could be more pleasing than the ride which I had this day. I ferried over the Schuylkill, about three miles below Philadelphia; from whence to the city the whole country is covered with villas, gardens, and luxuriant orchards."[3]

Philadelphia must have seemed a marvelous place indeed to a young man who, until the moment he rode down Market Street toward the State House (later Independence Hall), had never seen a city even one tenth the size of the Quaker metropolis. In 1769 it contained perhaps 25,000 people, making it nearly as large as any city in the British Empire except London. Madison saw for the first time such wonders as stone sidewalks and paved streets lighted at night, row on row of three-story brick dwellings, churches of eight different denominations within a few blocks of each other, and many other public buildings, including two libraries, the Pennsylvania Hospital, the Academy of Philadelphia, the State House, and a barracks for nearly two thousand soldiers.

When the Madison party reached the London Coffee House (operated by the family of William Bradford, Madison's soon-to-be college friend), the center in Philadelphia for news, travelers, and anti-British conniving, they heard excited talk about actions in Charleston, Williamsburg, and Boston to oppose the Townshend duties—as well as angry talk about a certain Philadelphia merchant who had bought up calfskins to send to England, thus driving up the cost of shoes; did not this undercut the nonimportation agreements by making it necessary to buy shoes in England or go barefoot? News of the "Wilkes and Liberty" riots in London gave American radicals a sense that their grievances and goals were shared by many on the other side of the Atlantic. *The Pennsylvania Journal* announced proudly that a boy in New York had recently been christened "John Wilkes," after the famed English radical leader. On Monday, July 17, perhaps while Madison was in Philadelphia, a "general meeting of the inhabitants" at the State House had condemned the importation of a shipload of malt and announced that anyone who purchased any of it "has not a just sense of liberty, and [is] an enemy to this country." Madison's awe at such a city as Philadelphia must have been heightened by the accident of his arriving there at a time of commotion against Great Britain. He agreed fervently with the patriot measures, and doubtless hiked around town to follow the activities of Charles Thomson and others who took the lead in them. He may even, as a good Whig, have purchased "A Fine Large Mezzotinto Print of Mr. PITT, In the character of a ROMAN Orator," on sale at the printing office, to take to Nassau Hall.[4]

Eager to get to Princeton, and traveling on the best and most heavily used road in the colonies, the Madison party probably hurried to make the forty-mile trip from Philadelphia in one day. The road went along the Delaware River through Frankford and Bristol to the ferry to Trenton, New Jersey, which in 1759 had contained "nothing remarkable": about one hundred houses, three churches, and a small barracks. Twelve miles farther on, the weary travelers reached Princeton, and Madison first saw Nassau Hall, the "convenient, airy, and spacious" three-story stone building that was to be his home for the next three years. He said

goodbye to tutor Martin and the slave Sawney, and since the summer
term was half over, began immediately on his own to read Horace and
otherwise prepare for examinations to permit him to enter the sophomore class in the fall. Madison wrote Martin on August 10, 1769 (probably after about two weeks at Princeton), that "I am perfectly pleased
with my present situation; and the prospect before me of three years
confinement, however terrible it may sound, has nothing in it, but what
will be greatly alleviated by the advantages I hope to derive from it. . . .
The near approach of examination occasions a surprising application to
study on all sides."[5]

Madison was studying hard so he could take the exams with the freshman class, which were to be given shortly before commencement in late
September. As a new statement of admissions rules made clear, he would
be required as well to meet the usual college entrance standards: "render
Virgil and Tully's orations into English and to turn English into true and
grammatical Latin, and to be so well acquainted with the Greek, as to
render any part of the Four Evangelists [Gospels] in that language into
Latin or English . . . be acquainted with vulgar arithmetic . . . [and
master] reading English with propriety, spelling the English language,
and writing it without grammatical errors." Madison not only passed
the freshman examination, but compressed the work of the next three
years into two, so that he graduated in September 1771. After observing
commencement in September 1769, Madison wrote his father knowingly
about college activities, and in response to a plea from home to be
thrifty, since the drought had severely damaged crops in Virginia, remarked on an experience he shared with college youths of every generation: "I am under a necessity of spending much more than I was apprehensive, for the purchasing of every small trifle which I have occasion
for consumes a much greater sum than one would suppose from a
calculation of the necessary expenses."[6]

Two lively dissenting traditions nourished the College of New Jersey
at the time of James Madison's matriculation in 1769. Founded by
Presbyterians anxious to assure that educated ministers would fill the
pulpits of their rapidly increasing churches, it was strongly influenced by
the "New Lights," who, following Jonathan Edwards, the Tennents,
and Samuel Davies, sought to make Presbyterianism a vital, personally
felt force in the lives of increasing numbers of laymen. Thus in the
seventeen-sixties the leaders of the college at Princeton had little use for
the established Congregationalism of New England, the moribund
Anglicanism of the College of William and Mary, or "Old Side" Presbyterianism, which forbade itinerant preachers to upset complacent clergymen or congregations.

An equally important wind of change stirred at Princeton as a result of the close connection the college had had from its inception in 1746 with the English dissenting academies. The universities at Oxford and Cambridge were stagnant in the eighteenth century; all but orthodox Anglicans were rigidly excluded from the faculty. Creative, questing persons therefore went elsewhere and established often short-lived academies where new ideas could flourish and where curricular experiments were easily tried. When the authorities at the College of New Jersey sought advice and precedent from Great Britain they turned to these dissenting academies rather than to Oxford or Cambridge. Two early leaders, Samuel Davies and Gilbert Tennent, toured the academies in 1754, and President Aaron Burr corresponded faithfully with the most influential of the academy masters, Philip Doddridge, on curriculum, textbooks, and methods of instruction. Though the staple ingredients of higher education everywhere in the Western world, Greek, Latin, and divinity, were sacrosanct at the College of New Jersey, the guise in which they appeared and the additions which might be made to them were negotiable. As a result, it seems certain that at Princeton Madison experienced relatively little of the dull, uninspired, rote-memory teaching of dead subjects that characterized so much "higher education" in the English-speaking world.[7]

The freshman studies at the College of New Jersey, which Madison bypassed by examination in the summer of 1769, consisted of "reading the Greek and Latin languages, especially Horace, Cicero's *Orations*, the Greek Testament, Lucian's *Dialogues*, and Xenophon's *Cyropaedia*." Sophomores applied themselves further to the ancient languages, especially Homer and the late Roman literary critic Longinus, and began to study "the sciences, geography, rhetoric, logic and mathematics." The next year, studies in mathematics and natural philosophy (science) continued, and moral philosophy (ethics and what we now call social studies), metaphysics, and chronology (history) were begun. Ministerial students also took Hebrew, though, since this was "unhappily unpopular," it was not required of all pupils. Seniors had their time "entirely employed in reviews and composition, improving parts of the Latin and Greek classics, parts of the Hebrew Bible, and all the arts and sciences." The emphasis in the last year seems to have been on written and oral expression, partly in Latin but primarily in English. "Promiscuous audiences" listened to syllogisms, forensic contests, debates, orations, and harangues in the chapel, and theses and compositions were "critically examined with respect to the language, orthography, pointing, capitalizing, with the other minutiae, as well as more material properties of accurate writing."[8]

From this description of the curriculum, and from the favorable comments of Madison and others who studied at Princeton before the American Revolution, it is apparent that the College of New Jersey was relatively progressive and stimulating. The ancient languages occupied less time than they did at many colleges, and students were introduced to modern science, living languages, and a study of contemporary society. Furthermore, though religious instruction was incessant, especially on Sunday, the college with pride guaranteed "free and equal Liberty and Advantage of Education [to] any Person of any religious Denomination whatsoever." Teaching methods, too, seem to have been less deadening than usual. Madison doubtless spent considerable time memorizing textbooks, copying and recopying lecture notes, and preparing for class recitations, as students in his day were forced to do, but at the same time he did encounter new and exciting ideas, and he had again and again to formulate his own thoughts orally and in writing. In 1769 Princeton was a happy choice for a student with intellectual promise and curiosity.

The College of New Jersey, the fruit of Presbyterian zeal and moral concern, did not conceive its mission to be merely or even principally intellectual, however. Nassau Hall had been built in the rural village of Princeton in 1756 so that "the students might be boarded as well as taught, and live always under the inspection of the college officers, more sequestered from the various temptations, attending a promiscuous converse with the world, that theatre of folly and dissipation." The building accommodated 147 students if three lived in a chamber "20 feet square, having two large closets, with a window in each, for retirement." A first-floor hall, forty feet square, contained an organ and portraits of King William III ("that great deliverer of *Britain*, and assertor of protestant liberty") and former Governor Belcher of New Jersey. It was used for speeches, services, exhibitions, and assemblies. A second-floor library and a large dining hall on the "lower story" were the other public rooms.

Madison lived in Nassau Hall for three years, subject to the rules of the college intended "to direct the conduct and studies of the youth; and to restrain them from such liberties and indulgencies as would tend to corrupt their morals, or alienate their minds from a steady application." The authorities sought, they said, to steer a middle course "between too great a licentiousness on the one hand, or an excessive precision on the other," and to mete out punishment "of the more humane kind." They shunned fines as penalties, because this afflicted parents (especially poor ones) more than students, but tried instead to reason with offenders and to impose public humiliation, restriction to quarters, and expulsion only on extreme and unrepentant lawbreakers. The goal, Professor Samuel Blair stated, was "to grant every innocent liberty, and, at the same time, to restrain every ensnaring indulgence: to habituate [pupils] to subjugation . . . without insolence or servility. . . . In a word, to inspire them with such principles, and form them to such conduct, as will prepare for sustaining more extensive connections, with the grand community of mankind; and introduce them on the theatre of the world, as useful servants of their country."⁹

The daily schedule of the college was itself a prime source of the discipline so earnestly sought. A bell at five o'clock in the morning awoke the students, and another, at six, summoned them to morning prayer, where the college president expounded a passage of Scripture. Pupils then studied for an hour (by candlelight in the winter) before breakfast, and at nine they had recitation, followed by study until dinner at one. The time until three was free, then recitation and study until five, when bells pealed for evening prayers, where the students took turns singing psalms. Supper was served at seven, and by nine a room check required all pupils to be in their rooms either studying or asleep. At the recitation periods each class sat together with its tutor, reciting for him, listening to his explanations, and responding to his questions.¹⁰

Though college education in the eighteenth century was everywhere prescribed and authoritarian by modern standards, the stated goal at Princeton was remarkably liberal: "In the instruction of the youth, care is taken to cherish a spirit of liberty, and free enquiry; and not only to permit, but even to encourage their right of private judgment, without presuming to dictate with an air of infallibility, or demanding an implicit assent to the decisions of the preceptor." Juniors and seniors "were allowed the free use of the college library, that they may make excursions beyond the limits of their stated studies, into the unbounded and variegated fields of knowledge; and, especially, to assist them in preparing their disputations, and other compositions." Examinations were held at the end of each year to determine which pupils might pass on to the next class. Quarterly exams permitted the instructors to "observe the gradual progress" of the students, apparently a somewhat unusual procedure, but one which Professor Blair thought encouraged "the assiduity and carefulness of the students in their daily preparations." Firm insistence on increase in knowledge and growth in self-discipline were the marks of education at Princeton during Madison's attendance there.¹¹

As one might expect in a school founded primarily to train ministers but also producing many lawyers and politicians, effective expression, especially in speaking, received constant attention. The three underclasses declaimed weekly on the stage, sometimes with their own compositions and sometimes pronouncing "select pieces from Cicero, Demosthenes, Livy, and other ancient authors; and from Shakespeare, Milton, Addison, and such illustrious moderns, as are best adapted to display the various passions, and exemplify the graces of utterance and gesture." Seniors "disputed" regularly and discussed "two or three theses in a week; some in the syllogistic, and other in the forensic manner," the former in Latin and the latter in English. Religious debates on Sunday completed the exceedingly thorough training in public discussion at Princeton.[12]

Madison seems to have been fortunate in his teachers at the College of New Jersey. Ebenezer Pemberton, only twenty-five years old in 1769, but one of the most renowned and beloved teachers in New England at his death at age ninety in 1835, helped Madison prepare for his freshman examinations. Madison remembered him as an expert classicist and as a teacher of the most admirable scholarly and personal qualities. His successor as freshman tutor, Tapping Reeve, later founded the famous Litchfield law school in Connecticut. Madison's teacher for his first year in college was James Thompson, a tutor at Princeton since his graduation in 1761, and characterized by Madison as "remarkable for his skill in the sophomore studies." He preached occasionally at the Presbyterian church in Trenton and left the college the year after Madison enjoyed his instruction. In the junior year Madison had William Churchill Houston, who remained on the Princeton faculty until 1783. He was also a member of various revolutionary bodies in New Jersey in 1776, of the Continental Congress (1779–1781 and 1784–1785), and of the Annapolis and Constitutional conventions. He must, therefore, have been far more able and aware of the real world than the proverbial dull, droning pedagogue of the eighteenth-century recitation room. More shall be said below of Madison's instruction as a senior and as a postgraduate by President John Witherspoon.[13]

Except for what can be gleaned from notes taken by Witherspoon's students in Madison's day, only a notebook of 122 pages in Madison's schoolboy copyist's hand entitled "A Brief System of Logick" and a commonplace book survive to document his student career. He compiled "A Brief System of Logick" from notes taken while listening to Thompson, Houston, or Witherspoon, perhaps most likely Thompson, since logic seems to have been taught at Princeton during the sophomore year. The traditional notes follow closely Isaac Watts's exceedingly popular handbook, *Logick: or the Right Use of Reason in the Enquiry after Truth*, first published in London in 1725 and in its twelfth edition by 1763. Watts did not invent his logical method, of course, but rather reworked skillfully and clearly the great tradition in logic going back through Petrus Ramus and the scholastics to Aristotle, Plato, Socrates, and the sophists. Madison's notes thus begin with attention to definitions of words and ideas and the use of language and figures of speech; they then proceed to a study of "Judgment and Proposition," analyzing different kinds of statements; and they concluded with "Discourse and Syllogism," about the various forms of argument and syllogism, the uses of each, and the pitfalls to be avoided in reasoning.

Though to a modern reader the mode of thought seems excessively formal, a student who took such notes must nevertheless have achieved a considerable mental discipline. Careless habits of thought were exposed and proper methods of inquiry insisted upon. Biblical and classical illustrations abounded; a knowledge of Greek and Latin were taken for granted; and references to such authorities as Hobbes and Locke show that the tutor was familiar with more recent philosophers. Though the notebook displays almost nothing original about Madison's mind, it is impressive evidence that he was a diligent student and had a thorough training in traditional logic. If he kept similarly careful notebooks in his other subjects, he would certainly have been among the best prepared, most well-informed students in his class.[14]

The students, tutors, and sometimes the president at Princeton ate together in the dining hall, which was managed by a steward who supervised the living quarters as well. The students drank tea and coffee at breakfast, and at dinner "almost all the variety of fish and flesh the country here affords, and sometimes pyes were served." "Small-beer and cyder" were the usual table drinks, though milk was provided at supper. Variety and wholesome nourishment were promised, but prospective students were warned not to expect "luxurious dainties, or costly delicacies," and private meals were not permitted in student chambers. Some "young gentlemen," however, were allowed "to make a dish of tea in their apartments, provided it be done after evening prayer [and does] not interfere with hours of study."[15]

Most likely to have interfered with study were the demands and pleasures of undergraduate "foibles" listed by Philip Fithian: "giving each other *names and characters*; Meeting and Shoving in the dark entries; Knocking at Doors and going off without entering; Strowing the entries in the night with greasy Feathers; freezing the Bell; Ringing it at late Hours of the Night; Picking from the neighborhood now and then a plump fat Hen or Turkey for the private entertainment of the Club; Parading bad Women; Burning Curse-John; Darting Sun-Beams upon the Town-People; Reconnoitering Houses in the Town, and ogling Women with the Telescope—Making Squibs, and other frightful compositions with Gun-Powder, and lighting them in the Rooms of timorous Boys, and new comers."[16]

We may assume that Madison generally followed the prescribed student routine during the years he spent at Princeton as an undergraduate, but little specifically is known of his day-to-day activity there. He sometimes went home for a few weeks during the spring and fall recesses. Purchase of clothes and other personal business took him occasionally to Philadelphia. He once complained to a tailor there that he had been given "the remnant instead of the measured piece" in a cloth purchase. He did not have a horse of his own except for trips home, but he hired one when required for short trips or rides in the vicinity. In one letter he asked for more money because with all his "frugality," he had not been able to meet the expenses "consistent with my staying here to the best advantage." He also enclosed "the measures of my Neck and rists," but asked his mother not to rush in making his shirts because he needed only three or four, and besides, "I should chuse she would not have them ruffled 'till I am present myself." Perhaps then, as now, college students, anxious to dress precisely in the fashion of the moment, distrusted parental taste. Principally, though, we may imagine Madison a rather more serious student than average, but nevertheless enjoying the informal and convivial aspects of college life. He always remembered his student friends with affection and thought well of the College of New Jersey and its faculty.[17]

Of Madison's close friends at Princeton, one, Philip Freneau, became the leading American poet of his generation, while another, Hugh Henry Brackenridge, was the first American novelist of note. Both were in Madison's class (1771), may have been his roommates, and were in the same student literary-social club, the American Whig Society. They were fervent revolutionists in 1776 and continued to share Madison's liberal political views as long as each lived. Another member of Madison's class, Gunning Bedford, Jr., of Delaware, served at the Federal Convention in 1787 and otherwise had a distinguished public career, but there is no evidence that he and Madison were friends except that both were American Whigs. Two other classmates, Charles McKnight and Samuel Spring, served valiantly in the Revolution and had notable professional careers, McKnight as a surgeon in New York and Spring as a Congregational minister in Newburyport, Massachusetts. Madison's most intimate study companion, Joseph Ross, died a year after he graduated. Two close friends in the class of 1770, Caleb Wallace and Nathaniel Irwin, entered the Presbyterian ministry after graduation; later though, Wallace moved to Kentucky, where he became an important lawyer and judge. Samuel Stanhope Smith of the class of 1769 remained at Princeton as a tutor and spent hours in philosophic discussion with Madison. In the seventeen-seventies the two young savants saw each other in Virginia, where Smith founded Hampden-Sydney Academy before returning to Princeton to serve for over thirty years as professor and president.

In the classes of 1772, 1773, and 1774, Madison's closest friend, perhaps his favorite of all Princeton associates, was William Bradford of the famous Philadelphia printing family. Bradford had a distinguished career as a lawyer and became Attorney General of the United States shortly before his untimely death in 1795. Madison must have known as well the remarkable number of men in those classes who later gained fame as public officials (Aaron Burr, Henry Lee, Morgan Lewis, Henry Brockholst Livingston, and Aaron Ogden), and as preacher-educators (James

Francis Armstrong, Thaddeus Dod, James Dunlap, John McKnight, John Blair Smith, John McMillan, Samuel E. McCorkle, William Linn, Andrew Hunter, Joseph Eckley and Moses Allen). In the decade before the American Revolution the College of New Jersey attracted many exceptionally able students who must have contributed substantially to Madison's intellectual growth.[18]

To understand Madison's place in this talented circle, one must contend with President Witherspoon's oft-repeated remark that "during the whole time [Madison] was under [my] tuition [I] never knew him to do, or to say, an improper thing." In the seventeen-eighties Witherspoon apparently said this to Jefferson, who subsequently delighted to embarrass Madison with it at every opportunity. Benjamin Rush made it part of an admonition to his son at Princeton in 1802, adding, in urging the lad to shun plays and idle amusement, that "the celebrated Mr. Madison when a student at the Jersey College, never took any part in them. His only relaxation from study consisted in walking and conversation." Luckily for Madison's standing as a "normal" college student, a notebook survives proving conclusively that he took part enthusiastically in "idle amusements" and student ribaldry.[19]

When collegiate exuberance reached the brim in Madison's day it spilled over in rivalry between the American Whig Society and the Cliosophian Society. Though no deep ideological differences divided them, Southerners and Pennsylvanians predominated among the Whigs; New Englanders among the Cliosophians. Furthermore, the Whigs generally assumed a condescending attitude toward what they conceived was the social inferiority of the Clios, and the Clios seem to have been rather more pious than the Whigs. The societies met separately for discussion and camaraderie, and directed their self-generated enthusiasm at each other in a "paper war" whenever the college authorities could be tricked or talked into permitting one. A paper war raged when one society attacked the other in writing, usually doggerel, to which the other would then reply. At least occasionally the verses were read aloud in the prayer hall before the entire student body, which presumably heard them with much cheering and chortling. The exchanges lasted until banned by the faculty; one went on for as long as two weeks.

About the time of Madison's graduation in September 1771, a furious paper war broke out in which Brackenridge, Freneau, and Madison were the chief writers and spokesmen for the Whigs. Of nineteen satires in a notebook copy made by Bradford, thirteen are by Brackenridge, three by Freneau, and the last three, the poorest poetry and most scurrilous in content, are by Madison. Since Madison did not have a strong speaking voice, he may not have declaimed his lines in the prayer hall, but he was fully engaged in the "war" and received "credit" for his sophomoric assaults. Following Brackenridge's hard-hitting though proper roastings

of the Clios and Freneau's slashing, vituperative attacks, Madison's verses
seem weak though not at all deficient in vulgarity. He wrote satirically,
for example, of the dream adventures of the Clio "poet laureate," Samuel
Spring, describing, allegedly in Spring's own words, an encounter with
the Muses:

> Urania threw a chamber pot
> Which from beneath her bed she brought
> And struck my eyes and ears and nose
> Repeating it with lusty blows.
> In such a pickle then I stood
> Trickling on every side with blood
> When Clio, ever grateful muse
> Sprinkled my head with healing dews
> Then took me to her private room
> And straight an Eunuch out I come
> My voice to render more melodious
> A recompence for sufferings odious . . .

Turning to Moses Allen, Madison aimed undistinguished couplets
which must nevertheless have made him a champion among his colleagues
in abuse:

> Great Allen founder of the crew
> If right I guess must keep a stew
> The lecherous rascal there will find
> A place just suited to his mind
> May whore and pimp and drink and swear
> Nor more the garb of Christians wear
> And free Nassau from such a pest
> A dunce a fool an ass at best.

These verses, of course, were not taken seriously by the combatants
(Madison was friendly with Spring and Allen as long as each lived), and
have meaning only within the context of undergraduate horseplay. They
demonstrate abundantly as well what Madison never doubted: he was no
poet. He wrote John Quincy Adams in 1822 that he had "never . . . been
favored with the Inspiration of the Muses." The verses are, however, an
early revelation of the broad sense of humor which so many of Madison's
associates testified came bubbling forth when he was in a small circle of
good friends.[20]

The political atmosphere at Princeton and Madison's growth in it,
however, are more important than the good-natured, rather typical social
life. He had not been at Princeton a month before he sent his tutor in
Virginia a pamphlet championing the English radical John Wilkes. After
attending his first Princeton commencement in September 1769, he

wrote his father that he saw honorary degrees awarded to John Hancock, John Dickinson, and Joseph Galloway, all at that time popular leaders in the resistance to British measures in America. The next year, after New York merchants had repudiated nonimportation agreements, Madison wrote approvingly of Princeton indignation: "We have no publick news but the base conduct of the Merchants in N. York in breaking through their spirited resolutions not to import. . . . Their Letter to the Merchants in Philadelphia requesting their concurrence was lately burnt by the Students of this place in the college Yard, all of them appearing in their black gowns and the bell Tolling." Furthermore, Madison reported, the seniors were to appear at commencement dressed only in "American cloth."[21]

Exercises at the September 1770 commencement, all surely approved or at least permitted by the faculty, showed how much politics filled the minds of the students. James Witherspoon, the president's son, defended in Latin the thesis that the law of nature obliged subjects to resist tyrannical kings. John Ogden upheld the nonimportation agreement as "a noble Exertion of Self-denial and public Spirit," and Mathias Williamson supported the proposition that "Every religious Profession, which does not by its Principles disturb the public Peace, ought to be tolerated by a wise State." Frederick Frelinghuysen "pronounced an Oration on the Utility of American Manufactures," doubtless a brief favoring American economic independence from Great Britain. Thomas McPherrin argued "*Omnes Homines, Jura Naturae, liberti sunt,*" and John Blydenburgh assrted that freedom of religion served the state by acting as "a *Censor Morem.*" Finally the valedictorian, Robert Stewart, orated on "Public Spirit," probably an appeal to patriotism. Though one of the speakers addressed complimentary remarks to Governor William Franklin, who sat on the platform, that staunch loyalist could not have been wholly pleased with the tenor of the exercises.[22]

At Madison's own graduation, a year later, the atmosphere was less heated, but the audience nevertheless heard an oration by Samuel Spring on "The idea of a Patriot-King," and listened to the fervently patriotic poem "The rising glory of America" written by Brackenridge and Freneau. In 1772 Madison's close friend William Bradford delivered a valedictory address on "The Disadvantages of an Unequal Distribution of Property in a State," and other orators discussed the virtues (or lack thereof) of a mixed monarchy, independence of spirit, obedience, and resistance, and the advantages of political liberty. Such radicalism was too much for one member of the audience, who wrote a public letter protesting the "improprieties" he had observed; college students should stick to Greek and Latin and not concern themselves with public issues which required "an eminence of knowledge which the unfledged wings of youth cannot soar to." He warned colleges against nurturing "the *dogmas* of any political party," and questioned the soundness of any institution whose commencement exercises consisted of the *"exotic productions"* he had just witnessed. The distinguished revolutionary careers of so many College of New Jersey graduates of Madison's day are clear evidence that doctrines of resistance and freedom were taught exceedingly well there from 1769 to 1776.[23]

In defending the college against charges of radicalism, President Witherspoon proclaimed his pride in "the spirit of liberty [which breaths] high and strong" among students and faculty and declared himself "an opposer of lordly domination and sacredotal tyranny." Witherspoon's habits of mind are, in fact, the keys to the climate of opinion which so impressed Madison during his years at Princeton. Madison stayed there for six months following his graduation to read with Witherspoon, and always admired and respected "the old Doctor," as he called Witherspoon.[24]

Witherspoon arrived in America in 1768 to be president of the College of New Jersey with a reputation for learning and eloquence, but more particularly for hostility to ecclesiastical hierarchy. For years in Scotland Witherspoon fought the power of the synods of the Presbyterian Kirk over individual congregations. He developed habits and doctrines of resistance to authority which, as many New England clergymen also demonstrated, needed little translation to be used against political authority. Thus when Witherspoon found American Calvinists such as William Livingston (author of *The Independent Reflector* and *The American Whig*, both greatly admired by Madison) protesting ecclesiastical control, and saw many Americans deeply alarmed at efforts to plant an Anglican bishop in the colonies, he understood the threat and responded vigorously. Though Witherspoon was orthodox enough in his theology and in his sense of family and social authority, his instinctive suspicion of "lordly domination and sacredotal tyranny," his spirit of self-righteous defiance of evil, and his sturdy conviction that temporal power must bow to conscience and God's law were bound to help create a climate in which, as the breach between Great Britain and her colonies widened, the seeds of revolution and independence would spawn and grow.[25]

In a way, when Madison went to the middle colonies and to the Presbyterian stronghold at Princeton, he placed himself at the center of the English dissenting tradition in North America. He found there that enlightened men took for granted the pattern of thought which from Cromwell's day had opposed religious establishment, ecclesiastical hierarchy, courtly influence, and every other manifestation of privileged and therefore easily and inevitably corruptible power. The heroes of this tradition were Milton, Algernon Sidney, Locke, and, most widely read of all in the American colonies, the authors of *Cato's Letters*, first published in London in the seventeen-twenties, John Trenchard and Thomas Gordon. Obsessed with an almost paranoid suspicion that all power in human hands would be abused, and on guard against exaggerated pretensions to authority, those who read the dissenting writers were ready to enlist, as Witherspoon had done in Scotland and would do again when he signed the Declaration of Independence, in any campaign to resist "domination and tyranny." In the presence of this eternal vigilance James Madison undertook his college studies.

We have seen already that Madison knew the ancient authors well, and had probably read such currently fashionable writers as Swift, Addison, and Steele, before he reached Princeton. It is likely, too, that he had begun early his lifelong addiction to newspapers, so he was familiar with the public issues that agitated the colonies. During his youthful reading, he kept, as diligent students in his day normally did, a commonplace book, wherein he copied quotations from what he read and occasionally made paraphrases of or reflected on his reading. The twenty-four surviving pages of this book (undoubtedly only a small portion of what he must originally have compiled) contain selections from five works, probably for the most part read at Princeton: *Memoirs of the Cardinal de Retz* (1723), *The Essays of Michael Seigneur de Montaigne* (1595), a poem printed in *The American Magazine* (Philadelphia, July 1758), *Critical Reflections* . . . by the Abbé Du Bos (1748), and *The Spectator*, Number 551 (1712). Madison read the three French authors in English translation, though presumably he could have read the originals by the time he reached Princeton.

Most of the commonplace book reflects a careful reading of the *Memoirs* of Cardinal de Retz, telling of the swirling riots and political maneuvers of the Frondist era in France, 1648–1652, just before Cardinal Mazarin and then Louis XIV gave firm direction to the French state. De Retz played a complicated role in these events, ambitious, obviously, to wield the power once exercised by Cardinal Richelieu. He acted sometimes as an agitator of the populace of Paris, and sometimes as a Machiavellian behind-the-scenes manager. In fact, de Retz admired Machiavelli and reflected his views more than those of any other political philosopher. Madison paid particular attention to the comments de Retz made on the nature of man and society as he described his role in the power struggles. Madison copied down such statements as "Irresolute minds waver most when they are upon the point of Action," "I have all my Life time esteem'd Men more for what they forebore to do than for what they did"; and "The Talent for insinuating is more useful than that of persuading. The former is often successful, the latter very seldom." At times Madison fashioned his own epigrams about human conduct from events de Retz related. At one critical juncture, for example, de Retz observed that timid counselors advised doing nothing about a popular riot while rash ones advised severe repression, both acting from the premise that the disturbances were not serious. In each case the result was to encourage the rebellious mood rather than to dampen it. On this circumstance Madison observed, "A Blind Rashness and an excessive timorousness cause the same Effects when the Danger is not known. For both endeavour to persuade themselves that the Danger is not real." Throughout, de Retz urged prudence, a shrewd calculation of consequences, a willingness to admit mistakes, and the ability to use power, or the appearance of power, effectively. In fact, there is an uncanny similarity between Madison's aphorisms and quotations from de Retz and the precepts that often guided Madison's long public career.

From Montaigne's *Essays* Madison drew more epigrams about human nature. He wrote, for example, following one of the essays, "People who are too tender of their Reputation, and too deeply piqued by Slander, are conscious to themselves of some inward Infirmity." Madison occasionally added Latin quotations or illustrations from ancient history to his gleanings from Montaigne. From Du Bos' *Critical Reflections*, a work concerned chiefly with differing tastes in the fine arts and their diverse expression and degree of excellence at various times and places, Madison again culled epigrams about man and society. He filled one section of the commonplace book with reflections on "National Characters": the French were wiser than they seemed, and the Spanish seemed wiser than they were (Madison included this observation from Francis Bacon's *Essays*); the English were unexpressive, while the slightest event animated the Italians; the English had little creative genius but were skilled at improving the inventions of others; and so on. Madison largely ignored the narrations and specific illustrations that de Retz, Montaigne, and Du Bos used in their essays, but rather filled his copybook with bits of wisdom he wished to absorb and remember.[26]

In addition to passages on the three French writers, Madison copied verbatim an anonymous poem "Upon the Tropes of Rhetoric" from the July 1758 *American Magazine*, and a section from *The Spectator*, Number 551 containing poetic epitaphs on five ancient authors. Neither entry reveals anything of Madison except his interest, in choosing to copy it, in canons of literary criticism. In fact, all the works from which he compiled the surviving fragment of his commonplace book are "polite literature"—polished pieces designed to display and encourage high standards of expression, taste, and conduct. In writing late in life of his own acquaintance at about age twelve with *The Spectator*, Madison said that it was "peculiarly adapted to inculcate in youthful minds, just sentiments, an appetite for knowledge, and a taste for the improvement of the mind and manners." He recommended *The Spectator*, especially Joseph Addison's contributions, to a young nephew because it encour-

aged "a lively sense of the duties, the virtues and the proprieties of life.'
Furthermore, Madison counseled, it was an excellent example of correct
writing, meeting Jonathan Swift's standard that good style consisted "of
proper words in their proper places." Like Benjamin Franklin, Madison
highly approved Addison's intention "to enliven Morality with Wit, and
to temper Wit with Morality." He admired as well *The Spectator*'s desire
to retain Puritan moral zeal without its fanaticism, and to enjoy Restoration urbanity while shunning its degeneracy. Thus in a very direct and
self-conscious way Madison absorbed concepts of public life in vogue
among enlightened Englishmen in the age of Addison, Swift, and Pope.[27]

It is apparent from this commonplace book, as we might have guessed
from what we know of reading habits in Madison's day, that he gleaned
much of his first wisdom about human nature and political obligation
from works that two centuries later are not commonly thought of as
prime sources for such concepts. *The Spectator*, for example, is limned
with support for moderation, the need to encourage good manners,
hostility to any form of fanaticism, the necessity of high standards of
public ethics, and the usefulness of good humor in a cultivated society.
These were *the* social virtues, which, of course, the state had a responsibility to encourage, because it could not prosper without them.
Madison's thinking about government and society very likely had such
sentiments firmly embedded before he read Locke and other political
philosophers. In the same way, Du Bos may have been as important as
Montesquieu in forming Madison's notions of national character,
Montaigne may have been his preceptor in understanding the human
condition, and de Retz may have contributed more than Hobbes to
Madison's understanding of the uses of fear, power, and avarice in statecraft. Madison probably first gleaned principles of politics from the
"popular" authors of his day rather than from the philosophers who are
now considered the towering intellects of the seventeenth and eighteenth
centuries.

Though there is no direct evidence of what Madison read or learned as
a college student beyond what has been suggested above, we do know
something of what he must have heard in John Witherspoon's lectures
and what he might have read in the college library. Notes taken by
William Bradford, Andrew Hunter, and John E. Calhoun, all students at
Princeton in Madison's day, survive and suggest what went on in
Witherspoon's classes.* He presided over most of the work of the senior

---

* Madison knew each of these students, heard the same lectures, and probably
compiled notebooks, now lost, similar to theirs. Witherspoon's lectures were
published in Edinburgh in 1815, but there are major differences between the
student notebooks of 1772 and 1774 and the printed lectures, which, for ex-

year, reviewing earlier lessons, and under the broad title "Moral Philosophy," commenting on what now might be called ethics, economics,
political science, history, and current events. He usually raised a general
question—about the utility of religious toleration, for example, or the
extent of paternal authority in the family, or the sufficiency of a merely
utilitarian ethic—explained the views of various authorities on the question, criticized these views, and then left no doubt of his own conclusions
on the subject.

Witherspoon sought especially to leave his students well instructed on
the major concern of eighteenth-century moral philosophers: the proper
relation between religion and ethics, between faith and being a good
person. As the Earl of Shaftesbury, Witherspoon's favorite whipping
boy, put it, the basic inquiry was "what *Honesty* or virtue is, consider'd
by itself; and in what manner it is influenc'd by Religion: How far
Religion necessarily implies Virtue; and whether it be a true Saying, that
it is impossible for an Atheist to be Virtuous, or share any real degree
of Honesty, or Merit." In this inquiry Witherspoon was unequivocally on
the side of religion. He told his classes that "the whole Scripture is agreeable to sound philosophy," meaning that he rejected rationalist insinuations that the Bible contained passages absurd to reasonable men and
therefore best denied or at least passed over. He persistently held Shaftesbury up for criticism and ridicule, often opposing to him the more
orthodox doctrines of Francis Hutcheson, an early exponent of the
Scottish "common-sense" philosophy.[28]

The "old Doctor" saved his sharpest barbs, however, for David Hume.
This "infidel writer," as Witherspoon called him, had "a system of morals
that is peculiar to himself. He makes everything that is agreeable and
useful virtue and vice-versa by which he entirely annihilates the distinction between moral and natural qualities." Witherspoon insisted that
some essentials of morality, revealed by Christian doctrine, were difficult
and even disagreeable, and that therefore the easy world of Hume and
the rationalists was a fool's paradise that earnest, faithful young men
would shun. Witherspoon also blasted Mandeville's *The Fable of the
Bees* for its ridicule of "industry, sobriety, and public spirit," and
repudiated Plato and Sir Thomas More for their implication that perfection and utopia might be achieved on earth. Throughout, Witherspoon
insisted on the orthodox Christian view that life was real and earnest and
that the only salvation for sinful men was a devout Biblical faith.

In commenting on government and society Witherspoon followed
very closely the analysis in Aristotle's *Politics*, though the Princeton
students recorded almost no explicit references to that vastly influential

---

ample, reveal much less concern to reconcile faith and reason than Witherspoon showed at Princeton while Madison was there.

work. Witherspoon outlined the three forms of government, monarchy, aristocracy, and constitutional polity, and the perversions of each, tyranny, oligarchy, and democracy, and he distinguished between the noble and perverted forms, just as Aristotle did, according to their attention to the common good or to selfish, factional ends. Thus Madison had at the foundation of his political education a supreme emphasis on the *ends*, not the *means*, of government. Rule by one or by a few could be good if conducted justly, while rule by the many could be bad if not so conducted. Democracy, in the Aristotelian sense of government by the multitude where the will of demagogues, not the law, is supreme, was, when Madison first heard it, a term of disdain and reproach. Witherspoon drove home again and again that the purpose of government was to encourage and nourish not life alone, but the good life, the life of virtue. As Madison came to accept as well the Lockean concepts of representation and government by consent, he *added* them to his earlier education in the politics of virtue. A great gulf, therefore, separates the thought of Madison (and the other Founding Fathers) from that of believers in such later concepts as Benthamite utilitarianism and simple majoritarian democracy, who denied that principles of justice and virtue can be identified and made the foundation of government, and therefore have a higher sanction than the will of the majority.

Though Witherspoon was orthodox in morality and conventional in his political analysis, the notes on his lectures reveal none of the narrow-mindedness, intolerance, or thought repression with which he has sometimes been charged. He chastised Plato for banishing orators and scored Plato and Sir Thomas More in terms similar to those used by modern critics of "the closed society." Among the rights of man he included "a right to private judgment in matters of opinion." He warned particularly "against persecution on religious account . . . because such as hold absurd tenets are seldom dangerous. Perhaps they are never dangerous, but when they are oppressed." Though this statement is closer to the Lockean concept of toleration than Madison's own later creed of complete liberty of conscience, the last sentence signals the end of religious persecution.

Witherspoon also lectured on some of the seventeenth- and eighteenth-century political writers, especially those emphasizing jurisprudence and international law. He recommended his students read "Grotius, Puffendorf, Barbeyrac, Cumberland, Selden, Burlamaqui, Hobbes, Machiavelli, Harrington, Locke, Sidney, and some late books" if they would understand government and politics. Montesquieu, Adam Ferguson, Lord Kames, and Hume appear elsewhere on his reading lists. Madison probably read every one of these authors either at Princeton or a few years after he left it. We need not suppose, therefore, that he had to overcome a narrow orthodox education in order to learn the latest social thought.

There was no such division either in Witherspoon's own thought or in his lectures to Princeton students.[29]

Witherspoon's lectures on history and eloquence were filled with literary criticism and advice on effective expression. He remarked, for example, that "of the ancient writers, the poets are the most instructive. . . . There is a clearer idea of the state of Asia and Greece in Homer's works and of Rome in Horace's satires than in the history of those times." All the ancient authors are cited over and over again as models both of just sentiments and good writing. Among modern authors, he favored Shakespeare, Swift, Fielding, Addison, Steele, Arbuthnot, and above all, Pope. He thought the style of William Robertson's *History of Scotland* (1759) and *History of the Reign of Charles II* (1769) "as just a mixture of strength and elegance as I know in the English language." On the other hand, Witherspoon said, reflecting a hostility second nature for a Scotsman, "I cannot help cautioning you against one author of some eminence—Johnson the author of the rambler—in his manner and such a lover of hard words, that he is the worst pattern for young persons that can be named." He exhorted each student, in writing and speaking, to discover the style best suited to him, to use his special talents to best advantage, and to be modest because "nothing more certainly makes a man ridiculous than an over-forwardness to display his excellencies."[30]

The impression is inescapable that Madison had in Witherspoon a remarkably able, learned, and eloquent teacher. He was thoroughly acquainted with ancient and modern learning, had no hesitation in exposing his students to its full range, and made his lectures to them a stimulating confrontation of ideas. When set beside the usual drillmaster, Witherspoon seems a lively pedagogue indeed. Little wonder, either, that he himself took a leading role in the American Revolution and that his students were intensely alert to current political issues, entered the disputes eagerly, and made important contributions to them. The College of New Jersey in Madison's day *was* the seedbed of sedition and nursery of rebels Tory critics charged it with being, but that is not all: it was as well a school for statesmen trained to seek freedom and ordered government through the pursuit of virtue.

The library of the College of New Jersey in 1769 contained perhaps two thousand books, twelve hundred of which had been presented by Governor Jonathan Belcher in 1755. Though Belcher prided himself on his orthodoxy and stocked his library with sermons and theological tracts, his bequest nevertheless gave Princeton students access to a wide world of learning. All the standard authors were represented, from the Greeks and Romans to Bunyan, Dryden, Tillotson, Locke, Newton, Milton, Watts, Defoe, Montaigne, Bacon, Shakespeare, Montesquieu, Addison, John Trenchard and Thomas Gordon (authors of *Cato's Letters*), Pope,

Johnson, and Whitefield. For the future statesman there were histories of
Ethiopia, the Reformation, the Jews, the Stuarts, Scotland, the Quakers,
commerce, New England, Virginia, the Duke of Marlborough, the
Church at Geneva, Holland, King Philip's War, Germany, New Jersey,
the Mogul Empire, the Roman Catholic Church, the Primitive Church,
the Puritans, Queen Anne's reign, the Turks, Rome, Greece, the Rebellion (Cromwell's), France, the Czar of Russia, and in case anything had
been missed, several universal and world histories. Such volumes as the
laws of Massachusetts and New Jersey, the journals of the House of
Commons, abridgments of law codifications, compilations of statistics,
and atlases were there for students interested in the raw materials of history and political understanding. The presence of Wollaston's *Religion of
Nature*, Butler's *Hudibras*, and Pope's *Essay on Man* indicates that
Belcher had not excluded works expressing new and heretical currents of
thought from his library.[31]

The college library grew slowly until Witherspoon arrived in 1768,
bringing with him perhaps five hundred volumes, including the latest
works by the Scottish writers then flourishing. We know from
Witherspoon's reading lists that Robertson, Smollett, Hume, Hutcheson,
Kames, Adam Smith, Ferguson, and others were familiar to him, and
that he brought their books to America. Though he had firm convictions of his own about which authors were "right" and which were
"wrong," and was perfectly willing to argue down those inclined toward
the "wrong" ones, there is no evidence that he believed "wrong" ideas
had to be *suppressed*; rather, they had to be *combated*. In Witherspoon's
day orthodox Presbyterianism was vigorous and self-confident, unneed-
ful of proscription to maintain its doctrines. Through Witherspoon's
lectures and library we may assume that Madison came to know fully
and freely of the issues agitating the world of Franklin, Hume, and
Voltaire.[32]

When Madison graduated from the College of New Jersey in 1771 he
was a paragon of the well-educated scholar. He had learned an enormous
amount, but more than that, he had acquired a great thirst for knowledge,
so great, in fact, that he injured his health by studying almost to the
exclusion of sleep; for weeks at a time as an undergraduate he slept only
four or five hours a night. For the rest of his life Madison had a reputation as a scholar: his college friends came eagerly to him for philosophic
discussions; Jefferson turned to him repeatedly for help in research and
in compiling bibliographies; and even his political foes admitted that on
nearly every question before any legislative body in which he sat he was
likely to be the best-informed member.

Madison's learning, like that of nearly all formally educated men in
the Western world between the Renaissance and the beginning of the
twentieth century, had its foundation in the lore and history and wisdom

of Greece and Rome. Madison mastered Latin well enough to correct
English translations of Grotius, and he knew enough Greek to read
Aristotle and Thucydides and Plutarch in their native tongue. He must
have known Cicero and Virgil by heart. Moreover his mind had been
saturated with them *before* he paid much attention to serious works in
English. His first visions of virtuous government, for example, probably
came from Livy's idealized account of the Roman republic. After reading, translating, and very likely declaiming from memory Cicero's
Orations, Madison would have known very well the dangers posed by
popular military heroes such as Caesar, and the poison injected into the
body politic by intriguers like Catiline. Demosthenes' *Philippics* would
have roused his patriotic zeal to resist an alien tyrant, and from Thucydides he could have learned how disunion and fratricidal strife corroded
morality and brought great states to ruin. Plutarch may have been Madison's first preceptor in the virtues necessary for statesmanship and in
the qualities of responsible citizenship. Furthermore, any reader of
Tacitus knew very well the absurdities sometimes caused by hereditary
monarchies and the abuses attendant on absolute and arbitrary power.

Though modern historians have shown that the actualities of ancient
history were different from the picture left by the great classical authors,
in Madison's day the towering figures of Greece and Rome and the
priceless books of the ancient sages and historians were very nearly
sanctified as an incomparable source of insight into human affairs. To
understand Madison's mind, it is necessary to sense in some way the
broad and primordial impact upon it of the Greek and Latin authors.
Though, like most of his contemporaries, he did not often "footnote" the
ideas he took from his classical studies, it is apparent that again and again
he accepted many of them as axiomatic when he considered public problems in Williamsburg, Philadelphia, and Washington. For Madison's
generation the wisdom of Greece and Rome furnished, so to speak, the
folklore, the "morality plays," and the schoolboy texts on fundamental
concepts of human nature and society.[33]

The other foundation stone of learning in Madison's day, and of his
education, was the Christian tradition. Down through his graduation
from college every one of Madison's teachers, as far as we know, was
either a clergyman or a devoutly orthodox Christian layman. In fact, so
pervasive was Christian influence, especially in rearing children, that an
education under other than Christian auspices was virtually unknown.
Even the technically nonsectarian College of Philadelphia founded by
Franklin gave its students the usual training in Christian morality and was
presided over by a zealous Anglican minister. Though much of the
Christian aspect of Madison's schooling was relatively perfunctory and
he seems never to have been an ardent believer himself, he nonetheless
year after year undertook his studies from a Christian viewpoint. Fur-

thermore, he never took an antireligious or even an anti-Christian stance, and he retained the respect and admiration of the devoutly orthodox young men with whom he studied at Princeton. It seems clear he neither embraced fervently nor rejected utterly the Christian base of his education. He accepted its tenets generally and formed his outlook on life within its world view.

Though the substance and significance of this Christian orientation for a rather passive believer such as Madison defy precise formulation, certain elements of Christian thought had almost universal acceptance in colonial America and are important to an understanding of Madison's intellectual growth. The Christian affirmation, for example, that each human soul has infinite worth, and the emphasis in the Protestant tradition that the essence of this worth is the relationship of each individual to the Almighty, were of vast significance. There were, therefore, limits to the claim the state could make upon the individual. Whatever Christians disagreed about and however their conduct might fall short, they all affirmed that in any ultimate confrontation between mere human dictates and the law of God, the former must give way. In accepting this view, Madison acknowledged that there is a nontemporal source of values, he insisted that the state live up to them, and he affirmed that individuals in a society were bound by more-than-earthly obligations. Such doctrines pervaded Witherspoon's sermons and chapel talks.

Furthermore, as practiced and expounded in colonial America, Christianity came to have an exceedingly individualistic tone. Witherspoon's evangelical Presbyterianism proclaimed that the supreme good for each person was to find a faith that would give him victory over death. All the essential requirements for traveling this road had a personal definition: proper (personal) beliefs, correct (personal) day-to-day habits, charitable (personal) relationships, and all the rest. An individual moral accountability filled every waking moment, making each Christian conscious that every step he took might be right or wrong. Akin to this concern for eternal salvation and moral awareness was an insistence that life be made to count for something, that a wasted life was a sinful life.

At the community level, the compulsion to make life count for good expressed itself in numerous humanitarian enterprises, of which the Quakers furnish the most notable examples. Significantly, Benjamin Franklin's career in Philadelphia, the best individual expression of this impulse, had its origin, he tells us in his autobiography, in the clubs organized in Boston by Cotton Mather to encourage a brotherly concern among Christians. Though this outreach could and did have its less commendable watch-and-ward aspects, a citizenry conditioned to attitudes of concern for fellow citizens and experienced in the methods of humanitarianism nevertheless would have priceless habits and skills for the tasks of revolution and nation building. The last step in the path marked out

by moral awareness, taken often in New England pulpits and elsewhere
in America, was to insist that *nations* likewise will be held accountable in
the final judgment. The American colonies especially, in a common
figure of speech, were conceived as a city set upon a hill to shine for all
the world to see. An incalculable dynamism and sense of purpose is
imparted to a people which so sees itself.

Entirely apart from theology or personal fidelity to any church ritual,
then, Madison's Christian education gave him an extremely important
overview of man and society, within which his more self-conscious
political philosophy grew. Moreover, it united him with nearly all the
leaders in revolution and nation building, including the heterodox Franklin and Jefferson, in commitment to certain moral standards. To them all,
the Ten Commandments, the Sermon on the Mount, and the twelfth
chapter of Paul's Epistle to the Romans were canonical. As Madison
studied under Donald Robertson, Thomas Martin, and John Witherspoon, all clergymen, he learned the essentials of Christian morality and
social theory. Though he did not long continue to express them in the
same way as his teachers, it is not possible to understand the purpose and
earnestness of Madison's public life without sensing its connection with
the Christian atmosphere in which he was raised.

The large place polite, "popular" literature had in Madison's reading
and education has already been described. Its cultivated style, ease of
expression, and emphasis on manners and morals had a continuing and
profound effect on Madison. He absorbed this outlook so thoroughly
that even though he lived far into the age of Wordsworth and Coleridge,
he showed not the slightest sign of abandoning the world view of *The
Spectator*. In the correspondence among Madison, Bradford, and Freneau
immediately after they left Princeton, the works of Fielding, Hume,
Pope, Kames, Swift, and Samuel Butler are referred to with that easy
familiarity that assumes writer and reader have a thorough knowledge of
the authors mentioned. Madison's intense training in the classics, of
course, reenforced his partiality for English neoclassical learning and
culture. In his conventional religious views, in his sense of political obligation, in his manners, in his literary and aesthetic tastes, and in his habit of
prudence and moderation in all things, he was the model Augustan gentleman. In fact, except in certain realms of political theory where the events
of his public career required creativity, Madison was very little inclined to break away from the conventional climate of opinion in basic
matters. Thus the thorough education he had in the writers who created
that climate appears persistently throughout his life.

Madison did read, of course, the philosophers who dominated intellectual life in the eighteenth century. By the time he left college he almost
certainly had read all of Locke's major works, particularly *Essay*

Concerning Human Understanding, the *Letters on Toleration*, and the *Second Treatise on Civil Government.* He accepted, apparently with little question, the epistemology of the *Essay* asserting that the mind is blank at birth and that it receives all its furnishings through the senses. From this Madison followed Locke in supposing that the minds of men were continually growing and could hold an infinite variety of insights and opinions. Thus an open, tolerant attitude toward beliefs was necessary, and more than that, legitimate civil power could derive only from a mode of government where infinitely varied persons could in some way register their consent. Three paragraphs—two from *Essay Concerning Human Understanding* and one from the *Second Treatise*—set forth the basic understanding of man and society Madison acquired from Locke:

> . . . the various and contrary choices that men make in the world do not argue that they do not all pursue good: but that the same thing is not good to every man alike. This variety of pursuits shows that everyone does not place his happiness in the same thing, or choose the same way to it. . . .
>
> Hence it was, I think, that the philosophers of old did in vain inquire, whether *summum bonum* consisted in riches, or bodily delights, or virtue, or contemplation: and they might have as reasonably disputed whether the best relish were to be found in apples, plums, or nuts, and have divided themselves into sects upon it. . . . It is not strange nor unreasonable that men should seek their happiness by avoiding all things that disease them, and by pursuing all that delight them; wherein it will be no wonder to find variety and difference. . . . Though all men's desires tend to happiness, yet they are not moved by the same object. Men may choose different things, and yet all choose right. . . .[34]
>
> Men being, as has been said, by nature all free, equal, and independent, no one can be put out of this estate, and subjected to the political power of another, without his own consent, . . . which is done by agreeing with other men to join and unite into a community for their comfortable, safe, and peaceable living one amongst another, in a secure enjoyment of their properties, and a greater security against any that are not of it. . . . When any number of men have so consented to make one community or government, they are thereby presently incorporated, and make one body politic, wherein the majority have a right to act and conclude for the rest.[35]

Locke's thought influenced Madison early and remained always the foundation of his personal and public philosophy.

These formative influences on Madison's mind, of course, came from the earlier, empirical, largely British phase of the Enlightenment. He seems never to have been much impressed by Hume's devastating analysis of the contradiction between empiricism and reason, by Kant's recon-

struction following Hume, or by the more elegant "Heavenly City" built
and furnished largely by the French *philosophes* in the second half of the
eighteenth century. Madison took the Newton-Locke world view at
face value: the universe was marvelously harmonious; the discovery of
facts about man and society would lead to progress and enlightenment;
empiricism and dependence on laws of cause and effect were not incompatible; and moral and social, as well as physical, understandings would
benefit from the application of human study and reason. Madison saw at
Princeton David Rittenhouse's intricate orrery, demonstrating the clock-
like precision of the heavenly bodies as they moved in their perfectly
predictable orbits. Its patterned motion was always the metaphor for
Madison's concept of the way his world operated. Though classical
realism, Scottish "common-sense" dependence on intuition, and Presbyterian soberness all had their impact on Madison, at bottom he responded
to the optimisim about reason and progress generated in the Western
world by the discoveries of Newton and the speculations of Locke.

In summary, Madison's education at Princeton furnished him, from the
wisdom of Greece and Rome, a lifelong realism about human nature, a
comprehensive concept of political obligation, and an instinctive admiration of patience, prudence, and moderation. From the Christian tradition,
he inherited a sense of the prime importance of conscience, a strict personal morality, an understanding of human dignity as well as depravity,
and a conviction that vital religion could contribute importantly to the
general welfare. From Locke, he learned that to be fully human, men had
to be free, and that to be free, they had in some way to take part in their
government. From Addison and other polite writers, he absorbed a sense
of manners, a life style, a mode of expression, and an impression of what
civilized society should be like. These elements of his thought were, of
course, not wholly compatible. For one not a systematic philosopher,
this proved not to be a serious handicap. Madison stood upon whatever
aspect of his basic learning seemed to him relevant for the intellectual
problem or political necessity at hand. His thought was eclectic, sensible,
and reasonable, if not always wholly consistent, and directed toward
effective encouragement of the large goals of freedom and government
by consent.

CHAPTER IV

The Search for a Vocation

MADISON asked his father's permission, after graduating from the College of New Jersey in September 1771, to remain "in Princeton this winter coming," and perhaps to return again after a spring visit home. He later wrote that he stayed because intense study had left him too weak to make the journey home. His intentions, in any case, were to study Hebrew and miscellaneous subjects, perhaps including law, under Witherspoon and to be with stimulating friends who were to be in Princeton during the winter: William Bradford, Hugh Henry Brackenridge, Samuel Spring, Samuel Stanhope Smith, and probably Philip Freneau and Nathaniel Irwin as well. He thus remained at Princeton until April 1772, in delicate health, but deepening a commitment to the life of the mind that he never relinquished.[1]

When Madison finally returned to Orange County, he confronted two major uncertainties: he was so sickly that he feared an early death, and he had not yet decided on a career. Madison's health presents perplexing problems. He was described frequently as "feeble," "pale," or "sickly," and he wrote repeatedly of bouts of illness and fears that poor health would prevent his doing something or other, yet he lived to be eighty-five years old and until his last years seems not to have suffered seriously or chronically from an identifiable disease. Of Madison's illness upon leaving Princeton, Irving Brant argues cogently that the young scholar suffered from a functional ailment modern medicine calls epileptoid hysteria. Madison himself described the disease as "a constitutional liability to sudden attacks, somewhat resembling Epilepsy, and suspending the intellectual functions. They continued thro' [my] life, with prolonged intervals." Among the papers of Madison's father is a list of drugs "For

an Epilepsy," dated October 11, 1753. If these drugs were for the future
President, and if the attacks suffered throughout his life were similar to
those complained of between 1772 and 1776, the disease probably was
not epileptoid hysteria, which is associated with the years immediately
following puberty. In any case, Madison's unwillingness to call the disorder epilepsy, and the uncertain diagnosis of it in his day, leave the
possibility that he suffered from a nervous disorder not now identifiable
and which for some reason plagued him more severely after he left college than at any other time.

The tendency of the disorder to appear at times of strain and tension,
and Madison's inclination toward hypochondria, strengthen the impression that its cause was in part functional. Madison wrote Jefferson in
1785 that he couldn't come to Europe because "I have some reason to
suspect that crossing the sea would be unfriendly to a singular disease of
my constitution," and late in life he told a young friend of the ailments
of the chest and nerves he had suffered from as a youth. Whatever the
proper diagnosis of the disease, it caused him moments of serious anxiety
in the early seventeen-seventies and all his life deterred him from sea
voyages and other physically arduous undertakings.[2]

When Madison and William Bradford parted on their way home from
Princeton in April 1772 they agreed to write often, for "pleasure and
improvement." Bradford wrote first (to "My dear Jemmy") explaining
that he had deferred writing while he knew Madison was at the Berkeley
warm springs (north of Winchester, Virginia)—a further sign of Madison's need to restore his health. Bradford lamented his recent graduation
and departure from Princeton: "If a collegiac-life is a state of bondage,
like the good old Chinesian I am in love with my chains. . . . I leave
Nassau Hall with the same regret that a fond son would feel who parts
with an indulgent mother to tempt the dangers of the sea." He then set
the theme for much of the correspondence by confessing he had not
decided "what business I shall follow for life," but, apparently to help
him decide, he proposed to study history and morality during the winter
so that he might better know himself.[3]

Madison replied promptly (to "My dear Billey") approving Bradford's
intended course of study, but, assuming a grave air, he advised his friend
to "season [your studies] with a little divinity now and then" and
warned him that "a watchful eye must be kept on ourselves lest while we
are building ideal monuments of Renown and Bliss here we neglect to
have our names enrolled in the Annals of Heaven." He argued further
that Bradford shun "those impertinent fops that abound in every City to
divert you from your business and philosophic amusements. . . . I am
luckily out of the way of such troubles, but I know you are cirrounded
with them for they breed in Towns and populous places, as naturally as

flies do in the Shambles." Madison reported that he was "dull and infirm" and had "little spirit and alacrity . . . [because] my sensations for many months past have intimated to me not to expect a long or healthy life." He urged Bradford, full of "Health Youth Fire and Genius," to prepare for a career in the service of mankind. Madison's sobriety, surprising even in an age when young men enjoyed affecting the weight of years, reflected both his health worries and the boredom of being back on the family farm. He was teaching his brother William (age ten) and his sisters Nelly (age twelve) and Sarah (age eight) "the first rudiments of literature," which, though tedious, by no means occupied all his time. He beseeched Bradford to send him letters and books, because Bradford was his only source for "an account of all literary transactions in your part of the world."[4]

Before the Bradford correspondence resumed, Madison received a lively letter from Philip Freneau, then teaching school on the eastern shore in Maryland. He too longed for the stimulating, studious days at Princeton, expecially since he found school teaching such drudgery: he had taught in Long Island for two weeks and found his pupils a "brutish brainless crew . . . void of reason and of grace," and after five weeks of teaching in Maryland, plagued by thirty students "who prey upon me like Leaches," he vowed to forsake pedagogy forever. Had Madison needed any push to turn his scholarly inclinations away from the class-room, Freneau's letter would have sufficed. Freneau hoped he might soon be in Virginia, where he looked forward to a visit with Madison, one of the "few Persons . . . whose conversation I delight in, [and] regret the loss of it."[5]

Bradford had returned to Princeton when he answered Madison's letter of foreboding about his ill-health. "I believe you hurt your constitution while here, by too close application to study," he wrote, and hoped that by taking care of himself Madison might live long and thus fulfill Witherspoon's oft-repeated petition in the college chapel that God "Spare useful lives." This letter took nearly eight weeks to reach Madison, who agreed immediately with Bradford that each ought to forbear explicit professions of friendship and excessive apologies for not writing punctually because such language should be interpreted thus: "As I have no real esteem for you and for certain reasons think it expedi-ent to appear well in your eye, I endeavor to Varnish Falsehood with politeness which I think I can do in so ingenious a manner that so vain a Blockhead as you cannot see through it." He thanked Bradford for send-ing him books and pamphlets ("You being at the Fountain-Head of Political and Literary Intelligence and I in an Obscure Corner"), and reported "My Health is a little better owing I believe to more activity and less Study recommended by the Physicians." As a sign of improved

spirits, Madison said he looked forward to a trip to Philadelphia in a year
or two.[6]

Again home in Philadelphia, Bradford replied he had abundant news
because several "Nassovian Friends" were seeking licenses to preach from
the Presbyterian synod then meeting there. He complained about so
many Princetonians "running their heads against the Pulpit who might
have done their country excellent service at the Tail of the plow" (those
so described were members of the Cliosophian Society), and reported
that another of their acquaintances had married a girl thoroughly and
scandalously known to Princeton students. The marriage, however, had
not been "acknowledged till the Fruits of it appeared in a fine Daughter." No place, Bradford remarked, was "so overstocked with Old-
Maids as Princeton." Turning from gossip, Bradford asked Madison for a
copy of the list of books he had drawn up "such as are proper for a
private Gentleman's Library."[7]

One of the hopeful young preachers at the synod meeting was Madison's close friend, Caleb Wallace, a Virginian, a College of New Jersey
graduate, class of 1770, and an American Whig. The synod assigned him
to "supply" some churches in Virginia and North Carolina, so he took
Bradford's letter with him and stopped at Montpelier for two days in
early June 1773. In September another Princetonian, Nathaniel Irwin,
visited Madison and preached at the Brick Church, where he won the
praise of everyone in Orange "for an excellent Discourse." Madison's
college friends, it seems, were important in the zealous Presbyterian
invasion of Anglican Virginia preceding the American Revolution.[8]

In reply to Bradford's letter, Madison wrote condescendingly of the
born plowmen attempting to batter their way into the pulpit and of the
idle, dissipated chap who had to marry the college party girl. He also
sent Bradford a list of books he had culled from a catalogue Witherspoon
had sent him, as well as a shorter list of books he had noticed as ones he
wanted to read sometime. Unfortunately the lists do not survive, but the
discussion of them shows how dependent Madison continued to be on
Witherspoon's advice and how serious the two young Princetonians
were in their self-imposed course of study. When Bradford wrote again,
in August, his search for a life's work had reached a crisis. If he thought
himself qualified, he said, he would choose the ministry, because "a
divine may be the most useful as well as the most happy member of
society." Since "insuperable objections" barred him from the ministry,
the remaining choices were "Law, Physic [medicine] and Merchandize
[business]." He felt little inclined toward medicine and most drawn toward law, so he sought to convince himself it was a proper choice in spite
of the common charge that legal work was "prejudicial to morals." He
argued that though "the conduct of the generallity of lawyers is very
reproachable," not all were that way, and besides, merchants on the

whole were no better. Furthermore, as Witherspoon had observed, a reputation for honesty was useful to a lawyer, and, Bradford asked, "Can there be a nobler character than his whose business it is to support the Laws of his country and to defend the oppressed from the violence of the Oppressor?" Yet, Bradford complained, there were already too many lawyers. He asked Madison's "open and unreserved" advice.[9]

Madison responded with his usual gravity. He offered condolences to "the Church on the loss of a fine Genius and persuasive Orator," and urged Bradford to "always keep the Ministry obliquely in View." Perhaps someday he might be moved to reject his prosperous temporal profession and become "a fervent Advocate in the cause of Christ," thus giving "Evidence . . . more striking" than that of a "Cloud of Witnesses." Though this might reflect Madison's own preference for a career had he felt qualified to undertake it, it is also possible he simply repeated sentiments about vocations he had heard Witherspoon express often at Princeton. Madison then pronounced "Law the most eligible" profession for his friend, since it required his eloquence and broad knowledge more than did medicine or business. Furthermore, "the objection founded on the number of Lawyers should stimulate to Assiduity rather than discourage the Attempt." The only drawback, as far as Madison could see, was that whatever Bradford's zeal to be honest, "misrepresentation from a client or intricacy in a cause" would almost surely debauch his good intentions at times. Madison closed with an apology for commenting on the severe deflation in Virginia: "I do not meddle with Politicks but this Calamity lies so near the heart of every friend of the Country that I could not but mention it."[10]

In his next letter Madison revealed his own plans and state of mind:

I intend myself to read Law occasionally and have procured books for that purpose so that you need not fear offending me by Allusions to that science. Indeed any of your remarks as you go along would afford me entertainment and instruction. The principles and Modes of Government are too important to be disregarded by an Inquisitive mind and I think are well worthy of a critical examination by all students that have health and Leisure. I should be well pleased with a sketch of the plan you have fixed upon for your studies, the books and the order you intend to read them in; and when you have obtained sufficient insight into the Constitution of your Country [Pennsylvania] and can make it an amusement to yourself, send me a draught of its Origin and fundamental principles of Legislation; particularly the extent of your religious Toleration. Here allow me to propose the following Queries. Is an Ecclesiastical Establishment absolutely necessary to support civil society in a supreme Government? and how far it is hurtful to a dependent State? I do not ask for an immediate answer but mention them as worth attending to in the course of your reading and consulting experienced Lawyers and Politicians upon.

When you have satisfied yourself in these points I should listen with pleasure to the Result of your researches.

You recommend sending for the Reviews as the best way to know the present State of Literature and the Choicest Books published. This I have done and shall continue to do; but I find them loose in their principles and encouragers of free enquiry even such as destroys the most essential Truths, Enemies to serious religion and extremely partial in their Citations, seeking them rather to justify their censures and Commondations than to give the reader a just specimen of the Author's genius."[11]

Clearly, Madison's interest in public affairs had become irrepressible. Furthermore, he meant to study government and public law to deepen his understanding of public affairs, not to master technical courtroom law. He never intended to practice, and he never qualified as a counsel-at-law. Madison's general ill-health, his weak speaking voice (he did not participate in commencement exercises at Princeton on that account), and perhaps some moral reservations deterred him from such a career.

It is significant as well that Madison's point of departure in discussing religious freedom was the conventional one for his day; support of religion was an essential function of a good government. Madison's strictures on "free enquiry" which threatened "essential Truths" and "serious religion" seem even more startling from one who later gained fame as a defender of freedom of expression, but this, too, was conventional in the eighteenth century. Madison had heard it from Witherspoon and his other teachers, and he had read it in countless guises, in newspapers, pamphlets, and books. He had much to learn.

Madison's reticence after this time on religious questions has encouraged claims both that he was seduced from a youthful piety by skeptical politicians such as Paine and Jefferson and that he retained the intense religious concern of his youth even though he ceased to write or speak of it. There is no evidence that he was ever more than conventionally religious as a youth or as a college student. His authorship of the blasphemous Whig doggerel confounds any supposition of particular devoutness. On the other hand, at Princeton his attention to religion did increase, intellectually at least, and perhaps even spiritually if he had been affected by the pervasive religious awakenings there in 1770 and 1772. His postgraduate study of Hebrew and theology, some surviving scholarly notes he took on scriptural commentaries in about 1772, a surviving prayer book he used in conducting family devotions, and the tone of his letters to Bradford all suggest a deep religious concern. The letter quoted from above, however, probably marks the shift of his attention to public affairs, a change probably spurred by his improved health and the passing of adolescent introspections. Madison seems simply to have dropped his interest in doctrinal questions, troubling, so far as we know, neither to reject nor to reaffirm his religious tenets thereafter. Furthermore, he never attacked religion or religious men and he always saw "good religion" as a useful support for republican government.[12]

When Madison wrote Bradford in January 1774, he approved the principle if not the violence of the Boston Tea Party and denounced the "obduracy and *ministerialism*" of the governor of Massachusetts, but he was preoccupied with his study of religious history. He noted that "Union of Religious Sentiments begets a surprising confidence and Ecclesiastical Establishments tend to great ignorance and Corruption, all of which facilitate the Execution of mischievous Projects." If the Church of England had been established in the northern and middle colonies as well as in the South, Madison declared, "it is clear to me that slavery and Subjection might and would have been gradually insinuated among us." A nasty situation close to home troubled Madison most, however: "That diabolical Hell conceived principle of persecution rages among some [people] and to their eternal Infamy the Clergy can furnish their Quota of Imps for such business. This vexes me the most of any thing whatever. There are at this time in the adjacent County not less than 5 or 6 well meaning men in close Gaol for publishing their religious Sentiments which in the main are very orthodox. I have neither patience to hear talk or think of any thing relative to this matter, for I have squabbled and scolded abused and ridiculed so long about it, to so little purpose that I am without common patience. So I leave you to pity me and pray for Liberty of Conscience to revive among us."[13]

Madison complained as well about the "Poverty . . . Luxury . . . Pride . . . Ignorance . . . Knavery . . . Vice and Wickedness" which prevailed in Virginia, and longed again "to breathe [the] free Air" of Philadelphia. When past eighty Madison wrote that he had been "under very early and strong impressions in favor of liberty both Civil and Religious [and had] spared no exertion to save [persecuted Baptist preachers] from imprisonment." He probably referred to the imprisonment of several Baptist clergymen in neighboring Culpeper County for preaching without a license. A Baptist elder had been jailed for praying in a private home; for good measure, his host was committed as well. Elijah Craig, later to work with Madison for constitutional guarantees for religious liberty in Virginia, had been arrested while "at the plough," jailed, and fed rye bread and water. He preached to all who came to the jail, but after a month was released. At another time he was arrested in the pulpit. The details of Madison's activity on behalf of these men are not known, but obviously he felt strongly about this first venture into public affairs. It is apparent, too, if Madison wrote precisely when he spoke of "religious Toleration" in December 1773, and of "Liberty of Conscience" a little over a month later, that his study and the scolding and disputing over the persecutions helped move him from the condescending idea of toleration to the more liberal concept he was to implant in the Virginia Bill of Rights in June 1776.[14]

It is further apparent that Madison's experience outside Virginia heightened his outrage at religious persecution near home. The Baptist preachers jailed in Culpeper had done no more, really, than Caleb Wallace and Madison's other clergymen-classmates sought to do throughout the South: bring vital religion to the unchurched or to indifferent Anglicans. Madison had doubtless heard the respected Witherspoon exhort his students repeatedly to go out and save souls—the precise intent of the imprisoned Baptists. Though Madison disdained "enthusiasts" whose religion led them to wanton acts, and did not himself respond to revival preaching, at this time he clearly approved the zeal of his friends and other preachers who sought to envigorate Southern Christianity. To one who looked upon the ministry as the highest calling, who had many friends in that profession, and who admired the open society the dissenting religions encouraged in the middle colonies, nothing was more absurd, unwise, and unjust than the spectacle of a moribund Anglican establishment using civil power to imprison "well-meaning men" who sought no privilege other than to preach their faith to those who would listen. Madison came later to broaden his defense of religious liberty to include the wholly secular ground that it was a fundamental human right of all men to believe, or not believe, whatever their conscience dictated, but his impulse to defend freedom of religion originated in his sympathy for his dissenting friends and others who encountered resistance from a religious establishment for which he had little respect.

When he next wrote to Bradford, in April 1774, defining and defending religious liberty still commanded Madison's attention. He hoped the Virginia Assembly would respond to the petitions of Baptists and Presbyterians for "greater liberty in matters of Religion," but he saw little chance for success. "Incredible and extravagant stories were told in the House of the monstrous effects of the Enthusiasm prevalent among the Sectaries," and the "Zealous adherants to [the Anglican] Hierarchy" did not have "that liberal catholic and equitable way of thinking as to the rights of Conscience, which is one of the Characteristics of a free people." Some Virginians had "generous Principles," but the clergy, numerous and powerful, had enough "influence at home [in England] by reason of their connection with and dependence on the Bishops and Crown," to keep Virginia's intolerant laws in force. Madison then congratulated Bradford on living in a land which had "long felt the good effect of . . . religious as well as Civil Liberty. . . . I cannot help attributing those continual exertions of Genius which appear among you to the inspiration of Liberty and that love of Fame and Knowledge which always accompany it. Religious bondage shackles and debilitates the mind and unfits it for every noble enterprize, every expanded prospect."[15]

The desire "again to breathe the free air" of the middle colonies, the prospect of seeing Bradford and other college friends, and the need to place twelve-year-old William Madison in a preparatory school (Donald Robertson's school had closed), were reasons enough for Madison to travel north in the spring of 1774. George Luckey, another Princetonian preaching in Virginia, spent Christmas 1773 at Montpelier, and he and Madison planned to be at the meeting of the Presbyterian synod in Philadelphia in mid-May of the following year. Madison's ill mother recovered enough to permit James and William to leave with Luckey late in April for Philadelphia. With his restored health, awakening interest in public affairs, and excitement at seeing old friends, not even the unseasonable hot spell, which drove temperatures in Philadelphia to 84 degrees, could have wilted Madison's high spirits as he traveled the now-familar road.

In Philadelphia, Madison just missed the spectacle of seeing five persons hanged at a public execution (and two given last-minute reprieves), but he probably was among the "vast concourse of people" who on May 3 paraded effigies of British Solicitor General Alexander Wedderburn and Governor Thomas Hutchinson of Massachusetts through the streets to the Bradford coffeehouse where they were hung and burned with "Electric Fire." The sign on Wedderburn (scorned in Philadelphia for his abuse of Benjamin Franklin before the Privy Council, news of which filled the newspapers) must have delighted Madison and any other veterans of Whig-Clio "paper wars" present:

> The infamous Wedderburn
> A pert prime prater, of a scabby race,
> Guilt in his heart, and famine in his face.

The sign also proclaimed that "the base-born SOLLICITOR" and Hutchinson were "horrid Monsters, a disgrace to human nature, and justly merit our utmost detestation, and the GALLOWS." The next day a freak snowstorm and severe cold wave doubtless chilled patriotic ardor, but the steady arrival of ships carrying news of harsh words spoken about America in the House of Commons would have given Madison and his friends plenty of politics to talk about as they waited for the synod to convene on May 18.

Sometime on Friday, May 13, though, a rider dashed into town from New York with news that Parliament had passed an act closing the port of Boston to punish that city for its Tea Party. The next day, the Bradford paper, *The Pennsylvania Journal*, published in an "extra" the text of the act, together with news that ships and troops were on the way to enforce it. Madison shared the consternation of the largest city in the colonies at word of "Coercive Acts" that, unless withdrawn, were almost certain to mean war between Britain and her colonies. One doubts whether even the meeting of the synod could very long have sidetracked

excited discussions of the challenge to liberty; the infamy of the British
Prime Minister, Lord North; and the need for union among the colonies.
Madison probably tarried long enough in town to attend the meeting at
City Tavern on May 20, which resolved that calling a "Congress of
deputies of all the colonies" was the only way to confront Lord North.
The days in Philadelphia, from the burning of the effigies to the meet-
ing at City Tavern, must have been among the most memorable in
Madison's life.[16]

In late May and early June, leaving brother William at the Princeton
preparatory school, Madison went on, apparently alone, to New York
and Albany and back. There seems to have been no motive for the
journey other than a desire to "see the country" and perhaps visit a
portion of America where social conditions were very different from
those in Virginia. The beautiful trip from New York to Albany and
back on the Hudson River, judging from Bradford's note in his letter
copybook that Madison was gone from Philadelphia only two weeks,
must have been made with good luck on wind and tide. The solitary
journey perhaps gave Madison an opportunity to ponder the fateful
events he had just witnessed, and to resolve to take what part he could in
the looming crisis. He observed the fast proclaimed for June 1 to mourn
the closing of the port of Boston, and he may have seen towns all along
the way meeting to pass resolutions supporting the stricken city.[17]

When Madison returned to Philadelphia entertainments competed for
attention with political news. The Jockey Club of Philadelphia held a
series of races "over the Centre Course," June 7 to 9, which, if Madison
had already acquired the zest for horse racing he later demonstrated, he
probably watched eagerly. On the seventeenth a "Grand Concert and
Ball" was held at the "Assembly Room in Lodge Alley" in honor of a
distinguished French musician and concertmaster visiting Philadelphia.
He played a series of "symphonies" and performed dance exhibitions,
which, if Madison paid the $1-a-ticket cost, doubtless seemed elegant
indeed to one used to the irregular performances of dancing master
Francis Christian. A meeting of 1,200 "Mechanics" at the State House
(Independence Hall) on June 9, and a larger "General Meeting" nine
days later, both organized by radical leaders to support the call for a
continental congress, kept political excitement high. When Madison left
Philadelphia for the ride home (about June 20), he held a keenly sharpened sense of the great struggle the colonies faced, and he plainly envied
his friend Bradford's excellent seat for the impending events. Madison
was surely both more a revolutionist and more a nationalist than he had
been when he left home two months earlier.[18]

For a year following July 1774, the correspondence between Madison
and Bradford was largely an exchange of news about revolutionary moves

in Pennsylvania and Virginia. The young men supported radical measures and took turns upbraiding Tories and moderates. Madison reported on July 1, 1774, that though most Virginians were "very warm" in support of the Bostonians, many "Europeans, especially the Scotch, and some interested Merchants among the Natives," shamefully held back from measures of resistance to Great Britain. He agreed with Josiah Tucker that, for her own economic benefit, England ought to relinquish political control of the colonies, but he had only contempt for Tucker's argument for Parliamentary supremacy: its "misrepresentations" reminded the Virginian of how "the specious Arguments of Infidels have established the faith of Enquiring Christians." Madison adhered to what he termed "Political Orthodoxy": Parliament had no legitimate authority in the colonies.[19]

As delegates gathered in Philadelphia for the First Continental Congress, Bradford denounced Pennsylvania's choice of two representatives "known to be inimical to the Liberties of America," while Madison found the Virginia delegation mostly "glowing Patriots and men of Learning and penetration." "One or two," though, probably Peyton Randolph and Richard Bland, Madison thought too timid. He longed to be in Philadelphia to listen to the debates, which he hoped would "illuminate the minds of thinking people among us" and display sufficient ability "to render us more respectable at Home [in England]." Madison agreed with Bradford's prophecy that the invasion of "our Liberties . . . by a corrupt, ambitious and determined ministry is bringing things to a crisis in America and seems to foretell some great event." Affairs in Europe "seem to be looking forward to some great revolution and . . . lead us to imagine there is something at hand that shall greatly augment the history of the world." The two earnest students could scarcely contain themselves as they saw some prospect that their country, perhaps even they themselves, faced a providential moment.[20]

Bradford next wrote while Congress was in session, reporting that "Philadelphia has become another Cairo; with this difference that the one is a city swarming with Merchants the other with politicians and Statesman." He told his fellow student that the delegates made "great and constant use" of the city library, especially the works of Vattel, Burlamaqui, Locke, and Montesquieu. Madison replied, pleased with the conduct of the learned delegates and sure that the "Liberty and Patriotism [that] animates all degrees and denominations of men" in Virginia would result in faithful adherence to the trade embargo and support for the Bostonians even if that meant violence and war. He criticized Quakers in Pennsylvania and Virginia for their "passiveness," which he supposed had material as well as religious motives. He reflected a persisting interest in religious freedom, however, by asking if Baptist charges of persecution in New England had been aired in Philadelphia.

Bradford replied in January 1775, praising the "zeal" and "silent spirit of courage" of the Virginians, bewailing that Pennsylvania's numerous Quakers "will always prevent our doing much" in the military way, and castigating Tory pamphleteers and printers centered in New York, which, he said, "has the least public Virtue of any City on the Continent." Later that month Madison reported that throughout Virginia "thousands of well trained High Spirited men [are] ready to meet any danger," and he predicted that "extreme events" were likely in view of British "Wickedness."[21]

Politics did not wholly exclude other topics, however. One mutual friend had had "a run away match" with the daughter of a prominent New Jersey landowner, and Princeton clergyman Moses Allen (the lampooned "Great Allen," leader of the Cliosophian Society), had stopped at Montpelier for several days just before Christmas 1774 and "preached two sermons with General Approbation." Madison approved his performance, though he made fun of Allen's "considerable equipage. . . . [He] seems willing to superadd the Airs of the fine Gentleman to the graces of the Spirit." He also felt constrained to tell fellow Whig Bradford that this once-ridiculed Clio was, despite his "primitive Levity," of "a friendly and generous Disposition." When Bradford wrote of the marriage of a college associate who "put the Cart before the horse: he was a father before he was a husband," Madison replied that although "the World needs to be peopled . . . I should be sorry it should be peopled with bastards as my old friend [Thaddeus] Dod and [his bride] seem to incline. Who could have thought the old monk had been so letcherous. I hope his Religion, like that of some enthusiasts, was not of such a nature as to fan the amorous fire."[22]

Madison and Bradford also had the unpleasant task of telling their friend Brackenridge that a long poem he had written, "On Divine Revelation," was faulty in style, and unhappily, ill-timed. Madison found its subject "frightful" and the "Antiquated Phraseology" disgusting to modern taste. He wished instead that Brackenridge had written a "Political or humorous Composition" that might have made the author famous. Bradford hoped Brackenridge would publish some poems attacking the Tories "to counterbalance several satires . . . published . . . against the Congress and patriotic party." Madison and Bradford were able to keep up with this and other news of Princeton friends through the travels of Samuel Stanhope Smith, yet another college friend on a preaching mission to the South, who stopped at Montpelier twice in the first six months of 1775. That spring and summer, however, he doubtless approached Orange with apprehension—dysentery raged in the county. Madison's seven-year-old sister, Elizabeth, died on May 17 and his four-year-old brother, Reuben, on June 5. Further "Irruptions" in late June and July "carried off" many slaves, and on July 3 Madison's mother came down with the disease, though by that time it was less severe and she recovered. As he was to do repeatedly throughout his life, the apparently sickly Madison escaped entirely from the widespread epidemic. But gossip and even a dreaded scourge could not in those months long detract Madison from revolution. At age twenty-three he had subscribed defiance to the authority of the King of England.[23]

The First Continental Congress had resolved that every county, city, and town in the colonies choose a "Committee of Safety" to enforce the ban on trade approved by the Congress. Violators were to be named in the newspapers and "universally condemned as the enemies of American Liberty." From their formation in 1774 and 1775, these committees were the effective government in most of the colonies, and through them the coming revolution had its impact on the people. James Madison was elected to the Orange County committee on December 22, 1774, along with his father (chosen chairman) and nine of their neighbors. All were substantial planters who had long guided the affairs of the county, and in organizing under the resolves of Congress they simply agreed to enforce its measures in Orange. James Madison, Jr., was by eleven years the youngest committeeman.[24]

Though Madison did not tell Bradford of his election, the tone of his letters reflected his change from observer to actor. He wrote on January 20, 1775, for example, that county residents were asked to sign the embargo agreement so the committee could, by noting those who refused, "distinguish friends from foes and . . . oblige the Common people to a more strict observance" of the agreement. Two months later Madison wished he and his fellow committeemen could have some New York Tory pamphleteers in Orange County for a while—to give them a coat of tar and feathers. He took part in the humbling of the Reverend John Wingate, rector of St. Thomas Parish in Orange County, for his refusal to surrender to the committee some "seditious" pamphlets in his possession. They were, he said, his personal property and could not be taken from him legally. The committee nevertheless seized the "execrable" documents and burned them before the militia. Madison then gloated that the clergyman, "finding his protection to be not so much in the law as the favor of the people, is grown very supple and obsequious." As for an offending "Scotch Parson" in Culpeper County who refused to preach on a fast day, Madison noted approvingly that "his Church doors [are] shut and his salary . . . stopped." He added threateningly that "I question, should this insolence not abate if he does not get ducked in a coat of Tar and surplice of feathers and then he may go in his new Canonicals and act under the lawful Authority of Gen. Gage [British commander in Boston] if he pleases." Madison obviously had no compunction about summary measures against those who defied the will of the committee.[25]

Madison was equally zealous in building the military muscle of the county. Helping his father, who, as county lieutenant, had charge of the militia, he procured and distributed arms and supplies. Companies practiced close-order drill and men trained in markmanship. "You would be astonished," Madison wrote Bradford two days after the battle of Bunker Hill, "at the perfection this art is brought to. The most inexpert hands reckon it an indifferent shot to miss the bigness of a man's face at the distance of 100 yards. I am far from being the best and should not often miss it on a fair trial at that distance." Though Madison was commissioned a colonel in the Orange County militia on October 2, 1775, and did participate in some drills and marches, he did not serve in the field and was in no sense a veteran of the Revolutionary War. As stated clearly in his autobiography, his feeble health and liability to sudden attacks prevented him from entering the army.[26]

As Virginia more and more openly defied British authority, there were many daring and adventurous things for young men to do. In April 1775 six hundred militiamen, possibly including Madison, gathered at Fredricksburg and threatened to march on Williamsburg to recover a large quantity of powder Governor Dunmore had taken from the colony's magazine and stored on board a British warship. Had the militiamen marched, an armed clash would almost certainly have followed. Four Virginia delegates to Congress—Peyton Randolph, Edmund Pendleton, Richard Henry Lee, and George Washington—fearing civil war, persuaded the men to return home. Patrick Henry resolved nevertheless to take action, and on May 2, when public opinion was inflamed by news of the bloodshed at Lexington and Concord, he assembled the Hanover County militia and marched toward Williamsburg, determined to force Dunmore to pay for the gunpowder; he apparently knew he could not retrieve it from under the guns of the warship. At the same time, the militia of Albemarle (Jefferson's home) and Orange counties, also anxious to act against Dunmore, mustered and marched. According to one of the Albemarle men, Philip Mazzei, in an account written long after the event, James Madison and one of his brothers were among the Orange militiamen. Mazzei may have had in mind a fall gathering of militia to repulse British landings around Hampton, but in any case, Madison marched at least once as a revolutionary militiaman.[27]

When the Orange men discovered Henry had received royal money for the powder, they adopted resolves applauding his action and opposing any effort to return the money to the King's treasury. The committee then, on May 9, approved a letter to Henry, probably drafted by Madison, proclaiming among other things that "we take this occasion . . . to give it as our opinion, that the blow struck in the Massachusetts government [at Lexington and Concord] is a hostile attack on this and every other colony, and a sufficient warrant to use violence and reprisal, in all cases where it may be expedient for our security and welfare." Madison then hurried off a letter to Bradford, telling him of these events and castigating tidewater gentlemen who, he thought, held back from vigorous measures because they feared reprisals on their property by British warships or other forces commanded by Dunmore. These gentlemen, said the hotheaded young Madison, displayed "a pusilanimity little comporting with their professions or the name of Virginia." Madison then seems to have ridden with the two letters to Port Royal, where on May 11 he delivered them both to Henry on his way to the meeting of Congress in Philadelphia. Henry responded to the committee letter, thanking the committee for its support, and carried the letter to Bradford on to Philadelphia.[28]

Madison's zeal for the patriot cause left him suspicious of anyone who showed, or seemed to show, the slightest backwardness or caution. Bradford wrote him, for example, that rumors were rife in Philadelphia that Benjamin Franklin, just returned from ten years' residence in England, "came rather as a spy than as a friend, and that he means to discover our weak side and make his peace with the minister [Lord North] by discovering it to him." Madison swallowed this, and likewise was willing to believe that Richard Bland, a Virginia delegate to Congress and long a foe of British oppression in America, had "turned traitor and fled from Philadelphia" for love of money. "Little did I ever expect to hear," wrote Madison, "that Jeremiah's Doctrine that 'the heart of man is deceitful above all things and desperately wicked' was exemplified in the celebrated Dr. Franklin. . . . It appears to me that the bare suspicion of his guilt amounts very nearly to a proof of its reality. If he were the man he formerly was . . . his conduct . . . on this critical occasion could have left no room for surmise or distrust. . . . His behavior would have been explicit and his Zeal warm and conspicious." Madison feared that "some Golden prospects will be opened to the Congress by the ministry before they make their ultimate appeal to the Sword. A prospect that could captivate the heart of a Franklin could almost make me shudder for the tempted." Madison was confident, nonetheless, that the "Integrity and attachment to Liberty [of Congress] both in their private and Confederate capacities must triumph over Jealousy itself."[29]

Actually, Franklin had already withstood severe temptation from the ministry in London, and acted inconspicuously for a month after his return to America in May 1775, while he tried in vain to convince two influential American Loyalists, his son, Governor William Franklin of New Jersey, and his long-time friend Joseph Galloway, to support the patriot cause. Franklin himself was at least as vigorous a foe of Great Britain as Madison, as he soon proved. Bland had left Congress because of ill health, and in July was completely exonerated of any taint of wrongdoing by the Virginia Revolutionary Convention. The problems of rev-

olution and statecraft were obviously more complex than they appeared
to the ardent but inexperienced Madison. Significantly, though, he began
his participation in public affairs with an attachment to the cause of
liberty and independence so strong that tar and feathers seemed a proper
means of persuasion or punishment, and even the revered Franklin came
under swift suspicion for a brief failure to parade his zeal in public.

As if to give depth to his revolutionary spirit, Madison read avidly the
works of English radical Whig writers, and we may assume he read every
scrap on the crisis he could find in American pamphlets and newspapers.
He sought from Bradford, first, a copy of Adam Ferguson's *An Essay
on the History of Civil Society* (Edinburgh, 1767), and later, Joseph
Priestley's *An Essay on the First Principles of Government: and on the
Nature of Political, Civil and Religious Liberty* (London, 1768). Madison
asked as well for Josiah Tucker's *Tracts* which argued that "owning" the
colonies was a disadvantage to Great Britain, and Philip Furneaux's
Essay on Toleration, supporting the petitions of English dissenters for
greater religious liberty. Though Ferguson was himself a conservative
Whig and no friend of the American Revolution, his *Civil Society* explored corruptions in the Roman Empire which led to its decline, and
which, to a colonial reader, must have held ominous and obvious implications for Great Britain. Furneaux's essay extended the doctrine of religious liberty to its ultimate limit, arguing that a magistrate had no right
whatever to restrain expressions of conscience, and that the whole concept of blasphemous libel, supposing the good reputation of religion, like
that of government, needed the protection of laws, was inadmissible.
Madison's recent experience with persecution left him receptive to such
views, and Furneaux's reasoning foreshadowed that used by Madison
himself in 1776, 1785, and 1800 to defend freedom of expression.

Priestley, though, would have furnished Madison with the most immediately welcome propositions. He sought, he wrote, to set the thought
of such honored English writers as Locke, Sidney, and John Trenchard
"in a new or clearer point of light," exactly what we may suppose
Madison worked toward in his own mind. Priestley restated familiar
propositions about hopes for progress, the need for freedom, and the usefulness of a government responsive to the will of the people. Officers
were pictured as servants of a public capable of rational discussion and
intelligent choice. He insisted that taxes could be levied justly only with
the consent of those taxed, and that the administration of laws had to be
uniform and predictable. Priestley's *First Principles* was, for a practicing
revolutionist, an admirable "refresher course" in the meaning of liberty.
In reading it, Madison capped his training in the Whiggish dissenting
tradition, his main resource ever since he had first thought seriously
about problems of government.[30]

In Madison's last known letter before his election to the Virginia Convention of 1776, to Bradford on July 28, 1775, he hailed the stirring addresses and papers of the Second Continental Congress. "For true Eloquence," he said, they rivaled "the most applauded Oration of Tully himself." He also approved "The Preparations for War . . . every where going on in a most vigorous manner," and hoped that "Overtures" were already being made to secure desperately needed munitions from foreign powers. He approved, in short, the declarations and the climactic domestic and foreign measures that could have but one meaning: the country in which Madison lived was soon to declare itself a new, independent nation, the first in human history to do so in a deliberate, self-willed way. As the correspondence with Bradford makes clear, Madison sensed some of the earth-shaking significance of this, and he was passionately involved in helping it come to pass. From the uncertain, introspective, affectedly grave youth he had been in the year after he graduated from college, he had become a man consumed by a cause. He had henceforth his vocation: he was a nation builder. During the galvanizing years before 1776, when the great revolution in loyalty took place (what John Adams called the *real* American revolution), James Madison shared, emotionally and intellectually, a traumatic excitement vital to the founders of the new United States. By the time of the battles of Lexington and Concord, Madison had found the purpose and adopted the ideals that were to motivate and guide him during forty years in public life and twenty years as his country's authentic sage.[31]

CHAPTER V

Virginia Revolutionist

O N Thursday, April 25, 1776, perhaps one of those heart-lifting spring days in the Virginia Piedmont when the world seems boundless in prospect, the freeholders of Orange County met before the courthouse to choose "two of the most fit and able men" in the county to represent it at the general convention to assemble at Williamsburg eleven days later. Everyone knew the convention was especially important: it was time for Virginia to declare formally what for a year had been true in fact, that Britain no longer ruled the Old Dominion, and to draft a new frame of government. Events during the winter of 1775–6 made it virtually certain the May convention would take these steps. British warships had cannonaded and partly burned the city of Norfolk on New Year's Day 1776. Tom Paine's *Common Sense* had been disabusing Americans of any vestiges of loyalty to the British Crown. "A few more of such flaming arguments as were exhibited at Falmouth [Maine] and Norfolk, added to the sound doctrine and unanswerable reasoning contained in the pamphlet *Common Sense*," wrote George Washington, "will not leave numbers at a loss to decide upon the propriety of a separation."[1]

The delegates elected in Orange County were twenty-five-year-old James Madison and his thirty-six-year-old uncle, William Moore. The delegates to the previous conventions had been Thomas Barbour and James Taylor, experienced leaders in county affairs and lifelong friends of the Madisons. The shift to the two younger men had little political significance, however, because all four served on the county Committee of Safety, where the shift in representation had probably been planned beforehand. Thus, as the hundreds of men stopped gossiping and drinking long enough to come before the candidates and Sheriff Barbour to shout out their choices, there was little sense of contest. By the end of the day, Madison knew he was to be a representative of Orange County, a career which, though often interrupted, did not end until at age seventy-eight he was a delegate to the Virginia Constitutional Convention of 1829.

Shortly after the first of May, Madison and William Moore began the long trip to Williamsburg, probably Madison's first to the little village, capital of Virginia since 1699. The journey began amid unseasonable, crop-damaging frost and drought, but as the two men moved from the red soil of the upcountry into the gray sand of the tidewater, it began to rain. After four days of steady downpour the farmers were relieved, but the travelers were harassed by quagmires and rivers or ponds swelling from every brook or low place in the road. Glad at last to be in the crowded town, and two days late for the opening of the convention, the Orange delegates found that the members had already replaced the defunct House of Burgesses as the colony's legislative body, and had elected Edmund Pendleton their presiding officer. Madison was doubtless pleased to find this trusted family connection and friend in a position of influence. Pendleton had won election as convention president over the opposition of the more radical Patrick Henry and his followers, and as chairman of the colony's Committee of Safety, had, in effect, already replaced the fugitive Dunmore as chief executive. A member of the old House of Burgesses since 1752 and chairman of the previous convention, held in December 1775, he clearly was the man Virginians most trusted to carry out the difficult tasks of revolutionary government. He and Madison came early to admire each other and were on the same side of nearly every major political question save Church establishment until Pendleton died in 1803.[2]

Other old leaders present were Robert Carter Nicholas, long the treasurer of the colony and foremost among those who opposed independence at this time, and Richard Bland, the intrepid, no-longer-suspect foe of British oppression in America. Slightly less venerable were John Blair, Archibald Cary, Paul Carrington, and William Cabell. Present as well were many men in the prime of life who were to be Madison's associates in Virginia public life for years to come: Meriwether Smith, Joseph Jones, Samuel McDowell, Issac Zane, Thomas Mann Randolph, Thomas Ludwell Lee, Bolling Starke, Mann Page, Dudley Digges, and of course, Patrick Henry. Two delegates, Edmund Randolph and Henry Tazewell, were younger than Madison and likewise destined to have notable public careers. Missing in person but very much present in the thoughts and proceedings of the convention members were General Washington and the Virginia delegates to the Continental Congress who were soon to sign the Declaration of Independence: Richard Henry Lee,

Carter Braxton, Benjamin Harrison, George Wythe, Thomas Nelson, Francis Lightfoot Lee, and Thomas Jefferson. In taking his place in the convention, Madison accepted habits and traditions which he was to retain and admire as long as he lived.[3]

The convention had first to act on formal resolves such as those from Cumberland County voters, who had instructed their representatives to "Use your best endeavors that the delegates which are sent to the General Congress be instructed immediately to cast off the British yoke." Madison knew the people of Orange County expected the same of him. All the delegates, except Nicholas and perhaps a few others, firmly favored independence, but many, including Patrick Henry, thought a formal confederation of the colonies and an alliance, or at least an assurance of one, with a friendly foreign power (obviously France) should precede a declaration of independence. Otherwise, what would prevent the colonies from falling out with each other? Or Britain from organizing a partition of North America by European powers, as had recently happened with Poland? The sentiment for independence soon overcame the hesitation and strategies of delay, though, and on May 15 the convention resolved unanimously that the Virginia delegates to Congress "be instructed to propose to that respectable Body to declare the United Colonies free and independent states." As a result, Richard Henry Lee moved in Congress on June 7 that independence be declared, and Thomas Jefferson drafted the famous document proclaimed on July 4, 1776.[4]

The convention cast aside the last symbol of British dominion in Virginia when, still in session, on July 5, 1776, it deleted from the Anglican prayer service petitions that God save the King, and every other reference to the royal family, and substituted prayers for "the magistrates of the commonwealth." Between May and July, Purdie's *Virginia Gazette* carried on its masthead first the ancient seal of the colony of Virginia, then a plain box containing the words "The Thirteen United Colonies. United, we stand—Divided, we fall," and finally the new seal of the commonwealth over the motto "Don't tread on me." Virginians were no longer subjects of George III.[5]

Madison took no part in the floor debate, but he approved the resolution for independence and went the next day to the great celebration at Waller's Grove. Since some gentlemen of the community had "made a handsome collection for the purpose of treating the soldiery," such companies as were in town paraded before the convention delegates, and then everyone "partook of the refreshments." After the resolve for independence was read, toasts were given to "The American independent states, the Grand Congress . . . and to General Washington." "The Union Flag of the American States waved upon the Capitol during the whole of [the] ceremony," the newspapers reported, and "the evening concluded with illuminations and other demonstrations of joy; every one seeming

pleased that the domination of Great Britain was now at an end." A
fast proclaimed by Congress for the next day gave too-indulgent cele-
brators a chance to recover and others an opportunity to repair to
Bruton Parish church, where the zealously patriotic rector preached
from the text "Harken ye, all Judah! . . . Be not afraid, nor dismayed,
by reason of this great multitude, for the battle is not yours, but God's."
We may imagine Madison stirred and exhausted by these celebrations
as he had not been since the excited demonstrations against the Coercive
Acts in Philadelphia two years earlier.[6]

The resolve calling for independence had been followed by one that
"a committee be appointed to prepare a DECLARATION OF RIGHTS, and
such a plan of government as will be most likely to maintain peace and
order in this colony, and secure substantial and equal liberty to the
people." A large committee, including Patrick Henry and other notable
delegates, was named to draft documents. The next day Madison and two
others were added, and on May 18 Pendleton added the recently arrived
George Mason to the committee. A wealthy planter, often aloof from
colonial politics, Mason was nevertheless widely acknowledged as having the most profound understanding of republican government of any
man in Virginia. Madison and Jefferson always deferred to him as their
mentor in matters of political theory. Thus he assumed immediately the
leadership of the committee, and his proposals became the basis for the
famous declaration of rights and plan of government subsequently
adopted by the convention. Presumably Madison did not know the stout,
gouty Mason until his late appearance in Williamsburg, but from that
moment on, Madison's admiration for the older man scarcely ever
wavered.

Jefferson, Richard Henry Lee, and others sent proposals to aid the
committee in its novel task of drawing a rational frame of government
for free men. It also had available John Adams' *Thoughts on Government* and the works of the great European theorists. Perhaps the shy,
scholarly Madison was able occasionally to make small contributions on
particular points, though as he often acknowledged, his lack of seniority
prevented him from playing more than a minor role. On many clauses of
the declaration of rights and the plan of government, members differed
very little; except for weakening the executive and otherwise repudiating
devices associated with British tyranny, the members showed themselves
generally satisfied with the mode of government long in use in the
colony.

The historic first sentence of the declaration—". . . all men are by
nature equally free and independent, and have certain inherent rights, of
which they cannot by any compact deprive or divest their posterity . . ."
—was, however, objected to by Nicholas and others "as being the fore-

runner or pretext of civil convulsion." What would prevent this clause, they asked, from being used by slaves to claim their freedom? Or non-freeholders to claim the right to vote? Thomas Ludwell Lee wrote in the midst of the debates of "a certain set of Aristocrats . . . monsters . . . [who] have kept us at Bay on the first line which declares all men to be born equally free and independent." They sought to perpetuate in Virginia what Lee termed "their execrable system," which would founder on that famous first line. Pendelton, as usual, made the key conciliating suggestion, by proposing that the phrase "when they enter into a state of society" be added after the word "which." Thus, since in Virginia political thought of that time, slaves were held to be outside "a state of society," the declaration would not apply to them. Madison undoubtedly favored the broad declaration proposed by Mason; whether his own instinct for conciliation, later so characteristic of his politics, caused him at this early date to support Pendleton's strategem is not known.[7]

Madison did, however, play a key role in one liberalization of the declaration of rights. The drafting committee adopted an article by Mason on religious freedom which stated that since reason and conviction, not force and violence, governed belief, "all men shou'd enjoy the fullest Toleration in the Exercise of Religion, according to the Dictates of Conscience." Mason thus expressed the enlightened view opposing religious persecution widely current in the Western world, at least since John Locke's famous *Letters on Toleration* (first published in 1667). Madison's experience at Princeton and his struggle against persecution of Baptists in Virginia had convinced him that "toleration" was an invidious concept. It was, as Thomas Paine later put it, "not the opposite of intolerance, but . . . the counterfeit of it. Both are despotisms. The one assumes to itself the right of withholding liberty of conscience, the other of granting it." Madison therefore sought to have the noxious word stricken from the declaration and to prepare the way for complete liberty of conscience and separation of church and state in Virginia.

When the convention took up the article on religion, Madison apparently persuaded Patrick Henry to propose that its main clause be changed to read "all men are equally entitled to the full and free exercise of [religion] according to the dictates of Conscience; and therefore that no man or class of man ought, on account of religion to be invested with peculiar emoluments or privileges." Since this clause, if adopted, would have wiped out the establishment of the Anglican Church, it alarmed enough men to cause its defeat. Forced to abandon the premature effort at disestablishment, Madison offered another amendment, declaring that "all men are equally entitled to enjoy the free exercise of religion, according to the dictates of conscience, unpunished and unrestrained by the magistrate, Unless the preservation of equal liberty and the existence of the State are manifestly endangered." This change evidently satisfied the convention, and on the motion of Pendleton, who probably was glad enough to accept a general statement not directly attacking the establishment he stoutly defended, the key part of Madison's revision was adopted. The article thus read: "That religion, or the duty which we owe our Creator, and the manner of discharging it, can be directed only by reason and conviction, not by force and violence; and therefore, all men are equally entitled to the free exercise of religion, according to the dictates of conscience; and that it is the mutual duty of all to practise Christian forbearance, love, and charity towards each other."[8]

Madison's revision, after the defeat of the disestablishment clause, probably caused no great controversy in the convention; Pendleton's support is strong evidence the pro-Church forces did not particularly object to it. Madison wrote late in life that Mason had used the word "Toleration" in the original draft because it appeared in the English code, but that "on a suggestion from myself [he] readily exchanged phraseology excluding it." The change was crucial, however, because it made liberty of conscience a substantive right, the inalienable privilege of all men equally, rather than a dispensation conferred as privilege by established authorities. Madison had made possible complete liberty of belief or unbelief, and the utter separation of church and state. He demonstrated, too, the tendency during the American Revolution to give parochial statements of "the rights of Englishmen" a more universal expression, in effect making them relevant to all men everywhere. As Madison wrote late in life, he proposed the change "with a view, more particularly to substitute for the idea expressed by the term 'toleration,' an absolute and equal right of all to the exercise of religion according to the dictates of conscience." George Bancroft called Madison's amendment "the first achievement of the wisest civilian in Virginia."[9]

One must not, though, imagine the convention only as a forum for debating great constitutional questions. The immediate broke in upon the delegates from all sides; war and rumors of war swirled about them. While the convention sat, Lord Dunmore moved his motley collection of soldiers, refugees, and runaway slaves northward from Norfolk to Gwynn's Island in Chesapeake Bay. Virginia militia pursued and eventually drove him away. At the same time, his ships blockaded Chesapeake Bay, capturing vessels bringing desperately needed supplies to Virginia. The Virginia Committee of Safety made strenuous efforts to erect foundries and salt works, manufacture saltpeter, collect scrap metal, establish a powder mill, and otherwise provide the means of war. General Charles Lee, continental commander in the Southern Department, came through Virginia seeking aid for his campaign in South Carolina. The ill-trained troops, called by a veteran chaplain "the most profane and disorderly of any I ever met with," were alternately the bane and glory of the harried civilian leaders. In an effort to improve discipline, the convention declared on June 24 that "gaming is at best an idle amusement, when carried to excess is the parent of avarice, dissipation, profaneness, and every other passion which can debase the human mind, particularly improper at this time, when our important struggle for liberty and freedom renders the practice of the most rigid virtue necessary." The delegates then resolved that the commander of the continental troops in Virginia ban "profane swearing, all manner of gaming, as well as every other vice and immorality." One can imagine the guffaws and chortles such piety likely called forth in the camps around Williamsburg.[10]

To these local concerns were added the even more nerve-wracking rumors, favorable and unfavorable, from around the world. Newspapers carried exaggerated accounts of the tens of thousands of Hessians and other mercenaries Britain had hired to crush and despoil the rebellious colonies. Equally wild stories of an imminent French declaration of war on England raised American hopes. Every letter from the West Indies told of huge amounts of cheap munitions at the French and Dutch islands, waiting only for ships to carry them—all this while British warships patroled Chesapeake Bay. In June came news of the crushing defeat of the American forces in Canada. Virginia also had to bear the "insult," as Madison wrote his father, of a Maryland request that she give an obnoxious Tory governor safe passage to return to England. Fanciful reports of Indian massacres and of a British-organized alliance of all the great nations of Europe to sack and partition North America received a credence made possible only by the emotion and excitement of revolution. Madison had a good taste early in his career of the distraction chaotic events and wild rumors can cause in councils of state.

Madison nevertheless found time to write Bradford for information about the constitutions of Pennsylvania and of Connecticut, "which might be useful to . . . a member of Convention." Madison also sought advice from Pendleton and Henry about the settlement of an estate in which his father was involved. To keep his constituents informed, the young delegate used a slave named Troilus as a messenger to Orange, and another time sent a letter by the once-persecuted Elijah Craig, a Baptist minister representing the interests of his denomination at the convention. Madison also reported to his father that bills of exchange brought from Orange were severely discounted in Williamsburg, and that most of the members of the convention "seem determined to go home to their Harvests . . . though it is obvious the Business will be by no means finished by that time [July]." As for his fellow delegate Uncle William Moore, he was "well as usual [and] grunts as much and eats as hearty as any man in Williamsburg."[11]

When Madison left Williamsburg after the convention adjourned on July 5, he sensed with a clearness unimaginable four years earlier a congenial and challenging task in life. He had taken sure steps along the customary path toward a political career in Virginia. As the scion of a substantial family, he had a firm political base. Moreover, he had sat honorably in a historic convention, whose members, as the years passed, would more and more acquire a hallowed place in Virginia history. His associations with Pendleton, Henry, Randolph, and many others placed him strategically among the men of influence in the new commonwealth. Though diffident and shy, he had supported a rising republicanism in Virginia politics, and he had impressed the foremost republican theoretician of the convention, George Mason. Events conspired, it seemed, to heighten Madison's zeal to be a nation builder and to increase his opportunities to be a good one. One doubts that even the torpor of a July journey under the Virginia sun could have wilted his excitement. We may imagine a prideful family greeting a much-matured son when twenty-five-year-old James Madison reached Montpelier.

A mood of watchful expectation prevailed in Orange County during the summer of 1776. Congress considered weighty matters of confederation and foreign alliance, while Washington's army in New York received harsh and nearly disastrous lessons in warfare from General William Howe's heavily reinforced British troops. But as Madison read the newspapers and letters from Bradford about these events, and probably took his annual visit to Berkeley Warm Springs, he thought mainly of the first session of the Virginia legislature in which, as a member of the 1776 convention, he was to sit during the fall.

Madison and William Moore arrived in Williamsburg on October 14, a week after the House of Delegates had been called to order, and were appointed immediately to the Committee on Religion. The committee had already received the first of many appeals to end religious establishment in Virginia. Some inhabitants of strongly Presbyterian Prince Edward County petitioned the Assembly to fulfill the plain implication of the clause on religion in the declaration of rights and relieve them from "a long night of Ecclesiastical bondage." They beseeched that "without delay, all Church establishments . . . be pulled down, and every tax upon conscience and private judgment be abolished . . . [that] Virginia [may become] an asylum for free inquiry, knowledge, and the virtuous of every denomination." Madison in fact may have had a hand in this petition, probably drawn by his close friend Samuel Stanhope Smith, then at work founding Hampden-Sydney Academy. Madison had been a trustee of the academy since November 1775 and his brother William was an early student there.[12]

Thomas Jefferson took the lead in proposing the disestablishment, but friends of the Church, led by Edmund Pendleton, opposed effectively. Jefferson wrote, referring to this session of the Assembly, that "taken

all-in-all [Pendleton] was the ablest man in debate I have ever met with.
. . . He was cool, smooth, and persuasive . . . never vanquished; for if he
lost the main battle, he returned upon you, and regained so much of it as
to make it a drawn one, by dexterous manoeuvres, skirmishes in detail,
and the recovery of small advantages which, little singly, were important altogether. . . . Add to this, that he was one of the most virtuous
and benevolent of men, the kindest friend, the most amiable and pleasant
of companions," and you had the measure of his stature in the
assembly.[13]

Two other senior members of the Committee on Religion, Carter
Braxton and Robert C. Nicholas, were also staunch friends of the establishment. After inconclusive deliberations, on November 9 the assembly
discharged the committee without receiving a report. Ten days of debate
in the Committee of the Whole led to a statement of principles such as
Jefferson and Madison favored, but no bill. Debates in the Committee of
the Whole are not recorded, but the delaying tactic bears a Pendletonian
stamp. The statement of principles—abolishing British statutes of religious
bigotry, supporting the desire of dissenters to be free of church taxes,
and declaring against state support of the clergy while promising to let
the Church retain its substantial properties—went to another committee
including Madison, which reported a bill substantially disestablishing the
Church. Pendleton reduced the key clause, withdrawing state pay to the
clergy, to a mere year's suspension—but once suspended the pay was
never reinstated, so the net effect was disestablishment.[14]

Madison's shyness and inexperience prevented him from taking a forward role in the "battle of titans, subtle and calm, with all the amenities
of cultured behavior but deadly nevertheless," but he undoubtedly took
Jefferson's side, and learned prodigiously about debate and legislative
procedure as well. He also watched Jefferson strike against the law of
entail, plan to revise the statutes of Virginia, and otherwise define the
social reforms needed to stamp upon Virginia society at large the principles of the American Revolution. Under royal government, Jefferson
wrote, Virginia law "had many very vicious points," so he was persuaded
"that our whole code must be reviewed, adopted to our republican form
of government; and now that we had no negatives of Councils, Governors, and Kings to restrain us from doing right, it would be corrected,
in all its parts, with a single eye to reason, and the good of those for
whose government it was framed." Madison's persistent effort over the
next ten years to enact this ambitious plan leaves little doubt that his own
understanding of the nature of the revolution in Virginia agreed with
Jefferson's.[15]

Generally, though, Madison's work in Williamsburg was routine. As
he served on the standing Committee of Privileges and Elections, and on
special committees to settle claims against the state arising from Lord

Dunmore's war against the Indians in 1774, to prepare a letter to the Virginia delegates to Congress, and to examine the enrolled bills, he began to acquire the skills and habits of a legislator. In these tasks, his scholarly, well-disciplined mind, zeal for the revolution, effectiveness in conversation, and skill in drafting papers enough impressed his senior colleagues for them within a year to elect him to the governor's council. He surely sensed the good impression he had made, and left Williamsburg in late December eager to continue his public career.[16]

As far as we know, James Madison spent the year 1777 at home. In an event unique in the fifty years during which he stood for elections in Orange County, his neighbors defeated him in the annual canvass for the Assembly held at the courthouse on April 24, 1777. According to his own third-person account:

> In the election of Delegates to the Legislature for . . . 1777, he was an unsuccessful candidate. Previous to the Revolution the election of the County representatives was as in England, septennial, and it was as there, the usage for the Candidates to recommend themselves to the voters, not only by personal solicitation, but by the corrupting influence of spirituous liquors, and other treats having a like tendency. Regarding these as equally inconsistent with the purity of moral and of republican principles; and anxious to promote, by his example, the proper reform, he trusted to the new views of the subject which he hoped would prevail with the people; whilst his competitors adhered to the old practice. The consequence was that the election went against him: his abstinence being represented as the effect of pride or parsimony.

Unwilling to concede the victory of these antirepublican forces, Madison's backers petitioned the legislature to annul the election. The winner was one Charles Porter, a landowner, tavernkeeper, and eventually a veteran of seven years in the Assembly, despite what Madison termed "deficient pretentions." He had, the petitioners alleged, "made use of bribery and corruption." The Committee on Elections appointed commissioners to investigate, but dismissed the petition when by June 9 no proof of the charges had been presented. From the rather cursory attention given the petition, one suspects the Assembly could ill-afford to unseat a member for doing what most of the House had probably done to secure their own elections.[17]

Madison continued, however, to take part in the revolutionary government of Orange County. In late March 1777, near the courthouse, two travelers, one a French officer in the Continental army, and the other "a man of decent figure," happened upon a boisterous fellow, one Benjamin Haley, who abused the Committee of Safety and swore his allegiance to George III. Alarmed, the travelers informed the committee. Nothing could be done, however, since the travelers could not remain to testify, and the committee no longer had its summary jurisdiction of two years before. As the two men resumed their journey, the imprudent roisterer repeated his oath to the Crown before a larger company, and was promptly clapped in jail, where he refused for five hours to post bail. Madison took the whole affair very seriously and asked his father, then in Fredericksburg, to "take the advice of some Gentlemen skilled in the Law, on the most proper and legal mode of proceeding against him." A severe anti-Tory law, passed with Madison's assent in the October 1776 session of the legislature, provided that offenders such as Haley might be fined £20,000 and imprisoned for five years, but the Orange court let him off with token punishments—a 12s. fine and one hour's imprisonment. Either revolutionary zeal in Orange had cooled since the harsh proceedings of 1775 against the unfortunate Parson Wingate, or the court thought Haley too harmless a rowdy to take seriously, ex-Delegate Madison to the contrary notwithstanding. Beyond this, of Madison's year of involuntary retirement we know only that he supervised the bleeding of a slave who had a badly infected arm, and that with 104 other Orange County planters he petitioned the legislature to limit by law the amount of tobacco any farmer could produce, in order to encourage "the raising and Manufacturing of those Articles which are necessary for the accommodation of our Army and the Prosecution of the War." The Assembly declined to refer the petition to committee.[18]

Governor Patrick Henry, the members of his overworked Council of State, and the Virginia House of Delegates, however, remembered Madison's service in the Assembly, when a vacancy occurred in the governor's council in November 1777. "James Madison the younger, of Orange, Esq.," received 61 votes in the House of Delegates to 42 for Meriwether Smith. News of the election was hurried to Montpelier; Madison packed promptly; and after a journey of less than a week, took his seat at the council table in Williamsburg on January 14, 1778, a clear, pleasant day with temperatures in the fifties, according to the weather journal kept by his cousin. He spent from then until July 1778, from November 1778 until July 1779, and from October 1779 until about the end of that year in Williamsburg as a member of the council.[19]

When Madison entered the council chamber in the capitol building (a plain structure with a columned, two-story portico—the quite different building now at Colonial Williamsburg is a restoration of the "old" capitol, which burned in 1747), he may have been somewhat awed and nervous. In the chair sat the redoubtable Patrick Henry, ill-suited to the meticulous tasks of war administration, but then, as he would be for ten more years, the most powerful, popular figure in Virginia politics. Madison had known Henry for at least two years and had looked upon him as *the* great spokesman and leader of the revolution. Henry again and again espoused causes Madison supported, and his oratory must have thrilled the new councilor, as it did nearly everyone who came within its range. Yet, in Madison's months of service with Henry, he very likely began to sense the limitations that in a few years were to estrange the two men. Henry came to stand for all that Madison detested in public life; he was, in Madison's epithet, "a forensic member," skilled at harangue but utterly neglectful of the labor of legislation and always ready to trim his sails to the popular winds he sensed so uncannily. Madison's later strictures on Henry and the orator's notorious aversion to disciplined labor were probably the source of exaggerated stories that Madison wrote Henry's state papers during his term as governor. Like the other councilors, Madison helped plan and draft papers, but there is no reason to suppose Henry was a mere figurehead. He was, rather, a willful, careless, somewhat vain, difficult man, who nevertheless had a steadfast zeal and a supremely persuasive voice still of great value to the revolution.

The councilors present when Madison took his seat were Dudley Digges, John Blair, Nathaniel Harrison, and David Jameson. Digges, from an old tidewater family, was, at age sixty, near the end of a long public career as a legislator, militia officer, and revolutionist. Blair, forty-six years old, had already had a distinguished judicial career, and would subsequently serve as rector of the College of William and Mary, member of the Federal Convention of 1787, and associate justice of the United States Supreme Court (1789–1796). Harrison was nearly seventy, but in addition to being on the council, would serve eight more years in the state Senate before his death. Jameson, at twenty-one, was six years younger than Madison, and judging from their correspondence after Madison went to Congress, they had much in common. An absent councilor, John Page of Rosewell (Jefferson's close friend), became an intimate and a political ally of Madison's during a long public career, including terms as United States Representative (1789–1797) and governor of Virginia (1803–1805). The council minutes shed no light on the disputes and discussions among these men, but since the Virginia constitution permitted the governor to act only with the advice of his council, they were forced to work together and reach agreement if anything was to be done. Furthermore, though the executive powers were in theory very restricted, the exigencies of war placed important matters in the hands of the council. Madison and his colleagues had plenty to do and played a major role in the conduct of war and revolution in Virginia.

The business of Madison's first day on the council is revealing. It first approved a purchase, costing £100 (Virginia paper currency), of provisions for the army. Next, in response to a pitiful letter from Washington, lamenting that his army would *"Starve Disolve or Disperse"* unless it received food immediately, Henry and the council ordered that "Eight or ten thousand Hogs and several thousand fine Beeves" be driven from northwestern Virginia "to Camp in the most Expeditious Manner." At the same time, galleys were designated to seize 2,600 bushels of salt from the works along Chesapeake Bay to be sent to the army, presumably to cure the meat after it had reached camp on hoof. These orders seem simple and urgent enough, but behind them were many tangled problems: disputes between state and Continental supply agents; the power of Congress, the army, and the states to impress goods and services needed for the war; difficulties in purchasing supplies with inflated currency; and increasing resistance, after more than two years of strife, to making sacrifices for the war effort.

The council then approved a letter Henry had drafted about Virginia's vast western empire, which at this time included, according to her claim, the states of West Virginia and Kentucky as well as all of the Northwest Territory. Two weeks before Madison became a councilor, George Rogers Clark, acting for the State of Virginia, had set out on his spectacularly successful expedition to capture the British posts in the Illinois country. Now the council approved the dispatch of David Rogers and thirty men at double pay to go to Pittsburgh and down the Ohio and Mississippi rivers to New Orleans to escort some badly needed supplies back to Virginia. Rogers also carried letters to the Spanish governor at New Orleans, suggesting, among other things, that the Gulf Coast between Pensacola and Mobile might be "united . . . to the Confederation of the United States of America" to help destroy British power in the region. The Virginia expeditions in the Mississippi valley challenged the plans of Congress, the claims of other states, and the speculations of rival land companies, all matters long destined to occupy Madison's attention. The overtures to the Spaniards were either disarmingly bold or unbelievably naïve, considering their own interest in the west Florida coast, and only complicated Franklin's efforts to form an alliance with France: pressing American interests in the Mississippi valley would dampen the zeal of the Bourbon monarchs of Spain and France to aid the upstart nation. In taking his seat on the Council of State in the seemingly provincial town of Williamsburg, Madison in fact found himself entangled almost immediately with most of the major, persisting problems of the revolution. His day-to-day work there gave him a practical grasp of these issues a mere observer, or even a legislator, would not likely attain.

A contributing reason for Madison's election to the council appeared in the letter Henry wrote to the governor of Louisiana on January 14, 1778. Henry explained in a postscript that a French version of the letter sent earlier contained some faults in translation. When the letter was dispatched "we [had] no persons sufficiently acquainted with the French language . . . [therefore] the meaning of [the letter] was omitted." The errors in translation had been spotted by the new councilor, who continued to serve as the French expert on the council until March 25, when the news of the French alliance persuaded the council to hire the delightful Italo-American Charles Bellini to handle the "growing communication with foreigners." Though Madison was always embarrassed by what he thought was a "Scotch burr" imparted to his spoken French by his teachers Robertson and Witherspoon (poor pronunciation caused by a lack of oral practice of any kind was probably the trouble), he read French easily and accurately. Such a talent and its quick use in the council doubtless heightened Madison's scholarly image in Williamsburg, and hastened his acceptance in the cultivated circle of Jefferson, George Wythe, John Page, Bellini, and the faculty of the College of William and Mary.[20]

Madison was fortunate to find upon reaching Williamsburg that the Reverend James Madison (1749–1812), his second cousin, had recently been chosen president of the college and therefore had at his disposal "the President's house," a pleasant steep-roofed, Georgian building with high, many-paned windows, which still stands today in the tree-shaded college yard, much as it must have done two centuries ago. At the Reverend Madison's "earnest invitation," Councilor Madison took "lodgings in a Room of the President's house which is a much better accommodation than I could have promised myself." (Rooms in Williamsburg were always scarce when the assembly was in session.) The educator-clergyman provided such good room and board that at the end of Madison's service on the council he felt he could repay "singular favours" only by supplying his host with a large quantity of Orange County flour. Earlier the councilor had asked his father to send dried fruit (of which the Reverend Madison was especially fond) and other "such rarities as our part of the Country furnishes" in order to return "the Culinary favours I receive."[21]

In the way of an Enlightenment scholar and gentleman, the Reverend Madison sought universal knowledge and had a special interest in the natural sciences. He was elected to the American Philosophical Society in 1779, for example, upon submitting a careful journal of the wind, atmospheric pressure, and temperature in Williamsburg for a period of fourteen months (half of the time, his councilor kinsman was living with him and presumably sharing in his experiments). Jefferson made simultaneous observations in Albemarle County to determine the effect of altitude and distance from the sea on the weather. The Reverend Madison concluded as a result of his observations that the circulation of dry air to carry off moisture from the skin had more to do with the sense of coolness a person felt than did a few degrees change in temperature. With American pride, he noted that Benjamin Franklin had first written correctly on this question after he had observed wind and temperature readings on a hot day in Philadelphia. Thus, wrote the Reverend Madison, "Franklin sitting in his chair, like Newton reasoning upon the figure of the earth, could shew what must cost others infinite labour and fatigue." In June 1778 the Reverend Madison made elaborate preparations with David Rittenhouse to observe an eclipse of the sun shortly before noon on the twenty-fourth. In Williamsburg there was "total Darkness," resulting, the Reverend Madison wrote Jefferson, in "something awful in Appearance which all Nature assumed. You could not determine your most intimate Acquaintance at 20 yds. distance. Lightening Buggs were seen as at Night."[22]

Councilor Madison sat in session that morning wrangling over commissions for officers of a state volunteer battalion, as did John Page, who assisted the Reverend Madison in the celestial observations. The session must have been short, and we may suppose the councilor joined Page and the clergyman as they took notes on their telescope and chronometer readings. Even these crude observations, helpful in the eighteenth century in determining terrestial distances, must have seemed exciting to Councilor Madison, who probably observed with pleasure that two who were as active in public affairs as Rittenhouse and Jefferson and a devout clergyman were at the same time experimental scientists. Madison's own devotion to the Enlightenment ideal of progress and freedom through knowledge is evident in his eulogy of his second cousin: "He was particularly distinguished by a benevolence, a politeness of mind, and a courtesy of manner . . . [of] intellectual power and diversified learning. . . . He was a devoted friend of our Revolution and to the purest principles of a Government founded on the rights of man." Living with his learned kinsman and sharing in Williamsburg's intellectual "renaissance" helped make the values of the age of reason a way of life for Madison.[23]

Of Madison's routine in Williamsburg we know only of his faithful attendance at Council of State meetings at ten o'clock six mornings each week. From January through July 1778 he missed only one week in May and one day in June, when the minutes record that he was sick but in town. He also took care of such family and personal affairs as he could from his vantage point in the capital. He sent quinine for his mother's malaria, ordered two bearskins from Orange for a friend in Williamsburg, and wrote to straighten out a mix-up of his laundry with his father's. Each letter home contained, of course, the latest war news, some accurate, but much that reflected high hopes more than reality, such as a report that news of the battle of Saratoga might turn out Lord North's ministry. Madison also warned his father during the winter Washington's army spent at Valley Forge not to resign as county lieutenant. Such an act would be viewed by state authorities as "unfriendly" and as betraying "at least a want of patriotism and perserverance." Father and son worried over the education of William Madison, who, driven from Princeton to Hampden-Sydney to William and Mary by the fortunes of war, had to be withdrawn from the latter institution because, under a recent reorganization, only "the higher and rarer branches of Sciences" were to be taught there. Hence, Madison advised his father, in 1779, "Willey" should be "put under the instruction of Mr. Maury rather than suffer him to be idle at home . . . till he is prepared to receive a finish to his Education at this place." The Madisons' opinion of William and Mary had changed since James Madison's own entrance in the College of New Jersey ten years earlier.[24]

Like a busy politician, or perhaps a preoccupied scholar, Madison had trouble keeping track of his belongings in Williamsburg. He advertised in *The Virginia Gazette* in October 1779 that his twelve-year-old sorrel horse "14 hands high, with a hanging mane and switch tail" had strayed or been stolen "from the common of this city." He offered $100 to anyone returning the animal to him. Another theft (or misplacement?) furnished Madison with a favorite anecdote. Nicholas P. Trist set it down as he said Madison told it: "Did I ever tell you of the loss of my hat? 'No.' Well sir, I was staying at Bishop Madison's in Williamsburg (he was not yet Bishop, by the way), and my hat was stolen out of a window in which I had laid it. It was about a mile from the house to the palace, and I was kept from going to the latter for two days, by the impossibility of getting a hat of any kind. At last, however, I obtained one from a little Frenchman who sold snuff—very coarse—an extremely small crown and broad brim, and it was a subject of great merriment to my friends."[25]

Shortly after Madison's election to the council, Samuel Stanhope Smith wrote to congratulate him and to offer a change of pace: "Perhaps it may prove a relaxation to you in the midst of other business, to attend a few metaphisical [speculations]. I would not have troubled you on such subjects, if I had not known your taste for them, and your quick discernment of every error or mistake; and even of every hint that may lead to the discovery of any truth." After noting that "you have frequently attacked me on that knotty question of *liberty* and *necessity*," Smith undertook in a long dissertation to show that men did have freedom of will, because they were able to choose from among their conflicting motives and desires. Smith admitted he could not prove this syllogistically, but he thought it fully confirmed in the experience of mankind. Thus Smith expressed the Scottish common-sense philosophy he and Madison had learned from Witherspoon at Princeton.

Madison's reply is lost, but its argument is visible in Smith's next letter. "I have read over," he wrote, "your *theoretical* objections against the doctrine of moral liberty; for *practically* you seem to be one of its disciples. I remember the manner in which you have formerly ex-

pressed yourself upon that intricate subject." Madison had confronted
Smith with the reasoning of Jonathan Edwards and others that even
though men thought they chose freely from among conflicting impulses, in fact their choice or inclination was *determined*, whether they
were conscious of it or not, by a chain of antecedent forces over which
ultimately they had no control. Then Madison apparently conceded that
in practice he agreed with Smith that men exercised free will. Madison
thus revealed in "metaphysics" as in other kinds of inquiry little interest
in the hairsplitting polemics so dear to many of his contemporaries. He
was content instead to accept what were to him clear, practical, humane
postulates, even though logicians might confute them. His correspondence with Smith, reminding him of long and relatively fruitless discussions of "intricate subjects," may have confirmed an inclination (important to the practicing politician he had become) to shun syllogisms
at odds with common sense.[26]

   Thomas Jefferson's election, in June 1779, as governor of Virginia
began, as he and Madison both affirmed, an "intimacy" lasting until
Jefferson's death on July 4, 1826. During their brief meetings before 1779
the difference in their ages (in 1779 Jefferson was thirty-six and Madison
twenty-eight) and Jefferson's prominence and Madison's shyness inhib-
ited close association, but when the two were together daily at the
council table, they soon responded warmly and enthusiastically to each
other. Foremost, they shared a zeal for the revolution and for ordered
liberty. Both had a fondness for words and ideas and books that over
and over gave them reason to seek each other out for the sheer joy of
learning. To each the life of the mind was pre-eminent. Finally, they
shared a cultural heritage, a social grace, and a day-to-day way of life
which, taken together, made them in every way congenial. The growth
of their friendship is a principal theme in the life of each. We may
imagine it taking seed daily as Councilor Madison made intelligent suggestions about problems posed by Governor Jefferson, and as the older
man impressed the younger with the orderly, thoughtful execution of his
public trust. Soon, presumably, they came to share private interests and
enthusiasms, and more and more sought each other's unofficial company. By the time Madison left Williamsburg in December 1779, the two
men had formed the bonds of respect, devotion, and affection which
would make their collaboration both a joy to themselves and a boon to
the new nation.

   As the friendship with Jefferson flourished, Madison's political stature
increased. In April 1778 the freeholders of Orange County had elected
him to the House of Delegates. The vindicated Madison declined the seat
in order to remain on the Council of State, whereupon the freeholders
promptly chose the treat-providing Charles Porter to fill the vacancy.

In October 1778 Richard Henry Lee had proposed that Madison go with Philip Mazzei to Genoa to borrow money for Virginia's war effort; Madison refused this office, as he did every proposal throughout his life that he serve overseas, though he did take a leading role in supporting Mazzei for the mission. Eight months later Madison declined, for reasons unknown, to have his name placed in nomination as a Virginia delegate to the Continental Congress. In December 1779, however, he accepted appointment to Congress, along with three other new delegates chosen in response to pleas from Washington and others that Virginia send her "ablest and best men to Congress" to replace the "indifferent" representatives elected after Jefferson, Pendleton, Wythe, and others had returned to service within the state. Madison left Williamsburg promptly, expecting that he would soon be on his way to Philadelphia, where Congress, in defeat and despair and but a shadow of the inspirited body which had led the nation in 1775 and 1776, needed all the zeal and willingness to work and more that he might bring to it.[27]

The worst winter anyone could remember, however, kept Madison snowbound in Orange until March 1780. Continental troops marching to Charleston, South Carolina, in December were delayed by "the extreme cold [and] the deep snows." The next month the British Navy virtually had to suspend operations because of "tempestuous weather," and Washington's army, encamped at Morristown, New Jersey, suffered more than it had at Valley Forge from severe frosts and six-foot banks of snow. Madison took advantage of his enforced leisure to study the vexing problem of how to pay for the Revolutionary War. With sound financing, the army could be recruited and supplied, and the new governments could achieve respect and authority at home and abroad; without it, chaos and defeat threatened on all sides.

As early as January 1778, a shortage of money had made necessary clumsy taxes in kind. Madison explained to his father how the "one pair of Shoes, Stockings, Gloves or Mittens" to be furnished by every county for each soldier enlisted from it were to be gathered by the county lieutenant. The food and clothing needed by the army, though abundant in the countryside, increasingly could not be pried loose with offers of depreciated paper currency. Stringent laws that the currency be accepted at par led to evasion and hoarding. During 1778 and 1779 Continental and state paper currencies depreciated rapidly, falling in some cases to less then 1 per cent of their face value. Sensing that finances would be the most urgent question he would face in Philadelphia, Madison sat down before the fireplace at Montpelier, his books around him, to compose his thoughts and write an essay he entitled simply "Money."[28]

Madison first attacked the widely held opinion that the *quantity* of money in circulation determined its value, the degree of inflation, and the price level. Madison thus took direct issue with two books that were at his elbow and which had enormous prestige in America in 1780: David Hume's *Political Discourses* (1752) and Montesquieu's *Spirit of Laws* (1748). The basic error of these men, Madison concluded after a careful study of the examples of price fluctuations they cited from British and ancient history, was to suppose that the amount of money in a country represented its total real wealth and that therefore an increase in the money in circulation automatically diminished its value per unit if one assumed the country's real wealth remained the same. Contrarily, Madison asserted that the speed and assurance with which a country's paper currency might be redeemed in specie or any other easily negotiable media determined its value. Even the value of government-issued paper currency, Madison wrote, "Does not depend on its quantity. It depends on the credit of the state issuing it, and on the time of its redemption; and is no otherwise affected by the quantity, than as the quantity may be supposed to *endanger* or *postpone* the redemption."

Applying this axiom to the financial woes of Congress, Madison noted that with little or no specie, the new United States necessarily resorted to a paper currency undergirded only by a promised redemption at a later date. Though this paper was bound to be less valuable than specie, the degree of depreciation, Madison insisted, varied not with the amount printed but with the confidence the people had in its redemptibility at a specified time. The apparent fluctuation with quantity was caused by the diminished confidence that Congress would in fact be willing or able to redeem huge amounts as promised. As soon as a farmer, asked to accept Continental currency for, say, a wagonload of wheat, seriously doubted the time and degree of recovery in specie, or his ability to persuade a merchant to accept the paper at its face value, inflation began. Reviewing the history of revolutionary finance, Madison observed that "a train of sinister events during the early stages of war . . . contributed to increase the distrust of the public ability to fulfill their engagements. . . . The quantity [of paper currency] itself soon . . . begat a distrust of the *public disposition* to fulfill their engagements; as well as new doubts, in timid minds, concerning the issue of the contest. From that period, this cause of depreciation has been incessantly operating. . . . [The inflation] has not been the effect of the quantity, considered in itself, but considered as an omen of public bankruptcy."

Madison concluded with an attack on the resolve of Congress in September 1779 to discontinue large-scale emissions of paper currency while at the same time emitting loan-office certificates, bearing a large interest, for which the paper currency might be exchanged. The certificates only further undermined the public credit by increasing the public obligation without diminishing at all the doubts about the time and completeness of redemption. "No expedient," Madison asserted, "could perhaps have been devised more preposterous and unlucky. . . . Instead of paying off the capital to the public creditors, we give them an enormous interest to change the name of the bit of paper which expresses the sum due to them; and think it a piece of dexterity in finance, by *emitting loan-office certificates*, to elude the necessity of *emitting bills of credit.*"

In studying public finance sufficiently to feel confident in challenging the redoubtable Hume and the oracular Montesquieu, Madison developed a theory of money and credit accounting for economic and political realities and as applicable today as it was in 1780. He cast aside the enormous amount of vacuous theorizing and technical gibberish that befogged the study of money and credit in his day. The lessons of the essay on money made Madison sure only loans of hard money from abroad, the determination of Congress and the states to lay and collect taxes, a rise in public confidence that the war would be won, and faith that the United States would fulfill its obligations would provide the needed fiscal strength. Mere "pieces of dexterity" would never undergird public confidence. No understanding could have been more pertinent to the practical problems he was soon to face.[29]

CHAPTER VI

In the Continental Congress

I N early March 1780 the severe winter weather broke enough for Madison to start northward. Due to "the extreme badness of the roads and frequency of rains," Madison and his servant, Billey, were twelve days making the 260-mile trip, for which Madison received in inflated paper currency $20 a day, $2 per mile, and $122 for ferriage. Mud-spattered, weary, and frustrated from numerous waits while ferrymen stuggled to cross swollen streams or while teamsters hauled carriages out of the quagmire, Madison arrived in Philadelphia on March 18, 1780. He had not visited the nation's capital and principal city for nearly six years. He spent two days at a public inn and then took lodgings at the home of Mrs. Mary House at Fifth and Market streets, a block from the Pennsylvania State House (later Independence Hall), where Congress met on the second floor. The House lodgings, usually the residence of five or ten delegates to Congress, proved a happy choice for Madison; he quickly became good friends with the family and always stayed there, when in Philadelphia, until Mrs. House died in 1793. The members of the household included Mrs. House (an elderly widow), her son, Samuel (a merchant), her daughter, Eliza Trist, Eliza's husband, Nicholas, and their son, Hore Browse. Members of Congress there at different times during 1780 included James Duane, William Floyd, Robert R. Livingston, and John Morin Scott of New York; William Sharpe of North Carolina; Isaac Motte and John Mathews of South Carolina; and Joseph Jones, James Henry, and John Walker of the Virginia delegation. Largely through the "good sense and good heart" of Eliza Trist, this household became for Madison, as it did for Jefferson and many other Virginia politicians, a pleasant and relaxing home when in Philadelphia.[1]

Madison generally, though, found himself among strangers both in Philadelphia and in the halls of Congress. He probably knew the lone Virginia delegate in attendance, Cyrus Griffin, and he must have been glad to see his old Princeton tutor, William Churchill Houston, a delegate from New Jersey, but otherwise he went through the ordeal (as it probably was for one of Madison's shyness) of meeting one unknown person after another. Among the more prominent delegates were Oliver Ellsworth and Roger Sherman of Connecticut, Thomas McKean of Delaware, James Lovell of Massachusetts, Livingston, Scott, and Philip Schuyler of New York, Thomas Burke of North Carolina, Frederick Muhlenberg of Pennsylvania, William Ellery of Rhode Island, and Mathews of South Carolina. To these men the new Virginia delegate was "young Madison," small (five feet six inches tall and slightly built) and so immature looking that even a year later one delegate spoke of him in his diary as "just from the College." As the youngest delegate in fact (four days past his twenty-ninth birthday when he took his seat), and even more so in appearance, he was, we may assume, reticent in every public gathering, probably just able at first to cope with his official responsibilities. Though French Minister La Luzerne exaggerated when he reported that Madison took no part in the debates in Congress until he had been there for two years, the remark underscores Madison's reputation for reserve.[2]

Awkwardly shy as Madison was in his new world, he grasped quickly its public issues and soon wrote knowingly to Virginia about them. He told his father of the act of Congress on March 18, 1780, to reduce the $200 million of outstanding Continental currency to $5 million by recalling it all and replacing it, at a ratio of 1 to 40, with new currency to be issued by the states and based on "permanent and specific" funds. It was hoped this new currency would escape depreciation and thus stabilize Congressional finances, though Madison recognized that it would "create great perplexity and complaints in many private transactions." After a week in Congress Madison wrote despairingly to Jefferson of the state of the revolution:

Our army, threatened with an immediate alternative of disbanding or living on free quarter; the public treasury empty; public credit exhausted, nay the private credit of purchasing Agents employed, I am told, as far as it will bear; Congress complaining of the extortion of the people, the people of the improvidence of Congress, and the army of both; our affairs requiring the most mature and systematic measures, and the urgency of occasions admitting only of temporizing expedients, and those expedients generating new difficulties. Congress from a defect of adequate Statesmen more likely to fall into wrong measures and of less weight to enforce right ones, recommending plans to the several states for execution and the states separately re-

judging the expediency of such plans, whereby the same distrust of
concurrent exertions that has damped the ardor of patriotic individuals,
must produce the same effect among the States themselves. An old
system of finance discarded as incompetent to our necessities, an untried and precarious one substituted, and a total stagnation in prospect
between the end of the former and the operation of the latter: These
are the outlines of the true picture of our public situation. I leave it
to your own imagination to fill them up. Believe me Sir as things now
stand, if the States do not vigorously proceed in collecting the old
money and establishing funds for the credit of the new, that we are
undone; and let them be ever so expeditious in doing this, still the
intermediate distress to our army and hindrance to public affairs are
a subject of melancholy reflection. General Washington writes that a
failure of bread has already commenced in the army, and that for any
thing he sees, it must unavoidably increase. Meat they have only for
a short season and as the whole dependance is on provisions now to
be procured, without a shilling for the purpose, and without credit
for a shilling, I look forward with the most pungent apprehensions.[3]

Yet the act stopping the Continental currency presses took power
from Congress precisely when it needed more to prosecute the war. As
Madison wrote Jefferson early in May:

It is to be observed that the situation of Congress has undergone a
total change from what it originally was. Whilst they exercised the
indefinite power of emitting money on the credit of their constituents
they had the whole wealth and resourses of the continent within their
command, and could go on with their affairs independently and as
they pleased. Since the resolution passed for shutting the press, this
power has been entirely given up and they are now as dependent on
the States as the King of England is on the parliament. They can
neither enlist pay nor feed a single soldier, nor execute any other
purpose but as the means are first put into their hands. Unless the
legislatures are sufficiently attentive to this change of circumstances
and act in conformity to it, every thing must necessarily go wrong
or rather must come to a total stop. All that Congress can do in
future will be to administer public affairs with prudence, vigor and
oeconomy.[4]

Washington observed later the same month that "I see one head gradually changing into thirteen. . . . I see the powers of Congress declining
too fast for the consideration and respect which is due to them as the
grand representative body of America, and am fearful of the consequences." This unfortunate abdication of power and the consequent
threat to the hope of victory in war and strength in new nationhood
gave to Madison during his four-year service in Congress the vital impulse to imbue that body with the authority and prestige he, with Washington and many others, thought it had to have to fulfill the revolution.

In moving from the Orange County Committee of Safety to the Virginia Convention, to the Council of State, and then to the Continental Congress, Madison kept his goal fixed; he changed only his sphere of action and his comprehension of the means of effective nation building.[5]

Madison's first weeks in Congress found him submerged in the onerous, petty, and frustrating tasks of running a war with neither power nor resources, against an enemy which in the spring and summer of 1780 won victory after victory. Two days after he took his seat he was elected to the Board of Admiralty, a three-man body charged with the thankless job of equipping and directing an almost nonexistent navy. Judging from Madison's quick appointment to the board, its utter impotence, and his inexperience in naval affairs, one suspects service on it was a duty imposed on junior members. During Madison's two and one half months' service the board handled typically intractable problems. It wrote to the officer commanding four puny vessels seeking to guard Charleston, South Carolina, from a vastly superior British fleet that the board had neither flour and bread to send him nor vessels to carry supplies, which was perhaps just as well, because were they to sail, the enemy would probably capture them. It resolved to trust instead in the commander's "Zeal . . . prudence and Oeconomy." An agent in North Carolina reported he could not outfit ships there because "some villaens with false keys" had stolen "the public Canvass." Though two of the offenders had been hanged, the board did not consider this adequate compensation for the loss of its supplies, especially since it had ordered the agent six months before to deliver the canvas to Continental officers and he had refused, implying that the canvas did not belong to the public. The board retorted that "If you thought it was not our property when demanded you will not, we hope, think it our loss now it is stolen," and asked for "an explanation of this dark business." The board also wrangled endlessly with its agents in Boston over disposition of prizes captured by privateers, seemed always to move too late to get Continental ships to sea usefully, and faced repeated insubordination from agents and officers. Madison was doubtless relieved when on June 6 Congress accepted his resignation from the board.[6]

Quarrels within the army, defeat, and treason plagued Madison and his colleagues during 1780. The British capture of Charleston on May 12, opening the Carolinas to invasion, required immediate action, but Quartermaster General Nathanael Greene, considered by Washington the officer best qualified to command in the South, was enmeshed in disputes over profiteering. Instead, General Horatio Gates received the Southern command, in time to suffer humiliating defeat at Camden on August 16. He fled through North Carolina with less than a thousand half-starved troops, all that remained of the Southern army. A little over a month later, news of Arnold's treason further shook the army and American confidence. The war had reached its darkest hour.

In Congress Madison supported resolves censuring the disgraced Gates and helped reorganize the Quartermaster's department, which led to Greene's resignation. Washington soon thereafter appointed Greene to command in the South, and Madison became a member of the committee of Congress to "correspond" with him—that is, be both a watchdog and means of support. In all of these measures Congress exhibited its weakness, ineptitude, and quarrelsomeness. Listening to the debates during these perilous months, doing what little a junior member could do on committees and executive boards, Madison learned hard lessons about the conduct of government. He saw how stirring words and high resolves would not win revolutionary wars. He saw how personal jealousies and international disputes undermined even the noblest causes. He experienced the baffling crosscurrents that swirled in Congress because it was the place where the thirteen states had to reconcile conflicting interests. He saw for the first time the stresses in a free deliberative body when the members, unlike those in the Virginia House of Delegates, did not know each other and when few if any members had firsthand knowledge of the whole country. These strains convinced Madison that only "greater authority and vigor [in] our councils" could prevent chaos and defeat. Effective federal power in the constitution of 1787 grew from the alarm and despair Madison felt in Philadelphia that summer of discontent as the dispatches came in from Charleston, Camden, and West Point.[7]

Madison soon turned, however, to crucial and divisive questions of foreign affairs, especially relations with France under the terms of the alliance of 1778. The need for French aid dominated all assessments of American prospects for winning the war. French gold was needed to support the conduct of government, her munitions and supplies were needed to arm and clothe American soldiers, her troops were needed to help defeat British regulars, and perhaps most vital of all, her navy was needed to give the United States some relief, at least temporarily, from the British blockade and from the enormous military advantage Britain derived from the quick movement of her forces by sea. Nearly all Americans recognized these needs and in some measure appreciated French help, but there agreement stopped. Some delegates trusted France, thought the alliance with her a wholly good thing, and looked forward to many-sided, long-range cooperation with her. Others, however, suspected France, supposed her ready to betray America at the first opportunity, and thought that beyond desperately needed military aid, little good could result from the alliance.

About a year before Madison entered Congress, the two groups had become openly hostile because of sensational charges by one American commissioner in France, Arthur Lee, that another one, Silas Deane, in collusion with certain Frenchmen, had defrauded the United States by seeking payment for arms and supplies that had in fact been a free gift from the French government. Deane defended himself with Benjamin Franklin's support, and the two diplomats together stood behind the intricate web of contracts and agreements linking the two countries and channeling aid across the Atlantic. The risks of war and the intrigues of revolution made some of the arrangements irregular and scandalously profitable, but on the whole, Deane and Franklin insisted, the agreements were honest, extraordinarily useful to the United States, and the best attainable under the circumstances. With the help of Conrad Alexandre Gérard, the first French minister to the United States (1778–1779), Deane and Franklin got Lee's charges sidetracked in Congress, and although Deane was recalled and eventually disgraced, the apparatus of alliance with France, under Franklin's management, remained intact, a strong buttress for the revolution. Lee's principal supporters in Congress were his brother, Richard Henry Lee, and Sam Adams, both of whom commanded wide support among other delegates, especially those from New England. This group, usually called the Lee-Adams faction, was outspokenly anti-French after mid-1779. In opposition was a less clearly identifiable group, largely of Middle State leaders—particularly James Duane, Robert R. Livingston, and Robert Morris—with some southerners, including in 1780, Madison, Joseph Jones, and occasionally one or two of the other Virginians who took the seats of R. H. Lee and his friends that year.[8]

Thus the matter stood when Arthur Lee and his colleague, Ralph Izard, returned to Philadelphia in the summer and fall of 1780, justifying themselves and hurling charges at Franklin and France. Madison was a member of a committee that in August thanked Izard rather unenthusiastically for his services abroad and approved his expense account. Izard smoldered until Lee arrived two months later and asked Congress for a vindication of his conduct in Europe. This time Madison was chairman of the committee, and he knew he had been handed a touchy job—how could he be approving enough to satisfy fellow Virginian Lee and yet not endorse the anti-Franklin vendetta? Madison wrote Edmund Pendleton of his difficulty: "Doctor Lee and Mr. Izard . . . have been here some time, and I believe are not very reserved in their reflections on the venerable Philosopher [Franklin] at the Court of Versailles. . . . I have had great anxiety lest the flame of faction which on a former occasion [that of the Deane-Lee controversy] proved so injurious should be kindled anew."[9]

The Madison committee reported on October 30, but as a smothering tactic Congress procrastinated for a month. The committee had thanked Lee for his "zealous and faithful exertions" and assured him his recall carried no censure; it was, rather, "a necessary measure to put a stop to differences subsisting among [American] Commissioners in Europe." The committee did not undertake, it said, to judge those disputes. Infuriated by these evasions, Lee assailed Franklin in a letter to Congress: the aged diplomat neglected the public business, profiteered through his nephew and a French banker, tolerated Tories and British spies, and was "more devoted to pleasure than would become even a young man in his station." Lee recommended Franklin's removal, the appointment of a new minister more zealous for the American cause, and an approach to the Empress of Russia for aid. The letter created a sensation in Congress. Its effect, plus the desperate desire of the Southern states to have even more French aid to rescue them from British occupation, resulted, temporarily, in a coalition convinced that Franklin was not doing enough. Lee's letter, sent to a committee of his friends, received a hearing its slander hardly deserved. A day after its presentation, Congress resolved to send an envoy extraordinary to France to solicit money and supplies —a direct affront, of course, to Franklin, who had handled such appeals in the past.[10]

Madison did everything he could to support Franklin. To outmaneuver the opposition, he and James Duane had a few days before written and pushed through Congress an appeal to Louis XVI for more aid and an expression of confidence that Franklin would present the appeal effectively. The day Lee's angry letter was read, Congress rejected a motion by Madison to reconsider sending the new envoy to France. Appointed to the committee to draft instructions for John Laurens (elected to undertake the mission), Madison sought to make Laurens' appearance in France seem an effort to bolster rather than to undermine Franklin's position; working with Franklin, Laurens would supply new, urgent information and act alone only if Franklin were ill. Madison also instructed Laurens to consult with the Chevalier de La Luzerne (French minister to the United States, 1779–84), Lafayette, and Washington before he left for France—that is, not to leave the country filled only with the charges of Arthur Lee and his friends. Next, Madison and Duane helped secure election of Francis Dana—not Lee, who wanted the job—as minister to Russia; this would, they hoped, keep Lee out of Franklin's hair in Europe. Then Madison and Duane combined to reduce Laurens' title from "envoy extraordinary" to "minister," thus making him subordinate to Franklin. At the same time, explicit directions to work with Franklin were deleted from Laurens' instructions; possibly this was a move forced by Franklin's foes, but it was probably agreed by his friends, who probably considered the deleted directions superfluous, since Laurens' reduced rank left him no choice but to work with Franklin. To see further that the right ideas were planted in the right places, Madison served on committees to confer with Laurens and with La Luzerne about the mission.

Finally, a committee of which Duane was a member wrote additional instructions to Franklin, making clear that the Laurens mission was no reflection on him; in fact the committee authorized him to seek the money and supplies on his own if Laurens was delayed or captured. The anti-Franklin forces won a final victory, however, when they secured deletion of a clause praising Franklin for his work in Paris.[11]

Unfortunately the debates in Congress over these complicated moves were not recorded, but Madison's intent and major role are nonetheless evident: he was appointed to nearly every committee that considered important motions and papers, he drafted crucial documents, and with Duane he initiated and guided moves supporting Franklin. By the end of 1780 he had risen from an exceedingly shy junior delegate to be chief lieutenant to James Duane, a Congressional veteran who seemed at the time to be "floor leader" for the pro-Franklin and pro-France forces. By taking a clear stand on the major, divisive question, and in playing a key role in a floor fight over it, Madison indicated that he had come of age and would henceforth be an influential figure in Congress.

Though the defense of Franklin and the consequent repudiation of Arthur Lee were important and showed more clearly than anything else Madison's place in Congressional politics, his own principles in foreign relations and his skill in drawing state papers are best displayed in his support of the American right to navigate the Mississippi River. According to the Treaty of Paris (1763), Great Britain owned the east bank of the Mississippi and had navigation rights. Spain owned the west bank and controlled its mouth, at New Orleans. Upon declaring independence, the United States claimed *all* British rights and territories in the Mississippi valley. When Spain declared war on Great Britain in 1779, she pointedly failed to recognize the American claims and obviously expected, as a result of her war with Britain, to increase her holdings on the Mississippi and in Florida. The United States and Spain were thus suspicious and uneasy allies against Britain. With no direct interest in the West, but seeking a full tripartite alliance against England, France tried behind the scenes to help Spain and to persuade the United States to relinquish her excessive claims. Virginia, of course, had a special interest in the Mississippi question because her western counties (now Kentucky and West Virginia) needed free use of the river to survive.[12]

Thus the matter stood when, in August 1780, John Jay, American representative in Spain, asked for a clarification of his instructions, and British victories in South Carolina sharpened the need for Spanish help. Madison's effective co-worker on the Virginia delegation, Joseph Jones, drew a committee report reasserting the full American claim to the Mississippi. After Jones left Philadelphia in September, Madison saw the report through Congress, on October 4, and was appointed to draft a letter to Jay explaining the reaffirmed instructions. The letter, Madison's first state paper on foreign affairs, set forth principles that in some sense guided him the rest of his life. He first argued that the rights of George III in the American West under the treaty of 1763 devolved in full upon the people of the United States when, in the Declaration of Independence, they took from him the powers of their own governments. So much, Madison said in effect, for kingly claims that the people had no right to powers granted monarchs in treaties. After asserting a technical right based on colonial charters, he turned to practical reasons supporting the American claim: (1) the Mississippi was "a more natural . . . more precise boundary than any other that can be drawn eastwardly of it," and therefore less likely to cause disputes; (2) American citizens were almost sure to settle the territory, so Spanish possession of it would only cause trouble; (3) since individual states claimed territory in the Mississippi valley, for Congress to relinquish it would cause disaffection in them and thus hurt the common fight against England; (4) for the United States to impose a foreign sovereignty over the American citizens in the West would be a "manifest violation of the common rights of mankind and of the genius and principles of the American governments"; (5) the United States could make better use than Spain of the resources of the Mississippi valley in the war with Britain.

Madison then turned to the proposed stoppage of navigation. Since the United States had an unquestioned right to lands in the Mississippi valley, "the circumstance of Spain's being in possession of the banks on both sides near its mouth, cannot be deemed a natural or equitable bar to the free use of the river. Such a principle would authorize a nation disposed to take advantage of circumstances to contravene the clear indications of nature and providence, and the general good of mankind." Natural rights, in Madison's estimation, placed free and efficient use of natural resources above the restraining claims of national boundaries. As Franklin commented when he learned that Spain had asked the United States to agree to stoppage of the Mississippi, "a neighbour might as well ask me to sell my street door." Finally, in pointing out that the Mississippi valley would surely become a rich farming region, Madison noted that if trade down the Mississippi was stopped, Spain and France would lose the benefit of it. Trade would instead turn northward to the Saint Lawrence valley, which would be an immense asset to Great Britain, possibly making secure her "maritime tyranny," which all nations sought so desperately to break.[13]

In applying natural rights principles to international relations, Madison had in mind the more liberal natural law theorists (he quoted Vattel in the letter to Jay), who held that the rights of man furnished the only just foundation for *all* human relations. Apparent too, though, is a readiness to equate American "manifest destiny" with natural law. Hence Madison asserted, as though stating a natural right, that vast areas of the American West would be settled inevitably by the energetic peoples of the seaboard states. The presumption of this equation was as lost on Madison as it was on most of his compatriots. In asserting that the growth and expansion of the new United States was synonymous with the spread of liberty and the rights of man, Madison expressed a sense of the "mission of America" accepted unhesitatingly by millions of people on both sides of the Atlantic in the succeeding century.

Madison spoke for American claims in the Mississippi valley amid a confusion of voices in Philadelphia. Almost the day Congress reaffirmed its instructions to Jay (in a supposedly secret session), Madison received from the French chargé, François de Barbé-Marbois, a carefully reasoned paper explaining why Spain might rightfully resist the American claims. Barbé-Marbois probably received aid from a Maryland delegate and land speculator, Daniel of Saint Thomas Jenifer, in drawing the paper, and he talked to Madison about it while Madison was drafting the letter to Jay. Though Madison seems not to have softened the claim much as a result, he had abundant opportunity to see how strong French influence was in Philadelphia. Despite the obvious long-range dangers, he nevertheless continued to think that influence generally was helpful to the patriot cause.[14]

Madison discovered as well how conflicting state interests could affect a decision on national policy. The dire need of Georgia and the Carolinas for Spanish help caused their delegates to abandon a habitually aggressive posture toward Spain. They faced drastic measures more readily, too, because rumors circulated in Congress that major European powers had proposed to mediate the Anglo-American war on a basis of *uti possidetis*: each side to retain in peace what it possessed as a result of the war. This, of course, would have left most of Georgia and the Carolinas under British rule. Thus delegates from those states were the first to propose in Congress that the United States abandon her claims on the Mississippi if necessary to secure Spanish aid and to resist the rumored mediation. The Middle States, especially Maryland, New Jersey, and Pennsylvania, which did not claim extensive Western lands, were more willing than most of their neighbors to abandon American rights there. Anxious to reinforce her own claim to Vermont, New York viewed unfavorably any measures breaking up a state by act of Congress, exactly the effect on Virginia of any proposal to abandon American claims to the Ohio valley. Though New England was little concerned with the West, she had a vital interest in the Grand Banks fisheries and feared that by being "soft" on the West she might lose support for fishing rights. Even Madison's colleague in the Virginia delegation, Theodorick Bland, was enough impressed with the immediate need for Spanish aid to be willing to defer to some future time the assertion of the American right to navigate the Mississippi.[15]

British military success in the South, including invasion of Virginia from the sea in January 1781, made Spanish aid seem so important that the Virginia legislature authorized its delegates in Congress to agree that the right to navigate the Mississippi might be ceded "if insisting on the same is deemed an impediment to a treaty with Spain." In February 1781, Madison complied, though he himself clearly felt the relinquishment neither useful nor necessary. Luckily for the eventual settlement of American claims in the West, Jay's inclination to defend them to the utmost, and the Spanish capture and suppression of the rescinding instructions, prevented any formal relinquishment. In May 1781, at the direction of Congress, Madison wrote Jay praising his stalwart defense of American rights. Perhaps Madison understood Jay's inclination and concluded such expressions of support from Congress, despite the revised instructions, would suffice to prevent him from backing down. Jay in any case approved: "I do not recollect to have ever received a letter that gave me more real pleasure. . . . It appearing to me that the communication . . . to this Court could not be better made than in the very words of this letter, which seemed exceedingly well calculated for the purpose, I recited them in a letter which I wrote two days afterwards to the minister." Madison's skillful insistence on American rights in the West, together with Jay's firmness, helped maintain important national interests in the face of panic at military reverses.[16]

Closely related, of course, to the assertion of American claims in the West, and indeed to nearly every question before Congress in 1780 and 1781, was control of the settlement and exploitation of the vast, rich lands of the Mississippi valley. Though Americans generally agreed in claiming title to the lands, they differed on details. Seven states had more or less valid claims to large portions of the West. Virginia, for example, by virtue of a vaguely worded colonial charter, claimed all the trans-Appalachian regions north of the westward extension of her southern boundary. From 1776 on, though, many leaders had felt that the national welfare required cession of Western lands to the general government, which would eventually create new states from them. Disposition and settlement of the West would be an essential bond of union after independence had been won. The states with land claims conceded the impracticality of extending state government over such vast regions and agreed that under national control the lands would provide resources and strength for the Union. The states without claims of course insisted cession was necessary to keep the states from becoming even more disparate in population and influence than they already were.

All might have been settled amicably if there had been no land companies eager to validate claims to vast tracts of Western lands. More or less valid titles to areas in West Virginia, Kentucky, Ohio, Indiana, and Illinois had been sought or secured from colonial governments, Great Britain, the Indians, state governments, and more recently, by confirmation of grants, from Congress. By and large, speculators within the "landed" states had claims validated by them, while speculators in "landless" states, especially Pennsylvania and Maryland, had claims based on Indian treaties or grants by British officials. Which, if any, of these overlapping or dubiously grounded claims would be upheld depended in large measure on the political authority eventually governing the territory of the land claims. Thus each land company used what pressure it could—often including bribery in the form of shares in the company offered to legislators and other officials—to secure validation of its claims by as many of the potential seats of sovereignty as possible.[17]

The first case to come to Madison's attention was the Indiana Company's claim, based on a 1768 Indian purchase, to nearly two million acres in present-day West Virginia. After the Virginia legislature declared its deed "utterly void," the company applied to Congress for validation, including in its appeal support from, among others, Benjamin Franklin, Patrick Henry, and the Earl of Camden. The company's influence in Congress secured referral of its petition to a committee, but there, due mainly to Virginia opposition, it languished. A company agent wrote the Virginia delegates, seeking arbitration of the matter, but was rebuffed. Madison explained: "We have given [the agent] for answer that as the State we represent had finally determined the question, we could not with any propriety attend to his proposition." At the same time, Madison made clear his opinion of the speculators: "I do not believe there is any serious design in Congress to gratify the avidity of land mongers, but the best security for their [Congressmen's] virtue in this respect will be to keep it out of their power." That is, Virginia, in ceding her Western lands, should stipulate that deeds such as that of the Indiana Company were void.[18]

Questions of control of the Western lands had a crucial impact on the ratification of the Articles of Confederation, pending in Congress at the time Madison rebuffed the Indiana Company. Maryland had for two years refused to ratify until Virginia and the other "landed" states ceded their claims. Her delegates argued that the general welfare and the equality of the states required that the lands be the common property of all the states. Actually, Maryland and Pennsylvania promoters of the Illinois-Wabash Company sought to exclude the unfriendly sovereignty of Virginia from the Northwest Territory, where their huge claims were, thus clearing the way for validation of the claims by a hopefully more tractable Congress. La Luzerne's predecessor as French minister, Gérard, had been given shares in the company in hopes he

would use his influence on its behalf. Virginia speculators had claims in
the Northwest conflicting with those of the Illinois-Wabash Company.
The effort to ratify the Articles came down, in one sense, then, to a
struggle between Virginia and Maryland land speculators.

In the summer of 1780 disaster on the battlefield brought this question,
like so many others, to a head. La Luzerne made it clear to Maryland
delegates that French aid would flow more abundantly if the Articles
were ratified. Partly to secure support for her claims to Vermont but
also, as she said, "to accelerate the federal alliance," New York offered to
relinquish her exceedingly dubious claims to Western lands. All now depended on Virginia. Acting on suggestions from George Mason, Joseph
Jones and Madison undertook to persuade Virginia to cede her claims in
the Northwest, subject to certain conditions, and to persuade Congress
to accept the conditions. The three Virginians proposed that new states
be created by Congress in the Northwest, that Virginia be repaid for the
expenses of the George Rogers Clark expedition, that her promise of
land bounties in the area to her soldiers be honored, that the ceded lands
be "a common fund for the use and benefit of . . . the United States," and
that deeds of land based on purchases from Indians be "absolutely void."
Jones and Mason went to Richmond to get the cession through the Virginia legislature, while Madison sought Congressional approval of the
Virginia conditions.[19]

The Virginia legislature passed the conditional cession on January 2,
1781, but Madison could not persuade Congress to approve complementary resolves. The matter dragged on for more than three years and was
settled finally, with minor changes, according to the Mason-Jones-
Madison plan of 1780. Thus important foundations were laid: the principle of cession of Western lands for the common good had been agreed
to by all the states, and the idea of new, fully equal states acceding to
the union of the original thirteen opened the way for, in Jefferson's
famous phrase, the "empire of liberty" to spread across the continent.
Though Madison's role in these events was at first subordinate to that of
Mason and Jones, he agreed wholeheartedly with their plan to strengthen
the union and thwart the speculators, and he accepted readily the Congressional leadership on the question when Jones returned to Virginia.

Altogether, Madison's first year in Congress was one of remarkable
growth. Though in Orange and in Williamsburg he had been fully committed to the revolution, and though his election to Congress signified
his increasing stature among Virginia leaders, it was not until he reached
Philadelphia that he experienced the larger, more complex issues. During
the spring and summer of 1780, as a sense of crisis and military reverses
drove Congress to one difficult, almost frantic decision after another,
Madison had to act full time as a *national* leader. He was at first hesitant

and silent, but with surprising speed for one as young and shy as he was, he soon gained respect and influence. As early as August 1780, for example, he was proposed for an overseas post, perhaps as Franklin's secretary in Paris, and the next winter, after he had prepared important diplomatic papers, some members thought that Madison, "a young gentleman of industry and abilities," might be made secretary for foreign affairs.[20]

The note of alarm in Madison's first letters to Virginia suggests that things were worse in Philadelphia than he had anticipated. The revolution was much closer to defeat or collapse, apparently, than had seemed possible in Virginia, not yet a theater of war when Madison left home. Inflation had been a persisting nuisance at home, but in the national capital it was a monster consuming the strength and integrity vital to the cause. Congress seemed a quarrelsome, inept body rather than the group of zealous, high-minded statesmen Madison and William Bradford had written about in 1775. Letters read almost daily in Congress from Washington and other commanders aroused more pity and frustration than pride. Dispatches from abroad were filled with ill omens: diplomats quarreled in Paris; profiteering agents held up supplies; British influence outweighed American in Madrid; and the sources of loans seemed to dry up at the moment of greatest need. Thus Madison was required to exert every ounce of energy to sustain the revolution when it appeared most hopeless, and his devotion to it, his sense that its fulfillment was his vocation, grew even stronger. As he learned that his insights, his pen, and his political skills were extraordinarily useful in Congress, he knew he had found his place. He thus served in the Continental Congress almost every day for nearly four years, a record of steady attendance unsurpassed by any other delegate in its fifteen-year history. Not once until after the peace treaty had been signed and the army disbanded in late 1783 did Madison take a leave of absence from Congress or return to Virginia.

As Madison's commitment to the revolution deepened, so too did his sense of its scope and meaning. It was not a mere matter of resisting unjust taxes, seeking religious liberty, or even avoiding debts to British merchants. At stake in one sense was the direction of future events in the Western world and the place the new United States would have in that world. The American Revolution stirred both great hope and dark foreboding in Europe; how Americans acted there and what attitude they took toward the stirrings might be matters of considerable consequence. As Madison saw these reactions in dispatches from Franklin, Adams, and Jay, heard his fellow delegates express their own hopes and fears, and then saw emotions and prejudices burst forth following Arthur Lee's assault on Franklin, he took his stand with those who, like Franklin and Jefferson, wanted the United States, as an experiment in

free government, to play a significant role in the world. This did not
mean neglect of domestic concerns or entangling alliances of the traditional European sort, but rather that the country should be united and
strong, and that, given the existing state of international affairs, American
interests should for the immediate future at least, be closely bound with
those of France. That country could be both a counterweight to England
and sponsor and guide to the United States in world affairs. Madison
seems never to have shared the insular view that the United States could
"go it alone." The notion of a pure, republican America utterly cut off
from the rest of the world except for some unavoidable commerical ties
seemed to him timid.

Thus when he observed French Minister La Luzerne seeking to persuade Maryland to ratify the Articles of Confederation, or saw, through
Franklin's dispatches, that an adroit mixture of deference and realistic
suggestion yielded rich dividends in French aid, Madison's impulse was to
applaud, confident that neither French influence nor Franklin's courtly
tact would harm the cause; on the contrary, each could aid it substantially. Furthermore, by 1780 the French stake in the success of the revolution was very great indeed. If Britain subdued her former colonies,
France, weakened by dissension and financial chaos at home, would
surely feel the full force of Britain's emboldened power. Madison saw,
therefore, that French influence would in most ways help make the
United States the kind of nation Madison wanted it to become: united,
powerful, and able to play a significant role in world affairs. When Madison found he enjoyed the company of the French minister and his urbane
countrymen who visited Philadelphia, and as he had more and more
reason to abhor and revile England, his disposition to look kindly on
Louis XVI and his subjects increased. Madison, in short, became a friend
of France as a means of enlarging his American patriotism. The impulse
of Madison and other revolutionaries to form a more powerful union
had important roots in their sense of the *domestic* dangers of weakness
and disunion. Equally important, however, was the need to build national
strength so that the United States might fulfill a wider destiny in the
world.

In adopting this attitude toward France, Madison took sides on a question far more complex and divisive than any he had encountered in Virginia. His hesitation at returning a report he knew would infuriate
Arthur Lee, and his fear that "a spirit of faction" would thus be aroused,
reflected the greater intricacy. He hesitated only momentarily, however,
for within a month he stood forthrightly for Franklin's mission in France
and for close cooperation with the French legation in Philadelphia. For
this, Lee offered the opinion that Madison "ought to lose his head." If he
had not experienced it previously, Madison had from Arthur Lee and his
friends a good lesson in personal partisan politics. Confirmed in his con-

victions, Madison became partisan himself and wrote persuasive reasoned documents sustaining his side. The arguments presented to John Jay defending American claims in the West and the document drawn on Franklin's behalf for use in Congress were the first in a long series of papers and polemics from Madison's pen defending American interests and upholding positions he favored. Madison had not been in Congress a year before he was marked as a "laboring" rather than a "forensic" legislator, one adept at committee work and reasoned argument, one who could be depended upon to speak and to write with precision and force what others could express but vaguely and in part.[21]

Madison learned very quickly, of course, that votes in Congress turned less on careful arguments than on a bewildering variety of special interests. He himself at times ducked the larger issues and worked as hard for his own state as any partisan. His special skill, though, was in bringing local and general interests together, as he did in his stands on both navigation of the Mississippi and the conditional cession of Western lands. In grappling with these matters, he listened day after day in Congress to the flow of opinions from such diverse persons as earnest, upright Sam Adams of Massachusetts, cagey Dr. Witherspoon of New Jersey, land company spokesman Jenifer of Maryland, and flamboyant John Mathews of South Carolina; and what he heard—petty, wise, provincial, magnanimous—must have enormously increased his understanding of the problems of federal union. The obvious and often legitimate bias of these men and others for their home states, the far more subtle and often suspect influence of the French minister, and the certainly sinister (in Madison's view) operations of the land company agents enlarged Madison's sense of political realities. He had further lessons, too, in the emotions aroused by personalities—whirlpools of envy, distrust, and adoration swirled around such figures as generals Gates and Greene, Franklin, Arthur Lee, Robert Morris, and Lafayette. Having read Tacitus, Cardinal de Retz, and many others on the machinations of government and diplomacy, Madison could not have been startled by these struggles and passions, but in Congress he saw them operate firsthand in ways shaping the destiny of nations. He came to understand them well and soon dealt realistically and effectively with them.

Before the Articles of Confederation were ratified, in March 1781, the Continental Congress possessed, without carefully defined limits, all the powers of a federal government—legislative, executive, and judicial. As a member of Congress Madison served on bodies exercising each of these functions. The Board of Admiralty was in effect an executive navy department. Madison was on committees that judged conflicting state claims and interpreted laws enacted by Congress. In writing instructions to Jay he acted as a secretary of foreign affairs. The Jones-Madison resolution on Western lands was legislation of the most important kind.

Thus involved in all the powers of government, he had an opportunity to see the nature of each, what each required for effective conduct, and the dangers and advantages of mingling them in a single body. The Continental Congress was therefore an extraordinarily flexible laboratory of government, abundantly supplied with pressing revolutionary problems on which to experiment. Madison's membership in it completed the education in *ad hoc* government by consent he had begun as a member of the Orange County Committee of Safety in 1774 and the Virginia Convention of 1776. By his thirtieth birthday, on March 16, 1781, then, Madison not only understood republican theory, but he had had a unique experience to give him a "feel" for the problems of free government.

Along with performing the official duties which so fully engaged his attention, Madison had to learn to live the life of a prominent bachelor in the nation's capital. His private life centered in the House-Trist lodgings where, besides his fellow Virginians, he came particularly to know the New York delegates. There he probably met for the first time Robert R. Livingston, five years his senior, wealthy, cultured, and importantly connected with Madison in public life until his death in 1813. Blustery General John Morin Scott was there during much of Madison's first year in Philadelphia. Most important for Madison's public career, however, was James Duane, a Congressional veteran described as "of good and even temper, attentive to business, of a low soft voice, not eloquent nor designing, but upon the whole a good republican." Duane was perhaps the most influential member of Congress during Madison's first year there and normally took the lead in moves to strengthen the power of Congress, aid the army, and maintain good relations with France. He had been a moderate in 1776 and therefore probably was among the "timorous gentlemen" Madison then disdained, but as the revolution progressed and constructive tasks of government became pressing, he proved to be a valued colleague of Washington and other national leaders. Madison seems to have moved to a position of influence in Congress first as a supporter and then as a lieutenant of Duane's. They must have spent many hours in their lodgings talking over the moods and measures of Congress.[22]

In the fall of 1780 Madison took time from politics to deal with some housing problems. Joseph Jones asked him to rent a country home from one of the Pembertons to prepare for Jones's return to Philadelphia in January 1781. Madison did so obligingly, and in the process, may have met Mary Payne, his future mother-in-law, who visited her Quaker friends the Pembertons that fall. He also watched with great interest the efforts of one Joseph Bulkley, a scoundrel who on some technicality had sued Mrs. House for her boardinghouse, or at least its furnishings. Scott and Duane took the lead in defending her, eventually winning their case when, among other things, Bulkley was jailed for debt. In the process Duane made what may have been one of the first pleas on behalf of Congressional immunity: he wrote President Reed of Pennsylvania, claiming Bulkley had no right to interfere at the House establishment because of the "publick Characters" who lived there. In the meantime, Madison gathered huge quantities of inflated paper currency needed to pay the bills for his first six months' lodging and other expenses (all chargeable to the Commonwealth of Virginia): over $21,000 to Mrs. House for room and board, $2,459 for "liquors, sugar [and] fruit not included in board," $6,034 for care of his three horses "at the Continental Stables," $1,776 for laundry, $1,020 to his barber, and $605 for wood. His December accounts showed payment for the same items, plus candles, a sign probably of shorter days as well as long evenings at his writing table drafting diplomatic papers.[23]

Meeting Americans and Europeans with ways new to him must have enlivened Madison's first months in Philadelphia. He had not been there a month before he had his first encounter with the New Englanders whom Virginians in Congress so often found a strange, sober lot. Samuel Holten, delegate from Massachusetts, recorded in his diary that on March 30, 1780, "Mr. Maderson and Mr. Killosh [Kinloch of South Carolina] dined with us"—that is, at the house where a group of Northern (or Eastern, as they were more commonly called in the eighteenth century) delegates lodged. Four days earlier Madison may have attended the funeral of James Forbes of Maryland. His illness and death created the vacancy permitting Madison's "sentence" to the Board of Admiralty. On May 8, at the invitation of French Minister La Luzerne, members of Congress attended a requiem mass at the Roman Catholic chapel "for the repose of the Soul," Madison wrote, of Spanish agent Don Juan de Miralles. This may have been Madison's first attendance at a Roman Catholic service.[24]

Perhaps most significant among Madison's broadening experiences were the elegant dinners at the French legation in John Dickinson's great mansion on Chestnut Street. There is no record of when Madison went to these functions, but in view of his sympathy for France and her citizens, we may suppose he went once a week or so, as did Samuel Holten and others. Delegate John Armstrong was pleased with the "simplicity and temperance" of La Luzerne's table, though he thought there was "a great redundance . . . of Sweet Meats and Desserts." The "civility" of the Frenchman, it seems, simply overwhelmed the somewhat provincial delegates. For example, Ezekiel Cornell of Rhode Island wrote of "the ease and comfort every one enjoys, that has the honour to dine at his table, free from every kind of ceremony or formality, every one left to eat and drink as he pleaseth, stay as long as he pleaseth, and go away when he pleaseth."[25]

On December 13 Madison dined with some distinguished French
gentlemen visiting Philadelphia, including the Chevalier de Chastellux
("a man of sense, politeness and letters") and "Baron de Montesquieu,
grand son to the great Montesquieu." Chastellux noted in his journal
simply that he had sat near Mr. "Mutterson" and had been "much satisfied" with the conversation. The French nobleman, however, was obviously much more impressed with the "gay . . . amiable . . . well informed
. . . graceful . . . witty" daughters of prominent Philadelphia families,
and regretted not having met them earlier, presumably to relieve him of
the tedium of grave political discussions. There can be no doubt that the
dazzling style of the French noblemen, their habit of flattering American
aspirations, and the ample expense account La Luzerne had at his disposal helped importantly to earn good will for France. Yet there were
those, too, who opposed and feared French influence in Philadelphia,
and understood well the significance of La Luzerne's social activities.
Delegate Thomas Smith once complained on the floor of Congress that
"while some members held an intercourse with the French minister and
were constantly seen at his table and entertainments, others were wholly
excluded." La Luzerne's dinners and the attentions of French noblemen were Madison's first substantial experience of the social graces of
cultured Europeans; he obviously enjoyed and appreciated them very
much. He was pleased, not apprehensive and embarrassed, as were some
of his countrymen, to have the aid of such men in the fight for
independence.[26]

The fourth anniversary of American independence occurred during
Madison's first year in Congress, and "was observed as a Day of Joy and
Festivity." Members of Congress, La Luzerne, and other public dignitaries who attended the commencement exercises of the College of
Philadelphia held on that early Fourth of July made, a local newspaper
reported, "a most genteel, respectable, and brilliant assembly of Ladies
and Gentlemen." The throng listened to, among others things, a patriotic ode by three of the graduating seniors:

> . . . Four years has independence (once our fear)
> Stood like a rock against the rage of Britain.
> And may it stand united in its parts,
> As long as stands the world.
> How like a tree just planted in the soil,
> And striking root, did independence bear
> The black and bellowing blasts of seventy-six.
> The shaking did her good,
> And fix't her but the faster in her place.
> May ev'ry shaking have the same effect.
> And so it ever will.

Though a Princetonian could not entirely approve effusions coming from the rival Philadelphia college, Madison doubtless welcomed the sentiments and the break from labors in Congress afforded by the ceremony.[27]

Before another Fourth of July came around, Madison experienced more dangerous fireworks right at home. *The Pennsylvania Packet* reported that on the night of June 26, 1781, "several houses in the city, and a vessel in the harbour, were damaged by lightning. The building which suffered most is that in which Mrs. House lives, at the corner of Market and Fifth Streets. The lightning entered near the chimney, and passed through several rooms, but no person was injured by it, nor was the house as much damaged as might have been expected, the lightning having been conducted by a bell wire, which it melted. This incident affords an additional proof of the utility of the electrical rods invented by the ingenious Dr. Franklin." If Madison was at home when the lightning struck (he probably was), he may have taken added satisfaction in his defense in Congress of the aged diplomat whose wisdom had so dramatically protected the House boarding establishment.[28]

Recorders of Madison's conduct in Philadelphia during his first year there are divided—either critics of his personal behavior or admirers of his political talents. Thomas Rodney, a delegate from Delaware, asserted that Madison "possesses all the self-conceit that is common to youth and inexperience . . . but it is unattended with that gracefulness and ease which sometimes makes even the impertinence of youth and inexperience agreeable or at least not offensive." Twenty days after this unflattering characterization, Martha Bland, wife of Virginia delegate Theodorick Bland, and one who swooned over the attentions of the chivalrous Frenchmen in Philadelphia, scored Madison's social conduct: he was "a gloomy, stiff creature, they say he is clever in Congress, but out of it he has nothing engaging or even bearable in his manners—the most unsociable creature in existence." At the same time Louis Otto, private secretary to La Luzerne, met Madison and found him, he later reported, "well-educated, wise, temperate, gentle, [and] studious."[29]

Rodney and Mrs. Bland were but the first of many persons who, only slightly acquainted with Madison and seeing him only in large social gatherings, found him stiff, reserved, cold, even aloof and supercilious. Numerous persons wrote during Madison's presidency of attending receptions where they were as repelled by his personality as they were charmed by Dolley Madison. Also numerous, however, are the characterizations of Madison as warm, humorous, and amiable in small groups of close friends. Impressions of Madison from his first years as a nationally important politician were, in fact, remarkably uniform: he was thought awkward at formal events, congenial in small groups, and skillful in public councils. He overcame his habitual shyness and reserve only when among people he trusted and when he felt in such command of public issues that he spoke and acted with confidence to support measures he favored. He therefore seldom made a good first impression, seldom overawed a legislative body at his first appearance, and seldom figured in the spicy or dramatic events of which gossip and headlines are made.

Until late in Madison's career as a member of the Continental Congress, nothing is known of his romantic interests. A tradition in the family of Philip Freneau has Madison in love with the poet's sister, Mary, and being spurned by her during visits to their home while he was at Princeton; but this is unsupported by other evidence, and sounds like one of the fanciful stories that always gather about the early years of famous men. Curiously, no such traditions connect Madison with any Virginia belles; if he courted or had amorous adventures in Virginia, the secret has been kept perfectly. Though he and William Bradford wrote of the loves and courtships of their friends, there is no hint of any such exploits on Madison's part. Bradford was nevertheless interested in his friend's matrimonial prospects; he wrote in 1784 to his fiancée, Susan Boudinot, that "I have waited two days for Mr. Madison's departure. I wished to have the satisfaction of writing to my dear Susan, by this old friend, companion and classmate. At length I enjoyed it—and I feel a pride in reflecting that he will now converse with and contemplate you as the charming woman that is to bestow happiness on his friend. Besides he is a bachelor still—and I would wish to allure him to a happier state by presenting him with a prospect of the sweet scene that opens on your happy B."[30]

In the winter of 1782–3, however, Madison fell from his niche as an apparently confirmed bachelor. William Floyd, a New York delegate who had long lived at the House lodgings, returned with his wife and three children, the youngest of whom, Catherine, called Kitty, was fifteen. Madison may have noticed her before, as a child, perhaps even as an uncommonly attractive and interesting one, but now his attention was of another sort and soon had a particular objective. Thomas Jefferson spent the month of January 1783 in Philadelphia, where Madison introduced him to "the Family" at the Houses. During winter evenings in the drawing room, the gentlemen were charmed by Kitty as she played the harpsichord. Especially infatuated were a nineteen-year-old medical student, William Clarkson, and Congressman Madison. By the time Jefferson left Philadelphia, on January 26, Madison and the girl were at least close enough for Jefferson to send his "complements to Miss Kitty" via Madison. When Madison replied, on February 11, John Adams' "venom against . . . Franklin" so irritated him he made only vague mention of the "Ladies and Gentlemen" who returned Jefferson's compliments. On February 14 Jefferson expressed "warmest wishes for your happiness," probably a discreet way of saying he hoped Madison's romance went well.[31]

When Jefferson returned to Philadelphia in late February, he lodged again at Mrs. House's and observed with pleasure that the Madison-Floyd affair flourished. After his next departure, in mid-April, Jefferson wrote in code of what he knew was uppermost in his friend's mind: "I desire [my affectionate compliments] to Miss Kitty particularly. Do you know that the raillery you sometimes experienced from our family strengthened by my own observation, gave me hopes that there was some foundation for it." Obviously, during Jefferson's February absence Madison and Kitty Floyd had been together enough to cause gossip and pleasant banter, while in March the signs of attachment were unmistakable to Jefferson. He hoped something would come of the courtship, he wrote, because "it would give me a neighbor [Kitty] whose worth I rate high, and as I know it will render [you] happier than you can possibly be in a single state. I often made it the subject of conversation, more exhortation, with her and was able to convince myself that she possessed every sentiment in your favor which you could wish."[32]

Madison replied in a letter he must have written in as great a state of excitement and anticipation as he ever experienced. He had given Kitty Jefferson's particular greetings, he wrote, and proceeded to the big news: "Your inference on that subject [impending marriage] was not groundless. Before you left us I had sufficiently ascertained her sentiments. Since your departure the affair has been pursued. Most preliminary arrangements [public announcement of the engagement], although definitive, will be postponed until the end of the year in Congress [November 1783, when Madison's term ended]." Kitty Floyd had her sixteenth birthday at Mrs. House's on April 24, two days after Madison had written so expectantly, and five days later he set out with the Floyd family for New Brunswick, New Jersey, sixty miles away. The journey, Madison's first away from Philadelphia in more than three years, must have been perfectly delightful—a ride with his betrothed at the height of spring, up the fertile Delaware valley and past the familiar buildings at Princeton. After a day or two with the Floyds, Madison left Kitty, expecting that they would soon be making plans for the wedding. He rode back alone carrying with him a letter from Kitty to eleven-year-old Patsy Jefferson containing a "copy of a song." Had it not been lost we might have had a glimpse of Kitty's feelings as she left her fiancé.

But the happy days in New Jersey were the end, not the beginning, of the marriage plans of delegate James Madison and the young beauty he had courted that winter and spring. While Madison went ahead with plans to travel to Virginia to arrange for his homecoming as a married man, retire from Congress, go north for the wedding, and thus begin a new pattern for his life, Kitty brooded over her courtings of the winter before. For reasons unknown, she decided to break her engagement to Madison. Her heart had turned, apparently, to the young medical student, William Clarkson, whom she married in 1785. She wrote Madison a letter in July 1783, containing, as he wrote Jefferson, a "profession of indifference," and sealed it, according to Floyd family tradition, with a piece of rye dough.[33]

Back in Congress Madison had no hint at first of the change in his fortunes. He told friends in Virginia that reelection to Congress would not "coincide with my private conveniency." On June 1, Jefferson, at Monticello, requested Madison to furnish "a safe more than speedy conveyance" for a letter to Kitty from Patsy—that is, Madison could wait and take it with him when he went to see Kitty. By June 10 Madison suffered doubts caused by delay of the mail—or, dreadful thought, had Kitty not written? He wrote Jefferson that the time of his departure for Virginia was uncertain, but "cannot now be very distant." On July 17, after Congress had been forced by mutinous soldiers to flee from Philadelphia to Princeton, Madison still spoke of forwarding mail to Miss Floyd, and reported again that his movements depended "on some circumstances which in point of time are contingent." *Why didn't he hear from Kitty?* Eleven days later he had heard; he cryptically wrote to Edmund Randolph that "contrary to my intentions I shall be detained here several weeks yet, by a disappointment in some circumstances which must precede my setting out for Virginia." Rather, he would stay in Philadelphia to await a chance to repair his fortunes. We may imagine Madison spending anxious, lonely days of despair after hearing disturbing word from Kitty and during the absence of Congress in Princeton.[34]

At last, on August 11, he wrote Jefferson of his shattered romance. The account is only partially legible under the heavy overlinings made by Madison in old age to obscure all clear reference to Catherine Floyd in his letters. Phrases of disappointment can still be made out, however: " . . . one of those incidents to which such affairs are liable. . . . The necessity of my visiting . . . New Jersey [or New York?] no longer exists. . . . It would be improper by this communication to send particular explanations . . . profession of indifference . . . more propitious turn of fate." Jefferson offered such comfort as he could: "I sincerely lament the misadventure which has happened from whatever cause it may have happened. Should it be final however, the world still presents the same and many other resources of happiness, and you possess many within yourself. Firmness of mind and unintermitting occupations will not long leave you in pain. No event has been more contrary to my expectations, and these were founded on what I thought a good knowledge of the ground. But of all machines ours is the most complicated and inexplicable." Jefferson hoped Madison would keep busy by attending the Virginia legislature or undertaking an intensive course of private study in Philadelphia.[35]

Understandably, Madison never wrote anything more—and probably said very little—about this painful experience. One might guess that it was not his first such disappointment, and that it therefore heightened an already strong tendency to push aside romance for the public work he now did so well. His reticence on this matter (as on all personal affairs), together with Catherine Floyd's extreme youth, might lead to the conclusion that they were an absurd match and therefore could not have taken each other seriously. The correspondence with Jefferson, straightforward, and surely about a matter each thought of considerable importance, belies this conclusion. Furthermore, presuming Kitty emerged rapidly and radiantly into young womanhood at age fifteen, it was not unusual in her day for such blossoming to be a prelude to early marriage, particularly to a man of such respectable standing as Madison, who, though sixteen years older than Kitty, was boyish in appearance. At some time in their courtship, probably just before he and Kitty left Philadelphia in April, the betrothed pair had miniature portraits painted by Charles Willson Peale, which if they followed the usual custom, they then exchanged. Madison's shows him as a sandy-haired, bright-eyed, rather mischievous youth, while Kitty seems a pretty, oval-faced girl. In these portraits, Madison looks, if anything, younger than Kitty.* Thus we need not picture Madison, the "older man," peeping hopefully at her as he conversed gravely with her father, while she made eyes at her true love, the handsome young medical student. The rivals each courted Catherine, and as long as all were present in person, Madison clearly had the better of it. For whatever reason, Kitty rejected Madison, thereby losing her chance to become First Lady. And Madison had before him the ten most fruitful years of his public career—unencumbered and unblessed with wife or family.

* The miniature of Madison is owned by descendants of his sister Nelly, so apparently he got it back from Kitty after she broke the engagement. Kitty's portrait is now owned by her descendants. See illustrations following p. 288.

CHAPTER VII

Emergence as a National Leader

W HATEVER the pleasures and disappointments of Madison's private life in Philadelphia, they fade when set beside the quick, sure grasp of public problems that made certain his increasingly large role in Congress. After observing his conduct for nearly four years, French Minister La Luzerne found that Madison was regarded as "the man of soundest judgment in Congress. . . . He speaks nearly always with fairness and wins the approval of his colleagues." As the military phase of the revolution concluded successfully, Madison turned to large questions, of the structure of government, of finance, and of foreign relations. All needed resolution before the new nation could enjoy real independence and republican government.[1]

When Madison took his seat in March 1780, Congress was experiencing a rapid decline in the vast, ill-defined powers it had exercised since 1774. Its original power came from the united zeal of the colonies to resist Great Britain and from the need to act created by the outbreak and expansion of war. As the instrument of this zeal and necessity, Congress raised armies, concluded alliances, issued paper currency, and otherwise did whatever the exigencies of war required. As the struggle wore on, and resources were strained, spirits flagged, and selfish or hard-pressed groups began in many ways to question and deny the authority of Congress. Furthermore, according to the prevailing Whig orthodoxy, for a government to be reckoned just, its powers had to be defined and carefully limited. Otherwise its actions would be arbitrary and unpredictable, the very essence of tyranny. Therefore, Congress had had under consideration since 1775 plans of union or confederation that would define the powers of the general government. It had approved the Articles of

Confederation in November 1777, but they were not ratified and implemented until March 1, 1781. Even as ratification approached, Congress bowed more and more to the demands of those who opposed its broad powers—a wariness culminating, in 1779 and 1780, in the voluntary stoppage of the paper money presses. Congress had deprived itself of financial independence.

Members of Congress consequently watched the beginning of government under the Articles with mixed feelings. Some, like Thomas Burke of North Carolina, looked to the Articles to restrain the power-grabbing instincts of Congress and thus preserve the sovereignty of the states and the liberty of the people. Others thought that the Articles would furnish an orderly government competent to win the war and establish peace. Still others, Madison among them, were troubled from the outset by the lack of power given Congress, the easy prospect of obstruction, the dependence upon the states for money, and perhaps most important of all, the failure to specify how Congress might enforce the few powers granted it. As Alexander Hamilton wrote to James Duane:

> The fundamental defect is a want of power in Congress. . . . The confederation itself is defective and requires to be altered; it is neither fit for war, nor peace. The idea of an uncontrollable sovereignty in each state, over its internal police, will defeat the other powers given to Congress and make our union feeble and precarious. There are instances without number, where acts necessary for the general good, and which rise out of the powers given to Congress must interfere with the internal police of the states, and there are many instances in which particular states by arrangement of internal police can effectually though indirectly counteract the arrangements of Congress. . . . The first step [in revising the Articles] must be to give Congress powers competent to the public exigencies.

Though Madison did not know Hamilton at this time—the letter came to Duane when he and Madison lived together—they doubtless each read it, approved generally, and marked its author as an able champion of increased national power. For Madison the letter began almost exactly ten years of substantial agreement with Hamilton on the weaknesses and needs of the new United States.[2]

On March 12, 1781, after but twelve days of government under the Articles, Madison proposed an amendment containing fateful language: ". . . a general and *implied power* is vested in the United States in Congress assembled to enforce and carry into effect all the articles of the said Confederation against any of the States which shall refuse or neglect to abide by such their determinations." Madison sought as well to make the mode of the enforcement explicit: Congress was authorized "to employ the force of the United States as well by sea as by land" to compel obedience to its resolves. A month later he explained further, to Jefferson:

The necessity of arming Congress with coercive powers arises from the shameful deficiency of some of the States which are most capable of yielding their apportioned supplies, and the military exactions to which others already exhausted by the enemy and our own troops are in consequence exposed. Without such powers too in the general government, the whole confederacy may be insulted and the most salutary measures frustrated by the most inconsiderable State in the Union. At a time when all the other States were submitting to the loss and inconveniency of an embargo on their exports, Delaware absolutely declined coming into the measure, and not only defeated the general object of it, but enriched herself at the expence of those who did their duty. . . . It may be asked perhaps by what means Congress could exercise such a power if the States were to invest them with it? As long as there is a regular army on foot, a small detachment from it, acting under Civil authority, would at any time render a voluntary contribution of supplies due from a State an eligible alternative. But there is a still more easy and efficacious mode. The situation of most of the States is such, that two or three vessels of force employed against their trade will make it their interest to yield prompt obedience to all just requisitions of them.[3]

When the states' rights forces in Congress blocked amendments explicitly expanding its powers, Madison became more devious. During the first three months of government under the Articles, he moved successfully to give Congress power to prohibit trade with Great Britain, to pay soldiers from Continental funds, and to permit impressment of supplies. Unsuccessfully he sought to expand the power of federal courts and to compel states to redeem Continental currency. These moves set the pattern for the rest of his service in the Continental Congress. Recognizing that explicit expansion of national power was virtually impossible, he used every stratagem to expand it indirectly. Whenever possible, he put federal rather than state authority behind important war measures. He had key proposals referred to committees dominated by nationalist-minded delegates. He himself more and more drew reports on matters most likely to expand federal power. In short, Madison sought to make the Articles of Confederation an effective instrument of national government. His frustration and piddling success more than anything else pointed toward the constitution of 1787.[4]

For Congress to have proper dignity and prestige, Madison saw it had to adopt efficient rules for its own proceedings. The Articles required that major questions of war, peace, international relations, and finance be approved by the vote of at least nine state delegations in Congress. Amendments required unanimous consent of the states. For lesser matters, however, including appointment of committees and preliminary moves on the major questions, the Articles vaguely required the assent of the "votes of a majority of the United States, in Congress assembled." Did this require an absolute majority of seven? Or merely a majority of the states present and voting? If the former, Congress would be severely handicapped, because states not represented would in effect be voting no, as would states with only one delegate present (the Articles required two delegates be present for a state's vote to be counted) and states whose delegations were divided. In short, to get seven affirmative votes in the face of absent, undermanned, or split delegations would be exceedingly difficult.

For four days in early March 1781 Madison, Duane, and others fought for a rule to permit action by a simple majority of the states present and voting. Those who feared any easy exercise of power combined with those who wanted especially to hamstring Congress to defeat the Madison-Duane plan, thus shackling Congress with a procedure which again and again left effective power, even on minor matters, in the hands of two or three or sometimes even one state. If only nine were present, and two divided, the negative vote of one state could block a measure favored by six. The few did indeed exert their will on the many, but, of course, not in the way those who favored "the rule of seven" professed to fear. By leaving a state certain its absence from Congress would not hamper its ability to block measures it opposed, and by making it easy for absent members to obstruct irresponsibly, "the rule of seven" insured that Congress would have great difficulty conducting even the most routine business. We may imagine Madison time and time again angered and frustrated as two or three states could defeat five or six, and as tardiness, sloth, and indifference could join malice and self-interest to defeat "acts necessary for the general good."[5]

As important as rules to permit Congress to legislate efficiently was a reorganization so that it might fulfill its executive function. During Madison's first year in Congress plans had been approved to replace the burdensome executive committees with departments or agencies of foreign affairs, finance, war, and marine headed by administrative officers, not delegates to Congress. By February 1781 the chaos, especially in the handling of finances and war supplies, was so bad that republican suspicions of executive officers as instruments of corruption and tyranny were forced to give way. Madison supported the appointment of Robert Morris as Superintendent of Finance and urged Congress to meet his conditions, including the provision of an adequate staff under his control, for accepting the office. Madison opposed the long delay in selecting a Secretary of War, and finally, after the election of Benjamin Lincoln in October 1781, he sought unsuccessfully to create the office of Assistant Secretary, to provide someone to act in Lincoln's absence. Madison was not among those fearful men who suppose that any man given the power to do anything will act badly. To him the revolution meant creating and constructing as well as resisting and opposing.

Madison sought delay, however, in appointing a Secretary for Foreign Affairs as long as the cloud over Franklin caused by Arthur Lee's charges remained. Until then, Lee was the leading candidate, hostile to France and Franklin, and determined to pull back as rapidly as possible from the European connections implicit in the French alliance. French Minister La Luzerne made it clear that Lee's appointment was utterly unsatisfactory to his government. After six months' delay, an opportunity arose to elect Robert R. Livingston of New York, one of the inner circle of nationalist-minded friends of France who often met in Mrs. House's drawing room. In August 1781 Madison neutralized Virginia's vote by having it cast for a Virginian who had no chance of election (the state could under no circumstances support a New Yorker against native son Arthur Lee). La Luzerne persuaded New Jersey to switch from Lee to Livingston, thus giving Livingston the seven votes needed for election. He overcame much of the inattention and obstruction that under the old committee system had often irritated the French.[6]

Financial matters, however, most occupied Congress, most concerned the public, and most required Madison's attention in Philadelphia. In March 1780 Congress devalued Continental currency by a ratio of 40 to 1, but the move, a desperate effort to prevent further inflation, failed completely. By the end of the year the actual depreciation had reached 100 to 1; in the spring of 1781 the states began to repeal their laws designed to support the Continental paper, and in May the bottom fell out —$1 in specie would purchase $1,000 of currency—and soon thereafter the phrase "not worth a Continental" meant literally "worth nothing." Thus shorn of the vital source of its financial independence, the power to emit negotiable paper currency, Congress essentially had to beg for funds.

Help was available from four sources, all in some way demeaning for Congress to solicit. First, the Articles of Confederation provided that Congress "requisition" the states for money, but since there was no way it could compel compliance, and since each state assumed it could judge the fairness or necessity of the requisition and therefore whether or not to meet it, the method was doomed. Second, Congress could impress supplies, but while this was effective when the army was in the field, it caused resentment against national authority and was not in the long run consistent with the principles of free government for which the revolution was being fought. Third, Congress could seek to enlist the resources and credit of private citizens; this was done increasingly while Robert Morris was Superintendent of Finance, but it opened the way for corruption, introduced countless conflicts of interest, and seemed sure to give certain powerful financial interests a mortgage on the government and even the nation itself. Fourth, Congress could continue and increase its appeals through Franklin for loans from France. Already, however, the loans burdened France severely, and many Americans feared giving her the increased influence in affairs in Philadelphia that further financial dependence would entail.

Madison saw the disadvantage of each of these recourses, but he nevertheless supported resort to each when it seemed the only way to prevent total collapse of the revolution. Again and again he helped work out intricate appeals to the states for funds, and he did his best to secure Virginia's compliance. Though it might seem strange that some of the motions to permit impressments came from one who later fathered the Bill of Rights, and in 1798 wrote the Virginia Resolutions, limiting federal power to restrain states or individuals, Madison was in fact consistent in approving strenuous, even highhanded measures when unavoidable in wartime, and in opposing them when, in peacetime, they threatened the gains of the revolution. He approved the enlistment of the fortunes of Robert Morris and other wealthy men in the patriot cause, but he knew this would neither sustain the government nor be morally defensible in the long run. Finally, though Madison feared French influence far less than did most of his colleagues, he never doubted that once the revolutionary emergency had passed and French interest in supporting a war against Great Britain had ceased, American self-respect required independence from the French treasury as much as in 1776 it had required independence from British officials and soldiers.

Only one thing would do ultimately: Congress needed the authority to lay and collect taxes. The four expedients might willy-nilly keep Congress limping along for a while, but even so, Madison became more and more convinced that the power to tax was essential to effective, stable government. Furthermore, as influential creditors saw Congress powerless to fulfill its war-caused obligations, they urged the states to assume the debts insofar as they were owed to citizens within the state. As the states did this, of course, they were strengthened and the federal government weakened in the eyes of the people. The end result could only be the dissolution of the general government. As long as Robert Morris served as Superintendent of Finance, he made do by combining the pitifully small sources of public credit, loans from France, and his substantial private credit to retain some authority in Congress and to discharge its most critical obligations—day-to-day maintenance for the army, salaries for public officials, and interest on some of the debt. Madison offered him wholehearted support in these efforts, though the Virginia farmer's son probably had some reservations about the growth of Morris' already vast commercial interest throughout the country.[7]

During 1782 Madison, Morris, Alexander Hamilton (out of the army and a delegate to Congress by late November), James Wilson, and other nationalists sought repeatedly to turn the impetus created by Morris' success into long-range financial independence for Congress. Under Madison's leadership, Congress moved slowly during the winter of 1782–3 toward a plan to furnish it with the revenue, if not from the 5 per cent impost on all imports, then from a differentiated levy, or other, more complex tax. To make the plan as acceptable as possible to states' rights men, the states were given the power to appoint the collectors and to retain the funds until requisitioned by Congress; furthermore, all the revenue was pledged to discharge war obligations, and the impost was limited to a period of not longer than twenty-five years. The only strongly nationalist provision was the stipulation that the collectors, once appointed, "shall be amenable to and removable by the United States in Congress assembled alone." In drafting the full financial plan submitted to Congress on March 6, 1783, Madison also included a provision that the debts of the states resulting from the "reasonable expenses" of war should in justice and equity be assumed by the general government. He sought to "sweeten" the impost further by linking it with measures especially favored by the different states. Most of them, especially those important to Virginia, were stricken, however, along with the assumption of state debts, before the plan passed Congress on April 18, 1783, with Rhode Island and in effect New York opposed. The measure as amended gave so little effective power to Congress, though, that Hamilton opposed it—because, Madison wrote, of his "rigid adherence . . . to a plan which he supposed more perfect."[8]

Madison's own strictures on the plan as adopted indicate he, too, felt it defective, but he saw that in furnishing Congress with its own source of revenue, and in giving it a substantial control over the collectors, the plan established the rudiments of a genuine federal government. As news of the preliminary articles of peace with Great Britain and of a new mutiny in the army agitated Congress, and as Kitty Floyd's charms and impending departure from Philadelphia preoccupied Madison, he wrote a stirring address to gain from the states the unanimous approval required by the Articles of Confederation for the impost amendment. Madison explained the necessity and practicality of the plan and pointed out that the most nationalistic provisions of earlier, rejected imposts had been eliminated or softened. He had as well to defend amendments to the plan he had opposed in debate. Congress sought, Madison said with some double meaning, "to attend at all times to the sentiments of those whom they serve . . . [and] in some way or other [provide] for an honorable and just fulfillment of the engagements which they have formed." In a plea that would haunt him seven years later, when he opposed Hamilton's plan for funding the public debt, he rejected any discrimination between the various kinds of creditors; all had lent in good faith and any distinctions would be "equally unnecessary and invidious." Madison concluded the address with an appeal to the idealism and the sense of national purpose always to him the essence of the revolution:

Let it be remembered finally that it has ever been the pride and boast of America, that the rights for which she contended were the rights of human nature. By the blessing of the Author of these rights on the means exerted for their defence they have prevailed against all opposition and form the basis of thirteen independent States. No instance has heretofore occurred, nor can any instance be expected hereafter to occur, in which the unadulterated forms of Republican government can pretend to so fair an opportunity of justifying themselves by their fruits. In this view the citizens of the United States are responsible for the greatest trust ever confided to a political society. If justice, good faith, honor, gratitude and all the other qualities which enoble the character of a nation and fulfill the ends of government be the fruits of our establishments, the cause of liberty will acquire a dignity and lustre, which it has never yet enjoyed, and an example will be set, which cannot but have the most favourable influence on the rights of Mankind. If on the other side, our governments should be unfortunately blotted with the reverse of these cardinal and essential virtues, the great cause which we have engaged to vindicate, will be dishonored and betrayed; the last and fairest experiment in favor of the rights of human nature will be turned against them; and their patrons and friends exposed to be insulted and silenced by the votaries of tyranny and usurpation.[9]

For Madison, the ceaseless quarrels among states and the Congressional indecision in facing foreign enemies carried an unmistakable lesson: the people of the thirteen former colonies would have gained nothing if, in place of British tyranny, they experienced the chaos and insecurity bred by weakness. Madison assumed, of course, as did most of his contemporaries, that such instability always resulted in the imposition of a new tyranny.

Some patriots even noted ironically that the successful conclusion of the war seemed likely to be the beginning, not the end, of American misery. The tendency to dilute the authority of government as the needs of war subsided would only bring more grief. Gouverneur Morris wrote that the

. . . vigor, organization and Promptitude [needed] to render [the United States] a considerable Empire . . . can only be acquired by a Continuance of the War which will convince People of the necessity of obedience to common counsel for general purposes. War is indeed a rude, rough Nurse to infant States, and the Consequence of being committed to her care is that they either die Young or grow up Vigorous. . . . The Confederation has not given Congress sufficient authority. This becomes daily sensible and that Sense will remedy the Evil. But if the War cease the Conviction of our Weakness will also cease until shown by another War, and then perhaps it may be too late.

Though Madison would not likely have reflected the cynicism of this letter, he would have agreed with Morris on the need for increased authority, and the impetus military exigency gave to it. Madison sought in 1783, as he did throughout his public career, to find in peace, prosperity, and freedom the same sense of purpose and resolve evident during the Revolutionary War. The struggle for the solvency of Congress, which Madison bespoke in his address to the states, provided the crucible in which, more than in any other, he forged his understanding of the requirements of effective government.[10]

Equally as urgent, and as corrosive of national unity as financial weakness, were questions of alliance and foreign policy. In June 1781 peace overtures came from Europe, and a British army under Cornwallis roamed the Virginia countryside. The arrival of a French fleet convinced Washington that the time had come for a decisive encounter with the British in New York or in Virginia. In either case, close cooperation with French forces was necessary. At the same time French Minister La Luzerne reported the peace feelers from England, Russo-Austrian mediation seemed to offer a new opportunity to end the long war. La Luzerne's communications to Congress assumed that the military situation required diplomatic concessions by the United States. Meanwhile, letters had arrived from John Adams accusing France of a betrayal of American interests; French flattery, he thought, blinded Franklin to this duplicity. English plots to sow dissension between America and her European allies and French willingness to end the costly war by sacrificing vital American interests vied with each other for Adams' contempt and heightened his suspicions. When Adams' friends in Congress used his dispatches to arouse resentment against France, La Luzerne countered that Adams was *persona non grata* to French officials in Paris and that the Franco-American alliance stood in grave danger if Adams became its custodian as well as the chief peace negotiator. New American peace commissioners, with new instructions, were needed.[11]

Madison faced the problem in Congress sure of his objectives but uncertain how best to seek them. Preservation of the French alliance, protection of territorial claims in the West and South, and complete independence from Great Britain were the goals. To forestall efforts to split America and France, and to insure that the suspicious Adams would not act secretly against French interests, La Luzerne proposed that Congress instruct the peace commission "to conform yourself to the advice and opinion" of the French negotiators. He also urged that America be "flexible" about territorial claims—that is, be willing to relinquish as much of British-occupied Georgia, South Carolina, and New York, and the lands west of the Appalachian Mountains as circumstances might require.

Madison fought any reference to territorial concessions and hoped the American negotiators would be able, when the time came, to bargain from a position strong enough to secure for the United States all the land east of the Mississippi River except Florida and New Orleans. He did not consider France hostile to these objectives, though he recognized she had no particular stake in promoting maximum American claims. Working closely with his old teacher, Witherspoon, Madison agreed to the clause making the American negotiators dependent on the French, and approved adding Franklin, John Jay, and Henry Laurens to the peace commission to restrain the anti-Gallic Adams. Fear of British intrigues to divide her enemies, confidence in French good will and in Franklin's diplomatic finesse, and recognition of American need for French support combined to make Madison accept most of La Luzerne's proposals. In fact, he saw in the French minister's hostility to Great Britain a useful antidote to the tendency among some Americans to fear England less as anti-French rumors revived ancient prejudices. To Madison, the vastly greater danger of British hostility made the almost humiliating subservience to France necessary, while his long-range confidence in American power convinced him the dependence could be made temporary.[12]

The victory at Yorktown (October 1781), by diminishing the threat posed by England and therefore easing the need for help from abroad, intensified the campaign in Congress against the connection with France. Arthur Lee and Ralph Izard, now delegates to Congress, took every opportunity to raise suspicions against France and Franklin. They complained about La Luzerne's influence in Congress, played up every hint, real or fanciful, of French intrigue in Europe, questioned Franklin's financial transactions, and encouraged the innuendos about the "wickedness of that old man" amid the ladies of Paris. Through 1782 Madison continued working with James Duane and other nationalist delegates to thwart every attack. When Arthur Lee left Congress in early October, Madison wrote in code that "he left this place I believe in not the best of humours. In Congress he has been frustrated in several favorite objects."[13]

Two days before Christmas 1782 letters arrived from Jay charging that France sought "to postpone an acknowledgment of [American] independence by Britain" until after Spain and France had achieved their war aims in Europe, notably Spanish conquest of Gibraltar. Furthermore, both France and Spain would, if they could, exclude the United States from the Mississippi valley. To support his charges, Jay enclosed a copy of a letter from the French chargé in Philadelphia, Madison's friend Barbé-Marbois, to French Foreign Minister Vergennes. Barbé-Marbois proposed that before the British evacuated New York, France should make known her opposition to American fishing off Newfoundland and American claims to Western lands. He clearly intended to make

French support of the evacuation contingent upon American abandonment of the fishing rights and land claims. To thwart these schemes,
Jay wrote, he had taken the lead in peace negotiations with Great Britain,
without consulting Vergennes, thus violating the explicit instructions of
Congress and possibly arousing the suspicions and enmity of France.[14]

While Madison thought Barbé-Marbois' anti-American letter a forgery
(he was mistaken), and France still a true and faithful ally, he did recognize the "peculiarly delicate" position of that nation in seeking at once
to satisfy her two allies, Spain and the United States. As Madison explained in notes on debates in Congress he began to take about this time:

> . . . the claims and views of Spain and America [in the Mississippi
> valley] interfere. The . . . attempts of Britain to seduce Spain to a
> separate peace, and the ties of France with the latter whom she had
> drawn into the war, required her to favor Spain, at least to a certain
> degree, at the expense of America. Of this Great Britain is taking
> advantage. If France adheres to Spain, Great Britain espouses the
> views of America; and endeavours to draw her off from France. If
> France should adhere to America in her claims, Britain might espouse
> those of Spain and produce a breach between her and France, and in
> either case Britain would divide her enemies. If France acts wisely she
> will in this dilemma prefer the friendship of America to that of Spain.
> If America acts wisely she will see that she is with respect to her great
> interests, *more in danger of being seduced by Britain than sacrificed
> by France.*[15]

Madison thus set forth guidelines he followed as long as he sat in the
Continental Congress. The United States had a paramount interest in
the Mississippi valley, which, if Spain would not recognize, France
should. It would be wiser for her to back the stronger—that is, the
American—interest. Since Great Britain was the only sure gainer in any
quarrels among France, Spain, and the United States, those who agitated
such disputes were in fact helping Great Britain (so much for trouble-
making Americans). American policy should have as its foundation, at
least as long as threatened by England, the French alliance. Though some
possibility of a French betrayal existed, it was more remote than many
other dangers faced by the weak new nation. To act suspiciously, un-
gratefully, or deceitfully toward France would only encourage forces
hostile to American independence. These propositions were essentially
Benjamin Franklin's; perhaps Madison's own position took shape as he
read Franklin's dispatches to Congress from Europe.

In February 1783, while Congress awaited definite word on peace negotiations, a number of delayed letters from John Adams, written the
previous September, led Madison to some strictures on the doughty
New Englander. The correspondence was, Madison wrote Jefferson,
"not remarkable for anything unless it be a display of [Adams'] vanity,
his prejudice against the French Court, and his venom against Doctor

Franklin." Madison had never met Adams and knew him only through his letters, which came in cascades while he sat in Holland, frustrated, suspicious, and neglected after his rejection by the French court. The letters contained valuable information, patriotic exhortations, and occasionally some good judgment, but for a reader such as Madison, convinced of French good will, page after page seemed wrongheaded and dangerous. Jefferson, on the other hand, had known Adams during his heroic work for independence in 1775 and 1776, and had a deep appreciation of his mind and heart. "I am nearly at a loss," Jefferson replied to Madison's disdainful comments,

> to judge how [Adams] will act in the negotiation. He hates Franklin, he hates Jay, he hates the French, he hates the English. To whom will he adhere? His vanity is a lineament in his character which had entirely escaped me. His want of taste I had observed. Notwithstanding all this he has a sound head on substantial points, and I think he has integrity. I am glad therefore that he is of the commission and expect he will be useful in it. His dislike of all parties, and all men, by balancing his prejudices, may give the same fair play to his reason as would a general benevolence of temper. At any rate honesty may be extracted even from poisonous weeds.

Madison's harsh judgment of Adams' personality and prejudices nevertheless reveals important grounds for the Virginian's view of the peace negotiations in Paris.[16]

In March 1783 the long-awaited preliminary peace treaty with Great Britain arrived. "The terms granted to America appeared . . . on the whole extremely liberal," Madison observed. Independence, the fishing rights, the lands east of the Mississippi, and its navigation had all been guaranteed to the United States. Two matters, however, alarmed Madison and other friends of France: the preliminary treaty had been signed before Vergennes had been informed of its terms, and it contained a separate, secret article providing that should Great Britain get West Florida as a result of her peace treaty with Spain, the United States agreed to a northern boundary to that province one hundred miles above the one designated if Spain had possession. That is, the United States was willing to grant her enemy what she would not grant her friend. The peace commissioners, Madison observed, had been "ensnared by the dexterity of the British Minister. . . . Writing sentiments unfriendly to our Ally, [served] . . . the insidious policy of the Enemy. The separate Article was most offensive, being considered as obtained by Great Britain not for the sake of the territory ceded to her, but as a means of disuniting the United States and France." In Madison's view the bilateral proceedings of the American commissioners had sown enough distrust, to say nothing of the repercussions sure to come from the secret article. The commissioners had very nearly destroyed all basis for confidence between America and France, thereby making "the safety of their Country depend upon the sincerity of [British Prime Minister] Lord Shelburne."[17]

After confiding to Edmund Randolph the differences among the American commissioners (Jay had taken the lead in secret approaches to the British negotiators; Adams "followed with cordiality"; and Franklin was "dragged into it"), Madison wrote of the "infinitely perplexing . . . dilemma to which Congress are reduced. If they abet the proceedings of their Ministers, all confidence with France is at an end which in the event of a renewal of the war, must be dreadful as in that of peace it may be dishonorable. If they disavow the conduct of their Ministers . . . the most serious inconveniences also present themselves." To add to Madison's pain, La Luzerne and Barbé-Marbois hinted to him of the anger of Vergennes at the peace negotiations, and pointed out that though great powers might not *complain*, they "*felt* and *remembered*." Furthermore, shortly after the treaty arrived, Congress learned that Washington's army threatened to mutiny, the measures to bolster the public credit seemed doomed to defeat, and the day of Robert Morris' resignation as Superintendent of Finance drew near. All of these circumstances, Madison reported, "gave peculiar awe and solemnity to the present moment, and oppressed the minds of Congress with an anxiety and distress which had been scarcely felt in any period of the revolution."[18]

The debate in Congress centered upon Foreign Secretary Robert R. Livingston's proposals to tell the French minister of the secret article, to explain Congress' embarrassment over it as best he could, to inform France (and Spain) that they would be granted the same favorable boundary for West Florida as Great Britain, and to declare America's intention to delay its ratification of the treaty until France had made her own peace with Great Britain. Clark of New Jersey argued that Congress ought not to interfere at all; the commissioners had made a very good treaty and should be allowed to explain their actions in France in their own way. James F. Mercer, Madison's colleague from Virginia, spoke hotly of the betrayal of France and of his "inexpressible indignation" at the commissioners' "stooping, as it were, to lick the dust from the feet of a nation whose hands were still dyed with the blood of their fellow-citizens." Rutledge of South Carolina and Williamson of North Carolina opposed any rebuke, direct or implied, to commissioners who "had shown great ability," and argued that agreements with France had not been violated. Arthur Lee defended the commissioners and blamed all the trouble on what he insisted were the humiliating instructions of June 1781. He was not, he said bitingly, and perhaps looking at Madison, "surprised that those who considered France as the Patron rather than the Ally of this Country should be disposed to be obsequious to her, but he was not of that number."

We may imagine Madison indignant and intent on gathering his thoughts while Virginian Theodorick Bland and Stephen Higginson of Massachusetts supported Lee's innuendos, and Alexander Hamilton, together with two Pennsylvanians, James Wilson and Richard Peters, defended the need somehow to allay legitimate French resentments and suspicions. Then Madison, but thirty-two years old, yet the member of Congress most experienced in defending the French alliance, rose to repudiate the anti-French arguments. He was surprised at the attacks on the instructions of June 1781, enacted during the dark days of the revolution and acquiesced in, he recalled, looking at Lee and Bland, by those who now so gleefully approved their violation. It was absolutely necessary that the United States communicate immediately to France the secret article and other details of American negotiations with Great Britain; otherwise all nations would regard the United States as "devoid of all Constancy and good faith." The difficulty of France in conciliating the interfering claims of Spain and the United States, not deceit or hostility, had caused the indecisive delaying tactics of French diplomats. The United States, then, "instead of cooperating with Great Britain in taking advantage of [French] embarrassment . . . ought to make every allowance" for the problems of a faithful ally. The secret and hostile aspect of the separate article would "be regarded by the impartial world as a dishonorable alliance with our enemies against the interests of our friends." Only complete disclosure of the treaty and the negotiations leading to it, and profuse explanations and even apologies to France, could restore American honor and leave her in a strong enough position to renew the war against Great Britain should the peace negotiations break down. By so doing, the United States might be able to retain the favorable terms of the preliminary treaty, the confidence of France, and the respect of the rest of the world.[19]

Madison was sure that unless the United States, weak and dependent next to the great nations of Europe, could establish a realistic position balancing in some way among them, her independence would be incomplete. Commercial and cultural links to Britain were, despite the revolution, still far stronger than those with any other foreign country. France was, therefore, an indispensable counterpoise to British power and influence. This realism, together with a conviction, shared with Franklin, that new nations needed especially the respect and good will that honorable dealings in world affairs could bring, were Madison's guideposts in the debates over the peace treaty. He was pleased, then, when Congress ratified the treaty in a way maintaining Franco-American good will.

Though the positions Madison took on the peace treaty and other issues, and the principles upon which he stood, were remarkably honest and candid for one to whom the term "politician" can properly be applied, back-home pressures, factional interests, and emotional biases,

not logic and justice, often influenced his acts. Beyond the special interests of each state, the most important forces influencing Congress
during Madison's service were the friendly reaction of many delegates
to French support of the revolution, the spread of the financial empire
of Robert Morris, and the effort to strengthen national authority by
enlarging the powers of Congress. These forces were, moreover, linked
tightly, suggesting collusion and party spirit to those opposed to them:
French military and commercial officials worked closely with Morris' network of partnerships and agents, and together they sought their ends by
enlarging the powers of Congress.[20]

The dispute in 1779 between Arthur Lee and Silas Deane about the
early contracts for French support, and the debate a year later over
Franklin's mission to France (see Chapter VI), had shown Congress divided along more than merely sectional lines. Though the dispute broke
out over a specific issue, its roots ran deep into colonial history and
into the emotions of the revolution. Many Americans, like Madison,
welcomed an association with France beyond mere military support.
Through her, they felt, America might maintain the cultural ties with
Western civilization in one sense severed by the Declaration of Independence. Furthermore, they saw in the French *philosophes*, who greeted
the American Revolution so enthusiastically, earnest co-workers in the
mission to spread the blessings of liberty around the world. They had
little fear that Europe would corrupt America; more likely America
would infect Europe with its promise of human freedom. Clearest in
Franklin and Jefferson, this view influenced many delegates to Congress,
and other relatively cosmopolitan Americans. Madison probably first
sensed it directly from Spaniards and Frenchmen in Williamsburg who
at once embodied ancient culture and Enlightenment hope for the future.
In Philadelphia the elegant, brilliant circle at the French legation reinforced Madison's Francophile tendencies. At the same time, he realized,
of course, that self-interest was France's basic reason for helping the
United States.

On the other hand, many Americans, especially New Englanders,
could not shed a centuries-old Anglo-Saxon animosity toward Catholic,
despotic France. They were, in a way, early American isolationists: they
wanted the new United States to shun as much as possible any connection with Europe. They were sure that France wanted only to humble
Great Britain and would therefore desert America as soon as it suited her
to do so. Furthermore, Americans who sought to deal with her would
inevitably be corrupted by the intrigues of her court and end betrayed
and defeated. Hence the only safe course for the United States was to
depend as little as possible on France and to have nothing but the most
formal relations with her in order that the republican experiment in
America might flourish free from European contamination. Sam Adams,

the Lees of Virginia, and somewhat later, John Jay most clearly reflected this point of view.

These two contrary predispositions were by no means perfectly distinct, but the general cleavage was significant enough to be the foundation for the first great division in American national politics. Patriotism,
of course, was not an issue. Those who feared France believed that *only*
by being on guard against her would the United States be genuinely free
to work out her unique destiny. Those who welcomed her support
thought the United States could become independent and great *only* by
finding through France ways to stay in the mainstream of Western civilization. They also regarded as chimerical any thought that a weak,
essentially dependent nation could remain aloof from international
politics (such a luxury would come only with the strength acquired
after the War of 1812).

Decades of strife between France and England lay behind this division
in American politics. Nursing the humiliation of the Seven Years' War,
Frenchmen had eagerly watched as trouble brewed between England and
her colonies. French agents were active in America and American emissaries went to France a year before the Declaration of Independence.
French munitions and supplies were vital to the revolution even before
the conclusion of the French alliance in February 1778. After that,
France played an active, often open role in American affairs. Her minister in Philadelphia supported Silas Deane when the sensational charges
against him were brought before Congress, adding fuel at home to the
rising conflagration of suspicion that already consumed Arthur Lee and
his friends over what they thought were corrupt, treasonable contacts
and contracts between Americans and Frenchmen in Europe. By the
time Madison took his seat in Congress in 1780, a new French minister,
La Luzerne, and his artful private secretary, Barbé-Marbois, had become
powerful figures in Philadelphia. As American financial and military
collapse seemed imminent in 1780 and 1781, their leverage increased.

La Luzerne's pressure on friendly delegates helped secure support for
the act of March 18, 1780, to devaluate and then stabilize Continental
currency. Together with Barbé-Marbois, he played an important role in
restraining the American claims for Western lands so important to Madison in the fall of 1780. At the end of that year, the Frenchmen helped
turn aside Arthur Lee's assault on Franklin. La Luzerne's influence with
Daniel of Saint Thomas Jenifer, and other Maryland delegates, furnished
the final push for that state's vital ratification of the Articles of Confederation. The establishment of the permanent executive departments under
Congress and the appointments of Robert Morris and Robert R. Livingston were all effected with La Luzerne's support. His foes in the Lee-
Adams faction were sure, moreover, that without French "conniving,"
as they saw it, different decisions would have been made. La Luzerne

again and again thwarted Morris' enemies by stipulating that French funds would be available to the United States *only* if disposed of as Morris wanted. La Luzerne helped friendly delegates (probably including Madison) draft the controversial June 1781 instructions that the American peace commissioners be guided by the "advice and opinion" of the French foreign ministry. In all these moves, except those about the Western lands, Madison approved La Luzerne's efforts, and he almost certainly acted often in Congress with his advice and counsel. Delegates James Wilson, Richard Peters, and Thomas Fitzsimons of Pennsylvania, Joseph Jones and Edmund Randolph of Virginia, James Duane of New York, and John Sullivan of New Hampshire, together with Morris, Livingston, Jenifer, and Madison were the core of the "French party," as their foes labeled it, in Philadelphia. The Reverend Samuel Cooper of Boston, Thomas Paine, Hugh Henry Brackenridge, and perhaps Dr. Benjamin Rush were paid by the French ministers to write on behalf of good will for France in the United States, and Sullivan was much beholden to La Luzerne for loans.

Persons predisposed to distrust France, of course, saw nothing but danger and disaster for America in La Luzerne's influence. Inheriting a hard core of delegates who even before 1775 had looked to Richard Henry Lee and Sam Adams for leadership, opponents of French influence drew together as "evidence" of pro-French collusion mounted. Every deference paid by Franklin to French interests or sensibilities, every intervention by La Luzerne in American affairs, every sumptuous dinner he gave for members of Congress, and every proposal by Madison or others to adhere to the letter and spirit of the French alliance, seemed to the anti-French party part of a conspiracy to sink American virtue and republican independence in a cesspool of French corruption and absolutism. The mood of the anti-French party is apparent in a letter about Robert R. Livingston from Arthur Lee to the American minister in Russia: "Whatever you see or receive from him you may consider as dictated by the French Minister. He made him what he is, and policy, or gratitude, keeps him from disobeying or renouncing his maker."[21]

In the spring of 1782, amid innuendos and even open charges that the connection with France was pernicious and disgraceful to America, Madison collaborated with Barbé-Marbois in a written defense of the French alliance. It was printed in the newspapers as a letter from an American official, and summarized the view of those who felt as Madison did. The severe defeat of the French fleet in the West Indies (in April 1782), the two men wrote, gave the United States a chance to show her gratitude for French aid. "Four years have elapsed since the date of the happy alliance which unites us with France; we have every year received new benefits from this nation, without being able to make any other return than barren acknowledgments; and like one friend who is constantly obliged by another, without having it in his power to render reciprocal services, we waited with impatience an opportunity of demonstrating that our professions of attachment and gratitude were graven on our hearts. . . . This opportunity has happened." By continuing to fight and by refusing "perfidious" British proposals of a separate peace, the United States could prove herself "activated by principles of justice, of constancy and fidelity." Barbé-Marbois and Madison rejoiced in a recent repudiation by both countries of separate British peace over-tures. "This was the proper conduct," they wrote, "to do honour to the two nations. . . . [Britain] hoped, by sowing seeds of jealousy and dis-trust, to divide us: she flattered herself that the two allies, or at least one of them, might listen to her propositions; that the other would conceive suspicions therefrom; that discontent would succeed, and that a rupture would eventually take place. . . . Her project has miscarried, the artifice is detected. . . . [It] serves to evince the mutual fidelity and attachment of the allies; and the necessity of an unlimited confidence and constant communication of every thing which relates to our mutual interests." Accept France as a trusted friend, and British arrogance and deceit would fail. Should the allies split, British "subjugation" would return. Madi-son and Barbé-Marbois concluded with a plea for "the courage to TAX ourselves" and thus provide the sinews of war still desperately needed.[22]

The division over attitudes toward France might have remained rather remote and theoretical had not many of the friends of France also been deeply involved in the mercantile affairs of Robert Morris, the dominant figure in American trade and finance during the revolution. Though historians have not yet unraveled all of Morris' complicated business activities, and probably never will, part of his story, at least, is clear enough. He began poor, then enjoyed moderate success as a merchant, mostly in shipping, before the revolution. His energy and experience made him a key figure in the secret committees which, beginning in 1775, managed the effort to secure arms and supplies for the American armies. Whatever their deficiences, these arrangements, more or less secret, all improvised, and all characterized by contracts susceptible to great loss as well as great profit, did equip the army. Morris thus gained valuable political contacts, an amazing command of revolutionary fi-nance, and mercantile connections of vast use in his private ventures.[23]

In 1778 he retired from public life and for three years devoted his energy and skill to his private affairs. Benefiting from his prestige, and using capital partly accumulated while he was in office, he began an incredible expansion of his activities. By 1780 he was the undisputed "Prince of Merchants" in America, and if not the richest man in the country, at least the one best able to command its credit and resources. A dozen partnerships and many more less formal arrangements gave him a role in hundreds of trading ventures, most in some way related to the war. He had especially large and lucrative enterprises in the West Indies, the Southern states, and in the towns and cities south and west of the Hudson River. When Congress came to select a Superintendent of Finance in February 1781, Morris was "the only man for the job." He and he alone seemed able to master the riddle American trade and finance had become in six years of separation from the systematic, experienced counting houses of Britain.

Any man who became rich as fast as Morris inevitably aroused opposition, envy, and suspicion; when he had been deeply involved, at the same time, with politicians, the suspicions increased tenfold. Morris' partners included James Wilson, Thomas Fitzsimons, and Gouverneur Morris, all members of Congress at various times. Another partner, William Bingham, also served as American consul at Martinique in the West Indies. Morris' connections with the Harrisons and Braxtons in Virginia gave him a strong hold on the trade of that state. His connections in the other Southern states were as strategic and widespread. Most sensitive politically, the Morris empire was deeply involved with France. He and Silas Deane were partners. John Holker, purchasing agent for the French navy and the most active French merchant in America, worked mainly through Morris. The web of trade connecting France, the West Indies, and the American mainland, expecially south of New York, was more and more in Morris' hands. Thus, when a vessel reached an American port, or a contract to supply arms was fulfilled, or a cargo of American rice or tobacco reached Europe, enormous profits often ended in his coffers.

To the east, toward Boston, however, Morris' enterprises were less dominant, and since his business did not become large until after 1775, he did not have the extensive connections with Great Britain characteristic of colonial merchants. New Englanders both feared his encroachments and were not as dependent on him as were trading men in the rest of the country. Furthermore, to older merchants, accustomed to British trading patterns and perhaps anxious to revive them, Morris was a parvenu of the worst sort, having built a fortune on their ruin by becoming master of the new trade routes dictated by the revolution. That Morris' empire was largely a product of the revolution was a persistent vexation to the Lee-Adams group, many of whom were traditional-minded New Englanders and old-line Virginia aristocrats who often stigmatized their foes as lowborn, socially and morally inferior *nouveaux riches*. Yet the Morris group had, by whatever means, provided the sinews of war, and no one else had energy, will, and resources to keep the revolution solvent. This fact, crucial and undeniable, was the making of Morris as a revolutionary statesman and the reason why Madison always backed him.

A man like Morris was bound to deal in Western lands, and these ventures, in turn, were bound to make his foes all the more sure that he improperly mixed public and private affairs and that his dealings with alien (French) entrepreneurs somehow betrayed the revolution. Among the stockholders in the Illinois-Wabash Company, for example, which claimed title to 60 million acres of land, were Morris, James Wilson, Silas Deane, French purchasing agent John Holker, delegates to Congress from Maryland, and Franklin's banker and landlord in Paris, Le Ray de Chaumont. Furthermore, 12 per cent of the shares were set aside "for purposes most conducive to the [company's] general interest"—that is, they might be given to anyone who could help persuade Congress to validate the company's dubious land titles. Conrad Alexandre Gérard, first French Minister to the United States, was among those so "honored." To outsiders, most of whom considered the Illinois-Wabash claims fraudulent in the first place, the company seemed obviously a conspiracy by Morris and his French friends to make even more fast money by a discreet oiling of congressional palms.[24]

Though Madison fought doggedly, and in the end successfully, to defeat the extravagant claims of Illinois-Wabash and other land companies, he seems nevertheless to have objected neither to Morris' technique of combining public and private affairs nor to the leading role of Frenchmen in the land speculations. As the United States government had no financial institutions or purchasing agencies of its own, it had necessarily to use private means. In fact, without the private merchants who "lent" their credit and connections to the public, both government and the war would have collapsed. The crucial question was not whether formal "conflict of interest" opportunities existed (they usually did), but whether any particular merchant cheated the government, whether he used information obtained in confidence as a public official for his personal gain, or whether his operations in balance gave the public a "fair" return for its money. That Madison understood these matters and that he by and large thought Morris operated within justifiable limits is apparent in the following letter (bracketed words were written in code) commenting on the charges that circulated against Morris.

I own I can not [invent an excuse for] the [prepense malice] with which the [character and services of this gentleman are murdered]. I am persuaded that [he accepted his office] from [motives which were honourable and patriotic]. I have seen [no proof of misfeasance]. I have heard of many [charges] which [were palpably erroneous]. I have known others somewhat [specious vanish on examination]. Every [member in Congress] must be sensible of the [benefit] which has [accrued to the public from his administration]. No intelligent man [out of Congress can be altogether insensible of it]. The [Court of France has] testified [its satisfaction at his appointment] which I really believe [lessened its] repugnance to [lend us money]. These consid-

erations will make me cautious in lending an ear to the suggestions
even of the impartial; to those of [known and vindictive enemys]
very [incredulous]. The same fidelity to the public interest which
obliges those who are its appointed guardians, to pursue with every
vigor a [perfidious or dishonest servant of the public] requires [them]
to confront the imputations [of malice against the good and faithful
one].[25]

Clearly, Madison thought Morris a patriot whose intentions were honorable and whose business skill was a boon to the cause. Furthermore,
his close ties with France were a mark in his favor, not a sign of treachery or near treason as the Lee-Adams faction assumed. Of Madison's
career in the Continental Congress Arthur Lee wrote: "It is his political
conduct which I condemn, that without being a public knave himself
he has always been a supporter of public knaves, and never, in any one
instance, has he concurred to check, censure, or control them—that has
had such vanity to suppose himself superior to all other persons, conducting measures without consulting them and intolerant of all advice
or contradiction—that in consequence he has been duped by the artful
management of the rapacious Morris and the intriguing Marbois." Lee's
charges embody the persisting suspicions and self-righteousness of the
Lee-Adams faction. That Lee identified Madison as "always a supporter"
of the Morris–Barbé-Marbois combine is a sure sign that Madison played
an important role in the party struggles dividing Congress during his
service there.

To Madison the heart of the matter was national power. In February
1783 he had argued the vital need of Congress to possess a revenue of
its own. Otherwise the general government would be impotent, and
the states divided into hostile factions where finally "foreign aid would
be called in by first the weaker [and] then the stronger side, and finally
both be made subservient to the wars and politics of Europe." Arthur
Lee had responded that Madison's theories were "pregnant with danger."
Lee raised the specter of the "ship money" of Charles I, and declared,
to charges that without revenue power Congress was a "rope of sand,"
that he "had rather see Congress a rope of sand than a rod of iron."
Both men knew there were dangers in such arrangements as joint "help"
from Morris and the French: it might become corrupt, collusive, and
inimical to American liberty and independence. The crucial difference
between them was in *where* each saw the *greatest* danger. To Lee it came
from combinations of power able to subvert American freedom. Put another way, the Lee-Adams faction feared power more than impotence;
they suspected those in authority would be unable to withstand or overcome corrupting influences. Madison, on the other hand, believed that
men of good will, given power, could guard against its corruption and
use it to fulfill the revolution. This faith was the essential foundation of
Madison's nationalist decade, 1780 through 1789.[26]

Tension between the Madison–Morris–La Luzerne group and its adversaries was heightened because the Lees and the Adamses and their supporters had by and large reached the culmination of their careers in the events of 1776. These were the colorful revolutionary heroes who had spent a good part of their adult lives resisting British measures. Casting off the British yoke was for them the climax, the successful conclusion, of a long struggle. Most of them had for perhaps a generation been active in their native states as the leaders of local resistance movements. Habitually they thought in state terms and opposed more central authority. They conceived of Congress as a league formed to coordinate the various state struggles for independence—a natural view for them because under British rule there had been no intercolonial authority except London's. Though the colonies had long recognized the need for unity to defend their rights, the acts of resistance for men who had been adults in the generation before 1776 had usually been generated by one colony or one city. These same men, furthermore, had been adults during the last great, glorious war, against France (many of them had fought in it), and therefore had, in the same way that millions of men in the United States and western Europe in the 1960s were still hostile to Germany, an often irrepressible animosity toward France. Finally, they had known and often benefited from the old British Empire trading patterns, which Robert Morris and his associates frequently displaced. Most of the leaders of the Lee-Adams faction had been born before 1740: Sam Adams (1722), Henry Laurens (1724), William Whipple (1730), Richard Henry Lee (1732), Thomas McKean (1734), Francis Lightfoot Lee (1734), John Adams (1735), James Lovell (1737), and John Rutledge (1739).

Madison's colleagues, on the other hand, were mostly younger: they had come of age with the revolution, which was to them the beginning, not the culmination, of their careers. The purpose and meaning of their lives were tied up with the growth and greatness of the nation the revolution had brought into being. Though they, like Madison, had usually been active in state resistance movements, and had perhaps served briefly in state conventions and legislatures, their habits had not been formed there, and they easily transferred their loyalty to the national scene. For them France was less an ancient foe than a friend who might sponsor the new nation in foreign affairs, as, in a way, Britain had done under the colonial system. The emotions of these young men were geared not to local measures of resistance and revolution, but to deeds of nation building. They could find fulfillment for their ambitions and public careers only if the United States became a great and powerful nation. Though these men had powerful support from older leaders (Franklin, Robert Morris, James Duane, and Washington) they had for the most part been born in the seventeen-forties and seventeen-fifties: Thomas Fitzsimons (1741), James Wilson (1742), Thomas Jefferson

(1743), Richard Peters (1744), Robert R. Livingston (1746), Madison (1751), Gouverneur Morris (1752), Edmund Randolph (1753), and Alexander Hamilton (1755).[27]

These men turned to an enlargement of national power as naturally, and in time, as habitually as the older men turned to the state legislature. Madison, for example, sought on two important questions to use "national reasons" to persuade the Virginia legislature to do something older, state-oriented men were inclined to oppose. He urged that Virginia cede her Western lands to the general government, and he pleaded repeatedly for Virginia to fulfill her obligations to Congress and to approve the desperately needed power to lay and collect federal taxes. Robert R. Livingston accepted appointment as a delegate to Congress and joined the nationalist group in part to put pressure on the New York state government. He sought measures in Congress to restrict or even forbid the states from exercising taxing power he opposed in New York. If La Luzerne, Barbé-Marbois, and Morris could help, so much the better. When the Pennsylvania legislature refused to charter a bank Morris and James Wilson had organized in the grim days of 1780, they sought and received support from Congress for the Bank of North America. Again and again as the young nation builders sought measures they believed essential to national well-being, they encountered opposition from state legislatures and resistance from members of Congress dominated by them. Little wonder, then, that they formed their own "nationalist party" and became leading federalists in 1787, 1788, and 1789.[28]

Madison's analysis in 1782 of the effect of state interests on the "two great objects which predominate in the politics of Congress," the status of Vermont and the disposition of Western lands, reveals further his impatience with localism. The New England states, excepting in some degree New Hampshire, which claimed parts of Vermont for itself, favored admission of Vermont as an independent state "from ancient prejudice against New York," partly to benefit land interests of New Englanders in Vermont, but mostly to add another New England vote in Congress. Pennsylvania and Maryland favored Vermont in order to add a vote against the claims of Southern states, especially Virginia, to Western lands. New Jersey and Delaware had the same motive, plus the additional one of adding another "small state" to the Confederation. Both of these motives worked as well on Rhode Island. New York claimed Vermont for herself and therefore, of course, vehemently opposed independence. Opposition from the four southernmost states rested upon "an habitual jealousy" of New England, suspicion that Vermont would oppose their Western claims, disinclination to "admit so unimportant a state" to an equal vote in Confederation councils, and fear that "carving" Vermont from New York and New Hampshire would be a precedent for dismembering other states.

On the other great question, New Jersey, Pennsylvania, Delaware, and Maryland opposed the Western land claims, especially Virginia's, because of "the intrigues of their Citizens" who were interested in the land company grants not recognized by Virginia. Furthermore, these states, plus Rhode Island, envious of the "superior resources and importance" of the Southern states, wanted the Western lands as a fund for *national* revenue in which they would share. Connecticut and Massachusetts subordinated their position on Western lands to that on Vermont: they perceived that Maryland and Pennsylvania, with no fundamental interest in Vermont, would cease to support her pretensions once they no longer needed New England to oppose Western land claims. Therefore, Massachusetts and Connecticut refused to settle the land claims issue until after resolution of the Vermont question. New York, on the other hand, with very flimsy Western land claims, would tend toward New England once the Vermont question ceased to divide her from that region. As the pressures of war and calamity eased, increasing the influence of state-oriented coalitions and factions in Philadelphia, Madison had little hesitation in supporting the nationalist inclinations of La Luzerne and Morris against such forces.[29]

In the first three years or so of the revolution, patriotic zeal muffled the disputes in Congress. However, as the hardships of war mounted in 1778, 1779, and 1780, and foreign influence increased, party patterns emerged. The Lee-Adams coalition dominated the controversy over Silas Deane's activities in France, but as its localistic bias seemed unsuitable either for waging war or for bringing a stable peace, and as Madison and other younger nationalistic delegates gained in influence, the tide turned slowly: Franklin was vindicated, cooperation with France was strengthened, and Morris took over as Superintendent of Finance. During 1782 La Luzerne wrote in almost every dispatch to Vergennes of the growing power of the Madison-Morris group, and he boasted at the end of that year that "the Eastern [Lee-Adams] party had lost its great influence over Congress."[30]

Morris' threatened retirement, the defeat of the impost, the signing of the peace treaty, and the decline of French interest in American affairs, all in 1783, undercut the supremacy of the nationalist party. No longer facing the clamorous pressures of war, and riding a reaction against the sometimes desperate measures they had produced, the Lee-Adams faction reasserted itself, and remained dominant as long as the Articles of Confederation lasted. The alarming chaos of 1786 revived the nationalist party, and its adherents almost to a man became leaders in the move for a new constitution; they dominated the Federal Convention, waged the successful fight for ratification, and took the lead in establishing the new government. The best sign, beyond the continuity of persons, of the close relationship between the friends of national power in 1782 and in 1789 is the near identity of the financial measures proposed by Morris in 1782 and those proposed at the later date by Hamilton. The government created under Washington's leadership in 1789 provided, finally, the strong national authority Morris, Hamilton, and Madison had sought during the chaotic days at the end of the Revolutionary War.[31]

Though, like most of his contemporaries, Madison disdained faction and party—words meaning to him combinations for selfish purposes— he saw that if such forces coalesced, organization was necessary to oppose them. He worked easily, effectively, and without remorse in joint efforts for political purposes. He was effective in Congress in large part because he had both a program and a party. By the end of 1783 Madison had had abundant experience in the politics of revolution and nation building. He knew the difficulties and pitfalls as well as the prospects and opportunities. To a youthful revolutionary zeal, he had now added necessary political skills. A sure grasp of the public problems of the new nation and a keen sense of the modes of government appropriate to those problems were the result.

Anxious concern and the press of business dominated Madison's years in Philadelphia, but there were periods of pleasure, excitement, and even exultation. One day in September 1781, for example, Madison stood on the steps of Independence Hall with Washington, Rochambeau, and members of Congress as, first, three thousand lean, ragged Continentals and then two divisions of French troops paraded up Chestnut Street on their way to Yorktown. The French soldiers saluted "Congress as a crowned head, and [its] President as the first Prince of the blood." Madison reported that "nothing can exceed the appearance of this specimen which our ally has sent us of his army, whether we regard the figure of the men, or the exactness of their discipline." Then John Laurens arrived with cash, supplies, and arms from France, and, at the gala dinner held for the French and American officers, news came that a French fleet had appeared in Chesapeake Bay to blockade Cornwallis. The stage was set for the decisive military action of the war.[32]

On October 24, Washington's aide-de-camp, after four days of furious riding, reached Philadelphia with news that the British army at Yorktown had surrendered. Pennsylvania officials, members of Congress, and French Minister La Luzerne forgot their feuds as they heard artillery salutes boom across the State House yard. They marched solemnly to the Dutch Lutheran church where Congressional chaplain George Duffield, whose sermons John Adams reported "filled and swell'd the Bosom of every Hearer," gave thanks to Almighty God for the providential victory. That evening windows in Philadelphia shone with candles, and crowds celebrated in the streets. Madison offered "fervent congratulations" to Edmund Pendleton "on the glorious success of the combined arms" at Yorktown, and hoped that the "severe doses of ill fortune would cool the phrenzy and relax the pride of Britain." A month later Madison reported that Washington ("our illustrious General") had arrived in Philadelphia and would try to resolve quarrels in Congress over army arrangements for the coming year. His four-month stay, Washington wrote, was "divided between parties of pleasure, and parties of business." He visited Madison, Duane, and his other friends at Mrs. House's. Madison probably went to the Southwalk Theatre on January 2, 1782, to a performance of Beaumarchais' comedy *Eugénie* (in French) and David Garrick's *The Lying Valet*, offered in Washington's honor, as well as to La Luzerne's party for the general, where the "first serious American attempt at grand opera," Joseph Hopkinson's *The Temple of Minerva*, was presented. Madison's close association with Washington, the mutual respect and admiration between the two Virginians, and their fundamental agreement on the needs and character of the new nation probably date from this winter of planning and, for Washington, "respite from the fatigues of war."[33]

The most elaborate Franco-American celebrations, however, took place during the spring and summer of 1782, after news had arrived that after twelve years of waiting, and only girl babies, the queen of France had given birth to a dauphin. On May 13 Congress received La Luzerne with elaborate ceremony, cannons were discharged, and a vast company was entertained at City Tavern that evening. The French minister was delighted that Americans celebrated "the birth of the heir of the crown of France with more éclat than the birth of a Prince of Wales ever elicited in the eras of British rule," while Madison, more soberly, observed that "it was deemed politic at this crisis to display every proper evidence of affectionate attachment to our ally." Two months later La Luzerne, at the height of his personal influence and at the time of the greatest French involvement in American affairs, sponsored a lavish festival to celebrate the royal birth. Hairdressers and fancy clothiers were busy for weeks grooming Philadelphia ladies for the greatest social event in the city's history. Numerous Frenchmen in attendance charmed members of Congress and provided, as they had on an earlier occasion, "a swarm of French beaux . . . marquises, counts, viscounts, barons, and chevaliers" to escort American belles. La Luzerne built a pavilion to accommodate his six hundred invited guests, while twelve thousand others watched French fireworks or enjoyed favors handed out by La Luzerne's servants. The affair was a huge success and furnished Madison and other pro-French Americans a marvelous opportunity to praise the courage and fidelity of Louis XVI and to exalt the virtues of Gallic civilization. Though Benjamin Rush enjoyed the occasion, he nevertheless noted its irony: "How new the phenomenon for republicans and freemen to re-

joice in the birth of a prince who must one day be the support of
monarchy and slavery! Human nature in this instance seems to be turned
inside outwards." Rush's ambivalence reveals why many Americans hesitated to link their fortunes too closely with those of despotic France.[34]

Probably more satisfying to one with Madison's dislike for large, formal occasions, however, were the joys of the family circle at Mrs.
House's and the deep pleasure Madison took in close friendships with
those who shared his political convictions. By the time Madison left Congress he was very close to the sensible and sociable Eliza House Trist,
whose partiality for Virginians resulted in, among other things, the
marriage of her grandson to a granddaughter of Jefferson's in 1824. She
wrote Jefferson soon after Madison left Congress, hurt that she had not
heard from him: "We . . . expected Mr. Madison would have wrote a
few lines. . . . I can't help thinking he might have said a few words by
way of comfort to his old friends." Madison's eventual letters to Eliza
return the affection. He joked over her disparagement of his clothes,
advised her on the education of her children, and warned that her ambitious travel plans were "more likely to break down a good constitution
than to reestablish an infirm one."[35]
A later letter from Eliza to Jefferson reveals the effect of Madison's
personality on his friends and the regard in which he was held by his
Philadelphia family. To a hint that Madison might become governor of
Virginia, she replied, "He deserves everything that can be done for
him, but . . . I think it rather too great a sacrifice. . . . He has a soul
replete with gentleness, humanity and every social virtue and yet I am
certain that some wretch or other will write against him. . . . Mr. Madi-
son is too amiable in his disposition to bear up against a torrent of abuse.
It will hurt his feelings and injure his health, take my word." To Eliza,
Madison was too valued a friend to be thrown to the political wolves.
"I have no idea," she wrote, "that men are to live only for the Publick.
They owe something to themselves."[36]
Though Madison enjoyed the company of French officials and delegates from all the states, his closest friends were Virginians. Joseph
Jones, dark complexioned, severe, and taciturn, was a close and congenial colleague. A generation older than Madison and a confidant of
Washington and Pendleton, he lent experience and prestige to the many
enterprises he and Madison jointly sponsored. On July 16, 1781, Edmund Randolph, two years younger than Madison, yet attorney general
of Virginia since 1776, took his seat in Congress and became Madison's
closest co-worker. Handsome, eloquent, and brilliant, he was already one
of the most distinguished lawyers in Virginia and must in many ways
have outshown the less spectacular Madison. During Randolph's long absences from Congress, the two young statesmen corresponded at length

about moves to be made in Richmond and in Philadelphia to support Virginia's cession of Western lands, her approval of the impost, and other measures of national importance. Acquainted since 1776 and friends since their service together in Williamsburg during 1778 and 1779, Madison and Randolph became the axis upon which Virginia support for national needs depended.

They also worked together to defend the special interests of Virginia. Their elaborate arguments supporting Virginia's claim to Western lands were used to resist Eastern hostility to expansion toward the Mississippi, to establish Virginia's title to Kentucky, and to thwart land speculators who wanted to exclude Virginia from the Northwest Territory in order to strengthen their own fraudulent claims. Madison also worked with other Virginians to have the permanent national capital located on the Potomac. Arguing that a site there was geographically central and would be most accessible to the West and therefore most likely to bind the trans-Appalachian territory to the union, Madison sought as well to gain for his state the commercial advantages of locating the national capital on or within its borders. His work for Virginia was persistent enough for La Luzerne to note that "he is not free from prejudice in favor of the various claims of Virginia, however exaggerated they may be; but that is a general failing." Madison was especially quick to resent aspersions on Virginia or acts of Congress infringing her prerogatives. He conceded, for example, that Kentucky would eventually separate from Virginia because, joined, they made too large a territory to be governed from Richmond, but Virginia, not Congress, had the right to judge the mode and time of separation. Repeatedly while in Congress Madison skillfully maintained his political base in Virginia by effective attention to her interests; at the same time, he presented national needs to his home state in a way which reconciled them with local interests.[37]

Madison's closest companion in Philadelphia, though, was Thomas Jefferson. Their friendship, begun in Williamsburg during Jefferson's governorship, enriched their large official correspondence as long as Jefferson retained office (until June 1781). Then, for a year and a half Jefferson retired. He resented legislative censure (later withdrawn) of his conduct as governor; and he had, first, to care for a sick wife, then to mourn her passing. Madison took the lead in seeking his return to public life. He wrote in January 1782, regretting that Jefferson had refused appointments to Congress but nevertheless enlisting his aid in researches to establish Virginia's title to Western lands. In April Madison assumed Jefferson would accept election to the Virginia House of Delegates, but he refused, still resentful at the censure of the previous year. Madison observed that "great as my partiality is to Mr. Jefferson, the mode in which he seems determined to revenge the wrong received from his Country, does not appear to me to be dictated either by philosophy or patriotism." It was unjust, Madison wrote, to visit the faults of the legislature on the public at large by retiring entirely to private life. After Martha Wayles Jefferson died, in September 1782, Madison tried again to reenlist Jefferson in the public service, by moving in Congress that Jefferson join the American peace negotiators in Paris. Congress approved and Jefferson accepted immediately. By late December 1782 he was with Madison at Mrs. House's, and the two men resumed at the national level the marvelously useful collaboration they had begun in Williamsburg.[38]

They were together in Philadelphia for roughly three months in 1783 (January, March, and November), first while Jefferson sought unsuccessfully to embark for Europe, and later when he returned North as a Virginia delegate to Congress. During the first month, the time of Madison's courtship of Kitty Floyd, the two scholarly Virginians happily pored over book catalogues. Congress had appointed Madison to draw up a list of books which might be useful to its deliberations—that is, to establish a library of Congress. The methodical Jefferson at the same time sought to catalogue his own books and to list hundreds more he meant to buy in Europe. Depending on the resources of the Library Company of Philadelphia, the catalogue of William Byrd's library, then for sale in Philadelphia, and Jefferson's lists, Madison compiled a comprehensive list of 307 works, comprising fourteen hundred or more volumes on international law, treaties, political theory, geography, war, languages, and history, as well as an exhaustive list of books and tracts "related to American antiquities and the affairs of the U.S." Beginning with Diderot's *Encyclopédie Méthodique*, Madison included many of the new and often radical Enlightenment writers (Bayle, Voltaire, Gibbon, Barbeyrac, Mably, Hutcheson, Hume, Adam Smith, Price, and Priestley), as well as such authorities as Plato, Aristotle, Locke, Hooker, Bacon, Montesquieu, Grotius, Harrington, Coke, and Blackstone.

Madison and Jefferson must have spent hours savoring the contents of these books and relishing the prospect of having the debates of Congress guided by them, but the design was frustrated. Madison presented the list to Congress on January 23 and moved that the secretary "procure the same." Madison argued that the treatises would enable Congress to "render their proceedings . . . comfortable with propriety" in international relations, and observed that "the want of this information was manifest in several important acts of Congress." Furthermore, the works on America, "many of the most valuable of [which] were every day becoming extinct," were needed to refute Spanish territorial claims in the New World. The "economy bloc" prevailed, however, and defeated Madison's motion as well as a substitute one by James Wilson "to confine the purchase for the present to the most essential part of the books." The list of books in Madison's hand still exists among the papers of the Continental Congress. He and Jefferson doubtless recalled this early scholarly collaboration when, in Jefferson's Presidency, a library of Congress came into being, and in Madison's, Congress agreed to buy Jefferson's superb library to replace the public one burned by the British.[39]

In November the two men dicussed the hoped-for revision of the constitution of Virginia and studies in natural science and public law Madison would undertake after his retirement from Congress. They also planned for Jefferson to fulfill such Madisonian programs as the creation of new states in the West and the strengthening of commercial ties with France. Two of Jefferson's most notable acts of statesmanship during the seventeen-eighties, the drafts of the Northwest Ordinance and the consular convention with France, gave effect to programs long sought by Madison. Madison, for his part, agreed that if he had a chance, he would promote Jefferson's revision of the laws of Virginia. The letters between the two men during their absences from each other in 1783 testify to a growing personal warmth, a mutual respect for each other as public servants, and an extraordinary meeting of minds on a wide variety of subjects. Jefferson's confidence in Madison is apparent in his instructions, shortly after Madison's return to Virginia, to a young nephew studying in Orange County: "Mr. Madison's judgment is so sound and his heart so good that I would wish you to respect every advice he would be so kind as to give you, equally as if it came from me." Perhaps even more than the governor's palace in Williamsburg, Mrs. House's drawing room and the yard of Independence Hall saw the cementing of the most important and fruitful partnership in American political history.[40]

Though by and large Madison lived pleasantly while a delegate to Congress, he did suffer from two common plagues of congressmen during the revolution—lack of funds and poor accommodations when Congress convened outside Philadelphia. During the inflation of 1780 and 1781 Virginia delegates could scarcely haul currency to Philadelphia fast enough to keep up with rising prices. At times Virginia was unable to pay his salary, and at other times Madison did not want it, because it would have been paid in nearly worthless paper. By the end of 1782 the state owed him nearly £900 specie. Madison struggled along by borrowing from his father and from indulgent Philadelphians. He wrote Randolph in August 1782 that "I cannot in any way make you more sensible of the importance of your kind attention to pecuniary remittances for me than by informing you that I have for some time past been a pensioner on the favor of Haym Salomon, a Jew Broker." A month later Madison wrote warmly of Salomon's help: "The kindness of our little friend in Front Street . . . is a fund which will preserve me from extremities, but I never resort to it without great mortification, as he obstinately rejects all recompense. The price of money is so usurious that he thinks it ought to be extorted from none but those who aim at profitable speculations. To a necessitous Delegate he gratituously spares a supply out of his private stock." By the time Madison left Congress, however, he had received nearly all his back pay from the state and presumably was no longer in debt to Salomon. Madison always remembered the Jewish broker fondly and used his patriotic conduct to defend Jews generally against slanderous charges of selfish profiteering during the revolution.[41]

In June 1783 some soldiers, tired of waiting for back pay, actually drove the Continental Congress from Philadelphia. As they gathered noisily in front of the State House, Madison and the other delegates watched from inside, determined not to promise anything until the angry men dispersed peacefully. The delegates feared "no danger from premeditated violence," Madison reported, "but it was observed that spirituous drink from the tippling houses adjoining began to be liberally served out to the Soldiers, and might lead to hasty excesses." The soldiers taunted the delegates when they left the State House, and after state authorities failed to offer firm pledges to restore order, Congress fled to Princeton. One military officer wrote contemptuously that "the grand Sanhedrin of the Nation, with all their solemnity and emptiness . . . have removed to Princeton, and left a State, where their wisdom has long been questioned, their virtue suspected, and their dignity a jest."[42]

In Princeton Madison found little to soothe wounded dignity. "In this village," he wrote, "the public business can neither be conveniently done, the members of Congress decently provided for, nor those connected with Congress provided for at all. . . . We are kept in the most awkward situation that can be imagined; and it is the more so as we every moment expect the Dutch Ambassador. . . . Mr. Jones and myself . . . were extremely put to it to get any quarters at all, and are at length put into one bed in a room not more than 10 feet square . . . without a single accommodation for writing. I am obliged to write in a position that scarcely admits the use of any of my limbs." If Madison had needed any incident to dramatize for him the absurdly weak and unstable condition of Congress and the general government, the humiliating flight to the inconveniences of Princeton would have served perfectly. Federal authority in the United States has many lesser roots than Madison's indignation as he sat cramped in his room at Princeton.[43]

Madison last appeared as a delegate to Congress on October 25, 1783. Four weeks later he had shipped his clothing and books to Virginia and left Mrs. House's with Jefferson to go to Annapolis, where Congress was scheduled to convene on November 26. The four-day ride to Annapolis, Madison's first south of the Mason-Dixon line in nearly four years, was the last chance the two Virginians had for long talks until after Jefferson returned from France late in 1789. Madison stopped briefly in Annapolis, but hurried on to take advantage of more of the good weather they had enjoyed on the trip from Philadelphia. The fine autumn ended, however, forcing Madison for nine days to fight his way over mud-clogged roads and across swollen rivers to reach Orange. The red quag-mire of the Piedmont and the sodden skies hovering over the Southwest Mountains and blotting out the Blue Ridge must have dampened his spirits and heightened his eagerness to reach the comfortable fireside at Montpelier, but they did not prevent him from thinking about his four-year service in Congress. Shortly after he got home he wrote to Jefferson of his visit at Gunston Hall on the Potomac:

> I took Col. [George] Mason in my way and had an evening's conversation with him. I found him much less opposed to the general impost [to support Congress] than I had expected. . . . He seemed upon the whole to acquiesce in the territorial cession [of Virginia's western lands to the general government] but dwelt much on the expediency of the guaranty [of resistance to speculators' claims]. On the article of a convention for revising [Virginia's] form of government he was sound and ripe and I think would not decline a participation in the work. His heterodoxy lay chiefly in being too little impressed with either the necessity or the proper means of preserving the confederacy.[44]

Madison and Jefferson had agreed, clearly, on the need to strengthen both the state and national government, and were anxious to enlist the staunchly republican Mason in the cause. Mason agreed on the principles, but the older man, secluded in his study, did not have Madison's acute sense of the means required to sustain the principles. The impost, fidelity to the French alliance, and revision of the Articles of Confederation, had for Madison precise usefulness as means. When he had ridden down the road from Orange to Fredericksburg at the end of the bitter winter of 1780, he was shy, inexperienced, and perhaps, like Mason, unaware of the measures required to fulfill the revolution and build a nation. The brief, confident paragraph to Jefferson on the conversation with the learned, liberal man they respected and admired is a measure of Madison's growth in Philadelphia. He was now ready to speak up to anyone in the land and able to take the lead in any legislative body in pursuing programs to protect the newly won independence and build a strong national union of the states. He returned to Montpelier one of the nation's acknowledged, creative leaders.

CHAPTER VIII

Virginia Legislator and Traveler

WHEN Madison reached Montpelier in December 1783, after being away for nearly four years, he faced many uncertainties. Though he was sure his main interest was politics and public life, questions remained about how to make a living and where to live. Even had there been some prospect of being able to live on his public earnings (there was virtually none), tradition forbade it. A politician dependent on his salary would, many felt, be tempted to sacrifice the public good to his own needs. To have a respectable foundation for his political career, Madison needed a steady income from some private source. The family plantation up until now had paid his way, and the support and good will of his father and brothers assured him that, if he chose, he could continue to serve the public while depending on them, a common practice in a state where substantial planters took political obligations seriously.

This prospect, however, made Madison uneasy. He objected in a way to being dependent on his family for financial support. Furthermore, his uncertain health and long absences from home ever since he had gone to Princeton in 1769 meant he was far less acquainted with management of the plantation than one might expect of an eldest son more than thirty years old. Though he came in middle and old age to enjoy farming, in the seventeen-eighties his interests were elsewhere. He often lingered for months at a time in Philadelphia or New York or Richmond to enjoy the company of men who shared his relish for books and with whom he could keep fully up to date on public affairs. He wrote Edmund Randolph after his first winter at home that his legal studies had "been much retarded by the want of some important books, and still more by that of some living oracle for occasional consultation." He added that being in Richmond near Randolph had "its full influence" in reconciling him to service in the state legislature.[1]

Though Madison studied law as best he could in Orange and Richmond during 1784, 1785, and 1786, he was in fact no more intent on a legal career than in 1773, when he had discussed the prospect with William Bradford. He remarked casually in a letter to Jefferson in April 1785 that if he interrupted his legal studies then, he would "probably never" resume them. Three months later a career at the bar had receded even further; he wrote Randolph that though his "course of reading" continued, he was "far from being determined ever to make a professional use of it. My wish is if possible to provide a decent and independent subsistence, without encountering the difficulties which I foresee in that line"—that is, the often quibbling, devious nature of a lawyer's practice. This, plus Madison's weak voice and lack of confidence in his oratory, persuaded him that a legal career was not the way to be free of dependence on the family plantation. The sole advantage for Madison of many years' intermittent study of the law, aside from the general increase in knowledge, was a technical familiarity with the world of torts and suits inhabited by so many of his political colleagues.[2]

In the letter admitting his inability to become a lawyer, Madison also wrote of "several projects from which advantage seemed attainable." One, "in concert with a friend" in Orange, would, the young politician hoped, "yield a decent reward for our trouble," after which Madison would not have to be "ostensibly concerned" in it. The friend and the nature of the particular project are not known, but almost certainly, judging from the direction Madison's pursuit of wealth took at this time, some form of land speculation was involved. Though Madison himself and even the rest of his family were far less inclined toward "land-jobbing" than were most Virginians of their day, they did not ignore the prospects of profit and improved farming open to them in the vast unsettled Western lands. From the seventeenth century on, Madison's ancestors had bought lands in the West as they were opened for purchase, and the family owned, typically, lands in a number of counties in Virginia. Trade in land was as much a part of plantation management as trade in tobacco or corn.

Between May 9, 1780, and March 15, 1781, James Madison, Sr., and his sons Ambrose and William, bought between them over sixteen thousand acres of lands near the mouth of Panther Creek, which flowed into the Green River between what are now Henderson and Owensboro, Kentucky. Madison purchases in the vicinity continued in 1782 and 1783, and even down into the seventeen-nineties. James Madison may have heard of the lands and begun negotiations for his family to speculate in them in 1778, when George Mason accepted the judgment of Richard

Henderson that the richest lands in Kentucky were on Panther Creek. Madison was in Williamsburg on the governor's council and knew Mason well. At any rate, Hancock Lee (Ambrose Madison's brother-in-law) scouted the lands and filed claims on nearly forty thousand acres for Mason, the Madisons, and William Moore, Madison's uncle. All the surveys were based on a tract previously patented in Mason's name at the mouth of Panther Creek. The Madisons probably paid about $15,000, largely on credit, for their share, a substantial risk, even in inflated currency, for farmers chronically short of cash, but theirs was still a relatively modest speculating venture. James Madison's personal share in these purchases is not known, but it makes little difference, since, in fierce litigation which lasted until 1804, the original survey, upon which all the other patents depended, was invalidated. The Madisons seem never to have profited significantly from the Kentucky speculations, though as long as James Madison lived, he owned some lands in that state.[3]

Madison's main hope in the seventeen-eighties for the wealth that would make him independent, however, rested on lands in the Mohawk valley which Madison had seen in 1784 (see pages 154–157). During a visit to Mount Vernon in October 1785, Madison discussed the Mohawk project with George Washington, who had wide experience as a surveyor and speculator in Western lands. The general approved enthusiastically. The Mohawk valley was "the very Spot which his fancy had selected of all the U.S." for land purchases, and he had, in fact, recently bought a tract there himself. Madison then began to arrange with James Monroe for a purchase. They agreed to buy about a thousand acres for $1.50 per acre on the Mohawk across from the mouth of Oriskany Creek, between what are now Utica and Rome, New York. Unfortunately, both men were short of cash, so first Madison and then Monroe had to plead for time and juggle finances. On terms of one half down and one half two years later, Madison's initial share was just $337.50. It is apparent, therefore, that he had very little capital for speculation, but he was eager to proceed. He agreed with Monroe on enlarging the purchase and planned a trip to examine the lands more carefully.[4]

In April 1786 Madison reminded Monroe that they should be careful about the proportions of "low grounds and uplands" in their proposed purchase, because though the upland was thought to be generally good, "there must be both degrees and exceptions to its quality." A journey to the Mohawk valley with Monroe fell through, but Madison's conviction that the area offered the best hope for large profits nevertheless led him to propose a really big deal to Jefferson, whose post as American minister to France afforded a potential access to capital undreamed of in North America. The soil in the Mohawk valley, Madison wrote, is "scarcely inferior to that of Kentucky, it lies within the body of the Atlantic States and at a safe distance from every frontier, it is contiguous to a branch of Hudson's River which is navigable with trifling portages which will be temporary [the Erie Canal passed the lands in question within forty years] to tide-water, and is no more than ten, 15 or 20 miles from populous settlements where land sells at £8 to £10 per Acre. . . . We have made a small purchase, and nothing but the difficulty of raising a sufficient sum restrained us from making a large one. In searching for a means of overcoming this difficulty one has occurred. . . . It is that the aid of your credit in your private capacity be used for borrowing say [$16,000 to $20,000] . . . on interest not exceeding six percent." Madison proposed he, Jefferson, and Monroe share the purchase, which Madison was sure would in ten or twenty years return them at least five or six times their investment. Everything, Madison urged, favored the plan: the lands were owned by speculators who needed cash desperately; they would sell large amounts at bargain rates; the scarceness of specie would increase the value of a loan obtained in France; and the prospects on the Mohawk were much brighter than those in the more landlocked James River area in Virginia where Jefferson had often centered his plans. "Scarce an instance," Madison concluded, "has happened in which purchases of new lands of good quality and in good situations [on the Mohawk] have not well rewarded the adventurers."[5]

This great plan, if successful, would furnish Madison his eagerly sought financial independence. His share of the profit might be as high as $40,000—an amount of capital that in that day was virtually certain, with careful investment, to support him comfortably for the rest of his life. Jefferson's discouraging reply, then, must have been a heavy blow. To benefit the Potomac Canal, he had sought recently to borrow money in France, on the terms Madison had proposed, but despite the added advantage of endorsements from General Washington and the Virginia Assembly, his efforts had been without success. French bankers could loan all the funds at their disposal to their government and receive 6 per cent interest, paid quarterly without fail. Further, they also received "sweeteners" (bribes) and would not loan money across the Atlantic except at much higher interest. The only hope, Jefferson said, was to take French bankers as partners, but even this was "only possible, not probable." Thus, unable to launch a really significant speculation, Madison hung on to his modest purchase through the depression and panics of the next ten years, and eventually sold the land for a net profit of nearly 200 per cent, a respectable transaction, but with so small an investment scarcely enough to make him a rich man.[6]

The Mohawk speculation was not Madison's only plan to move from the family plantation. He responded longingly to Jefferson's invitation that he buy a farm near Monticello which would "support a little table and household," and thus make him a neighbor of Monroe, and Jefferson's protégé, William Short, as well. Madison declined because he was not sure he could make a living in Albermarle County. In August 1785 Madison wrote an old college friend who had moved to Kentucky that though he had no immediate plan to migrate, he favored frontier settlement and had "no Local partialities which can keep me from any place which promises the greatest real advantages." Three years later Madison was enthusiastic about Henry Lee's proposal that he take a one-third share in a five-hundred-acre tract through which the Potomac Canal would be built. He would be delighted to take part, Madison responded—but he could not put up any cash. When Lee's partners pressed for payment, Madison reluctantly dropped out of the scheme. The plain hard fact was that Madison had neither the capital nor the reckless speculative spirit required to free himself from the family plantation. Despite repeated efforts, at the end of the decade he was as dependent on Montpelier as ever. In retrospect, both Madison and his compatriots may be thankful that Orange, Virginia, ever remained his home. His mind and energies were spared the demands a move and great business enterprises would have made on them, and he remained in the peaceful, healthy, attractive surroundings he had always enjoyed and came increasingly to cherish.[7]

Madison's motivation to be independent of Montpelier was moral as well as a financial, however. Though brought up among slaves and dependent on their labor, he abhorred the institution of slavery and sought to have as little as possible to do with it. Madison, like Jefferson, Washington, George Mason, and other liberal Virginia leaders of the revolution, came to believe slavery was immoral, in the long run uneconomic, and destined gradually to disappear. That Madison saw the incongruity between slavery and the professed ideals of the revolution is apparent in his response to a plan to give slaves as a bounty to army recruits. "Would it not be as well," he asked, "to liberate and make soldiers at once of the blacks themselves as to make them instruments for enlisting white Soldiers? It would certainly be more consonant to the principles of liberty which ought never be lost sight of in a contest for liberty." In 1783, as Madison prepared to return to Virginia from Philadelphia, he discovered that, after nearly four years in the company of free servants, his slave Billey was "too thoroughly tainted to be a fit companion for fellow slaves in Virginia." Madison decided to sell him in Philadelphia, where he would be free in seven years, rather than ship him, as other Virginians often did to slaves rendered "uppity" by a Northern residence, to the West Indies. Why, Madison asked his father, should Billey be punished "merely for coveting that liberty for which we have paid the price of so much blood, and have proclaimed so often to be right, and worthy the pursuit, of every human being?"[8]

Thus, himself "tainted" with abolitionist sentiments, after almost two years back in Virginia Madison wrote Edmund Randolph that he wished "to depend as little as possible on the labor of slaves." The cruelty and injustice of the slave system, which he had been away from for four years, so affronted him that he undertook uncongenial law studies and land speculations in order to be free from it. His difficulties and ultimate failure in the effort are a measure, of course, of the hold slavery had on Virginia and her sister Southern states. In 1785 Madison spoke in the Virginia Assembly favoring a bill Jefferson had proposed for the gradual abolition of slavery (it was rejected), and helped defeat a bill designed to outlaw the manumission of individual slaves. Of this effort a French observer wrote that Madison, "a young man [who] . . . astonishes . . . by his eloquence, his wisdom, and his genius, has had the humanity and *courage* (for such a proposition requires no small share of courage) to propose a general emancipation of the slaves." Finally, though, Madison saw no practical way to fight the system, and more and more seems to have acquiesced in it. Nevertheless, he maintained his concern and throughout his life took part in largely futile efforts to rid the country of the moral and economic millstone he thought slavery to be.[9]

Though Madison's restless search for a vocation, a place to live, and a support divorced from slavery caused him to travel considerably during the years from 1784 to 1787, he lived for months at a time at Montpelier, perhaps helping his father and brother Ambrose manage the plantation, but spending most of his time studying and writing. Toward the end of this period, his father's cousin Francis Taylor began to keep a diary in which he recorded something of the social life in Orange County. On March 2, 1786, for example, he and other notables of the county were at Montpelier discussing the entailed estate of Harry Beverley, which for twenty years had plagued James Madison, Sr. Taylor reported that "Col. Madison Jr. while we were here [at Montpelier], came to breakfast of which he ate sparingly, and then went to go to his room till a little before dinner. After dinner played at Whist for half bits till bed time. Smart snow." Other entries in Taylor's diary suggest that Madison usually retired from any assembled company until dinnertime, and then joined the evening festivities. Often a dozen or more people would stay two or three nights, talking, dancing, feasting, and playing cards. Madison was considered important enough for Taylor to record his movements, his participation in the family gatherings, and his opinions on public policy of special concern locally. The diary makes clear that Taylor took pride in the political prominence of his kinsman, and considered him a respected leader in county affairs.[10]

Madison chafed under the demands dinner-table conversations, visiting, and cardplaying made on his time, however. He wrote after he retired from Congress that he undertook his planned study "as soon as the necessary attention to my friends admitted." In the spring, he reported regretfully, his time was "much less [his] own than during the winter

blockade." He worked industriously on *Coke upon Littleton*, Edward
Coke's elaborate commentary on Thomas Littleton's treatise on tenures,
which was long the standard authority on real property in England and
America. Its dry, crabbed text doubtless bored Madison, as it had Jefferson, John Adams, and countless other fledgling lawyers, but Madison may
have learned nevertheless to respect Coke's meticulous, responsible treatment of English law.[11]

Though the severe winter of 1783-4, with "a greater quantity of
snow than is remembered to have distinguished any preceding winter,"
saved Madison from interruptions in his law studies, it also deprived him
"entirely of the philosophical [scientific] books I had alloted for incidental reading; all my trunks sent from Philadelphia . . . being still at
Fredericksburg." Madison nevertheless began immediately to correspond with Jefferson in the fashion of the Enlightenment man fascinated
with the physical world around him. The two scholarly Virginians had
conversed during their late fall ride from Philadelphia to Annapolis about
the explanation of the great French scientist Buffon of why the earth
seemed warmer near its center than at its extremities. Madison proposed
that the "oblate figure of the earth" furnished the best opportunity to
test the theory: if the earth was indeed cooler at points farther from its
center, there should be a measurable difference in temperature between
the end of the longer, equatorial, radius and the end of the shorter,
polar, one. Jefferson supposed both Madison and Buffon in error; the
earth should be thought of as a hot body being cooled by its surroundings. Therefore the *distance from the surface* was the critical thing,
whether at the poles or the equator, or on mountains or in valleys.
Madison replied that Jefferson had "rectified his misconception" of the
matter and that he would "forbear" further comment, "as I ought perhaps formerly to have done . . . at least until I have seen [Buffon's] work
myself."[12]

Madison also pointed out to Jefferson an obscure reference to some
bones found in South America of an animal which in the *Notes on
Virginia* Jefferson had supposed not to have existed "to the South."
Jefferson thanked Madison for the reference, but said he would not be
convinced the animal was native to South America unless more remains
were found: the Spaniards, or perhaps the Indians, may have carried a
few of the species southward. In the same letter Jefferson wished that
Madison had a thermometer so he could join with him and the Reverend
James Madison to test further Jefferson's hunch that small latitude variations were less important than altitude or distance from the sea in determining temperature. He suspected, therefore, that Orange would usually
be colder than Annapolis, and wished to have simultaneous temperature
readings to test the hypothesis.[13]

While Jefferson was in France, he and Madison sought to understand the relation between North American and European animals—especially to test, and hopefully to refute, Buffon's theory that of animals common to both continents, those found in America were smaller due to unfavorable climate. Madison made thirty-three careful measurements of the parts of a dead female weasel found at Montpelier, and sent the data to Jefferson in a table comparing them with similar measurements of two European animals, called in French the *belette* and the *hermine*. Madison concluded that the weasel was a variety of the *belette*, somewhat larger in nearly every way. Therefore, Buffon's theory of relative sizes was wrong, as was his supposition that "no animal is common to the two continents [America and Eurasia] that cannot bear the climate where they join." Madison also sent similar measurements of the mole, the skins of all common and some rare quadrupeds, and the seeds or striplings of nearly two dozen varieties of trees. In return, to satisfy "a little itch to gain a smattering in chymistry," Madison asked for "two Boxes, called *Le necessaire chemique*" and "a good elementary treatise" on the subject. He received these, and as well, a pedometer, a watch, some phosphoretic matches ("a great treat to my curiosity"), and an excellent reading lamp Madison thought well worth the two guineas it cost. In the correspondence with Jefferson, in the wonderful books and equipment he received from Europe, and in his own careful observations of nature at Montpelier, Madison broadened his contact with the new learning and showed his full sympathy for the exciting world view of Newton, Franklin, Buffon, and other scientists.[14]

To mark Madison's standing as a scientist, in January 1784 he was nominated for membership in the American Philosophical Society. When Jefferson saw a list of those elected, he observed with surprise Madison's omission and complained that the twenty-one "new philosophers" by no means had qualifications superior to those of "my countryman Madison." Francis Hopkinson hastened to explain: "The case of Mr. Maddison was this—the Candidates for Election were enter'd on two different pieces of paper. When the Election came on, one of those Papers was missing, in which was Mr. Maddison's Name, with the Names of other worthy Persons. This Paper has never been found. A Debate ensued and it was finally agreed to put the Names on the Paper in hand alone to Vote. I have at last Meeting, again enter'd Mr. Maddison as a Candidate. The Election will be in April [1784] and I doubt not but every Voter will be glad of such a Member." Neither this slight nor further delay seems to have bothered Madison, for he accepted his election as a member on January 22, 1785, along with, among others, Thomas Paine, Richard Price, Joseph Priestley, Manasseh Cutler, and his old college friend William Bradford.[15]

Madison and Jefferson also wrote about economic problems, notably poverty and overpopulation. Following a trip in the French countryside, Jefferson remarked on the "unequal division of property which occasions the numberless instances of wretchedness which I had observed." Uncultivated land was held by great nobles for hunting, while living beside it were landless peasants unable to find work to maintain their families. "The consequences of this enormous inequality producing so much misery to the bulk of mankind" led Jefferson to declare to legislators that they could not "invent too many devices for sub-dividing property." The abolition of entails and primogeniture, and other laws in the United States encouraging the wide distribution of property, he asserted, were the foundations of her prosperity and republican institutions. In reply, Madison both revealed the essential way his thought differed from Jefferson's and anticipated Malthus by twelve years:

> . . . I have no doubt that the misery of the lower classes will be found to abate wherever the Government assumes a freer aspect, and the laws favor a subdivision of property. Yet I suspect that the difference will not fully account for the comparative comfort of the mass of people in the United States. Our limited population has probably as large a share in producing this effect as the political advantages which distinguish us. A certain degree of misery seems inseparable from a high degree of populousness. If the lands in Europe which are now dedicated to the amusement of the idle rich were parcelled out among the idle poor, I readily conceive the happy revolution which would be experienced by a certain proportion of the latter. But still would there not remain a great proportion unrelieved? No problem in political economy has appeared to me more puzzling than that which relates to the most proper distribution of the inhabitants of a Country fully peopled. Let the lands be shared among them ever so wisely, and let them be supplied with labourers ever so plentifully . . . there will . . . remain a great surplus of inhabitants, a number greater by far than will be employed in cloathing both themselves and those who feed them, and in administering to both, every other necessary and even comfort of life.[16]

Three years later, when Jefferson proclaimed his famous doctrine that "the earth belongs always to the living generation," Madison again posed practical limitations. To the question, "Has one generation of men a right to bind another?" Jefferson responded that "the dead have neither power nor right over" the property and privileges of succeeding generations. "On similar ground," Jefferson held, "no society can make a perpetual constitution, or even a perpetual law." Since personal liberties and property were the "sum of the objects of governments," there could be no just law interfering with the right of each generation to determine for itself the *entire* disposition of these objects. Should not, therefore, every law lapse after one generation? Were not national debts funded

over many decades unjust? Should not all laws governing the descent of
lands be abolished? "Turn this subject in your mind," Jefferson wrote
Madison, "particularly as to the power of contracting debts; and devel-
ope it with that perspicuity and congent logic so peculiarly yours. Your
station in the councils of our country gives you an opportunity of producing it to public consideration."

Madison received the letter, appropriately, while he was a member of
Congress considering Hamilton's plan for funding the national debt. He
was, he replied, dubious and skeptical. The injustice Jefferson feared from
retaining old laws Madison thought less dangerous to society than
"pernicious factions that might not otherwise come into existence" if
laws remained in effect until repealed. As to the obligations between
generations, "if the earth be the gift of Nature to the living, their title
can extend to the earth in its natural State only. The *improvements*
made by the dead form a charge against the living who take the benefit
of them. This charge can no otherwise be satisfied than by executing the
will of the dead accompanying the improvements." As to the debts of the
United States, they were incurred in a war beneficial to subsequent
generations, which should therefore not resent paying their due share.
"There seems then," Madison summarized, "to be a foundation in the
nature of things, in the relation which one generation bears to another,
for the *descent* of obligations from one to another. Equity requires it.
Mutual good is promoted by it. All that is indispensable in adjusting the
account between the dead and the living is to see that the debits against
the latter do not exceed the advances made by the former. Few of the
incumbrances entailed on nations would bear a liquidation even on this
principle."

Jefferson's mistake, Madison added, had been to conceive too narrowly
the concept of tacit consent. It had to be broad enough not only to bind
the minority to the acts of the majority but also to imply acceptance of
all old laws not specifically repealed by a popular legislature. Madison
nevertheless approved Jefferson's speculations and wished the United
States would declare in principle that the earth belonged to the living to
restrain one generation "from imposing unjust and unnecessary burdens
on their successors." Upset by the power and arrogance of Hamilton's
supporters in Congress, however, Madison saw little chance such
"philosophical legislation" would soon be considered: the feared "weakness in Government, and licentiousness in the people, have turned attention more towards the means of strengthening the former than of nar-
rowing its extent in the minds of the latter."[17]

Thus Madison shared the ideals and high hopes of Jefferson's enlightened, *philosophe* circle in Paris, but his political tasks in the United States
gave him a turn of mind inclined to dampen or amend Jefferson's speculations. Madison thought the unfortunate yet relentless way overpopula-

tion caused human misery meant laws, though helpful in parts of the United States, would never be able to abolish poverty. Likewise, the noble principle that the earth belonged to the living generation, drawn from the doctrine of consent, needed to be restrained and amended, lest it upset vital and useful aids to order and stability. Enlightenment, faith in experiment, and reason had only limited application in human society. Madison came to understand very well the new science and the vision of the age of reason, but he grasped, too, perhaps better than Jefferson, the need to blend high hopes with sobering reality when applying the maxims to public policy.

In the years from 1784 to 1787 long journeys often interrupted Madison's studies at Montpelier. He attended three winter sessions and one spring session of the Virginia Assembly in Richmond (each lasting two or three months), and each fall he traveled northward for two months to Philadelphia and New York, partly on business, but also because he needed to "exercise after a very sedentary period [and to] ramble into the Eastern States which I have long had a curiosity to see." In New York he saw members of Congress. In Philadelphia he sojourned pleasantly at Mrs. House's, and he seldom failed to stop at Mount Vernon as he traveled along the Potomac. One time he took the inland route northward to Winchester, Virginia, and thence through the fertile "Pennsylvania Dutch" farm country around Gettysburg, York, and Lancaster to Philadelphia. He marveled at the rich harvest (hurt by heavy rains in Maryland and Virginia), and wrote of the "magnificent scene" at Harpers Ferry. He climbed the mountain at the confluence of the Shenandoah and Potomac rivers, but the fatigue of an ill-chosen trail and poor visibility during a thunderstorm prevented full enjoyment of the spectacular sight. He reported favorably on "the progress of the [canal] works on the Potowmac," and on the cooperation between the states to combine canal and road routes over the Appalachian Mountains. Madison thought such activity a "fruit of the Revolution" in its nation-building phase.[18]

Madison's longest trip, however, was in the fall of 1784, with Lafayette to Fort Stanwix (near what is now Rome, New York) for an Indian treaty. Traveling northward in September, Madison "fell in" with the young Frenchman at Baltimore and accompanied him to Philadelphia. The journey was marked by "the most flattering tokens of sincere affection [Lafayette received] from all ranks." In New York Madison was delighted with the four days of feasting and celebration in honor of Lafayette. It must have pleased Madison especially to see Mayor James Duane, his old mentor and associate during dark days in the Continental Congress, presiding over festivities which symbolized the union of the states and "furnished occasion for fresh manifestation of these sentiments toward France which have been so well merited by her, but which her enemies pretended would soon give way to a returning affection for G. Britain." Lafayette took pleasure in the same observation. "The English here make long faces at our gathering, and the racket with which the city resounded . . . must have been a scarcely agreeable celebration for them." Buoyed by the excitement, anxious to prolong his visit with Lafayette, and curious about the lands in the Mohawk valley, Madison decided to join the dignitaries headed up the Hudson River for Fort Stanwix.[19]

Fair winds and tides for two days carried the party on a sailing barge past the Palisades, through the wide Tappan Zee, and into the narrows between Peekskill and West Point. Then the weather changed. For three days rain, violent winds, and turbulent waters held the vessel at anchor most of the time. A nearby sloop capsized; Madison lurched about seasick; and for its trouble, the party found it had covered barely ten miles —it was near Newburgh, still in sight of massive Storm King Mountain, which had come into view seventy-two hours earlier as the barge had passed West Point. Despite occasional fog and high winds, the rest of the trip, past the great patroon houses to Albany, was rapid and relatively pleasant.

At Albany, Madison's old friend and collaborator from the French legation in Philadelphia, François de Barbé-Marbois, joined the party. Madison and Lafayette and his aide, the Chevalier de Caraman, piled into Barbé-Marbois' four-wheeled phaeton, and accompanied by their servants, took the rough road west. They spent the first night at the Shaker village of Niskayuna, where they found 140 believers gathered in a large hall. The trembling, fitful behavior of the Shakers, their total sexual abstinence, their serious, rational sermons, and the diligence of their workers fascinated the visitors. They left the next morning, convinced, as Barbé-Marbois reported, that despite the eccentricities of the Shakers they were useful citizens.

Signs of war and Indian raids were grim reminders all along the way of the hard effect of the revolution in that part of New York, but the superb country, the rapid growth in population, and the enterprise of the people left little doubt of the region's future prosperity. Madison and his companions were a curiosity in a countryside not used to travelers, least of all noble Frenchmen, and were everywhere welcome. They found pioneer cabins where families of ten or twelve children slept in one bed; Barbé-Marbois often made them a "delicious" soup, which, added to the abundant native butter and milk, furnished a great feast for the entire household. Finding the roads "worse than we could have imagined," the party abandoned the phaeton at German Flats and proceeded the remaining fifty miles on horseback. Lafayette had charge of the horses; Caraman saw to the lodgings; Barbé-Marbois was the cook; and Madison "directed the march." We may picture him in the van urging the servants and horses onward, trying hard not to lose the way as they left the settled parts of the lower valley and plunged into the wilderness. After three days of rough going, the party passed the ravine near the mouth of Oriskany Creek, where seven years earlier General Nicholas Herkimer had rallied his ragged militia after being ambushed by the British and their Indian allies. Perhaps, too, Madison noticed rich lands across the Mohawk which he would purchase in 1786. Finally, six days from Albany, the weary travelers reached Fort Stanwix. It was run down, ungarrisoned, and at the time consisted of two crude cabins presided over by the famous missionary Samuel Kirkland.

When Lafayette and his companions discovered that neither the Indian nor the American negotiators had arrived, they set out to satisfy their curiosity about Indian life by journeying to the chief village of the Oneidas, eighteen miles southwest of the fort. The "road . . . [was] really barbarous and wild." On horseback, they could scarcely follow the Indians who in the "gloomy, rainy weather" once even lost the way. Fording streams where they had to dismount and swim the horses, the party arrived at the Oneida village "very wet and very tired." They were greeted hospitably, treated to a feast of fresh salmon, milk, butter, fruit, and honey, and watched an Indian dance until they were so tired Lafayette asked a Frenchman living among the Indians to get them to stop. The white men then retired to the cabin provided them, without, so Barbé-Marbois asserted, "getting married to one of the Indian squaws" for the sake of hospitality, as was the custom among the Indians. Some of the servants succumbed, however, and in the morning "several squaws [were] adorned with wedding ribbons, and the separation was very touching." Altogether, the debauched, half-civilized condition of the Oneidas shocked the Frenchmen: "These children of nature are not at all what the writers of Europe say, who have never seen them." Their deplorable state, though, Barbé-Marbois observed, came from contact with European civilization, because Indians from remote parts of the continent were "less corrupted and more robust" than the Oneidas.

The group returned to Fort Stanwix the next day, and though the American commissioners had not yet arrived, Lafayette decided nevertheless to begin negotiating the treaty. Luckily, the commissioners then appeared; Lafayette made an impressive conciliatory speech; and negotiations commenced which led eventually to the first general treaty beween the English-oriented Iroquois and the new United States. The night before the conference opened the temperature dropped to 26 degrees, freezing a basin of water three feet from the campfire. Everyone shivered except Lafayette, who seemed impervious to the cold in his great, gummed tafetta coat—the envy of all the assembled company, white and red. Seeing the negotiations well begun, and anxious to be on their way, Madison and the Frenchmen procured a boat, and as the

leaves turned to brilliant reds and yellows, "comfortably . . . descended
the Mohawk . . . in the finest weather in the world." Shortly after the
portage around Little Falls, the party picked up Barbé-Marbois' phaeton,
and on October 7, once again viewed the Dutch gables of Albany.[20]

Madison reported to Jefferson that he had enjoyed the trip immensely
and that it had "rather inflamed than extinguished [my] curiosity to see
the Northern and Northwestern Country." But, in fact, he never again
ventured so far into the wilderness, nor was he ever again as remote from
his Virginia home. Typically, the political implications of the events at
Fort Stanwix most interested Madison. The British, he wrote Jefferson,
obviously connived to keep the Indians hostile, to retain possession of
Niagara and other Western forts, and to monopolize the fur trade.
Madison felt that the United States could counteract these designs only
with the French backing that Lafayette's influence with the Indians
symbolized. Yet some of the American commissioners at Fort Stanwix
resented Lafayette's presence and seemed unwilling to depend any longer
on French support. Madison saw this as part of the continuing delusion
of the "British partizans" in Congress that Great Britain would be a
better friend to the United States than France. Hence, Commissioner
Arthur Lee, Madison's old antagonist and a leading "British partizan,"
sought to exclude Lafayette from a formal role at the treaty. Madison
nevertheless advised Lafayette to exert his influence, which he accordingly did. He was, Madison wrote, "the only conspicuous figure. The
Commissioners were eclipsed. All of them probably felt it. Lee complained to me of the immoderate stress laid on the influence of
[Lafayette], and evidently promoted his departure." Fascinated as were
most Americans with Lafayette's colorful, dramatic personality, Madison
wrote a candid, cautiously coded account to Jefferson of the impressions
gathered during a month of constant association with the Frenchman:
"With great natural frankness of temper he unites much address; with
very considerable talents, a strong thirst of praise and popularity. In his
politics he says his three hobby horses are the alliance between France
and the United States, the Union of the latter, and the manumission of
the slaves. The two former are the dearer to him as they are connected
with his personal glory. The last does him real honor, as it is a proof of
his humanity. In a word, I take him to be as amiable a man as his vanity
will admit, and as sincere an American as any Frenchman can be; one
whose past services gratitude obliges us to acknowledge and whose
future friendship prudence requires us to cultivate." Lafayette desired to
make a speech at the treaty, Madison asserted, because it would "form a
bright column in the gazettes of Europe."

During the eighteen-twenties, as Madison arranged his papers for
publication (including his original letters he had retrieved from his
friends), he changed this probably accurate assessment to conform with

the heroic reputation Lafayette had by then acquired. Madison changed the decoding of the words "his vanity will admit," to read "can be imagined." To compound the deceit, he sought to imitate Jefferson's writing in the decoding, and he changed the number code to obscure his original intention. Thus he altered the number 706 to 786, changed each of the other four numbers less cleverly, and added a new number, 359, standing for "d" at the end of the line, so that even a person who knew some of the code might suppose the phrase ended with "imagined" rather than "admit." In fact, the new numbers inserted by Madison when decoded are nonsense: "nine then in turn total d."* The substance of the change, and the motive behind it, represent no serious blot on Madison's character; he sought only to remove what he believed was an unnecessary aspersion on one who had a deserved reputation as a hero of French and American liberty. Nevertheless, the picture of the aged Madison conniving to deceive users of his letters is most disturbing, casting doubt, as it must, on the integrity of the records he bequeathed to posterity. We would be less alarmed had he, as so many of his contemporaries did, merely blotted out or destroyed the offending remarks.[21]

During the years of study, travel, and relative retirement from public life, Madison was an Orange County delegate to the Virginia Assembly. At four sessions, in 1784, 1785, and 1786, he spent eleven months in Richmond, as leader of the group anxious to continue the reform in the laws of Virginia Jefferson had begun in 1776 and to add Virginia's weight to measures strengthening the union of the states. Many in Richmond hoped Madison would lead a group of newly elected Assemblymen who had a chance to rescue that body from its perennial, dramatic, but unfruitful forensic contests between Patrick Henry and Richard Henry Lee. As Edmund Randolph explained to Jefferson, "the increase of new members has introduced some of the children of the revolution, who labour to satisfy themselves and disdain dependency. . . . It was manifest through our last session, that Henry had one corps, Richard Henry Lee . . . another. . . . The new legislative [members] will want a general to

* This shrewd detective work by Julian Boyd enabled him for the first time to print Madison's letter as Jefferson received it. Only one other case of such devious tampering has been discovered. On February 11, 1783, Madison wrote Jefferson in code of "a display of [John Adams'] vanity." Late in life Madison made the phrase read "a fresh display of his vanity" in his interlinear decoding, thus increasing the aspersion on Adams. In view of the close scrutiny the documents left by Madison have received by Boyd, Irving Brant, the editors of *The Papers of James Madison*, and others, with only isolated instances of tampering uncovered, it is most unlikely that Madison made major, wholesale changes in his papers late in life, as William W. Crosskey has charged in *Politics and the Constitution in the History of the United States* (2 vols., Chicago, 1953).

enable them to make head against those of the other parties. . . . This renders it probable, that our friend of Orange will step earlier into the heat of battle, than his modesty would otherwise permit, for he is already resorted to, as a general, of whom much has been preconceived to his advantage." William Short wrote that the new members had "formed great Hopes of Mr. Madison," and Franklin's neighbor in France, William Alexander, visiting Richmond, reported to the old diplomat of "a rising young man" named Madison, of whom much was expected.[22]

In early May 1784 Madison arrived in Richmond, a city of about three hundred, mostly frame, buildings, described by a German traveler that year as almost "an Arabian village. . . . The whole day long [there were] saddled horses at every turn, and a swarming of riders in the few and muddy streets, for a horse must be mounted if only to fetch a prise of snuff from across the way." At the small Assembly House the door-keeper "incessantly and with a loud voice called out for one member after another. In the ante-room is a tumult quite as constant; here they amuse themselves zealously with talk of horse races, runaway Negroes, yesterday's play, politics, or it may be, with trafficking." In the evening the inns were filled with "generals, colonels, captains, senators, assembly-men, judges, doctors, clerks and crowds of gentlemen, of every weight and caliber and every hue of dress. [They] sat all together about the fire, drinking, smoking, singing, and talking ribaldry."[23]

When the Assembly finally made a quorum, on May 12, Madison began immediate consultations. On the evening of the fourteenth, he, Henry, and Joseph Jones left the rowdy fireside of the inn for the quiet of the coffeehouse where they decided "that Mr. Jones and Mr. Madison should sketch out some Plan for giving greater Powers to the federal Government, and that Mr. Henry should support it on the Floor. It was thought a bold Example set by Virginia would have Influence on the other States." Henry's support encouraged Madison, though he was irritated that the orator, as usual, held back from endorsing "any precise plan." Henry was equally vague on revising the Virginia constitution, which Madison thought too weak to provide effective government. Nevertheless, he reported hopefully that Henry's "general train of thoughts seemed to suggest favorable expectations."[24]

At first everything went smoothly. The Assembly approved Henry's motions (probably drafted by Madison) that the state comply with federal requisitions and that her delegates to Congress support forcible collection in noncomplying states. A petition from Augusta County for revision of the constitution, supported by Richard Henry Lee, caused Madison to reconsider his determination "to be silent on the subject"; instead, he decided to "stir the matter." He therefore made a speech outlining eleven reasons for changing the constitution, among them that the 1776 document had not been ratified by the people, that the legislature had a "Union of powers" not guarded by checks and balances, that the "priveleges and wages of members of Legislature [are] unlimited and undefined," that representation was not equal, that the rights of suffrage were not sufficiently assured, and that the experience of Massachusetts, New York, and other states suggested other important improvements which might be made.[25]

The high hopes of Madison and the other new members faded, however, when Patrick Henry showed "a more violent opposition than we expected" to the revision proposed, and R. H. Lee "unluckily" left the Assembly, because of illness, the day before the crucial vote. Though the motion for revision was defeated overwhelmingly, Madison consoled himself that its supporters "included most of the young men of education and talents." When it came to laying taxes to pay federal requisitions, the levys were "much short" of what was needed. Henry's fulminations against higher taxes were the principal cause of the niggardly measures. He frustrated Madison's hopes a third time when his "talents . . . preserved from a dishonorable death" a bill to support all religions in Virginia from funds collected by a state-wide tax. Little wonder, then, that Madison wrote disdainfully of "Mr. Henry and . . . the forensic members" of the Assembly, exulted at Henry's removal from the Assembly to the relatively important governorship, and feared that however foolish the measure, "should [Henry] erect the standard [for it] he will certainly be joined by sufficient force to accomplish it." Madison doubtless shared Jefferson's severe judgment that the inadequate constitution was, "while Mr. Henry lives . . . saddled forever on us. What we have to do I think is devoutly to pray for his death." Indeed, long after Henry's death, remembering the many hours spent listening while his oratory doomed vital measure after vital measure, Madison and Jefferson continued to disparage him, agreeing that "neither in politics nor in his profession [law] was he a man of business; he was a man of debate only." Nothing reveals more characteristically Madison's earnest way in politics than his growing contempt for the havoc wrought by Henry's flamboyant, overpowering bombast.[26]

Two extremely important matters, however, were saved from parochial politics and transfixing oratory. Madison and three other men were appointed to negotiate the conflicting claims of Maryland and Virginia along the Potomac River—the first move for interstate conferences which, through meetings at Mount Vernon (1785) and Annapolis (1786), led to the Federal Convention of 1787. Also, though defeated on the move to revise the constitution, Madison managed to revive work on the systematic reform of the laws of Virginia undertaken seven years before by Jefferson, Edmund Pendleton, and George Wythe. Five hundred copies of their proposed revisions were ordered (a "frivolous economy," in Madison's opinion, prevented a larger printing) for the study and use of the legislators. Invigorating the government in Virginia would not, Madison knew when the Assembly adjourned on July 1, 1784, be easy. For three years he worked to fulfill the revolution by at once liberalizing and giving authority to the state government, and by strengthening the union of the states.[27]

Reform of the laws of Virginia progressed smoothly in the fall of 1785. For three days each week the Assembly, prodded by Madison, considered one by one the modernizations and liberalizations in the 117 statutes proposed by Jefferson and his colleagues. Bills on minor matters passed easily, and it was soon apparent that about half of the proposed revisions would become law, amounting altogether to a reform of Virginia statutes proper for her change from an Empire colony to an independent state. A legislator, observing Madison's work, asked, "Can you suppose it possible that Madison should shine with more than the usual splendor in this Assembly? It is, Sir, not only possible but a fact. He has astonished Mankind and has by means perfectly constitutional become almost a Dictator. . . . His influence alone has . . . carried half . . . the Revised Code." After a month, Madison told Washington that "we have got thro' a great part of the revisal, and might by this time have been at the end of it had the time wasted in disputing whether it could be finished at this Session been spent in forwarding the work."[28]

Efforts to reform the courts, however, largely fell victim to the forces arrayed against Madison. The old system, based on inefficient justices of the peace and an overworked court of appeals, made litigation in Virginia long and costly, resulting in injustice to the principals and lucrative fees to the lawyers. Jefferson's proposal called for courts of assize, standing between the local justices and the general court, in order to prod and supervise the former and to relieve the backlog of cases confronting the latter. The "old courthouse crowd" first killed the clauses giving effect to the new courts, next offered a fake reform, amounting to no more than entrenchment of the local justices, and then wholly vitiated the reform by providing that dockets be cleared quarterly, when there had long been an unenforced law on the books that they be cleared monthly. Finally, the opponents of any change put forward a measure so sweeping that it had no chance of passage. Madison observed ruefully that "the greatest danger is to be feared from those who mask a secret aversion to any reform under a zeal for such a one as they know will be rejected."[29]

Madison found that the foes of the revisal "exerted their whole force" against the bill to reform the penal code, making punishments proportional to the crime. In the fall of 1785 they managed to postpone action on the new code by pleading that the session was too near an end to permit the full discussion so important a measure required. A year later "opponents contested . . . every innovation inch by inch . . . [with] vigorous attacks" in the Assembly, and in the Senate placed even higher hurdles before the bill. It lost, by a single vote, in the Assembly, because "the rage against horse stealers" made the legislators unwilling to let murder and treason be the only capital offenses. Madison reported regretfully to Jefferson that "our old bloody code is by this event fully restored." At the same session the bill to establish a public school system in Virginia fell before timorous men who thought the state too poor for such a plan. A year later Madison wrote Jefferson that further progress on the revised code was impossible in view of Patrick Henry's "inveterate" opposition. In spite of the stubborn resistance and important failures, Jefferson nevertheless hailed his friend's accomplishment: due to "the unwearied exertions of Mr. Madison, in opposition to the endless quibbles, chicaneries, perversions, vexations and delays of lawyers and demi-lawyers, most of the bills were passed by the legislature, with little alteration."[30]

Madison won overwhelming victories in the defeat of a tax to support teachers of religion in Virginia and the enactment of Jefferson's famous bill for religious freedom. In the spring of 1784 the legislature indicated it might favor some kind of establishment, and in the fall, in response to many petitions from tidewater counties and a torrent of eloquence from Patrick Henry, it resolved to support "teachers of the Christian religion" by a general tax. Harking back to colonial days, when Anglican churches enjoyed the comfortable patronage of the government, and stimulated by Henry's perfervid exclamations about the "moral decay" of Virginia since the disestablishment, the forces favoring state support of religion surprised Madison by their strength. Along with many others, he supposed that the discredit of the Anglican Church during the revolution, the growth of other denominations, the clause in the Virginia Bill of Rights (drafted by Madison; see Chapter V) guaranteeing liberty of conscience, and the demise of church taxes in 1777, had ended religious establishment in Virginia. Many influential men, including George Washington, Edmund Pendelton, Richard Henry Lee, Joseph Jones, John Marshall, and Benjamin Harrison, in addition to Henry, nevertheless retained the hallowed ideas that religion was essential to the well-being of society and that the well-being of religion required state support. Though the bill for a religious tax, as presented by the legislature, did not require citizens to support religions in which they did not believe, and was otherwise tolerant and permissive, Madison thought it "obnoxious on account of its dishonorable principle and dangerous tendency."[31]

In November 1784 Madison marshaled the arguments against the bill in a speech before the Assembly. The proposal, he said, would neither make religion more vital nor cure the alleged "moral decay" in Virginia. It would, moreover, violate the natural right to liberty of conscience and involve the state in questions of heresy and orthodoxy entirely outside its province. Henry's eloquence, and a "pathetic" appeal by former governor Benjamin Harrison, however, overcame Madison's dispassionate exposition. Fighting for time, he agreed to support a bill (repealed three years later) to incorporate the Episcopal Church in order to gain votes to postpone final action on the religious tax until the next session of the Legislature.[32]

Madison and his colleagues thus had nearly a year to muster opposition to the bill. First, Madison supported Patrick Henry's election as governor; the orator's departure from the Assembly would be "a circumstance very inauspicious to his offspring," Madison reported to James Monroe. The wide interest aroused by the religious assessment soon brought protests from around the state, especially from the Piedmont and the Shenandoah valley, where the establishment tradition was less strong than on tidewater. In April 1785, many supporters of the assessment lost their seats in the Assembly. Madison was delighted that the people did "not scruple to declare [the assessment] an alarming usurpation of their fundamental rights" and a violation of the Virginia declaration of rights, which it thus obliged them to resist. He felt the dreadful bill "warranted this language of the people."[33]

Non-Episcopalians rose up in opposition to the assessment. The Baptists and Methodists, at this time growing rapidly, especially in the western part of the state, opposed on principle and remembered as well their harsh treatment at the hands of the established church before 1776. Presbyterians, who had for a time supported the bill as a source of financial assistance to themselves, soon switched sides when it became apparent that most laymen feared the measure's dangerous tendencies. Even many Episcopalians suspected the privileges conferred on the clergy would undermine the traditionally strong lay control of their church in Virginia. These attitudes showed fundamentally that the churches had become so splintered and liberalized that there was no practical way for the state to support them, even if it wanted to, a circumstance of which Madison took note and advantage.

To channel this tide of opposition, Madison agreed to draft a "Memorial and Remonstrance against Religious Assessments" to circulate as a petition against the pending bill. In June 1785, at home in Orange among his books, he had time to think the subject through and set down an argument in defense of freedom for the human mind worthy of Milton, Jefferson, or Mill. He assembled a host of reasons supporting religious liberty and a complete separation between church and state:

1. Religious liberty was "in its nature an unalienable right . . . because the opinions of men, depending only upon the evidence contemplated by

their own minds, cannot follow the dictates of other men. . . . Religion is wholly exempt from the cognizance [of Civil Society]."

2. Since civil society itself had no right to interfere with religion, certainly the legislature, its creature, had no such right.

3. "It is proper to take alarm at the first experiment on our liberties. . . . Who does not see that the same authority which can establish Christianity, in exclusion of all other Religions, may establish with the same ease any particular sect of Christians, in exclusion of all other Sects?"

4. The free exercise of religion implies the right to believe in no religion at all, so even the most permissive tax to support religion might violate some consciences.

5. Civil magistrates can properly neither judge religious truth nor subordinate religion to public purposes.

6. The Christian religion did not need civil support; it had often "existed and flourished, not only without the support of human laws, but in spite of every opposition from them."

7. "Ecclesiastical establishment," far from promoting religious purity and efficacy, had nearly always corrupted and stultified it.

8. Rather than promoting order and freedom in civil society, religious establishments had ordinarily been malignant and oppressive.

9. The assessment marked a first step toward bigotry, differing from "the Inquisition . . . only in degree," and would make Virginia no longer an asylum for the persecuted.

10. Good and useful citizens would be driven from the state or deterred from coming there by a religious tax.

11. Religious strife and violence would be encouraged by laws touching religion.

12. "The policy of the bill is adverse to the diffusion of the light of Christianity. . . . The bill with an ignoble and unchristian timidity would circumscribe it, with a wall of defence, against the encroachments of error."

13. An attempt to enforce a religious assessment obnoxious to many citizens would weaken respect for law and order generally.

14. Evidence was strong that a majority of the people opposed the assessment.

15. "Because, finally, the equal right of every citizen to the free exercise of his Religion according to the dictates of conscience is held by the same tenure with all our other rights. If we recur to its origin, it is equally the gift of nature; if we weigh its importance, it cannot be less dear to us; if we consult the Declaration of those rights which pertain to the good people of Virginia, as the basis and foundation of Government, it is enumerated with equal solemnity, or rather studied emphasis. Either then, we must say, that the will of the Legislature is the only

measure of their authority; and that in the plenitude of this authority, they may sweep away our fundamental rights; or, that they are bound to leave this particular right untouched and sacred: Either we must say, that they may control the freedom of the press, may abolish the trial by jury, may swallow up the Executive and Judiciary Powers of the State; nay that they may despoil us of our very right of suffrage and erect themselves into an independent and hereditary assembly: or we must say, that they have no authority to enact into law the Bill under consideration."[34]

George Mason had the "Remonstrance" printed in Alexandria, and hundreds of copies were circulated throughout the state. In August, Madison reported candidly to Jefferson: "The opposition to the general assessment gains ground. At the instance of some of its adversaries I drew up the remonstrance herewith inclosed. It has been sent thro' the medium of confidential persons in a number of the upper Counties, and I am told will be pretty extensively signed. The Presbyterian clergy, have at length espoused the side of the opposition, being moved either by a fear of their laity or a jealousy of the Episcopalians. The mutual hatred of these sects has been much inflamed by the late Act incorporating the latter. I am far from being sorry for it, as a coalition between them could alone endanger our religious rights, and a tendency to such an event has been suspected."[35]

Madison must have been confidently jubilant as he took his seat in the Assembly that fall: "The table was loaded with petitions and remonstrances from all parts against interposition of the Legislature in matters of Religion." A Presbyterian convention had petitioned for a law establishing religious freedom, and Baptists and Methodists declaimed against a religious tax. The assessment bill of the previous session died silently, and Madison quickly proposed adoption of Jefferson's eloquent "Bill for Establishing Religious Freedom." After its enactment, Madison wrote its author that "I flatter myself [we] have in this country extinguished forever the ambitious hope of making laws for the human mind." Of all his accomplishments as a legislator, Madison took greatest pleasure and pride in this victory.[36]

In fact, religious liberty stands out as the one subject upon which Madison took an extreme, absolute, undeviating position throughout his life. The phrases he proposed for the first amendment to the federal Constitution—"the full and equal rights of conscience [shall not] be in any manner, or on any pretext, infringed," and "no State shall violate the equal rights of conscience"—were less equivocal than the language finally adopted. He opposed inquiring about a man's profession in the national census because for clergymen to respond to such questions might infringe upon the absolute privacy of religious opinions. He opposed chartering a national bank partly because he feared the broad interpretation of federal incorporating power it required might lead to establishing religious corporations. In 1798, 1799, and 1800 he made the threat to religious liberty an important part of his protest against the Sedition Act. To strengthen the wall of separation between church and state, he opposed having the government pay chaplains for Congress or for the armed forces. He opposed presidential proclamations of religious holidays, and as President he vetoed a Congressional grant of land to a Baptist church in Mississippi because it comprised "a principle and precedent for the appropriation of funds of the United States for the use and support of religious societies." Religious liberty, Madison wrote, ought to be defined "as distinctly as words can admit, and the limits to [religious laws] established with as much solemnity as the forms of legislation express. . . . Every provision for [such laws] short of this principle, will be found to leave crevices at least through which bigotry may introduce persecution; a monster feeding and thriving on its own venom, gradually swells to a size and strength overwhelming all laws human and divine."[37]

The part played in the defeat of the assessment by the various religious sects, each jealous that others would derive special benefit from it, helped impress upon Madison the protection afforded to liberty by competing factions. He recognized that without this competition his forceful arguments in the "Remonstrance," and even the declaration in favor of religious liberty in the state constitution, were, in his words, mere "parchment barriers." He asked and answered the crucial question before the Virginia Convention of 1788: "Is a bill of rights a security for [religious liberty]? . . . If there were a majority of one sect, a bill of rights would be a poor protection for liberty. Happily for the [United States] they enjoy the utmost freedom of religion. This freedom arises from the multiplicity of sects, which pervades America, and which is the best and only security for religious liberty in any society. For where there is such a variety of sects, there cannot be a majority of any one sect to oppress and persecute the rest." Madison quoted often—"with great approbation," according to his neighbor and biographer, William Cabell Rives—Voltaire's comment in the *Dictionnaire Philosophique* that "if one religion only were allowed in England, the government would possibly be arbitrary; if there were but two, the people would cut each other's throats; but, as there are such a multitude, they all live happy and in peace." Madison's experience in finding that religious diversity confounded those inclined to seek privilege or to oppress dissent, helped importantly in forming his more general theory that freedom was safest in the presence of a multitude of counterbalancing forces, which acted to check the tyrannical impulses of any one of them.[38]

Late in life Madison had frequent opportunity to comment on what he thought was the benign effect of complete liberty of conscience. He wrote a Lutheran clergyman that "a due distinction . . . between what is due to Caesar and what is due God, best promotes the discharge of *both* obligations. . . . A mutual independence is found most friendly to practical religion, to social harmony, and to political prosperity." Asked to compare the state of religion and public virtue in Virginia under the colonial establishment with its state after forty years of religious freedom, Madison replied:

> That there has been an increase of religious instruction since the revolution can admit of no question. The English church was originally the established religion. Of other sects there were but few adherents, except the Presbyterians who predominated on the West side of the Blue Mountains. . . . At present the population is divided, with small exceptions, among the Protestant Episcopalians, the Presbyterians, the Baptists, and the Methodists. . . . Religious instruction is now diffused throughout the Community by preachers of every sect with almost equal zeal, tho' with very unequal acquirements; and at private houses and open stations. . . . The qualifications of the Preachers, too, among the new sects where there was the greatest deficiency, are understood to be improving. On a general comparison of the present and former times, the balance is certainly and vastly on the side of the present, as to the number of religious teachers, the zeal which actuates them, the purity of their lives, and the attendance of the people on their instructions. It was the Universal opinion of the Century preceding the last, that Civil Government could not stand without the prop of a Religious establishment, and that the Christian religion itself, would perish if not supported by a legal provision for its Clergy. The experience of Virginia conspicuously corroborates the disproof of both opinions. The Civil Government tho' bereft of everything like an associated hierarchy possesses the requisite stability and performs its functions with complete success; Whilst the number, the industry, and the morality of the Priesthood, and the devotion of the people have been manifestly increased by the total separation of the Church from the State.[39]

There is no evidence that Madison's defense of religious liberty reflected any hostility to religion itself or to its social effects. On the contrary, he argued repeatedly that freedom of religion enhanced *both* its intrinsic vitality and its contribution to the common weal. He believed that attitudes and habits nourished by the churches could and did help importantly to improve republican government. He believed just as strongly that complete separation of church and state saved the church from the inevitably corrupting influence of civil authority. From his early reading of the *Memoirs of Cardinal de Retz* and observation of religious persecution in Virginia, he had gained firm impressions of the ill effects of any connection between church and state. Throughout his long public career he received cordial support from Protestants, Catholics, and Jews who admired his forthright stand on religious liberty. In turn he respected the constructive contribution unfettered, variegated religion made to the well-being of society. Madison bespoke fully and cogently what came to be the characteristically American attitude toward the relation between religion and politics.

Madison spent most of his time in the Virginia legislature, however, dealing with matters less congenial to an Enlightenment philosopher than liberalized law codes and religious freedom. As chairman of the Committee on Commerce he confronted the disadvantageous terms of trade in Virginia. Planters, especially those with wharves on tidewater, were inclined to revert to the colonial pattern of direct trade with England. To Madison this had four major disadvantages: It re-established the old cycle of favors, credit, and debt which bound Virginians to the British mercantile system; it meant Virginians bought dearer and sold cheaper than they would be able to do in a large commercial center; it siphoned off the profits of trade to such out-of-state cities as Baltimore and Philadelphia; and by permitting Britain easy access to the full profits of the American trade, it robbed Virginia (and ultimately the United States) of any effective leverage against British regulations excluding American vessels from the important West Indian trade. As evidence of Virginia's disadvantage, Madison pointed out that even though tobacco in Philadelphia was as far from European ports as it was on tidewater wharves, it sold for 20 per cent higher in the city. Similarly, imported goods were cheaper in the trading centers than they were when brought directly to Virginia plantations.

To combat the liabilities, Madison, Jefferson, and Washington favored a plan to establish Norfolk as the only port of Virginia's foreign trade. Norfolk would then soon become a great commercial metropolis where Virginia planters could trade advantageously and where Virginia merchants would reap the middleman's profits. Madison termed arguments opposing the proposal as a blow to free trade "decoys" used by those hungry for the long-term credits available in London and Liverpool. The trade-regulating plan, violating Madison's own inclination to favor the free flow of commerce, shows him perfectly willing to depart from that principle when national self-interest so required.

Madison soon discovered, however, that though Virginians were anxious to resist British commercial monopoly and to refuse profits to Philadelphia and Baltimore merchants, there was almost no agreement about means, and particularly about which Virginia port to favor. First, it was decided that Alexandria should be an approved trading center for the north, but this broadened proposal still threatened too many special interests: "We were obliged," Madison reported, "to add York, Tappahannock, and Bermuda Hundred [as entry ports] in order to gain any-

thing." Even this measure, he suspected—correctly—would be rescinded
before it took effect. Virginia planters remained utterly exposed to whatever profits British or out-of-state merchants chose to extract; the
humiliation of British discrimination persisted; and Virginia continued
unable to earn any significant revenue from her flourishing trade. Madison had for his exertions only bitter lessons in the threat special interests
posed to any regulation for the common good, and the need for effective
nation-wide control over commerce if the United States was to participate advantageously in international trade. He stated the general precept
ruefully to Monroe: "If it be necessary to regulate trade at all, it surely
is necessary to lodge the power where trade can be regulated with effect;
and experience has confirmed what reason foresaw, that it can never be
so regulated by the States acting in their separate capacities. They can no
more exercise this power separately than they could separately carry on
war, or separately form treaties of alliance or commerce." Even in Richmond, struggling with the trade problems of Virginia planters, Madison
could not keep his feet off the path leading to the Federal Convention
of 1787.[40]

The need for interstate cooperation was further impressed on Madison
in the difficulties between Maryland and Virginia over use and navigation of the Potomac River. According to Maryland's charter, her boundary extended to the *southern* shore of the river. Interpreted strictly, this
might preclude Virginia from any use of the river or from any regulation
of the trade in her ports on the Potomac. In June 1784 Madison persuaded the Virginia legislature to appoint commissioners, including himself, to seek with Maryland "a harmonious settlement." Prodded by
Washington and Jefferson, Maryland appointed commissioners for the
same purpose, and they met in March 1785 at Mount Vernon. Poor
communications and executive inefficiency deprived Madison of notifica-
tion until after the conference had adjourned, but led by George Mason,
the commissioners settled major problems facing the two states: the
Potomac was declared a common highway; regulations for its use were
agreed upon; and Virginia acceded to Maryland's wishes in certain trade
problems in Chesapeake Bay. The conference also pointed out that the
commercial potential of the Potomac could be exploited fully only by
cooperating with Pennsylvania to link it with the waters of the Ohio.[41]
Madison secured approval of the Mount Vernon compact in the Virginia legislature, and sought quickly to take advantage of its recommendations about interstate cooperation and an additional conference. He
inspired a motion by John Tyler that Virginia press for Congressional
regulation of interstate commerce, and he persuaded the Assembly to
appoint himself and others "commissioners who . . . shall meet such
commissioners as may be appointed by the other states in the Union . . .

to consider how far a uniform system in their commercial regulations may be necessary to their common interest and their permanent harmony." This motion resulted eventually in the Annapolis Convention.[42]

But Madison's concern for Virginia's commercial health and his zeal to increase federal power over trade had deeper roots than the desire to settle disputes over seacoast trade. Like many other Virginians, he never relinquished the vision of a Western empire. The great question was that of how best to open the lands of the Ohio valley to settlement and to channel the potentially fabulous trade of that region to the East Coast. Madison and other Virginians, of course, sought ways to bring the trade through Virginia, but they did not conceive that this goal conflicted in any way with national objectives. Rather, they thought of Virginia as in the vanguard of expansion movements to benefit and strengthen the Union as a whole. With typical ambivalence, Washington wrote Patrick Henry that the canal systems linking Virginia with Albemarle Sound and the Ohio valley would "open channels of convenience and wealth to the citizens of this state that the imagination can barely extend to and render this the most favored country in the universe." Madison endorsed enthusiastically Washington's support of internal improvements: "He could not have chosen an occupation more worthy of succeeding to that of establishing the political rights of his Country, than the patronage of works for the extensive and lasting improvements of its natural advantages; works which will double the value of half the lands within the Commonwealth [Virginia], will extend its commerce, link with its interests those of the Western States, and lessen the emigration of its Citizens, by enhancing the profitableness of situations which they now desert in search of better."[43]

Washington surveyed canal routes over the Appalachian Mountains, secured the cooperation of promoters in other states, and raised money, while Madison, depending on the general's enormous prestige, guided measures through the Virginia legislature. In January 1785, Madison sought state support, in cooperation with Maryland, for a plan to connect the Potomac, by widening and deepening it and by building canals and roads, with the headwaters of the Monongahela River. Thus, with a portage of no more than twenty or thirty miles, produce could be transported entirely by water (on shallow draft bateaux) from the far northern and western reaches of the Mississippi and Missouri rivers to the Atlantic Ocean. To soothe sectional jealousy, Madison carried through with the Potomac Canal charter a similar measure to make the James River navigable and to connect it by short portages with the upper reaches of tributaries of the Ohio and Tennessee rivers. At the same time, he secured funds to survey a canal from Norfolk via the Elizabeth River through the Great Dismal Swamp to Albemarle Sound. This furnished an inland link between Virginia and North Carolina, and opened up vast lands in southern Virginia drained by the Roanoke River. In all of these promotions Madison sought, with some success, to keep public participation high and protect public needs against the avaricious and monopolistic schemes of private speculators and entrepreneurs. To him the essential need was to build transportation bonds which would enhance the general prosperity and eventually become sinews of union too powerful for divisive forces to break.[44]

Finance, however, was the most vexing matter to Madison during his three years in the Virginia legislature. Unsound measures threatened Virginia's solvency and the survival of the Union itself. In 1784 Madison fought unsuccessfully a Henry proposal that the collection of taxes be postponed for a year. Such a move, especially when high tobacco prices made specie relatively plentiful in Virginia, would, Madison wrote, unnecessarily confuse state finances and subordinate public wisdom to popular foolishness. Furthermore, he asserted, "we shall make a strange figure, after our declarations with regard to Congress and the Continental debt, if we wholly omit the means of fulfilling them." The next year, with tobacco prices down, Madison managed to defeat outright cancellation of taxes by urging a postponement and payment of taxes in tobacco and other produce instead of in specie. Next, he felt sure, Henry and his followers would call for paper money, a resort Madison felt had already done much damage in other states.[45]

Another measure of Virginia's financial irresponsibility, in Madison's view, was the persistent effort to circumvent the treaty of peace with Great Britain. To fulfill the treaty, Virginia had to pass laws permitting actions in her courts to recover the substantial prerevolutionary debts owed to citizens of Great Britain. To Madison, never one to repudiate or depreciate debts, both national honor and national self-interest required fidelity to the treaty. Skillful maneuvering enabled Madison and his cohorts to push through the Assembly repeal of measures preventing collection of the debts, but before the bill was signed and enrolled, an act of nature—and perhaps some collusion by debt-ridden legislators—nullified the hard-won victory. Madison explained to Jefferson: the day before the Assembly was to adjourn, "several of the members went [across the James River] to Manchester . . . with an intention it is to be presumed of returning the next morning. The severity of the night rendered their passage back . . . impossible. Without them there was no [quorum]. The impatience of the members was such as might be supposed. . . . The next day presented the same obstructions [ice] in the river. A canoe was sent over for enquiry by the Manchester party, but they did not choose to venture themselves. The impatience increased. . . . On the morning of the third day the prospect remained the same.

Patience could hold out no longer and an adjournment . . . ensued."
Madison's bill therefore was lost.[46]

Since, as Irving Brant has remarked, no study has been made of the
British debts owed by the marooned delegates, we do not know whether
they took advantage of the severe weather to defeat the measure providing for payment. Madison's longing looks across the ice-clogged river
might have been even more anxious had he known that in the next two
legislatures bills to provide for the debts would not come close to passage.
The result heightened Madison's conviction that the states, left to their
own devices, would never display the harmony, integrity, and stability
required if the United States was to achieve domestic solvency and
international self-respect.[47]

In 1786, as Virginia's shifting financial policies and commercial depression caused widespread hardship, the "itch for paper money" spread
ominously in the Assembly. A resolve that Virginia join the states which
had issued paper money was introduced at the beginning of the November 1786 session. Madison rose at once, marshaling an impressive barrage
of arguments to combat it: paper money would only drive what little
specie remained in Virginia away, thus further embarrassing foreign
trade, for which specie was essential; it was unjust to creditors forced to
accept inflated payments for debts honestly contracted; it was antifederal,
because it infringed the power of Congress to regulate coinage; it was
unnecessary, because "the produce of the country will bring in specie, if
not laid out in superfluities"; and finally, it was pernicious, because it
fostered luxury, enriched "sharpers," vitiated morals, created dissension
among the states, reversed the "end of government which is to reward
the best and punish the worst," and tended "to disgrace Republican
Governments in the eyes of Mankind."[48]

The next day, by an overwhelming vote of 85 to 17, the House rejected paper money, resolving that it was "unjust, impolitic, destructive
of public and private confidence." Madison reported to Washington and
Jefferson, hoping that the empty state treasury and repeated defaults in
payments to Congress might now be overcome, but he had second
thoughts over the measure permitting payment of taxes in tobacco:
"This indulgence to the people as it is called and considered was so
warmly wished for out of doors [of the House] and so strenuously
pressed within that it could not be rejected without danger of exciting
some worse project of a popular cast." "Mania" for paper currency and
the inclination of legislative leaders to favor it and other measures un-
dermining financial integrity, despite their obvious injustice and foolishness, were to Madison unmistakable examples of the operation of faction:
selfish, unwise measures all too easily swept through small popular assemblies. Though he managed to defeat the worst paper money bills,
Madison had no illusions about either the strength or the severity of the

fever for them. As his argument about the "antifederal" nature of the currency resolve hinted, he thought the only antidote for the "raging disorder" was federal control of currency.[49]

Thus, even in Richmond, Madison's attention strayed persistently to national concerns. Religious freedom, internal improvements, and interstate cooperation, though state measures, had in Madison's mind highly significant national implications. Almost his every speech and every act in Richmond marked him as a nationalist. With James Monroe and other Virginia delegates to Congress, he worked for state laws vital to the dignity and authority of the nation. He seized every opportunity to highlight the blessings of strength and the perils of weakness in the federal union. He moved patiently to put Virginia in the vanguard of the states favoring increased national power, and eventually, a revised, possibly even a new, federal constitution. His experience with state government from 1784 to 1787 confirmed his conviction, gained in Philadelphia from 1780 through 1783, that the future glory of America required a strong central government.

CHAPTER IX

Toward the Constitution

M ADISON'S concern for a stronger Union impinged on almost
every issue he faced while out of Congress. He was delighted,
for example, when in May 1784 Patrick Henry offered resolves in the Virginia legislature that money due to the Confederation
be based on population rather than land valuation and that unpaid requisitions be forcibly collected by "distress on the property of the defaulting
States or of their citizens." Madison observed pointedly the next year
that "a single frigate under the orders of Congress could make it the
interest of any one of the Atlantic States to pay its just quota." Con-
federacy-wide measures and the power to compel obedience were also
necessary to prevent ultimately self-defeating commercial disputes among
the states. Moreover, foreign humiliation often resulted from the opportunity other nations had to intrigue and play one state off against
another. Madison wrote indignantly to Monroe:

> The policy of Great Britain (to say nothing of other nations) has
> shut against us the channels without which our trade with her must
> be a losing one; and she has consequently the triumph, as we have
> the chagrin, of seeing accomplished her prophetic threats, that our
> independence should forfeit commercial advantages for which it would
> not recompence us with any new channels of trade. What is to be
> done? Must we remain passive victims to foreign politics, or shall we
> exert the lawful means which our independence has put into our hands
> of extorting redress? The very question would be an affront to every
> Citizen who loves his Country. What, then, are these means? Retali-
> ating regulations of trade only. How are these to be effectuated? only
> by harmony in the measures of the States. How is this harmony to be
> obtained? only by an acquiescence of all the States in the opinion of

a reasonable majority. If Congress as they are now constituted, can not be trusted with the power of digesting and enforcing this opinion, let them be otherwise constituted. . . .[1]

The same vicious circle, with the same enervating effects, in Madison's opinion, operated in state emissions of paper money. In the summer of 1786 Madison reviewed the situation for Jefferson. In each of the six states having paper currency, there was some measure of depreciation. In North Carolina public officers gave twice as much in paper currency as in specie for purchases of tobacco, and since the paper was legal tender, debtors "ran" to sell tobacco to the public officers and then forced the inflated paper on their creditors, who "paid the expense of the farce." Public pressure prevented serious depreciation within New Jersey, but in New York and Philadelphia, "where all the trade of N.J. is carried on," depreciation went on apace. In Rhode Island laws making depreciated paper legal tender kept supplies from the market, closed shops, and left the state "in a sort of convulsion." Worst of all, paper currency emissions were "producing the same warfare and retaliation among the States as were produced by the state regulations of commerce." State-designed laws either to protect citizens against paper money or to force it on them paralyzed commerce.

In Madison's mind the need was not particularly to protect creditors from inflationary debtor relief laws. The object, rather, was to increase the real wealth of the country by encouraging hard work, proper use of resources, and trading centers where Virginians (and all Americans) would get a fair return for their produce. "The intrinsic defect of the paper," Madison wrote, was that "this fictitious money will rather feed than cure the spirit of extravagance which sends away the coin to pay the unfavorable balance [in foreign trade] and will therefore soon be carried to market to buy up coin for that purpose. From that moment depreciation is inevitable. The value of money consists in the uses it will serve. Specie will serve all the uses of paper. Paper will not serve one of the essential uses of specie. The paper therefore will be less valuable than specie." Accusations that Madison's undeviating "hard money" views identify him with the interests of rich men, insensitive to the oppressions of the poor and debt-ridden, miss the mark. He was well aware of the farmer's difficulties, and he had no interest in or little sympathy for the rising commercial classes. In fact, he opposed a fluctuating and chaotic money system because he had so often seen that "sharpers," speculators, and other parasites were the main beneficiaries of an unstable currency. He opposed deflation for its equally harmful social effects. This had been his position in the 1780 essay "Money"; it was his argument consistently in the Continental Congress; and it remained his opinion throughout his life. To Madison a stable currency would be equally useful to industrious citizens at home and to foreign traders and investors willing to deal fairly with the new nation.[2]

Though the economic distress, commercial warfare, and paper money "depravity" of the Confederation may have been exaggerated by Madison and others at the time, and by "critical period" historians ever since, it is important to remember that Madison's anxiety and concern rested as much on tendencies as on actuality. The amicable settlement of some disputes among states was to him less significant than the looming unresolved issues. He declaimed not about the lack of patriotism of the defenders of state supremacy, but against their unwisdom and their failure to envision the inevitable debilitation that would result from the deficient authority of the general government under the Articles of Confederation. Whatever the growth and achievements of the Confederation period, Madison was convinced that in the long run the United States required government over, not negotiation among, its constituent parts.[3]

The need to protect American access to the Mississippi revealed to Madison a vital connection between the effective conduct of foreign affairs and a stronger Union. American weakness invited foreign highhandedness. In 1784 Madison explained to Jefferson why he thought the renewed Spanish attempt to close the river to navigation was "impolitic and Perverse." "She can," Madison asserted, "no more finally stop the current of trade down the river than she can that of the river itself." Though "justice and the general rights of mankind" were often disregarded in international relations, he noted, it was "no small advantage that these considerations" were on the American side in the navigation dispute. "Even the most corrupt councils," he believed, would be somewhat touched by "the progress of philosophy and civilization." Should such considerations fail, Spanish national interest, Madison thought, required her to permit free navigation; for (1) New Orleans would then become a great trading center, loyal to Spain for permitting the trade upon which her prosperity depended; (2) the friendship of the United States, important to Spain as American power increased, would thus be assured; (3) the aggressive power of England, which Spain had so much feared in the Mississippi valley, would be replaced by an unaggressive United States, and "the complexity of our federal government and the diversity of interests among the members" would hinder American moves dangerous to Spain; (4) many of the great nations in the world would resist claims such as Spain's of the right to block the mouths of rivers; (5) if bottled up east of the Appalachians, the United States would turn to sea commerce and manufacturing and thus increase her naval potential (a threat to Spain) and her competition with the nations of Europe, but if left to expand through the Mississippi valley, America would become a land of farmers and therefore a rich market and an abundant granary for Europe.[4]

Seven months later, in persuading Lafayette to write French Foreign Minister Vergennes on behalf of American claims to the Mississippi, Madison reviewed the arguments he had earlier sent to Jefferson and emphasized appeal to the rights of man in a way he knew would touch the young Frenchman:

> Nature has given the use of the Mississippi to those who may settle on its waters, as she gave to the United States their independence. The impolicy of Spain may retard the former as that of G. Britain did the latter. But as G.B. could not defeat the latter, neither will Spain the former. Nature seems on all sides to be reasserting those rights which have so long been trampled on by tyranny and bigotry. Philosophy and Commerce are the auxiliaries to whom she is indebted for her triumphs. Will it be presumptuous to say that those nations will shew most wisdom as well as acquire most glory, who instead of forcing her current into artificial channels, endeavour to ascertain its tendency and to anticipate its effects? If the United States were to become parties to the occlusion of the Mississippi they would be guilty of treason against the very laws under which they obtained and hold their national existence.

Only Britain, the "watchful adversary" of Louis XVI, Madison concluded, would benefit from a Spanish-American quarrel over the Mississippi.[5]

In the spring of 1786 Foreign Secretary John Jay, despairing of efforts to persuade Spanish Minister Gardoqui to settle the dispute between the two nations by opening the Mississippi, proposed that the United States agree for twenty-five years to abandon claims for navigation of the river in exchange for a commercial treaty guaranteeing American fishermen access to the huge Spanish market and favoring American merchants suffering from British discrimination. This, Jay argued, would yield immediate advantages in exchange for a postponement that, given the remoteness of most of the lands in the Mississippi valley, would not for years have much practical effect on American expansion. Jay's view reflected, ominously, a much keener awareness of the interests of the Eastern, trading, portion of the new nation than of the agricultural regions. To Southerners and Westerners, of course, the Jay-Gardoqui project was anathema, a sectional measure proving that a stronger federation would sacrifice the vital interests of some parts of the Union. It would be better, thundered Patrick Henry and others, for Virginia and her Southern neighbors to stand alone than to strengthen a union neglectful of their rights and interests.[6]

Jay's proposal disgusted Madison. "The measure in question," he wrote Monroe, "would be a voluntary barter in time of profound peace of the rights of one part of the empire to the interests of another part." It was shortsighted and dishonorable to betray Americans who had crossed the mountains, to doubt French ability, on behalf of the United States, to influence Spain, and to seek a humiliating alliance with a nation impotent to help Americans against Britain's still unabated enmity. Why embrace a nation, Madison protested, "who has given no proof of regard for us and the genius of whose Government, religion, and manners unfit them of all the nations in Christendom for a coalition with this country." The contemplated American guarantee of Spanish possessions in the New World was "still more objectionable. If it be insidious we plunge ourselves into infamy. If sincere, into obligations the extent of which cannot easily be determined. In either case we get farther into the lab-yrinth of European politics from which we ought religiously to keep ourselves as free as possible." As for the Spanish guarantee of American territory, the United States did not need it, or if it did, "will any man in his senses pretend that . . . the arm of Spain is to save it?"[7]

Madison explained further ill effects to Jefferson. "Figure to yourself," Madison suggested pointedly, the impression of the Jay-Gardoqui proj-ect "on the assembly of Virginia, already jealous of northern policy and which will be composed of about thirty members from the western waters. . . . Figure to yourself its effect on the people at large on the western waters . . . who will consider themselves as *sold* by their Atlantic brethren. Will it be an unnatural consequence if they consider themselves as absolved from any federal tie and court some protection for their betrayed rights? This protection will appear more attainable from the maritime power of Britain than from any other quarter; and Britain will be more ready than any other nation to seize an opportunity of embroiling our affairs." The obvious goal of the Spanish negotiator was "a total separation of interest and affection between western and eastern settlements and to foment the jealousy between the eastern and southern states." Furthermore, Madison added, "my personal situation is rendered by this business particularly mortifying. Ever since I have been out of Congress I have been inculcating on our Assembly a confidence in the equal attention of Congress to the rights and interests of every part of the republic, and on the western members in particular, the necessity of making the Union respectable by new powers to Congress if they wished Congress to negotiate with effect for the Mississippi." Jay's proposal killed Madison's argument. Far from being a vital reason *for* a strength-ened Union, the conduct of foreign relations threatened to be an irresisti-ble argument *against* it. To defeat the proposed treaty with Spain, Mad-ison planned to secure a protest against it from the Virginia legislature and then its repudiation by Congress. Though he did not think Congress would approve the treaty, even a narrow failure, he wrote, would "be fatal I fear to an augmentation of the federal authority if not to the little now existing."[8]

In Richmond Madison found "as much zeal as could be wished" among members of the legislature to defend navigation of the Mississippi. Petitions from Kentucky (still part of Virginia) threatened secession if the Jay-Gardoqui project was approved. Madison sought to channel anti-Jay feeling usefully by leading the Assembly to resolve unanimously that to surrender the right to use the Mississippi would "destroy . . . confidence in the wisdom, justice and liberality of the federal councils . . . and undermine our repose, our prosperity and our Union itself." Madison wrote Washington that unless these resolves were respected, "the hope of carrying this State into a proper federal system will be demolished." Many leading Virginia federalists were "extremely soured with what has already passed." Patrick Henry, who "had hitherto been a champion of the Federal cause, had become a cold advocate, and in the event of an actual sacrifice of the Mississippi by Congress, will unquestionably go over to the other side." Madison accepted election to Congress to fight the Jay proposal.[9]

In late January 1787 Madison began on horseback the long, cold journey to New York, bypassing Montpelier entirely in his haste. He switched to the stagecoach in Fredericksburg, avoided a delay there by not stopping to visit Monroe and his new bride, and on January 25 stopped at Mount Vernon, where Washington paused from farm chores to talk politics with his guest. Heartened at the firm Virginia resolves on the Mississippi question, they discussed the coming Federal Convention, to which each had been elected to the Virginia delegation. Washington hesitated to go, but Madison urged him to, since the Union so desperately needed strengthening. As they said goodbye the next day, Madison was more sure than ever of Washington's confidence in him, and especially aware of his need to maintain the general's effective support of federal measures. Madison then crossed the Potomac, stopped briefly at the House lodgings in Philadelphia, and fought a northeast blizzard that made the roads almost impassable. The rivers, he complained, were "clogged with ice and a half congealed mixture of snow and water which was more in the way than the ice itself." On February 9 he crossed the Hudson River from Paulus Hook to Manhattan, glad at last to join the only Virginia delegate in New York, William Grayson, who had partly recovered from a nervous breakdown, but was still the "frequent prey" of his hypochondriac illusions.[10]

Madison was pleased at the status of the Mississippi question. New Jersey had withdrawn its support of Jay's proposal; Pennsylvania was soon expected to do the same; and there was even hope that some of the New England states also would. Madison supposed, therefore, that Jay would "not venture to proceed in his project."[11]

Since Jay was not required to report to Congress on his negotiations with Gardoqui, Madison decided to find out what he could from the

Spaniard. He called on Gardoqui in the company of William Bingham, a wealthy Philadelphian with important foreign commercial connections, and a ravishingly beautiful wife especially skilled at impressing titled Europeans. Gardoqui nevertheless was absolutely unyielding on the Mississippi question: Spain had nothing to fear from England, and threats from state legislatures and pugnacious frontiersmen would serve only to draw more Spanish soldiers to New Orleans. Though dismayed at Gardoqui's attitude, Madison was relieved to learn what he could not discover on the floor of Congress—that Jay and Gardoqui had not conferred since the previous October. "The Spanish project sleeps," he wrote Jefferson.[12]

Jay's outlook, as it was gradually revealed in Congress, was nevertheless alarming. He viewed the plundering lawlessness of George Rogers Clark and other Americans in the Illinois country as compelling evidence that an agreement with Spain, however compromising, was necessary to preserve order in the Mississippi valley. Madison wanted instead to use the disturbances to frighten Spain into opening the river. When Madison finally persuaded Congress to ask Jay for a report, the Foreign Secretary revealed enough inclination to make concessions to Spain to set Pennsylvania and Rhode Island against him. Congressional rules favoring inaction shielded Jay from an open repudiation by Congress, but Madison had made it perfectly clear that a majority of the states would not acquiesce in the river closure.[13]

As Madison prepared in April 1787 to leave New York for the Federal Convention, the Spanish negotiations remained in a "very ticklish situation." Madison and others had failed in a move to transfer negotiations to Madrid, where they would be under Jefferson's firm guidance, because, with only eight states present in Congress, two, Massachusetts and New York, were able to block action. Though Madison hoped "the paucity of States who abet the obnoxious project" of closing the Mississippi was clear to everyone, he nevertheless asserted that "the consequences of [Jay's] intention and the attempt are likely to be very serious." Not sure of Congress' resolve to retain Mississippi rights, Patrick Henry had refused to attend the Federal Convention. The Southern states were furious at the neglect of their opinions, and "the people living on the Western waters, . . . already in great agitation, [were] taking measures for uniting their consultations." British agents fomented disunion in the West. France was as constrained as she had been in 1780 from seeming to favor the United States over Spain.[14]

Madison readily projected the pernicious effects of the proposal to close the Mississippi to broader questions of political theory. In his view, stopping American trade on the Mississippi River was as clearly unjust as were the British misdeeds that had caused the American Revolution.

What could be made of the fact that a Congress of freely elected delegates had nearly sanctioned such a depravity? Six months earlier Madison had thought out loud in a letter to Monroe:

> Should the measure triumph under the patronage of 9 States or even of the whole thirteen, I shall never be convinced that it is expedient, because I cannot conceive it to be just. There is no maxim in my opinion which is more liable to be misapplied, and which therefore more needs elucidation than the current one that the interest of the majority is the political standard of right and wrong. Taking the word "interest" as synonymous with "ultimate happiness," in which sense it is qualified with every necessary moral ingredient, the proposition is no doubt true. But taking it in the popular sense, as referring to immediate augmentation of property and wealth, nothing can be more false. In the latter sense it would be the interest of the majority in every community to despoil and enslave the minority of individuals; and in a federal community to make a similar sacrifice of the minority of the component States. In fact it is only re-establishing under another name and a more specious form, force as the measure of right; and in this light the Western settlements will infallibly view it.[15]

Madison had struggled with this tension between government by consent (which seemed ultimately to mean majority rule) and the idea of inalienable rights, implanted in successive phrases of the Declaration of Independence, ever since 1776. Was there any way to guard against the majority consenting to a violation of such rights? A positive answer to this question would, in Madison's mind, solve the fundamental problem of republican government. To him, concepts of right and justice were paramount to expressions of majority rule. Foolish or unjust measures sanctioned by the majority were no more legitimate than such measures decreed by despots. An entire region or state in a large federation could be as much oppressed as individuals or groups in a small republic. To join in one government the principle of consent and a belief in inalienable rights would not be easy.[16]

Jefferson had faced the same dilemma in 1783, when he had drafted a new constitution for Virginia, to replace the 1776 document both he and Madison considered defective. The lack of a proper separation of powers, the absurdly deficient powers of the governor, and the insecure standing of the constitution as supreme law were the main flaws in the existing government, in Jefferson's view. Madison agreed. In June 1784, sensing a mood in the Assembly favoring amendment, Madison rose to propose some changes. The lower house of the legislature, since it elected the governor, appointed the judges, and otherwise had predominating authority, he declared, violated the principle of separation of powers laid down by Montesquieu and others as essential to the preservation of liberty. The governor was so hampered by an ill-conceived council that he could scarcely be held accountable for executive actions, and the Senate, barred from initiating legislation and otherwise subservient to the House of Delegates, was a mere cipher in the frame of government. Eight years of experience with the Virginia constitution of 1776 had convinced Madison and Jefferson that it would neither protect liberty nor promote the public welfare.[17]

After the amendment effort proved to be premature in Virginia, Madison offered his advice to friends in Kentucky who were looking ahead to the day when Kentucky would draft its own constitution. The legislative department, he began, "ought by all means . . . to include a Senate constituted on such principles as will give *wisdom* and steadiness to legislation. The want of these qualities is the grievance complained of in all our republics." The intense concern in 1776 to prevent infidelity to the wishes of the people, which had characterized the last years of British rule, had led Virginia to give too much power to the annually elected lower house. A strong senate, elected for a term of perhaps six years, and requiring a higher property qualification for its electors, was needed to assure "wisdom and steadiness." Madison also commended the Maryland system of having the people choose electors, who in turn elected the senators.[18]

To further encourage *good* laws, Madison opposed a strict definition of "the extent of Legislative power." He did, however, urge that the constitution exempt from legislative attention religion and other matters usually protected in a bill of rights. He also approved the provision in the New York constitution for a council of revision as "a further security against fluctuating and indigested laws." Even better would be "a standing committee of a few select and skillful individuals" to advise the Assembly. One session of the Virginia legislature had convinced Madison that members chosen by local constituencies were often inexperienced in public affairs, and left to their own devives, were not likely to legislate wisely and prudently. No proposal Madison ever made showed more clearly his insistence that the *quality* of legislation, not the nature of the enacting body, however popular, was proper grounds for judging legitimacy.

Regarding the executive department, Madison merely warned that Virginia's was "the worst part of a bad Constitution." In assessing the judiciary system, he compared that in Virginia unfavorably with British courts, which maintained "private Rights against all the corruptions of the two other departments," because executive appointment, fixed salaries, and life tenure gave the judges genuine independence. Furthermore, judges' salaries should be liberal, to make a term on the bench preferable to service at the bar. Again Madison sought to protect rights from popular interference.

Finally, Madison accepted the traditional view that property owners had a special stake in society and therefore should have special suffrage rights; those without property would be inclined either to abuse their vote or sell it to "the rich who would abuse it." Nevertheless, since *all* citizens had personal rights requiring political protection, he favored "a good middle course," with suffrage limited in the upper house and widespread in the lower. Recollecting his own defeat at the public poll of the liquor-influenced voters of Orange County eight years earlier, Madison urged the secret ballot as "the only radical cure for those arts of Electioneering which poison the very fountain of liberty." He favored representation in the lower house according to population, adjusted from time to time to account for "the disproportionate increase of electors in different Counties."

Though he recommended annual elections for the lower house, he noted heretically that "some of the ablest statesmen and soundest Republicans" advised longer terms. Finally, he approved re-eligibility for members of the legislature, and perhaps even for the governor and other executive officers, to insure effective authority and responsibility—by 1785 for Madison as essential to "sound republicanism" as preventing tyranny and abuse of power.

To better understand these basic principles, and especially to learn more about the complexities of federated government, at Montpelier in the spring and summer of 1786 Madison turned to the "literary cargo" of books on history, politics, and commerce sent by Jefferson from Paris. In them Madison found information about nearly every experiment in republican or federal government of which there was any historical record. The "cargo," Madison reported, was "perfectly to my mind," so brilliantly did it illuminate his researches. Madison found support, for example, for his often-stated argument that the federal Union needed to be strengthened, lest some members of Congress or of the state legislatures become "instruments of foreign [British? Spanish?] Machinations," and thus undermine and finally overthrow the country. Philip of Macedon had done precisely that to the weak and quarrelsome Amphictyonic confederation in ancient Greece, Madison read in Fortuné Barthélemy de Felice, *Code de l'Humanité, ou La Législation Universelle, Naturelle, Civile et Politque* (13 volumes, published in France in 1778).[19]

Madison poured over Felice, Diderot's stupendous new *Encyclopédie Méthodique*, Abbé Millot's *Éléments d'Histoire Générale* (11 volumes), Abbé de Mably's *De l'Étude de l'Histoire*, Jacques-Auguste de Thou's *Histoire Universelle*, and other French works (most of them recent and reflecting the critical spirit of Voltaire and the *philosophes*), as well as such traditional works as Plutarch's *Lives*, the orations of Demosthenes, and the histories of Polybius. From this study Madison compiled a lengthy paper, "Of Ancient and Modern Confederacies," outlining the structure and history of the Lycian, Amphictyonic, and Achaean confederacies of ancient Greece, and of the Holy Roman Empire, the Swiss Confederation, and the United Provinces of the Netherlands in more recent times. He catalogued the various devices for financial support, diplomatic representation, cooperation in time of war, regulation of commerce, coercion of members who disobeyed confederacy orders, and other matters that had troubled the United States under the Articles of Confederation. He sought especially to identify the constitutional bonds of union, the way these bonds worked or failed to work in practice, and the particular causes of the demise or enfeeblement of the confederation. He concluded the account of the several leagues with a section entitled "Vices of the Constitution."

In this study Madison accepted deliberately the Age of Reason concept that "the past should enlighten us on the future: knowledge of history is no more than anticipated experience. . . . Where we see the same faults followed regularly by the same misfortunes, we may reasonably think that if we could have known the first we might have avoided the others." Chief among the "regular faults" of the ancient and modern confederacies were the jealousies and animosities among the members and the lack of a sufficient central authority to arbitrate or control them. The inevitable "misfortunes" were domestic turmoil and international humiliation. In the Amphictyonic confederation, "the Deputies of the strongest cities awed and corrupted those of the weaker," and Greece thus "was the victim of Philip . . . [and later] proved [no] Barrier to the vast projects of Rome." In the United Provinces of the Netherlands Madison noted that though the confederacy *seemed* on paper to be strong enough, "the Jealousy in each province of its sovereignty renders the practice very different from the theory." Furthermore, there were "numerous and notorious" examples of foreign ministers who intrigued with deputies and otherwise interfered in the internal affairs of the Netherlands. Everywhere, Madison found that weak unions courted disaster.[20]

He recorded the facts and lessons about the ancient and modern confederacies in a booklet of forty-one pocket-sized pages, easy to use in debate or writing. He probably referred to the notes during the Federal Convention and the Virginia ratifying convention. He also inserted large parts of his notes almost verbatim in the eighteenth, nineteenth, and twentieth *Federalist Papers*, concluding that "a sovereignty over sovereigns, a government over governments, a legislation for communities, as contradistinguished from individuals; as it is a solecism in theory, so in practice, it is subversive of the order and ends of civil polity, by substituting *violence* in place of *law*, or the destructive *coercion* of the *sword*, in place of the mild and salutary *coercion* of the *magistracy*." Madison's intense study at Montpelier in 1786, after his sparse breakfasts and before the evening games of whist for half bits, left him as well informed on the workings of confederate governments as any man in America. It also confirmed his conviction that the United States would be torn by faction within and be a farce in the family of nations unless she took heed of what history could teach her and strengthened her bonds of union before it was too late.[21]

In August 1786 Madison left his study of ancient and modern confederacies for a firsthand lesson in the problems of federation at the Annapolis Convention, called for September 1786. On the way, he found "Federal affairs" gloomier than ever: "[N]o money comes into the public treasury, trade is on a wretched footing, and the states are running mad after paper money." Delegates gathered slowly in Annapolis at George Mann's tavern, famous for the "elegant and profuse" celebration it had furnished when Washington resigned his commission nearly three years before. Only two delegates were present when Madison arrived on September 4, and by the eleventh, only twelve in all had appeared. The New Jersey, Delaware, and Virginia delegations each had a quorum, while Pennsylvania and New York were represented unofficially. Obviously the convention could not execute its commission "to examine the trade of the states . . . and consider . . . a uniform system in their commercial regulations," so the like-minded delegates (those opposed to increased federal power had boycotted the meeting) decided to issue a call for a convention the following May in Philadelphia to consider more generally the ills of the Union.[22]

Madison endorsed the proposal wholeheartedly, but observing Edmund Randolph's hesitation to impugn too severely the conduct of Congress or paint too darkly the conditions existing in some of the states, he persuaded Alexander Hamilton to put more tactfully his lucid and stirring call to the states to appoint delegates to the Philadelphia convention "to render the Constitution of the federal government adequate to the exigencies of the Union." Thus Madison, Hamilton, John Dickinson, Tench Coxe, and other nationalist delegates moved shrewdly toward the comprehensive reform they felt absolutely necessary. Madison and Hamilton, further, had time for long conversations considering the prospects for union and beginning three years of close cooperation. They knew, for example, that the Adams-Lee faction, their old adversary in the Continental Congress, remained strong and would oppose moves toward greater federal power. One of its leaders, Stephen Higginson of Massachusetts, had written that the Annapolis Convention "originated in Virginia with Mr. Madison" and seemed to be a plot of the "great aristocrats" against legitimate and hard-pressed merchants, such as himself, who opposed any plan that might result in federally collected import duties. The two young nationalists knew they faced hard battles.[23]

During the winter of 1786–7, Shays' Rebellion in Massachusetts heightened the possibility that, as Washington put it, "the prediction of our transatlantic foe [Great Britain] 'leave them to themselves, and their government will sure dissolve' " would soon be fulfilled. The "great Commotions" alarmed Madison, though he was careful not to condemn the insurgents before considering their grievances. If the rebels sought "abolition of debts public and private, and a new division of property," however, he had little sympathy for them. While orderly processes for change remained open, armed men closing courts and capturing government arsenals were not likely to win Madison's approval. In midwinter the situation in Massachusetts became more ominous: "It is pretty certain," Madison wrote, "that the seditious party have become formidable . . . and have opened a communication with the viceroy of Canada." After reaching New York, Madison had better sources of information, soon discounted the rumors of treason, and took heart that the government's expedition against the Shaysites had "restored calm." He feared, though, that the harsh measures contemplated, "*disfranchising*" as well as disarming the rebels, would revive the commotions. On the other hand, granted the vote, the former insurgents seemed bent on "sheltering . . . their wicked measures . . . under the forms of the Constitution." Irresponsible men were likely to control both branches of the legislature; paper money was in the offing; and John Hancock, "tainted by a dishonorable obsequiousness to popular follies," had been elected governor. To Madison Shays' Rebellion demonstrated fully the dangers of a weak republic. Insufficient authority would produce a cycle of commotion, harsh measures, and demagoguery fatal to good government.[24]

In New York between mid-February and mid-April 1787, attending the desultory, ineffectual sessions of Congress, reflecting on existing and incipient disorders and follies evident in nearly every state, and observing the contempt of foreign nations for the new United States, Madison sharpened his thoughts on the deficiencies of the federal government. In a paper on the "Vices of the Political System of the United States," he summarized the telltale results of the experiments in government conducted in America since the Declaration of Independence. The thirteen independent sovereignties had quarreled with each other, defied federal measures, and violated solemn international agreements. Imperative national measures, such as internal improvements and regulation of commerce, were thwarted by the "perverseness of particular States." The states, as Shays' Rebellion showed, were, without federal help, prey to internal violence and subversion. Furthermore, numerous confusing and unstable statutes passed by the states brought all law into disrepute.

The root evil, though, was the overwhelming tendency of the existing governments, obsessed with their selfish interests, to lose sight of the general welfare and the need for disciplined respect for law. "Is it to be imagined," Madison asked, "that an ordinary citizen or even Assemblyman of Rhode Island in estimating the policy of paper money, ever considered or cared in what light the measure would be viewed in France or Holland; or even in Massachusetts or Connecticut? It was a sufficient temptation to both [ordinary citizen and Assemblyman] that it was for their interest; it was a sufficient sanction to the latter that it was popular in the State; to the former, that it was so in the neighbourhood." In Congress, a similar small-mindedness, the real hardships on some states of almost every federal measure, the temptation to "the courtiers of popularity" to exaggerate these hardships and to whine about nonexistent ones, and a reluctance to honor federal recommendations for fear other states would default, all corroded the Union. In Madison's opinion, federal measures would always be abortive as long as the Articles of Confederation were "a mere treaty of friendship. A sanction is essential to the idea of law, as coercion is to that of Government. The federal system being destitute of both, wants the great vital principles of a Political Constitution."

The necessity, then, was a government that could overcome pettiness and give effect to, not just preach about, "the general and permanent good of the community." Madison's persistent inclination to find safety for freedom in a multiplicity of forces (as he had done, for example, in the early seventeen-seventies regarding religious liberty), and his sense of the virtues of union, foreshadow his solution. At the crystallizing moment in New York, he may have read David Hume's "Idea of a Perfect Commonwealth," an explicit rejection of the notion, hallowed by Aristotle and Montesquieu, that "no large state . . . could ever be modelled into a [republican] commonwealth." The contrary, Hume asserted, was probable. Democracies, prone to turbulence, became more so in small territories because, there, passions were readily communicated and easily became dominant. In a large republic, on the other hand, the greater number of factions, and the physical difficulties of effective collusion on prejudices and passions, would hinder hasty, irrational measures against the public interest. Madison adopted this view and concluded: "The great desideratum in Government is such a modification of the sovereignty as will render it sufficiently neutral between the different interests and factions, to controul one part of the society from invading the rights of another, and at the same time sufficiently controuled itself, from setting up an interest adverse to that of the whole Society." Madison added that indirect modes of election, properly devised, might "extract from the mass of the society the purest and noblest characters which it contains." These "desiderata" guided him in his leading role at the Constitutional Convention.[25]

Madison wrote letters to George Washington and to Governor Edmund Randolph outlining a plan of government embodying the insights of his recent studies. The virtues of Hume's "Perfect Commonwealth" permitted Madison's master stroke: he could at once support Randolph's insistence that state prerogatives be protected and Washington's insistence on a thorough reform giving dignity and authority to the national councils. "Conceiving that an individual independence of the States is utterly irreconcileable with their aggregate sovereignty, and that a consolidation of the whole into one simple republic would be as inexpedient as it is unattainable, I have sought for middle ground, which may at once support a due supremacy of the national authority, and not exclude the local authorities wherever they can be subordinately useful." The essence was what Madison later called a "mixed government," a unique blend of the federal principle (a government whose constituents were *states*, not the people) and of national government designed to preserve at once freedom, national dignity, and local self-government. Madison knew that a plan suitable to Randolph's local biases and to Washington's sense of national needs might just have a chance of adoption.

The foundation had to be a shift from equal representation by states in the national councils to representation according to population. Not only did justice and the republican principle of government by consent require this, but the large states would not agree to an increase in national power unless they would have due weight in deciding national questions. Furthermore, Madison hoped the New England states, presently most populous, and the Southern states that expected to become so, would all favor such a foundation. Next he urged both an enlargement of the powers of the general government, especially over commerce among the states, and a veto on acts of the states by some national power. This would prevent violations by the states of treaties and national laws and also bar such foolish and unjust state measures as emissions of paper money. The national government, Madison supposed, would have the "disinterested and dispassionate" character inherent in a properly devised "extended republic." Some form of national judiciary would be necessary to give force, uniformity, and equity to law, and an executive department with its own administrative officers and control over the militia and national defense would likewise be indispensable. He proposed a bicameral legislature, the lower house based on population, the upper on some more restricted principle. The states should be guaranteed protection against subversion and invasion, he concluded, and to give the new federal constitution the sanction of supreme law, it should be ratified by conventions of the people in the various states.[26]

Thus, on the eve of the Constitutional Convention Madison outlined to two influential Virginians the thoughts on government soon laid before the convention as the "Virginia Plan," the basic framework for the document that became the Constitution of the United States. He had, by this time, Jefferson wrote, "acquired a habit of self-possession, which placed at ready command the rich resources of his luminous and discriminating mind, and of his extensive information, and rendered him the first of every assembly afterwards, of which he became a member. Never wandering from his subject into vain declamation, but pursuing it closely, in language pure, classical, and copious, soothing always the feelings of his adversaries by civilities and softness of expression, he rose to the eminent station which he held in the great National Convention of 1787." He was ready, too, with a galvanizing idea that enabled him to neutralize the flaws that for centuries had doomed republican federations.[27]

Madison realized that *weak* government and *free* government were not synonymous; meaningful freedom required authority and stability. From the study "Of Ancient and Modern Confederacies" he knew the pitfalls of trying to join strength and survival in freedom in enlarged states. The intrigues and cynical sacrifice of vital interests surrounding the Jay-Gardoqui project to close the Mississippi to American trade, and such follies as Rhode Island's repudiation of every sound principle of finance and Shays' Rebellion in Massachusetts, had made Madison sure only a stronger Union could prevent the United States from adding another black chapter to the history of republican government. The key insight was to turn the charges that popular governments were too turbulent and that they could only exist in a small territory against each other by arguing that in an "extended republic" the larger number of interests and the increased opportunity to find able public officials would confound the turbulence of the demos and the passion of demogogues. This was Madison's formula for at once protecting "inalienable rights" and basing government on "the consent of the governed."

CHAPTER X

The Federal Convention

MADISON arrived in Philadelphia on May 3, 1787, to take part in the "grand convention of the states." He stayed, as usual, at the congenial House-Trist lodgings at Fifth and Market streets, just a block from the Pennsylvania State House. Like the other delegates, he was apprehensive and hopeful by turns about the challenge ahead. He agreed with Washington that "no morn ever dawned more favorably than ours did; and no day was ever more clouded than the present. Wisdom and good examples are necessary at this time to rescue the political machine from the impending storm." Though "the probable diversity of opinions and prejudices" to be represented at the convention had made Madison cautious, he nevertheless noted that "the whole community is big with expectation, and there can be no doubt but that the result will in some way or other have a powerful effect on our destiny." Benjamin Franklin warned further that if the convention "does not do good, it must do harm, as it will show that we have not wisdom enough among us to govern ourselves; and will strengthen the opinion of some political writers that popular governments cannot long support themselves."[1]

The weather was gloomy in Philadelphia during much of May; its public atmosphere, anything but. On the eighteenth *The Pennsylvania Packet* (long Madison's favorite newspaper) observed that "perhaps this city affords the most striking picture that has been exhibited for ages. Here, at the same moment, the collective wisdom of the continent deliberates upon the extensive politics of the confederated empire, two religious conventions [Presbyterian and Baptist] clean and distribute the streams of religion throughout the American world, and those veterans whose valour accomplished a mighty revolution [the Society of the Cincinnati] are once more assembled." The paper might have added that the American Philosophical Society, the Pennsylvania Society for the Abolition of Slavery, and the recently formed Society for Political Enquiries, all sponsored by Franklin, and often gathering at his house, held meetings during the month. If ever a free society was to demonstrate its capacity to increase in prosperity and virtue, it should, it seemed to the many distinguished men coming together in Philadelphia in May 1787, do so there.[2]

Madison arrived early for the convention, to talk informally with as many delegates as possible. He renewed his acquaintance with Robert Morris, Thomas Fitzsimons, Gouverneur Morris, and George Clymer, all members of the Pennsylvania delegation and known to Madison since his service in the Continental Congress. They all favored a stronger Union. Dinner at Robert Morris' elegant mansion, which was a block from the House lodgings, and staffed by liveried servants, including a French butler, was probably among Madison's first social gatherings, and undoubtedly an occasion for the financier and his guest to discuss the practical necessities facing the convention. Though Morris was not a political theorist and took almost no part in the debates of the convention, his influence was immense. No one had a clearer idea of the powers and agencies of government required to invigorate the credit and commerce of the nation. A block in the other direction, Madison likely called on James Wilson, "a tall, solid man, thick-muscled, inclined a little to stoutness, with a ruddy complexion, a neat white wig, and thick-lensed glasses." Wilson agreed with Madison on most of the great principles of government debated in the convention, and the two men together far outdistanced their colleagues as political theorists. Wilson, one observer noted, "ranked among the foremost in legal and political knowledge. . . . Government seems to have been his peculiar Study, all the political institutions of the World he knows in detail, and can trace the causes and effects of every revolution from the earliest stages of the Grecian commonwealth down to the present time." We may imagine the two men in long, scholarly conversations before Wilson's fireplace in Philadelphia.[3]

Madison also met Benjamin Franklin. He had persistently and resourcefully defended Franklin's reputation and mission in France during the dark days of the revolution, and of course, Franklin was for Madison an authentic sage and hero. Eighty-one years old, Franklin had received a propitious reprieve from his painful gout and bladder stone, and called upon his marvelous reserves of energy to attend every session of the convention for four months. At his newly enlarged home on Market Street a block and a half from the House lodgings, he frequently entertained delegates in his courtyard, where he sat under a large mulberry tree surrounded by grass plots, gravel walks, and flowering shrubs. On

May 16, Madison and the other twenty or so delegates then in town assembled comfortably in the pleasant, airy dining room, around a long mahogany table set with silver and fine porcelain Franklin had gathered during twenty-five years' residence in Europe. As the company enjoyed a cask of London stout and ale which all declared "the best porter they had ever tasted," talk of government, the trials of revolution, and the prospects of nationhood filled the room. Foreshadowing his role on the convention floor, Franklin offered sage advice and told stories to emphasize the need for an accommodation that would secure the blessings and benefits of union. Madison delighted in Franklin's steady devotion to the cause of stronger government and matchless skill at finding points of agreement amid discord. The two men were in fact kindred spirits and deeply respected each other.[4]

Madison's main task in Philadelphia, however, was to bring the Virginia delegation solidly behind the plan for strong government he had outlined the month before to Washington and Randolph. Forceful leadership by Virginia, still the largest and most influential state, would help enormously to set the convention on the proper path. On Sunday, May 13, Madison rejoiced to hear that General Washington had arrived. Amid chiming bells, booming cannon, and cheering citizens, the Philadelphia Light Horse escorted him into town. Months of patient, skillful encouragement by Madison, and almost equally persistent hesitation by the former commander in chief, had ended as Madison had hoped: Washington had agreed to be present and thus lend his vast prestige to the convention. Without his presence and support, the other delegates could have but scant hope for their labors. He alighted first at the House lodgings, intending to stay in quarters arranged for him by Madison, but he yielded to the urgings of Robert Morris and remained his guest during the convention.[5]

Washington's arrival gave Virginia a quorum, and with the Pennsylvania delegates in town, permitted the convention to gather on its appointed day, May 14, in the white-paneled, high-windowed chamber on the first floor of the State House where, eleven years before, the Declaration of Independence had been signed. Though too few states were present to begin business, there was, Madison wrote Jefferson, "a prospect of a pretty full meeting." George Wythe, the lean, learned judge, professor of law, and ardent revolutionist whom Madison had come to know and respect during his service in Williamsburg, and John Blair, another learned jurist, a close friend of Madison's, and a supporter of strong central government, were the other Virginians present on the fourteenth. The following day Governor Randolph arrived, the official head of the delegation, and in view of his "eloquence . . . most harmonious voice, fine person, and striking manners," a man to reckon with in and out of the convention chambers. He and Madison were intimate personal friends, though the latter knew very well it would be necessary to handle the governor carefully, lest he become frightened at the strong Union favored by the majority of the delegation. Guiding Randolph's conduct and opinion would be one of Madison's most delicate tasks. By May 17, with the arrival of Dr. James McClurg, a physician little accustomed to debate, but nevertheless an influential backer of Madison's proposals, and the redoubtable republican theorist and elder statesman George Mason, the Virginia delegation was complete.[6]

Washington's decision to stay at Robert Morris' turned out to be but the first exception to Madison's plan to have all the Virginians live at Mrs. House's. With all the space there taken or reserved by mid-May, George Mason had to stay at the old Indian Queen Tavern on Fourth Street, where he was "very well accomodated" for what he considered the "cheap" amount of 25s. a day, including board and room for himself, a companion, their servants, and horses. By the middle of the summer so many delegates lodged at the Indian Queen that its common rooms were virtual convention annexes, and Madison so often visited them that travelers thought he lived there. Randolph stayed a few days at Mrs. House's but moved when his pregnant wife arrived, so they could have two rooms. A Delaware delegate quickly took Randolph's room for John Dickinson, who had neglected to make reservations in advance.[7]

Though the refusal of Mason and Randolph to sign the Constitution may have caused Madison to rue the day they had "escaped" from him at Mrs. House's, there was surely some benefit in having the Delaware delegates, suspicious of large-stage power, near at hand to persuade and influence. At any rate, as the delegates settled in and sought "to grow into some acquaintance with each other," they found time to ride out to the beautiful country estates that lined the Schuylkill and to attend mass at "the Romish Church," as Washington put it in his diary. Gouty Anglican George Mason went to the mass "more out of curiosity than compliment," he said, and soon reported himself "heartily tired of the etiquette and nonsense so fashionable in this city." Altogether, though, the delegates were pleased to be meeting in so attractive a city, second in size only to London in the English-speaking world, where they all lived within a few blocks and could easily exchange visits. We may imagine Madison enjoying the social life and taking advantage of it to build helpful personal relationships for the hot, difficult summer to come.[8]

Among the twenty-nine delegates in attendance by May 25, in addition to the Pennsylvanians and Virginians, were many men Madison already knew well. Alexander Hamilton, elegant, eloquent, brilliant, and strong willed, not only agreed with Madison on the need for a stronger national union but sought a completely centralized government. Madison's Princeton tutor and colleague in the Continental Congress, William Churchill Houston, and the jurist and Princeton gallant William Paterson, arrived to lead the New Jersey delegation. From North Carolina came Alexander Martin, recently governor of the state and Madison's companion on his first trip to Princeton in 1769, and Hugh Williamson, a good-humored physician, man of wide learning, and a member of the Continental Congress. William Few of Georgia had also been a member of Congress for two years during Madison's service there. Heading the South Carolina delegation was John Rutledge, its foremost revolutionary leader, former governor, and long Madison's colleague in the Continental Congress. Rufus King of Massachusetts, George Read of Delaware, and Charles Pinckney of South Carolina were among the important delegates present who were more or less new to Madison.

Altogether fifty-five men attended the convention at one time or another. Of the latecomers, the New Englanders were most important. John Langdon and Nicholas Gilman of New Hampshire, Elbridge Gerry and Nathaniel Gorham of Massachusetts, and Roger Sherman, Oliver Ellsworth, and William Samuel Johnson of Connecticut had had long careers in the Continental Congress, were well known to Madison, and had a large impact on the convention's deliberations. William Livingston from New Jersey and John Dickinson of Delaware had for more than twenty years been among Madison's intellectual guides, though neither played a role in the convention commensurate with the reputation he brought there. Gunning Bedford, Jr., of Delaware had been Madison's classmate at Princeton. Daniel Carroll and Daniel of Saint Thomas Jenifer of Maryland had served with Madison in Congress and were staunch friends of a stronger Union. Also from Maryland and known to Madison since his Princeton days was the brilliant, effusive Luther Martin, the most persistent and vehement of the foes of a more powerful national government. There were usually about thirty delegates in attendance on any given day and never more than eleven states present and able to vote at one time. The burden of debate on the floor, and of influence behind the scenes too, was carried principally by perhaps eighteen men: Gerry, Gorham, and King; Ellsworth, Johnson, and Sherman; Hamilton; Paterson; Franklin, Wilson, and Gouverneur Morris; Luther Martin; Washington, Madison, Mason, and Randolph; and Rutledge and Charles Pinckney. These were the men of "ability and intelligence" of whom Madison said late in life that "individually and collectively . . . there never was an assembly of men, charged with a great and arduous trust, who were more pure in their motives, or more exclusively or anxiously devoted to the object committed to them."[9]

In the eleven-day interval between the date set for the convention to open and the arrival of a quorum of delegations, the Virginians met at three o'clock each day for two or three hours "to form a proper correspondence of sentiments." They soon agreed that Madison's plan, previously described to Washington and Randolph, should be presented to the convention by Randolph as its basic working document. Madison and his colleagues also talked incessantly with men from other states, eagerly sounding out each new delegation as it arrived. Surprisingly, the New Englanders seemed most "anti-republican"—probably, George Mason thought, because their greater experience with purer forms of republican government had left them "tired and disgusted with . . . unexpected evils," and they had therefore "run into the opposite extreme." On the whole, though, the delegates were highly pleased with the seriousness of their preliminary discussions. Benjamin Rush reported that the fortunate arrival of copies of the first volumes of John Adams' *Defence of the Constitutions of the United States* had "diffused such excellent principles among us, that there is little doubt of our adopting a vigorous and compounded [bicameral] federal legislature." Franklin told Rush that the convention was "the most august and respectable assembly he was ever in in his life." Mason was relieved that "fine republican principles" generally prevailed over opinions "soured and disgusted" by the failures of democratic governments, and thought that "America has certainly, upon this occasion, drawn forth her first characters." Madison shared Mason's feeling that even the "certain degree of enthusiasm which inspired and supported the mind" during the revolt from Great Britain was "nothing compared to the great business now before us. . . . To view, through the calm, sedate medium of reason the influence which the establishment now proposed may yet have upon the happiness or misery of millions yet unborn, is an object of such magnitude, as absorbs, and in a manner suspends the operations of the human understanding."[10]

During a downpour on Friday, May 25, the convention for the first time made a quorum and organized itself for business. As the delegates entered Independence chamber, Madison "chose a seat in front of the presiding member, with the other members on my right and left hand. In this favorable position for hearing all that passed, I noted in terms legible and in abbreviations and marks intelligible to myself what was read from the Chair or spoken by the members; and losing not a moment unnecessarily between the adjournment and reassembling of the Convention I was enabled to write out my daily notes during the session or within a few finishing days after its close in the extent and form preserved in my own hand on my files." No one asked Madison to record the debates in this way. It was the long hours of study leading to this momentous day, and his own sense of history, that made him do it. *This* time, at least, for *this* effort to form a federal government, there would be a better record than the ones he had had to pore over and try to learn from, for future generations to use. As he explained it:

The Curiosity I had felt during my researches into the History of the most distinguished Confederacies, particularly those of antiquity, and

the deficiency I found in the means of satisfying it, more especially
in what related to the process, the principles, the reasons, and the
anticipations, which prevailed in the formation of them, determined
me to preserve as far as I could an exact account of what might pass
in the Convention whilst executing its trust, with the magnitude of
which I was duly impressed, as I was with the gratification promised
to future curiosity by an authentic exhibition of the objects, the opinions, and the reasonings from which the new System of Government
was to receive its peculiar structure and organization. Nor was I
unaware of the value of such a contribution to the fund of materials
for the History of a Constitution on which would be staked the happiness of a people great even in its infancy, and possibly the cause of
Liberty throughout the world.[11]

After electing Washington chairman, the convention adopted its rules.
One required that "nothing spoken in the House be printed, or otherwise published, or communicated without leave." On May 29 Randolph
laid before the delegates Madison's "Virginia Plan"—fifteen resolutions,
which for the next two weeks were the foundation of the debates, and in
fact formed the essential frame of government finally offered to the
people of the states. Noticing Randolph's severe strictures on the ade-
quacy of the Articles of Confederation and the supremacy in the Virginia
Plan of the national authority over the states, Hamilton proposed at once
that the convention debate "whether the United States were susceptible
to one government, or [whether each state] required a separate existence
connected only by leagues." Hamilton's incisive mind and disdain for the
states led him immediately to question the incongruity of sovereign
states existing within a truly *national* government. By a surprising
majority, 6 states to 1 (the others absent or divided), the convention
agreed with Hamilton, and voted that "a national Government ought to
be established consisting of a supreme Legislative, Executive and Judiciary." The convention intended to create a new constitution, not merely
to tinker with the old.[12]

The next resolve, however, disclosed what became the most difficult
question the convention would face: should the states each have an equal
vote in the national legislature, or should representation there be according to population? George Read of Delaware, of "feeble voice . . . low
stature, and a weak constitution," pointed out that his instructions forbade a departure from the principle of state equality; therefore, if the
convention so departed, it might become his "duty to retire from the
Convention." Gouverneur Morris and Madison saw immediately the
danger in Read's threat, and sought to calm him, but they nevertheless
insisted that the equality of the states was incompatible with a centralized
republican government. They moved to postpone the question of state
equality as such, and the convention instead debated whether or not the

lower house of the legislature "ought to be elected by the people of the several states." Roger Sherman urged that the state legislatures elect the members of the lower house, because the people "want information and are constantly liable to be misled," and therefore should have as little *direct* voice in the government as possible. Elbridge Gerry agreed, proclaiming that "the evils we experience flow from the excess of democracy." He had once been more purely republican, he said, but "the popular clamour in Massachusetts [Shays' Rebellion] . . . [had] taught [him] the danger of the levelling spirit."[13]

A powerful phalanx rose immediately to defend direct representation. Mason, "able and convincing in debate, steady, and firm in his [republican] principles," argued that the lower house ought to be "the grand depository of the democratic principle." He admitted the dangers of democracy, but cautioned against running to the opposite extreme. The convention, he asserted, "ought to attend to the rights of every class of the people." Wilson, stiff and florid-faced, "contended strenuously" that the stability of the government depended upon it having "as broad a basis as possible. No government could long subsist without the confidence of the people." Using what became his favorite metaphor, Wilson asserted that popular government was like a pyramid, stable because of its broad base. Madison concurred, asserting that the popular election of one branch of the legislature was "essential to every Plan of free Government." He favored "refinements," he said, especially in electing the second branch, the executive, and the judiciary, but he did not want "the people . . . lost sight of altogether." The delegates then resolved, 6 states to 2 (2 were divided), that the lower house be elected by the people. Madison was elated.[14]

The rest of that day and the next (May 31 and June 1) the delegates bypassed disputed points and acted on matters of general agreement. Thus they left "a chasm" by not settling the mode of electing the upper house of the legislature, agreed that the legislative power should extend to all matters where the individual states were "incompetent," accepted unanimously Franklin's suggestion that states be forbidden to enact laws contrary to treaties "subsisting under the authority of the Union," and on Madison's motion, postponed considering the clause authorizing the use of force against "delinquent" states. Such force, he argued, "would look more like a declaration of war, than an infliction of punishment," and would therefore virtually dissolve the Union. He apparently had already talked to Wilson and others who saw that a supreme-law clause, bringing national authority to bear against offending *individuals*, would have greater efficacy than the punitive measures against states as a whole he had supported only a year before.[15]

The convention next debated the composition, powers, and election of the executive. When Wilson and Randolph clashed over a single or plural executive (Randolph asserted that "a unity in the Executive [was] the foetus of monarchy"), Madison moved to postpone the question; he agreed with Wilson but thought good will in the convention and a tender regard for Randolph's sensitive feelings were for the moment the prime considerations. The delegates then accepted a very general definition of executive powers, set seven years without re-eligibility as the term of office, and turned to the method of election. Wilson renewed his plea for election by the people (Sherman opposed this as "the very essence of tyranny"), but as the shadows had begun to lengthen, Mason moved that the tired delegates defer consideration of so momentous a proposal until the next day, when Wilson could argue his case more fully. When Madison got back to Mrs. House's that evening, he was probably pleased to find Dr. William Samuel Johnson had temporarily moved in with John Dickinson and would the next day take his seat as a delegate from Connecticut. His learning, eloquence, and habit of accommodation would be most welcome. Within his state's delegation he would help restrain the excessive emphasis on the legislative department advocated by Roger Sherman.[16]

The next day (June 2), following defeat of Wilson's proposal for an executive chosen by an electoral college, the convention resolved that the national legislature elect the executive. Though Madison and other nationalists thought this better than having the states choose the executive, it seriously impaired the independence of the executive and thus the separation of powers. Its reconsideration was virtually certain. Franklin then moved that executive officers receive no salary, and since his gout and bladder stone made standing painful, he had Wilson read for him a short speech reflecting his long experience, especially in England, with the venality introduced into government by officers competing for money. Better to have no salaries and depend on public-spirited persons willing to serve without pay, he asserted, than usher in a greedy scramble for offices. Madison listened intently, but like most of the other delegates, experienced only with government in America, he had less fear of corruption than the aged diplomat, and a stronger sense of the worthy persons who would be unable to accept public office if not paid. Hamilton graciously seconded Franklin's motion, but no debate ensued. Madison recorded that "it was treated with great respect, but rather for the author of it, than from any apparent conviction of its expediency or practicability." After a long debate on impeachment, and further inconclusive discussion of a plural as opposed to a unitary executive, the convention adjourned for the weekend.[17]

Madison must have been pleased with the first week of debate. The convention had supported unequivocally a stronger national government; the talents displayed in the speeches and proposals had been very bright indeed; and perhaps most gratifying, there had been a remarkable disposition to seek agreements rather than to aggravate differences. The "working members," in Madison's favorite phrase, were many, and the search for light had been most serious. True, Read's threat to walk out unless state equality was preserved, Sherman's dogged insistence on legislative supremacy, and Randolph's sensitivity foreshadowed difficulties, but very likely a crucial mood had been established: the delegates, protected by the rule of secrecy, would be able to *deliberate*, most of them intent on a substantial increase in national power and willing to accommodate divergent views. As Madison walked about the pleasant, cobblestone streets on a fair, warm Sunday morning (perhaps attending services at beautiful Christ Church, where Bishop William White made clear that in America the Episcopal Church was no longer Anglican), the earnest Virginian took quiet pride in being one of the intellectual and tactical leaders of the convention about which all Philadelphia buzzed.[18]

When the convention reconvened, Wilson resumed powerfully his defense of a single executive: all the states had such a governor, and any division of authority would open the door for intrigue and irresponsibility. In the crucial vote, only New York, Delaware, and Maryland withstood Wilson's arguments. Madison managed to cast Virginia's vote, 4 to 3, for Wilson's proposal, by carrying with him the usual nationalists in the delegation: himself, the faithful McClurg, Wythe (voting in absentia), and Washington. In fact, the general's presence led many wavering delegates to support Wilson. If, as all assumed, Washington would head the new national government, there could be little initial danger in a single powerful executive. Mason, Randolph, and cautious Judge Blair nevertheless expressed what was already a characteristic mark of anti-federalism: especially fearful of any seemingly unchecked power in corruptible human hands, they thought it vitally important to guard against the lures of ambition and glory, even at the risk of diminishing the "energy" of the government. A major thrust of Madison's arguments for the next year sought to persuade such sincere republicans as Mason and Randolph that effective authority in the hands of a government responsible to the people had a wholly different relationship to tyranny than such authority invested in a king.[19]

After a long debate over the veto power of the executive, in which Mason argued passionately that an absolute veto in the hands of a unitary executive would create a more tyrannical power than that wielded by the hated George III, the convention accepted, with Madison's support, the provision that the legislature might, by a two-thirds vote, override an executive veto. Moving on to the judiciary, the convention resolved readily to institute national courts, but upon objection by Rutledge of South Carolina and the relentless Sherman, postponed the Wilson-Madison proposal that the executive or perhaps the Senate appoint the

judges. Over the protests of those tender about state interests, Wilson
and Madison were narrowly able to preserve the power of the national
legislature to establish federal district and circuit courts. The sinews of
effective national government grew stronger.[20]

On June 6, the convention debated again whether the people should
elect the lower house of the legislature. The South Carolinians, supported by Elbridge Gerry, still panicky over Shays' Rebellion, declaimed
anew that the people were seldom "fit judges" of legislators; they therefore proposed some indirect mode of election. Sherman pleaded again
for election by the state legislatures, in order to preserve their pre-
eminence and thus insure that the powers of the general government
would be limited strictly to the few matters the states were not competent to handle. Liberty and virtue would disappear, he argued, if the
states were in any way dominated by the national government. Wilson
responded first, restating his argument that unless the people had a direct
voice in the government, they would not have the requisite attachment
to it. "The Government ought to possess not only . . . the *force* but . . .
the *mind or sense* of the people at large," he asserted. Mason followed,
admitting the dangers of "democratic elections," but he asked his colleagues not to be too alarmed at this because "no Government was free
from imperfections and evils." The dangers were offset, he said, by the
advantage of direct elections "in favor of the rights of the people, in
favor of human nature." Representatives "should think as [the people]
think, and feel as they feel."[21]

Madison then delivered his most important speech of the convention.
The direct election of the lower house by the people was, he asserted,
"a clear principle of free Government." Furthermore, the objections
Sherman and others raised against it were largely specious. The national
government had not only to deal with the few matters the Connecticut
member had assigned to it, but had as well to "provide more effectually
for the security of private rights, and the steady dispensation of Justice."
Interferences with these, rampant in the states, had been responsible for
calling the convention together. Would not, then, preserving the present
powers of the states preserve as well the contingent evils? Madison then
projected Sherman's concession that the worst government was in tiny
Rhode Island to the general proposition that smallness and poorness of
government were very often directly proportional. An enlarged republic "was the only defense against the inconveniences of democracy
consistent with the democratic form of Government." Next, Madison
presented to the convention for the first time the argument that since
honesty, respect for character, and conscience had proven insufficient
guards against faction and oppression of the minority, only the inclusion
within a government of a multitude of interests, sentiments, and sections,
each with power to resist the others, would prevent majority tyranny.

History proved conclusively that "where a majority are united by a common sentiment, and have an opportunity, the rights of the minor party become insecure." The only remedy, he concluded, "is to enlarge the sphere, and thereby divide the community into so great a number of interests and parties, that in the first place a majority will not be likely at the same moment to have a common interest separate from that of the whole or of the minority, and in the second place, that in case they should have such an interest, they may not be apt to unite in the pursuit of it. It was incumbent on us then to try this remedy, and with that view to frame a republican system on such a scale and in such a form as will controul all the evils which have been experienced."[22]

Thus, in controverting both sides of the Gerry-Sherman argument, that republics had to be small and that they were prone to anarchy and misrule, Madison slew the twin enemies of popular government by turning them against each other. Republican weaknesses were not compounded in an enlarged country; rather, by counteracting each other, they were diminished and controlled. He admitted what his colleagues accepted as gospel, that turbulence and depravity were very real dangers in the as yet little-tried experiment of republican government, and then pointed to an enlarged sphere, to the principle of consent, and to an increase in the powers of the general government as each being an essential part of the defense against those evils. When the convention, shortly after Madison's synthesizing speech, agreed to the election of the lower house directly by the people, it laid the strongest possible foundation for democratic government: an assessment of human nature so sober that if found unsafe not governments representing many factions (which could counteract each other), but authoritarian ones, where a greedy, unchecked minority could oppress everyone else. Madison and his colleagues thus went beyond the dangerous, oversimplified, yet enticing position of many republican theorists that faith in the people is the only necessary reliance of popular government. Madison's role in attaining this wisdom won for him the assessment that "he blends together the profound politician with the scholar. In the management of every great question he evidently took the lead in the convention. . . . From a spirit of industry and application which he possesses in a most eminent degree, he always comes forward the best informed man of any point in debate."[23]

Following this important decision, the convention resolved, despite Madison's opposition, not to join a council of judges to the executive in exercising the veto power, and then turned to the knotty question of choosing the Senate. Wilson and Madison again sought elections independent of the state legislatures, but in the end were defeated overwhelmingly. On June 8 the convention could not agree on how national power might negate state laws. Madison argued for an explicit, unlimited power, and sought to allay the fears of the small states by asking whether "if the large States possessed the avarice and ambition with which they were charged, would the small ones in their neighbourhood, be more secure when all controul of a General Government was withdrawn?" In addressing this question to his old college classmate Gunning Bedford of Delaware, Madison devised another of his shrewd arguments to persuade delegates that local interests would be served by an effective national government.[24]

On Saturday, June 9, the convention again considered the looming question of state equality in the national legislature. Thus far, Madison and others who supported representation by population had had things deceptively easy. The small-state forces were waiting for a full representation of their champions. On June 1, the strongly nationalist James McHenry left the Maryland delegation, to be replaced a week later by the redoubtable Luther Martin, tenacious of states' rights, powerful in debate, and sometimes governed by a heat and passion heightened by whisky. He was able to deadlock the Maryland delegation and occasionally to carry it into the small-state column. On June 5, Governor William Livingston of New Jersey arrived, lending his prestige to that state's somewhat lackluster but always vigilant representation.

During the heat of the day on the ninth, the fateful issue was joined. William Paterson of New Jersey, squat and unassuming, but one whose "powers break in upon you, and create wonder and astonishment," rose and demanded that the Massachusetts credentials be read. These revealed what all the delegates knew: they were empowered only to amend the Articles of Confederation. To institute a national rather than a confederate government would place the convention delegates technically at odds with their constitutents. A confederacy, Paterson asserted, "supposes sovereignty in the members composing it and sovereignty supposes equality." The convention's sole task was to "mark the orbits of the States with due precision, and provide for the use of coercion, which was the great point." Paterson then threw down the gauntlet to Wilson, who had hinted that should the small states prove balky, the large ones would unite among themselves. Go ahead, the New Jersey lawyer thundered, but let Wilson and his cohorts remember that they "have no authority to compel the others to unite." New Jersey would never join a union where she would be "swallowed up," a fate worse than monarchy or despotism. Stunned and flush-faced, Wilson reasserted the arguments for representation by population, and turning to the defiant Paterson, proclaimed that "if the small States will not confederate on this plan, Pennsylvania and he presumed some other States, would not confederate on any other. We have been told that each State being sovereign, all are equal," Wilson continued, but the equality of *individuals* was a superior principle, so the states would have to give way. "If New Jersey will not part with her Sovereignty," he concluded vehemently, "it is in vain to talk of Government."[25]

Madison must have listened with a sinking heart to these strong words, much more charged than any thus far spoken in the convention. He was probably relieved when Paterson moved for an adjournment for the weekend. The "promising spirit," which Madison had written three days before pervaded the debates, had become rancorous; delegates were soon writing home for more money to see them through what seemed sure to be "a Summer's Campaign." And the temperature rose with the rancor. As Philadelphia began to suffer from the first of a series of intense heat waves, the talk among the delegates at Mrs. House's, in Dr. Franklin's courtyard, and at the bustling Indian Queen Tavern reflected a concern and apprehension not felt before. The next three weeks would be the most critical of the convention.[26]

When the delegates, already sweltering even in the morning, reassembled on June 11, Madison bent silently over his notes, waiting cautiously for a propitious moment to enter the tense debate. Canny Roger Sherman proposed at once what became the "Great Compromise": let representation in the lower house be according to "the respective numbers of free inhabitants," and in the upper house let the states be equal. When the Southerners protested Sherman's substitution of "free inhabitants" for the "three-fifths rule" (five slaves to count as three whites in determining representation) that had applied under the Articles of Confederation, Franklin saw that another deeply divisive issue had been raised. He then made the first of his many pleas for conciliation. "We are sent here to *consult*, not to *contend*, with each other," Wilson read soberly from a paper in Franklin's neat hand, "and declarations of a fixed opinion, and of determined resolution, never to change it, neither enlighten nor convince us." Franklin then argued that having "the number of Representatives . . . bear some proportion to the number of the Represented," a principle he supported, would not endanger the small states because the large states had no common interests that would lead them to combine against the small ones. As an accommodating gesture, he then proposed an intricate, probably impractical plan to let the states have an equal voice in determining payments to the general government.[27]

The large states, Massachusetts, Pennsylvania, and Virginia, supported, as Madison had foreseen, by the Southern states (the Carolinas and Georgia) that expected to become large, nevertheless ignored the conciliatory pleas, and by votes of 6 to 5 first rejected the Connecticut compromise and then rammed through a resolution that "the ratio of representation [be] the same in the second as in the first branch." For two days a number of minor issues were debated, and some of them settled. The votes, unyielding, and conforming more and more to the large-state–small-state division, caused the delegates to fidget apprehensively. In supporting terms of three years for Representatives and seven years for Senators (both were approved), Madison argued that the convention "ought to consider what was right and necessary in itself for the attainment of a proper Government," not merely, as some delegates asserted, what the people were thought to favor. Madison declared further that far from being inconsistent with republican theory, the long terms would increase stability and thus counteract the alleged volatility of republican governments.[28]

On June 13, Madison persuaded Sherman and Pinckney that the lower house would be "too much influenced by partialities" to permit it to appoint judges, after which the Committee of the Whole rose and reported nineteen resolutions, embodying the Virginia Plan of May 29 as amended during two weeks of debate: that a national government of three branches be established; that the legislature consist of two houses, each to be apportioned according to population (including three-fifths of the slaves); that the lower house be elected by the people and the upper house by the state legislatures; that the term in the lower house be three years and in the upper seven years; that the legislature have the power "to legislate in all cases to which the separate States are incompetent" and to negate state laws contrary to the Constitution or to treaties; that the executive be a single person chosen by the legislature for a term of seven years; that he be ineligible for re-election; that he have a veto power, which the legislature might override by a two-thirds vote; that the judges in the national courts be appointed by the upper house to serve during good behavior; that an amendment process be included; and that ratification be considered by conventions elected by the people expressly for that purpose. Though some important changes had been made, Madison's plan was still essentially intact, and his assessment of the tenor of the convention had proven largely correct. The delegates almost unanimously supported a stronger general government, and they agreed with few exceptions on a tripartite frame embodying checks and balances. Only the question of state equality seemed seriously to threaten the constructive possibilities of the convention.[29]

The delegates received a day off on June 14, when Paterson asked for more time to prepare a plan based on state equality. The next day, he laid the so-called New Jersey Plan before the convention, stating that several delegations (Connecticut, New York, New Jersey, Delaware) and Martin of Maryland wanted it "substituted in place of that proposed by Mr. Randolph." The convention agreed to submit it, along with the recommitment of the Virginia Plan, to a committee of the whole, and then adjourned so that members might copy and study the new proposals. Scornful of the doctrines of the New Jersey Plan, Madison was dismayed as well that it forced the convention to reconsider the important decisions already taken. Paterson proposed that the Articles of Confederation be retained with a few simple but important changes: that Congress be given the power to lay and collect certain taxes for its own support; that Congress have power to regulate interstate and foreign commerce; that executive and judicial branches be established; that acts and treaties of the United States be "the supreme law" of the land; that the state courts be obliged to uphold that supremacy; and that if they did not, the federal executive might "enforce and compel an obedience." Though these were steps in the right direction, in Madison's judgment they did not go nearly far enough. If they were the only fruits of the convention, the fatal flaws in the Articles would remain, and the nation would have lost its best, and perhaps its last, chance to adopt an effective government.[30]

June 16 luckily produced some relief from the week-long hot spell; tempers were heated enough without the midsummer sun that had streamed in so relentlessly all week. Madison must have winced with each pen stroke as he took notes on the blunt speech of Abraham Lansing of New York condemning the Virginia Plan as "totally novel," beyond the powers of the convention, unacceptable to the states, and repugnant to the people. New York, he was certain, would never accept it. Paterson then defended the New Jersey Plan, asserting emphatically that only the unanimous consent of the states could take from them their equal sovereignty under the Articles of Confederation. Wilson's principle of equality among the people, he suggested craftily, could be reconciled with state equality by "throwing the States into Hotchpot"—that is, by chopping them up into equal units. Knowing that the large states, especially "Big Knife" Virginia, bristled at the faintest suggestion that Congress might tamper with their boundaries, Paterson taunted them: would they agree to "Hotchpot" in order to attain their cherished principle of representation according to population? The redoubtable Wilson, as he did repeatedly during the summer, spoke first in rebuttal. He upheld the right of the convention to *propose* what it pleased, even though it could *conclude nothing*, and denied that Lansing and Paterson could say with confidence what the people wanted. In a lengthy discourse on the differences between the two plans, and on how the lessons of history stood behind the Virginia Plan, he underscored his conviction that "inequality in representation poisons every government." Randolph ended the day's debate, arguing eloquently that the New Jersey Plan would cure none of the evils of the Confederation that had called the convention into being. Madison sat silent and disheartened.[31]

When the convention reconvened on Monday, Alexander Hamilton rose for the first time, perhaps hoping that the near deadlock might make the delegates receptive to a bold new departure. In a brilliant speech, lasting the full five or six hours the convention sat that day, Hamilton expressed the ideas about strong, stable, energetic, centralized government for which his name has become a symbol. He spoke not of compromises or patchwork amendments, but of a theory and frame of government he thought would best suit the nation, "a model which we ought to approach as near as possible." Hamilton sought as well to establish institutions, notably a senate, that would encourage the rich, the well-born, and the able to provide the wise, stabilizing, and creative guidance he thought unassured in Randolph's "democratic senate." The plan he offered called for the President, the Senate, and the national judges to hold office during good behavior, the President to have an absolute veto and other broad powers, and the legislature to have "power to pass all laws whatsoever." To assure national supremacy, the state governors would be appointed by the national government and would have as their special duty vetoing state laws contrary to the national constitution or laws. Though Madison sympathized with Hamilton's zeal for a vigorous general government, the Virginian thought it unrepublican for officers to have life tenure, and Hamilton's hostility to the states exceeded Madison's. Tactically, though, the speech and plan might be useful. It cast the Virginia Plan in a moderate role between the Paterson and Hamilton proposals. On the other hand, the fright of staunch republicans and states' rights men at Hamilton's exposition might aggravate already dangerous suspicions and tensions.[32]

The next day Madison addressed the convention for the first time on the New Jersey Plan. All his past research on federalism, all his past practical political experience, had made him intellectually ready for almost any debate, but he was beginning to be able to do even more than reason well—he was beginning to deal subtly with other men's unreason, to help others see the difference between their phantoms and real fears. He thus spoke not to reinforce the prejudices of those who already agreed with him, but rather to crumble away what he hoped were the soft edges of the small-state bloc. After denying, as Wilson had done, that in even considering the Virginia Plan the convention exceeded its powers, Madison questioned whether the New Jersey Plan would serve the urgent needs of the United States. In leaving the states "uncontrouled" in their power to violate laws and treaties, the plan opened the door for foreign intrigue and internal dissension, "the greatest of national calamities." It left the states free to continue encroaching on the general government, which history showed was the great evil to be feared in federal systems. It left the states free as well to prey on each other, and free to continue such follies as printing paper money and indulging in trade wars. It contained no effective restraints against such internal tumults as Shays' Rebellion. Madison then pointed out to the small states that the coercion clause in the New Jersey Plan would be effective only against themselves; it would, he said, "be the sport of the strong." Finally he asked the small states to consider their plight should their "pertinacious adherence to an inadmissable plan . . . prevent the adoption of any plan." The Union would disintegrate, perhaps to re-form into regional confederacies, but in any case, the small states would be left defenseless before the "ambition and power of their larger neighbours" they professed so much to fear. Madison here anticipated the grounds for the early and unanimous federalism of Delaware, New Jersey, and Georgia during the first months of the ratification struggle. After pointing out the practical difficulties of the "Hotchpot" scheme, and raising before tiny Delaware and New Jersey the specter of a multitude of small Western states overwhelming their influence should state equality be preserved, Madison sat down. The convention promptly rejected the New Jersey Plan. Significantly, of the five small states, Maryland divided and Connecticut preferred the Virginia Plan, thus giving it a substantial 7 to 3 majority. Unless this decision was reversed, the Articles of Confederation were dead. Listening to Madison, delegate William Pierce of Georgia formed the opinion that of "the affairs of the United States, he perhaps, had the most correct knowledge of any man in the Union."[33]

From June 20 until July 2, the convention, in plenary session, considered the clauses of the Virginia Plan as approved and reported by the Committee of the Whole. All seemed to sense that the critical moment had arrived. Luckily cool days alternated with hot spells as Madison and the other lodgers at Mrs. House's walked the block to the State House each morning shortly before eleven o'clock, and then in late afternoon adjourned to talk into the evening or to relax over a good meal or a bowl of punch. Madison often left the convivial groups to sit hours at his desk at Mrs. House's writing out the speeches of the delegates from the cryptic notes he had taken at the convention. The task was so laborious that late in life Madison said it "almost killed" him, but he was determined, he wrote Jefferson in mid-July, "to go on with the drudgery, if no indisposition obliges me to discontinue it." His feeling that this convention somehow represented *his* moment of special destiny grew stronger and gave him reserves of energy for which he had repeated need during the weeks before and after the Fourth of July.[34]

At first, the plenary sessions skirted the hard issues. The Wilson-Madison forces agreed to delete the word "national" from the first clause, to placate the states' rights men, a point Madison conceded because he was ready to accept a novel "composite" of national and federal principles. The convention reaffirmed the bicameral principle (only New York, New Jersey, and Delaware opposed), refused to let the state legislatures direct the election of the lower house, and reduced its term from three to two years. Madison again denied the popular notion that only small, local governments could preserve freedom. "A citizen of Delaware was not more free," he declared, "than a citizen of Virginia, nor would either be more free than a citizen of America." In each case, he insisted, the crucial question was not the size, but the *character* of the government. The next day Madison supported successful moves to make the salaries of federal legislators independent of the state governments and to prevent Congressmen from increasing their own salaries or creating offices for their own benefit. Franklin's heavy frame stirred with approval at these restraints on office mongering.[35]

After a weekend adjournment, the difficult question of the Senate came up again, on June 25. Aristocratic Charles Pinckney advocated a senate founded on professional, merchant, and landed interests. Gorham of Massachusetts favored giving the small states some advantage, though not complete equality, in the upper house. Read of Delaware hinted that should the small states be given a fair share of the wealth of the vast Western lands, the matter of state equality might become more negotiable. Clearly, substantial differences persisted. The convention agreed merely that the state legislatures elect the upper house, and then deadlocked on the remaining issues. Another day of wrangling over the Senate led only to resolves that the minimum age for Senators be thirty and that the term be reduced from seven to six years. Madison lectured the convention about the delicate problem of constructing a proper senate: it must at once be prevented from betraying its trust and yet have power to stand for "wisdom and virtue" when "fickleness and passion" had misled the people and the lower house. The Senate should be "a portion of enlightened citizens, whose limited number and firmness might seasonably interpose against impetuous counsels." Madison here expressed fundamental propositions most delegates accepted, but hard issues of power remained unresolved.[36]

The next day, June 27, was hot and dispiriting. Luther Martin spoke all day (and much of the next), rambling so that Madison and Robert Yates of New York, who was also taking notes that day, had great difficulty. With characteristic understatement, Madison recorded that Martin spoke "at great length . . . with much diffuseness, and considerable vehemence," while Yates, even though he agreed with Martin, was more blunt: "[H]is arguments were too diffuse, and in many instances desultory. . . . It was not possible to trace him through the whole, or to methodize his ideas into a systematic or argumentative arrangement." One of Martin's hostile listeners later wrote publicly to the Marylander of his "eternal volubility," and alleged that "you . . . might have continued two months, but for those marks of fatigue and disgust you saw strongly expressed on whichever side of the house you turned your mortified eyes." Beneath all the rhetoric and the long quotations from Locke, Vattel, Somers, Priestley, and others with which Martin bored his hearers, however, his message was simple: that the convention had no authority to diminish in the least the power of the states, and that the three large states were plotting to oppress all the rest. Maryland, he left no doubt, would bitterly resist both moves. Since Martin had arrived late, and had not until this lengthy speech taken a major part in the debate, his vehement performance seemed to poison the whole patiently nourished air of good will in the Independence chamber.[37]

After Martin sat down, the small states moved again to reverse the decision against state equality. Madison then undertook patiently to refute the aspersions cast on the large states. After asserting the fundamental justice of representation according to population, he asked whether Massachusetts, Pennsylvania, and Virginia had any common interest distinguishing them from the rest of the states. None, he declared, and in fact with fish, flour, and tobacco respectively as their "staples," there were no conceivable grounds for their collusion. Rather, they would, like all large political units, be more inclined to jealousy than coalition. Then, turning Martin's argument upside down, Madison pointed out that the small states would be the losers in a weak confederation. They would be sacrificed in clashes among the large states. "The more lax the bond [of union], the more liberty the larger will have to avail themselves of their superior force," Madison admonished. Furthermore, only a strong union offered any hope to the small states that the large states would agree to partitions or that the Western lands would be a bounty for all. Without such a union, the large states would surely cling to all they had, and they would, moreover, have sufficient force to exert their will. The small states should, therefore, be the strongest advocates of a firmer union.[38]

The small states remained unbudged, since what they fought was not so much a stronger union as a decrease of their power within it. Franklin, sensing the deep divisions and the acrimony introduced by Martin's speech, then made his famous plea that the sessions be opened with prayer. After alluding to the prayers which had so moved the Continental Congress in 1775 and affirming that "*God Governs in the affairs of men,*" Franklin beseeched his fellow delegates not to let "local partial interests" destroy the convention and thus lead mankind to "despair of establishing Governments by Human wisdom and leave it to chance, war and conquest." Fearing that suddenly to invite in a clergyman for prayers would alarm the public, the convention did not adopt Franklin's suggestion, but he had probably accomplished much of his purpose: he had dramatized his intense concern that tempers be calmed and that amiable deliberation be resumed.[39]

On June 29 and 30, the delegates went over, again and again, the by now well-known representation arguments. When votes showed that the large-state bloc of six states remained firm, the small states turned anxiously toward the absent New Hampshire delegation. Why not write urging its immediate attendance? The large states defeated the effort. Johnson of Connecticut renewed the compromise proposal for proportional representation in the lower house and state equality in the Senate, but the large states still insisted this was not compromise, but surrender to a principle already discredited under the Articles of Confederation. Wilson, Madison, and Hamilton argued powerfully that the gross inequities of giving the states equal power would soon introduce all the corruptions and intrigues of Britain's "rotten borough" system, or of the councils of the Holy Roman Empire. Wilson declared that no one had refuted Madison's argument that the large states had no common interest to oppress the small. The Virginian then, with some trepidation, pointed out that the most serious division in the Union probably was that between slave and free states. This difference, perhaps, should be the basis of the crucial compromise: let the slaves be counted in determining representation in one house and excluded from the determination in the other. Consumed and upset by one deeply divisive issue, none of the delegates had the heart to respond to this suggestion.[40]

On Saturday, June 30, toward the end of a very hot day, the convention reached its low point. Gunning Bedford of Delaware, "impetuous in temper . . . precipitate in judgment . . . and very corpulant," and therefore perhaps suffering especially from the heat, hurled threatening thunderbolts. He had no doubt that, given the power they sought, the big states would not "fail to abuse it." "I DO NOT, GENTLEMEN, TRUST YOU," he shouted defiantly. He refused to yield to "dictatorial airs," implying that the small states must join a stronger union or die. The larger states would not "dare dissolve the Confederation," he declaimed, because the small states had a final recourse: "sooner than be ruined, there are FOREIGN POWERS WHO WILL TAKE US BY THE HAND." Intent on his notes, Madison winced at such a divisive, almost treasonable threat. From the dais, Washington glared sternly at the perspiring, perhaps already regretful, Delawarian. Rufus King gathered his composure and responded in even tones: "I am concerned for what fell from the gentleman from Delaware—'Take a foreign power by the hand'! I am sorry he mentioned it, and I hope he is able to excuse it to himself on the score of passion. Whatever may be my distress, I never will court a foreign power to assist in relieving myself from it." The fearful specters of Philip of Macedon intriguing among the Greek city-states and of the recent dismemberment of Poland haunted the delegates and held them back from the precipice of disunion.[41]

After a fretful Sunday, the delegates gathered again on July 2. They voted immediately on the question of state equality in the Senate. The absence of two Georgia delegates divided her vote and reduced the large-state bloc to five, thus leaving the issue deadlocked, 5 to 5. In a mood of discouragement, numerous delegates proposed compromises, and Gouverneur Morris delivered a long, brilliant, sometimes cynical speech arguing for an aristocratic government, which would reflect realistically the various interests in the country. With an air of resignation, the convention finally agreed to adjourn until after the Fourth of July celebrations and to place the representation matter in the hands of a grand committee composed of one delegate from each state. Madison objected unsuccessfully. When he and Wilson were not put on the committee, they must have suspected that their despairing colleagues favored exactly the compromise they had so long resisted.[42]

In preparation for the holiday, the delegates sought hard to be in a festive mood when, following their adjournment, they met at a dinner sponsored by "the Gentlemen of the Convention at the Indian Queen." Franklin and Washington were there, weary from the long debates, but as veteran campaigners used to setbacks and discouragements, they nevertheless talked confidently and reassuringly with their colleagues. After dinner the general drank tea with William Bingham, a wealthy federalist merchant, and his wife, Anne, reckoned by many connoisseurs of femininity in Europe and North America as one of the truly remarkable beauties of the age. Before returning to Robert Morris', in the lingering summer twilight, Washington "walked . . . in the State house yard," thinking about what he had written the day before to a friend in Virginia. "The primary cause of all our discontents," he had asserted, "lies in the different State Governments." As long as "independent sovereignty" and the local interests of each state refused to "yield to a more enlarged scale of politicks," the United States would be weak at home and disgraced abroad. He hoped, though, that the "Demogogues and interested characters" would be defeated and a strong general government approved. He and Madison had talked long and earnestly about this, and the two men continued to be in almost perfect agreement.

On the Fourth of July, all Philadelphia was festive. Madison watched the Philadelphia militia and the city cavalry parade on the commons south of the State House, and followed them to the Reformed church on Race Street, where James Campbell addressed the convention delegates as "Illustrious Senate." He exhorted them to shun monarchy and to prove to the country and to the world that free men could govern themselves. "How fallen," he exclaimed, "would be the character we have acquired in the establishment of our liberties, if we discover inability to form a suitable Government to preserve them!" If Madison was not too exhausted from his labors to be attentive, he nodded in agreement. The Society of the Cincinnati, dining in the State House and feeling the same need, toasted "The Grand Convention—may they form a Constitution for an eternal Republic."[43]

The Grand Committee, meeting on July 3, had adopted motions by Franklin that in the lower house each state be allowed one member for each forty thousand inhabitants (each state to have at least one member), that all money bills originate in the lower house, and that the states have an equal voice in the upper house. When it reported to the convention on July 5, the large-state forces immediately made plain their dissent. Wilson protested that the committee had exceeded its powers. Madison refused to bow to the threats of the small states or to the will of what he was sure was a minority. "The Convention," he declared, "with justice and the majority of the people on their side, had nothing to fear. . . . [It] ought to pursue a plan which would bear the test of examination, which would be espoused and supported by the enlightened and impartial part of America, and which they could themselves vindicate and urge. . . . The merits of the system alone can finally and effectually obtain the public suffrage." Madison sought desperately to avoid a patchwork compromise, which would, in his view, embody unjust and unrepublican principles of representation. The so-called Great Compromise was to him unconditional surrender to the notion of state equality, which would leave the United States saddled forever with a "rotten borough" system. He and Wilson refused to yield.[44]

For over a week, during the most oppressive heat of the summer, the delegates belabored the report of the Grand Committee. Gouverneur Morris spoke more and more frequently, openly skeptical of reliance on the good sense of the people. With the support of Georgia and South Carolina slaveowners, he argued that while life and liberty might be the great goals among savages, in civilized societies, due protection of property stood first among the objects of government and should therefore be the basis of representation. Republicans like Franklin and George Mason resisted this, but it was apparent that the ill temper engendered by the debate on representation had emboldened many delegates to bring forward schemes of special interest. The adamant New Yorkers, Yates and Lansing, disliking the compromise as much as Madison and Wilson, but for diametrically opposed reasons, left the convention, thus depriving their state of any further vote in its proceedings. Sure now that any plan the convention might propose would enlarge the general government and thus, among other things, restrain New York's commercial domination of her neighbors, Yates and Lansing sought only to disband the convention, or failing in that, to discredit its recommendations. On the day the New Yorkers left, Washington wrote discouragingly to Hamilton: "The state of the Councils . . . are now, if possible, in a worse train than ever. . . . I *almost* despair of seeing a favourable issue to the proceedings of the Convention." Repeating Madison's arguments, he asserted that the "Narrow minded politicians . . . under the influence of local views" masqueraded when they claimed to speak for the people; the convention should seek "the best form" to offer to the country, and trust in the people to recognize its merits.[45]

In the convention, skirmishing continued over the apportionment of representatives in the lower house, over its size, over how to deal with slaves, and over the relative strength to be allotted to the Northern and Southern and to the Eastern and Western interests. Madison stood with the South and with the West in these debates, seeking principally to insure that the new states in the West would have rights and privileges equal to those of the seaboard states. To him, and to Wilson, the cardinal principle was that of consent, which came increasingly for them to mean eliminating discriminations among voters; the power of a vote should be the same whether cast in Virginia or in some new, as yet unformed state in the Mississippi valley, whether in New Jersey or in Pennsylvania. Any other foundation, they insisted, was unjust and sure to be corrupted. Madison supported a compromise plan for modified proportional representation in the Senate. He raised again the specters of large-state refusal to join a union equating them with tiny Delaware and Rhode Island, and of the ominous division between Northern and Southern interests. But all was to no avail, because the small-state forces, together with Franklin, Mason, Caleb Strong of Massachusetts, and other large-state delegates willing to compromise, had become predominant.[46]

On Monday morning, July 16, the convention at once made the fateful decision: by a 5 to 4 vote (Massachusetts divided) it agreed to "the whole of the report from the grand Committee." The states, therefore, were to have equal representation in the upper house. New York had departed; New Hampshire had not arrived; and Rhode Island took no part in the convention; so ten states made the decision. With Massachusetts divided and Wilson and Madison holding Pennsylvania and Virginia firmly in opposition, the victory was clearly one for the small states: Connecticut, New Jersey, Delaware, Maryland, and their new-found ally, North Carolina. Madison was so perturbed at the result that he recorded in his notes the vital lost votes. Strong and Gerry of Massachusetts had deserted, as had at least one of the four North Carolina delegates, perhaps following an agreement with Rutledge to protect Southern interests. Had either Strong or Gerry stayed with the large states, and any one of the North Carolina majority changed his vote, Madison calculated, the vote would have been 5 to 4 *against* state equality. Randolph immediately declared his unwillingness to accept the narrowly approved Grand Committee report, and moved an adjournment, obviously to gather strength to reverse the vote. Stung at this stubborn unwillingness to accept the long-sought decision, Paterson shouted that it was indeed "high time" to adjourn, *sine die*, he hoped, so the people could be told how Randolph and his cohorts had sought to subvert the states. Calmer voices prevailed, and adjournment was voted merely for the rest of that day,

but not before John Rutledge had proclaimed that "he could see no
chance of compromise."[47]

That afternoon and evening the Madison-Wilson forces consulted
informally about the grave problem before them. They had been beaten
on a crucial vote. Could they in fidelity to the spirit of the convention
refuse to accept it? Would not such an attitude insure the collapse of the
convention, leaving the country weaker and more bitterly divided than
ever? Yet the principle they considered indispensable to a just government had been repudiated. Pondering the dilemma, they decided to call
a meeting of the large-state delegates the next morning. Some of the
small-state delegates were asked to come too, to ease their fears about
large-state conspiracy and domination. At the meeting, opponents of
state equality disputed whether they should be firm and seek a large-
state plan to which the small states would have to accede (Madison
favored this), or whether they should agree to the "imperfect and exceptional" compromise. Madison knew the cause was lost when he saw
the small-state men sit smugly during the wrangle. They knew, Madison
wrote acidly, "that they had nothing to apprehend from a Union of the
larger [states]". They had divided and conquered their enemies. Madison
gave up and, after a moment of fresh air on a blessedly cool day, returned
to the Independence chamber resigned to the obnoxious "Great Compromise." That afternoon, when Washington came to Mrs. House's for
dinner, he doubtless commiserated with Madison over the defeat, but
perhaps urged as well that preventing the dissolution of the convention
was, for the moment, the paramount concern.[48]

As Madison reflected upon the forces at work in the convention, it
was apparent that with the adoption of the "Great Compromise" a key
change would occur. Resistance to the essentially national government
proposed in the Virginia Plan had centered among small-state delegates
fearful of large-state power. The Western lands were an especially sore
point. New Jersey, Maryland, and other small states had been most
reluctant to join even the Articles of Confederation unless the vast Western claims of some states were ceded to the Union as a whole. Virginia,
claiming at one time all the Northwest Territory, as well as the present
states of West Virginia and Kentucky, seemed especially grasping and
arrogant. Speculators in Virginia and other states with substantial claims
had exerted their enormous influence to acquire huge tracts of land.
Equally ambitious operators in the small states, unable to press for patents
through their own legislatures, had turned to federal and foreign governments for entree to the West. Many of the delegates had a personal
interest in these conflicting efforts, and even those who did not, such as
Madison, were well aware of the pressures they generated.

Thus, when Paterson or Read or Martin challenged the claims and powers of the large states, their hearers understood them readily. They were determined to deny the large states, and the speculators who had influence in them, a monopoly on the riches of the West. The determination could only have been hardened when such notorious land operators as Gorham of Massachusetts, Wilson and Robert Morris of Pennsylvania, and Mason and even General Washington of Virginia, argued strenuously in the convention for large-state power. Hints about dismembering the large states were likewise understood immediately in terms of the rival speculative ambitions. Since the convention itself had no direct effect on land claims, the issue was largely one of the future exercise of power. As Irving Brant has put it, "it was easy to see that the states with the most votes in Congress would be best able to get what they wanted."[49]

Therefore the question of whether this or that *power* should be vested in the general government depended on the allocation of votes in its councils. As long as representation by population seemed likely, the small states resisted every effort to increase the general powers, and the large states on the whole favored such an increase. However, the moment the states were made equal in one branch of the legislature, the small states became by and large supporters of increased national authority. Madison late in life explained this point to Martin Van Buren: "The *threatening contest* in the Convention of 1787 did not, as you supposed, turn on the degree of power to be granted to the federal government, but on the rule by which the states should be represented and vote in the government." He told George Bancroft that "from the day when every doubt of the right of the smaller states to an equal vote in the Senate was quieted they . . . exceeded all others in zeal for granting powers to the general government."[50]

After approval of the "Great Compromise," Paterson, for one, backed every effort in the convention to extend the powers of the general government, and was for the rest of his life a staunch federalist. The power the small states gained in the Senate became in them one of the two great self-interest foundations for federalist power in the ratification controversy. (The other, the frailty of some of the states as economic and political entities, will be discussed in the next chapter.) Madison's nationalism, on the other hand, had reached its peak during the weeks when it seemed likely representation would be according to population. After the meeting on the morning of July 17, though, Madison, suspicious of land speculators' influence in small-state legislatures, solicitous of the interests of his native state, and earnestly believing that state equality in the Senate was unjust and antirepublican, became more cautious about the powers granted to the general government. Though he and Wilson continued to champion the new plan of government, they now had to withstand dangerous new crosscurrents: powers rightfully belonging to the people might be captured by "rotten borough" states through their "agents" in the unjustly apportioned Senate, and the whole delicate system of checks and balances might be improperly manipulated.

Though engrossed in these intricate issues, Madison and the other delegates managed to find some time for relaxation and conviviality. On July 12, he was among the delegates gathered for the evening at the Indian Queen when the Reverend Manasseh Cutler arrived for a visit with the Massachusetts delegation. Madison may have been sitting under the mulberry tree in Dr. Franklin's courtyard the next day, when the famous sage sought good-humoredly to encourage a spirit of conciliation. Franklin talked mainly of science, but it was perfectly clear he thought the dispassionate, truth-seeking attitude of the natural philosopher could with equal utility hold sway in the convention. Madison attended the meeting of the American Philosophical Society at Franklin's house on July 20, discussing with his fellow members the new hall the society intended to build in the State House yard (the building still stands). On the morning of July 14 he rose at dawn, and with Cutler, Hamilton, and a few other delegates, rode out along the Schuylkill River. The "large and gay company" found William Bartram, the famous naturalist, barefoot among the trees and plants in the amazing garden begun by his father. They probably stopped as well at Richard Peters' estate, where they may have heard Peters recite some of the notorious bawdy poems Madison always found so amusing. After breakfast at Gray's Ferry Tavern, on a high porch overlooking the river, the delegates hurried back to town for their morning session. What little we know of Madison's daily habits and movements when he was not sitting in the convention suggests that he and the other delegates thoroughly enjoyed each other, the magnificent homes of Philadelphia, and its busy social life. Happily lodged at Mrs. House's, absorbed by the momentous debates in the Independence chamber, and surrounded by a remarkably learned and congenial group of men from all over the country, Madison doubtless found the summer a rewarding experience.[51]

Following the acquiescence of the Virginians and Pennsylvanians in the "Great Compromise," the delegates turned to other major unresolved questions and many matters of detail. Having decided on the composition of the national legislature, the convention next considered its powers. Madison urged again that the national legislature be empowered to "negative" state laws, but most of the delegates had come to favor a more subtle, less humiliating, and probably more effective means of controlling the states. They approved clauses making national legislative acts and treaties "the supreme law of the respective states," and subordinating the courts and legislatures of the states to this supreme law. Madison sat silently while the convention again rejected popular election of the executive. Such a procedure, Mason scoffed, would be as unnatural as referring "a trial of colours to a blind man." The country was too large, he said, for the people to have "the requisite capacity to judge of the respective pretentions of the Candidates." A decision to make the executive eligible for re-election alarmed Madison. Since the legislature was to elect the executive, such a provision would make him utterly dependent on it. To dramatize this concern, Madison renewed, through his quiet colleague Dr. McClurg, a tactical proposal that the executive serve "during good behavior." When Gouverneur Morris supported the motion on aristocratic grounds, Madison had to maneuver carefully. He was as opposed to monarchy as any delegate, he declared, but that hated principle would more probably emerge from throwing all power into "the legislative vortex," than from anything else. The independence of the executive from legislative domination was absolutely essential. Though Madison did not really favor life tenure for the executive, and his support of McClurg's motion later proved embarrassing, Madison had emphasized his concern for independence and succeeded in delaying the decision on election of the executive to a more propitious time.[52]

The next day the convention agreed to establish a supreme national judiciary, but it could not agree on how the judges should be appointed. Madison and Gorham of Massachusetts persuaded their colleagues not to leave appointment wholly in the hands of the legislature, but the convention refused for the present to permit appointment by the executive with approval of the Senate. In a long debate on July 19, Madison again opposed vehemently election of the executive by the legislature. Still unwilling to approve popular election, the convention moved slowly toward the electoral college scheme. During two more days of inconclusive debate on the executive and judicial departments, Madison sought further to establish their capacity to restrain the legislature by having them share the "revisionary," or veto power. Such an association, he declared, would help the legislature "in preserving a consistency, conciseness, perspicuity and technical propriety in the laws, qualities peculiarly necessary; and yet shamefully wanting in our republican Codes. It would moreover be useful to the Community at large as an additional check against a pursuit of those unwise and unjust measures which constituted so great a portion of our calamities." Remembering the tumultuous proceedings in the Rhode Island legislature and the often disastrous influence of the demagogic Patrick Henry in Virginia, Madison never doubted that great care would be needed to prevent domination of the general government by a misled or selfish majority in the legislature. Madison had devoted more than a week almost wholly to a search for effective checks and balances.[53]

In four days of debate (July 23–26) the next week, the first at which delegates from New Hampshire were present, the convention decided the important question of how the members of the Senate would vote. Under the Articles of Confederation, and in the convention itself, each state had from two to seven delegates, who voted among themselves to see how the single vote of the state would be cast. The tally of votes was then by states, not by individuals. This system, of course, emphasized the states as entities, and also frequently left them divided or unrepresented (ordinarily a single delegate could not cast the ballot for a state) in votes. The agreement (concurred in by Madison) that each state should have two Senators, and that each should cast an individual vote, diminished the position of the states as the foundation of the new constitution.[54]

The convention took another step in this direction when it decided "to refer the Constitution . . . to assemblies chosen by the people." Small-state delegates, led by Paterson and by Oliver Ellsworth, moved for ratification by state legislatures. A phalanx bore down on them, however, using arguments Madison had espoused for two or three years. "Whither must we resort," George Mason asked, in seeking authority to establish fundamental law. "To the people with whom all power remains that has not been given up in the Constitutions derived from them," he answered. Rufus King, by now well established as one of the most effective delegates, pointed out that ratification by conventions would be "the most certain means of obviating all disputes and doubts concerning the legitimacy of the new Constitution; as well as the most likely means of drawing forth the best men in the States to decide on it." Madison concluded the debate by noting that approval of the new constitution by existing state legislatures would make it comparable to "a league or treaty" rather than to a fundamental law operating on the people themselves. With remarkable prescience, he pointed out that under a treaty judges would be obliged to respect "perfidious" laws, while under a constitution such laws might be declared null and void by the courts. Furthermore, though under a treaty a breach of one article freed the parties of any obligation under other articles, "in the case of a union of people under one Constitution, the nature of the pact has always been understood to exclude such an interpretation."[55] No statements of the Convention of 1787 reveal more clearly Madison's understanding of the nature of the federal Constitution. Its provisions were to be supreme, the courts were to judge statute law by its conformity to the Constitution, and a state was not to have the right to nullify a law or secede from the Union whenever it deemed a clause of the Constitution had been violated. Madison intended unreservedly that a nation, not a league of states, be established by the new constitution.[55]

On July 25, Madison made a characteristic speech analyzing the knotty and much-debated question of electing the national executive. Either men already in office or especially chosen electors, he began, might elect the executive. If the former, the possibilities were five: the state legislators, executives, or judges, or the national legislature or judiciary. Madison quickly disposed of executive or judical election, and then repeated his argument against legislative election. In addition to the threat to executive independence, Madison emphasized the opportunities for intrigue, holding up before the delegates the corrupt and foreign-dominated elections in Poland and the Holy Roman Empire. Obviously in his mind, too, were the powerful influence French Minister La Luzerne had exerted over selection of officials by the Continental Congress during the revolution and the influence English agents sought to resume in American councils. In fact, Madison argued, election by any "standing body" would find its members being "courted and intrigued with by the Candidates, by their partizans, and by the Ministers of foreign powers." Thus eliminating "standing bodies," Madison turned to the remaining modes: election by a body chosen especially for that purpose by the people, or direct popular election. He pointed out his preference for the first mode, but refrained from arguing the point, he said slyly, since the convention had recently voted against it. He concluded with a theoretically sound defense of popular election, but, shrewdly, he also mentioned practical aspects he knew would defeat that method: candidates from small states would have little chance in such elections, and the North would have an advantage because of its "disproportion of qualified voters." Madison sought (successfully) a reconsideration of the electoral college scheme by discrediting all alternate proposals, a habit of argument he used throughout his life. He had used his acute powers of analysis to summarize debate and to identify the least imperfect alternative, thus making a key contribution to the executive branch and the actual conduct of government, areas where he otherwise seldom displayed creative or independent thought.[56]

On July 26, the convention adjourned for ten days while a committee on detail, consisting of Rutledge of South Carolina, Randolph of Virginia, Gorham of Massachusetts, Ellsworth of Connecticut, and Wilson of Pennsylvania, "arranged and systematized," as the Philadelphia newspapers put it, "the materials which that honorable body have collected." Many of the delegates took advantage of the break to go home or to New York, where some of them were also members of the Continental Congress. Washington went fishing for trout with Gouverneur Morris near Valley Forge (he had never seen the encampment area in the summer), tried more successfully for some Delaware perch a few days later, and made careful notes on how the farmers near Philadelphia grew such bountiful crops of buckwheat. We do not know what Madison did other than snatch time to write encouraging though rather cryptic letters home, but we may assume he worked diligently on his notes of debate and talked with Randolph and Wilson about the work of the committee on detail. He heard the absurd rumor that the convention intended to call the second son of George III to "the American throne," and aware that unrefuted charges of antirepublicanism could vitiate the convention's good work, he doubtless approved the statement given to Philadelphia newspapers that the delegates "never once thought of a king." Madison was pleased, generally, both with the progress of the convention and with his success in molding its resolves to what he considered sound principles of free government. If only the momentum, good sense, and accommodating spirit could be maintained, he now dared to hope, the United States might be placed on a solid foundation.[57]

When the convention reconvened on August 6, the committe on detail laid before the delegates a plan of government embodying the decisions thus far made. The basic outline still followed the Virginia Plan. The most significant departure, and a surprise to most of the delegates, was the substitution of enumerated powers of Congress for the blanket power "to legislate in all cases to which the separate States are incompetent." Now, probably with Madison's approval, the convention, especially the large states that dominated the committee on detail, sought to define the powers of a legislature liable to control by the inequitably apportioned Senate. The convention adjourned for the day to let delegates study the report.

The next day the delegates began a clause-by-clause consideration one delegate thought likely to be "tedious [rather] than difficult." In fact, it turned out to be both. The delegates imposed on themselves six- or seven-hour sessions six days a week. Madison summoned his last reserves of strength to add this burden to his committee assignments and note taking. When Gouverneur Morris moved to limit the right to vote for representatives to freeholders, Madison and others bristled. Wilson, Ellsworth, and Mason protested resting the federal legislature on a narrower base than that of the state legislatures. Morris raised the hoary fear that if the poor were enfranchised, they would sell their votes "to the rich who will be able to buy them," thus making the lower house a plutocracy. Mason urged the convention to shed "antient prejudices" and partiality toward British modes and give meaning to the principle of consent by broadening the suffrage. Franklin pointed out that Morris' proposal would "depress the virtue and public spirit of our common people" so important to the vitality of a republican government.

Madison added that though theoretically "the freeholders of the Country would be the safest depositories of Republican liberty," he could not sanction departure from "the fundamental principle that men can not be justly bound by laws in making of which they have no part." Perhaps property qualification in voting for one house was desirable, but certainly in the other the rights of man required a general suffrage. When, late in life, Madison reviewed this debate, he noted that his "more full and matured view" left him even further from Morris' position: though the threat to property by enfranchised nonfreeholders was very real, the mechanisms of government in an extended republic would usually prevent "combining and effectuating unjust purposes," and in any case, if a conflict arose, it was more just to weaken property rights than personal rights. Madison, though, always held devices to insure good government more sacred than universal suffrage. Furthermore, since he insisted on the natural (universal) right to acquire property, he would not have recognized the distinction later made between "human rights" and "property rights," nor would he have assumed they were generally opposed to each other. At the same time, however, he consistently regarded the doctrine of consent as more vital than mere protection of property. The insights that under a properly constructed government in a generally egalitarian society wide suffrage would not endanger property, and that in fact natural rights were most secure when both suffrage and property were protected, slowly broadened the foundation of Madison's republicanism. In 1787, therefore, he voted against Morris' motion to limit the franchise to freeholders.[58]

For six days (August 9–11, 13–15) the convention debated the tenure and qualifications of Congressmen, the rules for their election and meeting, and other details. Madison generally supported long terms and re-eligibility, but opposed lengthy exclusion of immigrants from Congress: "great numbers of respectable Europeans; men who love liberty and wish to partake its blessings, will be ready to transfer their fortunes hither" if they are not marked unjustly with "suspicious incapacitations." Franklin agreed. "When foreigners after looking about for some other Country in which they can obtain more happiness, give a preference to ours it is a proof of attachment which ought to excite our confidence and affection." Madison and Franklin also favored rapid, easy naturalization of immigrants to full citizenship privileges. In disparaging the xenophobia and paranoia of some of their colleagues, they held up a vision of growth in freedom in an open society offering asylum to all who shared its principles.[59]

On August 16, worn by the petty, sometimes irritable debate over details, and another spell of hot weather, the delegates discussed the vital clauses enumerating the powers of Congress. Madison supported a broad revenue power, including that of taxing exports. He argued that the fears of some Southern delegates that their states might be injured by such a power should be allayed by their greater need for the naval protection revenue thus raised could provide. He supported Elbridge Gerry's little-noticed but fateful amendment to add power over "post roads" to Congress' right to establish post offices, and he acquiesced in deleting the specific power to emit bills of credit, since he was confident Congress had an implied power to do so. The next day Madison and Gerry again combined, to change the clause granting Congress the power to "make" war to read "declare war"; the executive, they argued, should have "the power to repel sudden attacks" without prior consent from Congress. Though Madison probably did not foresee or intend the use made in the twentieth century of this change of one word, he did intend that the President have the authority to cope with emergencies and exigencies. A hamstrung government would be unable to protect the interests of the people. To further enable Congress to act in the public interest, Madison proposed granting power to govern the territories, control a federal district, grant patents and copyrights, establish a university, and promote "useful knowledge and discoveries." The proposals were referred to a committee, after which the convention, in view of the "impatience of the public and the extreme anxiety of many members" to go home, moved to convene an hour earlier, at ten o'clock each day, and to allow no motion to adjourn before 4 P.M. Madison agreed and turned more diligently to his notes.[60]

When the convention reconvened on August 20, after a Sunday break, it referred proposals for a bill of rights and a cabinet to the committee on detail. The clauses affected the structure and powers of the executive department, about which the delegates had as yet failed to form any precise or united opinion. Discussion of the militia and of prosecutions for treason skirted the same subject. At the end of the week the convention considered the article on the executive department clause by clause. It voted first that Congress elect the President in a joint ballot, but then agreed to consider an electoral college scheme. The mode of electing the President thus remained unsettled. A further contentious and inconclusive debate on the appointive power evidently persuaded the delegates their late afternoon sessions frayed tempers for no useful purpose; they agreed unanimously to adjourn at three rather than four o'clock.[61]

Occupied with disputes over slavery and trade regulation, the convention left pending the organization of the executive, and finally referred it, on August 31, to a grand committee (including Madison) on unfinished parts. Though the committee's proceedings are not recorded, Madison would have sought to make both the election and the conduct of the President more independent of the legislature. The committee's report on September 4 included provisions Madison thought vital: the President to be chosen by an electoral college, not by any ballot of Congress, and to have a term of four years and be eligible for re-election, thus making him more responsive to the wishes and interests of his constituents. Furthermore, the President was given power to appoint judges, ambassadors, and other officials, subject only to the advice and consent of the Senate.[62]

In the debate on the report, Wilson foresaw that even with the Electoral College, "Continental Characters will multiply as we more and more coalesce"; thus he anticipated the system of nation-wide attention to a few candidates which developed so quickly. Other delegates agreed that the Electoral College was an ingenious improvement over previous proposals. Serious objections arose only to the provision that the Senate rather than the House of Representatives choose the President when the Electoral College failed to give a majority to one candidate. While Mason and Gerry displayed their growing hostility to the constitution by quibbling over every point, the other delegates, led by the increasingly confident Madison, Wilson, and Morris, more and more felt the merits of the draft constitution heavily outweighed its defects. Largely to placate Mason and others who objected to the Senate taking part in presidential elections, the convention agreed that the House of Representatives, voting by states, choose the President when the Electoral College failed to find a majority candidate. Two more days of debate settled the power of the President to make appointments and treaties with the advice and consent of the Senate (a two-thirds majority needed for treaties), and the power of the Senate to try impeachments. As Morris put it, the President thus would be responsible for the conduct of the executive department, and the Senate would have power to prevent abuses. The convention had solved its most vexing structural problem and fashioned an office wholly without precedent either in the old Confederation or in the history of large federal governments anywhere in the world. Though Madison took little part in the "tedious and reiterated" debate, he approved the new office as indispensable to a vigorous national government.[63]

As the delegates thus resolved structural problems, a nagging sectional conflict threatened the convention with failure: Southern states, fearing Northern commercial domination, sought a veto over laws regulating trade by making a two-thirds vote in Congress necessary for such acts; and Northerners, suspicious of growing slave power, sought to abolish the slave trade. As the delegates tried one accommodation after another, tempers became short; the issues were of immediate, practical, and (so some delegates conceived) life-and-death importance. Evidence accumulated, moreover, of a "deal" between Rutledge of South Carolina and Sherman of Connecticut to satisfy slaveowners, Southern importers, shippers, and land speculators alike. Madison wrote his father on August 12 that the convention might be "spun out . . . [for] months." Three days later *The Pennsylvania Herald* reported "agitated" sessions lasting until five in the evening. On the nineteenth Washington fretted over the slowness of the proceedings, the "contrariety of sentiments" that prevailed, and the tendency toward "a mere nihility" in the decisions of the convention. David Brearley of New Jersey complained two days later of the "earnestness and obstinacy" with which settled questions were reopened, and pleaded with the absent William Paterson to "come down and assist" with the burdensome labors. Paterson wrote on the 21st that he had heard the convention, "Full of Disputation and noisy as the Wind . . . [is] afraid of the very windows and have a Man planted under them to prevent the Secrets and Doings from flying out." He dreaded "going down again to Philadelphia."[64]

In late August and early September illness added to cumulating fatigue forced Madison to restrict his part in the debates and reduce his note taking by 30 per cent. He nevertheless dragged himself to the State House for every session. On August 31, Mason declared he "would sooner chop off his right hand than put it to the Constitution as it now stands," to which Gouverneur Morris retorted hotly that he, too, would be content for the convention to dissolve without result so another could convene "to provide a vigorous Government, which we are afraid to do." Another crisis had been reached.[65]

Mason's anger arose from the repudiation on the convention floor of the provision that trade regulation require a two-thirds vote in Congress, a point he deemed due the South because of her concessions on other matters. New England interests hostile to the two-thirds clause had perceived, however, that Georgia and South Carolina cared less about it than they did about protecting the slave trade. The New Englanders agreed to countenance this trade in return for repudiation of the two-thirds clause. Virginia and Maryland objected strenuously, because they suffered from both provisions: they had no use for more slaves (in fact they already had a surplus of slaves for export south- and west-ward), and they had most to lose from trade regulations favoring Northern shippers. In late-night drinking sessions Luther Martin not only drew confession of the New England maneuver from inebriated delegates, but he encouraged an increasingly dangerous group of malcontents to wreck the convention. Mason, furthermore, had deep moral objections to slavery. Like his Roman hero, Cato, Mason called for attention to principle: the slave traffic was "infernal." Slavery itself discouraged arts and manufactures, caused the poor to despise labor, prevented the immigration of industrious persons, had a "most pernicious effect on manners," and made every master "a petty tyrant." He begged his colleagues to move against this evil, at least by restraining its growth. Only thus could the United States avoid "the judgement of heaven," and national calamity. A country dominated by an alliance of slave traders and grasping merchants had little appeal to the intrepid old republican.[66]

Sharing Mason's moral revulsion, Madison sought to limit the duration of the slave trade and keep direct reference to or support of the evil institution out of the Constitution. He was, however, less insistent on the two-thirds clause. He expected Southern commercial activity to increase. Regulation of trade by a simple majority would permit quicker retaliation against foreign trade laws. The agricultural interest would grow as the West was settled. An increase in the coastal trade would benefit the South. Finally, he added in a magnamimous and far-reaching insight, "if the Wealth of the Eastern [states] should in a still greater proportion be augmented, that wealth would contribute the more to the public wants, and be otherwise a national benefit." He was willing, therefore, to trust to majority rule on commercial regulation and concede, if necessary, on the slave trade. The benefits from union were to his mind so immense, and the progress made thus far by the convention in framing a government so remarkable, that he would not now throw over the whole business. The New England–South Carolina axis had its way, and the final conflict of interest compromise found its way into the Constitution, with all the fateful consequences against which Mason had warned so eloquently.[67]

The delegates, now certain they could offer a document to the people, turned to final polishing and last-minute efforts to gain the acquiescence, if not the support, of the four hostile delegates, Martin of Maryland, Gerry of Massachusetts, and Mason and Randolph of Virginia. Madison was probably glad enough to see the abrasive, loquacious Martin go home on September 4, but he was most anxious to reconcile his Virginia colleagues. If they persisted in opposition, Virginia was unlikely to ratify the document. With Gerry, and with Martin until he left, however, the objecting Virginians viewed with alarm and raised specters at every turn as the convention disposed of the remaining "unfinished parts." Martin objected to the terms for admitting new states to the Union, opposed the broad power of the general government to suppress domestic insurrection, and sought the unanimous consent of the states in order to implement the new constitution. The convention brushed him aside on all counts, as it did Mason and Gerry when they supported Martin in the last motion. For three or four days the convention hurried through many changes in the clauses on ratifying treaties, defining treason, and trying impeachments, pausing only to give brief and increasingly impatient attention to its relentless objectors. Madison had frequently to omit the roll call on the votes, and he made more mistakes in his tallies than he did at any other time. Exhausted and half sick, he was engulfed by the "precipitation" he noted so often characterized the last sessions of a deliberative body.[68]

On Saturday, September 8, the convention felt its work sufficiently complete to appoint a committee on arrangement and style. Elder states-

man William Samuel Johnson of Connecticut presided over a committee
of the convention's bright young penmen: Hamilton, King, Madison,
and Gouverneur Morris. They labored three days at their important
task, apparently entrusting the actual draft of the Constitution to Morris.
Madison wrote late in life that "the *finish* given to the style and arrangement of the Constitution fairly belongs to the pen of Mr. Morris; the
task having, probably, been handed over to him by the chairman . . . with
the ready concurrence of the others. A better choice could not have
been made, as the performance of the task proved." Morris reduced
twenty-three unwieldy articles to three, with sections and subsections
defining the great departments of government, plus four additional, and
more miscellaneous, articles. He polished the language throughout and
wrote the graceful preamble, beginning simply "We, the people," followed by the list of general purposes. On Monday the convention
further directed the committee to prepare a covering letter from Washington to Congress, a task apparently assigned to Madison, judging from
its style and language. The convention met on Tuesday only to adjourn
so the committee could complete its work, and the next day saw for the
first time a document in reasonably complete and final form. The end
was in sight. The delegates turned eagerly to the printed broadside laid
before them.[69]

In four days the convention went through the Morris draft clause by
clause. A proposal to reduce from three-quarters to two-thirds the vote
in Congress necessary to override a presidential veto troubled Madison.
The veto was supposed to defend executive rights and "prevent popular
or factious injustice." The difficulty was that it might be abused or overawe the legislature. "We must compare," Madison admonished, "the danger from the weakness of ⅔ with the danger from the strength of ¾.
. . . On the whole the former was the greater." On a vote Madison
considered important enough to record in detail, he joined Washington
and Blair to cast the Virginia ballot for a three-fourths veto, but the
convention voted 6 states to 4 for the smaller figure. No action in the
convention shows more clearly Madison's skepticism of legislative supremacy and belief in a powerful national executive.[70]

The delegates next brushed aside a Gerry-Mason motion for a bill of
rights, on the grounds, accepted at this time by Madison, that in a constitution of limited powers no such explicit statement was necessary. The
federal government had no power to interfere with rights, because none
was granted to it. This set the pattern for a series of changes rejected as
unnecessary. Provisions thus lost would have empowered Congress to
establish a university (moved by Madison), prohibited interference with
the liberty of the press, and asked the convention to prepare an address
to the states. Franklin, Wilson, and Madison moved to empower Congress to build canals and otherwise act to promote the general welfare.

Sherman thought such a provision would be too expensive, and Rufus King thought it unnecessary, so down it went. Madison noted that many members were "very impatient" and immediately and repeatedly called for the question. He and King were, however, able to defeat a motion that persons impeached be suspended from office until tried. Such a stipulation, they asserted, would subject the President and other officials to harassment and intimidation by a mere majority of the House of Representatives. Executive independence had to be preserved.[71]

On Saturday, September 15, the convention hurried through the final two dozen or so votes approving the draft constitution. The week had been a grueling one, and on a dark, cloudy day the delegates were anxious to gather around the punch bowl at City Tavern, but it was necessary to hear the final speeches of the "committee on fears and objections." Mason tried once more for a two-thirds clause on navigation laws, but the New England–South Carolina coalition again held firm. Randolph objected to the "indefinite and dangerous power" given to Congress, and moved that the Constitution be submitted to the states with provision for a second "general Convention" to follow. Mason seconded the motion, warning that "monarchy or a tyrannical aristocracy" would result from the present document. He would not sign it. Pinckney of South Carolina expressed the view of Madison and a majority of the delegates when he exposed the second convention plan as an effort to kill by introducing "confusion and contrariety." Gerry foreshadowed antifederalist arguments by objecting to practically every clause enhancing the energy and stability of the general government. He, too, wished for a second convention. Two hours past dinnertime, and after seven hours of continuous session, Madison recorded the convention's impatience: "On the question on the proposition of Mr. Randolph, all the states answered —no. On the question to agree to the Constitution as amended. All the states ay. The Constitution was then ordered to be engrossed. And the House adjourned."[72]

Over the weekend, at Franklin's urging, the delegates searched once more for a strategy to persuade the dissenters to sign the document. The aged diplomat spoke frankly of his own objections and showed a group gathered at his house a speech he planned to make asking all delegates to join him in suppressing their reservations in the interests of unanimity. Gouverneur Morris suggested an ambiguous form of approval, "done in Convention by the Unanimous Consent of the States present," to permit delegates with personal objections nevertheless to sign. This was approved, and Wilson agreed to read Franklin's speech when the convention met on Monday morning.[73]

As the delegates gathered for the last time in the Independence chamber, Wilson rose with Franklin's speech. The eloquent plea that each delegate "doubt a little of his own infallibility," the well-known story

about the French lady who, in a dispute with her sister, said, "I don't
know how it happens, sister, but I meet with no body but myself that's
always in the right," and other sage comments from Poor Richard,
failed to move the objectors. Even agreement to Washington's personal
appeal, his only one on the convention floor, that the maximum ratio of
representatives to the people be reduced from 1 to 40,000 to 1 to 30,000
had no effect. Mason sat silently, determined to withhold his signature.
Gerry and Randolph proclaimed a similar refusal, insinuating resentment
at Franklin's speech, which they "could not but view" as aimed at them.
Randolph's remarks that he would not necessarily "oppose the Constitution without doors," and that he meant only to reserve the right to
decide later what attitude to take, heartened Madison to hope that in
this instance, as in so many others, he would be able to exert a decisive
influence over his vacillating friend. The delegates "then proceeded to
sign the instrument," and Franklin made his famous observation that the
sun painted on the back of the president's chair was "a rising and not a
setting Sun." The convention adjourned *sine die*, and the members repaired to City Tavern, where, Washington wrote in his diary, they
"dined together and took a cordial leave of each other." The old soldier
then returned to his lodgings "to meditate on the momentous work
which had been executed."[74]

As Madison walked back to Mrs. House's he, too, meditated. The
document finally approved was in some ways very different from the
plan he had proposed in May. The small states had imposed what Madison
persistently regarded as the unjust and impractical principle of state
equality in the Senate. The clause empowering Congress to "negative"
state laws, long thought by Madison to be the only effective way to
prevent state encroachment on national authority, had been dropped in
favor of the less explicit supreme-law clause. Persuaded by Wilson's
brilliant arguments, Madison came gradually to see the virtue of this
change. An enumeration of the powers of Congress was substituted for
the broad power "to legislate in all cases to which the separate States
are incompetent." After the decision in favor of state equality in the
Senate, Madison more and more approved enumeration as a necessary
check on a poorly constructed Congress. Finally, the office of the
President, unified, largely independent of Congress, and vested with
broad appointive and treaty-making powers, furnished an unforeseen
capstone for the federal government. By the end of the convention,
Madison heartily endorsed the unprecedented office, both because he
favored an energetic executive and because the President was to be
elected roughly in proportion to population. Though Madison would
have been willing to create an even more powerful national government
had it not been flawed by state equality, he was by and large content

with the balance of powers finally agreed upon both between the state and federal governments and among the three departments. In fact, he increasingly admired the structure of the new government.

In attending to every detail of this structure, and in being sensitive at every point to the effect of blending the various parts, Madison played his most critical role, and earned the title later bestowed upon him, Father of the Constitution. Next to him in influence and understanding was James Wilson. The Pennsylvanian's intrepid insistence on "a broad base," the need in the name of stability and authority to have as many of the agencies of government as possible rest directly on a large electorate, contributed immensely to the thoroughly republican character of the Constitution. He was also especially creative in devising the executive department. George Mason's confidence in the people, and Franklin's steady advocacy of their responsibility, strengthened Wilson's position. Madison by and large agreed. Furthermore, Wilson's sense of the efficacy of the supreme-law clause implanted another subtle and exceedingly significant principle: a composite government, both parts of which rested directly on the people, had been formed. Gouverneur Morris and Hamilton led Wilson, Madison, King, and others in insisting on an energetic government. Morris, like Hamilton, was willing to sacrifice the direct influence of the people to the need for strong, even aristocratic government, but watched by the convention's purer republicans, especially Mason and Franklin, the effect of their advocacy was to counteract Paterson, Dickinson, Martin, and others who upheld restraints and states' rights. Conciliators like Franklin and the Connecticut delegates Sherman, Ellsworth, and Johnson repeatedly eased tensions and suggested compromises permitting the convention to continue its work. Only a handful of delegates—the New Yorkers Lansing and Yates, the garrulous Martin, and late in the convention, the apprehensive Mason and Gerry—walked out, sulked, or merely obstructed.

Throughout, of course, special concerns of particular states and the economic interests of the delegates or their constituents were in view and had an influence on the debates and the decisions. Slavery received careful but limited protection; commercial interests were placated; and creditors were guarded against inflation or debt repudiation. Yet, although many of the delegates had a personal financial interest in the decisions of the convention, the most thorough comparison of these interests with votes in the convention indicates almost no significant correlation along lines of economic self-interest. Those with wealth in land and slaves and those with wealth in commerce and securities did not form separate blocs. The clauses against paper money and repudiation of contracts received mixed backing. Public creditors among the delegates failed to act together. Many members of the convention were heavily in debt, and many had voted for debtor relief laws in their states. Two of the nonsigners, Gerry and Mason, were respectively the largest holder of public securities and the wealthiest creditor and landowner. One concludes that the economic interests of the delegates were exceedingly complex and ambiguous and probably seldom decisive in their effect on the debates and votes of the convention.[75]

Madison, as a member of the propertied class, perhaps selfishly befriended property rights, but every word and deed of his public career suggest as well that he believed strongly, in the Lockean manner, that free republican government depended on the right to at least acquire property. In his mind, human rights and property rights complemented and buttressed each other. It is a gross perversion to picture his work and that of his fellow delegates as a sinister plot to feather their own nests. Their decisions cannot be explained under such a view, and the primary concern of the delegates for matters of *government* is manifest on every page of their surviving debates and votes. As Madison reflected upon the fruits of his labors during the summer of 1787 he had no reason to fear exposure as a plutocrat. He had acted as a republican and as a nation builder. As he stated in the letter transmitting the Constitution to the Continental Congress, "In all our deliberations . . . we kept steadily in our view . . . the consolidation of our Union, in which is involved our prosperity, felicity, safety, perhaps our national existence. . . . The Constitution, which we now present, is the result of a spirit of amity, and of that mutual deference and concession which the peculiarity of our political situation rendered indispensable."[76]

CHAPTER XI

Ratification

A FTER a few days in Philadelphia spent writing letters and completing his notes on the convention debates, Madison left Mrs. House's in late September for New York. Passing through Princeton a few days before commencement, he probably learned that his alma mater would then confer upon him an honorary doctorate of law, recognizing the high place he now occupied in the nation's life, and especially, the key role he had played in the Federal Convention. Transmitting Madison's diploma, his old teacher President Witherspoon wrote that "all concerned in this college were, not barely willing, but proud . . . [to honor] one of their own sons who had done them so much honor by his public service. And, as it has been my peculiar happiness to know, perhaps more than any of [the trustees], your usefulness in an important public station, on that and some other accounts, there was none to whom it gave greater satisfaction."[1]

Preoccupied with the ratification question, however, Madison hurried on. His colleagues sitting in Congress in New York had warned him that enemies of the new constitution, including the influential Richard Henry Lee, threatened its prompt transmission to the people of the states. When Madison and other convention delegates took their seats, however, they soon squashed the objections, and by agreeing to omit any commendation of the new constitution, persuaded Congress to resolve unanimously that the states elect conventions to consider the new document. Madison wrote dispassionately to Washington that despite the comfort antifederalists in some states would derive from the failure of Congress to praise the Constitution, "the circumstance of unanimity" would be favorable everywhere. Indeed, in states such as Virginia, inclined to do the opposite of what Congress might recommend, the simple referral would help the federalists,* as the friends of the new constitution now began to call themselves.[2]

In New York, comfortably settled at 19 Maiden Lane, in the lodging-house of Mrs. Dorothy Elsworth, which he shared with other Virginians, Madison was at the center of the ratification fight. He corresponded with people all over the United States, and with Jefferson and other friends in Europe, about the prospects. He placed discreet hints and telling arguments where he thought they would most effectively aid ratification. He kept Washington fully informed and guided the general in doing and saying what would best utilize his vast influence. Madison's most ticklish task, however, was to bring the hesitant, curiously wavering, yet earnest Edmund Randolph from his qualified opposition to the Constitution to a position of approval before the gathering of the Virginia convention a few months hence. If, as seemed more and more certain, the fight in Virginia would be close, Randolph's position and considerable influence could well be decisive. Madison waited eagerly for news from his associates in Virginia and kept a detailed record of the changes in attitude of every political leader in the state.[3]

In New York, the federalists had a mighty band of generals to plan and lead the compaign for ratification. Hamilton, Rufus King, Madison, William Samuel Johnson, Gouverneur Morris, and other framers were there. Henry Lee of Virginia and other delegates to Congress who favored the Constitution took up the cause, and influential New Yorkers such as John Jay, William Duer, and Robert Livingston also helped. Little is known of the meetings among these men, but their letters when absent from each other leave no doubt that they had laid careful plans. Though they organized no formal party, they coordinated activity in the various states, acted as a clearinghouse for information, and planned responses to the increasingly active antifederalist publicists. Their superior unity of purpose, organization, communications, and propagandists' skill were exceedingly important to the eventual victory. Madison and Hamilton were, throughout, the strategic and intellectual chieftains of this able group. Though the ratification controversy was in fact thirteen contests rather than one, best understood in terms of the special circumstances in each state, federalists everywhere received valuable intelligence, encouragement, and ideological ammunition from "headquarters" in New York.[4]

* This word, uncapitalized, will refer to those who, from 1787 to 1789, supported the new constitution, while "Federalist," capitalized, will refer to the political party that emerged in the early 1790s and controlled the national government until 1801. Madison was never a "Federalist," but was, and in one sense always remained, a "federalist."

During the last weeks of the Federal Convention, delegates more and more had in mind as they spoke the effect of this or that clause or provision on ratification prospects. As the delegates left Philadelphia, each knew what his colleagues from other states thought of the probabilities at home. Madison was encouraged that in Philadelphia both local parties (that is, the friends and the foes of the state constitution, who had ever since 1776 made Pennsylvania politics the most contentious and highly organized in North America) at first favored the new federal constitution, but he foresaw correctly that "a country party [might] spring up" in opposition. Traveling across New Jersey, Madison heard only words of support, and predicted the nearly unanimous approval of the Constitution there. In New York, the outlook was clouded: though in the city "the general voice coincided with that of Philadelphia," the state's dominant politicans, headed by Governor George Clinton, had already begun a vigorous opposition. In New England, the early reactions from Boston were favorable (but Madison admitted "more will depend on the Country than the Town"); the first impressions from Connecticut seemed "auspicious"; and in New Hampshire members of the legislature were "extremely pleased" with the new constitution. Only in Rhode Island, the perverse bane of federal measures for nearly a decade, did Madison hear of "violent opposition," fomented, as might be expected, he wrote Washington, by the same disorderly crowd that had passed the recent paper-currency measures.

From southward, news arrived more slowly. At first it seemed as favorable as that from New England. No opposition at all appeared in Delaware, and in Maryland, despite Luther Martin, Samuel Chase, and a few others, popular sentiment, especially in the city of Baltimore, was favorable. In Virginia, too, early news was encouraging. Edmund Pendleton enthusiastically endorsed the new document; the town of Alexandria approved; and the dissenting George Mason had been treated rudely when he expressed his opposition. Indications that Mason, Randolph, R. H. Lee, and Patrick Henry might join in opposing, however, left Madison with but "very faint hopes" that his home state would offer the overwhelming support for the Constitution her sponsorship of the convention might have indicated. This was the more regrettable since there were signs the states south of her would follow her lead. Nevertheless, word that seaboard North Carolinians were favorably disposed, the support of the powerful South Carolina leaders who had attended the convention, and a feeling that Georgia's exposed position would make her a friend of a stronger federal government left Madison moderately optimistic about the Southern states. For a few weeks the federalists enjoyed remarkably favorable prospects. The widespread dissatisfaction with the Articles of Confederation had created a climate receptive to change.

By late October, however, the opposition everywhere had had a chance to form, and in key states serious dissension appeared. In Massachusetts, some of the "old Revolutionists," stimulated by delegate Elbridge Gerry's strictures, began to hint objections. The powerful, popular Samuel Adams–John Hancock combination seemed on the verge of open opposition. Madison agreed readily with Rufus King and other Massachusetts federalists that such opposition would be fatal and had at all costs to be prevented. Though Madison refused to concede defeat, in New York the enlarging campaign of Governor Clinton's party made victory there less and less likely. In Pennsylvania the rough tactics used by Assembly sergeants-at-arms to maintain a quorum during the vote to call a convention seemed to Madison "an unlucky ferment," auguring a more protracted struggle there than had been anticipated. Led by James Wilson, the federalists had the support of the city of Philadelphia, the Quakers, and most of the Germans, but it became more and more evident that their opponents in state politics, whatever their opinion on the merits of the new constitution, felt obliged for local reasons to oppose what their traditional foes endorsed. Combined with strong antifederal sentiment in the western parts of the state, this resulted in a substantial, though apparently still minority, opposition. Nevertheless, Madison was distressed at the bitterly partisan nature of the contest in what had at first seemed to be an overwhelmingly federalist state.

Most alarming of all, antifederalist sentiment grew stronger in Virginia. George Mason's published *Objections to the Proposed Federal Constitution* carried him far beyond the moderate criticisms he had expressed on the convention floor. Upset and feeling betrayed, Madison appealed plaintively to Washington whether "it be candid to arraign the Convention for omissions which were never suggested to them—or prudent to vindicate the dissent by reasons which either were not previously thought of, or must have been willfully concealed." Mason was, Madison reported, in "an exceedingly ill humor," angry enough to espouse schemes to weaken the Union which in a less passionate mood he would not countenance for a moment. Governor Randolph continued to urge a second convention (a move sure to lead to stalemate and disunion in Madison's opinion), so Madison maintained his campaign of tactful persuasion. Richard Henry Lee published the widely distributed *Letters from the Federal Farmer*, attacking the Constitution, joined heartily in Virginia antifederal politics, and of course, carried with him the large influence of his family. Many others, including ex-Governor Benjamin Harrison, the Cabell family, James Mercer, and most of the bench and bar, were antifederal. Even three of Madison's closest friends, President Madison of William and Mary College, Joseph Jones, and James Monroe, "criticized [the new constitution] pretty freely."[5]

As if this were not enough, Patrick Henry, after hinting to Washington that he might approve the Constitution, revealed himself, as Madison had feared, an extreme, inveterate opponent. Madison's dismay and disgust at Henry's conduct grew steadily through the fall and winter. At first, in mid-October, he noted merely that "much will depend on Mr. Henry." A week later he "took for granted" that the orator would oppose. Then Madison learned that in the Virginia Assembly, "Mr. Henry has upon all occasions however foreign to his subject attempted to give the Constitution a side blow." By December Madison's alarm reached new heights as he discovered more about Henry's tactics in the Assembly. Madison called its actions "several mad freaks," passed as Henry worked up "every possible interest into a spirit of opposition." Shrewdly favoring special interests in the state, the orator backed laws that would be proscribed by the new federal constitution and painted a pathetic picture of Virginians being hauled off for trial before federal courts hundreds of miles distant. He sought to bend other states to Virginia's will, and hinted in private conversation and by innuendo in debate that the Southern states might be better off in a confederacy of their own than united with the North so disadvantageously as the new constitution provided.

A month later, still attempting to woo Randolph away from the antifederalists, Madison warned him about Henry: he sought a Southern confederacy, and all his support of amendments was a mere cover for his divisive plans. In February Madison wrote Jefferson of Henry's "very bold language," which stressed Virginia's self-sufficiency and even hinted at "external props"—that is, support by foreign powers. To Madison, recently in receipt of letters from Jefferson telling of British and Prussian interference with republican patriots in Holland, such hints were threatening indeed. Though Henry probably never planned or even desired secession or foreign intervention, his encouragement and use of the threat posed by such moves, together with the unnerving agitation his speeches and tactics produced in the Assembly, stirred dangerous, volatile, and to Madison, all too familiar currents in Virginia politics. In return, he and other federalists sought to reduce Henry's influence by exaggerating his intrigues and disaffection. Clearly, a major battle loomed in Virginia, with the highest possible stakes. It was also apparent, by midwinter, that Madison himself would have to go to Virginia to engage the redoubtable Henry and his numerous band.[6]

As he watched the forces at work in the ratification struggle, Madison noticed, as did many other observers, some nation-wide patterns overlaying the peculiar circumstances affecting the controversy in each state. Early reports that Boston, New York, Philadelphia, Baltimore, Alexandria, and other seaboard towns were federalist suggested an important basis for support of the Constitution: those concerned with trade, those affected by the opinion held by foreign powers of the United States, those who needed a stable currency, those who sensed the dazzling prospects before the several states if united under an energetic government, those impressed with the links between law, order, and civilization, those keenly aware of the dangers a weak, disunited, country faced in international relations—these people by and large rallied behind the Constitution. As Madison put it, in the Northern and Middle states, "the men of intelligence, patriotism, property, and independent circumstances" nearly all favored the Constitution. By this Madison meant not so much to suggest that sharp economic lines divided the parties as to underscore his conviction that only selfish, parochial, ignorant, or unscrupulous men could fail to see that every legitimate interest in the country would benefit from the energetic, more purely republican government provided by the Constitution.[7]

He put the matter more directly, if not without bias, when, with carefully chosen words, he asked Edmund Randolph to consider who his allies would be if he continued to oppose the Constitution. In New York the opponents were men who "notoriously meditate . . . a dissolution of the Union." In Connecticut and Massachusetts they were "people who have a repugnance in general to good government." Some in the latter state even "aim at confusion, and are suspected of wishing a reversal of the Revolution." In Pennsylvania the foes were governed by no principle other than "an habitual opposition to their rivals." In Virginia the "mad schemes" of Patrick Henry should warn people against an alliance with him. Nothing, Madison continued, "can be farther from your views than the principles of [these] different setts of men who have carried on their opposition under the respectability of your name." After the narrow federalist triumph in Massachusetts in February 1788, Madison wrote to Pendleton that there "the men of abilities, of property, of character, every judge, lawyer of eminence, and the clergy of all sects" were nearly all for the Constitution. The foes "looked no farther than to reject the Constitution in toto," and they had not a single leader capable of reasoned and logical opposition to it on its merits.[8]

Though there undoubtedly was, as Madison's letters make clear, an economic cleavage on the ratification question—most rich men favored the Constitution, and relatively more poor men opposed it—it does not follow that it was a document calculatingly designed by men of wealth for their own self-protection, or that its ratification amounted to a triumph of "plutocracy" over the "common man." There were many honest opponents who envisioned the future of the United States in rather simple, idyllic terms, harking back to the small city-republics of antiquity. By and large they viewed every extension of government as dangerous to liberty and tending toward enlargements of ambition and commerce that would end in corruption and militarism. The *political* force behind antifederalism, however, consisted principally of groups who saw their own future in terms of power they exerted within and through the existing and often admirable state governments. In New York the Clintonians controlled a viable government effectively serving their interests. Why should they give it up or agree to its restraint by a stronger general government? In Massachusetts the antifederalists derived much strength from the fear in the back counties, recently the scene of Shays' Rebellion, that adherence to the new constitution would strengthen their political foes. Opposition in Pennsylvania rested in part on a similar foundation. In Virginia, Henry rallied support among those who believed in Virginia's self-sufficiency, in her ability to cope effectively with her own problems, and in the bright future the state had in exploiting, on her own, her vast western lands.

In short, antifederalism flourished where states, or groups within states, saw no need, in terms of the matters then facing them, for a stronger central government. Federalism, on the other hand, was strong in the states least able to deal individually with their problems (hence the overwhelming federalism of the small states—Delaware, New Jersey, Georgia, Connecticut, New Hampshire, and Maryland), among groups frustrated and stymied by existing state governments, and among men like Rufus King, Hamilton, Washington, Madison, and James Wilson, who, both in their personal careers and in a broad consideration of the future of the United States and its place in the world, saw an energetic general government as the only path to greatness. More than any other thing, the substantial unity of the leading federalists in this vision, together with the debilitating effect on the antifederalists of their irreconcilable particularisms, explains the ultimate victory of the former. Madison's letters throughout the controversy reflect this vital factor.[9]

As Madison observed the clash of interests over ratification, and especially the differences in Virginia among men he respected, he reflected on some important principles of free government. Noting, for example, that Mason, Randolph, R. H. Lee, Monroe, and Joseph Jones, devoted patriots, and often his able coworkers, opposed the Constitution, he commented that "the diversity of opinion on so interesting a subject among men of equal integrity and discernment is at once a melancholy proof of the fallibility of the human judgement and of the imperfect progress yet made in the Science of government. . . . Companies of intelligent people equally divided . . . [urge] on one side that the structure of the government is too firm and too strong, and on the other that it partakes too much of the weakness and instability of the Government of the particular states. What is the proper conclusion from all this? That unanimity is not to be expected in any great political question." Nonetheless, Madison thought the people at large, despite the

pernicious influence of Henry and other leaders, and the intricacy of
the question, "which certainly surpasses the judgement of the greater
part of them," had in their own "sober and steady" way come to favor
the Constitution. They were tired, Madison was sure, "of the vicissitudes,
injustice, and follies, which have so much characterized public measures,
and are impatient for some change which promises stability and
repose."[10]

In January 1788, after observing the disillusioning picture of a majority of the Virginia Assembly responding to Henry's demagoguery, and
the rising strength everywhere of what Madison considered was an
obscurantist antifederalism, he was more sober. "The great body of
those who are both for and against [the Constitution]," Madison wrote
Randolph,

> must follow the judgement of others, not their own. Had the Con-
> stitution been framed and recommended by an obscure individual . . .
> it would have commanded little attention from most of those who now
> admire its wisdom. Had yourself, Colonel Mason, Colonel Richard
> Henry Lee, Mr. Henry, and a few others, seen the Constitution in the
> same light with those who subscribed it, I have no doubt Virginia
> would have been as zealous and unanimous, as she is now divided, on
> the subject. I infer from these considerations that, if a government be
> ever adopted in America, it must result from a fortunate coincidence
> of leading opinions, and a general confidence of the people in those
> who may recommend it. . . . Human opinions [are] . . . as various and
> irreconcilable concerning theories of government, as doctrines of reli-
> gion; and give opportunities to designing men which it might be
> impossible to counteract.

Though Madison held steadily to the Lockean principle of government
by consent and knew that some confidence in the judgment of the people at large was its necessary corollary, he understood as well that the
people needed able, responsible leaders if they were to judge wisely.[11]

In the debates over the new constitution, Madison undertook early to
help the public form its mind intelligently. Before the Federal Convention adjourned, publications in New York, inspired by the reports of
Yates and Lansing on the form of government likely to be proposed,
began the opposition. Anonymous defenders responded acrimoniously.
In mid-October Madison reported that the papers in the Northern and
Middle states had begun "to teem with vehement and violent calumni-
ations of the proposed Government." Federalist preparations for a
countercampaign began informally in Philadelphia before the convention
delegates dispersed. Tench Coxe, a young Pennsylvanian who partici-
pated in the evening discussions of government at Franklin's home, in
late September 1787 sent Madison some "Remarks on the Proposed
Constitution" (published over the signature "an American Citizen") as

well as some papers intended for Hamilton, then attending court in Albany. Through October Coxe continued to feed materials supporting arguments for the Constitution to Madison, who promised to consult with Hamilton about them. Pleas poured in on Madison, Hamilton, and the other federalist leaders to write and publish a comprehensive, reasoned defense of the new constitution.[12]

When Hamilton returned to New York City, about October 10, he may have had with him a draft of the first number of *The Federalist*, written, according to family tradition, on shipboard as he sailed down the Hudson River from Albany. He consulted immediately with John Jay about the work, and the two sought Madison's collaboration. Gouverneur Morris, invited to participate, declined, pleading the pressure of other business. William Duer was also asked to help, but his "intelligent and sprightly" essays, as Madison wrote of them—too charitably—in old age, proved inadequate to be printed over the pseudonym, Publius, selected for the essays. Thus, in late October 1787, Hamilton, Jay, and Madison undertook what became the authoritative commentary on the Constitution and the best-known work of political theory ever written in the United States. A severe attack of rheumatism incapacitated Jay for most of the winter and limited his contribution to only five of the eighty-five essays. Madison wrote twenty-nine, Hamilton the other fifty-one.*

Though the three authors, especially Hamilton and Madison, met to plan the work, and perhaps discussed matters of substance, it is doubtful that they prepared any detailed outline or agreed fully on its doctrines in advance. Time was too short, and the purpose was to promote ratification in New York and other states, not to write dispassionately for posterity about the great questions of government. The first essay, by Hamilton, appeared in the New York *Independent Journal* on October 27, 1787, barely fifteen days after he returned to the city. The next eight essays, by Hamilton and Jay, appeared between October 31 and November 21, and Madison's first contribution, the to-be-famous Number 10, appeared in the New York *Daily Advertiser* on November 22. Publication was needed too fast for the essays to come out first

---

* The introduction to *The Federalist*, Jacob E. Cooke, ed. (Cleveland, 1961), describes the writing of *The Federalist*, and discusses with full bibliographical citations the long dispute over its authorship. Though Cooke considers the matter not fully settled, he concedes that Madison's claim to the disputed numbers (49–58 and 62–63) is substantially stronger than Hamilton's. This seems unnecessarily cautious, however, since in fact Madison's authorship of all the essays he claimed in 1818 has been established by every technique of modern scholarship—including computers, as described by Frederick Mosteller and David L. Wallace in *Inference and Disputed Authorship: The Federalist* (Reading, Massachusetts, 1964). What follows assumes Madison wrote numbers 10, 14, 18–20, 37–58, 62–63. All quotations from *The Federalist* are from the Cooke edition, cited by number and without further source notes.

in only one newspaper (there were, actually, no *daily* newspapers in New York at this time), so they appeared, three or four a week, first in one New York paper and then another, between November and April 2, 1788, when Number 77, the last to be printed in a newspaper before the book publication of the entire series, appeared in the *Independent Journal*. The haste was so great, Madison reported, that there was "seldom time for even a perusal of the pieces by any but the writer before they were wanted at the press, and sometimes hardly by the writer himself."[13]

Madison's first five essays, appearing in the last two months of 1787 and prepared from notes drafted a year earlier, were written under relatively little pressure. Three of these, 18–20, on the deficiencies of other attempts at confederation, were written with the assistance of notes supplied by Hamilton, though Madison drafted the essays and sent them to the press without further consultation with Hamilton. The main burden was Hamilton's until January 11, 1788, when, with Number 37, Madison began a series of twenty-two essays which appeared in less than six weeks. Madison's final two essays appeared just before he left for Virginia in early March. From mid-November 1787 until late February 1788, then, and especially under the heavy pressure of late January and early February, Madison divided his attention between his concern for the progress of ratification in Massachusetts and elsewhere and the notes and books on his desk before the fire in his room. Until he left for Virginia, he shared the writing evenly with Hamilton; of the sixty-four essays printed while Madison was in New York, he wrote twenty-nine, Hamilton thirty, and Jay five. In 1787 and 1788, though, *The Federalist* appeared in part in only a dozen papers outside New York state—a very small distribution compared, for example, to the more than fifty newspapers (of a total of about ninety in the states) that reprinted Franklin's final speech at the convention. Furthermore, *The Federalist* appeared *in toto* too late to be influential in many states and was too complex to be widely popular. Nevertheless, it helped importantly to make stronger and more consistent the arguments of federalist leaders and delegates in critical conventions from Massachusetts to South Carolina. *The Federalist* was remarkable for its speed of composition, brisk cogency, and overwhelming thoroughness.

Though some analysts have found in the parts of *The Federalist* written by its two principal authors very different political philosophies, the work is best understood as a whole and in its pressing context. Its explicit purpose, to persuade the people of New York and other states to ratify the new constitution, supplied the unifying theme of the work. The authors provided a full, balanced, and largely candid expression of their theoretical views on government, but of more immediate concern, they expounded the specific document before them, presented it to the public in the most favorable possible light, and met the most effective arguments of their opponents. The Constitution was, as the convention debates demonstrate fully, not Madison's notion of an ideal government, and Hamilton considered it an exceedingly imperfect form, worth supporting only because it was better than the existing Articles of Confederation. These doubts and reservations, of course, do not appear in *The Federalist*. The appeal of antifederalist arguments defending the powers of the states under the Articles caused the authors of *The Federalist* to soften their rather forthright nationalism, and to present the new constitution as a plan for a more federal and a less national government than each had sought, and to a lesser extent, thought had been formed during the summer of 1787. There are some differences in emphasis between the principal authors, especially in Madison's greater concern for representative republican government, and Hamilton's stronger emphasis on energy, but considering only what appears over the pseudonym Publius, the unity and consistency is impressive and significant.[14]

Hamilton set the theme for the work, and expressed "Publius' " sense of mission and enlightened outlook, when he wrote in the opening essay that "it seems to have been reserved to the people of this country, by their conduct and example, to decide the important question, whether societies of men are really capable or not, of establishing good government from reflection and choice, or whether they are forever destined to depend, for their political constitutions, on accident and force." The issue, in short, was whether or not the ideals of the Declaration of Independence were mere dreams—could they be embodied in a workable frame of government suitable for human beings as they existed in fact rather than in the speculations of "closet philosophers"? In the next eight essays, Jay exposed the fatal weaknesses of the United States in world affairs if it did not strengthen the Union, and Hamilton painted a similarly bleak picture domestically unless great changes were made. The first nine essays sought to banish any lingering, fanciful hope that the United States could prosper and survive in freedom under the weak, ineffective Articles of Confederation.

In Number 10 Madison summarized the argument—until this time he had not done so publicly—that a large republic was not a contradictory concept, as so many writers, leaning on Aristotle, Montesquieu, and a host of English radicals and dissenters, insisted. Unless the connection between a large nation and tyranny could be broken, the antifederalist argument that a stronger Union threatened republican principles would remain persuasive, perhaps even decisive. Madison asked his readers to consider the likely result of extending the representative principle to a large territory. He granted that this would result in great diversity of interests in the government, but then pointed out what other theorists had overlooked: in a system which fairly represented the people, this would *preserve* freedom rather than threaten it, because no one interest would be able to control the government; each interest—economic, religious, sectional, or whatever—would be a natural check on the domineering tendencies of others. Thus Madison made a virtue of human diversity and neutralized the selfishness of mankind.

Furthermore, a large republic would not be subject to the demagoguery so fatal to small democracies, because the representative principle would "refine" the expression of the people's consent, and the large extent of the country would prevent any faction (a self-interested, passion-dominated group, whether a minority or a majority of the people) from coalescing and exerting its will. Madison pointed out particularly that though the "republican principle" in a simple form could restrain minority factions, only a mixed government over a large territory could prevent "the public good and private rights" from being sacrificed to the "ruling passion or interest" of a majority faction. "Hence," he concluded, "it clearly appears, that the same advantage, which a Republic has over a Democracy, in controlling the effects of faction, is enjoyed by a large over a small Republic. . . . In the extent and proper structure of the Union . . . we behold a Republican remedy for the diseases most incident to Republican Government." Madison had thus turned the tables on the antifederalists: it was now up to them to refute his argument that a strong, enlarged Union, far from being the foe of freedom, was rather its only sure defense. Madison stated for the federalists the critically significant position that the power, energy, and size necessary for national survival and prosperity would not subvert the principles of the revolution. They were, in fact, essential to their fulfillment.

After Hamilton set forth the agricultural, commercial, and tax-gathering advantages of a stronger Union, Madison, in Number 14, upbraided his opponents for failing to meet the argument he had presented in Number 10. By citing Aristotle and Montesquieu on the dangers of large republics, the antifederalists "availed themselves of a prevailing prejudice . . . in order to supply by imaginary difficulties, the . . . solid objections" they seemed unable to produce. Madison then sought to clarify a troublesome point in eighteenth-century political thought. In a democracy, as the term was then used, he explained, "the people meet and exercise the government in person; in a republic they assemble and administer it by their representatives and agents. A democracy consequently will be confined to a small spot. A republic may be extended over a large region." The objections to applying the principle of consent to a large territory, however true for a democracy, were invalid for a republic. Even the westward extension of the nation, given the improvements likely in transportation, would not prevent the speedy and frequent assembly of representatives. Therefore Madison exhorted his countrymen to "hearken not to the voice which petulantly tells you that the form of government recommended for your adoption is a novelty in the political world . . . that it rashly attempts what it is impossible to accomplish. . . . Why is the experiment of an extended republic to be rejected merely because it may comprise what is new?" The nation and the world were indebted to the heroes of the American Revolution for "numerous innovations . . . in favor of private rights and public happiness." The remaining task was to persist in this bold spirit and correct the errors in the structure of the Union. Again Madison stated for the federalists the forward-looking position, seeking, with faith in the ingenuity of mankind, to give meaning and reality to the noblest and most humane sentiments of the day. Madison had contrasted sharply federalist confidence in republican virtue and in national greatness with antifederal timidity.

After Hamilton wrote the next three essays, on the specific deficiencies of the Articles of Confederation, he gave Madison his notes on the dreadful consequences of similar weakness in other confederacies. Then, using his own notes, "Of Ancient and Modern Confederacies," Madison outlined in three essays the pattern of anarchy followed by tyranny or foreign domination evident in the weak confederacies of ancient Greece, the Holy Roman Empire, and the Netherlands. The lesson of these experiences was unequivocal, he asserted, and ought therefore to be regarded as "conclusive and sacred." A strong Union, exerting itself directly upon the people and not merely on the states, was essential to domestic happiness and national dignity.

The groundwork was now complete. "Publius" had demonstrated thoroughly and systematically the general efficacy of an extensive union. In view of the tight ratification contest, Hamilton and Madison pressed ahead to defend each article of the Constitution. Delaware, New Jersey, and Pennsylvania had ratified, but the issue was in doubt in many states, and the Convention pattern seemed to be one of clause-by-clause debate of the new constitution. Federalist delegates would need every argument "Publius" could provide to allay the prospects of tyranny and corruption the antifederalists found lurking in its every provision: the states would be abolished; a standing army worse than Cromwell's would arise; the President would become a monarch; the people would be impoverished by taxation; Congress would favor the commerce of one section over that of another; because there was no bill of rights, federal courts would conduct inquisitions; and so on. In sixteen essays, largely on the taxing and military authority of the federal government, Hamilton discussed the powers of Congress and the President most complained of by the antifederalists. He argued that these powers would not result in tyranny, but rather were the necessary foundation of energetic, stable government, which was itself the only sure defense against the twin dangers of anarchy

and despotism. Hamilton was at his best—lucid, forceful, and earnest—
expounding the requirements of effective government.

Madison then took his turn and wrote the next twenty-one essays. In
Number 37, after reminding his readers of the extraordinarily difficult
questions faced in the Federal Convention, especially that of "combining
the requisite stability and energy in Government, with the inviolable
attention due to liberty, and to the Republican form," Madison addressed
the query so often raised by his opponents: was the Constitution "strictly
republican"? The essential criterion of a republican government was
that it derive "all its powers directly or indirectly from the great body
of the people." The Constitution conformed "in the most rigid sense"
to this standard, since nowhere did it provide an office or bestow a
power not resting ultimately on the people. In fact, he observed, in
numerous ways the Constitution was more strictly republican than were
the constitutions of some of the existing state governments. In distinguishing between a democracy and a republic, Madison (and his compatriots, whether federal or antifederal) very carefully *equated* them
insofar as each embodied the principle of consent. Thus, in Lockean
terms there was no moral distinction between those who favored a democracy and those who favored a republic; all were wholly faithful to
the *sine qua non*. They disputed whether direct or representative consent
was more likely to result in good government, which form would be
most tumultuous, which would best reflect the public will, and so on.
Therefore assertions that those who disparaged democracy were neo-
aristocrats seeking to subvert rule by the people, and that the founders
intended to establish a "republic" only partly responsible to the public
will, though in a way accurate, missed the point. No one, in fact, in
eighteenth-century terms, would have supposed it either desirable or
possible for a country as large as the United States to be a democracy.

In the next essay Madison examined the charge that the new constitution established a national, not a federal, government, a charge the more
confusing because the supporters of the Constitution, by calling themselves "federalists," attached that name to the form of government established by the Constitution. In fact, in 1788, a federal government was
universally understood to be one in which sovereign states acted as the
participating units, a form then and ever since often referred to as a
confederacy. (In 1788, "federation" and "confederation" were virtually
synonymous terms.) Since the people of the United States by and large
associated the federal form with the preservation of their liberties, the
proponents of the new constitution were tactically shrewd if not strictly
accurate in calling themselves "federalists." Madison admitted this in
Number 39 when he noted that the Constitution was partly national and
partly federal. The House of Representatives, elected by the people was

national, while the Senate, elected by the states, was *federal.* The direct action of the laws of Congress on the people was a *national* characteristic, while the limited extent of Congressional jurisdiction was a *federal* feature. The election of the President mixed federal and national principles. The Constitution was therefore, Madison concluded, neither strictly national nor strictly federal, but a *composite,* unprecedented perhaps, but not in any way unrepublican. Though admitting this composite quality was a tactical liability, Madison hoped the innovating spirit of the country would approve the Constitution's unique characteristics. Though it did not provide for a democracy, it was strictly republican, and therefore completely consistent with the principle of consent, and it was a composite of the national and federal forms, seeking to blend the best features of each into a government especially suited to the requirements and "genius" of the United States.

In the next two essays (40 and 41) Madison interrupted his exposition to meet two accusations made repeatedly by the antifederalists. In answer to the charge that the Federal Convention had exceeded its legal powers, Madison pointed out its broad, or at least ambiguous, authority, and quoting the Declaration of Independence, urged the right of the people to "abolish or alter their governments as to them shall seem most likely to effect their safety and happiness." Then, since the antifederalists continued to press the point, Madison returned to the insinuations about military despotism and standing armies Hamilton had earlier exposed. Far from being the *cause* of standing armies, Madison asserted, only a strong Union able to preserve external and internal tranquility could save the country "from as many standing armies as it may split into States or Confederacies." Small, quarreling principalities, easily the prey of aggressive neighbors, were more likely to incur oppressive military burdens than were stable and respected nations.

Madison next inquired whether the powers given to the general government were necessary and proper and whether they in fact threatened the states with extinction. In three long essays (42–4) Madison paraded all the absurdities of the Confederation he had so long railed against in the Continental Congress. Every provision granting power to Congress or denying it to the states was absolutely essential to avoid the errors and deficiencies of the past. Madison's long experience in Congress gave overwhelming force to his exposition of these clauses.

To deny that the new constitution did not "eclipse" the states was more delicate for Madison. Though less ardently nationalist than Hamilton, and deeply attached to Virginia, Madison had for eight years been disgusted with the abuse of power by the states and had in the convention proposed far more severe limitations on them than were finally approved. Yet the politics of the ratification debate obliged the federalists to resist stoutly the charge that the new constitution reduced the

states to impotence. After he reminded his readers that any useful structure of government, whether founded on state or national sovereignty,
had to promote "the public good," Madison argued (in Number 45) that
the provisions of the new constitution and the experience of other confederacies both suggested that the states were more likely to encroach on
the general government than the general government on the states. "The
powers delegated by the proposed Constitution to the Federal Government are few and defined. Those which are to remain in the State
Governments are numerous and indefinite. . . . The powers reserved to
the several States will extend to all the objects, which, in the ordinary
course of affairs, concern the lives, liberties and properties of the people;
and the internal order, improvement, and prosperity of the State." Next
Madison pointed out the many devices available to the states for resisting
federal authority, most of which have been used repeatedly, especially
before the Civil War, in just the way Madison foresaw. Though in 1788,
and frequently thereafter, he did not fully approve of these "weapons"
left to the states, he recognized they were part of the Constitution
(nullification and secession, however, were *not*) and conceded the right
of the states to use them.

In the next five essays (46–50), Madison sought to untangle the crucial but often misunderstood question of separation and balance of
powers. All revered the concept, he stated, but the antifederalists had so
distorted it that any government conforming to their interpretation
would be unworkable. The great authority on separation, Montesquieu,
had for his model the British constitution, which in fact embodied far
more mixing of powers than did the proposed American one. Furthermore, Madison asked, how could the great departments of government
check and balance one another if they were completely separated? The
antifederalists complained that the presidential veto power violated the
separation of legislative and executive functions, that Congress should
not be empowered to impeach judges, and so on. At the same time, they
claimed to find numerous opportunities for tyranny and oppression resulting from insufficient *checks* on the exercise of power. Madison
showed that all the state constitutions, so much appealed to by the antifederalists, contained provisions giving the departments mutual checks
similar to those provided for in the new federal constitution. Shrewdly,
he quoted Jefferson's strictures on legislative supremacy in the Virginia
constitution to refute antifederal invocation of that concept, and he
examined at length the difficulties caused in Pennsylvania by a similar
supremacy. The opponents, Madison declared, engaged in slogan-
mongering, misunderstood the great writers on government, and used
contradictory arguments.

The real problem, he asserted, was to so contrive "the internal structure of the government, as that its constituent parts may, by their mutual relations, be the means of keeping each other in their mutual places." *Real* balances, not verbal declarations, were necessary to assure proper separation of powers. Besides being able to control society at large, a republican government also had to be obliged to control itself. In the division of powers between the states and the general government and in the intricate, prudent provision for checks and balances between the departments of government, the diverse interests and private rights of the people would find their only secure protection. Madison branded mere statements that powers should be separate as useless "parchment barriers"; only properly devised mechanisms of government, ingeniously arranged to afford meaningful leverages, would provide the flexibility, fluidity, and dispersal of power the preservation of freedom required (Number 51). To Madison, the *effect* of specific provisions in the federal system on the actual forces at work in the extended republic of the United States was critical; pious phrases and shibboleths were not.

Having thus explained the powers and general structure of the federal government, "Publius," still using Madison's pen, turned (in 52–6) to the specific parts, first the House of Representatives. Since antifederalists in Massachusetts had thundered against the alleged "aristocratic" features of the Constitution, Madison needed to emphasize the purely republican nature of the lower house. He noted first that the electorate of the House was fixed on as broad a base as that of the much-admired lower houses of the state legislatures. Though his confident statement that "it cannot be feared that the people of the States will . . . abridge the right [to vote]" proved too sanguine in Virginia and elsewhere a century or more later, it met effectively current antifederalist insinuations. Essay Number 53 disposed of the bugaboo that without annual elections tyranny would soon follow: states with legislative elections every two or four years had as much "rational liberty" and were as well governed as those with annual elections. Then, in three narrowly polemical essays (54–6), Madison defended the three-fifths ratio, the number of Representatives assigned to each state, and the high ratio of people to Representatives, all features under heavy antifederalist attack.

He explored the basic issue in responding to charges that the Representatives would be "most likely to aim at an ambitious sacrifice of the many to the aggrandizement of the few." After pointing out, as "Publius" had to do again and again, that such cynicism and fearfulness about representatives to be elected by the people "strikes at the very root of republican government," Madison examined (in Number 57) the goals of representative government and the prospects of achieving them in the proposed House of Representatives. The aims were to "obtain for rulers, men who possess most wisdom to discern, and most virtue to pursue the common good of the society; and . . . to take the most effectual precautions for keeping them virtuous, whilst they continue to hold their public trust." The republican principle required that "the great body of the people" be free to choose as a representative anyone "whose merit may recommend him to the esteem and confidence of his country." The vital question was whether this principle would encourage selection of wise, virtuous men who would remain so in office. Madison probed for factors that might yield the desired result. Representatives would ordinarily be above normal wisdom and virtue in order to be distinguished by their fellow citizens for election; sentiments of honor and fidelity were not wholly lacking in human nature and would perhaps be in more than normal abundance in elected representatives; vanity and pride would impel some men to serve earnestly in office; and most important, frequent elections would require a faithfulness to the public trust. Though some might scorn such observations as visionary, republican government had no foundation other than such human possibilities. "What are we to say," Madison asked, undercutting hundreds of pages of antifederalist croaking, "to the men who profess the most flaming zeal for Republican Government, yet boldly impeach the fundamental principle of it; who pretend to be champions for the right and the capacity of the people to chuse their own rulers, yet maintain that they will prefer those only who will immediately and infallibly betray the trust committed to them?" Though antifederalist charges that the House of Representatives provided no real, substantial representation for the people probed genuine difficulties, there was nevertheless a negative quality to their fears about popular elections, which Madison here relentlessly and clearly exposed.

After one more essay (Number 58), on enlarging the House of Representatives as the country grew, Madison rested for a few days while Hamilton, again back in New York after attending court in Albany, contributed three essays defending the right of Congress, in the last resort, to be the regulator and judge of its own elections. Madison then submitted his last two essays, Numbers 62 and 63, on the Senate, as he prepared to leave for Virginia. Again he was obliged to defend a body whose composition and method of election he had opposed vehemently in the convention. As to election by the state legislatures, he observed merely that that mode seemed "most congenial with the public opinion." Refusing again to express arguments to which he did not subscribe, on the equality of the states in the Senate, Madison noted simply that this provision was known to be the result of a compromise in the convention, and should therefore, in the spirit of amity and mutual concession always necessary among free men, be accepted by all. In defending the notion of a senate in general, composed of a few men with long terms of office, Madison resumed earnest argument. The Senate would check the

passions and impulses of the lower house and lend continuity and stability
to the government. Like the idealized senate of the Roman republic, so
familiar to men reared on Livy and Cicero, it would be the place where
long-range national interests and the common good of all could receive
calm, rational discussion. The House of Representatives, moreover,
would be able to check Senatorial attempts at usurpation or corruption.

Called home to contest an unexpectedly close election to the Virginia
ratifying convention, Madison left the remaining portion of *The Federalist* (notably sections on the federal judiciary and the absence of a bill
of rights) in Hamilton's willing and capable hands. The two men had
helped significantly to sustain and reinforce the arguments being used by
federalists throughout the country on behalf of the Constitution, their
avowed purpose in undertaking the exacting series of essays. More important, however, they had given the new Constitution the exposition
which has ever since been considered uniquely authoritative. The work
was so viewed even in the lifetime of its authors. Jefferson proclaimed
The Federalist the "best commentary on the principles of government
which ever was written." Whether or not the work deserves this superla-
tive, it displays cogently Madison's political thought, for he wrote his
contributions at a peak of concern and with reference to a specific
document. Again and again he had to assess the difficult particulars
ordinarily overlooked in more theoretical works.[15]

When Madison returned to New York in September 1787, he expected
to stay there, serving in the Continental Congress and acting as a strategist and propagandist in the ratification contest. At first he thought it
improper for members of the Federal Convention to sit as judges of their
own work in the state ratifying conventions, but as antifederalist sentiment strengthened, Madison reconsidered. Rhode Island was hopeless
from the beginning, and it became increasingly apparent that New York
would oppose. If Patrick Henry exerted his often irresistible influence in
Virginia, and if North Carolina followed her example, the margin became perilously close. Though the victory in Massachusetts, known in
New York in mid-February 1788, was heartening, its narrowness nevertheless seemed an ill omen, and in early March news that only an adjournment without a vote had prevented defeat in New Hampshire further
alarmed the federalist high command in New York. Madison reported to
Washington that the prospects made "a very disagreeable subject of communication," and another Virginia delegate wrote that he feared these
events "operating together . . . will prevent the noble fabrick from being
erected."[16]

Madison's news from home also became bad as the winter wore on.
By November 1787 he had received many requests that he be a member
of the Virginia convention so he might correct misconceptions about the

new constitution. "For God's sake," pleaded one associate, "do not disappoint the anxious expectations of your friends and let me add of your Country." On November 8 Madison put his local "political machine" into low gear by asking his brother Ambrose to inform the people of the county, "as my father or yourself may judge best," that he "would be honored" to accept an appointment to the convention. Madison learned somewhat later that "slanders" against the new constitution had aroused opposition to it even in Orange County; he was urged to be home "some time before the election," obviously to campaign. In January 1788 Henry Lee, assessing the opposition in Orange, considered it formidable enough to suggest that "several counties in Kentucky" would be glad to elect Madison should he fear defeat at home. At the end of the month Madison received particulars from his father: Colonel Thomas Barbour, a neighbor and long-time friend of the Madisons, had been infected by antifederalist propaganda and had publicly declared himself an opposition candidate. Most alarming, Barbour had a considerable following among the numerous Baptists in Orange who were offended that the Constitution contained no guarantee of religious liberty. At the February court day in Orange, Madison's cousin observed, there was "much talk amongst the people about the Constitution, the Baptists and ignorant part of them against it." By mid-February Madison had determined to go to Orange and even campaign if necessary, despite "the laborious and very irksome discussions" entailed, the danger of jeopardizing "greatly prized" friendships, the disagreeable appearance of soliciting votes for himself, and the long journey required "at a very unpleasant season."[17]

Madison left New York March 4, and after a week in Philadelphia, he hurried southward, reaching Mount Vernon on March 18, in time to enjoy dinner at Washington's hospitable table. The two men had not seen each other since the Federal Convention had adjourned, and though they had been in close touch by mail, there was much to discuss, especially the increasingly critical situation facing the federalists. Washington interrupted his spring planting, fence mending, and other farm chores to "remain at home all day" to talk with his serious guest. After the cold winter in New York, Madison enjoyed the early signs of spring along the Potomac as he and his host visited in the pleasant parlors of Mount Vernon. Madison persuaded Washington to make even clearer his wholehearted support of the new constitution, and continued the delicate, subtle task of preparing the general for his indispensable role as the first leader of the new government. The years from 1786 to 1789 marked the height of the intimate association between the two men. Madison stopped regularly at Mount Vernon, often for several days, on his journeys back and forth to Philadelphia and New York, and he gained Washington's confidence as the best-informed, wisest, and most effective political leader in the country. Anxious to reach Orange, Madison took Washington's carriage the next morning to meet the stage at Colchester. Washington wrote John Langdon several days later that "I am still strong in the expectation of [the Constitution] being adopted here notwithstanding the unjust and uncandid representation, which have been made by the opponents to inflame the minds of the people and prejudice them against it."[18]

On his way from Fredericksburg to Orange, with the election now but a few days away, Madison stopped to see the influential Baptist preacher John Leland, who had drawn a vigorous memorial protesting, among other things, the failure of the new constitution to guarantee religious freedom. He told Madison he could not support it unless an appropriate amendment was added. The meeting was cordial, since the fiery preacher and the soft-spoken politician had worked together in Richmond in 1784 and 1785 to defeat Patrick Henry's plan for state support of religious instruction (see Chapter VIII). Furthermore, as a leader of the great Baptist revival in Virginia that had accompanied the revolution, Leland knew very well of Madison's early and continuing support of religious liberty. Since the two men agreed completely in principle, they needed only to reach an understanding on how best to secure the maximum protection for freedom of conscience. Madison pointed out that demanding prior amendments would serve only to defeat the Constitution, thus losing not only the admitted advantages of the new government but any chance for advance on the religious question as well. In return for Leland's promise to withdraw his objections, Madison reaffirmed what he and other federalists had increasingly agreed to: they would support a bill of rights, including a firm article on religious freedom, as amendments to the Constitution *after* its ratification. Assured of Leland's good will, Madison hurried on, to be home in time for the election. He had not seen his family since his departure for the Annapolis Convention more than eighteen months ago. Those months, the most productive and important in his life, had placed him among the great leaders of the revolutionary era.[19]

At the traditional court day election, the fourth Tuesday of the month (March 25), planters and tradesmen, despite a "very cold wind," gathered early, and "Colonel" Madison, Francis Taylor noted, "addressed himself in a speech to the people in defense of the new Constitution, and there appeared much satisfaction." As the voters filed before the sheriff one by one to declare their preference, it was soon apparent that Madison would be an easy winner; he received 202 votes, to 56 for Thomas Barbour. Madison was doubtless further pleased that the other defeated antifederalist was Charles Porter, who eleven years earlier had beaten Madison by treating the voters to large amounts of liquor. It was revolutionary indeed if words had replaced whisky as the decisive factor in

Virginia elections. When other Virginia federalists learned of Madison's victory, they congratulated him on having turned "the sinners of Orange from their wicked ways," and foiled "some unwarrantable proceedings." The encouraging result confirmed Madison's conviction that ignorance and antifederalist distortions were the main foes of the new constitution. The need, then, was to explain to the people.[20]

At Montpelier for two months, Madison enjoyed spring rides and rambles about the countryside amid the redbud and fruit blossoms, and in a burst of social activity which distracted diarist Taylor from his usual fixations on weather and the price of crops, the now-distinguished politician exchanged visits with his neighbors. During a cool, pleasant spell in April, Madison and his father toured leisurely about the country, staying overnight with cousin Charles Taylor, Colonel Lawrence Taliaferro, and Captain Charles Conway. In early May they had a big dinner at uncle James Taylor's, where Madison visited with cousin Lucy Taylor Balmain, wife of the Winchester clergyman who six years later would marry him to Dolley Payne Todd. On May 14, Madison and his intimate friend William Moore examined the scholars at "Mr. Goodlett's school." Visiting around home also gave Madison more opportunity than he had had in New York, absorbed in his books and notes writing *The Federalist*, to sense that ratification depended on more than arguments over political theory. Though the severe winter had caused "short crops" of grain, prices remained steady. Tobacco, on the other hand, fell so low that planters on both sides of the Potomac had trouble paying their debts. Maryland antifederalists sought to use this circumstance to frighten debtors about the clauses in the Constitution proscribing paper currency, but generally the federalists were able to blame the bad conditions on the weaknesses of the Articles of Confederation.[21]

More trouble brewed in Kentucky (still part of Virginia), where Patrick Henry had used the aborted Jay-Gardoqui agreement (see Chapter IX) as proof that a strengthened federal union would soon close the Mississippi River to American trade. Unless this insinuation could be squelched, the expected federalist majority in Kentucky would vanish. Madison wrote a long letter to Kentuckian John Brown, then in New York, to dissuade him from writing home too darkly about the prospects of Mississippi navigation under the new government. Madison stated the essence of his argument to George Nicholas, a Virginian about to move to Kentucky: "The successors [of the old Congress] if the new government take place, will be able to hold a language which no nation having possessions in America will think it prudent to disregard; and which will be able to have a due effect on Spain in particular." Foreshadowing the Monroe Doctrine, Madison always emphasized the vastly increased power to act positively in the public interest which the new constitution would make possible. He also noticed earlier a pointed reminder of the disastrous result of a weak union in news from Europe: the Dutch patriot movement had collapsed in the face of French duplicity, Prussian pressure, and English bribes. "The want of Union and a capable Government," Madison observed, "is the source of all [the Dutch] calamities; and particularly of that dependence on foreign powers which is dishonorable to their character as it is destructive of their tranquility." Rather than *fear* the international transactions of a strengthened union, Madison urged his countrymen to see its power as their only salvation in foreign affairs.[22]

To further bolster the federalist cause in Virginia, Madison ordered a large supply of the first volume of the newly printed book edition of *The Federalist* for distribution among delegates to the convention, who, George Nicholas asserted, were "without information" about the new constitution. Madison also wrote friends in Maryland and South Carolina, urging them to carry through as soon as possible their expected federalist victories to increase the pressure on Virginia to join her southern neighbors in the new government. Ratification in those states in April and May encouraged Madison to think that "the nice balance of the parties" in Virginia might be tipped in favor of the federalists. He continued his delicate effort to bring Governor Randolph into the federalist fold, urging that Randolph's plan for a second convention would play into the hands of Patrick Henry and others "who secretly aim at disunion." Since nothing was "more remote" from Randolph's intentions, Madison insinuated that Randolph's own purposes would be best served if he joined a "coalition among all the real federalists" to espouse ratification of the Constitution as it stood, with amendments to be recommended for later adoption. By late April Madison's campaign had been successful enough for him to report that "the Governor . . . cannot properly be classed with" the enemies of the Constitution. As the Virginia convention opened in early June, Randolph was an avowed federalist, and Madison felt otherwise in a favorable position to confront Patrick Henry and his allies in the most difficult and critical debate of Madison's public career.[23]

When Madison reached Richmond the evening of June 2, the date set for the meeting of the convention, he discovered to his surprise that a quorum had gathered on time and had already elected Edmund Pendleton chairman. The importance of the convention, and perhaps the annual races of the Richmond Jockey Club being held at the same time, had caused a rare promptness in attendance at a Virginia political gathering. Though Pendleton's perennial chairmanship of Virginia conventions meant his election was not actually a federalist victory, Madison was pleased to have the respected old judge, now a staunch friend of the Constitution, in the chair. Madison also learned that the assembly hall in the State House had proved too small for the 170 delegates, so the convention had moved across the street to the "New Academy on Schockoe Hill," a hall built two years earlier by Alexander Quesnay as a place for an elegant, French-style school as well as "balls, concerts, theatrical and other public entertainments." Despite the opposition of worriers over public morality, the famous Henry and Hallam Theatrical Company had presented *Romeo and Juliet, The Merchant of Venice, School for Scandal, The Beggar's Opera,* and other popular plays in the Quesnay building in the two years before the convention gathered there. Madison was familiar with plans for the large, wooden building, but he had not seen it until he entered on the morning of June 3 to take part in the convention.[24]

Madison's first two days on the floor were ones of important, perhaps crucial, advantages gained for the federalists. They surprised the antifederalists by agreeing that the convention should debate the Constitution clause by clause. With his unmatched knowledge, Madison would be at his best in such discussion and might be able to convince by the force of his arguments the few uncommitted delegates whose votes would be decisive in the evenly balanced convention. The motion to proceed in committee of the whole both prevented the convention from taking any hasty final votes under the spell of Henry's oratory and added chairman Pendleton to the federalist advocates on the floor. He intervened sharply when Henry charged that the Federal Convention had exceeded its authority. The business of the Virginia convention, Pendleton said, was to judge the results, not investigate the powers, of the Federal Convention, and moreover, under republican theory the people had a right to form their government in any way they saw fit. Henry retreated immediately, unwilling to challenge Pendleton, the peerless parliamentarian, on a procedural question. When it appeared that Henry and Mason took "different and awkward ground" in opposing the Constitution, Madison could not suppress being "a good deal elated by the existing prospect," as he wrote Washington in the first of his careful reports to Mount Vernon on the progress of the convention. Both sides conceded that the now wavering delegates from the Ohio valley would be decisive. Madison wrote that they were "extremely tainted" and were being subjected privately to seductive appeals to their local prejudices, while an antifederalist foresaw victory if he could win over the delegates from four counties in what is now West Virginia.[25]

The next day (June 5) the delegates sparred cautiously at first. Randolph dispelled lingering antifederalist hopes by giving unequivocal support to the Constitution. Paraphrasing Madison's argument in *The Federalist,* as advocates of the Constitution were to do repeatedly throughout the convention, George Nicholas began the clause-by-clause debate by defending the mode of elections to the House of Representatives. Henry and Mason ignored the rules by assaulting the Constitution generally and by skipping down to an attack on the federal taxing power. Henry Lee, the famous "Light-Horse Harry" of the revolution, an intimate of Madison's since their college days at Princeton, and now a vehement federalist, felt it necessary, as did Pendleton, to reply to the sweeping antifederalist assaults before resuming the clause-by-clause debate. This unfortunate strategy gave Henry exactly the opening he sought: the discussion had become amorphous, the agenda seemed forgotten, and the delegates were restless, perhaps waiting to hear a compelling voice.

"The forest-born Demosthenes," as his first biographer inaccurately dubbed Henry, arose and began a passionate oration lasting the rest of the day. He decried the "consolidating" tendency of the new government and paid some attention to the specific provisions of the Constitution, but principally he thundered emotionally about endangered rights and the threat of tyranny the people of Virginia would face if they ratified. Trial by jury, the cherished right of "our glorious forefathers of Great Britain" (strange language from one who thirteen years before had pledged "liberty or death" when faced with so-called British justice), would be forefeited; many other traditional rights of Englishmen would perish; local control of the militia would vanish; and federal tax collectors and sheriffs would infest the land, plundering and oppressing the poor. Worst of all, the new constitution would lead to monarchy. Henry orated so grandiloquently that the shorthand reporter, overcome by the torrent of words and the magnificently effective grimaces and gestures, recorded simply that Henry "strongly and pathetically expatiated on the probability of the President's enslaving America, and the horrid consequences that must result." Henry concluded with a shrewd tactic he had used often in prerevolutionary tirades against British measures: though disclaiming any thoughts of disunion himself, he asserted such was "the language of thousands," thus leading his listeners to entertain exactly these thoughts themselves.[26]

The performance, marvelous in its own right, acquired heightened force from the impression, cleverly cultivated by Henry, that this was his last great effort to defend with his matchless voice the rights and liberties of the people of Virginia. A few of his listeners had heard Henry's electrifying assault on the Stamp Act twenty-three years earlier and many had heard his ringing, roaring denunciations of the tea tax, the "coercive" Acts, and other measures. These speeches, of course, had placed Virginia in the van of the revolution and made Henry its most popular civilian hero. Dozens of the delegates had sat in the House of Delegates, spellbound by his words, and accustomed to finding them irresistible when the votes were tallied. Furthermore, Henry's oration, typical for him, and characteristically antifederal, used the familiar lan-

guage of a century of English and American radical Whiggism. He
paraded all the shibboleths of the struggles of Parliament and the dissenting churches against monarchy and establishment. Since those campaigns had been waged *against* the powers of government, the slogans
were readily used against a constitution proposing an increase in the
authority of government. Listening with apprehension and perhaps even
despair, Madison knew the gauntlet had been thrown down. If he was
forced to argue abstractly *for* the authority of government in opposing.
Henry's denunciations, the federalist cause was doomed. Madison saw
that his task was to bring Henry down to particulars, to engage him in a
point-by-point examination of whether the horrors he foresaw were
in fact inherent in the structure and powers of the new government.
Though Henry had often overwhelmed such reasoned efforts in the
past, the attempt nevertheless had to be made.

The federalists talked that evening of their next steps. With Henry's
words ringing in the delegates' ears, it seemed hopeless to resume the
clause-by-clause discussion immediately. Henry had to be answered, lest
his charges and insinuations seem true by default. The federalists were
convinced that ultimately they would have to rely on Madison's un-
rivaled command of the issues, but the contrast in lung power and his-
trionics between him and Henry seemed too stark to be set immediately
adjacent. Seeking also to capitalize further on Randolph's recent conversion to their cause, the federalists decided that he—big, eloquent, and
prestigeful—could best counteract the *impression* as well as the argument
of Henry's speech. Then Madison would make his first major contribution to the debate, undertaking to refute Henry point by point, and
hopefully reviving in the convention the calm, dispassionate atmosphere
the federalists saw was essential for them.[27]

The next morning, as Randolph sat down, Madison arose, diffidently
and if we may judge from his usual procedure, with his notes in his hat.
He was too short to be seen from all parts of the house, and he spoke in
tones so low that the stenographer "could not hear distinctly." The only
sign of Madison's intense concern for the debate was the "more or less
rapid and foreward seesaw motion of his body." He quickly warmed to
his task, however, and soon spoke so that the recorder managed to put
down his remarks fully and clearly. Eschewing at the outset Henry's
declamatory tactics ("professions of attachment to the public good . . .
ought not to govern . . . us now"), Madison pleaded for an examination of
the Constitution "on its own merits solely." He hoped, looking at Henry,
"that gentlemen, in displaying their abilities on this occasion, instead of
giving opinions, and making assertions, will condescend to prove and
demonstrate, by a fair and regular discussion." Following his own advice,
Madison asked the convention to consider Henry's charge that the Con-

situation "endangered the public liberty." Exactly how and in what way? Madison queried. What clauses, on careful examination, could fairly be expected to result in tyranny? Consider the assertion that tyranny usually resulted from usurpation of power by rulers who then would not relinquish it. However true this might be in monarchical or oligarchical societies, Madison said, approaching ground he knew better than any man in America, in republics all experience pointed another way. "On a candid examination of history, we shall find that turbulence, violence, and abuse of power, by the majority trampling on the rights of the minority have produced factions and commotions, which, in republics, have more frequently than any other cause, produced despotism." Henry had failed, Madison pointed out, to see a vital distinction: ". . . by this [Constitution] powers are not given to any particular set of men, they are in the hands of the people." Here, therefore, a grant of power was not despotism, but rather was a fulfillment of the principle of consent. To clinch his point, Madison reviewed for the convention "the various means whereby nations had lost their liberties," correcting, as he went along, Henry's misconceptions of Swiss and English history.

Madison also exposed Henry's illogic. The orator had viewed with alarm the provision that three quarters of the states must approve amendments. What, he had asked, with the air of protecting a sacred principle, had happened to majority rule? On the other hand, he had protested against the ratification process itself, which permitted nine states to change the government, thus violating the clause in the Articles of Confederation requiring *unanimous* consent for alterations. Had the federalists no regard for sacred principles? he had asked. Did they cast aside lawful procedures, as they seemed inclined to do, when it suited their suspicious purposes? Madison reminded the delegates of the humiliation and iniquity the Union had suffered because one tiny state, Rhode Island, had again and again used this clause to thwart the other twelve; then he observed pointedly that it was Henry and his followers, not the federalists, who seemed determined to permit "a trifling minority" to bind the majority. Such, at least, would be the case if the Articles of Confederation remained the frame of the union. This exchange perfectly illustrated Madison's problem and method in debate. Though there was some point to Henry's argument, he also declaimed endlessly that the Constitution violated this or that aspect of republican doctrine, without attention to whether his denunciations were consistent or whether, if heeded, *any* practical structure of government was possible. Madison had to challenge and deflate cogently enough to lift the veil from Henry's enveloping rhetoric.

While urging that federal control over the army and militia was necessary in order to insure a proper respect among foreign nations, Madison reminded his listeners, especially those from the Ohio valley, that during the revolution American claims to the Mississippi had been endangered only when certain Southern states had sought to barter navigation rights in exchange for Spanish aid to defend their territories (see Chapter VI). What, Madison asked, would prevent weak states from finding themselves again in that position? Obviously, only a strong union could properly defend American claims in the West. Delegates turned anxiously to see the reaction of the Kentuckians. If they accepted this agrument, federalist victory was virtually assured.

Madison concluded with patient arguments about taxing power, consolidation of the states, and the nature of the House of Representatives, taken directly from *The Federalist*. As he sat down, he reminded his listeners that they need not be frightened by Henry's parade of bogeymen. If the patriotism of the people continued, they would long enjoy their liberties. Federalist Bushrod Washington (Madison told Jefferson that he was "considered as a young gentleman of talents") wrote his uncle at Mount Vernon that Madison spoke "with such force of reasoning, and a display of such irresistible truths, that opposition seemed to have quitted the field. However, I am not so sanguine as to trust appearances, or even to flatter myself that he made many converts. A few I have been confidently informed he did influence, who were decidedly in the opposition." With long experience in how seldom cogent speeches changed men's minds, Madison shared young Washington's doubts, but he took heart from the careful attention he had received. Henry's passionate oratory of the day before had not stampeded the delegates. The federalists would have an opportunity to present their case.[28]

Sensing that further remarks on the flaws in the existing Union would be useful, Madison the next day resumed a favorite subject: the absurdities of government under the Articles of Confederation. He outlined the paralysis at home and disgrace abroad that had been the lot of the United States since their adoption. It was sheer fantasy to suppose, as the antifederalists did, that the United States could exist indefinitely in peace and freedom under the Articles. Then, rather abruptly, Madison ended his speech. Worn out from two long sessions of public speaking, and perhaps upset by the strain of the closely divided convention, he had to leave the assembly, and spent the next three days in bed, suffering from a "bilious indisposition." Even writing was "scarcely practicable and very injurious," he reported. Though by this time Madison had overcome the sickliness of his early manhood and was able to endure long periods of exacting labor, as his performance the previous summer in Philadelphia showed, he tended throughout his life to come down with "bilious indispositions" at times of tension and strain, especially during the hot months. He could not have served so continuously in public office or lived to be eighty-five without a fundamentally sound constitution, but he never displayed the boundless vitality of some of his more robust colleagues and had always to guard himself against undue strain and exposure.[29]

Luckily there were many able federalists to carry the debate during Madison's illness. Henry Lee, George Nicholas, and Edmund Randolph continued to parry the jibes of Henry, Mason, and William Grayson, and younger members began to join in, notably James Monroe against and John Marshall for the Constitution. Madison later remarked that Marshall had shown "a great deal of ability" when he entered the debates. George Nicholas, so grotesquely fat that Madison once laughed until tears came to his eyes at a caricature representing Nicholas "as a plum pudding with legs on it," battered antifederal inconsistencies, and with his keen wit, managed more often than any other federalist to meet Henry on his own ground. Though still "extremely feeble," Madison returned to the convention, with careful outline notes in his hat, on June 11, and was soon on his feet, swaying back and forth, defending the direct taxing power of the proposed government. Henry played on fears of this clause repeatedly. Unless it was defended forcefully, vital votes would probably be lost. In a typical performance, examining and refuting all the alleged objections, Madison argued that the power was necessary, practical, safe, and economical. Though the subject was technical and undramatic, in this long speech, and in another one on the same subject the next day, Madison laid out, for any delegate seriously concerned, the most plausible significance of the power of direct taxation: it would enable the people, through their elected representatives, to command equitably the resources of the nation for the general welfare. He also pleaded again that the convention proceed in an orderly fashion so "we can finish . . . in one week [rather] than one month."[30]

Perhaps appalled at Madison's invincible preparation in clause-by-clause debate, on June 12 Henry and Mason continued their sweeping random attacks, seeking always to revive and strengthen doubts and fears they noted in a delegate's puzzled face or anxious queries. Therefore, Madison said irritably, despite his earnestness to proceed with the "regular discussion," it was necessary to answer Henry's miscellaneous objections. Madison protested first against antifederalist insinuations that Jefferson was on their side. Aware that the delegates knew he was Jefferson's most intimate correspondent, Madison denied the claim categorically. "I believe, that were that gentleman now on this floor, he would be for the adoption of this constitution." Specifically, Madison asserted, Jefferson would favor the federal taxing power, "because it enables the government to carry on its operations." Madison then reminded the delegates, indirectly but unmistakably, that the absent Virginian of most towering influence (Washington) strongly favored the new constitution. Next he neutralized Henry's protests that the Constitution contained no statement on freedom of religion by alluding to the orator's support four years earlier of a tax for religious education, in spite of the sweeping clause in the Virginia Bill of Rights proclaiming liberty of conscience. Mere declarations would less effectively promote freedom of religion than the "multiplicity of sects" to be included in the strengthened Union, which would have the power to block moves such as that Henry himself had sponsored. Madison then pointed out that antifederal cries against the cost of maintaining so many offices of government and pleas for more representatives were contradictory. In the five minutes before he sat down, Madison scored Henry's inconsistencies on the secrecy of proceedings in Congress, the Mississippi question, the collection of taxes, the activities of stockjobbers, and the dominance of landed or commercial interests in the proposed government. If taken seriously and altogether, Henry's fears made government itself impossible.[31]

The next day, Friday the thirteenth, and near the end of two weeks' debate, Henry and Mason had by and large maintained an air of turbulent apprehension. They returned to the sensitive Mississippi question, and, during a "Hail Storm [that] made the House . . . thoroughly wet," painted lurid pictures of Spanish emissaries distributing gold to Congressmen to betray the West. Madison took the floor again to set the record straight. Luckily, from the time of his earliest service in Congress (1780), he had been an ardent, unswerving defender of American rights on the Mississippi. He reviewed the conduct of Congress on the navigation right, concluding that the project to cede it to Spain "will never be revived," and emphasized again that with the claim maintained, only an energetic government would be able to defend it. Would a strong or a weak government, a united or a divided country, be more likely to be tempted by Spanish gold? "A weak system produced this project. A strong system will remove the inducement," Madison concluded.[32]

Whatever the logical superiority of federalist arguments, Madison knew Henry's machinations and oratory had been extremely effective. Madison reported gloomily to Mount Vernon: ". . . appearances at present are less favorable than at the date of my last. Our progress is slow and every advantage is taken of the delay, to work on the local prejudices of particular sets of members. . . . The Kentucky members . . . seem to lean more against than in favor of the Constitution. The business is in the most ticklish state that can be imagined. . . . I dare not encourage much expectation that [the majority] will be on the favorable side." The "local prejudices" most worked upon were fears among debtors to British merchants that under the Constitution they would be compelled to pay their creditors, the fears of Virginia speculators that rival land claims would be validated by Congress, and the fears of Mississippi valley delegates that the new government would connive to close the river. Furthermore, antifederal agents from New York and Philadelphia were in Richmond, ominously "closeted with Henry, Mason, etc. . . . The chief mischief is effected . . . out of doors," Madison wrote Rufus King. Obviously, nefarious schemes of obstruction and perhaps disunion were smoldering, which needed only an antifederal victory in Virginia to burst forth in a calamitous national conflagration. Despite the threatening aspect at the convention's mid-point, Madison thought a favorable result still possible, and given the enormous stakes—in his view, the fate of the new constitution and therefore of the survival of the Union depended on the decision in Virginia—he resolved to persevere. Informal polls indicated ten or a dozen uncertain delegates, enough to decide the issue, so Madison and his colleagues set about to make them federalists.[33]

On Monday morning the federalists took heart as the convention finally resumed the clause-by-clause debate. In seven speeches in one day Madison responded to reasonable inquires about the modes of electing members of Congress, their compensation, the origin of money bills, command of the militia, the alleged control of purse and sword by Congress, and the right of Congress to regulate its own elections. Again he borrowed from *The Federalist* to combat the standard antifederal assumption that any power in any hands would be abused to oppress the people. The next day of debate Madison defended again the need for some federal control over the militia, and could not suppress his exasperation over antifederal assertions that "black crimes" were likely if Congress had exclusive power over the seat of the national government. The horrors the antifederalists pictured, Madison said testily, were possible only under an absurdly wide construction of that power. He pleaded for an end to such flights of fancy, but he was still so shaky from his recent illness that three times in one day the reporter was unable to hear his words. Though weakened "in a degree which barely allows me to cooperate in the business," Madison remained at his place and during the next two days (June 18 and 19) spoke briefly on the importation of slaves, the election of the President and the Vice President, and the treaty power. The days of orderly debate led Madison to report to Washington that "great moderation as yet marks our proceedings." Even though he thought the federalists had a slight majority, he feared Henry's assaults on the executive and judicial departments would tip the balance again.[34]

In the debate over the judiciary on June 20, Pendleton, Randolph, and Marshall, all experts in legal matters, carried the main burden. Madison intervened only to explain the view taken of the judicial power at the Philadelphia convention, and to protest, as he had so often, antifederalist suppositions about the awful abuses which would be made of the powers granted. He appealed to the humane republicanism of the delegates:

"Gentlemen suppose, that the general legislature will do every mischief
they possibly can, and that they will omit to do every thing good which
they are authorized to do. . . . I consider it reasonable to conclude, that
they will as readily do their duty, as deviate from it. . . . I go on this great
republican principle, that the people will have virtue and intelligence to
select men of virtue and wisdom. Is there no virtue among us? If there
be not, we are in a wretched situation." We do not depend alone on the
virtue of the elected representatives, or place sole confidence in them,
Madison concluded, "but in the people who are to choose them." Antifederal objections were so often founded on a lack of faith in public
virtue that Madison, without either embracing the visionary notion that
the people could do no wrong or espousing the self-controlled system
explained in *Federalist* Number 10 as an all-sufficing mechanism for
good government, thought it necessary to remind the delegates that they
were, after all, heirs of the American Revolution, which had no other
foundation than a conviction that the people could be trusted with their
own government.[35]

Amid cautious federalist optimism (Madison calculated on "a majority
of 3 or 4, possibly of 5 or 6") as the clause-by-clause debate ended,
Madison spent most of the time in his room, still fighting the "bilious
indisposition." The convention set Tuesday, June 24, as the day for
concluding speeches and crucial motions by the opposing sides. George
Wythe, the revered law teacher of Jefferson and perhaps dozens of the
convention delegates, and a liberal leader in Virginia for two generations,
moved unconditional approval of the Constitution and proposed a brief
bill of rights to be added later as amendments. Henry attacked this
proposal, and at the same time, placed before the convention forty
amendments, many of them sponsored by George Mason, including
both a bill of rights and substantial alterations in the frame of government. Virginia's ratification, he insisted, should be made conditional upon
acceptance of these amendments. Other states would bend to Virginia's
will in this respect, Henry assured the delegates. Since such a conditional
concurrence was clearly no ratification at all, the motion in effect was
one of rejection.[36]

Toward the end of the day, Madison rose to summarize the federalist
position in a debate in which even his opponents conceded he had taken
"the principal share." He rejected utterly the idea of previous amendments, and stated again his conviction that the Constitution did not in the
least threaten fundamental rights. Since the federal government had only
specified powers and no others, and since the Constitution did not provide
expressly for the violation of the cherished rights, they were unthreat-
ened by it. He also pointed out that the proposals to make the armed
forces and the regulation of commerce depend on a two-thirds vote in
Congress were likely to paralyze the nation at times of greatest need,

and of course, they violated the principle of majority rule for no sufficient reason. The time for detailed argument and analysis having passed, however, Madison reminded the delegates that the constitution before them had been formed in a convention remarkable for its "calm and dispassionate" discussion, and that even then only "mutual deference and concession [made] agreement on a general system" possible. Another such meeting of minds, to say nothing of a superior result, was most unlikely, Madison asserted. One should not be fooled by antifederalist arguments that a second federal convention would solve everything. Therefore, he pleaded, let the United States excite the astonishment and admiration of the world by "peacefully, freely and satisfactorily" establishing a general government over a vast and diverse territory. Only thus could the promise of the American Revolution be fulfilled.[37]

Henry rose in reply, reaching heights of "lofty and pathetic eloquence": "The gentleman has told you of the numerous blessings which he imagines will result to us and the world in general from the adoption of this system. I see the awful immensity of the dangers with which it is pregnant. I see it—I feel it. I see *beings* of a higher order anxious concerning our decision." Shortly, according to a federalist witness long a close friend of Madison's, as if responding to Henry's invocation, "a storm suddenly arose. It grew dark. The doors came to with a rebound like a peal of musketry. The windows rattled; the huge wooden structure rocked. . . . Henry [seemed to have] seized upon the artillery of Heaven, and directed its fiercest thunders against the heads of his adversaries. . . . The scene became unsupportable. . . . The members rushed from their seats with precipitation and confusion." Madison shared the climactic excitement of the afternoon thundershower so amazingly suited to the roaring voice of his mighty adversary.[38]

June 25 was the day of decision. The tense debates and the oppressive heat of a Virginia June had left the delegates restless and exhausted, ready to cast their ballots. The visitors' gallery was crowded. James Innes, almost Henry's equal in florid oratory, reputed to be the biggest man in Virginia, and a friend of Madison's since they had attended Donald Robertson's school together, gave a final speech for the federalists, while Monroe, John Tyler (also a student at Robertson's school), and Henry concluded for the opposition. The first vote, and the key one, was on Henry's motion for previous amendments. The clerk began the roll call, alphabetical according to the name of the county. Madison frowned as the first 28 votes were recorded; the antifederalists led by 5; a key Kentucky county was in opposition; and southside Virginia remained firmly antifederal. Things brightened when Fayette County in Kentucky divided its vote and Loudoun County, thought to be wholly under Mason's influence, also divided. Madison and his fellow Orange delegate, James Gordon, voting after another crucial western county had gone federalist, took the same side joyously. Madison probably nodded expectantly and sadly as his constant opponents for ten years, Meriwether Smith and Theodorick Bland voted antifederal. As the roll call neared its end, 9 of 12 votes going for Henry's motion made an antifederalist victory possible, but Madison knew he had won: 6 straight Tidewater votes, including those of Lee, Bushrod Washington, Wythe, and Innes, gave the federalists an 88 to 80 victory. Immediately thereafter the convention approved, 89 to 79, Wythe's motion for ratification with amendments recommended for later adoption. In two days of anticlimactic debate, Madison sought to delete "several . . . highly objectionable" amendments from the Mason-Henry proposals, but enough federalists took pity on their foes to defeat Madison's effort. The convention therefore recommended the full list of forty proposals for the consideration of Congress and adjourned *sine die*.[39]

Although immensely pleased and heartened at this victory, Madison did not for a moment think everything was settled. During the last days of debate he had worried about the temper of the opposition. Mason had hinted once, in an almost threatening way, that "civil convulsions" would result from "obtruding the [proposed] Government on the people." In free government much depended, Madison knew, upon a loyal opposition working within the constitution. Henry's graceful speech on June 25, pledging that he would "be a peaceable citizen . . . [and seek only to] remove the defects of [the Constitution] in a constitutional way," and the acquiescent if not cordial attitude of the bulk of the antifederalists were encouraging. Yet on the day the convention adjourned, Madison wrote Washington of expected antifederalist moves to get two thirds of the state legislatures to seek a second convention and to elect a Congress "that will commit suicide on their own authority." Though these efforts would be within the frame of government, and therefore not technically disloyal, Madison thought they lacked fairness in not permitting the new constitution a chance to prove itself. He hoped to dissuade all but the most extreme antifederalists from collusion in such schemes and to bring the new government into being quickly and effectively. The coming months would be busy, excited, and anxious ones.[40]

In assessing the results of the ratification struggle in Virginia and throughout the country, Madison knew, of course, that speeches, newspaper essays, and arguments over political theory were but part of the picture. The federalists did not win solely because they were more profound students of government or were more able propagandists— though most contemporary observers agreed that they did excel in these areas. Madison's own letters recognize repeatedly economic and regional divisions of great significance. He reported again and again that seaboard cities were firmly federalist. He knew that creditors often favored the Constitution; that certain classes of debtors opposed it; and that "men of property," merchants, and professional people by and large favored it. Since he had no fear of what these classes of men might seek to accomplish—indeed, he had often found such men enlightened and public spirited—he had no reason to discount their reasoning or to feel their support in any way compromised the federalist cause. He would have had little use, for example, for the suspicion of some observers in 1788, and ever since, that because the undisputed prince of American trade and finance, Robert Morris, was ardently federalist, the new constitution must be a clever plot by him and his cohorts to serve their own selfish interests. In fact, Morris was in Richmond during the Virginia convention, on business. He talked with "knowing ones," undoubtedly including Madison, about the likely results of the convention. Antifederalists could not regard his presence as wholly coincidental. Madison had the intellectual confidence and objectivity, however, to judge Morris, and others like him, by less stereotyped and simplistic standards. He was well aware that these men sought a government that would protect profits already made and the prospect of future gains. It was also possible, as Hamilton later asserted—too categorically for Madison—that a frame of government favorable to Morris would also be a good one for the country at large.[41]

It was likewise true, as Madison had observed repeatedly during the seventeen-eighties, that poor men, simple farmers, and the like, could be mistaken or weak in their understanding of government. There was, in short, no good way to judge the *merit* of constitutional proposals in terms of the economic interests of those who made them. Furthermore, Madison never supposed that political agencies and decisions were always subservient to economics. The intent, in fact, of Madison's *Federalist* Number 10, often admired by economic determinists, was to devise *political* means to control the economic forces described so realistically in the essay. He was sure properly devised government should and could recognize and work toward concepts of the public good which were beyond the ken of "the factious spirit." Therefore Madison worked easily and candidly with the various forces—some selfish, some unfathomable, and some ambiguous—that in different ways helped secure the ratification of the Constitution. He knew very little could be done about the opposition of interests which conceived themselves injured by the new constitution, except to ease such apprehensions as were based on misunderstandings. He knew as well, though, that there were varying degrees of rationality and disinterestedness among different individuals and groups throughout the country that would in some measure be open to reasoned persuasion. To those so open—possibly a decisive group, Madison thought—he addressed himself. There is considerable evidence that this assessment in fact led him to do just the things crucial to victory.

Within Madison's native county and state the forces at work were typically complex. Ever since the whisky-influenced defeat in the 1777 election for the House of Delegates, Orange County had been "safely Madisonian." Then, in 1788, Madison faced a challenge from his neighbor Thomas Barbour, a man whose economic interests were virtually identical to Madison's and who had long been allied with him in conducting the public affairs of the county. The grounds of Barbour's antifederalism are not known beyond his probably earnest fears for American liberty under the proposed constitution and a hint that on a visit to Richmond he had been persuaded by Patrick Henry and his associates. Barbour may have felt the issue a good one to use to displace the absent "young Colonel Madison" as Orange County's leading politician, or he may have conceived that his Western land interests (on Panther Creek in Kentucky, near lands owned by the Madisons) were endangered by the new constitution. Whatever, we know Madison won the election handily by a skillful, though honestly reasonable, cultivation of the local Baptists, and probably most importantly, by his own return to the county to re-establish his personal contacts and explain the new constitution clearly and authoritatively. Thus Madison won a victory in the Piedmont region which, as he had written Jefferson, was "much chequered" in its federalism. Presumably the other contests in the region turned on largely personal, somewhat capricious elements akin to those deciding the election in Orange County.[42]

In the state at large, Madison recognized the same "geographical view" of the election for the June convention which subsequent students have set forth in detail: the northern neck and tidewater areas north of the James River were firmly federal; the region south of the James was antifederal; the Piedmont was "chequered"; the Great Valley was federal; and the western counties in the Ohio valley were divided but leaning toward the federalists. As in other states, towns and areas dependent on trade, and especially regions along navigable rivers, tended to be federal, while more isolated sections were largely antifederal. Important specific interests affected those who favored the Constitution because it might enforce 1783 peace treaty terms on return of slaves or payment of debts, and those who opposed it because it might enforce treaty provisions for return of sequestered loyalist estates. Farmers in the Great Valley were federal because their livelihood depended on interstate commerce on the Potomac River. Obviously in some sections neighboring planters would find themselves pulled in opposite directions by these interests, and there were many cases of individuals torn in many ways. Perhaps most important of all was the conviction of delegates from the Ohio valley, largely from what is now West Virginia, that British retention of posts in the Northwest Territory contrary to the terms of the peace treaty was the great obstacle to their growth and prosperity. They consequently favored a constitution pledged to fulfill the treaty. Slaveholders, landowners (large and small), and public security creditors were found in roughly equal numbers on each side of the ratification question. There was virtually no commercial interest as such in Virginia. Two of the leading Virginia antifederalists, Richard Henry Lee and George Mason, were very wealthy northern-neck tidewater planters, exactly in the category sometimes held to be most overwhelmingly federal. Sectional and personal considerations seem clearly to have been more important than class or wealth divisions, and economic interests were complex enough to permit just the opportunity for debate Madison needed. He played a crucial role because he both recognized the factional forces at work and spoke persuasively to the ambiguities and disinterestedness intertwined among them.[43]

The "heartland" of Virginia antifederalism, south of the James, probably took its stand because of the influence of Henry, the Cabells, and its other leaders, its opposition to tidewater and northern-neck politics, and its relative isolation. Henry and others persuaded southside citizens that a stronger central government would be "a menace" and that a sovereign Virginia could best solve her own problems. Federalism in Virginia, on the other hand, rested largely on forces apparent in Madison's own outlook. Many who supported the Constitution undoubtedly did so because they thought it would better protect property, insure the payment of public and private debts, and restrain the issue of paper currency and other inflationary schemes. The antifederalism of many wealthy planters, large slaveowners, public creditors, and land speculators, however, suggests that some such men, insofar as they were guided by economic interests, thought a powerful state government, perhaps pliant to their influence, would better protect their interests than a strengthened federal government guided by unknown, possibly hostile, forces. Another important factor was that to men of Madison's generation, who had grown to manhood amid the stirring national deeds of the revolution, and who, unlike Henry, Mason, and many antifederal leaders, had little remembrance of Virginia as a separate colony, the need for a strong Union seemed perfectly clear. At the same time, they were often disillusioned with the conduct of state government.

The decisive issue in Virginia, however—the one on which wavering delegates were open to persuasion—was almost certainly the Mississippi question. Because there were vast territories on the western waters, with great numbers of energetic Virginians (including the Madisons) looking to them for their future prosperity, the right of navigation on the Spanish-controlled portions of the Mississippi River was viewed as of transcending importance. Had the federalists failed to quiet fears that a stronger Union would somehow compromise this right, and especially to

counteract the suspicions aroused by the abortive Jay-Gardoqui project, ratification would have been impossible in Virginia. The telling
federalist argument on this point, reiterated by Madison at least since
1780, was the essentially political one that a strong central government
would have both the will and the power to assure American access to the
Mississippi.

Finally, the figure of General Washington looming in the background
was to many the basic argument for ratification. Monroe wrote Jefferson shortly after the Virginia convention adjourned, ". . . be assured
his influence carried this government." The powers of the new government, and especially the office of the President, had been framed in part
according to what would suit Washington, and the people judged the
Constitution with the same thought in mind. His presence and universally admired patriotism gave the plans and debates of 1787 and 1788 a
specific, personal quality that had an immense influence on the results.
Though some leaders raised the disquieting question of what would happen after Washington passed from the scene, by and large the federalists
managed to keep attention on what powers of government could safely
be entrusted to the hero of the revolution. More than anything else this
vitiated antifederal specters of rampant corruption and tyranny under
the new constitution.[44]

Still a Virginia delegate to the Continental Congress, and anxious to
attend to the final phases of ratification, Madison left Richmond shortly
after the convention adjourned, and headed northward without stopping
in Orange. In Fredericksburg he found a box from Jefferson, containing seeds for "Cork, Acorns, Sulla and peas," which he forwarded to
Orange with instructions for planting. He traveled with Dr. David Stuart,
a federalist delegate from Fairfax County, and William Lee, moving
slowly because Madison had a return of the "bilious lax" that had sticken
him during the convention. On the afternoon of the Fourth of July the
party reached Mount Vernon, where Washington greeted the travelers
and presumably joined in exultant toasts to the ratification by Virginia
of a constitution that would at last give energy and stability to the new
nation born twelve years before. News that New Hampshire had ratified
further cheered the company. Establishment of the new government was
now certain; the three holdout states (New York, North Carolina, and
Rhode Island) would be forced eventually to ratify, or find themselves
increasingly isolated and enfeebled. The discouragement and anxiety
Madison and Washington had felt the previous March were dispelled as
the two men turned to the difficult transition from the old to the new
government. Washington wished, as he had ever since 1783, that no
further public service would be required of him. One doubts, though,
despite the repeated, soulful hopes expressed in his letters, that he ever

really supposed the country would fail to call him again or that he would fail to respond.[45]

The two men first reviewed the dangers still posed by the opponents of the Constitution. They were sure Henry and Mason, though peaceful, were "not reconciled" to the new government and would do all they could to hinder its inauguration. Antifederalists in Maryland and Pennsylvania seemed only to wait for leadership to give form and direction to their mischievous inclinations. Since nothing helpful could be expected from the three states which had not ratified, the obstructionist forces seemed formidable. They could not prevent the transition from taking place, but at a time when unity and good will were vital, Madison and Washington saw all too much discord. The now-intimate soldier-planter and scholar-statesman also began to talk of administering the new government: where its seat would be, what offices it might require, what laws should first be passed, what its foreign relations might be, and so forth. Three days of friendly discussion as Madison sought to throw off the effects of his illness helped both men see what the tasks ahead were.

It was not easy amid the tavernlike atmosphere of Mount Vernon, though, to find time for serious conversation. Washington's diary for early July reads like a hotel register. Madison's party of three arrived the fourth. The next day Dr. Stuart left, and Washington's trusted aide and secretary, David Humphreys, returned. On the sixth, a Colonel Fitzgerald and Dr. James Craik, Jr., came for dinner at noon, and two more men came in the afternoon to discuss the affairs of the Potomac Canal Company. Washington added with relief that they "all went away in PM," permitting him to return to his talks with Madison. On the seventh, after the evening meal, Washington put Madison and William Lee into his carriage to go to Alexandria where they were to catch the stage for New York the next morning. Madison could scarcely have helped reflect, as he continued the hot, uncomfortable journey northward, that Washington's cordial support was a most precious resource in the effort to bring the new government into being, and that one of his most delicate tasks would be to nourish and use this vital reservoir of support in the most effective way possible.[46]

CHAPTER XII

Establishing the New Government

W HEN Madison reached New York on July 14, 1788, he happily laid Virginia's ratification of the Constitution before Congress. He also learned that at the New York convention, meeting in Poughkeepsie, Hamilton had read Madison's adverse opinion of the antifederal proposal to ratify on condition that unless certain amendments were accepted by a specified date, the ratification would be considered void. Such a plan would "as effectually keep [New York] . . . out of the New Union as the most unqualified rejection," Madison noted. Though he rejoiced when New York did ratify unconditionally, he thought its call for a second convention, to amend the Constitution, would have "a most pestilent tendency." Such a gathering, he said, would "be the offspring of party and passion, and . . . the parent of error and public injury." After North Carolina refused to ratify, Madison began to hope it and other antifederal states, likely to elect obstructionists to the new Congress, would stay out until after the government had been organized by its friends. Six or eight thousand people in New York City celebrating Virginia's ratification with a grand parade and a feast of roast oxen, cows, and sheep (with drinks furnished by the city's brewers), convinced Madison, though, that the *people* of the Union were for the Constitution, whatever the schemes of self-seeking politicians in some state legislatures.[1]

In its last, dying days the Continental Congress agreed in two months of haggling (Madison saw antifederal plots behind every delay) that states should choose Senators and Representatives under the new constitution as soon as convenient, that presidential electors be chosen in January 1789, that the electors cast their ballots in February, that Congress meet in March, and that New York be the temporary capital. Only the last decision caused any serious debate. A dozen towns and locations from New York to Virginia sought the capital, since enormous prestige, financial advantage, and influence on the government hinged on its location. As a Virginian and a Southerner, Madison wanted ultimately to have the permanent capital on the banks of the Potomac, but he thought Philadelphia's centrality and accessibility from the West made it the best choice for the temporary seat. He considered "accomodation of the Western Country particularly essential," since that was the direction of growth and the most likely source of disunionist sentiment should its interests be ignored. Furthermore, selection of New York would be used by Henry and other Southern antifederalists as evidence that New England dominated the new government. Nonetheless, the New York–New England coalition, abetted by scattered Southern votes, held firm. To Madison's disgust, Congress made the temporary capital New York, only three hundred miles from the northern extremity of the Union and over four times that far from the southern limit.[2]

Madison disclosed his fears in code to Jefferson: "the Western Country [keeps] a very jealous eye [on matters] . . . involving a seeming advantage to the eastern States which have been rendered extremely suspicious and obnoxious by the Mississippi [closure] project. There is even good ground to believe that Spain is taking advantage of this disgust in Kentucky, and is actually endeavoring to seduce them from the union. . . . This is a fact as certain as it is important but which I hint in strict confidence." The ties with the West across the Appalachian Mountains were tenuous at best, and should the East seem neglectful, disunion, helped along by Spanish intrigue, would blot out the federalists' vision of a great continental republic. If the West resolved to secede, the East could not prevent it, and a pattern of petty, squabbling nations instead of a "United States" would be set. To calm Western fears, Madison supported a resolve in Congress "that the free navigation of the River Mississippi is a clear and essential right of the United States, and that the same ought to be considered and supported as such." He knew, though, that only *deeds* showing that national and not local interests would prevail in the councils of the new government would cement East and West. This theme was important in Madison's public policy from the time of the revolution through the debate over Jay's Treaty to the reaction to Burr's conspiracy and the War of 1812.[3]

When not busy with his public duties, Madison enjoyed New York society, especially the sophisticated French community there. He resumed his friendship with Louis Otto and other Frenchmen he had known for nearly ten years, greeted Jefferson's French friends who came to America, and visited with the French consul, J. Hector St. John

Crèvecoeur, soon to be famous as the author of *Letters from an American Farmer*. He was "a very worthy man and entitled, by his philanthropy and zealous patronage of whatever he deems useful, to much esteem and regard," Madison wrote Washington when the Frenchman applied, like all other foreign visitors, for an introduction to the master of Mount Vernon. Madison also read the works of Condorcet, DuPont de Nemours, and other French philosophers.[4]

Madison was sorry, therefore, that the new French minister, Count de Moustier, soon after his arrival in January 1788, incurred a series of near-fatal social liabilities; by the end of the year Madison wrote Jefferson he was a "most unlucky appointment." He was embroiled with the French community itself, and by an "unsocial, proud and niggardly" manner, and "fastidiousness" toward the United States, he irritated many Americans as well. Worst of all, he had brought with him Madame de Bréhan, an artist and bright conversationalist, introduced as his sister-in-law, but in fact his mistress. Adjusted to the casual Parisian attitude on such matters, Jefferson had written Madison simply that she was "goodness itself . . . well disposed. You must be well acquainted with her," he added. Madison apparently did so, for during his spring absence in Virginia, his colleague Cyrus Griffin kept him posted, with obvious relish, on "the Marchioness": she entertained a high opinion of Madison; she made "a thousand inquiries" about him; and she received and returned his compliments "with great pleasure." When Madison returned to New York, he responded to Madame Bréhan's desire for a Negro boy servant by getting one for her from Virginia. Clearly delighted with the cosmopolitan, ingratiating way of the French noblewoman, who made most American women seem dull and provincial, Madison accepted Jefferson's suggestions that he receive her "as an acquaintance of a thousand years standing." Furthermore, Jefferson added, since she spoke little English, Madison "must teach her more, and learn French from her."[5]

Her "illicit connection" with the count (they neglected "the most obvious precautions for veiling their intimacy") soon became well known, however, and was universally "offensive to American manners." The ladies of New York "withdrew their attentions from her," and in Boston a tangle of etiquette resulted in the social isolation of the count and his "sister-in-law." She was "deeply stung" by the snubs and became "perfectly soured" toward the United States. Even worse, she vented her rancor on "her paramour over whom she exercises despotic sway," Madison reported sorrowfully to Jefferson. Though the social scandal wore off after a few months and Madison was broad-minded about it, Moustier was never able to become an effective French emissary in the United States. Through Jefferson and Lafayette, Madison helped to obtain Moustier's "retirement" to France the next summer.[6]

Less compromised by hauteur over etiquette (which always made Madison impatient) was the pleasure of greeting Brissot de Warville on his travels through New York. At a dinner given by Madison, they toasted the shining ideals shared by American revolutionists and French *philosophes*, and spoke hopefully of the prospects for "liberty and humanity in general." Brissot described Madison glowingly: "He distinguished himself particularly at the time that the conventions met to vote on the new Federal Constitution. For a long time Virginia hesitated to join the Union, but by his logic and his eloquence Mr. Madison persuaded the convention to favor acceptance. . . . He looked tired, perhaps as a result of the immense labors to which he had devoted himself recently. His expression was that of a stern censor; his conversation disclosed a man of learning; and his countenance was that of a person conscious of his talents and of his duties." Madison seemed to Brissot to be six or eight years younger than Hamilton, who was actually four years younger than Madison. Hamilton had "the determined appearance of a republican; Mr. Madison the thoughtful look of a wise statesman. . . . [They were] worthy rivals as well as collaborators," Brissot thought.[7]

Jefferson and Madison sought assiduously to cultivate good relations between France and the United States and thus to reduce cultural, and especially commercial, dependence on Great Britain, not because they were doctrinaire Anglophobes, but because they were sure that the United States could could not be independent as a nation while British merchants dominated her vital trade. Thus while Jefferson sought consular and commercial treaties with France, Madison worked with Moustier in New York to see if the French and American economies could be made more complementary. Though Madison saw little hope that French products could compete with English "courser woolens . . . hardware, and leather," he saw a flourishing potential trade of French "wines, brandies, oil, Fruits, silks, cambricks, Lawns, printed goods, Glass, Kid gloves, ribbons, [and] superfine broadcloaths" for Virginia "tobacco, naval stores, ready-built vessels, flax-seed . . . wheat, and flour." The Virginians never succeeded, however, in overcoming the disadvantages of La Luzerne's judgment given to John Adams ten years earlier that, compared to British merchants, the French agents in America were "a Parcell of little Rascals. . . . Adventurers who have sold the worst merchandises, for great Prices."[8]

The two Virginians also dared to suppose that France might become the European beacon for the ideals of the American Revolution. Jefferson's circle in Paris and the Frenchmen Madison knew in New York and Philadelphia began to see real hope for this in 1788, as changes in the old regime became imminent. Madison expressed his world-wide sense of mission to Edmund Randolph: "There is good reason . . . to presume, that, as the spirit which at present agitates [France] has been in a great measure caught from the American Revolution, so the result of the struggle there will be not a little affected by the character which liberty may receive from the experiment now on foot here. The tranquil and successful establishment of a great reform by the reason of the community, must give as much force to the doctrines urged on one side as a contrary event would do to the policy maintained on the other." Thus when French chargé Louis Otto wrote in 1788 that Madison was "*ami intimé de M. Jefferson et sincèrement attaché à la France*," he had no illusions that Madison was in any way subservient to French interests or intoxicated by French ideas. Rather, Madison saw improved Franco-American trade and the cooperative pursuit of liberty as both necessary counterweights to British domination and useful supports for American national purpose.[9]

In speculating about the world-wide prospects for freedom, Madison wrote Jefferson that while he still did not consider the omission of a bill of rights from the federal constitution "a material defect," he had no serious objection to adding one. He warned, though, that mere "parchment barriers" would not protect cherished rights from overbearing power: "Wherever the real power in a Government lies, there is the danger of oppression. In our Governments the real power lies in the majority of the Community, and the invasion of private rights is *chiefly* to be apprehended, not from acts of Government contrary to the sense of its constituents, but from acts in which the Government is the mere instrument of the major number of the constituents." Nonetheless, in popular governments bills of rights might serve two purposes, Madison noted, anticipating their subsequent usefulness in American history: (1) rights solemnly declared might become so "incorporated with the national sentiment" as to deter violations, and (2) on occasions when the government might exceed its limits, a bill of rights would "be a good ground for an appeal to the sense of the community."[10]

Responding again to friends in Kentucky, which was expecting soon to draft its constitution as a separate state, Madison assessed further the proper structure of republican government. Senators elected for six years at large in the state, he thought, could better supply "knowledge and experience," better represent "the interest of the whole society," and otherwise correct "the infirmities of popular Government," than those elected for shorter terms. A freehold franchise for the upper house and one "more at large" in the lower house would protect both "the rights of persons, and the rights of property." Though Madison was sure clergymen should have neither special exclusion from nor privilege to public office, and that a re-eligible executive would encourage "faithful administration . . . perserverance, and system," how properly to lodge the power to revise or veto laws still puzzled him. No "council of revision" yet proposed seemed satisfactory, but to give the courts final power over the validity of legislation, he said, "makes the Judiciary Department paramount to the Legislature, which was never intended and can never be proper." Thus Madison emphasized the need for devices to insure "wisdom and steadiness" in the legislature and a strong, responsible executive more than he had three years earlier (see Chapter IX), while he remained attached to a liberal suffrage, secret ballot, and representation according to population. Also, the perplexing question of blending popular control with proper restraint remained at the center of Madison's political thought as he prepared for a role second only to Washington's in establishing the new federal government.[11]

In the fall and winter of 1788 all eyes turned to the elections under the new constitution. "The Presidency alone unites the conjectures of the public," Madison wrote Jefferson. The vice presidential candidates Madison and Washington had spoken of most highly in their private conversation, John Jay and General Henry Knox, were unwilling, Madison discovered, to accept such "an unprofitable dignity." The other choices, John Hancock and John Adams, were both objectionable to Madison. Hancock was "weak, ambitious, a courtier of popularity, given to low intrigue, and lately reunited by a factious friendship with Samuel Adams," while John Adams was vain, overly ambitious, and had made himself "obnoxious to many . . . by the political principles avowed" in his recently published *Defence of the Constitutions of Government of the United States*. In the elections to Congress, the federalists were everywhere so triumphant that by December 1788 Madison reported joyfully the new government would have a "peaceable commencement in March next, and . . . be administered by men who will give it a fair trial." Only in Virginia, ironically, were opponents of the Constitution in control. Patrick Henry had engineered the election of antifederalists Richard Henry Lee and William Grayson to the Senate, and he was cleverly arranging districts for the House of Representatives to favor foes of the new government. To humiliate Madison, Henry managed his rejection by the Assembly for a seat in the Senate, referring to him as one "unworthy of the confidence of the people," whose election to office "would terminate in producing rivulets of blood throughout the land." In an attempt to exclude Madison from the House of Representatives as well, Henry, a master of the "gerrymander" long before that term had been invented, placed Orange County in a Congressional district otherwise composed of counties considered heavily antifederal.[12]

Faced with this hostility, Madison pondered his next move. He was eager to take part in launching the new government, though according to the convention of his day, he had to profess indifference or even reluctance, and he actually preferred the House of Representatives to the Senate. When he heard of Henry's successful efforts against him, he was inclined to view the situation in Virginia as hopeless. He would, he wrote, simply stay in New York and see what happened in the Virginia elections. If defeated, he was sure of an important post in the new administration, though he and Washington had hoped he would be a leader in Congress. Madison soon gave in to the pleas of his political associates in Virginia, however, and resolved that despite his distaste for "electioneering," he would go home to do whatever he could to gain a seat in the House. Suffering from piles and a recurrence of the "bilious indisposition" of the previous summer, he regretfully exchanged the comforts of New York for the rigors of a winter journey to Virginia.[13]

Madison stopped at Mount Vernon for seven days, and Washington recorded that, as usual, he "remained at home with Mr. Madison." On Christmas Eve he entertained Henry and Charles Lee and two or three others at dinner and talked earnestly about inaugurating the new government: what should Washington say in his inaugural address? what legislation should he recommend? who should head the executive departments? what etiquette should guide the head of state? what should be his relations with Congress? Washington made clear his intention to have Madison at his right hand as the new government got under way, and doubtless agreed to aid discreetly, as he had opportunity, in Madison's election to the House of Representatives.[14]

When Madison arrived home, shortly after Christmas 1788, he found "the calumnies of the antifederal partizans" far more widespread than he had anticipated. Baptists throughout his district, but especially around Fredericksburg, and a group of Germans in Culpeper County, had been alienated by reports that Madison was "dogmatically attached to the Constitution in every clause, syllable and letter," and that he would therefore oppose all amendments, including one to protect liberty of conscience. Upon the advice of his brother William, Madison wrote to an influential Baptist preacher, George Eve, declaring unequivocally his support for amendments guaranteeing "the rights of conscience in the fullest latitude, the freedom of the press, trials by jury, security against general warrants, etc." Persuaded of Madison's good faith, Eve attended a Baptist meeting antifederalists were using for political purposes, and by reminding the people of Madison's repeated services to Baptists and others who sought freedom of religion, gave "a great wound" to antifederal pretensions.[15]

Madison also wrote a public letter to Thomas Mann Randolph, published in the *Virginia Herald and Fredericksburg Advertiser*, January 15, in the *Virginia Independent Chronicle*, January 28, and elsewhere, explaining his moderate federalism and his approval of amendments incorporating a bill of rights. John Nicholas' "Decius" articles supported Madison's cause, as did numerous other broadside and newspaper publications. The reappearance of many of these pieces in Pennsylvania newspapers attested to the widespread interest in the election. Madison thus pursued his electioneering "much further than he had premeditated," and was soon convinced that his personal appearance and strenuous activity were "more necessary" than he and his friends had calculated beforehand.[16]

The election was the most memorable in Madison's career, however, because he was opposed by his close friend James Monroe in a large district drawn by Patrick Henry to give Monroe the advantage. Supposedly only Madison's home county of Orange was safely federalist. The rest of the district included Monroe's home, Spotsylvania County, and the antifederal stronghold of Amherst, ruled by Patrick Henry and his allies. Baptists and other dissenters in Louisa and Culpeper counties were supposed to swell the antifederal ranks. To overcome these liabilities, Madison agreed to face-to-face debates with Monroe in several courthouses and churches. At the Culpeper courthouse on January 19 and at Louisa somewhat later, Madison "contradicted the erroneous reports propagated against" him. On the twenty-sixth the candidates spoke before Madison's friends and neighbors in Orange. On one wintery day they journeyed twelve miles to the church of a "nest of Dutchmen who generally voted together and whose vote might probably turn the scale." According to Madison's own account, he and Monroe sat through the service, at which two fiddles provided the music, and afterwards the two candidates kept the people standing in the snow, listening as the constitutional issues were earnestly debated. On the long ride home that night, Madison's nose froze, leaving a scar he bore for the rest of his life. Throughout the debates, despite intemperate charges made by the supporters of each, there was "no atom of ill-will" between Madison and Monroe. Madison wrote Jefferson that keeping politics and personal views separate "saved our friendship from the smallest diminution."[17]

On February 2, the voters went to the polls, and as the returns came slowly to Orange, an impressive victory for Madison took shape. Orange, as expected, went for him, 216 to 9. Supposedly hostile Culpeper and Louisa each gave him pluralities of over 100, and Albemarle was his 174 to 105. Monroe carried his home county by 74 votes and Amherst overwhelmingly, but Madison still had a total plurality of 336 votes—a resounding federalist victory and a remarkable personal tribute to Madison in a district "rigged" against him. Washington rejoiced in Madison's election "by a respectable majority of the suffrages of the. District for which you stood," and looked forward to an early visit of the new Congressman-elect to Mount Vernon. Madison left Orange for the opening of Congress with a political base in his home district so solid that he was never again challenged there.[18]

Since it was apparent that neither house of Congress would have a quorum by the appointed date, March 4, Madison heeded his "own convenience" as well as Washington's request for aid and stayed at Mount Vernon for a week on his northward journey. Washington had sent to

Montpelier a draft of a long inaugural address explaining his feelings
upon assuming high office and recommending a detailed legislative program to Congress. Madison had queried whether such a lengthy performance would be appropriate and whether the legislative proposals
might not violate the separation of powers. At Mount Vernon the two
men, together with Washington's aide and secretary, Colonel David
Humphreys, discarded the draft, and Madison wrote for Washington's
approval the short, dignified speech eventually delivered at the inauguration ceremonies in New York, April 30. They talked, too, of vexing
social precedents: should the President accept invitations to dine out?
should he return calls? how should he arrange to see the multitudes of
people, official and unofficial, who sought meetings and visits with him?
where should he live in New York? Madison left Mount Vernon instructed to find answers to these questions.[19]

The journey to New York was one of discomfort and frustration as
well as excitement and anticipation. Heavy snow, swollen rivers, and
"the unparalleled badness of the roads" had delayed Madison's trip to
Mount Vernon, and the ride from there to Baltimore, ordinarily only
two days, took twice that long amid snow and rain and on more bad
roads. The winter session of Congress had been set in the hope that import duties could be passed soon enough to be collected on the heavy
influx of spring shipping. As members of Congress struggled to reach
New York, they wondered whether it was worth it, and resolved, if
possible, to avoid such unseasonable sessions in the future.

Despite the cold, Madison enjoyed the company of more and more
Congressmen and the air of triumphal procession that accompanied their
northward journey. At Mount Vernon, John Page, long Madison's
friend and colleague in science as well as politics, joined the party, and at
Alexandria they found Richard Bland Lee waiting for them. The three
men were staunch supporters of the new constitution and surely talked
all the way of their strategy in the House of Representatives. Nearing
Baltimore, they met the bearers of Georgia's electoral votes for President and Vice President (the former unanimous for Washington, and
the latter "thrown away" on favorite sons) and learned that the Georgia
Congressional delegation would be ardently federal. In Philadelphia the
Congressmen discovered that their business in New York could not
possibly begin for nearly two weeks, so they tarried to enjoy the social
life of the city. At a dinner at the home of Dr. William Shippen, Jr.—a
house still standing at the corner of Fourth and Locust streets—the
company discussed the prospects of the new government. Some guests,
including Chief Justice Thomas McKean and the wealthy merchant
William Bingham, argued that noble titles and other symbols of authority would be required to give the government proper respect and dignity. Madison asserted that in a republic the simple title "Mr. President"

was the most dignified and appropriate; anything else was unnecessary and unbecoming. He saw that the high-toned aristocratic notions often popular in the fashionable drawing rooms of Philadelphia and New York could undermine the republican character of the new government. Much, therefore, would depend on the attitude and social customs Washington would adopt, so Madison resolved to exert his considerable influence on Washington in favor of a republican simplicity in manners.[20]

During this visit, too, Madison may have first seen Dolley Payne, the niece of his fellow Congressman from Virginia, Colonel Isaac Coles, who stopped in Philadelphia to visit Dolley's mother, his sister. Though Colonel Coles, like his kinsman Patrick Henry, was not a friend of the new constitution, this would not have prevented visits with his federalist colleagues and his relatives in Philadelphia. Age twenty-one, and very much an eligible belle (and within a year to be married to John Todd), Dolley Payne would have been a welcome guest at the afternoon teas then so popular, and would have been thrilled to meet the congenial Virginians (she had grown up in Virginia herself) traveling with her uncle.

Reaching New York in mid-March, Madison found only eighteen Representatives and eight Senators assembled, two weeks after the date set for Congress to convene. In worried letters to Washington and Jefferson, Madison fretted over the bad impression such dalliance would create in Europe, and lamented as well over the chances for effective action in Congress. As he reviewed the list of Congressmen, he could find but "a very scanty proportion who will share in the drudgery of business"; speechmakers unhappily predominated. Probable "contentions first between federal and antifederal parties, and then between Northern and Southern Parties" added to the disagreeable prospects. Furthermore, news that Spanish agents and scheming Americans conspired to detach Kentucky and other Mississippi valley settlements from the United States seemed to assure bitter and divisive debates. Preserving the Union, it seemed clear, depended on the measures of the new government. Despite all the dangers, Madison dared to hope to Jefferson that "conciliatory sacrifices will be made in order to extinguish opposition to [the new Constitution] or at least break the force of it, by detaching the deluded opponents from their designing leaders," and that predictions of "antidemocratic" measures by the new Congress would prove unfounded. The time of theorizing and planning had passed; the critical moment of execution had come.[21]

Finally, on April 1, a quorum of Representatives assembled at City Hall in New York, and six days later the Senate, too, was able to convene. The electoral ballots for President were counted, and as everyone knew, Washington was the unanimous choice. John Adams, though bitterly disappointed that he received less than half the number of ballots

cast for Washington, became Vice President. Messengers started for
Mount Vernon and for Quincy to summon the winners to New York
for their inauguration. As the city waited expectantly for Washington's
appearance, the House of Representatives began its business. Eight members, including Madison, had been delegates to the Federal Convention.
Many others were also known to Madison. Among the members new to
national politics was the brilliant, youthful Fisher Ames of Massachusetts, soon to distinguish himself as the finest orator in Congress as well as
one of its most caustic and candid judges of character. The disputes and
dissensions Madison had foreseen appeared in close votes electing
Frederick Muhlenberg of Pennsylvania Speaker of the House, and
Madison's long-time friend and political confidant John Beckley clerk.
For the present, power seemed centered south and west of the Delaware.

On April 8, Madison opened the legislative business by moving that
Congress establish a revenue system to enable the nation as soon as
possible to pay its debts and meet the expenses of government. He
proposed high import duties on items regarded as luxuries (rum, liquors,
wine, molasses, tea, sugar, spices, coffee, and cocoa), a lower, ad valorem
duty on all other imports, and a system of tonnage duties favoring
American ships and ships of nations that had commercial treaties with
the United States. Though the duties were primarily to raise revenue, as
members agreed unanimously, they also regulated trade and therefore
affected special interests throughout the country. Pennsylvania members
sought protection for infant industries; New Englanders argued that a
high duty on rum would ruin their profitable West Indies trade; and
Southerners feared higher duties on foreign shipping would leave them
at the mercy of Northern merchants.

Madison asserted that though he was a "friend to a very free system of
commerce, and [held] it as a truth, that commercial shackles are generally
unjust, oppressive, and impolitic," nevertheless, tariffs were in some cases
justifiable: to protect, temporarily, new industries against foreign competition, to discourage luxury spending, to develop certain self-
sufficiencies necessary for national defense, and to retaliate against
unfair commercial regulations by other countries. The need, Madison
argued, was to enact duties that would serve these ends but otherwise
interfere as little as possible with the free flow of trade in the long run
vital to national prosperity. Though the House yielded some here and
there to sectional demands, especially to arguments for protection of
steel- and cloth-making and indigo, Madison and others managed generally to preserve free trade.[22]

More dangerous disputes arose over the proposal to discriminate
against countries not in treaty with the United States. Britain, without a
treaty, forbade the repair of her ships in American harbors, excluded
American ships from her West Indian islands, and reserved most of the
carrying trade through British ports for British ships. British shippers

and merchants thus enjoyed advantages against which their competitors were helpless. These regulations, together with the generally high quality of British goods, the tradition of American trade with Britain, and the relatively easy credit available from her commercial houses, promised to put the United States forever at the mercy of British mercantilism, contributing enormously to Britain's power and prosperity. Madison and Jefferson sought at the same time to encourage American trade with France, the only nation in their view capable of capturing enough of the commerce with Great Britain to give the United States the independence and flexibility inherent in a nearly equal competition between the two European powers for American markets.

Some opponents of discrimination against Britain simply preferred British goods, felt more comfortable working with British traders, and saw nothing to fear in close commercial connections with her. Included in this group were many who still had strong emotional and cultural ties with the former mother country and thus welcomed any strengthening of the bonds loosened between 1776 and 1783. Others either had interests in British companies or needed the credit available only in London or Liverpool, and thus benefited themselves from increasing trade with Great Britain. Still others considered the United States too weak to stand up so boldly to the world's greatest maritime and trading country. Since America would surely lose in an open commercial war with Britain, they argued, prudence and national prosperity demanded cooperation with, not resistance to, the English system. Finally, some Congressmen argued that retaliatory measures would restrain trade and thus deprive the country of desperately needed income from the import duties. What did it matter, they asked, whether the cash needed for national solvency came from British or French merchants? They asserted, plausibly, that for years to come, no trade channels could yield the volume of imports available through the familiar, trusted, and generally satisfactory merchants of the British Isles, and that therefore nothing should be done to interrupt that trade.

Madison argued the matter patiently and persistently in three separate debates in the House of Representatives. "Long possession of our trade [by Great Britain], their commercial regulations calculated to retain it, their similarity of language and manners . . . all concurring have made their commerce with us more extensive than their natural situation would require it to be. I would wish, therefore," he concluded, "to give such political advantages to those nations" that might eventually take from England the "unnatural" portion of her American trade. "Is it not also of some importance," Madison asked, "that we should enable nations in treaty with us [France] to draw some advantage from our alliance, and thereby impress those Powers that have hitherto neglected to treat with us [Great Britain], with the idea that advantages are to be gained by a reciprocity of friendship?" It was the duty, Madison concluded, "of those to whose care the public interest and welfare is committed, to turn the tide [of trade] to a more favorable direction."

Though the House of Representatives approved Madison's discrimination proposals, the Senate rejected them, and in the rush of business at the end of the session, accommodation failed, so the measure was lost. Madison had, nonetheless, laid down principles of foreign and commercial policy from which he never departed: though he favored free trade as the surest way to greater prosperity, he saw that in a world of hostile, greedy nations, each seeking its own advantage, positive action by the United States to protect its own interest was both permissible and necessary. Any other course, Madison asserted persistently, was dishonorable and would leave the United States with the form, not the substance, of independence.[23]

The debates on commercial discrimination also revealed fundamentally different attitudes toward France and Great Britain that aroused memories of similar disputes between Americans before the peace treaty of 1783 (see Chapter VII). Fisher Ames, the most effective opponent of discrimination, though conceding that Madison was "a man of sense, reading, address, and integrity . . . our first man," charged that the Virginian was nevertheless "very much Frenchified in his politics." Ames meant not to asperse Madison's patriotism, but rather to complain of his too-ready inclination to connect American interests with those of France, a charge first leveled at Madison nine years earlier, when he had defended Franklin and the French alliance during the revolution. Madison, on the other hand, blamed much of the opposition to his anti-British policy on "the spirit of this city [New York], which is steeped in anglicanism." By this he meant the atmosphere created by the inclinations of merchants with British connections, the appeal British aristocracy and government still had for some people, the influence of British agents, and the presence in New York of many whose Tory sympathies had persisted throughout the revolution. The danger, more apparent to Madison each day he remained in fashionable New York society, was that pro-British sentiments might coalesce around domestic and foreign policies which would turn the new nation from its independent republican course, back toward a shameful alliance, no less real for its informality, with the corrupt, aristocratic former mother country. The conditions were present, and the groundwork had been laid, for the party battles of the coming decade.[24]

Before the debates had reached a decisive state, however, Congress forgot its differences to join in the acclaim and celebration of the inauguration of the first President of the United States. George Washington had completed his triumphant procession to New York on April 23, when he crossed the bay from New Jersey on an elegant barge made and decorated for the occasion. Landlubber Madison, glad he wasn't one of the Congressional delegation chosen to accompany the new President on the windy barge voyage, was in the throng that cheered Washington's arrival at the foot of Wall Street and then, amid bells, cannon salutes, and huzzas, followed the procession up Queen Street to the executive residence. A state dinner given by Governor Clinton, brilliant fireworks, and candles in windows all over town concluded the day's celebrations. Excitement gripped the city until Inauguration Day, April 30, when at noon Madison went to Washington's residence on Cherry Street (now lost in the approaches to the Brooklyn Bridge) to march in the formal procession, immediately behind the President, as one of five delegates from the House of Representatives. At City Hall (henceforth called Federal Hall), Washington and his Congressional escort went inside, where the new chief executive was introduced to the legislature. Then he went to the portico, where Chancellor Livingston of New York administered the oath of office. Madison and other Congressmen joined the crowd at the junction of Wall and Broad streets below as shouts of "God bless our President" filled the air. Washington bowed his acknowledgements, and followed by members of Congress, returned to the Senate chamber to read the short address he and Madison had prepared at Mount Vernon two months earlier.

Washington stood awkwardly in dark brown dress, left hand thrust into a high pants pocket, and right hand nervously turning pages; he was more "agitated and embarrassed," one observer noted, "than ever he was by the leveled cannon or pointed musket." He spoke in a deep, low voice, and ventured only one gesture, "a flourish with his right hand, which left rather an ungainly impression . . . when he came to the words *all the world*." Though the sentiments he expressed were conventional, and his delivery was monotonous, it was nevertheless "a very touching scene and quite of the solemn kind," reported Fisher Ames, sitting next to Madison. "I, pilgarlic, sat entranced," wrote the Massachusetts orator, who was overwhelmed by Washington's sincerity and filled with "emotions of the most affecting kind. [The speech] seemed to me an allegory in which virtue was personified, and addressing those whom she would make her votaries." The less emotional Madison, better acquainted with Washington and aware of what he would say, listened more calmly, and gladly left the crowded chamber to walk half a mile to St. Paul's Church, where the assembled dignitaries heard Bishop Prevost lead a short Episcopal service, familiar to Washington and Madison since boyhood. Watching the fifty-seven-year-old Washington during the prayers, Ames thought, "time has made havoc on his face." Since the arrangements committee had mercifully spared the weary hero-statesman any further ceremony, he rode from the church to a private dinner at home. That evening Madison went to Battery Park to watch an ingenious fireworks display. A large illumination with a portrait of Washington in the center, an emblem of fortitude above him, justice personified by the Senate on his left, and wisdom, the House of Representatives, on his right, burned brightly and then faded into the night. The press of people was so great even Washington had to walk home. Carriages couldn't move. Tired, but pleased at the display of affection for Washington, Madison walked slowly back to Mrs. Elsworth's on Maiden Lane with his fellow lodgers.[25]

Washington's inaugural address was referred by the House of Representatives for response to a committee headed by Madison. He drafted the brief reply subsequently approved by the committee and by the House. When Washington received this message, he wrote confidentially to Madison, "Notwithstanding the conviction I am under of the labor which is imposed upon you by the public individuals as well as by public bodies; yet as you have begun, so I wish you to finish, the good works." That is, Madison had undertaken every part of the business: he had drafted Washington's address in the first place, managed its delivery, and written the reply of the House of Representatives; "to finish the good works," he not only drafted Washington's reply to the House, but the one to the Senate as well. Though these messages were routine, they did set a certain simple republican tone, and marked Madison as the principal architect of precedent-setting measures and procedures.[26]

The formalities of the inauguration raised again the difficult question of titles for the President and other officers of the new government. Since the British government was both the most familiar one in America and the only example in a major power of communication between an executive and a genuinely powerful legislature, it came first to mind. Moreover, nearly all members of Congress had served in state legislatures, where the customs by and large followed English precedent. Yet all were aware that a government founded on a republican revolution could not adopt unchanged the habits of a hereditary monarchy, especially one that had been ridiculed and reviled ever since 1776, when Tom Paine had observed in *Common Sense* that the English crown descended from "a French bastard [who] with an armed banditti" had conquered and oppressed the people. Vice President John Adams and Senator Richard Henry Lee nevertheless thought majestic titles corresponding to those used in the courts of Europe would be absolutely necessary to give the new government proper "dignity and splendor" in the eyes of the people. Adams believed in "the efficacy of pageantry" and declared that "a royal or at least a princely title will be found indispensably necessary to maintain the reputation, authority, and dignity of the President. His Highness, or, if you will, His Most Benign Highness, is the correct title that will comport with his constitutional prerogatives and support his state in the minds of our own people or foreigners." Lee concluded a plea for titles asserting that since "all the world, civilized and savage, called for titles; . . . there must be something in human nature that occasioned this general consent." They persuaded the Senate to address the chief executive as "His Highness, the President of the United States of America, and Protector of the Rights of the Same."[27]

The House of Representatives, led by Madison, had agreed that the simple title President of the United States was both most appropriate and fully dignified. When the Senate proposed differently, some defiant republicans in the House sought to rebuke the upper chamber for its aristocratic airs. Madison opposed titles, but pleaded for compromise. He did not "conceive titles to be so pregnant with danger as some gentlemen apprehend," because in Europe, in absurd little principalities and dukedoms, "superb and august" titles did not confer power or influence or even respect. But, Madison said, titles "are not very reconcilable with the nature of our Government or the genius of the people. . . . Instead of increasing, they diminish the true dignity and importance of a Republic. . . . The splendid tinsel or gorgeous robe [of pompous courts] would disgrace the manly shoulders of our chief [Washington]. The more truly honorable shall we be, by showing a total neglect and disregard to things of this nature: the more simple, the more Republican we are in our manners, the more rational dignity we shall acquire." Madison then urged, successfully, that the House confer with the Senate, and as chairman of the House conferees, he managed to defeat the Senatorial pretensions. The messages to the chief executive were addressed simply to "the President of the United States."[28]

Madison rejoiced in the plain title, he wrote Jefferson, because it would show "the friends of Republicanism that our new Government was not meant to substitute either Monarchy or Aristocracy, and that the genius of the people is as yet adverse to both." Use of elaborate titles would, moreover, "subject the President to a severe dilemma," because Washington had, with Madison's firm support, resolved to shun all the pretensions of monarchy. The impressive titles were proposed "without any privity or knowledge of it on my part, and urged after I had apprized of it contrary to my opinion," Washington asserted.[29]

As party strife intensified in the seventeen-nineties, Madison and Jefferson sought to use the urging of pompous titles by Adams as proof that he and other Federalists were in fact monarchists in disguise, and historians have been inclined to see in the proposals evidence of powerful antirepublican sentiment in the country. In fact, as Madison had admitted candidly on the floor of the House of Representatives, the matter was not vitally important. Adams and Lee, the radical revolutionists of 1776, believed that a purely republican government, perhaps even more than a despotic one, needed all the support for its authority pageant and ceremony could provide. "I am as much a republican as I was in 1775," Adams protested to Benjamin Rush. In fact, he considered himself a

prudent republican, wise enough to see the forms and ceremony necessary to make the new government work. The Representatives who
declaimed against titles were to Adams foolish men whose naïveté would
destroy the republic for which they spoke so earnestly. Though Madison's suppositions that the people abhorred the trappings of monarchy
(no member of the House of Representatives dared speak or vote publicly for fancy titles) and that titles borrowed from foreign courts would
diminish rather than enhance republican dignity were probably sound,
Adams and his allies need not be vilified for supporting in the United
States ceremonials of government almost universal in the eighteenth century. Few leaders of American government in 1789 (and certainly not
John Adams) were antirepublican, though some did favor, to insure the
order and authority Madison himself so earnestly sought, familiar symbols for government. The dispute was over means not ends.[30]

Of all the burdens of his new office, none troubled Washington more,
and in fact none was more delicate and potentially explosive, than that of
appointments. "If injudicious or unpopular measures should be taken . . .
with regard to appointments," he observed, "the Government itself
would be in the utmost danger of being utterly subverted." "The eyes of
Argus are upon me," he added, "and no slip will pass unnoticed that can
be improved into a supposed partiality for friends or relatives." Merit,
therefore, was his first criterion, and then service during the revolution,
firm support of the new constitution, and equity among the states.
Though Washington had to fill every office from his cabinet and the
justices of the Supreme Court to the lowliest clerks and revenue agents,
there were nevertheless a hundred applicants for every job, supported by
a staggering weight of letters and other recommendations from respectable persons throughout the Union. Since each appointment would tend
to establish a precedent and create vested interests among sections, professions, and parties, Washington agonized exceedingly at every designation. All his prestige, tact, incorruptibility, and sense of fairness were
needed.

Here, as in everything else, Madison stood highest in Washington's
confidence. Senator William Maclay of Pennsylvania wrote, in July 1789,
of rumors that Madison "affected to govern" the President's appointments, and a month later, when the Senate sought to direct patronage,
members discovered that Madison was "deep in this business" of protecting the executive from undue legislative interference. Considering their
common objectives and Washington's keen sense of responsibility for
the judgments made, the case was not one of insidious or improper influence by Madison, but rather one of an effective working arrangement.
The two men had discussed appointments generally even before Congress
had created the offices, and the nature of the executive and judicial

departments was in part fashioned in Congress under Madison's leadership in terms of the persons Washington had in mind appointing.

From the beginning Madison favored Alexander Hamilton to head the vitally important Treasury Department, because he was "best qualified for that species of business and . . . preferred by those who know him personally." Madison knew, long before appointments were made, that Robert R. Livingston "would not succeed" in his application for the treasury office, and that General Henry Knox would be continued in the War Department. John Jay, widely known and respected and very much in Washington's confidence, could have had virtually any office: continuation as Secretary of Foreign Affairs, the Treasury Department (which Madison, probably with relief, thought he would reject), the chief justiceship of the Supreme Court, or a foreign appointment. When Jay wrote Washington in August that he preferred the court, Madison concurred readily and moved carefully toward an objective he and Washington had long cherished: to persuade Jefferson to relinquish his stated preference for continued service in France and to return home to be Secretary of State. Though professing deference to Jefferson's inclinations as he prepared to come to the United States for a visit, Madison hinted with increasing directness during 1789 that Jefferson's obligation lay in New York, not Paris. At Washington's request, Madison helped persuade Edmund Randolph to accept appointment as Attorney General. In Virginia, the new government had to be protected against antifederalists. Egotistical Arthur Lee, for ten years a troublemaker in Madison's view, sought appointment to the federal bench. Washington agreed that he should be rejected, but how could this be done without alienating his powerful family? Only by tendering the appointments to truly distinguished Virginians to whom there could be no objection, so Washington proposed John Blair as Associate Justice and Edmund Pendleton as district judge for Virginia. These decisions were made in New York during the first session of Congress and before there was any cabinet or executive department with which Washington could consult or act. Madison had throughout been at the President's right hand, at once his aide, grand vizier, and prime minister.[31]

One decision, made after Hamilton had been appointed Secretary of the Treasury and just before Madison left New York, however, found Washington rejecting Madison's advice in favor, apparently, of Hamilton's. The unresolved issues arising from the peace treaty with England, and the prospect that Congress would soon pass Madison's commercial regulations aimed at Britain, increasingly embittered Anglo-American relations. The President felt pressed to appoint an agent to go to London to settle outstanding differences. Jay and Hamilton approved the idea (in fact may have aroused Washington to consider it) and recommended that Anglophile Gouverneur Morris be given the mission at once. Wash-

ington asked Madison's opinion, and received three cogent reasons for
delay: it would be better to wait until Jefferson, to be Secretary of
State, had returned; appointing Morris would imply a perhaps unwise
commitment to him to be minister to Britain or France; and Morris
might therefore conduct his first, temporary agency "with an eye" to
obtaining a permanent one. Washington recognized the force of these
arguments and delayed a week. Meanwhile, British secret agent George
Beckwith so alarmed Hamilton and other friends of England about her
probably harsh response to Madison's commercial regulations that the
"Anglomen" stepped up their pressure on Washington. They were anxious, too, to secure Morris' appointment before Jefferson, who, one
Federalist Senator told Beckwith, was "too democratic . . . and a frenchman," could assume his duties and stop it. Washington's appointment of
Morris gave Hamilton an important victory, but because the secret
conversations with Beckwith were unknown to Madison, he was more
puzzled than alarmed that his advice had been rejected.[32]

In Congress Madison persistently sought to defend the authority of the
executive department, since, judging from the conduct of the state governments and the Continental Congress, legislative domination, not executive tyranny, was the chief threat to republican government. The issue
came to a head in the debates over the removal power of the President.
There were, Madison acknowledged, four ways to view the matter:
first, that Congress had the power to create the offices, so it had and
ought to retain the power to decide the tenure of the holders of the
offices; second, that removal ought to be only by impeachment, the
sole mode mentioned in the Constitution; third, that removals ought,
like appointments, to require the approval of the Senate; and fourth,
that the power of removal, being an executive function not proscribed
by the Constitution, ought to rest unrestrained in the hands of the President. After stating practical and constitutional objections to the first
three positions, Madison defended the final one. He pointed out that in
the state governments and "in the political writings of the most celebrated [theorists] . . . [it] is everywhere held as essential to the preservation of liberty, that the three great departments of Government be kept
separate and distinct. . . . If the federal Government should lose its
equilibrium," Madison declared, "that effect will proceed from the Encroachments of the Legislative department." The structure of the Constitution, then, required executive independence in terminating
appointments.

Madison sought most, however, to insure *responsible* leadership in the
new government. It was fatuous, he admonished, harking back to the
debates over ratification, to dwell excessively on the abuse of the removal power by the President. There might be abuses, Madison conceded, but to paralyze the administration because of this fear was simply

to admit that republican government itself was unsafe. Under the careful processes defined by the Constitution, vesting ultimate authority in the people, he asserted, it was "extremely improbable" that a President "not highly distinguished by his abilities and worth" would be elected. Therefore, it would be *safe* to give him substantial authority. Furthermore, it was *necessary*, because giving the Senate a voice in removals would "abolish at once that great principle of unity and responsibility in the Executive department, which was intended for the security of liberty and the public good. If the President should possess alone the power of removal from office, those who are employed in the execution of the law will be in their proper situation, and the chain of dependence be preserved; the lowest officers, the middle grade, and the highest, will depend, as they ought, on the President, and the President on the community. The chain of dependence therefore terminates in the supreme body, namely, in the people." Any other arrangement, Madison insisted, would create "a two-headed monster," leaving the government uncertain of its direction and the people unable to fix responsibility. Persuaded by these arguments, which Fisher Ames asserted were utterly conclusive, Congress confirmed the President's full removal power. It thus set in place an essential prop of what in the course of nearly two centuries was to become the most powerful executive office in the world. Equal in importance to the effectiveness imparted to the government, in Madison's view, was the republican rationality of the removal power. If the people were to judge the conduct of the President, his responsibility for the executive department had to be clear and absolute. Such a system gave the breath of life, not the kiss of death, as the prophets of doom insisted, to the principle of government by consent.[33]

Four days after Washington's inauguration, Madison began in Congress to fulfill his promise, made repeatedly since February 1788, to add a bill of rights to the Constitution. Though there was no open opposition in Congress or in the country to provisions that would prohibit federal interference with such basic personal liberties as freedom of expression, trial by jury, and protection against excessive bail, unregenerate antifederalists still hoped for amendments to limit federal power to tax, to regulate commerce, to make treaties, and to interfere with state laws or court decisions. Any of these changes would, in Madison's view, seriously and perhaps fatally weaken the Constitution. Members of Congress devoted to them resisted the personal liberty amendments, hoping by delay to find an opportunity to enact their drastic structural alterations. Federalists who still thought any amendments unnecessary and unwise sometimes voted with the die-hard antifederalists in opposing Madison's moderate course. Despite the apparent large majority in favor of the personal liberty amendments, Madison saw that resourceful guidance would be required in Congress.

To forestall antifederalists and to fulfill his campaign promises, Madison announced, on May 4, 1789, that as soon as other pressing business permitted, he intended to introduce a bill of rights. "If we can make the Constitution better in the opinion of those who are opposed to it, without weakening its frame, or abridging its usefulness in the judgment of those who are attached to it," Madison told his fellow Congressmen a month later, "we act the part of wise and liberal men to make such alterations as shall produce that effect." He advocated measures to satisfy the large number of people who objected to the Constitution only because it lacked a bill of rights. If these people could be won to the Constitution without weakening it, the effect of adopting a bill of rights, Madison reasoned, looking at his strongly federalist colleagues, would be to strengthen the authority of the new government. He hoped as well that federalist support of a bill of rights would convince North Carolina and Rhode Island to ratify the Constitution.

Madison himself, however, had gone far beyond tactical reasons for supporting a bill of rights. Though he had once agreed with James Wilson and others that the carefully enumerated grant of powers in the Constitution automatically guaranteed all the personal liberties, and that any listing of them might by implication deny some rights, Madison now defended the usefulness of an explicit declaration. First, he said, the British bill of rights, usually considered still operative in the United States, raised a barrier only against executive interference. Furthermore, freedom of the press and of conscience had come to have a much wider meaning in America than in England. These extensions, Madison suggested, ought to be stated clearly in a bill of rights specifically suited to the United States. It was also necessary, especially in a republican government resting ultimately upon the people, to define the limits to the powers of the legislative branch and even of the majority itself. As Madison explained it, "the prescriptions in favor of liberty ought to be levelled against that quarter where the greatest danger lies, namely, that which possesses the highest prerogative of power. But this is not found in either the Executive or Legislative departments of Government, but in the body of the people, operating by the majority against the minority. It may be thought that all paper barriers against the power of the community are too weak to be worthy of attention; . . . yet as they have a tendency to impress some degree of respect for them, to establish the public opinion in their favor, and rouse the attention of the whole community, it may be one means to control the majority from those acts to which they might be otherwise inclined."

Madison sought also to prevent broad construction of some powers of Congress from encroaching on the rights of the people. Suppose, for example, Congress asserted that general search warrants were necessary to properly carry out its power to collect taxes. An explicit proscription of general warrants in the Constitution, Madison observed, would surely make it easier to resist such an inadmissible interpretation. It would help, too, to give the federal courts ("independent tribunals of justice") as well as the state courts clear authorization to be "guardians of the people's liberties." A bill of rights in the federal constitution would add this protection in states having their own bills of rights, and would supply some protection in states having none. Madison's argument rested on an intention to make the rights of the people as secure as possible. Explicit statement of them, in as many constitutions as possible, taking care not by omission to exclude any rights, would afford maximum legal protection for them and help fasten them in the public mind.

The amendments proposed by Madison had been culled largely from the hundreds proposed at the state ratifying conventions. His suggestions were referred to a committee, shortened, clarified, and reported back to the House. In mid-August, when the House found time to return to the amendments, obstruction persisted. New Englanders intent on preventing Congressional interference with their state-supported churches, and others who still cherished government assistance to religion in general, sought a clause on religious liberty merely prohibiting establishment of a *national* religion and restraining Congress from prescribing "articles of faith or a mode of worship." Some Congressmen sought to require Representatives or Senators to abide by instructions given them by their constituents, and others wanted the word "expressly" added to the amendment reserving to the respective states "the powers not delegated to Congress." Madison argued that a contradictory tangle of binding instructions would paralyze the legislature and prevent rational deliberation, while to restrict the general government to powers expressly granted in the Constitution would require impossible foresight and an impractical amount of detail in the Constitution. By insisting that the essential powers of Congress be preserved, that rights not be lost by timorous statement of them, and that only amendments likely to meet with overwhelming approval be submitted to the states, Madison and his supporters managed to secure the support of two thirds of both houses of Congress to twelve amendments before the end of its first session in September 1789. Thus the base of support for the new government widened substantially, and what has come to be a cherished part of the Constitution received nearly final definition.

Madison's devotion to natural rights is evident in the portions of his original proposals that Congress or the states rejected. He had, for example, suggested the bill of rights begin with the Lockean principles stated in the Virginia declaration of rights and the Declaration of Independence: that the legitimate powers of government were derived from the people, that government existed to promote the happiness and safety of the people, and that the people had "an indubitable, unalienable, and indefeasible right to reform or change their Government, whenever it be found adverse or inadequate to the purposes of its institution." These

clauses were omitted as unnecessary, because the Constitution in no way
denied them, and because they had been a solemn foundation of American government since 1776. Madison had also proposed that "no person
religiously scrupulous of bearing arms shall be compelled to render military service in person." He sought both to give the widest possible scope
to freedom of conscience and to demonstrate the diversity a republican
government could safely accommodate. Finally Madison had sought an
amendment unmentioned by any state convention: that "no state shall
violate the equal rights of conscience, or the freedom of the press, or the
trial by jury in criminal cases." Convinced that state legislatures were
at least as likely as Congress to enact illiberal legislation, Madison attempted an enormously significant enlargement of the protection
afforded basic rights of the people. He sought so forthrightly to use
national power to insure maximum personal freedom that the nation at
large refused to follow him. More clearly than any of his colleagues in
nation building, Madison saw that effective, authoritative government
and genuine liberty for the people were not only compatible but were
in fact essential props for each other.[34]

Before adjournment of the fruitful, precedent-setting first meeting of
Congress—a session whose "great moderation and liberality," Madison
said, "disappointed the wishes and predictions of many who have opposed
the Government"—Congress resumed the heated quarrel over location
of the capital. Again the public discussion was about whether the permanent capital should be near the center of "wealth, population, and territory," as would be a site on the Delaware River (possibly Trenton), or
closer to the geographic center of the country and accessible to the
future western expansion of the country, as would be the head of
navigation on the Potomac. All agreed that the temporary capital, for
ten years or more, had to be in a centrally located city able to accommodate Congress and the offices of government. This meant Philadelphia, or
slightly less practical, New York. Intense behind-the-scenes negotiations
went on among members of Congress, with each state delegation, and
even factions within the delegations, seeking both a temporary and a
permanent location favorable or convenient to it.

Madison acted as a Virginian, seeking a temporary location in Philadelphia and a permanent capital on the Potomac. He resisted particularly a New York–New England coalition working for New York and
Trenton as temporary and permanent sites. If united, Pennsylvania and
all states south of her could prevent this, but they disputed whether the
permanent site should be on the Potomac or the Susquehanna. Some
New Englanders and New Yorkers sought Southern aid in keeping the
temporary capital in New York in exchange for permanent location on
the Susquehanna, while Pennsylvanians sought to play off Southerners

against Northerners to secure both temporary and permanent capitals for their state. To emphasize the dangers in such sectional cabals, Madison reminded Congress of the suspicions the year before in the Virginia ratifying convention among members from Kentucky and Appalachia that a strengthened national government would neglect their interests. Had the distrustful members from western Virginia been able to foresee the cynical arrangements now pending, Madison warned, they would have voted against the Constitution, and Virginia thus would have remained out of the Union. When coalitions hostile to the Potomac seemed near victory, Madison managed to gather enough uncertain and discontented votes to prevent any action. Fearing the effect of the acrimonious debate on other legislation, Madison sought postponement until a more propitious occasion presented itself. It was clear, nevertheless, that members considered the location of the capital a crucial question, and that its settlement could have an important effect on other major policy decisions soon to be made.[35]

The stalled debate on the national capital permitted Congress to adjourn until January 1790. It had set in motion the administration of the new government: revenue was assured; executive departments were provided for; a federal judiciary was established; and a bill of rights designed to consolidate support for the new government had been offered to the states. Except for the judiciary act, fashioned in the Senate, Madison had taken the lead at every stage, and the resulting legislation was largely as he wanted it to be. When he set out for Orange in the fall of 1789, he could view the work of the last six months in New York with satisfaction. The long task of framing and ratifying a new constitution had had its decisive fulfillment as the great departments of government acquired form and personnel. Madison knew, too, that his role throughout had been uniquely creative, and that excepting only Washington, his support of the new constitution had been more influential than that of any other leader. He was at the pinnacle of his career as a nation builder.

This intense activity matured Madison's political thought. Had a respite from his public duties permitted him in the fall and winter of 1789 to write a treatise in political theory, he would have been at the peak of his power to do so. For three years the happy conjunction of study, debate, planning, exhortation, advising, and legislating had furnished an ideal experience for sharpening useful political concepts. He had a chance to *do* what other philosophers of government could but speculate about.

Like Jefferson and Franklin, Madison rested his political thought on the moral standards of John Locke's *Second Treatise on Civil Government*—primarily that reason requires all men be esteemed free and equal. By this Madison understood that to regard man, or any group of men, a priori, as "unfree," was immoral—that is, could not be defended rationally. There was nothing about the "nature" of any men that could be grounds for depriving them of freedom or that could entitle one man to rule another. A man could become fully human only insofar as he was free. Likewise, there was nothing in the nature of men that conferred upon some of them special privileges. Considered rationally, men were equal in rights and in the esteem to which they were entitled on earth and in heaven. When Madison spoke of man in a state of nature he meant simply to express a moral requirement that men ought to be free and equal. He meant to deny the immemorial traditions of government that some men were "by nature" slaves or subjects, that classification of men into unequal orders was both just and inevitable, that obedience was the only duty in government of the mass of men, and that social order required the subjugation of man to authoritarian control.

Madison did not need to suppose that in some primeval age, before the rise of unjust social institutions or tyrannical governments, a society had once existed where all men had enjoyed the full freedom and equality of the state of nature. The concept "state of nature" was moral or normative, describing the condition that ought to be, rather than historical, having reference to a society which might once have existed. Nor did Madison use the terms "free" and "equal" in any absolute or literal sense. He knew perfectly well that any society, especially a complex, civilized one, imposed many legitimate, unavoidable limitations on the right of a man to do as he pleased. Furthermore, since men obviously were unequal in talents and abilities, they would necessarily differ in their achievements in life. The moral imperative of equality required, for example, not that Isaac Newton and his stablekeeper be equal in fame or wisdom or wealth, but rather that one could not justly rule the other and that each had the same "natural" right to life, liberty, and the pursuit of happiness. When Madison spoke of the natural rights of freedom and equality he had in mind ideals, or standards, in terms of which societies and governments could be judged and toward which men should aspire.

In applying these moral imperatives, Madison and other men of reason on both sides of the Atlantic insisted, to begin with, that the state existed to protect and expand freedom and equality of opportunity, and that the surest way to prevent betrayal of this purpose was to rest the powers of government on the consent of the governed. This concept did not always mean in Madison's day, as it might seem to do in the twentieth century, universal suffrage or the elimination of such unrepublican features as a house of lords or a hereditary monarch. Rather, it meant, in the English Whig formulation following Locke, which Madison knew by heart, that there had to be a powerful *portion* of the government responsive to the people, ordinarily through a legislative body composed of their elected representatives. The antiroyalist sentiment of the American Revolution, and the absence of a hereditary nobility in the United States, caused American theorists to lay aside Lockean formulations that the people might consent to hereditary forms, but Madison and most of his colleagues in nation building continued to accept Whiggish limitations on the subsequently hallowed dictum of "one man, one vote," and to work earnestly at "refinements" in government capable of restraining the majority. The essence of consent for Madison was to insure that the government could not ignore or oppose ultimately the will and interests of the people being governed; this was *his* hallowed "republican principle," to which all just governments had to conform. Madison's chief purpose as a political theorist and statesman was to find the mechanisms that would provide such insurance while maintaining order and virtue in government.

Also implied in the doctrine of consent was the right of national independence. Locke had scored the injustice of domination by conquest, the clearest and most complete denial of freedom and equality. The harsh rule of alien armies, wherein some were absolute masters and others abject slaves, was in the political literature of the Age of Reason always the prime example of injustice and denial of the rights of man. When the resistance to British oppression in North America became a movement for independence and a war to expel occupying armies, the sense of connection between natural rights and nationhood increased immensely. Then, as a means to realize both national independence and the principle of consent, the natural-rights theorists insisted on the right of revolution. They reasoned that since government existed to nourish and insure freedom and equality, and indeed had no other purpose, when it betrayed those obligations it lost its legitimate authority and in a sense annulled itself, leaving the people free to replace it. The right of revolution, in fact, was inseparable from the insistence that government, far from being an absolute or divine institution recognizing no superior authority, was subordinate to certain purposes or principles, which those being governed could discern and judge for themselves. A divergence between the acts of government and rationally discoverable natural rights required that the government be changed or abolished.

To give effect to "the republican principle" within a nation, Madison asserted that the freedom least subject to social restraint was freedom of expression, including the rights to believe, speak, and write according to one's own lights. Without these rights, so often denied by allegedly legitimate governments, freedom meant very little. Put positively, man could not be the kind of being Enlightenment philosophers insisted he should or might be without these opportunities of expression. To give further reality to freedom, Madison also considered certain personal immunities sanctioned in English law to be natural rights—trial by jury, confrontation of witnesses, freedom from general warrants, seizures, excessive bail, and cruel punishments, a guarantee of habeas corpus, and subjugation of armies to civil control. Though freedom meant more than these things, the arbitrary, oppressive acts of the Stuarts, Bourbons, and other mighty rulers around the globe made it clear to Madison that substantial success in achieving them would bring mankind immeasurably closer to the moral imperatives.

Madison normally assumed or implied these fundamentals. He seldom discussed them explicitly or argued for them as opposed to other basic principles. They were the sentiments John Adams said were "hackneyed in Congress" in 1774, 1775, and 1776 and which Jefferson said, explaining his objective in drafting the Declaration of Independence, were "an expression of the American mind" at that time. The authority of the Declaration, Jefferson wrote, rested "on the harmonizing sentiments of the day, whether expressed in conversation, in letters, printed essays, or the elementary books of public right, as Aristotle, Cicero, Locke, Sidney, etc." These sentiments guided Madison's efforts to frame, ratify, execute, and expound a free government for the United States.[36]

As a realist and as a practical politician, Madison sought to give meaning to the moral requirements of the natural-rights doctrine in a way relevant to the actual character of man and the society in which he lived. In understanding the nature of man, Madison followed John Locke's *Essay concerning Human Understanding*, which, by insisting that sensory impressions were the sole source of human knowledge, emphasized the diversity of mankind. Each human being was the product of a unique pattern of sense impressions, and therefore in some measure different from other humans. Since this limitless variety resulted from the very nature of the human mind, the life of man had to be organized in ways permitting expression of this diversity. To do otherwise would impose an unjust contradiction on human society. Hence the emphasis on freedom in the thought of Locke and all those who followed him. Furthermore, since, as Locke had put it, after describing the inclination of men to cherish or value different things, "men may choose differently, and yet all choose right," a good society had to be tolerant, flexible, receptive to change, open. Privilege and hierarchy arbitrarily restraining the choices, opportunities, and inclinations of any person were inadmissible. In accepting Lockean epistemology and its understanding of the diversity of mankind, Madison in fact accepted the essential foundation of an open society and the burden, as a theorist of government, of blending variety, change, and uncertainty with more fixed and orderly political concepts.

Madison's political experience confirmed this diversity. He saw the good and bad sides of human nature and all the infinite gradations that could exist between the extremes. The contrast between the benign religious freedom of Pennsylvania and the persecuting bigotry of Virginia had led him to favor liberty of conscience. During the revolution he had experience with both patriots and knaves. In seeking to correct the weaknesses in the Union, he had suffered the opposition of such perversely selfish men as those who dominated the Rhode Island legislature, and he had enjoyed the support of the men gathered in Philadelphia in the summer of 1787, whom he thought "pure in their Motives, . . . [and] devoted to the object committed to them." Near the end of his life, reflecting on over half a century of experience with public affairs, Madison observed that "some gentlemen, consulting the purity and generosity of their own minds, without averting to the lessons of experience, would find a security against [tyranny and malice] in our social feelings; in a respect for character; in the dictates of the monitor within. . . . But man is known to be a selfish, as well as a social being. Respect for character, though often a salutary restraint, is but too often overruled by other motives. . . . We all know that conscience is not a sufficient safeguard; and besides, that conscience itself may be deluded; may be misled . . . into acts which an enlightened conscience would forbid." Such was the diverse nature of man.[37]

Madison insisted, as he remarked during the Federal Convention, that in framing governments, "we must not shut our eyes to the nature of man, nor to the light of experience." Following Locke's empirical method, he studied as fully and carefully as he could the experience of mankind recorded in the histories of his day. From these books, and from the generalizations of philosophers from Aristotle to David Hume, Madison absorbed a sober view of human history. The record was generally one of war, tyranny, violence, stupidity, and corruption, with distressingly few instances of peace, prosperity, and enlightenment. The thought of Machiavelli, Calvin, and Hobbes, known to, though largely rejected by, Madison, helped keep him in mind of human depravity. Unlike some Enlightenment thinkers, who emphasized human goodness to the point of blaming all evil on social conditions, Madison sought always to recognize and take into account the limitations of human nature.

Shunning the extreme attitudes on human nature helped Madison avoid simplistic and impractical theories of government. "If men were angels," as he had pointed out in *Federalist* Number 51, "no government would be necessary." On the other hand, if men were absolutely evil, as he told the Virginia Convention of 1788, "we are in a wretched condition . . . [where] no form of government can render us secure." The real and difficult problems of government existed precisely because of the mixed character of mankind. There was sufficient reason, virtue, and charity among men to afford some prospect that good government might result from the principle of consent, but there was also sufficient greed, corruption, and ignorance to require the lawful restraints traditionally associated with government. Madison took seriously both modest hopes and grave dangers. The problem was to devise a government giving maximum scope to the former and raising the surest barriers against the latter. In working his way toward this moderate position, Madison may have recalled Aristotle's comment on the place of "the mean between two extremes": "We may add that it is a good criterion of a proper mixture of democracy and oligarchy that a mixed constitution should be able to be described indifferently as either. When this can be said, it must obviously be due to the excellence of the mixture. It is a thing which can generally be said of the mean between two extremes: both of the extremes can be traced to the mean [and it can thus be described by the name of either]." Such a recollection would also have comforted Madison as he heard some critics call the Constitution too "aristocratical" and others label it too "democratic."[38]

Madison had both reservations about democracy and confidence that republican government was far better suited to the nature of man than any other form. He wrote Jefferson in 1787 that

> those who contend for a simple Democracy, or a pure republic, actuated by the sense of the majority . . . assume or suppose a case which is altogether fictitious. They found their reasoning on the idea, that the people composing the Society enjoy not only an equality of political rights; but that they have all precisely the same interests and the same feelings in every respect. . . . We know however that no Society ever did or can consist of so homogeneous a mass of Citizens. . . . In all civilized societies, distinctions are various and unavoidable. A distinction of property results from that very protection which a free Government gives to unequal faculties for acquiring it. . . . [There are also] differences in political, religious or other opinions, or an attachment to the persons of leading individuals. However erroneous or ridiculous these grounds of dissention and faction may appear to the enlightened Statesmen, or the benevolent philosopher, the bulk of mankind who are neither Statesmen nor Philosophers, will continue to view them in a different light.

It was delusive, in Madison's view, to suppose that simple majoritarian democracy would overcome all the contentions and difficulties of civil society. He saw with special clarity that appeals for unity of feeling (Madison probably had in mind repudiating Rousseau's "general will" in the letter to Jefferson), neglected and even often tended to suppress the vital diversities born of freedom.[39]

Late in life he used the same understanding of human nature to refute more dogmatic theorists:

> It has been said that all Government is an evil. It would be more proper to say that the necessity of any Government is a misfortune [a thrust at Paine and Rousseau]. This necessity however exists; and the problem

to be solved is, not what form of Government is perfect [a thrust at Plato], but which of the forms is least imperfect; and here the general question must be between a republican Government in which the majority rule the minority, and a Government in which a lesser number or the least number rule the majority. If the republican form is, as all of us agree, to be preferred [because of the moral requirements of natural rights], the final question must be, what is the structure of it that will best guard against precipitate counsels and factious combinations for unjust purposes, without a sacrifice of the fundamental principle of Republicanism [the task of the federal government]. Those who denounce majority Governments altogether because they may have an interest in abusing their power, denounce at the same time all Republican Government and must maintain that minority governments would feel less of the bias of interest or the seductions of power [a thrust at Hobbes and apologists for monarchy].[40]

Madison would have agreed with Reinhold Niebuhr's dictum that "man's capacity for justice makes democracy possible; but man's inclination to injustice makes democracy necessary." (Madison, of course, would have used "republican government" to indicate what Niebuhr meant by "democracy.") The very flaws in human nature pointed to by authoritarians to confound theories of government by consent provided for Madison the surest defense of republicanism. He turned against the authoritarian theorists their often effective claim that the weaknesses of human nature made government by consent impractical and absurd. By pointing out that absolute power wielded by tyrants not exempt from human failings would be far more dangerous than a republican *dispersal* of power into the hands of the people, Madison made government by consent seem the most realistic and prudent form, as well as one morally preferable.[41]

Madison used the recognition of human diversity and tendency toward faction—"sown in the nature of man" he had asserted in *Federalist* Number 10—to explain the dynamics of the forces he supposed would be at work in the enlarged republican government created by the constitution of 1787. The existence of many interests and factions would in the United States prevent the domination of any one. Thus, Madison prepared to diminish the danger, all too real in small simple democracies as well as in various forms of minority government, that unjust and selfish interests would control the state. Madison's key contribution to the political dialogue of his day was to show that a republican government over a large territory, by dispersing power, provided the surest guard against the corruptions and abuses of power feared by federalists and antifederalists alike.

Some commentators, impressed with the realism of this position and its reliance on selfish interests to defend freedom and government by consent—nowhere does it seem to require virtue in the people, or to propose noble purposes for the nation as a whole—have supposed that Madison therefore too much neglected concern for "the good life." The realistic doctrine of selfish interests restraining each other was, however, but part of Madison's political theory. First, the moral requirements of the Lockean natural-rights theory, founded as they were on human dignity and fulfillment, proposed a profound concept of "the good life." To insist on freedom and equality excluded practices that had for centuries in all parts of the world denied most of mankind any hope of fulfillment. Madison insisted repeatedly that the future of republican government was hopeless without *some* confidence in human virtue, and despite his inattention to the need for virtues in free government in the famous *Federalist* Number 10, his interest in education (to produce *good* rulers and citizens), his concern that the national economy provide virtue-sustaining occupations, and his attention to the virtue-demanding processes of local government all testify to his moral approach. Perhaps even more basic, though, was his acceptance, in part, if not in its full meaning, of the classical dictum that "a state exists for the sake of the good life, and not for the sake of life only." Aristotle insisted that the state nourish the primary ethical principle, "the golden mean," and argued that fortitude, temperance, justice, and prudence were the qualities that made a man happy. A man "afraid of the flies that flew around him," a man who would "murder his dearest friend for a farthing," or who had no more understanding than "an infant or an idiot," would, thus lacking virtue, be miserable. "It is evident," Aristotle declared, that "that government must be the best which is so established that every one therein may have it in his power to act virtuously and live happily." Witherspoon's Aristotelean "Introduction to Government" lectures at Princeton rested upon these axioms from the *Politics*.[42]

The axioms were also inherent in *The Spectator* and other commentaries on public and private life available to Madison. Though he seldom paid explicit attention to them, they nevertheless constituted the underlying *purpose* for which he worked so diligently in devising mechanisms of government. His admiration for George Washington rested squarely upon his embodiment of the Aristotelean (or Addisonian) virtues. A clever structure of government or a shrewd notion of political dynamics meant nothing, in Madison's view, separated from the intention that it protect and provide ways to enlarge the private virtues and public blessings associated with a traditional understanding of "the good life." The first without the latter was mere cynical opportunism, while the latter alone was mere idle dreaming. Like many antifederalists, Madison's ideal was the virtuous republic, a concept he thought compatible with a large nation, though not, as his subsequent break with Hamilton showed, with one *dominated* by selfish commercialism. Madison's quarrel with an antifederalist such as George Mason was over means, not ends. They would have agreed readily on the goal of a virtuous republic, but then differed on whether this was compatible with a centralized government including the commercial Northern states, whether such a government would too much vitiate virtue-producing local responsibility, whether a strong executive would dominate and debauch the representatives of the people, and so on. Madison stood between a Mason and a Hamilton precisely in supposing that with sufficient political ingenuity, the ideals of a virtuous republic and an enlarged, energetic government were not only compatible but helpful to each other.

Madison's political principles revealed themselves in responses to dozens of particular problems during the busy years from 1786 to 1789. As he saw repeatedly how concentration of power inclined toward tyranny or the triumph of selfish interests, his devotion to checks and balances and the doctrine of separation of powers increased. He disliked the legislative domination in the Virginia constitution almost as much as he had the executive domination of the deposed royal government. Each resulted in foolishness and injustice. To Madison, however, separation of powers did not mean *paralysis* of powers. He ridiculed the impotent office of governor created by the Virginia constitution, and he scorned the incapacity of the general government under the Articles of Confederation. His zeal for efficient government at all levels arose from the frustration he felt in seeking to do the things necessary to fulfill the revolution. The domestic chaos and internal quarreling among the states was to him at least as great a threat to freedom and progress as the "sceptre of tyranny" antifederalists saw haunting every move to strengthen government. Even more fatal was the weakness of the country in the face of the formidable threats from abroad. The intrigues of Spain, England, and France, to say nothing of hints of direct aggression, could only be met by a strong, united nation. Madison discerned, as Jefferson was to proclaim in his first inaugural address, that an enlarged republican government, "where every man, at the call of the laws, would fly to the standard of the law, and would meet invasions of the public order as his own personal concern, [is] . . . the strongest government on earth."[43]

In seeking separation of powers Madison meant not only to prevent simple tyranny but to tap more fully the latent increment to power for constructive action afforded by the republican principle. In this insight Madison transcended the traditional dogma, so strong in English radical Whig rhetoric, reacting against royal prerogative, that freedom meant *release* from the authority of government. Under a government of consent, properly constructed to prevent domination by faction, freedom could mean the *use* of power in the public interest. The antifederal

assumption that the powers of republican government were just as oppressive as those of monarchy utterly missed the new dimension, which
was in fact the freedom-extending basis of Madison's vigorous nationalism. A large republic, could, under a properly constructed constitution,
combine its inherent strength with an inherent protection against faction
to realize the fulfillment under self-control implicit in Jefferson's phrase
"an empire of liberty."

Almost as revealing as Madison's unchanging opinions are three vital
matters on which he revised or enlarged his views during the work of
nation building. First, he abandoned his insistence that the federal government have explicit power to void state legislation and accepted instead James Wilson's argument that a clause declaring federal acts
supreme would be more consistent with free government, and in the
long run, fully as effective. Aware of the repeated, flagrant contempt of
various states for the acts and requisitions of the Continental Congress,
and sure that state power and ingenuity would thwart or evade anything
other than a perfectly clear coercive authority vested in the federal government, Madison had gone to Philadelphia in May 1787 determined to
place such coercive power at the heart of the new constitution. First,
however, he came to see that efforts to enforce a federal veto of a state
law would result in "a scene resembling much more a civil war than the
administration of a regular government." More subtly effective and more
consistent with national principle would be an administrative insistence
throughout the nation upon the supremacy of federal laws. Hamilton's
understanding of the use and efficacy of federal judges, marshals, collectors, and other officials in upholding federal law against state encroachment or defiance, evident in *The Federalist*, further reconciled Madison
to the omission of the coercive clause. By making federal law supreme
within its defined sphere, and by making it apply as such directly to the
people, it established a mixed government with limited sovereignty at the
federal level rather than a crude league of states empowered to punish
recalcitrant members. Furthermore, by creating direct bonds of consent
and of obedience between the people and the federal government, it
enhanced the republicanism of that government itself rather than allowing it to be merely reflective of republican states.

Second, Madison switched during the Federal Convention from support of a broad power of the federal government to act and legislate in
the public interest to a belief that its powers ought to be enumerated. He
first supported enumerated powers after the convention had adopted the
"Great Compromise," assuring the states equality in the Senate. Regarding the compromise at first as unjust and unwise, Madison thought it
imprudent to invest such a poorly devised Congress with undefined
powers. The shift reflected as well Madison's aversion as a large-state

delegate to placing large-state interests at the mercy of small-state power in the Senate. Madison's nationalism, in fact, began to recede the moment the nation committed itself to what he considered an unrepublican state equality. His devotion to the principle of consent forbade granting unlimited power to a flawed government. Soon, though, and especially during the fight against Federalist programs in the seventeen-nineties, Madison came to see that the enumeration of the powers of Congress reinforced the concept of the rule of law and was therefore useful, perhaps even necessary, in a republic. In fact, the acceptance of a Senate based on state equality (and thus dependent on a basically different constituency from the House of Representatives), coupled with enumerated powers, expanded substantially the checks and balances implanted in the Constitution. Madison's eventual support of the Senate and of enumeration demonstrated the depth of his distrust of "the idea of a government in one center, as expressed and espoused by [Condorcet], . . . a concentration of . . . power," Madison asserted, "universally acknowledged to be fatal to public liberty."[44]

Madison's final shift, to support of an explicit bill of rights in the federal constitution, was at first tactical, but finally principled as well. Reading Jefferson's persuasive arguments, he came to believe a bill of rights would make the Constitution a better instrument of free republican government. The clear statement of important liberties would help engraft them in the public consciousness and provide a ready defense against future assaults on them. Madison, of course, had never opposed the rights themselves, but rather changed his mind about the surest means of their protection. Again the effect was to deepen his understanding of the devices of government most likely to preserve the moral imperatives of the good society he had learned from Aristotle, John Locke, Joseph Addison, and John Witherspoon, and from half a lifetime of freedom and opportunity in the new world.

Shortly after Madison undertook the labors which earned for him the title Father of the Constitution, Edmund Burke wrote in his *Reflections on the Revolution in France* that: "To make a government requires no great prudence; settle the seat of power, teach obedience; and the work is done. To give freedom is still more easy. It is not necessary to guide; it only requires to let go the rein. But to form a free government, that is, to temper together the opposite elements of liberty and restraint in one conscious work, requires much thought; deep reflection; a sagacious, powerful, and combining mind." Solution of this paradox was the focus of Madison's political thought from 1786 to 1789. That the Constitution of the United States has endured for nearly two hundred years is the measure of his wisdom and success in the endeavor.

CHAPTER XIII

Party Leader

ADISON was at home in Orange County the last three months
of 1789. He had every reason to suppose his work in the
next session of Congress would be much like that in the one
recently adjourned. He would be the floor leader of essentially nonpartisan programs necessary to further establish the new government,
especially to provide funding and repayment of the huge national debt.
He also looked forward to further consultation with Washington and
the executive department, a prospect the more alluring since, with his
wholehearted approval, Alexander Hamilton had been appointed Secretary of the Treasury and Thomas Jefferson Secretary of State. Madison
had then moved in Congress that Hamilton present a plan to fund the
debt and revive the public credit. The two secretaries were friends of
Madison's, and he was sure they would be brilliant, efficient executive
officers. Hamilton wrote Madison in October, cordially and confidently:
"May I ask of your friendship to put to paper and send me your thoughts
on such objects as may have occurred to you for an addition to our revenue; and also as to any modifications of the public debt which could be
made consistent with good faith, the interest of the Public, and of its
Creditors?" Madison replied urging an excise on home distilleries, a higher
duty on imported liquor, and a land tax to increase revenue. The land tax
would have the added advantage of "pre-occupying" for the national government a source of revenue the states would otherwise acquire. On the
debt, Madison suggested vaguely that it be extinguished rather than per-
petuated, because the public expected that, and because otherwise it would
fall into the hands of foreigners. Madison concluded with "affection and
regards." Obviously, Madison and Hamilton each expected further cooperation.[1]

At the same time Hamilton wrote asking for advice on the debt, however, he held secret conversations with British agent George Beckwith, in which he indicated grounds for party opposition and Madison's place in them. According to notes taken by Beckwith and sent to his superiors in London, Hamilton had explained his own well-known preference for close relations with England. *"We think in English,"* Hamilton observed, "and have a similarity of prejudices, and of predilections." Beckwith then observed with regret the effort in Congress to discriminate against British trade, and especially his surprise at finding Madison, a man "of good sense, and other qualifications, . . . so decidedly hostile to us." Hamilton replied "I confess I was likewise rather surprised at it," and added that although Madison was "a clever man, he is very little Acquainted with the world. That he is Uncorrupted and Incorruptible I have not a doubt; he has the same End in view that I have, And so have those gentlemen, who Act with him, but their mode of attaining it is very different." Though Hamilton sought to allay Beckwith's fears about Madison, the secretary had nonetheless revealed a division he would not have thought merely one of means had he known the depth of the Madison-Jefferson conviction that the United States needed more, not less, independence from England. Had Madison known of Hamilton's conversations with Beckwith, the Virginian would have been very alarmed indeed, and probably would have moved more quickly than he did in opposing Hamilton's influence.[2]

Just before Christmas 1789, Jefferson returned to Monticello after five years as minister at the court of Versailles. He hoped and expected to go back to France after attending to some pressing personal problems, but Washington's determination (strengthened by Madison's advice and pleas) to have him in the cabinet left him with little choice; "it is not for an individual to choose his post," Jefferson wrote the President, but "you are to marshal us as may be best for the public good." Still hoping Washington would change his mind, Jefferson greeted Madison joyfully when the Congressman rode to Monticello for a brief visit at the year's end. Amid eager conversations about the great events each had witnessed and acted in during the five years of separation, the two men spoke cautiously of the difference between Jefferson's inclination and Washington's wishes. Jefferson was worried that domestic duties—record keeping, handling patents, issuing commissions, supervising territorial governments—would, though routine, be a heavy burden. Not so, Madison said, adding that should the task prove beyond Jefferson's considerable talent for managing such matters, the office could be divided and the secretary relieved of his domestic duties.[3]

Franklin was too old for the job, Madison pointed out, John Adams had been elected Vice President, and John Jay appointed Chief Justice; no other American approached Jefferson in experience or skill in foreign affairs. Furthermore, Madison argued, Jefferson's great objects in returning to Europe—improving Franco-American commercial relations and encouraging the hopes for liberty stimulated there by the French Revolution—could be promoted more effectively by a policymaker at home than by a mere agent abroad. It was essential, therefore, that Jefferson submit to the President's decision. After the conversation, Madison urged Washington to persist in the appointment, predicting Jefferson's acceptance, finally transmitted formally to Washington in mid-February 1790. Implications that Jefferson and Madison sought partisan political objectives in these discussions are far-fetched, since neither man at this time foresaw the disputes that would arise over Hamilton's as yet undisclosed plans for establishing the public credit. Nor was there yet any partisan dispute in the United States over the merit or methods of the French Revolution. The talks at Monticello seem to have been entirely about Jefferson's desire to return to France, Washington's need for his assistance in the cabinet, and Madison's conviction that Jefferson's republicanism, understanding of foreign affairs, and administrative skill were exactly the combination required to launch the new Department of State. That the two friends looked forward to working together in New York and expected continuing agreement on nearly all public questions goes without saying, but such amity does not necessarily amount to partisan scheming.[4]

Confident that Jefferson would soon be in New York, Madison returned to Montpelier and set out on another uncomfortable winter journey northward, already late for the scheduled opening of Congress on January 4, 1790. He had delayed his departure until assured that his mother would recover from a critical illness, but he did not indulge himself to stay for the wedding a few days later of his sister Sarah to Thomas Macon. In Georgetown Madison suffered a severe dysentery attack. A stopover of a few days and some powerful medicine cured him, but left a bad outbreak of piles, still troublesome when he arrived in New York and took his seat in Congress on January 20. On the twenty-fifth he consulted with Washington about British and Spanish intrigues to detach Kentucky from the union, and on the twenty-eighth he dined at the President's house with a large company of Congressmen and government officials. Another busy legislative season was under way.[5]

The major business was Hamilton's comprehensive plan to establish the public credit of the United States, laid before Congress on January 14 in an impressive pamphlet of fifty-one folio pages. The secretary discoursed at length on the need for a strong credit structure if the new nation was to attract the trade and investment necessary for sound, swift economic growth. Madison agreed wholeheartedly; in fact, Hamilton quoted a portion of an appeal for payment of the war debts Madison had written in 1783. In particular, Hamilton proposed the full, prompt payment of the principal and interest of the portion of the debt owed abroad, principally to the French and Dutch governments. This amounted to nearly $12 million of a national debt calculated to be about $54 million. Madison approved completely, as did nearly all members of Congress. The loans from abroad had been made in good faith by friendly governments and bankers in "hard" currency at a time of great need during the revolution. National honor required the immediate discharge of this obligation.

The other parts of the report took Madison by surprise and excited grave misgivings. Hamilton proposed to pay current holders of the more than $40 million owed to citizens of the United States the full face value of the principal and all accrued interest. These debts included certificates issued during the revolution to pay soldiers and to buy supplies and services required by the army, bonds owned by citizens who loaned money to the Continental Congress, and certificates issued to redeem Continental currency. The difficulty was that the threatened bankruptcy of the general government and the long defaulted interest payments had led to severe depreciation of all of this paper; the market value of some certificates had at times been 10 per cent or less of the face value. Moreover, those who had suffered most in becoming creditors of the nation, especially veterans of the Continental army paid in irredeemable certificates, when they had no choice but to accept them, had in most cases been forced to sell their certificates at greatly depreciated rates. Speculators stood to profit enormously under a plan providing payment at face value to current holders. Madison had supposed that some effort would be made to compensate the original holders by taking into account the depreciated prices at which the later purchasers had obtained the certificates.

The third part of Hamilton's plan, that the federal government assume all the still outstanding Revolutionary War debts incurred by the states (estimated at $25 million), also disturbed Madison. These debts were even more confused than the national debt. In some states, including Virginia, the debts had been incurred so hastily and chaotically, and records which survived the ravages of war and fire were so sketchy, that state officials had no clear idea of their obligations. Some states had either largely discharged their debts or made sound provision for repayment, while others, especially Massachusetts and South Carolina, owed huge, unfunded sums. Furthermore, Madison observed, the cost and desolation of the revolution had impinged on the states most unequally—should not an accounting of these injuries be made and states be compensated accordingly in any plan to settle the finances of the revolution?

On February 11, a Massachusetts Congressman reported, "Mr. Madison who has hitherto been extremely reserved came forward in a long speech" announcing his opposition to Hamilton's plan for payment at face value to current holders of the national debt. The Virginian proposed instead that original holders who had kept their securities be paid in full, but holders who had purchased certificates at depreciated rates be paid at the highest market rate (plus interest), with the difference between that rate and the face value devolving upon the original holders. Madison sought no total reduction in the payments due from the government; this would be in bad faith. Rather, he proposed a *redistribution* of the payments, to benefit those who had suffered from the government's earlier defaults, and to scale down the profits of the speculators who had gathered the depreciated certificates. Hamilton's supporters pointed out that inadequate records of original purchasers and the difficulty of determining the "highest market rate" of the securities made Madison's plan utterly impractical; Madison retorted that if a fraction of the energy and zeal lavished on speculation was applied to solving the practical difficulties, a substantial measure of justice could be secured. Friends of the Treasury plan argued as well that those who had bought the depreciated certificates should not be wholly excluded from public gratitude; their purchases had sustained what little was left of the public credit during dark days when the chance that the certificates would become utterly worthless was very great indeed. As the tide ran strongly against Madison, he explained to his father that "the proposition for compromizing the matter between original sufferers and the stockjobbers, after being long agitated, was rejected by a considerable majority, less perhaps from a denial of the justice of the measure, than a supposition of its impracticality."[6]

Madison more successfully rallied resistance to the plan for assumption of the state debts. He proposed that the federal government assume responsibility for the debts as they had existed in 1783, at the close of the revolution. To simply assume the debts outstanding in 1790 would benefit the delinquent states and penalize those that had sacrificed to fulfill their obligations. Madison further insisted on an accounting and equalization of the total expenses and losses incurred during the revolution by all the states. Though such changes would add one third to the amount of the debt assumed, "rendering the measure more just and satisfactory . . . would more than compensate for this," Madison asserted. On April 22, Madison spoke for over an hour against assumption, using arguments Fisher Ames said "seemed to have [been] framed . . . with great care, [though] the reasoning is specious [and] will not bear a strict examination." Supported by all but one of the Virginia delegation, and representatives from other states calculated to suffer under the assumption plan, Madison blocked Hamilton's measures four times between February and July 1790.[7]

During the months of stalemate Congress renewed debate over the location of the national capital. The self-interested arguments and complicated maneuvers of the previous session were resumed, until many began to despair of a solution. "The business of the seat of Government is become a labyrinth," Madison wrote, "for which the votes printed furnish no clue, and which it is impossible in a letter to explain." Bitter articles, some perhaps written by Madison, filled the newspapers, charging members of Congress with corruption, selfishness, and inconsistency. As warm weather and warm debate frayed nerves, an epidemic of "influenza or something like it" spread in New York. A "dangerous" attack kept Madison at home for several days in late April, and in May Congressman Theodorick Bland (of course, this old nemesis of Madison's had been the lone supporter in the Virginia delegation of Hamilton's assumption plan) died of the disease. Jefferson had "a tedious spell of the headache," and Washington himself was "at the point of death" before he recovered. In late June, "somber, haggard, and dejected beyond description," according to Jefferson's account, Hamilton approached the recently arrived Secretary of State on the street in front of the President's house and proposed that the two cabinet officers, vitally concerned with the successful administration of the government, seek to settle the vexatious assumption and seat-of-government questions. Sensing Hamilton's distress, and himself aware of the animosities in Congress, Jefferson decided to ask his colleague to dine with him and Madison the next day, when they might "by some mutual sacrifices of opinion . . . form a compromise which was to save the Union."[8]

When Hamilton appeared at Jefferson's table in a newly rented house on Maiden Lane, Madison was the only other guest. Over some of Jefferson's good Madeira, the three men spoke candidly of the dilemma. Madison was disposed to compromise, but he insisted that the assumption plan in some way reward the efforts several states had made to pay their debts and compensate Virginia for the destruction in the state during the Revolutionary War. A proposal for federal payments to Virginia and some other states that had made substantial efforts to discharge revolutionary obligations, which in Madison's view meant that financially assumption was "no longer of much consequence to Virginia," seemed acceptable, so it was agreed the Virginians would persuade two Congressmen whose districts bordered the Potomac to vote for assumption. Hamilton agreed, for his part, to persuade Pennsylvania Congressmen (through Robert Morris) to vote for the permanent capital on the Potomac, if it was agreed as well that the temporary capital should be Philadelphia. Madison said, Jefferson reported, that though he would not vote for assumption "nor entirely withdraw his opposition, yet he would not be strenuous, but leave it to its fate." Before Congress adjourned in August the compromise measures passed. One Philadelphia newspaper announced that "Miss Assumption" had given birth to two illegitimate children, "Philadelphia" and "Potowmacus," as a result of the seductive attentions of "Mr. Residence."

Though there undoubtedly was a "bargain" made, we need not suppose it corrupt. In insisting on the modifications in the assumption plan, Madison secured much of what he had been urging in the debates in Congress for four months. He had never opposed the idea of assumption itself, but only the inequities of the plan first proposed by Hamilton. The Secretary of the Treasury, for his part, agreed to the sacrifice of a sectional interest that in his judgment had no particularly principled foundation. Jefferson thought merely that he had presided over a compromise without which, he had written Monroe, "our credit . . . will burst and vanish, and the states separate to take care everyone of itself." Through the long final session of Congress in New York the sense of urgent need to close ranks until the new government was safely under way proved strong enough, once again, to united men soon to be bitterly opposed party leaders.[9]

Private letters and remarks reveal differences in sectional interests and in attitudes toward government far deeper than those suggested in the rather restrained debates over the alleged inequities and impracticalities of funding and assumption. Even before Madison spoke openly against the funding plan he wrote alarmingly to Jefferson of "the avidity for stock" that had greatly raised security prices, and of "emissaries . . . exploring the interior and distant parts of the Union in order to take advantage of the ignorance of holders." Members of Congress were alleged to have dispatched ships southward laden with money to buy up depreciated certificates. Senator Maclay of Pennsylvania asserted, "There is no room to doubt but connection is spread over the whole continent on this villainous business [of stock speculating]." From Philadelphia Benjamin Rush wrote Madison indignantly of Hamilton's unjust and immoral plan, hatched in the New York nest of "British agents, . . . Tories, and antifederalists." Madison responded approvingly and elicited from Rush the further charge that Congress "appear as if they were legislating for British Subjects." "I sicken," Rush concluded, "every-time I contemplate the European Vices that [Hamilton's] gambling report will necessarily introduce into our infant republic." Obviously, corrupt and ulterior motives, not concern for the public welfare, were widely held responsible for some of the enthusiasm for Hamilton's plans.[10]

The hostility aroused by the plans, on the other hand, alarmed their backers. Hamilton himself, according to arch-Federalist Manasseh Cutler, viewed Madison's opposition as "a perfidious desertion of the principles which [Madison] was solemnly pledged to defend," or so the Secretary of the Treasury had interpreted Madison's previous support for full payment of the national debt. Apprehensive that Madison would oppose assumption as well, Cutler hoped the Virginian might be appeased by "a particular modification in favor of his own state." Massachusetts Congressman Theodore Sedgwick expressed more complex reservations: "Mr. Madison who is the leader of the opposition [to Hamilton's plans] is an apostate from all his former principles. Whether he is really a convert to anti-federalism, whether he is actuated by the mean and base motive of acquiring popularity in his own state, . . . or whether he means to put himself at the head of the discontented in America, time will discover. The last, however, I do not suspect, because I have ever considered him a very timid man. Deprived of his aid, the [opposition] party would be weak and inefficient." Less than a month later, Fisher Ames complained bitterly of the "uncommon want of prudence as well as moderation" among the Southerners, who had "teased and bullied the House out of their good temper." Characteristically, Vice President John Adams expressed most acidly the Federalist disdain for Madison's new role: "Mr. Madison is a studious scholar, but his Reputation as a man of Abilities is a Creature of French Puffs. Some of the worse Measures, some of the most stupid Motions stand on Record to his Infamy."[11]

Thus, though the nonpartisanship sought by Washington had not entirely disappeared, Madison's break with Hamilton divided "administration" ranks and gave an immense boost in prestige and ability to the opposition. The first sign of the split is visible in Madison's hint to Hamilton in November 1789 that he disliked an expensively financed long-term debt, an outlook sharply at odds with the secretary's belief that a national debt was a blessing that, as in Great Britain, would bind the interests of a substantial part of the community to those of the nation at large. In January 1790 the activity of speculators, some with advance information about the report, leaked through Assistant Secretary of the Treasury William Duer, alarmed and disgusted Madison. A notorious New York speculator, Andrew Craigie, who lived in a lodginghouse with six New England Congressmen, had boasted that "I know no way of making safe speculations but by being associated with people who from their Official situation know all the present and can aid future arrangements either for or against the funds." Living in the same neighborhood, Madison heard such talk on all sides. By mid-February he had decided upon what he surely knew could be a fateful dispute with Hamilton and his supporters.[12]

Most obvious among Madison's motives for opposing the funding and assumption plans, beyond their intrinsic inequities, is that each (especially assumption as originally proposed) seemed little suited to the special interests of Virginia. The speculators in depreciated currencies and the holders of public securities were mostly from the financial houses of New York, Boston, and Philadelphia and almost all from north of the Mason-Dixon line. Even the public securities of the Southern states were owned largely by Northerners. Thus the plan to redeem these holdings at face value would enormously enrich the North, perhaps giving that section a critical advantage which in the future would result in economic bondage for the South. Furthermore, the assumption plan favored Massachusetts, Connecticut, and other Northern states (plus South Carolina) that had borrowed heavily during the revolution, but it offered no compensation to Virginia and other Southern states that had suffered severe physical damage during the war. Funding, and especially assumption, therefore, were unpopular in Virginia, and as one of her Representatives in Congress, Madison sensed some need to seek changes in the plans, both to protect the interests of his neighbors and to maintain his political strength in the state. Certainly a tenderness for the interests of Virginia and of the South generally played a part in Madison's decision to break with Hamilton, and hence subsequently in the basic orientation of the Jeffersonian Republican party.[13]

One need not suppose, however, that Madison's motives for opposing Hamilton's plans were solely or even principally sectional and tactical. The plans encouraged a tendency in economic development and a structure for the national economy for which Madison had little sympathy. Hamilton thought a consolidated business community, tied to the national interest by privileges granted to it, would afford the surest, most effective economic leadership. Hamilton further believed only government stimulation of commercial and industrial expansion could make the nation strong and self-reliant. A largely agricultural nation, he was convinced, would never, given the patterns of trade and technology apparent in 1790, achieve the glory and power of the great eras of the past Hamilton so much admired: the Athens of Pericles, the Rome of Augustus, and the France of Louis XIV. Hamilton supposed that the welfare of the nation as a whole, including the agricultural interest, would follow and keep pace with the favored commercial community, but he was sure only the encouragement of the latter would yield the leadership necessary to prevent domination by provincials with the sort of bucolic lack of vision evident so recently among antifederalists.

Self-interest, sectional hostility, and opposition to republican government seem not, as the secretary's critics, beginning with Jefferson, have sometimes charged, to have been among Hamilton's motives for the plans. His personal fortunes declined during his secretaryship; he was probably the least sectionally oriented of the founders; and he thought his bold measures were the minimum needed to give the republican frame of the Constitution a chance to survive and endure. His ambition, arrogance, and will to dominate the government, all more marked from 1792 through 1794 than in 1790, together with disinterested differences on issues, spawned the partisan disputes which soon developed. Each side could reasonably claim its program enhanced the national interest.

Madison shared some of the pastoral predilections of Aristotle, Virgil, the English gentry, the physiocrats, his friend Jefferson, and a host of others who sung the praises of country life. Madison certainly saw no superior virtue in cities or among merchants. He thought the soundest pattern of economic development, and the surest path toward national self-reliance, was to continue the vigorous agricultural expansion that had always been basic to North American growth. The economic foundation for "the good life," in Madison's estimation, already existed in the Virginia Piedmont, in the Pennsylvania "bread basket," and on the farms of the Connecticut valley. He had always supported as well a balanced commercial and industrial growth bestowing economic advantages equitably throughout the Union and resisting British domination, but the reckless stimulation of a new merchant class to lead the nation was to him at best unnecessary and at worst likely to lead to distortions and corruptions in every way disastrous. Though the issue was not clearly drawn in 1790, Madison's opposition to portions of the Report on Public Credit bespoke a concept of the national economy far different than that of the Secretary of the Treasury and his followers. The implications of the report revived and strengthened Madison's instinctive but undogmatic agrarian bias.[14]

Most significant, however, was Madison's conviction that Hamilton's program would result in an unrepublican concentration of power and dynamic of government. Madison thought, for example, that the program pressed inequitably on veterans of the revolution who had been forced to sell certificates at depreciated rates, on states, such as Virginia, that had discharged some of their war debts, and on the agricultural portion of the community, which had little to gain directly, and perhaps much to lose, from the privileges accorded to trade and manufacturing. Conversely, current holders of public securities, states (mostly in the North) with large war debts, and the commercial classes generally stood to reap immense benefits from Hamilton's plans. The result would be a regional and class concentration of power Madison could only view with alarm. Hamilton's candid admission that he intended the concentration in order to bring to the federal government a self-interested support he thought it desperately needed to become an effective means of government only increased Madison's apprehensions. Though the secretary expressed regret at the misfortunes of those whose interests suffered under his plans, he saw them as a small price to pay for the vital strengthening of the Union he thought made them necessary. As Madison observed the Hamiltonian "phalanx" in Congress, the eager support given the program in New York financial circles, the often arrogant comments by men of wealth about their superior capacity to lead and govern the country, and the tendency of backers of the secretary's report to exalt the executive over the legislative department, his concern for the survival of republican principles grew rapidly. Jefferson's famous charges, made in old age, that "Hamilton's financial system . . . had two objects; 1st, as a puzzle, to exclude popular understanding and inquiry; 2nd, as a machine for the corruption of the legislature," and that "men thus enriched by the dexterity of a leader [Hamilton], would follow of course the chief who was leading them to fortune, and become zealous instruments of all his enterprises," reflect the bitter animosities of years to come more than the emerging suspicions of 1790. Nonetheless, Madison and Jefferson saw that deep political differences separated them from the Secretary of the Treasury.[15]

Though charges that Hamilton's program would bring "the British system" to the United States in one way reflect little more than the lingering prejudices of the Revolutionary War, in fact Benjamin Rush, William Maclay, and other supporters of Madison had much more in mind when they railed against "Anglicanism." Schooled on years of revolutionary propaganda about the corruption of Parliament, the arrogance of George III and his ministers, the sinister machinations of British merchants, and the oppressive perpetuity of the British national debt, Rush, Madison, Jefferson, and others recoiled at the dynamics of the Hamiltonian program: were not Congressmen who traded in public securities as much "bought" by the secretary as members of Parliament given royal sinecures were bribed by the English Crown? would not the forty- or fifty-year funding of the United States debt subject the federal government to as much improper influence as resulted from the huge British debt? was not the guidance Hamilton attempted in Congress, and the influence he seemed likely to attain as a result of his program, as serious an encroachment on legislative prerogatives as Lord North ever achieved in London? Though John Adams and some other friends of strong government as well as of separation of powers reserved the highest praise for the British constitution as described *ideally* by Montesquieu, the glorification by Hamilton of the *reality* of British government, with all its corruption, arrogance, and dependence on selfish interests, appalled Madison.

In drawing back from Hamilton's program, Madison took another step back from the nationalism he had expressed so firmly in May 1787 and from which he had first retreated after the decision to make the states equal in the Senate. Hamilton's use of federal power to encourage the commercial interests gave Madison further reservations about the wisdom of reposing unlimited authority in the national government. His nationalism waned as he saw the federal impotence of the last days of the old confederation replaced by the sweeping national possibilities envisioned by the Report on Public Credit. Separation and balance of powers seemed utterly lost. Though Hamilton and others judged correctly Madison's changing attitude toward national power, and perhaps had some grounds for feeling betrayed by him, in fact Madison shifted his view of the powers that could be safely consigned to the federal government in order to *preserve* consistency on the vastly more important matter of republican freedom. In 1786 the threat came from *state* foolishness, jealousies, and encroachments. In 1790 the threat came from a sectional and oligarchical domination nourished by the Treasury Department of the federal government. Madison shifted (consistently) to block the danger, whatever the source.

Amid the central controversy over Hamilton's financial plans, Madison attended to a number of other matters during the long second session of Congress. He continued a busy schedule of consultations and social meetings with the President. In April, for example, Washington recorded a conversation with Madison on the President's obligation to consult the Senate before making diplomatic appointments. The chief executive was relieved to discover the Congressman as well as the Secretary of State (Jefferson) and the Chief Justice (John Jay) agreed it would be "unwise" to consult in advance; the Senate was entitled merely to approve or disapprove nominations. On a hot Sunday afternoon in August, Madison and Edmund Randolph (in New York as Attorney General) stopped at Washington's house after a horseback ride in the countryside for tea and a two-hour conversation. Thus close to the nation's patriarch, Madison also took the lead in commemorating the death of its sage, Benjamin Franklin, in April. Madison moved a month's mourning be observed officially "as a mark of veneration" due to the memory of "a citizen whose native genius was not more an ornament to human nature than his various exertions of it have been precious to science, to freedom, and to his country."[16]

Franklin's last public act, sponsoring a petition to Congress to abolish slavery and the slave trade, thrust upon Madison a delicate dilemma. Though opposed to slavery, and willing to support gradual, practical plans for its demise, he nevertheless foresaw correctly that petitions that Congress take such action immediately would serve only to inflame Georgia and South Carolina Congressmen. They denounced abolitionist petitions violently, threatening to "blow the trumpet of sedition in the southern states." Madison's embarrassment at refusing to support futile moves against an institution he regarded as evil, in order to soothe Congressional tempers, is evident in his response to an anti-slave-trade memorial sent him by a Philadelphia Quaker: "I am much obliged by the friendly communication. The number of vessels employed in the trade to Africa is much greater than I should have conjectured. I hope it will daily diminish and soon cease altogether. . . . Should the evil still go on, it continues to be my opinion that the interposition of the General Government ought to be applied as far as may be constitutional. . . . At present I not only flatter myself that the necessity may not exist, but apprehend that a revival of the subject in Congress would be equally unseasonable and unsuccessful. Future opportunities cannot be more and will probably be less so."[17]

Though Madison was pessimistic about the prospects of federal action against slavery, and perhaps temporized too much in the presence of this gross denial of freedom, he had high hopes that the revolution in France might result in dramatic victories for liberty abroad. He commented to Edmund Pendleton on events in Europe: "France seems likely to carry thro' the great work in which she has been laboring. The Austrian Netherlands [Belgium] have caught the flame, and with arms have renounced the Government of the [Holy Roman] Emperor forever. . . . All Europe must by degrees be aroused to the recollection and assertion of the rights of human nature. . . . The light which is chasing darkness and despotism from the old world, is but an emanation from that which has procured and succeeded the establishment of liberty in the new." A month later he asked Pendleton for information about the origins of the American Revolution, because "its foreign and future consequences [make] every circumstance connected with it" a matter of great interest to mankind. Madison saw more and more that liberty in the United States would be easily and profoundly affected by events abroad.[18]

As adjournment approached, in August, Madison also attended to his re-election to Congress. Since no opposition candidate had appeared, he wrote his father he would not even bother to hurry home to be present at the polls. Instead, he wrote a circular letter to a key supporter in each of the eight counties in his district, explaining that assumption had been settled "in a manner more favorable to Virginia than was hoped," that the permanent seat of the government would be on the Potomac, and that the national debt had been funded in a way making direct taxes unnecessary. Madison hoped this record would be sufficiently attractive to the voters to insure easy re-election, but just in case late opposition or a behind-the-scenes plot to defeat him might emerge, he requested that his brother Ambrose attend the election in Louisa County and brother William in Culpeper. Thus Madison's campaign amounted to eight short letters, and his party machine consisted of two dependable brothers. The result was overwhelming victory.[19]

Before heading home, Madison also played a key role in the Nootka Sound alarm, which burst upon New York in the midst of the controversies over assumption and location of the capital. In the Pacific Northwest, a Spanish officer had fired on British vessels. Britain responded with threats against Spain, which if carried out, and if France supported Spain, would lead to a general war in Europe. The United States was surrounded by the possessions of two of the powers, and in alliance with the other. Washington asked Jefferson to confer with Madison on the posture the government should take. They agreed, as did Washington's other advisors, that neutrality was the proper course, but they noted that should Britain conquer Louisiana and Florida, the United States was in a bad position: "Instead of two nations balancing each other [on our borders], we shall have one, with more than the strength of both." The United States therefore, should seek to prevent war, but use its possibility as a lever to let England know that an Anglo-American treaty could only be one of "perfect reciprocity," and that the United States had it "infallibly . . . in our own power" to stand up against British commercial discrimination. Madison was also one of two Congressmen in on the secret mission of David Humphreys to Spain to gain from the crisis the long-sought goal of free navigation of the Mississippi. Madison and Jefferson, with the President's support, wanted to use neutrality as a means of gaining concessions from both Britain and Spain, not as a step, as Hamilton sought, toward an alliance with Great Britain.[20]

Madison delayed his departure to be in New York during the diplomatic crisis, but also to avoid the journey home during uncomfortable, sickly August weather, and to be able to make the journey leisurely, in Jefferson's company. The two men left New York on September 1, in Jefferson's phaeton. They probably visited as usual with Madison's teacher, the aged and nearly blind Dr. Witherspoon, at Princeton, and then stayed for a week in Philadelphia at Mrs. House's. Madison joyfully engaged a room there for the coming session of Congress (an arrangement he continued until Mrs. House died in 1793), and Jefferson made detailed plans to renovate a house he had rented three blocks farther west on Market Street. With his usual liberality and expensive taste, the Secretary of State had arranged spacious quarters for the elegant furnishings he expected from France. He soon asked Madison to move in with him, but content at Mrs. House's, fearing Jefferson would not accept adequate rent, and perhaps unwilling to feed the rumors of collusion between the legislative and executive branches, the Congressman refused the generous invitation. To vary the journey and take advantage of the pleasant late summer weather in the Chesapeake Bay country, the Virginians traveled down the eastern shore to Chestertown and sailed across the wide bay from there to Annapolis. Forced to wait nearly a day for a boat, the two men, joined by young Thomas Lee Shippen, rowed about the rivers and inlets and ate some of the "delicious crabs" for which the region is still famous. In Annapolis, waiting for their horses, on a slower boat, to catch up with them, the travelers climbed to the top of the state capitol (still standing and in use) to view a magnificent panorama of bays, rivers, and islands dotted with superb country seats. Before leaving the next day, they feasted on the most perfectly prepared turtle Shippen had ever eaten, a repast which seemed all the more wonderful when they found themselves the next night at a country inn where the food was atrocious and "mosquitoes, gnats, flies and bugs" pestered them unmercifully.

Refusing to breakfast at such a squalid place, the travelers went on to Bladensburg, to an inn kept by "an old black woman," where a few

nights before, President Washington had lodged. Jealous of this preference shown such a lowly person, irate townspeople had the next day
torn down her outhouse. Madison and Jefferson heard the story from the
woman's lips and viewed the shambles left by the mob. They stayed the
next two nights in Georgetown, where, with a large party on horseback,
led by Madison's old friend Congressman Daniel Carroll, they explored
carefully the rolling country soon to be the site of the national capital,
and went by boat four miles upstream to the Little Falls of the Potomac.
Young Shippen left the Virginians as they crossed the river. He had
derived "infinite pleasure" from his journey with "those charming men
Jefferson and Madison," but he was also impoverished from the high style
in which they traveled. He begged his father for $50 more to continue
his travels.[21]

Madison and Jefferson arrived the next afternoon at Mount Vernon,
where they talked with the President about the federal district they had
just surveyed and reported to him on the conferences with Carroll and
others. The next day they visited George Mason at Gunston Hall. The
old statesman suggested many reasons why the "Federal City" should be
built near Georgetown rather than Alexandria. Two days later, on
September 18, the travelers arrived in Orange, almost three weeks after
they had left New York. The season was an especially pleasant one at
Montpelier, but Jefferson stayed only one night before going on to
Monticello, an easy one day's journey (about twenty-five miles) to the
southwest. A horse Madison loaned his friend for the short trip was
later the subject of a long mock-serious negotiation between the two.
Jefferson wrote he would like to buy the animal, but the "many disputes
on our journey," in which each man had sought to pay more than his
share of the expenses, persuaded the master of Monticello that he knew
"nobody with whom it is so difficult to settle a price" as the master of
Montpelier. Therefore, he wrote jokingly, he hoped a third party could
set the price, to prevent Madison from defrauding himself. Before it
could be paid for, the horse died. Jefferson insisted the sale was nevertheless bona fide, that the death was no fault of Madison's, and that he
(Jefferson) should therefore pay for the horse. Madison refused, asserting he would not be a cheating trader who sold worthless animals. He
had discovered, in fact, that the horse had been drenched and ill while
still under the care of his servant. Jefferson persisted, however, observing
that "I should as soon think of filching the sum from your pocket as of
permitting the loss to be yours." When Jefferson sent the money, Madison could do no more than return an overpayment resulting from the
Secretary of State's faulty arithmetic.[22]

In November Jefferson was back at Montpelier, to join Madison for
the return to Philadelphia. Again the two men traveled slowly, taking

fifteen days for the trip. At the temporary capital, they were pleased to find two changes in the Virginia delegation, caused by the deaths the previous spring of cranky old Senator William Grayson and odd, cross-grained Representative Theodorick Bland, each an obstructing antifederalist. In their places came two brilliant young men. James Monroe replaced Grayson in the Senate, moved to Philadelphia with his young wife, and soon took a leading role in the emerging Jeffersonian party. William Branch Giles (1762–1830), introduced to Madison by John Marshall, took Bland's place, and began a stormy, pugnacious career as a fervent republican during the seventeen-nineties, an administration leader during Jefferson's presidency, a troublesome opponent during Madison's administration, and an extreme state's rights governor of Virginia in the eighteen-twenties. Though Madison seems to have been personally close only to Monroe, the two young legislators added "weight" and republican zeal to the Virginia delegation.

For nearly two months relative calm prevailed. As usual, Madison drafted (with assistance now from Hamilton) Washington's "State of the Union" address. When the President read the noncontroversial speech to a joint session of Congress, assembled in new quarters in the west wing of the Pennsylvania State House, he spoke so softly that Vice President Adams read the speech again to be sure it was understood. In their own chamber on the ground floor, the Representatives proceeded rather informally, members wearing their hats, reading newspapers, and whispering to each other during debates. Occasionally they gathered in small groups to warm themselves before the large fireplace at the back of the room. Madison drafted the reply of the House to the President's speech, but he did not otherwise take the leading role he had played in earlier sessions. He successfully supported Hamilton's plan to tax domestic and imported liquors to pay off the assumed state debts, but he was defeated when he sought to exempt conscientious objectors from militia duty.[23]

Hamilton's proposal for a national bank, however, ended the tranquility and brought Madison to his feet in the House. After raising some rather piddling questions about the merits of the proposed bank, he turned to its constitutionality. He pointed out that a proposal to grant the federal government power to charter corporations like the national bank had been rejected in the Federal Convention. Furthermore, the Constitution was "a grant of particular powers only." Efforts to enlarge the specified powers of Congress by loose construction endangered the very notion of *limited* government. He then insisted that the arguments voiced in the state ratifying conventions were the proper guide in interpreting the Constitution, because in them could be found the understanding of the people of the fundamental law. In a number of conventions, Madison noted, defenders of the Constitution had denied Congress had the power to charter corporations. Furthermore, they had denied that the clause giving Congress the power to enact legislation "necessary and proper" to effect its stated obligations, the clause upon which the national bank rested, had in any way broadened the matters on which Congress might legislate. Under this interpretation, generally accepted by federalists in 1787 and 1788, the "necessary and proper" clause merely permitted Congress to pass laws explicitly and necessarily related to its enumerated powers.

Madison then moved to the critical matter:

> The doctrine of implication [broad construction] is always a tender one. The danger of it has been felt in other Governments. The delicacy was felt in the adoption of our own; the danger may also be felt, if we do not keep close to our chartered authorities. Mark the reasoning on which the validity of the [national bank] bill depends! To borrow money is made the end, and the accumulation of capitals implied as the means. The accumulation of capitals is then the end, and a Bank implied as the means. The Bank is then the end, and a charter of incorporation, a monopoly, . . . implied as the means. If implications, thus remote and thus multiplied, can be linked together, a chain may be formed that will reach every object of legislation, every object within the whole compass of political economy.

In short, Madison argued, the doctrine of implied powers struck "at the very essence of the Government as composed of limited and enumerated powers." The only safe role of interpretation was to take the word "necessary" seriously. If, as in the case of a national bank, there were other ways, clearly constitutional, to tax, to borrow money, and to regulate the currency, then a national bank was not necessary, and was therefore not constitutional. To argue, as Hamilton's supporters did, that the bank's "convenience" justified it was in Madison's view to abolish all limits to federal power.[24]

Despite these objections, the Hamiltonians pushed the bill through the House after but a week's debate. Fisher Ames wrote that Madison's speech was "full of casuistry and sophistry," and that his reading of long extracts from the proceedings of the ratifying conventions was "a dull piece of business, and very little to the purpose." Of 39 votes in its favor, 33 were from states north of the Potomac, while 15 of 20 negative votes came from south of the river. Though party organizations had not yet emerged, and opposition came from local banking interests likely to be hurt by the national bank as well as from noncommercial groups, a split between a Southern, agrarian interest and a Northern, commercial one had nonetheless appeared. When the President received the bill, he asked Jefferson and Hamilton to submit opinions on it. In response they drafted the famous conflicting papers considered ever since as the great defining statements of strict and broad construction of the Constitution. In fact, each restated arguments Madison and Fisher Ames had already made during the debate in Congress.* Jefferson wrote a relatively compact opinion, which the President transmitted to Hamilton, who, in a long argument of nearly fifty pages, expounded the doctrines of broad construction and the supremacy of the Union used subsequently by Marshall, Webster, Lincoln, the two Roosevelts, and other advocates of federal power.[25]

Before he received Hamilton's brilliant and persuasive treatise, Washington seriously enough considered a veto to ask Madison to draft for him messages of rejection based on constitutionality and on merit. In several lengthy conversations, Madison thought he had detected that the chief executive accepted the reservations about the bank. The Congressman therefore compressed his argument against the bank's constitutionality into a single phrase the President might use in returning the bill to Congress: authority to create a national bank could not be inferred "from any express power [granted in the Constitution] by fair and safe rules of implication." Washington decided, however, to accept Hamilton's argument, and on the very last day available to him, signed the National Bank Act into law. An important "engine" in the Hamiltonian system had been set in motion, and a grave constitutional dispute had been added to the moral and economic differences of the previous session.[26]

Furthermore, in declaring the national bank unconstitutional, Madison took another important step back from his nationalism of 1786 to 1788. He had written in *Federalist* Number 44, for example, explaining the "necessary and proper" clause, that "no axiom is more clearly established in law, or in reason, than that wherever the end is required, the means are authorised; wherever a general power to do a thing is given, every particular power necessary for doing it, is included." (Hamilton quoted this passage, with obvious relish, in his opinion to Washington.) Now Madison sought to impose severe limitations on the means Hamilton and Congress had chosen to execute the financial powers of the federal government. This retreat, like the earlier withdrawals from general powers for Congress (1787) and assumption of state debts (1790), reflected his conviction that the republican character of the Constitution had been compromised. The national bank, given special privileges by law, yet placed under a board of directors composed largely of private individuals, seemed to Madison a means to further enrich the commercial classes

---

* As Dumas Malone has pointed out, the opinions of Hamilton and Jefferson were expressed in private papers submitted to the President and seem not to have been known to the public in any form until John Marshall summarized them in his *Life of George Washington* (1807), and it was much later than that before they achieved the definitive position they now hold. The speeches of Ames and Madison, on the other hand, were widely reprinted at once in the newspapers.

Hamilton favored so candidly and a device to further corrupt Congress and bend it to the will of the Secretary of the Treasury. To Madison the chain of power seemed dangerous: a privileged financial aristocracy, led and encouraged by an officer of the executive department, had acquired a dominant influence over a Congress that acted under an interpretation of the Constitution virtually abolishing restraints on its authority. As Madison described the matter to Jefferson, "the stock-jobbers will become the praetorian band of the Government, at once its tool and its tyrant; bribed by its largesses, and overawing it by clamors and combinations." Republican newspapers charged repeatedly that Lord North and George III had had no greater power in London during the seventeen-seventies. This specter, and the shambles the Hamiltonian system made of the doctrines of consent and separation of powers, drove Madison to a strict construction of the Constitution otherwise ill-suited to his positive concepts of the *uses* of republican government. For Madison, both national authority and broad construction of the Constitution were subordinate to a conviction that only under pure republican forms, free from oligarchical influence and corruption, was strong government compatible with freedom and the rights of man.[27]

The sectional nature of the vote against the national bank, the eager, almost frenzied support of Hamilton's program among certain commercial groups in Boston, New York, and Philadelphia, and the physiocratic views of Jefferson and others opposed to the program have led many students to emphasize the class or sectional origins of "Jeffersonian democracy." Madison's motivations in formulating the attitudes soon to be the program of the Jeffersonian party, plus the strong *commercial* opposition to the national bank, in the North as well as in the South, reveal this interpretation to be an important though incomplete insight. That Madison had little use for Hamilton's program for federal direction of national economic growth and that he believed the agricultural interests of his native state would suffer as a result are abundantly clear. It is equally evident that his own future as a political leader would have been threatened gravely had he continued to support Hamilton. Congressman Benjamin Bourne of Rhode Island added the charge that Madison's arguments against the bank would not have been expressed "did not the Gentlemen of the Southward View the [national bank] as adverse to the removal of Congress, ten years hence, to the Powtowmack." These very real concerns and pressures undoubtedly encouraged Madison to break with Hamilton, but there is every indication that had the self-interested motives conflicted with Madison's concepts of republicanism or of sound national policy, he would have stood by the latter, or at the very least retired from public life. In the very session when he opposed the bank, for example, Madison had voted for the excise tax on whisky, a measure often more bitterly opposed by the agrarian interest than the bank. Earlier Madison had supported import duties only very incompletely suited to the special interests of Virginia. Furthermore, by 1791, Madison had for nearly twenty years expressed and acted upon principles of free republican government thoroughly consistent with the fears and objections raised against the Hamiltonian programs and inter- pretation of the Constitution. Madison the farmer and Virginian had substantial grounds for opposing assumption of state debts and the na- tional bank, but Madison the apostle of free government had even more fundamental reasons for opposing the web of oligarchy he saw spreading through the federal government.[28]

After the First Congress expired, on March 3, 1791, Madison stayed in Philadelphia for a month or so, attending to family business and enjoying spring rides and rambles into the countryside with Jefferson. He also talked with the British agent George Beckwith, who had taken up lodg- ings at Mrs. House's. At the request of Jefferson and Washington, Madison questioned Beckwith about British support for hostile Indians in the Northwest Territory. The agent denied any British incitement and otherwise refused to give the American officials any satisfaction; he was already in intimate communication with Hamilton and others much more favorably disposed toward Great Britain than the Secretary of State. In late April, having planned a further trip northward with Jeffer- son and perhaps David Rittenhouse, Madison left for New York. He stopped at Princeton, but was disappointed to find both Samuel Stanhope Smith, now president of the college, and Dr. Witherspoon out of town on vacation. In New York, again settled at Dorothy Elsworth's board- inghouse on Maiden Lane, he relaxed for three weeks, talking politics with Philip Freneau, Aaron Burr (recently elected Senator from New York), Robert R. Livingston, Rufus King, and others, but also explor- ing plans to extend his Northern trip to Boston and perhaps Portsmouth, New Hampshire.[29]

On May 19 Jefferson arrived at Mrs. Elsworth's. After a day of visit- ing with Freneau, Burr, Livingston, and others, the two Virginians em- barked on the always beautiful voyage up the Hudson, which Madison had made in 1774 and again ten years later, with Lafayette, on the way to negotiate the Indian treaty at Fort Stanwix. This time the travelers switched to Jefferson's phaeton at Poughkeepsie and three days later were in Albany, where they were the guests of Hamilton's father-in- law, General Philip Schuyler, whom Burr had just replaced as United States Senator. Riding through the lush countryside, past the great estates of the Livingstons, the Van Rensselaers, and others, the two planters, with two mounted servants and Madison's saddle horse trotting along behind the phaeton, presented an elegant sight. Three more days carried the party through Saratoga, where General Schuyler's son John guided them about the battleground, and Fort Edward, to Fort George at the head of Lake George. Writing to his youngest daughter, Polly, on a piece of birch bark in a canoe in the middle of the lake, Jefferson described it as "the most beautiful water I ever saw"—the green islands of Paradise Bay near its center, towering Black Mountain on the rugged eastern shore, and near the northern end, precipitous Roger's Rock, which recalled a slide to safety into the lake of a hero of the French and Indian War, and "Mad Anthony's Nose," named for its likeness to the physiognomy of revolutionary stalwart General Anthony Wayne. The party caught speckled trout, salmon trout, and bass in the cold, crystal-clear waters of the lake, and in their camp on its shores they shot three red squirrels and two rattlesnakes. "Rich groves of thuja, silver fir, white pine, aspen and paper birch" covered the mountainsides, and huge clusters of a red shrub Jefferson thought resembled azalea, and fragrant honeysuckle, lined the banks of the lake. Pussy willows, wild gooseberry, wild cherries, and "strawberries in abundance" likewise delighted the Virginians.

At the northern end of the lake, they traversed the short portage down to Lake Champlain, where they explored the dilapidated forts at Ticonderoga and Crown Point and studied the famous battlefields surrounding them, which, Jefferson wrote his son-in-law, "have been scenes of blood from a very early part of our history." Pleased with their sail on Lake George, they set out again on Lake Champlain, but, Jefferson wrote, "after penetrating it about 25 miles, we [were] obliged by head winds and high sea to return having spent 1-½ days on it." In the only surviving portion of Madison's diary of the trip, he noted that the east shore of Lake Champlain was pretty generally settled, but that east of Lake George the only inhabitant was "a free negro" who had a fine farm of 250 acres, "which he cultivates with white hirelings and by his industry and good management turns to good account." Used only to blacks degraded in slavery, Madison was surprised to find he was "intelligent, reads, writes, understands accounts, is dextrous in his affairs," and had served in the commissary department during the revolution. The travelers returned via Lake George and Fort Edward to Saratoga, where John Schuyler again entertained them. They had had a "prosperous and pleasant" trip thus far, Jefferson wrote, marred only by excessively sultry weather, which surprised the Virginians, who were used to stories of the severe weather in the northern mountains.

After leaving Saratoga, Madison noticed that the scattered farms were small and plain "according to the plan of New England," and the houses, handsome wooden structures, "very scantily furnished within." In Bennington, Vermont, on Sunday, June 5, they stayed with Governor Moses Robinson, long a political friend, who, according to his own account, took the two deists to the Congregational church. Asked how they liked the music, Jefferson and Madison reportedly replied that they had no basis for comparison, since they hadn't been to church anywhere else for several years. Able to travel again after the sabbath, they rode down the

great valley of the Housatonic River, past the new college at Williams-
town, to Pittsfield, and thence over the Berkshires to the Connecticut
valley town of Northampton. When Jefferson's granddaughter wrote
him of her wedding journey through the same countryside in 1825,
describing its prosperous, well-settled appearance, he replied that in 1791
between Saratoga and Northampton there had been "mostly desert; now
it is what 34 years of free and good government have made it." The trip
down the Connecticut valley to Springfield, Hartford, and Middletown,
and then to Guilford on Long Island Sound took Madison for the first
and only time through an old, thriving section of New England, very
different, with its small farms, many villages, and white wooden
churches, from his native Virginia. Here was the plain, egalitarian countryside of which New Englanders so often boasted when they experienced what seemed to them to be "aristocratic airs" in a Philadelphia
drawing room or on a Southern plantation. In Springfield the Virginians
marveled at two huge elm trees, one nearly seven and the other nearly
eight feet in diameter.

The afternoon of June 11, the travelers boarded a sloop in the small
fishing village of Guilford for the forty-mile voyage across Long Island
Sound to Oysterpond Point on the northeastern tip of Long Island. As
the vessel worked its way at high tide past the shoals and rocks of the
harbor, the bluffs of Sachem Head disappeared astern, and soon the hulk
of Faulkner's Island, grim and desolate in the middle of the sound,
loomed to starboard. Madison was fearful of the sea as unfavorable to
his bilious disposition, and his apprehensions at what was probably the
longest sea voyage of his life may have prevented his full enjoyment of
the lingering twilight of the long summer evening. In any event, the two
men soon retired, and in the morning, marveled at the skill of the sailors
as they maneuvered the boat through the treacherous tide currents of
Plum Gut. Snug in the harbor, the Virginians, followed by their horses,
servants, and phaeton, climbed ashore and traveled across Long Island
through Southold and Riverhead to Moriches on the south shore. On
June 14, at Mastic, they visited the home of their old Continental Congress colleague General William Floyd, where Madison could scarcely
have suppressed thoughts of his dashed hopes eight years earlier of claiming Floyd's daughter, Kitty, as his bride (see Chapter VI). Later that day
the travelers stopped at an Unquachog Indian settlement, and the next
day at a well-known nursery in Flushing, where Jefferson left a large
order for trees and shrubs he wanted shipped to Monticello. He was
especially enthusiastic about the beauty and delicious products of the
sugar maples he had seen in such abundance throughout the trip, but
most of the varieties sent to Virginia from Flushing soon died, as did
those requested earlier from Vermont. After crossing Brooklyn ferry to
New York, Jefferson hurried back to Philadelphia, but Madison returned
to Mrs. Elsworth's. As Jefferson wrote, Madison was tired after "the

journey to the lakes," but nevertheless "in better health than I have seen him."[30]

Events conspired to thwart Madison's hope for more travel in New England. House clerk John Beckley, his intended companion, set out before Madison could leave New York, and he was unwilling to go alone in the uncomfortable stage, which, in any case, "travelled too rapidly" for his purposes. Furthermore, his horse was sick, and his own summer biliousness was soon too severe to make another journey alluring. Instead, he settled down, for nearly eight weeks, in New York, where the political controversies impending since before his vacation trip reached new intensity. The first public expression of the differences in political ideology beginning to affect public affairs had occurred after Madison passed along a copy of Thomas Paine's *The Rights of Man* to Jefferson. The Secretary of State in turn sent it, at the request of John Beckley, who had lent it to Madison, to a Philadelphia printer who intended its republication. In transmitting the pamphlet, Jefferson remarked he was "extremely pleased . . . something is at length to be publickly said against the political heresies which have sprung up among us. I have no doubt our citizens will rally a second time round the standard of Common Sense." In early May 1791, Jefferson was embarrassed and thunderstruck to find his remarks printed in the preface of the republication. In castigating "political heresies," Jefferson had particularly in mind John Adams' *Discourses of Davila*, published the previous year, but he never meant such criticism to appear in public over his name. Madison, on the other hand, seemed almost pleased. He "comforted" his troubled friend: "Mr. Adams can least of all complain. Under a mock defence of the Republican Constitutions of his Country, he attacked them with all the force he possessed. . . . Since he has been the 2nd magistrate in the new Republic, his pen has constantly been at work in the same cause. . . . Surely if it be innocent and decent in one servant of the public thus to write attacks against its Government, it cannot be criminal and indecent in another to patronize a written defence of the principles on which that Government is founded."[31]

Madison had a much greater part in the plan, conceived early in 1791, to induce his old college friend Philip Freneau to establish a lively, ardently republican, and nationally significant newspaper in Philadelphia to counteract the influence of John Fenno's *Gazette of the United States*, which Madison and Jefferson regarded as "a paper of pure Toryism, disseminating the doctrines of monarchy, aristocracy, and the exclusion of the influence of the people." Jefferson offered Freneau the vacant post of State Department translating clerk and such minor printing jobs as the department had at its dispensation, if that would help him establish a press in Philadelphia. The income from these tasks, however, was but a fraction of that needed by Freneau to support his growing family, so the project languished, and Freneau investigated starting a paper in his native New Jersey. Disappointed, Madison feared that "those who know [Freneau's] talents and hate his political principles have practiced some artifice" to frighten the poet off. Madison nonetheless persisted, and soon persuaded Freneau's former publisher in New York, Francis Childs, to underwrite a newspaper in Philadelphia. Henry Lee, another Princeton friend of Freneau's, together with Madison and Jefferson, sent a stream of letters soliciting subscriptions. Yet another Princetonian, Hugh Henry Brackenridge, agreed to add his trenchant pen to the considerable talents already enlisted for the venture. Freneau moved to Philadelphia, began his duties at the State Department, and on October 31, 1791, the first issue of the soon-to-be-famous, immediately controversial *National Gazette* appeared in Philadelphia.

Since Hamilton soon charged that the *National Gazette* had been founded by Jefferson and Madison as a party organ to mount systematic assaults on him and the administration, and that the newspaper thus *began* party warfare in the United States, the Virginians were often at pains, sometimes protesting too much that they did not entertain partisan intentions in bringing Freneau to Philadelphia. Jefferson's place in the cabinet made him especially open to Hamilton's charge, so except for offering the State Department support (too trivial to have been decisive) and assisting in gathering subscriptions, he left the negotiations with Freneau to the Princetonians, Madison and Henry Lee. Madison worked assiduously to bring Freneau to the temporary capital, and although perhaps he did not anticipate or approve the heights to which Freneau's antiadministration invective would soon rise, he certainly knew Freneau well enough to know that the fervent poet would write pointedly and effectively, and therefore would be a storm center.

Jefferson doubtless believed, as he explained to the President, that "no government ought to be without censors; and where the press is free, no one ever will," and that therefore there could be no principled objection to an opposition newspaper. Madison preached similarly to the Attorney General: in aiding Freneau he "entertained hopes that a free paper meant for general circulation, and edited by a man of genius, of republican principles, and a friend to the Constitution, would be some antidote to the doctrines and discourses circulated in favor of Monarchy and Aristocracy and would be an acceptable vehicle of public information in many places not sufficiently supplied with it." It was also true, however, that the anti-Hamiltonians needed a newspaper outlet, that Freneau was aided and encouraged to serve that end, and that party disputes, consequently, would be exacerbated.[32]

Madison may have agreed, as part of the negotiation to persuade Freneau to come to Philadelphia, to write a series of essays for the *National Gazette* on political economy and fundamental republican principles. His first essay, "Population and Emigration," appeared on November 21, 1791, in the seventh newspaper Freneau published. In it Madison pursued further Benjamin Franklin's speculations about the very rapid increase of population in the New World. The human species, Madison wrote, had reproductive capacities which far outreached the ability of the earth to feed and maintain. Infanticide, famine, pestilence, and war had normally restored the balance between man and nature. The open lands of America, however, offered another, far less grim alternative to mankind: emigration. The free movement of peoples first across the Atlantic and then across the continent bestowed benefits everywhere. It relieved population pressure in old centers, provided markets to give employment to those who stayed behind, opened new lands for cultivation, gave opportunity to enterprising men, and improved public morals by restraining the growth of crowded cities. Therefore, Madison concluded, the United States ought to encourage both immigration from Europe and emigration to the West.[33]

In later essays Madison returned to political economy. In December 1791 he published his treatise "Money," written in 1780 (see Chapter V). Its warnings about speculative finance and a national debt seemed worth repeating in the face of the recently enacted Hamiltonian program. Early in February 1792 Madison ridiculed Rousseau and other "visionary philosophers [and] benevolent enthusiasts" who entertained hopes for "universal and perpetual peace." He nevertheless scored the folly and wickedness of war and insisted, following orthodox republican theory he shared with Jefferson, that by making war possible only with the consent of the people, and by requiring each generation to pay for its own wars, bloodshed and violence could be substantially reduced. With these safeguards, human reason would seldom if ever resort to war. In March Madison argued that the best "republican distribution of citizens" would be in occupations that favored "*health, virtue, intelligence* and *competency* in the *greatest number* of citizens." He then expressed the conventional physiocratic doctrine that the life of the farmer best nourished those qualities and that therefore it was in the public interest to encourage agriculture. Two weeks later Madison lamented about the poor workers of England, whose livelihood often depended on the fashionable whims of the aristocratic classes, as was shown in the instance of twenty thousand buckle makers in Birmingham being thrown out of work by the caprice of the Prince of Wales in wearing only slippers or shoes with laces. How much better off were the self-sufficient farmers of the United States! In these essays Madison revealed his tenderness for the economic interests of his native region and his personal predilection for rural life, as well as his persistent concern for the social and economic foundations necessary for republican government, a concern increased, of course, by Hamilton's growing political power.[34]

Ten other essays written during the winter of 1791–2 expressed more directly the heightened liberalism induced in Madison by his apprehensions about the political consequences of the Hamiltonian program. He sought to turn the tired debate over state versus national government into an argument that each should guard public liberty and the public welfare: let state enthusiasts prevent federal, especially executive, encroachments, and let nationalists work to eradicate "local prejudices and mistaken rivalships," each thus helping "our complicated system" to be both efficacious and freedom preserving. He then defended the *National Gazette* by arguing that a free press would help mold a "sovereign," nation-wide public opinion and therefore cement the bonds of union. Next Madison restated the lesson of *Federalist* Number 10 that only a "confederated republic" could preserve a large country from despotism, by making every citizen the "centinel" of his rights and the legitimate source of authority in the various governments. In another essay Madison, noting "the daring outrages committed by despotism on the reason and the rights of man," urged his countrymen to be faithful to the charters of government under which they lived. Only such fidelity could defend "liberty against power, and power against licentiousness." Though stated in general terms, each essay in fact reflected charges Madison and his colleagues had leveled at the Hamiltonians, and the essays were undoubtedly understood in that context by Madison's readers.[35]

Madison then discussed even more explicitly the "party issues" before the nation. Aiming directly at Hamiltonian arguments that the government ought to favor the wealthy to consolidate the Union, he asserted that a republican government should insure political equality, encourage an equitable distribution of property, abstain from granting special privileges, and thereby diminish the *unnecessary* party strife caused by partisan measures. A balance of parties based on natural and inevitable differences would then serve the cause of freedom. Madison next asserted that the British government, far from being a good example of a balance of "king, lords, and commons," in fact was virtuous only insofar as public opinion influenced it. So much for John Adams and other misguided admirers of Britain, Madison meant his readers to think. The true model for a balance of powers that would prevent abuses was the American system, with its separation of the departments in the federal government and the division of powers between it and the states. Madison counseled that "those who love their country, its repose, and its republicanism, will study to avoid the alternative" of disunion or tyranny by observing scrupulously the prescribed limits, and particularly by desisting from acts that would heighten jealousies and animosities. So much for Hamilton's programs to favor the commercial classes and to consolidate power in the federal government. In another essay Madison was even more

pointed: "a government operated by corrupt influence; substituting the
motive of private interest in place of public duty," and depending on
bribes, privileges, and selfishness, was an "imposter." He hoped such a
government (obviously he had Great Britain in mind) would never be
established in America, though he clearly meant to warn his readers that
the Hamiltonian system led inexorably in that direction.[36]

In a remarkable essay entitled "Property," Madison explained the full
republican meaning of the maxim invoked by Locke and others that the
purpose of government was the protection of property. The particular
meaning of property, Madison stated, was the "domination which one
man claims and exercises over the external things of the world, in exclusion of every other individual," but its "larger and juster meaning . . .
embraced every thing to which a man may attach a value or have a
right; and *which leaves to everyone else the like advantage*." Thus a
man's land or merchandise or money were his property, but so were his
freedom of expression, his liberty of conscience, his safety of person, and
his opportunity to use his faculties as he chose. "In a word," Madison
concluded, "as a man is said to have a right to his property, he may be
equally said to have a property in his rights. . . . Government is instituted
to protect property of every sort; as well that which lies in the various
rights of individuals, as that which the term particularly expresses. This
being the end of government, that alone is a *just* government, which
impartially secures to every man, whatever is his *own*." According to
this standard, a government that protected possessions but did not protect human rights deserved little praise. In fact, Madison hinted, the
preservation of rights was, because more basic and more universally
applicable, more important than mere protection of possessions. Inequitable taxes, arbitrary seizures, and special privileges bestowed by law
were, because they weighed unfairly on some citizens, likewise unjusti-
fiable. Even under the narrow meaning of property, the need, as Madison
had observed in *Federalist* Number 10, was to protect "unequal faculties
for acquiring property." To this liberalized understanding of the obligation to protect property in its "particular" meaning, he added the equal
or possibly prior claims of the "property in rights." He thus rejected the
obsession with material possessions immemorially characteristic of merely
plutocratic governments.[37]

Having expressed this vital republican principle, Madison turned on the
Hamiltonians: the real enemies of the free union of the American states
were those who favored measures pampering speculators, those who
promoted unnecessary accumulations of the national debt, those who by
"arbitrary interpretations and insidious precedents" perverted the Constitution, and those who avowed cynical, aristocratic, or selfish maxims
of government. On the other hand, the *real* friends of the Union were
the supporters of the principles of free government that were the true
bonds uniting the people of the United States.[38]

In the fall of 1792, as party lines hardened during the effort to supplant John Adams from the vice presidency and during a bitter paper war between Hamilton and defenders of Jefferson, Madison wrote two final essays, expressing clearly partisan views. Examining political disputes in the United States, he declared that unhappily one party "from particular interest, from natural temper, or from the habits of life, are more partial to the opulent than to the other classes of society; and having debauched themselves into a persuasion that mankind are incapable of governing themselves, it follows with them, of course, that government can be carried on only by the pageantry of rank, the influence of money and emoluments, and the terror of military force. Men of those sentiments must naturally wish to point the measures of government less to the interest of the many than of a few, and less to the reason of the many than to their weaknesses." Another party retained faith in the people and believed in government by consent. For the first time using the word "Republican" in a formal sense to describe his party, Madison concluded his essays in the *National Gazette* with a dialogue on "Who Are the Best Keepers of the People's Liberties?" In it he repudiated the assertion that liberty was something bestowed on the people by a firm, paternalistic government and asserted instead that the people themselves, controlling their own government, were the best protectors of their rights. On this point, Madison said, the growing party disputes turned.[39]

Thus the author of the "Memorial and Remonstrance" against religious persecution and the chief architect of the Constitution expounded the theoretical bases of the emerging Republican party. Though public interest during 1792 centered on the war of words between the partisans of Hamilton and of Jefferson, Madison's essays helped importantly to clarify the broader principles that separated the two factions. Furthermore, in the earlier essays, in supporting a liberal emigration policy, frugal, simplified government finance, practical fashions, and an agrarian society, Madison summarized the essential political economy of the Republican party. His deep commitment and unquestionably partisan propagandizing purpose, however, resulted in oversimplification and distortion; the Federalists, for example, were not monarchists or corrupt spoilsmen. Nonetheless, the essays reflect accurately both Madison's apprehensions about the direction of Federalist policy and the Republican "party line" as it appeared in the newspapers.

In 1791 and 1792, Madison's partisanship, hinted at in his objection to important parts of Hamilton's financial plans, steadily intensified as more organized political opposition to "the Treasury system" appeared in many parts of the nation. His roles as a friend of the administration, supporting a wide variety of programs necessary to establish the new government, and as President Washington's chief advisor became minor. Disgust over the greedy quest for stock in the national bank, the increasing arrogance of Hamilton's followers in Congress, an unpleasant association with the British agent Colonel George Beckwith, and a growing conviction that Hamilton connived with Beckwith to form an unwise Anglo-American alliance all heightened Madison's willingness to become openly partisan. Without systematic intention, he took steps establishing one of the two great political parties dividing the nation during the seventeen-nineties. He worked to bring Philip Freneau to Philadelphia to found a partisan newspaper, and he talked with Aaron Burr, Robert R. Livingston, and perhaps with Governor George Clinton himself, to prepare the groundwork for the Virginia-New York anti-Hamilton alliance that became the core of the Republican party. Hamilton's friends saw evidence of a "passionate courtship" between the republican leaders of the two states, and Connecticut Federalists saw devious political purposes in the Madison-Jefferson trip through western New England in June 1791. Nathaniel Hazard reported they "scouted silently through the Country, shunning the Gentry, communing with and pitying the Shayites, and quarrelling with the Eatables; nothing good enough for them." Though their main purposes were "health, recreation, and curiosity," the two Virginians systematically strengthened the personal foundations for future policy organization. Madison, too, proved himself a good politician in learning to work with such former antifederalist leaders as Monroe and Clinton in the new partisan groupings.[40]

During the first session of the Second Congress, October 1791 to May 1792, votes were increasingly along party lines. In analyzing thirty-three roll votes, Noble E. Cunningham, Jr., has shown that about half of the sixty-five Representatives voted regularly either for or against measures favored by Madison. (Madison's vote was taken as the "party stand" because he consistently opposed Federalist programs and was acknowledged by both sides as the "opposition leader.") In the Madisonian "party" were the Virginia and Georgia delegations, all but one North Carolinian, about half the Maryland contingent, a few New Yorkers, and scattered members such as Thomas Sumter of South Carolina and William Findley of Pennsylvania. The Federalists included New Englanders and South Carolinians, portions of the New York and Pennsylvania delegations, and such individuals as Elias Boudinot of New Jersey and John Steele of North Carolina. Though there was no formal party apparatus, the coalitions were clear enough to require only organization and coordinated leadership to become self-conscious parties.[41]

Madison's conversations with Benjamin Rush, another firm federalist of 1787 to 1789 turned Republican, were increasingly partisan. In March 1792 Rush recorded that he "spent a long and agreeable evening with Mr. Madison in his room at Mrs. House's. We talked about the evils introduced into our country by the funded debt of the United States, and in praise of republican governments. He said that he could at all times discover a sympathy between the speeches and pockets of all those members of Congress who held certificates." Federalist Fisher Ames was equally partisan in noting that "most of the measures of Congress have been opposed by the Southern members. . . . Faction glows within like a coal-pit." In January 1792 he asserted that "the hatred of the Jacobites towards the house of Hanover" was no worse than the enmity between the parties in Congress, and in May he spoke of the anti-Hamiltonians as "a regular, well-disciplined opposition party, whose leaders cry 'liberty,' but mean, as all party leaders do, 'power.'" Eight months later the charge was more specific: "Virginia moves in a solid column, and the discipline of the party is as severe as the Prussian. Deserters are not spared. Madison is become a desperate party leader. . . . He opposes, *vi et armis*." When Madison and Jefferson visited Albany in May 1791, a reporter noted that the Secretary of State was accompanied by "the Charles Fox of America, the celebrated Madison," thus implying that Madison was the leader of the opposition in the United States, the liberal legislative spokesman against the sometimes oppressive acts of the administration. At a banquet in Richmond the next year, celebrating Washington's birthday, diners toasted "James Madison, the Congressional defender of the rights and happiness of the people."[42]

In the summer of 1792, party differences erupted in a vituperative newspaper war. Freneau's *National Gazette* blasted Hamilton's policies, and Fenno's *Gazette of the United States* imputed selfish motives and devious tactics to the opposition. In July, while Jefferson, Madison, and Washington were in Virginia, Hamilton, anonymously, accused Jefferson of having brought Freneau to Philadelphia to attack the administration. Freneau denied this and charged in turn that Fenno enjoyed Hamilton's patronage. Hamilton deluged Philadelphia newspapers with attack after attack on Jefferson, using a variety of pseudonyms that fooled no one, least of all Jefferson's friends. Edmund Randolph, in Philadelphia, kept Madison and Monroe informed of Hamilton's handiwork and, convinced that the assaults could not go unanswered, offered his services. He wrote briefly in Jefferson's defense, but Monroe and Madison planned the main reply in Virginia, where they had access to Jefferson's advice and files. In a long series of articles signed "Vindicator," published before the end of the year in Philadelphia newspapers, Monroe and Madison denied that Jefferson had opposed the Constitution, that he had mishandled American finances while in Europe, and that he had bribed Freneau to start an opposition newspaper in Philadelphia. Though Jefferson himself refrained from writing for the newspapers, the hardhitting but relatively dignified "Vindicator" series, and Freneau's own slashing poems and essays, did indeed vindicate the Secretary of State.[43]

Washington's response to the quarrel, of course, would be decisive. Observing it from Paris, Gouverneur Morris thought Washington "never had a very high opinion" of Jefferson, but would be sympathetic to the Secretary of State because he (Washington) was "attached to [Madison] immeasurably," due to "some local circumstances." Actually, the bitter public quarrel between supporters of his two chief cabinet officers alarmed and disgusted the President. In late August he wrote both men, pleading "that instead of wounding suspicions, and irritable charges, there may be liberal allowances, mutual forebearances, and temporising yieldings on *all sides*." From the perspective of the chief executive it was inexcusable "that internal dissensions should be harrowing and tearing our vitals" while the new nation was surrounded by enemies. The secretaries replied, deferring to the President's desire that public contention cease, but each justified himself and made it perfectly plain that the differences between them could not be glossed over. Washington's agony at the newspaper polemics and at the bitter struggle between two men he admired and had hoped would work together amicably dramatized the great change since the balmy inauguration of the government. The nonpartisan pursuit of the public good, Washington's persistent ideal, had by the summer of 1792, become impossible. For Madison, who in *Federalist* Number 10 had shown a deep understanding of factional politics, the development was unwelcome but hardly surprising. In becoming a party leader, he reluctantly accepted the partisan character of free government and came to see that what was at least a necessary evil could perhaps become an effective way to achieve constructive public goals.[44]

The national elections in the fall of 1792 inevitably reflected the heightened political disputes. Washington, anxious to retire, in May had asked Madison to draft a "valedictory address" for him. Madison urged the President to remain in office another four years, since only he could safely pilot the country through the troubled seas ahead. Washington persisted, so Madison drafted for him a few paragraphs subsequently included in the famous "Farewell Address" of 1796. When Jefferson and others also pleaded that Washington postpone his retirement, the weary, aging general agreed and thus stopped intrigues for the succession. If Washington would serve, his unanimous election was assured.[45]

No such unanimity existed on the vice presidency, however. In fact, John Adams had made himself obnoxious to many republicans by favoring elaborate titles for the President and other officers of government, and by his candid approval in the *Discourses of Davila* of the aristocratic features of the British constitution. Though he deeply distrusted the Secretary of the Treasury personally and had no part in the speculative ventures attending the financial plan, Adams had supported them, and he was a New Englander. Southern and Western agrarians, therefore, counted him an opponent, as did Northern foes of Hamilton's measures. Madison had never warmed at all to Adams and was willing, in any case, to displace a man who had very little support in Virginia and southward. To fight local contests in New York and Pennsylvania, and to prepare to supplant the Vice President, Republican leaders corresponded with each other, printed electioneering broadsides, and agreed on "tickets" to be supported throughout each state. They won substantial victories: Republicans were elected in nine of eleven districts in Pennsylvania; George Clinton defeated John Jay in a bitterly contested, possibly fraudulent election in New York, and Republicans consolidated their hold on the legislature in that state.

The Republican leaders, however, could not agree on a candidate to oppose Adams. Jefferson, the most likely candidate, would not oppose his long-time personal friend John Adams, and there were, besides, major constitutional and sectional obstacles to having both national offices filled by residents of the same state. Since Clinton of New York had just won an important election, standing as a Republican, and was in addition a well-known leader of the revolution, he had impressive qualifications. Yet he had been antifederalist in 1787 and 1788; his recent victory was tainted; and he was not especially anxious to serve nationally. Certain New York leaders, therefore, promoted Burr's candidacy and dispatched discreet inquiries to Virginia: would Madison and Monroe support Burr? The two Virginians consulted, and replied that in view of Burr's youth and inexperience, it would be ludicrous to stand him against such an experienced, respected, and patriotic hero of the revolution as John Adams. All things considered, they said, Clinton offered the best chance to give the country a more firmly republican Vice President than the now suspect author of the *Discourses of Davila*.[46]

Further correspondence and consultation took place among Republican leaders. Benjamin Rush introduced Madison's political confidant John Beckley to Aaron Burr: "This letter will be handed to you by Mr. Beckley—he possesses a fund of information about men and things, and what is more in favor of his principles, he possesses the confidence of our two illustrious patriots, Mr. Jefferson and Mr. Madison." Beckley found New York Republicans eager to cooperate to unseat Adams. Emissaries were sent to New England and southward to seek agreement on candidates and campaign methods. Word arrived of the Virginia preferance for Clinton over Burr. On October 16, Beckley, Melancthon Smith of New York, and Pennsylvania Republican leaders met in Philadelphia, Beckley wrote Madison, "to conclude *finally* and *definitively* as to the choice of V.P." They settled on Clinton, and messengers again departed for all parts of the Union to inform Republican electors of the "party decision." Beckley asked Madison and Monroe to write "principal republicans" in Virginia and to ask Patrick Henry to "influence" his friends in North Carolina. Though the New Yorkers took the initiative, and functionaries like Beckley did most of the traveling and letter writing, Madison aided in every way he could. The coordination was clear in the result: though Adams won with 77 electoral votes, Clinton received 50 of the 55 anti-Adams votes, including the entire vote of New York, Virginia, North Carolina, and Georgia. Madison thought that, coupled with substantial Republican gains in Congress, the strong challenge to Adams would "satisfy him that the people at large are not yet ripe for his system." The results of the election were "promising," Jefferson wrote, for "the republican interest . . . [and] the true principles of the Constitution."[47]

The national unity of 1789 had disappeared. Hamilton explained the party split entirely in terms of Jefferson's insidious influence and Madison's apostasy: "When I accepted the Office, I now hold," the Secretary of the Treasury wrote, "it was under full persuasion, that from similarity of thinking, conspiring with personal good will, I should have the firm support of Mr. Madison. . . . Aware of the intrinsic difficulties . . . and of the powers of Mr. Madison, I do not believe I should have accepted under a different supposition." Hamilton knew for certain, he said, that a "primary article" of Madison's creed was that "the real danger in our system was the subversion of the National authority by the preponderancy of the State governments." Yet from the beginning of the debate over the funding system, he had opposed measures Hamilton regarded as vital to establishing national authority. By 1792 Hamilton thought Madison's character "peculiarly artificial and complicated," rather than candid, simple, and fair. Furthermore, by slipping pro-Republican insinuations into addresses drafted for Washington, Madison had "abused the President's confidence in him." Finally, "entertaining an exalted opinion of the talents, knowledge, and virtues of Mr. Jefferson," whose opinions were "more radically wrong" than Madison's, the latter, "seduced by the expectation of popularity, and possibly by calculation of advantage to the state of Virginia," had become "the head of a faction decidedly hostile to me and my administration; and actuated by views in my judgment subversive of the principles of good government." Madison, for his part, had become thoroughly alarmed at Hamilton's political system and was increasingly disgusted personally with the secretary's arrogant, overbearing manner. Though Hamilton's brilliance, energy, and great influence in the government sometimes discouraged Madison and perhaps made him, as Hamilton charged, "a very discontented and chagrined man," the Virginian was willing, despite misgivings, to be a party leader to meet the challenge.[48]

CHAPTER XIV

A New Nation Faces World War

Iɴ the same letter that scorned Madison's apostasy on domestic issues, Hamilton recorded concern over an issue that dominated the rest of Madison's service in Congress: "In respect to foreign politics," Hamilton wrote, Madison's and Jefferson's views were "unsound and dangerous. They have a womanish attachment to France and a womanish resentment against Great Britain." Always impressed with the need to cultivate French friendship and trade as a counterweight to Great Britain, and grateful for French support during the American Revolution, Madison admired France increasingly through the early years of the French Revolution. He agreed with Washington that the revolution was "wonderful in its progress and . . . stupendous in its consequences," and that acceptance of the 1790 constitution by Louis XVI promised "happy consequences . . . [to France] as well as to mankind in general." Furthermore, his "resentment against Great Britain," expressed each year in Congress in proposed resolves to retaliate against her commercial regulations, grew as he observed the cynical intrigue of her agents in American affairs and the uncritical enthusiasm of Hamilton and many of his friends for British ways. Far from feeling that moral support for the French Revolution in the United States would lead to a dangerous entanglement, Madison believed a dynamic, republican France would insure a genuine balance of power congenial to a weak new nation. Entanglement and loss of national independence would result from French impotence and British aggrandizement, not from the triumph of the revolution. As long as the revolution remained largely internal, however, events in Paris were of great interest, but they were not of vital importance to the United States. Vice President Adams and a few others from the beginning had had little use for the French Revolution, but it did not divide Americans sharply during its first three years.[1]

In the fall of 1792, however, the pace of the drama in Paris quickened, and it was soon apparent that the fate of all Europe for years to come would be deeply affected by forces generated there. Americans learned in October that Louis XVI had been shorn of all his powers, and that Lafayette had deserted the revolution and been imprisoned by the Austrians. Two months later more momentous news arrived: France had proclaimed herself a republic, a wave of massacres had swept Paris, and French revolutionary armies had won an important victory over the Prussians at Valmy. Madison fretted over the uncertainty of the reports and deplored "the follies and barbarities which prevail in Paris," but he was pleased that the French nation was "united against Royalty" and hoped that France's armies would overcome her reactionary enemies. Leaders not impressed with the need for a counterweight against Britain were, on the other hand, alarmed. Fisher Ames wrote that "France is madder than Bedlam, and will be ruined," while John Adams lamented that so many Americans were "so blind, undistinguishing, and enthusiastic of everything that has been done by that light, airy, and transported people."[2]

During the winter session in 1792–3, Congressmen listened more intently for news from Europe than to their own acrimonious debate of the Giles resolutions condemning Hamilton's conduct of the Treasury Department. Madison approved the resolutions, and despite tactical reservations, he defended them on the floor of the House. After Hamilton submitted long technical reports justifying his conduct, though, Congress overwhelmingly rejected the resolutions. Disheartened, Madison blamed the defeat on the blind devotion of some members to administration policy and on the self-interest of many other members in Hamilton's fiscal arrangements. More than ever, Hamiltonians seemed to dominate the federal government.[3]

It is not surprising, then, that the spontaneous enthusiasm that greeted the news of Valmy and the founding of the French Republic seemed in many ways to Madison most propitious. The celebrations of French victories in American cities during January 1793 indicated that a larger public might respond to foreign issues than to arguments over banks and financial plans. Madison saw—and it added to his geopolitical and philosophic reasons for approving events in France—that the wave of pro-French enthusiasm might revive republican fortunes in the United States. With the growing certainty of a general war in Europe again pitting France against Great Britain, Madison knew it would be possible as well to enlist the still potent American Revolutionary prejudices against the pretensions and armies of George III. The exciting news from Europe and its alluring political possibilities eased and overshadowed the frustration of seeing the Hamiltonian phalanx bury the Giles resolutions.

The important emotional overtones were apparent in a letter Madison received from a Virginia friend in February 1793, noting that "the fate of human nature is involved in Europe. . . . The Reign of Despotism in whatever form it may appear in Europe will scarcely survive the 18th Century. . . . The Rent in the great Curtain" of despotism made in America would soon widen and spread the light of freedom everywhere. With an eye to the solid Federalism of New England, the correspondent wished that "the same spirit reigned in the bosoms of our Eastern Brethren that inspired their Breasts in 1776–77." Indeed, he concluded, if such were so, "endless Funding Schemes, etc.," would not be necessary. To perceptive Republicans, the sympathy for France, the concern of the United States for the spread of republican principles throughout the world, the supposed apostasy of New England from the "Spirit of '76," and the pernicious influence of Hamilton's financial plans all pointed, as war loomed in Europe, in the same direction: the time was ripe for a great crusade against the forces of plutocracy, arrogance, Anglomania, and stockjobbery that since 1789 had seduced the new nation from its revolutionary ideals and purpose.[4]

Madison had a chance to express his ideological enthusiasm when he received notice that, along with Joseph Priestley, Tom Paine, Bishop Wilberforce, Pestalozzi, Kosciusko, and a bit ironically, Washington and Hamilton as well, he had been elected an honorary citizen of France. In his letter of acceptance Madison applauded "the renunciation of [national] prejudices," evident in this cosmopolitan galaxy, as among the "sublime truths and precious sentiments recorded in the revolution of France." He took "peculiar satisfaction as a citizen of the U. S. which have borne so signal a part towards banishing prejudices from the world and reclaiming the lost rights of mankind, [in] the public connection with France . . . endeared by the affinities of their mutual liberty." He concluded with "anxious wishes for . . . the prosperity and glory [of] the French Nation," and the complete triumph of liberty over all its adversaries. Warily, Washington and Hamilton let their elections go unnoticed.[5]

In March 1793, responding to a friend in Kentucky who had deep misgivings about the course of events in France, Madison explained his own sense of the profound importance of those events to the United States:

The war in which [France] is engaged seems likely to be pushed by her enemies during the ensuing campaign. As yet her conduct has been great both as a free and [as a] martial nation. We hope it will continue so, and finally baffle all her enemies, who are in fact the enemies of human nature. We have every motive in America to pray for her success, not only from a general attachment to the liberties of mankind, but from a peculiar regard for our own. The symptoms of disaffection to Republican government have risen, and subsided

among us in such visible correspondence with the prosperous and
adverse accounts from the French Revolution, that a miscarriage of
it would threaten us with the most serious dangers to the present
forms and principles of our governments.[6]

Thus, shortly before he learned that England had joined the war
against revolutionary France (an extension sure to bring the war to
North America and have a perhaps catastrophic effect on American
trade), Madison saw that world war would soon dominate American
public life. The celebrations of French victories during the winter of
1793, and an increasing Federalist tendency to identify American and
British interests, made the new issue perfectly clear: did the national
interest of the United States consist in a strict neutrality, acquiescent
to the British maritime hegemony, that would permit the vital revenue-
producing trade with Britain to grow and prosper, as the Federalists
urged, or did it consist in a neutrality that would resist British naval
supremacy and trade monopoly and thus be able both to nourish world-
wide republican forces and to provide the United States with a counterweight to British pretensions, as Madison and the Republicans sought?
While the party division was thus basically geopolitical, the public often
responded to a sentimental preference for either the former mother
country or the ally of the American Revolution. Only among intellect-
uals such as Jefferson and John Adams were ideological differences at
first important. The rival understandings of national interest each had
honest, substantial foundations. Neither side wanted direct American
entanglement in European wars. It was nevertheless unavoidable that a
life-and-death struggle between France and England would overshadow
all other issues in Philadelphia.

At home in Orange during the spring and summer of 1793, Madison
saw mounting evidence that the turbulence in Europe was a boon to
Virginia farmers. As early as February 1790 he had written his father
that the European troubles would probably keep prices for Virginia
wheat high for several years. Five months later Joseph Jones wrote from
Virginia of bountiful crops and the "comfortable prospects to America"
of selling them in a strife-torn Europe. In the next year France's laws
putting its tobacco trade in defiance of British navigation acts pleased
Madison, and late in 1792, as news arrived that Europe was at war, he
renewed his reports of high prices and continued good prospects for
farmers. Clearly, the demand created by the European war enriched
Madison's family and friends in Virginia, and thus added to their pleasure at the progress of French arms. The war-born agricultural prosperity (shared by many merchants, of course) enabled Madison and other
Virginians more readily to follow the path marked out by their geopolitical premises and sentimental attachments.[7]

At the same time, Madison's friends in Kentucky, almost all of them

Virginians who had recently been his neighbors, wrote him of their own special reasons for partiality toward France. Spanish closure of the Mississippi and the work of Spanish agents in the Southwest and British agents in the Northwest to rouse the Indians against American settlements were life-and-death matters in the West. The Kentuckians wrote repeatedly that an outlet for their crops and safety from the Indians were vital to them, and unless the United States could protect these interests, the West might be forced into the arms of Spain or Great Britain. Anxious to remain under the American flag, however, the Kentuckians saw Spain and Great Britain as the enemies, and with no immediate fear of France, they responded enthusiastically to the French victories over the allied powers, especially after the formal alliance between Spain and Great Britain in May 1793. Madison saw in the Western reaction, including the veiled threat of secession should British power seem irresistible, another reason for identifying American national independence with the cause of republican France. British ascendency would threaten disunion as well as commercial enslavement.[8]

Thus when Madison learned, in late March 1793, that Louis XVI had been beheaded, he considered the effect in the United States. Though sorry personally at the fate of this friend of the American Revolution, Madison quickly overcame his regrets when he saw "Anglomen" attempt to turn sympathy for Louis into hostility toward a France that had murdered him. Madison was soon glad to hear "plain men" saying that "If [the King] was a traytor, he ought to be punished as well as another man." The countryside, Madison was sure, would be "universally and warmly right . . . with regard to Liberty and France," however much "the fiscal party in Alexandria" and other towns on the post road might give a "heretical tone" to the reaction there. Madison agreed with Jefferson's proposal that the United States respond to the war of Great Britain and the other naval powers on French trade by "instantly excluding from our ports all the manufactures, produce, vessels, and subjects of the nations committing this aggression." Though the Virginians did not want the United States to enter the war, they sought unhesitatingly a definition of neutrality that would aid France and harm her enemies. Madison proposed that American grain be given to France as a symbol of sympathy for her cause and as a guard against the threat of famine. Sure that a "miscarriage" of the French Revolution would most seriously endanger free government in the United States, Madison was willing to overlook the execution of a king and to take sides, nonbelligerently, in a European war.[9]

From Philadelphia, Secretary of State Jefferson wrote of the grave questions President Washington faced: should Congress be called to decide on war or neutrality? how far was the United States bound by the French alliance? what should the rules of neutrality be? how should the

United States receive Edmond Genêt, the dynamic, self-confident new
envoy from republican France? Through Jefferson, Madison learned of
the tense cabinet discussions in which Edmund Randolph sought to find
a middle ground between Hamilton's desire to repudiate the French
alliance and Jefferson's effort to fulfill its spirit by upholding nonbellig-
erent rights useful to France. Jefferson objected to an *executive* declaration of peace, to the repudiation of France implied by the word
"neutrality," and to a hasty declaration that, if delayed, might be used
as a lever to extract from the belligerents, especially Great Britain, safeguards vital to the commerce of neutral nations. For three days the
President listened as Hamilton and Jefferson argued brilliantly, and then
adopted Randolph's middle course. The Proclamation of Neutrality, issued on April 22, declared the United States would be "friendly and
impartial" toward the belligerents, and warned American citizens to
avoid any acts that might "contravene such disposition." Though, at
Jefferson's insistence, the word "neutrality" was not included in the
text of the proclamation, Jefferson approved unenthusiastically, fearing
"a mere English neutrality" that would be "a disagreeable pill to our
friends."[10]

In Virginia, less restrained than Jefferson by official responsibilities,
and deeply impressed with popular sympathy for France, Madison insisted that the alliance of 1778 (he was indignant that its validity should
even have been discussed) required a privileged status for France. "The
term *impartial* in the Proclamation," wrote Madison, was an unnecessary
and improper affront to France and compromised American honor and
good faith. The United States should of course avoid war, but her vital
interests were so clearly linked with French success that impartiality was
unwise and wrong. Even worse was a timid, technical neutrality that in
fact acquiesced in British control of the seas. "The proclamation was in
truth a most unfortunate error," Madison concluded in June. "It wounds
the national honor, by seeming to disregard the stipulated duties to
France. It wounds the popular feelings by a seeming indifference to the
cause of liberty. And it seems to violate the forms and spirit of the
Constitution, by making the executive Magistrate" decide issues of peace
and war. Furthermore, the President himself was falling prey to "the
unpopular cause of Anglomany." It was "mortifying," Madison wrote,
that Washington "should have anything to apprehend from the success
of liberty in another country, since he owes his pre-eminence to the
success of it in his own."[11]

Madison hoped a warm reception for the new minister of the French
Republic, Edmond Genêt, would strengthen the bonds between France
and the United States. He read with delight in Freneau's *National
Gazette* of the "elegant civic feast" given for Genêt in the largest banquet hall in Philadelphia. Guests toasted the "spirit of seventy-six and

ninety-two—may the citizens of America and France, as they are equal in virtue, be equal in success." Crowds sang the "Marseillaise"; the tricolor and the stars and stripes hung side by side everywhere; the poet Freneau supplied new words to the British national anthem, beginning with "God save the Rights of Man"; and a huge throng on the Philadelphia waterfront "burst into peals of exultation" when a French frigate brought in a British prize flying the tricolor above the inverted union jack. Genêt, Jefferson informed his friend in Orange, "offered everything and asks nothing. . . . It is impossible for anything to be more affectionate, more magnanimous than the purport of his mission." For about a month Genêt basked in Jefferson's favor and buoyed republican enthusiasms.[12]

Soon, however, Genêt's highhanded excesses alarmed even his most ardent admirers. From his first arrival in the United States he had issued commissions to American privateers, enlisted American seamen for service on French warships, and promoted expeditions against Spanish and English possessions in Canada, Louisiana, and Florida, all compromising the "impartiality" of the neutrality proclamation. When President Washington seemed to lag behind the public and the Secretary of State in sympathy for Genêt's efforts, the flamboyant minister appealed directly to the people. As the officer most responsible for enforcing the neutrality proclamation, Jefferson found Genêt's activities more and more unacceptable, and he had no doubt of the offensiveness and folly of the Frenchman's presumption that Americans would follow him rather than their revered President. Jefferson also opposed such unneutral acts as the arming of French ships in American ports. By mid-June Genêt's letters to the Secretary of State had become insulting. Jefferson feared Genêt's attitude would "enlarge the circle of those disaffected to his country," and he deplored Genêt's misapprehension that "the people of the U. S. would disavow the acts of their government."[13]

Washington's patience with Genêt was nearly exhausted. "Is the Minister of the French Republic to set the acts of this Government at defiance with impunity? And then threaten the Executive with an appeal to the people?" he asked Jefferson when Genêt disobeyed orders that a French warship illegally fitted out in Philadelphia remain in port. Jefferson shared the disenchantment. He wrote Madison that "never . . . was so calamitous an appointment made, as that of the present Minister of France here. Hot-headed, all imagination, no judgment, passionate, disrespectful and even indecent toward the President. . . . He renders my position immensely difficult." Genêt would, Jefferson wrote, "sink the republican interest" unless abandoned. Madison was appalled. "Your account of Genêt is dreadful," he replied to the Secretary of State. "He must be brought right if possible. His folly will otherwise do mischief which no wisdom can repair." Jefferson and Madison knew perfectly well what Genêt blithely and disastrously ignored: though popular sympathy for France was widespread, and many Americans saw important strategic reasons for friendship for her, other propositions were even more firmly fixed—the nation did not want war and would insist on genuine independence of action. French interference in American councils was utterly unacceptable, and appeals to the people over either the President or the Congress would be deeply resented. Perhaps most unforgiveable of all was the inference that Americans might prefer the appeals of Genêt to the judgment of Washington.[14]

By late summer Jefferson had concurred in Washington's decision to ask for Genêt's recall. Gloomily, Madison observed that the rupture between the President and the French minister "will give great pain to all those enlightened friends of those principles of liberty on which the American and French Revolutions are founded, and of that sound policy which ought to maintain the connection between the two countries." Unfortunately, people who in Madison's view disliked republican government and the French alliance (Federalists) were attempting "to turn the public [revulsion] . . . in respect to Genêt against the French Nation." They sought also to use "the public veneration for the President to produce . . . an animosity between America and France, [then a] dissolution of their political and commercial union, . . . [consequently a] connection with Great Britain, and [finally], under her offices, a gradual approximation to her form of government." The only antidote to this "poison . . . of the Anglican party," Madison wrote Jefferson, was to distinguish between France and her indiscreet minister, between principles and the unhappy events Genêt had precipitated, and "to impress the well meaning that the enemies of France and liberty" sought to subvert republican government.[15]

The Federalists acted exactly as Madison foresaw. Hamilton leaked information to Rufus King and John Jay, who made public accusations against Genêt, and King arranged for the New York Chamber of Commerce to adopt resolves hostile to France. By the end of August 1793 over twenty towns in New England and the Middle States had followed suit. In a major political coup, Hamilton persuaded John Marshall and Edward Carrington to have a meeting in Richmond; chaired by the respected George Wythe, it adopted anti-Genêt resolves. The Federalists undertook a wide-ranging, carefully coordinated campaign to use sympathy for the President to injure the Republicans.[16]

To combat these tactics and crystallize "the genuine sense of the people" still friendly to "France and liberty," Madison and Monroe met at Monroe's home near Charlottesville in late August. Responding to information from Jefferson, and convinced that they faced a potent Federalist "cabal," they drafted some resolutions they hoped would be approved at public meetings in counties all over Virginia and perhaps elsewhere. After endorsing the Constitution, peace, and "the eminent virtues and services" of Washington, the proposed resolves addressed the real issues: that the United States ought to remember gratefully French aid during the American Revolution; that the cause of liberty in America was tied to the same cause in France; and that the Tories and monocrats in America who showed an "active zeal [to] . . . assimilate our Government to the form and spirit of the British Monarchy . . . ought to be . . . reprobated." At Madison's suggestion, John Taylor of Caroline, whose writings against the national bank had left Jefferson "in raptures," had the resolves sponsored in his county by "the very respectable old gentleman" Edmund Pendleton. Monroe carried a stronger set of resolves with him on court circuit in the valley. By late September eight Virginia counties had passed the resolves, made to differ slightly, Taylor wrote Madison, "to avoid suspicion of their being coined in the same mint." The efforts on both sides had been incomplete and *ad hoc*; nevertheless each party had for the first time appealed to the public to influence and crystallize opinion. Madison marked John Marshall as the leading Federalist. Since he had borrowed money from the national bank or people connected with it, Madison reported, Marshall was in "absolute dependence on the monied interest, which will explain . . . the active character he is assuming." A newspaper war in the *Virginia Gazette and General Advertiser* between Monroe, who signed himself Agricola, and Marshall, who wrote over the pseudonyms Aristides and Gracchus, continued through the fall.[17]

At the national level the outcry against Genêt threatened to engulf the Republican interest. Meetings in cities in the Middle and Northern states proclaimed support for the President and anger at Genêt, and increasingly, at his country. Federalists exulted. Fisher Ames wrote that Boston had blessedly become "less frenchified," and Stephen Higginson congratulated Hamilton on the anti-Gallican spirit sweeping Massachusetts. A series of newspaper articles over the pseudonym Pacificus, written by Hamilton, upheld high Federalist notions of executive prerogative in foreign affairs and defended the policy of neutrality, with all its implicit dependence on the commercial system of Great Britain. Jefferson had detected antirepublican "heresies" at once, and had urged that Hamilton be "cut to pieces in the face of the public." "For God's sake, my dear sir," Jefferson pleaded with Madison, "take up your pen. There is none else who can and will enter the lists with him."[18]

Madison agreed that "Pacificus" needed to be answered, but in Orange Madison had neither the books nor the full record of facts necessary for an effective reply. He would look for someone else to do the job, he wrote Jefferson, perhaps having in mind Monroe or John Taylor of Caroline. A few days later, after reading more "Pacificus," Madison again complained of his "ignorance of some material facts," but he had reconciled himself to attempting the "solid, prudential" response required. He complained to Jefferson: "I have forced myself into the task of a reply. I can truly say I find it the most grating one I ever experienced; and the more so as I feel at every step I take the want of counsel on some points of delicacy as well as of information as to sundry matters of fact. . . . Being obliged to proceed in scraps of time, with a distaste to the subject, and a distressing lassitude from the excessive and continued heat of the season, I cannot say when I shall finish. . . . Delay I know is bad; but vulnerable parts that would be seized for victories and triumphs would be worse."[19]

Thus harassed and disadvantaged, Madison wrote five long essays signed Helvidius, all directed at Hamilton's argument in the first "Pacificus" paper that the executive had wide prerogatives in conducting foreign affairs, including the rights to interpret treaties, receive envoys, declare "peace" or "neutrality," and even take actions that might later limit Congressional options in declaring war. Altogether, Madison's papers show the ill-effects of his isolation and reluctance. They appear labored and pedantic beside Hamilton's vigor and confidence, and at times the Virginian returned partisan diatribe when understatement might have been more effective. He began harshly *ad hominem*: "Several pieces with the signature of Pacificus were lately published, which have been read with singular pleasure and applause, by the foreigners and degenerate citizens among us, who hate our republican government, and the French revolution." Near the end of the first essay, Madison renewed the invective against the "un-American" character of Hamilton's executive encroachments: these prerogatives were *"royal prerogatives in the British government*, and are accordingly treated as *executive prerogatives* by *British commentators*." "Pacificus," then, was simply another Anglophile, trying to subvert American republicanism by aping British practices.[20]

Hamilton's strategy had been to defend the legality of the neutrality proclamation by upholding the broad implied powers of the executive in the areas of diplomacy and war. Madison objected to the proclamation as both unwise and unconstitutional, but aware that pressing these points reflected directly upon President Washington, Madison concentrated his fire on Hamilton's definition of executive prerogatives. Following the method of his attack on the national bank, Madison insisted that every exercise of power by a branch of the federal government rest clearly and plainly on a specific clause of the Constitution. Madison granted that the executive was obliged to maintain peace until Congress declared war, and to fulfill the terms of valid treaties, but these duties did not *require* executive proclamations or clever rationalization in interpreting treaties. Therefore, under the doctrine of strict construction, the President should desist from actions that would in any way prejudice treaty obligations or Congressional power to declare war—or to declare peace. Madison quoted from *Federalist* papers written by Hamilton denying precisely the broad powers he now defended. Madison perceived correctly that the doctrine of implied powers would have hindered the ratification campaign of 1788, and that its subsequent avowal was therefore in some sense an imposition. His narrow construction was also probably closer to the intent of the ratifying conventions than Hamilton's assertion of implied powers. Yet from the standpoint of effective government, on the specific issue of the proclamation of neutrality, Hamilton's arguments seem less exceptionable than Madison's tight, legalistic, almost tortured constructions.

Madison's own sense that "Helvidius" was not among his best efforts is apparent in his repeated pleas to Jefferson for help and correction before the papers went to the printer. How did the French interpret the terms of the alliance of 1778? What was the President's understanding of the word "impartiality"? Were the citations from Montesquieu, made from memory, correct? Was quoting *The Federalist* good strategy? At that, Madison feared he was being too "prolix" and straying "too much into the wilderness of books." Furthermore, the papers had been drafted hastily, while Montpelier was "full of particular friends who will stay some weeks and receive and return visits from which I cannot decently exclude myself." Lest there be "vulnerable" sections "Pacificus" could "seize for victories and triumphs," Madison begged the Secretary of State to "look over what is said critically, and if you think there will be anything of importance wrong, or that may do more harm than good, that you will either erase it, where that will not break the sense or arrest the whole until I can make the correction." Jefferson praised the work and actually changed very little, but Madison nevertheless gave up the task after answering only one of Hamilton's essays.[21]

Madison was as much concerned, however, with the long-range effect of Hamilton's interpretations of American government as with the immediate issue of the neutrality proclamation. He had protested Hamilton's financial and banking plans because of their tendency toward privilege, plutocracy, and centralization; he objected to the doctrines of "Pacificus" because they subverted the limitations on power inherent in Madison's understanding of republican government. "We [may] regard it as morally certain," Madison insisted, that if Hamilton's theories become "the creed of government" acquiesced in by the public, "every power that can be deduced from them, will be deduced, and exercised sooner or later by those who may have an interest in so doing. . . . A people . . . who are so happy as to possess the inestimable blessing of a free and defined constitution cannot be too watchful against the introduction, nor too critical in tracing the consequences, of new principles and new constructions, that may remove the landmarks of power." This watchfulness was nowhere more important than in full maintenance of Congress' war powers:

In no part of the constitution is more wisdom to be found, than in
the clause which confides the question of war or peace to the legislature, and not to the executive department. . . . In war, a physical
force is to be created; and it is the executive will, which is to direct it.
In war, the public treasures are to be unlocked; and it is the executive
hand which is to dispense them. In war, the honours and emoluments
of office are to be multiplied; and it is the executive patronage under
which they are to be enjoyed. It is in war, finally, that laurels are to
be gathered; and it is the executive brow they are to encircle. The
strongest passions and most dangerous weaknesses of the human breast;
ambition, avarice, vanity, the honourable or venial love of fame, are
all in conspiracy against the desire and duty of peace.[22]

To Madison, war and executive aggrandizement undermined every
foundation of free government. He was alarmed to find the father of the
national bank, the organizer of the Federalist phalanx in Congress, and
the theorist of the "special relationship" between wealth and centralized
government, enlarging the executive power over peace and war.
"Helvidius" is a major demonstration of Madison's preoccupation during
the momentous spring and summer of 1793 with the threat posed to
republicanism by the use the already suspect Federalists might make of
the great war in Europe to stifle liberty at home and abroad. Spared the
dire perils and emotional excesses of war, Madison had been relatively
sanguine that the basic republicanism of the American people would
resist illiberal pretensions. Now he was not sure. The next few years
were to be vexatious and frustrating as the storm of war in Europe
threatened repeatedly to engulf the republican experiment in the United
States.

The Philadelphia to which Madison returned in November 1793 had
just emerged from the worst ordeal of its history: since August, yellow
fever had ravaged the city, killing perhaps five thousand people, about
one tenth of the total population. During the worst period, in October,
over one hundred a day died, and many people feared Philadelphia would
never again be inhabitable. In late October, however, blessed frosts came,
the fever subsided, and officers of government moved back into the
afflicted city. When Congress assembled on December 3 to hear President
Washington's fifth annual address, a momentary calm and unanimity
prevailed, reflecting the mood of the city at its deliverance. The President
explained his reasons for issuing the proclamation of neutrality, denied
any infidelity to the French alliance, called upon Congress to "correct,
improve, or enforce" his measures, and in the face of world war, asked
that the national defense be strengthened: "If we desire to avoid insult,
we must be able to repel it; if we desire to secure peace, one of the most
powerful instruments of our rising prosperity, it must be known that
we are at all times ready for war." Madison, as usual, drafted the reply

of the House, praising the President's virtue and wisdom, and promising to join him in the measures of defense and vigilance necessary for peace. Moreover, the nation rejoiced in the skill and firmness with which Washington and Jefferson had managed the troublesome Genêt business during the preceding summer. The long correspondence with the French and British ministers, made public in late fall, had "faithfully maintained the reputation of the country" against French "impertinent aggressiveness" and against British "supercilious arrogance," wrote Vice President Adams' grandson many years later. Even dyspeptic Fisher Ames thought the horizon calm, the new members of Congress "good natured," and the future "hopeful."[23]

Jefferson's long-postponed resignation as Secretary of State, to become effective at the end of 1793, saddened Madison but opened again the opportunity of high executive office. He was Washington's first choice to succeed Jefferson, but inclined to limit rather than expand his public duties, Madison refused the offer. After considering Chief Justice John Jay, Washington elevated Attorney General Edmund Randolph to the post, thus placing another trusted Virginian at his right hand. Madison's old friend, Philadelphian William Bradford, replaced Randolph. Though Madison had once been exceedingly intimate with the new cabinet members, in fact their appointments were unwelcome politically. Randolph had earned the suspicion and even enmity of Jefferson and Madison by what they regarded as his vacillating, unprincipled, compromising course during the preceding year, and Bradford had become as staunchly Federalist as the Boudinot clan into which he had married. Increasingly Madison feared the President, surrounded by Federalists, would become their unwitting tool.[24]

Before Jefferson left Philadelphia, however, he delivered to Congress the long-delayed "Report . . . on the Privileges and Restrictions on the Commerce of the United States in Foreign Countries," on which he and Madison had worked for over two years. It presented a full record of American trade, showing conclusively what Jefferson and Madison had long held: the United States was still an economic dependent of Great Britain. Britain took over half of American exports (twice as much as France) and supplied over three quarters of all imports (seven times as much as France). Moreover, Britain re-exported most of her American imports, thus enriching British middlemen at the expense of American producers. Even worse, more than twice as much trade from France was carried in American ships as was true from England, evidence that British ships monopolized the huge Anglo-American commerce. All of this was made possible, to Britain's immense benefit, by her discriminatory regulations, which, among other things, wholly excluded American ships from the British West Indian trade and from the carrying trade in British products. Jefferson also argued *for* expanded commerce with France and pointed out the benefits American manufacturers would derive from anti-British regulations. Though Jefferson favored free trade ideally, he believed only reciprocal regulations against Great Britain would bring redress. "Free commerce and navigation [should] not be given," Jefferson insisted, "in exchange for restrictions and vexations, nor are they likely to produce a relaxation of them."[25]

On January 3, 1794, to implement the report, Madison introduced in Congress seven resolves calling for higher duties on goods imported from "nations having no commercial treaty with the United States," higher duties on vessels of such nations, reciprocal restrictions against nations that forbade portions of their trade to the United States, and compensation to Americans injured by illegal, discriminatory regulations of other countries. In every case, of course, the resolves aimed at Great Britain. In supporting the resolves, Madison echoed the hallowed argument popularized by Franklin before the revolution that America could exert its will on other nations through commercial regulations because she exported necessities (food, raw material, ships) and imported the luxurious products of European factories. Any "contest of self-denial" the United States would certainly win, Madison insisted, because it would merely give up superfluities, while Great Britain and her island possessions would lose the bread needed for survival. In long speeches during January 1794, Madison urged the Republican doctrine of resistance to Britain through retaliatory regulations that would force that shopkeeping nation to her knees and vindicate American virtue and economy without resort to war or costly armaments. Madison wrote out his speeches for the newspapers, in which they were distributed throughout the nation, and he probably defended his resolves in public letters signed "Columbus."[26]

Federalists replied that the British trade was vital to American economic life and public finance, that the trade with her was not so one sided or unfair as Jefferson's report alleged, and that commerce with a chaotic, industrially underdeveloped France could not possibly replace the prospering trade with England. To support these arguments, Hamilton, who was doubtless aware that Jefferson's report was in preparation, had drafted, with help from British Consul Phineas Bond, an opposing view of Franco-American and Anglo-American trade, emphasizing British beneficence. Representative William Smith of South Carolina used Hamilton's notes in a long, powerful speech opposing Madison's resolves. In private, the Federalists charged that "all French" was spoken in support of Madison's resolves, and that their defenders, driven from arguments that the resolves would benefit American commerce, turned to assert that the regulations were necessary to "reach the tender sides of our enemy [Great Britain], which are not to be wounded in any other way." "It is surprising to me," wrote a New England Congressman who admitted admiration for Madison's "neat and elegant" speeches, "that we will not see that this [attack on English commerce] is French policy and French intrigue, and especially when we know that the *learned Madison* and his coadjutors are the constant associates of the disgraced Genêt whose conduct here must inflame the heart of every honest, independent American." A Boston newspaper repeated the charge about Genêt and added that Madison had been "a corrupt tool of France" ever since he first entered the Continental Congress in 1780. Madison's friends, on the other hand, congratulated him on his spirited defense of American interests. General Horatio Gates wrote of wide support in New York, where "the Murmurings of rank Tories and Interested Factors [agents] serve only to increase your popularity," and Joseph Jones praised Madison's "saucy" resistance "to the insolent and overbearing hand of [British] oppression." Gates wrote later that there was "not a Sound Whigg from the River St. Croix to the River St. Mary's, that does not Honour and applaud" Madison for his resolves.[27]

Soon, however, calamitous news overwhelmed the debaters. Under British orders in council of June and November 1793, her warships captured American vessels carrying provisions to France and trading with her colonies in the West Indies. Hundreds of fully laden American ships were carried into British ports, where their cargoes spoiled or were condemned. Ruin threatened thousands of merchants and mariners. Moreover, a new treaty between Britain and her ally Portugal, and the Barbary powers, left American ships the chief victims of the "dreaded Algerines." Finally, British authorities in the West incited the Indians and hatched secessionist plots with disgruntled settlers. Clamor against England buried Madison's resolves under demands for trade embargoes, army and navy expansion, and even war.

Though Madison and other Republicans welcomed the anti-British zeal, they refused to support the army and navy increases urged by the Federalists. Great Britain would not declare war, Madison insisted, because it would stop her prosperous trade with the United States. "I conclude therefore," he wrote, "that [Britain] will push her aggressions just so far and no farther, than she imagines we will tolerate. I conclude also that the readiest expedient for stopping her career of depredation on those parts of our trade which thwart her plans, will be to make her feel for those which she cannot do without." To Jefferson, he echoed "Helvidius'" suspicion of the real Federalist intent in expanding the armed forces: "You will understand the game behind the curtain too well not to perceive the old trick of turning every contingency into a resource for accumulating force in the government." Madison therefore voted in favor of two temporary embargoes and sought unsuccessfully to enact his resolves and a stringent nonimportation law against Great

Britain. New York Republicans went further, clamoring for preparedness and war. Madison held firm, though, voting against recruiting a
large army, building a navy, or raising excise taxes to pay for the defense
measures. Fear of armies and Caesarism and faith in commercial coercion
were for Madison cherished axioms.[28]

War news and events in France continued to excite the public. Though
the execution of Marie Antoinette and the Reign of Terror alarmed
Madison, the great victories of the revitalized French revolutionary
armies pleased him and others who saw Britain as the most dangerous
foe of the United States. He was delighted when the new French Minister, Fauchet, reported "the Revolution firm as a Rock." General Gates
hoped for "the promised Millenium" if war privations should "finally
produce a Republic in England." Madison replied that if French victories
continued, "the public attention may possibly be called off from the
French to the British Revolution. You may then renew your prophetic
wishes [for] . . . a Millenium under the auspices of the three great Republics," he concluded.[29]

Alarmed that the bitter resentment at England might pit a virtually
defenseless United States against the awesome aggressive might of the
British navy, Hamilton and other Federalists urged a special mission to
England, empowered to settle differences between the two countries.
Washington considered the proposal during March and early April. As
heightened tensions in the West made damping the crisis more urgent,
news from London that the most offensive orders in council had been
withdrawn, brightening prospects that Britain might welcome a rapprochement, persuaded the President to make the attempt. Though
many Federalists favored Hamilton for the mission, Washington refused
to consider his deeply partisan, widely mistrusted Secretary of the
Treasury. By mid-April Washington had decided upon John Jay, the
Senate approved in one day's debate, and Jay left for England on
May 12. The President had chosen the path of peace through reconciliation with the former mother country.[30]

Madison had little use for either the intent or the agent of the mission
to England. He considered supplication to the former mother country
unnecessary, misguided, and humiliating. If England yielded anything, he
wrote later to Monroe, it would be from fear that the retaliatory resolves
might otherwise succeed or from weakness imposed by the triumphs of
French arms. Thus, since England understood only power, persistence
in the resolves and cultivation of French friendship would *increase* the
chance of a settlement with the overbearing British. John Jay, therefore,
hostile to France since his service as a peace commissioner in 1782 and
1783, and by 1794 deeply involved in Federalist politics, was almost
certain to yield too much to England, upset Franco-American friendship, and thus destroy the balance between the two great powers vital
to American independence.[31]

To allay French suspicions and to placate Republicans at home, Washington also decided to send a friendly envoy to France. Madison, as usual, was offered the post, and as usual, he declined. Anxious to cement relations with New York Republicans, he then supported either Aaron Burr or Robert R. Livingston. When the latter declined and the President refused to consider the former, attention turned to James Monroe, who as Senator from Virginia had assumed an increasingly important role in Republican councils. Monroe agreed, and received instructions from Secretary of State Randolph contrary to at least the spirit of Jay's mission to England. Monroe was to assure France that she was "our first and natural ally," that the United States had no intention "to sacrifice our connection with France to any connection with England," and, explicitly, that the Jay mission was not in the least anti-French, since its *only* objects were "compensation for our plundered property, and restitution of the [Western] posts." Though Randolph sought to be subtle, even-handed, and conciliatory to the Republicans and to France, his naïve supposition that Monroe's friendly words would reconcile France to any concessions Jay might make to England set a dangerous trap for the Republicans: they would appear as the pliant deceivers of the French.[32]

In June 1794, with misgivings about the Jay and Monroe missions, and little to be politically joyful about, Madison rode toward Virginia, and in Baltimore, put Monroe on board a ship bound for Europe. Though public meetings, newspaper campaigns, and better organization had strengthened the Republicans at the local level, in Congress army and navy appropriations had passed, a carriage tax Madison thought unconstitutional had been levied to meet the expense, and everywhere invocation of the President's name carried measure after measure favored by the Federalists. This manipulation, and "the public confidence in the President," Madison had written gloomily, "are an overmatch for all the efforts Republicanism can make. The party of that sentiment in the Senate is completely wrecked; and in the House of Representatives in a much worse condition than at an earlier period of the Session." The Federalist ability to arouse the public to endorse war preparations, the consequent enlargement of executive power, and Washington's growing deference to Federalists, or at best, to compromising Republicans such as Randolph, made Madison's public duties seem irksome and unrewarding. The session just closed, begun in high hopes but ended in calamity, concluded Madison's active leadership of the Republicans in Congress. Furthermore, he was at that very time courting an attractive, vivacious widow, Dolley Payne Todd, and would in three months marry her. Old tasks lost their lure and fresh prospects cast their spell.[33]

When Madison returned to Philadelphia in November 1794, foreign concerns abated as the country awaited news of the Jay and Monroe missions. Meanwhile, the long-smoldering Western resentment against excise taxes, especially that on whisky, had, in the summer of 1794, become open resistance to federal tax collectors in western Pennsylvania. In August and September, amid efforts by moderates among the "rebels" to make the protests peaceful, and conflicting reports in Philadelphia of armed defiance in Pittsburgh, President Washington resolved to act in support of the law. In October he marched with more than ten thousand militiamen to Bedford in the Allegheny Mountains. Hamilton was with him, hoping to suppress the insurgents with a show of force that would enchance substantially the power and authority of the federal government. Amid signs of conciliation from the West, however, Washington restrained his zealous aides and returned to Philadelphia, where Congress was soon scheduled to convene. The "federal army" marched to Pittsburgh, met no resistance, and after arresting twenty unimportant "rebels," returned home, thus ending the "Whisky Rebellion."[34]

Madison had no sympathy with the "rebellion," but he thought the business a tempest in a teapot, dangerous only if manipulated by Hamilton and his friends to "accumulate force" in the federal executive. Reporting on the events to Monroe, Madison noted "the tendency of insurrections to increase the momentum of power," as had happened after Shays' Rebellion in 1786, and which was "to be dreaded on a larger scale in this Case." Luckily, however, the people of western Pennsylvania, "with a spirit truly Republican . . . condemned the resistance to the will of the majority" and agreed peaceably to obey the laws. Except for this prudent behavior, Madison was sure "a formidable attempt would have been made to establish the principle that a standing army was necessary for *enforcing the law*." Hamilton's military zeal against the "rebellion" left no doubt that he was the "Cromwell" in Madison's mind. The hostility of New England to standing armies, and Washington's calmness, dampened the zealots, but Madison felt nonetheless that military despotism might some day threaten American liberty.[35]

Washington had decided to speak out against the "Democratic societies" formed in many parts of the country to express sympathy for the revolutionary ideals of France. "Certain self-created societies" had served as focal points of the "rebellion," the President told Congress, implying with unmistakable meaning, that the societies were extralegal and in opposition to the established agencies of government. Fisher Ames made the usual invidious connections when he charged that the societies, modeled on the Jacobin club in Paris, "were born in sin, the impure offspring of Genêt . . . [and] everywhere the echoes of factions in Congress." To Madison, the societies were simply political clubs—at worst, harmless and inevitable in a free society, and at best, worthy devices for strengthening republican principles. They were, moreover, often valuable in organizing support for Republican candidates. He therefore condemned Washington's hostile reference to them as "perhaps the greatest error of his political life," making him the tool of the Hamiltonians. "The game was," Madison explained, "to connect the democratic Societies with the odium of insurrection—to connect the Republicans in Congress with those Societies—to put the President ostensibly at the head of another party, in opposition to both," and by that means to strengthen the Federalist party.[36]

The "game" succeeded in the Senate, which commended Washington's aspersions on the "self-created societies," but in the House, Madison, who as usual chaired the committee to draft a reply to the President, chose instead to emphasize the devotion of the great majority of the people to the Constitution and to the laws made under it. In the debate over the proposed reply, Madison asked if it was not unjust and tyrannical for government officials to censure societies "innocent in the eyes of the law." "If we advert to the nature of republican government," he admonished, "we shall find that the censorial power is in the people over the government, and not in the government over the people." Overriding Federalist objections, the House ignored the President's pointed reference to "self-created societies," and instead merely condemned "individuals or combinations of men" who defied the law. The whole "spectacle" of the pitiful "insurrection" and the overwhelming support of the country for the government, "when viewed in its true light," the House told the President, using Madison's words, displayed "in equal luster the virtues of the American character and the value of republican government." To Madison the issue was clear: a free government could in justice neither proscribe lawful political societies nor set itself up as the judge of what censures on its conduct were permissible. In these arguments, Madison outlined doctrines of free association, free speech, and political opposition more libertarian than those prevailing even among republican theorists, and of immense importance to the expansion of civil and political liberty in the United States.[37]

As mild Christmas weather gave way to heavy snow and bitter cold in January, Madison again defended liberal principles. He introduced a naturalization bill that required of prospective citizens only five years' residence, renunciation of foreign titles, and an oath of "attachment" to the Constitution. Federalists sought a longer residence, hinting darkly about dangers from hostile aliens. When Samuel Dexter of Massachusetts held up visions of potential "Popish intrigue" and made fun of Catholicism generally, Madison called him to order: "He [Madison] did not approve the ridicule attempted to be thrown on the Roman Catholics. In their religion there was nothing inconsistent with the purest republicanism. . . . Americans had no right to ridicule Catholics. They had, many of them, proved good citizens during the Revolution."[38]

Generally, however, as Vice President Adams wrote his wife, "the business of Congress [was] dulness, flatness, and insipidity itself." Members attended more to the election returns for the next session than to their own proceedings. Madison was pleased that the few Republican candidates in New England had done well, that New York had elected at least half Republicans, including the brilliant young Edward Livingston, that Pennsylvania was calculated to be three-fourths Republican, and that in the South, only two or three seats in South Carolina remained Federalist. Among other things, high prices for farm products, 50 per cent above the previous winter, Madison reported to Jefferson, kept Southerners happy. Overall, though, Madison seemed only mildly interested in the large growth in Republican political power these successes signaled. He did, however, agree to run once more for Congress himself, and again merely asked his father and brother to "see or drop a line" to a friend in each county in his district, indicating his candidacy. Francis Taylor reported the foregone conclusion in Orange: "I went to Court House, it being the day for Election of Representatives for Congress—But few people met, the number who voted did not amount to 30, all for J. Madison."[39]

Congress marked time, though, because members knew that the really momentous public business, relations with France and Great Britain, depended on news of Jay's mission in London and the reaction in Paris to it. Though Jay had signed a treaty in November 1794, no reliable news of its terms reached Philadelphia before the Third Congress expired on March 3. Ames noted that Congress maintained "a pouting silence, an armed neutrality, that does not afford the animation of a conflict, nor the security of peace. We sleep upon our arms." Republicans sought to prepare the people to be indignant should Jay return with a treaty in the least subservient to England, while Federalists "spared no industry to prepare the public mind to echo the praises" of Jay should he return with an agreement assuring peace with Great Britain. When news that Jay had signed a treaty reached Philadelphia in late January, but before its terms were known, Madison sought to assure French Minister Fauchet that the treaty would not be hostile to France. Nevertheless he remarked to Jefferson that though "it is wrong to prejudge, I suspect that Jay has been betrayed by his anxiety to couple us with England and to avoid returning with his finger in his mouth." Madison's partisan fears underscored Ames's reaction: "The success of Mr. Jay will secure peace abroad, and kindle war at home. Faction will sound the toscin against the treaty. I see a little cloud, as big as a man's hand, . . . that indicates a storm."[40]

When, on March 7, Washington finally saw Jay's Treaty, he knew that the forebodings of Madison and Ames were not in the least exaggerated. Though the treaty did provide for British withdrawal from the Western forts on American territory, all the other stipulations and omissions were ambiguous or favored Great Britain. Her traders were guaranteed free access to the Northwest Territory and to the Mississippi River. Commissioners were to examine pre-Revolutionary debts, boundary confusions, and recent British seizure of American ships, but with no assurance of redressing American grievances. The United States agreed, at least implicitly, to support British abridgments of neutral rights on the high seas, notably the repudiation of the doctrine that "free ships make free goods." Claims against British capture of American slaves during the revolution and resentment against impressment of American seamen by British warships were ignored completely. A trifling breach in the exclusion of American ships from the British West Indian trade was both humiliating and virtually worthless. Worst of all, in Madison's view, was the extension to Britain of "most favored nation" status without insisting on any change in her navigation laws. The effect was to repudiate the Republican program of commercial retaliation and to perpetuate American trade vassalage to Great Britain. Furthermore, France was certain to take offense at the favorable terms given England, thus making impossible the republican cooperation long cherished by Madison and Jefferson. To them Jay's Treaty was a complete disaster.[41]

His suspicions thoroughly aroused in advance, Madison exploded indignantly when, in the summer of 1795, he learned the terms of the treaty, that the Senate had ratified it, and that the President had, despite his own distaste for the treaty, and after long delay, signed it. Vigorous protests against the treaty throughout the country strengthened Madison's objections. As Jay remarked, he could have found his way the length of the land by the light of bonfires burning his effigy. Madison thought the treaty "a ruinous bargain," and concurred in Robert R. Livingston's warning to Washington: "I see in it not the slightest satisfaction of our wrongs. . . . I dread in the ratification . . . an immediate rupture with France. . . . I dread a war with France as a signal for a civil war at home." So unequal was the treaty that Madison could explain Jay's agreement to it only by "referring his conduct to the blindest partiality to the British Nation and Government and the most vindictive sensations toward the French Republic. Indeed the Treaty from one end to the other," the Virginian charged, "must be regarded as a demonstration that the Party to which the Envoy belongs . . . is a British party systematically aiming at an exclusive connection with the British Government and ready to sacrifice to that object as well the dearest interests of our commerce as the most sacred dictates of National honour." The treaty ignited the smoldering party feelings about the place the United States should take in a world at war.[42]

In a circular letter to Alexander J. Dallas and to other friends and party leaders in many parts of the country, Madison explained why, in view of Republican principles of foreign policy, he condemned the treaty. First, it overlooked the realities of international trade. "What can be more absurd," Madison asked, "than to talk of the advantage of

securing the *privileges* of sending raw materials to a manufacturing
nation, and buying merchandizes which are hawked over the four quarters of the globe for customers?" Even worse was the argument that "we
must take the treaty or be punished with hostilities." Besides being
ignoble, this supposed Great Britain would destroy deliberately the trade
she needed so desperately to carry on the war in Europe. The article
which gave Britain most favored nation status, without withdrawal of
her own unfair trade regulations, would in effect restrict or perhaps
bar altogether expanding trade with other nations, especially France.
Furthermore, the treaty accepted "the arbitrary maxims" of Great
Britain hostile to neutral nations in time of war, thus putting the United
States in the scale "against the fundamental rights of nations and duties
of humanity." Some of the "arbitrary maxims" now accepted had been
explicitly repudiated by the United States in previous negotiations with
France and were hostile to her. Thus, the United States concurred
voluntarily "in the scheme of distressing a nation in friendship with this
Country, and whose relations to it, as well as the struggles for freedom
in which they are engaged, give them a title to every good office not
strictly forbidden by the duties of neutrality." The clauses on the peace
treaty of 1783 required full, immediate compliance by the United States,
only delayed, partial fulfillment by England, and still left her free to
intrigue among Indians in the Northwest Territory. Even the suspension
by the Senate of the humiliating article permitting the trifling West
Indian trade in American vessels did not help. Should Britain agree to the
suspension, American commerce with the Indies merely reverted to the
inequitable status Jay had been instructed to correct. Jay's apology, repeated endlessly by defenders of the treaty in the press, that the treaty
was the best obtainable from Great Britain at this time, was unacceptable
even if true: no treaty would have been preferable to a bad one. Madison
concluded with a rousing appeal: "Nor is any evidence to be found,
either in History or Human nature, that nations, are to be bribed out of
a spirit of encroachment and aggressions by humiliations which nourish
their pride, or by concessions which extend their resources and power.
To do justice to all nations; to seek it from them by peaceable means in
preference to war; and to confide in this policy for avoiding that extremity; or securing the blessing of Heaven, when forced upon us, is the
only course of which the United States can never have reason to
repent."[43]

Had Madison known that Hamilton had secretly assured the British
Minister that the United States would not under any circumstances enter
into agreements of armed neutrality hostile of Great Britain, and that,
learning this, the British negotiators of the treaty were emboldened to
resist every American claim, Madison's fury and disgust at "the British
Party" would, of course, have been even more intense. An unlettered
New Englander summed up Republican contempt: Federalists spread

about "a colection of the most horred and frightful falsehoods that ever was invented by the Divel . . . to fright the peopel . . . that unless the trety took place Britain would sartainly make war with us, and that their power over us and Vengance upon us would be such that they would rouse off a grate gun 3000 miles distance and blow all our brains out if we stept out to piss."[44]

Perhaps recalling the unsatisfactory "Helvidius" papers, Madison refused Jefferson's plea to "For God's sake take up your pen" against defenses of Jay's Treaty written by Hamilton, the "colossus of the anti-republican party, . . . an host within himself." Madison knew nonetheless that a mighty battle awaited him when he returned to Philadelphia in November 1795. Certain provisions of Jay's Treaty would require support in the House of Representatives, so that body could, indirectly, thwart it. Madison did not hesitate to accept the Federalist challenge there. As he greeted old colleagues and met new ones, important changes were evident. In the cabinet, two personal friends were unexpectedly missing: Attorney General Bradford had died during the summer, and Secretary of State Randolph had been forced to resign when his cabinet colleagues persuaded the President that Randolph had intrigued treacherously with the French minister. In their places were Virginian Charles Lee and Timothy Pickering, both firm Federalists. New secretaries of War and the Treasury, James McHenry and Oliver Wolcott, were utterly devoted to Hamilton, who had returned to New York to practice law, but was still vastly influental. With such a cabinet, Madison wondered, "Through what official interstice can a ray of republican truths now penetrate to the President?"[45]

In Congress Republican prospects were less gloomy. The Virginia stalwarts, Page, John Nicholas, Josiah Parker, and Giles, were back, as were Findley of Pennsylvania, Macon of North Carolina, and Abraham Baldwin of Georgia, all firm Republicans. Furthermore, such newcomers as Joseph B. Varnum of Massachusetts, John Clopton of Virginia, and Edward Livingston of New York added talent as well as numbers to the Republican interest. Most important of all, the brilliant Albert Gallatin, a resident of Philadelphia during the last five sessions of Congress, briefly a Senator, and already highly prized as a sound Republican, had been elected to the House of Representatives by his western Pennsylvania district. Madison eagerly welcomed him to the House, soon pronounced him "a real treasure," and shared with him the burden of leadership the Virginian had carried for six years and was now increasingly anxious to lay down. Without clear party labels, the exact disposition of the new Congress could not be measured until key votes were taken, but Madison hoped the House would offer steady opposition to Federalist domination of the cabinet and Senate.[46]

Federalists nonetheless showed increasing confidence that they could

humble the once mighty Madison. Congressman Zephaniah Swift of
Connecticut had written the previous winter of the "undeserved
celebrity" of "the great Maddison." Even when he had "full time to collect his ideas, arrange his arguments, and round his periods," Swift asserted, he was

> a child in comparison with Ames. A hollow, feeble voice—an awk-
> ward, uninteresting manner—a correct style without energy or copi-
> ousness—are his distinguishing traits. Tho' correct in expression and
> solid in judgment, yet he is wholly destitute of vigour or genius,
> ardour of mind, and brilliancy of imagination. He has no fire, no
> enthusiasm, no animation; but he has infinite prudence and industry;
> the greatest apparent candor, he calculates upon everything with the
> greatest nicety and precision; he has unquestionably the most personal
> influence of any man in the House of Representatives. I never knew
> a man that better understood [how] to husband a character and make
> the most of his talents; and he is the most artificial, studied character
> on earth.

Some of this characterization would have pleased Madison, who had
disdained the "forensic" members of legislatures ever since his over-
exposure to Patrick Henry, but it reflects as well Madison's waning influence, an impression the debates begun in November 1795 would
confirm.[47]

Though Washington's seventh annual message was mild in tone,
Madison persuaded the House in reply to delete a reference to "the un-
diminished confidence" it had in the President, because, Madison wrote
Monroe, it was "not true in itself and . . . squinted too favorably at the
Treaty." Madison and his colleagues laid plans to ambush the treaty, but
uncertain of opposition strength on the main question, they postponed a
confrontation. Though Edward Livingston wrote he derived "great
entertainment and instruction from [Madison's] conversation," and
recognized the Virginian as the Republican leader, he fumed at the
cautious tactics: "Madison's . . . great fault as a politican appears to me a
want of decision and a disposition to magnify his adversary's strength—
a habit of considering the objections to his own plans so long and so
frequently that they acquire a real weight, and influence his conduct.
. . . He never determines to act until he is absolutely forced by the pressure of affairs and then regrets that [he] has neglected some better
opportunity." Ominously, Livingston's strictures reflected as well a continuing split among Republicans that found the New Yorkers more extremely hostile to Britain and more willing to countenance war than the
Southerners. The Republicans sparred cautiously in Congress for three
months over the new year, sure that a majority in the House opposed the
treaty, but equally certain that to raise the issue in a way implying a
challenge to the President would be fatal. In the meantime Madison rejoiced at French victories under an exciting new general named Bona-

parte, at severe food shortages in England, and at consequent soaring prices for American wheat. On March 2, 1796, after Washington had sent the ratified treaty to the House for its information, Edward Livingston moved that the President be requested to furnish papers related to the negotiaton of Jay's Treaty. The Federalists fell immediately upon both the request for papers and the debate over the treaty: the first infringed executive prerogative, and the latter invaded treaty-making power reserved in the Constitution to the President and to the Senate. Jay's Treaty, pugnacious Roger Griswold of Connecticut asserted, "is become law, and the House of Representatives have nothing to do with it, but provide for its execution." Gallatin retorted that this reminded him of a British bishop's maxim that "the people have nothing to do with the laws but obey them." Members girded themselves for the most important, dramatic debate thus far in the House's history.[48]

Still not certain of Republican strategy, Madison affirmed cautiously, on rather technical grounds, the right of the House both to request executive papers, and by passing or rejecting legislation to carry out the treaty, to pass upon the treaty's validity. Without these powers, the House could neither deliberate as the people's representatives nor protect their interests. Fisher Ames, writing on the floor of the House while Giles spoke intemperately and interminably, thought Madison had "spun cobwebs," had flinched from the implicit anarchy of his doctrines, and had been "strangely wary in giving his opinion." On March 24, the House approved Livingston's resolves, 62 to 37, but six days later, bolstered by strong opinions from Chief Justice Ellsworth, Secretary of State Pickering, and the absent but still omnipresent Hamilton, the President refused the requested papers. The need for "caution and secrecy" in diplomacy made it "pernicous" and "extremely impolitic" to condone the doctrine of the House that it had a *right* to see diplomatic papers. Not content with this, Washington asserted further that the convention of 1787 had explicitly rejected a proposal that treaties require "ratification by a law," and that its debates as he remembered them contradicted the Republican interpretation of the powers of the House of Representatives.[49]

Madison's opinion that "the tone and tenor of the message are improper and indelicate," was underscored by the embarrassing position thrust upon him. Many of his colleagues in the House knew that *he alone* had full notes on the debates of the convention of 1787, and that he had there defended executive powers similar to those now upheld by Washington. Federalists taunted him to admit his earlier position, and Republicans implored him to use his notes to repudiate Washington's reference to the debates. At a caucus of House Republicans on April 2, the first such formal meeting in Congressional history, the Republicans decided to submit resolves defending the right of the House to pass upon treaties and to call for executive papers (still refused by Washington), without detailing reasons for so doing. Madison's 1787 notes were at Monticello, and the debate was over before Madison could make use of information supplied by Jefferson from them. In any case, Madison insisted again that an appeal to the *private* debates preceding the Constitution was less relevant to its interpretation than one to the public discussion after it had been submitted to the people. He therefore evaded the questions hurled at him about the Convention debates. Though the Republican resolves passed easily, the Federalists raged at the embarrassed Virginian: "The conduct of Mr. Madison," Jonathan Trumbull, Jr., wrote, "has been insidious and uncandid in a high degree. . . . Although repeatedly called upon by Members to inform the House what was the understanding on this head in the Convention for framing the Constitution—and tho' known to be perfectly conversant and particularly active in all that passed in that body—yet he has been reserved and silent as the Grave— not one explanation could be drawn from him—this conduct will serve to plunge him in infamy—and ruin his hard-earned and long-continued reputation." Ames declared Madison "irrevocably disgraced, . . . devoid of sincerity and fairness."[50]

With the rights of the House thus upheld, for nearly a month it debated the central question: should the House enact the laws necessary to put Jay's Treaty into effect? Madison made long speeches on April 14 and 15, restating fully his arguments against the treaty of the summer before: it gave everything and secured nothing; it was hostile to France; it supported British violation of neutral rights; it harmed American trade; and it surrendered the vital weapon of commercial retaliation. Furthermore, the arguments for executive and Senatorial prerogative set forth on behalf of the treaty endangered republican government at home as much as cleaving to British "monocracy" threatened it abroad. For two more weeks the debate raged. Giles, Nicholas, Livingston, and Findley spoke long and effectively against the treaty, while a host of New Englanders, supported by William Smith and Robert G. Harper of South Carolina, defended it. Federalist charges that rejection of the treaty at this late stage meant insult to Washington, humiliation to the nation's honor, and war with Great Britain, together with a cascade of protreaty petitions inspired by Hamilton and other Federalist leaders, corroded the Republican majority. Samuel Smith of Maryland declared that despite his personal objections, he would respond to petitions from his constituents and vote for the treaty. Madison thought the antitreaty majority of perhaps 20 on April 18 had diminished to 8 or 9 by the twenty-third, and threatened to "daily melt" until the vote was taken. The critical moment was at hand, and the result uncertain.[51]

To conclude the debate, the Republicans depended upon Gallatin, whose widely circulated speeches on Jay's Treaty had so "enchanted" Jefferson that he thought them "worthy of being printed at the end of

the Federalist [Papers]." In a calm, even voice tinged with a politically
unfortunate French accent, Gallatin dissected the treaty itself and Federalist jeremiads over the effect of its rejection. What was so marvelous,
he asked, about the provision restoring the Western posts? It merely
repeated a commitment already made in the treaty of 1783. The need
even to mention it eleven years later was evidence of British unworthi-
ness. What possible excuse could there be for abandoning neutral rights
the United States had insisted upon for twenty years? And so on. He had
only contempt for the "conjured fears" under which the treaty had been
negotiated, signed, and ratified. The United States, a stable republic
secure in the devotion of its citizens, had no reason to cringe before an
arrogant Britain that was, at the very moment, hard pressed on the
battlefields of Europe.[52]

The Federalists feared Gallatin's brilliant, powerful speech might
arrest the decline of the antitreaty forces. But their most redoubtable
champion had not yet spoken: "Is Ames sick?" asked an absent partisan.
"I hope he will attend and . . . make a display of that eloquence and
intelligence so rare in this country." On April 28, word spread that the
Massachusetts man, weak and emaciated from a long illness, would take
the floor in a final, fervent appeal for the treaty. Vice President Adams,
most of the Senate, and justices of the Supreme Court crowded the galleries for the finest oration in Congress before the days of John Randolph
of Roanoke, Clay, and Webster. Frail and ashen, in neat, dark clothes,
Ames accentuated the drama with his opening words: "Mr. Chairman,
I entertain the hope, perhaps a rash one, that my strength will hold me
out to speak a few words." He spoke for an hour and half without
notes, eloquently and imaginatively. After scolding the Republicans for
their excessive claims of treaty power for the House of Representatives,
and for their persistent opposition to the defense appropriations that
refusal of Jay's Treaty would make especially necessary, Ames un-
leashed a torrent of oratory on the awful consequences of rejection.
Bloody Indian strife would blaze along the frontier. Could any opponents
of the treaty, Ames asked, assume responsibility for an Indian peace? No,
rejection would lead to savage warfare, and any honest legislator would
have to say to the frontier inhabitants "in the daytime, your path through
the woods will be ambushed; the darkness of midnight will glitter with
the blaze of your dwellings. You are a father—the blood of your sons
shall fatten your corn-field. You are a mother—the warwhoop shall
wake the sleep of your cradle. . . . By rejecting [the treaty and the frontier forts] we light the savage fires, we bind the victims. . . . I can fancy
that I listen to the yells of savage vengeance, and the shrieks of torture;
already they seem to sigh in the western wind; already they mingle
with every echo from the mountains." Vice President Adams and many
others wept. Madison sat glumly, and some Republicans "grimaced horri-

ble ghastly smiles." Justice Iredell blurted out, "Bless my stars, I never
heard anything so great since I was born."[53]

Ames then asked whether the government would "be able to temper
and restrain the turbulence" that would result in the country should the
treaty be rejected. He accused its foes of being impractical philosophers
who assumed "that our union, our peace, our liberty, are invulnerable
and immortal; as if our happy state was not to be disturbed by our
dissensions, and that we are not capable of falling from it by our un-
worthiness." Ames asserted that governments, especially new republican
ones, needed most urgently the blessings of peace, and needed most
earnestly to cultivate internal unity and respect for authority. All this
the Republicans ignored. "The great interest and general desire of the
people," Ames declared, was "to enjoy the advantages of neutrality. . . .
[The treaty] affords America that inestimable security. . . . When the
fiery vapors of war lowered in the skirts of our horizon, all our wishes
were concentrated in this one, that we might escape the desolation of the
storm. This treaty, like a rainbow on the edge of the cloud, marked to
our eyes the space where it was raging, and afforded at the same time
the sure prognostic of fair weather. If we reject it, the vivid colors will
grow pale; it will be a baleful meteor portending tempest and war."
Exhausted and with the palor of death on his face, Ames concluded
pathetically: "There is, I believe, no member who will not think his
chance to be a witness of the consequences greater than mine. If, however, the vote should pass to reject, . . . even I, slender and almost broken
as my hold upon life is, may outlive the Government and Constitution."
Justice Iredell exclaimed in tears, "My God, how great he is!" Adams
replied, "It is divine." Joseph Priestley declared Ames the equal of Pitt,
Fox, and Burke. Federalists on the floor cried, "The question," but
Republicans, dazed and fearful, shouted, "Committee, rise," and managed
to adjourn the House. Madison walked home in despair. Not since
Patrick Henry's heyday had he seen demagoguery so stampede a
deliberative assembly.[54]

The next day, Christie of Maryland, Speaker Dayton of New Jersey,
and even George Hancock of Madison's twenty-member "Virginia
phalanx," declared for the treaty. The antitreaty majority had disappeared. The fateful roll call in the committee of the whole tied, 49 to 49.
Chairman Frederick Muhlenberg, long a foe of the treaty, also switched
and voted for it. The next day in formal session the House voted 51 to 48
to pass the appropriations necessary to carry Jay's Treaty into effect.
The Republicans were shattered and defeated. For four years, until
President Adams approved the 1800 convention with France, the
Federalists allied the nation with Great Britain and carried it to the brink
of war with France. Internally, higher taxes, mobilization for war, and
repression of dissent followed. All that Madison had feared and opposed
had come to pass.

Reflecting on the debacle, Madison could see little to be hopeful about. The petitions favoring the treaty had been wrung out of the people by threats of ruin and terror. "The banks, the British merchants, the insurance companies were at work in influencing individuals. . . . Scarce a merchant or trader but what depend on [their] discounts. . . . Under such circumstances, a bank director, soliciting subscriptions, is like a highwayman with a pistol, demanding the purse." Furthermore, Madison noted, "The people have everywhere been made to believe that the object in the House of Representatives in resisting the treaty was war, and have thence listened to the summons 'to follow where Washington leads.' " In New England, "The exertions, and influence of Aristocracy, Anglicism, and Mercantilism . . . perfectly overbalanced . . . Republicanism." In the House itself, "a few wrongheads" disagreed on strategy. As a result, "before some were ripe" for a plan to accommodate all antitreaty sentiment, "others were rotten." Altogether, Madison reported, "the progress of this business throughout has to me been the most worrying and vexatious that I have ever encountered."[55]

Jubilant, and with their opponents in disarray, the Federalists sensed that at last they had the troublesome apostate Madison on the run. Ames gloated, "I attend Congress daily, but crack jokes instead of problems, and think as little of the proceedings as the doorkeeper." Henry Knox implored Jeremiah Wadsworth, "Do let your Hartford Wits loose upon Madison, French always, staunch French, as well in the days of despotism as of anarchy." A Boston newspaper, noting Gallatin's dominant role in the debates, dismissed Madison as a mere "file-coverer to an itinerant Genevan," and the Federalists increasingly referred to their foes as "Gallatin and Co." The new champion of Federalist venom, "Peter Porcupine" (William Cobbett), wrote an epitaph: "Citizen Madison was formerly reckoned as a sort of chief, but he has so sunk out of sight this campaign that we can look upon him, at least, no more than an aide-de-camp . . . without even the hope of repairing his reputation. As a politician he is no more; he is absolutely deceased, cold, stiff and buried in oblivion for ever and ever." When Madison left Philadelphia in June 1796, not he, his colleagues, nor the country at large still pictured him as *the* great Republican champion. Tired and discouraged, he longed to retire from public life. He had, in fact, played an important role in a national legislative assembly for the last time.[56]

Madison attended the inconsequential lame-duck session of Congress during the winter of 1796–7, but he took little part in its proceedings. Federalists excluded him from his usual role as chairman of the committee to reply to the President's annual message. He cooperated for a final time with Washington in attempting to found a national university, but the economy bloc defeated the plan. He resisted defense appropriations and higher taxes, but a temporary international lull made even these debates halfhearted and inconclusive. English insults to American commerce had declined, and French reaction to Jay's Treaty had not yet become unmistakably hostile.[57]

All eyes, in fact, were on the presidential election. Washington had made known his intention to retire in the summer of 1796, and in September had presented his "Farewell Address" to the nation. The first part followed closely the paragraphs of general solicitude for the national welfare Madison had drafted during more congenial days in 1792, but most of the address, guided by Hamilton, was a defense of the Federalist view of executive authority, of the dangers of "political societies," and of the place of the United States in a world at war. Even the famous warning against "permanent alliances," in the context of the pending elections, was a rebuke to friends of France and a commendation of Jay's Treaty. Disgusted at Washington's "suspicion of all who are thought to sympathize with [the French] revolution and who support the policy of extending our commerce" with France, Madison was amazed that the honored chief executive had "his own mind wrought up to the tone that could dictate or rather adopt some parts of the performance." Madison would not speak publicly against the general and President he had so long revered and in whose confidence he had once held the first place, but in fact he agreed with Benjamin Franklin Bache's Philadelphia *Aurora* on the political effect of the President's retirement: "Every heart in unison with the freedom and happiness of the people ought to beat high with exultation that the name of Washington from this day ceases to give a currency to political iniquity and to legalized corruption."[58]

With Washington out of the picture, the presidential contest was between an inactive, unanxious, but perfectly willing Jefferson, and Vice President John Adams, who, though unwilling to campaign, thought the presidency rightfully his at this time. Partisans of each man exerted themselves in what became a largely sectional contest: apart from Pennsylvania, Jefferson was to gather but five votes north of the Potomac, and Adams received only two votes south of it. At Montpelier during September and October, Madison took little part in the campaign beyond making sure Virginia remained wholly Republican and responding helpfully to reports from John Beckley, who "managed" Republican strategy from Philadelphia.[59]

When Madison returned to the capital in late November, it seemed likely Adams would win, but the curious electoral machinery and the embryonic state of the political parties left many uncertainties. Though unanimous for Jefferson, internal divisions caused the Republicans to give less than half their strength for their leading vice presidential candidate, Aaron Burr. More important, Hamilton led a move secretly to withhold some electoral votes from Adams (principally in South Carolina) to let the more pliant Thomas Pinckney, the Federalist vice presidential can-

didate, win over Adams. New Englanders who learned of the plot resolved to withhold their votes from Pinckney. Therefore, Madison
informed Jefferson he should be prepared for a first-, second-, or third-
place finish. Jefferson must accept the vice presidency not only from
a general sense of duty, Madison wrote, but because "your neighbourhood to Adams may have a valuable effect in his councils. . . . His
censures of our paper system [Hamilton's financial plans] and the intrigues at New York for setting Pinckney above him, have fixed an
enmity with the British [Hamiltonian] faction. . . . He is said to speak of
you now in friendly terms and will no doubt be soothed by your acceptance of a place subordinate to him."[60]

Though reluctant to leave his retirement, Jefferson expressed his
willingness to serve under Adams, since "he had always been my senior,
from the commencement of my public life." Jefferson therefore wrote a
letter congratulating Adams, and incidentally, inveighing against the intrigues of "your arch-friend of New York [Hamilton]." Jefferson sent
this letter under cover to Madison, "open for your perusal," so that it
might remain undelivered if it seemed "ineligible" in any way. Jefferson's
view was that "if Mr. Adams can be induced to administer the government on its true principles, . . . [it might be] for the public good to come
to a good understanding with him. . . . He is perhaps the only sure
barrier against Hamilton's getting in." Impressed with his delicate responsibility, Madison gave six reasons why he decided not to deliver the
letter: (1) Adams already had full confidence in Jefferson's friendship
and good will; (2) the air of Jefferson's letter betrayed an embarrassment
Adams might misunderstand or resent; (3) Adams was "fully apprized"
of Hamilton's treachery and might think Jefferson sought only to cause
trouble among Federalists by mentioning it; (4) Jefferson's joy at *not*
being President might seem to reflect on one of a "ticklish temper" who
was himself to be President; (5) ought the honest efforts of Jefferson's
supporters be "depreciated" by "implying the unreasonableness of them,"
as the apologies to Adams seemed to do? and (6) if Adams acted badly
as President, it might be politically embarrassing to Jefferson for Adams
to have in writing so much "compliment and confidence." In fact, Madison did not share Jefferson's personal confidence in Adams and could not
persuade himself "to augur much that is consoling from him."[61]

As he sought to be sure Jefferson would accept public office, Madison
was just as insistent on his own final retirement. He refused re-election
to Congress from his "safe" Virginia district. Though Madison and other
Republicans had never doubted that Jefferson should be their candidate,
the "retired" farmer at Monticello wrote that "the first wish of my
heart" was that Madison should become President in 1797. In a desperate
effort to halt the deterioration of Franco-American relations, leading
Federalists proposed that Madison be sent to France as a minority member of a special conciliatory commission. On inauguration eve President-

elect Adams approved the plan and talked to Jefferson about it: would Madison undertake such a mission? Staying with Madison during the ceremonies, Jefferson knew his friend's mind perfectly, and told Adams of Madison's unalterable opposition to any appointment requiring a long sea voyage. At about the same time Madison rejected an offer from powerful leaders of the Virginia Assembly that he be elected, unanimously, governor of Virginia. In a final move to insure his retirement, Madison warned his father that if Jefferson should stop at Montpelier, urging Madison's election to the Virginia legislature, the proposal was "merely expressive" of Jefferson's wishes and should "not be allowed to have the least effect." His determination to retire was "sincere and inflexible," Madison asserted.[62]

After the March winds had dried the roads, Madison left Philadelphia for a leisurely journey to Virginia with Dolley (his wife now for two and a half years), her sister Anna, her five-year-old son, Payne, and his own twenty-two-year-old sister, Fanny. The party stopped at Harper's Ferry, at Berkeley Springs, at Harewood to visit Dolley's mother and sister, and in Winchester to see Madison's sister Nelly. The pleasant trips among friends in warm spring weather doubtless increased Madison's joy at being free from public duties, with no immediate prospect of re-employment, for the first time since he had been elected to the Orange County Committee of Safety in December 1774. The increasing frustration and disappointment of the last few years in Congress heightened his relief. Since the first session of Congress in 1789, when there had been substantial unity behind Madison's leadership in measures to launch the new government, the trend had been toward more and more bitter partisanship, and from Madison's vantage point, more and more power in the hands of wrongheaded leaders. Hamilton had saddled the country with a financial system suited to speculation and intrigue, not simple republicanism. Bending to his powerful arguments, the Constitution itself had become a dangerous instrument of centralization and executive domination. Washington's name had been used to overawe and befog rational deliberation and to slander democratic societies. Worst of all, the nation had been tied to the commercial system and maritime arrogance of Great Britain in a way that compromised genuine independence and poisoned friendship with republican France. For nearly three years, ever since the defeat of the commercial retaliation resolves in 1794, Madison had increasingly left leadership of Congressional Republicans to others. He now did so completely; Gallatin, Livingston, Nicholas, and Giles were to fight the battles for the next four years. Before Madison was to return to politics, first in the Virginia Assembly, to oppose the Alien and Sedition Acts, and then in the cabinet of Thomas Jefferson, he found full absorption in his roles as Virginia planter and family man.[63]

CHAPTER XV

Montpelier and Dolley Madison

D URING the seven years between Madison's departure from Montpelier in August 1786, to attend the Annapolis Convention, and
the end of the Second Congress in March 1793, he spent only
sixteen months in Orange County. During the four years of the next two
Congresses (1793–1797), he spent twenty-six months in Virginia, and during the following four years he did not once leave the state. Those years
settled a pattern of private life that lasted for Madison until his death in
1836. The frustrating search for vocation, the qualms about being tied to a
slave-worked plantation, and the restlessness of bachelorhood were, finally,
to be exchanged for the contentments of becoming a master farmer in
Orange County, and of a superbly happy marriage to the Quaker widow
Dolley Payne Todd.

When drafting the Constitution and establishing the new government
took Madison away from home in 1786, he had not finally decided how
and where he would earn a living (see Chapter VIII). Fitful studies of
law continued, temptations to find a land base in Albemarle County, in
Kentucky, or even in the Mohawk valley in New York State lingered,
and judging from his tendency to stay on for months at a time in New
York or Philadelphia between sessions of Congress, the society and
sophistication of the growing cities beckoned. Had Madison achieved
success at the bar, or earned financial independence in Western land
ventures, he might, in the fashion of Hume, Burke, Franklin, and many
others in the English-speaking world in the eighteenth century, have left
the provinces for the pleasures and excitement of the capital. During
the years of full commitment to public affairs, however, Madison's ties
to Montpelier, whether or not he wished it, actually became stronger,
and finally unbreakable.

The family of small children and younger brothers for whom Madison acted as schoolmaster in the early seventeen-seventies (see Chapter IV), had by the seventeen-nineties outgrown the plantation James Madison, Sr., still managed profitably. Besides the three children who had died in infancy and the two carried away by dysentery, James Madison had three brothers and three sisters. Francis, two years his junior, is a shadowy figure almost never mentioned in family correspondence. No letters survive between him and his older brother. He married a local girl in 1772, established himself on a farm a few miles from Montpelier, and before his death in 1800 had at least four sons and five daughters, who together with their children, shared in James Madison's estate in 1836. Otherwise, Francis Madison leaves no mark and apparently had little to do with his father's other children or with their affairs. The next younger son, Ambrose (1755–1793), on the other hand, was until his early death a close, congenial, and valued colleague of his politician brother. In 1780 he married Mary Willis Lee, and soon built his own home, Woodley, on land adjacent to Montpelier but on the opposite, east-facing slope of the Southwest Mountains. His daughter, Nelly Conway (1781–1865), named for her paternal grandmother, lived at Woodley all her life, and according to family tradition, was James Madison's favorite niece. Ambrose helped manage Montpelier, and in every way took part in family affairs and enterprises. He acted as one of his brother's political lieutenants locally, but was not otherwise active in public life. As James Madison, Sr., grew old and feeble, and his eldest son turned to politics, Ambrose became increasingly the capable, dependable heir to family responsibilities in Orange County. His sudden death in October 1793 left a chasm that probably was of major importance in turning James Madison's attention more toward family affairs.

The other brother, William (1762–1843), was, until the seventeen-nineties, too much younger than James Madison to be an adult companion. He was, however, bookishly inclined and shared his eldest brother's political interests. He studied at the Princeton preparatory school, Hampden-Sydney Academy, and William and Mary, and read law for a time under Jefferson's guidance. He also served briefly in the revolutionary army, perhaps even at the seige of Yorktown. In 1783 he married Frances Throckmorton and settled on a farm, Woodbury, a few miles north of Montpelier, and soon began to duplicate his parents' fecundity: in the twenty years following their marriage, William and Frances Madison had ten children, all of whom survived at least until adolescence. Raising a family and farming seem to have distracted William from the law, but from 1791 to 1794 and again from 1804 to 1811 he served in the Virginia legislature. Though there is no contemporary evidence during the seventeen-eighties and nineties of difficulties between William and the rest of the family, later disputes may reach back to those

Montpelier as it was after Madison's enlargement in 1809. Taken from *Chesapeake and Ohio R.R. Illustrated Guide and Gazetteer, 1884.* (*Courtesy of the Virginia State Library and Archives*)

The President's House, Washington, D.C., according to an 1807 plan; drawing by Benjamin H. Latrobe. (*Courtesy of the Library of Congress*)

James Madison, 1782, sil-
houette by Joseph Sansom.
(*Courtesy of the Historical Society
of Pennsylvania*)

*James Madison Esqr. Representative
in Congress for the State of Virginia
Aged 30*

James Madison, ca. 1790,
engraving by W. R. Jones;
T. Gimbrede, printer. (*Courtesy of the Historical Society of
Pennsylvania*)

James Madison, 1792, replica
of marble bas-relief by Gui-
seppe Ceracchi. (*Courtesy of
The Art Museum, Princeton
University*)

James Madison, 1833, portrait by Asher B. Durand. (*Courtesy of The New-York Historical Society, New York City*)

James Madison, 1825, plaster life mask by J. H. I. Browere. (*Courtesy of the New York State Historical Association, Cooperstown*)

James Madison, 1817, portrait by James Wood. When the Madisons' close friend Eliza Collins Lee saw this portrait, she exclaimed: "The likeness . . . almost breathes, and expresses much of the serenity of [Madison's] feelings at the moment it was taken; in short, it is, *himself.*" (*Courtesy of the Virginia Historical Society*)

Dolly Madison, 1817, portrait by James Wood. (*Courtesy of the Virginia Historical Society*)

Dolly Madison, 1804, portrait
by Gilbert Stuart. (*Courtesy of
the Pennsylvania Academy of
Fine Arts, Philadelphia, Harrison
Earl Fund*)

Dolly Madison, 1825, plaster
life mask by J. H. I. Browere.
(*Courtesy of the New York
State Historical Association,
Cooperstown*)

Anna Payne Cutts, copy
by Charles B. King from a
portrait by Gilbert Stuart.
(*Courtesy of the Virginia
Historical Society*)

Elizabeth Patterson Bonaparte, *ca.* 1804, copy of a portrait by Gilbert
Stuart, made by Georges D'Almaine, 1856. (*Courtesy of the Maryland Historical Society, Baltimore*)

George Mason, portrait by
Louis M. D. Guillaume. (*Courtesy of the Virginia Historical
Society*)

James Monroe, portrait by an
unknown artist, probably taken
in the 1780s. (*Courtesy of the
James Monroe Museum and Memorial Library, Fredericksburg,
Virginia*)

Edmund Randolph, copy by
Flavius J. Fisher of lost original
by an unknown artist. (*Courtesy
of the Virginia State Library and
Archives*)

Chevalier de La Luzerne, portrait by Charles Willson Peale. (*Courtesy of Independence National Historical Park*)

James Duane, 1806, portrait by John Trumbull. (*Collection of the City of New York, City Hall, Governor's Room*)

William Pinkney, portrait attributed to Bouche, *ca.* 1795. (*Courtesy of the Hammond-Harwood House Association, Annapolis, Maryland*)

James Wilson, portrait by Philip Wharton. (*Courtesy of Independence National Historical Park*)

Albert Gallatin, American Bank Note Company engraving, from portrait by Gilbert Stuart. (*Courtesy of The New-York Historical Society, New York City*)

Henry Clay, portrait by Charles B. King. (*Courtesy of the Corcoran Gallery of Art*)

John Randolph of Roanoke, silhouette from life by William Henry Brown. (*From Brown's* Portrait Gallery of Distinguished American Citizens, *1845*)

A North-West Prospect of Nassau-Hall, with a Front View of the President's House, in New Jersey.

Nassau Hall, College of New Jersey at Princeton, 1764. (*Courtesy of the Princeton University Library*)

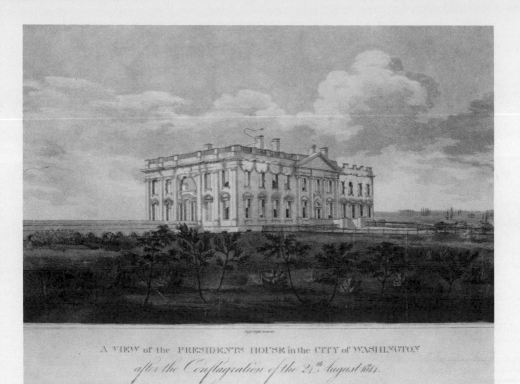

A VIEW of the PRESIDENTS HOUSE in the CITY of WASHINGTON
after the Conflagration of the 24th August 1814.

The President's House in ruins, 1814, engraving by William Strickland.
(*Courtesy of the Library of Congress*)

Flyglarna af Capitolen i Washington år 1819.

The Capitol, Washington, D.C., after its destruction by British soldiers,
August 1814. (*Courtesy of the Library of Congress*)

Philadelphia, from *The Columbian Magazine*, January 1790.
(*Courtesy of The New-York Historical Society, New York City*)

Account of some Public Buildings in the City of Philadelphia. 25

FOR THE COLUMBIAN MAGAZINE.

EXPLANATION *of the* PLATE, *exhibiting a
View of several* PUBLIC BUILDINGS *in the
City of* PHILADELPHIA.

THE plate represents a south-west
view of a group of the following
public buildings in the city of Philadelphia, situated in the vicinity of each other.

No. 1. The back part of the Protestant Episcopal Academy ; a large, handsome brick building, fronting on Chesnut-
street, between Sixth and Seventh-streets
from the Delaware—Not entirely finished.

No. 2. The County Court-house ; a large,
new building, finished in a neat and elegant style. It is situate on the northwest angle of the State-house square (the
corner of Chesnut and Delaware-Sixth-
streets, with the front on Chesnut-street.
The view here given, exhibits the west-
side, on Sixth-street, and the back part,
extending into the State-house square.

No. 3. The State-house, towards the square.
This spacious and venerable structure, which
was erected in the year 1735, is situate on
the south-side of Chesnut-street, midway
between Delaware-Fifth and Sixth-streets.
Though plain, it has an air of magnifi-
cence. It was furnished with a lofty steeple,
which was taken down a few years since.
A north-west view of this building, as it
appeared in the year 1778, is given in the
Columbian Magazine for July 1787, accompanied with a description.

It is intended to erect a City Courthouse, on the north-east angle of the State
house square ; of the same dimensions and
appearance (*externally*, at least), as the
County Court-house, on the other end of
the State-house. The accomplishment of
this design will render the whole *front* of
the square, noble and uniform. And,
should the State-house itself be put in
thorough repair ;—the doors be somewhat
ornamented,— the wings be rebuilt in a better style,—and the steeple restored ;—the
appearance of this front would, then, be
really magnificent.

No. 4. The Hall of the American
Philosophical Society. This is a large,
neat and commodious brick building ; situate on the East-side of the State-house
square, in Fifth-street, between Chesnut
and Walnut-Streets. It has a garden-
front towards the square, being that which
is represented in the annexed view.

An account of the institution, to which
this building belongs, is contained in our
last month's Magazine and in the Supplement.

COL. MAG. VOL. IV. No. 1.

No. 5. A front view of the Hall of the
Library Company of Philadelphia. This
is an elegant and stately edifice, of brick ;
and was begun in the course of last summer.
It is situate in Fifth-street, nearly opposite the Hall of the American Philosophical Society. Over the front-door of
the Library-Hall is a niche, in which it
is designed to place a marble statue of the
celebrated Dr. Franklin, the principal
promoter of this valuable institution : and
a gentleman of this city has, it is said,
offered to have it executed by an eminent
artist, at his own expense.

No. 6. The Carpenter's Hall. This is
a roomy brick building ; fronting a small
avenue or court, leading to it, from the
south side of Chesnut-street, between
Third and Fourth-streets. The City Library, before mentioned, is kept here
at present, and some of the apartments
are occupied for public stores and offices.
—This edifice, though more humble in
its architecture, and less conspicuous in
its situation, than some of the others, is,
nevertheless, rendered famous, by being
the place in which that august body,—the
first general Congress of America, assembled, and held their councils.

The State-house square, already mentioned, is bounded on the north by Chesnut-street, on the south by Walnut-street,
on the east by Fifth-street, and on the
west by Sixth-street. It is inclosed, on
three sides, by a brick wall ; the State-
house, County Court-house, &c. con-
stituting its boundary towards Chesnut-
street. This area has, of late, been judi-
ciously improved, under the direction of
Samuel Vaughan, Esq. It consists of a
beautiful lawn, interspersed with little knobs
or tufts of flowering shrubs, and clumps of
trees, well disposed. Through the middle of the gardens, runs a spacious gravel-
walk, lined with double rows of thriving
elms, and communicating with serpen-
tine walks which encompass the whole area.
These surrounding walks are not uniform-
ly on a level with the lawn ; the margin
of which, being in some parts a little
higher, forms a bank, which, in fine
weather, affords pleasant seats. When
the trees attain to a larger size, it will be
proper to place a few benches under them,
in different situations, for the accommodation of persons frequenting the walks.

These gardens will soon, if properly attended to, be in a condition to admit of
our citizens indulging themselves, agreeably, in the salutary exercise of walking.

D

Madison addressing the Virginia Convention of 1829–30. He is surrounded by ninety of his colleagues including Monroe, John Marshall, and John Randolph of Roanoke. Watercolor by George Catlin. (*Courtesy of the Virginia Historical Society*)

Montpelier today, as restored by the National Trust for Historic Preservation. (*Courtesy of the National Trust for Historic Preservation, Montpelier*)

years. In any case, William Madison seems never to have been consistently successful in his various starts and enterprises, nor could he, apparently, replace the steady, congenial Ambrose in family councils.

The two oldest Madison girls, Nelly (1760–1802) and Sarah (1764–1843), also began raising families during this period. In 1783, Nelly married Isaac Hite (1758–1836), of a prominent German pioneer family of the Great Valley, and settled with him near Winchester, Virginia. Nelly seems always to have been close to her eldest brother, inheriting pieces of furniture he made and the miniature painted at the time of the ill-fated Kitty Floyd romance. Isaac Hite became a close friend and supporter of James Madison, and even after his wife's death at age forty-two, his home provided a welcome stopping place in northern Virginia. The frail Nelly bore but two children who lived to maturity. Sarah Madison married Thomas Macon in 1790 and settled with him on a plantation, Somerset, just across Blue Run from Montpelier on the road to Charlottesville, where for nearly fifty years they were Madison's neighbors. They seem to have been good, substantial people, occupied with farming, local social activities, and naturally, a large family. Between 1791 and 1808, Sarah Madison Macon gave birth to at least nine children, seven of whom reached maturity.

The four children born to Madison's mother between 1766 and 1771 died in childhood; her last child, a daughter, Frances Taylor (1774–1823), was ten years younger than Sarah. Fanny, as she was called, was therefore, very much the baby of the family, and to her eldest brother, twenty-three years her senior, more like a daughter than a sister. She was a playful child when her increasingly famous brother spent months at a time at Montpelier from 1784 to 1786, and during the seventeen-nineties, when he was again often home, she was a maturing young lady, interested in music, something of a belle, and doubtless very much aware that her brother's stature in the nation opened for her prospects far wider than those customary for girls raised on Piedmont plantations. In 1800, she nevertheless married a local doctor, Robert H. Rose, and soon she, too, was raising a large family. She had at least ten children, of whom at least six reached maturity. By the seventeen-nineties, then, James Madison was surrounded by the huge families of his brothers and sisters: they had altogether some fifty children, of whom over thirty survived to adulthood. Though James Madison was himself childless, wherever he turned among his relatives, fertility abounded. To him, as to another early American theorist of the "population explosion," Benjamin Franklin, "the increase of mankind so remarkable in the new world" was an omnipresent fact in his own immediate family.

The progenitors of this numerous brood, James Sr. and Nelly Conway Madison, observed their fiftieth wedding anniversary in 1799, in feeble health, but full of amazement at the transformations they had seen in their lifetime. The half-cleared frontier farm James Madison, Sr., had helped his mother manage in the seventeen-forties had become the largest plantation in the county, now worked by more than one hundred slaves, nearly all of whom had been born at Montpelier. The Indian raids so near and so terrifying in 1755 had become tales of a bygone era as Virginians pushed into Kentucky and even across the Mississippi. The allegiance to George III, and the old trade dependence on Clay and Midgely of Liverpool and other English merchant houses, had given way to diversified commerce through Richmond, Fredericksburg, Baltimore, and Philadelphia. As the old couple more and more turned affairs over to their sons and sons-in-law, traveled to the spas to ease the aches and pains of advancing age, and enjoyed their grandchildren (at least a dozen arrived during the seventeen-nineties), they were pleased to have their renowned eldest son fully committed to the management of the family plantation.[1]

We do not know exactly how James Madison came into possession and effective management of the Montpelier plantation. Since he was the eldest son, despite his absorption in public life, Virginia tradition strongly favored his assumption of that privilege and responsibility. In the seventeen-eighties, his letters to his father and to his brother Ambrose show clearly that they were in charge at Montpelier. Cousin Francis Taylor's diary likewise pictures James Madison as a politician and scholar who until the mid-seventeen-nineties really only visited in Orange County. He rode about the plantation during visits home, encouraged scientific farming methods, purchased supplies in Philadelphia, and sometimes oversaw the marketing of Montpelier produce, but otherwise he left things to his father and brother. As late as 1787, he held virtually no property in his own name, a fact which has led some students to rank him among the least substantial members of the Federal Convention. Forrest McDonald, for example, using Orange County land, personal property, and tax records, places Madison's wealth in 1787 at "560 ill-kept acres . . . valued at $725, six adult slaves and three slave children, and five horses. . . . Madison owned no personalty, held no paying job, and owned no public securities." In fact, the 560 acres were a gift from the father, part of a long-term plan for gradual transfer of the Montpelier estate to his eldest son. By 1790 Madison had title to and special responsibility for a section of lowland near the Rapidan River and an upper section extending over the Southwest Mountains. Except as evidence that Madison was more and more committed to Montpelier, these legal transfers indicated very little about his total wealth.[2]

The overall growth and prosperity of the family holdings is a better measure of Madison's economic standing. The Madisons owned and farmed perhaps ten thousand acres of land in Orange County, of which five thousand acres formed the core of the Montpelier estate, running compactly from the top of the Southwest Mountains to the Rapidan. This made them the largest landholders in the county. Though too-intensive cultivation, especially of tobacco, had somewhat depleted the fertile land, a sharp decline in tobacco prices most seriously threatened the prosperity of Montpelier. During 1787, while Madison attended the Federal Convention, the price dropped 20 per cent. Less than a year later it had fallen nearly another 50 per cent. This price collapse, common throughout Virginia, squeezed planters, made cash scarce, heightened the concern of Virginians over the evils of debt, and increased their reluctance to make full payment on old debts owed British merchants without compensation for their own losses in slaves and other property during the revolution. Sharing Jefferson's opinion that the culture of tobacco was "productive of infinite wretchedness," because it yielded no food, required excessive labor, and rapidly impoverished the soil, Madison was glad, though, in one sense, to see reasons to limit its cultivation.[3]

Luckily, events in Europe soon opened up a profitable, and to philosopher-farmers, a morally welcome alternative. Madison wrote his father from New York in early 1790 that the "run" on the American grain market from Europe was increasing. Jefferson noticed the high price of wheat in Virginia when he returned from France. "If the alarm [of revolution and war] be not artificial in France, England, etc., which cannot altogether be the case," Madison concluded, "it is probable that the price will be high for several years." This prediction proved accurate enough, so until after the Napoleonic Wars, Madison, Jefferson, Washington, and other Virginia enthusiasts for scientific agriculture had a favorable market for testing their cherished theories of grain culture, crop rotation, the use of clover on fallow fields, and the abandonment of the exhausting tobacco economy. Wheat raised in abundance on the broad fields, carted in great barrels or floated in barges to Fredericksburg or Richmond, and there loaded on ships to feed the war-torn nations of Europe, gave the Madisons a cash crop to replace tobacco. By 1792, Madison wrote happily that wheat "has effectually supplanted tobacco in the conversation and anxieties of our cropmongers, and is rapidly doing so in their fields." A French traveler visiting the Virginia Piedmont in 1796 reported that "the culture of tobacco [is] now almost entirely relinquished in this part of Virginia." Madison's instructions to his overseers and letters to his father during the seventeen-nineties show increasing attention to testing new seeds, interplanting grain and fruit trees, contour plowing, and building dams, mills, and tools. He gradually developed a crop rotation, similar to Jefferson's, that called for a seven-year cycle—five of wheat, corn, peas or potatoes, vetches, wheat, and then two years in clover. The Virginians hoped to double the productivity of their exhausted fields and thus make farming the profitable, aesthetically satisfying, and morally edifying occupation republican social philosophy required it to be.[4]

Madison corresponded frequently while in public life about farm matters in Orange. He and his father exchanged "weather diaries" to continue an experiment of ten years' standing to understand temperature variations caused by differences in altitude, latitude, and distance from the sea. He sent "a few grains of *upland* rice, brought from Timor by Captain Bligh," all that the intrepid master of the *Bounty* had "saved out of a fine collection" during his forty days at sea in a lifeboat. Setting politics aside, or perhaps making a shrewd bid for support, Madison asked his father to send Jeremiah Wadsworth, an arch-Federalist and avid speculator, "a Barrel or half Barrel of the best Peach brandy," for which Orange County seems to have been renowned. The older the better, he instructed, "provided the quality be excellent," and its cask was to be "of wood that will give it no ill taste." On departing for Philadelphia one fall, he instructed his overseer to supervise the building of a loom, two good wheelbarrows, three wagons, and three carts. He was further to plow "all around each parcel [of land], instead of the common way," up and down, which encouraged soil erosion. Finally, he was "to take particular care of the horses and stock, [and] to avoid riding the horses without the approbation of my father." And of course, like all farmers, Madison wrote often of the price of crops.[5]

Evident, too, in Madison's farm papers is his continuing humaneness toward his slaves, as well as his deepening dependence on them. He told his overseer to "treat the Negroes with all the humanity and kindness consistent with their necessary subordination and work," and to be sure they had milk cows and meal for their sustenance. One slave, the same Sawney who had accompanied Madison on his first trip to Princeton in 1769, and would serve his mother until her death in 1829, was by the seventeen-nineties a trusted overseer of one section of the plantation. Madison wrote him (some Montpelier slaves, at least, were taught to read) to set out apple trees, plant corn, and replace tobacco fields at the top of the Southwest Mountains with fields of Irish potatoes. Each year, Sawney marketed farm produce in Fredericksburg and bought supplies for the coming year. Another Montpelier Negro, the slave Billey whom Madison had brought to Philadelphia in 1780 and then left to be freed because he took the words of the Declaration of Independence seriously, had by 1793 become "Mr. William Gardner," a merchant's agent who handled much Madison business in Philadelphia. Two years later Madison wrote regretfully to his father to "let old Anthony and Betty know that their son Billey was no more." He had gone to sea and been swept overboard on a voyage to New Orleans. Anthony was probably the same household servant whom Madison had bled and cared for when he served as family doctor in 1777. A notice in a Richmond newspaper in 1786, about another Anthony, perhaps Billey's brother, indicates, though, that freedom had its lure despite good treatment at Montpelier: "Run away

. . . a Mulatto Slave, named Anthony, about 17 years old, low, but well made, had very light hair and grey eyes; . . . he has been used to house business, and as a waiting servant. Ten Dollars Reward will be given, if he be secured so that I get him again. . . . N. B. It is probable he has secured a pass, or a Certificate of his Freedom; and has changed his name and clothes. James Madison [Sr.]." Though by the seventeen-nineties Madison had been forced to abandon his hope to be free of the slave system, and even had to take part in maintaining it, he still did what he could to lessen its harshness and degradation.[6]

Although the Madisons increasingly centered their activities in Orange County, they continued to speculate in frontier lands. In the summer of 1793, James and Ambrose Madison purchased seven thousand acres of land in Kentucky to supplement earlier family purchases made there in cooperation with George Mason (see Chapter VIII). Relatives Hancock Lee and Hubbard Taylor were to oversee their survey, development, and resale. Ambrose's death in October 1793, fluctuations in the value of Kentucky lands, and the discovery of an error in the survey and deed of the original Madison purchase, however, threatened the whole adventure. Kentucky land sharks, abetted by Madison's erstwhile friend George Nicholas, and by a future brother-in-law of John Marshall, took deliberate advantage in the error to file technically more proper claims to most of the Madison lands. Though District Judge Harry Innes (a friend of Madison's since their student days together at the Donald Robertson school) threw out the obviously collusive claim, when the case finally reached the Supreme Court in 1804, Chief Justice Marshall, with no hint of embarrassment at the conflict of interest, reversed the decision by rigid application of an old English precedent that one man may protect himself from loss by taking advantage of another's error. Madison was thus deprived of his richest Kentucky lands; the relatively small claims remaining were scarcely more than a nuisance to him. In 1829, after his agents had suffered, from a rapacious tenant, "more abuse than I ever heard poured forth from a female tongue," Madison finally sold all his holdings for less than $3,000. Bad luck, and one suspects, distaste and ineptitude for speculation, kept Madison from reaping the profits of the widespread "get rich quick" pattern of his day.[7]

Madison's decision in 1794 to sell his Mohawk valley lands (see Chapter VIII) to furnish capital for a gristmill at Montpelier is further evidence that a prosperous, attractive farm in Orange County had become Madison's first priority. The mill was so "particularly favorable to the interest of my brothers as well as myself," the Congressman wrote his father, that he was willing to sell the Mohawk lands even though keeping them a few years longer would almost surely double or triple their value. He sold the nine-hundred-acre tract for $5,250 in 1796. At about the same time, he advised his father to dispose of his few public securities, then selling comfortably above par. Besides the mill, scientific farming experiments, and the routine demands of growing families, the Madisons needed cash for extensive remodeling and enlargement of the Montpelier mansion. Orders of windowpanes for French doors, fancy hardware, and fine flooring and payments to skilled workmen for plastering and building fireplaces suggest that at this time the house changed from being merely comfortable to being elegant. Nails were ordered in large quantities from Jefferson's home factory at Monticello, and the two planters discussed Palladian designs for porticoes: Jefferson added the front section to Monticello between 1796 and 1801, and Madison built or rebuilt the four-columned front of Montpelier at the same time. Madison asked Jefferson to inquire "whether there be known in Philadelphia any composition for encrusting Brick that will effectually stand the weather: and particularly what is thought of common plaister thickly painted with white lead overspread with sand. I wish to give some such dressing to the columns of my Portico, and to lessen as much as possible the risk of the experiment." Apparently nothing judged "effectual" by the prudent Madison was soon discovered, because an 1804 visitor describing the mansion reported that "Mr. Madison himself superintended the Building which he had executed by the Hands of common workmen to whom he prescribed the Proportions to be observed. It is of brick which requires and is intended to be plastered. . . . [It] was executed by [Madison] without the assistance of an Architect and of very ordinary Materials; but he had cases made for the Shape of the Pillars, of wood, and filled them up with the Mortar and bricks according to measure." Though the building of a Virginia plantation home was a never-ending process, Madison clearly used the prosperity of the seventeen-nineties, the availability of Jefferson's advice and assistance, and his own respite from public labors to build at Montpelier a farm and home of usefulness, taste, and dignity. Not coincidentally, he had at the same time, at long last, married.[8]

In May 1794 a twenty-six-year-old Quaker widow, Dolley Payne Todd, wrote excitedly to her best friend: "Thou must come to me. Aaron Burr says that the great little Madison has asked to be brought to see me this evening." The attractive young woman who thus found opening to her the world of a Virginia planter and famous politician was herself a Virginian of no mean background and heritage. Though born in North Carolina, where her farmer father had moved for a few years, her roots were in Virginia, and she remembered only her childhood in Hanover County, twenty miles north of Richmond. One great-grandfather was Isaac Winston, an early Quaker settler in Virginia and the grandfather of Patrick Henry. Her maternal grandfather was William Coles, an immigrant from Wexford County, Ireland, who had, some years before his marriage to Lucy Winston, become a Quaker. Their daughter, Mary, Dolley Madison's mother, in 1761 married John Payne, of respectable but undistinguished yeoman stock. Soon after their marriage John Payne converted to his wife's Quaker faith, and he was thereafter strongly influenced by its conscientious convictions. He made the brief move to North Carolina to try the experiment of living in an isolated Quaker farming community. Back in Virginia with his growing family (his eldest daughter, Dolley, born in 1768, had two elder and two younger brothers born before the Declaration of Independence), he lived for a time at Scotchtown, a plantation once owned by his wife's cousin Patrick Henry. Though the farm prospered, John Payne abhorred the slave system upon which it was based. He joined fellow Quakers in urging that Virginia seize the "favorable juncture" of its 1776 declaration of rights to abolish slavery, and like most of his Quaker brethren, he refused to serve in the revolutionary army. When, in 1782, the manumission of slaves became legal in Virginia, John and Mary Payne gave freedom to the many Negroes who worked their farm. Dolley, at age fourteen, doubtless understood the great economic sacrifice her parents had made for the sake of their faith.[9]

Deprived of a living in Virginia, and perhaps reprobated by his neighbors, John Payne took his family, in 1783, to Philadelphia, where his children could "be educated in their religion." They were welcomed by the Quaker community, but John Payne, skilled only in farm management, found it impossible to earn a living as a starchmaker. He went bankrupt in 1789, and rejected by his Quaker meeting for failing to pay his debts, he died two years later, broken and dispirited. Dolley, however, found life in America's largest city as exciting as could be for a girl brought up in strict Quaker fashion. She enjoyed Quaker outings, and blooming into womanhood, soon had the young men competing for her attention. She sympathized with girl friends who "eloped to effect a union with the choice of their hearts"—that is, to marry non-Quakers—but she herself, shortly after her father's bankruptcy, married a young Quaker lawyer, John Todd, who, one of Dolley's friends wrote, "had been so solicitious to gain her favor many years." The match so pleased leading Quakers that eighty of them came to the Pine Street Meeting House on January 7, 1790, to solemnize the union and sign the marriage certificate. John and Dolley Todd moved into a fine house at the corner of Fourth and Walnut streets (now restored and open to visitors as the Dilworth-Todd-Moylan House); the conscientious lawyer gained many clients; and by the summer of 1793, there were two children.[10]

The terrible yellow fever epidemic of 1793, which had nearly driven the federal government from Philadelphia, destroyed the young family. Dolley, her year-and-one-half-old son and newborn baby, and her widowed mother and her three youngest children, Anna (fourteen), John (eleven), and Mary (eight), took refuge in the suburbs, while

John Todd stayed in the stricken city, caring for his parents, ministering
to the sick, and drawing dozens of wills. Dolley wrote on October 4, of
the "dread prospect, . . . a reveared Father [in-law] in the Jaws of
Death, and a Loved Husband in perpetual danger." The warm weather
continued into October, mosquitoes droned, and Todd's mother and
father succumbed to the plague. John Todd himself pressed his luck too
far: after two months among the sick and dying, he took the fever, and
died in his wife's arms the same day her infant son died. Mary Payne
wrote that "My Poor Dear Dolley, . . . the same day [consigns] her
Dear husband and her little babe to the silent grave." Finally, though,
frost silenced the deadly carriers. Dolley, desperately ill herself, friend-
less, and with only $19 to her name, struggled to survive. She and her
mother slowly nursed the remnants of the sick and devastated family
back to health.[11]

In the late fall, Mrs. Payne, with John and Mary, went to live in
Virginia with her daughter Lucy, who earlier that year had married
George Steptoe Washington. Dolley returned to the vacant house on
Fourth Street with her little son, John Payne Todd, and her fourteen-
year-old sister, Anna, who was from this time on, Dolley's ward and
closest companion. Through the bequests of her husband and his father,
Dolley was not long in great need. To a suggestion that her late husband's library be sold to pay debts, she replied, "Books from which he
wished his child improved, shall remain sacred, and I would feel the
pinching hand of Poverty before I disposed of them." Left though, for the
first time in her life, without family to guide her, she needed help from
friends to manage finances and raise her son and sister. She turned first to
a respectable Quaker attorney and friend of her late husband's, William
Wilkins. He advised conscientiously, but soon fell under the spell of her
charms, and in the way of a gallant, called her by a private name, Julia.
In the picture, too, was Aaron Burr, an ambitious, charming Senator
from New York who had lived at Mrs. Payne's boardinghouse while
Dolley was married to John Todd. Dolley turned to him for legal aid
and advice in educating her son and her sister. Though Burr's wife was
fatally ill in New York, and died five days after Dolley made him the
sole guardian of her son in case of her death, there seems to have been
no romantic connection between him and Dolley. In a day when widows,
especially young, attractive ones, did not remain single very long, however, Dolley was a center of attention. Her close friend Eliza Collins,
soon to be the bride of Virginia's Congressman Richard Bland Lee, later
recalled that "gentlemen would station themselves where they could see
her pass." Eliza remonstrated: "Really Dolley, thou must hide thy face,
there are so many staring at thee." Clearly, the widow Todd (in comfortable circumstances, vivacious, handsome, bright eyed, full bosomed,
and well educated) was one of *the* eligible women of Philadelphia in the
spring of 1794.[12]

Congressman James Madison, forty-three years old, was highly eligible but, so some of his friends feared, perhaps a confirmed bachelor. Very little is known of his relationships with women between the Kitty Floyd fiasco (see Chapter VI), and May 1794, when he asked Aaron Burr to take him to see Dolley Todd. No hints or even rumors connect him in any way with Virginia belles during those eleven years. He obviously had been impressed by Madame de Bréhan, the companion and mistress of French Minister Moustier, during long sojourns in New York in 1788 and 1789 (see Chapter XII), and he was reported to have been "fascinated by the celebrated Mrs. Colden," the widow of a British army officer and renowned for her "masculine understanding and activity, as well as for feminine graces and accomplishments." Madison's only surviving comment about Mrs. Colden is his remark, in recommending her son to Jefferson, that she was "an amicable lady . . . within the circle of my acquaintance" in New York. Though these glimpses show that Madison had overcome his social awkwardness, and that he could even be somewhat intriguing to cultivated ladies, it is nonetheless likely that during the years of fullest commitment to public affairs (1786–1792) he was little distracted by romance. As politics became less engrossing, however, and when, especially after the death of his brother Ambrose in October 1793, he undertook more responsibilities at Montpelier, the attractions of marriage heightened. Furthermore, Mrs. Mary House, keeper of the boardinghouse that had been Madison's home in Philadelphia since 1780, died ("went out like a candle," Jefferson reported) in June 1793. Her establishment soon closed, so Madison spent an unsettled, perhaps lonely winter in Philadelphia during the 1793–4 session, the first, also, since Jefferson's retirement from the cabinet. Madison had probably known Dolley Payne Todd at least since visiting Philadelphia with her uncle, Congressman Isaac Coles, in 1789, and probably long before that he knew of the Virginia family that for the sake of conscience had manumitted its slaves and moved to Philadelphia. Madison said late in life he "was indebted for his matrimonial success to the friendly aid" of Coles. Aaron Burr and others doubtless spoke of Dolley in Madison's presence, and he had very likely met her occasionally at the innumerable tea visits Philadelphians exchanged during the late afternoon and early evening. (Likely, too, Dolley by look or word had encouraged the earnest Virginian.) Madison's request to Burr for a formal introduction to the beautiful widow, then, was a declaration of serious intent.[13]

Though the romantic meeting at Dolley's house has often been pictured and written of, nothing in fact is known of it except that things proceeded amicably if not decisively. Dolley is said to have worn a mulberry-colored satin dress, a silk kerchief at her neck, and a tiny cap, while Madison doubtless had with him his new "Round Beaver" hat (size 7¼), purchased on April 3 from Quaker merchant Isaac Parrish. According to family tradition, Martha Washington soon asked her distant kinswoman Dolley if it was true that she and the Congressman her husband so much admired were engaged. Dolley stammered, no, she thought not, and might have added, "Yet. . . ." In any case, the First Lady approved the match. By mid-June, when Congress adjourned and Madison left for Virginia, he had said nothing of his romantic plans to Jefferson or Monroe, but almost conclusive arrangements were under way: Dolley had left to visit her Winston relatives in Hanover County, Virginia, to consider the prospect before her and, obviously, to be near her husband-to-be in case she should decide on marriage. Catherine Coles, the young wife of Dolley's uncle, Congressman Isaac Coles, wrote her of a disappointed suitor, one Mr. Grove, being "in the Pouts" about her, and that "Poor Colonel Burr had lost his wife [and] gone to New York." Otherwise, all the teasing news was of the leading aspirant for Dolley's affections: "Now for Madison. He told me I might say what I pleased to you about him. To begin, he thinks so much of you in the day that he has lost his Tongue; at Night he Dreames of you and starts in his sleep a Calling on you to relieve his Flame for he Burns to such an excess that he will be shortly consumed and he hopes that your Heart will be calous to every other swain but himself. He has consented to everything that I have wrote about him with sparkling Eyes. Monroe goes to France as Minister Plenipotentiary. Madison has taken his House. Do you like it"? Though Catherine obviously had connived with Madison to amuse his beloved, it is equally apparent that she expected her "Cosen" would soon be married and living with her new husband in the recently vacated Monroe house.[14]

In Virginia, Madison attended to sick visitors and to a sick mother at Montpelier, and Dolley became seriously ill in Hanover. By early August, however, she was well enough to travel, and wrote letters making final and public her decision to marry James Madison. Her agent and disappointed suitor, the Philadelphia lawyer Wilkins, replied manfully:

> Mr. Madison is a man whom I admire. I know his attachment to you and did not therefore content myself with taking his character from the Breath of popular applause—but consulted those who knew him intimately in private life. His private Character therefore I have every reason to believe is good and amiable. He unites to the great talents which have secured his public approbation those engaging qualities that contribute so highly to domestic felicity. To such a man I do most freely consent that my beloved sister be united and happy. . . . That I have not been insensible to your Charms ought not I think be regarded as a fault—few persons in similar Situations would not have felt their irresistible influence: but none I would venture to say could have mingled in their emotions more true Respect and more Fraternal Affection than I have.

Wilkins urged a generous property settlement for Dolley's son, possible, he said, because Madison was "a man of genteel though not of large property." This would protect her from "Enemies [that] have already opened their mouths to censure and condemn you"—a reference to the strict Quakers in the Pine Street meeting who on December 12, 1794, would disown Dolley for marrying a non-Quaker "before a hireling priest." In thus discarding the pious ways of John and Mary Payne, Dolley imitated her elder brothers and sister Lucy, and thus virtually wiped the family name from Quaker rolls. Dolley Payne Todd underwent a sharp change when she committed herself to a Virginia planter and to his way of life.[15]

At Lucy Washington's home, Harewood, in northern Virginia, Dolley received Madison's ardent reply to her letter saying yes to his proposal: "I received some days ago your precious favor. . . . I cannot express, but hope you will conceive the joy it gave me. The delay in hearing of your leaving Hanover, which I regarded as the only satisfactory proof of your recovery, had filled me with extreme . . . inquietude, and the confirmation of that welcome event was endeared to me by the style in which it was conveyed. I hope you will never have another deliberation on that subject. If the sentiments of my heart can guarantee those of yours, they assure me there can never be a cause for it." While waiting to see if his ailing mother would recover sufficiently for him to join Dolley, Madison made a hasty trip to Monticello, where, though delighted his friend was to seek the "joys perpetual" of marriage, Jefferson was alarmed at the apparently contingent desire to retire from Congress. About the first of September, probably with his youngest sister Fanny, now twenty, Madison departed for Harewood, near what is now Charles Town, West Virginia, and the famous Berkeley Springs, to which Madison had been going for more than twenty years. They stopped to see their old aunt Frances Madison Hite, near Winchester, but hastened on to the wedding site.[16]

Harewood was the home of nineteen-year-old George Steptoe Washington, nephew and ward of President Washington, who, at his uncle's expense, had attended the University of Pennsylvania while Madison served in Congress. After his marriage in August 1793 to Dolley's sister Lucy, then a budding fifteen-year-old beauty, the young couple moved to the fine Harewood estate George Steptoe inherited from his father. Dolley's mother and her two youngest children, John and Mary, soon came to live with them, as, apparently, did George Steptoe's sister, Harriot. This was the family that welcomed the prospective bridegroom on a warm, bright late summer day. Eager now for marriage, Madison "urged many conveniences in hastening the event which I had solicited," and on September 15, 1794, his cousin Lucy Taylor's husband, the Reverend Alexander Balmain of Winchester, pronounced the solemn words that began forty-two years of devotion in marriage for James Madison and Dolley Payne Todd. Only the immediate families attended the ceremony in the large Palladian Harewood drawing room, which was

fully paneled from floor to ceiling, with each window and door opening
framed with Doric pilasters, and with a richly carved green marble man-
tlepiece at one end. There was abundant gaiety, of course, and the
vivacious Payne sisters, Dolley, Lucy, and Anna, plus Fanny Madison
and Harriot Washington, placed the bridegroom in the midst of a lively
feminine circle. He expressed his gratitude to his cleric-kinsman by giving him a fee of £5 4s. 10d., the largest save one recorded by Balmain
for that year.[17]

Throughout the day, the bride could not forget that in marrying the
famous Congressman and Virginia planter, she was stepping into a world
far different from that of her father, the pious starchmaker, and of her
deceased husband, the earnest Quaker lawyer. Before the ceremony she
wrote seriously to her friend Eliza Collins Lee, who had been censured
by the Quakers for her recent marriage to a Virginia Congressman: "I
have stolen from the family to commune with you—to tell you in short
that in the course of this day I give my hand to the man who of all
others I most admire—you will not be at a loss to know who this is as I
have been long ago gratified in having your approval. In this union I
have every thing that is soothing and grateful in prospect—and my little
Payne will have a generous and tender protector. . . . How shall I express
the anxiety I feel to see you? . . . Tell your dear Lee that he must not
supplant DPT in your affections but suffer her whilst she deserves it to
share with him your ever valuable esteem. adieu! adieu! . . . Dolley Payne
Todd." After the ceremony, before going to her husband, the bride
scribbled a hasty postscript: "Evening—Dolley Madison! alass! alass!"[18]

Four days after the wedding, James and Dolley, accompanied by Anna
Payne and Harriot Washington, stopped overnight in Winchester with
the Balmains. They were on their way to Belle Grove, a few miles
farther up the valley, the farm home of Madison's sister Nelly, her
husband, Isaac Hite, and their two children, five-year-old Nelly and
one-year-old James Madison. The "great pleasure" of the visit with the
congenial relatives was marred, however, by a return of the fever and
chills that had afflicted Dolley earlier in the summer, at Hanover. The
attack, apparently malaria, was so severe that Madison called a physician
from Winchester, who "by a decisive administration of the Bark soon
expelled the complaint." After nearly two weeks at Belle Grove, a handsome limestone house with four large porticoes overlooking mountain
valley vistas, Dolley was able to travel, and the newlyweds returned to
Harewood, where ten days of further rest and visiting left them with no
time to go to Montpelier before heading north for Philadelphia. Madison
apologized to his father: "Your daughter-in-law begs you and my
mother to accept her best and most respectful affections, which she
means to express herself by an early opportunity. She wishes Fanny also
to be sensible of the pleasure with which a correspondence with her

would be carried on. . . . I must ask the favor of my mother to make me a memorandum of the clothing to be obtained at Mr. Dunbar's for the Negroes, and of yourself to have it transmitted along with a list of other articles such as salt, iron, etc., which may be wanted for winter's use. . . . With my sincere prayers that perfect health and every other good may attend you both, I remain, Your affectionate son, J. Madison, Jr." Though Madison left in mid-October for the meeting of Congress, his thoughts were of his family and the farm in Orange, and of course, of Dolley, her sister, and son, who rode beside him through the brilliant fall colors, over roads so rough that his new carriage was "a perfect wreck" when he reached the waiting house in the capital city still more "home" to the new family than any other place.[19]

The Madisons spent three winter seasons in Philadelphia, living first in the vacated Monroe house, then in a large, fashionable dwelling on Spruce Street, and finally, during a season when Fanny Madison joined the family, in a house further crowded by the arrival of a water-soaked shipment of furniture Monroe had sent from Paris and which was intended ultimately to give Montpelier touches of the French taste so much the vogue during the seventeen-nineties. Spruce Street in front of the Madison's house was paved with cobblestones, had brick sidewalks, gutters for drainage, elm trees, and posts every ten feet or so for hitching horses and keeping wagons off the sidewalks. Though this seemed very elegant to Virginians and other "provincials" coming to the flourishing Quaker city, a Frenchman who moved to Philadelphia in 1794, Moreau de St. Méry, found much to complain about: the poor water, the mosquitoes sheltered by the trees, and the "lunacy" of scrubbing sidewalks and front steps every Wednesday and Saturday, "even in winter [which] exposed the passers-by to the danger of breaking their necks." Moreau thought the houses ill-designed, gloomy, excessively hot in the summer, furnished without taste, and usually dirty and in disrepair. Furthermore, "each house has a toilet, a small room set apart from the house, but it is far away. One often gets wet going to it."
Dining habits seemed to Moreau equally barbaric:

They breakfast at nine o'clock on ham or salt fish, herring, . . . coffee or tea, and slices of toasted or untoasted bread spread with butter. At about two o'clock they dine without soup. Their dinner consists of broth, with a main dish of an English roast surrounded by potatoes. Following that are boiled green peas, . . . then baked or fried eggs, boiled or fried fish, salad [of] thinly sliced cabbage, . . . pastries, sweets to which they are excessively partial and which are insufficiently cooked. . . . The entire meal is washed down with cider, weak or strong beer, then white wine. . . . They keep drinking [Bordeaux or Madeira] right through dessert, toward the end of which any ladies who are at the dinner leave the table and withdraw by themselves, leaving the men free to drink as much as they please, because the bottles then go the round continuously, each man pouring for himself. Toasts are drunk, cigars are lighted, [and] diners run to the corners of the room hunting night tables and vases which will enable them to hold a greater amount of liquor. . . . In the evening, round seven or eight o'clock (on such ordinary days as have not been set aside for formal dinners), tea is served, . . . but without meat. The whole family is united at tea, to which friends, acquaintances and even strangers are invited.

Though the Madisons doubtless had more style than the critical Frenchman commonly observed, the daily routine he described was well known to them during the winters they spent in Philadelphia.[20]

Americans immersed in the social life of the capital, however, seldom expressed the aspersions cast upon it by the snobbish and perhaps ignored Frenchman. Letters of Congressmen are filled with accounts of balls, parades, and festivals celebrating such events as the President's birthday and the opening of Congress. The Madisons, together with an excited Anna Payne, attended the lavish Washington's birthday ball given by the City Dancing Assembly under the direction of Benjamin Franklin Bache in 1795. Four hundred and fifty people crowded in to honor the "great chief [who] rises over enemies like the sun scattering the mists," Fisher Ames wrote. Parades celebrating the end of the Whisky Rebellion and General Anthony Wayne's victory over the Indians at Fallen Timbers, numerous great fires that attracted throngs of watchers as well as fire fighters, and the almost nightly dances, plays, or exchanges of visits also must have kept life in Philadelphia busy if not a bit exhausting for James and Dolley Madison. John Adams wrote his wife in February 1796: "I dined yesterday with Mr. Madison. Mrs. Madison is a fine woman, and her two sisters [Anna and Lucy] are equally so. . . . These ladies, whose name is Payne, are of a Quaker family." The hard-to-please, often prophetic Vice President doubtless would have been delighted to know that he had set down the earliest known "official" praise of the woman who for fifty years was to be the nation's premier hostess.[21]

The most exciting part of Philadelphia social life, though, was that of the young set. Between Dolley's old girl friends and the popular Anna Payne, who in her mid-teens was at the age when Moreau said Philadelphia women were most "charming and adorable," the Madisons saw plenty of courting and partying. Sally McKean, daughter of a prominent Pennsylvania Republican, and soon to be the wife of a Spanish nobleman, in 1796 wrote breathlessly and tantalizingly to Anna who was at Montpelier:

Philadelphia never was known to be so lively at this season as at present. . . . All our beaux are well; the amiable Chevalier [Sally's future husband] is perfectly recovered, and handsomer than ever . . . and

desired that I should give his best love to you. . . . You can have no
idea, my dear girl, what pleasant times I have; there is the charming
Chevalier, the divine——, the jolly——, the witty and agreeable——,
the black-eyed Lord Henry, the soft, love-making Count, the giggling,
foolish——, and sometimes the modest, good——, who are at our house
every day. We have fine riding-parties and musical parties. . . . Signor
Don Carlos has given me a few lessons on [the guitar]. . . . We have
a famous Italian singer . . . who can play any instrument, and is moreover the drollest creature you ever saw. He sings divinely, and is the
leader of our fine concerts. I am serenaded every night with divine
music. I must say divine, for it is so much above the common music.
. . . For Heaven's sake make as much haste to town as you can, for
we are to have one of the most charming winters imaginable. . . .
——told me to be sure to give his best and most sincere love to you;
he looks quite handsome, and is smarter than ever.

Little wonder that Madison's young sister Fanny took up piano playing
and persuaded her brother to take her to Philadelphia for "the season"
in 1796–7.[22]

Fashions competed with beaux for the attention of the ladies, young
and old. Sally glowingly described the new French mode of dress to
Anna, and was especially ecstatic about eighteenth-century décolletage.
Waistlines were high, necklines low, and ". . . there is no such thing as
long sleeves. They are half way above the elbow, either drawn or
plaited in various ways, according to fancy; they do not wear ruffles at
all, and as for elbows, Anna, ours would be alabaster, compared to some
of the ladies who follow the fashion; black or a colored ribbon is pinned
around the bare arm, between the elbow and the sleeve." Dolley Madison, radiant and full bosomed, had her portrait painted in just such a
dress a few years later by Gilbert Stuart. Abigail Adams, though, took
no such gay, innocent view of the new fashions:

The stile of dress . . . is really an outrage upon all decency. . . . A
sattin peticoat of certainly not more than three breadths gored at the
top, nothing beneath but a chemise. Over this thin coat, a Muslim
sometimes, sometimes a crape made so strait before as perfectly to
show the whole form. The arm naked almost to the shoulder and
without stays or Bodice. A tight girdle round the waist, and the "rich
Luxurience of nature's Charms" without a handerchief fully displayed.
. . . Every Eye in the Room has been fixed upon a certain lady [Marie
Bingham] and you might litterally see through her. But in this stile
of dress, she had danced nor regarded the splitting out of her scanty
coat, upon the occasion. I asked a young Gentleman if Miss [Bingham]
was at the dance last Evening. The replie was: yes, most wickedly.
. . . Most [ladies] wear their Cloaths too scant upon the body and too
full upon the Bosom for my fancy. Not content with the *show which*
nature bestows, they borrow from art, and litterally look like Nursing
Mothers.

Harrison Gray Otis ogled Marie Bingham more appreciatively: "I have been regaled with the sight of her whole legs for five minutes together, and do not know 'to what height' the fashion will be carried." Since Dolley Madison and her sisters adopted the new fashions and seemed in every way delighted with the French-influenced manners of Philadelphia society, we may assume ex-bachelor Madison enjoyed fully the "luxurient" feminine displays for which "the Republican Court" of the seventeen-nineties was famous—or infamous.[23]

The letters that would have described the Madison domestic circle itself in some detail, those of Dolley and Anna to their mother and sister Lucy at Harewood, have disappeared, so our knowledge of it can only be vague and inferential. James Madison, of course, wrote very little of it. In a characteristically indirect understatement, he wrote to Monroe in Paris of his marriage: "Present my best respects to Mrs. Monroe and Eliza, and tell them I shall be able on their return to present them with a new acquaintance who is prepared by my representations to receive them with all the affection they merit, and who I flatter myself will be entitled to theirs. The event which puts this in my power took place on the 15th of September." Old friends offered formal best wishes for a happy marriage, but little else. Retired General Horatio Gates, to whom Madison had recently prescribed "a long journey, at a mild season, through pleasant country, in easy stages [as] the best medicine in the world," wished the newlyweds "every Earthly Felicity." Princeton classmate Philip Freneau promised them a kind, if not a costly, welcome to his rural retreat in New Jersey, and Jefferson offered merely "a thousand respects to Mrs. Madison and joys perpetual to both." Many years after the marriage Charles Pinckney, who recalled discussions of matrimony with Madison during the Federal Convention, wrote that he had "heard everything I could wish" of Dolley Madison, and hoped that she did not exercise "petticoat government," for "if ever a man deserved a good wife," James Madison did, and there was no man the South Carolinian "should have pitied more . . . [or] more sincerely wept over" had he been henpecked.[24]

Friend and foe alike, of course, could not ignore the political aspects of the marriage of so prominent a public figure as James Madison. Fearing the joys of matrimony would distract him from his Congressional duties, Jefferson implored, "Hold on then, my dear friend. . . . I do not see . . . a greater affliction than the fear of your retirement; but this must not be, unless to a more splendid and efficacious post [the presidency]. . . . Pray [Mrs. Madison] to keep you where you are for her own satisfaction, and the public good, and accept the cordial affection of us all." Another old college friend, Governor Henry Lee of Virginia, heard "with real joy" of the marriage, but revealed his own growing Federalism in his hope that Dolley would "soften . . . some of your political asperities." Connecticut Federalist Jonathan Trumbull, Jr., thought he saw the partisan hope becoming real: "Mr. Madison has been married in the course of last summer—which event or some other, has relieved him of much Bile—and rendered him much more open and conversant than I have seen him before." Whatever the brightening effect of marriage on Madison's personality, the event had no impact on his political principles, though it almost certainly did, as Jefferson feared, quicken his desire to retire to private life.[25]

Impenetrable, too, is the effect of the infertility of the Madison marriage. Since Dolley had had children by her first husband, it seemed apparent that the reason for the barrenness of the new marriage was in her new husband. No record of any disappointments or tensions thus caused has survived, other than a brief sentence in a letter from Aaron Burr to James Monroe, eighteen months after the marriage—"Madison still childless, and I fear like to continue so"—and a remark by Jefferson in 1801 to an old friend of Madison's that he was "not yet a father." Clearly the matter was of concern to close friends like Burr, Monroe, and Jefferson, and the comments may even indicate Madison discussed it with intimates. Some students, especially those hostile to him, have implied that Madison's disappointment at his lack of offspring warped and embittered him in important ways: turned him inward, away from public life, turned him against the expansive nationalism of the prolific Hamilton, and left him generally irascible in his reaction to people and events. Such interpretation, however, is wholly speculative, and offers no substantial insights. Madison's inclination to retire had worried his friends *before* his marriage, and his hostility toward Hamilton had also long predated that event, and had quite sufficient political foundations. Furthermore, Madison's return, after 1801, to both high public office and farsighted, even grand, visions of national destiny refute any suggestion of significant "psychological damage" inflicted by his and Dolley's infertility. Their failure to fill their home with their own children was doubtless a deep personal disappointment, but there is no reason to suppose extraordinary psychic impact or harmful political consequences.[26]

Home in Orange after his retirement from Congress in March 1797, Madison managed the family plantation and superintended the remodeling of the Montpelier mansion. He, Dolley, five-year-old Payne Todd, and Anna Payne formed a family of their own, probably living in the northern half of the house, apart from the aging senior Madisons and sister Fanny in the south wing. Dolley soon assumed the role of a Virginia plantation hostess she might have filled much earlier had her father not freed his slaves and moved to Philadelphia fourteen years before.

Though Dolley was born in North Carolina, and sometimes pictured as a "Quaker maid," her family ties were to Virginia. Amid interruptions by carpenters rebuilding the mansion, the four slow-paced years spent in Virginia (1797–1801) gave her time to perfect the natural aptitude that soon made Montpelier one of the great centers of Virginia hospitality.

In Southern-plantation fashion, the Madisons visited friends and relatives all over the county and state. Soon after they returned from Philadelphia in May 1797 excited messages went out among the Taylors, Moores, Barbours, and Pendeltons that "Col. Madison Jr. and wife" were expected here or there for dinner, and would Uncle George, Cousin Reuben, etc., please join the party? During a three-day rainy spell in June 1798, the Madisons, with Anna Payne, Fanny Madison, and niece Nelly Madison, dined, visited, and partied at three different Taylor farms. That fall the same group gathered at Robert Taylor's. On a pleasant, sunny Sunday the next spring they partied at the farm of Major William Moore, Madison's old colleague in the Virginia Assembly. Madison had introduced the Moore's son, John, a few years earlier to Dickinson College in Carlisle, Pennsylvania. Longer visits were made to Dolley's mother and sisters and to the Hites in northern Virginia, to the Winstons in Hanover, and to many friends and relatives in the James River region when Madison went to Richmond for sessions of the Virginia Assembly in 1799 and 1800. Jefferson stopped at Montpelier as often as possible on his journeys between Philadelphia and Charlottesville, and the Madisons began the pattern of twice-yearly visits to Monticello that lasted as long as Jefferson or his family lived there. After Monroe returned from France in 1797, he began to build a house a few miles from Monticello, and thus furnished the Madisons with another reason for pleasant visits in that direction. We may imagine long talks of farming and house building, as well as of war and politics, when the three republicans got together amid the fields, forests, and hills they loved so much.[27]

By the time Madison returned to national politics, as Jefferson's Secretary of State in 1801, the gradual, perhaps unsought, transformation from semiresident in Orange to family patriarch was complete. The death of dependable brother Ambrose in 1793, and the death of his wife five years later, left his plantation on the east slope of the Southwest Mountains the possession of his teenage daughter, who thus became James Madison's ward. Her mother, who had died on March 14, 1798, was not buried until April 7, when on a mild, cloudy day, "a considerable large number of genteel people" gathered for the interment in the family cemetery. The sun came out in time for the many guests who stayed for supper to watch it set behind the Blue Ridge. The good weather continued the next day, when a "tolerable number of people" heard the

famous blind preacher James Waddel deliver the funeral sermon at
Orange Court House. "The young colonel," as Orange neighbors continued to speak of James Madison as long as his father lived, now knew
that the major family responsibilities were his. The declining health
of sister Nelly Madison Hite, the death of shadowy brother Francis in
April 1800, leaving numerous young children, and the marriage that
same year of "baby sister" Fanny to Dr. Robert H. Rose, all heightened
Madison's standing as the first citizen of the county. Though he did not
write of the evolving status, and his relatives and neighbors accepted it
as a matter of course, the change nevertheless had an important bearing
on Madison's public career. In 1790 he had been a bachelor, as much at
home in New York or Philadelphia as in Orange, with only minor farming duties, and deferential to his father and brother Ambrose in family
affairs. By 1800 all of these circumstances had changed drastically. Except when required to be in Washington on public business, he lived always at Montpelier. Except for a visit to Philadelphia in the summer of
1805, made necessary by Dolley's health, Madison is not known to have
left the State of Virginia and the environs of Washington after he made
his commitment to the family plantation in the seventeen-nineties. He
had become in occupation and love of his home "the complete Virginian"
his political foes increasingly accused him of being in his public
prejudices.[28]

The main reason for Madison's assumption of the role of "squire of
Montpelier," though, was his father's declining health. For more than
fifty years the elder Madison had been the leading citizen of Orange
County, its guide through revolution and war, often its sheriff, and related to virtually every substantial landowner in it. His wife, in chronic
ill-health, but like her eldest son, apparently shielded by dearly bought
immunities to the common fatal diseases, shared his last years, traveling
with him for several weeks each summer to the healing springs where
pure waters and a leisurely atmosphere revived body and spirit. While
his parents were away, Madison wrote to them of crops, house building,
slave illnesses, and politics. During the tense winter of 1800–1801, however, while the nation speculated about the tie vote between Jefferson
and Burr in the electoral college, seventy-seven-year-old James Madison,
Sr., fell gravely ill. Ten days into the new year Madison wrote Jefferson
that "the age and very declining state of my father are making almost
daily claims on my attention, and from appearances it may not be long
before these claims may acquire their full force." The old man hung on
to life, but knowing the end was near, he settled accounts with his
long-time friend and neighbor Thomas Barbour. Reference to wagon
wheels, salt, beef, and brandy furnished the revolutionary army, and
great bundles of nearly worthless Continental currency, recalled the
leading role the "old Colonel" had played in community affairs. He
asked Barbour to say what he thought some old mill equipment was

worth, and to remember some "good rum" due the Madisons for "four gallons of brandy" loaned a dozen years earlier. Friendly trust, good will, and common sense pervaded the account, likely suggesting the way the elder Madison had always sought to deal with his neighbors.[29]

On February 28, Madison wrote Jefferson of "a melancholy occurrence": "My father's health for several weeks latterly seemed to revive, and we had hopes that the approach of milder seasons would still further contribute to keep him with us. A few days past however he became sensibly worse, and yesterday morning rather suddenly, tho' very gently, the flame of life went out." Thus ended for his fifty-year-old son decades of trust, reliable support, and admired example. His letters to his father, covering a span of over thirty years, and invariably opening with an "Honored sir" and closing with "Your dutiful son," never showed the slightest ill-will or irascibility, and scarcely ever even any misunderstanding. The father had made an immense contribution to the moral and practical education of his son, and deserves therefore an important share of the credit for the sensible, humane qualities of the son's statesmanship. Had the younger man written of the "person and character" of his father as Benjamin Franklin did of his, the assessment might in many respects have been similar: "He had an excellent Constitution of Body . . . but his great excellence lay in a sound Understanding, and solid Judgment in prudential Matters, both in private and publick Affairs."[30]

Though Jefferson urgently needed Madison in Washington to get the new administration under way, Madison, noting the "crowd of indispensable attentions . . . necessarily due from me" in settling his father's estate, stayed in Orange for nearly two more months. As executor of the will, Madison decided to bring a friendly suit against all the other heirs as the simplest way to ratify the father's wishes in the courts. Shares were settled upon the surviving children, sons James and William Madison, and daughters Nelly Hite, Sarah Macon, and Frances Rose, as well as on the living heirs of the deceased sons, Ambrose and Francis Madison. Trust provision was made for the widow, who continued to live in the southern wing of the Montpelier mansion for twenty-eight years. The children further agreed that a bag of gold found in the father's desk should be made an outright gift to their mother. Family-owned mills and other property were divided; claims to lands in Kentucky and western Virginia were devolved upon the Roses; and thousands of acres of Orange County lands were settled permanently upon the other children. James Madison retained the Montpelier mansion, about a hundred slaves, and five thousand acres of land running from the woodlands at the top of the Southwest Mountains westward through gently rolling hills to the Rapidan River. With the family business thus settled amicably, and his own future home base marked out clearly, James Madison pleaded "the political lien" incumbent on him, made his brother William acting executor, and turned his own attention again to national politics.[31]

CHAPTER XVI

Triumph Over Federalism

B EFORE Madison assumed his post at Jefferson's right hand, he suffered
the agonies of responding at long range to the administration of
John Adams, and he took a leading role in the Republican protest
culminating in the famous Virginia Resolutions of 1798 and the "Report
on the Resolutions" of 1800. Though Madison and Adams had lived in
the same city for eight years during sessions of Congress, shared a Whiggish faith in separation of powers, and had good mutual friends in Jefferson and Benjamin Rush, in fact they were never close, personally or
politically. Jefferson had once told Madison that Adams "is so amiable,
that I pronounce you will love him if ever you become acquainted with
him," but Madison, without the bond of common labors in 1776 that
united Jefferson and Adams, could see only the President's pompous vanity. At home in Virginia, Madison reacted to every letter from Jefferson
or Virginia Congressmen about the Adams administration, and to every
fervent message from the President printed in the newspapers, with disgust and derision. The personal style, the sympathy for aristocratic
government, and the geopolitics of the New Englander were all anathema to the Virginia farmer. Removed from the scene, and unaffected by
responsibilities felt only in the capital, Madison spent four years "viewing with alarm." He thought often of his critical reaction (almost twenty
years ago) to Adams and his Francophobic friends in Congress as the
nation, under his leadership, fought an undeclared war with France.[1]

Upon assuming the presidency, John Adams felt a heavy burden. He
had to provide for an orderly succession in the executive branch, seek
his predecessor's goal of leadership above party, and achieve an honorable neutrality in a world at war. He wrote his wife shortly after his
inauguration that he saw before him "a scene of ambition beyond all my

former suspicions and imaginations." He feared that "at the next election England will set up Jay or Hamilton, and France, Jefferson, and all the corruption of Poland will be introduced, unless the American spirit will rise and say, 'we will have neither John Bull nor Louis Baboon.' " Since Adams thought Jay's Treaty had established peaceful relations with England on a tolerable basis, his chief concern in 1797 and 1798 was to come to a reasonable understanding with a France that viewed Jay's Treaty as a hostile act and that was swollen with power and pride as a result of Napoleon's great victories. Adams felt France's hostility unwarranted and her pride exceedingly dangerous. He was therefore unwilling to be obsequious to France, but instead sent diplomats, who stood on their own dignity, to treat with her, and urged military preparedness at home. His horror at events in France since 1789, and his certainty that her course would lead to tyranny at home and aggression abroad, strengthened his determination to accept no nonsense or arrogance from the imperious Directory ruling in Paris. At the same time, he sought no war with France and no more connection with England than commerce made necessary and useful.[2]

Madison, of course, thought the President's premises mistaken, his biases dangerous, and his fiery truculence absurd. Less than a year after his retirement from Congress, Madison scathingly compared Washington and Adams: "The one cool, considerate and cautious, the other headlong and kindled into flame by every spark that lights on his passion: the one ever scrutinizing into the public opinion, and ready to follow where he could not lead it, the other insulting it by the most adverse sentiments and pursuits. Washington a hero in the field, yet overweighing every danger in the Cabinet—Adams without a single pretension to the character of a soldier, a perfect Quixote as a statesman. . . . The avowed exultation of Washington in the progress of liberty of every where . . . the open denunciations by Adams of the smallest disturbance of the ancient discipline, order, and tranquility of despotism." Finding Adams' messages to Congress a parade of "violent passions and heretical politics," Madison urged defeat of preparedness measures, and public protests against the "war policies" of the administration. He accused Adams of "a wish to seize pretexts for widening the breach between the two Republics," France and the United States, rather than a desire for reconciliation.[3]

Little wonder, then, that Madison refused to view the "X Y Z Affair" and its insults to American diplomats by French officials as a cause for even undeclared war against France. He regarded Talleyrand's intrigue and bribes as incredibly stupid, and even depraved, but the antidote was to talk sense and seek explanations, not to shout "vile insults and calumnies," as the President and the Federalist press were inclined to do. Adams had proclaimed, for example, that "the arts and agents [of foreign nations] . . . must be resisted and exterminated, or it will end in America, as it did anciently in Greece, and in our own time in Europe, in our total destruction as a republican government and independent power." After observing street scuffles between pro- and anti-French youths and reading assaults by Benjamin Bache's *Aurora* on the President, Abigail Adams wrote that "Bache is cursing and abusing daily. If that fellow and his [puppet editors] and all is not suppressed, we shall come to a civil war," she concluded, and hoped for strong alien and sedition bills. Madison was outraged when he saw Adams' address printed in the newspapers: "His language . . . is the most abominable and degrading that could fall from the lips of the first magistrate of an independent people, and particularly from a Revolutionary patriot." The address displayed, Madison remarked, Adams' belief "that there is not a single principle the same in the American and French Revolutions." Madison still accepted Monroe's dictum that "republics should approach near to each other."[4]

The passage of the Alien and Sedition Acts in June and July 1798, as Madison learned of them through Jefferson's alarmist letters, confirmed all his worst fears. Madison called the act permitting imprisonment or deportation of suspected aliens "a monster that must forever digrace its parents," and a sign that "a majority of the House of Representatives and ⅔ of the Senate seem to be ripe for everything." He could not, he said, believe republican assemblies of free men could contemplate such measures. Another bill permitting capture of French privateers was virtually a formal commencement of hostilities, and yet another suspending commerce with the French West Indies, "begotten" by Jay's Treaty, was in effect a "coalition" with Great Britain for starving the French people. The scene in Philadelphia, as viewed from Montpelier, was a "grotesque tragicomedy." When the sedition bill came before Congress in June, Jefferson called it an "enormity . . . so palpably in the teeth of the Constitution as to show [the Federalists] mean to pay no respect to it." Though justified by their Congressional sponsors as necessary in the face of dire peril to the nation, the Alien and Sedition Acts were, Jefferson insisted, designed to drive away such zealous "foreign" Republicans as Joseph Priestley and perhaps even Albert Gallatin, and to silence the Republican press. Madison observed soberly that "perhaps it is a universal truth that the loss of liberty at home is to be charged to provisions against danger real or pretended from abroad." Though Edward Livingston and Gallatin spoke out against the Alien and Sedition Acts in Congress, and Bache's *Aurora* continued to chastise the administration, at one time calling the President "old, querulous, bald, blind, crippled, toothless Adams," Federalist-engendered war hysteria nearly overwhelmed the Republicans in the spring and summer of 1798.[5]

Vice President Jefferson was deeply disturbed, perhaps even fearful, when he left Philadelphia in late June, but a public dinner in Fredericksburg, where toasts were drunk to him, and to Madison, Monroe, and Elbridge Gerry, bouyed his spirits. More than ever, he rejoiced to be back in Virginia. On July 2, after a hot ride in the sun, Jefferson reached Montpelier, where he and his host had long, earnest conversations about the state of their country and party. As they sat on the porch, they watched lightning flicker over the Blue Ridge, heralding the "loud thunder and brisk rain" that after dark relieved the sticky heat of the day. They agreed that an appeal to the public was the proper remedy and that, as Jefferson had written John Taylor of Caroline, responding to a hint that the South might have to secede, with "a little patience . . . we shall see the reign of witches pass over, their spells dissolved, and the people recovering their true sight, restoring their government to its true principles." The difficult question was one of means and timing, however. With the federal courts already moving against editor Bache and clearly prepared to challenge public officials, as the arrest of Congressman Matthew Lyon soon showed, the Vice President and the former Representative thought it necessary to be careful not to expose themselves to prosecution under the Sedition Act, which forbade conspiring "with intent to oppose . . . measures of the government," or bringing either Congress or the President "into contempt or disrepute." It was also necessary to let the Federalist hysteria run to excess, to the point of arousing public disgust at the war measures and the laws and taxes enacted to support them. On the other hand, the people and the Republican press needed some rallying point, some statement of principles and policy that could crystallize antiadministration sentiment. Probably before Jefferson left Montpelier on July 3, the two men had agreed that the state legislatures might be the most effective and legally invulnerable organs of protest. Such proceedings, of course, were second nature to men who had lived through the 1765-to-1775 era of assembly appeals against acts of tyranny.[6]

During the summer of 1798 the two Virginians read of the final passage of the Sedition Act (July 14, 1798), of the first prosecutions under it, and of the elaborate preparations for war under the nominal leadership of Washington, but actually directed by Alexander Hamilton, second in command as inspector general of the army. There is no record of correspondence between Madison and Jefferson in the three months following the early July visit at Montpelier, nor are they known to have met again until Madison went to Monticello in mid-October. Though Madison's neighbor, Francis Taylor, observed that "the people do not appear pleased with political matters," the farmers of Orange County were generally occupied with their own affairs: a cockfight at Colonel Maury's, visitors on the way to Kentucky or to the Springs, a quart of whisky traded for a peck of onions, church audiences so thin the parson sometimes didn't bother to preach, and in late July, a heavy rain that was "very acceptable" after a seige of "fair, warm, dry, and windy" weather. Busy house building, Madison and Jefferson nonetheless suspected that Federalist agents tampered with the mails, and they feared the rumors their enemies would circulate should they seem to be "conspiring." The mood was reflected by another neighbor of Madison's, who wrote that "the greatest feuds, animosities and divisions" agitated the country, that many people took opposition to the Alien and Sedition Acts to be "a mark of hostility to the Government itself," and that the federal Senate was meeting "in dark conclave, plotting mischief, with the President at their head."[7]

Since by early October, when Jefferson had already drafted the Kentucky Resolutions, it was apparent he and Madison knew each other's minds perfectly, it is entirely possible, despite the obstacles and lack of records, that they were in touch through the summer. On September 21 Jefferson's neighbor Wilson Cary Nicholas wrote his brother in Kentucky that "everything depends upon the firmness of the state governments," and on October 4 he wrote Jefferson about a draft of some resolves he had already received from the Vice President for adoption by a state legislature, either North Carolina or Kentucky. Though nothing was said of Virginia in these exchanges, it is inconceivable that her legislature would not take part in protests planned by Jefferson and Madison. The *Aurora*, in fact, had reported on August 6 that the Virginia Assembly would act in defense of freedom of expression. Madison had probably already been designated as the draftsman for Virginia. On September 24, at Orange Court House, "James Barbour and Robert Taylor spoke in behalf of sundry Resolves to be presented to the next session of the Assembly"—probably the first public airing of a draft of the resolutions Madison was preparing for the November meeting of the legislature.[8]

Though Jefferson urged Nicholas to show his resolutions to Madison, from whom, he said "of course I have no secrets," Nicholas was unable to do so, so Madison may not have seen them until his mid-October visit to Monticello. By mid-November he had a copy of Jefferson's draft, and perhaps before he made his final draft of the resolutions intended for the Virginia legislature, he had seen the Kentucky Resolutions as adopted on November 16, 1798. Jefferson outlined, forcefully and at length, the doctrine of strict construction the Republicans had voiced increasingly for seven or eight years: the Constitution was a compact among the states delegating certain specific powers to the general government, whose *legitimate* acts could not exceed or contravene those powers. Thus far there was no disagreement among Republicans, and in fact very little dissent by Federalists either. Jefferson quickly moved to fateful implications, however: that when the general government assumed undelegated powers, its acts were "unauthoritative, void, and of no force"; that the general government was not the exclusive or final judge of the limits of its powers; and that each state had "an equal right to judge for itself, as well of infractions as of the mode and measure of redress." Following long resolves explaining how the Alien and Sedition Acts were both outside the limited powers of Congress and in violation of explicit clauses of the Constitution, the Kentucky Resolutions proclaimed that state's rejection of the tyrannical acts and called upon other states to join in declaring them "void and of no force." Furthermore, in an extreme expression, deleted before adoption by the Kentucky legislature, Jefferson had affirmed that "where powers are assumed which have not been delegated, a nullification of the act is the rightful remedy; that every state has a natural right in cases not within the compact to nullify of their own authority, all assumptions of power by others within their limits."[9]

Though Madison agreed entirely with the specific condemnation of the Alien and Sedition Acts, with the concept of the limited delegated power of the general government, and even with the proposition that laws contrary to the Constitution were illegal, he drew back from the declaration that each state legislature had the power to act within its borders against the authority of the general government to oppose laws the legislature deemed unconstitutional. Madison began immediately to point out the dangers to Jefferson. "Have you ever considered thoroughly," he asked, "the distinction between the power of the *State* and that of the *Legislature*" in deciding constitutional questions? It might be wise, he counseled, to use "general expressions," to permit flexibility in response and to avoid usurpation by the legislatures "in the very act of protesting against the usurpations of Congress." The exchange was typical. Jefferson had sought, perhaps a bit heedlessly, to state as strongly and as eloquently as words allowed, a doctrine he thought would be useful in defending what were to him vital republican liberties. As his response to Madison's reservations show, he apparently had not considered very seriously the threat the doctrine might pose to the valid and useful powers of the federal government, or the abuses state governments might make of it.[10]

In a final draft of the Virginia Resolutions, probably done in late November 1798, Madison therefore began with statements of "warm attachment" to the Constitution and to the Union, but immediately asserted the compact and strict construction theories and protested that the Alien and Sedition Acts subverted "the general principles of free government, as well as the particular organization and positive provisions of the Federal Constitution." He deplored especially the Sedition Act, "levelled against the right of freely examining public characters and measures, and of free communication among the people thereon, which has ever been justly deemed the only effectual guardian of every other right." He thus agreed with Jefferson that the main objective was to defend vital civil liberties against Federalist measures obviously and inevitably tending "to transform the present republican system of the United States into an absolute, or, at best, a mixed monarchy." As to means, Madison insisted merely that in case of "deliberate, palpable, and dangerous exercise" of unconstitutional powers by the federal government, the states "have the right and are duty bound to interpose for arresting the progress of the evil, and for maintaining within their respective limits, the authorities, rights and liberties appertaining to them." Finally Madison appealed to other states to join Virginia "in declaring that the acts aforesaid are unconstitutional," and that necessary cooperative measures be taken to maintain the liberties of the people. When John Taylor of Caroline introduced Madison's resolves in the Virginia House of Delegates, he had added, at Jefferson's suggestion, the words "null, void, and of no effect" after "unconstitutional"; but, almost certainly at Madison's urging, these words were dropped before the resolutions were adopted on December 24, 1798. Thus the Virginia Resolutions, due largely to Madison's astute understanding of constitutional pitfalls, were a moderate statement shunning the centrifugal tendencies of the more categorical resolves Jefferson had sent to Kentucky.[11]

Though the Kentucky and Virginia resolutions did provide a rallying point for Republicans, they themselves were challenged, and the other states refused to concur in them. Even in Virginia sixty-three members of the House of Delegates voted against the resolutions. This minority promptly commissioned John Marshall to defend the constitutionality of the Alien and Sedition Acts, which the future Chief Justice did in a powerful pamphlet addressed to the people. Massachusetts and several other states adopted resolutions upholding the acts, Massachusetts declaring that the Virginia Resolutions reduced the Constitution to "a mere cipher . . . without the energy of power . . . [unable to resist] the ambitious projects of a particular state." Fisher Ames expressed the view of many Federalists: "Virginia, excited by crazy Taylor, is fulminating its manifesto against the federal government." More threatening to the Virginia Republicans were rumblings from Mount Vernon. Washington wrote Patrick Henry on January 15, 1799, that the doctrines of the Virginia Resolutions, if "systematically and pertinaciously pursued [will] . . . dissolve the Union or produce coercion." The old general then begged the old orator to return to the Assembly to stop the "torrent that carries away others." Though sick and dispirited, Henry agreed to stand in the spring elections. With these heroes of the revolution arrayed against them, Madison and Jefferson knew they faced stiff battles.[12]

Jefferson wrote from Philadelphia that "the season for systematic energies and sacrifices" had arrived. He asked Madison to write once a week for the press, an "incalculable service [which will] lessen the effect of our loss of your presence here." Madison apparently declined. Two days later, six Virginia Congressmen urged him to enter the Virginia legislature to resist the usurpations of the federal government. Writing after hearing of Patrick Henry's decision to return to public life, John Taylor of Caroline joined in the entreaty to Madison: "Consider that Virginia is the hope of Republicans throughout the Union, and that if Mr. Henry prevails in removing her resistance to monarchical measures the whole body will be dispirited and fall a sudden and easy prey to the enemies of liberty. If you will not save yourself or your friend—yet save your country." Madison yielded and agreed to stand for election. After a large gathering of Moores, Taylors, Barbours, and Madisons at Major William Moore's farm on Sunday, April 14, 1799, had revived Madison's political machine, the freemen of Orange County met at the courthouse ten days later for the election. Francis Taylor described the day: "Fair, except some broken clouds. . . . Breakfasted with the boys who came last evening. We all went to the Election. There was no poll taken for the County Delegates—Colonel James Madison [Jr.] and Captain James Barbour Elected. About 200 votes and upwards for Mr. [John] Dawson [for Congress] and French Strother for State Senator." Madison thus prepared for a battle royal that never took place. Patrick Henry died in June 1799, before the legislature met.[13]

While Jefferson and Madison made plans to arouse the public against the Federalist measures, events abroad, on the high seas, and in the Quincy and Philadelphia sitting rooms where President Adams took counsel with himself, conspired to transform the forces against which they contended. Nelson's victory at Abukir in August 1798, dooming Napoleon's Egyptian campaign, and the French defeats in Germany and Italy in 1799 during Napoleon's absence, diminished French arrogance and thirst for war with the United States. Furthermore, American naval victories, war preparations, and patriotic fervor had made it clear that, despite fundamental weaknesses and internal dissension, the new nation was determined to uphold its honor. Thus a flood of "peace feelers" reached Adams during the fall and winter of 1798 and 1799, and in February, to the consternation of his cabinet and other Hamiltonian Federalists, who had grand domestic and foreign plans for which war measures were vital, he announced his intention to send another peace mission to France. Throughout the spring and summer of 1799 Adams remained firm, and the departure of the envoys in October terminated the war crisis. "The end of war is peace," the President declared, "and peace was offered me." The battle Adams fought on this issue with the high Federalists was in fact the vital one then going on in the country. His triumph in it crippled his party but preserved peace and cooled political tempers. For this the country at large, and the ungrateful Republicans as well, owed the "always honest and sometimes wise" President a great deal.[14]

In early September 1799, after another summer of house building, Madison, Monroe, and Jefferson met at Monticello to "consider a little what is to be done." "The principles already advanced by Virginia and Kentucky are not to be yielded in silence, I presume we all agree," Jefferson wrote in inviting his friends. The Vice President wanted to state clearly the rights reserved to the states when the federal government exercised powers "to which we have never assented." Though he professed "warm attachment to union," and said he was "not at all disposed to make every measure of error or wrong a cause of scission," he proposed that Kentucky and Virginia declare themselves "determined . . . to sever ourselves from that union we so much value, rather than give up the rights of self government which we have reserved, and in which alone we see liberty, safety and happiness." Alarmed at this reasoning, Madison argued, as he was to do again in 1830, opposing Calhoun, that "we should never think of separation except for repeated and enormous violations," which if committed, would put an end to the Constitution and leave the people, as they were in 1776, in a natural state of revolution. But such a state, in Madison's view, dissolved the Constitution, and therefore it was wrong to speak of nullification and secession as a legitimate process *within* the frame of government. Jefferson readily accepted this vital revision. When, shortly after the meeting, he again outlined "what is to be done," he merely urged generally that the people declare they would not suffer forever the violation of their rights. Perhaps recognizing Madison's surer grasp of the interlocking problems of freedom and union, the three friends agreed that he should draft the Republican manifesto and present it for approval by the Virginia legislature at its winter session.[15]

About December 1, 1799, Madison left Orange to take his seat in the House of Delegates, then gathering in Richmond. "A dysenteric attack," plus the labor "of preparing a vindication of the Resolutions of last Session against the replies of the other States, and the sophistries from other quarters," left him "in a state of debility" through most of the month. The political atmosphere of the House seemed staunchly republican, however, and even more propitious, French reverses in Europe brightened prospects for peace, Madison thought, "if our Executive and their Envoys be sincere in their pacific objects." Thus encouraged, Madison drafted a "report on the Resolutions" of the previous session, his most important statement of the principles that should guide republican governments in protecting civil liberties during a national crisis. Secondarily, of course, it was an electioneering and states' rights manifesto.[16]

Madison defended the resolutions one by one against the assaults on them by state legislatures and others during the year. The first two resolves, pledging devotion to the Constitution and to the Union, required little comment. The next, asserting that the Constitution was a compact valid only insofar as its terms were honored, and that the states must "interpose" in cases of "deliberate, palpable, and dangerous" abuse of powers granted to the general government, Madison defended under the hallowed doctrine of government by consent. What did this mean if not that governments were limited by the charters from the people creating them? Since the states, in their sovereign capacity, were parties to the compact, and were more intimately the instruments of the people than the federal government, they were the obvious, legitimate agencies of "interposition" to defend civil liberties. Though Madison emphasized that the states would not "interpose" for light or transient reasons, he was nevertheless perfectly clear in asserting their primacy, in judging constitutionality, over the federal courts. They themselves, he observed, might aid and abet usurpations, an argument with special relevance at the time because federal judges such as Samuel Chase were so obviously partisan in upholding the Alien and Sedition Acts. Thirty years later, though, Calhoun used the argument, to Madison's embarrassment and disgust, in upholding nullification.

Next, Madison outlined the persistent tendency of the Federalist administration "to enlarge its powers by forced constructions of the constitutional charter." Madison cited the national bank, the carriage tax, and the arguments of Hamilton's *Report on Manufactures*, as well as the Alien and Sedition Acts, as examples of encroaching federal power. The trend was toward "consolidation of the states into one Sovereignty," enlargement of the executive, "excessive augmentation of . . . offices, honors, and emoluments," and "the transformation of the republican system of the United States into a monarchy." Since Madison's first speech against the national bank, nine years earlier, this argument had been a distinguishing feature of the popular image of "Jeffersonianism"; it remained so for a century or more.

Madison turned his heaviest fire, however, on the Alien and Sedition Acts as unconstitutional assaults on rights and liberties inseparable from the very concept of free government. He asserted that the Alien Friends Act permitted exactly the kind of highhanded measures, devoid of procedural safeguards, that Whig doctrine had long regarded as the essence of tyranny. It gave the executive discretionary judicial powers incompatible with the liberalism inherent in the American Revolution. Even worse, the Sedition Act exercised a power not given by the Constitution, a power expressly forbidden by the first amendment, and a power fatal to the free examination of "public Characters and Measures," which was "the only effectual guardian of every other right." Madison had first to destroy the notion that the English common law on sedition and free expression was in force in the United States, because under the dicta of Blackstone and Mansfield, the Sedition Act was not only admissible, but was liberalizing in that it permitted truth to be a ground for defense against prosecution. Madison argued that a major purpose of the revolution, to throw off the oppressive opinions of British judges, and the very nature of the new governments under written constitutions would both be subverted if the common law, "with all its incongruities, barbarisms, and bloody maxims [is] saddled on the good people of the United States." Without the common law, and without strained construction of implied powers, Madison concluded, there was no warrant in the Constitution for such an enormity as the Sedition Act.

Even worse, the Sedition Act clearly violated the First Amendment provision that "Congress shall make no law . . . abridging the freedom of speech or of the press." Again, defenders of the act appealed to English common law. The First Amendment meant, they said, that Congress could not abridge *the common-law meaning* of freedom of the press, which merely assured freedom from licensing or previous restraint, and did not upset prosecutions for seditious libel. Moving beyond his technical invalidation of the common law in the United States, Madison argued that the common-law doctrine was incompatible with the nature of republican government. It was, in the first place, "a mockery to say that no laws should be passed preventing publications from being made, but that laws might be passed for punishing them in case they should be made." The essential difference between British and American government, however, placed the subject "in the clearest light," Madison observed. In Britain "the danger of encroachment on the rights of the people" was understood to be from the king. Hence the key freedom was from previous restraint by his officers. Parliament was held to be omnipotent, so such "ramparts" as the Magna Charta and the Bill of Rights were not erected against it. In the United States, on the other hand, the people were sovereign, and the legislature as well as the executive was under limitations of power. "The great and essential rights of the people . . . are secured, not by laws paramount to prerogative, but by constitutions paramount to laws." Furthermore, in Britain the king, a hereditary, not a responsible magistrate, could "do no wrong," and the House of Lords as well had no constituent responsibility. They were therefore in some sense sanctified, and thus perhaps not to be subjected to unrestrained criticism. In the United States, though, the executive was not held to be "infallible" nor the legislature omnipotent. Each was responsible to the people, and therefore "a peculiar freedom" was necessary in examining and criticizing their conduct. The value of this freedom was evident, Madison observed, to anyone who reflected "that to the press alone, chequered as it is with abuses, the world is indebted for all the triumphs which have been gained by reason and humanity over error and oppression. . . . That to the same beneficent source the United States owe much of the lights which conducted them to the ranks of a free and independent nation, and which have improved their political system into a shape so auspicious to their happiness."

Madison then asked, noting that the Sedition Act was to be in effect during a national election, whether its rigid execution might not repress "that information and communication among the people which is indispensable to the just exercise of their electoral rights." The very language of the act, he insisted, proscribing "false, scandalous, and malicious writing" against the government or its officers, and any attempt to "defame . . . or bring them into contempt or disrepute," ignored the character of free government. In debating the deeds of the administration, it was obvious that "opinions and inferences, and conjectural observations, are not only in many cases inseparable from the facts, but may often be more the objects of the prosecution than the facts themselves." Therefore the provision that truth was a valid defense offered little protection. Furthermore, "It is manifestly impossible to punish the intent to bring those who administer the Government into disrepute or contempt, without striking at the right of freely discussing public characters and measures; because those who engage in such discussions must expect and intend to excite those unfavorable sentiments, so far as they may be thought to be deserved." To prohibit the *intent*, then, was to prohibit the "actual excitement" of derogatory attitudes toward government, which, further, was to prohibit *discussion*, and finally, to protect the administration against criticism even when it "deserves the contempt or hatred of the people." The existence of the Sedition Act at election time thus made the ballot unequal, because of restraints on the opposition party, and unfree, because the people "will be compelled to make their election between competitors whose pretensions they are not permitted . . . equally to examine, to discuss, and to ascertain." After asserting again that the Virginia Resolutions had proposed no intention to flout federal law and made no appeals to treason or disunion, Madison concluded the "Report" with renewed "protest against the Alien and Sedition Acts as palpable and alarming infractions of the Constitution."[17]

In exposing the sharp contradiction between the Sedition Act and the principles of republican government, and in asserting the enlarged need for free expression under the new constitution of the United States, Madison added substantially to the theory of free government he had been evolving for a generation or more. Surprisingly little had been said during the revolution, except in general terms, about the place of a free press in a republic, and indeed practices were often not at all "libertarian." Even during the ratification debate and the discussion of the federal Bill of Rights in the First Congress, the ancient doctrine of seditious libel was not repudiated. Thus from 1798 to 1800 arguments based on it were still current, and even after 1801 the Republicans, though not Madison himself explicitly, countenanced seditious libel proceedings in *state* courts. But the Virginia report of 1800, drawn by Madison and given official endorsement by a state legislature, pointed unequivocally toward the place of free expression in a democratic government given classic formulation by John Stuart Mill half a century later. The argument of the 1800 report is thoroughly consistent with the Jefferson-Madison concept of the human mind and their assumptions about government by consent, but not until the report had either of them developed the libertarian theory in detail. Thus, a recent student has observed, Madison took "a major step in the evolution of the meaning of the free-speech-and-press clause" of the First Amendment.[18]

In retrospect it seems true, as John Quincy Adams put it (and one suspects, as Madison himself must have agreed privately in 1832), that Madison "admitted rather too many of [Jefferson's] premises" about the "sovereign powers" of the states. However, the states' rights theory in the Virginia Resolutions and the report, especially in view of Madison's moderation of them in the face of the more extreme expressions of Jefferson and John Taylor of Caroline, is incidental when set beside the signal advance in civil liberties theory. Partly under the brilliant reasoning of the 1800 report, the Sedition Act died ignominiously a year later, and ever since, those attempting to restrict free expression have had to confront Madison's words, while friends of free expression have found aid and comfort in them. The report is an entirely consistent last chapter in Madison's public exposition of the theory of free government. That he drew back from his nationalist position of ten years earlier is certainly true, but that he did so to maintain a principle he thought paramount to any particular structure or interpretation of national government is equally evident. Limited government according to the freely given consent of the people and the protection of their natural rights was always for Madison the greatest good. In 1800 acts of the federal government threatened this free consent and these rights, so Madison spoke and acted to resist them. As he was to admit himself in old age, in so doing he adhered to a theory of the Constitution not wholly consistent with its uniform interpretation throughout the Union. But this embarrassed him much less than it has his most zealous defenders ever since: he knew that evolving the modes of free government was a process one learned in part by trial and error. The need regarding the Constitution, he wrote at the time of the nullification controversy, was to resist those who would "squeeze it to death" as well as those who would "stretch it to death." The most inadmissible "error" was to betray the very principles of freedom one adopted constitutions and made laws to uphold. The vindication of these principles, not states' rights theory, was for Madison the great issue of 1798 to 1800. The "Report" was, as John Dickinson wrote Jefferson, "an inestimable contribution to the cause of liberty."[19]

Ten days after the adoption of the "Report" on January 11, 1800, Madison attended a meeting in Richmond of over one hundred Virginia

Republicans to lay plans to insure Jefferson's victory in the coming presidential election. Federalist gains during the previous year, including John Marshall's election to the House of Representatives, presented a powerful challenge. Feeling confident of a state-wide majority, but uncertain of their strength in some districts, the Republicans had, with Madison's support, pushed through the legislature a plan to choose the state's presidential electors on a general ticket. At the January 21 meeting, and at three more meetings within a week, therefore, the Republicans nominated a "general ticket" of electors and chose a five-man central committee "to communicate useful information to the people relative to the election, . . . to repel every effort which may be made to injure . . . the ticket in general . . . [and] to keep up a regular intercourse" with subcommittees in each county in Virginia. Madison paid $1 dues to the central committee, served as chairman of the Orange County subcommittee, and along with such "venerable patriots" as George Wythe and Edmund Pendleton, appeared as a Republican elector on the general ticket ordered printed and distributed by the committee. Thus Madison, despite his eighteenth-century distaste for electioneering and party organization, helped make formal and public the close-knit coordination he and others had provided for the Republican interest in Virginia for nearly ten years.[20]

Though home in Orange, fretting about crop damage caused by heavy snow that covered the ground from early February to mid-March, and working to finish the portico on the remodeled Montpelier mansion, Madison attended as well to the presidential election. Not only did he believe the very survival of republican government depended on Jefferson's victory, but he knew the results were likely to be as close as they were in 1796, when Adams had won by only three electoral votes. Federalist gains in the 1799 Congressional elections, general prosperity, and public support for President Adams' peace policy made Republicans anxious, but the split between Adams and Hamilton, resentment against the increasing highhandedness of Federalist administrations, improved Republican party organization, and especially, public resistance to high taxes, favored the Jeffersonians. With New England solidly Federalist and the South and West strongly Republican, the result, as in 1796, seemed to turn on critical elections in the large middle states, New York and Pennsylvania. In many states electors were chosen by the legislatures; vital news reached Madison in April that the Republicans, led skillfully by Aaron Burr, had gained control in New York: her electoral votes, which had provided Adams' margin of victory in 1796, would swing to Jefferson. Through the summer and fall, returns came gradually to Virginia and to the new Federal City, where Congress gathered for the first time in November 1800: New Jersey and Delaware had gone Federalist, and although the Republicans swept Virginia, Georgia,

Tennessee, and Kentucky, the district system of choosing electors imposed a 5 to 5 split on them in Maryland and gave them only an 8 to 4 victory in North Carolina. On November 30 Jefferson calculated he had 58 votes and Adams 53. A week later the loss of Rhode Island, which Burr had predicted would go for Jefferson, evened the scale, with only Pennsylvania and South Carolina unreported. A deadlock in the Pennsylvania legislature seemed sure to nearly neutralize her vote, so everything depended on South Carolina, the most Federalist of Southern states, and also the home of the Federalist Vice Presidential candidate, General Charles C. Pinckney. The Republican manager there, Charles Pinckney, who had been in close touch with Madison all year, promised patronage and otherwise strained every effort for Jefferson. When the legislature finally cast its ballots, on December 2, the Republican electors all won by small majorities. By mid-December Madison knew his party was victorious.[21]

Republican discipline, however, had been so firm that Jefferson and Burr, the intended *vice* president, each had 73 votes, thus unexpectedly throwing the election into the House of Representatives. Southern Republicans, including Madison, had counted on Burr's assurance of victory in Rhode Island and his promise that one of her electors would vote for Jefferson but not for Burr. They had agreed, therefore, to demonstrate loyalty to Burr by voting solidly for him as well as for Jefferson. Though charges were made in 1801 (and have been often revived since) that Burr deliberately deceived the Southerners because he knew Rhode Island would go Federalist, the extreme danger of throwing votes away in such a close election could just as well have been the cause of the tie. Madison went to Richmond in late November 1800 to cast his ballot as a Virginia elector inclined to withhold one vote from Burr, but appeals to the "honor and integrity" of Virginia dissuaded him; he held the Republican electors solidly behind both their candidates. Though Burr professed loyalty to Jefferson and to the intention of the people, especially as long as he believed Jefferson would in fact receive more electoral votes than any other candidate, the New Yorker would not withdraw categorically. He held that if the House could not settle on Jefferson, he would not refuse election if the alternative were anarchy or Federalist domination. Whether, as Madison charged in old age, Burr had schemed for months to secure his own election, remains uncertain. Ironically, his temporizing began the split with the Virginians that eliminated him from the succession to the presidency and thus virtually assured Madison's own standing as the Republican heir apparent. In any event, the stage was set for two months of uncertainty and intrigue, ended on February 17, when enough moderate Federalists abstained to permit Jefferson's election.[22]

During the winter months of suspense, Madison suffered "from several complaints" including an attack of rheumatism which even "temperance and flannels" could not cure. This, plus his father's illness and the impropriety of appearing to seek office, caused him to decline Jefferson's suggestion that he come to Washington while the contest for the presidency remained unsettled. Madison nonetheless kept in close touch with developments. When extreme Federalists spoke of using the tie as an excuse for excluding both Republicans and turning the government over to a Federalist designated by the Senate, Republican governors of the strategic states of Virginia and Pennsylvania made clear that they would resist such a usurpation by all means at their disposal. Federalist attention then turned to intrigues with Burr and to strategies of delay or confusion. Fortunately, almost all their responsible leaders, Hamilton, Ames, Jay, Gouverneur Morris, and President Adams, rejected extralegal moves, and in fact preferred Jefferson to Burr, whom Hamilton called "the Catiline of America" and Adams scorned as a "dexterous gentleman." Madison proposed to Virginia Congressman John Dawson "a complete counter-project" should the Federalists prevent an election of a new President: "Messrs. Jefferson and Burr, one of whom must certainly be President, should issue a joint [proclamation] for the convening of the [new] Congress, who should then proceed to a choice." This would frustrate both Federalist intrigue and Burr's ambitions, because the new House of Representatives was overwhelmingly Republican. Madison soon exulted at Jefferson's election under constitutional forms and the rejection of military force and usurpation: "What a lesson to America and the world, is given by the efficacy of the public will when there is no army to be turned against it!"[23]

Madison's continuing ill-health and the settlement of his father's estate prevented him from being in Washington a day or two after Jefferson's inauguration to accept his appointment as Secretary of State (made on March 5), and to help the President "put things under way." Jefferson fretted: "I am still at a loss, Mr. Madison not having been able to come yet, Mr. Gallatin not agreeing to join us until my return [in May], and not knowing yet where to get a Secretary of the Navy." Thus frustrated, he left the capital and "passed an evening with Mr. Madison" on his way to Monticello. Though Madison's health was still "very indifferent," the two men talked of the vexing, "not yet decided . . . rule of conduct" about appointments to office and the possible removal of Federalists from key positions. They decided, tentatively, to seek repeal of the new judiciary act enlarging the federal courts, to eliminate the holders of the new offices created under it, and to nominate only good Republicans until the heavy preponderance of Federalist officeholders had been corrected. Jefferson again spent a night at Montpelier on April 26 on his way back to Washington, but to his dismay, he found

Madison sick in bed. The President invited the Madisons, and Dolley's sister Anna, to stay with him until they could find a house, and sent back word on the roads to take to avoid mudholes and carriage-tipping bumps.[24]

On May 1 Madison finally arrived in Washington, "better than when he left home," according to Jefferson. The next day William Cranch, one of John Adams' "midnight judges" (and his wife's brother-in-law), administered the oath of office to the new Secretary of State, and by May 14 the President reported "the organization of our new government complete." A month later he wrote Monroe that "Mr. Madison's health is sensibly improved, and we hope it is the effect of the application of his mind to things more congenial to it than the vexatory details of a farm." After three or four years of lagging interest in national politics and four more years of relative seclusion in Virginia, Madison was again in a seat of power, eager to translate republican theory into administration policy. A young Virginian destined to play a large role in Madison's later years, Edward Coles, described the new Secretary of State, whom he first met at about this time:

> I never knew him to wear any other color than black; his coat being cut in what is termed dress-fashion; his breeches short, with buckles at the knees, black silk stockings, and shoes with strings or long fair boot tops when out in cold weather, or when he rode on horseback of which he was fond. His hat was of the shape and fashion usually worn by gentlemen of his age. He wore powder on his hair, which was dressed full over the ears, tied behind, and brought to a point above the forehead, to cover in some degree his baldness, as may be noticed in all the likenesses taken of him. . . . In height he was about five feet six inches, of small and delicate form, of rather a tawny complexion, bespeaking a sedentary and studious man; his hair was originally of a dark brown color; his eyes were bluish, but not of a bright blue; his form, features, and manner were not commanding, but his conversation exceedingly so and few men possessed so rich a flow of language, or so great a fund of amusing anecdotes, which were made the more interesting from their being well-timed and well-told. His ordinary manner was simple, modest, bland, and unostentatious, retiring from the throng and cautiously refraining from doing or saying anything to make himself conspicuous.[25]

CHAPTER XVII

Secretary of State

W HEN the Madisons reached Washington in May 1801, they
stayed for three weeks with Jefferson at the unfinished "President's House," described by John Adams' Secretary of the
Navy as a "large, naked, ugly looking building, . . . a very inconvenient
residence for a Family." Other observers, though, found it a pleasing,
well-proportioned building. The city itself was "almost a wilderness,"
and the house to which Madison took his wife, sister-in-law, and stepson
"stood unenclosed on a piece of waste and barren ground, separated from
the capital by an almost impassable marsh." Conceived on a grand scale,
in 1801 the city was too scattered to be "pleasant or even convenient."
The unfinished Capitol, surrounded by "seven or eight boarding houses,
one tailor, one shoemaker, one printer, a washingwoman, a grocery shop,
a pamphlets and stationery shop, a small dry-goods shop, and an oyster
house," formed one center; the President's House, a mile and a half away,
formed another; and the town of Georgetown, equidistant in the other
direction, was yet another center. Intervening were rivers, swamps,
"thick groves and forest trees, wide and verdant plains, with only here
and there a house along the interesting ways, that could not yet be properly called streets." Albert Gallatin, preparing his sophisticated New York
wife for the trials of life in such a country town, wrote that the small
stream between the Capitol and the President's House, "decorated with
the pompous appellation of 'Tyber,'" fed rather than drained the swamp,
making it certain that any house built on the forest path called "Pennsylvania Avenue" would consign its "wretched tenants to perpetual
fevers." The pastoral Jefferson, on the other hand, wrote after three
months in his new house that "we find this a very agreeable country

residence, good society and enough of it, and free from the noise, the heat, the stench, and the bustle of a close built town."[1]

For two more months, while the Republicans sought to set their administration in motion, the Madisons lived in one of a row of houses, "Six Buildings," a few blocks from the President's House on the road to Georgetown. Six Buildings also temporarily housed the offices of the Department of State. The next fall, after staying with Jefferson a few days until their "freshly plaistered" house was dry, they moved into the house, which was at what is now 1333 F Street NW, two blocks east of the President's House, and next door to the residence of William Thornton, who supervised the work on the new building for the absent secretary. It was a comfortable, three-story brick home, complete with a cupola for fire escapes, four dormer bedrooms on the third floor, wine and coal rooms in the cellar, and a coach house and stables for four horses in the rear. This house, later occupied by John Quincy Adams, became, under Dolley's presiding genius and amid the excitement of the "young set" surrounding Anna Payne, one of the bright gathering places of the new Federal City during the eight years the Madisons lived in it.[2]

Like all others connected with the new administration, the Madisons furnished gossip for the ladies of Washington. Margaret Bayard Smith, both the arbiter and chronicler of early Washington social life and a devoted admirer of Madison and Jefferson, wrote of the Montpelier family for the first time on May 26, 1801: "Our city, is now as gay as in the winter; the arrival of all the secretaries, seems to give new animation to business, and the settlements of their families, affords employment to some of our tradesmen. . . . Mrs. Madison is at the President's at present; I have become acquainted with and am highly pleased with her; she has good humor and sprightliness, united to the most affable and agreeable manners. I admire the simplicity and mildness of Mr. Madison's manners, and his smile has so much benevolence in it, that it cannot fail of inspiring good will and esteem." Two days later Mrs. Smith reported that Dolley and Anna were so "open" that one immediately felt them to be personal friends, and "Mr. Jefferson's and Madison's manners were so easy and familiar that they produced no restraint. Never were there a plainer set of men, and I think I may add a more virtuous and enlightened one, than at present forms our administration." The informality insisted upon by Jefferson at the President's House, the unpretentious beginnings of housekeeping by his ministers, and the country-town atmosphere of the new capital were not mere personal idiosyncracies or unwelcome necessities; they were essential parts of republican social theory. To Virginia planters, used to an easy mixing of work, pleasure, and politics, and fascinated with physiocratic doctrines, the social environment of the government would, of course, be of intense concern. Republicanism to them was a way of life.[3]

The State Department on May 2, 1801, when Madison assumed its direction, consisted of eight clerks inherited from the Federalists, housed temporarily in some crowded offices in the Six Buildings. Slowly, over a course of months, the department moved into a new, square building next to the President's House and shared with the War Department. In his new quarters, Madison "received foreign ministers in a very indifferent little room into which they were ushered by his clerk," a British diplomat reported. The clerk was probably Jacob Wagner, the chief among four "complete picaroon" (*i.e.*, followers of high Federalist former Secretary Timothy Pickering) employees with whom Madison had to contend. In an economy move he discharged one of them, but the others he kept on. The four "non-picaroons" were described by vitriolic editor William Duane as "a Hamiltonian, a nothingarian, a modest man, and a nincumpoop." The "nincumpoop" was Daniel Brent who nevertheless still held his job in 1837. Connections may have helped him: he came from an old Virginia family and he had a brother who was mayor of Washington, two cousins prominently allied politically with Madison and Monroe, and an uncle who had served in Congress with Madison and was United States Senator from Virginia from 1809 to 1814. Wagner, on the other hand, proved able and honorable, though unregenerately Federalist until he resigned six years later, despite Madison's appreciation of his efficient service.[4]

With this uneven staff, Madison turned to the business of his department, which in 1801 included many laborious domestic responsibilities. Madison had to draw reports for Congress when requested, correspond with governors, territorial officials, judges, marshals, and attorneys, preserve public papers, print and distribute the laws, supervise the patent office and the census, and keep the Great Seal of the United States, used to authenticate documents. As foreign minister, the secretary had to correspond with American ministers and with dozens of consuls scattered around the world, deal with foreign embassies in Washington, issue passports and ships' papers, and act as savior and/or truant officer for stranded American seamen. At first, despite his almost legendary methodical application, Madison was nearly overwhelmed: "I find myself in the midst of arrears of papers, etc. etc., which little accord with my unsettled health." Two months later he explained to a Virginia friend why he hadn't written: "Having brought with me to this place a very feeble state of health, and finding the mass of business in the department, at all times considerable, swelled to an unusual size by sundry temporary causes, it became absolutely necessary to devote the whole of my time and pen to public duties, and consequently to suspend my private correspondences altogether, notwithstanding the arrears daily accumulating. To this resolution I have thus far adhered." His continued adherence, expecially while in Washington, in fact altered sharply the character of his previously informal, discursive, and political correspondence. From

1801 to 1817, he received thousands of impersonal, routine reports and letters, and wrote hundreds of official replies to them. For the first time in his life, he had clerical assistance. With resignation, and with some regret, no doubt, he became an administrator. As the hot tidewater summer closed in on him, one suspects Madison, chained to a desk piled high with papers, pondered ruefully on the course of his public career.[5]

Much more to his liking, and far more important, were his informal responsibilities as a member of the "Republican triumvirate." None, friend or foe, had the slightest doubt that Jefferson would select Madison as his Secretary of State and Gallatin as Secretary of the Treasury. Each appointee was by experience and ability well-suited for his post, and each had, in six years of Republican leadership in Congress, matchless training in politics. The three men were, as well, in close agreement on what each regarded as fundamental republican principles. Among themselves they made all the great decisions of Jefferson's administration. The other cabinet members, though they were, according to the President's testimony, unfailingly amicable and helpful, functioned more strictly as department heads than as top-level counselors. Jefferson deferred to Gallatin on fiscal questions and always asked him to prepare the financial portion of the annual message. On other matters, especially appointments, political strategy, and foreign affairs, Gallatin was a trusted advisor, valued for his understanding and mastery of every matter placed before him. "The stern integrity and firm republicanism of this veteran politician," as *The National Intelligencer* put it when Gallatin retired from the cabinet after twelve years' service, were of immense value to the new nation.[6]

Though Gallatin's office and abilities made him coequal with Madison as an advisor to the President, the personal intimacy between the two Virginians made Madison in fact the first minister and in every respect Jefferson's most trusted counselor. For eight or nine months of each year, they were in daily contact in the capital—consulting, exchanging notes, and enjoying each other's company. During the other months, they lived twenty-five miles apart in Virginia. Couriers took letters and documents back and forth between them, and they exchanged visits, sometimes lasting a week or two, at least once a year. Jefferson wrote two months after he left office that "Mr. Madison is justly entitled to his full share of the measures of my administration. Our principles were the same, and we never differed sensibly in the application of them." Jefferson's position as President gave him the ultimate responsibility, and the Constitution required that acts of the executive department come forth under his authority, but the voluminous correspondence between him and Madison reveals clearly that as often as not Madison initiated important policies, and his opinions again and again changed the President's mind. The oft-repeated phrase in Madison's letters to American diplomats, "the President has determined," meant not that literally, but that the two men had consulted and agreed on a decision. As had been true for over twenty years, the two men regarded each other as colleagues in every way and were fully open, candid, and respectful with each other. Jefferson's colorful pen and personality, his genius for warm human relationships, and the passionate devotion he inspired among his followers made him, in the eyes of the public and of history, loom over his self-effacing friend, but in fact Jefferson's administration was very nearly as much Madison's as his. They were coarchitects and coexecutors of a Republican policy to which they were equally devoted.[7]

Friends and supporters clamoring for jobs and other favors were more immediately vexatious to the new administration than were its enemies. Madison's own relatives and almost forgotten acquaintances deluged him with applications: one to be Secretary of the Treasury, another to be United States marshal for Kentucky, and another for "any little place in the post office." The applications of one intemperate Republican editor began hopefully with a request for a territorial governorship, gradually descended to pleas to be appointed a port collector or postmaster, and ended finally, as Madison often retold the story with great relish, with a request for castoff clothing! Madison turned these pleas aside as the administration pondered its dilemma: for twelve years the Federalists had filled offices with their partisans; Jefferson and Madison believed earnestly in a merit system, so they had no thought of turning out all Federalists; but how could the imbalance be redressed and the public protected from the highhandedness of some federal officials? Since, as Jefferson was to observe ruefully in July, "Vacancies . . . by death are few, by resignation, none," how was the public service to receive its needed Republican infusion? The President sought to conciliate moderate Federalists, and at the same time, encourage and reward deserving Republicans. After consulting with Madison and Gallatin, he decided on three grounds of removal he hoped would gradually adjust the balance: first, all appointments made by Adams after he knew of his defeat, except those protected by the Constitution, would be "considered as nullities"; second, "officers who have been guilty of *official* mal-conduct are proper subjects of removal"; and third, United States marshals and attorneys, "being doors of entrance into the courts," and therefore vital in protecting the rights of the people, might have to be changed in some cases "from zealous Federalists to mild Republicans." Nonetheless, Jefferson warned his partisans, ". . . good men, to whom there is no objection but a difference of political principle . . . are not proper subjects of removal."[8]

By midsummer, confronted with intense pressure from insistent, sometimes beleaguered Republicans, especially in New England, the leaders in Washington retreated to a more subtle political view of the patronage problem. A letter from twenty-four prominent Connecticut Republicans had set their case before the President: "The season has now arrived, when it is necessary for us to organize, and to adopt measures for Conveying to our people just sentiments respecting the motives, Measures and objects of the present administration. . . . The operating republicans here are few: they need every aid in advancing the cause—the Federal leaders are numerous, they have the influence of the Clergy, of federal papers, State offices, and federal officers. Without the aid of these last, the republicans cannot encounter the others." A remonstrance from some New Haven merchants protesting the removal of a Federalist port collector spurred Jefferson and his cabinet to frame a public reply pointing out that "nearly the whole offices of the U.S. were monopolized by [Federalists]," and hinting at "prompter correctives" than mere attrition would secure. After that, the nation could "return with joy to that state of things, when the only questions concerning a candidate shall be, is he honest? Is he capable? Is he faithful to the Constitution?" Contrary to the intentions of the cabinet, the effect of this letter was to encourage hungry Republicans to expect patronage benefits as a result of the "prompter correctives."[9]

Ignoring these expectations, Gallatin drafted a circular letter to Treasury Department officers, insisting that they and their appointees stay out of politics and that the "door of office be no longer shut against any man merely on account of his political opinions." In sending the draft to Jefferson, Gallatin observed further that "talent and integrity are to be the only qualifications for office," and that "an electioneering collector is commonly a bad officer as related to his official duties." Jefferson replied that "Mr. Madison happened to be with me when I opened your circular," and that, "restrained by some particular considerations," he and Madison thought Gallatin should withhold the circular until the "equilibrium" forecast in the New Haven letter had been achieved. Regretfully Gallatin desisted, and apparently never did send the circular, because three years later, responding to a suggestion from Jefferson that federal officers be ordered not to meddle in elections, Gallatin observed smugly that he had always favored such a policy but had set it aside because ". . . you, as well as Mr. Madison, thought [it] premature."[10]

Though we do not know what Jefferson and Madison said to each other in discussing patronage, one suspects Madison brought up the "particular considerations" making adoption of the ideal system "premature." Before the summer was over, he helped withhold a lucrative appointment from a lieutenant of Aaron Burr's, largely because the Virginians increasingly distrusted Burr and were unwilling to strengthen his hold on New York politics by favoring his friends. To their great distress, the Jeffersonians discovered they faced political pressures and tempests that were to prove less rather than more resistible as years went by. Thus, though unable to eliminate political patronage, the Republican administration in Washington did adhere to the merit system sufficiently to cause howls, and ultimately serious defections among its followers. In dismissing probably less than 10 per cent of the federal officeholders for purely political reasons, Jefferson and Madison discovered their task was not simply to put republican theory in practice, but rather to be as faithful as possible to it amid the give and take of politics.[11]

As Madison looked to Europe in assuming his direction of foreign affairs, relative calm prevailed. The omnipotent arbiter of American destiny in world politics, the great war between France and Great Britain, had slackened and was moving steadily toward the peace of Amiens, agreed to in September 1801. The recent convention with France and the amicable relations with England, skillfully cultivated in London by Federalist Minister Rufus King, raised hopes that the United States might at last have peace. With no thought of recalling so able an envoy, Madison instructed King to ease British fears that the new American government would be as hostile as the Republican press. He was to convey "the sincere desire of the United States . . . to see every obstacle removed to that entire confidence and harmony and good will between the two countries, which can be firmly established on no other foundations than those of reciprocal justice and respect." Madison expressed his "very great and sincere pleasure" at the progress made in King's negotiations and the "disposition to cultivate good will and liberal intercourse" shown by Britain, but he warned sternly against continued spoliations and impressments by arrogant officers of the Royal Navy, and hinted broadly of American action "more remedial" than her previous responses. Though the immediate scene called for no diplomatic manifestoes, Madison made it clear that he and Jefferson intended to adhere to the Republican doctrine, propounded by Madison for more than twenty years, of peace through equitable, reciprocal relations with all nations.[12]

Before leaving the stifling heat of his Washington office, Madison talked agreeably with both the French and British chargés, and found them reasonable men, each anxious to cultivate the good will of the new administration. At an early cabinet meeting it was agreed to pay the tribute owed the Dey of Algiers, but at the same time, four American warships were dispatched to protect commerce in the Mediterranean, and Great Britain agreed to let American vessels operating against the pirates use her ports. The Barbary wars were in the offing.

The most pressing issues, though, arose from the great slave revolt in Santo Domingo that had given control of the former French colony to the Negro General Toussaint L'Ouverture. The United States and

Britain had agreed with Toussaint on trade relations, but French concern that Santo Domingo not be recognized as an independent country and American reluctance to encourage slave revolts created delicate problems. Tobias Lear was sent to Santo Domingo with vague credentials, and instructions to preserve American neutrality and to protect American commerce. Madison followed John Adams' basic policy that American concern was first to prevent the island from falling into British hands, and thus behind the wall of Britain's navigation system, but at the same time, to hint to France that the island should not be viewed as a base for reviving French imperial interests in North America. Madison spoke evasively to French Chargé Louis Pichon, and then raised the really vital question: did French designs on Santo Domingo have any relation to the rumor, accepted as true by Madison, that in a secret treaty Spain had retroceded Louisiana to France? Such designs would place France and the United States in a confrontation that would necessarily throw the United States into alliance with Great Britain. Madison used this unwelcome prospect as a threat to temper French ambitions in the Caribbean. Though in 1801 the matter was temporarily in abeyance, Madison knew perfectly well that then and foreseeably, as had been the case since his first concern with foreign affairs in 1780, the vital interest of the United States was free access to the Mississippi. As long as a weak Spain controlled New Orleans, the United States could feel confident, but if arrogant, aggressive Great Britain, or imperial France under Napoleon, gained control, then the United States would face a grave threat to her national survival, and equally dangerous, would become dependent on the great power *not* athwart her life line in the West. "The day that France takes possession of New Orleans," Jefferson later wrote, dramatizing, with characteristic hyperbole, propositions already outlined by Madison, "we must marry ourselves to the British fleet and nation."[13]

The heat and hard work of the Washington summer were too much for Madison's delicate health. Jefferson wrote on July 11 that "Madison has had a slight bilious attack." He advised the Secretary of State to "get off by the middle of this month," but added that "we who have stronger constitutions shall stay to the end of it." Madison's collapse strengthened the determination of the Virginians to spend at least August and September of each year in the Piedmont, whatever the press of public duties. When Gallatin, who was usually the senior official in Washington during the summer, wrote of complaints about the long absences of the President and the Secretary of State, Jefferson expressed sentiments in which Madison wholly concurred: "I consider it as a trying experience for a person from the mountains to pass the two bilious months on the tidewater. I have not done it these forty years, and nothing should induce me to do it. . . . Grumble who will, I will never pass those months on tide-water." In Virginia from late July until mid-October, the Madisons relaxed to revive their strength, settled further details of the estate of James Madison, Sr., and exchanged the usual visits with the Monticello family. By the time Madison returned to the capital, his health was restored and he accepted a full share of the burdens of the new administration.[14]

In the fall of 1801, with peace restored in Europe, Madison turned to the tempest still raging in Santo Domingo and its immense significance for the future of North America. He instructed Tobias Lear to help the island obtain its vital food supplies from the United States, but at the same time, to avoid formal recognition of Toussaint's regime. Letters to American ministers in Europe worrying about Bonaparte's intentions now that he had peace in Europe brought responses during the winter of 1801–2 that treaties had acknowledged the retrocession of Louisiana. Furthermore, a huge French army commanded by Napoleon's brother-in-law, General Leclerc, descended on Santo Domingo, obviously the first step toward French occupation and exploitation of Louisiana. Napoleon had tried to conquer Egypt, and was already master of half of Europe; peace with the British navy now gave him his chance at North America. Though the United States was alarmed by these imperial intentions, friendship with France, suspicions of Great Britain, distrust of black rebels, the need to be neutral, and a desire for profit led the administration to send supplies to Leclerc's initially successful armies. When Leclerc responded to the high prices of monopolizing American merchants by requisitioning their stores and forcing inflated currency on them, American opinion turned against the highhanded general. Not even shrewd French attempts to play on American fears of slave insurrection helped. Lear returned to the United States in May 1802, expelled for his attempts to aid plundered American merchants and sea captains. Madison listened to his sad tales and upbraided French Chargé Pichon: didn't Leclerc's outrages undercut all the professions of Franco-American friendship, and prove that "Bonaparte is the proper successor to the cashiered dynasty"? Pichon agreed and protested Leclerc's actions to Paris, but the general's angry accusations that Pichon was a tool of the Americans buried the sober observations of the unfortunate chargé.[15]

Madison's stance was deliberately evasive: as matters stood, no visible resolution in Santo Domingo seemed propitious for the United States. French defeat would encourage British intrigue or create a "Caribbean Algiers," while her triumph would whet Napoleon's appetite. Indeed, in response to the first news of Leclerc's victories, the First Consul decreed the re-establishment of slavery in the French West Indies and ordered another armada destined for Louisiana to gather in Dutch ports. The triumph in Santo Domingo was short-lived, however. The Negro forces fought tenaciously and tellingly on their home ground, and yellow fever swept through Leclerc's army. By mid-September he wrote that of his original army of 28,000 men, only 4,000 remained fit for service; to subdue the island would require another army as large as the one he had lost. Leclerc himself succumbed on November 1, 1802.[16]

Amid the startling news from the Caribbean and the wild rumors of Napoleon's machinations that reached Washington during the "peaceful" year 1802, concern turned to alarm at the prospect of having a strong, aggressive France as a Western neighbor. Furthermore, Madison told Pichon, French secrecy about the retrocession raised disquieting suspicions. Did Napoleon suppose he could separate the Western states from the Union and attach them to a French empire in the Mississippi valley? Perhaps protesting too much, Madison insisted this would never happen. Rather, he asserted, "France cannot long preserve Louisiana against the United States," because France's presence there would cause the American states to draw together, and would as well unite them with Great Britain. In ten years the two nations would have the power to divide all the French and/or Spanish possessions in North America between them, or if they wished, to monopolize their trade. Madison painted a gloomy picture of French prospects. A long Franco-American border along the Gulf Coast would cause frictions bound to strengthen Anglo-American ties. The astounding rate of American influx into the Mississippi valley— Kentucky had grown from 60,000 to 250,000 people in fifteen years— would soon settle all questions of authority there, and renewal of the war in Europe would leave French possessions in the New World at the mercy of restive slaves, expansive pioneers, American food producers, and the British navy. Thus Madison argued "with much coolness, much method," Pichon reported to Talleyrand. The chargé also advised accepting Madison's advice to France: "To be resigned to [the Americans'] future power, to conciliate them and acquire the merit, useful in other respects, of acceding to that which the force of events will give them in spite of us." Madison had made the French envoy himself the proponent of the message he intended for the ears of Talleyrand and Bonaparte.[17]

While French and American leaders acted as though the destiny of the empire on the Gulf of Mexico was theirs to settle, Spain in fact retained possession of the Floridas as well as of New Orleans and Louisiana. Napoleon sought to entice Spain to cede the Floridas to him. American diplomats, including Madison, assumed he would succeed. Spain, however, delayed and delayed again turning over her Mississippi valley possessions to France. Robert R. Livingston, the new American minister in Paris, and for twenty years Madison's colleague in seeking to strengthen Franco-American ties, was in the odd position of seeking an understanding with France about one province (Louisiana) she refused to acknowledge she possessed, and another (Florida) she had not yet gained. For a year, therefore, he suffered Talleyrand's evasions and smug silence. Since the immediate need of the American West was free use of the rivers draining through the Floridas as well as the Mississippi, American diplomacy moved increasingly to seek cession, for appropriate compensation, of the Floridas and of New Orleans. Little attention was given to the vast lands west of the Mississippi, title to which was regarded as uncertain, and which Madison was sure in the long run would be settled by American pioneers. Thus through most of 1802, Washington, Paris, and Madrid seethed with rumors, threats, evasions, and innuendoes about the North American empire the abatement of war in Europe had thrust into the foreground. On the sidelines, London watched complacently as her potential enemies quarreled. British ministers knew that resumption of the war, never far from anyone's mind, would again subject all pretensions to the authority of the Royal Navy.

Amid these crosscurrents Madison was startled in November 1802 by news that the Spanish intendant at New Orleans had closed the port to American commerce. The closure, violating the Spanish-American treaty of 1795, seemed especially ominous, coming just as Spain agreed to give France possession of New Orleans. Would the French then claim that they would not grant the United States privileges Spain had denied them? The Spanish minister in Washington saw the folly of the closure, assured Madison it was an unauthorized act by the intendant, and sent a protest to New Orleans by special messenger. Madison wrote angrily to American Minister Charles Pinckney in Madrid: should the intendant "prove as obstinate as he has been ignorant or wicked," the residents of the West would demand "the most ample redress. . . . The Mississippi is to them everything. It is the Hudson, the Delaware, the Potomac and all the navigable rivers of the Atlantic States formed into one stream." Believing that Napoleon's hostile designs lay behind the edict, Madison wrote even more pointedly for Livingston's guidance:

> The holders, whoever they may be, of the mouth of the Mississippi [must know that] justice, ample justice, to the Western citizens of the United States is the only tenure of peace with this country. There are now or in less than two years will be not less than 200,000 militia on the waters of the Mississippi, every man of whom would march at a moment's warning to remove obstructions from that outlet to the sea, every man of whom regards the free use of that river as a natural and indefeasible right, and is conscious of the physical force that can at any time give effect to it. This consideration ought not to be overlooked by France and would be alone sufficient if allowed its due weight to cure the frenzy which covets Louisiana.[18]

As denunciations of the Spanish act and of French designs swelled throughout the country, the administration decided to send James Monroe as special envoy to France, authorized, with Livingston's assistance, to purchase New Orleans, and if France had indeed acquired the Floridas, to buy them as well. This, plus the protests to New Orleans and Madrid, placated the West, and made more clear than ever the administration's conviction that possession of the mouth of the Mississippi had become an American *sine qua non*. Again, the administration denied explicitly any interest in land west of the Mississippi. Madison wrote long instructions for his ministers and outlined elaborate draft treaties to suit a variety of circumstances they might confront, all holding in the long run that cession of New Orleans to the United States for a fair price was the only rational, just solution.[19]

Madison's cogent arguments and Livingston's assiduous work in Paris, however, were of little use unless the master of France abandoned his plans for a North American empire. Events during the winter and spring of 1803 conspired to that end. News of the French disaster in Santo Domingo reached Paris. The armada destined for Santo Domingo and Louisiana lay icebound in Dutch harbors. The King of Spain refused to cede the Floridas to France. American and British diplomats, in London and in Washington, asserted more and more openly that French designs on the shores of the Gulf of Mexico, if not abandoned, would be grounds for an Anglo-American alliance. Britain even hinted that she might occupy New Orleans. Finally, Napoleon had tired of peace, and confronted with British resistance to his ceaseless encroachments and deceits, he moved toward a war, which broke out in May 1803. Although as late as February 1803 Napoleon still talked of sending vast armaments to North America, the drain Santo Domingo imposed on his resources, the geopolitical disadvantages of possessing New Orleans, and his preoccupation with the impending war in Europe, had in fact put him in a disposition most useful to the United States. Happily, the Americans most intimately concerned, Jefferson, Madison, Livingston, and Monroe, were ready to take advantage of Bonaparte's change of mind.[20]

On April 11, 1803, the day after Monroe arrived in Paris, Talleyrand summoned Livingston to his headquarters. Would the United States like to buy *all* of Louisiana? he asked. The day before, Napoleon had declared the colony "entirely lost" and ordered his ministers to get what they could for it. Livingston was dumbfounded. Adhering to his instructions he said, no, the United States wished only New Orleans and the Floridas. Without indicating Napoleon had already made his decision, Talleyrand hinted the price would be high and asked Livingston to discuss the matter with Monroe. Two days later Barbé-Marbois, Madison's old friend and antagonist in Philadelphia during the seventeen-eighties, made more definite overtures. Livingston and Monroe gradually realized the fabulous prize was almost within their grasp. After a midnight talk with Barbé-Marbois, Livingston sat down at three in the morning to write Madison: "The field open to us is infinitely larger than our instructions contemplate. . . . We shall do all we can to cheapen the purchase but my present sentiment is that we shall buy." During the two weeks the negotiators haggled over price, the Americans were disadvantaged by broad hints that unless they agreed quickly to the French terms, Napoleon might withdraw the offer. Finally on April 29, 1803, they agreed that for $15 million the United States should acquire possession of the entire province of Louisiana from the Gulf of Mexico to the Minnesota forests and from the Mississippi to the Rockies.[21]

When news of the purchase reached Washington in July, Madison wrote the envoys of Jefferson's "entire approbation," and added, to Monroe, that the purchase was "a truly noble acquisition." It would prevent the evils of foreign entanglement and of a domestic military establishment, and "favor liberty" by opening a vast tract for settlement. In congratulating a Western supporter on the purchase, Jefferson pointed out that the future inhabitants of the Mississippi valley "will be our sons," and that when the country east of the Mississippi should be settled, "we may lay off a range of states on the western bank from the head to the mouth, and so, range after range, advancing compactly as we multiply." To the Republican leaders, startled as they were by the timing of the Louisiana Purchase, the acquisition was not, in their long-range expectations, either surprising or unwelcome, but rather was a wonderfully fitting extension of the "Empire of Liberty." By diminishing the prospects of war and foreign dependence, and by more than doubling the land area open for eventual settlement by yeoman farmers, the Louisiana Purchase perfectly suited Republican political and social theory.[22]

Having acquired Lousiana, the administration had to decide how to explore and define its limits, take possession, pay for it, and provide for its incorporation into the United States according to a Republican view of the Constitution. An expedition, to be led by Meriwether Lewis, up the Missouri River and across the continental divide to the Pacific had been planned the previous winter to explore unknown territory; now it could become a survey of the vast new purchase. Though there were doubts for a time about Spain's willingness to relinquish New Orleans to France or to the United States, though Gallatin and others grumbled about the stiff terms of payment, and though some Congressmen opposed the purchase as an unwise and unmanageable extension of the Union, these proved passing difficulties, and by December 20, 1803, the double change of sovereignty from Spain to France to the United States was complete. The American flag at last flew over New Orleans.

Throughout 1803 the Republicans had been troubled by the conflict between a strict interpretation of the Constitution and the power of the executive, or even of Congress, to acquire new territory. There was no express power to do so, nor was it *necessary* to the fulfillment of a delegated power, so, according to solemn pronouncements by both Jefferson and Madison during the seventeen-nineties, the power did not exist within the Constitution. In contemplating the acquisition of New Orleans and the Floridas, Jefferson had asked the cabinet for opinions on the constitutionality of such an act. Madison agreed with Gallatin that "the existence of the United States as a nation presupposes the power enjoyed by every nation of extending their territory by treaties," and that the President and Senate could conduct such treaties, as the Constitution provided. If the Constitution had intended to prohibit such a universal right, Gallatin added, it was "a provision sufficiently important and singular to have deserved to be expressly enacted." Jefferson admitted the force of this, but remembering the dangerous use the Federalists had made of enlarged executive powers, he added nonetheless that "it will be safer not to permit the enlargement of the Union but by amendment of the Constitution." He stuck to this position through the summer as he waited for Congress to assemble in special session to ratify the purchase, but alarms that France might change her mind before the slow amendment process could be completed showed Jefferson that *his* course was dangerous and unsafe. He would, he said, in a letter written while Madison was with him at Monticello, "acquiesce with satisfaction" in the mere legislative ratification his friends thought fully legal, and necessary, to gain Louisiana. The Senate then quickly ratified the treaty; Congress enacted enabling legislation; and Jefferson forgot his qualms in the joy of acquiring so vast a territory.[23]

The importance of the Louisiana Purchase, the most significant event of Jefferson's presidency, has led to two persisting questions regarding it: to whom should credit go for the accomplishment? and doesn't Jefferson's "surrender" to broad construction show that the Federalists rather than the Republicans had the only workable interpretation of the Constitution? Madison himself answered the first question in declaring officially to Livingston and Monroe, who had quarreled over credit for the purchase, that they each deserved a just portion of merit, but that "the state of things" which led Napoleon to abandon his designs on North America was mainly responsible. Jefferson added that though his administration made no pretense of having *caused* the crucial events in Europe, especially the renewal of the war, "We said with energy what would take place when it should arise [and] we availed ourselves of it when it happened." Following Madison's initiative, the administration had from its inception, in writing and in conversation, impressed upon all the European powers, but especially on France, that the United States had special, irresistible interests in the Mississippi valley, which it was to the advantage of all nations to recognize. This insistence, coupled with a patient, skillful diplomacy of acquisition by purchase rather than conquest, and a shrewd realism about the character of European power politics, were the vital ingredients. At his desk in the State Department and in the drawing rooms of Washington, Madison proved himself an able secretary and advocate in bringing off the historic purchase.[24]

On the constitutional question, Madison never really doubted the power of the United States to add to its territory by treaty, but in deference to Jefferson, after he and Gallatin had expressed their views in January 1803, he was generally silent or vague. He saw the point of Jefferson's effort at consistency, and if an amendment would please important segments of the party and strengthen public acceptance of the purchase, Madison was perfectly willing to seek an amendment. When Senator John Quincy Adams asked him if the administration intended to submit an amendment, Madison admitted that the Constitution didn't cover the case of the Louisiana Purchase, but that it was necessary to remember "the magnitude of the object," and to trust "the candor of the country" to approve the deed. In effect, Madison joined Jefferson (perhaps led him) in insisting that the circumstances surrounding particular acts must guide the degree to which strict construction was carried. This, of course, made the doctrine not abstract and legalistic, but rather calculating and politically attuned. Thus a sedition act, passed by a Federalist administration bent on creating war hysteria and silencing its political foes, could not be afforded the same stretched construction of the Constitution as could a treaty, passed by cautious Republicans, that vastly extended the domain of the United States at a trifling cost. Jefferson's scruples over the Louisiana Purchase, and his ultimate compromise of them under the pressure of events and the advice of his trusted colleagues, prove *not* that he was unprincipled and that the Republicans had no more constitutional purity than their opponents, but rather that the Republicans were not blind doctrinaires. They remained cautious about broad construction and desisted on principle from countless acts of aggrandizement about which the Federalists would have had no qualms, while at the same time they recognized that the Constitution was not a strait jacket, but rather was an instrument for *governing* a *nation*. One suspects that in their discussions at Monticello in September 1803, Jefferson and Madison covered these points, and that more than once the secretary brought the President around to his more flexible view.[25]

Madison closed his letter congratulating Livingston and Monroe on the Louisiana Purchase by asking them what understanding "prevailed in the negotiation with respect to the Boundaries of Louisiana," particularly the eastern border along the Gulf of Mexico, which would determine control of the great rivers between New Orleans and Pensacola. Before 1763, when France owned Louisiana, its boundary was the Perdido River, 150 miles east of New Orleans, but between then and the retrocession of 1800, whether under Spanish or English rule, Louisiana had included only the island of New Orleans east of the Mississippi. The Gulf Coast settlements of Mobile, Pascagoula, and Biloxi had been considered part of a province called West Florida. In the retrocession, France had sought to restore the old Perdido River boundary for Louisiana, but negotiations were incomplete when the transfer was made to the United States.

Madison took a characteristically "carrot and stick" approach in seeking a favorable settlement. The United States still sought full possession of the Floridas, especially West Florida (between New Orleans and the Apalachicola River), and she offered again to purchase the provinces from Spain. Should Spain prove reluctant, however, Madison urged his minister in Madrid to point out her weak position: Florida in the hands of Spain "must ever be a dead expense in time of war, and at all times a source of irritation and ill blood with the United States." Amicable relations between the two countries could only come when "the manifest indications of nature" replaced "the artificial and inconvenient state of things now existing"—that is, when the American hinterland had free access to the sea. Unless Spain ceded Florida to the United States, Britain would soon conquer it and use it in her own negotiations with the United States. In any case, Spain would lose out. Furthermore, Madison added, "we are the less disposed to make sacrifices to obtain the Floridas, because their position and the manifest course of events guarantee an early and reasonable acquisition of them." Spain would be well advised, Madison concluded, to follow the prudent example of France in removing sources of conflict with the United States. "What is it Spain dreads?" Madison asked. "She dreads . . . the growing power of this country, and the direction of it against her possessions within its reach. Can she annihilate this power? No. Can she sensibly retard its growth? No." Therefore she should agree to sell the Floridas, lest by truculence and "obnoxious precautions" she bring upon herself "prematurely the whole weight of the Calamity which she fears."[26]

Protected by good relations with France and Britain, Madison adopted a firm, even arrogant attitude toward the weak and declining giant of the new world. He never doubted that all of Florida would some day be part of the United States, and he never doubted that despotic, corrupt Spain was unfit to possess it. This was manifest destiny. As long as he was in public office, Madison maintained a steady, sometimes aggressive pressure on Florida. He insisted on the dubious claim that Louisiana extended to the Perdido River, and when Spain refused to negotiate, Madison used the claim to support American authority in Mobile and elsewhere along the coast. In fact, France and Britain were for reasons of their own less hostile to Spanish pretensions in Florida than Madison supposed, and Spain had a deeper interest in the province than Madison seemed capable

of recognizing, so the negotiations dragged on for years. Madison sought
to be patient and in some instances he resisted the depredations of American adventurers along the Gulf Coast, but there was no doubt that officially and unofficially he moved inexorably toward American possession
of first West Florida and then East Florida.[27]

Though war between France and Great Britain resumed in May 1803,
it seemed at first that the United States might avoid the dangers and
insults it had faced during the war of the seventeen-nineties. The convention of 1800 and the Louisiana Purchase treaty had removed major points
of dispute with France, and in any case, Napoleon's continental power
offered little opportunity for conflict with the United States. During
eight useful years in London, Rufus King had soothed many of the
irritations which had rankled Anglo-American relations ever since 1783.
Furthermore, the Addington ministry of 1801 was, as Madison wrote
Monroe in 1804, "more liberal and cordial toward the United States
than any preceding one." Recent admiralty court decisions had been
favorable to neutral shipping, so only impressment remained as a looming
issue.[28]

     With some optimism, therefore, Madison sent a draft of a proposed
Anglo-American convention to James Monroe, who had been transferred from Paris to London upon King's retirement in the summer of
1803. The snag remained the claimed right of officers of the Royal Navy
to board American ships on the high seas, and even in American harbors,
to examine their crews, ostensibly to find deserters from British ships,
and then, with no recourse for the American vessel standing under
British guns, to remove any seamen they claimed were British subjects.
This humiliation to the American flag was bad enough even if the British
officers removed only British sailors, but, as Madison put it to Monroe,
"the similarity of language and of features between American citizens
and British subjects are such as not easily to be distinguished," so Americans were often summarily removed and impressed into service under
the harsh and dreaded discipline of the Royal Navy. On the other hand,
acquisition of American citizenship was so casual, and service on American ships was so much easier and more profitable than on British naval
vessels, desertions were sometimes wholesale, and would have unmanned
the fleet if not opposed resolutely. No British ministry that gave up the
power of impressment could last a day. Thus Monroe met only evasions
and coolness from the Foreign Office, and as the weak Addington ministry gave way to Pitt ministries determined to prosecute the war more
vigorously, the matter seemed bound to deteriorate.[29]

     As Madison, then, finished his first term in the State Department,
troubles and difficulties crowded out triumphs. In June 1804 an arrogant
Royal Navy captain impressed some seamen off an American vessel in

New York harbor. In an angry exchange with Madison, the British Minister defended the captain and demanded that American officials act themselves to prevent desertions from British ships in American harbors. Madison learned at the same time that Talleyrand had scoffed at American claims to the Perdido River boundary to Louisiana. This increased the already shrill Spanish protests at the so-called Mobile Bay Act, passed in February 1804, which seemed to place that area under American civil jurisdiction. For the moment, neither London, Paris, nor Madrid was much impressed with American diplomacy. Only from the Barbary coast, where American naval vessels won spectacular victories over the Tripolitanians, did good news come to Madison's desk. He and Jefferson took pleasure in the abolition of the ancient patterns of bribery and tribute, and in the heroic deeds of Preble, Decatur, and Rodgers, but even there, quarrels among American prima donnas left many tangles for the Secretary of State to unsnarl.[30]

By the time of Jefferson's second inauguration, Madison's "style" as Secretary of State had become clear. He and the President agreed on a "republican theory of foreign affairs": their conception of American "national purpose"—the growth of a peaceful, prosperous society resting on the virtue and industry of its yeomanry and guaranteeing maximum personal liberty—required the nation to shun the military adventures that led inexorably to the tyranny of a Caesar or a Cromwell, to avoid entanglements in foreign wars, to seek reciprocal trade agreements and the free flow of goods, to use the power of its prosperous commerce to resist foreign depredations, and to wait for the stupendous growth of American wealth and population to make the nation impregnable to its enemies. Thus Madison and Jefferson sought to purchase Louisiana and the Floridas, resisted impressment, rejected the tribute system of the Barbary pirates, and upheld neutral rights as foreign policies implicit in their understanding of republican government.

To implement policy, however, Madison had to try to play the great nations off against each other, and to make the best use he could of such elements of American power as tough pioneers in the Mississippi valley, daring naval officers in the Mediterranean, and commercial retaliation in Europe. Madison's fault in this game was not timidity, inexperience, or naïveté, but rather an inclination to overplay his hand. In warning Napoleon of the dangers of empire building in the Mississippi valley, for example, Madison was doubtless lucky the First Consul's attention turned elsewhere, thus rescuing the Republicans from the considerable task of opening the Mississippi River against the power of a few of General Victor's regiments entrenched at New Orleans. Similarly, as Madison found out in his highhanded West Florida policy, when France and Britain favored Spain, American threats rang hollow and very nearly entangled the new nation in exactly the kind of adventure the Republicans castigated when undertaken by other nations—or other parties in their own nation. Though in appearance diffident and reserved, in diplomacy Madison often spoke louder than the weight of his nation could sustain in a world dominated by Nelson's fleet and Napoleon's army.

Madison's diplomatic instructions were analytical and tough-minded, time and time again furnishing his ministers abroad with exactly the facts and arguments they needed to best set forth the American position. American diplomacy was more often thwarted by force and will than by right and reason. In conversations with foreign envoys to the United States Madison was blunt or reserved according to his own need. In response to French greed in the West and British naval arrogance in the Atlantic, for example, Madison called the respective chargés on the carpet and issued stern rebukes that enough impressed them to elicit letters home urging exactly the policy Madison asked for. At the height of the Santo Domingo crisis, on the other hand, when any clear statement of American policy would have been embarrassing, the French envoy explained in despair to Jefferson that "from the equivocal and reserved language of Mr. Madison, I did not know" whether or not the United States supported France. All in all, Madison's handling of the secretary-ship caused Jefferson to say in old age that he would never have accepted the responsibilities of the presidency if he had not been assured of Madison's help in performing them.[31]

Except for the drama of the Louisiana Purchase, however, personalities and the social scene were often as interesting and important as diplomacy and other official business. The President went to Monticello twice each year, usually for a month in the spring (April preferably) and again for August and September. The Madisons went to Montpelier for the late summer, but apparently not so regularly in the spring. While in Virginia, Jefferson and Madison visited each other and entertained a stream of guests from Washington and elsewhere. At Montpelier the only recorded out-of-state guest in 1801 was uninvited, Aaron Burr's lieutenant, Matthew L. Davis, seeking a political appointment. When Davis stopped in Washington, Gallatin hinted broadly at the rudeness of going to Montpelier and Monticello, but Davis "was not easily diverted from his purpose," the secretary complained. "To want of early education and mixing with the world I ascribe his want of sense of propriety on this occasion, and his going is the worst thing I have known of him," Gallatin added. At Montpelier Davis found Madison as cool as Gallatin toward his zealous job hunting. By the time Davis got to Monticello, he was a bit shaken. He enjoyed Jefferson's hospitality, but did not "open" about his intentions after the President made it clear he would not settle patronage questions until he returned to Washington.[32]

The next summer more welcome guests were the Madison's Washington neighbors, Dr. William Thornton (in Madison's department as director of the patent office), his French wife Anne Marie, and her mother. Mrs. Thornton recorded in her diary that Montpelier was "in a wild and romantic country, very generally covered with fine flourishing timber. . . . The House [was] plain but grand . . . rendered more pleasing by displaying a taste for the arts which is rarely to be found in such retired and remote situations. . . . The House is on a height commanding an extensive view of the blue ridge, which by constant variation in the appearance of the clouds, and consequently of the mountains, form a very agreeable and varied object, sometimes appearing very distant, sometimes much separated and distinct and often like rolling waves." After two weeks of viewing this scene from the front porch, the Madisons and Thorntons greeted more Madisons, Bishop James and his son, and the entire company rode off for a week to Monticello, which as always was torn up with rebuilding. There another Thornton arrived, British Chargé Edward, and Jefferson showed everyone his marvelous library and collection of fine prints. The Madisons enjoyed the daily routine at Monticello when, as was usual, company crowded all the rooms:

> The family breakfast hour was at eight. After breakfast Mrs. Randolph [Jefferson's daughter] and her amiable daughters as well as the other female relations of the house set about cleaning the tea things and washing the alabaster lamp. . . . After this operation the President retired to his books, his daughter to give lessons to the children, . . . and the guests were left to amuse themselves as they pleased til four o'clock, walking, riding or shooting. . . . At four dinner was served up and in the evening we walked on a wooden terrace or strolled into the wood. Mr. Jefferson played with his grandchildren til dusk when tea was brought in, and afterward wine and fruit of which the peaches were excellent. At nine o'clock our host withdrew and everybody else as they pleased.

Madison probably went with the President to the library ("not thrown open to guests . . . disposed to be indiscreet"), to talk informally and make important decisions.[33]

The British diplomat who described this routine at Monticello, Sir Augustus John Foster, had stopped at Montpelier on the way. "The Secretary of State," Foster commented, "was a man of good family and had a considerable estate. . . . No man had a higher reputation among his acquaintances for probity and good honorable feeling, while he was allowed on all sides to be a gentleman in his manners as well as a man of public virtue." Foster enjoyed the "very fine woods about Montpelier," but regretted that there were "no pleasure grounds"—that is, formal gardens such as surrounded great estates in Europe. The heat in Virginia, Foster supposed, caused ladies to prefer "a high situation from which they can enjoy an extensive prospect [to] venturing out of their houses to walk or to enjoy beautiful scenery." He regretted, too, that he had not brought his fowling piece to hunt the wild turkeys that were "in great numbers in the woods." Madison, Foster noted with surprise, had no guns to lend his guests. Most interesting to the Englishman, though, were the slaves, of whom there were well over one hundred at Montpelier at this time. Madison told him that the annual expense for supporting a Negro was $25 or $30, and that only about half of them were "fit for service at any given time."

> The Negro habitations [Foster wrote] are separate from the dwelling house both here and all over Virginia, and they form a kind of village. . . . When at a distance from any town it is necessary [the slaves] should be able to do all kind of handiwork; and, accordingly, at Montpelier I found a forge, a turner's shop, a carpenter, and wheelwright. All articles that were wanted for farming or the use of the house were made on the spot, and I saw a very well constructed waggon that had just been completed. . . . The Negro women . . . preferred by a great deal working in the fields to spinning and sewing. They appeared to me to be a happy thoughtless race of people when under a kind master as was the Secretary of State.

Though Montpelier's situation and view were beautiful, the grounds and countryside, at least by European standards, were surprisingly wild, even unkempt. Madison's Virginia plantation was a working farm, not a country estate; less than one hundred years old, it still exhibited the disorder of growth, abounding in the smells, dirt, and bustle of agriculture. Probably remembering tough conversations with Madison in Washington, Foster found his host rather too much "a disputatious pleader," but "better informed" than Jefferson, "and, moreover, a social, jovial and good-humored companion full of anecdote, and sometimes matter of a loose description relating to old times, but oftener of a political and historical interest. . . . [He] was a little man, with small features rather wizened when I saw him, but occasionally lit up with a good-natured smile." Mrs. Madison, on the other hand, was "a very handsome woman and tho' an uncultivated mind and fond of gossiping, was so perfectly good-tempered and good-humored that she rendered her husband's house as far as depended on her agreeable to all parties."[34]

Less settled in its routine than the hospitality of the Virginia country-side, however, was the burgeoning social life of the new capital. When Jefferson opened his house for large receptions on New Year's and the Fourth of July, and on many other occasions, Dolley Madison and Anna Payne served as hostesses for the widower President. He wrote once, apparently in a last-minute jam, "Thomas Jefferson begs that either Mrs. Madison or Miss Payne will be so good as to dine with him today, to take care of female friends expected." So many Congressmen brought their daughters and other female relatives to Washington for the social season that one time representative Samuel L. Mitchell of New York had "to escort several of the fair creatures in succession to their carriages." The Madisons' good friend Margaret Bayard Smith wrote the day after Christmas 1802 that in the past two weeks she had dined twice at the President's, three times at French Chargé Pichon's, four times at the home of Navy Yard commandant Thomas Tingey, and once at General John Mason's (perhaps at his island home in the Potomac), and that twice the Pichons had dined with the Smiths. In addition, Mrs. Smith had "drank tea out three or four times and declined several invitations to balls." Six months later, during a rage of playing loo, her husband reported winning $2 from Dolley Madison and another lady. Loo, a card game, was "an innocent diversion," said Sir Augustus Foster, "of the ladies who, when they were looed, pronounced the word in a very mincing manner." In the game a player was "looed" when he had supposed his hand was good enough to win, but then discovered it was not. At a dinner party at Secretary of War Henry Dearborn's that same spring, Smith spent some highly agreeable hours: "After a few bottles of champagne were emptied, on the observation of Mr. Madison that it was the most delightful wine when drank in moderation, but that more than a few glasses always produced a headache the next day, [he] remarked with point that this was the very time to try the experiment, as the next day being Sunday would allow time for a recovery from its effects. . . . Bottle after bottle came in. . . . Its only effects were animated good humor and uninterrupted conversation."[35]

A few days after Smith had beaten the ladies at loo, by lucky coincidence the news of the Louisiana Purchase arrived on the eve of Independence Day. The next day, he reported, "at an early hour the city was alive—a discharge of 18 guns saluted the dawn, the military assembled, . . . at 12 company began to assemble at the President's, . . . enlivened by the presence of 40 and 50 ladies clothed in their best attire, cakes, punch, wine, etc., in profusion. . . . At dinner our toasts were politics, our songs convivial. . . . Part of the company remained, I believe, till day light."

The next winter was the most notable social season of Jefferson's administrations. Celebrations over the Louisiana Purchase continued. At one of them, given by members of Congress and attended by the heads of departments, Senator William Plumer of New Hampshire reported, "a number of guests drank so many toasts that in the night they returned to their houses without their hats." A month later the Madisons had, for a large company, "An excellent dinner. The round of Beef of which the Soup is made is called *Bouilli*: It had in the dish spices and something of the sweet herb and Garlic kind, and a rich gravy. It is very much boiled, and is still very good. We had a dish with what appeared to be Cabbage, much boiled, then cut in long strings and somewhat mashed [water or land cress]; in the middle a large Ham, with the Cabbage around. It looked like our country [New England] dishes of Bacon and Cabbage, with the Cabbage mashed up, after being boiled till sodden and turned dark. The Dessert good; much as usual, except two dishes which appeared like Apple pie, in the form of the half of a musk-melon, the flat side down, tops creased deep, and the color a dark brown." Though Foster, used to European formality, criticized the Madison table for being "more like a harvest-home supper, than the entertainment of a Secretary of State," Dolley Madison made no apology: "As profusion so repugnant to foreign customs arose from the happy circumstance of the abundance and prosperity of our country, she did not hesitate to sacrifice the delicacy of European taste, for the less elegant, but more liberal fashion of Virginia." This same informality caused Jefferson's son-in-law to find "the sweet simplicity of Mrs. Madison's conversation at an afternoon visit" a welcome respite from the "noisy disputations" that dominated most Washington gatherings.[36]

In the spring, the Madisons celebrated the wedding of Anna Payne, by this time a daughter to them, to Congressman Richard Cutts from the Maine district of Massachusetts. The wedding was "a fine affair," though the presents "were tokens of love or friendship made by the hand of the friend, elaborate embroideries from sleeves to pin cushions, paintings, and original poetry," rather than lavish, expensive gifts. The Madisons were grieved to lose the gay Anna, but her husband soon became a devoted personal and political friend, and their family of small children were always very close to the Madisons. Only the arrival in Washington of Baron von Humboldt cheered them after Anna's marriage. "We have lately had a great treat in the company of a charming Prussian Baron," Dolley Madison wrote. "All the ladies say they are in love with him, notwithstanding his want of personal charms. He is the most polite, modest, well-informed, and interesting traveller we have ever met with." Humboldt reported his pleasure not only with the ladies, but also with the conversation of the philosopher-statesmen of Washington.[37]

The most remarked-on personalities of the new capital, however, were the ministers of the great powers, who alone, in a way, could introduce to Washington the habits and customs of European diplomacy. Fully accredited ministers were slow in arriving; none were there when Madison took office in 1801. A year later the new Spanish minister, the Marquis de Casa Yrujo, arrived with his wife, the former Sally McKean, a close friend of the Madisons since their residence in Philadelphia (see Chapter XV). Madison hoped this would help cultivate agreeable relations with Spain, but Yrujo's sharp reaction to Madison's tough stand on

West Florida soon caused rancor and bitterness, and led to his recall. On one occasion Yrujo stormed into Madison's office branding the Mobile Bay Act an "atrocious libel" on Spain and an "insulting usurpation on the unquestionable rights of his sovereign." Madison indicated clearly and calmly that such "intemperance and disrespect" was unacceptable, and soon made Yrujo *persona non grata*. After the blowup, Dolley Madison wrote her sister that she "felt a tenderness" for the Yrujos "independent of circumstances." Late in 1804 General Louis-Marie Turreau arrived as French minister. He was a bald-headed, red-faced, mustachioed man whose visage, Senator Plumer said, "indicates a ferocious disposition and an obstinate fixed determination of mind." He had gained an infamous reputation for brutality and highhandedness during the wars of the French Revolution. Madison found him reasonably easy to deal with, but the ladies of Washington, who encountered him through his treatment of his wife, agreed with Senator Plumer. Dolley Madison wrote of hearing "sad things" about Turreau: "that he whips his wife, and abuses her dreadfully. I pity her sincerely; she is an amiable, sensible woman." For as long as the Turreaus remained in Washington, they furnished abundant gossip.[38]

Even more exciting than the ferocious French general, however, was the marriage of Napoleon's nineteen-year-old brother, Jerome, to the beautiful Betsy Patterson of Baltimore, daughter of a wealthy merchant, and niece of influential Senator Samuel Smith of Maryland. The marriage was altogether against Napoleon's dynastic plans and was sure to be annulled by him, Chargé Pichon said, but the prospect of family alliance with the Bonapartes was too much for the Marylanders to resist. They had such an *"inconceivable infatuation"* for the match, John Quincy Adams wrote, that "it was really the young man who was seduced." The administration was hopeful the marriage might improve Franco-American relations; the President gave a ceremonial dinner honoring the bridal pair, and Madison wrote the American minister in Paris, explaining the affair and directing him to make what use of it he could. At "a large and splendid ball" given for the Bonapartes at Uncle Robert Smith's (Secretary of the Navy), though, politics and family alliances were banished by a sight that astounded one observer: "Madame Bonaparte made a great noise here, and mobs of boys have crowded around her splendid equipage to see what I hope will not often be seen in this country, an almost naked woman. . . . No one dared look at her but by stealth; the window shutters being left open, a crowd assembled round the windows to get a look at this beautiful little creature, for everyone allows she is extremely beautiful. Her dress was the thinnest sarcenet and white crepe without the least stiffening in it, made without a single plait in the skirt; . . . there was scarcely any waist to it and no sleeves; her back, her bosom, part of her waist and her arms were uncovered and the rest of her form visible." A group of ladies agreed that they would attend no more parties with Madame Bonaparte unless she "promised to have more clothes on." The Madisons were among the wide-eyed celebrants, though judging from criticisms made of Dolley Madison for not always having a discreet handkerchief at her bosom, and from her lifelong friendship with Betsy, one suspects that they were more pleased than horrified at the remarkable display.[39]

Also at the ball was Mrs. Anthony Merry, the wife of the new British minister in Washington, whose snobbish sense of precedence and disgust at social life in the United States had created a storm threatening the peaceful relations between the two countries. At a dinner at the President's on December 2, 1803, the first at which the Merrys were present, Jefferson conducted Dolley Madison to the dinner table, "a personal compliment," he said, "to the lady who was so kind as to take charge of my company of the other sex." Madison and the other cabinet officers each turned to the nearest lady and went informally to the table. The Merrys, used to the formal order on such occasions in Europe, were surprised and insulted. They tagged along to dinner as best they could. Four days later the performance was repeated at the Madisons. Following the "rule of pele-mele," the Merrys found the head of the table occupied. Mr. Merry nonetheless conducted his wife there, where it happened Mrs. Gallatin sat. She offered her place to Mrs. Merry, "who took it without prudency or apology." Thus unnerved, the Merrys accepted no more invitations from the Republican leaders. Only Federalists seemed to enjoy Mrs. Merry's company. Manasseh Cutler, for example found her "a remarkably fine woman [who] entered instantly into the most agreeable conversation." Margaret Smith spotted the disadvantage in her volubility: "She is so entirely the talker and actor in all companies, that her good husband passes quite unnoticed." For a month or two Washington society was in an uproar. Things reached such proportions that Madison thought it necessary to explain to Monroe (American minister in London) "this display of diplomatic superstition, truly extraordinary in this age and in this country." Madison was afraid Merry might ascribe the alleged insults to an American contempt for Great Britain now that the Louisiana Purchase had resolved difficulties with France. Such was not the case, Madison said, as anyone who knew the informality of American manners would have no doubt.[40]

There was, of course, a certain amount of calculation in Jefferson's etiquette. He intended, he said, to change the practices of his predecessors, "which savoured of anti-republicanism" and to demonstrate that "the principle of society with us, as well as of our political constitution, is the equal rights of all; and if there be an occasion where this equality ought to prevail preeminently, it is in social circles collected for conviviality." Republican resentment at the "high tone" of the Federalist administrations, their charges of "monarchy," and their disgust at the pompous titles suggested for federal officials arose from a conviction that genuine republicanism required a revolution in manners and customs as well as in government. Thus Jefferson's refusal to hold formal levees and his reception of foreign ministers in slippers were part of a studied campaign to create a republican atmosphere in the capital. Since social life so often revolved around treatment of ladies, as the Merry incident showed, Dolley Madison's position as Jefferson's hostess placed her and her husband in key positions. They agreed entirely with Jefferson, and sought with him to make Washington social life consistent with their political principles. Far from being neglectful of customs, the Republican leaders set out most deliberately to reform them. To do so was for them an essential task of their administration. Though Madison regarded the Merry business as an unfortunate tempest in a teapot, in one perspective it is both a significant and appropriate part of the story of the first years of Republican rule.[41]

Political partisanship, regarded by Jefferson and Madison as an unfortunate necessity acceptable only in the face of the Federalist challenge, provided as many complexities as battles over etiquette. Deep policy differences between Federalists and Republicans, the continued strength, in New England at least, of the Federalists, and the struggle for power and offices among the Republicans, however, doomed the nonpartisan hope from the start. The Federalists looked upon the repeal of the judiciary act of 1801 as an assault on the principle of law and order itself. The Republicans saw the need to reduce the national debt and the nation's armed forces as essential to the very survival of free government. Nonetheless, peace, prosperity, the Louisiana Purchase, the shrill extremism of the Federalists, and the generally mild character of Jeffersonian government were all the Republicans needed to win the presidential election of 1804, 162 electoral votes to 14, carrying even the Federalist bastion of Massachusetts by a comfortable margin. In the new Congress the Federalists could claim but 7 of 34 Senators and 25 of 142 Representatives. Madison and Vice President Burr cooperated in 1802 in a fundraising effort for their alma mater to replace Nassau Hall, destroyed by fire, but their old intimacy had been ruined by Burr's equivocations in 1801. For that and other reasons, Burr was removed from the ticket in 1804. His demise enhanced Madison's standing as Jefferson's heir apparent, but the danger arose of the new Vice President becoming a rival for the succession. The selection of Governor George Clinton of New York, old, ill, but a respected hero of the revolution, seemed a good maneuver, maintaining a North-South balance, while at the same time, introducing a man whose age alone made him an unlikely candidate for the presidency four years later. Madison wrote Monroe in July 1804 that "our affairs continue in a prosperous train. The tide of opinion is more and more favorable to the administration. . . . If we can avoid the snares which our folly or foreign arts may spread for our peace, we can scarcely fail to flourish and to effect by degrees more of concord than has for some years been seen or thought practicable by the great body of the nation." Republican politicians took great pride in their record and promised that "The Tree of Liberty will take deep root, grow high, spread wide and be well matured under Jefferson and Clinton in the next four years."[42]

Amid the euphoria of victory and public acclaim, however, lurked dissensions that would cause the Jeffersonians, and Madison in particular, immense trouble during the coming decade. Extreme Federalists, led by Senator Timothy Pickering of Massachusetts and Congressman Roger Griswold of Connecticut, angry and frustrated at the Republican successes, in the winter of 1804 had talked among themselves of detaching New England and perhaps New York and New Jersey from the Union as the only way to salvage anything from the tyranny of Jefferson and Virginia. Since one of the purposes of the proposed secession was to insure close relations with Great Britain, the extremists told British Minister Merry of their plans, hoping for support, which he willingly gave. Furthermore, since Burr had by this time broken completely with the administration, Pickering and his friends supported Burr in his campaign for the governorship of New York. Burr could "break the democratic phalanx" in New York and combine it and New Jersey with New England "if a separation should be deemed proper," Pickering theorized. Burr's defeat in the April 1804 election and the opposition of Hamilton, the Adamses, King, and other prominent Federalists, doomed this scheme, but signs of danger remained: extreme Federalists in New England were enough disaffected with government by "the Virginia faction" to countenance secession; a British minister welcomed the scheme eagerly; and some dissident Republicans seemed willing to take part to gain personal or political advantage.[43]

Stymied in New York by his defeat and by Hamilton's intrepid opposition, Burr killed Hamilton in a duel and turned his ambitions westward. In August 1804, and again in March 1805, Burr approached Merry, seeking British support for vague plans to establish an independent power in the Mississippi valley. He also intrigued with the Spanish Minister, Yrujo, and with the American army commander in the West, General James Wilkinson, who was already a paid informer for Spain. Burr assured all his various cohorts that detachment of the West from the Union would lead as well to rupture between North and South. However bizarre, improbable, or contradictory these various schemes might appear in retrospect, at the time, in a nation still uncertain of its cohesion, and spread so thin geographically that it took months sometimes to get messages from remote parts to the capital, ambitious leaders, fanning discontent among citizens used to depending on their own initiative and resources, and willing to intrigue with foreign powers, could indeed threaten the union. Madison lived with this possibility from 1780 until 1815, when all the great powers finally conceded nationhood to the United States, and American settlers, tied together increasingly by steam transportation, grew secure in their nationality. He agreed with Jefferson in prosecuting Burr for treason in 1807 because, amid world war and internal threats of secession, the danger of disunion was in fact grave. Madison had confidence that "the general sentiment" would support neither Burr nor a collusive agreement with a foreign power, but confronted with so many imponderables, it was nevertheless necessary to act forthrightly. Far from being careless about national cohesion, the Republicans adopted firm policies both to expand the Union equitably and to prevent its disruption.[44]

The challenge politically most troublesome to Jefferson and Madison, however, came from within the party, from groups that had been valued allies in the great victory of 1800. First, some politicians from the Middle States, mostly from New York and Pennsylvania, for reasons of patronage disappointments, regional pride, and personal ambition, more and more opposed the administration. Since they saw 1808 as their first chance to score important national victories, they deferred to Jefferson and concentrated their hostility on Madison as the major contender for the presidency that year. Though from 1801 to 1809 Republican newspapers in Philadelphia and New York (especially James Cheetham in the New York *American Citizen*) often became violently antiadministration, and Vice President Clinton rallied anti-Madison sentiment as the 1808 election approached, by and large, forces loyal to Madison and Jefferson remained in control.[45]

More threatening were rumblings of discontent with the "apostasies" of the Jeffersonians in power that began among "Old Republicans" in the South and West, and especially in Virginia, almost as soon as the new administration took office in 1801. Instigated by John Taylor of Caroline, Edmund Pendleton had in October 1801 written an essay entitled "The Danger Not Over," calling upon Republicans to restrain executive power, limit federal authority to borrow money, respect the rights of the states, and eliminate the "wiles of construction." Doctrinaire Republicans such as Taylor, John Randolph of Roanoke, and Nathaniel Macon of North Carolina were increasingly unhappy over the obvious intention of Jefferson and Madison to *govern*, and in so doing, to retain much of the Federalist system. The dissidents objected as well to Jefferson's moderate course, designed to reconcile all but the extreme Federalists to the Republican administration. To those who took the Republican statements and slogans of the seventeen-nineties literally and rigidly, this was sheer betrayal. Jefferson's popularity and unique place in the affections of Republican leaders cast Madison in the role of the evil genius who debauched the President from his principles and made the party neo-Federalist. John Taylor of Caroline, closely allied with Madison during the seventeen-nineties, wrote in 1808 that he had reservations about Madison that arose "chiefly from an opinion . . . that the book called the *Federalist*, is full of Federalism" which Taylor "thought wrong," and to which Madison seemed partial as an executive officer. *The Federalist* espoused "the obnoxious doctrines of John Adams," Taylor added in final condemnation. Another old political associate of Madison's, John Beckley, wrote in 1806, that "Madison, is deemed by many, too timid and indecisive a statesman, and too liable to a conduct of forbearance to the Federal party, which may endanger our harmony and political safety."[46]

All of this might have remained muted and behind the scenes but for the flamboyant, domineering, eccentric, embittered genius of John Randolph of Roanoke. Though Madison had known Randolph, his family, and his connections (the Blands and Tuckers) for years, the two men were never close personally. Between the retirement of Fisher Ames and the rise of Webster, Clay, and Calhoun, Randolph's brilliant, slashing, high-pitched oratory dominated the House of Representatives. He quickly assumed leadership of the large, undistinguished Republican majorities in the House during Jefferson's first administration, and as chairman of the Ways and Means Committee he guided many Republican measures through Congress. His temper and unbalance, however, made him an unlikely legislative leader. By 1805 he had alienated many of his colleagues, and feeling, justifiably or not, slighted and unappreciated by the administration, he turned increasingly on it. Almost with relief he resumed the roles of critic and prophet in the wilderness. Genuinely devoted to what he referred to as "Old Republican" principles, aware of Jefferson's relative invulnerability, and perhaps personally envious of Madison's social and political successes, Randolph assailed the Secretary of State.[47]

The earliest and most unrelenting charge Randolph made against Madison was that he was a "Yazoo Man," a designation earned as a member of a commission (also including Gallatin and Levi Lincoln) appointed to arrange a cession of Georgia's western lands, title to which had been hopelessly snarled after a bribed Georgia legislature in 1795 had sold millions of acres of rich land to speculators. A year later, after exposure of the fraud, the legislature repealed the sale. Difficulty arose because between sale and repeal, most of the lands had been sold to perhaps innocent third parties, including many New Englanders. To completely repudiate the claims would injure innocent people, but to uphold them all would earn millions for dishonest speculators, so the commission arranged a compromise, setting aside the proceeds from the sale of a small fraction of the land to divide among the claimants, thus giving them a value roughly equivalent to their aggregate investment. The settlement also arbitrated between the interests of Georgia and New England Congressmen. For attacking Madison, the issue was perfect: charge him, the other commissioners, and their supporters with collusion, bribery, deceit, and "compromise of principles."[48]

Randolph at first cleverly opposed the commission's report as an invasion of the sovereignty of the State of Georgia, whose legislature repealed the sale. He next inveighed against an administration that sanctioned such "atrocious public robbery." He could not, he said, understand men who admitted wholesale fraud and then would dispense public funds to the perpetrators. Senator Plumer, who, with most of the Senate, could not resist going to the House galleries when Randolph spoke, reported that the lean Virginian "pronounced two or three very bitter and very personal phillippics," filled with "course and vulgar . . . allusions to brothel-houses and pig stys . . . [and] arraigning the motives of members, charging them with speculation, bribery, and corruption." The next year (1806) Randolph attacked Jefferson and Madison for, he alleged, asking Congress to appropriate $2 million that in effect would be used to bribe France to persuade the Spanish to give up West Florida. Actually the uncertain status of West Florida, the secret Franco-Spanish negotiations over it, and Napoleon's growing influence in Madrid made American efforts to acquire the province necessarily ambiguous. Randolph insisted that American occupation of West Florida was the only forthright, honorable course. In a speech filled with "energy, eloquence, and biting sarcasm," Randolph "most explicitly declared that most of the evils which the United States now suffered proceeded from the measures of the Executive—from the weak, feeble, and pusillanimous spirit of the keeper of the Cabinet—the Secretary of State." Having identified the culprit, Randolph flung down the challenge: "I considered it a base prostration of the national character, to excite one nation [France] by money to bully another nation [Spain] out of its property, and from that moment, and to the last moment of my life, my confidence in the principles of the man entertaining these sentiments, died, never to live again." A week later Randolph announced his formal opposition to the administration.[49]

John Quincy Adams recorded the gossip that "Mr. Randolph's object in his present denunciation is to prevent Mr. Jefferson from serving again, and Mr. Madison from being his successor. Mr. Randolph's man is said to be Mr. Monroe." Randolph was writing at about the same time to Monroe: "Everything is made a business of bargain and traffic, the ultimate object of which is to raise Mr. Madison to the presidency. To

this the old Republican party will never consent. . . . They are united in
your support." The day before, Randolph had written pointedly: "In
Madison, the man of Rufus King and Gouverneur Morris, we have no
confidence." Some months later, after Monroe had told Randolph there
were "older men . . . having higher pretentions" to the presidency than
himself, men for whom he had an "ancient friendship" he was loath to
endanger, the dogged Congressman resumed the attack:

> To the great and acknowledged influence of [Mr. Madison] we are
> indebted for that strange amalgam of men and principles which has
> distinguished some of the late acts of the administration and proved
> so injurious to it. Many, the most consistent of the old republicans, by
> whose exertions the present men were brought into power, have beheld
> with immeasurable disgust the principles for which they had con-
> tended, and (as they thought) established, neutralized at the touch of
> a cold and insidiuous moderation. . . . [They] ascribe to the baleful
> influence of the Secretary of State that we have been gradually relax-
> ing from our old principles, and relapsing into the system of our
> predecessors. . . . They are determined not to have a Yazoo president.

Randolph then hinted to Monroe of some Federalist-inspired slanders
against Dolley Madison and her sisters: "You, my dear Sir, cannot be
ignorant—although of all mankind, you perhaps have the least cause to
know it—how deeply the respectability of any character may be impaired by an unfortunate matrimonial connexion—I can pursue this subject no farther. It is at once too delicate and too mortifying."[50]

Thus, with nearly three years left of Jefferson's second term, he, and
particularly Madison, had found the brilliant Randolph turned from
difficult friend to bitter enemy. The Federalists gloated, of course, but if
the President and Secretary of State were very worried, they failed to
reveal any signs of it. Doubtless aware that Randolph's plans included
promotion of Monroe as a presidential candidate, Jefferson wrote his old
friend, at this time Minister to England, that the House of Representatives, with but half-a-dozen exceptions, was "solidly united" behind the
administration, and that Randolph, recently "so eminent a leader [was]
at once and almost unanimously abandoned," when he went into opposition. Jefferson was pleased at this "steady, good sense in the Legislature,
and in the body of the nation," and was sure "that no *ignis fatuus* will
be able to lead them long astray." More pointedly, Jefferson told Monroe
that "the great body of your friends here are among the firmest adherents of the administration," and referring to Randolph, "it is unfortunate
for you to be embarrassed with such a *soi-disant* friend. You must not
commit yourself to him." Though Madison was so weighted with work
that he was "robbed of any leisure for writing my friends," and hobbled
by a sprained ankle suffered in a fall down his front steps, he was nevertheless cheerful and unconcerned. At a summer picnic at the Smiths'

farm home near Washington, he "was in one of his most sportive moods" and passed the afternoon "sans ceremonie," swinging in the hammock and inspecting Mrs. Smith's milkhouse. For dinner they sat outdoors at a large table set "with nice white cloth, plates, knives, home made bread" and some delicious farm-churned butter, "as hard as in the middle of winter."[51]

Though Randolph's following was small, and Republican prospects were generally flourishing, the seeds had been sown for troubles Madison was to reap in anguish and despair during his own presidency; of recalcitrant Federalists, ambitious politicians, greedy Senators, and of Randolph's bitter spleen he was to see more than enough in the next ten years. Jefferson and Madison took most seriously, however, the charge that they had betrayed republican principles. At many specific points it had substance: implied powers were used to justify the Louisiana Purchase; many offices and officeholders of Federalist origin were retained; no amendments limited federal borrowing or spending power; and in the Yazoo case, federal law and federal commissioners had overruled a state legislature. Part of the difficulty, of course, was that the Jeffersonians discovered many Federalist measures, including even the much-reviled national bank, were more useful than they had supposed. Furthermore, the opposition rhetoric of 1793 to 1800 made people forget that Jefferson and Madison had each long been proponents of effective, forceful government for legitimate republican goals. States' rights theorists who expected them to reduce the federal government to impotence simply ignored the burden of the thought and career of each. A firm posture in foreign affairs, a sense of national needs in settling domestic disputes, a concern to reconcile all sections and shades of opinion to the national government, and a quick willingness to take advantage of such golden opportunities as the Louisiana Purchase were, to Jefferson and Madison, in no sense anti-republican. In fact they were *necessary* to build a republican nation. To have boggled, as Taylor and Randolph did, at rhetoric and technicality would have been foreign to both the impulses and vision of two men who since 1776 had been nation builders. If this meant that they accommodated themselves, admittedly or otherwise, to programs and achievements of their political foes, this was to them less harmful than betraying national interests. It suggests, too, what Jefferson himself declared in his inaugural address—that among moderate Republicans and moderate Federalists there was a good deal more in common than one would gather from campaign oratory.

Madison's role in the administration as conceived by Randolph and other "Old Republican" critics is ironic in view of the charges later made about his relationship with Jefferson in the seventeen-nineties. In that decade Madison is pictured as the dupe of Jefferson, seduced from his nationalism of 1787 to 1789 by the wily ex-minister to France, who had imbibed visionary notions in Paris. After 1801, however, Madison is the villain, seducing Jefferson from his Republican principles to turn the great victory of 1800 into a surrender to Federalism. A sense of perspective in viewing the records of the Federalist and of the Jeffersonian administrations, however, reveals little substance to the charges of inconsistency, seduction, and betrayal. Madison's "desertion" of Hamilton in the period from 1790 to 1792 had explicit foundations: he believed the Secretary of the Treasury had organized a system dangerous to republicanism and going far beyond the intent of the Constitution. Though Hamilton's program was consistent with one view of the national destiny under the Constitution, it is surely true as well that had the voters of 1788 been asked if they thought they had sanctioned such a program, many of them, including large numbers of federalists, would have said no. The war measures, hysteria, and suppression of the Adams administration were to Madison the logical conclusion of the arrogant, encroaching Hamiltonian system. Madison sought instead in 1788, 1790, 1793, 1798, 1801, and 1806, to define and carry out a program consistent with *his* federalism and *his* republicanism.

The cautious financing, the shrinking of the armed forces, the persistent effort to avoid commitment to the English commercial system, the restraint of the judiciary, the social informality, and the generally mild government of the Republican administration are in marked contrast to the preceding twelve years, and do indeed represent fundamental changes if one tries to project what the Federalists, especially Hamilton, might have done between 1801 and 1809. As Jefferson said in his inaugural address, republican government was the strongest in the world because of its support by the people. He and Madison intended to use this strength for the only purpose that would not diminish it: to achieve republican ends. The charges against Madison, particularly that he led the administration toward the principles of *The Federalist*, are in fact evidence that, of the Republican leaders, he was the most able and alert in devising ways to *use* government for republican ends. For this he earned Jefferson's praise and admiration. This was the crux of their relationship in 1806 and the essence of their cooperative effort for eight years.

CHAPTER XVIII

Confrontation with Great Britain

As Jefferson's second administration began, frustrations were darkening the rosy hue that had surrounded American foreign relations during Madison's first four years in office. Spain had refused to relinquish posts on the lower Mississippi and had ignored American spoliation claims, and the United States could get no satisfaction on either a boundary settlement for Louisiana or a purchase of the Floridas. The rebuff of American advances, more and more blatantly abetted by France, threatened American interests and pretensions in the West, and had raised among many a cry for war with Spain. At the same time, the renewed war in Europe had led to increased British depredations on American shipping, though there were fewer, Jefferson had told Congress in November 1804, "than on former occasions." Jefferson and Madison therefore decided to seek friendship and even alliance with Britain so they could deal bluntly with Spain, and even with her powerful neighbor across the Pyrenees. It soon became clear, however, that English help against Spain in Texas and Florida would entail the same compromise of American rights, interests, and even independence the Republicans had resisted for a dozen years. Through the summer and early fall of 1805, the cabinet remained in a quandary.[1]

Late in the fall new possibilities took shape. Napoleon began his great campaign in central Europe, thus both increasing his need for cash and making it certain, Jefferson assumed for a year at least, he would be little able to concern himself with the New World. At the same time, American merchants protested the British admiralty court decision in the *Essex* case making illegal the long-established, highly profitable, "broken-voyage" trade of neutral (American) ships between the West Indies and the Continent: the courts declared they would no longer accept the fiction that American ships bound from the West Indies to Europe, a trade illegal if undertaken directly, had made a "broken," lawful voyage if they entered American ports for some meaningless formalities before continuing eastward. The seizures thus authorized, especially if taken as a sign that Britain had renewed her old tough policy on the high seas, made her a most unlikely alliance partner. Madison counseled "a little delay," but Jefferson proposed to end the futile negotiations in Madrid, shelve the alliance with England, and instead, try to use Napoleon's need for cash to persuade him to extract concessions from Spain. Madison acquiesced reluctantly, and the cabinet spent November and December 1805 hammering out the new policy and drafting messages to Congress to effect it.[2]

The vacillations, however, were soon overwhelmed by news of momentous events in Europe: Nelson's victory at Trafalgar on October 21 and Napoleon's triumph at Austerlitz on December 2. Britain's rule of the sea was now absolute, and the Emperor of France was master of the European continent. The two powers also saw quite clearly at last the mortal nature of their struggle, and each had no doubt of its vital need: England, by controlling the sea, to strangle the continental giant; and Napoleon, by manipulating his control of Europe, to break the British blockade. The days of tender treatment of neutral commerce, fidelity to international law, and decent bargaining with third parties were past. The administration continued to give priority to its relations with Spain, and American negotiators continued to haunt the foreign offices in London and Paris, seeking agreements on the old problems, but in fact they faced a new era of total war.

In the summer and fall of 1805, Madison responded intellectually to the new threat in Philadelphia, where he had gone with Dolley, who was to be treated there by the famous Dr. Philip Syng Physick for "a complaint near her knee; which from a very slight tumor had ulcerated into a very obstinate sore." For months evidence had accumulated that under Pitt's firm leadership Britain had decided to drive American ships from the West Indies and from the European carrying trade. A major weapon was the so-called Rule of 1756, which declared that a trade closed to neutrals in time of peace was also closed to them in time of war. Under this rule and its interpretation in the *Essex* decision, American ships trading between Cuba, Guadaloupe, and Santo Domingo, and France and Spain, while those countries were at war, were subject to capture by British vessels. Madison had protested this rule in a letter to Monroe in April 1805, and thus triggered an influential and violent attack on American trade, James Stephen's *War in Disguise; or, The Frauds of the Neutral Flags*, but before this tract reached the United States, Madison aimed at the Rule of 1756 a 204-page pamphlet of his own, *An Examina-*

*tion of the British Doctrine, Which Subjects to Capture a Neutral Trade,
Not Open in Time of Peace.* During almost three months in Philadelphia,
settled "in excellent lodgings on Sansom Street," surrounded by books
he had brought with him and others borrowed from the learned lawyer
Peter S. Duponceau, Madison piled up evidence from international law
theorists, treaties, and admiralty court decisions that the Rule of 1756
had no legal foundation whatever. He quoted the standard theorists,
Grotius, Pufendorf, Bynkershoeck, Martens, and especially Vattel, corrected the translations of Grotius' Latin, employed a translator suggested
by Duponceau for German books, and otherwise indulged his scholarly
bent. The result was the longest single work he ever undertook. It was,
Madison wrote Monroe, "a pretty thorough investigation," and was to
prove five points.[3]

He began with his usual assumption that international law should
favor peace and free trade: "The progress of the law of nations, under
the influence of science and humanity, is mitigating the evils of war, and
diminishing the motives to it, by favoring the rights of those remaining
at peace, rather than those who enter into war." Then, discarding
eloquence, and with increasing unreadability, he took up the attack:
(1) the international law theorists rejected the Rule of 1756; (2) treaties,
many signed by Britain herself, repudiated it; (3) it could not be
found in the admiralty judgments of foreign nations; (4) even British
courts had repeatedly ruled against it; and (5) the reasoning used by its
defenders in Britain was fallacious. In examining treaties, Madison found
fifteen not involving Britain and thirty-two signed by her since the peace
of Westphalia in 1648 that at least by implication disavowed the infamous
rule. For sixty-two pages he quoted from British court decisions showing
that such influential jurists as Sir William Scott, Lord Mansfield, and
Sir James Marriot had often decided against it. Having thus destroyed
the legal claims of the rule, Madison pointed out its only remaining
justification:

> Finding no asylum elsewhere, it at length boldly asserts, as its *true
> foundation, a mere superiority of force.* It is right in Great Britain to
> capture and condemn a neutral trade with her enemies, disallowed by
> her enemies in time of peace, for the sole reason that her force is
> predominant at sea. And it is wrong in her enemies to capture and
> condemn a neutral trade with British colonies, because their maritime
> force is inferior to hers. The question no longer is, whether the trade
> be right or wrong in itself, but on which side the superiority of force
> lies? The law of nations, the rights of neutrals, the freedom of the
> seas, the commerce of the world, are to depend, not on any fixt prin-
> ciple of justice, but on the comparative state of naval armaments.[4]

The dilemma, and futility, of Madison's hard work is evident in his
conclusion. He had indeed, as Jefferson wrote, "pulverized [the Rule of
1756] by a logic not to be controverted," but the Royal Navy would

not, and perhaps could not have been expected to bow to logic and the niceties of law when the very survival of Britain depended on its violation. The plain fact was that had the claims of neutral commerce, as Madison upheld them in the *Examination* and in other state papers, been allowed by Britain, her only real weapon against Napoleon, the blockade of the continent he controlled, would have been rendered impotent. It was also often true, as British officials pointed out repeatedly, that eager American shippers took advantage of even the smallest leniency in British courts to flood Europe with produce that aided Napoleon and/or damaged British trade. The profits were so high that only the most stringent regulations could deter it at all. The trouble was that Madison's conclusion was all too valid: as long as the great war raged, access to world trade routes would depend "on the comparative state of naval armaments."[5]

The pamphlet, originally intended to be an official government document, was instead placed informally on the desks of all Congressmen in January 1806. On the whole it created little stir, except when John Randolph flung it contemptuously on the floor, calling it "a shilling pamphlet hurled against eight hundred ships of war." Learned Senator John Quincy Adams, after taking eight days to read it, recorded that "I am, on the whole, much pleased," but William Plumer of New Hampshire probably expressed a more general reaction when, also after eight days, he pronounced it "often obscure and sometimes unintelligible, . . . too prolix for common use, . . . yet I think it useful—it contains many facts, and . . . very justly exposes the fallacy and inconsistency of the British Courts of Admiralty." "I never read a book that fatigued me more than this pamphlet," Plumer added. The course of war in Europe moved too fast, and the passions of Congress were too intense for Madison's diligent labor to have much impact. Though the *Examination* furnished ammunition for propagandists and diplomatic instructions, it was soon forgotten, and Madison himself generally omitted it from lists of his writings.[6]

Before the escalating war in Europe claimed all of Madison's attention, he and Dolley enjoyed reunions with Philadelphia friends they hadn't seen in eight years, and in a rare period of separation from each other, exchanged personal letters. Amid worries that she would never walk again and fears of staying on the tidewater during "the sickly season," Dolley Madison finally agreed to spend the summer of 1805 in Philadelphia under Dr. Physick's care. At first her husband was not to go with her, but Dolley's "dread of the separation" and her increasingly serious condition changed the plan. In "dangerously hot weather" in late July they rode to Philadelphia. Dolley wrote anxiously to her sister after they reached Philadelphia: "I am on my bed, with my dear husband sitting anxiously beside me, who is my most willing nurse. But you know how delicate he is. I tremble for him; one night on the way he was taken very ill with his old complaint [a kind of fit "suspending bodily functions"] and I could not fly to aid him as I used to do. Heaven in its mercy restored him next morning, and he would not pause until he heard my fate from Doctor Physick." Physick decided immediately to treat the tumor with splints and caustics and without surgery. Her spirits transformed, Dolley was soon deep in the social round she admitted she liked "all too well." She had "the world to see me, and many invitations to the houses of the gentry." Her husband was "well, though besieged with callers." Dolley's old friends visited her sickroom and vied with each other to care for her. Only a scolding by a strict old Quaker for having too much company troubled Dolley: "This lecture made me recollect the times when our Society used to control me entirely and debar me from so many advantages and pleasures, and although so entirely from their clutches I really felt my ancient terror of them revive to a disagreeable degree." Obviously, Dolley had come to enjoy without remorse the gay social life attending her second marriage.[7]

James Madison enjoyed the mixture of visiting and work on his *Examination*, but in late October, with Dolley's recovery assured, business called him back to Washington. He and Betsy Pemberton, Dolley's most faithful nurse, teased and flirted; she wore Madison's hat to divert Dolley and sent him notes she refused to let the jealous wife read. Madison responded: "Miss Pemberton's postscript makes my mouth water. Cousin Isaac's would too, if he had ever had the taste which I have had." "Cousin Isaac" was probably Isaac Coles, Jefferson's private secretary, who was thought by many to be the handsomest man in Washington, and whose travels caused palpitations up and down the Atlantic coast. Dolley's almost daily letters to her husband were filled with tender concern and sorrow at the separation. Her visitors respected "the grief they know I feel at even so short a separation from one who is all to me." One night she couldn't sleep "from anxiety for thee, my dearest husband." Dr. Physick consoled his patient on the departure of her husband, whom the doctor "regards . . . more than any man he knows." She rejoiced at the first word from Madison and said she was "getting well as fast as I can, for I have the reward in view of then seeing my beloved." A few days later Dolley was well enough to inquire about the news. "You know I am not much of a politician," she wrote, "but I am extremely anxious to hear (as far as you think proper) what is going forward in the Cabinet." Two weeks later she did some shopping for the President, returned some visits, and prepared to return to Washington with Anna and Richard Cutts.

Dolley's letter announcing her imminent return brought a reply full of joy, instruction, and news: "Yours of the 1st instant my dearest gives me much happiness but it cannot be complete till I have you again with me. . . . I [will] make arrangements for paying the Dr. etc. . . . Don't forget to do something as to insuring the buildings [Dolley owned in Philadelphia]. . . . If a general war takes place in Europe, Spain will prob-ably be less disposed to insult us and England less sparing of her insults." Word that Dolley might leave sooner than planned left her husband "not without hope that this [letter] will be too late." Dolley's last letter was written after word from her husband saying that Payne Todd had been placed in a boarding school in Baltimore: "your charming letter, my be-loved, has revived my spirit, and made me feel like another being—so much does my health, peace, and every thing else, depend on your affec-tion and goodness—I am very grateful for the prospect you have opened for our child—and I shall now look forward to his manhood, when he will bless and do honour to his guardians. . . . Pray take as much relaxa-tion, and pleasure as you can—all together, business will not agree with you, and unless you amuse yourself as usual I may travel too soon. Betsy Pemberton . . . says she feels already your sweet kisses—what must somebody else do—farewell til tomorrow—your own D." In late November, after a month's separation, the Madisons were reunited when Dolley stepped from the Cutts carriage in front of the house on F Street.[8]

The "season" in Washington to which Dolley returned was one of special excitement. Gossip about General Turreau and his wife was more titillating than ever—and apparently more grounded on fact. Dolley Madison had reported that "the impression of him in Philadelphia is a sad one; he is remembered as the cruel commander of La Vendee, and the fighting husband." He had, Senator Plumer recorded, "most unmerci-fully beat and bruised his wife—tis however true that she gave him the first blow." He locked her up when he left town and upbraided neigh-bors who released her. Worst of all, "some days since as General Turreau was writing to his Government his wife came by him with a smoothing iron and struck him. He rose and beat her cruelly with a large cane. She cried murder—the children and servants came in crying— instantly the Secretary of Legation raised the windows, and to drown the noise played furiously on the French horn." Dolley Madison continued to feel sorry for the poor wife, and the Secretary of State "mediated" to bring the feuding couple together again, but according to Federalist Senator Plumer, who was horrified that his government should receive such a brutish minister, the cabinet wives were so fearful of offending Napoleon that they turned their backs on the unfortunate woman.[9]

Less fraught with diplomatic complications and even more exotically interesting were the simultaneous visits in Washington of a group of Indian chiefs and an ambassador from the Bey of Tunis, Sidi Suliman Mellimelli. The Indians included semi-civilized Creeks and Cherokee of the Southwest, accompanied by Madison's old friend Benjamin Hawkins, who had lived among them for many years, and tall, exotic Sauks, Sioux, and Osage chiefs sent from the Missouri country by Lewis and Clark. Mellimelli landed to a cannonade by a frigate and immediately presented his credentials to Madison, along with Arabian horses and other bizarre presents for American officials and their wives. According to Eastern custom, the United States government bore the expenses of the numerous retinue accompanying the ambassador, and as well, furnished some concubines, including one "Georgia a Greek." Madison quietly entered this expense on the books of the State Department as "appropriations to foreign intercourse." The terms were "of such latitude," the secretary remarked, that "urgent and unforeseen occurrences" might be provided for under them.

At the President's New Year's reception, he and the other officials paid so much attention to the strange guests that the sensitive British minister, Anthony Merry, felt slighted again, and in five minutes left in a huff. Crowds poured through all the rooms on the first floor, a band played, and guests helped themselves at "side boards . . . numerous and amply furnished with a rich variety of wines, punch, cakes, ice cream, etc." At this reception, and at elegant balls and dinners held later in the month, Mellimelli, a great, dark, turbaned man of about fifty, the Indians, and their American hosts discussed women and religion. The Indians declared bluntly that their women "were the handsomest on earth," while the Tunisian admitted American women seemed like angels, but somehow they didn't suit him. Then he spied a large black woman in the kitchen and embraced her enthusiastically, shouting that she reminded him of his best and most expensive wife, "a load for a camel." Mellimelli asked a group of Cherokee what God they worshiped. According to Plumer, "The Indians answered *The Great Spirit*. He then asked them if they believed in Mahomed, Abraham, or Jesus Christ? They answered neither [*sic*]. He then asked what prophet do you worship. They replied none. We worship the Great Spirit without an agent. [Mellimelli] then exclaimed you are all vile Hereticks." Though some Congressmen thought the honor paid these pagan emissaries indecent, none could help being fascinated by their exotic looks, strange ways, and startling opinions. After the excitement of their visit, the same winter, Randolph of Roanoke thundered against the Secretary of State, the Madisons, through whose house Indians had roamed during receptions and balls, may, in late February, have been glad for the more sedate evening, when they had to dinner Supreme Court justices John Marshall, Bushrod Washington, and William Johnson and Senator John Quincy Adams. The ladies withdrew to relax, playing loo.[10]

The State Department scene, as the tumultuous 1805–6 session of Congress drew to a close, Madison found disheartening indeed. He was alienated from the English and Spanish ministers to the United States, and on uncertain terms with the blustery French minister. In Europe an incompetent minister to Spain, Charles Pinckney, had been succeeded by an ineffective one, James Bowdoin, Jr. Spanish-American negotiations languished. Robert R. Livingston had been succeeded in Paris by his brother-in-law, John Armstrong, a firm-minded though pompous and lazy ex-general who was at a loss amid the intrigues and edicts of Talleyrand and Napoleon. In London the intrepid Monroe, discouraged by unsuccessful missions in Paris and Madrid, found Anglo-American relations deteriorating as the Foreign Office fell more and more under the influence of naval and commercial interests that insisted on a hard line toward the United States. British attacks on American shipping increased rapidly, and Jay's Treaty expired. Alarmed, the administration attempted once more to reach an accord with Britain on impressment and neutral trade by sending William Pinkney, a Maryland lawyer, to join Monroe in an extraordinary mission to London. Madison dared hope for success when he learned that the new British foreign secretary, Charles James Fox, long regarded as a friend of America, had written to Merry that the King wished without delay "to so arrange all matters liable to cause Dispute, that a ground may be laid for permanent Friendship and good Understanding between the two Nations."[11]

Madison instructed the envoys in London to seek amiable relations between the two countries based on "a friendly reciprocity." An American nonimportation act, he said, had been suspended to give time for further negotiations. Nonetheless, the matter of impressment, because of "the licenciousness with which it is still pursued, and the growing impatience of this country under it," had to be settled before the Nonimportation Act could be entirely withdrawn. He therefore insisted that impressment and intrusions by British warships into American waters be outlawed in the most explicit terms. Madison then called again for a liberal interpretation of the rights of neutral commerce: narrow definitions of contraband, elimination of the Rule of 1756, a disavowal of paper blockades, and a settlement of spoliation claims. With these issues settled, the envoys should seek a commercial agreement consistent with "the permanent object of the United States, to have the intercourse with [British colonies] made as free as that with Europe." Though the position of the United States and the need of the West Indies for American food would "necessarily" produce this freedom "at some no very distant period," Madison conceded that British obstinacy would probably prevent it for a time, so Monroe and Pinkney were told to do the best they could, taking care only to avoid the humiliations imposed on the United States in Jay's Treaty.[12]

In England, Monroe's uneasiness at the "rebuke" implied by giving him an unwanted colleague (Pinkney) in his negotiations, was heightened by frequent reports from John Randolph and others about Madison's alleged political intrigues. The secretary's intent, they said, was to appease the Federalists by appointing Pinkney, abandon the "true Republicans" in the bargain, and then ruin the reputation of his honorable rival (Monroe) by giving him instructions so unyielding as to make a treaty with Britain impossible. The friendly tone of Monroe's first conversations with Fox made Madison's ultimatum-like instructions, especially the demand that impressment be abandoned, most unwelcome. To Monroe the Secretary of State seemed to be trying to *prevent* his success. Fox's illness and death in the summer of 1806 at first suspended negotiations and then threw them into the hands of men whose power seemed likely soon to be transferred to hard-line Tories determined to use the Royal Navy to drive American trade from the high seas. Thus feeling rushed, and further alarmed by Napoleon's Berlin Decree, Monroe and Pinkney agreed to a treaty on December 31, 1806, utterly incompatible with their instructions: it ignored impressment and in many ways seemed to require the United States to help Britain enforce the Rule of 1756 and other obnoxious maritime regulations.[13]

Madison and Jefferson were dumbfounded at letters from the envoys indicating such a treaty had been signed. The cabinet agreed immediately that it "would rather go on without a treaty than with one which does not settle" the matter of impressment. There was no point in even sending a treaty omitting it to the Senate. Madison wrote at once, instructing the negotiators to resume their talks to obtain a better treaty, but lacking that, to withdraw from the discussions. He emphasized again the insufferable, arbitrary character of "the horrible practice of impressments." "The habits generated by naval command," Madison noted, made meaningless a British promise to exercise "the greatest caution" in reclaiming British seamen. Furthermore, the stipulations protecting British colonial trade had "no origin or plea but those of commercial jealousy and monopoly." Madison nonetheless tried to soften the blow to Monroe's pride. "The President and all of us," he wrote, "are fully impressed with the difficulties . . . as well as with [your] faithfulness and ability, . . . and are ready to suppose . . . that in your position we should have had your [view], as that, in our position, you would have had ours. . . . It has been a painful task with the President to withhold from the joint work of yourself and Mr. Pinkney the sanction which was expected, as it has been to me to communicate the event, with the considerations which produced it." Madison expressed his deep indignation, however, to agent George Joy: "That an officer from a foreign ship should pronounce any person he pleased, on board an American ship on the high seas, not to be an American citizen, but a British subject, and carry his interested decision on the most important of all questions to a freeman into execution on the spot, is so anomalous in principle, so grievous in practice, and so abominable in abuse, that the pretension must finally yield to sober discussion and friendly expostulation."[14]

Yet "sober discussion and friendly expostulation" is exactly what Monroe and Pinkney had undertaken in London for six months. They discovered, however, that Madison's ultimatums, especially regarding ending impressment, were of "a vital character" to Great Britain "at a time when the very existence of the country depended on an adherence to its maritime pretensions." More than ever, manning the Royal Navy was life or death to England, so the American negotiators had to yield that point or gain nothing. Furthermore, Monroe observed that "it is important for us to stand well with some power." With Spain arrogantly hostile, Napoleon flushed with new victories, and American diplomacy bankrupt everywhere on the Continent, it seemed again, as it had to John Jay in 1794, that even a poor agreement with the world's foremost maritime power was preferable to recriminations and probably war.[15]

In fact, the divergent views of the "realities" as seen by Madison in Washington and Monroe in London indicated the growing chasm between Britain's need in her war against Napoleon and the requirements of American commerce, independence, and self-respect. Ever since the publication of *War in Disguise* (1805), which with some justice branded the claims of neutral commerce a pious fraud to succor the tyrant Napoleon and to ruin British trade, British opinion and eventually cabinet policy more and more insisted that Britain unashamedly use the full power of the Royal Navy to uphold British commercial interests and to inflict maximum damage on Napoleon's continental economy—neutral rights to the contrary notwithstanding. The British prosperity needed to wage war, this argument held, could come only from the growth of Britain's trade, even with France and her allies on the Continent. If this meant laying heavy hands on American and other neutral ships, this could be justified under the necessities of a war that, English publicists never tired of saying, Britain waged on behalf of all the world not yet in the hands of the bloodthirsty despot Napoleon. Therefore, since the Royal Navy had the means to "regulate" all the trade of Europe and the Americas, she should do it strictly in accord with Britain's vital requirements. Spencer Perceval, the leading minister from 1807 to 1812, put the matter bluntly less than a year after the ill-fated Monroe-Pinkney treaty: "The short principle is that trade in British produce and manufactures, and trade either from a British port or with a British destination, is to be protected as much as possible. . . . [Neutral countries] will have no trade, or they must be content to accept through us. . . . Our orders say to the enemy . . . 'the only trade, cheap and untaxed, which you shall have shall be either direct from us, in our own produce and manufactures, or from our allies, whose increased prosperity will be an advantage to us.'" British newspapers and pamphleteers trumpeted this doctrine, edged with hostility to the United States, as the new, hard-line Tory ministry took office in April 1807.[16]

In Washington, Madison had full reports of these hostile words and ominous changes. The new policy said frankly that American trade and wealth would be plundered to the advantage of British competitors. Insofar as necessary, the Royal Navy would enforce this discrimination, and also, if necessary, press gangs would man the navy with seamen taken from the very American ships it preyed upon. The United States had only to suffer the disgrace of submitting to the sweeping orders in council to avoid the humiliation of search and seizure. To Americans who remembered British policy before the revolution, and British arrogance during the seventeen-eighties and nineties, submission to such arbitrary measures would forfeit independence. The existence and honor of the nation seemed to depend on resistance to the new policy. Thus, though Madison and Jefferson were willing to try again and again to reach an agreement with England, and to search for any kind of formula, or even evasion, that would preserve American self-respect, they simply could not submit.

Part of the darkening scene in the first months of 1807 was news of Napoleon's Berlin Decree (November 1806) and the British orders in council of January 1807. The first declared Britain in a state of blockade and subjected to French seizure any vessels trading with Britain or stopping at British ports, while the second subjected to British seizure any vessel engaged in trade between continental ports. Since American ships ordinarily stopped at a number of European ports, they were virtually certain to violate at least one of the edicts, and thus be liable to seizure merely upon entering a British or a continental port. During 1805 and 1806 British depredations had mounted. Under the new orders and strict enforcement of the Rule of 1756, seizures reached at least two per week in 1807. During the last half of 1807 Napoleon's officers in the ports of Europe began wholesale confiscations of American ships and goods. The administration made plans for improving the national defense and sent more tough words to guide its diplomats in Europe, but in fact, it was paralyzed at the profound contradiction between the abusive hostility it faced and the intense Republican commitment to peace and commercial retaliation. Discouragement reached new depths in late March 1807, when Madison, "very unwell with a cold," was just barely able to go to his office, and Jefferson had "a sick headache every day, and is obliged to retire to a dark room every morning by nine o'clock."[17]

The public, meanwhile, concentrated on the news of Aaron Burr's intrigues in the West, his capture and return East, and his sensational trial in Richmond, presided over by Chief Justice Marshall. As Secretary of State, Madison had for months received mysterious, ominous letters about the intrigues. He agreed fully with Jefferson that Burr had acted treasonably and that he ought to be prosecuted vigorously. Though generally attention centered on Burr's personality, the complicated nature of his schemes, and the battle among the famous lawyers at his trial, Madison was more concerned about the dangers of fomenting disunion and the disastrous effect of such moves on American diplomacy. Strong public support in the United States for the government would, Madison hoped, confound the French, Spanish, and British ministers, all of whom connived in the plots to dismember the Union. Upon a hint from Jefferson that "our Ministers at Paris, London, and Madrid [may] find out Burr's propositions and agents there," Madison warned Armstrong "to ascertain the Agents and intrigues of Burr at Paris." Burr's acquittal under Marshall's narrow construction of the the treason clause, coming as the position of the United States in Europe and on the high seas deteriorated, heightened Madison's sense of the danger the country faced.[18]

As Jefferson and Madison prepared for their 1807 summer sojourns in the Piedmont, news arrived that on June 22, a few miles from Hampton Roads, H.M.S. *Leopard* had attacked the unsuspecting American frigate *Chesapeake*, inflicting severe damage and killing or wounding twenty-one of its crew. Under orders from Admiral Sir George Berkeley, commander of the Royal Navy in American waters, to stop the *Chesapeake* and remove deserters, Captain Humphreys of the *Leopard* had hailed her, sent a boarding party, and been refused permission to search for deserters. Thus frustrated, for fifteen minutes he ordered his gunners to pour broadside after broadside into the *Chesapeake*, which had no time even to clear her gun deck. Defenseless, Commodore Barron struck his colors. The British boarding party returned, mustered the American crew, which in fact included many Englishmen and deserters, and dragged off four men. Three of them were Americans who had been impressed into the Royal Navy from an American ship some months earlier, escaped, and then enlisted aboard the *Chesapeake*. The other, a sharp-tongued Londoner who had deserted a British man-of-war and then reviled his former officers on the streets of Norfolk, was a legitimate prize of the boarding party and soon swung from a yardarm in Halifax harbor.[19]

Though the *Chesapeake* incident illustrated both the frustrations of the Royal Navy in retaining its crews in American waters and the arrogant outrages committed by its impressment boarding parties, the more flagrant enormity was the indefensible, deceitful attack on an American warship. The *Leopard* might as well have bombarded Norfolk itself. If Britain condoned this act, or if the United States suffered it, American honor and independence meant nothing. Though Jefferson and Madison were in Washington, Gallatin and Secretary of War Dearborn were not.

They were sent for immediately, and Jefferson warned the Governor of Virginia to be prepared to "prevent future insults within our harbors," a reference to the menacing presence of a strong British squadron in the Roads. On July 2, the day after the cabinet reassembled, it issued a proclamation ordering British warships out of American harbors and refusing to them all supplies or other aid.

Madison had urged a much more strongly worded proclamation, and succeeded in inserting more outraged, defiant language in the final pronouncement. He then wrote American diplomats in Europe new instructions. Monroe was informed that "this enormity is not a subject of discussion," and that he was to demand of the British government a formal disavowal of the deed, release of the impressed seamen, punishment of the offending officers, and "as a security for the future, an entire abolition of impressments." Thus Madison sought to use the "spirit . . . of ardent and determined patriotism . . . roused by this occasion . . . pervading the whole community . . . [and] abolishing the distinctions of party" to extract a vital concession from Great Britain. Should satisfaction not be obtained, Monroe was to advise all American ships in British ports and in the Mediterranean to "hasten home," obviously in preparation for war. Madison instructed American ministers in Madrid and Paris to suspend negotiations to purchase the Floridas from Spain, since the probability of war would strain American finances, and because the advantages to Spain and France of a rupture between the United States and England were so great that the price ought to be "greatly reduced." Furthermore, in case of war with England, military actions in the Gulf of Mexico would soon make American "protection" of the Floridas necessary. Far from feeling the crisis with England weakened American posture vis-à-vis France and Spain, Madison sought to use it to stiffen his bargaining with them. Whether those nations would find this justifiable remained to be seen.[20]

The cabinet decided, for the time being, to dampen the ardor in the country, to give Britain a chance to offer apologies and reparations, to permit American vessels to return home, and to let Congress, not the executive, settle the issue of war. In deciding not to summon Congress immediately, however, Jefferson took a crucial step toward peace at a time when the cry for war was strong. Meanwhile the menacing British squadron in Hampton Roads caused Jefferson to suppose Britain might be intending to shell Norfolk or undertake other hostilities. Similar assaults might be planned on other cities. He ordered Governor Cabell of Virginia to hold 100,000 militiamen in readiness and to use the meager forces available to him to apprehend any landing parties from the British warships. The cabinet planned diplomatic moves and considered the state of the nation's defenses. Gallatin drew a long memorandum on the status of fifteen seaports he thought easy to defend and seven others, in-

cluding New York, Washington, Norfolk, and New Orleans, that
"require particular attention and more powerful means of defense."
Gallatin also outlined military operations against Halifax and other
places in Canada, and gave estimates of the men and money necessary
for them. During July 1807 frantic plans (on paper) for war and
desperate hopes for peace at once occupied the cabinet as it encountered
the most serious threat of war since the "X Y Z Affair" of 1798.[21]

Though the Republican leaders were honestly scrupulous about
Jefferson's stated reasons for cooling the war fever, anxious remarks
reveal that the nation's pitifully weak and vulnerable condition preyed
heavily on their minds. Gallatin asked if pilot boats from New York or
Philadelphia could be dispatched to the entrance to the Chesapeake to
warn inbound American vessels to avoid Hampton Roads because of the
British squadron there. Jefferson urged the Secretary of War to rush
federal defense measures, because the Virginia militia at Hampton Roads
had neither artillery nor money to pay for it. Madison told Monroe, in
warning American ships to return home, to use "the mode least likely to
awaken the attention of the British Government," and he also admitted
that the administration delayed war preparations that might offend Great
Britain to "avoid stimulating British cruizers in this quarter to arrest our
ships and seamen now arriving . . . from all quarters." Clearly, the
administration held back from war in substantial part because it was so
ill-prepared to fight. The British warships already operating in American
waters, and two regiments of marines at Halifax, could have with impunity driven American ships from their own coastal waters and devastated
a dozen American cities.[22]

Had Albert Gallatin been inclined to say "I told you so," he might
have reminded his colleagues at one of the impromptu dinners served that
July at the President's House of his memo two years before on the
connections between military and foreign policies. "An efficient navy,"
the Secretary of the Treasury had stated then,

> would have a favorable effect on our foreign relations. . . . So long as
> we have none, we must be perpetually liable to injuries and insults, par-
> ticularly from the belligerent powers, when there is a war in Europe;
> and in deciding for or against the measure, Congress will fairly decide
> the question whether they think it more for the interest of the United
> States to preserve a pacific and temporizing system, and to tolerate
> those injuries and insults to a great extent, than to be prepared, like
> the great European nations, to repel every injury by the sword. The
> Executive will, from their decision, know the course which it behooves
> them to pursue in our foreign relations and discussions.

In 1807 the force of this exposition was abundantly clear—and the
bankruptcy of the Republican effort to dodge its harsh alternatives was
equally so. Lacking a sword, the Republicans were stuck with "a pacific

and temporizing system," and their blunt, threatening posture in Europe had received the disdain and ridicule it was bound to invite in the absence of any force to back it up. Acquiescing in the defense policy authorized by Congress was consistent with Republican theory developed during the party battles of the seventeen-nineties, but it did not excuse the administration from heeding the admonition of Gallatin's last sentence. Though Jefferson and Madison might argue cogently that a large navy would involve the nation in more wars and might reasonably rely on thousands of zealous militiamen springing to arms, hundreds of American privateers wreaking havoc among British ships, and dozens of Spanish and British colonies in North America falling easy prey to nearby American forces, these were long-range factors that afforded little comfort to a city under the muzzle of Royal Navy guns or to an unarmed vessel fired on by British frigates. The restrained (some newspapers said cowardly and dishonorable) response to the *Chesapeake* "enormity" may have been wise and humane, but it was as well, the cabinet ruefully discovered, virtually the only course open to it. French Minister Turreau wrote after a long dinner conversation with Jefferson "that the President does not want war, and that Mr. Madison dreads it still more. I am convinced that these two personages will do everything that is possible to avoid it."[23]

When Madison returned to Washington on October 5, 1807, after a summer of severe rains (twelve inches one day) that washed away his milldam on Blue Run, he found word from Monroe that British Foreign Secretary Canning seemed conciliatory, but there was otherwise little to be hopeful about. Admiral Berkeley, in Halifax, had executed one of the men "whose restoration was included in the demand of reparation" for the attack on the *Chesapeake*, thus inspiring "great distrust" Madison wrote, "of the temper and intentions of the British Government." Newspapers announced the unprovoked attack of the British navy on the defenseless city of Copenhagen and the outcry in Parliament by the "West India interest" for harsher measures against American commerce. French and British seizures of American ships had mounted alarmingly. American frigates were immobilized because the crews were to be discharged to save expenses. The Secretary of War found the militia in a "really deplorable [state] all over the Union"—seven cannon in all Pennsylvania, and one musket for each five men.[24]

Alarmed that this unpreparedness and the peaceful mood which had replaced the war fever of the summer might force an irresolute course on the administration, Jefferson and Madison drafted a message to Congress Gallatin thought "rather in the shape of a manifesto issued against Great Britain on the eve of a war, than such as the existing undecided state of affairs seems to require." After two weeks of Congressional inaction, Madison had some Congressmen, the cabinet, and half a dozen naval officers for dinner. Madison also invited British legation secretary Augustus John Foster, presumably so that he might sense American indignation and resolve. Apparently unimpressed with the conversation, Senator John Quincy Adams noticed only that Dolley Madison was absent, "having very recently lost her mother." Four days later the Senator added, "I observe among the members great embarrassment, alarm, anxiety, and confusion of mind, but no preparation for any measure of vigor, and an obvious strong disposition to yield all that Great Britain may require, to preserve peace, under a thin external show of dignity and bravery." Foster noted the same mood, and so informed his superiors in London. Congress spent November and half of December passing administration bills providing less than $2 million for harbor fortifications and for the virtually immobile gunboats preferred by Jefferson to oceangoing vessels. Since this was one-tenth the estimated cost of a year of fighting, clearly war was not in the offing.[25]

In mid-December, many vessels that had made fast passages—of about a month—from Europe brought bad news. Napoleon's orders to enforce the Berlin Decree were in vigorous execution; George III had issued orders to his naval commanders to continue impressments; and the English cabinet had agreed on sweeping Orders in Council requiring every neutral vessel trading with any port in Europe to stop first in a British port and to get a British license. Though the news was not known for some months in the United States, Napoleon's response was the Milan Decree, declaring any vessel submitting to English search or regulations, or stopping at a British port, lawful prize. The effect, of course, was to abolish entirely the concept of neutrality. France and Britain each declared nations were either for them or against them. The only news hinting at all of conciliation was that a British emissary was on his way to settle the *Chesapeake* incident.[26]

Since neither Congress nor the administration had prepared for war, only one response could be made to the drastic decrees abolishing neutral commerce. The time had come for a full trial of the hallowed Republican doctrine of commercial retaliation. Madison hastily drafted a message for Jefferson, calling for an immediate embargo on all American shipping. Not only would this protect American vessels from almost certain seizure, but it would, Madison thought, with the Nonimportation Act made effective December 14, deprive European nations of a trade they needed desperately, or at least in the case of Great Britain, was so important and profitable to influential merchants that she would soon accede to American demands. Congress agreed and passed the Embargo Act on December 22, 1807. In the cabinet, only Gallatin had expressed uneasiness. He had urged an embargo for a limited time, because "in every point of view, privations, sufferings, revenue, effect on the enemy, politics at home, etc., I prefer war to a permanent embargo. Governmental prohibitions do always more mischief than had been calculated and it is not without much hesitation that a statesman should hazard to regulate the concerns of individuals as if he could do it better than themselves. . . . As to the hope that it may . . . induce England to treat us better, I think it entirely groundless."[27]

Madison had been devoted to the doctrine embodied in the Embargo since he was a college student at Princeton, where he had believed non-importation agreements in the colonies, if strictly adhered to, would maintain American rights. After 1783, when Britain discriminated against American trade, Madison argued that only a growing commerce with other nations, and American counterdiscrimination, would end British arrogance. As a member of Congress from 1789 to 1794, he proposed repeatedly that the United States retaliate against Britain unless she rescinded her restrictive navigation laws. He felt commercial warfare would prove effective because British trade was fatally exposed at two points: hundreds of thousands of workmen and scores of wealthy merchants in England depended for their livelihood on goods sold to the United States, and the British West Indies depended on the adjacent mainland for food and lumber. Therefore, to shut off exports to the Indies and imports from Britain would bring the Empire to its knees. Since the United States, with but little inconvenience, could do without the manufactured goods, mostly luxuries, imported from Britain, the entire stopping of Anglo-American trade was to her no tragedy. With perseverance, the United States could work its will on Britain without firing a shot. This Madison and Jefferson called on their countrymen to do as the year 1808 began.

Before the effects of the Embargo occupied all attention, Madison spent a month in fruitless talks with George Rose, sent to settle the *Chesapeake* affair. Rose's rigid instructions required him to act as though England, because of the welcome given to British deserters on American ships and the hostile proclamation of July 2, 1807, against British warships, was the injured party. The United States must, Foreign Secretary Canning ordered, withdraw the proclamation and disavow its encouragement and harboring of Royal Navy deserters *before* reparations of any kind could be discussed. Madison receded from his earlier insistence that satisfaction on impressments and settlement of the *Chesapeake* incident be linked, but he could not consent to treat the armed attack as a mere part, admittedly excessive, of the British right to reclaim deserters from its navy. Rose, lionized by Federalists, was so disdainful of Congress that he thought its plebeian character proved "the excess of the democratic ferment, . . . the dregs having got up to the top." He tried halfheartedly to find an accommodation, but the chasm between his instructions and the minimum needs of American dignity was too great. Ill through most of the negotiations, the fatigued Madison returned Rose's passport in late March. "Mr. Rose's mission is abortive," Madison wrote Monroe. "He will depart, I understand, without delay." Rose had come, as Henry Adams has remarked, "not to conciliate, but to terrify. His apology was a menace." Madison's health improved, and American self-respect increased, as Rose's homeward-bound frigate fell down the Potomac.[28]

While the Rose negotiations occupied Madison, the Embargo and its enforcement engrossed the country. Congressmen and segments of the public that, in the haste and confusion of December 1807, supported the Embargo either as a temporary measure to safeguard American shipping or as a prelude to war, became opponents when the administration simply persisted in the Embargo. Gallatin's collectors of customs meanwhile struggled manfully with the virtually impossible task of policing thousands of miles of coast and land borders. Movement of goods by land across the Canadian border for reshipment overseas reached alarming proportions. Shipowners rushed hundreds of vessels to sea in the weeks that passed between enactment of the law and the establishment of detailed regulations and penalties. Other hundreds were dispatched to take more or less fraudulent advantage of such loopholes as the right to send vessels for goods bought before the Embargo and the permission granted for coasting vessels to enter foreign ports in case of bad weather. Vessels trading between Boston and New Orleans often found it "necessary" to put in at Havana or some other Caribbean port because of "damage"; while there, it was easy to load a cargo of enormously profitable sugar. Gallatin informed the President that absolute authority by port officials over the movement of every vessel in their jurisdiction, the power to inspect warehouses throughout the country, and the raising of "a little army" on the Canadian border would be required to make the Embargo effective. As it stood, it served only to distress American citizens, disorder the economy, and penalize honest, law-abiding merchants. Gallatin saw that to give the Embargo effect would require executive aggrandizement and even oppression contrary to every republican principle, and would create opposition in the country fatal to Republican political hopes, and perhaps even to the Union itself.[29]

As the member of the administration most zealous for the Embargo, Madison sought particularly to use it to compel either or both of the belligerents to rescind its edicts against American commerce. In March 1808 he wrote that the Embargo "continues to take deeper root in the public sentiment," and that Congress had agreed to effective enforcement rules. In early April Madison declared the continuing insults to American commerce and diplomacy showed France and England were in "great ignorance of the character of the United States," and later that month he said that "no pains have been spared to stop every leak by which the effect of the Embargo laws might be diminished." Lest the warring powers think the United States needed their wares, the Secretary of State observed that "we are less unripe for manufacturing establishments than has been supposed." Furthermore, the United States stood ready to resume trade with either power if it withdrew its illegal edicts. If only one power continued to offend, she would "force a contest with the United States," Madison added. Courage to resist depredations, national unity behind commercial coercion, and faith in the American economy were Madison's shields against aggression and world war.[30]

Madison's private letters to Minister William Pinkney in London, only recently discovered, reveal that Madison thought the insolence of French and British officials, by "exciting all the indignation which was to be presumed," would "rivet" the Embargo on the United States and "reconcile more and more all parties to it." Madison warned further that there was "not the slightest indication of a purpose to rescind" the Embargo while its cause, "the colonizing aspect of the British Orders," remained. On May 1, minimizing Gallatin's difficulties, Madison declared, "The public mind everywhere is rallying to the policy of the Embargo, . . . the efforts to render it unpopular are recoiling on the authors of them, [and] . . . an indignation against the smugglers is moreover beginning to cooperate with those charged with its execution." Madison noted, too, evidence that some people in England saw "no excuse for persisting in the follies" of the orders in council. "In a government like that of Great Britain," constitutional theorist Madison observed, where one branch published its proceedings and thus was connected with public opinion, it was "of great importance to know what that opinion is and what it is likely to be." Thus, if Britain "calculated on the efficacy as well as the duration" of the Embargo, heeded "the distresses of the West Indies, the discontents at home, [and] the alienation of [American] habits from her manufactures," and considered that France by rescinding her decrees could expose Britain to the embarrassment of alone persisting in unjust policies and the threat of war with the United States, she would abandon the orders. Only "the pride of the Cabinet" could resist these considerations, Madison concluded.[31]

Apparently confident of the nation's commitment to his long-cherished plan, Madison set out for a vacation at Montpelier. Gale winds stopping the Potomac ferry, muddy roads, high waters on the Rappahannock, three days rainbound with Dolley's Winston relatives, and a flood on the Rapidan forced the Madisons to take seven days for the hundred-mile trip. The Secretary of State wrote the President, "I got home Friday night by taking my carriage to pieces and making three trips with it over Porter's mill pond in something like a boat, and swimming my horses." Though Dolley wrote that "my limbs yet tremble

with the terrors and fatigue of our journey," she actually had inflam-
matory rheumatism that gave her "more extreme sickness and pain"
than she had ever known before. Madison's mother and his niece, Nelly
Willis, cared for her "with great attention and kindness." Dr. John
Willis, whom Nelly had married in 1804, bled Dolley and gave her
medicine. She was well enough to entertain Jefferson in early June, but
she had had to miss completely a gathering of fifteen or twenty Madison
connections a few days before. Later in the summer, half a dozen of
Dolley's relatives at Montpelier "clapped our hands in triumph" at the
news that Anna Cutts had given birth to her third son; a week earlier, at
Monticello, the Madisons had cheered the arrival of Martha Jefferson
Randolph's third son, Benjamin Franklin (her second was James Madison), and celebrated the forthcoming marriage of her eldest daughter,
Ann. They did not, however, go to see James Monroe, who had lent aid
and comfort to the increasingly open movement to put him into the presidency instead of Madison. Back at Montpelier "a large party" filled the
house as the usual round of September festivities concluded.[32]

Keeping an eye on public affairs, Madison thought that despite Federalist victories in Massachusetts elections (gained by "shameful misrepresentations" and even vote fraud, he declared), the embargo retained "a
solid support in the judgment and patriotic pride of the great body of the
nation." Fourth of July celebrations around the country gave overwhelming support, and resolves of the South Carolina legislature recommending the Embargo and American manufactures seemed especially
important, coming as they did from a state supposedly dependent on
trade with England. Indeed, "the astonishing zeal for homespun, . . .
the looms and wheels set up" and sure to remain in operation after the
crisis, and "Legislative patronage to support them" if needed, would soon
close the American market to British manufactures. The harvest in the
United States, especially of wheat, was good enough to be most helpful
"to the nations which may need and be willing to receive" it. The Secretary observed to Pinkney that should England withdraw the Orders in
Council, causing the Embargo to be suspended in regard to her but continued against France, the British blockade of the Continent would be
strengthened by the American law. If Britain yielded, therefore, to "the
plainest reason" and to the "powerful objections" to the orders at home,
trade with her could be resumed immediately. On the other hand, if
France relaxed her decrees and Britain persisted in the orders, they would
acquire "the inevitable character of war."[33]

In late summer, however, Madison wrote more and more of "malignant partizans" who "flinched from . . . duty": they encouraged the
opinion that the United States would abandon the Embargo and declare
war on France, while "at the same time [they] promoted every effort to
render the Embargo unpopular and ineffectual." He wrote of treasonable

"collusions with Canada" on Lake Champlain by "the party hostile to the Administration," of smugglers who mixed "force and fraud" to flout American law, and of the "no inconsiderable quantity of provisions smuggled into the West Indies." The public unity created by French and British hostility, and the hope that peaceful persuasion would suffice, were giving way to concern and dismay. Dolley Madison reported in late August that "the President and Madison have been greatly perplexed by the remonstrances from so many towns to remove the Embargo. . . . The evading it is a terrible thing. Madison is uneasy and feels bound to return to the seat of government."[34]

Grim letters from Gallatin increased the uneasiness. Since Federalists had prevented the Embargo "from becoming a measure generally popular" in New England and New York, he wrote, "arbitrary powers . . . equally dangerous and odious" had become necessary for its enforcement. "Congress must either invest the Executive with the most arbitrary powers and sufficient force to carry the Embargo into effect, or give it up altogether," he asserted. The Canadian border along Lake Ontario and the Saint Lawrence River seethed. Bad collectors and inactive district attorneys, combined with too few gunboats and revenue cutters, made violations around Cape Cod daily occurrences. Though distressed by these "maligant maneuvres for vexing the Executive," Madison wrote back that the "public mind in [Virginia] appears to be unshaken" in support of the Embargo, despite a drop in grain prices largely blamed on it. In reply, after another month of desperate and often losing struggles against Embargo violations, Gallatin pointed out that "patriotism and union" were not sufficient to enforce a measure "the people have been taught to view . . . less as a shield protecting them against the decrees and orders of foreign powers, than as the true if not primary cause of the stagnation of commerce and depreciation of produce." He concluded that "I had rather encounter war itself than display our impotence to enforce our laws." Madison fumed at Federalist exultation over a speech by Canning ridiculing the Embargo: such glee sought to make the American people feel its government had been "grossly negligent or insidious," and proved the British-Federalist connivance to vitiate the Embargo.[35]

American unwillingness to endure the privations of the Embargo, and the unpatriotic, if not treasonable, defiance of the measure by many leading Federalists were, as Madison asserted repeatedly, prime sources of the impending failure. Other factors, though, were important enough to raise doubts that even full compliance by American citizens would have yielded success. The need of the American economy for its export market was greater than Madison supposed. Also, the haste and confusion of the Embargo's enactment, the delay in its implementation, permitting hundreds of vessels to put to sea, and traditional Republican "executive mildness" placed it under a heavy handicap. In 1808 six hundred American vessels sailed for foreign ports under special permission granted by the government. Moreover, the law did not forbid imports in foreign vessels, though they by law had to return in ballast (many did not), and the law did not prohibit exportation of specie to pay for the arriving cargoes. Thus a lively import business continued. Arrivals at Philadelphia in 1808 fell by only one quarter from the average of the preceding years.[36]

Abroad, since the Royal Navy had already shut off most of France's international trade, and Napoleon had little use for his remaining West Indian possessions, the Embargo had almost no effect on him. The American minister to France wrote that Napoleon would "prefer to [the Embargo] a war on our part with Great Britain, but would prefer it, to any state of things, except that of war." By diminishing British trade, the Embargo served as a substitute for his nonexistent navy. The Embargo pinched some in Britain, especially in the linen industry, dependent on American flax, but Britain's economy proved resilient, resourceful, and lucky. Large reserves of cotton and wheat, augmented by some shipments from the United States and some from other parts of the world, prevented serious shortages. In the potentially more vulnerable export field, though the United States took only one seventh rather than the normal one third of Britain's trade, the revolt against Napoleon in Spain opened her large Latin American empire to British goods, almost exactly matching the market lost in the United States. Also, the British West Indies proved not to be utterly dependent on American grain. Prices rose steeply, and grain imports sometimes were but one-half normal, but reserves, smuggling from the United States, and increased shipments from England prevented famine or severe hardship. World trade and the economy of the British Empire simply were not as critically dependent on the United States as Jefferson and Madison theorized. Their analysis was statistically correct in that had the American trade been completely withdrawn without leakage or replacement, the hoped-for unbearable dislocations might have come to pass, but the passage of goods across seas controlled by the Royal Navy was, as the Republican leaders might have foreseen, far too flexible for that.[37]

Finally, there were the diplomatic weaknesses in the Embargo. Most serious was the insufficiently calculated possibility—or even probability—that in a mortal struggle, both sides would find the resources to resist, and the careful defense of neutral rights and firm adherence to American interests expressed so cogently by Madison would turn to empty bombast and make the United States a laughingstock. Madison's urgent pushing of his diplomats to persuade each belligerent of the benefits of rescinding its edicts only heightened this impression. To Canning and Champagny

(Talleyrand's successor), the disingenuous argument that the Embargo signified no hostility to other countries proved only that the Americans had no other weapon. Canning scoffed: "If the Embargo is only to be considered as an innocent municipal Regulation, which effects none but the United States themselves, . . . His Majesty does not conceive that he has the right or pretension to make any Complaint of it; and He has made none. But in this light there appears to be not only no Reciprocity but no assignable Relation, between the Repeal . . . of a Measure of voluntary Self-restriction, and the Surrender by His Majesty of his Right of Retaliation against his Enemies." American Minister William Pinkney squirmed helplessly before this telling thrust, and Madison's reaction was merely to declaim about Britain's "very determined enmity," her "sneering" officials, and the "great folly" of her course. Eight months earlier Champagny had similarly insulted the United States. He told Armstrong that France would confiscate all American vessels in its hands unless the United States made the declaration her honor required of war on Britain.[38]

Pinkney, though, reported that the Embargo had begun to have effect, and would "be felt with more severity every day." The wheat harvest was "alarmingly short"; manufacturers were sustained by "temporary causes"; and cotton prices were rising. The Embargo had not been decisive only "because we have not been thought capable of persevering in self-denial." Even if the United States relaxed the Embargo as applied to Great Britain, the prevailing "spirit of monopoly" there would not "under any circumstances tolerate [the United States] as rivals in navigation and trade," and in an alliance, the United States would be in a state of "vassallage and meanness." Giving up the Embargo, Pinkney asserted, would throw the United States "bound hand and foot, upon the generosity of a government that has hitherto refused us justice, [and] sanction too the maritime pretensions which insult and injure us."[39]

Madison praised Pinkney's "excellent views" and included his letter among documents sent to Congress, because it "coincided . . . so entirely with the sentiments of the Executive." Madison hoped that "a spirit of independence and indignation" would reinforce the Embargo, that the British would be disabused of their "miscalculations" about weakening American resolve, and that the "narrow limits of discontent" in the United States would be diminished further by public disclosure of insults from France and Britain. Madison drafted the portion of Jefferson's last annual message to Congress praising the "candid and liberal experiment" of commercial retaliation, and by inference at least, urging persistence in the Embargo despite its lack of effect so far on the belligerents. Privately Madison wrote Pinkney that though some Congressmen favored war "as most honorable or least unprofitable, [probably] measures short of war will prevail; such as an invigoration of the Embargo, a prohibition of imports, *permanent* duties for encouraging manufactures, and a *permanent* navigation act: with an extension of preparations and arrangements for the event of war." Madison meant for his minister to use the prospect of these measures as only slightly veiled threats in his talks with Canning.[40]

Though Jefferson approved this course, his pending reversion to being "but a spectator" made him feel unjustified in urging measures others would have to carry out. Since Madison's election as President was by this time certain, the House of Representatives committee on foreign affairs, in "great perplexity and confusion," asked him for advice. He in turn consulted Gallatin, who wrote desperately to the President:

> Both Mr. Madison and myself concur in opinion that, considering the temper of the Legislature, or rather of its members, it would be eligible to point out to them some precise and distinct course. As to what that should be, we may not all perfectly agree; and perhaps the knowledge of the various feelings of the members and of the apparent public opinion may on consideration induce a revision of our own. I feel myself nearly as undetermined between enforcing the Embargo or war as I was in our last meeting. But I think that we must (or rather you must) decide the question absolutely, so that we may point out a decisive course either way to our friends. Mr. Madison, being unwell, proposed that I should call on you and suggest our wish that we might, with the other gentlemen, be called by you on that subject. Should you think proper, the sooner the better.[41]

Jefferson persisted in being a "spectator," so the President-elect (Madison) and the supposed Secretary of State-designate (Gallatin) drafted a report for the Congressional committee, concluding with resolves that the United States could not with honor submit to the French and British edicts, that all vessels of France, Britain, and other nations "violating the lawful commerce and neutral rights of the United States" be excluded from American ports, that imports from such nations be prohibited, and that "measures ought to be immediately taken for placing the country in a more complete state of defence." Madison explained to Pinkney that the resolves presented war and nonintercourse (including the Embargo) as the only options. The latter was more likely, and Congress would soon "make the Embargo proof against the frauds which have evaded it which can be done with an effect little apprehended abroad." He hoped further that the inclusion of France in the ban on foreign warships in American harbors, and other equalizations between the belligerents, might provide "Canning himself, if he was as much of a statesman as he is a Bel-esprit, and had less of Upstart arrogance," a grounds for peaceful settlement.[42]

Ten days of fumbling in Congress undermined Madison's confidence; he soon wrote of the indecision in government councils and of outcrys against the Embargo in "the Eastern States." He could not believe, he said, that there was "so much depravity or stupidity" there among "the body of intelligent people" to make them prefer secession to submission to the Embargo, though he had no doubt "such a project may lurk within a junto ready to sacrifice the rights, interests, and honor, of their country, to their ambitious or vindictive views." Clearly, though, concern about the extent of disaffection in New England increasingly caused Madison to consider withdrawal from the Embargo. At the same time, he told British Minister David Erskine that the United States was "fully justified" in commencing war with either belligerent and hesitated only "from the difficulty of contending with both." Madison asserted that though the United States "are not at all prepared for war," the people were incensed and began to feel the Embargo was "too passive." War might soon be regarded as "less injurious to the interests, and more congenial with the spirit of a free people." Madison's intention, of course, was to heighten the efficacy of commercial coercion by making war its clear alternative. For this to be credible, Congress would have to act energetically.[43]

Instead, in January and February 1809, a "factious spirit" spread as pressure from New England against the Embargo mounted. Petitions poured in on Congress, breathing defiance of the stricter enforcement measures. Boston declared all those who enforced the Embargo "enemies to the Constitution . . . and hostile to the liberties of this people"; the town of Wells, Maine, deplored that the national purse strings were held by "a Frenchified Genevan, . . . a satellite of Bonaparte"; and the little town of Alfred warned that "oppression did sever us from the British empire; and what a long and continued repetition of similar acts of the government of the United States would effect, God only knows!" Madison acknowledged to Pinkney that "the Eastern seaboard is become so impatient under privations of activity and gain . . . that it becomes necessary for the sake of the Union that the spirit not be too much opposed. . . . What is called the Essex party in Massachusetts are strongly [suspected of plotting disunion]. . . . Such is the [hatred] of that [faction to this] administration and its [devotion] to [England] as to account for the most [desperate plans]. It is believed also that there is an understanding between its [leaders and] the [British Ministry]." (Bracketed words were written in code.) Though Madison's own faith in the Embargo remained unshaken, the news from New England and the suspicions of treason clearly were decisive in leading him to countenance other measures. Confronted with the threat of foreign intrigue to disrupt the Union, and stunned by the widespread resistance to laws enacted by a popularly elected legislature, Madison drew back from the Embargo.[44]

On February 2, New England Republicans, Pennsylvania Quids, Clintonites, and John Randolph's little band joined with Federalists in the

House to repeal the Embargo as of March 4. The vote was 76 to 40. Madisonian Congressmen, seeking to limit the humiliating submission as much as possible, urged that the Embargo be continued against Britain and France and that imports from those nations be banned. Madison had to be content, however, with a weak measure repealing the Embargo, excluding foreign armed ships from American waters, and banning imports from France and England beginning May 30, 1809. Erskine called it "rather a nominal prohibition than a rigorous enforcement. . . . Great advantages may be reaped from it by England. . . . The whole measure is a subterfuge to extricate [the administration] from the embarrassments of the embargo system." Only the addition by the Senate of a clause empowering the President to renew trade with any nation that rescinded its illegal decrees strengthened Madison's hand. The session left Congressional Republicans splintered and demoralized. Madison wrote less than a month before his inauguration that "on no occasion were the ideas so unstable and so scattered." He blamed repeal on "the disorganizing spirit in the East," which he nevertheless hoped would be repressed by "universal indignation" against it elsewhere in the country and by bad news from England that made her aid to New England in case of civil war less likely. Madison's gloom at the problems he faced was matched by Jefferson's joy at fleeing them. "Never," the retiring President wrote, "did a prisoner, released from his chains, feel such relief as I shall in shaking off the shackles of power."[45]

Intrigues and maneuvers looking toward the presidential election of 1808 complicated the debates over foreign policy and the Embargo. Jefferson and most Republicans throughout the country never doubted, apparently, that at the end of his two terms the Republican candidate would be Madison, the cofounder of the party and its coleader for more than fifteen years. Though no written record survives, Jefferson and Madison in conversation certainly had reached a complete meeting of minds on the succession. The Federalists would oppose, of course, and as Republican party fissures began to show during Jefferson's second term, it became clear that Middle State and New England dissidents would back aging Vice President George Clinton of New York, while John Randolph and other Southern "Old Republicans" favored James Monroe. With Jefferson gone, Republicans for the first time faced an intraparty struggle for leadership. The Clinton forces had shown their dissatisfaction with the Virginia leadership almost as soon as Jefferson took office. George Clinton's replacement of Burr as Vice President in 1804 was not so much a reconciliation with the Virginians as a play for better leverage to oust them in 1808. As personal and patronage disputes festered and sectional jealousies heightened, the Clintonians became more dangerous, because they showed a willingness to cooperate with the Federalists to gain their ends.

The Randolph-Monroe movement, proclaiming itself "true Republican" and Madison a Federalist in disguise, seemed serious both because of its ideological earnestness and its possession, in Monroe, of a nationally respected candidate. Its base, however, was almost wholly in Virginia, North Carolina, and Georgia. As feelings cooled between Monroe and the Jeffersonian administration after the rejection of the British treaty of 1806, Randolph skillfully secured Monroe's tacit consent to oppose Madison for the nomination in 1808. Monroe was presented as the only real Republican devoted to the principles of 1798 and at least less pro-French than Madison. Whispering campaigns pictured Monroe as having the presence, dignity, fortitude, and virility that the small, unprepossessing Madison lacked.[46]

With these candidates in the field, the Congressional nominating caucus met on January 23, 1808, amid charges that members had not been properly notified. Anti-Madison Republicans generally boycotted the caucus; only 89 of 149 invited members came. Of these, 83 voted for Madison as presidential nominee and 79 for Clinton for Vice President, thus giving each a majority vote of all Congressional Republicans. Clinton repudiated the caucus without refusing its nomination, thus putting himself in the curious position of running independently for the presidency while a regular party nominee for Vice President. Forces supporting Monroe also repudiated the caucus, declaring it an undemocratic cabal hostile to the Constitution, and its nominee "unfit to fill the office of President in the present juncture of our affairs." The Monroe group had higher hopes for support in Virginia, but even there, in hurriedly called caucuses of members of the legislature, a meeting dominated by Madison's friends cast 124 votes unanimously for the Secretary of State, while the caucus of Monroe's backers managed only a 57-to-10 vote in Monroe's favor. Though the challenge by Monroe hurt Madison personally, he was clearly in a commanding position as the election year opened.[47]

The "campaign" for Madison, beyond that carried on by the increasingly effective Republican state and local organizations, consisted of newspaper editorials on his behalf and release of some of the diplomatic correspondence of his eight years as Secretary of State. *The National Intelligencer* praised him as the man "best fitted to guide us through the impending storm, . . . [of] irreproachable morals, solid talents, intelligence, fidelity, and zeal. . . . He has invariably displayed a dignity and moderation which are at once the best evidence, and the surest preservative of republican principles." Responding to Randolph's assertion that the Secretary of State lacked energy, the Richmond *Enquirer* noted Madison's role at the Federal Convention, and his vanquishing of Patrick Henry in 1788. Madison's energy, the editorial concluded, "rested on the most solid and durable basis—conscious rectitude supported by the most profound and extensive information, by an habitual power of investigation which unraveled with intuitive certainty, the most intricate subjects, and an eloquence, chaste, luminous and cogent." Opposition newspapers, recalling Madison's support of the pro-French peace instructions of June 1781 (see Chapter VII), charged that his partiality caused him to respond to French insults as though they exhibited only "the disinterestedness of a friend and the tenderness of a lover." After disclosure of Madison's stern rebukes to France, the Philadelphia *Aurora* retorted that the "delusion is now passed [that Madison] . . . contenanced, winked at, or connived at the decrees of France; and that [he was] silent on the subject of the aggressions practiced under those decrees." Federalists charged Madison with being too meekly and diffidently republican and too much Jefferson's sycophant to be President, while "Old Republicans" accused him of being a crypto-Federalist. Altogether the campaign turned upon defense of the administration and Madison's role in it, and assaults on it from opponents on all sides.[48]

The publication of Madison's official dispatches began in March, with the long letters on the rejected Monroe-Pinkney treaty. The effect was to vindicate Madison's position that acceptance of the treaty would have compromised neutral rights and allied the United States shamefully with Britain. Disclosure of the letters between Madison and British envoy George Rose exhibited again the secretary's dogged insistence on American dignity and honor. The insulting letter from Champagny, made public in April, excited indignation against France and pride in the American officials who responded to it. In November, just before the electors balloted, Jefferson sent to Congress another package of Madison's official letters, showing again that the secretary had dealt equally and firmly with the great belligerents. He was not partial to France, frightened of England, or prejudiced against her; rather, he had displayed a resourceful concern for American national interests. These documents defined Madison's platform and program.[49]

As the campaign reached a climax, however, it was apparent that the Embargo was the key issue. Madison's friends supported it, and his opponents reviled it. The election returns reflected, in many ways, the relative popularity of the measure in different sections of the country. In New England the Federalist candidate, Charles Cotesworth Pinckney, carried all states except Vermont. He also won in Delaware, and took two of nine districts in Maryland and three of eleven in North Carolina, giving him 47 electoral votes. Clinton received only 6 of New York's 19 votes. Monroe, whose electors lost to Madison's in Virginia by a margin of more than four to one, did not receive a single electoral vote. Madison carried Vermont, New Jersey, and Pennsylvania solidly, most of New York, Maryland, and North Carolina, and he made a clean sweep of the rest of the South and West, to roll up 122 electoral votes. Confronted by a Federalist party revived by the pinch of the Embargo, and serious defections among Republicans, Madison nevertheless entered the presidency with impressive public support.[50]

There is perhaps no better measure of Madison's career as Secretary of State than Senator John Quincy Adams' evolving reaction to it. During the seventeen-nineties, Adams had opposed Madison at almost every point: the New Englander was hostile to the French Revolution, a friend of Jay's Treaty, and of course, a zealous defender of his father's administration. Called home from diplomatic service in 1801, Adams entered the Senate as a Federalist. On his third day in Washington he quarreled with Madison about his accounts while abroad. Madison made "difficulties beyond what I conceive to be reasonable or proper," Adams complained. His next visit to the State Department was more congenial. He and the secretary talked of Massachusetts Historical Society affairs and agreed that constitutional technicalities should not interfere with the Louisiana Purchase, which Adams then supported in the Senate. After that the Massachusetts Senator seldom disagreed with Madison on diplomatic questions. He agreed that impressment as practiced by Britain was insufferable, and he considered Madison's *Examination* a work of "elaborate research and irresistible reasoning." Madison for his part spoke very favorably to Benjamin Rush of Adams in Philadelphia in 1805. Adams agreed that the Monroe-Pinkney treaty was unacceptable, and by 1807 he was generally considered an administration supporter. Federalist partiality to Britain and willingness to countenance disunion were anathema to an Adams. When he backed the Embargo, the Massachusetts legislature demanded he change his views. He refused, resigned, and defended administration measures "to preserve from seizure and depredation the persons and property of our citizens, and to vindicate the rights essential to the independence of our country against the unjust pretensions and aggressions of all foreign powers." Madison could scarcely have stated his own position more concisely. On his third day as President he nominated John Quincy Adams as minister plenipotentiary to Russia.[51]

Adams' ostracism by the Federalists and Madison's repudiation by the "Old Republicans" suggests the understanding of the national interest upon which the two men had come to agree. They abhorred the commercial and political bias implicit in Federalist willingness to continue the old trading ties with Great Britain, and they shunned the agrarian, isolationist naïveté of the "Old Republicans." For Madison this was consistent with more than thirty years of resistance to Britain and hardheaded protection of American interests abroad. For him, every French victory that humbled England had contributed to American security. Though in retrospect Napoleon might seem the most dangerous aggressor and tyrant of the first decade of the nineteenth century, from Madison's desk, Austerlitz and Jena were far less ominous than Trafalgar and Copenhagen. The first two glorified an army thousands of miles away, while the others emboldened a navy in daily contact with thousands of American citizens on the high seas and actually in control of the harbors and coastal waters of the United States.

During Madison's years as Secretary of State, only Napoleon's campaign in Santo Domingo and designs on Louisiana placed French power athwart American vital interests. Madison immediately mobilized to counteract these moves and did not scruple to seek English support in his effort. Napleon's failure in the Gulf of Mexico and his consequent sale of Louisiana underscored the relative capacities of France and Britain to threaten the United States. Nonetheless, Madison did not hesitate to condemn France for her illegal assaults on neutral trade, and never considered seriously an alliance with the French Emperor as a tactic to resist Britain. In fact, the dilemma of 1808 and 1809, when Madison and Jefferson seemed to court war with both great powers, is a measure of their impartiality, if also of their failure. Their primary goal was undeviating: to assert American independence by peaceful means, according to a humane understanding of international law.

Their difficulties arose from the unprecedented fury of the European war, the weaknesses of their country, and the limitations they imposed on themselves in fidelity to their republican principles. Participants in the wars of 1792 to 1815 soon abandoned the restraints that had generally characterized conflict in Europe since 1648. With the advent of "total war," the belligerents ignored the concepts of international law Madison upheld in his long, closely reasoned state papers. Locked in mortal struggle, Britain and France respected no power or authority not imposed on them by force of arms. In such an arena republican precepts of international relations counted for little. Though Madison's approach exhibits his enlightenment, it was not always relevant to the hard realities he faced.

Furthermore, despite the vast extent and limitless potential of the United States, she was not in 1805 a major power. She played an important role in world trade, and she had a strategic position in a global war, but it is doubtful if at any time during the Napoleonic Wars her support or friendship was vital to either side. Madison's consternation that Canning and Talleyrand ignored alike his logic and his threats might have been less had he assessed his own nation more objectively. A shrewd understanding of the Louisiana Purchase, for example, would have revealed it as in many respects a lucky accident. Suppose disease had not leveled Leclerc's army in Santo Domingo, or the second fleet not been icebound in Dutch harbors: would American blandishments then have impressed Napoleon? Though Madison acted wisely in taking such advantage as he could of the crosscurrents of war and European power politics, he would at the very least have saved himself anguish and dashed hopes had he been less tied to an early version of what has since been called "the illusion of American omnipotence."

Finally, certain Republican axioms were ill-suited to the Napoleonic era. A belief in executive forbearance, fiscal predilections that abhorred debt, a faith that standing armies and navies necessarily corroded freedom, a reliance on militia, an adherence to commercial coercion, and a long-range view that America was impregnable were, however correct and virtuous by themselves, dangerous when insisted upon categorically in a world at war. Thus the Jeffersonians merely asked Congress for defense appropriations, and they tried every alternative to a regular army and to a fleet. They placed debt reduction above national defense, and they persisted in the Embargo long after both their countrymen and foreign powers had recognized its failure. The result was to leave the United States virtually helpless in a world it could not compel to accept its republican precepts. By learning too slowly the exigencies of power, the Republicans endangered national survival. The great miscalculation of the Jeffersonian administration, for which Madison shared general, if not direct, administrative responsibility, left a chasm between the principles it proclaimed and the power and means necessary to give them effect. The Jeffersonians' fault was not cynicism or lust for power or infidelity to constitutional principles or partiality toward France or agrarianism or sectional bias; rather, it was a republicanism that left them disarmed in a hostile world.

Conduct in high office in such perilous times revealed, too, something of Madison's personal strengths and weaknesses. His manner often created the impression that he was indecisive, irresolute, ineffective, and evasive—and led many people to think him unfit for executive leadership. Cold and reserved in the presence of strangers or large crowds, small in stature, and weak voiced, he made an indifferent first impression. Foreign envoys to the United States often wrote disparagingly of him at first, and implied that he would be an easy mark. Furthermore, by scholarly and intellectual habit, he weighed matters carefully, sought subtle and sophisticated insights, and suspended judgments as long as possible; this tendency caused many to see him as a "closet politician," too little in touch with the practical world and too much wrapped up in his own thoughts and theories. The total effect denied to him the charisma necessary for dynamic leadership.

On the other hand, he was regarded by friend and foe alike as well informed, keen minded, and brilliant. In private conversation, and in councils of government conducted over long periods of time, he was persuasive and effective. The same foreign envoys who initially depreciated Madison came in time to see that his opinions and positions were more often than not the reigning ones in the administration. In April 1806, Senator William Plumer recorded a conversation between himself and Senator John Adair: "Mr. Adair said the President wants nerve—he has not even confidence in himself. For more than a year he has been in the habit of trusting almost implicitly in Mr. Madison. Madison has acquired a compleat ascendency over him. I observed that I considered Mr. Madison an honest man—but that he was too cautious—too fearful and timid to direct the affairs of this nation." Reflecting years later on Madison's habits of mind, Plumer noted:

> No man was more tenacious of his opinions than he was—he would die sooner than give them up; but then no man was more ready to waive for the present, their application to existing circumstances; e.g., the embargo which he so often recommended [from 1812 to 1814]; he was confident it was the best measure which the U.S. could adopt, that it was necessary for the support of the war, and would prove destructive to the enemy; in short he would allow no man to argue against it in his presence. Yet if permitted to have the whole argument for himself, he seemed less anxious about the immediate adoption of the measure which he then deemed necessary. He would say "Gentlemen the embargo is a most efficient measure—true, it is an admirable weapon against the enemy; but perhaps we had better defer it a few months—well, if you think so postpone it until the next session, but you will find there is nothing of equal to the embargo." It was the same with all other measures—if you agreed with him in the abstract, he would not contend much with you about particulars. Nothing would have induced him to surrender the neutral rights for which he so ably contended in his pamphlet and in his correspondence with England—but he was willing to pass them over—to say nothing of them—to put 'em in abeyance—to waive them for the present—with a caveat as to our rights; to maintain the argument and assert our principles, but to forbear their application. Something of this disposition is no doubt seen in most men, but it was remarkably characteristic of Mr. Madison, and forms the true explanation of his conduct in more than one important transaction.[52]

This intricate quality of Madison's mind, and the way it detracted from the impression of force in his character, is evident, too, in a comparison Hugh Blair Grigsby, who knew Madison in old age, made of the styles of Jefferson and Madison in their diplomatic dispatches. They exhibited in common, Grigsby noted,

> . . . perfect self-possession, ample research, great aptness in disquisition, and vigor and elegance of expression, [but Jefferson] hastened rapidly to his conclusions, [while Madison was] more elaborate in his argumentation. . . . Force and point and rapid analysis are the characteristics of the style of Jefferson; full, clear, and deliberate disquisition carefully wrought out, as if the writer regarded himself rather as

the representative of truth than the exponent of the doctrines of a party or even of a nation, is the praise of Madison. . . . Every paper from the pen of Jefferson abounds with expressions easily separable from context, which become the tocsin of party; while it is difficult to cull from the papers or even the speeches of Madison, written purely on party topics, an adage or a maxim, or even a pointed phrase, as a weapon to be used in the existing contest.[53]

The perceptive Gallatin noted after working daily with Madison for eight years that "Mr. Madison is, as I always knew him, slow in taking his ground, but firm when the storm rises." This dual quality explains the reactions both of indecisiveness and of steadiness, as well as Plumer's observation of Madison's habit of negotiating particulars once the essential principle had been settled. It explains, too, the repeated accusations that Madison vacillated, or changed his mind, when he had in fact merely moved to another refinement within a general principle—a refinement that to less subtle minds might seem simply contradictory. Hence the different application of strict construction to the Sedition Act and to the Louisiana Purchase. Until a question had received careful study and had been turned around and around in his mind, and until the proper priorities had been settled, Madison was indecisive, and doubtless until then, he did evade and obfuscate. However, after study and reflection, Madison was able to take such strong, well-founded positions that he held them tenaciously, argued them persuasively, and usually prevailed in cabinet councils. In executive office this might serve him ill when fast action was needed or when political acerbations made reasoned consideration impossible, but it served him well when deliberation was in order and when national policy required long-range wisdom and consistency. Thus, as Madison entered the presidency, those who knew him well might have anticipated the bright and dark spots of his administration.[54]

CHAPTER XIX

War Looms

A FEW days before Madison's inauguration as President on Saturday, March 4, 1809, spring weather arrived in Washington, cheering the throngs of visitors, especially young ladies from Baltimore, who came for the parties at the Thorntons', the Gallatins', and the Navy Yard. At dawn on Inauguration Day army and navy bands awakened the city with stirring airs, and the militia assembled for escorting duty. Thousands crowded Pennsylvania Avenue and the Capitol grounds. By midmorning in the chamber of the House of Representatives, *pêle-mêle* reigned: "There was an attempt made to appropriate particular seats for the ladies of public characters," Margaret Bayard Smith noted, but "the sovereign people would not resign their privileges and the high and low were promiscuously blended on the floor and in the galleries." Jefferson arrived at the Capitol a few minutes before noon, and Madison soon rode up in a carriage escorted by the Washington and Georgetown cavalry. He entered the hall of Representatives accompanied by Secretaries Gallatin and Robert Smith, Attorney General Caesar Augustus Rodney, and Jefferson's secretary, Isaac Coles. A committee of Congressmen escorted Madison to the front of the chamber, where he occupied the central chair. President Jefferson was on his right with cabinet members, Senators, and foreign diplomats. Justices of the Supreme Court sat in front, and Representatives in their places on the floor.

In an inaugural address of less than ten minutes Madison restated conventional republican principles but gave no hint of new directions the government might take in a world situation "indeed without a parallel." One of the ladies in the gallery recorded that he "was extremely pale and trembled excessively when he first began to speak, but [he] soon gained confidence and spoke audibly." Near the end, he paid tribute to his predecessor for "exalted talents zealously devoted through a long career" to the welfare of his country whose citizens now bade him an affectionate and grateful farewell. After Chief Justice Marshall, glum at having to install a political foe in high office, administered the oath, the new President left the hall; guns roared, and the militia formed along the route to the residence on F Street, where the Madisons held open house. "The street was full of carriages and people," Mrs. Smith reported, "and we had to wait near half an hour, before we could get in—the house was completely filled, parlours, entry, drawing room and bed room. Near the door of the drawing room Mr. and Mrs. Madison stood to receive their company. She looked extremely beautiful, was drest in a plain cambrick-dress with a very long train, plain around the neck without any handkerchief, and beautiful bonnet of purple velvet, and white satin with white plumes. She was all dignity, grace, and affability. Mr. Madison shook my hand with all the cordiality of an old acquaintance." He wore a suit of black American-made cloth; one observer deemed it "not a bit smarter than Mr. Jefferson's"—perhaps because both suits had been ordered from the same Connecticut factory and demonstrated support for the Embargo and infant American industries founded in response to it. Dolley Madison's finery, on the other hand, had been imported from Paris. As the crowd continued to press, and Madison's discomfort grew, Jefferson, nodding toward the new President, remarked that he was "much happier at this moment than my friend."

When the F Street house had disgorged its visitors, Madison rested, and Dolley changed to "a pale buff colored velvet" dress; she retained her gaudy bonnet, and adorned her handkerchiefless bosom with a pearl necklace. They arrived at the grand inaugural ball at Long's Hotel shortly after Jefferson (by then a "plain, unassuming citizen"), and were led into the hall to the martial air of "Madison's March," composed for the occasion. All eyes were on Dolley, who "looked a queen," and displayed such manners as "would disarm envy itself, and conciliate even enemies." One of the managers of the ball escorted her, and the President came in with Anna Cutts. Mindful of etiquette troubles during Jefferson's presidency, the managers very carefully had French Minister Turreau, "in all the splendor of gold and diamonds," escort Dolley to dinner and the English minister, David Erskine, her sister. Mrs. Robert Smith, resentful of the precedence given to Anna Cutts, came next and with Madison sat across the cresent-shaped table from the First Lady. Jefferson watched so benevolently and so happily that Margaret Smith declared that "a father never loved a son more than he loves Mr. Madison." The new President, on the other hand, was by midevening "spiritless and exhausted." With "a most woe begone face, and looking as if he could scarcely stand," he wished earnestly, he told one guest, that he could be home in bed. He exchanged pleasantries about well digging and "made some of his old kind of mischievous allusions" to the ladies, but the evening had become too much for him. The crowd elbowed around, peering over shoulders to get a look at Dolley, and almost pressing her to death. Spectators stood on benches, and the upper panes of the windows were broken for ventilation. Jefferson retired after a couple of hours, and the Madisons left immediately after dinner; the increasingly uncomfortable celebrants danced until midnight. Senator John Quincy Adams, a veteran of many official functions on two continents, dismissed the affair with a sentence: "The crowd was excessive—the heat oppressive, and the entertainment bad."[1]

The new chief executive and his wife were the objects of intense curiosity. Jefferson's studied informality, remarkable personal style, and wifelessness, together with the unfinished physical state of the capital, had given his administration a unique and unsettled social aura. By 1809, as a peerless hostess became First Lady and as Washington reached some maturity, its society obviously expected more grace and elaborateness. The social and personal qualities of the Madisons, therefore, became important. Though most observers gave far more attention and praise to the vivacious Dolley than to her reserved husband, Gallatin's sister-in-law, Mrs. Frances Few, passed a woman's critical judgment on them both:

> Mr. Madison the President-elect is a small man quite devoid of dignity in his appearance—he bows very low and never looks at the person to whom he is bowing but keeps his eyes on the ground. His skin looks like parchment—at first I thought this appearance was occasioned by the small-pox but upon a nearer approach, I found this was not the case—a few moments in his company and you lose sight of these defects and will see nothing but what pleases you—his eyes are penetrating and expressive—his smile charming—his manners affable—his conversation lively and interesting. Mrs. Madison is a handsome woman —looks much younger than her husband—she is tall and majestic—her manners affable, but a little affected. She has been very much admired and is still fond of admiration—loads herself with finery and dresses without any taste—and amidst all her finery you may discover that in neatness she is very deficient. Her complexion is brilliant—her neck and bosom the most beautiful I ever saw—her face expresses nothing but good nature. It is impossible however to be with her and not be pleased. There is something very fascinating about her—yet I do not think it possible to know what her real opinions are. She is all things to all men—not the least of a prude as she one day told an old bachelor and held up her mouth for him to kiss.

To a restrained Northerner like Mrs. Few, Dolley's open, perhaps noisy and fulsome Southern enthusiasms did seem overdone, but to most people she was the perfect hostess and First Lady.[2]

Jefferson finally got his abundant belongings out of the White House (first so-called at about this time) on March 11, so the Madisons then left the house on F Street where they had lived for eight years. They occupied the southwest corner of the President's mansion, while Richard and Anna Cutts with their three sons, James Madison and Thomas, aged four and three, and the baby Richard (two daughters, Dolley Payne and Mary, were born during the next six years), had quarters in the southeast corner. Dolley Madison's son, Payne Todd, a handsome, frivolous seventeen-year-old, at this time attending a Catholic boarding school in Baltimore, and Edward Coles, Madison's private secretary and Dolley's cousin, were the other "regular" members of the White House family. Various cousins and friends lived for months at a time with the Madisons, especially eligible young girls eager to take part in the increasingly gay Washington social whirl. Winstons from Virginia, Morrises from Philadelphia, and Duvals from Maryland came for full seasons. Nephews and nieces of the President were among the visitors, and Lucy Payne Washington, recently widowed, with her three young sons lived with the Madisons most of the time until she married Supreme Court Justice Thomas Todd in 1812. Thus, though the Madisons were childless and often are pictured as adults completely taken up with politics and society, in fact they lived all their lives amid young people and swarms of growing children. The White House was a very busy place from 1809 to 1814, more often than not filled to overflowing with a multitude of "connections."

In an extraordinarily generous mood, Congress appropriated $12,000 for repairs and improvements to the White House and $14,000 more for furnishings, decorations, and landscaping, all to be spent under the direction of the able architect Benjamin Henry Latrobe. He was also extravagant, and Jefferson warned that "the reins must be held with a firmness that never relaxes." He spent $2,150 for three mirrors, $556.15 for china, $458 for a pianoforte especially requested by Dolley Madison, and $220.90 for "knives, forks, bottle-stands, waiters, and Andirons" in his first purchase. The First Lady and the decorator alternately quarreled and exclaimed over the exciting task. Latrobe wished to place a large mirror to "repeat the landscape through the center windows," but when Dolley disagreed he gallantly told her (in French) that her wish was his command. Imported yellow satin and damask in the drawing room and red velvet curtains, also selected by Dolley, would, Latrobe feared, "entirely ruin the effect" he sought, but the bright, flamboyant tastes of the mistress again prevailed. On the other hand, the state carriage made in Philadelphia, a superb reddish brown vehicle trimmed inside with yellow lace, with an "elegant Cypher" on the door, delighted both Dolley and Latrobe.[3]

The farmer-President was more interested in food, drink, books, and shrubbery than in draperies and mirrors. He hired the excellent French

maître d'hôtel and chef, John Sioussa, left behind by the snobbish British
Minister Anthony Merry. When the Madisons were away Sioussa was
sometimes drunk, but he was otherwise faithful and provided well for
the Madisons and their guests as long as they lived in Washington. Madison restocked his wine cellar with Madeira, port, and champagne imported from France, and purchased the ninety-three volumes of the
Encyclopédie Méthodique from Joel Barlow for $488.88. The White
House grounds, which in Jefferson's day had been forest and pasture,
were also to be "improved." The President watched Latrobe's men plant
fifteen native trees in lines, twelve other varieties for clumps and screens,
and more than two dozen flowering trees and shrubs about the White
House yard. Though many visitors continued to be displeased or even
disgusted with what they thought was the unkempt, disgraceful condition of the "Palace" and its grounds, Madison very clearly wanted a place
to live befitting the dignity of his high office and the honor of his
country.[4]

By May 31, 1809, Dolley Madison thought the redecorating far
enough along to have the first of her soon-to-be-famous Wednesday
"drawing rooms." Congressmen and their wives, socially prominent
Washingtonians, visiting belles, and foreign emissaries crowded the
White House rooms for a glimpse of the new furnishings and the new
presidential pair. Military music filled the house, and the guests helped
themselves from buffets loaded with punch, cookies, ice cream, and
fruit. Those who recorded their impressions of the Madisons joined in
praise of Dolley's elegant dress and hair style, ample figure, magnetic
personality, and gracious manner, while one of the few who noticed the
President recorded that he was "a very small thin pale-visaged man of
rather a sour, reserved and forbidding contenance. He seems to be incapable of smiling, but talks a great deal and without any stiffness. . . .
[He] was in black, his hair dressed in a very oldfashioned style—a large
club highly powdered, his locks long without any curl or fizzing and his
hair combed down on his forehead." Six months later, early in the next
social season, a guest reported that "Mr. Madison appears to be bending
under the weight and cares of office," but that "Mrs. Madison who
performed the duties of the Levee appeared a robust and hearty lady. . . .
[General Turreau] as usual was the finest, best dressed Man" present.
Since the President never quite reconciled himself to large, formal occasions, his wife more and more dominated White House gatherings. Washington society, on the other hand, still self-conscious and insecure,
continued to dote on and rave over the costumes and manners of visitors
from foreign courts.[5]

By mid-July 1809 the Madisons, accompanied by Anna and Richard
Cutts and their children, were ready to go to Montpelier in the new

traveling coach. They arrived amid another flurry of house building. Aided by Jefferson's brickmaker, Madison had kept his kilns busy supplying materials for rebuilding the foundations and chimneys of his house. Skilled carpenters built a colonnade over the sunken icehouse, one of the earliest in Virginia, that kept cool drinks and ice cream ready for the many visitors to Montpelier. Moreover, with aged mother Madison still occupying nearly half the original house, the Cuttses and Washingtons regular summer residents, and the number of guests sure to grow, an enlarged mansion was badly needed. According to plans drawn by William Thornton, a Washington neighbor and the architect of the Capitol, and with the aid of the industrious Latrobe, Madison added one-story wings on each side of the house. The wings preserved the symmetry of the house and gave it the spaciousness and grace scores of travelers remarked on during the next thirty years.[6]

On August 2 the summer season at Montpelier reached a peak with the arrival of Mr. and Mrs. Samuel Harrison Smith. Dolley asked immediately where their little girls were, and upon being told they had been left home, for "fear of incomoding my friends," the hostess said, "I should not have known they were here, among all the rest, for at this moment we have only three and twenty in the house!" Though leaving their adored friend Jefferson had made the Smiths sad during the twenty-five-mile ride from Monticello, their spirits were improved "instantly . . . by the cheering smile of Mrs. Madison and the friendly greeting of our good President." Mrs. Smith described the visit in her diary:

It was near five o'clock when we arrived, we were met at the door by Mr. Madison who led us in to the dining room where some gentlemen were still smoking segars and drinking wine. Mrs. Madison enter'd the moment afterwards, and after embracing me, took my hand, saying with a smile, I will take you out of this smoke to a pleasanter room. She took me thro' the tea room to her chamber which opens from it. Everything bespoke comfort, I was going to take my seat on the sopha, but she said I must lay down by her on her bed, and rest myself, she loosened my riding habit, took off my bonnet, and we threw ourselves on her bed. Wine, ice, punch and delightful pineapples were immediately brought. No restraint, no ceremony. Hospitality is the presiding genius of this house, and Mrs. Madison is kindness personified. . . . The house seemed immense. It is a large two story house of 80 or 90 feet in length, and above 40 deep. Mrs. Cutts soon came in with her sweet children, and afterwards Mr. Madison, Cutts, and Mr. Smith. The door opening into the tea room being open, they without ceremony joined their wives. They only peeked in on us; we then shut the door and after adjusting our dress, went out on the Piazza—(it is 60 feet long). Here we walked and talked until called to tea, or rather supper, for tho' tea hour, it was supper fare. The long dining table was spread, and besides tea and coffee, we had a variety of warm cakes, bread, cold meats and pastry. At table I was introduced to Mr. William Madison, brother to the President, and his wife, and three or four other ladies and gentlemen all near relatives, all plain country people, but frank, kind, warm-hearted Virginians. At this house I realized being in Virginia, Mr. Madison, plain, friendly, communicative, and unceremonious as any Virginia Planter could be—Mrs. Madison, uniting to all the elegance and polish of fashion, the unadulterated simplicity, frankness, warmth, and friendliness of her native character and native state. Their mode of living, too, if it had more elegance than is found among the planters, was characterized by that abundance, that hospitality, and that freedom, we are taught to look for on a Virginian plantation. We did not sit long at this meal—the evening was warm and we were glad to leave the table. The gentlemen went to the piazza, the ladies, who all had children, to their chambers, and I sat with Mrs. Madison till bed time talking of Washington. When the servant appeared with candles to show me my room, she insisted on going up stairs with me, assisted me to undress and chatted till I got into bed. How unassuming, how kind is this woman. How can any human being be her enemy. Truly, in her there is to be found no gall, but the pure milk of human kindness. If I may say so, the maid was like the mistress; she was very attentive all the time I was there, seeming as if she could not do enough, and was very talkative. As her mistress left the room, "You have a good mistress Nany," said I. "Yes," answered the affectionate creature with warmth, "the best I believe in the world—I am sure I would not change her for any mistress in the whole country." The next morning Nany called me to a late breakfast, brought me ice and water (this is universal here, even in taverns), and assisted me to dress. We sat down between 15 and 20 persons to breakfast—and to a most excellent Virginian breakfast—tea, coffee, hot wheat bread, light cakes, a pone, or corn loaf—cold ham, nice hashes, chickens, etc.[7]

Over their wine in the parlor and while smoking on the front porch, Madison and his male guests talked gravely of bad news—a "mixture of fraud and folly" on the part of England, the President wrote his predecessor, that placed him under "the mortifying necessity" of setting out at daybreak for Washington. In a whirlwind trip, Madison spent three days on the road each way and three days in Washington, where he conferred with his cabinet and studied "volumes of papers" from Europe. He had no time for visits, he wrote Dolley, and the period of his stay would, "you may be sure, . . . be shortened as much as possible. Everything around and within reminds me that you are absent, and makes me anxious to quit this solitude." A few days after Madison's return to Montpelier, the Gallatins arrived, and the entire company went to Monticello on August 24. They took the winding road up Jefferson's mountain, through "untamed woodland," and emerged on its cultivated summit to find "a noble pile of buildings, surrounded by an immense lawn, and shaded here and there with some fine trees." The ex-President rode out to greet them and took his guests to meet his family of twelve: his daughter and son-in-law, their nine children, and their eldest daughter's husband. The three statesmen mixed earnest conversation in the library with rambles about the plantation, leisurely meals, and games with the children, the only time, Jefferson said, "that a grave man can play the fool." Back at Montpelier during September, the Madisons continued the round of visits, and arrived in Washington in early October refreshed from "two months on our mountain."[8]

Clearly, under Dolley's presiding genius, and with her husband's entire approval, both in Washington and at Montpelier the years of Madison's presidency were a social triumph. The honor and dignity of the republic, never separate in Madison's mind from the success of the experiment in republican government, seemed to require some elegance and style in its social life. The deliberate informality of Jefferson's administration, necessary to deflate the courtly pretensions of the Federalists, could with Dolley's magic touch be discarded for dinners, receptions, balls, and visits that were graceful, and even magnificent, without being unrepublican. Though provincial Republicans remained suspicious and uncomfortable, viewing the elegance of Dolley's drawing room as further evidence that her husband had become a Federalist, in fact the Madisons set entertaining standards that dominated Washington social life until the Civil War. (James Buchanan, for example, learned etiquette at Dolley Madison's salon, and thought her the epitome of social grace.) The pattern reflected Madison's lifelong desire to unite cultured graces and the best of European tradition with attitudes, habits, and customs thoroughly republican. It also demonstrated his conviction that the new nation had a character so unique that every aspect of its life was worth the attention of those who cared for its future. Dolley Madison's memorable personality thus was consistent with her husband's comprehensive understanding of the nature of the republic.

Madison needed all this social serenity and family diversion because, even before his inauguration, he knew that the Republican party unity of Jefferson's administration, already frayed by John Randolph and a few other dissidents, threatened to unravel utterly. Aware of Gallatin's acute understanding of foreign affairs, and like Jefferson, anxious to have his chief counselor in the State Department, Madison had notified William B. Giles and other Senators that he intended to nominate Gallatin as Secretary of State. A powerful group of Republican Senators, led by Giles, Samuel Smith of Maryland, and Michael Leib of Pennsylvania, soon to be called the "Invisibles," opposed Gallatin. Backed by disaffected Clintonians, William Duane's powerful Philadelphia *Aurora*, and by individual Republican malcontents, and with the obstructing support of the Federalists, the "Invisibles" were in a strong position. Holding the balance of power in the Senate, they could block Gallatin's nomination and cause endless other difficulties for the President. Senator Giles apparently thought *he* should be Secretary of State, while Senator Smith thought his brother Robert, Jefferson's Secretary of the Navy, deserved the post. Others favored James Monroe, undoubtedly qualified, but he could not join the cabinet at least until the strains of his opposition to Madison for the presidency in 1808 had been eased.

Madison saw he had to compromise. He considered promoting Robert Smith to the Treasury Department in exchange for Senatorial support for Gallatin's switch to the State Department, but Gallatin demurred. During eight years with Smith in Jefferson's cabinet, Gallatin had come to enjoy the affable, generous Navy Secretary (as had the Madisons), but Smith's lazy incompetence was all too painfully evident. Gallatin knew he would have to do the work of the Treasury Department as well as the State Department under Madison's plan, so he preferred to remain at his old post. The only way, then, Madison could attain his primary goal, keeping Gallatin in the cabinet, was to retain him as Secretary of the Treasury, where he would not need confirmation by the Senate. Desperate to restore party harmony, Madison offered the State Department to Robert Smith, knowing that he himself would have to do what Gallatin had declined: continue to perform his old duties as well as discharge those of the presidency. John Randolph of Roanoke said with wise sarcasm of Smith, "as he can spell he ought to be preferred to Giles."

Political necessity and sectional balance seemed to force mediocrity on Madison for the rest of his cabinet. He retained Jefferson's Attorney General, Caesar A. Rodney of Delaware, a zealous Republican who served competently but who continued a private law practice in Wilmington that kept him away from Washington for weeks and even months at a time. The War and Navy departments, insignificant offices in peacetime, and according to republican orthodoxy, not to be aggrandized under any circumstances, were allotted sectionally. Jefferson's Secretary of War, General Henry Dearborn, had been given a really important (and lucrative) office, collector of the port of Boston, thus making way for another New Englander, William Eustis, a physician of note and a devoted Republican, who in two terms in Congress had become a congenial part of the Washington social scene. He was, moreover, the son-in-law of New Hampshire Republican stalwart John Langdon. With these advantages he apparently did not need to have any particular talents or experience qualifying him for the War Department. For Secretary of the Navy Madison chose Paul Hamilton, a former governor of South Carolina who had neither qualifications for the post nor political connections promoting him for it. He was, it seems, simply an unobjectionable Southerner.[9]

Thus at the outset Madison found himself saddled with one of the weakest cabinets in American history. Its only strong member, Gallatin, was restless in a post neither his nor the President's first choice and without the support of Congress. Thus situated, however much Madison valued his counsel, and however able his own labors, Gallatin was sure to be a political liability, as easy target for the disaffected press and Congressional critics. The weak appointments in the War and Navy departments might in normal, Jeffersonian times have been of little consequence; attending to a few hundred soldiers at frontier posts and directing a handful of frigates were not demanding jobs. As war impended, however, with the consequent build-up of the armed forces, the weakness became alarming. Smith's place in the State Department might have been tolerable too, had he merely done nothing and let Madison continue to handle the diplomatic correspondence and take the lead in delicate talks with foreign ministers in Washington. Madison did in fact undertake these tasks, but Smith's official position meant he could make embarrassing, contrary proposals and remarks, while his political position, tied to his brother's power in the Senate, made him a center of antiadministration intrigue within the cabinet itself.

Madison, of course, recognized these liabilities, and accepted them in an obvious bid for party unity and Congressional support. Perhaps he knew, too, that sooner or later, especially if war became more rather than less probable, he would have both to challenge the "Invisibles" and to insist upon more able colleagues, whatever the political price. For the time being, though, he chose to postpone the confrontation, hoping that time or changing circumstances would make it unnecessary. This course suited Madison's personal inclination to avoid crises and was as well essential to his concept of the presidency. He wanted desperately to lead an administration of national unity and of peace. He could not do this if at the outset he undertook a bitter struggle over offices and chose chiefs of the armed services looking toward war.

The astute Gallatin saw immediately that his own position was seriously compromised and that unless there was a miraculous return of peace and harmony, the President had rendered his own task almost impossibly difficult. During the August 1809 visit to Monticello the Republican triumvirate discussed the prospects. Gallatin, deeply wounded by the "unmerited" insults he had suffered from Congress, wanted to resign. Furthermore, he was worried about the tendency of the Republican administration to let expenditures exceed receipts, something permissible in wartime, but to Gallatin utterly repugnant otherwise. Madison's response to this warning is not known, but Jefferson agreed heartily, adding that on Madison and Gallatin alone hung the responsibility for the debt reduction so "vital to the destinies of our government." Assured of Jefferson's support, and feeling better that the situation had been fully

aired before the President, Gallatin "relinquished the idea [of resigning]
. . . in a great degree on account of my personal attachment to Mr.
Madison, which is of old standing, I am sure reciprocal, and strengthened
from greater intimacy." Furthermore, the native Genevan acknowledged that "gratitude . . . to the country which has received me and
honored me beyond my deserts, the deep interest I feel in its future welfare and prosperity . . . [and] the desire of honorably acquiring some
share of reputation . . . would induce me not to abandon my post."
Jefferson's rhetoric and a personal loyalty to Madison kept Gallatin in a
cabinet he thought certainly headed for treacherous political shoals and
perhaps even, with or without the grudging consent of the President,
willing to enact unrepublican measures.[10]

For two years Madison endured the political cross fire while laboring
patiently at tasks his incompetent Secretary of State should have undertaken. The "Invisibles" in the Senate continued their vendetta against
Gallatin, pictured by their editor-accomplice, William Duane of the
Philadelphia *Aurora*, as an evil genius filled with "horrible . . . duplicity
and cunning [who] sought to enhance his own interest, power, and
aggrandisement by the most insatiate avarice on the very vitals of the
unsuspecting nation." Gallatin's policies were called imbecile and mean.
More and more his foes revealed their deeper motive by inculpating
Madison as well and hinting that in 1812 Republican leadership would
have to pass to other hands. "If Mr. Madison suffers *this man* to lord it
over the nation," Duane proclaimed, "Mr. Gallatin will *drag him down*;
for no honest man can support an administration of which he is a member." Resentment at Gallatin's influence, envy of his keenness, anger at
his resistance to the spoils system, and a perception that his "foreignness"
made him politically the most vulnerable member of the administration,
combined to make hostility to him the rallying point for factions more
and more often able to frustrate Madison. Like Hamilton, the brilliant
Gallatin, administering the tax-gathering Treasury Department, seemed
to focus on himself all the negative, always-in-opposition attitudes left
over from the revolutionary struggle against Great Britain. Federalists
and the ever-querulous John Randolph, though they had no love for the
"Invisibles," nevertheless aided in moves to embarrass the administration.[11]

Had the opposition been confined to dissident Congressmen, angry
editors, and even considerable segments of the public, Madison might
have managed by girding his administration in united support of his
policies. Smith's presence in the cabinet, however, balked every such
effort. He was his Senatorial brother's willing accomplice, passing on
information to him (and to the press) that repeatedly undercut administration policy. Smith implied repeatedly to foreign representatives that
powerful forces in the country (*i.e.,* his brother's business and political

friends) disagreed with the President. Since Jefferson and Madison had each been Secretary of State before becoming President, Smith even fancied his standing off from the administration in a conciliatory posture toward England would (with Federalist support) put him in line for the presidency in 1812. The effect from Madison's standpoint was utterly debilitating. Both French and British ministers could, when confronted by his diplomacy, discount it, noting that not only Federalists but important Republicans and even cabinet members did not support the President. Madison's conversations with these same foreign agents, as well as common gossip in Washington, made Smith's disloyal indiscretions perfectly well known. Seeing no acceptable replacement readily available, and not willing to further jeopardize party unity by firing Smith, Madison carried on. John Randolph, as usual venomously perceptive, remarked that "our Cabinet presents a novel spectacle in the world; divided against itself, and the most deadly animosity raging between its principal members—what can come of it but confusion, mischief, and ruin?"[12]

Madison's main reason for delaying firing Smith, however, was that he wanted to replace him with James Monroe. Almost from the day of Madison's inauguration, Jefferson and others had worked to reconcile the two Virginians, who had, except for opposition in 1808, been personal and political friends for nearly thirty years. Madison valued Monroe's talents, his energy, his republican zeal, and the political support he could bring to the administration. Monroe, for his part, retained a deep admiration for Madison, knew that reconciliation was the only way to redeem his political fortunes, wanted to run the State Department, and saw increasingly that his policy differences with Madison were in fact over relatively trifling matters of means and emphasis. Only Monroe's pride and unwillingness to displease the Virginia and North Carolina "Old Republicans" who had supported him in 1808, and Madison's feeling of awkwardness in inviting Monroe to join him, prevented action. Monroe declared in April 1810 that "Mr. Madison is a Republican and so am I." Much of the personal coolness disappeared the following summer, when Monroe went to Washington. His reception by the President and the cabinet was "kind and friendly," and the Madisons later visited the Monroes in Albemarle. John Randolph, glad to have arrived himself after "the royal birds [the Madisons] had just taken their flight," reported that Monroe's mind was "wholly occupied . . . by public affairs whilst he would seem bent on private ones." Monroe's election as governor of Virginia in January 1811 underscored his eagerness to return to public life and provided him a prestigious place from which to move in response to a "call of duty" from Washington. Randolph saw what was coming and dismissed Monroe with the epithets "Traitor" and "Judas."[13]

The disarray in Washington during the session of Congress ending on March 3, 1811, made Gallatin's position impossible. The recharter of the Bank of the United States had failed, and warfare between Gallatin and Smith had intensified. Gallatin wrote the President that "under existing circumstances" he could no longer be useful in the cabinet. The adversities and embarrassments confronting the United States required "a perfect heartfelt cordiality" within the cabinet, Gallatin told his chief, while, in fact "new subdivisions and personal factions, equally hostile to yourself and the general welfare, daily acquire additional strength." The lack of confidence this caused at home and abroad made "a radical and speedy remedy . . . absolutely necessary." Since his presence in the cabinet "invigorated" the opposition to Madison himself and threatened to destroy Gallatin's own reputation, the secretary tendered his resignation, conscious nonetheless of his "personal attachment" to the President and of "the grateful sense I ever will retain of your kindness to me."[14]

Madison could hardly have been surprised at the letter (in fact it was probably part of a careful plan arranged by the two Republican leaders to strengthen their councils by substituting Monroe for Smith), and he instantly returned it. Newspapers and letters from Congressmen had for weeks hinted about an impending change in the State Department. Monroe, at the same time, had rejected third party suggestions and otherwise drawn nearer the national administration. The adjournment of Congress on March 3, permitting Madison to make a recess appointment effective for eight or nine months without Senate confirmation, together with Gallatin's formal "either Smith or me" ultimatum, allowed the plan to be set in motion. Through Senator Richard Brent of Virginia the President received assurances that Monroe would accept the State Department. Monroe was sure "the utmost cordiality would subsist" should he join Madison and Gallatin in Washington. Madison offered the post to Monroe on March 20, and Monroe immediately accepted, asking only that the President permit him to act as his own "judgment and conscience" dictated—that is, that the effort to find an accommodation with England (the purpose of his rejected 1806 treaty) be pursued earnestly. Madison reassured him that such an accommodation had been his purpose ever since he had become Secretary of State in 1801. Differences between them from 1806 onward, Madison wrote, "turned not a little on different understandings of certain facts and constructive intentions rather than on the merits of the questions decided." The President was sure "free consultation and mutual concession" would bring "the necessary unity" to the executive councils. Face thus saved, Monroe accepted what he termed "fair and liberal principles," and agreed to be in Washington in a week or two. By being courteously vague and by avoiding blame or recrimination, the two men were able to focus on underlying harmonies. Madison had, without diminishing his authority to guide foreign policy, gained a strong right arm and was free to do battle with his "Invisible" enemies.[15]

Smith's insufferable disloyalty and incompetence finally led to his dismissal early in 1811. The "straw" was telling British chargé John Morier that he (Smith) did not believe French assurances officially accepted by the United States government, that the American system of commercial retaliation against Britain should be abandoned, and that Britain "had a right to complain" about American diplomacy. Whatever the intrinsic merits of such positions, for a cabinet member to express them officially to a British representative could only be considered sabotage. Morier, of course, immediately wrote his government that cabinet dissension rendered American threats impotent. Madison heard of the talk almost at once and ordered the secretary to disavow it formally. Instead, Smith merely persuaded Morier to "withdraw" his first report (impossible, since a copy was already on its way to London) and send another omitting the account of Smith's remarks. Smith followed this indiscretion by questioning the new French minister in a way that destroyed any hope of persuading him of American resolve, candor, or good will.[16]

Smith, with hurt innocence, recounted that Madison had in February 1811 with a "high degree of disquietude, . . . fretful expressions, . . . [and] peevishness," complained of his blundering conversations with the French minister. In fact, Smith had witnessed Madison's last, and for him extraordinarily blunt—but still ineffective—attempt to persuade Smith to be quiet. Personal relations between Smith and the President were also cooling. Then, waiting only for Congress to adjourn, and for assurances that Monroe would join the cabinet, Madison again called Smith to his office. Admitting a "delicate and disagreeable" situation, the President nonetheless declared he meant to be "candid and explicit." It had become "notorious," he said, that despite "apparent cordiality" at meetings, a lack of "harmony and unity" in the cabinet sapped its strength and hindered its success. "Language and conduct out of doors counteracted what had been understood within to be the course of the Administration and the interest of the public." This state of affairs, Madison averred, "was exclusively chargeable" to Smith. The secretary expressed surprise that the President "should have yielded to such impressions; declared that he had given no cause for them," and expressed his undeviating desire to bring credit on the administration. Madison replied that he had "long resisted [unfavorable] impressions . . . but that . . . facts and circumstances [had been] brought to [my] knowledge from so many sources and with so many corroborations, that it was impossible to shut [my] mind against them." It was painful, he added, to have to believe that one to whom he had given "constant aids . . . in discharging his duties . . . should privately set himself against me." Smith again denied any "unfriendly conduct" and asked what motive he could have for so acting and what particular misdeeds the President had in mind. Madison said he could not possibly guess the motives, and then painfully recounted Smith's conversations with disgruntled Republicans, disaffected Federalists, angry newspaper editors, and foreign diplomats, undercutting administration policy and even divulging state secrets.[17]

Smith still denied everything. The President again insisted his sources were unimpeachable, and observed that "the labor I had taken upon myself in behalf of [Smith's] official duties, and for his credit . . . ought to have found" a return other than Smith's duplicity. When Madison pointed out the many ways the State Department "had not been conducted in [a] systematic and punctual manner," Smith retorted that this remark reflected only the President's excessive fastidiousness. Madison replied hotly that Smith was "in great error," reminding him of the "crude and inadequate" way his dispatches were brought to the White House, which, Madison said, "generally obliged [me] to write them anew myself, under the disadvantage, sometimes, of retaining thro' delicacy, some mixture of [your] draft." The President pointed out further that Smith neglected utterly to urge informally on Congressmen measures useful to the conduct of his department. When Smith denied the propriety of such executive initiatives, Madison remarked "that where the intention was honest, and the object useful, the conveniency of facilitating business in that way was so obvious that it had been practiced under every past administration, and would be so under every future one; that Executive experience would frequently furnish hints and lights for the Legislature; that nothing was more common than for members of Congress to apply for them; and that, in fact, such communications . . . were indispensable to the advantageous conduct of the public business."

Having thus expressed a positive theory of executive leadership not usually associated with his administration, Madison offered Smith a "lenient" way out: would he like to resign from the State Department to become American minister to Russia? Sensing this was "exile to Siberia," Smith asked for the similar post in London. Madison replied that even if he hadn't "another arrangement" in mind for that assignment, London was "a place of discussions and negotiations, calling for appropriate talents and habits of business." Madison spoke bluntly, he later noted, to "repress miscalculations" on Smith's part. Undaunted, the angry secretary inquired about a pending vacancy on the Supreme Court. The President noted Smith's slight acquaintance with the law, and "that the Senate would probably he hard to please in such a case." Smith then mentioned the main cause of the political troubles—"a body of firm friends, personal and political" (*i.e.*, brother Samuel Smith and his powerful allies in the Senate) which would stand with him against the President. Madison warned Smith not to overestimate his political power and again offered him the Saint Petersburg post, one that "tho' neither difficult nor laborious, might be important," and which in any case, was one where Smith's "private resources would . . . aid his salary in bearing the expensiveness of that Metropolis and Court." Seeming not to sense anything demeaning in this comment, Smith admitted his "inclination towards a trip to Europe," accepted the proffered post, and gained the President's approval to "let it be known that the mission was on foot." The interview ended in apparent agreement, in spite of Madison's uncharacteristic anger and bluntness during it.

For a few days Smith seemed pleased and passed notices to the newspapers that he had been offered the post in Russia. He wrote his brother, though, that armed with a commission to the Czar, he had not yet decided what to do. In fact, he was doing a slow burn—he and his wife, without notice, ignored an invitation to a White House dinner given explicitly to acquaint them further with Russian representatives in Washington. While the President and his guests dined, Smith again wrote his brother, this time calling the Saint Petersburg offer an "insidious" one he would treat with "silent contempt." Dolley Madison and her sisters, refusing to take offense at Smith's discourtesy, called twice on Mrs. Smith to smooth things over, perhaps at the very time the angry ex-secretary wrote of his intention to "humble Mr. Madison." "The course I have taken," he exclaimed, "I am confident will lead to the injury of Mr. Madison and to my advantage. . . . I will make . . . no compromise with him. His overthrow is my object and most assuredly will I affect it." Aware that something was amiss, Madison sent for Smith again. This time Smith called the Saint Petersburg appointment an obviously crude device "to get rid of [me] as Secretary of State." The President said that the offer was "as delicate and favorable to [Smith] as could be reconciled with what I owed to the public and to myself." After again pointing out Smith's impossible behavior, Madison renewed the Saint Petersburg offer, and Smith again scorned it, with more threats to appeal to his powerful friends and to the public. Madison replied that he hoped public discussion could be avoided, but felt himself "on firm ground, as well in the public opinion as in my own consciousness." The conversation ended with "cold formality," and, said Madison, "I did not see him afterwards." The dismissal, he concluded, "will be pretty sure to end in secret hostility, if not open warfare."[18]

The "warfare" smoldered during the spring of 1811 as Smith fed innuendos to the anti-Madison press, and burst into flame in late June with the publication of a forty-page pamphlet addressed to "the People of the United States" and soon copied in newspapers all over the country.

It accused Madison of devious, dishonorable conduct toward members of his cabinet, and of a treasonable bias toward France. Quotes from confidential state papers gave aid and comfort to those intriguing against the United States. Smith quoted as well from dispatches he claimed showed *his* firmness toward France. The President, Smith led his readers to believe, had overruled this stance in truckling to Napoleon. Drafts in Madison's hand of the very dispatches (signed by Smith) with which the President was supposed to disagree proved Smith's dishonesty. Madison made no public reply, but fumed to Jefferson about Smith's "wicked publication," luckily so inept that "his infamy is daily fastening itself upon him." Madison did furnish information, though, to William Lee and Joel Barlow (recently appointed American minister to France), who wrote a slashing "Review of Robert Smith's Address" printed in *The National Intelligencer*. Republican newspapers used this to abuse Smith, and even foes of the administration realized Smith had destroyed himself. Henry St. George Tucker, half-brother and confidant of John Randolph, wrote that Smith's pamphlet was a "rare instance of a man's giving a finishing stroke to his own character, in his eagerness to ruin his enemy. I hear but one opinion of Smith! He has signed his own death-warrant. . . . Bad as Mr. M[adison] is I should prefer him as the least of two evils." For Madison's friends, disgust soon turned to glee; Benjamin Hawkins, Madison's colleague for thirty years, wrote the pamphlet was "a weak, wicked and illjudged thing" sure to embarrass its author, while Attorney General Rodney joyfully paraphrased Job to his chief: "O that mine enemy would write a book!"[19]

Only an exceedingly patient man would have for so long done so much of Smith's work while also enduring from him so much disloyalty. As long as intraparty factionalism remained relatively quiescent or harmless, Smith, affable and powerfully connected, could be suffered, though not always gladly. It was not until he undermined vital policies (clear to Madison and Gallatin for a year before April 1811) that Madison slowly and definitely decided to replace him. Gathering an overwhelming case against him, and waiting until it became possible for Monroe to join the cabinet, caused the delay. Whether the damage done American foreign policy as war impended, probably more severe than Madison thought possible, was worth awaiting the propitious moment is difficult to judge. Madison faced a dilemma. To confront Smith openly was sure to exacerbate already bitter political dissensions, which would become more serious if Madison moved before being certain of public approval. Yet to keep Smith was to poison the administration. The incident reflected not so much timidity or impotence as a possible misjudgment by Madison of how much he needed loyal support in his councils, and what his chances were in open battle with Smith's "important" supporters. In retrospect, Madison's conduct is at least plausible, and he did bring off the dismissal in a way that strengthened his cabinet and his standing in the country.

Madison gained important support from "Old Republicans" who joined Monroe in reconciliation with the administration, and from Gallatin, who, though increasingly restless and apprehensive about financing defense measures, remained at his side. Also useful was the more open and clearly defined character of the political opposition; it now insisted that not only Gallatin but also Madison had to be replaced in 1812. Despite furious personal rivalries among themselves, opponents sought a common candidate who, hopefully, would also be acceptable to the Federalists. Vice President George Clinton, though old and ill, had made himself a hero in antiadministration circles by casting the deciding vote against the recharter of the Bank of United States, supported by Gallatin and Madison. But Clinton, despite, or perhaps because of, the shrewd ambitions of his nephew–heir-apparent, De Witt, could not even count on solid support from New York Republicans. The elder Clinton's obviously failing health only sharpened the battle among the dissident factions. Though Smith's dismissal kindled political passions often hostile to Madison, the opposition remained at least as divided as ever, and the "majority" Republican support for the President was, if anything, consolidated.

Behind all the political maneuvers and at the center of the country's attention, of course, were negotiations to find peace with honor in the midst of the Napoleonic Wars. Madison had guided these negotiations during eight years in Jefferson's cabinet, and he was in everything but name his own Secretary of State until Monroe joined the cabinet in April 1811. The root difficulty, beginning with the furor over the attack on the *Chesapeake* and culminating in the failure of the Embargo (see Chapter XVIII), was the waning prospect that a weak neutral might compel fair treatment from mighty belligerents locked in mortal combat. Madison therefore entered the presidency facing urgent but almost hopeless tasks. "Aversion to war, the inconveniences produced by or charged on the embargo, the hope of favorable changes in Europe, the dread of civil convulsions in the East [New England], and the policy of permitting the discontented to be reclaimed to their duty by losses at sea," Madison wrote Pinkney, all contributed to the weak Nonintercourse Act passed by Congress on March 1, 1809. He called the postponement of import prohibitions on British and French goods until May 30 "most unfortunate," because it "must produce an apparent submission to Foreign Edicts." "No measure was ever adopted by so great a proportion of any public body," the President observed, "which found the hearty concurrence of so small a one." Perhaps, he hoped, Congressmen would "derive some vigor" from being with their constituents during the adjournment, and be ready to undertake "fresh efforts to vindicate our rights or enforce our resentments." Madison saw some prospect of hurting Britain by encouraging American manufacturers, but Southern resentment at New

England betrayal of the Embargo, and the resolves of New England legislatures "so well calculated to pamper the views of Great Britain against us," made a firm, consistent policy almost impossible.[20]

Furthermore, whatever the United States did, both belligerents were likely to persist in their illegal and oppressive edicts. In that case, Madison faced the grim alternatives of a disgraceful withdrawal of American commerce from the high seas or measures of self-defense almost certain to mean war with, in Jefferson's words, "a conqueror roaming over the earth with havoc and destruction, [and] a pirate spreading misery and ruin over the face of the ocean." Deliberately minimizing this prospect, Madison hoped the provisions of the Nonintercourse Act, excluding French as well as British warships from American waters for the first time since 1807, and offering to restore trade with either belligerent that ceased its depredations, would gratify Britain. Since, however, French warships and commerce had been driven from the seas, American restrictive measures, though equitable under law, largely affected British vessels. Over the signature of his incompetent Secretary of State, Madison wrote identically to Pinkney in London and Armstrong in Paris that the United States remained determined "not to acquiesce in the edicts of either of the belligerents." If, when Congress met in May 1809, either side had revoked or modified its edicts so as to safeguard American rights, and the other had not, Congress would "authorize acts of hostility" against the offending nation. Though the empty threats bolstered American self-respect, and Madison showed a formal impartiality toward the belligerents, in fact alternatives to war or submission had virtually disappeared.[21]

For a time, economic distress in England (partially induced by the much ridiculed Embargo), and Napoleon's victories in Spain, had compelled the weakened English ministry to consider some accommodation with the United States. In January 1809, therefore, Foreign Secretary Canning instructed his American minister, David Erskine, to offer the United States satisfaction for the attack on the *Chesapeake* and withdrawal of the offending Orders in Council if: (1) American trade was opened to Great Britain but remained closed to France, (2) the United States accepted the Rule of 1756, closing even the indirect French colonial trade to American vessels, and (3) the British navy was authorized to seize American ships violating the ban on trade with France. The new instructions, received on April 7, 1809, posed a delicate problem. Anxious to find an accommodation with the United States but also aware of Madison's firm requisites for settlement, Erskine saw that Canning's conditions, if presented fully and rigidly and at once, would be unacceptable to the Americans and nullify the value of the substantial British concessions. He decided to risk a partial violation of his instructions in order to take advantage of the new flexibility.[22]

Erskine immediately told Secretary Smith of his new powers. The offer of reparations and restoration of captured seamen fron the *Chesapeake* pleased Smith, who added only that Madison might require assurances that the offending admiral, Berkeley, be punished. Erskine rejected this, and after a day's consultation, the President and cabinet acquiesced. Erskine ignored his instruction that the proclamation of July 1807 banning British warships from American waters be formally revoked, and offered to rescind the Orders in Council in exchange for exemption of Great Britain from the Nonintercourse Act. He did not, however, state explicitly the condition that Franco-American trade remain closed. When he asked about French trade, Madison and Smith replied that under the Nonintercourse Act it would, of course, continue to be proscribed, but as Gallatin later explained to Erskine, the state of Franco-American trade "was to result from our own laws, known or anticipated by [the British] government when they authorized an arrangement; and it was not proposed by us that the continuation of nonintercourse with France should be made a condition of that arrangement." Thus another source of misunderstanding crept into the pending agreement. The long-contested colonial carrying trade, the American negotiators said, could only be settled by a treaty in which the United States would relinquish the *direct* trade between the colonies and mother country in return for legalization of the "broken voyage" trade from the West Indies to the United States and thence to Europe. This position, of course, maintained American resistance to the Rule of 1756, which Erskine was instructed to end. He also accepted the American argument that British occupation of French islands in the West Indies made the rule largely irrelevant, and then omitted to Canning the crucial word "direct" in reporting the American willingness to relinquish the colonial trade, thus planting still another misunderstanding.

Finally, Madison and Smith rejected British naval enforcement of American laws. It was, Madison later said, a condition "too absurd and insulting ever to have been sincerely counted upon." Erskine apparently agreed, and hoped his superiors would also honor American self-respect. The negotiators, then, only eleven days after Erskine had reported his new instructions, signed a note accepting the principle for which American diplomats had worked for fifteen years: neutral trade was not to be sacrificed to efforts by belligerents to injure each other. Smarting from years of Royal Navy arrogance and unwilling to approve it even by silence, Madison insisted, in concluding the agreement, on condemning British failure to punish Admiral Berkeley. Such an example, Madison wrote tartly, little "comported with what is due from His Britannic Majesty to his own honor." Thirty-three years after the insults of *Common Sense*, George III still had much to suffer from his former subjects in North America.[23]

When Madison reopened Anglo-American trade as of June 10, 1809, more than six hundred American ships left for England, on the assumption that the Orders in Council were void. The long-sought recognition of American rights caused wild celebrations from Maine to Georgia. Republican newspapers heralded the President's skill and sagacity; Federalist papers conceded the popularity of the agreement; and even John Randolph approved Madison's "promptitude and frankness" in meeting the British overtures. Benjamin Rush expressed the prevailing euphoria in congratulating a British correspondent on the return of friendly relations between the two nations: "Our new President, Mr. Madison is very popular. Both the two great parties that have so long divided our country, have united in him. He possesses with uncommon talents [and] extensive knowledge, much of the prudence and common sense of General Washington."[24]

Rufus King noticed more realistically that "one side rejoice because they think that the Embargo, etc., has brought England to terms, and the other side rejoice because they believe that the opposition to the last Measures of Congress has obliged the administration to abandon their system, and to accept a Reconciliation with England." In May 1809 Madison asked Congress to remove all barriers to trade with England and declared the administration's intention to use the continuing restrictions on French commerce not as a step on the road to war with her, but as a lever to persuade Napoleon to rescind his decrees against American trade. Aware of Canning's supposition that British-American reconciliation would lead to more, not less, Franco-American hostility, Erskine must have squirmed uneasily at this passage in Madison's message.[25]

Madison recognized this privately in speculating to Jefferson that Britain must have changed her course "under a full conviction that an adjustment with this country had become essential; . . . mingled with . . . the hope that [the Erskine agreement] may embroil us with France." Steps deemed proper to doom this hope, Madison added, "will not be omitted." But on June 10, as the country celebrated the supposed end of British commercial hostility, word arrived of new Orders in Council, of April 26, 1809, which, though much less restrictive than those of 1807, imposed a paper blockade on Europe from the German North Sea ports to the Adriatic. Madison noted the inconsistency of the Orders with the more liberal Erskine agreement and wondered how the British cabinet could adhere to them and also approve the agreement. He hoped "the crooked proceeding" arose from "an awkwardness in getting out of an awkward situation," rather than from British insincerity, as some suspected, but he feared Britain pursued the "trickish" course of intending to void the Erskine agreement, and then, after declaring the Orders in Council had been only temporarily withdrawn, capture the hundreds of American vessels on the high seas, virtually hostages to the British navy.[26]

Madison left Washington for Montpelier in mid-July, still assuming, despite misgivings, Anglo-American reconciliation, but after he had spent a week on his plantation, thunderclap news arrived from Gallatin. London had repudiated the Erskine agreement and thus restored the discriminatory Orders against American trade. Madison fumed that Britain would negotiate with the United States while apparently adopting "openly a system of monopoly and piracy" designed principally "to prevent the legitimate trade of the United States from interfering with the London smugglers of sugar and coffee." Since British commercial warfare so clearly drove the United States toward France, Madison was sure only the rapacity of British merchants enriching themselves in violation of their country's laws could explain so foolish a policy. This unheard of "outrage on all decency," reinforcing as it did in Madison's mind the lessons of forty years' experience with the cynical selfishness and political power of that merchant class, more than anything else convinced him of England's implacable, unreasonable hostility. He returned to Washington, where, supported by the cabinet, he reapplied the restraints of the Nonintercourse Act to Anglo-American trade.[27]

With news of the disavowal of the Erskine agreement, Madison heard that while the British cabinet was inclined to accept the agreement, George III refused to "ratify anything in which he was so personally insulted," referring to Madison's gratuitous call for punishment of Admiral Berkeley. Though the King may have hardened his cabinet's resolve, in fact Canning and his colleagues, encouraged by reports of Napoleon's defeat in Austria, news of antiadministration sentiment in New England, and a realization that ships already on their way across the Atlantic would fill British warehouses with needed American goods for years, saw no reason to accept an agreement so favorable to the despised and troublesome former colonies. Furthermore, under the desperate strategy of using her navy to strangle Napoleon's empire, Britain could only recognize American maritime "rights" if the United States herself undertook to bar her trade from the European continent. Hence the condition in Erskine's instructions that the British navy be permitted to enforce American nonintercourse with France. Madison's outrage at this suggestion was a measure of the psychic distance between the two countries, just as his intention that the Erskine agreement be a lever to open trade with France, and Canning's contrary requirement that it be a step toward Franco-American war, measured the vastly different national policy needs.[28]

Though Madison understood perfectly well that the hostile Tory outlook of the Perceval government, backed by a strident press, demanded full use of Britain's naval supremacy to injure Napoleon and favor British commerce in every way possible, regardless of neutral rights, he nevertheless chose to encourage as much as he could the eloquent liberal voices in England by negotiating in good faith to renew Anglo-American trade. He did this at the considerable and fully recognized risk of raising possibly false hopes in the United States and of again exposing American commerce to British depredation. Though the risk soon proved a bad one —something Madison might have anticipated more certainly had he counted more heavily on cynical realities than on glimmering hopes— yet his course was consistent with the Republican policy of seeking every opportunity to implant liberal principles in international relations. Unhappily, however, with the repudiation of the Erskine agreement, Gallatin's gloomy analysis was all too accurate: "We are not so well prepared for resistance as we were one year ago. [Then] all or almost all our mercantile wealth was safe at home, our resources entire, and our finances sufficient to carry us through the first year of the contest. Our property is now afloat; England relieved by our relaxations might stand two years of privations with ease; we have wasted our resources without any national utility; and, our treasury being exhausted, we must begin any plan of resistance with considerable and therefore unpopular loans."[29]

When Madison returned to Washington in October 1809, he found a new British minister, Francis James Jackson, who had spent his month of waiting for Madison being lionized in Federalist parlors. Little was expected from this arrogant diplomat, notorious for his brutal order some years earlier to the British navy to destroy the city of Copenhagen. Jackson, for his part, had found Erskine's house in "a state of ruin and dirt," to be expected, the London snob supposed, in a dwelling occupied by "a Scotchman with an American wife." Madison received him coolly but politely, serving him punch and cake the Englishman found distinctly below European standards. The President, he reported, was "a plain and rather mean-looking little man, of great simplicity of manners, and an inveterate enemy of form and ceremony." About the same time, Mrs. Jackson, a former Prussian baroness, labeled Dolley *"une bonne grosse femme de ʾi classe bourgeoise*, very fit to grace the President's table; without distinction either in manners or appearance, but, to be just, she is also without pretensions." Her husband was even less impressed. He found Dolley "fat and forty but not fair," and repeating Federalist slander, noted that "she must . . . have been a comely person when she served out the liquor" at her father's Virginia tavern. Madison nonetheless hosted a White House dinner after which the surprised Jackson reported, "I do not know that I had ever more civility and attention shown me."[30]

The diplomatic negotiations foundered from the beginning on Jackson's condescension, his unyielding instructions, and Madison's insistence that Jackson and his government atone for the disavowal of the Erskine agreement. Insulting remarks dominated the exchange of notes. On October 19, in what Henry Adams termed "perhaps the best and keenest paper Madison ever wrote," the President declared "more than merely inadmissible" Jackson's claim that the American government had connived with Erskine to violate his instructions. A week later Jackson tried to talk seriously with the President on horseback at the Georgetown races, but only got pleasantries about thoroughbreds. Jackson wrote his brother Madison was "as obstinate as a mule." On November 1 Madison told Jackson he had made "irrelevant and improper allusions . . . inadmissible in the intercourse of a foreign minister with a Government that understands what it owes itself," and a week later, "no further communications will be received from you." Mrs. Jackson reported that her husband, "being accustomed to treat with the civilized Courts and governments of Europe, and not with savage Democrats, half of them sold to France, has not succeeded in his negotiation." Moreover, she found Washington-Baltimore cuisine "detestable; *nappage grossier*, no claret, champagne and Madeira indifferent." Society consisted of "rich merchants, who spent their mornings in their counting-house, and talk politics in the evening in their drawing rooms." As was so often the way with courtly Europeans visiting America during the Republican years, leering at Betsy Patterson Bonaparte was the most exciting entertainment capital society could offer. To Madison's relief, the Jacksons left hastily for the more civilized cities of New York and Boston.[31]

In the midst of the negotiations, Madison asked William Pinkney how "can a nation [Britain] expect to retain the respect of Mankind whose government descends to so ignoble a career?" Madison was satisfied that disgust at Jackson's "mean and insolent" behavior had resulted in considerable public support for American foreign policy, had led to Republican victories in Maryland and Vermont, and seemed likely to do the same in Massachusetts, New Hampshire, and Rhode Island, thus reversing elections "which took place during the fever which the Embargo was made to produce." The disappointment of Federalist merchants, who found "trade limited to the British dominions, is but a mouthful and not . . . a bellyfull," helped reverse the public sentiment: shipments to the West Indies proved ruinous; losses in the Mediterranean ran at least 25 per cent; and speculative voyages to the north of Europe were "still more entirely blasted." British friendship proved less profitable than Federalists had hoped and proclaimed. Madison was pleased, too, as he noted in every annual message during his presidency, at "the astonishing progress of manufactures, more especially in the Household way throughout the Middle, Southern, and Western countries," that enabled families to clothe and equip themselves "both cheaper and better than heretofore." He saw this as evidence that agrarian self-reliance and industry might achieve for the country what mercantile greed and speculation could never attain: genuine national independence and self-sufficiency.[32]

During the 1809–10 session of Congress Madison observed ruefully that "the diversity of opinions and prolixity of discussion [make clear that] few are desirous of war; and few are reconciled to submission; yet the frustration of intermediate courses seems to have left scarce an escape from that dilemma." The Nonintercourse Act had not induced either belligerent to rescind its hostile decrees and had been a disaster for American commerce and public finance. Bermuda, Halifax, and Amelia Island (between Georgia and Florida) became transshipment ports for goods prohibited direct entry into the United States. Since this illegal trade paid no duty and raised the cost of goods, both the Treasury and the consumer suffered. For the first time since 1801 the Treasury, denied tariff income, threatened to show an operating deficit. Secretary Gallatin, insisting on a balanced budget while the nation remained at peace, demanded that military expenditures be cut in half. Revealing long-cherished republican predispositions, he expostulated, "I cannot . . . consent to act the part of a mere financier, to become a contriver of taxes, a dealer of loans, a seeker of resources for the purpose of supporting useless baubles, of increasing the number of idle and dissipated members of the community, of fattening contractors, pursers, and agents, and of introducing in all its ramifications that system of patronage, corruption, and rottenness" Jeffersonians had always "execrated." At the same time, Madison received reports that the navy was unfit for sea, Jefferson's gunboats were fast rotting away, and the army was virtually nonexistent, its only substantial contingent having been ravaged by disease due to the insubordination and incompetence of its commander, General James Wilkinson.[33]

Confronting this unhappy scene, Madison felt obliged to let Gallatin recommend his economy budget in December (he threatened to resign rather than submit a different one), but a month later the President asked for an army increase of twenty thousand men and suggested that the navy be outfitted for active service. As for financing, he noted simply "the solid state of the public credit." "In point of obscurity," Senator William H. Crawford of Georgia remarked, the message resembled "a Delphic oracle." Thus uncertain of executive intent, Congress merely promised to "call into action the whole force of the nation" to maintain its rights. To replace the unlamented Nonintercourse Act, the lawmakers produced "Macon's Bill No. 1," barring all French and British vessels from American harbors, but lifting the ban for any power that rescinded its offensive decrees, a measure Madison thought "better than nothing, which seemed to be the alternative." British Minister Jackson, living idly among New York Federalists, exulted that Congress "have covered themselves with ridicule and disgrace. . . . [What] began in 'blood and thunder' [has] ended in a drunken frolic." His respect for Congress had not been heightened when earlier in the session one of its members had "been horsewhipped by the President's Secretary and another had been severely wounded in a duel." Both incidents struck close to the Madisons. The whip wielder was Dolley's handsome cousin Isaac Coles, while the wounded legislator was her brother-in-law John G. Jackson, who had risen to reject a slur on the Republican leadership.[34]

Congress took the executive lack of enthusiasm for Macon's Bill No. 1 as an excuse to emasculate it. The House then substituted "Macon's Bill No. 2," which opened American trade unconditionally unless one of the belligerents withdrew its decrees. In that case, if the other failed to do likewise within three months, nonintercourse would be revived against the remaining offender. This "botch of a bill," Madison thought, would "open too late the eyes of the people to the expediency and efficacy" of the 1808 Embargo. He nonetheless hoped the bill, which allowed Britain to enjoy the benefits of American trade while her navy blockaded the ports of Europe, might "become a motive with [France to rescind her decrees and thus] turn the tables on Great Britain, by compelling her either to revoke her Orders, or to lose the commerce of this country." Madison sought, in effect, to so favor Britain that Napoleon would withdraw his edicts and thus revive American nonintercourse against England, a move sure to produce an Anglo-American crisis unless Britain revoked her Orders. While Macon's Bill No. 2 was on the surface a "miserable, feeble, Puff," it was actually a step on the road to war, barring the unlikely possibility that both belligerents ceased preying upon American trade.[35]

In fact, the repudiation of the Erskine agreement and the great victory at Wagram so inflated Napoleon that he issued yet another edict against American trade, and stepped up his confiscations of United States vessels—measures, Madison fumed, that "comprise robbery, theft, and breach of trust, and exceed in turpitude any of his enormities not wasting human blood." To prepare public opinion for the day when war might become necessary, Madison released papers detailing French and British insults. Suspicions of France were not diminished when the country, used to gossiping over the dynastic entanglements of Europe, buzzed with excitement at the huge allowances Betsy Patterson Bonaparte received from her brother-in-law for her infant son. Was Napoleon planting his dynasty in the United States? The prospect became more alarming when it seemed that the youngster's uncles, the Secretary of State and a Senator from Maryland, might fancy themselves "prince regent for the future sovereign of America."[36]

Nonetheless, on the strength of the firm stand taken against Jackson and the feeling that the country should support the administration in a time of crisis, the Republicans scored impressive victories in the spring (1810) elections. "New York and New England are rallying to the Republican ranks," the President reported to his predecessor, and "in

New Jersey, every branch of the legislature is again sound." Results in Massachusetts forced the retirement of arch-Federalist Senator Timothy Pickering, and in New York Republicans increased their majority on the Congressional delegation from ten-to-seven to twelve-to-five. Madison may for a while have shared Jefferson's euphoria. "Our difficulties are indeed great," the ex-President wrote, "but when viewed in comparison to those of Europe, they are the joys of Paradise. . . . Ours is a bed of roses. And the system of government which shall keep us afloat amidst the wreck of the world, will be immortalized in history." On July 4, 1810, Madison listened in "the Baptist meeting house near the President's square" to passionate oratory praising the interlocking growth of freedom, education, internal improvements, and manufacturing in the United States, and then opened the White House to "a large and brilliant assemblage of both sexes," from which he heard effusive toasts to his leadership and patriotism. Despite international dangers and domestic uncertainties, the nation showed confidence in its rapidly rising strength and in its Republican helmsman.[37]

On the trip to Orange after the Fourth of July celebration, Madison sat in the sun much of the way, and came down with a fever that lasted a week. But he got up to cope with the burgeoning problem of West Florida, the territory along the Gulf Coast between New Orleans and the Perdido River including the key harbor and fort at Mobile, claimed dubiously by the United States as part of the Louisiana Purchase, but still occupied by Spain. As long as weak Spain retained possession and settlement by Americans continued unabated, Madison was certain of ultimate American possession by default, purchase, or occupation. By 1810 four fifths of the perhaps twenty thousand inhabitants were Americans, and Spanish authority crumbled as first France and then Great Britain threatened to occupy Florida and other territories under pretense of upholding their rival puppet governments of Spain. To forestall both foreign occupation and disorder among the ungoverned American settlers, in June 1810 Madison had asked Governor William Claiborne of the Orleans Territory to see if his friends in West Florida could organize a convention to "request" a United States occupation. Thus matters stood when Madison received word at Montpelier that irregular bands of Americans had gathered near Baton Rouge, Mobile, and other points and threatened to destroy what remained of Spanish power.[38]

The crisis offered Madison difficult choices. To do nothing would almost surely lead to anarchy in West Florida and was likely, at best, to end in a quasi-independent government controlled by unruly elements bent on appropriating for themselves the best lands in the territory, and at worst, to invite French or British occupation. To aid Spain in reasserting her authority would forfeit the American claim and require a politically unacceptable and militarily dubious campaign by American troops against their countrymen. To order occupation by American soldiers and officials, on the other hand, seemed an unauthorized executive act as well as a provocation to three foreign powers. Britain's "propensity to fish in troubled waters," made plain by her interference in the Spanish possessions of Buenos Aires and Caracas, and the threat of West Florida "passing into the hands of a third and dangerous party," the President explained later to Jefferson, nonetheless persuaded him to risk the "quadrangular contest" American occupation of the territory would bring on. Furthermore, the declared intention "of the temporary government to *grant* lands"—that is, to validate the huge patents given collusively by Spanish authorities to American speculators—was, the President wrote his Secretary of the Treasury, an additional reason "for the Executive to exercise authority" in West Florida immediately. Lands rightfully belonging to the public required public protection. Madison therefore sent word to West Florida that the extralegal forces must disperse and that the American government would protect its legitimate interests.[39]

Back in Washington in October, Madison learned that American irregulars, encouraged by his "request" for United States occupation, had captured the Spanish fort at Baton Rouge and asked that West Florida be made "an integral and inalienable portion of the United States." Madison noted that "a crisis has at length arrived," pointing toward anarchy or British occupation, desirable to neither Spain nor the United States, so he therefore proclaimed, "it right and requisite that possession should be taken of the said territory in the name and behalf of the United States." At the same time, he ordered Governor Claiborne to enter the territory with enough troops and officials to establish civil government, but not to attack Mobile or other forts where Spanish forces remained. In January 1811, Madison acted again to keep hostile powers away from the American doorstep by securing passage of a law authorizing him to occupy East Florida as well should local authorities there request aid or should foreign nations threaten invasion.[40]

In these actions Madison had, of course, "governed by executive proclamation," contrary to Republican prescriptions against implied powers. Though his queries to Gallatin show a concern for this "transgression," he never doubted that the United States government, like all governments, would on occasion have to act quickly and decisively to meet unforeseen situations. Thwarting extralegal domination of West Florida, and excluding foreign powers there, were sufficient justification for Madison. He explained the whole business privately to William Pinkney:

> The occupancy of [West Florida] was called for by the crisis there, and is understood to be within the authority of the Executive. East Florida, also, is of great importance to the United States, and it is not

probable that Congress will let it pass into any new hands. It is to be hoped Great Britain will not entangle herself with us by seizing it. . . . The position of Cuba gives the United States so deep an interest in the destiny, even, of that Island, that although they might be an inactive, they could not be a satisfied spectator at its falling under any European Government, which might make a fulcrum of that position against the commerce and security of the United States. With respect to Spanish America generally, you will find that Great Britain is engaged in the most eager . . . grasp of political influence and commercial [gain, extorting] . . . a preference in trade over all other nations . . . from the temporary fears and necessities of the Revolutionary Spaniards.

Reacting to a turbulence not settled until after promulgation of the Monroe Doctrine, Madison had enlarged the scope of American national interest and made clear the dangers of European inroads in the Western Hemisphere.[41]

Even more momentous than the swift pace of events in Florida was news in late September that Napoleon had—apparently in response to Macon's Bill No. 2—relaxed his edicts against American trade. The French foreign minister, the Duke of Cadore, had informed American envoy John Armstrong on August 5, 1810, that "the decrees of Berlin and Milan are revoked, and . . . after the 1st of November they will cease to have effect; it being understood that, in consequence of this declaration . . . the United States, conformably to the act you have just communicated, shall cause their rights to be respected by the English." Taken at face value, this seemed to be the good news so long awaited: one of the belligerents had agreed to open her ports and respect neutral trade. "We hope from the step," Madison wrote Jefferson, "the advantage at least of having but one contest on our hands at a time." The President expected, that is, England would not match French concessions—which, of course, would precipitate a crisis with England when nonintercourse was revived against her in three months, as provided for in Macon's Bill No. 2.[42]

Actually, however, Napoleon had presented to the President a tissue of uncertainties rather than an unequivocal response to Macon's Bill No. 2. That law called for *unconditional* revocation of belligerent decrees by one side, in response to which the United States would restore its restraints against the other power. Yet Cadore's letter of August 5 implied that the Berlin and Milan decrees were withdrawn only if the United States "cause their rights to be respected by the English." This vague language obviously was subject to French interpretation of what acts by the United States constituted such forcing of respect. Even more ominous was the failure to mention decrees other than those of Berlin and Milan hostile to neutral commerce, the fate of hundreds of American ships already sequestered by the French, and the possibility that French "domestic regulations" might be substituted for the withdrawn decrees.

The indirect and incomplete transmission of the letter of August 5 to the United States compounded the uncertainties. First news of it came, as often happened, by a fast ship carrying London newspapers. Though there was no reason to doubt its authenticity, the American government nevertheless had to bide its time while public expectations of a rapprochement with France rose. First formal word came almost a month later, on October 19, through Pinkney, who reported "written and official notice" from Armstrong of the French action. Entirely lacking were letters from Armstrong explaining the circumstances of Cadore's letter and evaluating its meaning and sincerity, vital information for the President to judge correctly what response he should make. Furthermore, Pinkney also reported British reaction to Cadore's letter: "Whenever the repeal of the French decrees shall have actually taken effect, and the commerce of neutral nations shall have been restored," Lord Wellesley, the Foreign Secretary, wrote, "His Majesty will feel the highest satisfaction in relinquishing a system, which the conduct of the enemy compelled him to adopt." Though this seemed conciliatory, obviously the British government took a skeptical "wait and see" attitude toward the crafty French Emperor's pronouncements. Pinkney's own assessment was that, overall, the cabinet still seemed committed to "that abominable scheme of monopoly, called the Orders in Council."[43]

Having pondered all this, the President wrote Armstrong in October that he hoped "France will do what she is understood to be pledged for, and in a measure that will produce no jealousy or embarrassment here. We hope in particular that the sequestered property will have been restored," as Madison had instructed Armstrong to insist months earlier. As to Wellesley's letter, Madison wrote Pinkney that it seemed "a promise only, and that in a very questionable shape. . . . The obnoxious exercise of [Britain's] sham blockades . . . discourage the hope that she contemplates a reconciliation with us." Thus, though the President realized both belligerents had written ambiguously, he clearly *chose* to place more credence in the French promise than in the English one. He did so in part because, as Jefferson had observed, "without something new from [one of] the belligerents, I know not what ground [Congress] could have taken for their next move." The whole American policy "for two or three years," Administration apologists later explained, had been "to divide the belligerents by inducing one or the other of them to revoke its edicts, so that the example would lead to a revocation by the other, or our contest be limited to a single one." On November 2, 1810, therefore, the day after formal notice arrived from Armstrong, the President proclaimed that "whereas it has been officially made known to this government that the edicts of France violating the neutral commerce of the

United States have been . . . revoked," nonintercourse would be revived against Great Britain in three months unless in that time she also withdrew her decrees.[44]

Madison's decision is understandable only when viewed as a last chance to remove "embarrassments . . . as afflicting as they have been unexampled," and to extricate the country "from the dilemma, of a mortifying peace, or a war with both the great belligerents." He knew perfectly well that, as Jefferson later put it, "Bonaparte hates our government because it is a living libel on his, [and] the English hate us because they think our prosperity filched from theirs." Madison knew, too, that Bonaparte was notoriously volatile and that any hesitation by the United States over his "offer" would likely cause him to issue more severely hostile edicts than ever. Thus the calculated risk was to take deliberately at face value the attractive ground opened by the French to put pressure on the English. The President informed the British chargé that unless England revoked her orders, revival of nonintercourse would be followed by measures that "would create the most serious collision between the two countries," and he told the French minister that "if . . . England does not renounce her system of paper-blockades and the other vexations resulting from it, [American] measures . . . will lead necessarily to war." Gallatin explained further to the French minister why war should be expected: "England could not suffer the execution of measures so prejudicial to her, and especially in the actual circumstances could not renounce the prerogatives of her maritime supremacy and of her commercial ascendency."[45]

Coupled with the threats of war was a final offer of the way of reason to the combatants. Madison thought Napoleon's self-interest would make him see the advantage of accepting the American "good faith" interpretation of the Cadore letter in order to unite America against England. That nation, on the other hand, seeing the United States driven into the arms of France by the Orders in Council, would see her stake in withdrawing them to save for herself the immense benefits of American commerce. These calculations, though, glossed over the two grim realities: Napoleon's intention to withdraw his revocations if *he* judged the United States didn't sufficiently resist English depredations, and England's intention, while the Royal Navy remained afloat, to prevent American ships from succoring Napoleon's war machine. The bloody needs of war for survival mocked reason, and by the end of 1810, had blocked all the avenues even an ingenious republican might search out in quest of peace with honor. It was not so much that a naïve Madison had been tricked by the clever French as that Madison accepted, knowingly, interpretations and risks he might have foreseen would make matters more, not less, dangerous. Instead of having removed afflicting embarrassments and mortifying dilemmas, he had probably precipitated even more excruciating quandries for his country.

Furthermore, had Madison known anything like the full story behind Cadore's August 5 letter, his reaction to it would have been different. When Napoleon learned of Macon's Bill No. 2, he noted that American vessels entering French ports and still subject to the Orders in Council would be sequestered as usual. He would, however, declare that the decrees of Berlin and Milan were repealed, but "this situation will have no effect on the customs regulations, which will always regulate arbitrarily duties and prohibitions. . . . Thus it is evident that we should commit ourselves to nothing." Strict licensing regulations and duties were announced, keeping the Continental System intact. French courts ordered wholesale confiscations of sequestered American ships. Cadore informed his minister in Washington that revocation of the decrees "will depend on the measures which the United States shall take if England persists in her Orders of Council." Thus Napoleon had not really acted unconditionally, as Macon's Bill required, nor did he accept Madison's reasoning that France could afford to deal justly with the United States in return for American resistance to British decrees. From England, Jefferson's friend William Short, a veteran of twenty-five years experience in European diplomacy, wrote of French wiles: "I really pity Mr. Madison. He does not know the wheel within the wheel on which they [France] roll him and from which they will let him down whenever they have no further need for him."[46]

Though Madison saw immediately the potential duplicity of Cadore's letter, Armstrong's first dispatches about it, received in Washington on November 1, merely conveyed Cadore's letter with no indication that he had pressed the Frenchman for clarification, perhaps because, as Cadore told Napoleon, Armstrong did not want to tarnish "the glory . . . he attaches to having obtained the note of August 5." The only ominous hint in these tardy dispatches, sent more than a month after Armstrong received Cadore's letter, was a report of "domestic regulations" being erected against American trade. A week later, after Madison's proclamation of November 2, new letters came from Paris, finally reporting crucial conversations with Cadore: American vessels captured before November 1, 1810, would not be released, and the emperor meant to use the licensing system to restrain American trade. These disclosures, of course, contravened Madison's interpretation of Cadore's letter used to justify the proclamation. Had Madison known this in October, as would have been possible if Armstrong had questioned Cadore at once in August and immediately reported to the President, he would probably have withheld the proclamation, but a week after its issuance, it seemed unwise to rescind it. Besides the embarrassment of so abruptly changing his course, Madison hoped against hope one more time that France might give him some leverage against England.[47]

The response to Cadore's letter, of course, revived charges of Madison's partiality to France. One Federalist editor declared that "Bonaparte knows as well how to manage James Madison as he does any of his vassal kings of Europe. In assisting to destroy English commerce, the President served the emperor faithfully." John Randolph pronounced the proclamation of November 2 "a bargain which credulity and imbecility enter into with cunning and power." Loyal Congressional Republicans nonetheless imposed nonintercourse against England, but dispirited by accumulating evidence of French hostility, they otherwise failed the administration. Congress permitted the Bank of the United States to go out of existence, omitted the taxes needed to forestall deficit financing, and cut army and navy appropriations. Though Madison had abandoned his 1791 opinion of the bank's unconstitutionality, because twenty years of usefulness and public approval "amounted to the requisite evidence of the national judgment and intention," the embarrassment of bank opponents quoting his old antibank speeches caused him to let Gallatin lead the fight for recharter. "Old Republicans" hostile for the old reasons, "new Republicans" hostile because of interest in state banks, and politicians eager to torment Gallatin and the administration combined to defeat the bank by a margin of one vote in each house. Furthermore, since revival of nonintercourse against England would cut Treasury receipts in half, Gallatin requested offsetting duty increases. Congress rejected this, and instead, authorized a loan of $5 million. The government therefore had neither funds in hand nor a bank to borrow them.[48]

Having thus in two blows virtually destroyed the nation's fiscal foundations, Congress, with support from Gallatin, in order to balance the budget, reduced already low defense appropriations, despite Madison's request for increases. The amount granted, less than $5 million, was only half that spent in 1809 in the war scare following repeal of the Embargo. The administration's insistence that France had withdrawn her decrees and that England must soon be forced to follow suit gave unfortunate credence to arguments that successful diplomacy had diminished the need for armaments. Altogether Madison found his administration dangerously exposed: in a desperate, last-chance effort to bring pressure against England, he had based his diplomacy on French relaxations that in fact he had increasing reason to doubt were genuine; if his doubts proved true, England was certain to reject similar relaxations and precipitate an Anglo-American crisis. At the same time, Madison saw ten years of Republican fiscal strength evaporate and the preparedness of the armed forces reach a new low. Though he had opposed the debilitating financial and military measures, he did share the responsibility for the gap between perils faced and preparations to meet them. Young

Washington Irving, visiting in Washington, conveyed some sense of the disarray and resulting cynicism: "As to talking of patriotism and principles, I have seen enough both of general and state politics to convince me they are mere words of battle—'banners hung on the outer walls,' for the rabble to fight by; the knowing leaders laugh at them in their sleeves for being gulled by such painted rags."[49]

While the "jumble of accounts from France" and lack of accurateness left Madison "on thorns, . . . prey to the ignorance and interested falsehoods which fill our newspapers," British warships responded to the renewal of nonintercourse by reappearing off New York harbor, capturing American ships bound for France, and impressing seamen. Madison ordered Commodore John Rodgers in U.S.S. *President* to stop these insults, especially the impressments. Off the entrance to the Chesapeake, in enveloping darkness, Rodgers overtook a British warship. Amid confusing signals, cannonading began, and in fifteen minutes the British vessel was helpless. In the morning Rodgers discovered to his chagrin, not the powerful *Guerrière*, known to be in the area, but the *Little Belt*, a corvette only half as powerful as the *President*. Inquiry failed to establish which vessel fired first, though evidence slightly favored Rodgers' charge that it was the *Little Belt*. In any case, each government backed its commander; newspapers demanded retribution for "dastardly assaults"; and Americans felt at long last that the insult to the *Chesapeake* had been returned. Madison accepted Rodgers' account of the engagement and let it be known publicly that naval commanders "in supporting the dignity of our flag . . . will be rewarded with the applause of the American government and nation." He wrote calmly to Jefferson that the encounter, "not unlikely to bring on repetitions, will probably end in an open rupture or a better understanding, as the calculations of the British government may prompt or dissuade from war." Since the incident increased substantially the chance of war, it was fortunate that it also boosted American morale and made plain public support for hostilities should events make them necessary.[50]

In late June the long-awaited frigate *Essex* arrived, carrying William Pinkney as well as dispatches from France, and H.M.S. *Minerva* reached Annapolis, bearing a new British minister to the United States, Sir Augustus John Foster, whom Madison knew well from his tour as secretary of the British legation (1804–1808). The letters from Paris displayed further the French tactic of furnishing some privileges to American commerce while also insisting that the Continental System would not die before Britain's Orders in Council. Foster also brought bad news: An offer of *Chesapeake* reparations would be withheld until the United States had made amends for the attack on the *Little Belt*. He also handed Monroe notice that the Orders in Council would remain in effect not only until Napoleon's decrees had been withdrawn "absolutely and unconditionally" but also until French "municipal regulations" having the same restrictive effect had been revoked. Polite conversations with Foster and the personally amiable new French minister, Louis Sérurier, failed to reveal grounds for accommodation with either country. With official business stalled, talk turned to French literature, which, Sérurier reported, Madison was "fond of and knows well." News in mid-July of the release of a large number of American vessels held in French ports since the previous November 2, however, was reason enough, the President thought, to dispatch Joel Barlow as minister to France to seek a full adjustment of Franco-American difficulties. Pinkney's return without replacement at the ministerial level notified Britain that the United States had marked her as the principal offending nation.[51]

Britain, of course, took added offense at American demands that the partially fraudulent French revocations be regarded as grounds for full and unconditional withdrawal of the Orders in Council. For Madison, however, two factors stood out: Britain was still the nation most able to injure the United States, and her deliberate insults to American rights, in ways that required permanent economic subservience to the former mother country, made Napoleon's merely selfish, tactical depredations seem petty by comparison. This firm conviction caused Sérurier to report that "Mr. Madison seems delighted to see himself confirmed in a system which is wholly his own. . . . I have never seen him more triumphant. . . . The President, superior to [the cabinet] in enlightenment as in position, governs entirely by himself, and there is no reason to fear his being crossed by them." With grim resolution, Madison called Congress to convene a month early to contend with the expected rupture with Great Britain, and departed for two months of "health and peace" at Montpelier.[52]

Conversations in Virginia during the summer among Monroe, Jefferson, and Madison confirmed the course toward war. While the old leaders talked, young Henry Clay wrote that if England persisted in the Orders in Council, and France was "honest and sincere in her recent measures, I look upon War with Great Britain [as] inevitable." Madison's old Princeton friend, "Light-Horse Harry" Lee, though a pillar of Virginia Federalism, pleaded that the President "take us out of the odious condition . . . of half war . . . by restoration of amity, or by drawing the sword." Reflecting this mood, the new Congress that gathered on November 4, 1811, had little patience for the vacillations of the past half-dozen years. This so-called War Hawk Congress, chosen in 1810–11 as the country approved the administration's resistance to British insults, was not notably younger or newer in membership than its two predecessors, and in many states, personalities and local issues had, as usual, dominated the elections, but in its ranks were decisive additions to the small group of "new Republicans" unbothered by "Old Republican" verities about peace, mildness, and frugality. To Clay, Richard M. Johnson, Peter Porter, and Langdon Cheves, were added Felix Grundy of Tennessee, William R. King of North Carolina, Jonathan Roberts of Pennsylvania, John A. Harper of New Hampshire, and William Lowndes and John C. Calhoun of South Carolina. For the first time in years Congress contained many able leaders upon whom Madison could depend. They would be capable of ending loquacious immobility and of galvanizing cautious colleagues to take fateful steps if necessary. Clay's election as Speaker heralded great changes: "He is a gentleman who commands respect and esteem, and keeps good order," a new member reported. *"Mr. Randolph has brought his dog into the House only once this Session*, and then the Speaker immediately ordered the Doorkeeper to take *her* out." In the past the House had cowered before Randolph's arrogant brilliance and "no one dared turn the dogs out."[53]

The President, back in Washington a month before Congress met, discussed his annual message with the cabinet. Determined to declare war on Great Britain if she persisted in her Orders in Council, Madison drafted a blunt paragraph threatening that unless her "direct and undisguised hostility" ceased, he would "authorize reprisals" amounting to war before the session of Congress "lapsed," as it would do in the spring. Alarmed, Gallatin urged the President to remember "the uncertainty in every respect of the effect of a war." "The measures necessary to carry on the war must be unpopular and by producing a change of men may lead to a disgraceful peace, to absolute subserviency hereafter to Great Britain and even to substantial alterations to our institutions," the secretary warned. He advised his chief to defer more to Congress and to make the reference to reprisals more vague in order that the potential enemy be less certain of American intentions. Madison did tone down his draft, but nonetheless accused England of "hostile inflexibility" and of measures having "the character as well as the effect of war on our lawful commerce," and he told Congress, "the period has arrived" to put the country "into an armor and an attitude demanded by the crisis." The President explained further that the new British minister, Foster, had stiffened rather than softened British demands and that "our coasts and the mouths of our harbors have again witnessed scenes not less derogatory to the dearest of our national rights than vexatious to the regular course of our trade." Though Madison avoided open threats, the nation correctly understood these words as a call to gird for war. Furthermore, since France had failed to follow her "amiable professions" with "prompt and ample" deeds of reconciliation, Congress should keep an eye on "the ulterior policy of the French government." To face the accumulating perils, Madison recommended enlarging the army, preparing the militia, finishing the military academy, stock-piling munitions, expanding the navy, and increasing the tariff to encourage trade and manufactures vital to the national interest. Finally, though the Treasury had a $5-million surplus for the year of restored trade under Macon's Bill No. 2, the reduced revenue resulting from nonintercourse with Britain and the costs of preparedness and war would require both new taxes and large loans.[54]

Though Federalists complained of "the overcharged colors" used to paint the conduct of Great Britain, and of the whitewash applied to "the most obvious injuries sustained from France," praise for the message came from all over the country. Ex-Federalist Senator William Plumer called it manly and energetic; John Adams asserted it did its author "great honor"; and Benjamin Rush said it "extorted praise . . . even from the Tories" in Philadelphia. Ex-President Jefferson termed it "most excellent, rational, and dignified," while President-to-be Andrew Jackson used its firmness to exhort his militiamen to make it "the pride and boast of every lover of his country to support the government in every measure it would take" in demanding justice from Great Britain. French Minister Sérurier reported happily that the message was considered by many "as equivalent to a declaration of war on Great Britain" and that the nation generally applauded the President's stance—"a thing decidedly unusual in this country," he added. The worried British minister, Foster, hurriedly concluded the long-delayed agreement on reparations for the *Chesapeake* incident, but he also asserted that the British government would not consider the French decrees revoked, nor would she withdraw her Orders unless the United States required France to admit British as well as American goods into Europe, and that nonintercourse would soon bring reprisals. When Madison responded that "anything was better" than the existing state of Anglo-American relations, and that he would be glad to negotiate a convention between the two countries requiring "no sacrifice of principle in Great Britain," Foster reported nervously to London that though the administration would "seize with avidity [any] pretext" for adjusting Anglo-American relations, it preferred war to its "present embarrassments."[55]

Madison wrote Joel Barlow via the fast dispatch vessel *Hornet* that since the British demand that the United States force France to open her markets to her enemy was "a fitter subject for ridicule than refutation," Congress would probably declare war, "unless a change in the British system should arrest the career of events." On the other hand, since the "crafty contrivance and insatiate cupidity" of France had aroused "as much irritation and disgust as possible" in the United States, Barlow should explain to French officials that unless she ceased her "folly and iniquity," the ill-will directed against her enemy would "be drawn off against herself." "Hostile collision," Madison noted, "will as readily take place with one nation as the other," unless depredations stopped. Meanwhile the United States would await the return of the *Hornet*, hoping, unexpectantly, that a British withdrawal of the Orders in Council would avert hostilities, and that word would arrive from France that Barlow's "remonstrances" had effected "a radical change of the French policy toward this Country." Madison's position was thus clear: Britain was to have one more chance to withdraw the Orders, and France another chance to cultivate American good will. In the meantime preparations for war would aim at being ready to fight, if necessary, in the spring of 1812.[56]

"A bilious fever . . . caused by an unfinished canal" had, Dolley Madison wrote, filled Congress with a "dread of contagion" at its opening, but after cold weather banished the fears, the social season became so busy that the First Lady wished she were in Paris "for a little relaxation." Instead, she asked Ruth Barlow in the fashion capital to send her "large head-dresses, a few flowers, feathers, gloves, and stockings, black and white, with anything else pretty" but not too expensive. Had Dolley known the impression she made two days later on a freshman Congressman from Pennsylvania, she might have plead even more earnestly for finery: "I got a sight of [Mrs. Madison] today—she appears to be about 45, of coarse if not masculine features. Her eyes dark and neither large nor brilliant—her cheeks I think were painted. The whole contour of her features was dull and uninteresting, her habit is too full to be graceful. She must be considered in ruins though I could trace no evidence that she was ever lovely or beautiful. No doubt she is ambitious, and may have intellect." A week later the same Congressman reported seeing Dolley and her sister doing their own shopping and seemed surprised that the President's wife so often mingled with tradesmen.[57]

Actually the Congressman, Jonathan Roberts, had observed an important part of Dolley Madison's daily routine. She rose early, dressed in plain clothes, and spent the morning shopping and attending to other domestic duties. Then, donning finer dresses, she graced the sitting rooms of the White House, where her husband often visited her, sure he said, "of a bright story and a good laugh . . . as refreshing as a long walk." Otherwise, Madison, his countenance "pallid and hard," labored incessantly, sleeping "very little, going to bed late and getting up frequently during the night to write or read; for which purpose a candle was always burning in the chamber." Despite committing White House social life as much as possible to his wife, Madison still found it made "sad inroads on his time." He was, therefore, "somewhat cold and stiff, taciturn in general society and preoccupied. After dinner, however, at which he usually took a liberal portion of wine, he became free and even facetious, telling with great archness many anecdotes" that displayed, one young house guest noted, the "habitual smut" common to men of

Madison's generation in Virginia. At one dinner Madison was doubtless moved to his anecdotal style by Madeira wine brought from Kentucky by Henry Clay, who had "had the mortification to have been present some years ago at the exhibition at Mr. Jefferson's table of some Kentucky wine which, having been injured in the process of fermentation, was of a most wretched quality." The new Speaker of the House hoped the new sample would "restore in some degree the credit" of Kentucky wine as it softened presidential austerity.[58]

Though the President, as he approached his sixtieth birthday, often seemed bowed and tired, and Dolley, seventeen years his junior, began at last to show signs of middle age, they continued to enjoy a houseful of youthful "connections." Nephews Alfred and Robert Madison lived with them for months at a time between 1810 and 1813. Though illness detained the Cuttses in Maine, widowed Lucy Payne Washington, still "a great belle . . . as lively and amiable as ever," was there, causing Washington Irving to remark that the three Payne sisters reminded him of the merry wives of Windsor. Dolley's young brother John C. Payne, her nineteen-year-old son Payne Todd, and her cousin Edward Coles (the President's private secretary) all lived at the White House during the winter of 1811–12. As if this were not enough, Dolley invited twenty-year-old Phoebe Morris, daughter of her long-time Philadelphia friend Anthony Morris, to spend "the season" in Washington. "My Husband and myself will receive you with open arms," the First Lady wrote, and added that the President "sends you a kiss" for her kind concern for his health. Phoebe came and stayed for several months, dazzled by the life of receptions and balls, not to mention the still scandalous and now richly pensioned Betsy Patterson Bonaparte. "How I wish you could see Madame Bonaparte in all the splendor of dress and all the attractions of beauty," Phoebe wrote her father. "I think I never beheld a human form so faultless. . . . She is truly celestial, and it is impossible to look on anyone else when she is present." Amid such company, the President did not lack for youthful diversion or pleasing respite for eyes tired by the piles of paper always on his desk.[59]

Meanwhile, on Capitol Hill Speaker Henry Clay appointed vigorous young chairmen (all under forty) and a solid majority of War Hawks to the major committees of the House. Three times, Secretary of State Monroe explained the President's views to the Foreign Affairs Committee as it considered key passages of the annual message. With full support from the White House and spurred on by news of General William Henry Harrison's bloody victory over Tecumseh's Indians at Tippecanoe, the committee reported on November 29 that the Congress would no longer suffer quietly the British outrages, and, echoing Madison's message, that "the period has arrived . . . to call forth the patriotism and resources of the country . . . to procure that redress which has been sought for by justice, by remonstrance, and forbearance in vain." The committee then offered six resolutions, calling for an increase of ten thousand in the regular army, a levy of fifty thousand volunteers, alerting the militia, full outfitting of the navy, and—certain to bring hostilities with England—the arming of merchant ships. The committee, like the President, intended war within a few months unless the Orders in Council were withdrawn.[60]

Debate in the House revealed less unanimity, however. Grundy of Tennessee asserted that "war if carried on successfully, will have its advantages. We shall drive the British from our continent. . . . I feel anxious not only to add the Floridas to the South, but the Canadas to the North of this empire." John Randolph of Roanoke condemned these ambitions and asked whether the United States could side with Napoleon, the successor to Attila, Tamerlane, and Kublai Khan, "malefactors of the human race, who ground man down to a mere machine of their impious and bloody ambition." He urged instead sympathy for Great Britain, "from whom every valuable principle of our own institutions has been borrowed, . . . our fellow Protestants identified in blood, in language, in religion with ourselves." While Randolph, gaunt and intense, stalked about the chamber for hours, pointing his bony finger and transfixing the crowded galleries with his "eloquence, . . . ingenuity and eccentricity," young John C. Calhoun, who was not afraid of Randolph's venom, pointed out that the issue was not expansionism, or even a choice between Britain and France, but rather a simple one of national self-respect. Though a few "Old Republicans" followed Randolph in opposition, most of them agreed with Nathaniel Macon to accept war measures for the limited purpose of resisting British depredations. The administration–War Hawk strategy was so successful that in mid-December the six resolves passed by votes ranging from 110 to 22 to 117 to 11. The day after the House adopted the last resolve, Dolley Madison wrote her sister of the "determination to fight for our rights. . . . I believe there will be war," she added. "Mr. Madison sees no end to the perplexities without it, and [Congress] seem to be going on with the preparations." British Minister Foster, however, listening as always to Federalists, reported himself in a "sea of uncertainty," and wrote in code to London that retaining the Orders in Council would help unseat the Republicans at the next election.[61]

Content with the response in Congress, Madison turned to other matters over the holiday season. His old colleague at the convention of 1787, Gouverneur Morris, and the ambitious young mayor of New York, De Witt Clinton, called at the White House, seeking support for their grand plan to build a canal from the Hudson River to Lake Erie. Though Madison had constitutional qualms, he commended the project to Congress, observing that the canal "comprises objects of national as well as more limited importance," and that its advantages "have an intimate connection with the arrangements and exertions for the general security." The appearance of the New Yorkers also brought the political pot to boil. Dolley Madison wrote during their visit, "The intrigues for President and Vice-President go on," with "the Clintons, Smiths, Armstrongs, et cetera, all in the field." The real danger, as British Minister Foster observed, was that the Federalists and disaffected Republicans might support De Witt Clinton for the presidency in 1812, creating a dangerous sectional split: New England and the Middle States against the West and South. Then, three days after Christmas, everything was blotted out by news of the fire in a Richmond theater: it killed seventy-two persons, including Governor George Smith, former Senator Abraham Venable, girls of the Mayo, Nelson, and Page families, and many others well known to the Madisons.[62]

As the new year began, reports arrived of continued French attacks on American ships—hostile actions, Madison told the French minister heatedly at the White House New Year's reception, "fully as pronounced as were those of England, against whom the Republic was at that moment taking up arms." While these depredations blunted indignation against England, the "Invisible" opposition in the Senate, declaring Madison's army expansion plans pusillanimous, pushed through instead a bill to enlarge the army by 25,000, not 10,000, men for five, not three, years. Faced with insinuations of cowardice, and no alternative, the administration majority in the House, and the President himself, reluctantly accepted the Senate bill. The trouble was that 25,000 men could not be enlisted for so long a term as five years, nor was Congress likely to levy taxes to support so large a force, nor was it needed to carry out tenable war plans. The Senate bill was a "pestilent scheme" so obviously impractical, Monroe later observed, that the people and the British would think "the Executive did not intend to make war, [thus] depriving our country of the effect which [sound preparations] might have had in the British cabinet." This devious opposition, added to Clintonian opportunism, Randolph–"Old Republican" doctrinaire opposition to war, and increasingly shrill Federalist hostility, frustrated and infuriated both ardent Congressional War Hawks and patient administration strategists trying to unite the country.[63]

Opposition in Congress to an enlarged navy, however, most hindered war preparations. Madison had recommended constructing twelve ships of the line and ten new frigates, reoutfitting the ten existing frigates, enlarging the Navy Yard, and stock-piling naval timber. Though the new ships would still leave the American navy tiny compared to Britain's, well manned and well fought the ships would provide substantial coastal defense and permit effective challenge to small squadrons of British ships anywhere on the high seas. Chairman Langdon Cheves of the House Navy Committee supported the administration proposals with arguments that caused a Massachusetts Federalist to observe that Cheves "has done himself honor . . . , but whatever he may be nominally he is in reality as high a toned Federalist as ever was Alexander Hamilton." Randolph noted this gleefully, observing that the young Republican apostates repeated all the pronavy arguments Federalists had used in 1798. Many moderate "Old Republicans," generally disposed to follow the administration, but alarmed by a recently revealed report by Gallatin recommending loans and internal taxes to pay for war preparations, could not bring themselves to swallow a navy they had so bitterly resisted fourteen years earlier. Knowing that Madison had agreed with them then, they refused to believe changed circumstances had changed his mind. Pointing out that the navies of "Tyre and Sidon, Crete and Rhodes, Athens and Carthage" had led to plunder, piracy, and perpetual war, Johnson of Kentucky asserted: "Navies have been and always will be engines of power, employed in projects of ambition and war." Nearly all landlocked and agrarian Western representatives were traditionally against policies of the Eastern, mercantile interests. Only Speaker Clay defended the navy expansion. The hated English Orders operated on the high seas, he pointed out, and could therefore only be resisted effectively by American sea power. Furthermore, Western prosperity, dependent on exports through New Orleans, ultimately required naval power to keep open that port. "A navy," Clay concluded, "will form a new bond of connection between the States, concentrating their hopes, their interest, and their affections." In the final vote, January 27, the most critical of the session, the navy was sunk, 62 to 59, by "Old Republicans," economizers, and army-conscious Western War Hawks. The war party was weakened internally and the administration, virtually without a navy, faced a war with the world's dominant sea power.[64]

With bitter sarcasm Madison wrote Jefferson that "the newspapers give you a sufficient insight into the measures of Congress. With a view to enable the Executive to step at once into Canada they have provided after two months of delay, for a regular force requiring 12 to raise it . . . [if] at all for that object." "The mixture of good and bad, avowed and disguised motives accounting for these things," he concluded, "is curious enough but not to be explained in the compass of a letter." Jefferson answered "that a body containing 100 lawyers in it, should direct the measures of a war, is I fear, impossible."[65]

Indeed, the cold weeks in January and February, when ice choked the Potomac and its estuaries, visible from Madison's desk, were gloomy and unportentous for the President. One of the "jobs on my hands" was reading hundreds of pages of testimony from General Wilkinson's court martial. "A month has not yet carried me thro' the whole," Madison reported wearily. Earthquakes, causing terrible death and destruction in Venezuela, shook the Eastern seaboard; a strong shock the morning of February 7 in Washington continued for five or six minutes, alarming the White House family and the rest of the city. Antiwar clergymen in New England proclaimed the quakes evidence of God's anger with bloodthirsty leaders in the nation's capital.

Charges in British newspapers, widely reprinted in the American press, increased Madison's fretfulness. "America fluctuates between her inclinations and her apprehensions," intoned the ministerial London *Courier*. "She seems always to stand TREMBLING and HESITATING on the slippery verge of war; and to be incessantly tossed about at the mercy of every event; a condition which, of all others, most directly tends to palsy the spirit, and to destroy the confidence of a nation." What Madison termed "the mad policy" of the British government, depending on American paralysis and indecision, missed entirely the basic determination behind the intricate combination of blandishment and conciliation he had directed at Britain. At a "family dinner" at the White House on a cold February evening, Speaker Clay, General Dearborn, Secretary Monroe, and the newly appointed Comptroller of the Treasury, Richard Rush, heard the President speak vehemently on impressment and other war issues. "The President," Rush wrote in one of the first of his long reports to friends in Philadelphia, "*little* as he is in bulk, is, unquestionably above [the cabinet and Congress] in spirit and tone. While they are mere mutes, . . . he on every occasion, and to every body, talks freely . . . [and] says the time is ripe, and the nation, too, for resistance." Contempt for England increased when stories arrived that the Prince Regent "had lately had his *nose pulled*, *been kicked down a pair of stairs*, and had his *ankle bruised* by Lord Holland who detected him in *crim*[inal] *con*-[versation, *i.e.*, conduct] with Lady Holland."[66]

Meanwhile, as Congress debated the army and navy increases, Treasury reports forecasting reduced tariff revenues and showing that American trade with England was twenty times that with France caused fiscal nightmares. Gallatin proposed doubling the tariff on such imports as continued to enter the country, as well as stamp duties, license fees, and excises on salt, spirits, carriages, and sugar. Even with these heavy taxes and a conservative estimate of war costs, Gallatin had to propose a loan of $10 million, likely to be subscribed only at ruinous interest rates. It would require a sharp turn indeed for such Representatives as William Findley and John Smilie of Pennsylvania, seventy-year-old soldiers of the revolution, antifederalists in 1788, and veterans of twenty years of battle with Federalists in Congress, to vote for a stamp tax, laws vastly expanding the powers of the federal government, and measures virtually identical to those fathered by Hamilton and John Adams in the seventeen-nineties and for which they had been rejected by the people. A Virginia Republican who supported the administration used the grim, revealing metaphor that he would take the whole draught (of taxes) even if it were hemlock. Gallatin reflected the soul searching going on among Republicans when he wrote Jefferson, "with respect to the war, it is my wish . . . that the evils inseparable from it should, as far as practicable, be limited to its duration, and that at its end the United States may be burdened with the smallest possible quantity of debt, perpetual taxation, military establishment, and other corrupting or antirepublican habits or institutions." Nonetheless, driven by Clay and others who argued that republican doctrine had to yield to the necessity to pay for measures already adopted, the House finally accepted Gallatin's proposals, including the taxes, to take effect in case of war "against a European nation." Pleased, Madison wrote Jefferson that "the House of Representatives have got down the dose of taxes. It is the strongest proof they could give that they do not mean to flinch from the contest to which the mad conduct of Great Britain drives them."[67]

In late February 1812 the frigate *Constitution* brought news that Joel Barlow in Paris was, Madison reported to Richard Cutts, "engaged in discussions that encourage his hope of doing something valuable." At the same time Madison and Monroe were dealing secretly with bizarre figures in Washington who, probably with the connivance of French Minister Sérurier, showed them letters between Governor Craig of Canada and agents in New England encouraging treason and disunion during the outcry against the Embargo. The sensational documents supported Republican suspicions: Britain conspired with disloyal New Englanders to embarrass the American government, prevent war with England, and dissolve the Union. Secretary Monroe paid the English agent, John Henry, and his accomplice, the self-proclaimed Count de Crillon, $50,000 for copies of the letters. On March 9, Madison laid them before Congress as proof that the British government employed an agent (Henry) in Boston "in fomenting disaffection to the constituted authorities of the nation, and in intrigues with the disaffected, for the purpose of bringing about resistance to the laws, and eventually, in concert with a British force, of destroying the Union and forming the eastern part thereof into a political connection with Great Britain."[68]

The effect, of course, was electric, charging a foreign power with intriguing to break up the Union—a long-dreaded specter. Dawning awareness that the letters revealed no names of Henry's American accomplices, and that the Count de Crillon was actually a notorious French con man, embarrassed the administration and caused anguished cries of foul play from Federalists, but the documents did make clear Britain's strategy to paralyze the United States. An editorial in the ad-

ministration newspaper, *The National Intelligencer*, revealed the intent
to stimulate Congress and the country toward war measures. The affair
"speaks in a voice of thunder which the very deaf shall hear," the
editor wrote, and warned against a foe "perfidiously stirring up rebellion
and . . . feeling for the vitals of the Republic, to which she might in the
dead of night direct her poisoned dagger." Richard Rush, eager for decisive action, exulted that the letters produced "a burst of indignation, new
strength to the patriotick party, and a visible increase in the war tone."
Monroe told the French minister that "we have made use of the Henry
documents as a last means of exciting the nation and Congress," while
Madison wrote that he hoped the documents, offering "formal proof of
the cooperation between the Eastern Junto and the British Cabinet, will
. . . not only prevent future evils from that source, but extract good
out of the past."[69]

The social season had its ups and downs during the long winter and
spring of movement toward war. The usual number of strange and
exciting figures crowded the drawing rooms. General Jean Victor Marie
Moreau, Napoleon's ablest officer, but exiled because of his ardent republicanism, discussed military strategy with American officers made
loquacious by wine, while his wife, an ambitious Creole of Josephine's
circle and an "incessant talker" who dominated her husband, shocked
Americans by dancing and playing cards on Sunday. Twenty-nine-year-
old Simón Bolívar, dark featured, grave, and eloquent, pleaded earnestly
for help against Spain in South America. Robert Fulton demonstrated
new weapons, steam frigates and catamarans, on the Potomac. Betsy
Bonaparte's young son, Napoleon's nephew, living in Washington, was a
constant reminder that the French Emperor had a "prince" in the United
States, ready to be made the center of intrigues aimed at French dominion over North America. French Minister Sérurier, living at Joel
Barlow's superb country estate, Kalorama, and British Minister Augustus John Foster, elaborately domiciled at the Seven Buildings, both
polished young bachelors, competed in entertainments. At one such
occasion Foster served caviar, taken from Potomac River sturgeon, to
New England Congressmen, who, mistaking it for black raspberry jam,
first gulped it down, then quickly spit it out, pronouncing it excessively
bitter and nasty. To a ball given on January 20 to celebrate the Queen's
birthday, Foster invited the many "handsome ladies" attracted to Washington, "one of the most marrying places of the whole continent." There
couples did "a great deal of billing and cooing"; the men played brag, the
ladies loo; and Foster did his best to keep peace among "several hot-
headed Irishmen in Congress who would have desired no better sport
than to shoot at Randolph or any other leading member of the
opposition."[70]

The President, following Washington's practice, accepted no invitations to dine out—in fact, during the whole 1811–12 session of Congress, he was seen outside only twice—but everybody flocked to special dinners and the regular Wednesday evening "drawing rooms" at the White House. At one dinner the impostor Crillon—"a thick-set man, monstrous thick legs, a little hair on his head," but with abundant whiskers—had pushed in to sit beside Dolley Madison and dazzled her with embroidered talk of parties in the palaces of Europe. Madison exchanged banalities with drunken Senator Richard Brent of Virginia, and found occasion to warn Foster that "it seemed quite necessary to become a belligerent in order to enjoy the advantages of commerce." Somewhat later, after a young Dutchman at a dinner at Madame Bonaparte's had accused Crillon of being a fraud, he appeared at the White House in a gaudy uniform. He ostentatiously challenged the Dutchman, who calmly asked "Crillon" to offer proof of his identity. The Frenchman equivocated, was exposed, and thenceforth shunned. For two weeks in March the White House receptions became partisan affairs, because Federalists, "affronted to a man" by Madison's use of the Henry letters, refused to enter the President's door. By the twenty-fifth, however, hostile news from England and the loyalty of Republicans who continued to crowd the White House drawing rooms, brought them back, "old and young," and "in a large body."[71]

Dolley Madison was doubly pleased that the social boycott ended before the marriage, on March 29, of Lucy Washington to Supreme Court Justice Thomas Todd, a forty-seven-year-old widower with five children who had been a boy in King and Queen County, Virginia, while Madison attended the Robertson school there. Lucy had apparently rejected Judge Todd along with her other suitors, but, impulsively, after he had left for his home in Kentucky, she changed her mind and sent word for him to return to marry her; the wedding took place the following Sunday in the White House. All the young people of the household were bridesmaids and groomsmen: Phoebe Morris, Monroe's kinswoman Miss Hay, Navy Secretary Paul Hamilton's daughter, Edward Coles, John Payne, and Dolley's son, Payne Todd. Dolley pronounced the groom "amiable, intelligent, in short . . . all that I could wish in a brother." Only Judge Todd's promise to bring his bride to Washington for the annual sessions of the Supreme Court reconciled the three sisters and the President to the dissolution of the exceedingly congenial group that had for three years enlivened the White House.[72]

Lucy's honeymoon letters to Dolley, though, reveal that all was not sweetness and light in the White House circle. John Payne was sent with the new couple, in hopes that a journey as well as "kindness and attention" might restore his mental health. Lucy hoped, too, that Dolley would soon be "relieved" of the "too *agreeable*" company of Phoebe and Anthony Morris, and thus prevent Phoebe and Edward Coles from coming to blows in their quarrels. Lucy also thought "Ned" would be jilted by Miss Hay, whom Lucy was sure was teasing him. The new bride was "very much provoked at that old hag Mrs. Duval [wife of a Supreme Court Justice, whose] . . . disposition to venom" was such that no one would side with her in a social tangle of which Dolley Madison had complained. As for an old suitor, Mr. Briscoe, Lucy insisted that "there can be nothing said but that I jilted him. . . . They had no business to expect I'd have him—everybody hooted at him for a fool." She hoped, though, that "my dear brother James . . . misses me at meals and when he takes his usual walk to and fro in the little sitting rooms in the evening—oh! and when he kisses you—he was always so fearful of making my *mouth water—tell him I get kisses now that would make his mouth run over.*" To surmises that the new groom was like "still champaign," Todd hinted that Lucy was already pregnant, to which she added "*he* is only in *hopes it* may be so." A month later Todd asked his wife to tell the President "*that he* [Todd] *has got the apple in the dumpling*" (the best of the Payne sisters), but left "the hows, and whens, for him [Madison] to conjecture." Lucy could add only, "O these men ——." To cheer her "exile" to Kentucky, Lucy urged Dolley to send on some promised wine, which would improve on the journey, "and I hope induce brother [Madison] to come [to Kentucky] and taste it with you, and *us* next spring." For Lucy, at least, the clouds of war did not entirely blot out gaiety.[73]

Louisiana's admission to the Union on April 15 led to just the sort of festivities Lucy hated to miss: great parties with much cork popping, ribald songs, and wild toasts by drunken Congressmen. The celebrations continued the next day when Senator Outerbridge Horsey of Delaware, "a general favourite," married Eliza Lee, "a very pleasing young lady" from a distinguished Maryland family. "Great numbers" of Congressmen and diplomats imbibed punch and wine until they joked extravagantly about prospects for peace or war. Even the death of Vice President George Clinton on April 20 only briefly dampened social life. Foster canceled a dinner for Archbishop John Carroll, and sent his magnificent coach with four horses to the funeral, while Madison looked on as riflemen fired volleys over the old revolutionist's grave in the Congressional cemetery. The Madisons probably intended no disrespect when two days later they held a widely disapproved Wednesday reception, but the quick return to normalcy may have reflected honest relief at being rid of the senile presiding officer of the Senate, whose judgment John Quincy Adams had found "neither quick nor strong" and who was "totally ignorant of all the most common forms of proceeding in [the] Senate."[74]

"Electioneering . . . beyond description," Dolley Madison wrote, went on for Clinton's office, even before he died. Everywhere, in fact, Madison faced the vexing question of staffing offices for war. In Congress, curiously, he had few close, dependable associates. The Virginia senators, alcoholic Richard Brent and bombastic, ambitious William B. Giles, were useless or worse, while the delegation in the House was more or less infected with "Old Republican" hesitancies about war measures. He was also deprived of the invaluable support of his two brothers-in-law: John G. Jackson had resigned from Congress, and Richard Cutts was sick in Maine. Although Madison and Speaker Henry Clay came to respect and enjoy each other, on the whole, the sixty-year-old President did not develop warm personal relations with the new under-forty members dominant in the Twelfth Congress. In the cabinet, Gallatin and Monroe were extremely able and very close personally to Madison, but each—Gallatin because of his deep distress over war expenditures and Monroe because of his still strong "Old Republican" ties—was in some sense disqualified to be first lieutenant in marching toward war. William Pinkney, who had replaced Rodney as Attorney General in December 1811, was an able, worthy colleague, but he continued to live in Baltimore, and the Postmaster General, Gideon Granger, never close to Madison, became a liability as he intrigued over patronage, and like so many New Englanders, opposed the war. The secretaries of War and the Navy, William Eustis and Paul Hamilton, continued, as John Randolph remarked, to cut pretty figures in the drawing room, but they were regarded by everyone in Washington except the President, Senator Crawford of Georgia reported, as "incapable of discharging the duties of their office." To compound the difficulty, Congress on May 6 rejected Madison's request for two assistant secretaries of war, thus leaving the entire build-up of the army to Eustis and eight inexperienced clerks. Dolley Madison revealed the incongruities when she wrote Anna Cutts that only Mrs. Eustis and Mrs. Hamilton had had parties, and that all the heads of the departments and their wives dined at the White House at the very time "my dear husband is overpowered with business."[75]

The "Old Republican" orthodoxies about frugal government and the tangled political crosscurrents that vitiated Congress' move toward war also hamstrung the President in organizing administratively for it. The army in January 1812 was at less than one-third its authorized strength of 10,000 men, and as Madison had foreseen, the grand-sounding increase of 25,000 men authorized by Congress proved impossible to recruit. Army "regiments" were scattered about the frontier, under either old veterans of the revolution or officers inexperienced except in Indian fighting. Republican disdain for standing armies had resulted, a careful student has observed, in a war capability that "lacked integration, responsibility, unity, and energy, and was utterly inadequate for even the most modest military operations." Madison appointed Henry Dearborn, a fat, sixty-one-year-old revolutionary veteran, Republican stalwart, and Jefferson's Secretary of War, as senior major general, and Thomas Pinckney of South Carolina, a year older than Dearborn, as the other major general in command of the Southern Department. Both appointments brought prestige, seniority, and earnest patriotism to the army, but no particular military distinction; virtually fatal, neither general was capable of even normal exertions. Commanding in the West was another revolutionary veteran, fifty-nine-year-old William Hull, who, though valiant as a youth, had become timid and fearful by 1812. Dearborn and Hull came to Washington in February to "lend a helping hand," and make war plans, but Dearborn suffered incapacitating illnesses, quickly earned the nickname "Granny," and was dubbed "Generalissimo of the Terrapin Army" by sneering Federalists. Hull had a phobia about the Indian menace that prevented him from considering seriously prospective campaigns against British forces in Canada. Secretary Eustis, meanwhile, had no sense of "forming general and comprehensive arrangements for the organization of his troops," but instead "consumed his time in reading advertisements of petty retailing merchants to find where he may purchase one hundred shoes or two hundred hats."[76]

The navy had suffered even more than the army, if that was possible, from Republican antimilitarism and budget cutting. The failure of the navy bill in January 1812 left the total American navy less than one sixth the size of Britain's squadrons normally stationed in North America. Only a few exceedingly able officers and men battle hardened in the quasi-war with France (1798–1799) and the Barbary Wars, some well-built frigates, and the "nursery of seamen" provided by New England's seafaring ways brightened the grim picture. Secretary of the Navy Paul Hamilton, an amiable planter with little maritime experience, was declared by Congressman Macon, "about as fit for his place as the Indian Prophet would be for Emperor of Europe." To make matters worse, since the navy had no staff officers, orders went directly from Secretary Hamilton to individual ship captains and to a mixed bag of agents and navy yard superintendents along the seacoast. Thus, as Madison conferred with the civilian and "professional" heads of the armed forces in the spring of 1812, he found both personnel and organization hopelessly deficient.[77]

Almost as counterproductive was the "politicking" for the coming presidential election. Madison's position, generally firm in the absence of a widely popular rival, was strengthened in the late winter, when Virginia and Pennsylvania chose solid slates of electors for him. Added to Republican strength farther south and west, this gave the President close to an electoral college majority even if he lost New York, New England,

and the smaller seaboard states. Early in May, however, Federalist victories in Massachusetts and New York revived opposition hopes generally, and in particular excited De Witt Clinton, whose uncle, the Vice President, fortunately for the younger man's political ambitions, was no longer alive. Casting about everywhere, Clinton's friends had sought Western support by suggesting a Clinton-Clay ticket, but the Kentuckian had rejected such a strange alliance. Southern "Old Republicans," from the rabid Randolph, who reviled Madison, to the moderate Macon, who remained steadily though unenthusiastically loyal to the administration, were equally unable to embrace a Clinton tainted with both "Invisibility" and Federalism. Thus, spurned by Western War Hawks and antiwar Republicans, Clinton was left to seek support from Federalists drawn to him only by hostility to Madison.

Faced with this motley opposition, and finally rid of the Clintons, the administration offered the Vice-Presidential nomination to seventy-year-old John Langdon of New Hampshire, a steady Republican, father-in-law of Secretary of War William Eustis, and known to Madison since their service together, twenty-five years earlier, in the Continental Congress. When Langdon sensibly refused the nomination because of poor health, the Congressional caucus that under Clay's leadership had renominated Madison, 82 to 0, assembled again to add ten votes for Madison and name Elbridge Gerry of Massachusetts his running mate. Though Gallatin feared Gerry was an eccentric who "would give us as much trouble as our late Vice-President," Madison was glad to have on the ticket a famous patriot able to draw Northern votes and, of more than incidental importance, too old to challenge heir-apparent James Monroe in 1816. When the New York legislature announced its support for De Witt Clinton despite the caucus nominations, Madison knew that though the New Yorker was virtually isolated among Republicans, the way was open for a bitter campaign if, as many expected, the Federalists also backed Clinton. Madison never had serious cause to worry about either renomination or re-election, but the rival ambitions generated by the pending election were a substantial distraction from the foreign crisis.[78]

Overshadowing the social season, the frustrations of preparing for war, and presidential politics, however, was the steady deterioration of relations with both belligerents. On March 21 Congressmen deserted committee hearings for the crowded anteroom of the State Department to learn about the latest dispatches from England. At first, hope gave rise to rumors that Britain had yielded, but in fact the ministry had become more rigid. Foster was instructed to "avoid . . . any suggestions of compromise," to warn the American government that the Orders in Council would not be withdrawn, and to threaten that trade restraints and the arming of American merchant vessels might "produce the calamity of war between the two countries." Madison wrote that since Britain preferred "war with us to repeal of their Orders in Council, we have nothing left . . . but to make ready for it."[79]

Two days later came news that, under orders to halt the vital flow of American grain to Wellington's armies in Spain, French frigates were burning American vessels on the high seas. Monroe exploded to French Minister Sérurier: "Well, sir, it is then decided that we are to receive nothing but outrages from France! And at what a moment too! At the very instant when we are going to war with her enemies." This news, the Secretary of State continued, coming as it did after the Henry documents had been used to excite the country against England, and after Congress was on the point "almost unanimously" of declaring war on Britain, "put the Administration in the falsest and most terrible position in which a government can find itself placed." The next day *The National Intelligencer*, echoing Madison's recent annual message, and, as always, speaking for the administration, called the nation to "no longer deceive ourselves; the period has arrived when the rights and honor of our country must be asserted by an appeal to arms." Dolley Madison wrote that "the world seems to be running mad," and told her sister to have her husband bring his vessels back to home port. Though Congressman Macon declared "the Devil himself could not tell which government, England or France, is the most wicked," and some cried for war with both belligerents, Madison insisted that French depredations not deter the country from its confrontation with the prime enemy.[80]

On March 31, Monroe met with the House Committee on Foreign Affairs and reiterated Madison's position that Congress should declare war on Britain before adjourning. The secretary urged an embargo for sixty days to keep American vessels beyond the reach of English warships, to permit further preparations for war, to allow time for the *Hornet* to arrive with a final round of dispatches from Europe, and to "leave the ultimate policy of the government in our hands." Even at this point, the President left the door barely open for peace. The House agreed to the embargo and reluctantly accepted its extension to ninety days by the Senate. The President was afraid this would be interpreted as weakness, but having no alternative, signed the measure. Incensed by timid Senators, Rush explained that "at Sparta the Ephori prosecuted persons who tamely suffered themselves to be insulted. How does this apply to our long-insulted nation!" In the same mood, Madison had Monroe write a stirring anti-British editorial for *The National Intelligencer*: "The final step ought to be taken. . . . Our wrongs have been great; our cause is just; and if we are decided and firm, success is inevitable. Let war therefore be forthwith proclaimed against England." Preparations were to "go on with alacrity," and war, "that terrible event," Dolley Madison wrote, was to follow the Embargo.[81]

Madison complained to Jefferson that "the *Hornet* still loiters," and worried that "the conflict of opinions here, and of local interests elsewhere" would vitiate the war spirit. However, bolstered by the war editorial in the *Intelligencer*, which British Minister Foster admitted created a "very great sensation" throughout the country, Clay's forces in the House on April 25 and 29 beat back Senate motions for adjournment, and Congressmen increasingly accepted the certainty of war. Madison was especially encouraged when old John Smilie, the dean of the House and the bellwether of moderate Republican feeling, declared that though war was against his conscience, he would vote for it, and when John Sevier, the tough Tennessee militiaman whose victory over the British at King's Mountain had so cheered Madison and his colleagues in Congress in the dark days of 1780, asserted that not "a shadow of doubt remained of war." Though Randolph and Northern Federalists asked sarcastically how the nation could "go to war without money, without men, without a navy, . . . when we have not the courage . . . to lay war taxes," Clay and other War Hawks visited the President to assure him that a majority of Congress would vote for war. At the same time, the war of words intensified on both sides of the Atlantic. A member of Parliament declared that "America . . . could not do without Birmingham—she could not even shave herself, or catch her mice without their aid." A Boston newspaper replied, ". . . if America cannot shave *herself*, she can *shave old England*, as the battles of Bunker Hill, Saratoga, etc., plainly evince: And as to *mousing*, we ask, who manufactured the mouse-traps in which BURGOYNE and CORNWALLIS were 'taken'?" Madison took heart, and guarded his health, while Dolley, lonely for her sisters, was, she wrote, "the very shadow of my husband."[82]

On May 19 the long-awaited *Hornet* arrived in New York. Three days later its dispatches reached Washington, and in two more days they were decoded. French Minister Sérurier then described the reaction: "The avenues of the State Department were thronged by a crowd of members of both Houses of Congress, as well as by strangers and citizens. . . . Soon it was learned that the *Hornet* had brought nothing favorable, and that Mr. Barlow had as yet concluded nothing with [the French government]. On this news, the furious declamations of the Federalists, of the commercial interests, and of the numerous friends of England were redoubled; the Republicans, deceived in their hopes, joined in the outcry, and for three days nothing was heard but a general cry for war against France and England at once. . . . I met Mr. Monroe at the Speaker's House; he came to me with an air of affliction and discouragement." On top of this news from France came tidings from the new British foreign secretary, Lord Castlereagh. He listed the crimes of Napoleon that justified continuing British measures against all the com-

merce, neutral and otherwise, of Europe. Madison and the cabinet went
into long sessions weighted with the knowledge that the continuing
French depredations made the now unavoidable war with England all
the more difficult to undertake. Eloquent patriotic appeals in Philadelphia newspapers heightened war crys, and plans circulated in Washington to bring Jefferson back into the government to uplift and unify the
nation by "the overruling ascendency of his name."[83]

Amid such frantic rumors and after some deliberation Madison put
the dilemma to Jefferson. To go to war with England and not France
would alienate the Federalists and divide the Republicans, many of whom
were angry equally with the belligerents. "To go to war against both,
presents a thousand difficulties; above all, that of shutting all the ports of
the Continent of Europe against our cruisers who can do little without
the use of them. It is pretty certain also, that it would not gain over the
Federalists, who would turn all those difficulties against the Administration." Finally, though the double war might bring peace and concessions
from one of the powers, they might prolong the war "with as little
reason . . . as has prevailed in the past conduct of both." As had been
true for eight years, Madison saw cause for war with both belligerents,
but he saw, too, the impracticality of a double war, and therefore chose
to act against the greater enemy.[84]

Henry Clay moved in the same direction. On May 24 he wrote there
would be war, "whether against one or both the Belligerents, the only
point on which I find any diversity of opinion," while three days later,
after Barlow's dispatches had been read in Congress, revealing Napoleon's ministers had been polite if not accommodating, the Speaker predicted "the Government will proceed in its course against England,
[but] wait a while longer before it takes any measure of a hostile character against France." As the President worked on his war message to
Congress and ignored hasty, too-late maneuvers by British Minister
Foster, who at last realized how his Federalist friends had underestimated
Madison's determination, he warned the country through *The National
Intelligencer* not to suppose "that the misconduct of France neutralizes
in the least that of Great Britain."[85]

Meanwhile, opponents of war made a last, desperate effort to bring
the country to their side. Dolley Madison wrote on May 29 that "John
Randolph has been firing away at the House this morning against the
declaration of war." In fact, with no motion before the House, Randolph
spoke for over an hour, stalking about the chamber charging that if war
were declared on England, "this government will stand branded to the
latest posterity . . . as panderers of French despotism—as the tools, the
minions, sycophants, parasites of France." Sick of debate and fearing the
enervating effect of Randolph's invective, Clay and Calhoun demanded
that the Virginian submit a motion before speaking further. Randolph

refused, knowing that the House would reject any motion he might make and then begin secret debate on a war declaration. Clay persevered and Randolph cried that to deny the privilege of "prefacing a motion by remarks" would destroy "the last vestige of freedom of debate." Hotheaded Robert Wright of Maryland, supporting Clay, accused Randolph of being so much under British influence that he sought to discuss national security before "British licensed spies within this hall." Clay ordered Wright to his seat and again insisted that Randolph submit a motion. Randolph cited his fourteen years in the House to support his interpretation of the rules. Clay retorted that "priority of seat on this floor . . . gives to the senior members of the House *no* right to which the junior are not *equally* entitled." The House then voted not to consider Randolph's proposition and went into secret session. Madison doubtless shared the joy of Republican newspapers that "My lord" Randolph, so long tolerated by the House that "he kicks and squeals monstrously . . . like a spoiled child . . . on being forced to discipline," had been put down by a Speaker "equal to his duty."[86]

On June 1, for over half an hour, a clerk droned out Madison's war message to a closed session of Congress. It was simple to compile grievances against Britain because, as Henry Adams observed, "for five years the task of finding excuses for peace had been more difficult than that of proving a *casus belli*." The President mentioned, first, impressment, subjecting Americans to being "dragged on board ships of war of a foreign nation and exposed, under the severities of their discipline, to be exiled to the most distant and deadly climes, to risk their lives in the battles of their oppressors." Second, British cruisers warred against American commerce within sight of its own harbors, and British edicts proclaimed "pretended blockades" violating every principle of international law. Third, Orders in Council directed against neutral ships had been "molded and managed as might best suit [British] political views, . . . commercial jealousies, or the avidity of British cruisers." In response to patient American efforts to adjust these differences, Britain had refused perversely to see the mutuality of English and American interests. "It has become sufficiently certain," the President observed, "that the commerce of the United States is to be sacrificed, not as interfering with the belligerent rights of Great Britain; not as supplying the wants of her enemies, which she herself supplies; but as interfering with the monopoly which she covets for her own commerce and navigation, . . . a commerce polluted by . . . forgeries and perjuries."

After charging that Britain had fomented "the warfare just renewed by the savages on one of our extensive frontiers," Madison asked Congress to consider "the spectacle of injuries and indignities . . . heaped on our country . . . which its unexampled forbearance and conciliatory

efforts have not been able to avert." Though he left the "solemn question" of war or peace to Congress, as the Constitution required, he was
sure the decision would "be worthy of the enlightened and patriotic
councils of a virtuous, a free, and a powerful nation." He concluded with
a brief summary of French offenses, but asked Congress to await further
dispatches from Joel Barlow before deciding on "definitive measures"
against France. Though Clay and others had assured the President that
Congress would follow his lead, Macon of North Carolina wrote on
June 2 that "it is doubtful this morning, . . . whether Congress are as
firm for war as they have been thought." The next day, news from England that the Prince Regent had declared his confidence in Perceval and
his father's other ministers revived indignation against England and
prepared the House to heed the plea of its Committee on Foreign Relations, now headed by Calhoun: "Relying on the patriotism of the nation,
and confidently trusting that the Lord of hosts will go with us to battle
in a righteous cause, and crown our efforts with success, your committee
recommend an immediate appeal to arms." Clay and Calhoun now
thought it permissible to resume public debate, but at Madison's request,
the doors of the House remained closed. Denied an audience, the Federalists accepted Calhoun's report silently, and the House adjourned
early, knowing the moment of decision had arrived.[87]

Meanwhile Madison and Monroe had exchanged long notes with
Foster, who was still trying to forestall hostilities. Seeing that the notes
again convicted Britain of evasion and arrogance, Madison ordered
Edward Coles to copy the exchange for immediate transmission to Congress. Foster found the President "very pale and extremely agitated"
during a tense conference the afternoon of June 3. Foster himself was a
bit rattled when, that evening at Dolley's reception, people anticipated
his departure by asking if they could buy his fine race horses and a large
tent used for outdoor entertainments. Exhausted and preoccupied, Madison made an even poorer impression than usual on visiting Federalists.
One, from New York, wrote to his mother: "Last evening I went to
court. I was presented to the king and queen, and had some conversation
with his majesty about green peas and strawberries. . . . He has a serious
look, devoid of penetration; his face is crooked and wrinkled; and his
countenance does not exhibit the least trait of sincerity or candor. He is a
little, old, dried up politician. He does not know how to behave in company; instead of going about among his guests and setting them at ease, by
saying something to each, he stands in the middle of the room, and expects
his visitors to approach him, if they want to be favored by his conversation." To strengthen public confidence, Madison went to church the
next Sunday, his first appearance outside the White House grounds since
the Vice President's funeral.[88]

The prompt 79 to 49 vote for war in a secret session of the House on

June 4 cheered Madison, but he had to endure two weeks of delay while motley forces in the Senate procrastinated. With six Senators expected to oppose war away from Washington, the committee appointed to consider Madison's message did not report a war bill until June 8. Waiting while "voices were heard thundering in the senate," Richard Rush reported himself "more than half undone with anxiety, tears, and hope . . . as the hour of trial arrives." Foster confidently expected the Senate to equivocate, and even attended to such details as assigning an aide to keep Senator Brent of Virginia too drunk to vote. Brent nonetheless staggered in for every roll call to support the administration. On June 10 a move to substitute naval reprisal and letters of marque for full war received approval, and two days afterward an effort to place France on the same footing as England, a strategy to prevent any declaration of war, failed by only two votes. Later that day, however, the Senate in a crucial tie vote, killed the naval reprisal resolve, putting the question of full war again on the floor. After a weekend adjournment, on June 15 all Senators in town splashed through rivers of rain, to defeat, again by narrow margins, efforts to delay or limit the war. Rush wailed "alas for the senate, the senate, the senate! The first to give the whoop . . . now to hold back," and complained of its foolishness in "raising armies and refusing to march them." The next day the war resolve stiffened as first eleven and then only nine Senators favored postponing the war until November or July. Senators opposed to war knew they were defeated, but outsiders still felt a suspense "worse than hell," and feared the "diabolical" Foster had "dropped . . . bills of exchange . . . in the Senate." On June 17, at last, the Senate voted, 19 to 13, for a declaration of war. Undaunted, Foster went that evening to Dolley Madison's drawing room, where, as usual, he bowed three times to the President, and exchanged pleasantries with him about British victories over Napoleon in Spain. Foster thought Madison "looked ghastly pale" and weighted down with "all the responsibility he would incur." The next day the House accepted minor Senate amendments, and Madison signed the war declaration, exhorting "all the good people of the United States, as they love their country . . . [to] exert themselves in preserving order, in promoting concord . . . and in . . . invigorating all the measures which may be adopted by the constituted authorities for obtaining a speedy, a just, and an honorable peace."[89]

Madison viewed the declaration with sadness and regret, though he had for nearly a year been working with his cabinet and with Clay and other Congressmen to prepare the country for battle. In reviewing the course toward war, Madison observed that Foster's "formal notice" of July 1811 that Britain would require humiliating concessions before withdrawing Orders in Council had made war virtually inevitable. Writ-

ing to antiwar John Taylor of Carolina even before the final declaration,
Monroe had explained that upon joining the cabinet in April 1811 he had
found erroneous his conviction that Britain would make concessions if
properly approached. Nothing, he added, "would satisfy the present
Ministry of England short of unconditional submission which it was impossible to make." Thus, after July 1811, "the only remaining alternative
was to get ready for fighting, and to begin as soon as we were ready.
This was the plan of the administration when Congress met [in November 1811]; the President's message announced it; and every step taken by
the administration since has led to it."[90]

Asked late in life to assess Madison's state of mind as the war approached, Edward Coles noted that "it was congenial alike to the life
and character of Mr. Madison that he should be reluctant to go to war,
. . . [a] savage and brutal manner of settling disputes among nations,"
while diplomacy afforded any peaceful hopes at all. Coles agreed with
Monroe that Britain's notice of July 1811 "closed the door to peace in
Mr. Madison's opinion," and observed further that during the long session of Congress from November 1811 to July 1812, "a class of irritable
men, . . . hotspurs of the day," declaimed for war, heedless of the need
for preparation and scornful of "sound, prudent and patriotic men" who
wanted delay and further diplomatic initiatives. Madison stood in the
middle, Coles said, trying "to moderate the zeal and impatience of the
ultra belligerent men, and to stimulate the more moderate and forbear-
ing; to check those who were anxious to rush on hastily to extreme
measures without due preparation and to urge those who lagged too far
behind." The President restrained his own determination to go to war to
bring to his side "tardy and over cautious members of Congress" and
thus be able to declare war "by a large and influential majority."[91]

Viewed in this perspective, Madison's course during the year preceding the war declaration, and even during the whole seven-year period
following full scale resumption of the Napoleonic Wars in 1805, appears
straight and consistent, if not always wise and well executed. He thought
throughout that his goal, a genuine, republican independence for the
United States, found its worst menace in the commercial and maritime
arrogance and power of Great Britain. To have submitted to her unilateral decrees, her discriminatory trade regulations, or her naval outrages
would have restored the colonial dependence Madison had fought for
half a century. It would, moreover, have ratified unjust principles in
international law and emboldened antirepublican forces in Britain and
the United States, thus threatening, in Madison's opinion, the survival of
free government anywhere in the world. Madison's sense of history reminded him, as it had Richard Rush, that the United States, in the War
of 1812, would be "the first genuine democracy engaged in a war since
the ancients." "Shall we not reenact the splendid valor of Athens, of
Thebes, of Rome?" Rush asked.[92]

But so corrosive was war to republican principles that only the direst emergency could condone it. Thus Madison tried every conceivable and even some inconceivable ways of peaceful resistance, until many men less patient, less subtle, and less earnestly republican than he thought him hopelessly irresolute, or a tool of Napoleon. Madison pronounced this latter charge "as foolish as it is false." If the war coincided with the views of the enemy of Great Britain and was favored by Napoleon's operations against her, he observed coolly, "that assuredly could be no sound objection to the time chosen for extorting justice from her. On the contrary, the coincidence, though it happened not to be the moving consideration, would have been a rational one; especially as it is not pretended that the United States acted in concert with [Napoleon], or precluded themselves from making peace without any understanding with him; or even from making war on France, in the event of peace with her enemy, and her continued violation of our neutral rights." Though in retrospect it may seem Madison underestimated Napoleon's global ambitions, he had no illusions about the French tyrant. Britain's greater capacity to injure the United States was the steady, realistic base of Madison's policy.[93]

Less defensible is Madison's relentless, sometimes innocently implausible reliance on peaceful coercion, which instead of persuading the belligerents to deal honorably with the United States, only convinced them they had nothing to fear from them. Thus insult followed depredation, year after year. Shifting from one kind of nonviolent coercion to another, and offering the carrot and then the stick first to one belligerent and then to the other, instead of persuading either of them to accept American support in exchange for commercial justice, led each country to think it could by intrigue and maneuver get all it wanted while granting nothing. As a result, by 1812 the United States was neither trusted nor respected by the warring powers. At home, Madison's patient, subtle efforts to unite the country behind him often had the doubly debilitating effect of disgusting those impatient for war and encouraging those opposed to it to think he would ultimately flinch from hostilities. Though, even in retrospect, better alternatives are not readily apparent, Madison's course seldom had the effect he intended.

Least defensible of all is the absurd unfitness of the nation for war in June 1812. Since Britain, not the United States, had to fight at long distance, and therefore would benefit from delay and warning, Madison insisted in response to this charge, "it was, in fact, not the suddenness of war as an Executive policy, but the tardiness of legislative provision" that left the nation unprepared in June 1812. He had, he pointed out, recommended a military build-up in early November 1811, and it was more than two months before Congress took even ill-conceived steps. Though Congress did indeed hang back in this and many other ways during the twelve years of Republican rule, Madison seldom did more than call vaguely for "attention to the nation's defenses," and Secretary Gallatin insisted repeatedly that military expenditures be limited by his plans to discharge the national debt. From 1805 on, while Madison talked loudly and unyieldingly of neutral rights, the chasm deepened between the obvious military peril of the European war and the pitiful state of the country's armed forces. He often spoke loudly while carrying no stick at all.[94]

Madison correctly pointed out the host of difficulties he faced in placing the nation on a war footing. Officers for the army had to be chosen from among "survivors of the Revolutionary band," many of whom "were disqualified by age or infirmities," or from among those untried on the battlefield. Furthermore, to appoint any executive officer, "an eye must be had to his political principles and connections, his personal temper and habits, his relations . . . towards those with whom he is to be associated, and the quarter of the Union to which he belongs." Add to this, Madison concluded, "the necessary sanction of the Senate" (often denied) and the large "*number of refusals*" of office by the most qualified prospects, and the reasons for a poorly staffed register were painfully obvious. Madison lacked not will nor understanding of what needed to be done nor courage to face war, but rather, as his own apologies verify, a capacity to disentangle himself from republican pieties, political crosscurrents, and organizational weaknesses. Calhoun wrote a friend in April 1812 that "our President tho a man of amiable manners and great talents, has not I fear those commanding talents, which are necessary to controul those about him. He permits division in his cabinet. He reluctantly gives up the system of peace." The South Carolinian observed further that "this is the first war that the country has ever been engaged in; there is a great want of military knowledge; and the whole of our system has to be commenced and organized." Eight months later, after disasters caused by "errors and mismanagement . . . [of] most incompetent men," Calhoun noted that the difficulties "lie deep; and are coeval with the existence of Mr. Jefferson's administration." Jeffersonian republicanism simply was not a vehicle designed for effective travel down the road to war. What Clay, Calhoun, and other War Hawks did in 1811 and 1812 was not browbeat the President into war or give the impulse to it from their expansionist predilections, but rather to provide the legislative leadership in Congress, the effective attention to preparedness, and the sharp propaganda sense needed to arouse the country. Madison saw too clearly all the variables of a complex situation, knew too well the traps awaiting him in every direction, and understood too profoundly the antirepublican tendencies of arming for war to accept readily the reckless and unsubtle needs of girding for battle.[95]

What undermined Madison's policy of upholding American rights by peaceful, republican means was, first and foremost, the absence of effective armed force, which again and again prevented him from being able to confront his opponents with a plausible threat, and altogether, made skeptics on both sides of the Atlantic doubt he could have any ultimate intention of going to war. Second, an impression of irresolution grew from the shifting terms of his policies of commercial retaliation and peaceful coercion—embargo, nonintercourse, nonimportation, and so on —which often, at the very moment of effective pressure, freed trade long enough for Britain to fill her warehouses. Madison underestimated, too, the flexibility of international trade, the endurance of the belligerents, and the amount of damage to the United States. Thus the nation at home, especially New England, saw no credible, effective course to which to rally. Though Madison, striving for domestic unity, both tempered his policy and manipulated his channels of communication, his stance was inevitably regarded as unwarlike. This opinion was illustrated by the *Connecticut Courant* when it declared the war "was commenced in folly, it is proposed to be carried on with madness, and (unless speedily terminated) will end in ruin." Reflecting on the causes of the war, Republican Congressman Jonathan Roberts wrote that "there had all along been an idea cherished by the opposition, that the majority would not have nerve enough to meet war. This I believe, mainly induced Britain to persist in her aggressions. If she could have been made to believe . . . that we were a united people, and would act as such, war might have been avoided." As the London *Independent Chronicle* pointed out, "In every measure of government, the [Federalist] faction have rallied in opposition, and urged the [British] Ministry to persist in their Orders. They forced the United States to the alternative, either to *surrender their independence*, or *maintain it by War*."[96]

Thus, though these misjudgments, too-subtle policies, and republican predilections may, paradoxically, have made more likely a war Madison tried to avoid, and certainly left the nation dangerously unprepared, he was perfectly clear, as he stated in his first wartime message to Congress, on the basic cause and ultimate need for hostilities: "The war in which we are actually engaged is a war neither of ambition nor of vainglory. . . . It is waged not in violation of the rights of others, but in maintenance of our own. . . . To have shrunk [from it] . . . would have struck us from the high rank where the virtuous struggles of our fathers had placed us, and have betrayed the magnificent legacy which we hold in trust for future generations. It would have acknowledged that on [water] . . . where all independent nations have equal and common rights, the American people were not an independent people, but colonists and vassals."[97]

CHAPTER XX

Wartime President

OR a month or two the war seemed to go well. Madison visited the
War and Navy departments, "stimulating everything in a manner
worthy of a commander in chief, with his little round hat and
huge cockade," and met with the cabinet to deploy the meager American
forces against the awesome might of Britain. Success depended on taking
advantage of shorter supply lines for quick movement of men and ships
before Britain, heavily committed in Europe, could reinforce the thin
line of three thousand regulars, some undependable Indians, and reluctant
Canadian militia scattered along the vast frontier from Montreal to the
Great Lakes region beyond Detroit. Madison decided on both land and
sea campaigns, so four days after the declaration of war Commodore
John Rodgers was ordered to sea, both to protect returning American
commerce and to engage British warships whenever success seemed at all
possible. He also ordered the invasion of Canada at Detroit, Niagara, and
toward Montreal. Madison hoped especially that troops under General
William Hull could capture British positions opposite Detroit to begin
the conquest of upper Canada, cut off British communication with the
Northwest, and most vital of all, reduce the substantial Indian forces
under Tecumseh that since the battle of Tippecanoe in November 1811
had been ready to join the British against the expanding American
frontiersmen.

General Hull at first advanced rapidly on Detroit, and supported by
eager Ohio and Kentucky militiamen, crossed into Canada, where he
boldly called on the people to join the United States against the oppressive British and the savage Indians. With the British commander scarcely
in control of his troops, American capture of Fort Malden, opposite

Detroit, seemed certain. Furthermore, only token British forces were available to oppose the deliberate preparations of General Henry Dearborn in New York state, supported there by militia called out by the zealous Republican governor, Daniel Tompkins. Finally, the American navy, though overall outnumbered fifty to one by the British, had enough occupied their foes to permit the safe return of hundreds of American vessels, and in late July word arrived of splendid seamanship that enabled Captain Isaac Hull in the U.S.S. *Constitution* to taunt and then elude a British squadron five times his size. Arrogant English threats to wipe out the United States navy and drive American ships from the high seas in a month had proved hollow. Rush wrote on July 17 that "we are all tranquil yet . . . but the republick will do well. There must soon be glorious deeds by day." The ardent young Philadelphian reported further that "I visit the President very frequently in the evenings, where, whether he is alone, or whether like myself, his secretaries or neighbors have strolled in to his tea table, I pass the time delightfully."[1]

Diplomatic maneuvers and domestic dissension were troublesome from the start, however. On the very day of the war declaration departing British Minister Augustus Foster had proposed a suspension of hostilities until response to the declaration could come from England. It was clear to Madison that Foster and his superiors in London had miscalculated: listening too intently to Federalist taunts that Madison was not bold enough to take the country into war, the British had supposed no concessions needed to be made to preserve a peace they in fact wanted very much to keep. Now with the step taken, Foster asked anxiously whether "if the Orders in Council were revoked and a promise of negotiation given on the question of impressment, it would suffice." Madison replied that an immediate armistice would forfeit the vital American military advantage of swift action for perhaps meaningless assurances. He therefore closed negotiations in Washington and sent instructions to London that repeal of the orders, renunciation of illegal blockades, stopping impressments, and return of those already impressed were the American terms for ending the war. Thus, though Britain could have avoided the war merely by revoking the Orders, to get out of it, once begun, she would also have to end impressments. Madison and Monroe were encouraged by Foster's obvious dismay at the outbreak of war, by news from England that the "hard line" Prime Minister, Spencer Perceval, had been assassinated by a lunatic, and by debate in Parliament about repeal of the Orders, but they remained suspicious of ambiguous peace feelers likely only to dampen American patriotic ardor and upset military plans.[2]

In mid-July it became evident that Napoleon was not the least inclined to be grateful for American hostility toward Britain. Orders to burn American ships headed for Iberian ports were strengthened, and Joel

Barlow confirmed that the controversial French revocation of the edicts of Berlin and Milan had indeed, as the British and Federalists had so often asserted, been fraudently issued and dated. Thus made to seem mere tools of Napoleon, willing to suffer any indignity from him while remaining implacable toward England, Madison and Monroe countered by writing stern anti-French editorials for *The National Intelligencer*. The President wrote on August 4 that "our government will not, under any circumstances that may occur, form a political connection with France. . . . It is not desirable to enter the lists with the two great belligerents at once; but if England acts with wisdom, and France perseveres in her career of injustice and folly, we should not be surprised to see the attitude of the United States change toward these powers." He sent the editorials to Barlow, observing that "in the event of a pacification with Great Britain, the full tide of indignation with which the public mind here is boiling will be directed against France, if not obviated by a due reparation of her wrongs. War will be called for by the Nation almost *una voce*. Even without a peace with England, the further refusals or prevarications of France on the subject of redress may be expected to produce measures of hostility against her at the ensuing session of Congress." Madison sought, as always, to extract justice from the belligerents by offering concessions to the one favorably disposed and hostility to the other, but the question remained whether either France or England could afford to modify the means of their mortal combat with each other in order to treat justly with or even respond to the blandishments of the fledgling United States.[3]

Even more frustrating and perilous was the mounting evidence, as Madison wrote his predecessor four days after the war began, that "the Federalists in Congress are to put all the strength of their talents into a protest against the war and that the party at large are to be brought out in all their force." Rush wrote in midsummer that "Massachusetts and half New England I fear is rotten." Scandalized by what they regarded as Madison's subservience to France, angered by a war sure to destroy their commerce, suspicious of frontier territorial ambitions, and alert to political advantages they might harvest from an unpopular or unsuccessful war, the Federalists had voted unanimously against the declaration of war, and saw neither moral nor practical reasons for supporting it once undertaken. A Vermont Congressman echoed common Federalist attitudes: "In addition to the strong French partialities and the desire to save the sinking party, the Southern people are determined on the acquisition of the Floridas etc., and the Western people covet the Indian possessions. . . . Poor Madison was threatened with abandonment in the Presidential election unless he would aid their views. . . . Thus by action and reaction [the Republicans] have many of them been forced I believe reluctantly to take this fatal step. We are now in a state of war unable to give satisfactory reasons why or wherefore, and destitute of the means to produce either a speedy or a favorable issue."[4]

Opposition to the war soon reached near-treasonable proportions. When Congress adjourned in early July, the Federalist minority published an "address" to their constituents, voicing British arguments on American maritime grievances, justifying votes against the war, and, ominously, calling on the people to obstruct its prosecution. Federalist Governor Caleb Strong of Massachusetts, carried into office on a swelling anti-Republican tide, called on his people to lament a war "against the nation from which we are descended, and which for many generations has been the bulwark of the Religion we profess." One Boston area clergyman declared from his pulpit that "if at the present moment no symptoms of civil war appear they certainly will soon," and another thundered that "as Mr. Madison has declared war, let Mr. Madison carry it on. . . . The Union has long since virtually dissolved: and it is full time that this part of the Disunited States should take care of themselves." John Lowell gave New England its name for the war in a pamphlet entitled *Mr. Madison's War*. He proclaimed the President solely responsible for a war "undertaken for *French* interests and in conformity with repeated *French* orders," urged militiamen to refuse to fight in an unjust, unconstitutional war, and asked for Madison's defeat in the coming election. Former Senator Timothy Pickering wrote that "to my ears there is no magic in the sound of Union. If the great objects of union are utterly abandoned—much more if they are wantonly, corruptly, and treacherously sacrificed by the Southern and Western States—let the Union be severed."[5]

Serious threats to the war effort materialized when New England courts ruled that state governors, not Congress or the President, had the power to declare an emergency warranting use of state militia. The governors of Massachusetts and Connecticut hence refused to furnish militia quotas called for by the President. In another legal trick, courts declared that recruits for the regular service and conscripted militiamen had "debts," and then arrested and bailed them, insisting that they stay home while under "court order." By mid-August Madison wrote Jefferson that "the seditious opposition in Massachusetts and Connecticut, with the intrigues elsewhere insidiously co-operating with it, have so clogged the wheels of the war that I fear the campaign will not accomplish the object of it." New England governors prevented the use of their militia in expeditions outside their states and even refused to muster it along the seacoast to permit regular troops to be transferred to the Canadian frontier. General Dearborn, expected to lead the campaigns against Niagara and Montreal, stayed in Boston until late July, seeking cooperation from New England, but left thwarted and pessimistic.[6]

Madison wrote candidly to a sympathetic New Englander, the Reverend Samuel Spring, one of the Princetonians who had visited Montpelier before the revolution: "I will not conceal the surprize and the pain I feel at declarations from any portion of the American people that measures resulting from the National will constitutionally pronounced, and carrying with them the most solemn sanctions, are not to be pursued into effect, without the hazard of civil war. This is surely not . . . a course consistent with the duration or efficacy of any Government." After scorning the charges of French partiality and pointing out the stake all sections of the country had in the war, Madison touched the critical point: "The way to make [the war] both short and successful, would be to convince the Enemy that he has to contend with the whole, and not a part of the Nation. Can it be doubted that if, under the pressure added by the war to that previously felt by Great Britain, her Government declines an accommodation on terms dictated by justice, and compatible with, or rather conducive to her interest, it will be owing to calculations drawn from our internal divisions?"[7]

For twenty years Madison had believed the partiality of Federalist New England for English trade and attitudes seriously compromised a national unity that alone could compel Britain to respect American rights. In 1808 he had been certain that New England's defiance of the Embargo had caused its failure, and now, as war began under his leadership, he encountered at every turn Federalist apathy, resistance, and even seditious opposition. As long as he lived, Madison placed primary blame for the ineffectiveness of American foreign policy during the Anglo-French wars of 1793 to 1815 on "internal divisions" that betrayed and disgraced the revolutionary national purpose. Of all the burdens of his public career, none was more galling or in his sight more grievously and unforgivably imposed than this cancer of discord.

Worried by diplomatic and domestic perils, Madison had increasing cause, as the sultry Washington summer sweltered through July and seeped into August, to fret about military operations. When General Dearborn reached Albany on July 26 to mount a campaign against Montreal, he found only twelve hundred unorganized and ill-equipped men. Furthermore, he found orders from Secretary of War Eustis assuming that operations in western New York were also under his command. Responding, Dearborn, the ranking general in the American armies, asked, after six months of high-level planning and consultation, an incredible question: "Who is to have command of the operations in Upper Canada [the Niagara frontier]? I take it for granted that my command does not extend to that distant quarter." He had made no plans to cooperate with Hull in the pincers movement against the British north of Lake Erie, nor had he provided at all for the army supposed to be gathering at Buffalo. Madison and Eustis saw at once that confusion and uncertainty, compounded by Dearborn's habitual caution, had already destroyed the hope for a series of swift strokes against Canada, and even threatened Hull's army at Detroit by leaving the way open for British reinforcements to reach that area. Madison wrote Dearborn that the "systematic operation having been frustrated, it remains only to pursue the course that will diminish the disappointment as much as possible." Dearborn should attack at Niagara, secure control of the eastern end of Lake Ontario, and march immediately against Montreal. If these movements became impossible, he should at least cut the trade route along the Ottawa River to the Huron country, a thrust Madison had long thought would most effectively end British intrigue among the Indians in the Northwest Territory.[8]

Faced with troop and supply deficiencies, and awed by the extended operations placed under his command, Dearborn quickly embraced what to him seemed a heaven-sent reprieve: on August 9 an emissary from the governor general of Canada reached Albany, offering an armistice along the entire New York frontier, pending final word on peace negotiations the British alleged were on the verge of success; Dearborn agreed, hoping to use the breathing spell to push his lagging preparations. When word of the armistice reached Washington on August 13, Dearborn was ordered to terminate it at once and "proceed with the utmost vigor in your operations." Dispatches had already gone out, however, extending the armistice to the Niagara region, and Dearborn talked of mounting the three-pronged invasion of Canada in October, three months late and after all advantage of surprise and mobility had been lost. The gap between Dearborn's belief at his field headquarters that an armistice would benefit *him* by permitting time to gather men and supplies and Madison's assumption that the *British* would gain from delay measures the confusion and inefficiency of American war preparations.[9]

With both Gallatin and Monroe on hurried visits home, Madison worked alone in the capital with his incompetent secretaries of War and Navy, and found himself "much worn down, and in need of an antidote to the accumulating bile, of which I am sensible, and which I have never escaped in August on tidewater." News from Orange of illness, drunken relatives, and family quarrels did not help. Meanwhile, dozens of Plains Indians, "remarkable for their gigantic figures and fine proportion of their forms," added to the confusion when they assembled in Washington for powwows with the "great father of the eighteen fires." "Any one of these grand productions of our grand forests," wrote Richard Rush, "would look upon such a fellow as Bonaparte . . . with disdain . . . and say, or think, he was no warrior to fight with *them*." They were entertained at the White House, followed by what Dolley Madison described as "a frolic." On August 19, the Indians held a "feast, war dance, and war whoop" at Greenleaf's Point. The ritualistic exchanges between Madison and the chiefs left no doubt, however, that the Indians deeply resented their treatment by American frontiersmen. After several days of talks, Big Thunder, chief of the Sioux, declared "I am tired of rolling around on the floor and wish to return home." This confrontation, plus accumulating evidence that the Northwest Indians remained under British influence, convinced Madison that "nothing but triumphant operations on the theater which forms [the Indians'] connection with the enemy will control their bloody inroads."[10]

Happily spared "bilious disorders," Madison stayed in Washington after mid-August to respond to a proposal for a general armistice following repeal of the Orders in Council. To Madison the "insuperable objections" to this were "obvious": it might interfere with Congressional power over war; it might dampen patriotic ardor; it would give the British time to bring reinforcements to Canada; and it might throw away the expected benefits of Hull's campaign on the Great Lakes. Hence the President and cabinet rejected the British proposals, but they did soften their previous demand that Britain *renounce* impressment by agreeing to suspend hostilities provided only that the British agree to negotiate a treaty about impressment. Pleased with Madison's firmness toward England, but impatient with his failure to strengthen the cabinet, Rush wrote that "the little gentleman [Madison] sticks *as obstinately* to his anti-impressment and American maritime creed as to his *secretaries*, so the thing works both ways. . . . We have great good in him; we can't have all things."[11]

The news from the West was at first puzzling, then irritating, then alarming, and finally disastrous. After Hull's promising movement into Canada, he "allowed himself two weeks" to prepare an assault on puny Fort Malden. Madison next learned that Mackinac Island, in the strategic straits joining lakes Huron, Michigan, and Superior, had fallen to the British. Hull later explained that this "opened the northern hive of Indians, [to] swarm down in every direction" on the strained supply lines to Detroit. At the same time, though known only incompletely in Washington, the energetic British commander in Canada, General Isaac Brock, scorning the chaotic American forces in New York State, had used his control of lakes Ontario and Erie to move a small, élite army to Detroit. By failing to do what he might have done easily in mid-July, Hull suddenly found himself in what Madison termed a "very ineligible" position: he faced a brilliantly led army capable of thwarting his invasion of Canada while his own lines of supply and reinforcement, stretching across the Ohio and Michigan wilderness, were about to be straddled by Indians emboldened by the scent of victory. The aging American general, estranged from his eager young subordinates, collapsed in a spasm of fear and indecision. He recalled his forces to the fort at Detroit, whereupon Brock promptly appeared at its gates, demanding surrender. To the astonishment of the British as well as most of his own officers, Hull capitulated, and by August 23 Brock was back at the Niagara frontier with Hull's army as captives. Beyond the settlements in Ohio, the entire Northwest Territory was abandoned to British-Indian domination, and a triumphant British army holding two thousand American prisoners looked across the Niagara gorge at green, nervous New York militiamen.[12]

News of the fall of Mackinac reached Washington on August 14; shortly thereafter came word of Hull's withdrawal from the east bank of the Detroit River. Madison saw the peril of land-dependent communications and belatedly ordered movements to see if Lake Ontario, at least, could be made safe for American vessels. Determined at last, though, to find respite and gain health in Virginia, the Madisons left Washington on August 28, after being delayed a day by high waters. That evening at Dumfries an express rider brought the astounding news that Hull had surrendered. The President returned the next morning to the capital and called a cabinet meeting. Since part of Hull's weakness, and much of Dearborn's strategic uncertainty, resulted from British control of lakes Ontario and Erie, Commodore Isaac Chauncey was given naval command there, with orders to build ships and assemble men to afford American forces fast and safe use of the lakes. This "ought to have been a fundamental point in the national policy" from 1783 on, Madison declared, since with naval ascendency on the lakes "we command the Indians, . . . control the companies trading with them," secure such posts as Detroit and Mackinac, and hold Canada "as a hostage for peace and justice." Richard Rush wrote John Adams that Madison was so convinced upon this subject, "that [he said] if the British build thirty frigates upon [the lakes] we ought to build forty." The navy-minded Adams, not given to kind words about his successors, responded that "no President of the United States ever said a wiser thing."[13]

The cabinet also decided to assemble eight thousand militiamen to march on Detroit and resume the conquest of upper Canada—thwarted, Americans from the Potomac to the Mississippi were sure, only by Hull's incompetence and cowardice. Rush decried Hull as a "gasconading booby! . . . a horrid coward" who had *hoped* the British would surrender "at the sight, I suppose, of his big belly." Instead, Hull "threw down his arms, and screamed out for mercy, to *fewer than his own numbers!* Without the least resistance! Ought not a just vengance to tare such a miscreant to pieces and give up his loathsome guts to the winds—to the dogs to prey upon!" Jefferson exploded that "Hull will of course be shot for cowardice and treachery." Sensing larger implications, Rush lamented "republican Americans exposed to the sneers of federalists, the exhultation of tories—the contempt, the deserved contempt, of the British here and in Europe, of the very Indians! It is sorrow indeed."[14]

At Montpelier for only two weeks instead of the hoped-for two months, Madison received a flood of mail attesting to Western fervor and condemning Hull, Eustis, and others held responsible for the catastrophe. General William Henry Harrison, commissioned to lead Kentucky militiamen back to Detroit, asserted that he had "an army competent in numbers, and in spirit equal to any that Greece or Rome have boasted," while Clay, watching the frontiersmen march off, wrote Monroe that "if you carry your recollection back to the age of the Crusades, and of some of the most distinguished leaders of those expeditions, you will have a picture of the enthusiasm existing in this country." The capitulation of Detroit had produced no despair, Clay declared, but "on the contrary awakened new energies and aroused the whole people of this State." Following news of the dramatic victory of the *Constitution* over the *Guerrière*, Monroe wrote that, even in New England, the national spirit soared: "Misfortune and success have alike diminished the influence of foreign attachments and party animosities, and contributed to draw the people closer together. The surrender of our army excited a general grief, and the naval victory a general joy." Isaac Hull, captain of the *Constitution*, Rush said, was to the other, disgraced Hull like "a living soul to a rotten carcase." As Madison hurried back to Washington in mid-September, fully aware of the trials ahead, this spirited response gave him confidence.[15]

Madison's most urgent, vexing problem was to find leadership for the armed forces. His foolishly indulged hope that the country's spirit and natural advantages in the war would permit it to get by with old mediocrities in key places had vanished before Isaac Brock's daring brilliance. In the frantic days following Hull's surrender, the zealous Monroe offered to take a military command and depart immediately for the West to lead the armies. With the President absent from the capital, Monroe and others there endorsed Rush's plan to at once rescue American fortunes in the West, satisfy Monroe's military ambitions, and avert the political defeat military disasters threatened to inflict on the Republicans in the fall elections: Monroe's call to the colors would leave the post of Secretary of State vacant, and Jefferson's return to that office would rally the people and bring his immense prestige to the embattled administration. "May not his venerable and almost canonized form be seen to step forth," Rush asked the President, "at such a time, at such a call?" But Madison knew Jefferson would never leave Monticello, and that in fact his return would revive Federalist animosities over his anti-navy views and charges of Madison's subservience to Jefferson and to France. The President therefore brushed aside the suggestion, and back in Washington, withdrew his tentative agreement to give Monroe field command. The West had rallied enthusiastically behind Harrison, the hero of Tippecanoe, so Madison kept Monroe in the State Department, where his advice and counsel were exceedingly valuable. Disappointed but loyal, Monroe accepted the decision, though both he and the President knew more far-reaching changes would soon be necessary.[16]

Meanwhile, war news continued to be bad. Brock's arrival on the Niagara frontier, flushed with victory, and with Hull's army in tow, unnerved the disorganized forces there. New York militia general Stephen Van Rensselaer, a wealthy Federalist landowner without military experience, wrote on August 31 that "alarm pervades the country, and distrust among the troops. . . . Many are without shoes; all clamorous for pay; many are sick. While we are thus growing weaker our enemy is growing stronger." General Dearborn responded with words unlikely to inspire confidence: "I am not without fear that attempts will be speedily made to reduce you and your forces to the mortifying situation of General Hull and his army. . . . It will be necessary for you to be prepared for all events, and to be prepared to make good a secure retreat as the last resort. . . . A strange fatality seems to have pervaded the whole arrangements. Ample reinforcements of troops and supplies are on the way, but I fear their arrival will be too late to enable you to maintain your position." Nevertheless, in early October, after a successful raid on British vessels opposite Buffalo gave the Americans temporary naval superiority, and after General Alexander Smyth had arrived with 1,650 regular troops, a victory to avenge the humiliation at Detroit seemed for a moment possible. Smyth's refusal to act under Van Rensselaer, and the latter's willingness to act alone to gain all the glory, though, resulted in an attack into Canada by only half the available force. The resourceful Brock placed his small regular corps before Van Rensselaer's inexperienced troops and repulsed them at Queenston Heights. Wounded men from this battle, returning across the river, so frightened the untried forces there that they refused to cross into Canada. The troops there, despite individual instances of great bravery, were overwhelmed and eventually captured, delivering to the British a second American army in less than two months. Only Brock's death on the battlefield gave some hope for the future.[17]

Disgraced, General Van Rensselaer requested, and was immediately granted, relief from his command. Smyth took over and issued bombastic proclamations insulting his predecessors and making preposterous claims about pending accomplishments under his direction. By late November he had carried out hesitant probes against Fort Erie, opposite Buffalo, but a failure to muster every last man he deemed necessary to mount a full-scale attack caused him to withdraw and disperse his army. Again American arms had been humiliated. Madison observed years later that Smyth's "talent for military command was equally mistaken by himself and his friends." To complete the record of failure, the army of six thousand men General Dearborn had gathered so slowly at Albany finally marched north to Plattsburg in late November for the long-awaited attack on Montreal. Though there were fewer than five hundred soldiers defending the city, memories of the disastrous 1775 winter campaign against Quebec caused "Granny" Dearborn to withdraw to quarters near Albany after a few small raids across the border. The London *Times* sneered: "The army . . . at Plattsburg is making a great show of the pomp and circumstance of war. . . . When cold weather sets in they will be volunteering it to their firesides. . . . [What if] one of the first orders of General Dearborn should be to advance backwards, and take up snug quarters in Greenbush?" Knowing this was precisely what happened, the weary, well-intended, but bumbling Dearborn wrote the President, "It will be equally agreeable to me to employ such moderate talents as I possess in the service of my country, or to be permitted to retire to the shades of private life, and remain a mere but interested spectator of passing events." Though Madison's response to this letter is lost, he surely thought Dearborn could best serve in the shades too.[18]

Affairs in the West also soon "left a military crisis," as Madison wrote Jefferson in mid-October. Command disputes between Harrison and the bungling senior officer of the regular army, General Joseph Winchester, had resulted in a dangerous division of their forces in the swamps west of Lake Erie. Harrison wrote that the "absolute impossibility" of getting wagons and pack horses through two hundred miles of swampy wilderness made it necessary to wait for the rivers and lakes to freeze into smooth highways. Therefore he was "not able to fix any period for the advance . . . to Detroit," which in any case, he wrote after seven more weeks of useless effort, was untenable as long as the British retained Fort Malden and control of Lake Erie. "Every man who has the least military information," Harrison told Monroe, could see that the President's politically inspired plan to recapture Detroit was obviously impractical and had as well become scandalously expensive due to "the imbecility and inexperience of the public agents and the villany of the contractors." In fact, it was the clamorous fears of Kentucky and Ohio that required movement against Detroit, symbol of supremacy over the Northwest Indians; Madison had long believed and patiently urged that naval control of the Great Lakes and capture of Montreal, not expeditions into the wilderness, were the keys to the conquest of Canada.[19]

While receiving the bad news from Ohio and Niagara, Madison observed that the pending presidential election brought "the popularity of the war, or of the Administration, or both, to the *Experimentum crucis*." His strong position in the country, reflected by the large Republican majorities in Congress, was threatened by a strange alliance of dissident Republicans, led by De Witt Clinton, and Federalists ready to go to any lengths to defeat the incumbent. Clinton's candidacy destroyed the Virginia–New York cooperation that had been vital to Republican power ever since it had been used by Madison and Aaron Burr to assure Jefferson's victory in 1800. Clinton had good prospects of allying with other antiadministration Republicans to dissipate Madison's strength elsewhere in the country, while the spring elections and anger over the war made it clear Madison could expect little from New England. A secret Federalist decision in August and September not to nominate their own candidate assured Clinton of the electoral vote of states under Federalist control. Only a handful of Federalists followed Rufus King in opposing Clinton. On the other hand, antiadministration Republicans such as editor William Duane, who could not stomach Clinton's unprincipled campaign, returned to the Madison camp. "No canvass for the Presidency," Henry Adams wrote, "was ever less creditable than that of De Witt Clinton in 1812. Seeking war votes for the reason that he favored more vigorous prosecution of the war; asking support of peace Republicans because Madison had plunged the country into war without preparations; bargaining for Federalist votes as the price of bringing about a peace; or coquetting with all parties in the atmosphere of bribery in bank charters—Clinton strove to make up a majority which had no element of union but himself and money."

In response, Madison's backers praised Republican achievements and rallied the country behind a war effort required by national self-respect. Only by continuing to permit the grain trade nourishing Wellington's armies in Spain, which enriched middle Atlantic and Southern farmers, did the administration compete with Clinton in political expediency. Watching the election returns come in over a period of weeks, Madison saw all of New England except Vermont, and then New York, New Jersey, and Delaware go to his opponent. A sweeping Republican victory in Pennsylvania, plus sure triumphs in Virginia and most of the South and West, however, restored Madison's strength, with only Maryland, Ohio, and North Carolina in doubt. Maryland divided its vote in mid-November; Ohio went Republican; and in a resistance to bribery surprising to many, the North Carolina legislature remained Republican. Madison thus won a 128 to 89 victory in the electoral college. Though the margin was far narrower than earlier Republican triumphs, and reflected strong dissatisfaction with the war and Madison's conduct of it, the President could, despite military setbacks, count on public support.[20]

With politics finally in the background, Madison tackled the delicate but urgent problem of appointments. The military debacles of the summer and fall had made Eustis' departure from the War Department certain despite Madison's personal liking for the blustery, congenial doctor. Gallatin's estimate was more to the point: Eustis' "incapacity and the total want of confidence in him were felt through every ramification of the public service." A Secretary of War with "knowledge and talents would save millions and the necessary business would be better done," Gallatin told his chief. Madison at first proposed to move Monroe to the War Department, and bring in Senator Crawford of Georgia as Secretary of the Treasury, but politically inspired charges of Monroe's ambition to become an American Cromwell and knowledge of heavy Congressional opposition to each of the appointments sidetracked the idea. Unwilling to risk the loss of either Monroe or Gallatin in changes the Senate might obstruct, Madison had to find a replacement for Eustis in a post Gallatin declared so surrounded with "horrors and perils . . . [that it] frightens those who know best its difficulties." Senator Crawford and General Dearborn both refused it. The choice narrowed to two New Yorkers, Governor Daniel Tompkins or General John Armstrong, the recently returned minister to France. Tompkins ranked low enough in Gallatin's judgment to cause him to offer to take the War Department himself and give Tompkins the Treasury, knowing the work of both jobs would fall on the experienced secretary. Monroe, politically jealous of Armstrong, found him as well personally disagreeable, while Gallatin thought he lacked "disinterested zeal" and doubted his loyalty to the administration. Madison decided Armstrong was the least objectionable choice and appointed him, with a reluctance Madison described years later: ". . . nor was the President unaware or unwarned of the temper and turn of mind ascribed to him [Armstrong], which might be uncongenial with the official relations in which he was to stand. But these considerations were sacrificed to recommendations from esteemed friends; a belief he possessed, with known talents, a degree of military information which might be useful; and a hope that a proper mixture of conciliating confidence and interposing control, would render objectionable peculiarities less in practice than in prospect."[21]

In the Navy Department a change was needed as urgently, though the brilliant victories at sea muted public complaints against Secretary Paul Hamilton. He was, like Eustis, an amiable incompetent of whom Madison was personally fond and who in normal times might have served tolerably. He had, however, become an alcoholic; he often appeared drunk at public celebrations, and for two years his work day had ended at noon. "Mr. Madison and his friends tried by every means to cure him," French Minister Sérurier wrote, "but it was useless." He finally recognized his own disability and submitted a resignation the President accepted gratefully. Madison had good luck finding a replacement: William Jones, a Philadelphia merchant, sea captain, and loyal Republican whom Jefferson had sought for the Navy post as early as 1801. Madison later pronounced him "the fittest minister who had ever been charged with the Navy Department." Thus in early 1813 the President, in his second major cabinet shuffle, surrounded himself with men capable of organizing an effective war effort. The only potential flaw was Armstrong's doubtful loyalty and "objectionable peculiarities." Rush declared that it was "delightful . . . to all those who for months past have been agonized at the imbecility of the two departments, to think that now probably the two most able men the nation has in it . . . are the two men appointed."²²

Furthermore, the second session of the "War Hawk" Congress, meeting in early November, got busy with measures to win the war. Representative William Lowndes, an influential South Carolina War Hawk, wrote that committee assignments would be arranged to support "the schemes of the Administration," and Federalists complained that "the will of the Cabinet is the law of the land." After a month of labor with Gallatin and Monroe, Madison presented his assessment of the war, and plans for its future prosecution, in his fourth annual message. Richard Rush feared that the President, "so learned . . . [and who] has so long wielded a *peace pen*," would speak too pedantically. What was needed, Rush told Madison, was "a blast of war against England." He should, as well, "thwack . . . not a little these gentlemen patriots among us who are perpetually aiding and abetting the enemy." Madison's first draft did hurl such vigorous and wounding thunderbolts, but, probably at Gallatin's urging, he toned down a bitter indictment of Hull's surrender, largely ignored the domestic opposition, and generally glided over past follies and difficulties to emphasize the few bright spots. The President recommended (over Gallatin's objections) a substantial enlargement of the seafaring forces, and for the army, higher bonuses and pay to revive flagging enlistments, greater federal control over the militia, more general officers, and the creation of a general staff.

On the diplomatic front, Madison noted the good relations existing with most of the nations of Europe, glossed over France's failure to in any way favor her new cobelligerent, and despite the repeal of the Orders in Council, scorned two British armistice proposals as not justifying the least relaxation of American hostilities. Impressment remained the unsettled, sufficient cause for war. In a cursory and even misleading financial summary, Madison merely reported the books balanced for the previous year with a $6-million loan and stated vaguely that revenue and loans would "defray all the expenses of this year." Actually Gallatin had figured that expenses would exceed receipts by $21 million, an amount he thought "altogether unattainable" in loans from either banks or individuals. Madison concluded with a peroration on British arrogance, American honor, and the need to carry to a glorious conclusion this second war for national independence.²³

Within two months Congress passed bills raising army pay 60 per cent, closing the enlistment loophole of "imprisonment for debt," reorganizing the recruiting service, and more than doubling the size of the navy. Later in the session, following recommendations by Monroe and Gallatin, they allowed presidential appointment of top officers for twenty new regiments as well as authorization for twelve new generals and the reorganization of the quartermaster's department. Only reduction of the enlistment bounty from $40 to $16 threatened plans to enlarge the army. Less to Madison's liking were laws on revenue and trade regulation. Gallatin's request for an additional $5 million in taxes was ignored, and instead Congress added that amount to the President's already overextended borrowing power. It also refused to tax the nearly $20 million of excess profits in merchants' pockets as a result of heavy summer shipments from England, repealed portions of the nonimportation law Madison hoped would press hard on British manufacturers, and prohibited exports profitable to many American farmers. By the time it adjourned, on March 3, 1813, the Twelfth Congress had given Madison nearly all he sought to conduct war operations, but no responsible financing, and it had seriously compromised the commercial regulations he had always considered of prime importance in pressuring England.[24]

Madison and Armstrong commissioned William Henry Harrison one of their new major generals, but the others were mostly old, selected more for political than military reasons, and even included the insubordinate and incompetent James Wilkinson. Four of the new brigadiers, however, Zebulon Pike, Lewis Cass, Duncan MacArthur, and George Izard, were young, able, and destined for notable service, while Colonels Winfield Scott and Jacob Brown, given greater responsibility, were eventually between them to command the United States army most of the time until the Civil War. The other new brigadiers, though, were two old, politically powerful revolutionary veterans and William H. Winder (the brother of the governor of Maryland), whose incompetence was to cost the nation its capital in August 1814. The army thus had some fine field commanders, but its strategic direction was still woefully inadequate.[25]

War news continued bad. After months of floundering about in the snowy wastes of western Ohio, a large portion of General Harrison's army had been defeated and massacred in late January on the banks of the River Raisin. By early spring, as the Kentucky and Ohio militiamen returned home, the recapture of Detroit was as far off as it had been six months before. Gallatin, meanwhile, had informed the President that "we have hardly money enough to last till the end of the month." Loans were unobtainable; tax receipts dwindled; and treasury reserves had disappeared.[26]

Naval victories, however, dispelled some of the gloom. In October the American sloop-of-war *Wasp* defeated the stronger British *Frolic* in a bloody battle in which fewer than twenty of the English crew of 110 escaped injury. In early December the colorful Stephen Decatur brought the defeated and captured frigate *Macedonian* to New London, the only such British warship ever carried as a prize into an American port. Later that same month the *Constitution*, this time commanded by William Bainbridge, destroyed the British frigate *Java* off the Brazilian coast. Upon receiving word of Bainbridge's victory, Madison declared to Congress that "the circumstances and issue of this combat afford another example of the professional skill and heroic spirit which prevail in the Naval service." "Is not this the retribution of Providence," Richard Rush exulted, "that on the element where [the British] have so long been robbing us of our property and our citizens, this nation of naval free booters should be thus signally chastized and disgraced?" Though, as expected, Britain had swept American commerce from the high seas and would soon blockade and bombard the Eastern seaboard, these pride-boosting victories at sea, plus the scores of captures made by American privateers, seriously injured British commerce and unexpectedly proved America's navy, ship for ship, at least the equal of Britain's, something no other navy in the world had been for centuries.[27]

News from abroad, delayed, fragmented, and contradictory, was more difficult for Madison to assess, though probably more ultimately important than dispatches from American generals and sea captains. Rapidly shifting fortunes of war, together with slow communications, changed British attitudes toward the United States very fast in the year that followed the outbreak of what was to England the side show of North American hostilities. In October 1812 nothing but bad news reached Britain: Napoleon had captured Moscow; Wellington had abandoned Madrid and retreated into Portugal; the harvest was poor; English credit sunk; the Americans had rejected armistice offers; and perhaps most chastening of all to British pride, the Royal Navy had thrice struck its colors to the warships of the former colonies. Nearly overwhelmed, the English public and government viewed American hostilities as a stab in the back, in obvious alliance with the French tyrant, a crime for which the United States would be made to pay dearly as soon as English hands were untied. Then, week after week as Parliament met in November and December, came the incredible news of Napoleon's disastrous retreat from Moscow. Thus reprieved and emboldened, the cabinet sent huge naval squadrons across the Atlantic with orders to stop all shipping and bombard seacoast towns. Members of Parliament, including nearly all those formerly sympathetic to the United States, competed in bitter attacks on Madison and his treacherous countrymen.[28]

Madison had learned of British intransigence on impressment from his returned London chargé, Jonathan Russell, in November 1812, but the momentous news from Europe did not reliably cross the Atlantic until two months later. A prophetic observation from the gifted minister in Saint Petersburg, John Quincy Adams, though, might have alerted Madison to what the French faced: "the Fabian system of warfare . . . is now systematically tried against [Napoleon]. . . . The modern Alexander may after all be destined like his predecessor to be arrested in his career of domination by the Scythians." Noting all the British misfor-

tunes prior to the French retreat, the President knew that "nothing but
the difficulty of their [British] affairs will open their ears, and that
without opening their hearts to peace." As for Napoleon's defeat, Madison feared that "the effect of such a catastrophe on his compulsory allies
may once more turn the tables quite around in the case between France
and England." A month and a half later, Napoleon's dramatic return to
Paris and efforts to rally another army raised Madison's spirits. "It does
not appear anything like despondence is felt at Paris," he wrote, "and so
many interests on the continent have become associated with the ascendency of Napoleon, that it will [not] be surprising, if, with the terrors of
his name, he should surmount his difficulties." As for England, "unusual
exultation," and "rage and jealousy" against America "accounted for the
gigantic force she is bringing against us on the water." Thus Madison
perceived the ominous results of the failure of the "fair calculation" of
June 1812 that "Napoleon . . . could find full employment" for all of
Britain's martial resources. "Had the French Emperor not been broken
down, as he was to a degree at variance with all probability, and which
no human sagacity could anticipate," Madison asked, reflecting years
later on the news of 1812 and 1813, "can it be doubted that G. Britain
would have been constrained, by her own situation and the demands of
her allies, to listen to our reasonable terms of reconciliation?" The harsh
words of Wellesley, Canning, and Castlereagh made it clear that the
United States would soon find out what an angry former mother country could do.[29]

On February 24, however, a messenger from Saint Petersburg brought
welcome news: Czar Alexander, victor over Napoleon, and England's
ally, had offered to mediate the war between Britain and the United
States. Though "Hawks" like Richard Rush at first thought even considering mediation while the war went badly an "ignoble" sign of weakness, Madison accepted immediately, but delayed publication of the news
until after Congress had completed action on military measures and he
had heightened the national war spirit in his second inaugural address.
Madison saw some hope in this offer from "the only power in Europe
which can command respect from both France and England, . . . [and
which] has a sympathy with our maritime doctrines," but he wondered
"whether England will accede to the mediation, or do so with evasive
purposes," since she knew Russia had for forty years opposed Britain's
violation of neutral rights on the high seas. But, mindful of Russia's
"collateral view . . . of deriving advantage from the *neutral* interference
with British monopoly in the trade with her," the President resolved to
"endeavor to turn the good will of Russia to the proper account." With
news of this offer, and the dispatch of American commissioners to aid it,
began two years of expectation by Madison of word from Europe that
peace had been restored. Thus, though months of warfare lay ahead,
Madison's anxious attention centered on his diplomats in Saint Peters-

burg, Göteborg, London, and Ghent at least as much as on the battlefields of upper Canada or even the shores of Chesapeake Bay.[30]

During the first of three war winters, the White House was the center of a social season, and seemingly oblivious to the perilous state of the
nation. Richard and Anna Cutts, along with their four children—James
Madison and Thomas, eight and seven years old and able to run around
after their uncle, sickly four-year-old Richard, who would soon die
from the measles, and a baby, Dolley P. Madison—spent their last winter
with the Madisons. Richard Cutts was a lame-duck Congressman, defeated in the antiwar mood that had swept Massachusetts, but in March
1813, the President made him Superintendent of Military Supplies, one
of the appointments that later caused Federalists to grumble that "now
every Relation or Connection not only of Mr., but Mrs. Madison is
provided for at the public expense." (At least eight "connections" were
on the federal payroll at some time during the war.) Late the following
fall and after a summer at Montpelier, the Cuttses, married ten years, and
at last on executive salary rather than Congressional per diem, for the
first time established their own household in Washington.

Along with the Cuttses, Edward Coles, soon to become a favorite
eligible bachelor in Washington, was a valued, intimate, virtually permanent member of the White House family. Heir to a large plantation near
Monticello, Coles had attended the College of William and Mary; there,
under the tutelage of President Madison's cousin and close friend the
Reverend James Madison, the able young student had come, as he put it,
to wonder how, under enlightened ideas of the rights of man, "can you
hold a slave—how can man be made the property of man?" He determined to free his own slaves by taking them to the Northwest Territory, but deferred action to accept Madison's invitation to be his private
secretary. He copied letters and prepared papers, carried messages to
Congress, and served as social secretary, assisting cousin Dolley with
her Wednesday receptions, and planning celebrations sponsored by the
administration. He was the sole functionary in the Office of the Presidency, paid out of the appropriation for maintaining the White House
in an amount decided by the President. His antislavery views grew
stronger as he became more aware of the chasm between Republican
liberal professions and the fact of slavery in the nation's capital and even
in Madison's own house. One day, "seeing gangs of Negroes, some in
irons, on their way to a southern market," Coles taunted the President,
"by congratulating him, as the Chief of our great Republic, that he was
not then accompanied by a Foreign Minister, and thus saved the deep
mortification of witnessing such a revolting sight in the presence of the
representative of a nation, less boastful perhaps of its regard for the
rights of man, but more observant of them." Coles noted sadly that
though Madison's principles were "sound, pure, and conscientious, and

his feelings sensitive and tender, . . . yet from the force of early impressions, the influence of habit and association, and a certain train of reasoning, which lulled in some degree his conscience, without convincing his judgment (for he never justified or approved of it), he continued to hold Slaves." Coles's observation that "a certain train of reasoning" lulled Madison's conscience despite his abhorrence of slavery shows clearly the root of his lifelong compromise with "the peculiar institution." Intimate association with slavery and constant observation of blacks in a degraded condition made Madison unwilling, or at least unable, to confront the convulsion and social trauma eradication of slavery would certainly entail. Coles's moral ardor, which impelled him to free his slaves, exposed both Madison's complacency and the nation's inconsistency.[31]

John Payne Todd, now twenty-one years old and finished with eight years at a Catholic boarding school in Baltimore, had reached a turning point and required more of Madison's attention. Handsome, dashing, and competent, though not brilliant, he needed a steady occupation or enrollment at Princeton to fix on him the good training he had received from Father Dubourg and to counterbalance the attentions of a doting mother and the flattery of the belles of Baltimore and Washington, to whom he was an American "prince." He carried out some duties for his stepfather during a long illness of Coles's in the first months of 1813, but mostly he graced Washington balls and parties, becoming more idle, dissipated, and foppish. In April Madison sent him to Europe as secretary to Albert Gallatin, appointed a commissioner to accept the Russian mediation offer. Gallatin also took with him his own sixteen-year-old son, James, and George M. Dallas, son of Madison's ardent supporter Alexander J. Dallas of Philadelphia. The younger Dallas was just Todd's age, and reckoned by everyone a brilliant, steady lad, so Madison hoped he and the earnest, responsible Gallatin would prove wholesome influences on the frivolous Todd. The President placed among Gallatin's papers a note containing the first of many underestimates of Todd's ability to spend money: "I enclose a draft for $800 to be a fund in your hands for J. P. Todd. He has in his own $200 more; which our estimate called for."[32]

A further care for Madison during the first war winter was his nephew Robert, an intelligent nineteen-year-old sent to live with his uncle to prepare for college and to have the broadening experience of being in the nation's capital. The President enrolled him to study under the Episcopal minister the Reverend James Laurie, during the winter, and then, in April 1813, sent him off to Dickinson College in Carlisle, Pennsylvania. Thomas Cooper, a long-time liberal intellectual friend of Madison's, had helped create there an atmosphere Madison hoped would prove stimulating. Letters were soon coming to the White House with the usual requests for money, stories of "great commotions among the students and Faculty," and complaints that the townspeople in Carlisle were "penurious, . . . illiberal, prejudiced, . . . and persecuting in their dispositions." The President and his wife responded with injunctions to be thrifty, "to be careful of your health," to avoid bad companions, and to take advantage of opportunities to learn. Robert stayed at Dickinson until he joined a militia company mustered to repel the rumored British invasion of the Delaware valley in the fall of 1814, always writing of public opinion and political developments he thought warranted his uncle's attention. Robert died of tuberculosis early in life, but until his death (and even afterward, special bequests in Madison's will provided for the education of his children) he was his uncle's special ward and, like the Cutts children, one of the presidential household.[33]

To complement the young men of the White House entourage (which in 1813 also included a nineteen-year-old Virginian, William C. Preston), Dolley Madison invited two Richmond belles to be her house guests for "the season." These were her cousin Betsy Coles, sister of Edward and the superhandsome Isaac, then serving with the army on the Niagara frontier, and Maria Mayo. Maria proved to be very much admired, marrying at the end of the war its foremost army hero after Jackson, young, handsome, gigantic, gallant General Winfield Scott. Betsy, too, was very popular, and with a special gift for easy banter with the President, she remained a favorite of the Madisons as long as they lived.

In November 1812 social events began in earnest. Naval officers, with an eye to pending appropriations in Congress, had, with Edward Coles's aid, planned a "grand entertainment" for Washington official society on board the frigate *Constellation*. Madison was rowed to the ship amid cheers and broadside salutes in a small boat commanded by the conquerer of the *Guerrière*, Captain Isaac Hull. On board, hundreds of guests, including the drunken Navy Secretary, Hamilton, caroused "in the utmost concord and hilarity." The following day the House naval committee approved the anticipated appropriation. Two weeks later there was another naval ball, held at Tomlinson's Hotel, but the President stayed home to await official dispatches confirming Decatur's victory over the *Macedonian*. He "generally took a long nap in his chair" until party-goers returned, talked with them of the festivities, and then often worked by candlelight at his desk until dawn. At the ball, as usually happened at Washington parties, the crowds were so great that "few ladies ever sit." One experienced hostess observed that "the consequence is, the ladies and gentlemen stand and walk about the rooms, in mingled groups, which certainly produces more ease, freedom and equality than in these rooms where the ladies sit and wait for gentlemen to approach to converse." Into this egalitarian scene came a naval lieutenant bearing the flag of the captured *Macedonian*. Under Coles's direction, it was paraded about the floor by the senior naval officers present and then laid triumphantly at Dolley Madison's feet. At the next gathering of naval dignitaries, for the launching of the rebuilt frigate *Adams*, Madison stood beside Federalist Congressman Thomas Gold, who remarked, "What a pity, sir, that the vessel of *state* won't glide as smoothly in her course, as *this* vessel does." The President replied drily, "It would, Sir, if the *crew* would do their duty as well."[34]

Almost as exciting as the balls and parties were the great gatherings in the galleries of Congress and the Supreme Court when famous orators were due to speak. Long addicted to the flashing diatribes of John Randolph of Roanoke, spectators during the War of 1812 adopted two new favorites, elegant, flamboyant Attorney General William Pinkney and Speaker Henry Clay. One day as Pinkney finished a plea before the court, "Mrs. Madison and a train of ladies entered—he recommenced, went over the same ground, using fewer arguments, but scattering more flowers." He bowed low to the ladies, and in the opinion of a critical observer, "thought more of the female part of his audience than of the court." The ladies responded by often leaving as soon as Pinkney finished, whether or not the court had adjourned.[35]

On January 8 and 9, 1813, Clay spoke for two days in a performance that packed the galleries and caused a flood of comment in newspapers throughout the country. The Speaker took the floor to squash the innuendoes of the Federalists, especially Josiah Quincy, against Madison generally, his alleged French partiality in particular, and the government of the country by "two Virginians and a foreigner." Rush regarded Quincy as "a complete Bully," worse that Randolph with his "insulting, disorganizing, jacobinical, *atrocious*" harangues, which cried out to be answered. Clay condemned the Federalists for their "hypercritical ingenuity," the "tacking with every gale," and the "one unalterable purpose, to steer, if possible, into the haven of power," which had for ten years impeded every effort of Republican administrations to find peace with honor. Clay scorned as well the "coarse assaults of party malevolence" from which not retirement from office, eminent services, nor advanced age could exempt ex-President Jefferson. Jefferson, Clay cried, would be "hailed as the second founder of the liberties of his people [when] . . . the howlings of the whole British pack set loose from the Essex Kennel, . . . the treasonable annals of a certain junto," would be remembered only with the infamy of the assassin of Henry the Great of France or the betrayer of Christ himself. In meeting the "preposterous and ridiculous" charge that "the administration of this country [is] subservient to France," Clay especially delighted the ladies from the White House. He cited the "incredible" episode of Richard Cutts having lost his seat in Congress in part because of a story circulated in his district that "he was the first cousin of the Emperor Napoleon." The foundation of the story, Clay said with heavy sarcasm, was that Cutts "had married a connexion of the lady of the President of the United States, who was an intimate friend of Thomas Jefferson, . . . who some years ago was in the habit of wearing red French breeches." When Clay sat down, to thunderous applause, everyone knew he had only begun. Doubtless the President exulted that evening as his "family" told him about the Kentuckian's performance, glad his administration had at last found a voice to answer the Randolphs and Quincys.

The next day, before a hushed and expectant audience, Clay took the floor again. He decried the "diabolical ambition" of the Federalists, "conspirators against the integrity of the Union," who propagated for "their nefarious purpose . . . the idea of Southern preponderance— Virginia influence—the yoking of the respectable yeomanry of the north, with the Negro slaves, to the cart of southern nabobs." He recalled sarcastically that many Northern and Western states had voted consistently for the Virginia Presidents, and pointed out that if Madison had been "designated to [the presidency] before his predecessor had retired," it resulted from "public sentiment which grew out of his known virtues, his illustrious services, and his distinguished abilities." Resuming the scorn of the previous day, Clay charged that opposition apologies for British impressment policies asked American citizens to accept British passes similar to those a "master grants to his Negro slave." After an able summary of the causes of the war, Clay perorated: "An honorable peace is attainable only by an efficient war. . . . [Let us] prosecute the war with the utmost vigor, strike wherever we can reach the enemy, at sea or on land, and negotiate the terms of a peace at Quebec or Halifax. . . . Haughty as [England] is, we once triumphed over her, and if we do not listen to the councils of timidity and despair we shall again prevail." Since Quincy and others had insinuated both the President's impotence and his wife's infidelity, Madison must have welcomed Clay's thundering vindication. His "artillery," one listener noted, was as well aimed as "the fire on board the *Constitution*, the *Wasp* or the *United States*, [and] . . . never was man [Quincy] more severely castigated or one who more richly deserved it."[36]

The last festivities of the season attended Madison's second inauguration, on March 4, 1813, the day after the War Hawk Congress had adjourned *sine die*. Marines, artillery, and cavalry escorted the President to the Capitol, where he addressed a large audience, including the Russian minister, who, though in full regalia, was squeezed in, Republican-style, among Congressmen and plain citizens. The French minister discreetly stayed away, because he thought "Mr. Madison, pursued more consistently than ever by the epithet of Vice Roy to his Majesty [Napoleon], . . . was not displeased to escape being so near" the French minister as he had been four years earlier. After the oath-taking, during which, according to Federalist newspapers, Chief Justice Marshall beheld the President with scorn, indignation, and disgust, Washington society repaired to the inaugural ball, graced by "a most lively assemblage of the lovely ones of our district." Celebrations continued the next night at a grand imperial ball given by Russian Minister Daschkoff, at which Dolley Madison "feasted and retired very late." Almost overlooked was Madison's lack-luster inaugural address, which attracted attention largely from opposition editors who scorned the "profound hypocrisy" of Madison having evoked "the smiles of Heaven" on the war effort. He did, after reviewing the just causes of the war, condemning British and Indian atrocities, and turning what good light he could on American military exploits, seek to stimulate war fervor. British responses to American peace offers had "been received in a spirit forbidding every reliance not placed on the military resources of the nation," he warned. Inherent American strength and the virtue and valor of the people were such, however, that only "the discipline and habits [of war] which are in daily progress" were needed to assure a final triumph.[37]

With Congressmen packing for home and the new Congress already called into special session for late May, Madison turned to the urgent problem of the empty Treasury, unfilled largely because American financiers, especially in New England, lacked faith in the administration's war effort. Gallatin warned the President that unless money was obtained immediately, military operations, especially those in the West, and all offensive efforts, would have to be curtailed. Since Congress had not protected the nation's credit by raising taxes, Gallatin was sure loans could not be floated except at excessive interest rates. Madison agreed and authorized the secretary to negotiate as best he could with any bankers able and willing to help. Luckily, through Alexander J. Dallas, Gallatin found three financiers, German-born David Parish and John Jacob Astor, and French-born Stephen Girard, who in April placed the entire $16-million loan just authorized by Congress at interest rates only slightly higher than normal. This saved the Treasury, and according to careful plans outlined by Gallatin, provided virtually all the money available to fight the war for the rest of the year. The failure of New England, which held most of the specie in the country, to subscribe more than 3 per cent of the loan, and the heavy reliance on rather unorthodox foreign-born bankers, measures the magnitude of the doubt and hostility Madison faced from most of the financial community of the nation.[38]

Diplomatic developments also demanded a new round of appointments. Madison filled the vacancy in Paris left by Joel Barlow's death by freezing in Poland with Senator William H. Crawford of Georgia. Though a popular appointment, it removed at an unfortunate time the most loyal and effective friend of the administration from a Senate already on the verge of falling under the sway of Madison's foes. More ticklish was arranging for the mission to accept the Russian mediation offer, presumably to do its business in Saint Petersburg. The American minister there, John Quincy Adams, would of course take part, and Madison selected Federalist Senator James A. Bayard of Delaware to represent the moderate opposition. Then, in a move that startled the nation, the President agreed to Gallatin's request that he be allowed to head the delegation. In fact, the time was propitious for Gallatin's departure. He was tired of Washington after twelve years as Secretary of the Treasury; he had obtained loans to finance the war for a year and had already laid tax proposals before Congress; Armstrong's presence in the cabinet was distasteful to him; and most important, Gallatin was the administration's most prestigious and skilled negotiator. His presence on the mediation commission would underscore as nothing else could the earnestness of Madison's desire for an honorable peace. Gallatin's "very precise and full instructions in all matters which he left behind, . . . [plus] the skilled clerks in his office drilled by long practice," Richard Rush noted, assured that the Treasury Department would function smoothly in Gallatin's absence. His manifold usefulness to the President, however, was not so easily replaced. Nonetheless James and Dolley Madison said farewell hoping for the best as their good friend of twelve years' standing departed on April 21, taking Payne Todd with him for the long journey to Russia.[39]

As Gallatin prepared to leave, he helped plan the campaign of American arms for the coming summer. Through the winter and spring of 1813 General Harrison's army in northern Ohio had endured British harassment, Indian massacres, cold, and starvation. Only the bungling of the British commander, Colonel Henry Proctor, to whom the great Indian warrior Tecumseh had once said, "Begone, go and put on petticoats," and some heroic though indecisive stands by American militiamen preserved American power south of Lake Erie at all. Through the late spring and summer Harrison conducted a holding operation while a newly appointed naval commander, Oliver Hazard Perry, completed his fleet at Erie, Pennsylvania, to do the only thing that would bring American victory in the Northwest: cut the water supply lines sustaining both British forces and those of Britain's Indian allies.

Forced to bide time in the West, the Washington "high command" again laid plans for campaigns in New York state. Though Madison and Armstrong agreed that the capture of Montreal remained the only effective way to conquer Canada, the long winter there permitted earlier attacks farther south around Lake Ontario, at Kingston, York (Toronto), and the Niagara frontier. Orders went out, therefore, still through General Dearborn's somnolent headquarters, to take these objectives. The attack on York succeeded; the United States discovered an able commander when Jacob Brown repulsed a British attack on Sacket's Harbor; and Winfield Scott and others fought well along the Niagara

River. But by midsummer American forces still did not control Lake Ontario, and hopes had been transferred to a fall campaign against Montreal. The timid Dearborn was finally retired, but, largely at Armstrong's insistence, he was replaced by the inept and untrustworthy Wilkinson. To complicate matters, he, Armstrong, and the other senior officer in the theater, General Wade Hampton, became embroiled in bitter personal disputes and recriminations. Incompetent, bickering commanders unable to mount concentrated, decisive campaigns brought another year of frustration on the battlefield.[40]

The sounds of war close to the nation's capital heightened Madison's concern as he pondered the campaigns along the Canadian frontier. By February 1813 British Admiral Sir John Warren, ordered to "bring the war home" to American cities, had blockaded the coast with an overwhelming force. He not only closed ports from New York southward to foreign commerce (New England ports were left untouched, to encourage disunion sentiment) but severely disrupted coastal trade. Even more alarming, in March and April squadrons entered Chesapeake and Delaware bays, where Rear Admiral Sir George Cockburn was becoming a legend for his daring and brutality. Described by Napoleon, whom he escorted to Saint Helena, as "rough, overbearing, vain, choleric, and capricious," Cockburn ravaged the area around Lynnhaven Bay (near Norfolk) and then destroyed military stores and many small vessels before burning the town of Havre de Grace, Maryland. Inhabitants who had joined the militia, he wrote Warren, should "understand and feel what they were liable to bring on themselves by building batteries and acting toward us with so much useless rancor." To emphasize the point, he destroyed Fredericktown and Georgetown on the Maryland eastern shore.[41]

Though Cockburn was still too weak to threaten Washington, his boldness and the exposure of the city caused Dolley Madison to write of "the fears and alarms that circulate" in Washington. A Swedish ship in the Potomac, it was said, had been boarded, but "our informer was too frightened to wait for further news. . . . One of our generals has discovered a plan of the British—it is to land as many chosen rogues as they can about fourteen miles below Alexandria, in the night, so that they may be on hand to burn the President's house and offices." Cockburn had, she added, "sent me word that he would make his bow at my drawing-room very soon." Undaunted, Dolley praised the "considerable efforts for defense" and added that "though a Quaker, . . . [I] always have been an advocate for fighting when assailed." She would, she said, "keep the old Tunisian sabre within reach." But Cockburn had returned to Lynnhaven to join Warren in major assaults on lower Chesapeake ports.[42]

To this scene of alarm came the newly elected Congress, called into special session to lay taxes its worn-out predecessor had had neither time nor strength to pass. Almost half of the old Congressmen—including the two bitterest critics of the war, Josiah Quincy and John Randolph of Roanoke—did not return. Randolph of Roanoke had been defeated in a close election by Jefferson's son-in-law John W. Eppes, a veteran of four earlier Republican Congresses, an earnest war advocate, and an intimate friend of Madison's. Returned were Dolley Madison's bellicose brother-in-law, John G. Jackson, as staunch a supporter of Madison's as ever, and Clay, Calhoun, Grundy, Lowndes, and other young War Hawks who, as part of a two-to-one Republican majority, assured the administration of a friendly House of Representatives. Equally pleasing were spring elections that found Republican candidates for governor only barely defeated in the supposed Federalist strongholds of Massachusetts and New Hampshire, and war supporter Daniel Tompkins defeating a mixed bag of Federalists and Clintonians for the pivotal New York governorship.

Less propitious for Madison was the appearance in the House of an old nemesis, disunion advocate Timothy Pickering, and two able new foes, twenty-seven-year-old editor Alexander C. Hanson, who had written the calumnies about Dolley Madison's infidelity, and a sturdy, eloquent young New Hampshire man named Daniel Webster. In the Senate the balance of power threatened to turn against the administration. Its firmest supporter, Crawford of Georgia, had departed for France, and friendly Senators from North Carolina and New Hampshire had been replaced respectively by an independent and the exceedingly able Federalist Jeremiah Mason. Most threatening of all, New York sent to the Senate eloquent, respected, well-informed Rufus King, an opponent of the war and sure to be an effective foe of the administration. These new voices, added to returned Federalists, Clintonians, and the implacable Giles-Smith-Leib faction, now emboldened with prospects of successful obstruction, were sure to cause trouble.[43]

Madison informed Congress he had accepted the Russian mediation offer, and that despite any sign of British acceptance, he had high hopes for it. He urged nonetheless, even while peace negotiations were under way, "the vigorous employment of the resources of war." After an account of what the President rather misleadingly called "the auspicious progress of our arms," he noted that the $16-million loan had carried the nation past a crisis. Nonetheless, "a well digested system of internal revenue" was necessary to make future borrowing possible at lower interest rates, to place on the home front burdens commensurate with those borne by the armed forces, and to demonstrate "to the world the public energy of our political institutions." The House Committee on Ways and Means took prompt action on the detailed tax proposals left by

Gallatin, reporting out on June 10 levies on salt, licenses, spirits, carriages, auctions, sugar refining, and stamps, machinery for assessing and collecting them, and a direct land tax that would bring in $3 million. Though such measures seemed astounding from a party that had for years, as one member said, taught its followers "to look upon a taxgatherer as a thief," the Republican majority accepted the needs of war and approved the entire tax program. This, together with authority to borrow an additional $7.5 million if necessary, would underwrite the war, it was hoped, for another year.[44]

Madison's political difficulties soon began, however—when the Senate took up diplomatic appointments. It quickly confirmed James A. Bayard and John Quincy Adams as members of the mediation commission, but balked on Gallatin and on appointment of Jonathan Russell as minister to Sweden. Resolves implying that Russell had connived to conceal Napoleon's devious course in 1811 in rescinding the Berlin and Milan decrees, and parallel resolves introduced in the House by Webster, sent Congress into weeks of bitter, futile debate over the origins and causes of the war. At the same time, Senator King charged that the President had no lawful authority to give Gallatin a diplomatic appointment while he remained Secretary of the Treasury. Designating Navy Secretary William Jones as acting head of the Treasury Department for such a lengthy period was also alleged to be illegal. King had in fact made serious charges of executive usurpation, which a jealous Senate would be quick to heed, and had as well offered the anti-Gallatin, antiadministration forces a lever they grasped readily. The Senate demanded executive explanation of the administration's "high-handedness," and solemnly appointed committees to consult with the President.[45]

During the debate on Capitol Hill, and while angry conferees strode across Washington's "magnificent distances" to the White House, Madison's bilious fever attacked him again. Congressman Webster, who had reported that after his first "bow to the President, I did not like his looks any better than his Administration," kept close track of Madison's illness as he sought to deliver the invidious House resolves to the executive mansion. On June 19 he wrote that "Madison has been several days quite sick—is no better—has not been well enough to read the resolutions [of] the Senate." Five days later Webster showed little patience and less sympathy: "Madison still sick . . . I went . . . to the Palace to present the [House] Resolutions—the President was in his bed, sick of a fever—his night cap on his head—his wife attending him—I think he will find no relief from my prescription." On June 29, sixteen days after Madison had taken to his bed, Webster reported that "the President is worse today."[46]

Madison was in fact enduring a near-fatal illness, which kept Dolley at his bedside day and night for three weeks, sometimes, she wrote, "with despair" for his recovery. He had had her write to the Senate on June 18 that his "indisposition" not only prevented him from meeting its committee that day but also from "fixing a day when it will be in his power." Always wary of spending the hot months in sickly tidewater regions, and still subject to bouts of the mysterious, exhausting fevers experienced in varying degrees all his life, Madison had by mid-June 1813 pushed his luck and stamina too far. In a period of nearly two years he had been away from Washington for only two weeks, working long, strenuous hours and enjoying none of the relaxation and mountain air of Montpelier he had always believed essential to his good health, if not to life itself. Monroe wrote Jefferson worriedly on the fifteenth day of Madison's illness that his fever had "perhaps never left him, even for an hour, and occasionally symptoms have been unfavorable." The three doctors attending the President had been able to give him "bark" (quinine) some in the past week and felt he would recover, Monroe added, but he nonetheless shielded the President from Congressional temper "at a time when [he is] so little able to bear it, indeed when no pressure whatever should be made on him."[47]

"The thought of [Madison's] possible loss strikes everybody with consternation," French Minister Sérurier wrote. "His death, in the circumstances in which the Republic is placed, would be a veritable national calamity." Congressman Charles J. Ingersoll of Pennsylvania proclaimed on the floor of the House that "the almost universal expression of fervent wishes" for Madison's recovery proved his "strong and pervading hold on the confidence and affections of his fellow citizens." Such eulogies and other excessively soliticious comments—including, toward the end, daily health bulletins in *The National Intelligencer*—had the effect of heightening the alarm. John Adams heard wild rumors that the President "lives by laudanum and could not hold out for four months."[48]

The opposition, meanwhile, moved in like jackals. Congressman Grosvenor pontificated that the old President, who would "soon appear at the bar of Immortal Justice," must recoil at the "bloody crime" of having tricked the country into a war with England. The Federalist New York *Evening Post* observed sarcastically that the Senate resolves had proved "rather too much for the delicate nerves of our Chief Magistrate." The editor concluded that, since at long last his conduct was to be fully investigated, "it is no wonder that he is sick." The *Maryland Gazette* wished that such a man as Senator Rufus King was "at the head of our government," instead of "those who pursue the idle phantoms of a distempered imagination." The Georgetown *Federal Republican* was even more tactless: Gallatin had fled the country like a rat deserting a sinking vessel; General Dearborn, near death, was unfit for his command; and the nation should consider its plight if the cadaverous Gerry, termed by one Federalist a "scant-patterned old skeleton of a French Barber," should "succeed to the throne by the demise of the lingering incumbent." The editor then hinted darkly that should a "certain individual," obviously Speaker Henry Clay, find himself in line for the presidency, the nation might witness deeds of ambition "not for the first time introduced by the Duke of Gloucester." Monroe reported that administration foes in the Senate "have begun to make calculations, and plans, founded on the presumed death of the President and Vice-President, and it has been suggested to me that Giles is thought of to take the place of the President of the Senate," the next in line to the presidency after the Vice President.[49]

Finally, Madison reached a crisis and the fever subsided. Though Madison was worse on June 29, by July 2 Dolley was able to write "that Mr. Madison recovers; for the last three days his fever has been so slight as to permit him to take bark every hour and with good effect. . . . Now that I see him get well I feel as if I might die myself from fatigue." In another week Madison resumed some public business and visited with company, looking pale and resting on a settee in a loose flannel gown. By mid-July he had left his bed, but "so precarious is his convalescence," Dolley wrote near the end of the month, that "even now, I watch over him as I would an infant." On August 2 Richard Rush wrote to John Adams that though Madison's "long sickness has pulled him down a good deal," he had been out riding and had resumed full attention to business. The aged ex-President remarked that he knew from "sad experience" that the "agitations of mind and incessant labors" of the presidency "must be too much for any but the most robust constitutions," and reported to Rush an anxiousness "for Mr. Madison's Health, because much depends on it. In his Intensions, Zeal and Industry, I have much confidence," Adams added. Madison himself wrote Gallatin, on August 2, that "I have just recovered strength enough, after a severe and tedious attack of bilious fever, to bear a journey to the mountains, whither I am about setting out. The physicians prescribe it as essential to my thorough recovery and security against a relapse at the present season." This return to health marked the end of the most serious presidential illness since Washington's severe infection and near death in May 1790.[50]

Before Madison could leave Washington, though, Admiral Cockburn returned to the lower Potomac with a large fleet, fresh from a landing at Hampton, Virginia, where French and other prisoners pressed into service on English warships had burned, pillaged, and raped, inspiring, one nervous Washington lady wrote, "a terror in us we should not otherwise have felt." Members of Congress rushed to join militia companies that gathered around the capital in great disorder and largely without arms. Even Secretaries Monroe and Armstrong rode off to the bivouacs. Actually, as level-headed Navy Secretary William Jones noted, the British ships were probably only making a show of strength while they took on water; shoals would prevent such large warships from approaching Washington, whatever the disarray among its defenders. Jones also took a cynical view of the "heroism" of his cabinet colleagues.

They had gone to the front, "full of zeal . . . running for the Presidential purse intent only on each other," while in their rear, enemies in the Senate were "preparing a mine to blow them both up." After taking soundings, setting channel buoys, and cannonading bold American scouting craft, Cockburn rejoined Warren's main fleet in the Chesapeake.[51]

The really dangerous threat to the administration, from Congress, had, as Jones hinted, survived both Madison's illness and Cockburn's menace. Throughout the President's confinement, the Senate had continued to insist that Gallatin's cabinet and diplomatic appointments were incompatible and that Madison confer with a Senate committee on the matter. As soon as he was able, Madison informed the Senate that for him to confer officially with a mere committee of the Senate lost sight of the "independent and coordinate" relations between the executive and legislative departments. He would, however, be willing to *see* a group of Senators on an informal basis. The Senate committee came, the members thinking they could in fact insist upon a formal conference, but Madison merely greeted them, and mentioned that apparently he and the Senate had different understandings of the relations between them. "After the Committee had remained a reasonable time for the President to make any other observations and he made none," the committee reported huffily, it retired without saying anything to the President. Thus, having skillfully added defenders of Senatorial dignity and malcontents at the President's coldness to the open opponents of Gallatin, King and other antiadministration Senators secured close votes to reject both Gallatin's nomination and Russell's mission to Sweden. The President thus felt the full force of Rush's observation of the previous summer: "Mr. Madison is not a Mr. Jefferson or a General Washington, either of whom, from their vast ascendancy over Congress and the publick . . . might be gratified in any little executive freak dear to their heart."[52]

After the vote Dolley Madison wrote Hannah Gallatin of the "disappointments and vexations heaped upon [Madison] by party spirit"— worst of all, Gallatin's rejection, caused by the "desertion of some whose support we had a right to expect, and . . . the maneuvering of others, always hostile to superior merit." Madison informed Gallatin in code that the Senate's "mutilation of the Mission to St. Petersburg" had resulted from a series of accidents and intrigues. Friends of Gallatin's nomination had not pressed its confirmation early in the session, when success was certain. Then, with the opposition organized, the Senate offered to confirm the diplomatic appointment if the President would declare the cabinet office vacant. "Besides the degradation of the Executive," Madison observed, such a deal "would have introduced a species of barter of the most fatal tendency." That is, the Senate would have set a precedent for direct interference with executive appointments that would have infringed his independence and the responsibility of his cabinet to him. Also, antiadministration Senators would intrigue to prevent a competent appointment in the Treasury Department, and Gallatin's friends in the Senate thought they could win anyhow. So the President remained inflexible, and to his mortification, finally lost. Only the obvious party rancor in the Senate, which had the effect of giving Gallatin "a stronger hold on the confidence and support of the nation" ("trebled his friends," Dolley Madison asserted), offered consolation. Nonetheless, partly because the Wednesday receptions at the White House and other highly useful contacts with Congressmen had been suspended during Madison's illness, the weakened administration forces in the Senate had bungled badly and had suffered a humiliating defeat sure to encourage the opposition. Gallatin's rejection had little effect on him, however, because he was confirmed as a peace commissioner before he left Europe—word of the Senate action did not reach him in Saint Petersburg until late October.[53]

Finally off to Montpelier for two months on August 9, after a short attack of influenza, Madison fretted for news that the summer campaigns had succeeded. The struggles on lakes Ontario and Erie were still in the hands of carpenters frantically building ships for both sides to achieve superiority before doing battle. On the Atlantic coast, meanwhile, the British navy slowly tightened its grip. It had even beaten the frigate *Chesapeake* in a ship-to-ship duel off Boston harbor, memorable in American naval history for Captain James Lawrence's famous order, "Don't give up the ship!" before he died of wounds. General Wilkinson, on his way to command in New York state, spent months making the journey from New Orleans to Washington, where he saw Madison and Armstrong and submitted unimaginative campaign plans. The general and Secretary Armstrong, believed to be ambitious political allies, finally left for Sacket's Harbor. Since Armstrong's presence with the army made it virtually impossible for Madison to interpose in operations planned at the field headquarters, he was at the mercy of a team in which he had little confidence. Again he risked relying on indifferent leaders and ambiguous command channels, and again he unwisely let slip to others prerogatives he should have insisted on retaining for himself.[54]

At the end of August Dolley Madison wrote that her husband was "perfectly well but will be better for another month on the mountain," so they would resist Secretary Jones's impatient calls for the President's return to Washington. Meanwhile Montpelier was filled with "a crowd of company"; Madison rode about the plantation; and the usual visits were exchanged with the Monticello family. Almost daily reports came of inaction and quarreling in New York state, but news from Lake Erie told of steady progress, and at last there came a dispatch from Perry, delivered to Montpelier by express rider on September 23: "it hath pleased the Almighty to give the arms of the United States a signal victory over their enemies on this lake. The British squadron . . . have this moment surrendered to the force under my command, after a sharp conflict." His report to General Harrison was simply, "We have met the enemy and they are ours." With American naval superiority assured, the British abandoned Detroit and Fort Malden, and Harrison, with fresh Kentucky militia, pursued the retreating enemy north of Lake Erie. On October 5, on Ontario's Thames River, Harrison defeated the British forces in a battle that saw as well the death of Tecumseh. This ended British and Indian power in the Northwest and drove their forces back to the Niagara frontier, something Madison and the country had expected from General Hull fifteen months earlier.[55]

Word of Harrison's victory reached Madison just before he left Montpelier for Washington, and, combined with bright fall weather, fully restored health, and news of Napoleon's victory at Dresden (to be his last), made for a joyous return to the capital. Richard Rush reported, "The little President is back, and as game as ever. He mounted his horse on Tuesday and attended by Mr. Monroe and General Mason spurred off to the [race] course Virginia-like—where too he saw a Virginia steed carry the day." John Adams wrote that "Perry's triumph is enough to revive Mr. Madison, if he was in the last stage of a Consumption," and wished that "he may long continue to live and be well; and to see the good work of the War prospering in his hands; for a more necessary War, was never undertaken. It is necessary against England; necessary to convince France that we are something: and above all necessary to convince ourselves, that we are not, Nothing."[56]

The euphoric mood evaporated, however, as dispatches arrived from the Saint Lawrence front. By mid-October Armstrong and Wilkinson had not yet decided whether Kingston or Montreal was their objective. Two weeks later Wilkinson and Hampton, moving ponderously toward Montreal—one down the Saint Lawrence and the other from Lake Champlain—had exchanged angry letters, making their cooperation impossible. Sensing defeat, Armstrong abandoned his generals as British forces outmaneuvered the Americans. By late November Madison knew the campaign had failed exactly as Dearborn's had a year earlier, with the American armies in retreat to winter quarters. By the end of the year, the British, emboldened by American blundering, had reoccupied York and driven American forces from both sides of the Niagara River, burning and plundering as they went.[57]

In response to New York Governor Tompkin's harrowing report of

British ravages at Buffalo and elsewhere, Madison observed simply that the events on the New York frontier "were as unexpected as they have been distressing." At the same time came news that the Allies had overwhelmed Napoleon at Leipzig, driving him in full retreat back across the Rhine. Richard Rush reflected vividly the mood in Washington. The nation was fighting, he wrote John Adams, "but alas, it seems to fight for nothing but disaster and defeat; and, I dread to add, disgrace. . . . What, Sir, should be done? The prospect looks black. It is awful. . . . Is not the torrent rolling too fiercely upon us to be turned back? . . . Where shall we find commanders? And may we not be doomed to pass yet another and another and another campaign in the school of affliction and disgrace? I cannot pursue the subject, and am sick at heart at the view of our publick affairs. Have we, Sir, even seen worse times, and survived them? And how?" The aged patriot replied that "the times are too serious to write." He did not know what prevented "the President's Pallace and the proud Capitol, from becoming the Head Quarters of British Principles." "The country must have a *Winnowing*," Adams added; "the Chaff must be separated from the Wheat. . . . The real military Genius and Experience have been neglected, and Chaff, Froth, and Ignorance have been promoted." But lest Rush be too discouraged, Adams pointed out that during the revolution there had been "infinitely more difficult and dangerous times." When Rush showed Adams' letter to Madison, the grateful President observed that "opinions from such a quarter had the smack of rich and old wine."[58]

As he considered the necessary "winnowing," Madison had to deal first with the regular session of Congress, which gathered in Washington in early December. He reported the British rejection of the Russian mediation offer, but without word from the American commissioners in over six months, he had little diplomatic news to offer. Though Madison could justly boast of the victories of Perry and Harrison, and the consequent return of peace to the Northwest, he had as usual otherwise to glide by inaction and ineptitude. He nonetheless heralded the good effect of the war on the nation: it had given great impulse to domestic manufactures; it had caused many expenditures permanently useful to national defense and prosperity; retaliation for assaults on American commerce had accelerated American maritime growth; the spread of "military discipline and instruction" assured a longer and more just peace "than could be expected without these proofs of national character and resources"; and finally, free government had again proved capable of strength and unity in a national cause. "In fine," Madison wrote, concluding his fifth annual message, "the war, with all its vicissitudes, is illustrating the capacity and the destiny of the United States to be a great, a flourishing, and a powerful nation, worthy of the friendship which it is disposed to cultivate with all others." Though on most occasions such words would have seemed mere rhetoric, in fact at a time of peril, when powerful groups in the country claimed the Union could not survive the conflict, Madison was pledging again his faith in republican government.[59]

Following a special message from the President, Congress passed an embargo shutting all ports of the United States in order to stop the flow of supplies to the British and to try again to create pressures for peace in London by closing the market for British manufactures. Since the British blockade had already ended sea-borne commerce from New York southward, and the export of supplies as well as the import of British goods transpired almost entirely in Northern ports, the new measures seemed, as one critic charged, "more levelled at New England than at Old England." Thus embittered, and emboldened as well by news of Napoleon's disaster at Leipzig, Federalists complained more loudly than ever of the foolishness and malice of the administration. Gouverneur Morris noted acidly that stopping the *sale* or *smuggling* of supplies to British forces would result only in their *taking* them by landing parties from defenseless towns, while the renewed effort to injure Britain's export trade, with all the ports of Europe now open to her, was like the action of a man "who would submit his members to the rack, for the pleasure of seeing his enemy bitten by a louse." Anyone, said Morris pointedly, who urged such a plan, "must have rather more nerve than intellect." It is possible, the President's old colleague of 1787 concluded darkly, "that Mr. Madison may blow up a civil broil into a civil war." Violent speeches by Federalists in Congress assured Madison that nearly two years of war had, far from diminishing internal dissension, heightened it among the unreconciled minority, and he knew only too well the truth of Calhoun's timely warning in Congress: "Without resort to violence, [a factious opposition] is able in a thousand ways to counteract and deaden all of the motions of government, to render its policy wavering, and to compel it to submit to schemes of aggrandizement on the part of other governments, or, if resistance is determined on, to render it feeble and ineffectual."[60]

In January 1814 Congress rejected Secretary Armstrong's unauthorized call for conscription and instead enacted an administration request for quintupled enlistment bounties to fill the ranks. At the same time, Congress passed appropriations for army and navy operations for the coming year at about the same level as the year just passed. The Treasury report reflected on the surface the solvent condition of war financing thus far, but it did not take account, as Congressional critics were quick to point out, of the steady drain of specie into New England bank vaults, and abroad, to pay—illicitly or otherwise—for imports. Allowed to hope for the best, Congress merely authorized borrowing to fill the gap between expected tax receipts and war needs. Since these

acts combined would not greatly expand American war-making potential for 1814, the effect was to place the country on the defensive,
because, as Washington was painfully aware, Napoleon's defeat would
release hundreds of warships and thousands of battle-hardened British
troops for service in North America.[61]

Diplomatic developments also took anxious account of the news from
European battlefields. The same dispatch vessel that brought word of
French defeats also brought official notice that Britain had rejected
the Russian mediation offer, but had instead suggested direct peace
negotiations in London or Sweden. British Foreign Secretary Lord Castlereagh had condescendingly let the American commissioners know
that he considered the Anglo-American war "a sort of family quarrel,
where foreign interference can only do harm," and that therefore the
two nations should negotiate their differences directly. At the same
time, however, the British remained adamant on impressment. Though
Madison resented the hauteur and rigidity of the British position, he
knew as well that the offer of direct negotiation had been made *before*
Napoleon's defeat and that, therefore, Castlereagh's attitude was simply
more of the persisting British arrogance to which the United States
had been subjected for thirty years, rather than a punitive threat born
of victory on the battlefields. Hence the President accepted the offer at
once, despite the coincidental effect of seeming to submit to peace
negotiations at a time when the enemy had every advantage.[62]

As peace commissioners, Madison appointed Gallatin, J. Q. Adams,
and James Bayard, already in Europe, and added Henry Clay and
Jonathan Russell, a very able negotiating team. All their diplomatic
skill would be necessary, because to Castlereagh's call for a settlement
"not inconsistent with the established maxims of public law, and with
the maritime rights of the British empire," Madison had countered
with a readiness to treat only "on conditions of reciprocity consistent
with the rights of both parties as sovereign and independent nations."
That is, Britain would insist on the *right* of impressment and continue
to view her former colonies condescendingly, while the United States
would insist on ending impressment and assume that the Declaration
of Independence was exactly that. These stiff positions, together with
Britain's rapidly growing predominance in Europe, did not, as Madison was painfully aware, offer much prospect for a quick or a favorable
peace. At a dinner in Washington honoring Commodore Perry, Madison
doubtless appreciated Henry Clay's rather tough mood as, before he
left for Europe, he toasted, "The policy which looks to peace as the end
of war—and to the war as the means of peace."[63]

Gallatin's permanent release from the Treasury Department, hints
that the Attorney General should live in Washington, and bitter patronage disputes spurred a new round of appointment hassles. Madison

sought unsuccessfully to get Gallatin's close friend Alexander Dallas, who had helped float the April 1813 loan, to take the Treasury post, but finally settled on Senator George W. Campbell of Tennessee, an ardent War Hawk. Portentously, Campbell had no particular talent for finance and was in ill-health. When an unwillingness to live in Washington caused William Pinkney's resignation as Attorney General, Madison appointed Richard Rush, a move personally gratifying, but which, in view of Pinkney's distinction at the bar and Rush's relative inexperience, did not strengthen the cabinet. Republican Congressman Ezekiel Bacon of Massachusetts replaced Rush as Comptroller of the Treasury.[64]

The death of the postmaster in Philadelphia let loose another storm. Madison had retained Jefferson's Postmaster General, Gideon Granger, and continued the practice of letting Granger appoint local postmasters with very little presidential interference and without need for Senatorial confirmation. This worked well as long as Granger was sympathetic to the administration. During Madison's presidency, however, Granger favored the "Invisibles" and had increasingly appointed postmasters to strengthen that group. When he made it clear that he intended to appoint the bitterly anti-Madison Senator Michael Leib, defeated for re-election, to the vacant and profitable Philadelphia post, Pennsylvania Republicans loyal to the administration howled. Hannah Gallatin wrote of "great uneasiness" and the "insult to the good citizens of Philadelphia" should Leib be appointed. Dallas, Congressman Jonathan Roberts, Senator Abner Lacock, and other administration Republicans wanted Franklin's grandson Richard Bache made postmaster. Dolley Madison wrote that "Mr. Madison has *counseled* Mr. Granger to appoint R. Bache," but Granger refused and decided to test his strength. He appealed to Jefferson hinting that should he be opposed, he would revive such old slanders as the stories of Jefferson's alleged affair with Mrs. Walker, and the rumors of the unchastity of Dolley Madison and Anna Cutts. After Madison had warned his predecessor of Granger's intentions, Jefferson wrote cordially to Granger, but gave him no encouragement in his plan to issue a public vindication, and warned him especially against spreading "gossiping trash."[65]

When Granger nonetheless named Leib, Madison dismissed Granger and appointed instead Return Jonathan Meigs, who as governor of Ohio had given vigorous support to the war. Though this move improved the administration's standing in the West, it added to charges of nepotism against Madison: Meigs's daughter had recently become the second wife of John G. Jackson, widower of Dolley Madison's sister Mary! When Meigs in due time replaced Leib with Bache, Madison had strengthened administration Republicans in Pennsylvania, and his own standing with them, but otherwise the picture was gloomy. Clay had gone from the House, and Crawford and Campbell from the Senate. Pinkney would no longer charm Supreme Court galleries arguing brilliantly for the government, and worst of all, Gallatin was permanently removed from the inner circle in Washington. "That Campbell and Rush are equal to Gallatin and Pinkney is not, I imagine," observed Congressman Nathaniel Macon, "believed by anyone who knows them." Moreover, the ill-will between the secretaries of War and State had reached the point where Armstrong intrigued with Federalists to disgrace Monroe, and Monroe wrote the President that Armstrong "if continued in office will ruin not you and the Administration only, but the whole republican party and cause."⁶⁶

Though troubled by Armstrong's ill-concealed disloyalty within the cabinet, Madison did see that in many ways Armstrong had invigorated the army. By January 1814 the old, timid generals had been retired or shifted to quiet stations, and a crop of new appointments readied. Madison and Armstrong agreed on capable, thirty-nine-year-old George Izard as senior major general, but the President set aside a politically motivated suggestion by Armstrong, and instead made thirty-eight-year-old Jacob Brown a major general. Then the civilian chiefs nominated six new brigadier generals (average age thirty-three years), including Alexander Macomb, Edmund Pendleton Gaines, Winfield Scott, and E. W. Ripley, all of whom were soon to win impressive victories. Finally, after Armstrong had harried William Henry Harrison into resigning from the army, Madison immediately commissioned Andrew Jackson, the recent victor over the Creeks in the Southwest, major general and sent him to command at New Orleans. With these appointments, in part creditable to Armstrong, but in the cases of Brown and Jackson reflecting Madison's own judgment, the armed forces at last had effective leadership everywhere but in the Chesapeake Bay region, where a timid politician-made-general, William H. Winder, was to command.⁶⁷

With Congress adjourned, important appointments made, and little likelihood of news from the American peace commissioners, the Madisons made a spring visit to Montpelier for the first time since they had gone to the White House. Heavy rains gave "a fine contenance to the country," the President reported, but so clogged the roads that "the utmost exertions" were necessary both ways on the trip and delayed the almost daily messages coming from the capital. Madison did not visit Monticello, but wrote Jefferson of his hopes that the dazzling trade prospects opened to Britain by Napoleon's defeat would make her anxious to end the American war, and that Republican victories in New York would "crush the project [for disunion] of the [Essex] Junto faction, so long fostered by and flattering the expectations of the British

Cabinet." Unfortunately, however, Gallatin's assessment in London was more realistic. There had been a

> total change in our affairs produced by the late revolution [in France, returning the Bourbons,] and by the restoration of universal peace in the European world, from which we are alone excluded. A well-organized and large army is at once liberated from any European employment, and ready, together with a superabundant naval force, to act immediately against us. How ill-prepared we are to meet it [is well known]; but, above all, our own divisions and the hostile attitude of the Eastern states give room to apprehend that a continuance of the war might prove vitally fatal to the United States. . . . The hope [in Britain], not of ultimate conquest, but of a dissolution of the Union, [and] the convenient pretence which the American war will afford to preserve large military establishments . . . throw impediments in the way of peace. . . . In the intoxication of an unexpected success, which they ascribe to themselves, the English people eagerly wish that their pride may be fully gratified by what they call the "punishment of America." They do not even suspect that we had any just cause of war, and ascribe it solely to a premeditated concert with Bonaparte at a time when we thought him triumphant and their cause desperate.

Madison and the United States were to endure, it seemed certain, one more ferocious effort by Britain to exert her will on the former colonies.[68]

Back in Washington in early June, Madison called a cabinet meeting "to decide on the plan of campaign which our means naval and military render most eligible"—and which, Madison might have added, but did not have to, since it was uppermost in everyone's mind, the gathering British forces would soon impose on the United States. The cabinet, according to Madison's notes, ordered American forces at Detroit to recapture Fort Mackinac and General Brown's army on the Niagara frontier to cross the river and campaign, as had been tried twice before, toward York. Monroe thought this hazardous because Commodore Isaac Chauncey, forever building ships but seldom sailing them, had not yet gained supremacy on Lake Ontario. Finally, the cabinet again ordered assaults down the Saint Lawrence and down Lake Champlain toward Montreal. This time, especially in the Niagara area, although the forces were not larger than those used previously, they had energetic leaders. On the other hand, just four days before the cabinet meeting the British had ordered ten thousand soldiers sent to Canada, and a month later fourteen regiments of Wellington's veterans had sailed from Bordeaux for North America. Since Quebec and Montreal would soon have fresh defenders, British forces in lower Canada were sent to Niagara. During July 1814, despite a British attack on Oswego that had shown her

ability to move forces about Lake Ontario with impunity, Brown, ably
supported by Generals Scott and Ripley, invaded Canada opposite
Buffalo, fought sharp battles at Chippewa and Lundy's Lane, and
proved for the first time that American regulars were more than a
match for Britain's. The growing power of the British, however, prevented the Americans from gaining strategic advantages.[69]

Meanwhile, the expedition to Mackinac had failed, and a new British
commander with large forces at Halifax and Bermuda alarmed the seacoast. Landings were made around Eastport, Maine, and threats, real
or apparent, frightened towns for a thousand miles southward. In mid-
June, to an anxious request by Governor James Barbour of Virginia for
federal aid in defending his state, Madison responded pathetically. It
was, he agreed, necessary to "be prepared as well as we can to meet
the augmented force which may invade us." Despite "general apprehensions," however, the government did not know where the enemy
would strike. Since to call out the militia from Eastport to Savannah
"would rapidly exhaust our pecuniary means, and soon put everything
at hazard," Madison urged reliance on "exerting all our vigilance on
discovering the particular views of the enemy, and, by not prematurely
or erroneously applying our means of defense, be more able to use
them with effect where and when they become necessary." "Nothing
more," Madison concluded regretfully, was in his power. Both he and
Governor Barbour (a neighbor in Orange County) were fully aware
that should Britain act vigorously with the force in *her* power, American
defenders were unlikely to have the miraculous combination of luck,
vigilance, and mobility that would be needed to meet it.[70]

Amid these apprehensions, dispatch vessels arrived from Europe,
bringing to Washington Gallatin's gloomy forebodings on Britain's hostile intentions and vastly augmented ability to make the United States
feel them. With no prospect of complete victory over Great Britain, but
with some hope that she might agree to a standoff peace, Gallatin and
Bayard suggested that the United States soften its stand on impressment, because with the European war over, that subject involved "little
more than questions of abstract rights." They requested as well permission to move the peace negotiations from remote Sweden to Ghent in
the Low Countries, where friendly governments might exert influence
on behalf of the United States and where close watch could be kept on
the European peace negotiations in Vienna. Though Rush and Monroe
had reservations, Gallatin's case was finally irresistible, and new instructions were sent along the lines he had requested. French Minister
Sérurier summarized the grim mood: "The Cabinet is frightened. It
continues, however, to keep a good face externally, but the fact is that
it has a consciousness of its weakness and of the full strength of its
enemy."[71]

CHAPTER XXI

Defeat, Victory, and Peace

Toward the end of July 1814 Dolley Madison wrote Hannah Gallatin of the unhappy city of Washington. It had been, she complained, "in a state of perturbation for a long time—the depredations of the Enemy approaching within 20 miles of the City and the disaffected making incessant difficulties for the government. Such a place as this has become I cannot describe it. I wish (for my part) *we were* at Philadelphia. The people here do not deserve that I should prefer it—among other exclamations and threats they say that if Mr. Madison attempts to move from *this House* in case of an attack they will *stop him*, and that he shall *fall with it*. I am not the least alarmed at these things, but entirely disgusted, and determined to stay with him." The month had indeed been an awful one for the President, aware, among other things, that remaining in Washington during the summer would probably cause another attack of the bilious fever nearly fatal to him the year before. News came fitfully from the Niagara frontier, displaying the valor of Scott, Brown, Ripley, and their men, but proving in the end that Chauncey's failure to control Lake Ontario had not only negated the army's heroism but threatened again to restore British domination of the region. In early August word came simultaneously that fifteen-thousand British veterans had landed in Montreal and that England so dominated European diplomacy American ministers could not even secure interviews with French and Russian leaders.[1]

Just as disturbing was accumulating evidence of Secretary of War Armstrong's deceit, insubordination, and incompetence. In May 1814, when Madison was at Montpelier, Armstrong had kept news from the

President and had written inaccurate and unauthorized dispatches to insure the retirement of General Harrison, and, at the same time, make it seem that Madison had tried to block the promotion of Andrew Jackson. Armstrong had, as well, reorganized army regiments, by law the President's responsibility. Learning of these moves, Madison ordered Armstrong to send him copies of all correspondence with military commanders. The President discovered, among other things, that despite his explicit orders to the contrary, the senior officers on the New York frontier, Generals Brown and Izard and Commodore Chauncey, had been corresponding through the Secretary of War rather than directly—and this at Armstrong's insistence. The failure of communication thus imposed had, Madison saw clearly, been in large measure responsible for the lost opportunities of Brown's valiant Niagara campaign.

Spurred on by Monroe, Madison admonished Armstrong in no uncertain terms. "I owe it to my own responsibility, as well as to other considerations," he began, "to make some remarks on the relations in which the Head of the [War] Department stands to the President, and to lay down some rules for conducting the business of the Department." Madison pointed out the dependent place of the Secretary and the need to clear all important decisions with the President and to pass on to him all important intelligence. An even nominally loyal secretary would have done this as a matter of course. Instead, there were many important decisions "first knowledge of which," Madison complained, "was derived from the newspapers." Furthermore, "letters expressly intended and proper for the knowledge and decision of the Executive" had been disposed of without being sent to the President. Madison laid down ten rules to regulate Armstrong's conduct and insure that the War Department would once again become a subordinate part of the executive branch. In old age, reviewing an attempt by Armstrong to vindicate himself, Madison observed that the secretary's "gross misstatements . . . will suffice to put everyone on his guard, and justify a general protest against the credibility of a writer capable of such perverted and deceptive views of facts." Under normal circumstances, of course, Armstrong would have been removed from office, but the presence of a powerful British force in Chesapeake Bay made it impossible to undertake the disruptions this would have made inevitable. Consequently Madison faced an extreme crisis with a worse than useless right arm.[2]

Madison had warned Armstrong as early as May 20 that communications from England "admonish us to be prepared for the worst the enemy may be able to effect against us." Britain had, furthermore, indicated "the most inveterate spirit against the Southern States," and could be expected to attack all vulnerable points, among which, Madison observed pointedly, *the seat of Government cannot fail to be a favorite one.*" At a cabinet meeting on July 1, before the main British force had entered the Chesapeake, Madison asked for a full discussion of the defense of the

East coast, especially the city of Washington. Navy Secretary Jones did not share Madison's apprehensions, but he, Rush, Monroe, and Campbell readily concurred in the President's plans. Armstrong, on the other hand, argued strenuously that Baltimore was of far greater strategic significance than Washington (admittedly true) and would therefore be the object of British attack. Madison understood Baltimore's importance but was aware as well that the destruction of Washington would better suit British vindictiveness and psychic needs. He therefore created, according to a plan drawn up by Monroe, a special capital military district under General William H. Winder, ordered ten thousand militiamen held in readiness, and instructed that arms be collected and defensive positions established in preparation for the expected assault.[3]

For seven weeks Armstrong and Winder accomplished nothing. The Secretary of War argued with state militia officers and attended to every detail except the defense of Washington, while Winder exhausted himself riding about his district in a frenzy of indecision over the likely place of attack. Though nearly 100,000 militiamen were on the rolls in neighboring states, they were, at Armstrong's insistence, neither called up nor organized in ways likely to be effective against a surprise attack. Madison watched this bungling anxiously and asked relevant, pointed questions about arms not gathered, troops not positioned, and road blocks not prepared, but received no satisfaction. Unwilling as a civilian to interfere any further in military plans, and perhaps still hoping that, as in the previous summer, the British would bluff and disappear, Madison permitted week after week to pass, knowing full well that the nation's capital was virtually defenseless. Though he took care, as Sérurier wrote, "to display great calmness and complete confidence in the power of the nation to face all dangers," Madison must have felt sick as he heard from an American prisoner exchange official that Admiral Cockburn had remarked: "I believe . . . that Mr. Madison will have to put his armor on and fight it out, I see nothing else left."[4]

On August 17, the time, place, and means of "fighting it out" became evident: a British fleet of more than fifty vessels, including twenty transports carrying four thousand troops, commanded by a tough professional, General Robert Ross, anchored at the mouth of the Patuxent River, thirty-five miles southeast of Washington. That very day, though Dolley Madison had written Mrs. Gallatin to "be of good cheer my precious," the Gallatin silver plate had been carried out of town for safekeeping. When news of the British landing reached Washington the next morning, Madison, Monroe, and Winder issued a flurry of orders to position the chaotic American forces before the enemy. Monroe rode off on scouting trips, reporting sometimes twice a day to the President. Armstrong, on the other hand, scorned the bustle, insisting still that the British would march toward Baltimore. In fact, Ross and Cockburn moved very slowly: four days after their landing, they were but twenty-five miles from their ships, on the road toward Bladensburg—fifteen miles away and on the only dry-land approach to Washington. Not a shot had been fired at the British forces, nor had even a tree been felled across their path. Their march through open country on a hot day, one soldier wrote, resembled a summer picnic. Four days after the landing, Madison still thought it unlikely the British would come as far as Washington without cavalry and artillery and with as few as four thousand troops—unless, he added warily, the enemy "count on the effect of boldness and celerity on his side, and the want of precaution on ours."[5]

The next morning, Monday, August 22, as the alarm that the British would move toward the capital increased, Madison ordered government archives taken from the city and moved Virginia and Maryland militia toward Bladensburg. That afternoon he decided to visit the army, to encourage it, by his presence, to defend the capital. He anxiously asked Dolley if she was afraid to stay in the White House alone. She said she had no fear but for him and that she would see that "Cabinet papers, public and private," were neither lost nor destroyed. Madison then rode off with Rush, Jones, and three aides. They crossed the east branch of the Potomac, then went about ten miles, to near Old Fields, Maryland, where shortly after dark they met Armstrong, Winder, and some of the troops. Madison, Rush, and Armstrong spent the night at the Williams house, a mile west of the camp, while Jones slept in the tent of Captain Joshua Barney, who commanded a group of five hundred tough sailors eager to fight the enemy. The next morning, Madison reported in a pencil-scrawled note to his wife, was spent "among the troops who are in high spirits and make a good appearance." At first, General Winder and the President expected the enemy to "retreat to their ships," but after Madison questioned two British deserters, he wrote more alarmingly to Dolley: she "should be ready at a moment's warning" to enter her carriage and leave the city, because the enemy was stronger than anticipated and "it might happen that they would reach the city with intention to destroy it." After a hurried dinner at Williams', Madison, Jones, and Armstrong returned to Washington, as Ross's army, unknown to them, moved to within three miles of the camp.

That night a stream of excited callers knocked at the President's door. Virginia militia officers, seeking arms and instructions, were sent to the armory or to Armstrong. At nine o'clock General Winder came by, utterly exhausted and still unable to collect his forces or decide where to post them; nor, as had been true for five days, had he harassed the enemy march in any way. After wearing out three horses that day, Winder injured himself by falling into a ditch on his way back to camp. He nonetheless stayed up, personally supervising plans to blow up the bridge over the east branch of the Potomac, and slept but an hour or two that night. About midnight a note reached the White House from the also exhausted Monroe, acting as chief scout. "The enemy are in full march for Washington," he reported, and advised destruction of bridges and removal of records. He then galloped off to Bladensburg, to alert forces there. Meanwhile Madison approved the carriage his wife had loaded with the cabinet papers, but saw that it would be impossible to get wagons to carry away their personal possessions. Alarming, too, was the hostility expressed toward the President, and the "disaffection" that, Dolley wrote, "stalks around us." She was determined, she told her husband, not to leave Washington until she knew he was safe and could leave with her. What few hours they were able to sleep that night were the last they ever had in the White House.[6]

Early the next morning, August 24, came a message from the distraught Winder: he had "very threatening" news, and needed, Madison saw as he read the note, "the speediest counsel." The President rode off at once to Winder's camp, near the Navy Yard bridge, southeast of the White House. Monroe, Jones, and Rush also arrived promptly, and Monroe was sent off to Bladensburg to help position the Maryland militia already there. At ten o'clock a scout rode up, announcing the British had broken camp at daybreak and marched toward Bladensburg. Secretaries Armstrong and Campbell finally arrived, Armstrong taking no further part in the consultations beyond remarking, Madison noted, that "as the battle would be between militia and regular troops, the former would be beaten." When Campbell spoke privately to the President of his concern at Armstrong's "great reserve . . . on so critical an occasion," Madison told Armstrong explicitly to proceed to Bladensburg to give Winder any aid he could, and that he (Madison) would come to remove any "difficulty on the score of authority." Armstrong left immediately, following Winder and his troops. The British, though, already had a crucial head start on the march to the place everyone knew would be the battlefield. Madison, carrying a pair of dueling pistols Campbell had given him, and Rush went to the marine barracks and approved Jones's order for Captain Barney and his sailors to go to Bladensburg, then set off themselves. On the way, Madison's horse went lame, and he borrowed an unfamiliar mount for the rest of the hour's ride to Bladensburg. The President's party rode past tired, hurriedly assembled militia, toward the center of town, where they expected to find Winder. Instead, a sentry warned them, barely in time to avoid their capture, that the British had reached Bladensburg first and that Winder and his staff were on a nearby hilltop.

There, overlooking the town, Madison and Rush joined Armstrong, Monroe, and the commanding general, who was in a state of near collapse. Madison asked the still sulking Armstrong if he had conferred with Winder; he said he had not, but would do so if ordered to by the President. The two men rode up to Winder, but Madison's strange horse, frightened by gunfire and rockets, plunged and reared so much he could not hear the conversation. Now, in early afternoon and with the battle begun, the President told the cabinet members they should withdraw, leaving matters to the military leaders. Actually, the battle took place in stages, without overall direction from the incapacitated Winder or anyone else. The British regulars pushed ahead, driving first one detachment of militia and then another before them. Almost twice as many American as British troops were on the field, but they were undisciplined, ill-armed, and positioned so badly that the British defeated them easily. Only Barney's sailors, the last to meet the enemy, fought resolutely and inflicted heavy casualties, but by then it was too late. The American army was soon in hasty retreat, while the British paused for two hours to gather their forces. Winder at first had some hope of making another stand, before the Capitol, but his army had dispersed in too many directions. Washington was lost after a battle costing its defenders twenty-six dead and fifty-one wounded. The attackers lost perhaps one hundred dead and three or four hundred wounded.[7]

Madison and Rush watched anxiously until "it became manifest that the battle was lost," and then, in late afternoon, as the hot, sultry prestorm weather became more stifling, returned to the capital on roads choked with soldiers and refugees. They found the White House deserted, though their supper was waiting on the table, as Dolley Madison had left it. She had departed hurriedly at three o'clock, having at the last minute found a wagon to carry off the silver, the much-admired velvet curtains, more papers, a few books, a small clock, and, cut from its frame, a full length portrait of General Washington by Gilbert Stuart. Left behind, Dolley later reported, was "everything else belonging to the public, our own valuable stores of every description, a part of my clothes, and all the servants' clothes, etc, etc." While Rush went to see his family, Madison and General John Mason, son of Madison's old friend George Mason, and a prominent, wealthy resident of the District of Columbia, took only a quick look about the deserted White House, knowing that almost certainly the great center hall with its handsome furnishings and large lamps, the huge sideboard in the dining room, Dolley Madison's delicate-appearing parlor, the "immense and magnificent" oval room with its red-cushioned chairs and large sofas, and the thousands of dollars worth of fine wines in the cellar would be reduced to rubble and ashes. The President sent a hurried note to Secretary Jones, who, after seeing to the removal or destruction of stores at the Navy Yard and the burning of the nearly completed warships on the ways, had gone to the Carroll residence in Georgetown to meet his family and Dolley Madison. With British forces expected momentarily, Madison asked everyone to meet at the nearest Potomac River crossing. Then, according to Sérurier, who watched from his embassy sanctuary across from the White House, Madison "coolly mounted his horse," and with Mason, Rush, and their servants, rode off to the ferry.

At the landing, not finding Dolley and the Joneses, and not sure whether they had already crossed or had gone elsewhere, Madison sent another note to them, appointing a rendezvous on the Virginia side, and crossed the river himself, in the gathering dusk. In the ferry and on the ride up the Virginia shore, as Rush later recalled, they saw "columns of flame and smoke ascending throughout the night . . . from the Capitol, the President's house, and other public edifices, as the whole were on fire, some burning slowly, others with bursts of flame and sparks mounting high up in the horizon. . . . If at intervals the dismal sight was lost to our view, we got it again from some hilltop or eminence where we paused to look at it." In fact, Ross and Cockburn, after entering the deserted city and finding the Navy Yard already in flames, had fired the Capitol about nine o'clock, and moved on to the White House. There the impudent Cockburn, who had exchanged insults with people around Chesapeake Bay for over a year, sat down to the meal still on the table and drank to "Jemmy's health, which was the only epithet he used whenever he spoke of the President," one Washingtonian reported. After taking as mementos an old hat of Madison's and the cushion off Dolley's chair, about which he "added pleasantries too vulgar . . . to repeat," he ordered his marines to surround the house, and with great torches, set a fire in each of the windows, "so that an instantaneous conflagration took place and the whole building was wrapt in flames and smoke." The next day the British burned other public buildings, the bridges across the Potomac, the printing office of *The National Intelligencer* ("so that the rascals cannot any longer abuse my name," Cockburn reported), and a few homes from which they had been shot at; otherwise they respected private property. Cockburn told some citizens that "you may thank old Madison for this [destruction]; it is he who has got you into this scrape. . . . We want to catch him and carry him to England for a curiosity."[8]

In a darkness relieved by the flames of Washington and a violent thunderstorm, Madison, Rush, and Mason rode around through Falls Church toward Wiley's Tavern, near the Great Falls, where they had arranged to meet Dolley Madison and the Joneses. The President stopped, however, about midnight at Salona, at the home of the Reverend John Maffitt, five miles short of Wiley's. Dolley, meanwhile, had, unknown to her husband, stopped only a mile away, at Rokeby, with her friend Matilda Love, whose husband was away with his militia company. Both the President and First Lady, at any rate, spent the night comfortably, with friends. The next morning Madison rode back to Falls Church, looking for his family, and then returned to Salona, where he learned Dolley, still with the Joneses, had gone by on the way to Wiley's. Though in a hurry, Madison and Rush were forced to take refuge for a time from a furious windstorm that had both fanned the flames in Washington and frightened the British forces back toward their ships. Riding on through the bluster and rain, they were overtaken by a Navy Department clerk seeking orders for disposal of 136 barrels of powder he had removed from Washington. In early evening the party finally reached Wiley's Tavern, where they found Dolley Madison, the Jones family, and others. Totally uncertain of the enemy intentions, and impeded by more violent weather, Madison had the women and children wait at Wiley's while, about midnight, after a brief rest, he, Rush, Jones, Mason, and some dragoon escorts set out for Conn's ferry, above the Great Falls, to return to Maryland and to find, and gather if necessary, the dispersed army. Unable to cross the raging storm-swollen river at night, Jones returned to Wiley's to see to the safety of the families, while the President and his companions waited, wet and tired, until daybreak, when they crossed to the Maryland side.

Learning that Winder and portions of his army were at Montgomery courthouse (Rockville) fifteen miles northwest of Washington, Madison pushed on to there, arriving about 6 P.M., only to find Winder (and Monroe, who had rejoined the army) had left a few hours before, headed toward Baltimore to help defend that city. Madison and Rush had been in the saddle for nearly eighteen hours, but they nonetheless rode another ten miles to Brookville, to the home of Henrietta Bentley, who though a Quaker pacifist, had cared for soldiers and refugees all day long. There, according to Margaret Smith, "at bedtime the President had arrived and all hands went to work to prepare supper and lodgings for him, his companions and guards—beds were spread in the parlour. . . . All the villagers, gentlemen and ladies, young and old, thronged to see the President. He was tranquill as usual, and though much distressed by the dreadful event which had taken place, not dispirited." Aware that the British were not pursuing northward, before going to bed Madison wrote hurriedly to Monroe, asking advice about joining the army (camped a few miles farther north) or returning to Washington. Riders went as well to Frederick, Maryland, ordering Secretaries Armstrong and Campbell to return toward the capital.

The next morning the good news arrived: the British "were out of Washington and on the retreat to their ships." Madison wrote his wife that he, Monroe, and Rush would return to Washington at once and that "you will all of course take the same resolution." The President left the hospitable Mrs. Bentley's, and about five o'clock in the afternoon of Saturday, August 27, re-entered the distressed, ravaged city, after an absence of slightly less than three days. Since the morning of August 22, when the President had inspected the army east of Washington, he had been in the saddle many hours each day for six days, often in a great hurry or agitation, and with but a few hours, if any, sleep each night. Though stories later circulated by political enemies of Madison's panic-stricken flight and refuge in a slave's hovel were fabrications, the strenuous days and restless nights were a severe trial to a sixty-three-year-old man always weakened by the heat and unhealthy air of a tidewater summer. Not knowing "where we are in the first instance, to hide our heads," as Madison had written Dolley, he accepted the devoted Rush's offer of a roof and went to his house in the Six Buildings. There, after a conference with Monroe assigning him military command in Washington in the absence of Armstrong and Winder, Madison finally had a good night's rest.[9]

The anxious days were not over, however, because the next morning, Sunday, August 28, Madison learned that the violent explosion heard the previous evening was Fort Washington, guarding the Potomac approaches to the District of Columbia, being blown up by its commanding officer, who never fired a shot at the approaching British warships. The city of Alexandria, defenseless under British guns, capitulated and gave as ransom to avoid bombardment the hundreds of tons of tobacco, flour, and merchandise aboard seventy-one ships in its harbor. Alarm spread anew in Washington. "Every hour brings a different rumour," Mrs. Smith wrote, and "the English frigates . . . it was supposed only waited for a wind to come up to the city." Madison, with Monroe and Rush, saddled up to inspect the damaged buildings and to plan again the defense of the city. Secretary Jones soon joined them, telling Madison his wife was safe, still at Wiley's Tavern awaiting word from her husband. The President stopped at his house on F Street, now occupied by the Cuttses, and wrote Dolley of the new alarm: bargeloads of British sailors might soon menace Washington, so "it will be best for you to remain in your present quarters" rather than have to flee again, "which I find would have a disagreeable effect." On the other hand, if the threat to Washington diminished, for the sake of the city's morale, "you cannot return too soon."[10]

Madison then rode past the White House, "in ashes, not an inch but its cracked and blackened walls remained," and other public buildings burned but not so thoroughly destroyed. On Capitol Hill dead horses still lay about the grounds where they had fallen, and four or five houses, including Gallatin's, were gutted. The Capitol, reduced to a shell, was a melancholy sight: "Those beautiful pillars in that Representatives Hall were cracked and broken, the roof, that noble dome, painted and carved with such beauty and skill, lay in ashes in the cellars beneath the smouldering ruins, [all was] yet smoking." While Madison observed this scene, Dr. William Thornton rode up, saying that many citizens of Washington and Georgetown were "violently irritated at the thought of our attempting to make any more futile resistance . . . [and] were preparing to send a deputation to the British commander for the purpose of capitulating." "The President," Monroe reported tersely, "forbade the measure."

He was determined to resist any further British invasion and rode about "animating and encouraging the troops and citizens not to despair." After he and Monroe had ordered cannon placed along the Potomac, they returned to the Cutts house, where they were surprised to find Dolley Madison, safe, well, and scornful of both British marauders and Americans who would surrender to them. She had left Wiley's upon receipt of Madison's letter from Brookville and, cheered on by people along the way, driven to the F Street house in a borrowed carriage. The Madisons decided to live with the Cuttses for the time being, and while Mrs. Thornton came over from next door to drink tea, eleven dragoons bedded down outside on straw to guard the humble headquarters of the United States government.[11]

Early the next afternoon, when Armstrong and Campbell reached Washington (nearly forty-eight hours after Madison, Monroe, and Rush had returned), the cabinet met to further encourage the defense of the city. Commodore Rodgers and other naval officers stiffened militia resistance and organized bands of sailors to patrol the Potomac. Monroe later testified that "if by any casualty the President's return had been delayed 24 hours," the populace of the district would have panicked and surrendered disgracefully. Less welcome was the return of Armstrong, whom the citizens blamed for the destruction of the city. Deputations came to Madison declaring "that every officer would tear off his epauletts if General Armstrong was to have anything to do with them," and one officer "refused [Armstrong's] proffered hand and denounced his conduct" when he appeared at the militia encampment. The President told the officers immediately that Armstrong would issue no further orders, and rode off at long last to confront the sulking, insubordinate secretary.

After pointing out that "threats of personal violence had . . . been thrown out against us both, but more especially against him," Madison asked Armstrong what could be done to prevent "any convulsion at so critical a moment." Armstrong alleged the charges against him were based on "the most palpable falsehoods," but he was, in the public interest, willing either to resign or simply "retire from the scene." Madison agreed that the latter course was preferable and prepared to end the interview, but Armstrong persisted in justifying his conduct. The President agreed in part, but said he "could not in candour say that all that ought to have been done had been done and in proper time." When Armstrong still "returned to an exculpation of himself," Madison spoke bluntly: the secretary had failed utterly to propose plans to defend the city, and by his petulance, had impeded the plans of others. He had, in particular, contrary to the decision of the cabinet, failed to bring arms and equipment from distant depots to ones convenient for the defense of the District of Columbia. The militia, Madison observed scornfully, had had to go all the way to Harper's Ferry for arms. After remarking that only his great desire to "preserve harmony and avoid changes" had so long reconciled him to Armstrong's insubordination, the President virtually ordered him out of town. He left the next morning and submitted his resignation from Baltimore. Monroe took over formally as Secretary of War.[12]

The angry removal of Armstrong, the easy British capture of Washington, and the sometimes ludicrous efforts and movements of those responsible for its defense have spawned charges of blame for its destruction. Of General Winder, the military commander, Henry Adams said he was incapable "either to organize, fortify, fight or escape. When he might have prepared defences, he acted as scout; when he might have fought, he still scouted; when he retreated, he retreated in the wrong direction; when he fought, he thought only of retreat; and whether scouting, retreating or fighting, he never betrayed an idea." Adams had no better opinion of Monroe: "As a scout the Secretary of State's services were hardly as valuable as those of a common trooper, for he was obliged to be more cautious; as a general his interference with the order of battle at Bladensburg" led justifiably to Armstrong's charge that he was a "busy and blundering tactician." Madison concurred in Monroe's severe judgment of Armstrong: "He wants a head fit for his station and, indolent except for improper purposes, he is incapable of that combination [cooperation] and activity which the times require." Finally, Leonard White, with his keen sense of administrative efficiency, has heaped abuse on Madison: as commander in chief he was "irresolute, weak in his judgment of men, unaware of his proper function, and incapable of giving direction to the course of events. . . . On horseback he followed Winder from place to place a couple of days, for what military or official purpose can hardly be imagined. . . . [He did not have] what Washington or Hamilton would have instantly supplied, a reasoned conception of function and duty that would have provided an intelligent means of coping with the emergency."[13]

Though the disastrous course of events affords substantial grounds for many of these charges, there was in each instance another side and extenuating circumstances. Winder was appointed late to his command, without any staff assistance, and utterly deprived of day-to-day support and counsel from the only man in a position to give it, the Secretary of War. Moreover, state authorities in Virginia, Maryland, and Pennsylvania, by jealously guarding their own militia, deprived Winder of control over the only substantial body of troops available. Consequently, when the crisis arrived, he had exhausted himself contending with problems virtually certain to be intractable. Nonetheless, his inability to surmount these difficulties, indeed his deterioration before them, is a mark of his merely ordinary capacities. Armstrong, on the other hand, was not so much incapable as invidiously placed. Monroe's incessant jealousy, perfectly evident to Armstrong, he knew undermined him with the President and left him feeling lost amid what he called "Virginia intrigue." Furthermore, as Jefferson observed, "were an angel from Heaven to undertake [the War Department] all our miscarriages would be ascribed to him. Raw troops, no troops, insubordinate militia, want of arms, want of money, want of provisions, all will be charged to want of management" in the Secretary of War. Though often Armstrong dealt amazingly well with these matters, his stubborn refusal to accept the opinion of his Virginia colleagues about the threat to the Chesapeake region, and his willingness to place his political advancement above either loyalty to the administration or success in the war effort, more than offset whatever virtues he brought to his office. The corroding uncertainty of his doubtful loyalty had by the summer of 1814 become an intolerable cancer at the administration's center.[14]

Monroe's role is more difficult to assess. He scouted, placed troops, and otherwise acted as a general or Secretary of War at least in part because there was desperate, obvious need. Loyally and earnestly he turned his hand to the tasks no one else undertook. As an officer under Washington and as governor of Virginia, he had had relevant military and executive experience. Possessing Madison's full confidence, and having in two years of war performed as *ad hoc* head of all departments of government, Monroe was a kind of executive vice president, invaluable to his chief and willing to undertake any assignment. On the other hand, he was ambitious and vain, willing to distort the record and blame others in order to justify his every deed. He tried especially to make it seem he had not sought promotions or undermined associates (especially Armstrong), when in fact he had done so. Furthermore, he wanted desperately to insure his standing as Madison's successor. Throughout the war, he hoped and worked for chances to do this by becoming a military hero. His uneven record as a planner and strategist suggests that he might have failed in such a role, but nevertheless his ambitions were honest: he thought his leadership would bring victory. His steadfast loyalty, his unceasing efforts, and his considerable capacities as an administrator and counselor were vital, making him Madison's indispensable right hand throughout the war. His faults, carefully self-controlled, never vicious, and usually resulting from too much rather than too little zeal, seem minor by comparison.[15]

Of the other members of the executive circle, only Treasury Secretary Campbell was weak. Though loyal and intelligent, he was too sick to meet the heavy demands upon him, and he knew virtually nothing of the intricacies of finance. Secretary of the Navy Jones was always cool, wise, and dependable, and Attorney General Rush, the President's constant companion throughout the crisis, was so thoroughly helpful and zealous that Madison henceforth considered him fully qualified for the most responsible government posts. Rufus King noted at this time that Rush "passes more time with . . . and is more consulted by the President than any other personage." Unhappily, neither Jones nor Rush was in a position to give crucial direction to the defense of the nation's capital. Dolley Madison, privy to all the President's anxieties, and as always the leader of the mood of the capital, acted with steady heroism from start to finish.

Madison's deficiencies were grave, though not always what his enemies and historians have charged. Sooner than any of his advisers, he warned of the likely motivation for and place of the British attack. As Monroe later observed, Washington "might have been saved, had the measures proposed by the President to the heads of departments on the first of July, and advised by them, and ordered by him, been carried into effect." Madison was, moreover, personally courageous during the crisis and exerted a steadying influence on those around him. For a man of sixty-three, in uncertain health, his physical exertions were remarkable if not foolhardy or heroic. His faults of conception lay mainly in supposing the militia could be mustered effectively *after* the British forces appeared, and in trusting military command to Winder. A Jackson or a Winfield Scott would almost certainly have foiled the hesitant, poorly executed British campaign against the capital. Madison must bear the blame for Winder's unfortunate appointment as well as for the retention of Armstrong during a period of crisis. Whatever uproar might have followed dismissal of the politically powerful Secretary of War, it would have been preferable to his vitiating presence. Furthermore, presuming, as is generally warranted by the record, that Madison *knew* the preparations he deemed essential to the defense of Washington were not being made, he failed as commander in chief in not correcting the situation by whatever means necessary. The dangers and liabilities of almost any course of action likely to lead to correction were as grave as Madison supposed, but it was nevertheless incumbent on him to *do something*. The events of the summer of 1814 illustrate all too well the inadequacy in wartime of Madison's habitual caution and tendency to let complexities remain unresolved when no clear course of action was available. Though such inclinations are ordinarily virtues, in crises, as a Churchill or a Franklin Roosevelt would sense immediately, they are calamitous.

Madison's fault, however, was more profound than personal predisposition or the accident of being in the wrong position at the wrong time. Shortly after the President's return to Washington, Navy Secretary Jones, who had worked with him closely for a year and a half and had been with him almost constantly during the preparations, attack, and flight, observed that "the President is virtuous, able and patriotic, but . . . he finds difficulty in accommodating to the crisis some of those political axioms which he has so long indulged, because they have their foundation in virtue, but which from the vicious nature of the times and the absolute necessity of the case require some relaxation." That is, it was, ironically, Madison's very republican virtue which in part unsuited him to be a wartime president. His understanding of executive conduct did

not require or even allow him *singlehandedly* to make up for the reluctance of the people to be ready to defend themselves, for the hesitations
of the states to adopt forthright measures, for the ineffectiveness of other
executive officers, or for the failure of Congress to authorize and pay for
a sufficient war machine. To have done so would, according to Madison's
"political axioms," have corroded every virtue necessary to republican
government: a responsible citizenry, vital state governments, self-reliant
public servants, and respect for legislative leadership. It was, of course, impossible for him to be a Caesar or a Cromwell, but it was also against his
nature and deeply held principles to become even a William Pitt or a
Hamilton.[16]

Earnest Congressmen such as Nathaniel Macon, ex-President Jefferson,
and even, in a lesser way, Gallatin himself managed, with good luck
and without becoming gravely irresponsible, to evade the confrontation
of republican pieties with the hounds of war thrust painfully and unavoidably on Madison by British arms in the summer of 1814. Madison believed,
with much justification, that he could not conduct a war to validate a republican independence in the manner of an imperial proconsul without
destroying that cause in the process. Had he done that, his failure would
have been a moral one, permanently disastrous to the country. As it was,
he only failed, pathetically in many ways, to find the proper blend, discerned by Washington and Lincoln, of stern, vigorous leadership and of
republican deference necessary in wartime. The result was a mere temporary anxiety and destruction, perhaps a small price to pay to save the
vital political character of the nation. Just before the war Richard Rush
had heard Madison observe that "the difference between our government
and others was happily this: that here the government had an anxious and
difficult task in hand, while the people stood at ease—not pressed upon,
not driven, . . . whereas elsewhere *government* had an easy time, and *the
people* to bear and do everything, as mere *ambition*, will, or any immediate impulse dictated." To Madison, whose mind Rush found "fertile and
profound in these sort of reflections," to preserve this blessing and this
bar to imperial oppressions and ambitions, was of transcending importance.[17]

On September 1, 1814, Madison issued a proclamation "exhorting all the
good people" of the United States "to unite in their hearts and hands . . . in
manful and universal determination to chastise and expel the invader."
Then, as the British forces withdrew from Alexandria and the Potomac,
he consulted with the cabinet on the annual message to Congress, summoned before the invasion of Washington to meet on September 19 to consider the grave state of the nation's finances. Despite panicky suggestions
that Congress meet in a safer place, such as Philadelphia or Lancaster, the
President insisted on a defiant meeting in Washington. He ordered the

Post Office and the Patent Office building, the only public structures not destroyed, made ready for Congress, and at the same time accepted French Minister Sérurier's offer to vacate Benjamin Tayloe's town house (now called the Octagon House, and still standing at New York and 18th) so it could be a temporary presidential residence. Other government offices were squeezed into neighboring houses as Washington residents moved temporarily to the country to make room for them and for Congressmen arriving for the early session. Within a month of its capture by the British, Washington was able, by making do, to accommodate the government, and by mid-October even Federalist Rufus King conceded that the capital might as well remain where it was. In thus carrying on, the Madison administration averted the flight and failure of confidence that was in fact the real objective of the British in attacking Washington.[18]

Not only did the administration prevent, as Madison put it in his message to Congress, anything more serious than a momentary interruption of "the ordinary public business at the seat of Government," but it learned as Congressmen rode into town, of three great victories. On September 13 and 14 the land and sea defenses of Baltimore, organized effectively by Madison's political foe, Senator-turned-General Samuel Smith, had turned back a determined British attack. Off Fort McHenry in Baltimore harbor on the early morning of September 14, Francis Scott Key, a Washington lawyer sent by Madison to arrange prisoner of war exchange, observed "by the dawn's early light" that the "star-spangled banner in triumph doth wave," proving that the British bombardment had failed. Then, on the morning Congress held its first session, came news that the powerful British force moving toward Albany from Montreal had been repulsed. Commodore Macdonough reported to the commander in chief, "The Almighty has been pleased to grant us a signal victory on Lake Champlain," and General Macomb wrote that after the British naval defeat, Wellington's 10,000 veterans under Sir George Prevost fought only a halfhearted battle and retreated "precipitately, leaving their sick and wounded behind." The most dangerous threat to American soil since the revolution had failed, and as Madison suspected, a turning point in the war had been reached.[19]

In his message to Congress the President took full advantage of these and other feats of arms in praising American military prowess and belittling British successes. The forces at Lake Champlain had been as intrepid as the immortal Perry on Lake Erie, while elsewhere the heroism of Brown, Scott, and Gaines attested to "the progressive discipline of the American soldiery." Jackson's "bold and skilful" operations in the South, furthermore, had taught the British and Indians they could not molest American settlements with impunity. Captain David Porter's gallant but losing defense of the *Essex* in a Chilean harbor led the President to proclaim that Porter had fought "till humanity tore down the colors which valor had nailed to the mast." Madison did not, however, underestimate the peril still confronting the nation: "Our enemy is powerful in men and in money, on the land and on the water. . . . He is aiming with his undivided force a deadly blow at our growing prosperity, perhaps at our national existence." The people, the President was sure, would face these dire and barbarous threats "with the undaunted spirit which in their revolutionary struggle defeated [Britain's] unrighteous projects." To give force to these exhortations, Madison called again for an enlargement of the regular army and reorganization of the militia to give "to that great resource for the public safety all the requisite energy and efficiency"— words that meant classifying the militia to make it subject to conscription.[20]

Madison made only passing reference to the most serious matter, the virtual collapse of the nation's fiscal system. He had known in midsummer, after a loan had failed, that further taxing or borrowing power would be needed to fight the war during the last half of 1814. Then, at the depths of the gloom over the capture of Washington, and before news of the successes at Baltimore and Lake Champlain, banks in New York and southward suspended specie payment. Moreover, without a national bank, the government was unable to summon or use efficiently the meager resources it did possess. The financial reports submitted to Congress by Secretary Campbell displayed both the desperate condition and his utter inability to contend with it. With Gallatin absent, and neither Madison nor Monroe qualified to handle fiscal intricacies, the adminstration floundered. Congress was equally helpless. It met in a bad temper, Secretary Jones reported, "grumbling at everything in order to avert the responsibility which they have incurred in refusing to provide the solid foundations for revenue and relying on loans, . . . and yet they expect the war to be carried on with energy." Senator Rufus King found disarray everywhere: "No plan for prosecuting the war, none for the restoration of the public credit are thought of or proposed. . . . Difficulties . . . proceed from the general want of confidence in the Administration. . . . [Congress] will authorize the President and his miserable assistants to call upon the Nation for their blood and money, reserving to themselves the exclusive direction of the expenditure of both. . . . Our rulers can neither make war, nor conclude Peace."[21]

Secretary of the Treasury Campbell reported to Congress that barely half of the money needed to pay for the war through 1814 was in hand, and that the whole of the cost in 1815 was unprovided for; the government needed desperately over $50 million more than it had any prospect of acquiring. Campbell offered no plan to Congress, and his resignation to the President. All proposals more or less foundered on the inability of the government to command the resources of the country and to avoid the vicious circle of inflation and lack of confidence feeding on each other. The plans, keen old Gouverneur Morris remarked, all were like "the project of putting a world on an Elephant's Back to stand on a Tortoise and he on nothing." As a new Secretary of the Treasury was soon to observe, "the wealth of the nation in the value and products of its soil, in all the acquisitions of personal property, and in all the varieties of industry" was very great indeed, but due to "a system of taxation . . . inadequate to form a foundation for public credit . . . and an absence of the means . . . to anticipate, collect and distribute the public revenue," the government suffered from "pecuniary embarrassment." Madison noted the "gloomy inferences," but relied on a combination of factors to tide the nation over the crisis. Paper money issued by a national bank would supply a medium of exchange, while an increase in taxes would "pump out" enough money to prevent serious inflation. With an eye toward confidence inspired by the recent victories, Madison thought some private capital would become available on terms, "though hard, not intolerable" and that the money market abroad would soon open up. These conjectures, vague hopes rather than clear plans of the sort Gallatin had so often furnished, circulated in Washington as Congress equivocated.[22]

Campbell's resignation, meanwhile, compelled Madison to make yet another major shuffle in his cabinet. Madison was pleased to learn that Alexander J. Dallas, an able, ardently Republican Philadelphia lawyer closely connected to Eastern financial circles, would accept a cabinet post now that the obnoxious Armstrong was gone. Madison appointed him to the Treasury on October 5. Dallas immediately proposed detailed and practical, if not miraculous, expedients—depending on a national bank to be controlled by the public—that both furnished guidance to Congress and restored some of the confidence Gallatin's ability had generally commanded from the nation's financiers. With diplomacy centering in Europe, Monroe chose to remain Secretary of War, and when New York Governor Tompkins declined the State Department lest political enemies at home destroy him in his absence, Monroe became acting Secretary of State as well. The faithful Jones, meanwhile, having performed services for nearly two years few other men in the country could have rendered, begged to retire to repair his health and private fortunes. In December Madison found a virtually unique specimen, a Republican, seafaring merchant from New England (and from Salem, Massachusetts, at that), Benjamin Crowninshield, and over his protestations, appointed him Secretary of the Navy. Crowninshield, Madison later observed, was not only of great value politically as a New Englander, but he "added to a stock of practical good sense, a useful stock of nautical experience and information, and an accommodating disposition." In these colleagues, and the increasingly valuable Rush, Madison had an able though not outstanding cabinet with which to conclude the war.[23]

While Congress frittered indecisively with war and fiscal measures, Madison waited impatiently for news from the peace negotiations at

Ghent. In June Gallatin, in London for two months in the spring of 1814, had observed firsthand Britain's intoxication with victory and read the daily diatribes of the British press. Madison was a contemptible tool of Napoleon, the *Courier* screamed, characterized by "exaggeration and falsehood, of coarseness without strength, of assertions without proof, of the meanest prejudices, and of the most malignant passions." The London *Times* intoned, "Oh, may no false liberality, no mistaken lenity, no weak and cowardly policy, interpose to save [the United States] from the blow! Strike! Chastise the savages, for such they are! . . . With Madison and his perjured set no treaty can be made. . . . Our demands may be couched in a single word—Submission!" Gallatin wrote of Britain's determination to persist in the war by mounting a fierce campaign against the American coast from Maine to New Orleans. He was sure, also, that no satisfaction could be obtained on impressment or other maritime grievances, and that the best the United States could hope for was "the *status quo ante bellum.*" Czar Alexander told Gallatin on June 17, moreover, that "England will not admit a third party to interfere in her disputes with you . . . on account of your former relations to her [the colonial state] which is not yet forgotten."[24]

Madison and Monroe recognized the force of Gallatin's reflections, and on October 4, instructed the peace commissioners that since restoration of peace in Europe made questions of maritime rights largely academic, they might ignore them and accept "the *status quo ante bellum* as the basis for negotiation." Word of this concession, proof that the administration would not let dogma prevent peace, was hurried off to Ghent and helped importantly to speed negotiations there when it arrived in late November. On October 8, however, as the President and his family sought unsuccessfully to make themselves comfortable in the Octagon House, George M. Dallas arrived from Ghent with bad news. At the first meetings in August with the American commissioners, their British counterparts had made demands that in effect treated the United States as a conquered nation: the United States was to cede to Britain most of Maine north of Penobscot Bay, to remove all fortifications and armed vessels from the Saint Lawrence River and Great Lakes, to give up its Newfoundland fishing rights, to acquiesce in an Indian "buffer state" including all the Northwest Territory except southern Ohio, and to yield to Britain a use of the Mississippi that would assure her domination of the Louisiana Territory as well of all lands to the west. The American commissioners unanimously rejected the British terms as "above all dishonorable to the United States in demanding from them to abandon territory and a portion of their citizens; to admit a foreign interference in their domestic concerns, and to cease to exercise their natural rights on their own shores and on their own waters." Gallatin wrote privately that Britain meant to acquire and hold New Orleans "as a sugar colony . . .

commanding all our Western country both in a political and in a commercial view. . . . [She] intends to strengthen and aggrandize herself in North America. . . . Our struggle will be longer and more arduous than I had anticipated." He and the other commissioners thought the negotiations had failed, and they expected to return home soon.[25]

Young Dallas also filled Washington drawing rooms with anecdotes of European personages. He declared that Czar Alexander was "the best bred gentleman in Europe." Compared to him, the British Prince Regent, who publicly insulted his estranged wife, was "a mere beefeater." Amid this gossip, Madison and Monroe struggled to find a means of honorable peace. They published both the "arrogant" British terms and their own conciliatory instructions to the American commissioners. Even Senator King recognized the absurdity of the British demands and admitted that their publication greatly strengthened the President's standing at home. Madison decided, as he wrote Jefferson, to rest on the *status quo ante bellum* instructions already sent to Ghent, and hope that "intelligence from this Country and the fermentations taking place in Europe" would compel the British cabinet to take a more moderate course. After hearing from Dallas that British Lord Chancellor Erskine had actually declared, "America is right and we are wrong in this war," Richard Rush expressed the administration's fondest wishes: "I am not without a hope that the events of Baltimore, Plattsburgh, and Champlain, with the drubbings that my Lord Wellington's heroes have received on the Niagara, will induce many people in England to Lord Erskine's way of thinking." Britain was in fact at this very time, and upon advice from Wellington himself, modifying her terms, but no word of this reached Washington for two more months. In the meantime, threats of domestic insurrection, feeding on fears of Britain and the prospect of a long, exhausting war, grew stronger.[26]

In early October 1814 Federalist members of the House and Senate met secretly at Crawford's boardinghouse near Capitol Hill to lay their course for the pending session. Under Rufus King's cautious guidance they decided to "unite in the adoption of vigorous measures to repel the invaders of the country and to protect its essential rights and honor." They would support granting of supplies, increasing taxes, and building "sloops of war . . . to cruize against the Enemy," but they declared against Monroe's "scheme of conscription" for enlarging the army. Though they called the declaration of war "unnecessary and highly inexpedient" and asserted that "the incapacity of the Executive Government" was so gross that "nothing short of an entire change of the Heads of Departments" would allow either victorious war or lasting peace, the majority of the Federalists in Congress had decided to be a responsible opposition. Many, however, including Congressman Pickering, disavowed this moderation.

To King's earnest advocacy of his course, for example, Gouverneur Morris replied bitterly, "Anything like a Pledge by Federalists to carry on this wicked War, strikes a Dagger to my Heart. . . . How often, in the name of God, how often will you agree to be cheated? What are you to gain by giving Mr. Madison Men and Money?" Morris concluded that "an Union of the commercial states to take care of themselves, leaving the War, its Expense and its Debt to those choice Spirits so ready to declare and so eager to carry it on, seems to be now the only rational Course."[27]

In much of New England the extreme opponents of the war and the administration held power. On October 17 the Massachusetts legislature issued the invitation to the Hartford Convention. Connecticut and Rhode Island accepted, but to Madison's great relief, Vermont and New Hampshire refused. Meanwhile, smuggling and collusion with the enemy continued on the land and sea frontiers; New England governors refused again to use their militia for national purposes; and in the fall elections Federalist candidates were triumphant. William Wirt, visiting Madison as these events became known in Washington, wrote his wife that "the President . . . looks miserably shattered and woe-begone. . . . His mind is full of the New England sedition. He introduced the subject and continued to press it—painful as it obviously was to him." Sérurier, in almost daily contact with Madison, observed a little later that only "the great firmness of the President and the wisdom of the counsel he is given" enabled a government so badly armed to fight alone against England "with so active a hostile faction at the heart of the nation." Madison and Monroe took the precaution of sending Colonel Thomas Jesup, the hero of Lundy's Lane, to Connecticut on "recruiting duty," with instructions to cooperate militarily with the loyal Governor Tompkins of New York in case of an armed uprising. The President, Monroe wrote Jesup, "has no doubt that if traitorous designs are disclosed, the virtuous citizens . . . will separate from and punish the traitors."[28]

At the same time, English newspapers arrived, exulting that Washington, "the proud seat of that nest of traitors," had been destroyed, and hinting broadly, as they had for years, that Britain counted on the good sense of the Eastern states to separate from the mad Virginians and renew connections with England that would assure peace and prosperity. Then Madison got sick again from working in Washington during hot summer and fall months usually spent at Montpelier. The sense of a house collapsing about him heightened on November 23 when he learned that Vice President Gerry had died of a lung hemorrhage while riding in his carriage to the Senate chamber. Federalists again scented power. "If Mr. President Madison would resign," one wrote, "now that Mr. Gerry is no more, a president of the Senate might be chosen, who would . . . do honor to the nation," but he added that "we however can hardly hope that Mr. Madison will have the magnanimity to give up his place." A Federalist newspaper hinted more darkly that many wished Madison "was quietly asleep with the late vice president," while Congressman Hanson intoned that "the cold, icy hand of death is on this people." Only if Madison stepped aside and let the Senate choose Rufus King its president pro tem, and thus let King become chief executive, Hanson declared, could the nation be saved. The election of John Gaillard of South Carolina, an uninspiring "Old Republican," to head the Senate frustrated the succession hopes of the Federalists, but did little to strengthen Madison's standing in the country.[29]

Beset by these difficulties, Madison opened his heart to an old friend, Wilson Cary Nicholas, newly elected governor of Virginia:

> You are not mistaken in viewing the conduct of the Eastern States as the source of our great difficulties in carrying on the war; as it certainly is the greatest, if not the sole, inducement with the enemy to persevere in it. The greater part of the people in that quarter have been brought by their leaders, aided by their priests, under a delusion scarcely exceeded by that recorded in the period of witchcraft; and the leaders are becoming daily more desperate in the use they make of it. Their object is power. If they could obtain it by menaces, their efforts would stop there. These failing, they are ready to go to every length. . . . Without foreign co-operation, revolts and separation will hardly be risked. . . . The best may be hoped, but the worst ought to be kept in view. In the meantime the course to be taken by the Government is full of delicacy and perplexity, and the more so under the pinch which exists in our fiscal affairs, and the lamentable tardiness of the Legislature in applying some relief.[30]

As Congress dawdled through November and December, neither passing nor rejecting administration proposals, word came from Ghent that though British demands still far exceeded anything the Americans could accept, enough vague signs of conciliation had appeared to keep the negotiations going. At the same time, the paralyzing anxiety over the destination of the powerful British forces aboard warships in the western Atlantic came to an end: about ten thousand elite troops under the Duke of Wellington's brother-in-law, Sir Edward Pakenham, well armed and with massive naval support, had gathered at Jamaica for a descent on the Gulf Coast, with New Orleans their obvious ultimate objective.

Luckily, the war on the southern frontier had recently taken a turn for the better, under the forceful Tennessean Andrew Jackson. Though American forces in 1812 and 1813 had wrested Mobile in the west and Amelia Island in the east from the weak, almost nominal authority of Spain, by mid-1813 Federalist cries of aggression against a nation not at war with the United States, and fears that invasion of Florida would hinder Russian mediation efforts, caused the administration to back off. Amelia Island was abandoned, and Jackson's forces, mobilized to take Pensacola, were halted. Jackson found full employment for his mixed army, including units led by Davy Crockett and Sam Houston, however, against the Creek Indians who had, at Tecumseh's urging, raised the tomahawk against the United States. Jackson revenged an Indian massacre at Fort Mims with a bloody victory at Horseshoe Bend, and by the summer of 1814 was a major general in the regular army with full authority in the Southwest. He had conquered the Creeks and forced them to sign a treaty ceding most of the present state of Alabama to the United States. Respected, and thought by his troops to be invincible, Jackson ignored Spanish nonbelligerence and proceeded to reinforce Mobile and neutralize Pensacola, thus dooming the last hope of the Indians for foreign support and thwarting British attempts to install themselves along the Gulf Coast.

Though still nervous that Jackson's forays in Spanish territory would impede peace negotiations in Europe, Madison and Monroe nonetheless admired his boldness and began sending men and supplies down the Mississippi to arm Jackson for the British attack known in November 1814 to be aimed at New Orleans. By the end of the year the splendid British army was ashore a few miles from New Orleans, and Jackson gathered his forces and fortified the city to meet it. The fate of the entire Mississippi valley was at stake.[31]

Through the holiday season and the first weeks of 1815 the Madisons were anxious, tormented, and often discouraged. Dolley Madison wrote the day after Christmas that "the prospect of Peace, appears to get darker and darker. . . . [Britain] will not make Peace unless they are obliged to, and it is their policy," she and her husband had just learned from a letter John Adams had forwarded from his son, "to protract [the negotiations] as long as they can." Three days later, after Congress had rejected conscription and greater federal control over the militia, Dolley lamented, "I *will yet* hope we may have no more war—[but] if we do alass alass we are not making ready as we *ought to do*—Congress trifle away the most precious of *their days*—days that ought to be devoted to the defence of their *divided* country." To make matters worse, "an alarming fever" raged in Alexandria. Madison, Dolley added, "has not been well since we came to this house and our servants are constantly sick, owing to the damp cellar to which they are confined." Thus the social season had been cramped and gloomy. Furthermore, the Madisons learned through Gallatin that Payne Todd had lived frivolously and extravagantly in Europe, accepting little responsibility and indulging in every dissipation. They would have been even more upset could they have seen one of many early morning entries in John Quincy Adams' diary about goings-on in Ghent: "September 8, 3:45 A.M.—Just before rising, I heard Mr. Clay's company retiring from his chamber. I had left him with Mr. Russell, Mr. Beutzon, and Mr. Todd at cards." The only sources of cheer were prospects of moving in March, after Congress adjourned, to the brighter, healthier Seven Buildings, and the birth of a baby girl, Mary, to Anna Cutts and a boy to Lucy Todd.[32]

With the fever severely restricting New Year's Day celebrations, Madison waited impatiently for news from Hartford, New Orleans, and Ghent. Governor Strong's refusal to call out the Massachusetts militia to defend the district of Maine deepened the sense of impending disunion, which was also evident in letters addressed to Madison printed in Boston newspapers: "The bond of Union is already broken, broken by you and the shortsighted, selfish politicians who compose your councils," one writer charged. When Colonel Jesup, observing the Hartford Convention, reported that open acts of hostility could be expected any time, the President ordered New York and New England volunteers alerted "to repel the enemy and put rebellion down." Immediately after Madison sent these orders, on January 9, however, the resolves of the Harford Convention reached him. The danger of rebellion or secession seemed abated; though the convention had issued angry denunciations and proposed amendments to the Constitution, it had drawn back from calls to action by merely proposing another convention in June if the war continued. While many extremists deplored this relatively innocuous result, and some, like Timothy Pickering, were sure British bayonets at New Orleans would soon sunder the Union anyhow, Madison could take grim satisfaction that curses aimed at him had been substituted for acts of treason.[33]

Sunday, January 8, the day of Jackson's victory at New Orleans, and two weeks after peace had been made at Ghent, in fact began a month of incredible tension as well as "unusual and intense Frost" in Washington. *The National Intelligencer* announced on that day that British forces were at the gates of New Orleans and that Jackson stood waiting to meet them. "We shall be held in awful suspense as to the fate of that city," the paper concluded. Five days later Madison learned that Jackson had received needed reinforcements from Kentucky and Tennessee, and that he had declared martial law and made a mass levy of militia in New Orleans. Federalist papers cried tyranny and hinted repeatedly that the lack of news meant the administration was in fact withholding tidings of defeat. Dolley Madison wrote on the fourteenth that "the fate of New Orleans will be known today—on which so much depends." A week later, as twenty guests waited for dinner at the Octagon House, a servant called the President out of the room. Everyone waited speechless for him to come back with word from New Orleans. Instead he "soon returned with added gravity and said there was no news! Silence ensued. No man seemed to know what to say at such a crisis . . . and said nothing at all." During the meal, though grave-faced, Madison talked humorously with young George Ticknor of Boston about "religious sects and parties." Ticknor had the impression the President held beliefs virtually making him a Unitarian. At the end of January Madison had Jackson's report of a sharp but indecisive engagement and the positioning of his six thousand militiamen, regulars, "free men of color," and pirates behind breastworks. News of Jackson's ill-health revived Federalist innuendoes that the city would surely be lost and brought charges that "Madison, this man, if he deserves the name," who had brought "dishonor, disappointment, and disaster" to the country, should be impeached and punished. Neither Madison's peace of mind nor his standing in certain financial circles was enhanced by his veto, on the day the tense news arrived from New Orleans, of a national bank which, though Madison generally approved a recharter, in the Congressional version so ill-guarded public interests that its dangers outweighed some few benefits.[34]

On Saturday, February 4, however, the astounding word arrived: in an early morning battle, courageous, disciplined redcoats had moved rank upon rank toward Jackson's men, who were ready and waiting, with rifles cocked and cannon loaded, behind their battlements, stretching less than a mile between the Mississippi and an impenetrable cypress swamp. Confined to a frontal assault, the British could hope only to overpower or frighten their enemy. Jackson's men held their ground and kept up a steady, thunderous fire. By 8:30 A.M. the British retired, having lost seven hundred killed (including Pakenham and most of the other senior officers), fourteen hundred wounded, and five hundred captured. Though artillery accounted for most of the slaughter, one observer reported as well that "the dead and wounded were many of them perforated by from two to four Rifle Balls." Only seven Americans were killed and six wounded. The disproportion, Jackson wrote Monroe, "must . . . excite astonishment, and may not everywhere be fully credited." Jackson's careful preparation, plus the British troops' brave disdain for death, learned in nearly ten years fighting Napoleon, had resulted in a carnage never before known on an American battlefield.[35]

For Madison, the result not only rescued his administration from despond and disgrace but also achieved a goal he had sought for thirty-five years. Since he had written to John Jay during the dark days of the revolution that "the clear indications of nature and providence, and the general good of mankind" dictated that American settlers should have free use of the Mississippi (see Chapter VI), Madison had worked for American possession of New Orleans and the great valley it controlled. Now, with Spain prostrate, France conquered, and Britain utterly defeated at the very gates of New Orleans itself, 150 years of strife and changing control had ended: the red sea of British dead created by the fire of Jackson's men dramatically and finally underscored American possession of the Western empire. Madison knew the cheering throngs that filled the streets of Washington, illuminated by thousands of candles and torches that Saturday night, were celebrating the most important triumph of American arms since Yorktown.

Then, nine days later, a messenger galloped into Washington with news that a British sloop-of-war had arrived in New York with a peace treaty signed by the commissioners and already ratified by the Prince Regent. Expecting a report that the negotiations had broken down, Madison was delighted at the treaty Monroe handed to him in the front hall of the Octagon House on February 14: it contained not one of the humiliating conditions insisted upon by the British the previous August, and thus restored all American territory occupied by British forces, recognized American rights on the Mississippi, the Great Lakes, and the Newfoundland fishing banks, placed the two countries on equal grounds commercially, and by neither confirming nor denying impressment and other maritime rights, left these matters to the almost surely benign consequences of peace. Madison learned further from Gallatin and John Quincy Adams that the British cabinet had withdrawn its tough terms after the Duke of Wellington had declared the conquest of the United States impossible and after it saw it could not maintain the war without vast, unpopular expenditures. The President thus knew that though the Treaty of Ghent seemed to settle nothing, merely returning to the *status quo ante bellum* and ignoring the maritime grievances so often proclaimed as the cause of the war, in fact the United States, by standing up to Britain, had won a second war of independence. The Senate ratified the treaty unanimously, and on February 17 Madison declared the conflict ended. Celebrations again resounded throughout the nation, as not only were its independence and honor vindicated but, with dazzling trade prospects opened, an era of growth and prosperity seemed assured.[36]

Dolley Madison wrote in early March that since "our glorious peace . . . my brain has been harried with noise and bustle. Such overflowing rooms I never saw before—I sigh for repose." Senator W. T. Barry of Kentucky, however, thought "Queen Dolley" was in high spirits, and her husband so "much elated [over the] glory" of American arms and the "glad tidings of peace" that he was "inspired . . . with new life and vigor." Others, though, enjoyed little presidential hospitality. Harrison Gray Otis, bringing the Hartford Convention resolves to Washington, wrote that "we have received no invitation from Madison—what a mean and contemptible little blackguard." At a reception, which Otis found "all tinsel and vulgarity," his scorn and disappointment reached new heights; Madison, "the little pigmy, . . . shook in his shoes at our approach," Otis thought. Actually, as Jefferson remarked, Madison's "silent treatment" of the Hartford Convention "has shown the placid character of our constitution. Under any other their treasons would have been punished by the halter. We let them live as the laughing stocks of the world, and punish them by the torment of eternal contempt."

French Minister Sérurier observed that the position of Otis and his colleagues was "awkward, embarrassing, and lent itself cruelly to ridicule," because the United States had in fact gained tremendously from the war. American naval victories were "a prelude to the lofty destiny to which they are called on that element," and American military progress was so impressive that "three great attacks saw Wellington's best corps fall before their militia." More important, "three years of warfare have been a trial of the capacity of their institutions to sustain a state of war, a question . . . now resolved to their advantage. . . . Finally, the war has given the Americans what they so essentially lacked, a national character founded on a glory common to all." John Adams observed simply that the President had shown the American government could declare and fight war, make peace, and stand fully respected in the community of nations, proof of Madison's "long, laborious, able, and successful services" to the country.[37]

In notifying Congress of peace, Madison commented on long-range prospects: "Peace, at all times a blessing, is peculiarly welcome . . . at a period when the causes for the war have ceased to operate, when the government has demonstrated the efficiency of its powers of defense, and when the nation can review its conduct without regret and without reproach." He sensed that one era, obsessed with foreign wars and fraught with danger to the new republic, had ended, and that another, devoted to vigorous, peaceful growth, could now begin. John Quincy Adams had observed to the British commissioners at Ghent that he hoped they were signing "the last treaty of peace between Great Britain and the United States." Later, at a banquet given by the mayor of Ghent, Adams toasted the host city: "Ghent, the city of peace; may the gates of the temple of Janus, here closed, not be opened again for a century!" Madison echoed these sentiments three years later, when he remarked that "if our first struggle was a war of our infancy, this last was that of our youth; and the issue of both, wisely improved, may long postpone if not forever prevent, a necessity for exerting the strength of our manhood."[38]

Despite the bungling and defeats early in the war, the grave weakness of the nation during it, and even the apparently armisticelike peace, the circumstances of its conclusion, mirrored in the excited events in Washington in February 1815, produced a dramatic, gratifying effect. The surprise signing of the peace, after the British withdrew humiliating demands in response to blunt advice from Wellington and stiff bargaining by the able American commissioners, in every way buoyed American self-respect. The amazing success of New Orleans, added to the victories of the navy, the valiant battles at Niagara and Plattsburgh, and the injury inflicted on English trade by American privateers, cast the United States as a country fully able to take care of itself, even in a confrontation with the world's mightiest nation, flushed with victory and bitterly hostile. Finally, these glorious events, coming as they did when internal dissension and financial chaos threatened, and before the Madison administration had had to take repressive steps, seemed to vindicate the whole republican concept of government. This, of course, was Madison's only real war aim, and the crowning achievement of his public life.

The return of peace, the collapse of domestic defiance of the government, and the revived popularity of the administration enabled the presidential family to look forward to the end of nearly four years of being chained to duty. The cheerful, airy Seven Buildings, with the Treasury Department moved out, was made ready so the Madisons, Dolley wrote, could "get into the sunshine." She decorated elegantly, with the Gallatins' furniture, and soon had her wardrobe restored with finery imported from Europe. From large windows overlooking the street, she watched the parades of soldiers being mustered out of the army, and according to her nieces, waved to neighborhood children who came by to watch her feed her parrots. The Madisons' thoughts turned, too, to longer absences from Washington. Since October 1811 they had been away less than four months. Dolley wished longingly she could go to Paris with the Gallatins, and at the very least "indulged some hope" of seeing them in Philadelphia in the spring of 1815. The President, however, weary of formalities any visit imposed on him, wanted only to get to "his farm" as soon, and to stay there as long, as he could. Dolley somewhat petulantly resigned herself. "I see plainly," she wrote Hannah Gallatin, "that I deceived myself" in hoping to travel. "Washington and Orange forever rise up to impede my *fairer prospects*."[39]

Appointments, though, required the President's attention before he could leave for Montpelier. He returned Monroe, exhausted from overwork, to the State Department, and until William H. Crawford came home from his unhappy mission as Minister to France, turned War Department duties over to Secretary of the Treasury Dallas. Four of the successful Ghent commissioners were made ministers—J. Q. Adams to England, Gallatin to France, Jonathan Russell to Sweden, and James Bayard to Russia—while Clay chose to come home and resume his powerful post as Speaker of the House. Madison appointed three naval heroes, Rodgers, Hull, and Porter, to the Board of Navy Commissioners, and sent two others, Decatur and Bainbridge, to the Mediterranean to exact justice from the Algerine pirates. In reducing the army to ten thousand men, the President retained the general officers who had gained glory in the war. He permanently commissioned Jackson and Brown major generals, commanding the Southern and Northern Department respectively, Gaines, Scott, Ripley, and Macomb brigadiers, and named all six to a board to reorganize the army and recommend officers to be retained in the lower grades. Madison thus designated those who would lead the armed forces until the Civil War.[40]

The Madisons left on March 21 for an eleven-week vacation at Montpelier. Frequent reports from double-Secretary Dallas kept the President informed of the relatively smooth conversions of the War and Treasury departments to peacetime routine. In late April Madison resumed his semiannual visits to Monticello, where, he wrote Dallas, "I shall keep hold of the thread of daily communication with Washington." With the industrious, learned, ex-President, he happily poured over ten thousand books being packed for the trip to Washington, where they would become the basis for a new Library of Congress, to replace that burned by the British. Back at Montpelier in early May, Madison received the astonishing news of Napoleon's return from Elba and triumphant reception in Paris. "Should war ensue between Great Britain and France," the President wrote, "our great objects will be to save our peace and our rights from the effect of it; and whether war ensues or not, to take advantage of the crisis to adjust our interests with both." He hoped again, as he had for ten years, that the "competition between [France and England] in aggressions on us will be succeeded by rival dispositions to court our good will, or at least to cultivate our neutrality." Madison was pleased, therefore, when word arrived that British officers showed "the utmost courtesy toward the crews of our ships," even in British ports, that the British minister in Holland had reprimanded a captain who had merely threatened impressment, and that Gallatin and his colleagues had signed a commercial convention with Britain. At long last Britain had apparently forsaken bullying the United States and accepted her as an equal in the family of nations.[41]

In Washington for six weeks in June and July, Madison agreed to evacuation of occupied forts by British and American forces, exchange of prisoners of war, and other details of demobilization. He also settled a dispute between the prestigious Navy Board, composed of seagoing heroes, and the inconspicuous Secretary of Navy, in favor of the latter. The principle of civilian supremacy, as well as the need to "preserve that unity of action which is essential to the Executive trust," the President insisted, required that the board be responsible to the secretary, who in turn "must be understood to speak and act with Executive sanction." Assured that the return of peace had completely revived confidence in the government and that a remarkable prosperity seemed about to overtake the country, the Madisons returned to Orange with Anna Cutts and her five children for the months of August and September. News soon arrived, first from Richard Cutts in Boston and then from Dallas in Washington, of the "dreadful battle" at Waterloo in mid-June where, in a "carnage exceeding . . . anything in the history of battles," Wellington had triumphed over Napoleon, but with such losses himself that "a few such victories would leave the British without generals, and probably without troops." Though Madison regarded Napoleon as a bloodthirsty adventurer the world was well rid of, he feared as always that the complete triumph of England and the continental allies would embolden them not only to crush liberty in Europe but to turn their attention as well to the

New World. He and Jefferson agreed in hoping, as they exchanged their usual summer visits, that "overgrown [nations] may not advance beyond safe measures of power, [and] that a salutary balance may be ever maintained among nations." In any case, they concluded, reaffirming a conviction they had held for nearly half a century, "the less we have to do with the amities or enmities of Europe, the better." Madison underscored this conviction when he ordered Rush and Dallas, in Washington, to "divert" Joseph Bonaparte, the deposed king of Spain, from his intended incognito visit to Montpelier. "There is no claim of merit in that family on the American nation," the President observed bluntly, "nor any reason why its government should be embarrassed in any way on their account." Madison refused to be "a party to [Bonaparte's] concealment"; the ex-king could expect "protection and hospitality" in America, like any other immigrant, but nothing more.[42]

Anxiety continued, meanwhile, for the fate of Payne Todd, who had been in Europe for over two years. Crawford and Bayard had left England precipitately, due to Bayard's critical illness, taking with them Todd's baggage, but leaving him in London with Gallatin and Clay. Crawford stopped at Montpelier on his way to Georgia in early August, and reported the baggage, together with an expensive array of "gems of art and painting" Todd had bought, had been put ashore. Todd finally left England in late July and reached New York with Gallatin on September 1. Madison learned that Todd had run up a bill of $6,500 in Europe, drawing on Madison's credit with British bankers. Not included in this amount was a further $1,500 Todd had borrowed through Richard Cutts—whose name Todd "found it necessary to make use of . . . in preference to the President's or my Mother's"—for reasons not stated, but almost certainly to cover gambling losses. Through Gallatin's good offices, the President was able to cover the debts, but he was displeased with Todd's "heavy demand for expenses." Even worse, when Todd reached Montpelier in mid-September, it was apparent that though he was more handsome and courtly than ever, he was also on the verge of becoming, irredeemably, a dissolute fop, always late, full of excuses, and adept only at losing money playing cards. Even the usually indulgent Henry Clay had been forced to ask Todd, after he had irresponsibly failed to attend to his baggage, "Will you never gain any thing by experience?" He had become a classic example of the young American, warned of by Franklin and Jefferson, who was so dazzled by the courtly graces of Europe that he became unfit for useful life in his own country. From this time on Todd was increasingly a financial drain and psychic strain on both his mother and stepfather.[43]

During a leisurely fall in Washington, Madison considered with his cabinet the state of the world and the state of the nation. Gallatin's arrival in mid-October evoked thoughtful discussions of foreign policy questions that had confronted the Republican quadrumvirate—Jefferson, Madison, Gallatin, and Monroe—since the seventeen-eighties and nineties. In their minds Napoleon was a "restless spirit [who] left no hope of peace to the world," and whose selfish cynicism left no room for republican government. His attempt to establish "another Roman Empire, spreading vassalage and depravity over the face of the globe is not," Jefferson hoped, "within the purposes of Heaven." Yet, as Gallatin observed, the French Revolution had not been "altogether useless. There is a visible improvement in the agriculture of the country and the situation of the peasantry. The new generation belonging to that class, freed from the petty despotisms of nobles and priests, . . . have acquired an independent spirit, and are far superior to their fathers in intellect and information. [Though] still too much dazzled by military glory, . . . no monarch or ex-nobles can hereafter oppress them long with impunity." The Republican leaders had no doubt, on the other hand, that England continued to possess both the will and means to injure the United States, and that the victorious allies, no less than Napoleon, had "plunder" for their object and "shuffled nations together, or into their own hands, as if all were right which they feel a power to do." The President and his friends hoped, therefore, for France's revival. Only the English conversion to free trade under the pressure of her own self-interest, and the collusion of France in the reactionary schemes of Metternich, would shatter the Republican axiom, formulated as early as 1775, that for the United States, a powerful, preferably republican France was a vital counterweight to British hegemony and arrogance. But this far-reaching revolution in international affairs affected Monroe's administration, not Madison's.[44]

The President outlined domestic plans in his seventh annual message, reflecting fifteen years experience in making republican principles, abstract and doctrinaire in 1801, effective in national affairs. Madison hailed the reduction of the army, but he urged retention of its staff system, and compensation and honors for those released from service sufficient "to inspire a martial zeal for the public service upon every future emergency." He asked as well for the "gradual completion of works of defense," continued development of naval armaments, improvement of militia organization, and an enlargement of the military academy. A quick view of the nation's finances showed that swelling receipts had restored the nation's credit and would soon permit resumption of specie payment. Though Madison merely hinted in his message to Congress that a national bank "merited consideration," it was apparent he would support a detailed plan to be presented to Congress by Dallas on December 24, 1815. Madison reported that the national debt had trebled as a result of the war, but observed calmly its "amount will bear a gratifying comparison with the objects which have been attained, as well as with the resources of the country."

In reviewing the tariff, Madison stated the principle that guided him during the rest of his life: "However wise the theory may be which leaves to the sagacity and interest of individuals the application of their industry and resources, there are . . . exceptions to the general rule." Hence, items likely to be unavailable from abroad during a national emergency, industries needing support in their infancy, and manufactures using materials "extensively drawn from our agriculture" might be protected by tariffs. Madison believed generally in free trade, but conceded that circumstances might at times require a modification. On internal improvements, Madison noted that there was no country "which presents a field where nature invites more the art of man to complete her own work for his accommodation and benefit." Not only was federal support necessary to do what the states alone could not, but canals and roads were economically beneficial, of universally acknowledged utility, and honored a "wise and enlarged patriotism [which] duly appreciates them." Finally, better transportation would "bring and bind more closely together the various parts of our extended confederacy." The President cautioned, however, that a constitutional amendment might be needed for the projects "which can best be executed under the national authority."

Finally Madison urged, as did every President from Washington to John Quincy Adams, that "a national seminary of learning" be established in the District of Columbia. Such an institution, Madison proclaimed, in fidelity to republican gospel, "claims the patronage of Congress as a monument of their solicitude for the advancement of knowledge, without which the blessings of liberty cannot be fully enjoyed or long preserved; as a model instructive in the formation of other seminaries; as a nursery of enlightened preceptors, and as a central resort of youth and genius from every part of their country, diffusing on their return examples of those national feelings, those liberal sentiments, and those congenial manners which contribute cement to our Union and strength to the great political fabric of which that is the foundation." Madison concluded his message by noting that "our highly favored and happy country, . . . [under] political institutions founded in human rights and framed for their preservation [and proved] equal to the severest trials of war, . . . [is] in the tranquil enjoyment of prosperous and honorable peace."[45]

To "Old Republicans" in Congress, the President's message, and the nationalistic fervor of Calhoun and others upholding it, was a complete surrender to Federalism. John Randolph of Roanoke, back in Congress after a two-year absence, declared that the President "out-Hamilton's Alexander Hamilton," and that the question was "whether or not we are willing to become one great, consolidated nation, or whether we have still respect enough for those old, respectable institutions to regard their integrity and preservation as part of our policy." Madison, Randolph insisted, was merely a Federalist in disguise, who had abandoned the Republican principles of 1798. Henry Adams, at the end of his long history of the Jefferson and Madison administration, noted with glee that Madison had become a friend of "strong government" and had at long last come to see the wisdom of his Federalist predecessors, Washington and Adams. To Randolph, as well as to Henry Adams, Nathaniel Macon took the only consistent stand for an "Old Republican" when he declared, simply and in spite of the powerful arguments of "necessity," that "I cannot vote for a bank."[46]

What Randolph and Henry Adams failed to grasp, however, was that though Madison had a keen sense of the limiting character of the Constitution and a conviction that generally government, especially at the national level, ought to be "mild" and to shun self-aggrandizement, he did not make dogma of either strict construction or laissez faire. These were respectively Southern states' rights and late nineteenth-century business fixations wholly subordinated in Madison's view to the far more important question of finding the structure and use of government best suited to a prosperous, happy, and free people. Thus, in the seventeen nineties, with the tone of the new government unsettled, Madison feared Hamilton's tendency to centralize power and to use every stratagem and rationalization to stretch the Constitution. This, combined with a Federalist phalanx partial to England and spearheaded by ambitious financiers, gave to federalist theory and use of the federal government implications deeply hostile to Madison's understanding of the needs of republican independence. Debt, funding systems, banks, tariffs, English treaties, armies, navies, enlargement of the federal government, loose construction, and the Sedition Act—taken together and joined to the Hamiltonian vision of a splendid commercial nation led by a proconsul—had meaning far beyond that attached to any of the devices taken singly and in a less ominous context.

By 1815, however, profound changes had occurred. Fifteen years of Republican leadership had harnessed the Hamiltonian engine, not by destroying, aimlessly and dogmatically, everything the Federalists had done, but by subjecting the bank, the debt, the armed forces, and the federal service to mild Republican guidance. In each case the effect was to insure subordination to the popular will and to make obvious utility, not visions of Augustan grandeur, the test of programs and institutions. Though the severe pressures of international peril, and finally war, forced Jefferson and Madison to abandon dicta fashioned while out of power in the seventeen nineties, they did so cautiously and without losing sight of republican objectives. The War of 1812, like any national emergency, required greatly increased central power, but Madison's careful avoidance of Cromwellism (or even what a later age would call Gaullism) can be contrasted easily and obviously with how Hamilton might have conducted the war. Madison accepted knowingly the liabilities of his republican approach, calmly confident that preserving the nation's free character was worth some travail and inefficiency. As a result, by 1816 Madi-

son was far more certain than he could possibly have been twenty years
earlier that the nature of American government was firmly free, united,
and republican, and that the successful conclusion of the war made America's national independence unassailable.

Within this context, the seventh annual message becomes a forward-
looking program for republican growth. The bank and a small standing
army, now safely subordinated to republican ends, are endorsed, while
tariffs, internal improvements, and a national university are proposed
to let a free people *use* their representative government to fulfill national,
objectives. The Madison of 1816 is a "reversion" to the Madison of the
seventeen-eighties, not, as his critics have charged, in that he abandoned
the beliefs of the Jeffersonian years, but in that he was sure in 1816
that the benefits of union and national power sought in the seventeen-
eighties could safely and wisely be pursued by the federal government
operating under the Constitution. In 1791, in the presence of bank stock
speculators, in 1795 when Jay's Treaty tied the United States to Britain,
in 1798 under the Alien and Sedition Acts, and even in Jefferson's administrations, when domestic and especially foreign affairs were unsettled
and unstable, this safety and assurance were not always so evident. Madison's fidelity was not to particular programs, but rather to viable republicanism. It should not be surprising that, in a new nation, under an
untried system of government, this commitment should result in changing
tactics and even reversals of course. An ability to so adjust might well be
regarded as wise and constructive rather than as vacillating and unprincipled. The critical standards would be determined by the reality of the
dangers to republican government, against which Madison fought in the
seventeen-nineties, and the healthiness of the republican government over
which he presided in 1816. If the dangers, in Madison's anxiety for the
character of the new government, had perhaps been exaggerated, the free
vigor, independence, and national confidence of 1816 were incontestable.
This was the measure of Madison's achievement, the foundation of his
national program, and the source of the adulation surrounding him during his last two years as President and his twenty years in retirement.

The new Congress that received Madison's message was inclined to
follow the President's lead. The war leaders, headed by Clay and Calhoun, were back in the House, while in the Senate, the old obstructionist
faction headed by Giles was gone. The tone was so strikingly different
that "Old Republican" Nathaniel Macon, transferred to the Senate, was
"quite lost. . . . I feel almost like I was in a foreign land." House committees promptly considered the bank, the tariff, taxes, and internal improvements. The Senate ratified the commercial convention with England. A
visitor from Maryland, Isaac Briggs, found high spirits reflected at the
President's dinner table:

I called on the President, found him polite, affable and friendly, as usual. . . . When our conversation was finished and I rose to take leave, he invited me to return to take *pot-luck* with him at 3 o'clock. I returned accordingly, and partook of an excellent family dinner— myself the only stranger present. Dolly attempted to open a bottle of Champagne wine, the cork flew to the most distant corner of the room with an explosion as loud as—the sound of a popgun. She looked scared, and the wine seemed to be in haste to follow the cork. She however dextrously filled 3 large glasses, one for me, one for her sister Lucy Washington [Todd], and one for herself. She handed the bottle to her husband, but he would not take more than half-a-glass; I re- marked, after tasting it, that it was very treacherous wine—yes, said the President addressing himself to Lucy, if you drink much of it, it will make you hop like the cork. Dolly and Lucy, however, each took two glasses, but they soon afterwards left the table and retired —one glass and a half was as much as my head could bear without feeling uncomfortable.[47]

In April 1816, the President signed bills rechartering the national bank, setting tariffs at a mildly protective level, retaining many war taxes, and maintaining both the army and navy at levels calculated to protect land and sea frontiers. In a move reflecting Congress' new dignity and confi- dence in itself, it approved for the first time an annual salary for its mem- bers ($1,500, compared to Madison's relatively high $25,000) to re- place the old per diem of $6 while in session. Though no bill emerged on internal improvements, sentiment ran strongly in favor of them. Only the plan for a national university had disappeared into a pigeonhole. Finally, endorsing Madison's leadership, the Republican Congressional caucus nominated Monroe for the presidency, virtually assuring his suc- cession, given the discredited, moribund status of the Federalists. As Con- gress adjourned, Madison observed that its measures would soon abolish all the difficulties left by the war and that "the nation seems determined to lose nothing of the character it has gained." The French chargé rhap- sodized about "giant strides toward an extension of strength and power" and predicted that "the advance of civilization, the increase in public revenue, and the development of wealth and industry" would soon bring a new era to the United States.[48]

In this euphoric mood the Madisons left for Montpelier on June 5, not to return to Washington until October 9, their longest absence from the capital in sixteen years. "A short pelting shower" hampered the first day's journey, but otherwise "the weather and the roads were peculiarly fav- orable," and the crops less damaged than Madison expected. During the next three months, however, the Virginia Piedmont endured "unexam- pled" drought and cold weather. According to Jefferson's records, in- stead of the usual fifteen or twenty inches of rain, the region had but two or three inches, while frosts had continued into late May and others, in

August, were severe enough to kill what little corn had grown. Altogether the summer was "as cold as a moderate winter." Then, in mid-September, came great rains that were almost too much for the maturing tobacco. The deluge was such that for ten days Madison was out of touch with Monroe, who lived on the other side of a swollen branch of the James River.[49]

The unseasonable weather seemed not to hinder the busy social season at Montpelier, however. On the Fourth of July, ninety people, mostly country neighbors, and all men except the President's mother, wife, sister, and niece, ate a "profuse and handsome dinner . . . at one table, fixed on the lawn under a thick arbor." Such large numbers of guests, most of whom didn't stay overnight, were less trouble during the cool summer, Dolley reported, than having twenty-five guests in Washington. Following the Fourth, the new French minister, Hyde de Neuville, and four other French officials, arrived for two days. Madison put his guests at ease by talking as if "Louis XVIII had just succeeded Louis XVI" and showing none of the alleged Republican partiality for Napoleon. Later that month the Monticello family arrived for its summer visit, returned by the Madisons in August. The President meanwhile exchanged a steady stream of letters with Dallas and others in Washington. Among other matters, Madison drafted a blunt note to the Dey of Algiers protesting the renewed efforts to levy tribute on American ships. Madison hoped this would cease, "because the United States, whilst they wish for war with no nation, will buy peace of none. It is a principle incorporated into the settled policy of America, that as peace is better than war, war is better than tribute."[50]

In September Baron de Montlezun, a veteran of Yorktown, was greeted warmly by Dolley Madison, who was, he said, "sweetness, honesty and goodness itself." The modest President, he found, had "an excellent tone in conversation, never dogmatic. . . . Work is easy for him; he reads and writes almost all day, and often part of the night." Most welcome of all, the Madisons possessed "to a high degree the precious and rare art of leaving to the persons who pay them a visit the comfort and freedom they enjoy in their own home." Throughout a summer when Madison still carried the heaviest public burden in the United States, he followed Jefferson's practice "of placing our guests at their ease; by showing that we are so ourselves and that we follow our necessary vocations, instead of fatiguing them by hanging unremittingly on their shoulders." Richard Rush found the routine delightful:

> I have never seen Mr. Madison so well fixed any where as on his estate in Virginia; not even before he was burnt out here [Washington]. His house would be esteemed a good one for many of our seats near Philadelphia, and is much larger than most of them. The situation is among mountains and very beautiful. A fine estate surrounds him, at

the head of which he appears to eminent advantage, as well in his great
as in his estimable qualities. He has the reputation of being an excellent manager, and is a model of kindness to his slaves. He lives with
profuse hospitality, and in a way to strike the eye far more agreeably,
than while keeping tavern here. . . . He was never developed to me
under so many interesting lights, as during the very delightful week
I spent under his roof. Perhaps I should add, that French cooking,
and Madeira that he purchased in Philadelphia in '96 made a part of
every day's fare!

Despite having first to watch corn shrivel and freeze and then to see tobacco drown in heavy rains, the summer of 1816 was one of the happiest
the Madisons ever spent at Montpelier.[51]

When Madison returned to Washington for the last time in early October, he found only hopeful news, assuring that his administration would
end peacefully and prosperously. Under Dallas' energetic promotion, the
new national bank would open in early 1817, and specie payments resume soon thereafter. Foreign trade, especially Southern exports, increased
rapidly, enriching the nation and filling the treasury with receipts from
the new tariff. In the fall elections, though many Congressmen lost their
seats due to public disgust over the bill increasing salaries, the Republican
hold on state governments tightened. Monroe swept to victory in the electoral college, losing only the votes of Massachusetts, Connecticut, and
Delaware to Rufus King. Even the White House and the Capitol, though
not ready for use before Madison's retirement, had begun to rise in new
splendor from the smoking ruins left by the British only two years before.[52]

After noting the farm distress caused by bad weather, and some commercial depression in New England, Madison turned in his last message to
Congress to the many difficulties overcome in the last year or so, the surplus of nearly $10 million accumulating in the Treasury, and the need
to complete his program of national progress, begun so enthusiastically
the previous session. He also recommended a series of measures dear to an
Enlightenment statesman: stronger laws against importation of slaves, improvement of the federal judiciary, a decimal system of weights and
measures, liberalization of the criminal code, and a paternalistic Indian
policy to establish "in the culture and improvement of [the soil] the true
foundation for a transit from the habits of the savage to the arts and comforts of social life." Noting that he would soon retire from public life,
Madison indulged "the proud reflection that the American people have
reached in safety and success their fortieth year as an independent nation;
that for nearly an entire generation they have had experience of their
present Constitution, the offspring of their undisturbed deliberations and
of their free choice; that they have found it . . . to contain in its combination of the federate and elective principles a reconcilement of public

strength with individual liberty, of national power for the defense of national rights with a security against wars of injustice, of ambition, and of vainglory in the fundamental provision which subjects all questions of war to the will of the nation itself, which is to pay its costs and feel its calamities." The President, whose career had spanned the full period of independence and had had the drafting of the Constitution as its finest hour, took further pride that the Constitution had, "without losing its vital energies" expanded over a vast territory and population. He then extolled "the character of the American people," living under a government "pursuing the public good as its sole object": they enjoyed pure elections, free speech and press, trial by jury, separation of church and state, security of persons and property, and a "general diffusion of knowledge." Madison hoped as well that the nation, "by appeals to reason and by its liberal examples, [may] infuse into the law which governs the civilized world a spirit which may diminish the frequency or circumscribe the calamities of war, and meliorate the social and beneficent relations of peace." "These contemplations," he concluded, "sweetening the remnant of my days, will animate my prayers for the happiness of my beloved country, and a perpetuity of the institutions under which it is enjoyed."[53]

Though Congress did very little to enact Madison's program, it had, by mid-February 1817, authorized general federal support for internal improvements, without a constitutional amendment. The "very extraordinary" measure, as Madison termed it, reached him just four days before he left office. When he told Calhoun and other friends of the bill he could not sign it, they were surprised and vexed. Clay said later that "no circumstance, not even an earthquake that should have swallowed up half this city, could have excited more surprise" than the intended veto of a bill its supporters considered an administration measure. They had not understood the earnestness of Madison's repeated hints that only a constitutional amendment could sanction federally subsidized internal improvements. Clay, politically dexterous, wrote confidentially to the retiring President: "Knowing that we cannot differ on . . . the *object* of the Internal Improvement bill, . . . will you excuse me for respectfully suggesting whether you could not leave the bill to your successor"?[54]

Anxious to make a point of fidelity to the Constitution he took very seriously, and perhaps assured that Monroe would not sign the bill either, Madison vetoed it in his last act as President. After pointing out that no clause of the Constitution in any way conferred on Congress power to build roads and canals, Madison insisted that the clause, "to provide for the common defense and general welfare," in the taxing power, could not be used to *extend* the powers of Congress beyond those enumerated. Such an interpretation, he said, "would have the effect of giving to Congress a general power of legislation instead of [a] defined and limited one." He agreed that federal laws for internal improvements might bring "signal advantage to the general prosperity," but this should be done under a constitutional amendment, lest, as Jefferson observed in approving Madison's veto, "strained constructions . . . loosen all the bands of the constitution." Though to Clay and others Madison's last-minute scrupulousness was painful and unnecessary, the retiring President considered it an important "last testament" in favor of exactly the form of limited republican government he had just praised in his annual message as responsible for the free, prosperous state of the nation. Madison was also, as he had done repeatedly during his public life, making a subtle point of emphasis and balance: though the bank, the tariff, and other national measures could, in 1816, be undertaken without loosening "all the bands of the constitution," Madison meant to make clear that truly republican, truly federal government had to remain in vital ways "defined and limited." To maintain this quality was to Madison a far more relevant kind of consistency than mere rigidity.[55]

Preparing to leave Washington for the last time, Madison ordered a train of wagons to come from Montpelier to carry his belongings into retirement. His wife, he reported, was so busy with the "intense occupations in the packing and other arrangements," that she was unable to write her friends. As the bustle reached its peak in February, the mild winter turned frigid: "The thermometer, on the North side of the House, under an open shed," Madison wrote the weather-conscious Jefferson, was early in the morning "at 4° above o. At this moment, half after 9 o'clock, it stands at 6½°. Yesterday morning about the same hour it was 8, and at 3 o'clock between 10 and 11." Meanwhile, during all the farewell receptions, the chief executive, who had so often appeared weary and tense to his guests, was transformed. He went ("a thing very unusual") to a gala Christmas ball at the French embassy, where there were "cotillon parties in one room, cards in another, those who neither played nor danced in a third, and a supper-table in the fourth." "I think the President never seemed so happy as now," the Secretary of the Navy wrote, "his term of service nearly expired, and with the applause of the nation, what more can a good man hope for!" So benign had the atmosphere in the capital become that even John Randolph pronounced Madison "a great man . . . in some respects." Elijah Mills, a Massachusetts Federalist who had doubted there could be anything "pleasant or agreeable about a man of [Madison's] political principles," found in him an "altogether very pleasant . . . mixture of ease and dignity in manners and conversation, [with] more the appearance of what I have imagined a Roman Catholic Cardinal to be" than a civil and military chieftain.

Dolley Madison's final Wednesday evening receptions were triumphant. In two rooms so jammed no one could sit down, "coffee and wine and punch were handed about . . . to all classes and conditions of society, from the minister plenipotentiary of the Emperor of Russia to the under-

clerks of the post office. . . . Members of Congress and officers of the
army and navy, greasy boots and silk stockings, Virginia buckskins and
Yankee cowhides, all mingled in ill-assorted and fantastic groups." The
First Lady "very tall and corpulent . . . [with] manners . . . easy rather
than graceful, and pleasant rather than refined, . . . distributed her attentions and smiles with an equal and impartial hand." At the last reception, Congressman Mills found the crowd more genteel and better dressed
than usual and "no small evidence of approbation for [Mrs. Madison's]
past conduct, and regret of her retirement. . . . It is said her liberality to
the indigent and unfortunate is unprecedented in this part of the country.
. . . A coterie of ladies . . . were lamenting, as I thought sincerely, her
approaching retirement; and recounting to each other instances that had
come within their own knowledge of her kindness and munificence."
Sensing the end of an era, Mills suspected "from her successor . . . neither
the fashionable world nor the suffering poor have much to expect."[56]

Amid the busy farewells, the Madisons found time to sit for portraits
by the popular New York and Philadelphia miniaturist Joseph Wood.
His likeness of Dolley reveals the usual friendly, wide-set eyes, long nose,
and ample figure, while that of her husband was the best ever painted
of him (see illustrations). When Eliza Lee, a lifelong friend of Dolley
Madison's, saw it, she exclaimed, "The likeness of your dear Husband almost breathes, and expresses much of the serenity of his feelings at the
moment it was taken. In short, it is, *himself*." Wood caught Madison in
the full vigor of maturity, calm, poised, and confident, every bit the statesman and patriot. His hair, gray, and almost gone on top, is combed
long on the back and sides, and his brows are bushy and prominent over
clear, light eyes. The mouth is firmly pleasant, while the chin and jaw,
though showing the signs of age, complete a countenance that is at once
affable, vital, and self-possessed. Wood thus preserved for Madison and his
friends, as well as for posterity, the image of the President whose administration had, John Adams wrote Jefferson, "notwithstanding a thousand Faults and blunders . . . acquired more glory, and established more
Union, than all his three Predecessors, Washington, Adams and Jefferson,
put together."[57]

Other tributes, public and private, poured in on the retiring chief executive. At the close of an inaugural address outlining the accomplishments of the United States since independence, Monroe praised his predecessor "under whom so important a portion of this great and successful
experiment has been made." In another, semiofficial eulogy, *The National
Intelligencer* declared that no statesman could have "a more honorable, a
more grateful termination of his official life than that which crowned the
administration of James Madison." The city of Washington, mindful that
Madison's "wisdom and firmness" had rescued it from "the tempest of
war," remembered with gratitude that the sword drawn under his guidance had been wielded "without the sacrifice of civil or political liberty."

Madison replied by expressing his special pleasure at such sentiments from those in a position "to mark . . . particularly the course of my public and personal conduct." Even more meaningful to the retiring President were the tributes of his long-time republican colleagues. Gallatin wrote from Paris that "few indeed have the good fortune, after such a career as yours, to carry in their retirement the entire approbation of their fellow citizens with that of their own conscience. Never was a country left in a more flourishing situation than the United States at the end of your administration; and they are more united at home and respected abroad than at any period since the war of the independence." Jefferson, looking forward to his friend's residence in Virginia, congratulated him on his "release from incessant labors, corroding anxieties, active enemies, and interested friends, and on your return to your books and farm, to tranquility and independence." Richard Rush, left by Monroe in charge of the State Department during the summer of 1817, rummaged through the papers there, largely drawn by Madison, and exlaimed "what history, what anecdote, what genius, what industry!"[58]

The Madisons had hoped to leave Washington immediately after Monroe's inauguration, but the continuing round of farewell celebrations as well as the packing delayed them a month. At the inaugural ball, attended by hundreds, the Madisons stayed only long enough, as Jefferson had done in 1809, to pay respects to the new President and then retired, leaving to him the limelight as well as the responsibility. The most elaborate party, given, one suspects, especially for the supremely sociable Dolley, was held by the citizens of Georgetown. The walls were hung with such marvelous "transparencies, paintings and verses executed on white velvet and most richly framed," that they were gathered and taken to Montpelier where they became part of the permanent décor of one of the rooms. With the parties finally over, however, James and Dolley Madison boarded a steamboat at the Potomac wharf in Washington to begin the journey to Orange. To Madison, whose first journey along the Potomac had been made slowly on horseback, over poor roads and across many ferries, on his way to Princeton nearly fifty years earlier, the swift, comfortable steamer ride was both a welcome pleasure and a measure of the incredible changes wrought in his lifetime. As the vessel glided past Mount Vernon, Madison "was as playful as a child; talked and jested with everybody on board," and reminded James K. Paulding, who accompanied him, "of a school Boy on a long vacation." At Acquia Creek, forty miles from Washington, the Madisons mounted their carriage for the rest of the familiar trip to Montpelier. This time, as the Blue Ridge came into view and they passed by Orange Court House on the way to the farm that had always been home to Madison, he felt as unmixed a joy as he had ever known in his life: a public career ended in glory and a useful and pleasurable retirement in prospect before him.[59]

CHAPTER XXII

Retirement

MONTPELIER in 1817 was very different from the house Madison had come to in 1797, the last time he had returnd to Orange to be a full-time Virginia planter. To the four-columned portico, the limestone plaster put on over the brick exterior, and other remodeling of 1800 had been added in 1809 the one-story wings on each side designed by Thornton and Latrobe (see Chapters XV and XIX). The space and graciousness thus gained had been complemented by what twenty years of care and prosperity could do to the surrounding grounds. A telescope on the west-facing front portico was used to "explore" residences on the Blue Ridge, and to "spy the road where carriages and large parties were seen almost daily" coming to Montpelier. To the north stood a columned icehouse, a frequent conversation piece as well as a source of ice cream and cold drinks during the summer months. Nearby was an immense mulberry tree, and beyond, silver poplar and weeping willow, which hid a mill and other farm buildings along a stream running down to the Rapidan River. In front, at a gate on a gravel path leading toward the mansion, was a large tin cup used to measure the amount of rainfall at every shower. On one side stood a well of pure, cool water, in use since Madison's grandfather first developed the land nearly a century before. Oak, cedars of Lebanon, boxwood, and willows completed the foreground of the scene across the downward-sloping lawn and rolling fields of grain and tobacco reaching toward the Rapidan and the Blue Ridge Mountains twenty miles beyond. Behind the house, a smaller, columned porch, entwined with roses and white jasmine, faced on a level yard with two large tulip trees in the center, surrounded by groves of oak, walnut, and pine that shielded a ravine, farm buildings, and slave quarters. The steep slope of the Southwest Mountains enclosed the scene. To the south, beyond the "kitchen garden," for table vegetables, and an orchard of pears, figs, grapes, and other fruits, was a formal garden laid out by the French gardener in the horseshoe pattern of the seats in the House of Representatives. Madison strolled there with his guests, and the always plentiful young people at Montpelier used it for courting, as Jefferson had the formal gardens of the governor's palace in Williamsburg a half century before.

Inside, from the vestibule with its semicircular window, divided into thirteen parts to symbolize the original union of the states, visitors entered a large central drawing room. This was sometimes called "the clock room," for the old-fashioned English clock that regulated family life, and sometimes "the hall of notables," for the many paintings there (several by Gilbert Stuart) and for the busts of Washington, Franklin, Jefferson, John Adams, Lafayette, Baron von Humboldt, and others. A bas-relief of Madison himself by Ceracchi hung among the likenesses of his famous friends. A Persian rug and sofas covered with crimson damask lent color, and tall French windows opening on to the back lawn flooded the room with sunlight during the morning and early afternoon. A marble mantelpiece sent from France by Jefferson completed the décor of the cheerful, elegant room. To the right of this hall Madison's eighty-five-year-old mother, Nelly Conway Madison, still alert and active, had her own rooms, where she lived separately, attended by her own servants. One was the octogenarian Sawney, who had accompanied James Madison on his first trip to Princeton nearly fifty years earlier. To the left of the central hall was a pleasant room with a large fireplace and windows looking out at the Blue Ridge. As Madison grew more feeble, it became his "sitting room." It contained an iron-posted bed covered with a heavy canopy of crimson damask, bought by Monroe "from the dismantled palace of the Tuileries," easy chairs, and a study table piled with books and papers. Adjoining was the dining room, where portraits of Napoleon in ermine robes, Louis XIV, Confucius, and others gathered by Payne Todd in Europe, plus family portraits and a water-color drawing of Jefferson, looked down upon a large mahogany table and two sideboards covered with family silver. Long halls, with highly polished floors, at the back of the house were also hung with portraits, and had carved oak stairways leading up to bedrooms and Madison's library. Here four thousand volumes were shelved around the sides of the room and on stacks filling the center, while books and pamphlets—some gathered by Madison, and others sent unsolicited to him in a steady stream—were heaped high on every available chair and table.[1]

Though this large, comfortable home had only three permanent residents, the ex-President, his wife, and his aged mother, others lived there for months at a time, and multitudes, it sometimes seemed to Dolley Madison, came to stay for weeks or days. Payne Todd tried fitfully for a few months now and then to learn the life of a Virginia planter, but he seemed never to feel at ease or at home at Montpelier, perhaps simply because it was so uniquely and utterly his stepfather's house. At any rate, Todd went through the years when he ordinarily would have married and found an occupation without doing either. Instead he drifted restlessly from New York to Philadelphia to Washington and back, sometimes showing his old charm in ways that caused happy reports of him to reach Montpelier, but more often making drinking, card-playing, and gambling rounds of hotels and taverns. During one spree, in 1824 and 1825, while his mother sent him money as fast as she could and also cleared $200 of his local debts, his stepfather paid a $500 debt at a Washington lottery house and received "unforeseen" board bills from Philadelphia. Postmaster Richard Bache, out of friendship for the ex-President who had got him his office, covered a worthless $300 draft of Todd's to keep him out of prison. This proved to be a small part of over $20,000 in debts Madison struggled to pay without his wife's knowledge, to save her grief and mortification. Madison wrote painfully to the thirty-three-year-old adolescent: "What shall I say to you? . . . Weeks have passed without even a line . . . soothing the anxieties of the tenderest of mothers, wound up to the highest pitch. . . . Whatever the causes of [your long absence and debts,] you owe it to yourself as well as to us, to withhold them no longer. Let the worst be known, that the best may be made of it. . . . You cannot be too quick in affording relief to [your mother's] present feelings."

Two years later, again only heroic, sacrificial efforts by Madison and his friends kept Todd out of prison. Madison reimbursed John Jacob Astor $600 loaned to Todd during a New York binge, and covered $1,600 in Georgetown and Philadelphia debts. Calamity threatened, however, when Todd diverted $1,300 sent him to pay old debts to make another round of the gambling tables. The defaulted obligation of $1,300 reached Richmond providentially, just as tobacco prices rose for one of the few times during these years. Madison's agent there was able to pay the bill. Sales of Kentucky lands and mortgaging of nearly half of his Orange County estate met other heavy drafts, while in another emergency Edward Coles loaned Madison $2,000 on Todd's behalf. "His career," Madison wrote the loyal Coles, "must soon be fatal to everything dear to him in life. . . . With all the concealments and alleviations I have been able to effect, his mother has known enough to make her wretched the whole time of his strange absence and mysterious silence." In 1829 Dolley Madison, longing for news "from or of my dear child," heard the worst: he was "boarding within prison bounds!" He was soon released, but a year later, Dolley's faithful friend Anthony Morris wrote that Todd was again in prison and that his creditors would release him for $600, which Madison promptly furnished. Characteristically, when Todd was in Virginia for a few months in 1832 he searched for gold and talked of getting rich quarrying marble. He began to build his eccentric residence, Toddsberth, across the Southwest Mountains from Montpelier, and to take the all-night drunken rambles with his kinsman Colonel John Willis, which are still legendary in Orange County. Though Todd resolved repeatedly to reform himself, and his mother maintained her faith in him (she wrote, "Love shown to my son would be the highest gratification the world could bestow upon me"), he remained, as he confessed on his deathbed in 1851, "my own worst enemy."

Shortly before his own death Madison bundled vouchers for $20,000 and gave them to Dolley's brother John C. Payne, suggesting that he might give them eventually to his sister, "as an evidence of the sacrifice he [Madison] had made to insure her tranquility by concealing from her the ruinous extravagance of her son." Payne apparently never did this, because he wrote after his sister's death, in passing the vouchers on his nephew, that "Mr. Madison assured me these payments were exclusive of those he made with her knowledge and of the remittances he had made and furnished her the means of making. The sum thus appropriated probably equaled the same amount," concluded Payne, who was in a position to know in detail of Madison's payments for Todd. Madison spent, then, about $40,000 between 1813 and 1836 on gambling debts and other expenses of his wayward stepson, a huge amount under any circumstances, but ruinous to a farmer during years of agricultural depression. This financial drain, together with the psychic pain inflicted on Dolley Madison by her son's dissipation, caused Edward Coles, reflecting on the wasted life of his handsome cousin, to declare Payne Todd at Montpelier a veritable "serpent in the Garden of Eden."[2]

Most of the visitors to Montpelier, of course, brought more joy and less grief than did Payne Todd. Madison's own relatives, especially the abundant crop of nieces and nephews, came often and stayed long at what was for them still the family home. The families of Madison's sisters Nelly Conway Hite (d. 1802) and Frances Taylor Rose lived respectively in northern Virginia and Huntsville, Alabama, so the squire of Montpelier saw little of them, but the children of his deceased brothers Francis and Ambrose had largely remained in Orange, and looked to their uncle for guidance and sometimes support. Most enjoyable of these relatives was Ambrose's daughter Nelly, whose husband, Dr. John Willis, had died in 1812, leaving her to raise her two children at her father's plantation, Woodley, a short drive through the woods over the Southwest Mountains from Montpelier. Nelly Willis, a good natured, sensible, outgoing, unaffected woman of the kind the Virginia countryside has always been proud, was at Montpelier for every family occasion. Her own home was so congenial to her uncle that the large tree in her front yard is still called "the President's oak," because his horse was so often tied there while he visited inside.

The most numerous connections in Orange, however, were the children and grandchildren of Madison's sister Sarah (Mrs. Thomas Macon) and his brother General (a militia title earned during the War of 1812) William Madison, both of whom outlived the ex-President. Though Madison's relations with Sarah and her family seemed warm and close, the same was not always true with William Madison and his family. Enervating efforts during the War of 1812 went unrecognized—perhaps William Madison blamed this in part on his brother in the White House—frustrating William's last chance to gain the fame and fortune he had hoped for in his youth. Then, before his first wife's death in 1832, nine of his children died, mostly of tuberculosis, and his plantation, Woodbury Forest (several miles north of Montpelier on the road to Culpeper), suffered severely in the agricultural depression. He became dissatisfied with the settlement of his father's and mother's estates, and presented unwarranted pension claims for his Revolutionary War service, which his brother apparently refused to endorse. Though he is mentioned occasionally as among the guests at Montpelier, and though he did not come into open conflict with the rest of the family before James Madison's death, an unmistakable uneasiness existed. The ex-President nonetheless continued his special attentions to William's son Robert, whom he had "put through" Dickinson College, and who in 1816 had married a beautiful Petersburg girl, Eliza Strachan. They had three sons (one named for Robert's favorite teacher, and his uncle's long-time friend, Thomas Cooper), and Robert served several terms in the Virginia Assembly. He succumbed in 1828, however, to the dreaded consumption. Madison provided in his will for the education of the three boys, the last of whom, born the year of his father's death, became the personal physician of General Robert E. Lee after the Civil War.[3]

Always closer to Madison than his own relatives, though, were the families of Dolley's sister Anna Cutts, and to a lesser degree those of her sister Lucy Washington Todd and her brother John C. Payne. Lucy visited regularly at Montpelier with her young children, sometimes staying all summer, until her husband, Supreme Court Justice Thomas Todd, died in 1826. John C. Payne, fourteen years younger than Dolley, had, after false starts at seafaring and military life, and some bouts of mental illness, married and settled down on a small farm in Orange, secured with Madison's help. The father of six girls and two boys, he supplemented his income by acting as Madison's secretary and amanuensis. His fine, distinctive handwriting appears everywhere among Madison's papers, evidence of the hours he spent copying, arranging, and taking dictation at Madison's behest. So close was his family to the Montpelier family that upon Madison's death, Dolley adopted his daughter Annie as her own, probably only formalizing what had already become a fond attachment.

After 1817 Anna Cutts and her five children lived in Washington, in a house partly owned by the Madisons, while Richard Cutts was supported by the Second Comptrollership in the Treasury, to which his brother-in-law had appointed him. His efforts to recoup his shipping fortune, lost during the War of 1812, failed, however, carrying away as well about $5,000 loaned by Madison. He went through bankruptcy, and even to debtor's prison for a time. Only desperate maneuvers saved the house on Lafayette Square, which ended up in Madison's hands and became Dolley's residence when she returned to Washington after her husband's death. For weeks at a time during the hot summers Anna and the children came to Montpelier. The older boys, James Madison and Thomas, reached maturity during the eighteen-twenties, while the two girls, Dolley Madison and Mary, were busy children running about the house and grounds after their Aunt Dolley. The most promising of the Cutts children, however, was the youngest, another Richard, born in 1817, who became the favorite of the playful old man he called "Uncle Madison." When Richard was about ten years old, Madison, whose fingers were "a little sore," dictated to Dolley a letter addressed to "Richard Cutts, Tobaco Planter, Washington." With mock seriousness Madison asked the "experienced" planter whether he wanted his "three-ounce [crop] . . . made into pigtail or twist for chewing—or if you think it best to make it into snuff." Madison urged the boy to bring "Miss Modesty, her sister taciturnity, and above all, their cousin good humour" on his next visit, but "you need not trouble to bring your appetite for bacon and chicken—nor for warffle butter, custard, nor honey—particularly you'd better leave behind your relish for grapes, figs, and water mellons." Harking back to events of his own education nearly seventy years earlier, the former President also advised young Richard to read *The Spectator* papers of Joseph Addison. Madison hoped his nephew would some day employ his pen "for the benefit of others and for your own gratification." He sent a copy of *The Spectator* "as a token of all the good wishes of your affectionate uncle."

This young man became Dolley Madison's helpful neighbor and dependable advisor after she moved back to Washington in 1837. In 1844 he married a connection of Jefferson's, with whom he became the progenitor of a distinguished line of lawyers, engineers, and army officers. The oldest Cutts boy, James Madison, in 1834 married Ellen O'Neale, and came on his wedding journey to Montpelier, where Dolley Madison arranged a huge lawn party for the newlyweds. Ill and barely able to appear on the piazza, the eighty-three-year-old ex-President mustered strength to raise his wine glass in a toast to the bride, but then, supported by a servant, returned to his couch and fireside. Mary Cutts, always fervently devoted to the Madisons, and the author of the most authentic, intimate sketch known of their family life, wrote that her "Uncle Madison" was "a dear lover of fun and children" who often told anecdotes of his nieces and nephews with a swift transition "from sternness to brilliant mirth" delightful to his listeners. During the twenty years of Madison's retirement, Montpelier was a congenial place for reminiscing adults, but it was also alive with the joys and vicissitudes of growing children who, as had been true throughout Madison's life, kept him in touch with youth in a way remarkable for a man himself childless.[4]

Madison's daily routine began as he was dressed and attended to by his personal valet, Paul Jennings, who served Madison faithfully for the last twenty-five years of his life. Jennings remained with Dolley Madison until 1845, when Daniel Webster, to aid the hard-pressed widow, purchased him and made him a freeman. After breakfast at eight or nine, Madison relaxed for a time on the portico with his guests, perhaps looking through the telescope at distant plantations and mountains. Then, on his pampered horse, Liberty, he rode about the plantation. The rides were described in 1818 by James K. Paulding:

> As he never encumbered himself with a servant on these occasions, it fell to his lot to open the Gates, which he did with a crooked stick, without dismounting, a feat which required no little skill. . . . Mr. Madison had undertaken to substitute Beer in the room of whiskey, as a beverage for his slaves in Harvest time, and on one occasion, I remember, stopt on a wheat field . . . to inquire how they liked the new drink—"O! ver fine—vere fine masser" said one old grey head— "but I tink a glass of whiskey vere good to make it wholesome!" He was excessively diverted at this supplement of the old fellow, and often made merry with it afterwards. On another occasion we rode to a distant part of the Estate bordering on the Rapidan River, . . . a ferocious stream, and subject to occasional inundations. There had been a very heavy shower the day before; the river had overflowed its banks, and covered two or three acres of fine meadow with gravel some inches deep, so that is was completely spoiled. "Why this is a bad business Tony," said Mr. Madison. "Yes Masser ver bad—ver bad indeed," answered Tony. . . . "I tell you what Masser—I tink The Lor almighty by and large, he do most as much harm as good."

On rainy days Madison walked back and forth on the porch for his exercise, sometimes even racing with Dolley, who, one guest reported, could run very well for a woman of her age.[5]

At two in the afternoon, before dinner, the Madisons visited the rooms of Nelly Madison, who usually took her meals separately. The old woman, nearly one hundred, and no more marked with age than her son, was seldom sick or in pain, and except for some deafness, retained full command of her senses. She passed her time knitting and reading and was always glad to visit for a while with her son's many guests. She adored and appreciated Dolley Madison, saying one time, looking at Dolley, "You are *my* Mother now, and take care of me in my old age." After this filial call, the Madisons dined with their company about four o'clock, in a meal that usually lasted two hours. At the table, Margaret Bayard Smith reported in 1828, "Mr. Madison was the chief speaker. . . . He spoke of scenes in which he himself had acted a conspicuous part and of great men, who had been actors in the same theatre. . . . Franklin, Washington, Hamilton, John Adams, Jefferson, Jay, Patrick Henry and a host of other great men were spoken of and characteristic anecdotes of all related. It was living History!" Only the presence of strangers, Mrs. Smith wrote, could make "this entertaining, interesting and communicative personage . . . mute, cold, and repulsive." "After dinner," she continued, "we all walked on the Portico . . . until twilight, then retreated to the drawing room, where we sat in a little group close together and took our coffee while we talked. Some of Mr. Madison's anecdotes were very droll, and we often laughed very heartily. . . . When I retired for the night [ten o'clock], I felt as if my mind was full to overflowing, . . . as if I had feasted to satiety."

Another visitor about the same time found when he arrived:

Mr. and Mrs. Madison were out having gone over to a relation's in the neighborhood. . . . In a little while, a fine portly looking lady, with a straw bonnet, and shawl on came in, whom I at once took for her ladyship. . . . Soon after Mr. Madison came in. . . . [He] is quite a short thin man, with his head bald except on the back, where his hair hangs down to his collar and over his ears, nicely powdered—he has gray but bright eyes, and small features—he looks scarcely as old as he is, . . . and seems very hale and hearty—the expression of his face is full of good humour—he was dressed in black, with breeches and old fashioned top boots, which he afterwards took off and sat during the evening in his white stockings, but the next day he had black silk on and looked very nice. Mrs. Madison slipped off to change her walking dress, and made herself quite stylish in a turban and fine gown—she has a great deal of dignity blended with good humour and knowledge of the world. A number of her relations were staying with them, a party I suppose of a dozen, and two or three pretty girls among them. . . . I talked with or rather listened to [Mr. Madison] almost exclusively while I remained. We sat up pretty late; . . . his favourite topic appeared . . . to be the early constitutional history of this country, the state of the confederacy originally, the points involved in the constitution, the errors relative to many facts which he pointed out, etc. We discussed too ancient and modern literature —Herodotus, Gibbon, Sir Walter Scott and the Reviews. . . . The next morning I was down sometime before the ladies but found him reading in the parlour.

An Italian traveler, Count Carlo Vidua, had similarly favorable impressions of Madison during a visit to Montpelier in May 1825. He found

Madison "a small, thin old man, but of a kindly and pleasant face; his bearing is very aristocratic, and without assuming the air of importance and dignity befitting one of his station, he displays an indescribable gentleness and charm, which I thought impossible to find in an American. I have heard few people speak with such precision and, above all, with such fairness." After visiting with the four living ex-Presidents, and with President John Quincy Adams, Vidua found aged John Adams precise and vivacious in answering questions but too old to sustain a long conversation, and of the others he reported that "Jefferson's intellect seemed . . . the most brilliant, Madison's the most profound, Monroe's the least keen, and [John Quincy] Adams' the most cultivated." Altogether, Vidua preferred Madison because his "reflections seemed . . . the most weighty, denoting a great mind and a good heart."

So contented were the Madisons at Montpelier with their daily round of life that the letters and diaries of those who visited them reflect euphoria. One lady found Dolley "a great soul—and her body not decreased." The old couple "looked like Adam and Eve in their Bower," she added. Another glimpsed an unpretentious ex-President, "quite the Farmer, enthusiastically fond of all its employments, and wearing Pantaloons patched at the knees." In no other country, the visitor said, could one find an ex-ruler living so quietly and so simply. Surrounded by an affectionate family, visited by streams of agreeable guests, serenely comfortable at last on his own farm, and able to bask in the adulation of his countrymen, Madison enjoyed a retirement often idyllic beyond what he had dared hope.[6]

The need to make a living, as well as Madison's agrarian convictions about the good life, required him to remain an active farmer. Jefferson himself had declared, John Quincy Adams wrote in 1807, that "the person who united with other science the greatest agricultural knowledge of any man he knew was Mr. Madison. He was the best farmer in the world." The Montpelier plantation had prospered during the Napoleonic Wars, despite the inattentions of Madison's overseers during his long absences in Washington. He had shifted his production as much as possible to wheat and other grains (see Chapter XV), but the decline of European demand after the wars caused Madison to depend again on tobacco for a cash crop. His earliest letters from Orange after his retirement are filled with talk of fields, crops, market prospects, and the weather, marking his absorption in the concerns of a farmer. His neighbors elected him president of the Agricultural Society of Albemarle, which Madison soon made a model of the scientific, practical, self-help organization he and Jefferson thought could be the salvation of American agriculture. Their goal was to sustain in the country the life of rural virtue and prosperity vital to its republican character.[7]

Madison delivered a long address to the society in May 1818. Speaking

James Madison : *A Biography*

before Jefferson, members of the Board of Visitors of the University of Virginia, and Piedmont farmers anxious to apply the lessons of science to fields threatened with impoverishment, Madison first considered some questions of agrarian philosophy: what caused men to change from hunters to farmers? what instincts, if any, inclined men to become civilized? what ratio of plants to animals best suited human progress? and finally, what balances of nature must man be careful not to upset, lest he make the world unfit for human habitation? Especially important was plenty of pure air. "In all confined situations, from the dungeon to the crowded work-house, and from these to the compact population of overgrown cities," Madison declared, "the atmosphere becomes, in corresponding degrees, unfitted by reiterated use, for sustaining human life and health." Despite the dangers of upsetting natural harmonies, though, Madison insisted that man's reason and will, "by which he can act on matter organized and unorganized," enabled him to improve species of plants and animals, restore exhausted soil, and increase the proportion of living things useful to him. He insisted, too, that "the enviable condition of the people of the United States is often too much ascribed to the physical advantages of their soil and climate, and to their uncrowded situation. Much is certainly due to these causes; but a just estimate of the happiness of our country will never overlook what belongs to the fertile activity of a free people, and the benign influence of a responsible Government." Madison always believed that human effort, right principles, and proper institutions were vital adjuncts to the bounties of nature, separating the free, prospering portion of mankind from the degraded part. This remained throughout his life the center of his political and social philosophy, and furnished the essential point of his lifelong agreement with Jefferson.

Applying his insights to Virginia agriculture, Madison recommended specific changes and improvements. First, he pointed out the futility of continued working of exhausted fields, which put both land and laborer in a downward spiral of diminishing returns. He then commended Thomas Mann Randolph's system of contour plowing as of "inestimable advantage," particularly in "our red hills" and in the cultivation of Indian corn. Madison also spoke learnedly, and in great detail, of the benefits of various kinds of animal manure and of the relative merits of grain chaff and corn stalks as soil rejuvenators. He anticipated both the source and doctrine of Edmund Ruffin's landmark *An Essay on Calcareous Manures*, in commending Sir Humphrey Davy's demonstration that chemical fertilizers could, if properly applied, be the salvation of Southern agriculture. Madison next noted the advantages of irrigation, the superiority of the ox to the horse for most farm purposes, and the need to rid the countryside of scraggly animals, especially milch cows. The milk, manure, and hides of these cattle, Madison observed, seldom paid for the cost of feeding them, while the same feed given to a few fat cows would provide rich returns in the milk pail and elsewhere. Madison concluded with a plea for conserving and restoring the wood lots, toward which in pioneer days "the great effort . . . to destroy trees" seemed to have created an "antipathy." Estimating, for Virginia, that each fireplace required an average of ten cords of wood annually, that an acre of woods yielded twenty cords, and that it took twenty years for a wood lot to restore itself, Madison urged that every farm maintain ten acres of trees for every fireplace it wished to fuel. Madison's recommendations for scientific agriculture in Virginia embodied the reasoned, practical approach his disciplined mind applied over and over again to human problems. His listeners voted him their thanks for his "enlightened and important address," and ordered it printed and distributed for the edification of farmers everywhere.[8]

Despite the confident tone of his address, Madison in fact faced, along with his neighbors, the calamitous consequences of agricultural depression. With the end of war-heightened demand for wheat in Europe, the bottom fell out of the grain market, and the revival in the tobacco trade immediately after the war proved shortlived. An unusual number of poor harvests during the eighteen-twenties, the steady exhaustion of the soil, and competition from rapidly opening rich farm lands in the West intensified the distress. Always short of cash, Virginia planters found it increasingly difficult to derive anything like the needed amount of coin from their crops. Farmers, large and small, faced grim alternatives: sale of land, sale of slaves, emigration, or impoverishment. Madison saw the results all around him: his sister Frances and her husband moved to Alabama; his nephew Robert Madison sought to go to New Orleans for his law career; his nieces increasingly married merchants and professional men living in cities; his Taylor cousins moved almost en masse to Kentucky. Edward Coles left first for Illinois, and then Philadelphia; many of Madison's neighbors were virtually reduced to being breeders of slaves for sale "down the river"; and both Jefferson and Monroe went broke. The prosperous way of life Virginia had known for nearly two centuries seemed in the eighteen-twenties to be near its end.[9]

For ten or fifteen years Madison avoided the worst effects of the depression. His salary as President, $25,000 annually, was for that time a handsome one, and permitted him not only to make improvements at Montpelier but also to build up a reserve to carry him over hard times. His lack of expensive and dissipating habits meant he was without a burden many Virginia planters imposed on themselves, and he was also free of the steady drain of a large family. Furthermore, the use at Montpelier of the best farm techniques, evident in Madison's letters from the seventeen-eighties on, made its fields unusually productive. Finally, Madison possessed in 1817 not only clear title to five thousand fertile acres at Montpelier, but also over a thousand acres of Kentucky lands, some stock in a turnpike company, a house in Washington, and other assets able to cushion him from the shock of crop failures. On the other hand a gracious way of life filled with company and entertainment, a refusal to traffic in slaves, and the vast expenditures needed to keep Payne Todd out of debtor's prison depleted Madison's cash reserves. Through his retirement he gradually sold his Kentucky lands, disposed of his stock and other convertible assets, and even mortgaged, with little hope of regaining clear title, nearly half of his Montpelier lands. Madison's credit and the prospects of Virginia agriculture were so poor by 1825 that even his personal appeal to Nicholas Biddle failed to procure a $6,000 loan from the Bank of the United States. Nothing can have been more disappointing for Madison than the inescapable fact that by the time of his death his lifelong efforts to make Montpelier in particular, and Virginia generally, a prosperous farmer's paradise had failed. Though he was spared the pain and humiliation of bankruptcy, the threat of economic ruin grew stronger during his years of retirement. "Since my return to private life," Madison wrote Jefferson in 1826, "such have been the unkind seasons, and the ravages of insects, that I have made but one tolerable crop of Tobacco, and but one of Wheat; the proceeds of both of which were greatly curtailed by mishaps in the sale of them. And having no resources but in the earth I cultivate, I have been living very much throughout on borrowed means."[10]

Struck by these grim realities, Madison admitted increasingly that social problems were unlikely to yield to panaceas. Echoing opinions expressed forty years before to Jefferson, for example, Madison reasserted his Malthusian insights against the extravagant hopes of the English theorist William Godwin. Though Madison admitted, as always, that enterprise and good government could vastly improve human life, he insisted generally that "all the . . . beings on the Globe, . . . animal and vegetable, . . . when left to themselves multiply until checked by the limited funds of their pabulum, or by the mortality generated by the excess of their numbers." In 1827, reflecting on Robert Owen's hope that socialist communities would eliminate want and evil, Madison wrote more bluntly. "Custom," he averred, "is properly called a second nature; Mr. Owen makes nature itself." Though Madison hoped Owen's "enterprise" would "throw light on the maximum to which the force of education and habit can be carried," he had grave doubts that any social reorganization could wholly overcome the "desire for distinction," the harmful effects of fashion, and the tendency of leisure to produce ennui or "vicious resorts." And after all, Madison noted, "there is one indelible cause remaining of pressure on the condition of the labouring part of mankind; and that is, the constant tendency of an increase of their number, after the increase of food has reached its term. The competition for employment then reduces wages to their minimum and privation to its maximum." Any checks to this iron law, Madison said, thinking of war, famine, and pestilence, were themselves only further and worse evils. He concluded that, since it was impossible to banish evil from the world, "We must console ourselves with the belief that it is overbalanced by the good mixed with it, and direct our efforts to an increase of the good portion of the mixture."[11]

Of all evils, however, none was for Madison more pregnant with danger, and more intractable, than that of Negro slavery. His conviction of its immorality, and its incongruity in a nation resting on the Declaration of Independence, had been formed early, and never slackened. His failure in the seventeen-eighties to free himself from dependence on slave labor, and to secure a law for gradual abolition in Virginia, doomed him, it seemed, to live within a system he abhorred. During the years of his public life the revived economic utility of slavery in the fast-growing cotton fields made its elimination, contrary to what Madison, Jefferson, Washington, and other eighteenth-century Virginians had supposed, more difficult as time passed. In retirement, Madison renewed his efforts to abolish slavery. Though he insisted in 1819 that liberal principles and improved conditions made slaves much better off than they were before the revolution, their degraded status was nevertheless intolerable under a supposedly free government. Any plan for emancipation, Madison declared, would have to be gradual, for only by gradual measures could any "deep-rooted and widespread evil" be corrected. Furthermore, since slaves were recognized as property under the Constitution, any emancipation plan would have to pay a fair compensation to the masters. This would also reconcile the masters and help prevent violence and bloodshed. It was further necessary, Madison reasoned, that the plan provide for the free Negro so that "a state of freedom [will] be preferable, in his own estimation, to his actual one in a state of bondage." Madison felt using money earned by the sale of Western lands to purchase slaves from willing masters, under supervision of the national government, would be a sufficient, fair, and efficacious means of gradual abolition.

The most serious problem in Madison's view, arose from "existing and probably unalterable prejudices in the United States [requiring that] freed blacks . . . be permanently removed beyond the region occupied by, or alotted to, a white population." "Physical and lasting peculiarities" among the blacks would mean, if they were "thoroughly incorporated" in white society, "a change only from one to another species of oppression." "Reciprocal antipathies" would, moreover, leave a constant "danger of collisions" if the two races, each free, dwelled together. Clearly, Madison thought that blacks, either innately or from long bondage in Africa and America, were so different from and possibly inferior to the white population generally, and that white prejudices against them were so indelible, that meaningful freedom and equality for

Negroes in an integrated society was not practical. He hoped, therefore, to find a refuge somewhere in the world where freed slaves could
develop their full human potentialities entirely removed from the scene
of their former degradation. For a time, both Madison and Jefferson
thought the American West might provide such a refuge, but by 1819
Madison looked upon thinly settled parts of west Africa as the best
place for a colony of freed slaves. To this end, he had joined with Henry
Clay, Bushrod Washington, John Marshall, and many other eminent men,
mostly from the upper South, to found the American Colonization Society, dedicated both to the freeing of slaves and to their transportation to
the west coast of Africa. This idea, discussed by Jefferson and others
ever since the seventeen-eighties, had been urged systematically by Dr.
William Thornton in 1804, in a pamphlet dedicated to Madison. Madison
thought the plan practical if the national government would, over the
course of a generation or so, appropriate perhaps $600 million, the sum
to be expected from a sale at $2 an acre of about one third of the
Western lands then available. Such a fund would yield $400 to free each
of the one and one half million slaves in the country, and omitting slaves
unwilling or too old and frail to go to Africa, would furnish a surplus
to pay for transportation and for capital to develop Liberia, the nation
founded in 1822 for the freed slaves. Madison challenged those who
raised objections to come forth with a better plan and to remember the
transcendent need to *do something* about the looming evil that mocked
the moral integrity of the nation and even threatened the Union itself.[12]

Shortly after thus expressing himself, Madison heard from his ex-
secretary, Edward Coles, whose own antislavery feelings had intensified.
On an official mission to Russia, he had observed that serfdom was "a
form of servitude . . . infinitely of a milder and less oppressive character" than Negro slavery in America. Coles then freed his slaves, took
them to Illinois, gave each some land, and helped them become good
farmers. Madison was pleased Coles pursued "the true course" of providing for his Negroes' happiness as well as their freedom, because "with
the habits of the slave, and without the instruction, the property, or the
employments of a freeman, the manumitted blacks, instead of deriving
advantage from the partial benevolence of their Masters, furnish arguments against the general efforts in their behalf." Madison wished also
that Coles could change the color as well as the legal condition of his
slaves, because without this "they seem destined to a privation of that
moral rank and those social participations which give to freedom more
than half its value." The two Virginians thus displayed again the vital
difference that separated them: Coles so strongly felt the moral evil of
slavery, and had enough faith in the ability of his blacks, with such help
as he could give, to become genuinely free men, that he went ahead, with
great personal sacrifice, to manumit his slaves; Madison, on the other

hand, "lulled," as Coles put it, by a lifetime of existence with slavery, and without Coles's zealous faith in the ultimate equality of the races, was unwilling to undertake the suffering and disruption, for him and his slaves, of individual manumission. Furthermore, he placed his faith in a colonization plan that had serious practical difficulties and had as well supporters who saw it as a way to preserve slavery by getting rid of free blacks. That a man of Madison's realism and integrity should in this instance adhere to such an insufficient and compromised program is painful evidence of the virtually insoluble dilemma slavery posed for him.[13]

In the agitation preceding the Missouri Compromise, Madison opposed the restriction on slavery in Missouri, both because it denied Missouri the right to determine the question of slavery for itself, as the other states had done, and because he thought the "diffusion" of slavery, once importation was firmly prohibited, was the best way to secure its eventual abolition. Its abolition, he observed, had proved attainable in proportion to the relative scarcity of blacks in the population of a state. He feared as well "a new state of the parties, founded on local instead of political distinctions, thereby dividing the Republicans of the North from those of the South." This tendency, so clearly encouraged in the inflamatory and widely publicized speeches of Senator Rufus King and others, and added to heightening Southern sectionalism, was to Madison, as to Jefferson, "a firebell in the night," gravely threatening the survival of the Union.[14]

Madison wrote grimly to Lafayette in 1820 of "the dreadful fruitfulness of the original sin of the African trade." When the liberal Frenchman made his triumphal tour of the United States in 1824, he stopped for four days at Montpelier, and never missed, according to his secretary, "an opportunity to defend the rights *that all men without exception have to liberty*." Lafayette spent hours visiting with slaves at Montpelier, and though full of praise for Madison's humanity toward them, he made clear to his old friend that their joint efforts over a course of fifty years simply could not be reconciled with the existence of human slaves on the very plantations of those who talked so loudly of human freedom.

A few months later, Frances Wright, who had traveled in Lafayette's entourage, wrote Madison of her plan to gather slaves destined for freedom on large, collectivized plantations, where they could be educated while working to earn their independence. Madison replied that he doubted whether, under such an arrangement, "a competent discipline" could be maintained or whether "the prospect of emancipation at a future day will sufficiently overcome the natural and habitual repugnance to labor" on the part of blacks as well as whites. He doubted, too, whether "there is such an advantage of united over individual labor" as Miss Wright took for granted. Malice and indolence, in Madison's judgment, tempered plans to abolish slavery, just as they did all aspirations for human reformation. Commenting to Lafayette on the Wright plan and one he regarded as better—government purchase and manumission of all "female infants at their birth"—Madison insisted again that "no such effort would be listened to whilst the impression remains and it seems to be indelible, that the two races cannot co-exist, both being free and equal. The great *sine qua non*, therefore, is some external asylum for the coloured race."[15]

In the eighteen-thirties, as hope dimmed for state action for abolition, and as arguments upholding the virtues of slavery spread, the American Colonization Society seemed to Madison more and more to have the best plan. He accepted the presidency of the society, and, in a letter written four months after the Nat Turner rebellion, thought colonization prospects "brightening," and hoped the "increasing . . . spirit of private manumission" would gradually end "the dreadful calamity" of slavery. A little over a year later, reading Thomas R. Dew's defense of slavery and effort to blame the ills of the South on the tariff, Madison turned again to Colonization Society plans as the best answer. The expense of wholesale manumission and transportation he thought within the resources of the Union, and he insisted that thinly settled portions of Africa, plus lands in the far West or asylums in the West Indies, would provide ample space for freed slaves to develop their own society and culture. Madison admitted that "I may indulge too much my wishes and hopes, to be safe from error," but he thought partial success in colonization preferable to giving up in despair or to turning instead, as Dew did, to embrace slavery. The aged ex-President, eighty years resident on a Virginia farm, concluded by demolishing Dew's argument that the tariff had caused agricultural depression. Slavery itself was to blame, Madison asserted, insofar as it resulted in poor farming practices and led to the exploitive development of lands in Alabama and Mississippi. Even a slow and uncertain progress toward abolition was preferable, Madison asserted, "to a torpid acquiescence in a perpetuation of slavery, or an extinguishment of it by convulsions more disastrous in their character and consequences than slavery itself."[16]

In February 1835, Harriet Martineau, deeply concerned about slavery in America, visited Montpelier. She found Madison had "an inexhaustible faith that a well-founded commonwealth may . . . be immortal," a faith that "shone brightly" on every subject but slavery, where he was in despair. So great was his concern that Madison "talked more on the subject of slavery than on any other, acknowledging, without limitation or hesitation, all the evils with which it had ever been charged." It debauched young slave girls, who were expected to be mothers by the time they were fifteen. The Northern states, as well as foreign nations, treated freed blacks abominably. Though Madison thought treatment of slaves in Virginia had improved, in the new lands they were handled like brutes. He pitied as well the "slavery" of conscientious Southern women who could not trust their servants and had to superintend them in every detail. Masters lived "in a state of perpetual suspicion, fear and anger." Thus Madison extolled again the plans of the American Colonization Society, something Miss Martineau could ascribe only to his "overflowing faith; for the facts were before him that in eighteen years the Colonization Society had removed only between two and three thousand persons, while the annual increase of the slave population in the United States was upward of sixty thousand."[17]

As Madison's financial plight worsened, Virginia laws against manumission tightened, and prospects for freed blacks deteriorated, he withdrew from his intention, promised to Edward Coles, to free his slaves in his will, as Washington had done and Jefferson, unsuccessfully, had sought to do. Learning of Madison's hesitation, Coles wrote urging him not to let the practical difficulties of manumission deter him from a act of freedom that would be "the consummation of your glory." Madison agreed again to seek a plan to free his slaves, but difficulties accumulated. His slaves were terrified of Liberia, and of those remaining on the reduced Montpelier estate, two thirds were too young, too infirm, or too old to make the uncertainties of freedom seem a blessing to them. In October 1834 Madison sold sixteen slaves, who gladly consented to the transfer to a kinsman known for his humaneness. By thus disposing of surplus hands, for whom there was no longer work on his shrinking lands, Madison hoped to make Montpelier profitable enough to sustain plans to free the remaining slaves. Even this hope, however, was doomed, and in his will Madison said of his slaves merely that none of them should be sold without the slave's consent as well as Dolley Madison's. A lifetime of opposition to slavery had thus been reduced in Madison's will to a gesture, likely to be ineffectual, not of freedom, but only of decent treatment. As happened again and again in slave states, the demands of creditors and estate legatees subverted Madison's intentions. In the twenty years after Madison's death, in litigation following the sale of Montpelier (1844) and the deaths of Dolley Madison (1849) and her children (1851 and 1852), Madison's slaves were subjected to the miseries and uncertainties of their chattel condition.[18]

Beyond his invariably humane treatment, which made a slave's life at Montpelier as tolerable as possible, Madison failed utterly to do anything about what he always regarded as a moral evil and an economic catastrophe. He depended all his life on the labor of slaves; he did nothing effective to diminish the baneful place of the despised institution in the social fabric of Virginia; and at his death, slavery in the United States was far more an anomaly, a curse to the nation, and an affront to the conscience of mankind than it had been in his youth. Furthermore, his sense of the immense gulf between the ways of life of blacks and whites, whether inherent or resulting from centuries of cultural difference, was impressed on him during a lifetime of contact with blacks always in a degraded condition, and it prevented him from envisioning a human brotherhood in which men of different color might live equally, freely, and congenially together. Hence to him the only moral solution, fair to each race alike, especially in order to lift from blacks the "indelible prejudices" of whites confident of their own superiority, was division into separate societies. This was necessary not only to give blacks the life of freedom and opportunity Madison never doubted was as much their natural right as it was that of any portion of mankind, but also to complete the republican character of the United States, which was impossible as long as some men were slaves and others masters.

In June 1824 an itinerant bookseller, Samuel Whitcomb, commented on two Virginia customers he had recently visited:

> Mr. Madison is not so large or so tall as myself and instead of being a cool reserved austere man, is very sociable, rather jocose, quite sprightly, and active. . . . [He] appears less studied, brilliant and frank but more natural, candid and profound than Mr. Jefferson. Mr. Jefferson has more imagination and passion, quicker and richer conceptions. Mr. Madison has a sound judgment, tranquil temper and logical mind. . . . Mr. Madison has nothing in his looks, gestures, expression or manners to indicate anything extraordinary in his intellect or character, but the more one converses with him, the more his excellences are developed and the better he is liked. And yet he has a quizzical, careless, almost waggish bluntness of looks and expression which is not at all prepossessing.

Whitcomb further observed that Madison took many newspapers and, much more than Jefferson, remained well informed on current issues. In fact, from the moment he left Washington, Madison remained an active elder statesman, fully abreast of public affairs and in close touch with the nation's political leaders.[19]

In the first years of Madison's "retirement," Monroe and Richard Rush, almost as if from force of habit, forwarded diplomatic dispatches to Montpelier and consulted Madison on Latin America, Florida border disputes, the tariff, internal improvements, and other matters. A stream of letters came back from Orange. Madison took special interest in the convulsions racking South America as the Spanish colonies sought independence, consciously and at almost every step seeking to emulate their revolution-founded northern neighbor. The ex-President urged his successor to give "every lawful manifestation" of United States approval of the revolutionaries, "whatever may be the consequences," and saw with pleasure Britain's inclination to prevent the other European powers from helping Spain retain control. In 1823, as the repressive intentions of the Holy Alliance became clear, French armies invaded Spain, and Russia declared her right to expand down the Pacific coast, Monroe sought his predecessor's advice on the crossroads confronting American foreign policy. Britain had proposed cooperation with the United States to prevent the Holy Allies from "reducing the Revolutionized Colonies . . . to their former dependence." Madison replied to Monroe's queries that United States sympathy with the "liberties and independence [of] . . . these neighbors . . . and the consequences threatened by a command of their resources by the Great Powers confederated against their rights and reforms" made it imperative "to defeat the meditated crusade." It was fortunate, too, he observed, that Britain, whatever her motives, sought the same object. "With that cooperation we have nothing to fear from the rest of Europe, and with it the best assurance of success to our laudable views." "In the great struggle of the Epoch between liberty and despotism," Madison observed to Jefferson, "we owe it to ourselves to sustain the former in this hemisphere at least." Madison suggested a joint proclamation with Great Britain on behalf of Latin American independence. "With the British fleets and fiscal resources associated with our own," he noted to Rush several days later, "we should be safe against the rest of the World, and at liberty to pursue whatever course might be prescribed by a just estimate of our moral and political obligations."

Though later dispatches from London, John Quincy Adams' distaste at the United States being "a cock-boat in the wake of the British man-of-war," and Monroe's own inclination toward a unilateral American proclamation resulted in the famous Monroe Doctrine rather than Madison's proposed joint statement, the effect was much the same. The United States, with implicit British support and approval, had declared against colonialism in the Americas. Madison congratulated Monroe a few months later that despite the enmity of the Holy Alliance toward "free Government everywhere," the British-American stand had had "a benumbing influence on all their wicked enterprises." Madison's support of Latin American independence and of United States action with whatever friendly powers that might care to cooperate to resist the spread of despotism were, of course, consistent with his lifelong views of foreign affairs. He had shown himself, as well, fully able to forget a half century of anti-British hostility should Britain prove by her conduct once again to be a friend of freedom. Madison expressed his basic faith to Lafayette: "Despotism can only exist in darkness, and there are too many lights now in the political firmament, to permit it to remain anywhere, as it has heretofore done, almost everywhere."[20]

Madison even speculated that "were it possible by human contrivance so to accelerate the intercourse between every part of the globe that all its inhabitants could be united under the superintending authority of an ecumenical Council, how great a portion of human evils would be avoided. Wars, famines, with pestilence as far as the fruit of either, could not exist; taxes to pay for wars, or to provide against them would be needless, and the expense and perplexities of local fetters on interchange beneficial to all would no longer oppress the social state." Madison nonetheless retained a skepticism about quick and easy solutions, as is evident in a remark to John Quincy Adams, who had delivered to Jeremy Bentham Madison's polite deflation of the English philosopher's scheme to rationalize and codify American law: "[Either] I greatly overrate or [Bentham] greatly underrates the task . . . not only [of digesting] our Statutes into a concise and clear system, but [of reducing] our unwritten to a text law." Blending high hopes, always important to Madison, with the limitations impressed on him by his experience in public life and his sense of human frailty was the supreme political task.[21]

Chief Justice John Marshall's opinion in the McCulloch vs. Maryland case also commanded Madison's attention. Spencer Roane of the Virginia Court of Appeals and other jurists incensed at Marshall's nationalist doctrines sought Madison's support. Reflecting thirty years of political opposition to Marshall, and seeing in his decisions, almost verbatim, Hamilton's arguments for the "latitudinary mode of expounding the Constitution," Madison objected to Marshall's obiter dicta indiscriminately extending the power of the national government. Madison insisted that to place no restriction on the *means* Congress might choose to achieve its constitutional ends destroyed the whole notion of limited government. "To give an extent to the . . . means [of government] superseding the limits of [its objects] is in effect to convert a limited into an unlimited Government," Madison held. He agreed with Marshall, though, that the state of Maryland had no power to tax the Bank of the United States.

Two years later, following the Cohens vs. Virginia decision, Madison again sympathized with Roane's disgust at Marshall's "practice of mingling with his judgments pronounced, comments and reasonings of a scope beyond them; . . . and an apparent disposition to amplify the authorities of the Union at the expense of those of the States." The great need, the ex-President declared, was to maintain impartially the constitutional boundary between the state and federal governments. Sometimes this required restraint on state encroachments and sometimes on federal invasions. Madison belittled Roane's wild fears of Marshall's "ingenious and fatal sophistries" and the Supreme Court's "usurpations," however, by observing that other agencies of government, when backed by the sense of the people, would be fully able to restrain the court. One such "usurping experiment," the Alien and Sedition Acts, had thus been "crushed at once." Then, aiming directly at Roane's argument that the federal courts had no power to set aside decisions of the highest state tribunals, Madison upheld the final jurisdiction of the federal Supreme Court: "Were this trust to be vested in the States in their individual characters, the Constitution of the U.S. might become different in every State, and would be pretty sure to do so in some; the State Governments would not stand all in the same relation to the General Government, some retaining more, others less of sovereignty, and the vital principle of equality, which cements their Union thus gradually be deprived of its virtue."

Jefferson on the other hand, had agreed with Roane. Madison waited two years to politely but firmly set Jefferson straight. His plan to call conventions to settle disputes over state and federal jurisdictions Madison called "too tardy, too troublesome, and too expensive, besides its tendency to lessen a salutary veneration" for the Supreme Court. To suppose in such questions equal authority in state and federal courts, would end, after consultations had left some matters still in dispute, in "a trial of strength between the Posse headed by the Marshal and the Posse headed by the Sheriff." Madison then reaffirmed his opinion (stated in *Federalist*, Number 39, thirty-five years earlier, he reminded Jefferson) that to prevent inequalities and appeals to the sword, a federal tribunal must "ultimately" draw the line between state and national power. He also insisted, ten years later, on the primacy of the judiciary over the legislature and the executive in *interpreting* laws: "Notwithstanding [the] abstract view of the coordinate and independent right of the three departments to expound the Constitution, the Judicial department most familiarizes itself to the public attention as the expositor, by the *order* of its functions in relation to the other departments. . . . It may always be expected that the judicial bench, when happily filled, will most engage the respect and reliance of the public as the surest expositor of the Constitution."[22]

While the split over interpreting the Constitution lingered in the background, letters from an old Federalist antagonist, Jedidiah Morse, revealed another difference between Jefferson and Madison. To lead the Indians into the ways of white civilization, Morse proposed a national society composed of ex-Presidents, virtually all officers of the federal government, an array of state officials, Indian agents, and military officers, as well as all the college professors and clergymen in the nation. Jefferson estimated that of the total of perhaps 8,500 people, nineteen twentieths would be clergymen. He wrote at once to

Morse, refusing cooperation because the "gigantic" organization, however laudable its intention, would "rivalize and jeopardize the government." Writing to Madison, hoping he too would spurn Morse,
Jefferson explained further that though voluntary organizations of "moderate" size were useful, and "general associations coextensive with the
nation" might be necessary in revolutionary times, in the United States,
where no abuses called for revolution, "voluntary associations so extensive as to grapple with and controul the government . . . are dangerous
machines, and should be frowned upon in every regulated government." The goal of Morse's society, Jefferson observed, was being pursued by the government "with superior means, superior wisdom, and
under limits of legal prescription," and he foresaw further that a few
persons "clubbed together" in Washington under Morse's direction
would use the society for their own, perhaps nefarious, and at any rate,
unrestrained, purposes.

Unknown to Jefferson, Madison had already accepted membership
in Morse's society, esteeming its benevolent goal of rescuing the Indians
from their own "vices" as well as from those "doubled from our intercourse with them." The Indians could not really be helped, Madison
observed, "without substituting for the torpid indolence of wigwams
and the precarious supplies of the chase the comforts and habits of
civilized life." Madison also thought the intention to gather information
about "the opinions, the government, the social conditions, etc. of this
untutored race [might reveal] . . . a just picture of the human character" in its natural state. As to Jefferson's fears, Madison thought Morse's
plan "rather ostentatious than dangerous." The proposed membership,
wrote Madison, recurring to a favorite theme, was "too numerous, too
heterogeneous, and too much dispersed, to concentrate their views in
any covert or illicit object." Furthermore, even the clergy, so apparently
dominant, were "themselves made up of such repulsive sects that they
are not likely to form a noxious confederacy, especially with ecclesiastical views." Madison did concede that Jefferson had spotted an excessive concentration of power in the small board of directors, but even
that, Madison thought, would be rendered harmless by the watchful
eyes "of so many of every description of observers" in Washington.
Madison here reflected the same sense of the self-regulating quality of
a free society that again and again made him support or at least view
with equanimity plans or associations to *do things*, wherein the less
subtle Jefferson could see only the threat of bad men combining for
evil purposes. Though Jefferson spoke, in dead earnest, on behalf of the
people and their government, Madison in a crucial way displayed more
faith in the beneficent effects of "the extensive republic."

Madison revealed further both his unquestioned conviction that the
civilized ways of agriculture, trade, and republican government were

best for all men and his sense of the value of other cultures when he wrote approvingly of another plan to improve the lot of the Indians. Though Madison acknowledged he was "less sanguine" of the result than its promoter, he said, "I do not despair, and join in applauding the philanthropy and zeal that labour and hope for it." He advised, in estimating Indian character, further study of the advanced Aztec and Inca civilizations and the ability of Indians descending from them to live successfully and equitably in stable, Europeanized societies. Only with such understanding, Madison believed, could the problem of the "red race on our borders . . . next to the . . . black race within our bosom, . . . the most baffling to the policy of our country," be handled with humanity and any hope of success.[23]

In the extended controversy over the tariff, Madison stuck to his support of mildly protective duties as explained in his annual message of 1815 (see Chapter XXI). When the tariff of 1824 was before Congress, Madison wrote Thomas Cooper that he considered the general principle of free industry and free trade "unanswerably established," and furthermore a policy "certainly most congenial with the spirit of a free people, and particularly due to the intelligent and enterprizing citizens of the United States." He therefore told Henry Clay that he could not concur entirely in the extent of the proposed tariff or "in some of the reasonings by which it is advocated." The only industries that might be protected indefinitely, Madison wrote Clay, were those producing military supplies, other "indispensable" strategic materials, and goods calculated to be so expensive in wartime as to justify the higher cost of tariff-protected domestic manufacture in peacetime. Furthermore, there might be a *"temporary* [protection to] introduce a particular manufacture, which once introduced will flourish without that encouragement." "In every doubtful case," Madison wrote, "the government should forbear to intermeddle"; foreseeing the heated sectional dispute of a few years later, he added that "particular caution should be observed, where one part of the community would be favored at the expense of another." A "moderate tariff," Madison asserted, would "answer the purpose of revenue and foster domestic manufactures" without an undue interference with the economically and politically beneficent principle of free trade. Remembering Hamilton's national economic planning schemes, which he had fought in Congress in the seventeen-nineties, Madison had little use for the grandiose aspects of Clay's "American System."[24]

In 1828, when Southern hostility to the so-called Tariff of Abominations engendered arguments denying the constitutionality of any protective duties and even asserting the right of states to nullify tariffs deemed injurious to themselves, Madison wrote long public letters addressed to Joseph C. Cabell reaffirming his arguments to Clay on the *advisability* of a tariff in some instances, and upholding the constitutionality of a protective tariff. With his usual thoroughness and unique authority, Madison pointed out that regulation of commerce in the *national* interest had been a prime reason for adopting the Constitution in 1787, that this power had not been questioned in the ratifying conventions, and that in the tariff debates during the First Congress, Southern states no less than Northern ones had sought protective tariffs useful to themselves. Forty years of "uniform and universal" acceptance by every state in the Union of national regulation of commerce, Madison insisted, settled that question. Finally, he noted that if one accepted the extreme states' rights doctrines, "there would be an end to that stability in Government and in Laws which is essential to good Government and good Laws; a stability, the want of which is the imputation which has at all times been levelled against Republicanism with most effect by its most dexterous adversaries." Though Madison's requirement that tariffs be brought "to the test of justice and the general good" implied objection to the inequitable burden the 1828 tariff imposed on the South, he was perfectly clear that the line of resistance taken by South Carolina and the "Richmond Junto" (a group of Virginia Republicans) countenanced far graver dangers.[25]

Publication of Madison's views had great influence in Richmond and in Washington, Attorney General William Wirt and others reported, while *Niles' Weekly Register* remarked that Madison had throughout the country "silenced the *constitutional* croakers [like] . . . frogs frozen up in a pond." Nevertheless, Madison wrote Clay in 1832 that he hoped the "deep and extensive discontent" caused by the tariff might be relieved by compromise. It was "impossible to do perfect justice in the distribution of burdens and benefits," Madison admitted, but "equitable estimates and mutual concessions are necessary to approach it."[26]

Madison's only formal resumption of public life during his retirement came in 1829, when he accepted election as a delegate from Orange County to a Virginia convention to draft a new state constitution. Then, as he had done in 1776 and in 1788, he journeyed to the state capital to consider the fundamental law under which free men would choose to live. Leaving the Orange-Charlottesville region for the first time in twelve years, in October 1829 the Madisons rode to Richmond, where for three months they lived with Dolley's cousin Sally Coles Stevenson, enjoying Richmond society while Madison attended the convention. George Tucker found Madison "rejuvenated; . . . his cheerfulness and amenity and abundant stock of racy anecdotes were the delight of every social board." Dolley, of course, was in her glory. Anne Royall, who came to interview the famous sixty-year-old hostess, was astonished to find instead of "a little old dried-up woman," one "tall, young, active and elegant." With a full, oval face, and large, expressive dark eyes set off by a silk checked turban and black glossy curls, Dolley Madison "captivated by her artless though warm affability." She was "as active on her feet as a girl," and seemed to Mrs. Royall to be "young enough for Mr. Madison's daughter." "Her power to please, the irresistible grace of her every movement shed such a charm over all she says and does," Mrs. Royall exclaimed, "that it is impossible not to admire her." A young man who came to visit Madison found him "in tolerably good health, thin of flesh, rather under the common size, and dressed in his customary black, old-fashioned clothes. His form [was] erect, his step firm but somewhat slow, walks without a staff, his visage pale, and abounding in small wrinkles, his features well-proportioned but not striking, his head bald on the top but excessively powdered showing a point in front. . . . His forehead of common size, his brow grey, heavy, and projecting, his eyes small and faded, his nose of ordinary size and straight, his mouth rather small, . . . his ears obscured by whiskers and hair, his sight and hearing both somewhat impaired."[27]

The convention itself gathered the surviving leaders of Virginia public life in the past half century. At the opening session Madison nominated Monroe as presiding officer, and then with Chief Justice Marshall, escorted him to the chair. Madison was the sole surviving member of the 1776 convention, while Monroe and Marshall, Washington's comrades in arms, had each served the state and nation for more than fifty years. Among those whose careers dated from the seventeen-nineties were three long-time antagonists of Madison's, Littleton W. Tazewell, John Randolph of Roanoke, and William B. Giles. Of the younger members, many of whom would remain active in public life through the Civil War, literally dozens saw the seventy-eight-year-old Madison as a demigod whose thought and career had been guides for them as long as they could remember. Thus pre-eminent among the distinguished company crowded into the old House of Delegates chamber in the capitol (now a restored museum room dominated by a statue of Robert E. Lee), Madison appeared daily for the convention sessions, taking his seat, as he had done so often before in deliberative bodies, near the front in order to pay close attention to the proceedings.

Two great issues faced the convention. On the first, whether to extend the suffrage to those who did not own land, Madison stopped short of advocating universal suffrage, but he did succeed in pushing through the committee on legislation he headed an extension of the vote to all householders and heads of families who paid taxes. Noting that the rapidly increasing population of the United States would, despite the vast expanses of unsettled land, force large numbers, possibly even a majority, and perhaps within a century, to live in cities, Madison declared that republican government could not, in justice or in safety, be rested on a minority. Therefore citizens who, even though they did not have freeholds, had "a sufficient stake in the public order and the stable administration of the laws" should be allowed to vote.

Insisting as he and Jefferson always had that in *good* government responsibility had to accompany the right to participate, Madison could not accept the simple solution of universal suffrage, but in urging the extension he did, he satisfied the demands of most of those who sought the vote, stood on the liberalizing side in the convention, and broadened his own understanding of the needs of majority government. To the safety gained by eliminating a large portion of the disenfranchised, and therefore potentially rebellious, citizens, Madison sought by extending "the partnership of power," to add the constructive "political and moral influence emanating from the actual possession of authority and a just and beneficial exercise of it." This position, accepting the beneficent effects of political participation, put Madison clearly on the road to advocating universal suffrage once it became clear that possessors of property were not always responsive to the public welfare, any more than those without it always acted irresponsibly. His theory of suffrage, far from seeking to protect vested interests by exclusions, in fact *required* a steady expansion, keeping pace with, and even encouraging the growth of, a citizenry responsible not only to the rights of property but, in a priority always insisted upon by Madison, even more to the natural and political rights inseparable from republican government.

On the even more divisive issue of whether to count slaves in apportioning the state legislature, Madison again advocated a liberalizing course. The portions of the state east of the mountains wanted their numerous slaves counted, to retain their heavy preponderance, while the western counties insisted on a "white basis" that would give them, with proportionally far fewer slaves, a much stronger voice in the legislature. Under the old constitution, counting slaves, white votes in the east had at least twice as much weight as white votes in the west. Madison managed, narrowly, to move through his committee on legislation a "white basis" for the lower house, while retaining the old provision in the less powerful Senate. Expecting Madison to stand with them, eastern delegates fumed about his "fatuity" and "treason." Madison's compromise caused hotheads on both sides to bemoan "the effect of putting old men in active life." Shaken by the violence of eastern denunciation, and sensing defeat, Madison shifted to advocate the use of the federal three-fifths ratio in apportioning the lower house. Monroe stood with him, while Marshall voted against any movement toward a "white basis." Petitions poured in on the convention from eastern constituencies, threatening disunion and violence unless their position was protected.

In this tense atmosphere, Madison, in old-fashioned powdered hair, black clothes, and shoe buckles, rose on December 2 to deliver his only speech before the convention. *"Members from all parts of the Hall* (with the exception of not more than ten) gathered round him to catch the lowest accents from his tongue," a Richmond *Enquirer* reporter wrote. "His voice was low and weak, but his sentences were rounding and complete; and his enunciation, though tremulous and full of feeling, was distinct to those who heard him." Madison began by noting that he was deeply sensible of the disqualifications imposed by his extreme age and long retirement; he asked time to make only "a few observations." He affirmed his lifelong insistence that "in republics, the great danger is, that the majority may not sufficiently respect the rights of the minority." Generosity, social feelings, and even conscience were insufficient guards against selfish drives, whether in minorities or majorities. Though the "favorable attributes of the human character are all valuable, as auxiliaries," Madison observed, repeating language he had used before the 1788 Virginia convention, "they will not serve as a substitute for the coercive provision belonging to Government and Law. . . . The only effectual safeguard to the rights of the minority, must be laid in such a basis and structure of the Government itself, as may afford, in a certain degree, directly or indirectly, a defensive authority in behalf of a minority having right on its side." Therefore Madison urged the convention to accept the three-fifths basis for the lower house, both to give a security to the "peculiar" property of the easterners, and to give some recognition, even though a degraded one, to the humanity of the Negro slaves. Madison hoped further that the interests of the slaves might receive a little protection, sometimes by eastern members anxious to protect them as property, and sometimes by western members sympathizing with them against the oppressive designs of their masters. Madison concluded with a plea for "the spirit of compromise" that found him, consciously and almost word for word, re-enacting the role played by the aged Franklin at the close of the 1787 Federal Convention. He asked his fellow delegates not to despair, "notwithstanding all the threatening appearances we have passed through," but instead to "agree on some common ground, all sides relaxing in their opinions, not changing, but mutually surrendering a part of them."[28]

Madison's efforts at compromise failed, however, in the face of unyielding pressure from eastern delegates determined to retain their favored position as slaveowners. With the help of westerners, now seeking to disrupt the convention rather than accept less than a full "white basis," eastern delegates defeated Madison's three-fifths compromise and then pushed through provisions maintaining eastern control of both houses of the legislature. Partly through his own shifting tactics and failure to stand resolutely for majority rule and against slavery, Madison had vitiated his own influence and helped put the convention under the control of men with less subtle, less ambiguous intentions. Though, at adjournment, universal respect for "the venerable Mr. Madison" led to an affecting scene where all members, some with tear-filled eyes, shook his hand, he admitted after he got home that the convention, "by indulging the party whose defeat would have been most pregnant with danger to it," had surrendered to those "fixed in their hot opinion." Dolley Madison wrote that there had been so much gaiety and "quiet but thorough hospitality" in Richmond that she would like to spend the winters there, but her husband was discouraged that Virginia had not insisted on majority rule. "A government resting on a minority is an aristocracy, not a Republic," he noted severely, "and could not be safe with a numerical and physical force against it, without a standing army, an enslaved press, and a disarmed populace." The 1830 Virginia constitution was not a document of which Madison was proud, nor did he admire the tenor of the convention debates. Though he maintained an outward equanimity, he must have sensed that in Virginia, and the rest of the South, slavery and its defenders had become, as he had always feared they would, a grave threat to the survival of republican government.[29]

Madison's most important and fateful confrontation with forces defending the South and its "peculiar institution," however, came during the South Carolina nullification crisis, 1828 to 1833. He saw at once that the doctrines of nullification and secession posed a fundamental threat, and he took an active part in the war of words waged against them. His public defense of the constitutionality of the tariff had aroused the ire of states'-righters, but was only a mild foretaste of the storm that broke over him when Giles, Calhoun, and others insisted that the doctrine of nullification rested on the Kentucky and Virginia Resolutions of 1798. In holding that the Constitution countenanced state nullification of federal laws deemed in violation of the Constitution, states' rights theorists asserted they did no more than Jefferson and Madison had done in resisting the Alien and Sedition Acts in 1798–1800. The South Carolina "Exposition" of December 1828 declared that Madison's 1800 "Report on the [Virginia] Resolutions" so ably upheld the doctrine of state sovereignty that no further argument was needed. William B. Giles, in anonymous newspaper articles defending nullification, quoted at length from Madison's "Report" and from Jefferson's recently published letters declaiming against expansion of federal authority. As if suspecting Madison's rebuttal, Giles asked his readers to "rely on [Madison's] opinions of fifty," rather than on any senile effusions at age seventy-nine.

To State Senator Joseph C. Cabell, who led the antinullificationists in Richmond, Madison outlined arguments against the doctrine. The *people* composing the states, not the state governments, were the parties to the constitutional compact, delegating certain powers to the general government and reserving others to the states. The Constitution further provided that the Supreme Court of the United States should decide disputes over the boundary between state and federal powers. Admissible remedies for "usurpations" concurred in by the court, Madison said, included remonstrances and instructions such as those used by Virginia in 1798, "recurring elections and impeachments," and amendments to the Constitution. Finally, the ultimate resort, the natural right of resistance and revolution, was available to states or to individual citizens, but this exercise dissolved government and could not be claimed under the Constitution. Short of such extremities, Madison insisted nuliification made a farce of national law and supposed the Constitution established a mere league rather than a government. "The awful consequences of a final rupture and dissolution of the Union," which nullification certainly foreshadowed, Madison declared, "must be shuddered at by every friend to his country, to liberty, to the happiness of man."[30]

Early in 1830 the Webster-Hayne debate heated up the controversy and drew Madison further into its center. Each orator claimed Madison's support. Webster noted Madison's "impregnable" defense of the constitutionality of the tariff in the published letters to Cabell and the certainty that the Father of the Constitution could not approve a nullification doctrine almost certainly fatal to the Union. Hayne cited the report of 1800 at length, quoting (out of context) phrases such as "[the federal constitution] is a compact to which the States are parties." Though Madison did not wholly approve Webster's sweeping insistence that "the people of the United States in the aggregate" had established the Constitution, he unequivocally took Webster's side in the argument. Madison was delighted to hear from his young friend Nicholas P. Trist, who had sat in the Senate galleries enthralled during the debate, that Webster had been "the mammouth deliberately treading the canebreak," so devastating was his reply to Hayne. To Senator Hayne, who immediately sent copies of his speeches to Montpelier, Madison acknowledged their "ability and eloquence," but then explained in detail why he was "constrained to dissent . . . from the doctrines espoused in them."[31]

Madison gradually gave in to the mounting pressure to speak out and thus arrest, as the Richmond *Whig* put it, "the deadly poison circulating under the authority of his name." In June 1830 South Carolina and Virginia newspapers printed a letter from Madison to a South Carolina Unionist warning against interpretations of the Constitution giving the federal government virtually unlimited powers but nonetheless denying that state sovereignty was supreme and indivisible or that states could revoke or alter federal laws or the federal constitution on their own authority alone. Richmond Juntoists began to shift ground and declared that Virginia, despite her belief in states' rights, would not join South Carolina in nullification. As a Madison-suggested alliance of Unionists and moderate states'-righters emerged in Richmond, Cabell pronounced that "nullification is dead in this state." Sensing the power of Madison's support, Congressman Edward Everett, also editor of the influential *North American Review*, asked permission to print Madison's rebuke to Hayne, which had somehow come to his attention. Madison agreed, but recast the letter into one to Everett. It was printed in October 1830, Madison's final, most carefully considered interpretation of the nature and powers of the federal constitution.[32]

The aged statesman, weak from an attack of bilious fever, began by pointing out again, as he had in *Federalist*, Number 39, that the Constitution established neither a consolidated (national) government nor a confederated one, but rather a composite, or mixture of both. Since this was a unique form, it had to be interpreted in and of itself, and could not be expounded by "similitudes and analogies." Since the Constitution had been formed by *the people* of the states (the same authority that established the state constitutions, Madison noted), it *shared* sovereignty with the state governments and, furthermore, could be altered or annulled only with the consent, according to the prescribed modes, of the other parties to it, all the states and the federal government itself. Turning to the division of powers between the federal and state governments, Madison pointed out that the general government was no less sovereign, supreme in its prescribed realm, than the states themselves. In the vital matter of "controversies . . . concerning the boundaries of jurisdiction," Madison insisted that the clauses of the federal constitution making federal statutes the supreme law of the land, binding state judges to the federal constitution, and giving the federal judiciary jurisdiction in all cases arising under federal law indicated clearly that the Supreme Court of the United States was to be the final arbiter. To give this power to the states would violate the "vital principle [of] . . . a uniform authority of the laws." To make it a matter of "negotiation" among the parties overlooked the resort to arms that was the only recourse among "independent and separate sovereignties" when negotiations broke down, as invariably happened occasionally. There were many provisions within the Constitution, such as state control of Senators and frequent elections that had proved effective against the Alien and Sedition Acts, to guard against federal usurpations. On the other hand, the doctrine of nullification allowed the general government no means to defend itself against state pretensions, and hence would lead certainly to its demise.

Turning to "the expedient lately advanced," Madison pointed out that the proposal that state nullifications stand unless rejected by three fourths of the states was hopelessly cumbersome and insisted instead that changes (nullifications) be made only *with* the approval of that proportion of states, a provision already existing under the Constitution. As to the claim that the Virginia Resolutions of 1798 and "Report on the Resolutions" (1800) sanctioned nullification, Madison apologized for language perhaps insufficiently guarded, but went on to assert that not the resolves nor the "Report" nor the debates in the Virginia legislature anywhere disclosed any "reference whatever to a constitutional right in an individual state to arrest by force the operation of a law of the United States." The intent was entirely to call for concurring statements from other states and other modes of cooperation among them, as soon transpired in the political campaign that ousted the government responsible for the offending laws. Nothing was said in the Virginia proceedings, Madison observed, "that can be understood to look to means of maintaining the rights of the states beyond the regular ones within the forms of the Constitution." Further action could be justified only under the *natural* right, "extra and ultra constitutional," of resistance and rebellion, which, of course canceled the constitutional compact and returned society to a state of nature.[33]

Antinullificationists thrilled at Madison's performance. Cabell called its effect "as great as ever was produced by any document in any age or country." Edward Coles thought it "the clearest exposition of the Constitution" he had ever read, and even Chief Justice Marshall wrote of his "peculiar pleasure . . . [that Mr. Madison] is himself again, [avowing] the opinions of his best days." Nullifiers, having depended so heavily on the "doctrines of '98," felt injured and betrayed. Some who had recently praised and revered Madison became "his most embittered revilers and denouncers," while others argued at length that the resolves and report of 1798 and 1800 *had* made the states the final arbiters of the meaning of the Constitution and that Madison's recent letter was therefore a tissue of sophistries, demonstrating only his own inconsistency and senility.[34]

Meanwhile, events conspired to place Madison's friends, and hence his ideas, close to President Jackson's ear. Nicholas Trist, appointed a State Department clerk by Clay in 1827, became a White House aide and finally, in 1830, Jackson's private secretary, through his intimacy with Jackson's nephew Andrew Jackson Donelson. From then through the early months of 1833, Trist wrote at length to Montpelier of the problems faced by the administration, while Madison supplied Trist, and hence the President, with arguments and information useful in resisting nullification. Trist filled Washington and Virginia newspapers with anonymous articles that were often little more than paraphrases of Madison's notes and letters to him. Madison also advised the increasingly influential Martin Van Buren on interpreting the Constitution. Perhaps most strategic of all, after Jackson's expulsion of the Calhounite, anti-Peggy Eaton members of his cabinet in April 1831, Edward

Livingston became his Secretary of State and draftsman for documents on nullification. Livingston had been Madison's cohort in 1798, resisting the Alien and Sedition Acts. Though not always political allies, by 1831 they were again on friendly terms, and Madison responded to Livingston's inquiries with helpful advice on the best formulations to use against the nullifiers. Finally, the hero-President himself, informed by Trist of Madison's personal responsibility for his appointment as major general in 1814, and grateful for Madison's refusal to speak out against him in the 1828 election, maintained an affectionate respect for his former commander in chief. Jackson's visit to Montpelier in the summer of 1832 strengthened the personal bond between the two old patriots, and afforded them a congenial opportunity to attune their defenses of the Union. At the same time, by retaining his ties to the leading anti-Jackson foes of nullification, Clay, Webster, and John Quincy Adams, Madison was the nonpartisan elder statesman, the "honorary chairman" of an informal national committee to preserve the Union. Madison's still-powerful mind and unique prestige permitted him, though past eighty and long retired, to perform a final, vital service to his country.[35]

Through 1831 and 1832, Madison wrote long letters, not published over his name but obviously intended for public use, upholding the constitutionality of the tariff but at the same time both resisting nullification and denying that the "general welfare" or "necessary and proper" clauses gave Congress virtually unlimited authority, as Clay, Webster, and others at times seemed to assert. Madison, the living sage of Montpelier, also wrote at length to repudiate efforts by nullificationists to claim for their side the dead sage of Monticello. Finding unguarded expressions of states' rights in Jefferson's recently published letters, and aware that the word "nullify" had been used in the Kentucky Resolutions, drafted by Jefferson, the nullifiers argued that Jefferson was their source and that insofar as Madison protested, he betrayed or misinterpreted his dead friend. Though letters in Madison's possession confirmed more certainly than he liked Jefferson's authorship of the incriminating Kentucky Resolutions and his unequivocal appeal at times to state sovereignty, Madison insisted that a fair overall view of Jefferson's public and private writings afforded little comfort to the nullifiers, who "make the name of Mr. Jefferson the pedestal for their colossal heresy . . . [and] shut their eyes and lips, whenever his authority is ever so clearly and emphatically against them." Further, Madison observed, "allowances . . . ought to be made for a habit in Mr. Jefferson, as in others of great genius, of expressing in strong and round terms, impressions of the moment." To Madison, the South Carolina doctrines of 1830 to 1833 echoed the peripheral and occasional rather than the essential, enduring Jefferson, who had in fact worked for half a century to establish a viable Union.

As the crisis deepened, Madison's concern for the Union and disgust at its foes grew. "The idea," he wrote Trist in May 1832, "that a Constitution which has been so fruitful of blessings, and a Union admitted to be the only guardian of the peace, liberty and happiness of the people of the States comprizing it should be broken up and scattered to the winds without greater than the existing causes is more painful than words can express. It is impossible that this can ever be the deliberate act of the people, if the value of the Union be calculated by the consequences of disunion." The "preposterous and anarchic" proposals of the nullifiers for state conventions to approve acts of the Union had "no shadow of countenance in the Constitution," Madison asserted, and contained "such a deadly poison" that the Union would not last a year under them. He begged for equitable distribution of burdens among the states and urged "mutual concessions," but all within prescribed constitutional modes.[36]

In December 1832 Madison read the recently passed South Carolina nullification ordinance defying the authority of the federal government to enforce the tariff within her boundaries and embracing, theoretically, the even more dangerous heresy of secession. He sent long treatises Trist used in newspapers campaigns against nullification, and approved the conclusion, if not all the arguments, of Jackson's antinullification proclamation of December 10, written by Livingston. Pleas from Richmond for help against states'-righters seeking to place Virginia at South Carolina's side prompted letters from Montpelier denying that the proceedings of 1798 in any way furnished a precedent for South Carolina's recent deed. Virginia withheld her vital support. In Washington, Senator William Cabell Rives of Virginia, recently returned from France, spoke brilliantly for the Union, using materials furnished by Madison. "Mr. Rives . . . has met Mr. Calhoun on his own ground," wrote one correspondent sitting in the galleries, "and by one of the ablest speeches delivered this session, has demolished the doctrine of nullification, root and branch. . . . You have no idea how Mr. Rives's facts and arguments made Mr. Calhoun wince in his seat." Madison declared Rives's speech "very able and enlightening" and hoped it would confound those who sought to label defenders of the Union "as Innovators, heretics and Apostates." It made perfectly clear that "whilst a State remains within the Union it cannot withdraw its citizens from the operation of the Constitution and laws of the Union"; nor was "the more formidable" doctrine of secession any more within the meaning of the Constitution. Madison also praised a speech by Webster that "crushes 'nullification,' and must hasten the abandonment of 'secession.' "[37]

Early in 1833, Henry Clay, claiming he "adhered to the doctrines of that ablest, wisest and purest of American statesmen, James Madison," arranged the compromise tariff that led to the repeal of South Carolina's nullification ordinance. Madison hoped this would be "an anodyne on the feverish excitement under which the public mind was laboring," but he was nonetheless alarmed by "the torch of discord" lighted by the South Carolinians and by Northern hotheads who proclaimed "unconstitutional designs on the subject of . . . slaves." With a deep emotional breach opening between the sections, Madison hoped that "as the gulf is approached the deluded will recoil from its horrors, and that the deluders, if not themselves sufficiently startled, will be abandoned and overwhelmed by their followers." "What *madness* in the South," Madison lamented, "to look for greater safety in disunion. It would be worse than jumping out of the Frying-pan into the fire: it would be jumping into the fire for fear of the Frying-pan." Calhoun's defensive "Exposition" of 1828 was as much anathema to the architect of the "extended republic" as was fearful antifederalism in 1788 or timorous New England Federalism from 1808 to 1814. It was fitting that virtually the last remnant of Madison's strength should be expended against an effort to deny to the nation the benefits of mutual accord that could only come in union.[38]

More congenial, less nationally significant, though not in Madison's view less deeply important, than the fight against nullification was the care and labor Madison lavished on the infant University of Virginia throughout the years of his retirement. In 1816 he was appointed, with Jefferson and Monroe, one of the trustees, or visitors, of the university, at first called Central College, to be established Jefferson hoped, in Charlottesville, with the support of the state of Virginia. Though Madison did not leave Washington in time to attend a meeting of the board called for April 8, 1817, he did go to Charlottesville on May 5 to meet with Jefferson, Monroe, and John H. Cocke to launch Central College, which, according to Jefferson's strategy, would soon become the University of Virginia, standing at the apex of the state's educational system. At the next board meeting, held at Montpelier in July, the visitors went ahead with building plans and agreed to ask Dr. Samuel Knox of Baltimore to "accept the Professorship of Languages, Belles Lettres, Rhetoric, History, and Geography." In October the visitors gathered in Charlottesville to lay the cornerstone, "with all the ceremony and solemnity due to such an occasion," and since Dr. Knox had refused an appointment, to increase professorial pay and privileges. Madison was present on October 7, when the board agreed to invite his long-time friend Thomas Cooper to be professor of chemistry, zoology, botany, and anatomy, but had to go home the next day, before the minutes could be copied, so Jefferson signed the secretary's book for him.[39]

During the following winter Madison watched anxiously as a fund drive progressed and the legislature in Richmond struggled with a general education bill providing for primary education throughout the state, colleges or academies in each of nine districts, and a university to cap the system. The fund drive soon had subscriptions of nearly $50,000, including a $1,000 pledge from Madison. It was enough to begin building in Charlottesville, even though sectarians hostile to "godless" higher education, sectional jealousies over location of the university, and provincial, economy-minded opposition to elegant plans for education in general and to Jeffersonian speculations in particular combined in the legislature to threaten the whole scheme. Joseph C. Cabell, sponsor of the bill in the legislature, found every effort to garner votes met "the imputation of management and intrigue," and despaired at one point that only the election of Madison and other "enlightened" men to the House of Delegates could ever secure passage of the bill. A letter supporting the plan, signed by Jefferson, Madison, and the other visitors, helped, however, and in late February 1818 the legislature authorized a general system of education, including a university, but referred the vital question of location to twenty-four "discreet and intelligent" commissioners to be appointed by the governor and to meet in August at Rockfish Gap in the Blue Ridge between Charlottesville and Staunton. Jefferson wrote Cabell that, of course, Madison would serve as a commissioner, but that since "fanatics both in religion and politics . . . consider me as a raw head and bloody bones, . . . I believe the institution would be more popular without me than with me." It was not "mock-modesty," therefore, Jefferson said, that caused him to urge his own omission from the list of commissioners. He and Madison were both appointed, however, and they hastened the building of Central College, pushed the fund drive, and otherwise sought to strengthen the claims of Charlottesville at the Rockfish Gap meeting.[40]

In May and June wagonloads of beds passed through Charlottesville on their way to Rockfish Gap, where, Jefferson heard, the commissioners would be "tolerably" accommodated in forty lodging rooms. On a hot day in late July Madison rode to Monticello, where he wrote Dolley of his "anxiety" to be again with her, and warned her that Monroe, *"with his family"* (emphasis Madison's), would probably soon be at Montpelier. The next day Jefferson and Madison began a two-day trip to Rockfish Gap, where they found the other commissioners assembling. At the comfortable but unpretentious inn, near a falls on a branch of the James River and commanding broad vistas in all directions, they gathered for four days on homemade split-bottom chairs around a large dining room table in a low-ceilinged whitewashed room. Present were twenty-one eminent Virginians, many of them long known to Madison, including his brother-in-law John G. Jackson, Senator Armistead T. Mason, Archibald Stuart of Staunton, and Judge Spencer Roane. Jefferson, of course, was the center of attention, "the soul that animated the meeting," one of his admirers reported. He was chosen both president of the commissioners and chairman of a committee to deal with all matters except that *of location*. The committee accepted, probably with little amendment, a carefully drawn, philosophical plan Jefferson had brought with him, both for education in Virginia generally and for organizing the university.[41]

Jefferson proposed that the primary schools established with public support throughout the state teach the rudiments of learning, so that all citizens would be able to transact their own affairs, understand the elements of morality, and be trained in the responsibilities of community life and of citizenship. He further envisioned preparatory academies scattered about the state in places other than Charlottesville, to teach "the easier authors" in Latin and Greek and the intermediate stages of mathematics and natural science. Such a plan, the commissioners noted, would enable the university to be truly an institution of *higher* learning, unbothered by "the noisy turbulence of a multitude of small boys" characteristic of preparatory schools. Then the commissioners reaffirmed their faith in education generally, against the opinion of "some good men, and even of respectable information, [who] consider the learned sciences as useless acquirements." Scorning "the discouraging persuasion that a man is fixed, by the law of his nature, at a given point; that his improvement is a chimera, and the hope delusive of rendering ourselves wiser, happier, or better than our forefathers were," the commissioners declared that "each generation succeeding to the knowledge acquired by all those that preceded it, adding to it their own acquisitions and discoveries, and handing the mass down for successive and constant accumulation, must advance the knowledge and well-being of mankind . . . indefinitely to a term which none can fix or foressee."

To accomplish this, the commissioners approved Jefferson's plan for ten divisions in the university, each to be taught by a distinguished professor: ancient languages, modern languages, pure mathematics, physics (including geography), chemistry (including geology), biology, anatomy and medicine, government (including history and economics), law, and a humanities division to teach philosophy, ethics, rhetoric, literature, and fine arts. In a startling innovation, Jefferson proposed that students be allowed to choose freely which of these divisions they would emphasize. In explaining his plan, Jefferson endorsed the ancient languages as "the foundation common to all the sciences," but insisted that French, Spanish, Italian, and German, and also Anglo-Saxon, "the earliest form [of the language] . . . which we speak," be taught with equal earnestness. He emphasized the practicality of his curriculum by pointing out that mathematics would include military architecture; chemistry, "the theory of agriculture"; and medicine, all studies necessary to that art except, temporarily, "practice at the bedsides of the sick." Finally, Jefferson observed that though Virginia laws on freedom of religion precluded a professor of divinity, the professor of ethics would teach those proofs of God and moral obligations "in which all sects agree," while otherwise leaving "the different sects . . . to provide, as they think fittest, the means of further instruction in their own peculiar tenets." Though this plan and the arguments supporting it were Jefferson's, Madison agreed entirely with the philosophy behind the University of Virginia, providing for modern, nonsectarian higher learning.

In regulating the university, Jefferson left broad discretion in the hands of the visitors, but he did seek to create an atmosphere of maturity, in which learning would go on easily and enjoyably, rather than under the usual stern discipline. He designed the buildings to provide tranquillity and comfort for professors and students, with congenial access to each other. Gymnastic exercise, "the use of tools in the manual arts," militia drill, and "the arts which embellish life, dancing, music, and drawing," would be encouraged to broaden the experience of all students. To govern the whole system, Jefferson hoped that "pride of character, laudable ambition, and moral dispositions," could replace "the degrading motive of fear." "Hardening [students] to disgrace, to corporal punishments, and servile humiliations cannot be the best process for producing erect character," he admonished with pointed understatement. "A police exercised by the students themselves," Jefferson thought, would also be useful to initiate the students "into the duties and practices of civil life." Following Jefferson's lead, the commissioners accepted a transforming vision of educational needs and practices in a self-governing republic. To realize it, Madison did all he could to help Jefferson while Jefferson lived, and then for eight more years, when more than seventy-five years old, Madison took the lead himself.[42]

Before and after philosophizing about education, however, the commissioners wrestled with the vexing question of site. They found all three proposed places, Lexington, Staunton, and Charlottesville, "unexceptionable as to healthiness and fertility." Lexington offered the advantages of an existing institution, Washington College, willing to transform itself into the state university, a subscription of nearly $18,000, and the will of John Robinson, conveying property worth perhaps $100,000 to the university *if* it located in Lexington. Jefferson noted shrewdly that debts of unspecified amount against Robinson's estate and other uncertainties compromised the value of the bequest, and that "questions may arise as to the power of the [Washington College] trustees

to make the [pledged] transfers." Furthermore Washington College
stipulated that its present faculty be used by the state university, a
provision fatal to Jefferson's hope to acquire really distinguished professors and an indication to skeptics that self-interest motivated the
Washington College offer. Against this Jefferson set the larger subscription in favor of Charlottesville, the buildings already completed
there, and the fully certified transfer of Central College properties to
the state university. Finally, in debate before the full Board of Commissioners, Jefferson demonstrated Charlottesville's more central location, and underscored the healthy climate of its vicinity by offering a
long list of the octogenarians, soon to include himself, who lived there.
The commissioners concluded, "after full inquiry, and impartial and
mature consideration," and by a 16 to 5 vote, that Charlottesville was
the "convenient and proper" place for the university. As the meeting
adjourned, Jefferson declared he had "never seen business done with
so much order, and harmony, nor in abler nor pleasanter society." He
went on to the Warm Springs seventy-five miles to the west, but Madison returned home, confident at last that the ground was now firm
beneath the truly republican institution of higher learning rising in the
"academical village" he passed as he rode through Charlottesville.[43]

Early the following winter the Virginia legislature approved the proceedings of the commissioners. The university thus came into being
much as Jefferson and Madison had hoped, though as Cabell pointed
out, "the very same interests and prejudices which arrayed themselves
against the location at Charlottesville, will continue to assail that
establishment, [and] seize upon every occasion, and avail themselves
of every pretext, to keep it down." Jefferson hastily called the Central
College visitors to a nearly snowbound midwinter meeting at Montpelier, where he, Madison, and John H. Cocke authorized additional
buildings in Charlottesville and passed their assets into the hands of
the new university. Then, on March 29, 1819, Madison went to Charlottesville for the first of many meetings of the Board of Visitors of the
University of Virginia. Dolley Madison, as usual, went with him, visiting with the Monticello family while the men conducted their business.
With the two ex-Presidents on the board were Joseph C. Cabell and
John H. Cocke, who from the first had been Jefferson's able and diligent
allies in planning the university, and who would remain among its
visitors into the eighteen-fifties. They were pre-eminent among the
younger generation of Virginians who retained Enlightenment liberality
and enthusiasm for reform, and always revered Jefferson and Madison
as paragons of virtue and statesmanship. Also on the board were
Chapman Johnson, representative of valley interests, but nonetheless
a warm friend of the university, Robert B. Taylor of Norfolk, and James

Breckenridge of Botetourt County, a cultivated Federalist, but long respected by his Republican colleagues.

The visitors immediately elected Jefferson the chairman, or rector, thus placing on him, as everyone had always assumed, the executive guidance of the university. The board quickly approved filling the offices of bursar, secretary, and proctor, and provided for Jefferson and Cocke to oversee the construction of buildings, which, it was agreed, should take precedence at first over hiring professors. The board nonetheless affirmed the Central College commitment to Thomas Cooper as professor of chemistry, despite Cabell's warning that this would greatly abet political opposition to the university. The board followed its rector on this point, partly out of "unaffected deference . . . for his judgment and experience," an early observer reported, "and partly for the reason often urged by Mr. Madison, that as the scheme was originally Mr. Jefferson's, and the chief responsibility for its success or failure would fall on him, it was but fair to let him execute it in his own way." Thus were fixed the informal relationships animating the board during its early years: Jefferson, as Madison put it, "the great projector and mainspring," Madison his trusted associate in everything, Cocke the executive assistant on buildings, Cabell the legislative liaison, and the other members friendly aides as well as watchdogs on the board for various sectional and political interests.[44]

Even before the first meeting of the visitors, Madison had pronounced himself "uneasy on the subject of Cooper." Though he agreed entirely with Jefferson that Cooper was "the greatest man in America, in the powers of mind, and in acquired information," his touchiness, his reputation (undeserved Jefferson insisted) for heavy drinking, and his unitarianism if not atheism seemed likely to arouse exactly the controversy and emotionalism so dangerous in launching a university under public sponsorship. The board stuck with Cooper for a time, but by the spring of 1820 "the hue and cry raised from the different pulpits on our appointment of Dr. Cooper, whom they charge with Unitarianism . . . as presumptuously as if it were a crime, and one for which, like Servetus, he should be burned," caused the visitors to accept Cooper's resignation. "For myself," Jefferson observed, "I was not disposed to regard the denunciations of these satellites of religious inquisition; but our colleagues, better judges of popular feeling, thought that they were not to be altogether neglected. . . . I do sincerely lament that untoward circumstances have brought on us the irreparable loss of this professor, whom I have looked to as the corner-stone of our edifice."[45]

The charges of irreligion at Charlottesville continued strong enough to endanger legislative support, so the board, in October 1822, approved Jefferson's recommendation "to give every encouragement" to religious instruction by permitting the various denominations to establish semi-

naries adjacent to the university and to use its library and other buildings. Jefferson hoped that "by bringing the sects together and mixing
them with the mass of other students, we shall soften their asperities,
liberalize and neutralize their prejudices, and make the general religion
a religion of peace, reason, and morality." Justifying this policy, Madison observed that "a university with sectarian professorships becomes,
of course, a Sectarian Monopoly; with professorships of rival sects, it
would be an Arena of theological Gladiators. Without any such professorships, it may incur for a time at least, the imputation of irreligious
tendencies, if not designs. The last difficulty was thought more man-
ageable than either of the others. On this view of the subject," Madison
concluded, "there seems to be no alternative but between a public
University without a theological professorship, and sectarian Seminaries
without a University." Though Jefferson and Madison intended no
hostility to religion, they were determined both to keep inviolate the
separation of church and state in Virginia and to nourish at the university an atmosphere of impartial, undogmatic inquiry rather than the
shrill defense of sectarianism that engulfed so many of the religiously
founded colleges of their day.[46]

Madison clarified his attitude toward theological learning when
Jefferson requested him to prepare a catalogue of books on religion for
the university library. Madison declared that "although Theology was
not to be taught at the University, its Library ought to contain pretty
full information for such as might voluntarily seek it in that branch of
learning." He therefore undertook the "extremely tedious" task, considering "the immense extent" of theological books, of separating the
"moral and metaphysical part" necessary for a university library, from
the unfruitful "doctrinal and controversial part." He had prepared a
detailed list of authors, covering the first five centuries of the Christian
era, before Jefferson's request for speed caused him merely to sketch
lists for later periods. For the early centuries he included the works
of the Alexandrian fathers, Clement, Athenagoras, Tertullian, and
Irenaeus, Latin authors, including Augustine, as well as Flavius
Josephus and other corroborative accounts. Among the books noted
hastily, only Thomas Aquinas, Duns Scotus, the Koran, and some
critical books on the popes and saints represented the Middle Ages,
while "Erasmus, Luther, Calvin, Socinius, Bellarmin, and Chillings-
worth" were listed to herald the modern era. The major speculative
works of the seventeenth and eighteenth centuries concluded the list,
with emphasis, of course, on the rationalists: "Grotius on the truth of
Christian Religion," Tillotson, Hooker, Pascal, Locke, and Newton
"works on religious subjects," Bishop Butler, Samuel Clarke, Wollaston's
Religion of Nature Delineated, Jonathan Edwards on *The Will and
Nature of True Virtue*, Cotton Mather's *Essays to Do Good*, William
Penn, John Wesley, Priestley, Price, Leibnitz, Paley, and even the

Boston Unitarian Joseph Buckminster. Madison intended students to have all the source materials they wanted to investigate religious doctrine and history, but he meant as well to emphasize the critical approach and the rational and deistical writings so influential in forming his own religious convictions. However much a Roman Catholic or a "Baptist enthusiast" might have felt slighted, Madison thought his list included all the books necessary for earnest youths seeking, rationally, to understand divinity and theology.[47]

To insure both freedom from narrow sectarianism and a genuinely learned faculty, Jefferson and Madison soon saw they would have to recruit European professors. Two brilliant New Englanders, George Ticknor and Nathaniel Bowditch, had refused good offers from the University of Virginia. The Board of Visitors concluded that "it was neither probable that [first-rate American professors] would leave the situations in which they were, nor honorable or moral to endeavor to seduce them from their stations; and to have filled the professorial chairs with unemployed and secondary characters" would not fulfill the needs and expectations of the university. To progress, the board was convinced, "we must avail ourselves of the lights of countries already advanced before us." Jefferson's young friend Francis W. Gilmer was dispatched to Great Britain, "the land of our own language, habits and manners," to find and entice to Virginia young men "treading on the heels" of the unobtainable "men of the first eminence" at Oxford, Cambridge, and Edinburgh. With the help of Richard Rush and others, Gilmer signed up five brilliant young scholars: George Long in ancient languages, Thomas H. Key in mathematics, Charles Bonnycastle in physics, Robley Dunglison in medicine, and George Blaettermann, a German previously recommended to Jefferson, in modern languages. Appointment of the young Irish-American John Patton Emmet as professor of natural history completed the scientific faculty. Though the enormous problems of settling these learned foreigners happily and fruitfully in the isolation of Charlottesville plagued Madison for years, he enjoyed their cultivated company and approved their youth. "They will be less inflexible in their habits, the more improvable in their qualifications, and will last the longer," he wrote Jefferson. Cabell too, exulted at "our corps of Professors . . . full of youth, and talent, and energy," while Jefferson declared "the five professors procured from England" so morally upright, congenial, zealous for the university, and learned in their fields that "as high a degree of education can now be obtained here, as in the country they left."[48]

To complete the faculty, Jefferson and Madison insisted on finding Americans for the chairs in ethics and in law, fields especially subject to legislative oversight and thought to embrace peculiarly American understandings best taught by natives. Congressman George Tucker of Virginia seemed an admirable choice for the chair in ethics and literature since, as Madison wrote, to a style of "acuteness and elegance" he added a wide understanding of philosophy, literature, and American history. He responded favorably, and became in his twenty years at the university a fervent admirer of both the ex-Presidents, writing, with Madison's help, a biography of Jefferson, and a two-hundred-page unpublished memoir of Madison. Six eminent Virginia lawyers and judges could not be persuaded to trade their public posts for academic ones, but the seventh, a Fredericksburg attorney, John Taylor Lomax, finally accepted, and served for four years as an able, fair-minded professor of law.[49]

Establishing the school of law, or government, confronted Jefferson with a delicate problem. He opposed the usual pattern of textbooks prescribed by the trustees, he wrote Cabell and Madison, "because I believe none of us are so much at the heights of science in the several branches as to undertake this [selection;] and therefore that it will be better left to the professors, until occasion of interference shall be given. But, there is one branch in which we are the best judges, in which heresies may be taught, of so interesting a character to our own State, and to the United States, as to make it a duty in us to lay down the principles which shall be taught. It is that of government." Jefferson would not allow "a Richmond lawyer [states' rights extremist], or one of that school of quondam federalism, now consolidation [like John Marshall]" to be the professor of government in an institution designed to produce the "aristocracy of talent and virtue" he hoped would provide leaders in a republican government. "It is our duty to guard against the dissemination of such principles among our youth, and the diffusion of that poison, by a previous prescription of the texts to be followed in their discourses." He therefore proposed to require that the Declaration of Independence, *The Federalist*, and the 1798 and 1800 Virginia Resolutions and "Report," together with works of Locke and Sidney, be the basic texts for the study of public law.

Madison saw at once that this was another notion formed in Jefferson's precipitate passion for republicanism rather than upon careful reflection. "It is certainly very material," Madison noted tactfully, "that the true doctrines of liberty as exemplified in our Political System, should be inculcated on those who are to sustain and may administer it." He was as convinced as Jefferson of the universal truth of their republican doctrines and of the need to insure that later generations of leaders remained steadfast in them. But it was difficult, Madison cautioned, "to find standard books that will be both guides and guards for the purpose." Though Madison thus appeared to propose only *practical* objections, he in fact proceeded to demolish Jefferson's whole notion of prescribed texts. The Declaration of Independence, like Sidney and Locke, "though rich in fundamental principles," did little to combat "constructive violations" of existing constitutions. *The Federalist*, "an authentic exposition" of the federal constitution, nonetheless failed to anticipate many "misconstructions" and moreover was not accepted as authoritative by everyone in either of the political parties. Its use at Harvard and Brown, Madison observed, furnished merely the precedent of *selection* by the faculty, not "injunction from the superior authority." The Virginia Resolutions and "Report" were even more partisan, being objectionable, probably, even to some of the visitors, and so obnoxious to "the more bigoted" as to cause them to "withold their sons" from the university. Madison finished his critique with a pointed comparison he knew would strike powerfully with Jefferson: "In framing a political creed, a like difficulty occurs as in the case of religion, though the public right be very different in the two cases. If the Articles be in very general terms, they do not answer the purpose; if in very particular terms, they divide and exclude where meant to unite and fortify."

Madison suggested instead a listing of "the best guides" to the distinctive principles of American government, hoping that this would set useful standards for both students and professors while relaxing Jefferson's impractical, absolute prescription. Furthermore, to balance the list, Madison proposed adding Washington's Farewell Address to the three documents chosen by Jefferson. Madison concluded, however, with a remark of his own, as unwelcome to later defenders of academic freedom as Jefferson's impulse to shelter youth from "poisonous" ideas: "The most effectual safeguard against heretical intrusions into the School of Politics, will be an Able and Orthodox Professor, whose course of instruction will be an example to his successors, and may carry with it a sanction from the Visitors." Madison's point, however, was not as restrictive as it might seem. Since in its early stages the university would have but one professor of government, it seemed necessary that he himself be disposed to present republicanism sympathetically. The diverse library, as well as teachers in other fields and an abundance of current magazines and newspapers, offered an easy hearing to critics, even those referred to by Madison and Jefferson as "heretical." Both revolutionists, moreover, retained a sense that the nation was still so new as to require special nourishment of its peculiar and still vulnerable principles and institutions. Madison's letter persuaded Jefferson that prescribing textbooks to guard against "poisonous opinions" was inadmissible in a university dedicated to free inquiry. Later libertarian concepts of "a market place of ideas," where no idea is regarded as heretical, were to Madison and Jefferson both impractical at their new, small institution and unacceptable in theory within a world view not yet relativistic, but still assuming, absolutely, that free, republican government was *best* for *all* mankind. They therefore meant to nourish its growth, and in fact did so, at the University of Virginia, in ways deeply and practically useful to the state and to the nation; and in no way relevant at the time did they give aid or comfort to enemies of academic freedom. In fact they stood firmly for an innovating, elective curriculum and insisted that scholarship, rather than national or religious standing, be the vital qualification for professors, liberalizing reforms not accomplished in most American colleges and universities until a half century or more later.[50]

In March 1825 the pavilions were ready, the European professors arrived, forty students were on campus, and the university began instruction. In the fall the number of students had increased to more than one hundred and seemed likely soon to exceed the 218 for whom accommodations were available in the dormitories. Cabell declared ecstatically that "the University will advance with rapid strides, and throw into the rear all the other seminaries of this vast continent." Before long, though, "incipient irregularities" under the loose code of discipline threatened to destroy the infant university. Disorder had erupted fitfully during the summer, and in late September, while Madison, Monroe, and other Visitors were at Monticello for the annual meeting, full-scale riots broke out. Undisciplined students, some of them wealthy and dissipated, left classes, attacked professors, caroused in Charlottsville taverns, and made gambling dens of the dormitories. One night they threw a stink bomb into Professor Long's room, and the next, surged about the campus shouting, "Down with the European professors!" When Emmet and Tucker challenged the masked leaders, drunken cohorts set upon the courageous professors with canes and bricks. Sixty-five of the rioters had the effrontery to sign a petition condemning Tucker and Emmet for ganging up on a lone student. Disgusted, and perhaps frightened, Long and Key threatened to resign unless the Visitors re-established order.

The Visitors then confronted the unruly students across a large table in the rotunda. Seeing before him three ex-Presidents and other men already legendary in Virginia, one of the students thought the Visitors, "the most august body of men I have ever seen." Jefferson rose to speak, Margaret Smith recounted, "with the tenderness of a father and it required an evident struggle to repress his emotions. . . . His lips moved, he essayed to speak—burst into tears and sank back into his seat. The shock was electric." Chapman Johnson, eloquent and austere, rose and delivered the admonition, but, one of the students reported, "It was not his words, but Mr. Jefferson's tears that melted the stubborn purpose" of the rioters. Jefferson subsequently asked the board to adopt a stricter code of discipline. In his annual report he noted merely that since the original regulations had proved incapable of preserving order, "coercion must be resorted to where confidence has been disappointed." He explained to his granddaughter that "four of the most guilty [students have been] expelled, the rest reprimanded, severer laws enacted, and a rigorous execution of them declared in the future." This gave the students "a shock and struck a terror," Jefferson concluded, "the more severe, as it was less expected." The new rules provided that henceforth "minor . . . irregularities alone" would be handled by student courts, while unlawful riots would be quelled "on the spot by imprisonment and the same legal coercions, provided against disorder generally, committed by other citizens, from whom, at their age, [students] have no right to distinction." Thus, though Jefferson's principle "of not multiplying occasions of coercion" proved too visionary to handle the fifteen or twenty students "disposed to try whether our indulgence was without limit," the new regulations remained, for their day, relatively permissive while, at the same time, allowing the proctor and faculty to deal rigorously with inveterate troublemakers. Madison voted for the new code, and his reputation while rector himself as "no visionary or enthusiast" leaves no doubt of his support of the firmer regulations.[51]

A few months after "perfect subordination" had been restored and "industry, order, and quiet the most exemplary" again prevailed, one of the frequent refusals of the Virginia legislature to grant funds Jefferson considered essential to the university, coinciding with ill-health, near bankruptcy, and the death of his eldest granddaughter, caused Jefferson, "overwhelmed with every form of misfortune," to write of his "comfort" at being able to leave the university under Madison's care. Madison replied protesting that however deep his interest in the university—"the Temple through which alone lies the road to that of Liberty"—to suppose he could be Jefferson's successor in guiding it "would be the pretension of a mere worshipper [replacing] the Tutelary Genius of the Sanctuary." Madison hoped Jefferson could live until "stability and self-growth" could replace the unique care lavished on the university by its founder. Jefferson's premonitions proved sound, however. He died on July 4, 1826, beginning for Madison eight years as rector of the university. Unless sick, he never missed meetings of the Board of Visitors or public examination periods, for which he traveled to Charlottesville with Dolley Madison. One student remembered the old couple walking arm in arm about the university campus, with the taller, more vigorous Dolley sometimes helping the frail, crippled man, and with each seeming somehow, in old-fashioned dress, to be a representative of a bygone era.[52]

Though Rector Madison kept well informed of university affairs and took reponsibility for major decisions, neither physically nor psychically could he replace Jefferson in the university's guidance. Increasingly he depended on much younger colleagues, especially Nicholas Trist, Jefferson's grandson-in-law, who even prepared the annual report for Madison for a time. Madison continued to seek in the United States or abroad for professors of distinguished, enlightened scholarship, to repel sectarian efforts to dominate the board, the faculty, or the campus, and otherwise to maintain the university in the character given to it by Jefferson. Under Madison's leadership the university maintained its enrollment, reaching 208 in 1834 (the year Madison retired as rector); its library acquired over ten thousand volumes; the number of graduates each year rose toward fifty, and the first master of arts degree was conferred in 1832. Though Madison's role in founding and sustaining the University of Virginia was in no sense comparable to Jefferson's, he provided constant support during Jefferson's lifetime, and he served much longer as rector of the university with students in attendance than did Jefferson.[53]

While reserving his primary attention and support for the University of Virginia, Madison also befriended other Virginia colleges, supported his alma mater, Princeton, sent money to infant Allegheny College, struggling to bring learning to western Pennsylvania frontiersmen, and in his will left $1,000 to a college in Uniontown, Pennsylvania, named in his honor. He left the bulk of his huge library to the University of Virginia and provided particularly for the education of three of his nephews. He summarized the grounds for his devotion to education in a letter advising an old friend from Kentucky on its school system:

Learned institutions ought to be favorite objects with every free people. They throw that light over the public mind which is the best security against crafty and dangerous encroachments on the public liberty. They are the nurseries of skilful Teachers for the schools distributed throughout the Community. They are themselves schools for the particular talents required for use of the Public Trusts, on the able execution of which the welfare of the people depends. They multiply the educated individuals from among whom the people may elect a due portion of their public Agents of every description; more especially of those who are to frame the laws; by the perspicuity, the consistency, and the stability, as well as by the just and equal spirit of which the great social purposes are to be answered. . . . Throughout the Civilized World, nations are courting the praise of fostering Science and the useful Arts, and are opening their eyes to the principles and the blessings of Representative Government. The American people owe it to themselves, and to the cause of Free Government, to prove by their establishments for the advancement and diffusion of Knowledge, that their political Institutions, which are attracting observation from every quarter, and are respected as Models, by the new-born States in our own Hemisphere, are as favorable to the intellectual and moral improvement of Man as they are conformable to his individual and social Rights. What spectacle can be more edifying or more seasonable than that of Liberty and Learning, each leaning on the other for their mutual and surest support?[54]

Increasingly as the twenty years in retirement stretched out, however, attention to public affairs and even to cherished educational projects gave way to the perennial concerns of old age: health, reminiscence, and reflection at the loss of lifelong associates. To an earnest plea in 1834 that he speak out against Jackson's war on the Bank of the United States, against nullification, and against the spoils system, Madison replied that those evils seemed to thrive despite his known opposition to them, and that, in any case, the public had "the habit now of invalidating opinions emanating from me by a reference to my age and infirmities." He insisted more and more that whatever the issues of the third and fourth decades of the nineteenth century, younger men, not one whose public life had begun as a subject of George III, would have to deal with them.[55]

Madison left the presidency at age sixty-six in excellent health, his system largely immune, it seemed, to tuberculosis, cholera, typhus, and other periodic scourges of the countryside. For ten years after 1817 visitors found him spry and active, he took daily rides to manage his farm, and he looked forward to short trips in the Piedmont countryside. Through 1826 and 1827, however, he had premonitions that the debilities of old age would soon be upon him. A severe attack of influenza before Christmas 1827 weakened him, and late the following summer his old complaint, "bilious indisposition," so prostrated him that he missed, for the first time, the fall meeting of the Board of Visitors. Though an exceptional period of good health allowed him to enjoy three months in Richmond attending the Virginia Convention of 1829, he less and less felt able to leave Montpelier. A year later, a painful rheumatism, especially bad in his hands, became a serious, if intermittent, disability. In April 1831, on a page covered with tiny, crabbed letters wholly different from his usual, rather hasty hand, Madison explained his "microscopic writing" to Monroe: "The older I get, the more my stiffening fingers make smaller letters, as my feet take shorter steps; the progress in both cases being at the same time more fatiguing as well as more slow." He tried a medication supplied by Dr. Carr of the University of Virginia, but with little success; by midsummer the stiffness had become so general he had again to miss the meeting of the Board of Visitors.[56]

In the fall and winter of 1831–32, as Dolley Madison wrote fearfully of Nat Turner's "insurrection," her husband was so weak from rheumatism and fever that she scarcely left his side for months at a time. His hands were so sore and swollen "as to be almost useless, and so I lend him mine," she wrote. She played a music box as they sat together before the fire, looking out at the snow on the mountains while the winter wind whistled "loud and cold." Wrapping his legs in oiled silk and taking tepid salt baths failed to give much relief. Though the coming of spring helped some, and Dolley even hoped her husband might be able to take the prescribed journey to the Warm Springs, this proved too optimistic; in late May Madison wrote, "I am still confined to my bed with my malady, my debility, and my age, in triple alliance against me. Any convalescence therefore must be tedious, not to add imperfect." That summer he was well enough to greet President Jackson and Senator Clay, each campaigning for the presidency, from his sickbed. Clay found his old friend "feeble in health but his mind and memory . . . perfectly sound. He spoke with more freedom than is usual on public affairs, and appeared to take a lively interest in passing events." Then, as cold weather again stiffened his joints, and after a year spent almost entirely in bed, Madison nevertheless wrote cheerfully to Andrew Stevenson (husband of Dolley Madison's niece, Sally Coles) thanking him for a gift of a cap:

> It is as comfortable as it is fashionable, which is more than can be said of all fashions. . . . [An] excellent pair of gloves [made by] Mrs. Stevenson . . . being the work of her own hands . . . will impart the more warmth to mine. . . . Mrs. Madison has also provided well for my feet. I am thus equipt cap-a-pied, for the campaign against Boreas, and his allies the Frosts and the snows. But there is another article of covering, which I need most of all and which my best friends can not supply. My bones have lost a sad portion of the flesh which clothed and protected them, and the digestive and nutritive organs which alone can replace it, are too slothful in their functions.[57]

The next three years Madison was a semi-invalid, having periods, especially in the spring and summer, when the stiffness in his joints eased, the fevers subsided, and he resumed work at his writing desk. In September 1833 he was well enough to "ride out every day, three or four miles," and the visits of the Riveses, the Stevensons, and others "on their way from the White Sulpher Springs" again became enjoyable. Dolley wished fondly she could get away to the springs herself, but even a journey five miles to Orange Court House was "quite an event." Madison during a day often "walked only from the bed in which he breakfasts to another." Both the Madisons suffered eye inflammations that robbed them of their favorite pastimes, and in the summer of 1833 Dolley joined her husband on the sick list, with "a violent though short illness brought on . . . by indulging a fancy for Raspberries and milk." Altogether, from his eightieth birthday on, Madison again and again failed to muster the strength to partake even vicariously in public affairs, and weeks and months passed with him able to do little more than nurse his aching limbs.[58]

He devoted much of his waning strength to arranging his papers and commenting on the past. A year after he retired he gave to a Washington printer a list assigning authorship to *The Federalist Papers* that has only recently been accepted as entirely authoritative. To validate his list Madison not only noted cogent interval evidence but remarked that Hamilton's conflicting lists had been jotted down hastily, and thus errors in them could be ascribed to oversight, while his own list, prepared upon full and careful consideration, had obviously superior claims, which he implied Hamilton himself would accept were he alive. Hamilton's misstatement, Madison declared, "was involuntary, and . . . he was incapable of any that was not so." In 1818 and 1819, Madison supplied information to John Quincy Adams for his edition of the *Journal of the Federal Convention of 1787.* Controversy aroused by its publication, and the appearance a year later of notes taken during the first five weeks of the convention by Robert Yates of New York, caused renewed interest in the much fuller record of the debates known to be in Madison's possession. He continued to insist that this record be made public only after the death of all members of the convention, including himself. Rumors circulated that Madison guarded his notes for narrow political purposes, or to write a history of the United States himself. He disclaimed the project, assigning it instead "to those who have more time before them than the remnant to which mine is limited." Since "a personal knowledge and an impartial judgment of things rarely meet in the historian," Madison observed, "the best history of our Country therefore must be the fruit of contributions bequeathed by contemporary actors and witnesses, to successors who will make an unbiased use of them." Nonetheless, curiosity remained intense over Madison's archives because, as Edward Everett declared, ". . . next to those of Washington, and in some respects not second even to his, your [Madison's] papers must possess a higher interest with your countrymen, than those of any of your contemporaries."[59]

One publication project Madison heartily approved was Jonathan Elliot's to publish the debates of the state ratifying conventions of 1788. Madison had long believed that these debates, as an insight into the people's understanding of the Constitution upon its adoption, were the vital source for aid in interpreting the document, rather than the debates of the convention of 1787. He supplied Elliot with scarce printed copies of the debates in North Carolina and Pennsylvania. When Elliot asked Madison to "correct" his speeches in the Virginia convention, however, he declined because "it might not be safe, nor deemed fair, after a lapse of 40 years . . . to undertake to make [the speeches] what it might be believed they ought to be. If I did not confound subsequent ideas, and varied expressions, with the real ones," Madison added, "I might be supposed to do so." Though Madison often approved excluding personal or prejudicial material from publication, he did not believe in altering records with the benefit of hindsight (see Chapter VIII, however, for one exception). Another way Madison encouraged publication of source material was in responding to dozens of appeals from editors, historians, and archivists for information about, or letters from, famous people Madison had known. He pronounced George Mason "a powerful Reasoner, a profound Statesman and a devoted Republican," and he extolled the "brilliant careers" of Generals Nathanael Greene and Henry Lee during the revolution. Requests for material about others not always favored by Madison, such as Gouverneur Morris, John Jay, and General William Winder, drew restrained but polite responses.[60]

To James K. Paulding, who asked about materials for biographies of Madison's most famous colleagues in nation building, he wrote sharp sketches. Madison noted he had not known Franklin until the convention of 1787, and that "he has written his own life, and no man had a finer one to write, or a better title to be himself the writer." Of Jefferson, Madison observed that "he was greatly eminent for the comprehensiveness and fertility of his Genius, the vast extent and rich variety of his acquirements; and particularly distinguished by the philosophic impress left on every subject which he touched." John Adams had "a mind rich in ideas of its own, as well as in its learned store; . . . an ardent love of Country, and the merit of being a Colossal Champion of its Independence." These qualities far overshadowed "the alloy in his Republicanism, and the fervors and flights originating in his moral temperament," Madison added, paraphrasing a characterization of Adams Madison had read in Franklin's letters from Paris fifty years earlier. Madison said political differences made him cautious in commenting on Hamilton, who "possessed intellectual powers of the first order, and the moral qualities of integrity and honor in a captivating degree." "If his theory of Government deviated from the Republican standard," Madison continued, recalling the furious battles of the seventeen-nineties, "he had the candor to avow it, and the greater merit of cooperating faithfully in maturing and supporting a System which was not his choice." His greatest disservice, Madison scolded, was in giving the Constitution "a constructive and practical bearing not warranted by its true and intended character."[61]

Madison's most sustained aid to a historian, however, was to Jared Sparks. The diligent young Bostonian impressed Madison during a brief visit to Montpelier in 1827, and thereafter received invaluable aid and support from the aged Virginian. Madison allowed him to use over twenty letters from Washington, which inexplicably, or perhaps purposely, had not been copied into the general's letter books. They exchanged information about the origins of Washington's famous state papers and commiserated that his archives had "been very extensively mutilated by rats" while on loan to Chief Justice Marshall. Then, in April 1830, when "the blossoms and verdure of the trees [were] springing into perfection," Sparks spent five delightful days at Montpelier. "The intellect and memory of Mr. Madison," Sparks noted, retained "all their pristine vigor," and in conversation he was "sprightly, varied, fertile in his topics and felicitous in his descriptions and illustrations." Sparks listened avidly to Madison "on general topics," copied frantically from the piles of unique and interesting papers Madison showed him, and recorded anecdotes of "revolutionary times." Some of the comments were candid remarks about famous people. John Jay's hostility to France, Madison observed, arose from "two strong traits of character, suspicion and religious bigotry." He thought Washington had never "attended to the arguments for Christianity" nor had any definite opinions on religion, but rather "took those things as he found them existing" and observed faithfully the Episcopal rituals "in which he was brought up." He also insisted that Washington had been most reluctant about both Hamilton's funding plans and the national bank, accepting them not because he approved them as such, but because there seemed no practical alternatives. Hamilton, though personally incorruptible, Madison said, was so "hostile to France" that at times he made "perverted" and deceitful uses of public money. He thought "the talents of Richard Henry Lee were respectable, but not of the highest order"— dim, in fact, when compared to those of John Adams, who "was a bold and decided champion of independence from the beginning." Sparks also recorded Madison's observations on the usefulness of secret sessions during the Federal Convention and on Washington's disgust at the pompous ceremonies arranged for him by his aides in 1789. Sparks set down some of Madison's quips and puns, including a favorite story of a French officer during the American Revolution who fancied himself quite a lady's man. A friend, tired of his boasting, who was asked to divulge what others thought of the vain fellow, replied, "The opinion of the world is divided; the men say you are an old woman, and the women say you are an old man." Altogether, Sparks was enthralled at the "social happiness" at Montpelier, and as a historian, was beside himself with excitement at the treasures residing in Madison's memory and archives.[62]

Among the papers Sparks pored over were Madison's letters, copies of which he had not retained, written to his contemporaries forty or fifty years ago. Even before retirement Madison had begun to gather them as best he could from the recipients or their heirs. By 1830 he had retrieved many of his letters to Jefferson, Joseph Jones, Monroe, Edmund Pendleton, Edmund Randolph, and Washington. These letters, added to ones he received and notes he had made for his own speeches and state papers, were virtually a documentary history of the nation from 1780 until 1817, and even subsequently, since Madison preserved copies of the hundreds of letters he wrote on public affairs during his retirement. Before his death Madison had arranged his papers through the convention of 1787. He used letters to supplement his notes on debates in the Continental Congress and, of course, the full, uniquely valuable account of the Federal Convention. Madison wrote an introduction to this record, and with the help of Dolley Madison and her brother John C. Payne, had selected and edited other papers to be published after his death. He was, therefore, virtually his own editor for the three volumes of *Madison Papers* published in 1840 under the supervision of Congress, to which Dolley sold domestic publication rights for $30,000. It was much less than the $100,000 or more Madison had expected his widow would receive from the posthumous printing of the eagerly awaited 1787 debates. He had also arranged a fourth volume, on constitutional topics, largely from his post-1787 correspondence, which appeared in 1853. Beyond that, he organized his papers in large bound folios or bundles, intending the publication of three or four additional volumes under Dolley Madison's supervision. Unable to make favorable contracts, though, Dolley sold the papers remaining in her possession to the federal government for $25,000 in 1848. Hundreds of the most valuable letters had already been withdrawn by Payne Todd, to pay gambling debts, however, and through him reached a Washington, D.C., collector, James C. McGuire. These papers, following sale by his heirs, and further boxes of Madison's letters, found among the papers of his editor and biographer, William Cabell Rives, have in the twentieth century been, with some major exceptions, reunited with the collections sold earlier to the federal government. Thus Madison's intention that his papers furnish a readily available resource for scholars has at long last been largely realized.[63]

Reflections on the past and a sense of settling his accounts with it, incessantly before Madison as he labored over his papers at Montpelier, became immediate and poignant as he had last meetings with old friends or heard of their deaths. Lafayette's visit to Monticello and Montpelier in November 1824 recalled vividly for the Frenchman and his two venerable hosts the lifetime each had devoted to human liberty. Madison went to Monticello to greet Lafayette, whom he had not seen since their wilderness journey in 1784 to negotiate the Fort Stanwix Indian treaty (see Chapter VIII). "My old friend embraced me with great warmth," Madison wrote his wife. "He is in fine health and spirits but so much increased in bulk and changed in aspect that I should not have known him." An orgy of conversation over port in Jefferson's salon preceded a great dinner with four hundred guests at the new rotunda of the university, where Lafayette sat between the two ex-Presidents. Madison, whom Lafayette's secretary thought excelled all the guests "for the originality of his mind and the delicacy of his illusions," offered the toast—"Happy the people who have virtue for their guest and gratitude for their feast"—but his subsequent remarks were lost to the reporters present amid the din of the banqueters.

Lafayette then went to Montpelier, where for a week he and Madison reminisced about the campaigns of Washington, about the great events of the French Revolution that were so fateful to Madison's career in the seventeen-nineties, and about the incomplete struggles for liberty and national independence in Europe, South America, and the United States so long linked to the careers of both of the old revolutionaries. At the close of his nationwide tour, in August 1825, Lafayette returned to Monticello, where Madison and Monroe came for long conversations. Jefferson's great feebleness (he had, he wrote, "one foot in the grave and the other uplifted to follow it") and the fact that all knew this would be the last meeting with the French hero made the occasion deepy affecting. Madison reported Lafayette "took his final leave [carrying] . . . with him the unanimous blessings of the free nation which has adopted him, [and deserved honor] . . . due to the nobleness of his mind and the grandeur of his career."[64]

A few months later, sensing the end, Jefferson wrote feelingly to Madison of "the friendship which has subsisted between us, now half a century, and the harmony of our political principles and pursuits, . . . sources of happiness to me through that long period." If there ever was a government "conducted with a single and steadfast eye to the general interest and happiness of those committed to it," Jefferson continued, "one which, protected by truth, can never know reproach, it is that to which our lives have been devoted." He pronounced Madison his "pillar of support through life," and asked that Madison "take care of me when dead, and be assured that I shall leave with you my last affections." Madison replied: "You cannot look back to the long period of our private friendship and political harmony, with more affecting recollections than I do. If they are a source of pleasure to you, what ought they not to be to me? . . . Wishing and hoping that you may yet live to increase the debt which our Country owes you, and to witness the increasing gratitude, which alone can pay it, I offer you the fullest return of affectionate assurances."

Though Jefferson rallied occasionally through the spring of 1826, Madison never saw him again, and in early July was prepared for the worst by a note from Dr. Dunglison postponing a visit to Montpelier for a more urgent one to Monticello: ". . . without some speedy amelioration," he wrote, "my worst apprehensions [about Jefferson] must soon be realized." Madison learned on July 6, 1826, that Jefferson had died two days before, the fiftieth anniversary of the Declaration of Independence he had written. Responding to Nicholas Trist's note, and offering any assistance he could after an event evoking feelings "I need not, . . . cannot express," Madison eulogized his friend: "He lives and will live in the memory and gratitude of the wise and good, as a luminary of Science, as a votary of liberty, as a model of patriotism, and as a benefactor of human kind. In these characters, I have known him, and not less in the virtues and charms of social life, for a period of fifty years, during which there has not been an interruption or diminution of mutual confidence and cordial friendship, for a single moment in a single instance." Thus closed the most useful political friendship in American history as well as one of the great collaborations of all time. After July 4, 1826, Madison sensed more and more that for him and his generation time was running out.[65]

Three years later Madison's mother died, in her ninety-eighth year. Except for the intervals away from home on public business, Madison and his mother had lived under the same roof at Montpelier for eighty years. Until the very end, she remained alert and able to read without glasses, visited every day in her rooms by her son and daughter-in-law, and always a pleasure and a marvel to the many guests who stopped for a few minutes to talk. She was less wrinkled in her last years than her eldest son, one of them observed. She maintained a proud interest in her famous son's career, and he, though there is little formal record of it, was dutiful and affectionate toward her. The family gathered for her funeral reminded Madison again how deeply he was rooted in the land and amid these people he had known for half a century or more. The deaths a year or so before of his cousin and bosom companion since boyhood days at Port Conway, Catlett Conway, and his favorite nephew and ward, Robert Madison, removed other fixtures in the aged squire's life. Then, in 1832, the Madisons learned that the vivacious Anna Cutts, always virtually a daughter to them, had died suddenly. "Madison partakes in our sorrows," Dolley wrote Anna's husband, and "the heart of your miserable sister mourns with you and for your dear children."[66]

In the spring of 1831 Madison heard that Monroe, fatally ill, had sold most of his Virginia property and gone to live out his days in New York under his daughter's care. "I deeply regret," the emaciated Monroe wrote, "that there is no prospect of our ever meeting again, since so long have we been connected, and in the most friendly intercourse, in public and private life, that a final separation is among the most distressing incidents which could occur." Madison replied that the prospect of their never "meeting again afflicts me deeply, certainly not less so, that it can you. The pain I feel at the idea, associated as it is with a recollection of the long, close, and uninterrupted friendship which united us, amounts to a pang which I cannot well express." When the expected news of Monroe's death arrived, three months later, Madison praised "the comprehensiveness and character of his mind; the purity and nobleness of his principles; the importance of his patriotic services; and the many private virtues of which his whole life was a model." Monroe's passing removed the last of Madison's close associations dating back to the revolutionary era itself. "Having outlived so many of my contemporaries," he observed sadly, "I ought not to forget that I may be thought to have outlived myself."[67]

Thus surrounded with death, and aware that his own could not be far distant, Madison recalled his own comment earlier to a friend who had lost two children: "Afflictions of every kind are the onerous conditions charged on the tenure of life; and it is a silencing if not a satisfactory vindication of the ways of Heaven to man that there are but few who do not prefer an acquiescence in them to a surrender of the tenure itself." Madison may have recalled, too, his response in 1825 to questions about the nature of the deity. "Belief in a God All Powerful wise and good," Madison noted, "is so essential to the moral order of the World and to the happiness of man, that arguments which enforce it cannot be drawn from too many sources." Always an empiricist, Madison thought reasoning from effect to cause, "from Nature to Nature's God," would be "more persuasive" than theological abstractions. As for his own views, he noted:

The finiteness of the human understanding betrays itself on all subjects, but more especially when it contemplates such as involve infinity. . . . The infinity of time and space forces itself on our conception, a limitation of either being inconceivable; that the mind prefers at once the idea of a self-existing cause to that of an infinite series of cause and effect, which augments, instead of avoiding the difficulty; and that it finds more facility in assenting to the self-existence of an invisible cause possessing infinite power, wisdom and goodness, than to the self-existence of the universe, visibly destitute of those attributes, and which may be the effect of them. In this comparative facility of conception and belief, all philosophical Reasoning on the subject must perhaps terminate.

Though not inclined to religious speculations, Madison adhered to a calm faith in a moral, orderly universe presided over by a God beyond the limited capacity of man to fully conceive or understand.[68]

As Madison's life drew to a close, however, he looked not only backward over it, but forward to new generations that might carry on the principles of his public life. Four young men especially were Madison's legatees. Richard Rush as a diplomat and cabinet officer nourished plans of national growth long urged by Madison. Edward Coles mingled Virginia courtliness with a moral fervor that resulted in a lifetime of effective opposition to slavery. William Cabell Rives, a Piedmont neighbor, sustained Madison's principles in Virginia public life until the Civil War and then preserved Madison's record by writing a three-volume biography of him and by editing four volumes of his letters and other writings. Nicholas Trist, half-a-century Madison's junior, great-grandson of Madison's Philadelphia landlady, Mary House, and married to Jefferson's granddaughter, by nourishing the University of Virginia, by fighting nullification and secession, and by treating honestly yet realistically to end the Mexican War, was thus a lifelong Madisonian.

Each of these four men, young and unformed when Madison knew them, declared unequivocally that Madison was for him the pre-eminent guide, in principles and conduct, for every public act. Each labored often, in the generation or more he survived Madison, to vindicate his memory and to defend his career against a host of detractors. They had learned from the master himself an understanding of the character and virtues of "the extended republic," which he had expounded and sustained throughout his own public life, and thus each stood out in some way against the divisive sectional tendencies so strong and catastrophic in the thirty years following Madison's death. The course of events, from their arrival on the public stage at about the time of Madison's retirement, did not always conform either to their hopes or to Madison's. In fact, the triumph of an often merely rapacious Jacksonian democracy, the growth of an often merely crass Northern industrialism, and the arrogance of an often merely defensive Southern slavocracy would have been as unwelcome to Madison as they were to his young associates. Insofar as Madison's wisdom had relevance for the future, however, they gave it effect, and projected him meaningfully into the middle of the nineteenth century and beyond. No legacy would have pleased Madison more.

Through 1835 and 1836, in Madison's own metaphor, the candle of life in the old man at Montpelier sputtered toward its socket. Dolley Madison wrote that "my days are devoted to nursing and comforting my sick patient," while a visitor observed that "her devotion to Mr. Madison is incessant, and he needs all her constant attention." In February 1835, Harriet Martineau found Madison weak in sight and hearing, but eager for conversation. He sat from nine in the morning until ten at night "in his chair, with a pillow behind him, . . . his little person wrapped in a black silk gown; a warm gray and white cap upon his head, which [Mrs. Madison] took care should always sit becomingly; and grey worsted gloves, his hands having been rheumatic." He drew his will in April 1835, leaving generous bequests to colleges, universities, charitable institutions, and his nieces and nephews, and the residue of his estate to his widow. A series of illnesses, including a painful, itching eruption over his whole body, so sapped his strength that his valet, Paul Jennings, recalled that "for six months before his death, he was unable to walk, and spent most of his time reclining on a couch." His mind, though, Jennings continued, "was bright and with his numerous visitors he talked with as much animation and strength of voice as I ever heard him in his best days." Madison told one of his invited guests that of the uninvited ones, "some were taxes and other bounties." Fever and fatigue so filled the winter of 1835–36 that by the spring a shortness of breath affected Madison's speech. The last visitor to record full impressions of him, Charles J. Ingersoll, who came in May 1836, was warned by Mrs. Madison to talk a great deal himself to keep Madison from overexerting himself in trying to speak. He roused himself one final time, however, and talked eagerly with his War of 1812 colleague. Ingersoll found Madison's "understanding . . . as bright as ever; his intelligence, recollections, discriminations, and philosophy all delightfully instructive." "A purer, brighter, juster spirit has seldom existed," concluded Ingersoll, who, eight years earlier, had first toasted Madison as "the Father of the Constitution."

The stimulation proved too much for Madison; the visit left him "unable to write," Dolley reported, "or even to exert his thoughts without oppressive fatigue." He felt himself "on the descending, not the ascending line," and begged his wife "to be composed if not cheerful" as the end approached. Dr. Robley Dunglison, moved to Baltimore from Charlottesville by the demands of his growing practice, was called to Montpelier in late May to attend the failing ex-President. Madison shared some recently arrived sherry with the doctor, but regretted his own palate was too vitiated for him to pass proper judgment on it. Though Dunglison pronounced the sherry "to be of the first chop," he saw the ravages of old age left his patient beyond help. Madison used his last strength looking at the manuscript of Professor George Tucker's life of Jefferson, and on June 27, spent several hours painfully dictating thanks for the dedication of the book to him. He managed a final summary of his friendship with Jefferson: "A sincere and steadfast co-operation in promoting such a reconstruction of our political system as would provide for the permanent liberty and happiness of the United States" had been their undeviating goal. The trembling signature, barely legible and tumbling off the side of the page, was the last mark of Madison's pen, made, Tucker noted, "about thirteen hours before his decease." He was ready to die at his appointed hour, having rejected suggestions that he take stimulants to extend his life a few days so he could die on July 4, 1836, the sixtieth anniversary of the Declaration of Independence, just as Adams and Jefferson had died on its fiftieth anniversary and Monroe on its fifty-fifth.

The morning of June 28 Jennings joined his master as usual, about six o'clock, and shaved him as he had every day for sixteen years. Sukey, as old as Madison, and his servant for nearly seventy years, brought his breakfast, and Nelly Willis, always at Montpelier at times of need, came to the sickroom to visit with her uncle as he ate. When he seemed to have difficulty swallowing, Mrs. Willis asked him what the trouble was. Jennings recalled that Madison replied, "nothing more than a change of *mind*, my dear," and then "his head instantly dropped, and he ceased breathing as quietly as the snuff of a candle goes out."[69]

The next day Madison was carried by his neighbors James and Philip Barbour, Charles Howard, and Reuben Conway to his grave in the family plot half a mile south of his house. Following Dolley Madison, the family, and friends from all over Orange County were one hundred Montpelier slaves, "decently attired," James Barbour recalled, who remained silent until the words "dust to dust" in the Episcopal service, when they "gave vent to their lamentations in one violent burst that rent the air." As word of Madison's death spread, eulogies poured into Montpelier and memorial services were held all around the country. *The National Intelligencer* reported that "the last of the great lights of the Revolution . . . has sunk below the horizon . . . [and] left a radiance in the firmament." At an Orange County memorial meeting James Barbour made the common judgment that Madison's services to the nation had been exceeded only by Washington's, and asked his listeners to compare Madison's useful labors and lamented death, when "every hill and every valley of this vast republic resound with benedictions on his name," with the bloody ambition and wretched end of Napoleon.

In Quincy, Massachusetts, John Quincy Adams labored for two months on a eulogy of Madison, delivered to a crowded audience at the old Federal Street Theatre in Boston in late September. To prepare the two-and-one-half-hour oration, Adams wrote Dolley Madison for information on Madison's early life and pored over Jefferson's recently published letters. Noting privately in his diary that Madison was "a greater and far more estimable man" than Jefferson, "Old Man Eloquent" turned his stirring phrases on the figure he had come to regard with the deepest veneration. Madison, Adams proclaimed, had "improved his own condition by improving that of his country and his kind." The orator summarized the triumphs of Madison's career, such as that at the Virginia Convention of 1788, during which "the all but irresistible power of his eloquence, and the inexhaustible resources of his gigantic mind [had overcome] . . . the dazzling but then beclouded genius . . . of Patrick Henry." After noting that Madison's death removed the last of the nation builders who had drafted and signed the great founding documents, Adams asked his listeners to shun the whirlwind of discord, the earthquake of war, and the fires of nullification and civil dissension to listen to "the still small voice . . . that spoke the words of peace—of harmony—of union. And for that voice . . . fix your eyes upon the memory, and listen with your ears to the life of James Madison."[71]

Henry Clay's judgment a few years earlier, when he was asked to compare the administrations of Jefferson and Madison, made a more subtle point. Jefferson, Clay thought, "had most genius—Madison most judgment and common sense." Jefferson's enthusiasms often led him into "rash and imprudent and impracticable measures, [while] Madison [was] cool, dispassionate, practical, safe." When a companion declared that Jefferson's "power and energy," superior to Madison's, had better carried the nation through difficulties and dangers, Clay responded that "prudence and caution would have produced the same results." He pronounced Madison "after Washington our greatest statesman and first political writer," but he agreed finally that Madison and Jefferson "both were *great* and *good*, and though *different*—yet equal." Madison did lack the dramatic and even reckless qualities sometimes useful in public life, but within his own chosen style of statesmanship, valuing prudence, wisdom, and judgment, he was without peer.[72]

In the fall of 1834, at a moment of both revived health and foreboding for the future, Madison wrote down for posthumous disclosure his own final "Advice to My Country":

> As this advice, if it ever see the light will not do it till I am no more, it may be considered as issuing from the tomb, where truth alone can be respected, and the happiness of man alone consulted. It will be entitled therefore to whatever weight can be derived from good intentions, and from the experience of one who has served his country in various stations through a period of forty years, who espoused in his youth and adhered through his life to the cause of its liberty, and who has borne a part in most of the great transactions which will constitute epochs of its destiny. The advice nearest to my heart and deepest in my convictions is that the Union of the States be cherished and perpetuated. Let the open enemy to it be regarded as a Pandora with her box opened; and the disguised one, as the Serpent creeping with his deadly wiles into Paradise.

Madison's life reveals that he cherished the Union because only the cooperative power it released could bring the social justice necessary to fulfill the legal and moral equality of man. He furthermore cherished liberty because only it could open to man the opportunities due his limitless potential. His life has meaning, therefore, as long as these equations themselves are cherished and as long as men conceive government as legitimate only in pursuit of these ends.[73]

SELECTED BIBLIOGRAPHY

Manuscript Sources

Mr. Jasper E. Crane, Wilmington, Delaware: miscellaneous JM papers.

Mr. and Mrs. George B. Cutts of Brookline, Massachusetts, and Mr. Charles M. Storey, Boston: Cutts family papers.

Historical Society of Pennsylvania, Philadelphia: William Bradford papers, Jonathan Roberts papers, William Jones papers, Rush-Ingersoll letters.

Library of Congress, Washington, D.C.: JM papers, DPM papers, Rives-JM papers, Todd memorandum book, JM notes of debates in Federal Convention.

Maryland Historical Society, Baltimore: Isaac Briggs papers, William Pinkney papers, Elizabeth P. Bonaparte papers.

Massachusetts Historical Society, Boston: papers of various Federalists, including Cobb, Elijah Mills, Pickering, Stone, and Trumbull.

New Hampshire Historical Society, Concord: Daniel Webster and William Plumer papers.

New York Historical Society, New York: Gallatin papers, including Hannah Gallatin correspondence.

New York Public Library, New York: JM papers and Monroe papers.

Presbyterian Historical Society, Philadelphia: Madison family papers.

Princeton University Library, Princeton, New Jersey: Belcher and Witherspoon library lists, Bradford and Calhoun lecture notes, JM papers, William Pinkney papers, Edward Coles papers.

University of Virginia Library, Charlottesville, Virginia: DPM papers, JM pamphlets, minutes of the Board of Visitors of the University of Virginia.

Virginia Historical Society, Richmond, Virginia: Nicholas P. Trist papers, genealogical papers.

Virginia State Library, Richmond, Virginia: Francis Taylor diary.

Primary Sources

Adams Family Correspondence, L. H. Butterfield and others, eds., 2 vols., Cambridge, Massachusetts, 1963.

The Works of John Adams, C. F. Adams, ed., 10 vols., Boston, 1856.

The Memoirs of John Quincy Adams, C. F. Adams, ed., 12 vols., Philadelphia, 1874–1877.

Proceedings of the American Antiquarian Society.

American State Papers, Foreign, Vols. I–IV.

Seth Ames, ed., *The Works of Fisher Ames*, 2 vols., Boston, 1854.

Annals of Congress, 1789–1817.

Samuel Blair, *An Account of the College of New Jersey*, Woodbridge, New Jersey, 1764.

Andrew Burnaby, *Travels through the Middle Settlements in North America in the Years 1759 and 1760*, New York, 1904.

Letters of the Members of the Continental Congress, Edmund C. Burnett, ed., 8 vols., Washington, D.C., 1921–1938.

[Cabell,] *Early History of the University of Virginia as Contained in the Letters of Thomas Jefferson and Joseph C. Cabell*, Richmond, 1856.

The Papers of John C. Calhoun, R. L. Meriwether and others, eds., Vol. I, Columbia, South Carolina, 1959.

Marquis de Chastellux, *Travels in North America in the Years 1780, 1781 and 1782*, Howard C. Rice, Jr., ed., 2 vols., Chapel Hill, 1963.

Allen C. Clarke, *Life and Letters of Dolly Madison*, Washington, D.C., 1914.

The Papers of Henry Clay, James F. Hopkins and others, eds., Vols. I–II, Lexington, Kentucky, 1959–1961.

The Making of the American Party System, 1789 to 1809, Noble E. Cunningham, Jr., ed., Englewood Cliffs, New Jersey, 1965.

Life, Journals, and Correspondence of Rev. Manasseh Cutler, W. P. and J. P. Cutler, eds., 2 vols., Cincinnati, 1888.

Lucia B. Cutts, ed., *Memoirs and Letters of Dolly Madison*, Boston, 1886.

Life and Writings of Alexander James Dallas, G. M. Dallas, ed., Philadelphia, 1871.

Jeffersonian America, Notes on the United States of America Collected in the Years 1805–6–7 and 11–12 by Sir Augustus John Foster, Bart., R. B. Davis, ed., San Marino, California, 1954.

Jonathan Elliot, ed., *Debates in the Several State Conventions on the Federal Constitution*, 2nd ed., 5 vols., Philadelphia, 1861.

Max Farrand, ed., *The Records of the Federal Convention of 1787*, 4 vols., New Haven, 1937.

The Federalist, Jacob E. Cooke, ed., Cleveland, 1961.

Philip Vickers Fithian Journal and Letters, 1767–1774, John R. Williams, ed., Princeton, 1900.

The Prose of Philip Freneau, P. M. Marsh, ed., New Brunswick, New Jersey, 1955.

The Writings of Albert Gallatin, Henry Adams, ed., 3 vols., Philadelphia, 1879 (New York, 1960).

Hugh B. Grigsby, *The Virginia Convention of 1776*, Richmond, 1855.

——, *The History of the Virginia Federal Convention of 1788*, 2 vols., Richmond, 1890–1891.

The Papers of Alexander Hamilton, Harold C. Syrett and others, eds., 13 vols., New York, 1961–1968.

Gaillard Hunt, ed., *The First Forty Years of Washington Society*, New York, 1906.

Lady Jackson, ed., *The Bath Archives: A Further Selection from the Diaries and Letters of Sir George Jackson*, 2 vols., London, 1873.

The Papers of Thomas Jefferson, Julian P. Boyd and others, eds., 17 vols., Princeton, 1950–1967.

The Writings of Thomas Jefferson, Paul L. Ford, ed., 10 vols., New York, 1892–1899.

The Writings of Thomas Jefferson, A. A. Lipscomb and A. E. Bergh, eds., 20 vols., Washington, D.C., 1903.

The Family Letters of Thomas Jefferson, E. M. Betts and J. A. Bear, eds., Columbia, Missouri, 1966.

The Autobiography of Thomas Jefferson, Dumas Malone, ed., New York, 1959.

The Complete Anas of Thomas Jefferson, F. B. Sawvel, ed., New York, 1903.

Cecelia M. Kenyon, ed., *The Antifederalists*, Indianapolis, 1966.

The Life and Correspondence of Rufus King, Charles R. King, ed., 6 vols., Boston, 1894–1900.

Lafayette et Amérique en 1824 et 1825, A. Levasseur, 2 vols., Paris, 1829.

Journal of William Maclay, E. S. Maclay, ed., New York, 1890.

Harriet Martineau, *Retrospect of Western Travel*, 3 vols., Saunders and Otley, London, 1838.

The Papers of James Madison, William T. Hutchinson, W. M. E. Rachal, and others, eds., Vols. I–VI, Chicago, 1962–1969.

The Writings of James Madison, Gaillard Hunt, ed., 9 vols., New York, 1900–1910.

Letters and Other Writings of James Madison, William C. Rives and Philip R. Fendall, eds., 4 vols., Philadelphia, 1865.

The Papers of James Madison, purchased by order of Congress . . ., H. D. Gilpin, ed., 3 vols., Washington, D.C., 1840.

Selections from the Private Correspondence of James Madison from 1813 to 1836, printed by J. C. McGuire, Washington, D.C., 1853.

Index to the James Madison Papers, Library of Congress, 1965.

Bernard Mayo, ed., "Instructions to the British Ministers to the United States, 1791–1812," *American Historical Association Annual Report*, 1936, III.

The Writings of James Monroe, Stanislaus M. Hamilton, ed., 7 vols., New York, 1898–1903.

Moreau de St. Méry's American Journey, 1793–1798, Kenneth and A. M. Roberts, eds., Garden City, New York, 1947.

The National Intelligencer, 1801–1817, Washington, D.C.

The Life and Letters of Harrison Gray Otis, S. E. Morrison, 2 vols., Boston, 1913.

The Pennsylvania Journal, 1769–1776, Philadelphia.

The Pennsylvania Packet, 1780–1787, Philadelphia.

The Letters and Papers of Edmund Pendleton, David J. Mays, ed., 2 vols., Charlottesville, Virginia, 1967.

Henry Wheaton, *Some Account of the Life, Writings, and Speeches of William Pinkney*, New York, 1826.

William Plumer's Memorandum of Proceedings in the United States Senate, 1803–1807, E. S. Brown, ed., New York, 1923.

Messages and Papers of the Presidents, comp. by James D. Richardson, 20 vols., Washington, D.C., 1897–1917.

The Letters of Benjamin Rush, L. H. Butterfield, ed., 2 vols., Princeton, 1951.

"Some Unpublished Correspondence of John Adams and Richard Rush, 1811–1822," J. H. Powell, ed., *PMHB*, LX (1936) and LXI (1937).

The Virginia Gazette, 1751–1780 (Williamsburg, Virginia, various eds.).

The Virginia Magazine of History and Biography, "Accounts of the Donald Robertson School," XXXIII (1925), "After-Dinner Anecdotes of James Madison: Excerpt from Jared Sparks' Journal for 1829–1831," LX (1952), "An Unpublished Sketch of James Madison by James K. Paulding," LXVII (1959), letter of H. D. Gilpin to his father, September 16, 1827, LXXVI (October 1968).

Journals of the Council of the State of Virginia, H. R. McIlwaine, ed., Vol. II, Richmond, 1932.

Diaries of George Washington, John C. Fitzpatrick, ed., 4 vols., Boston, 1925.

The Writings of George Washington, John C. Fitzpatrick, ed., 39 vols., Washington, D.C., 1931–1940.

The Revolutionary Diplomatic Correspondence of the United States, Francis Wharton, ed., 6 vols., Washington, D.C., 1889.

The William and Mary Quarterly, "James Madison's Autobiography," II (1945); "Madison's 'Detached Memoranda,'" III (1946).

Secondary Sources

Abernethy, Thomas P., *The South in the New Nation 1789–1819*, Baton Rouge, 1961.

——, *Western Lands and the American Revolution*, New York, 1937.

Adair, Douglass, "James Madison," in W. Thorp, ed., *The Lives of Eighteen from Princeton*, Princeton, 1946.

——, "The Authorship of the Disputed Federalist Papers," *WMQ*, I (1944).

——, "'That Politics May Be Reduced to a Science': David Hume, James Madison, and the Tenth *Federalist*," *The Huntington Library Quarterly*, XX (1957).

——, "The Intellectual Origins of Jeffersonian Democracy," unpub. Ph.D. dissertation, Yale University, 1944.

Adams, Henry, *History of the United States during the Administrations of Jefferson and Madison*, 10 vols., New York, 1889–1891.

Adams, Herbert B., *Thomas Jefferson and the University of Virginia*, Washington, D.C., 1888.

Adams, John Q., *The Lives of James Madison and James Monroe*, Boston, 1850.

Ammon, Harry, *James Monroe: The Quest for National Identity*, (forthcoming, 1970).

Anthony, Katharine, *Dolley Madison, Her Life and Times*, Garden City, New York, 1949.

Bemis, Samuel F., *The Diplomacy of the American Revolution*, Bloomington, Indiana, 1957 (1935).

——, *Jay's Treaty: A Study in Commerce and Diplomacy*, New Haven, 1962 (New York, 1923).

——, *John Quincy Adams and the Foundations of American Foreign Policy*, New York, 1949.

Bernhard, Wilfred, *Fisher Ames*, Chapel Hill, 1965.

Beveridge, Alfred J., *The Life of John Marshall*, 4 vols., Boston, 1916–1919.

Brant, Irving, *James Madison*, 6 vols., Indianapolis, 1941–1961 (one-volume edition, 1970).

Brown, Roger, *1812: The Republic in Peril*, New York, 1964.

Brown, Stuart G., *The First Republicans*, Syracuse, 1954.

Bruce, Philip A., *History of the University of Virginia*, 5 vols., New York, 1920.

Burnett, Edmund C., *The Continental Congress*, New York, 1964 (1941).

Burns, Edward M., *James Madison, Philosopher of the Constitution*, New Brunswick, 1938.

Butterfield, L. H., "Elder John Leland, Jeffersonian Itinerant: Leland and Madison: Ratification of the Constitution and the Bill of Rights," *Proceedings of the American Antiquarian Society* LXII (1952).

Carson, Jane, *Colonial Virginians at Play*, Williamsburg, Virginia, 1958.

Coles, Harry L., *The War of 1812*, Chicago, 1965.

Collins, Varnum L., *Life of John Witherspoon*, 2 vols., Princeton, 1925.

Crosskey, William W., *Politics and the Constitution in the History of the United States*, 2 vols., Chicago, 1953.

Cunningham, Noble E., Jr., *The Jeffersonian Republicans: The Formation of Party Organization, 1789–1801*, Chapel Hill, 1957.

——, *The Jeffersonian Republicans in Power, Party Operations, 1801–1809*, Chapel Hill, 1963.

Dangerfield, George, *Chancellor Robert R. Livingston of New York, 1746–1813*, New York, 1960.

Davis, Richard B., *Intellectual Life in Jefferson's Virginia, 1790–1830*, Chapel Hill, 1964.

Dewey, Donald O., "Constitutional Theory of James Madison, 1817–1836," unpub. Ph.D. dissertation, University of Chicago, 1963.

Diamond, Martin, "Democracy and *The Federalist*: A Reconsideration of the Framers' Intent," *American Political Science Review*, LIII (1959).

——, "The Federalist's View of Federalism," in *Essays in Federalism*, Claremont, California, 1961.

Elkins, Stanley, and McKitrick, Eric, "The Founding Fathers: Young Men of the Revolution," *Political Science Quarterly*, LXXVI (1961).

Ernst, Robert, *Rufus King, American Federalist*, Chapel Hill, 1968.

Ferguson, E. James, *The Power of the Purse*, Chapel Hill, 1961.

Freeman, Douglas, *George Washington*, 7 vols., New York, 1948–1957.

Gay, Sidney H., *James Madison*, New York, 1894.

Gilbert, Felix, *To the Farewell Address: Ideas of Early American Foreign Policy*, Princeton, 1961.

Gottschalk, Louis, *Lafayette between the American and the French Revolution*, Chicago, 1950.

Hunt, Gaillard, *Life of James Madison*, New York, 1902.

Jennings, Paul, *A Colored Man's Reminiscences of James Madison*, Brooklyn, 1865.

Jensen, Merrill, *The New Nation: A History of the United States during the Confederation, 1781–1789*, New York, 1965 (1950).

Ketcham, Ralph, "France and American Politics, 1763–1793," *Political Science Quarterly*, LXXVIII (1963).

——, "The Dictates of Conscience: Edward Coles and Slavery," *The Virginia Quarterly Review*, XXXVI (1960).

Koch, Adrienne, *Jefferson and Madison: The Great Collaboration*, New York, 1950.

——, and Ammon, Harry, "The Virginia and Kentucky Resolutions: An Episode in Jefferson's and Madison's Defense of Civil Liberties," *WMQ*, V (1948).

Levy, Leonard W., *Freedom of Speech and Press in Early American History: Legacy of Suppression*, New York, 1963 (Cambridge, Massachusetts, 1960).

Lynd, Staughton, *Class Conflict, Slavery, and the United States Constitution*, Indianapolis, 1967.

McDonald, Forrest, *We the People*, Chicago, 1958.

——, *E Pluribus Unum: The Formation of the American Republic, 1776–1790*, Boston, 1965.

Main, Jackson T., *The Antifederalists*, Chapel Hill, 1961.

Malone, Dumas, *Jefferson and His Time*, 3 vols. (to 1801), Boston, 1948–1962.

Mayo, Bernard, *Henry Clay, Spokesman for the West* (to 1812), Boston, 1937.

Mays, David J., *Edmund Pendleton, 1721–1803*, 2 vols., Cambridge, Massachusetts, 1952.

Meade, Robert D., *Patrick Henry*, 2 vols., Philadelphia, 1957–1969.

Miller, John C., *The Federalist Era, 1789–1801*, New York, 1964.

Mitchell, Broadus, *Alexander Hamilton*, 2 vols., New York, 1957–1962.

Morgan, Edmund S., *Virginians at Home*, Williamsburg, Virginia, 1952.

O'Donnell, William E., *The Chevalier de la Luzerne*, Bruges, Belgium, 1938.

Perkins, Bradford, *The First Rapprochement: England and the United States, 1795–1805*, Philadelphia, 1953.

——, *Prologue to War: England and the United States, 1805–1812*, Berkeley and Los Angeles, 1961.

Peterson, Merrill D., "Thomas Jefferson and Commercial Policy, 1783–1793," *WMQ*, XXII (1965).

Powell, John H., *Richard Rush, Republican Diplomat*, Philadelphia, 1942.

Randall, Henry S., *The Life of Thomas Jefferson*, 3 vols., New York, 1858.

Risjord, Norman K., *The Old Republicans: Southern Conservatism in the Age of Jefferson*, New York, 1965.

Rives, William C., *History of the Life and Times of James Madison*, 3 vols., New York, 1859–1868.

Rossiter, Clinton, *Seedtime of the Republic*, New York, 1953.

Smelser, Marshall, *The Democratic Republic, 1801–1815*, New York, 1968.

Smith, Abbot E., *James Madison, Builder*, New York, 1938.

Smith, Charles Page, *James Wilson, Founding Father, 1742–1798*, Chapel Hill, 1956.

——, *John Adams*, 2 vols., Garden City, New York, 1962.

Smith, T. V., "Saints, Secular and Sacredotal—James Madison and Mahatma Gandhi," *Ethics*, LIX (1948).

Stinchcombe, William C., *The American Revolution and the French Alliance*, Syracuse, 1969.

Sydnor, Charles S., *Gentlemen Freeholders, Political Practices in Washington's Virginia*, Chapel Hill, 1952.

Tucker, Glenn, *Poltroons and Patriots, a Popular Account of the War of 1812*, 2 vols., Indianapolis, 1954.

Van Doren, Carl, *The Great Rehearsal*, New York, 1948.

Ver Steeg, Clarence L., *Robert Morris, Revolutionary Financier*, Philadelphia, 1954.

Walters, Raymond, Jr., *Albert Gallatin, Jeffersonian Financier and Diplomat*, New York, 1957.

Wertenbaker, Thomas J., *Princeton, 1746–1896*, Princeton, 1946.

White, Leonard D., *The Federalists*, New York, 1948.

——, *The Jeffersonians*, New York, 1951.

The William and Mary Quarterly, "James Madison Bicentennial Number," VIII (1951).

Wiltse, Charles M., *John C. Calhoun, Nationalist*, Indianapolis, 1944.

Young, Alfred E., *The Democratic-Republicans in New York: The Origins*, Chapel Hill, 1967.

SOURCE NOTES

Chapter 1

1. Brant, I, 53; James Madison, Sr., account book, 1755–1765, Presbyterian Historical Society, Philadelphia.
2. Brant, I, 13–28, 33; Delma R. Carpenter, "The Route Followed by Governor Spotswood in 1716 across the Blue Ridge Mountains," *VMHB*, LXXXIII (1965), 405–412.
3. "Will of Ambrose Madison, 1732," *VMHB*, VI (1898), 434–5, and VII (1899), 302.
4. Family information gathered from a wide variety of published and unpublished sources by the Chicago and Richmond offices of *The Papers of James Madison. MP*, I (opposite p. 213), shows a Madison family tree.
5. Charles S. Sydnor, *Gentlemen Freeholders* (Chapel Hill, 1952; Collier paperback, 1962), pp. 60–65.

Chapter 2

1. Joseph Chew to James Madison, Sr., February 18, 1746, September 6, 1749, and May 21, 1750, MPLC.
2. Brant, I, 41–5; conversations with Mr. Chester Hazard, manager of the Montpelier estate, September 1954 and April 1964.
3. James Madison, Sr., account book, 1755–1765, Presbyterian Historical Society.
4. Brant, I, 48–9.
5. Rives, *Life of Madison*, I, 47–52.
6. John Madison to James Madison, Sr., August 19, 1755, MPLC.
7. Journal of James Maury, August 1755, letter, June 10, 1756, quoted in Richard L. Morton, *Colonial Virginia* (2 vols., Chapel Hill, 1960), II, 681; GW to Robert Dinwiddie, October 11, 1755, *Writings of Washington*, I, 203.
8. John Duffy, *Epidemics in Colonial America* (Baton Rouge, 1953); Wyndham B. Blanton, *Medicine in Virginia in the Eighteenth Century* (Richmond, 1931), pp. 60–66.
9. Joseph Chew to James Madison, Sr., April 10, 1761, account book, 1755–1765, Presbyterian Historical Society.
10. John to Abigail Adams, June 26, 1776, in L. H. Butterfield and others, eds., *Adams Family Correspondence* (2 vols., Cambridge, 1963), II, 23.
11. "Will of Ambrose Madison, 1732," *VMHB*, VII (1899), 434–5; Daniel J. Boorstin, *The Americans: The Colonial Experience* (New York, 1958),

pp. 301–4; Madison invoice, March 16, 1749, Presbyterian Historical Society.

12. James Madison, Sr., account book, 1755–1765, Presbyterian Historical Society; Edmund S. Morgan, *Virginians at Home* (Williamsburg, Virginia, 1952), pp. 14–15.

13. James Madison, Sr., account book, 1755–1765, Presbyterian Historical Society; H. D. Farish, ed., *Journal and Letters of Philip Vickers Fithian, 1773–1774* (Williamsburg, Virginia, 1945), pp. 44–6.

14. *MP*, I, 18–20.

15. "Accounts of the Donald Robertson School," *VMHB*, XXXIII (1925), 292; Jane Carson, *James Innes and His Brothers of the F. H. C.* (Williamsburg, 1961), pp. 12–18; David J. Mays, *Edmund Pendleton* (2 vols., Cambridge, 1952), I, 139–40; JM, "Autobiographical Notes," ca. 1816, Princeton Univ. Lib.

16. "Accounts of the Donald Robertson School," *VMHB*, XXXIII (1925), 194–8, 288–92.

17. John C. Payne to J. Q. Adams, August 1836, Adams mss., Massachusetts Historical Society; Brant, I, 60.

18. Farish, *op. cit.*, pp. 25–6.

19. Edmund Pendleton to James Madison, Sr., April 17 and December 11, 1765, February 15, 1766, in David J. Mays, ed., *The Letters and Papers of Edmund Pendleton* (2 vols., Charlottesville, 1967), I, 20–24.

20. Invoice, August 24, 1769, Presbyterian Historical Society.

21. Morgan, *Virginians at Home*, pp. 26–7; Dumas Malone, *Jefferson and His Time* (Boston, 1948), I, 50–52.

Chapter 3

1. *Virginia Gazette*, July 6, 1769; Brant, I, 411.

2. Andrew Burnaby, *Travels through the Middle Settlements in North America in the Years 1759 and 1760* (New York, 1904), p. 68n.

3. John Adams to Abigail Adams, February 2, 1777, in L. H. Butterfield and others, eds., *Adams Family Correspondence* (2 vols., Cambridge, 1963), II, 152; Burnaby, *Travels*, p. 88.

4. *Pennsylvania Journal*, July 13 and July 20, 1769.

5. Burnaby, *Travels*, p. 103; *MP*, I, 43.

6. Rules adopted May 4, 1769, printed in *Pennsylvania Journal*, July 13, 1769; *MP*, I, 46.

7. Thomas J. Wertenbaker, *Princeton, 1746–1896* (Princeton, 1946), pp. 80–86.

8. Samuel Blair, *An Account of the College of New Jersey . . .* (Woodbridge, New Jersey, 1764), pp. 23–26.

9. *Ibid.*, p. 9, 11–23.

10. Philip Vickers Fithian to his father, November 30, 1770, in John R. Williams, ed., *Philip Vickers Fithian Journal and Letters, 1767–1774* (Princeton, 1900), pp. 8–9.

11. Blair, *Account*, pp. 25–34.

12. *Ibid.*, pp. 25–6.

13. To Benjamin Waterhouse, November 28, 1835, to James Madison, Sr., September 30, 1769, *MP*; I, 47n, 45.

14. *MP*, I, 32–42.

15. Blair, *Account*, p. 38.

16. Douglass Adair, "James Madison," in W. Thorp, ed., *The Lives of Eight-*

een from Princeton (Princeton, 1946), p. 144, quotes Fithian on undergraduate "foibles."

17. To James Madison, Sr., July 23, 1770, and to John Boyle, May 17, 1771, *MP*, I, 50, 60.
18. Samuel D. Alexander, *Princeton College during the Eighteenth Century* (New York, 1872).
19. Benjamin Rush to James Rush, May 25, 1802, Rush Papers, Library Company of Philadelphia.
20. From a notebook compiled by William Bradford; *MP*, I, 61–65, 68n.
21. To James Madison, Sr., September 30, 1769 and July 23, 1770, *MP*, I, 45, 50.
22. *Pennsylvania Chronicle*, October 8–15, 1770; *New Jersey Archives*, 1st series, (Paterson, New Jersey, 1907), XXVIII, 275–9.
23. *New Jersey Archives*, XXVII, 582–4; XXVIII, 272–5, 277–80.
24. An appeal on behalf of the College of New Jersey printed in March 1772; Brant, I, 102.
25. Eugene Rich, "John Witherspoon in Scotland, 1723–1768." unpublished Ph.D. dissertation, Syracuse University, 1964.
26. *MP*, I, 4–22.
27. Madison's "Autobiography," 1832, *MP*, I, 32n; to Richard D. Cutts, January 4, 1829, original owned by Mr. and Mrs. George B. Cutts, Brookline, Massachusetts; *The Spectator*, No. 10, London, 1712.
28. Anthony, earl of Shaftesbury, "An Inquiry Concerning Virtue, or Merit," *Characteristicks*, II (London, 1714), 7; Witherspoon quotations in this and the following four paragraphs are from "Lectures on Moral Philosophy, delivered at Nassau Hall by John Witherspoon: A True Copy by John E. Calhoun, Princeton, N.J., 1774," Princeton University Library. Calhoun's notes are somewhat more complete than, but otherwise virtually identical to, those taken by Andrew Hunter and William Bradford in 1772.
29. Witherspoon's reading lists are much fuller in the 1772 notebooks than in the published versions of his lectures.
30. Quotations are from William Bradford's notes, taken in 1772, on Witherspoon's "Lectures on Eloquence," Princeton University Library; Bradford and Madison probably discussed the lectures in the notebook.
31. Manuscript catalogue of Belcher's library, Princeton University Library.
32. Manuscript catalogue of Witherspoon's books, Princeton University Library.
33. Richard M. Gummere, *The American Colonial Mind and the Classical Tradition* (Cambridge, 1963), describes the wide influence of classical learning in colonial America.
34. John Locke, *Essay Concerning Human Understanding*, Book II, Chap. 21, Sec. 54.
35. Locke, *Second Treatise on Civil Government*, Chap. 8, Sec. 95.

Chapter 4

1. To James Madison, Sr., October 9, 1771, *MP*, I, 68–9; "Autobiography," *WMQ*, II (1945), 197.
2. Brant, I, 105–9; ms. "Autobiography" with interlineations, Princeton University Library; Madison Family Papers, Presbyterian Historical Society.
3. From Bradford, October 13, 1772, *MP*, I, 72–3.
4. To Bradford, November 9, 1772, *MP*, I, 74–6.

5. From Freneau, November 22, 1772, *MP*, I, 77–9.
6. From Bradford, March 1, 1773, and to Bradford, April 28, 1773, *MP*, I, 79–84.
7. From Bradford, May 27, 1773, *MP*, I, 85–7.
8. To Bradford, June 10 and September 5, 1773, *MP*, I, 88–9, 93–4.
9. To Bradford, June 10, 1773, and from Bradford, August 12, 1773, *MP*, I, 88–92.
10. To Bradford, September 23, 1773, *MP*, I, 95–7.
11. To Bradford, December 1, 1773, *MP*, I, 100–101.
12. "Scripture Notes," *MP*, I, 51–9; prayer book in University of Virginia Library collection of Madison pamphlets.
13. To Bradford, January 24, 1774, *MP*, I, 106.
14. To Bradford, January 24, 1774; "Autobiography," 1832, *MP*, I, 104–6, 107n; Lewis P. Little, *Imprisoned Preachers and Religious Liberty in Virginia* (Lynchburg, 1938), pp. 421, 426–7.
15. To Bradford, April 1, 1774, *MP*, I, 111–13.
16. *Pennsylvania Journal*, May 4, 11, 18, and 25, 1774.
17. Bradford note, *MP*, I, 114n.
18. *Pennsylvania Journal*, June 8, 15, and 22, 1774; to Bradford, July 1, 1774, *MP*, I, 114.
19. To Bradford, July 1, 1774, *MP*, I, 114–16.
20. From Bradford, August 1, 1774, and to Bradford, August 23, 1774, *MP*, I, 117–22.
21. From Bradford, October 17, 1774, and January 4, 1775, and to Bradford, November 26, 1774, and January 20, 1775, *MP*, I, 125–37.
22. To Bradford, January 20, 1775, and April 1, 1774, *MP*, I, 136–7, 111–12.
23. From Bradford, March 1775, and to Bradford, March 3, June 19, and July 28, 1775, *MP*, I, 138–41, 156, 161.
24. *MP*, I, 147n, 148n.
25. To Bradford, January 20, March 20, and July 28, 1775, *MP*, I, 135, 141, 147n, 161.
26. To Bradford, June 19, 1775, commission, October 2, 1775, *MP*, I, 153, 163.
27. Brant, I, 178–80; "Memoirs of Philip Mazzei," *WMQ*, 2nd ser., IX (1929), 172–3; Robert D. Meade, *Patrick Henry* (2 vols., Phila., 1957, 1969), II, 84–5.
28. Orange County Committee of Safety to Henry, May 9, 1775, and JM to Bradford May 9, 1775, *MP*, I, 144–7.
29. From Bradford, June 2, 1775, and to Bradford, June 19, 1775, *MP*, I, 148–53.
30. Caroline Robbins, *The Eighteenth-Century Commonwealth Man* (Cambridge, Massachusetts, 1959), pp. 199–202, 347–53; Leonard W. Levy, *Freedom of Speech and Press in Early American History: Legacy of Suppression* (New York, 1963 [Cambridge, Massachusetts, 1960]), pp. 164–8.
31. To Bradford, July 28, 1775, *MP*, I, 159–61.

Chapter 5

1. GW to Joseph Reed, January 31, 1776, *Writings of Washington*, IV, 297.
2. David J. Mays, *Edmund Pendleton, 1721–1803* (2 vols., Cambridge, 1952), II, 103–8.
3. Charles S. Sydnor, *American Revolutionaries in the Making* (New York, 1952 [1962]) describes these practices.

4. Peter Force, comp. *American Archives*, 4th ser., V, 1035; Brant, I, 233.
5. *Virginia Gazette* (Purdie), May 17 and July 5, 1776.
6. *Virginia Gazette* (Purdie), May 17, 1776; *Virginia Gazette* (Dixon and Hunter), May 18, 1776; Brant, I, 226.
7. "Edmund Randolph's Essay on the Revolutionary History of Virginia," *VMHB*, XLIV (1936), 45; Mays, *Pendleton*, II, 120–22.
8. *MP*, I, 172–5.
9. Brant, I, 247–9; George Bancroft, *The History of the United States*, (6 vols., New York, 1883–5), IV, 416–17.
10. *Virginia Gazette* (Purdie), June 28, 1776; Mays, *Pendleton*, II, 111–17.
11. From Bradford, May 20 and June 3, 1776; to Bradford *ca.* May 21, 1776, and to James Madison, Sr., June 1–15, and June 27, 1776; *MP*, I, 180–85.
12. Mays, *Pendleton*, II, 133.
13. Dumas Malone, ed., *The Autobiography of Thomas Jefferson* (New York, 1959), p. 51.
14. Brant, I, 298–300; Mays, *Pendleton*, II, 133–7.
15. Mays, *Pendleton*, II, 135; Malone, *Autobiography of Jefferson*, pp. 50, 55–6.
16. *MP*, I, 186–90.
17. Madison's "Autobiography"; "Report of Committee on Elections," *MP*, I, 192–3.
18. To James Madison, Sr., March 29, 1777, and Orange County petition, *MP*, I, 190–92, 213–14.
19. Reverend James Madison, "Meteorological Observations, July 1777–August 1778," *Transactions, American Philosophical Society*, II (Philadelphia, 1786), 141–58.
20. Council Minutes, January 14, 1778, H. R. McIlwain, ed., *Journals of the Council of State of Virginia* (Richmond, 1932), II, 62–7; *MP*, I, 214–19; Brant, I, 317–20.
21. To James Madison, Sr., January 23, 1778, and December 8, 1779, *MP*, I, 222–3, 316.
22. *Transactions, American Philosophical Society*, II (1786), 143; Reverend James Madison to TJ, July 26, 1778; Boyd *PJ*, II, 205–6.
23. To Robert Walsh, August 22, 1831, Cong. ed., IV, 194.
24. To James Madison, Sr., January 23 and March 6, 1778, June 25 and December 8, 1779, *MP*, I, 222–4, 233–4, 298–9, 315–17.
25. N. P. Trist (story heard July 17, 1827), recorded in Henry S. Randall, *The Life of Thomas Jefferson* (3 vols., New York, 1858), II, 326n.
26. From S. S. Smith, November 1777, and August 15, 1778; *MP*, I, 194, 211, 253–258.
27. Election certificate, May 27, 1778, *MP*, I, 242–3; R. H. Lee to TJ, October 5, 1778, Boyd *PJ*, II, 215; GW to Benjamin Harrison, December 18 and 30, 1778, *Writings of Washington*, XIII, 464–7.
28. To James Madison, Sr., January 23, 1778, *MP*, I, 223–4; Brant, I, 365.
29. Essay written in early 1780, but first published in *National Gazette*, December 19 and 22, 1791, *MP*, I, 304–9.

Chapter 6

1. To James Madison, Sr., March 20, 1780, expense account, September 20, 1780, *MP*, II, 3, 97; TJ to Martha Jefferson, November 28, 1783, Boyd *PJ*, VI, 360.
2. Diary of Thomas Rodney, March 10, 1781; Edmund C. Burnett, ed.,

Letters of the Members of the Continental Congress (8 vols., Washington, D.C., 1921–1938); VI, 19.

3. To James Madison, Sr., March 20, 1780, and to TJ, March 27, 1780, *MP*, II, 3, 6.
4. To TJ, May 6, 1780, *MP*, II, 20.
5. GW to Joseph Jones, May 31, 1780, *Writings of Washington*, XVIII, 453.
6. Board of Admiralty to Abraham Whipple, March 24, 1780, and other admiralty papers *MP*, II, 4–25.
7. To Pendleton, September 12, 1780, *MP*, II, 81.
8. William C. Stinchcombe, *The American Revolution and the French Alliance* (Syracuse, 1969), pp. 32–48, 77–91; Ketcham, "France and American Politics, 1763–1793," *Political Science Quarterly*, LXXVIII (1963), 198–223.
9. To Pendleton, November 7, 1780, *MP*, II, 165.
10. Committee report, December 1, 1780, *MP*, II, 217–18; Arthur Lee to the President of Congress, December 7, 1780, Francis Wharton, ed., *The Revolutionary Diplomatic Correspondence of the United States* (6 vols., Washington, D.C., 1889), IV, 182–6.
11. Reports and motions in Congress, December 1–23, 1780, *MP*, II, 217–61; *Journals of the Continental Congress* (Washington, D.C., 1910), XVIII, 1114–99; Brant, II, 62–9.
12. Samuel F. Bemis, *The Diplomacy of the American Revolution* (Bloomington, Indiana, 1957 [1935]), pp. 81–104.
13. Instructions to Jay, October 17, 1780, *MP*, II, 127–35; Franklin to Jay, October 2, 1781, Albert Smyth, ed., *The Writings of Benjamin Franklin* (10 vols., New York, 1904), VIII, 142.
14. "Notes on Observations of Barbé-Marbois on Western Boundary," October 6–16, 1780, *MP*, II, 114–17.
15. To Joseph Jones, November 25, 1780, *MP*, II, 202–6.
16. Resolve of January 2, 1781, instructions to Jay, May 2, 1781, *MP*, II, 273, III, 101–7; Jay to President of Congress, October 3, 1781, Wharton, *Diplomatic Corres.*, IV, 748–9.
17. Thomas P. Abernethy, *Western Lands and the American Revolution* (New York, 1937); Merrill Jensen, *The New Nation . . . 1781–1789* (New York, 1965 [1950]), pp. 44–5, 351–6.
18. George Morgan to Virginia delegates, November 16, 1780, and JM to Jones, November 21, 1780, *MP*, II, 176–8, 190–91.
19. Mason to Virginia delegates, August 2, 1780, and Jones-Madison motion, September 6, 1780, *MP*, II, 52–3, 72–8 (including long editorial note on politics of land cessions).
20. From Reverend James Madison, August 3, 1780, *MP*, II, 54–5; Thomas Burke to William Bingham, February 6, 1781, Burnett, *Letters*, V, 562–3.
21. Arthur Lee to John Page, June 1, 1781, A. S. W. Rosenbach, *History of America in Documents*, catalogue, I, #455; Stinchcombe, *French Alliance*, pp. 104–117.
22. Thomas Rodney diary, March 10, 1781, in Burnett, *Letters*, VI, 19.
23. From Jones, October 2, 1780, to Jones, October 10, 1780, account of expenses, September 25 and December 20, 1780, *MP*, II, 107–9, 122–4, 97, 252; Mary Payne to Rachel Pemberton Parke, May 5, 1780, Pemberton papers, HSP.
24. "Samuel Holten Diary," *The Historical Collections of the Danvers Historical Society*, Danvers, Massachusetts, VIII (1920), 124; to John Page, May 8, 1780, *MP*, II, 22.

25. Holten diary, Armstrong to Horatio Gates, June 6, 1780, Cornell to William Green, August 15, 1780, in Burnett, *Letters*, V, 10n, 200, 328n.
26. To Jones, December 5, 1780, *MP*, II, 225, 226n; Howard C. Rice, Jr., ed., *Travels in North America in the Years 1780, 1781, and 1782 by the Marquis de Chastellux* (2 vols., Chapel Hill, 1963), I, 174–5, 327; Charles Thomson, "Notes on Debates in Congress," August 28, 1782, in Burnett, *Letters*, VI, 460–61.
27. *Pennsylvania Journal*, July 5, 1780; *Pennsylvania Packet*, July 8 and 15, 1780.
28. *Pennsylvania Packet*, July 5, 1781; *MP*, III, 183n.
29. Rodney diary, March 10, 1781, Burnett, *Letters*, VI, 20; Martha Bland to Mrs. St. George Tucker, March 30, 1781, *VMHB*, XLIII (1935), 43; Louis Otto to Vergennes, 1787, Brant, II, 14.
30. Bradford to Susan Boudinot, September 10, 1784, HSP.
31. From TJ, January 31 and February 14, 1783, and to TJ, February 11, 1783, Boyd *PJ*, VI, 226, 234–6.
32. From TJ, April 14, 1783, Boyd *PJ*, VI, 262.
33. To TJ, April 22, 1783, Boyd *PJ*, VI, 263; Brant, II, 283–7, tells the full story of the Kitty Floyd romance for the first time; the account here depends heavily on Brant.
34. To TJ, May 20 and July 17, 1783, from TJ, June 1 and 10, 1783, Boyd *PJ*, VI, 271, 273–4, 276; to E. Randolph, July 28, 1783, Hunt, II, 5.
35. To TJ, August 11, 1783, and from TJ, August 31, 1783, Boyd *PJ*, VI, 333–6.

Chapter 7

1. La Luzerne, "Liste des Membres du Congress depuis 1779 jusqu'en 1784," quoted in Brant, II, 14.
2. AH to Duane, September 3, 1780; Syrett *PH*, II, 401, 402, 407.
3. Motion in Congress, March 12, 1781 (italics added); to TJ, April 16, 1781, *MP*, III, 17–19, 71–2.
4. Motions in Congress, March–May 1781, *MP*, III, 22–5, 66–7, 115, 124–5, 143–4.
5. Rodney diary, March 5, 1781, Edmund C. Burnett, ed., *Letters of the Members of the Continental Congress* (8 vols., Washington, D.C., 1921–1938), VI, 7–9; Brant, II, 104–8.
6. Brant, II, 122–4.
7. E. James Ferguson, *The Power of the Purse* (Chapel Hill, 1961), pp. 3–145, explains fully the fiscal problems summarized in these four paragraphs.
8. "JM Notes on Debates in Congress," March 7, 1783, Hunt, I, 397–400; Brant, II, 227–43; to TJ, April 22, 1783, Boyd *PJ*, VI, 263.
9. Address to the states, April 18, 1783, Hunt, I, 459–60; typescript of material to appear in Vol. VI of *MP*, under dates March and April 1783.
10. G. Morris to Matthew Ridley, August 6, 1782, Ridley papers, Massachusetts Historical Society, quoted in Clarence L. Ver Steeg, *Robert Morris, Revolutionary Financier* (Philadelphia, 1954), p. 167.
11. Samuel F. Bemis, *The Diplomacy of the American Revolution* (Bloomington, Indiana, 1957 [1935]), pp. 189–90; Edmund C. Burnett, *The Continental Congress* (New York, 1964 [1941]), pp. 517–21; Richard Morris, *The Peace Makers* (New York, 1965), pp. 173–90.
12. Brant, II, 133–45; motions in Congress, and notes, May 28–June 15, 1781, *MP*, III, 133–4, 147–55; Stinchcombe, *French Alliance*, pp. 153–70.

13. Lee to Francis Dana, July 6, 1782, Burnett, *Letters*, VI, 379; JM to Randolph, October 8, 1782, *MP*, V, 187–8.
14. Jay to Livingston, September 18 and October 13, 1782, Wharton, *Diplomatic Corres.*, V, 740, 809.
15. Debates in Congress, December 24, 1782, *MP*, V, 441–2, italics added.
16. To TJ, February 11, 1783, from TJ, February 14, 1783; Boyd *PJ*, VI, 235, 241.
17. Debates in Congress, March 12–15, 1783, Hunt, I, 403–6.
18. To Randolph, March 18, 1783, and debates in Congress, March 15 and 17, 1783, Hunt, I, 406–8.
19. Debates in Congress, March 19, 1783, Hunt, I, 410–19.
20. William E. O'Donnell, *The Chevalier de la Luzerne* (Bruges, Belgium, 1938), pp. 34–181; St. George Sioussat, "Luzerne and the Ratification of the Articles of Confederation by Maryland," *PMHB*, LX (1936), 391; Kathryn Sullivan, *Maryland and France, 1774–1789*, (Philadelphia, 1936); transcripts of La Luzerne's dispatches to Vergennes, 1780–1784, LC; and Stinchcombe, *French Alliance*, pp. 118–52; furnish information for this and the following five paragraphs.
21. Lee to Francis Dana, July 6, 1782, Burnett, *Letters*, VI, 379.
22. Letter "By a Gentleman in Office," Philadelphia, June 9, 1782, first published in *Pennsylvania Packet*, June 11, 1782; *MP*, IV, 326–30.
23. Information in this paragraph and the next three from Ver Steeg, *Robert Morris*, and Ferguson, *Power of the Purse*.
24. Thomas P. Abernethy, *Western Lands and the American Revolution* (New York, 1937), pp. 211–15, 231–7; Charles Page Smith, *James Wilson, Founding Father, 1742–1798* (Chapel Hill, 1956), pp. 160–61.
25. To Randolph, June 6, 1782, *MP*, IV, 313.
26. Arthur Lee to Thomas Lee Shippen, April 25, 1790, Shippen papers, LC, quoted in Brant, II, 199; JM and Lee, speeches in Congress, February 21, 1783, Hunt, I, 380–83.
27. Stanley Elkins and Eric McKitrick, "The Founding Fathers: Young Men of the Revolution," *Political Science Quarterly*, LXXVI (1961), 181–216.
28. George Dangerfield, *Chancellor Robert R. Livingston of New York, 1746–1813* (New York, 1960), pp. 113–180; Smith, *James Wilson*, pp. 140–48.
29. "Observations," May 1, 1782, *MP*, IV, 200–203.
30. O'Donnell, *La Luzerne*, p. 223.
31. Ferguson, *Power of the Purse*, pp. 122–4, 171–6, 334–7, describes the nationalist decline and the continuity between the "Morris" and "Hamilton" parties.
32. Letters of various members of Congress, September 4–8, 1781, Burnett, *Letters*, VI, 205–13; to Pendleton, September 3, 1781, *MP*, III, 247.
33. John Adams to Abigail Adams, June 11, 1775, L. H. Butterfield and others, eds., *Adams Family Correspondence* (2 vols., Cambridge, Massachusetts, 1963), I, 215; to Pendleton, October 30 and November 27, 1781, *MP*, III, 296–7, 317–18; Brant, II, 164–7; James T. Flexner, *George Washington and the American Revolution* (Boston, 1967), pp. 472–5.
34. Report of form of public audience for La Luzerne, May 7–9, 1782, Virginia delegates to Benjamin Harrison, May 14, 1782, JM to Randolph, May 14, 1782, *MP*, IV, 211–14, 235–43; La Luzerne to Vergennes, May 14, 1782, Martha D. Bland to Frances B. Tucker, March 20, 1781, in Brant, II, 31, 170; Benjamin Rush to Elizabeth Graeme Feruson (?), July 16, 1782, L. H. Butterfield, ed., *The Letters of Benjamin Rush*,

I (2 vols., Princeton, 1951), 279–84; Stinchcombe, *French Alliance*, pp. 188–9.

35. Eliza Trist to TJ, December 8, 1783, Boyd *PJ*, VI, 375; JM to Eliza Trist March 14, 1786, Blumhaven Library, Philadelphia.

36. Eliza Trist to TJ, April 13, 1784, Boyd *PJ*, VII, 97–8.

37. La Luzerne, "Members of Congress, 1779–1784," cited in Brant, II, 14; Brant, II, 149–54.

38. To TJ, January 15 and April 16, 1782, Boyd *PJ*, VI, 149, 176–7; to Randolph, June 11, 1782, *MP*, IV, 333; Dumas Malone, *Jefferson and His Time* (3 vols., Boston, 1948–62), I, 394–9.

39. *MP*, VI, 62–115, gives JM's list in full, with complete bibliographical information; debates in Congress, January 23, 1783, Hunt, I, 319; Boyd *PJ*, VI, 216; Brant, II, 288–90.

40. TJ to Peter Carr, December 11, 1783, Boyd *PJ*, VI, 380.

41. To Randolph, August 27 and September 30, 1782, *MP*, V, 87, 170; Brant, II, 210–11.

42. Debates in Congress, June 21, 1783, Hunt, I, 482–3; John Armstrong, Jr., to Horatio Gates, June 26, 1783, Burnett, *Letters*, VII, 199n.

43. To TJ, September 20, 1783, and to Randolph, August 30, 1783, Hunt, II, 22, 13.

44. To TJ, December 10, 1783, Boyd *PJ*, VI, 377.

Chapter 8

1. To Randolph, March 10, 1784, Hunt, II, 31.

2. To TJ, April 4, 1785, and to Randolph, July 26, 1785, Hunt, II, 141, 154.

3. Brant, III, 357–8; patents listed in Willard R. Jillson, *Old Kentucky Entries and Deeds* (Louisville, 1926), 244, 246; information on George Mason's Western land holdings supplied by Mr. R. Carter Pittman, Dalton, Georgia.

4. To Monroe, March 19, 1786, Hunt, II, 232; Brant, II, 340–41.

5. To Monroe, Apr. 9, 1786, Hunt, II, 234; To TJ, August 12, 1786, Boyd *PJ*, X, 234–6.

6. From TJ, December 16, 1786, Boyd *PJ*, X, 605; Brant, II, 341–2.

7. From TJ, Feb. 20, 1784, and to TJ, March 16, 1784, Boyd *PJ*, VI, 545, VII, 39; to Caleb Wallace, August 23, 1785, to GW, November 5, 1788, to Henry Lee November 30, 1788, Hunt, II, 166, V, 301–2, 306–7.

8. To Joseph Jones, November 28, 1780, *MP*, II, 209; to James Madison, Sr., September 8, 1783, Hunt, II, 15.

9. To Randolph, July 26, 1785, Hunt, II, 154; Rice, ed., *Travels of Chastellux*, II, 653n (comment by George Grieve); Boyd *PJ*, II, 470–73; Brant, II, 360–61.

10. Diary of Francis Taylor, 1786–1799, Virginia State Library.

11. To Randolph, March 10, 1784, and to TJ, March 16, 1784, Hunt, II, 30–31, 43.

12. To TJ, February 11 and 17, 1784, from TJ, January 1, 1784, Boyd *PJ*, VI, 537, 541, 436–7.

13. To TJ, February 11, 1784, and from TJ, February 20, 1784, Boyd *PJ*, VI, 538, 544–5.

14. To TJ, June 19, 1786, Boyd *PJ*, IX, 659–65; Brant, II, 409–10.

15. TJ to Hopkinson, February 18, 1784, and Hopkinson to TJ, February 23, 1784, Boyd *PJ*, VI, 542, 556; *Proceedings of American Philosophical Society*, VII (1859–1861), 37.

16. From TJ, Oct. 28, 1785, and to TJ, June 19, 1786, Boyd *PJ*, IX, 21, 659–60.
17. From TJ, September 6, 1789, Boyd *PJ*, XV, 392–7. To TJ, February 4, 1790 (following text as received by TJ, rather than the better known revision by JM late in life), Boyd *PJ*, XVI, 146–50.
18. To TJ, September 7, 1784, and August 12, 1786, Hunt, II, 77, 257–9.
19. To TJ, September 7 and 15, 1784, Boyd *PJ*, VII, 416–17, 421; Lafayette to the Prince de Paix, September 15, 1784, in Louis Gottschalk, *Lafayette between the American and the French Revolution* (Chicago, 1950), pp. 93–4.
20. Eugene P. Chase, ed., *Our Revolutionary Forefathers, The Letters of François de Barbé-Marbois, 1779–1785* (New York, 1929), "Journey to the Oneidas," September 23, 1784, pp. 180–97; Gottschalk, *Lafayette*, pp. 101–9; diary of Griffith Evans, September 1784, Huntington Library; Brant, II, 328–34. Gottschalk's assumption (p. 101) that JM did not go to the Oneida village is refuted by his report to TJ, October 11, 1784, stating he did go.
21. To TJ, October 11 and 17, 1784, Boyd *PJ*, VII, 439–41, 444–52.
22. Randolph to TJ and Short to TJ, May 15, 1784, Boyd *PJ*, VII, 260, 257; William Alexander to Franklin, May 30, 1784, American Philosophical Society Library.
23. Johann D. Schoepf, *Travels in the Confederation* (2 vols., trans., Philadelphia, 1911), II, 55–64; Brant, II, 314–15.
24. Short to TJ, May 15, 1784, and JM to TJ, May 15, 1784, Boyd *PJ*, VII, 257–8.
25. Speech, June 1784, Hunt, II, 54–5.
26. To TJ, July 3, 1784, and January 9, 1785, from TJ, August 12, 1784, Boyd *PJ*, VII, 360, 558, 588–93; to James Madison, Sr., June 15, 1784, Cong. ed., I, 81; to Pendleton, April 22, 1787, Hunt, II, 357; conversation with TJ recorded by Daniel Webster, December 2, 1824, in Alfred Fried, ed., *The Essential Jefferson* (New York, 1963), 513.
27. To TJ, July 3, 1784; Boyd *PJ*, VII, 360.
28. To GW, December 9, 1785, Hunt, II, 199. Archibald Stuart to John Breckinridge, December 7, 1785, Breckinridge family papers, LC.
29. Brant, II, 356–7; to TJ, August 20, 1785, Boyd *PJ*, VIII, 413–17.
30. To TJ, January 22 and December 4, 1786, February 11 and December 9, 1787, Hunt, II, 215–16, 291–2, 308, V, 67; Malone, *Jefferson Autobiography*, p. 58; Brant, II, 357–8.
31. To TJ, January 9, 1785, Boyd *PJ*, VII, 588–99.
32. Speech, November 1784, Hunt, II, 88–9; Brant, II, 347–8.
33. To Monroe, November 27, 1784, and June 21, 1785, Hunt, II, 94, 146.
34. Hunt, II, 183–91.
35. To TJ, August 20, 1785, Boyd *PJ*, VIII, 415–16.
36. To TJ, January 22, 1786, Boyd *PJ*, IX, 194–6.
37. Elizabeth Fleet, ed., "Madison's 'Detached Memoranda,'" *WMQ*, III (1946), 554–5 (undated, but probably written in early seventeen nineties); Stuart G. Brown, "Plural Values and the Neutral State: the American Doctrine of the Free Conscience," *The Syracuse Law Review*, Fall 1953, pp. 35–58; JM veto message, February 29, 1811, Hunt, VIII, 132–3.
38. Speech, June 12, 1788, Hunt, V, 176; Rives, *Life of Madison*, II, 220–21.
39. To F. L. Schaeffer, December 3, 1821, Cong. ed., III, 242; to Robert Walsh, March 2, 1819, Hunt, VII, 430–32.
40. To TJ, July 3 and August 20, 1784, and to Monroe, August 7, 1785, Hunt II, 57, 65–6, 156.
41. Brant, II, 311, 375–6.

42. *Journal of the House of Delegates*, General Assembly of Virginia, January 21, 1786; Brant, II, 375–81.
43. GW to Patrick Henry, November 30, 1785, *Writings of Washington*, XXVIII, 333–5; to TJ, January 9, 1785, Boyd *PJ*, VII, 588–99.
44. Brant, II, 363–9.
45. To James Madison, Sr., June 15, 1784, Cong. ed., I, 81; Brant, II, 317, 361–2.
46. To TJ, January 9, 1785, Boyd *PJ*, 588–98.
47. Brant, II, 358–9.
48. Notes for speech, November 1, 1786, Hunt, II, 279–81.
49. Brant, II, 362; to TJ, December 4, 1786, Hunt, II, 293.

Chapter 9

1. Rives, *Life of Madison*, I, 303n; Brant, II, 316; to TJ, October 3, 1785, Boyd *PJ*, VIII, 579–82; to Monroe, August 7, 1785, Hunt, II, 157.
2. To TJ, August 12, 1786, Boyd *PJ*, X, 229–36.
3. Merrill Jensen, *The New Nation: A History of the United States during the Confederation, 1781–1789* (New York, 1965 [1950]), details the virtues of state and Confederation governments but misses the national vision of men like Madison in emphasizing their economic motives for seeking a stronger union.
4. To TJ, August 20, 1784, from copy received by TJ, partly in code, Boyd *PJ*, VII, 401–8.
5. To Lafayette, March 20, 1785, Hunt, II, 121–2.
6. Robert D. Meade, *Patrick Henry*, II, 325–7.
7. To Monroe, June 21, 1786, Hunt, II, 253–5.
8. To TJ, August 12, 1786, Boyd *PJ*, X, 229–36.
9. To Monroe, October 30, 1786, to James Madison, Sr., November 1, 1786, and to GW, December 7, 1786, Hunt, II, 275, 278, 296–7.
10. Freeman, *Washington*, VI, 123; Fitzpatrick, ed., *Diaries of Washington* III, 163; to Eliza Trist, February 10, 1787, and to Monroe, February 11, 1787, Brant, II, 400.
11. To TJ, February 15, 1787, Boyd *PJ*, XI, 152–5.
12. To TJ, March 19, 1787, Boyd *PJ*, XI, 219–25.
13. Brant, II, 403–7.
14. To TJ, March 19 and April 23, 1787, Boyd *PJ*, XI, 219–25, 307–10.
15. To Monroe, October 5, 1786, Hunt, II, 272–3.
16. Martin Diamond, "Democracy and *The Federalist*: A Reconsideration of the Framers' Intent," *American Political Science Review*, LIII (1959), 52–68.
17. From TJ, June 17, 1783, Boyd *PJ*, VI, 277; speech, June 1784, Hunt, II, 54–55.
18. To Caleb Wallace, August 23, 1785, Hunt, II, 166–77, is the source for this and the following four paragraphs.
19. To TJ, March 18, 1786, Boyd *PJ*, IX, 332–6.
20. JM, notes on "Of Ancient and Modern Confederacies," LC, printed in Hunt, II, 306–90; Duclos' *Histoire de Louis XI*, quoted in Carl L. Becker, *The Heavenly City of the Eighteenth-Century Philosophers* (New Haven, 1932), p. 95.
21. Federalist Number 20, Jacob E. Cooke, ed., *The Federalist* (Cleveland, 1961), pp. 128–9; Brant, II, 410–11.
22. To Ambrose Madison, August 7, 1786, quoted in Brant, II, 383; Broadus

          Mitchell, *Alexander Hamilton* (2 vols., New York, 1957–1962), I, 360.
23. Brant, II, 383–7; Mitchell, *Hamilton*, I, 360–69; Higginson to John Adams,
     July 1786, *Report of the American Hist. Ass'n.*, 1896, I, 734–5.
24. From GW, November 5, 1786, *Writings of Washington*, XXIX, 50–52;
     to James Madison, Sr., November 1, 1786, to Edmund Pendleton, Jan-
     uary 9, 1787, to TJ, March 19, 1787, to GW, April 14, 1787, and to
     Pendleton, April 22, 1787, Hunt, II, 277–8, 307, 331–2, 351, 354.
25. "Vices of the Political System of the United States," Hunt, II, 361–9.
     Hume quote from *Political Discourses*, first published in 1752; Douglass
     Adair, " 'That Politics May Be Reduced to a Science': David Hume,
     James Madison, and the Tenth *Federalist*," *The Huntington Library
     Quarterly*, XX (1957), 348–50.
26. To Randolph, April 8, 1787, and to GW, April 16, 1787, Hunt, II, 336–
     40, 344, 349.
27. Malone, *Jefferson Autobiography*, p. 55.

                                  Chapter 10

 1. From GW, November 5, 1786, *Writings of Washington*, XXIX, 50–52;
     to James Madison, Sr., April 1, 1787, and to TJ, June 6, 1787, Cong.
     ed., I, 286–7, 332; Franklin to TJ, April 19, 1787, Boyd *PJ*, XI, 301–2.
 2. *Pennsylvania Packet*, May 18, 1787; Carl Van Doren, *Benjamin Franklin*
     (New York, 1938), p. 743; Freeman, *Washington*, VI, 88.
 3. Smith, *James Wilson*, p. 202; William Pierce, "Character Sketches of Dele-
     gates to the Federal Convention," in Max Farrand, ed., *The Records of
     the Federal Convention of 1787* (4 vols., New Haven, 1937), III, 91–2.
 4. Carl Van Doren, *The Great Rehearsal* (New York, 1948), pp. 2–3, 12–13.
 5. Freeman, *Washington*, VI, 86–9.
 6. To TJ, May 15, 1787, and Pierce, "Sketches," in Farrand, *Records*, III,
     20, 95.
 7. Mason to his son, May 20, 1787, and George Read to Dickinson, May 21
     and 25, 1787, in Farrand, *Records*, III, 24–25, IV, 61–2.
 8. Mason to his son, May 20 and 27, 1787, in Farrand, *Records*, III, 23, 28;
     Freeman, *Washington*, VI, 89–90; Brant, III, 18.
 9. JM, "Preface to Notes on Debates," in Farrand, *Records*, III, 551.
10. Mason to his son, May 20 and June 1, 1787, and Benjamin Rush to Richard
     Price, June 2, 1787, in Farrand, *Records*, III, 23–4, 32–3.
11. JM, "Preface," in Farrand, *Records*, III, 550, 94.
12. James McHenry notes, May 29, and JM notes, May 30, in Farrand,
     Records, I, 15, 27, 35. Year designations will be omitted in citations of
     convention proceedings, and unless otherwise indicated, reference is to
     JM's notes for speeches, motions, and votes. JM recorded the proceed-
     ings in the third person, past tense.
13. Pierce, "Sketches," and Read and Gerry speeches, May 31, *Records*, III,
     93, I, 37, 48.
14. Pierce, "Sketches," and Mason and Wilson speeches, May 31, *Records*,
     III, 94, I, 48–50.
15. Debates, May 31, *Records*, I, 51–5.
16. Debates, June 1, "Johnson's Diary," June 1 and 2, *Records*, I, 64–9, III,
     552.
17. Debates, June 2, *Records*, I, 81–5.
18. Smith, *Wilson*, p. 224.
19. Debates, June 4, *Records*, I, 96–7.

20. Debates, June 4 and 5, *Records*, I, 97–104, 119–20.
21. Debates, June 6, *Records*, I, 132–4.
22. JM speech, June 6, *Records*, I, 134–6.
23. Pierce, "Sketches," *Records*, III, 94.
24. Debates, June 7 and 8; *Records*, I, 150–56, 168.
25. Pierce, "Sketches," *Records*, III, 90; debates, June 9, *Records*, I, 177–80.
26. To William Short, June 6, 1787, North Carolina delegates to Governor Caswell, June 14, 1787, *Records*, III, 37, 46.
27. Debates, June 11, *Records*, I, 196–201.
28. Debates, June 11 and 12, *Records*, I, 201–2, 215, 218–19.
29. Debates, June 13, *Records*, I, 232–7.
30. Debates, June 15, *Records*, I, 240–43.
31. Debates, June 16, *Records*, I, 249–56.
32. AH speech, June 18, *Records*, I, 282–93; Paul Eidelberg, *The Philosophy of the American Constitution* (New York, 1968), pp. 106–36.
33. JM speech, June 19, Pierce, "Sketches," *Records*, I, 314–22, III, 94.
34. Remark to Edward Coles, cited in Hugh B. Grigsby, *The History of the Virginia Federal Convention of 1788* (2 vols., Richmond, 1890–1891), I, 95n; to TJ, July 18, 1787, *Records*, III, 60.
35. Debates, June 20, 21, 22, and 23, *Records*, I, 335–6, 357–8, 373, 385–9.
36. Debates, June 25 and 26, Robert Yates's notes, June 25, Convention Journal, June 26, *Records*, I, 397–409, 411–12, 420–23.
37. Martin speech, June 27 and 28, JM and Yates's notes, *Records*, I, 437–9, 445; "The Landowner" (Oliver Ellsworth), first published in the *Maryland Journal*, February 29, 1788, *Records*, III, 271–2.
38. JM speech, June 28, *Records*, I, 446–9.
39. Debates, June 28, *Records*, I, 450–52.
40. Debates, June 29 and 30, *Records*, I, 461–70, 480–87.
41. Pierce, "Sketches," and Yates's notes, debates, June 30, *Records*, III, 92, I, 490–93, 500–502.
42. Debates, July 2, *Records*, I, 510–16.
43. Van Doren, *Great Rehearsal*, pp. 107–8; GW Diary, July 2, GW to David Stuart, July 1, 1787, *Records*, III, 51–2.
44. Debates, July 5, *Records*, I, 527–9.
45. GW to AH, July 10, 1787, *Records*, III, 56–7.
46. Debates, July 14, *Records*, II, 5, 8–10.
47. Debates, July 16, *Records*, II, 15, 17–19; Forrest McDonald, *E Pluribus Unum: The Formation of the American Republic, 1776–1790* (Boston, 1965), pp. 176–8.
48. Notes of meeting, July 17, and debates, July 16, *Records*, II, 19–20; GW Diary, July 17, *Records*, III, 52.
49. Brant, III, 62–5; see also McDonald, *E Pluribus*, p. 179.
50. JM to Van Buren, May 13, 1828; George Bancroft, *History of the Formation of the Constitution of the United States of America* (2 vols., New York, 1882), II, 88, cited in Brant, III, 103–4.
51. W. P. and J. P. Cutler, eds., *Life, Journals, and Correspondence of Rev. Manasseh Cutler* (2 vols., Cincinnati, 1888), I, 254–70; *Proceedings of the American Philosophical Society*, I (1886), p. 261.
52. Debates, July 17, *Records*, II, 25–36; Brant, III, 105–6.
53. Debates, July 18, 19, 20, and 21, *Records*, II, 40–49, 51–9, 74.
54. Debates, July 23, *Records*, II, 94–5.
55. Debates, July 23, *Records*, II, 88–93.
56. JM speech, July 25, *Records*, II, 106–8.

57. *Pennsylvania Herald*, August 18, 1787; Van Doren, *Great Rehearsal*, pp. 138, 145; Freeman, *Washington*, VI, 102–3.
58. W. R. Davie to James Iredell, August 6, 1787, debates, August 7, *Records*, III, 67–8, II, 201–4; JM, "Notes on Suffrage," 1821, *Records*, III, 450–55.
59. Debates, August 9, *Records*, II, 236–7.
60. Debates, August 16, 17, and 18, *Records*, II, 306–7, 318–19, 324–8.
61. Debates, August 24, *Records*, II, 400–406.
62. Debates, August 31 and September 4, *Records*, II, 481, 496.
63. Debates, September 4–8; *Records*, II, 497–554; to TJ, October 24, 1787, Hunt, V, 20.
64. To James Madison, Sr., August 12, 1787; *Pennsylvania Herald*, August 15, 1787; GW to Henry Knox, August 19, 1787, Brearley to Paterson, August 21, 1787, Paterson to Oliver Ellsworth, August 23, 1787, *Records*, III, 69–73; IV, 73; McDonald, *E Pluribus*, pp. 174–9.
65. Brant, III, 147; debates, August 31, *Records*, II, 479.
66. Debates, August 22, *Records*, II, 370; McDonald, *E Pluribus*, pp. 179–84.
67. Debates, August 25 and 29, *Records*, II, 417, 451–2.
68. Debates, August 30 and 31, *Records*, II, 461–9, 475–81.
69. JM to Jared Sparks, April 8, 1831, and debates, September 8, 10 and 11, *Records*, III, 499, II, 564, 585.
70. Debates, September 12, *Records*, II, 585–7.
71. Debates, September 13 and 14, *Records*, II, 608, 612–13, 615–16.
72. Debates, September 15, *Records*, II, 631–3.
73. Van Doren, *Great Rehearsal*, p. 167.
74. Debates, September 17; GW Diary, September 17, *Records*, II, 641–9; III, 81.
75. Forrest McDonald, *We the People* (Chicago, 1958), esp. pp. 86–110.
76. Letter (signed by GW) to Congress, September 17, 1787, *Records*, II, 666–7.

Chapter 11

1. From John Witherspoon, August 11, 1788, quoted in Rives, *Life of Madison*, II, 517–18.
2. To James Madison, Sr., and to GW, September 30, 1787, Hunt, V, 2–8.
3. Rufus W. Griswold, *The Republican Court, or American Society in the Days of Washington* (New York, 1855), pp. 166–7.
4. McDonald, *E Pluribus*, pp. 207–8.
5. To James Madison, Sr., September 30, to GW, September 30 and October 18, and to Randolph, October 21, 1787, to TJ, October 24, 1787, from Jones, October 29, 1787, Hunt, V, 3–17, 33–7, 47.
6. To GW, October 18, to TJ, October 24, and December 9 and 20, 1787, to TJ, February 19, and to Randolph, January 19, 1788; Hunt, V, 14–15, 36, 40, 67, 75, 80–81, 103–4.
7. To TJ, December 9, 1787, Boyd *PJ*, XII, 408–12.
8. To Randolph, January 10, 1788, to Pendleton, February 21, 1788, Hunt, V, 80, 108–9.
9. Forrest McDonald, *We the People* (Chicago, 1958), seems more persuasive on this point than Jackson T. Main, *The Antifederalists* (Chapel Hill, 1961).
10. To Archibald Stuart, October 30, 1787, to TJ, December 9, 1787, Hunt, V, 48–9, 66–7.
11. To Randolph, January 10, 1788, Hunt, V, 81–2.
12. From Coxe, October 21, 1787, MPLC; to Coxe October 1 and 26, 1787,

notes in calendar of Coxe papers, Wyoming Historical and Geological Society, Wilkes-Barre, Box 4, Nos. 564 and 565.

13. Jacob E. Cooke, ed., *The Federalist* (Cleveland, 1961), Introduction and notes; to TJ, August 10, 1788, Boyd, *PJ*, XIII, 497–9.

14. Alpheus T. Mason, "Federalist, a Split Personality," *American Historical Review*, LVII (1952), 625–43, and Douglass Adair, "The Tenth Federalist Revisited," *WMQ*, VIII, (1951), 48–67, emphasize differences between AH and JM, while Martin Diamond, "The Federalist's View of Federalism," in *Essays in Federalism* (Claremont, California, 1961), pp. 21–64, stresses Publius' single-mindedness.

15. From TJ, February 1, 1825, MPLC.

16. To GW, March 3, 1788, and from Cyrus Griffin, March 24, 1788, Hunt, V, 110–11.

17. From Archibald Stuart, November 2, 1787, to Ambrose Madison, November 8, 1787, diary of Francis Taylor, February 26, 1788, ms. in Virginia State Library; from Lawrence Taliaferro, December 16, 1787, from Henry Lee, January 1788, from James Madison, Sr., January 30, 1788, Hunt, V, 50–52, 71, 88–9; to GW, February 20, 1787, Hunt, V, 105–6.

18. *Diaries of Washington*, III, 313; Douglas Freeman, *George Washington* (7 vols., New York, 1948–1957), VI, 123–4; Brant, III, 186–8; GW to Langdon, April 2, 1788, *Writings of Washington*, XXIX, 452–3.

19. L. H. Butterfield, "Elder John Leland, Jeffersonian Itinerant: Leland and Madison: Ratification of the Constitution and the Bill of Rights," *Proceedings of the American Antiquarian Society*, LXII (1952), 155–242; John Leland to Thomas Barbour, Objections to the Federal Constitution, undated, reproduced in facsimile in (Julian P. Boyd, ed.) *"Let every Sluice of Knowledge be Open'd and set a Flowing,"* a Tribute to Philip M. Hamer (New York, 1960), Part V.

20. Taylor diary, March 25, 1788, Virginia State Library; from Edward Carrington, April 8, 1788, and from Cyrus Griffin, April 7, 1788, MPLC, quoted in Brant, III, 188.

21. Taylor diary, April 23, May 10 and May 14, 1788, Virginia State Library, to TJ, April 22, 1788, Boyd *PJ*, XIII, 98–9; Brant, III, 188–9.

22. To Nicholas, May 17, 1788, MPLC; to Pendleton, February 21, 1788, Hunt, V, 100–110.

23. From AH, April 3, 1788, from Nicholas, April 5, 1788, to GW and to Randolph, April 10, 1788, to TJ, April 22, 1788, Hunt, V, 114–21; Brant, III, 189–94.

24. William A. Christian, *Richmond, Her Past and Present* (Richmond, 1912), p. 21; Martin S. Schockley, "The Richmond Theater, 1780–1790," *VMHB*, LX (1952), 421–36.

25. To GW, June 4, 1788, Hunt, V, 123–4; Pendleton speech, June 4, 1788, David J. Mays, ed., *The Letters and Papers of Edmund Pendleton* (2 vols., Charlottesville, Virginia, 1967), II, 514–15; Hugh B. Grigsby, *The History of the Virginia Federal Convention of 1788* (2 vols., Richmond, 1890–1891), I, 102–4; William Grayson to Nathan Dane, June 4, 1788, Dane papers, LC, quoted in Brant, III, 197.

26. Grigsby, *1788*, I, 79–82; Brant, III, 197–8; Meade, *Patrick Henry*, II, 354–60.

27. Grigsby, *1788*, I, 96.

28. JM speech, June 6, Hunt, V, 123–37; to TJ, April 22, 1788, Boyd *PJ*, XIII, 98–9; Bushrod Washington to GW, June 6, 1788, Jared Sparks, ed., *The Writings of George Washington* (12 vols., Boston, 1835), IX, 378n.

29. JM speech, June 7, to GW, June 13, 1788, Hunt, V, 137–47, 179; to Rufus

King, June 9, 1788, in Charles R. King, ed., *The Life and Correspondence of Rufus King* (6 vols., Boston, 1894–1900), I, 331.

30. JM speech, June 11, Hunt, V, 148–64; Grigsby, *1788*, I, 79n; to Tench Coxe, June 11, 1788, MPLC, quoted in Brant, III, 205.

31. JM speech, June 12, Hunt, V, 174–9.

32. JM speech, June 13, Hunt, V, 179–84; Pendleton to R. H. Lee, June 14, 1788, *Letters of Pendleton*, II, 535.

33. To GW, June 13, 1788, Hunt, V, 179n; to Rufus King, June 13, 1788, King, ed., *Life and Correspondence*, I, 332; Meade, *Patrick Henry*, II, 346–7.

34. JM speeches, June 16, to GW, June 18, 1788, Hunt, V, 206–8, 211–12; to King, June 15, 1788, King, ed., *Life and Correspondence*, I, 334.

35. JM speech, June 20, Hunt, V, 223.

36. To GW, June 23, 1788, Hunt, V, 225–6n; to King, June 22, 1788, King, ed., *Life and Correspondence*, I, 337; Meade, *Patrick Henry*, II, 370–1.

37. Monroe to TJ, July 12, 1788, Boyd *PJ*, XIII, 352; JM speech, June 24, Hunt, V, 225–34.

38. Letter from Archibald Stuart to William Wirt, quoted in Grigsby, *1788*, I, 316–17.

39. Grigsby, *1788*, I, 328–32, 344–7; II, 363–6.

40. To GW, June 23, 25, and 27, 1788, Hunt, V, 225–7, 234; Grigsby, *1788*, I, 342–3.

41. Robert Morris to Horatio Gates, June 12, 1788, and to Alexander Montgomery, June 18, 1788, cited in Main, *Antifederalists*, p. 226n.

42. From James Madison, Sr., January 30, 1788, Hunt, V, 105n; to TJ, April 22, 1788, Boyd *PJ*, XIII, 98–9.

43. Jackson T. Main, "Sections and Politics in Virginia, 1781–1787," *WMQ*, XII (1955), 96–112; Main, *Antifederalists*, pp. 223–33; McDonald, *We the People*, pp. 255–83.

44. Monroe to TJ, July 12, 1788, Boyd *PJ*, XIII, 351–3.

45. To TJ, July 24, 1788, Boyd *PJ*, XIII, 412–13; to Randolph, July 17, 1788, Hunt, V, 237.

46. *Diaries of Washington*, July 4–7, 1788, III, 384.

Chapter 12

1. To GW, July 21 and August 15, 1788, to Pendleton, August 22, 1788, Hunt, V, 237–8, 249, 252; Brant, III, 230.

2. To GW, August 24, 1788, Hunt, V, 256–8.

3. To TJ, August 23, 1788, Boyd *PJ*, XIII, 540–41; resolves of Congress, September 16, 1788, sent to GW, September 26, 1788, Hunt, V, 263.

4. To GW, November 5, 1788, to Philip Mazzei, December 10, 1788, Hunt, V, 301, 314–16.

5. To TJ, December 8, 1788, Boyd *PJ*, XIV, 340–41; from Griffin, March 17 and 24, April 28, May 12 and 26, 1788, MPLC, quoted in Brant, III, 233–4; to James Madison, Sr., August 18, 1788, Hunt, V, 251; from TJ, October 8, 1787, Boyd *PJ*, XII, 218–19.

6. To TJ, December 8, 1788, Boyd *PJ*, XIV, 341; Malone, *Jefferson and His Time*, II, 197–8.

7. J. P. Brissot de Warville, *New Travels in the United States of America, 1788*, trans. by M. S. Vamos and Durand Echeverria, and ed. by Echeverria (Cambridge, Massachuetts, 1964), pp. 146–8.

8. To Moustier, October 30, 1788, Hunt, V, 281–4; Merrill D. Peterson,

"Thomas Jefferson and Commercial Policy, 1783–1793," *WMQ*, XXII (1965), 584–610; John Adams' diary, June 21, 1779, L. H. Butterfield, ed., *Diary of John Adams* (4 vols., Cambridge, Massachusetts, 1961), II, 388.

9. To Randolph, October 17, 1788, Hunt, V, 276; Max Farrand, ed., *The Records of the Federal Convention of 1787* (4 vols., New Haven, 1937), III, 237.

10. To TJ, October 17, 1788, Boyd *PJ*, XIV, 18–20.

11. "Observations" sent to John Brown, October 1788, Hunt, V, 284–94.

12. To TJ, October 17, 1788, to GW, November 5, 1788, and to TJ, December 8, 1788, Hunt, V, 270–71, 302–3, 309, 311; from Henry Lee, November 19, 1788, MPLC, quoted in Brant, III, 237.

13. To Randolph, October 17 and November 23, 1788, to Lee, November 30, 1788, to TJ, December 8, 1788, Hunt, V, 303–14.

14. To James Madison, Sr., December 18, 1788, Hunt, V, 317; Fitzpatrick, *Diaries of Washington*, III, 456–7; GW to Henry Lee, December 23, 1788, original owned by Dr. Joseph E. Fields, Joliet, Illinois.

15. To Edmund Randolph, March 1, 1789, to GW, January 14, 1789, to George Eve, January 2, 1789, Hunt, V, 326, 318–21; Benjamin Johnson to JM, January 19, 1789, MPLC, quoted in Brant, III, 240.

16. To GW, January 14, 1789, to Randolph, March 1, 1789, Hunt, V, 319, 326.

17. Diary of Francis Taylor, January–February 1789, Virginia State Library; JM told the story of the debate at the German church—quoted in Henry S. Randall, *The Life of Thomas Jefferson* (3 vols., New York, 1858), III, 255n—to N. P. Trist, December 3, 1827; to TJ, March 29, 1789, Boyd *PJ*, XV, 6.

18. Taylor diary, February 1789, Virginia State Library; from GW, February 16, 1789, *Writings of Washington*, XXX, 203–4.

19. Nathaniel E. Stein and Ralph Ketcham, "Two New Letters on Washington's Inaugural," *Manuscripts*, XI (1959), 54–60.

20. To James Madison, Sr., February 24, 1789, to GW, March 8 and 19, 1789, to TJ, March 29, 1789, Hunt, V, 324–35; Griswold, *The Republican Court*, p. 153.

21. To Randolph, March 1, 1789, to GW, March 8 and 19, 1789, to TJ, March 29, 1789, Hunt, V, 326, 328–9, 335–6.

22. *Annals of Congress*, April 8 and 9, 1789; Brant, III, 246–50.

23. JM speeches, April 21, 1789, Hunt, V, 347–50; John C. Miller, *The Federalist Era, 1789–1801* (New York, 1960), pp. 14–19.

24. Ames to G. R. Minot, May 3, 1789, in Seth Ames, ed., *The Works of Fisher Ames* (2 vols., Boston, 1854), I, 35; to TJ, May 9, 1789, Boyd *PJ*, XV, 114–15.

25. Newspaper accounts, April 23 to May 4, 1789, in William S. Baker, *Washington After the Revolution, 1784–1799* (Philadelphia, 1897), pp. 117–21; Ames to Minot, May 3, 1789, in Ames, *Works*, I, 34–5; Freeman, *Washington*, VI, 178–98.

26. From GW, May 5, 1789, original owned by Dr. Joseph E. Fields, Joliet, Illinois.

27. E. S. Maclay, ed., *Journal of William Maclay* (New York, 1890), May 8, 1789, p. 23; John Adams to William Tudor, May 3 and 9, 1789, quoted in Charles Page Smith, *John Adams* (2 vols., Garden City, New York, 1962), II, 753–5.

28. JM speech, May 11, 1789, Hunt, V, 355–7.

29. To TJ, May 9, 1789, Boyd *PJ*, XV, 115; GW to David Stuart, July 26, 1789, *Writings of Washington*, XXX, 362–3.

30. Adams to Rush, July 5, 1789 (Boston Public Library), quoted in Smith, *Adams*, II, 755.
31. GW to Bushrod Washington, July 27, 1789, *Writings of Washington*, XXX, 366. *Maclay Journal*, July 1 and August 16, 1789, pp. 97, 122; to TJ, May 27, 1789, Boyd *PJ*, XV, 153; Brant, III, 281–9; Freeman, *Washington*, VI, 233–8.
32. *Diaries of Washington* (October 7–14, 1789), IV, 15–20; to TJ, October 8, 1789, Boyd *PJ*, XV, 509–10; Freeman, *Washington*, VI, 238–9; Boyd *PJ*, XVII, 46–61, quoting conversations of Beckwith with AH and other Federalists.
33. JM speech, June 17, 1789, to Pendleton, June 21, 1789, Hunt, V, 395–402, 405–406n; Miller, *Federalist Era*, p. 30.
34. JM speech, June 8, 1789, Hunt, V, 370–90; Miller, *Federalist Era*, pp. 20–25; Robert A. Rutland, *The Birth of the Bill of Rights* (Chapel Hill, 1955), pp. 131–71; Brant, III, 264–75.
35. To TJ, May 27, 1789, Boyd *PJ*, XV, 154; Brant, III, 276–81.
36. Adams to Pickering, August 6, 1822, in C. F. Adams, ed., *The Works of John Adams* (10 vols., Boston, 1856), II, 514; TJ to Henry Lee, May 18, 1825, *Writings of TJ*, X, 343.
37. JM, Preface for "Debates in the Convention of 1787," in Farrand, *Records*, III, 551; JM speech, Virginia Convention of 1829, Hunt, IX, 361.
38. JM speech, June 20, 1788, Hunt, V, 223; Aristotle, *Politics*, Book IV, Chap. 9 (Barker trans., 1953, cited in Paul Eidelberg, *Philosophy of the American Constitution* (New York, 1968), p. 130).
39. To TJ, October 24, 1787, Boyd *PJ*, XII, 276–7.
40. JM essay on "Majority Governments," 1833, Hunt, IX, 523.
41. Reinhold Niebuhr, *The Children of Light and the Children of Darkness* (New York, 1944), viii.
42. *Politics*, Book III, Chap. 9, Book VII, Chaps. 1 and 2; Jowett trans., Modern Library, 1943.
43. *Messages*, I, 310.
44. To TJ, Oct. 24, 1787; Boyd *PJ*, XII, 275.

Chapter 13

1. John C. Miller, *The Federalist Era, 1789–1801* (New York, 1964), p. 39; from AH, October 12, 1789, to AH, November 19, 1789, Syrett *PH*, V, 439, 525–32.
2. AH, "Conversation with George Beckwith," October 1789, Syrett *PH*, V, 482–8.
3. TJ to GW, December 15, 1789, Boyd *PJ*, XVI, 34–5; Dumas Malone, *Jefferson and His Time* (3 vols., New York, 1948–62), II, 248.
4. To GW, January 4, 1790, MPLC; Brant, III, 288; to TJ, January 24, 1790, Boyd *PJ*, XVI, 125–6; Malone, *Jefferson*, II, 248–9.
5. To TJ, January 24, 1790, to James Madison, Sr., February 27, 1790, Hunt, V, 460n; from George Nicholas, November 2, 1789, MPLC; John C. Fitzpatrick, ed., *Diaries of George Washington* (4 vols., Boston, 1925), IV, 74, 82.
6. Benjamin Goodhue to Michael Hodge, February 15, 1790, Stone papers, Essex Institute, Salem, Massachusetts; JM speeches, February 11 and 18, 1790, to James Madison, Sr., February 27, 1790, Hunt, V, 438–58, 460n; Miller, *Federalist Era*, pp. 38–41.
7. JM speech, February 24, 1790, to Pendleton, March 11, 1790, Hunt, V,

458–81, VI, 5–7; Ames to John Lowell, May 2, 1790, Boston Public Library.

8. To Pendleton, June 22, to James Madison, Sr., May 5, and to Monroe, June 1, 1790, Hunt, VI, 17n, 13–15n; Henry Wyncoop to Reading Beatty, April 29, 1790, *PMHB*, XXXVIII, 195.

9. TJ memorandum, probably written in 1792, and TJ to Monroe, June 20, 1790, Boyd *PJ*, XVII, 205–8, XVI, 527; Malone, *Jefferson*, II, 297–306; Brant, III, 312–18; Miller, *Federalist Era*, pp. 45–50.

10. To TJ, January 24, 1790, Boyd *PJ*, XVI, 125–6; E. S. Maclay, ed., *Journal of William Maclay* (New York, 1890), p. 178 (January 15, 1790); from Rush, February 27 and March 10, 1790, MPLC; to Rush, March 7, 1790, original owned by Mr. J. William Middendorf of New York City.

11. Cutler to O. Everett, February 28, 1790, W. P. and J. P. Cutler, eds., *Life, Journals, and Correspondence of Reverend Manasseh Cutler* (2 vols., Cincinnati, 1888), I, 460, 462; Sedgwick to his wife, March 4, 1790, Sedgwick papers, Massachusetts Historical Society; Ames to G. R. Minot, March 23, 1790; Seth Ames, ed., *The Works of Fisher Ames* (2 vols., Boston, 1854), I, 76; Adams to John Trumbull, April 1790, A. W. S. Rosenbach catalogue, *For Librarians, Collectors, and Scholars*, Philadelphia, 1943, p. 5, item 3.

12. Craigie to Daniel Parker, May 1788, Joseph S. Davis, *Essays in the Early History of American Corporations* (Cambridge, Massachuetts, 1917), I, 188.

13. Whitney K. Bates, "Northern Speculators and Southern State Debts: 1790," *WMQ*, XIX (1962), 30–48.

14. E. James Ferguson, "Madison's Motives for Discrimination, 1790: Ethics or Political Maneuver?" paper at American Historical Association meeting, Chicago, 1958, emphasized JM's sectional and tactical motivation. Ralph Ketcham, *The Jeffersonian and Hamiltonian Traditions: "Visions" of National Character and Purpose* (Tiffin, Ohio, 1969), outlines the broader difference.

15. F. B. Sawvel, ed., *The Complete Anas of Thomas Jefferson* (New York, 1903), pp. 30–31.

16. *Diaries of Washington*, IV, 122 (April 27, 1790); Thomas Lee Shippen to William Shippen, August 12, 1790, quoted in Brant, III, 319; *Annals of Congress*, April 22, 1790.

17. Brant, III, 308–9; to John Parrish, June 6, 1790, Parrish-Cox-Wharton papers, HSP.

18. To Pendleton, March 4 and April 4, 1790, Hunt, VI, 7n, 9n.

19. To James Madison, Sr., August 14, 1790, and to A. Rose and others, August 13, 1790, Hunt, VI, 20–21n.

20. TJ, opinion to GW, "Concurred in by JM," July 12, 1790, Boyd *PJ*, XVII, 68–88; Malone, *Jefferson*, II, 319.

21. Thomas Lee Shippen to William Shippen, September 15, 1790, Boyd *PJ*, XVII, 464–5; Brant, III, 320–21; Malone, *Jefferson*, II, 319.

22. TJ report, September 14, 1790, TJ and JM to GW, September 17, 1790, Boyd *PJ*, XVII, 461–7; from TJ, September 20, and 23, 1790, and January 10 and 12, 1791, accounts, January 11 and 12, 1791, Brant, III, 321–2; Malone, *Jefferson*, II, 324.

23. Brant, III, 325–6; Charles Page Smith, *John Adams* (2 vols., Garden City, New York, 1962), II, 811.

24. JM speeches, February 2 and 8, 1791, to Pendleton, February 13, 1791, Hunt, VI, 19–44.

25. Ames to Thomas Dwight, February 7, 1791, *Works*, I, 94; Malone, *Jefferson*, II, 348.
26. "Memo for GW," February 21, 1791, Hunt, VI, 42–3n.
27. To TJ, August 8, 1791, Hunt, VI, 59n.
28. Bourne to Zephaniah Andrews, February 3, 1791, Peck papers, Rhode Island Historical Society; Alfred E. Young, *The Democratic-Republicans in New York: The Origins* (Chapel Hill, 1967), pp. 211–30.
29. To Ambrose Madison, April 11, and to TJ, May 1 and 12, 1791, Hunt, VI, 45–51n; Brant, III, 334–7.
30. JM diary, May–June 1791, excerpts in Henkels catalogue, No. 698, Philadelphia, J. H. Dubbs sale, March 21 and 22, 1913; TJ to Martha Randolph, May 31, 1791, to GW, and to T. M. Randolph, June 5, 1791, *Writings of TJ*, V, 337–42; recollections of Moses Robinson, *Vermont Historical Gazetteer*, I, 168–9; TJ to Ellen Coolidge, August 27, 1825, *Massachusetts Historical Society Proceedings*, I (1900), 353; TJ accounts, May 17–June 20, 1791, in E. M. Betts, ed., *Thomas Jefferson's Garden Book, 1766–1824* (Philadelphia, 1944), pp. 157–9, 165–70n; Philip M. Marsh, "The Jefferson-Madison Vacation," *PMHB*, LXXI (1948), 70–72; Edward Dumbauld, *Thomas Jefferson, American Tourist* (Norman, Oklahoma, 1946), pp. 172–7, 237–8; Brant, III, 336–8; Malone, *Jefferson*, II, 359–61; Philip Schuyler to J. B. Schuyler, May 26, 1791, Schuyler papers, New York Public Library, noted in Young, *Democratic-Republicans in New York*, p. 199.
31. To TJ, May 5, 1791, Hunt, VI, 50–51n; to TJ, June 23 and 27, 1791, MPLC, Malone, *Jefferson*, II, 354–9.
32. TJ to TM Randolph, May 15, 1791, and to GW, September 9, 1792, *Writings of TJ*, V, 336–7, VI, 106–8; JM to Randolph, September 13, 1792, Hunt, VI, 117n; accounts of establishing the *National Gazette* are in Brant, III, 334–6; Malone, *Jefferson*, II, 420–28; Lewis Leary, *That Rascal Freneau: A Study in Literary Failure* (New Brunswick, New Jersey, 1941), pp. 179–203; P. M. Marsh, "Philip Freneau and James Madison, 1791–1793," *Proceedings New Jersey Historical Society*, LXV (1947), 189–94; and Noble E. Cunningham, Jr., *The Jeffersonian Republicans: The Formation of Party Organization, 1789–1801* (Chapel Hill, 1957), pp. 13–19.
33. Hunt, VI, 43–66.
34. "Universal Peace" (February 2, 1792), "A Republican Distribution of Citizens" (March 5, 1792), and "Fashion" (March 23, 1792), Hunt, VI, 88–106.
35. Essays on "Consolidation" (December 5, 1791), "Public Opinion" (December 19, 1791), "Government" (January 2, 1792), "Charters" (January 19, 1792), Hunt, VI, 67–70.
36. "Parties" (January 23, 1792), "British Government" (January 30, 1792), "Government of the United States" (February 6, 1792), and "Spirit of Governments" (February 20, 1792), Hunt, VI, 80–95.
37. "Property," March 29, 1792, Hunt, VI, 101–3.
38. "The Union: Who Are Its Real Friends" (April 4, 1792), Hunt, VI, 104–6.
39. "A Candid State of Parties" (September 26, 1792), and "Who Are the Best Keepers of the People's Liberties?" (December 20, 1792), Hunt, VI, 106–23.
40. Robert Troup to AH, June 15, and Hazard to AH, November 25, 1791, Syrett *PH*, VIII, 478, IX, 529–37; JM to TJ, May 12, 1791, Hunt, VI, 51n; Young, *Democratic-Republicans in New York*, pp. 187–99.

41. Cunningham, *Jeffersonian Republicans, 1789–1801*, pp. 22–3, 267–72.
42. G. W. Corner, ed., *The Autobiography of Benjamin Rush* (Princeton, 1948), p. 217; Ames to Minot, November 30, 1791, and May 3, 1792, and Ames to Thomas Dwight, January 23, 1792, and January 1793, *Works*, I, 104–5, 110, 118–19, 127; *Gazette of the United States*, June 8, 1791, quoting an Albany item of May 30, 1791, cited in Malone, *Jefferson*, II, 361; J. P. Todd, "Memorandum Book," LC.
43. Brant, III, 360–63; Malone, *Jefferson*, II, 469–77; Cunningham, *Jeffersonian-Republicans, 1789–1801*, pp. 24–7; P. M. Marsh, *Monroe's Defense of Jefferson and Freneau against Hamilton* (Oxford, Ohio, 1948).
44. Morris to AH, October 24, 1792, Syrett *PH*, XII, 617–18; GW to TJ, August 23, 1792, and to AH, August 26, 1792, *Writings of Washington* XXXII, 130–33.
45. From GW, May 20, 1792, and to GW, June 21, 1792, MPLC.
46. Cunningham, *Jeffersonian-Republicans, 1789–1801*, pp. 35–45.
47. Rush to Burr, September 24, 1792, Burr papers, American Antiquarian Society; Beckley to JM, October 17, 1792, Cunningham, *Jeffersonian-Republicans, 1789–1801*, pp. 45–9; JM to Pendleton, December 6, 1792, Hunt, VI, 121; TJ to Thomas Pinckney, December 3, 1792, *Writings of TJ*, VI, 143–4; Young, *Democratic-Republicans in New York*, pp. 324–32.
48. AH to Edward Carrington, May 26, 1792, Syrett *PH*, XI, 426–45.

Chapter 14

1. AH to Carrington, May 26, 1792, Syrett *PH*, XI, 439; GW to La Luzerne, April 29, 1790, and to Lafayette, November 22, 1791, *Writings of Washington*, XXXI, 40, 426.
2. To Pendleton, December 6, 1792, Hunt, VI, 120–21; Ames to Dwight, October 4, 1792, Seth Ames, ed., *The Works of Fisher Ames* (2 vols., Boston, 1854), I, 121; Adams to Rufus King, October 11, 1792, quoted in Charles Page Smith, *John Adams* (2 vols., Garden City, New York, 1962), II, 829.
3. Dumas Malone, *Jefferson and His Time* (3 vols., Boston, 1948–62), III, 14–36.
4. G. L. Turberville to JM, January 28, 1793, MPLC.
5. To J. M. Roland, April 1793, Hunt, VI, 125–6.
6. To George Nicholas, March 15, 1793, original owned by Mr. Jasper E. Crane of Wilmington, Delaware.
7. To James Madison, Sr., February 27, 1790, and November 23, 1792, from Jones, July 12, 1790, MPLC; to TJ, June 23, 1791, Hunt, VI, 52.
8. From George Nicholas, December 31, 1790, MPLC.
9. To TJ, April 12, May 27, and June 13, 1793, from TJ, March 24, 1793, MPLC.
10. From TJ, April 28 and May 12, 1793, *Writings of TJ*, VI, 232, 251; Malone, *Jefferson*, III, 68–9; John Carroll and Mary Ashworth, *George Washington* (New York, 1957), pp. 44–56.
11. To TJ, June 19, 1793 (misdated June 10, 1793), Hunt, VI, 127–8.
12. To TJ, May 27, 1793, Hunt, VI, 129–30; from TJ, May 19, 1793, *Writings of TJ*, VI, 260; Malone, *Jefferson*, III, 93–6; John C. Miller, *The Federalist Era, 1789–1801* (New York, 1964), pp. 132–3.
13. TJ to Monroe, June 28, 1793, in Malone, *Jefferson*, III, 102–3, 109.
14. GW to TJ, July 9, 1793, *Writings of Washington*, XXXIII, 4; from TJ,

July 7 and August 3, 1793, *Writings of TJ*, VI, 338, 361; to TJ, July 18, 1793, Hunt, VI, 133.

15. To Archibald Stuart, September 2, and to TJ, September 2, 1793, Hunt, VI, 189–91.

16. Harry Ammon, "The Genêt Mission and the Development of American Political Parties," *The Journal of American History*, LII (1966), 728–32.

17. Monroe to Taylor, August 29, 1793, *Massachusetts Historical Society Proceedings*, XLII (1908–1909), 321; Monroe to JM, September 25, 1793, MPLC; JM to TJ, September 2, 1793, Hunt, VI, 191–6; Taylor to JM, September 25, 1793, W. E. Dodd, ed., "Letters of John Taylor of Caroline," *John H. Branch Historical Papers of Randolph-Macon College*, II (1905), 255–60; Harry Ammon, "The Formation of the Republican Party in Virginia, 1789–1796," *Journal of Southern History*, XIX (1953), 303–5; and Ammon, "Agricola vs. Aristides: James Monroe, John Marshall, and the Genêt Affair in Virginia," *VMHB*, LXXIV (1966), 312–20.

18. Ames to Dwight, August 1793, *Works*, I, 129; Higginson to AH, August 24, 1793, J. C. Hamilton, ed., *The Works of Alexander Hamilton* (7 vols., New York, 1850–1851), V, 577–9; from TJ, June 29 and July 7, 1793, *Writings of TJ*, VI, 327, 338.

19. To TJ, July 18, 22, and 30 and August 11, 1793, Hunt, VI, 135–41.

20. "Helvidius, No. I," *Gazette of the United States*, August 24, 1793, in Hunt, VI, 138–50.

21. To TJ, July 30, August 5, 11, 20, 22, and 27 and September 1, 1793, in Hunt, VI, 138–41, 177–9, 196–7.

22. "Helvidius, No. IV," *Gazette of the United States*, September 14, 1793, in Hunt, VI, 174.

23. John H. Powell, *Bring Out Your Dead* (Philadelphia, 1949), pp. 234–5, 280–82; GW, "Fifth Annual Message," December 3, 1793, and "Address of the House of Representatives," December 6, 1793, *Messages*, I, 130–33, 136–7; C. F. Adams quoted in Malone, *Jefferson*, III, 154; Ames to Minot, December 6, 1793, *Works*, I, 132.

24. Monroe to St. George Tucker, January 16, 1794, *Peck Catalogue*, S. T. Freeman Co., 1947, part III, item 101; Carroll and Ashworth, *Washington*, 146–7; Malone, *Jefferson*, III, 161–2.

25. TJ report, *Writings of TJ*, VI, 470–84; Malone, *Jefferson*, III, 154–9; Merrill D. Peterson, "Thomas Jefferson and Commercial Policy, 1783–1793" *WMQ*, XXII (1965), 584–610.

26. *Annals of Congress*, January 3, 13, 14, 16, 21, and 29, 1794; JM speech, January 3, 1794, Hunt, VI, 203–8; Brant, III, 393; John Randolph to St. George Tucker, January 26, 1794, remarking that "Mr. Madison's sentiments and those of Columbus are in perfect unison," Brock Collection, Box 6, Huntington Library, San Marino, California.

27. AH, "View of the Commercial Regulations of France and Great Britain in Reference to the United States," 1792, Syrett *PH*, XIII, 395–436; Ames to Dwight, January 17, and to Christopher Gore, January 28, 1794, *Works*, I, 132–4; David Cobb to William Eustis, January 31 and February 8, 1794, Cobb papers, Massachusetts Historical Society; to TJ, March 2, 1794, from Gates, February 3 and March 13, 1794, and from Jones, March 4, 1794, MPLC.

28. To Gates, March 24, MPLC; to TJ, March 14, 1794, Hunt, VI, 209; Alfred E. Young, *The Democratic-Republicans in New York: The Origins* (Chapel Hill, 1967), pp. 371–3.

29. To Gates, February 23 and March 24, 1794, and from Gates, March 13, 1794, MPLC.
30. Carroll and Ashworth, *Washington*, pp. 159–70.
31. To Monroe, December 4, 1794, Hunt, VI, 220.
32. "Instructions," June 10, 1794, *American State Papers, Foreign Relations*, I, 668–9; Brant, III, 399–400; Carroll and Ashworth, *Washington*, 171; Stuart G. Brown, *The First Republicans* (Syracuse, 1954), pp. 107–8.
33. To TJ, May 25 and June 1, 1794, Hunt, VI, 215–19; Young, *Democratic-Republicans in New York*, pp. 399–412.
34. Carroll and Ashworth, *Washington*, VII, 180–213; Miller, *Federalist Era*, pp. 155–9.
35. To Monroe, December 4, 1794, Hunt, VI, 220–21.
36. GW, "Annual Message," November 19, 1794, *Messages*, I, 155; Ames to Dwight, September 11 and November 29, 1794, *Works*, I, 150, 153; to Monroe, December 4, 1794, Eugene P. Link, *Democratic Republican Societies, 1790–1800* (New York, 1942), pp. 145–51; William Miller, "Democratic Societies and the Whisky Insurrection," *PMHB*, LXII (1938), 324–9.
37. *Annals of Congress*, November 24 and 25, 1794; "Address of the House of Representatives," November 28, 1794, *Messages*, I, 162–3; Brant, III, 418.
38. *Annals of Congress*, January 1, 1795; JM speech, Hunt, VI, 231n; Brant, III, 420–21.
39. John to Abigail Adams, December 14, 1794, and January 26, 1795, quoted in Smith, *Adams*, II, 869; to Monroe, December 4, 1794, to TJ, December 21, 1794, and to James Madison, Sr., February 23, 1795, Hunt, VI, 224–5, 228–9, 233; diary of Francis Taylor, March 16, 1795, Virginia State Library; Young, *Democratic-Republicans in New York*, pp. 419–28.
40. Ames to Dwight, December 12, 1794, and February 3, 1795, *Works*, I, 154, 166; JM to Monroe, December 4, 1794, and to TJ, February 15, 1795, MPLC; Fauchet to French Foreign Minister, February 8, 1795, F. J. Turner, ed., "Correspondence of the French Ministers to the United States, 1791–1797," American Historical Association *Annual Report*, 1903, II, 573.
41. Samuel F. Bemis, *Jay's Treaty: A Study in Commerce and Diplomacy* (New Haven, 1962 [New York, 1923]), pp. 451–84.
42. To Livingston, August 10, 1795, Hunt, VI, 234–6; Livingston to GW, July 8, 1795, in Carroll and Ashworth, *Washington*, VII, 268n.
43. To Dallas and others, August 23, 1795, Hunt, VI, 238–57; Bemis, *Jay's Treaty*, pp. 335–45.
44. S. E. Morison, ed., "William Manning's *The Key of Libberty*," (written in 1797), *WMQ*, XIII (1956), 236–7.
45. From TJ, September 21, 1795, *Writings of TJ*, VII, 32–3; to TJ, December 6, 1795, MPLC.
46. To TJ, January 31, 1796, MPLC.
47. Zephaniah Swift to David Daggett, December 13, 1794, *Proceedings American Antiquarian Society*, IV (1888), 374.
48. To Monroe, December 20, 1795, and February 26, 1796, to TJ, February 7, 1796, MPLC; Edward Livingston to R. R. Livingston, December 20, 1795, Haverford College Library; Brant, III, 434; *Messages*, I, 184; *Annals of Congress*, March 1796; Raymond Walters, Jr., *Albert Gallatin, Jeffersonian Financier and Diplomat* (New York, 1957), pp. 97–8; Young, *Democratic-Republicans in New York*, pp. 459–65.

49. Ames to Gore, March 11, 1796, *Works*, I, 189; message of March 30, 1796, *Messages*, I, 186–8.

50. To TJ, April 4, 1796, JM speech, April 6, 1796, Hunt, VI, 264–5, 272; from TJ, April 17, 1796, *Writings of TJ*, VII, 70–71; Trumbull to John Trumbull, April 2, 1796, Connecticut State Library; Ames to Minot, April 2, 1796; *Works*, I, 191; Noble E. Cunningham, Jr., *The Jeffersonian Republicans: 1789–1801* (Chapel Hill, 1957), p. 82.

51. *Annals of Congress*, April 14 and 15, 1796; to TJ, April 18 and 23, 1796, Cong. ed., II, 95–8.

52. From TJ, March 27, 1796, *Writings of TJ*, VII, 68; *Annals of Congress*, AG speech, April 26, 1796.

53. William Plumer to Jeremiah Smith, April 12, 1796, Plumer papers, LC, quoted in Wilfred Bernhard, *Fisher Ames* (Chapel Hill, 1965), pp. 267–8; *Annals of Congress*, Ames speech, April 28, 1796; John to Abigail Adams, April 30, 1796, C. F. Adams, ed., *Letters of John Adams Addressed to His Wife* (2 vols., Boston, 1841), II, 225–7.

54. *Annals of Congress*, Ames speech, April 28, 1796; Bernhard, *Ames*, pp. 168–70.

55. To TJ, April 23, May 1, 9, and 22, 1796, to Monroe, April 18 and May 14, 1796, Cong. ed., II, 97–101; Brant, III, 438–9.

56. Ames to Dwight, May 19, 1796, *Works*, I, 193; Knox to Wadsworth, May 4, 1796, Wadsworth papers, Box 141, Connecticut Historical Society; Boston *Columbian Centinel*, April 27, 1796; *Porcupine's Political Censor*, Philadelphia, May 1796, p. 195.

57. Brant, III, 445–51; Gerard Clarfield, "Postscript to the Jay Treaty: Timothy Pickering and Anglo-American Relations, 1795–1797," *WMQ*, XXIII (1966), 106–20.

58. To Monroe, September 29, 1796, Brant, III, 441; Miller, *Federalist Era*, p. 198; Felix Gilbert, *The Beginnings of American Foreign Policy* (New York, 1965), pp. 115–34; Alexander De Conde, "Washington's Farewell, the French Alliance, and the Election of 1796," *MVHR*, XLIII (1957), 641–58, and Samuel F. Bemis, "Washington's Farewell Address: A Foreign Policy of Independence," *AHR*, XXXIX (1934), 250–68, give contrasting interpretations of the address.

59. Cunningham, *Jeffersonian Republicans, 1789–1801*, pp. 101–6.

60. Young, *Democratic-Republicans in New York*, pp. 548–51; to TJ, December 19, 1796, Hunt, VI, 300–302.

61. From TJ, December 17, 1796, and January 1, 1797, TJ to Adams, December 28, 1796, *Writings of TJ*, VII, 91–100; to TJ, January 15 and 29, 1797, Hunt, VI, 302–4, 307.

62. From TJ, December 17, 1796, *Writings of TJ*, VII, 91; Brant, III, 445, 449–50; to James Madison, Sr., March 12, 1797, Hunt, VI, 307–8.

63. Brant, III, 451.

Chapter 15

1. Information on the Madison family, in many particulars uncertain, has been gathered from birth and death notices in newspapers, official Virginia records, entries in family Bibles, references in letters, tombstone inscriptions, genealogies, and records kept by descendants. Full details, so far as they can be known, are being gathered in the Richmond and Chicago offices of *The Papers of James Madison* and will appear as

needed in the annotation of those volumes. *MP*, I (opposite p. 213), offers a Madison family tree.

2. Forrest McDonald, *We the People* (Chicago, 1958), pp. 72–3; Brant, II, 322–3.

3. To TJ, April 22, 1788, Boyd *PJ*, XIII, 98–9; T. P. Abernethy, ed., *Notes on the State of Virginia* (New York, 1964), p. 159; Brant, III, 16, 188.

4. To James Madison, Sr., February 27, 1790, Hunt, V, 460n; to TJ, June 12, 1792, MPLC; Duc de la Rochefoucauld-Liancourt, *Travels through the United States of North America . . . 1795–1796, and 1797* (2 vols., London, 1799), II, 72.

5. To James Madison, Sr., May 2 and June 13, 1790, and April 17, 1792, Hunt, VI, 13–15, 105; Brant, III, 323–4.

6. Brant, III, 323–4, 380; *The Virginia Gazette, or, American Advertiser*, Richmond, November 8, 15, 22, 1786.

7. "George Wilson *vs* Richard Mason, Devisee of George Mason," and "Richard Mason, Devisee of George Mason *vs* George Wilson," 5 U.S. 45, 1 Cranch 45, 2 L. Ed. 29 (1804); information supplied by Mr. R. Carter Pittman of Dalton, Georgia; from John H. Lee, April 30, 1831, Brant, VI, 501–2, III, 357–8.

8. To James Madison, Sr., May 4, 1794, and February 23, 1795, to TJ, April 4, 1800, Hunt, VI, 213–15, 233, 409; Augustus B. Foster, "Notes on the U.S.A., 1804–1812," ed. by M. B. Tinkcom, *WMQ*, VIII (1951), 96–7; Brant, III, 444, 458–9; Dumas Malone, *Jefferson and His Time* (3 vols., Boston, 1948–62), III, 232–42.

9. Katharine Anthony, *Dolly Madison, Her Life and Times* (Garden City, New York, 1949), pp. 1–19, though often inaccurate and fanciful, tells of Dolley Madison's family background and childhood; genealogies of the Payne, Winston, and Coles families at the Virginia Historical Society provide further information; Brant, III, 401–3, recounts her childhood and establishes beyond doubt that the only name she ever had or used was "Dolley," spelled thus.

10. DPM to M. B. Smith, August 31, 1834, in Gaillard Hunt, ed., *The First Forty Years of Washington Society* (New York, 1906), p. 351; Dolley Payne to Eliza Brooke, *ca.* 1788, and Sarah Parker to Eliza Brooke (1789), quoted in Anthony, *Dolly Madison*, pp. 32–6.

11. Dolley P. Todd to James Todd, October 4, 1793, John Todd to James Todd, October 12, 1793, Mary Payne to Margaret Hervey, *ca.* October 24, 1793, papers owned by W. Parsons Todd, Morristown, New Jersey; Paul Sifton, " 'What a Dread Prospect . . .' Dolley Madison's Plague Year," *PMHB*, LXXXVII (1963), 182–8.

12. Dolley P. Todd to James Todd, October 18 and December 12, 1793, W. Parsons Todd papers; Cutts, *Memoirs*, p. 14–16.

13. Samuel L. Mitchell to Mrs. Mitchell, January 3, 1802, JM to TJ, May 23, 1789, Boyd *PJ*, XV, 147–8; Malone, *Jefferson*, III, 5–6; Edward Coles to H. B. Grigsby, December 23, 1854, Virginia Historical Society.

14. Cutts, *Memoirs*, pp. 15–16; Isaac Parrish accounts, Cox-Parrish-Wharton papers, vol. II, HSP; Catherine Coles to Dolley Todd, June 1, 1794, University of Virginia Library.

15. William Wilkins to Dolley Todd, August 22, 1794, DPM papers, LC; Anthony, *Dolly Madison*, p. 92.

16. To Dolley Todd, August 18, 1794, MPLC; Brant, III, 408; Malone, *Jefferson*, III, 187; to James Madison, Sr., October 5, 1794; 1794 deed,

Bowman-Hite papers, Indiana Historical Society, Bloomington, Indiana, places Frances Madison at her aunt's that year.

17. Anthony, *Dolly Madison*, pp. 44–5, 51, 84–91; Brant, III, 408–11; to James Madison, Sr., October 5, 1794, MPLC; Balmain account book, photostat, LC.
18. DPM to Eliza Collins Lee, September 15, 1794, DPM papers, LC.
19. To James Madison, Sr., October 5, 1794, MPLC; to James Madison, Sr., December 14, 1794, quoted in Brant, III, 411.
20. Brant, III, 412–29, 445; Kenneth and A. M. Roberts, eds., *Moreau de St. Méry's American Journey, 1793–1798* (Garden City, New York, 1947), pp. 257–66, recording impressions of Philadelphia, 1794–1797.
21. Ames to Thomas Dwight, February 24, 1795, John Carroll and Mary Ashworth, *George Washington* (New York, 1957), 235; John to Abigail Adams, February 11, 1796, Adams mss., Massachusetts Historical Society.
22. Sally McKean to Anna Payne, June 6 and September 3, 1796, Cutts, *Memoirs*, pp. 18–22.
23. Abigail Adams to Mary Cranch, March 18, 1800, Stewart Mitchell, ed., *New Letters of Abigail Adams, 1788–1801* (Boston, 1947), pp. 241–2; Otis to his wife, January 18, 1800, S. E. Morrison, *The Life and Letters of Harrison Gray Otis* (2 vols., Boston, 1913), I, 137.
24. To Monroe, December 4, 1794, Hunt, VI, 226–7; to Gates, February 23, 1794, Boston Public Library; from Gates, December 27, 1794, from Freneau, May 20, 1795, and from TJ, October 30, 1794, MPLC; from Pinckney, October 26, 1800, MPLC, in Brant, III, 413.
25. From TJ, December 28, 1794, *Writings of TJ*, VI, 519; from Henry Lee, September 23, 1794, MPLC; Trumbull to John Trumbull, November 10, 1794, Trumbull papers, Connecticut State Library.
26. Burr to Monroe, March 10, 1796, Monroe papers, LC; TJ to Benjamin Hawkins, March 14, 1801, *Writings of TJ*, VII, 437; Alfred J. Beveridge, *The Life of John Marshall* (4 vols., Boston, 1916–1919), II, *passim*, supposes JM's deterioration during the seventeen-nineties, and W. W. Crosskey in conversations, July 1960, suggested that JM's sense of his own impotence beside AH's fecundity and prowess with women played a major role in the inveterate hostility, extreme sensitivity, and feeling of inferiority Madison displayed toward AH.
27. Francis Taylor diary, 1794–1799, Virginia State Library.
28. Taylor diary, 1798.
29. To TJ, January 10, 1801, Hunt, VI, 415; Brant, III, 423, 444, 458; James Madison, Sr., to Thomas Barbour, February 15, 1801, New York Public Library, cited in Brant, IV, 37.
30. To TJ, February 28, 1801, Hunt, VI, 417; L. W. Labaree and others, eds., *The Autobiography of Benjamin Franklin* (New Haven, 1964), pp. 54–5.
31. Brant, IV, 37–8; JM to an unidentified person, March 7, 1801, MPLC, quoted by Brant, *Ibid.*

Chapter 16

1. From TJ, January 30, 1787, Boyd *PJ*, XI, 95.
2. John to Abigail Adams, March 15, 1797, quoted in Charles Page Smith, *John Adams* (2 vols., Garden City, New York, 1962), II, 920.
3. To TJ, February 1798, April 2 and 15, 1798, Hunt, VI, 310, 312, 315.

4. Adams to Citizens of Baltimore, May 2, 1798, C. F. Adams, ed., *The Works of John Adams* (10 vols., Boston, 1856), IX, 186-7; Abigail Adams to Mary Cranch, May 10, 1798, Stewart Mitchell, ed., *New Letters of Abigail Adams, 1788-1801* (Boston, 1947), pp. 171-2; JM to TJ, May 20, 1798, Hunt, VI, 321.

5. To TJ, June 10, 1798, and May 13, 1798, MPLC; from TJ, June 7, 1798, *Writings of TJ*, VII, 266-7; Smith, *Adams*, II, 959.

6. Francis Taylor diary, 1798, Virginia State Library; TJ to John Taylor, June 4, 1798, *Writings of TJ*, VII, 265.

7. Taylor diary, 1798; George C. Taylor to James Taylor, July 27, 1798, Kentucky Historical Society, Frankfort, Kentucky.

8. Taylor diary, 1798; Dumas Malone, *Jefferson and His Time* (3 vols., Boston, 1948-62), III, 401.

9. TJ's draft resolves, and resolves as passed in Kentucky, *Writings of TJ*, VII, 288-309; TJ to W. C. Nicholas, October 5, 1798, *Ibid.*, VII, 281-2.

10. To TJ, December 29, 1798, Hunt, VI, 327-9; Malone, *Jefferson*, III, 408-9.

11. Brant, III, 459-63.

12. Resolves of Massachusetts Senate, February 9, 1799, Jonathan Elliot, *Debates in the Several State Conventions on the Federal Constitution* (2nd ed., 5 vols., Philadelphia, 1861), IV, 534; Ames to Christopher Gore, January 11, 1799, *Works*, I, 250; GW to Henry, January 15, 1799, *Writings of Washington*, XXXVII, 87-90; Robert D. Meade, *Patrick Henry* (2 vols., Philadelphia, 1957-69), II, 446-8. Marshall's address is reprinted in John P. Roche, ed., *John Marshall: Major Opinions and Other Writings* (Indianapolis, 1967), pp. 32-48.

13. From TJ, February 5, 1799, *Writings of TJ*, VII, 344-5; from Walter Jones, *et al.*, February 7, 1799, Hunt, VI, 341n; from John Taylor, March 4, 1799, cited in Brant, III, 465; Taylor diary, 1799.

14. Smith, *Adams*, II, 994-1017.

15. From TJ, August 23, 1799, quoted in Adrienne Koch, *Jefferson and Madison: The Great Collaboration* (New York, 1950), pp. 196-8; TJ to W. C. Nicholas, September 5, 1799, *Writings of TJ*, VII, 389-91.

16. To TJ, December 29, 1799, Hunt, VI, 342-4n.

17. "Report on the Resolutions," adopted by Virginia legislature, January 11, 1800, and published at once in an 80-page pamphlet; reprinted in Hunt, VI, 341-406.

18. Leonard W. Levy, *Freedom of Speech and Press in Early American History: Legacy of Suppression* (New York, 1963 [Cambridge, Massachusetts, 1960]), esp. p. 282.

19. J. Q. Adams to Edward Everett, October 10, 1836, *VMHB*, LXVI (1958), 179-82; JM, comment on Constitution, 1833, cited in *MP*, VI, xix. Dickinson to TJ, March 18, 1800, quoted in Brant, IV, 15.

20. Noble E. Cunningham, Jr., *Jeffersonian Republicans: The Formation of Party Organization, 1789-1801* (Chapel Hill, 1957), pp. 150-52; P. N. Nicholas to TJ, February 1, 1800, in Cunningham, ed., *The Making of the American Party System, 1789-1809* (Prentice-Hall Spectrum Book, 1965), pp. 106-8.

21. Cunningham, *Jeffersonian Republicans, 1789-1801*, pp. 231-6.

22. Brant, IV, 23-6; John C. Miller, *The Federalist Era, 1789-1801* (New York, 1964), pp. 266-74.

23. To TJ, January 10 and February 28, 1801, Hunt, VI, 415, 418; Brant, IV, 37; Broadus Mitchell, *Alexander Hamilton* (2 vols., New York, 1957-1962), II, 490-93; Adams to Elbridge Gerry, December 30, 1800, *Works*,

IX, 577–8; George W. Erving to Monroe, January 25, 1801, Monroe papers, LC.

24. TJ to JM, February 18, 1801, *Writings of TJ*, VII, 494–5; TJ to T. M. Randolph, March 12 and May 14, 1801, *Massachusetts Historical Society Collection*, 7th ser., I (1900), 93, 95; Brant, IV, 39–41.

25. TJ to Monroe, June 20, 1801, Monroe papers, LC; Edward Coles to Hugh Blair Grigsby, December 23, 1854, Virginia Historical Society.

Chapter 17

1. Benjamin Stoddert to William Thornton, January 20, 1800, AG to his wife, January 15, 1801, Allen C. Clarke, *Life and Letters of Dolly Madison* (Washington, D.C., 1914), pp. 36–7, 42–3; Margaret B. Smith, in Gaillard Hunt, ed., *The First Forty Years of Washington Society* (New York, 1906), p. 384; TJ to T. M. Randolph, June 4, 1801, quoted in Brant, IV, 42.

2. TJ to T. M. Randolph, October 18, 1801, E. M. Betts and J. A. Bear, ed., *The Family Letters of Thomas Jefferson* (Columbia, Missouri, 1966), pp. 209–10; Thornton to JM, August 15, 1801, Clarke, *Dolly Madison*, p. 46; Brant, IV, 42–3.

3. Letters of May 26 and 28, 1801, in Hunt, ed., *First Forty Years*, pp. 27–9.

4. R. B. Davis, ed., *Jeffersonian America, Notes on the United States of America Collected in the Years 1805-6-7 and 11-12 by Sir Augustus John Foster, Bart.*, (San Marino, California, 1954), p. 13; Duane "notebook," 1801, Raymond Walters, Jr., *Albert Gallatin, Jeffersonian Financier and Diplomat* (New York, 1957), p. 158; Leonard D. White, *The Jeffersonians* (New York, 1951), pp. 371–3; Charles W. Upham, *The Life of Timothy Pickering* (4 vols., Boston, 1873), IV, 461.

5. White, *Jeffersonians*, pp. 187–8; to Monroe, May 6, 1801, and to W. C. Nicholas, July 10, 1801, Hunt, VI, 419, 425.

6. TJ to D. deTracy, January 26, 1811, *Fed. ed. Writings*, XI, 185; Walters, *Gallatin*, pp. 414–15, 263–5.

7. TJ to W. C. Nicholas, May 25, 1809, *Fed. ed. Writings*, XI, 108.

8. Letters to JM, March 27–August 2, 1801, MPLC, and George Tucker memoir of JM, Rives-MPLC, cited in Brant, IV, 49–50; TJ to W. B. Giles, March 23, 1801, *Fed. ed. Writings*, X, 238.

9. Pierpont Edwards and others to Levi Lincoln, passed on to TJ, June 4, 1801, Noble E. Cunningham, Jr., ed., *The Making of the American Party System, 1789 to 1809* (Englewood Cliffs, New Jersey, 1965), pp. 167–70; TJ to Merchants of New Haven, July 12, 1801, *Fed. ed. Writings*, X, 268–73.

10. AG to TJ, July 25, 1801, and September 18, 1804, *Writings of AG*, I, 28–30, 208–9; TJ to AG, July 26, 1801, and September 8, 1804, *Fed. ed. Writings*, X, 101.

11. Walters, *Gallatin*, pp. 156–7; Brant, IV, 53–5.

12. To Rufus King, June 15 and July 24, 1801, Hunt, VI, 423–35; Robert Ernst, *Rufus King, American Federalist* (Chapel Hill, 1968), pp. 245–46.

13. Bradford Perkins, *The First Rapprochement: England and the United States, 1795–1805* (Philadelphia, 1953), pp. 106–10; Brant, IV, 60–67; TJ to R. R. Livingston, April 18, 1802, *Fed. ed. Writings*, X, 313.

14. TJ to Levi Lincoln, July 11, 180 , *Fed. ed. Writings*, X, 266; TJ to AG, September 18, 1801, *Writings of AG*, I, 55.

15. Brant, IV, 73–83.

16. Adams, *Hist.*, I, 414–18.
17. Pichon to Talleyrand, July 7 and 31, 1802, summarized in Brant, IV, 90–93.
18. To C. Pinckney, November 27, 1802, Hunt, VI, 462–3; to R. R. Livingston, December 16, 1802, quoted in Brant, IV, 99.
19. To Livingston and Monroe, March 2, 1803, Hunt, VII, 9–34.
20. Perkins, *First Rapprochement*, pp. 159–71.
21. Livingston to JM, April 13, 1803; George Dangerfield, *Chancellor Robert R. Livingston of New York, 1746–1813* (New York, 1960), pp. 359–69.
22. To Monroe and Livingston, July 29, 1803, and to Monroe, July 30, 1803, Hunt, VII, 60–61; TJ to Monroe, January 13, 1803, and to John Breckinridge, August 12, 1803, *Fed. ed. Writings*, X, 344–5, 408–10.
23. AG to TJ, January 13, 1803, *Writings of AG*, I, 111–14; TJ to AG, January 1803, quoted in Brant, IV, 141–2; TJ to W. C. Nicholas, September 7, 1803, *Fed. ed. Writings*, X, 417–20.
24. To Livingston and Monroe, July 29, 1803, Hunt, VII, 62–3; TJ to Horatio Gates, July 11, 1803, *Fed. ed. Writings*, X, 13.
25. C. F. Adams, ed., *The Memoirs of John Quincy Adams* (12 vols., Philadelphia, 1874–1877), October 28, 1803, I, 267–8.
26. To Livingston and Monroe, July 29, 1803, and to C. Pinckney, October 12, 1803, Hunt, VII, 53–60, 71–4.
27. Brant, IV, 188–212.
28. JM to Monroe, March 8, 1804, cited in Perkins, *First Rapproachement*, p. 134.
29. To Monroe, January 5, 1804, Hunt, VII, 79–114; W. P. Cresson, *James Monroe* (Chapel Hill, 1946), pp. 205–7.
30. Brant, IV, 254–7; Adams, *Hist.*, II, 257–63, 425–37.
31. Brant, IV, 90–92, 115–18, 254–5, 64 (quoting Pichon to Talleyrand, July 22, 1801); Irving Brant, "Madison and the War of 1812," *VMHB*, LXXIV (1966), 51.
32. AG to TJ, September 12 and 14, 1801, TJ to AG, September 18, 1801, *Writings of AG*, I, 47–55; Brant, IV, 54–5.
33. Diary of Anne Thornton, September 5–October 6, 1802, quoted in Clarke, *Dolly Madison*, pp. 51–2; Brant, IV, 44–5; Davis, ed., *Notes by Foster*, pp. 146–7.
34. *Ibid.*, pp. 139–43, 155.
35. TJ to DPM, May 27, 1801, Cutts, *Memoirs*, p. 28; S. L. Mitchell to Mrs. Mitchell, January 4, 1802, Clarke, *Dolly Madison*, p. 50; M. B. Smith to Susan Smith, December 26, 1802, S. H. Smith to M. B. Smith, April 26 and July 5, 1803, in Hunt, ed., *First Forty Years*, pp. 33–8; Davis, ed., *Notes by Foster*, p. 88; Jane Carson, *Colonial Virginians at Play* (Williamsburg, Virginia, 1958), pp. 66–9, 278–80.
36. S. H. Smith to M. B. Smith, July 5, 1803, in the Hunt, ed., *First Forty Years*, pp. 38–9; E. S. Brown, ed., *William Plumer's Memorandum of Proceedings in the United States Senate 1803–1807* (New York, 1923), p. 123; diary of Manasseh Cutler, February 21, 1804, in W. P. and J. P. Cutler, eds., *Life, Journals, and Correspondence of Rev. Manasseh Cutler* (2 vols, Cincinnati, 1888), II, 154; list of garden vegetables available in D.C., E. M. Betts, ed., *Thomas Jefferson's Garden Book* (Princeton, 1953), p. 639; recollections of M. B. Smith, quoted in Clarke, *Dolly Madison*, pp. 64–5; T. M. Randolph to Harriet Randolph, December 7, 1804, collection of C. M. Storey, Boston, Massachusetts.
37. DPM to Anna Cutts, June 1804, Cutts, *Memoirs*, p. 45.
38. To Charles Pinckney, April 10, 1804, Hunt, VII, 125–6; DPM to Anna

Cutts, April 26, 1804, and June 4, 1805, Cutts, *Memoirs*, pp. 38–9, 51; Brown, ed., *Plumer's Memorandum*, p. 208.

39. Adams, ed., *Memoirs of John Quincy Adams*, I, 284–5, January 7, 1804; M. B. Smith to Mrs. Kirkpatrick, January 23, 1804, in Hunt, ed., *First Forty Years*, pp. 45–7.

40. Cutler to Mrs. Poole, February 28, 1804, *Life, Journals, and Correspondence*, II, 164; JM to Monroe, February 16, 1804, Hunt, VII, 118–21; TJ to William Short, January 23, 1804, *American Historical Review*, XXXIII (1928), 832–3.

41. TJ to Short, Jan. 23, 1804, *Ibid.*

42. Samuel S. Smith to Aaron Burr, March 13, 1802, Burr papers, American Antiquarian Society; Adams, *Hist.*, II, 201–2; Noble E. Cunningham, Jr., *Jeffersonian Republicans in Power, 1801–1809* (Chapel Hill, 1963), pp. 98, 103–5; JM to Monroe, July 21, 1804, Monroe papers LC, quoted in Brant, IV, 244; unsigned broadside addressed to Pa. voters, 1804, in Cunningham, ed., *American Party System*, pp. 160–61.

43. Brant, IV, 111; Adams, *Hist.*, II, 160–91, quoting Pickering to Rufus King, March 4, 1804.

44. JM memorandum, January 23, 1807, Cong. ed., II, 393–401; Marshall Smelser, *The Democratic Republic, 1801–1815* (New York, 1968), pp. 111–123.

45. Cunningham, *Jeffersonian Republicans in Power*, pp. 103–24, 205–35.

46. "The Danger Not Over," October 5, 1801, David J. Mays, ed., *The Letters and Papers of Edmund Pendleton* (2 vols., Charlottesville, Virginia, 1967), II, 695–9; Harry Ammon, "James Monroe and the Election of 1808 in Virginia," *WMQ*, XX (1963), 34–7; Taylor to W. C. Nicholas, February 5, 1808, and Beckley to Monroe, July 13, 1806, quoted in Cunningham, *Jeffersonian-Republicans in Power*, p. 232.

47. *Ibid.*, pp. 73–8.

48. Brant, IV, 234–8.

49. Brown, ed., *Plumer's Memorandum*, p. 269, and pp. 464–5, quoting Randolph's speech of March 31, 1806; Adams, *Hist.*, III, 164; Brant, IV, 317–18.

50. Adams, ed., *Memoirs of John Quincy Adams*, March 6, 1806, I, 418; Randolph to Monroe, March 20, 1806, and to an unidentified correspondent, March 19, 1806, Stan V. Henkels' catalogue, April 27 and 28, 1900, p. 58; Monroe to Randolph, June 16, 1806, and Randolph to Monroe, September 16, 1806, *Writings of Monroe*, IV, 467, 486–8.

51. TJ to Monroe, March 17 and May 4, 1806, *Fed. ed. Writings*, X, 237–8, 260–61; JM to Monroe, March 10, 1806, Cong. ed., II, 212; Brant, IV, 322–3; M. B. Smith to Susan Smith, July 31, 1806, in Hunt, ed., *First Forty Years*, p. 51.

Chapter 18

1. Annual Message, November 8, 1804, *Messages*, I, 369; Adams, *Hist.*, III, 56–65.

2. TJ cabinet notes, November 14–December 7, 1805, *Fed. ed. Writings*, X, 180–205.

3. To Monroe, April 12 and September 24, 1805, Hunt, VII, 176–83, 191; DPM to Anna Cutts, July 29 and 31, 1805, Cutts, *Memoirs*, pp. 53–5; Duponceau to JM (1805), MPLC; Brant, IV, 293–8.

4. *An Examination . . .* , Hunt, VII, 204–375, quotes on pp. 207 and 346.

5. TJ to Comte de Volney, February 11, 1806, *Fed. ed. Writings*, X, 227.
6. C. F. Adams, ed., *The Memoirs of John Quincy Adams* (12 vols., Philadelphia, 1874–1877), January 22, 1806, I, 389; to Monroe, January 13, 1806, Cong. ed., II, 216; E. S. Brown, ed., *William Plumer's Memorandum of Proceedings in the United States Senate 1803–1807* (New York, 1923), January 22 and March 6, 1806, pp. 387–9, 444.
7. DPM to Anna Cutts, July 29 and 31, 1805, papers owned by Mr. and Mrs. George B. Cutts, Brookline, Massachusetts.
8. From DPM, October 23, 24, 25, 26, 28, and 30, November 1, 15, 17, 1805, Cutts, *Memoirs*, pp. 55–62; from DPM, November 1805, original owned by Mrs. Edward Chavalier, Los Angeles, California; to DPM, November 5 and 23, 1805, Hunt, VIII, 76–7 (misdated), Brant, IV, 289; Richard Cutts to Thomas Cutts, November 19, 1805, H. S. Burrage, ed., "Cutts Letters," *Maine Historical Society Proceedings*, IX (1898), 26.
9. Brown, ed., *Plumer's Memorandum*, November 30, 1805, January 18, 1806, January 3, 1807, pp. 337, 383, 556.
10. *Ibid.*, December 13 and 23, 1805, January 1, 2, 18, 1806, pp. 336, 349, 358, 364–5; Cutts, *Memoirs*, p. 32; R. B. Davis, ed., *Jeffersonian America, Notes on the United States of America Collected in the Years 1805-6-7 and 11-12 by Sir Augustus John Foster, Bart.* (San Marino, California, 1954), pp. 22–3; Adams, ed., *Memoirs of John Quincy Adams*, February 27, 1806, I, 416.
11. To Monroe, June 4, 1806, Cong. ed., II, 224–5; Fox to Merry, April 7, 1806, Bernard Mayo, ed., "Instructions to the British Ministers to the United States, 1791–1812," *American Historical Association Annual Report*, 1936, III, 221.
12. To Monroe and Pinkney, May 17, 1806, Hunt, VII, 375–95; to Monroe, May 17, 1806, Cong. ed., II, 223–4.
13. W. P. Cresson, *James Monroe* (Chapel Hill, 1946), pp. 218–29; Bradford Perkins, *Prologue to War: England and the United States, 1805–1812* (Berkeley and Los Angeles, 1961), pp. 117–34.
14. To Monroe and Pinkney, February 3, 1807, Hunt, VII, 395–404; from TJ, February 1, 1807, *Fed. ed. Writings*, X, 374; to Monroe, March 20 and May 25, 1807, and to George Joy, May 22, 1807, Cong. ed., II, 403–7.
15. Monroe to TJ, January 11, 1807, *Writings of Monroe*, V, 2.
16. Perceval to Abbott, *ca.* November 30, 1807, quoted in Adams, *Hist.*, IV, 98–9.
17. Perkins, *Prologue*, pp. 73–4; TJ to Monroe, March 21, 1807, *Fed. ed. Writings*, X, 377; DPM to Anna Cutts, March 27, 1807, Cutts, *Memoirs*, p. 64.
18. Brant, IV, 340–58; from TJ, May 1, 1807, *Fed. ed. Writings*, X, 391; to John Armstrong, May 22, 1807, Hunt, VII, 448–9.
19. Adams, *Hist.*, IV, 1–26.
20. TJ to AG, June 26, 1807, and to W. H. Cabell, June 29, 1807, proclamations of July 2, 1807, *Fed. ed. Writings*, X, 432–47; to Monroe, July 6, 1807, and to Armstrong and Bowdoin, July 15, 1807, Hunt, VII, 454–62.
21. TJ to George Clinton, July 6, 1807, and to W. H. Cabell, July 8 and 27, 1807, *Fed. ed. Writings*, X, 433–8, 448–9; AG to TJ, with memo, July 25, 1807, *Writings of AG*, I, 340–53.
22. AG to TJ, July 7, 1807, *Writings of AG*, I, 337; TJ to Dearborn, July 13, 1807, *Fed. ed. Writings*, X, 459; JM to Monroe, July 6, 1807, Hunt, VII, 458–9.

23. AG to TJ, September 12, 1805, *Writings of AG*, I, 252–3. Turreau to Talleyrand, July 18, 1807, quoted in Adams, *Hist.*, IV, 37.

24. To Monroe, October 21, 1807, Hunt, VII, 466; to Pinkney, October 21, 1807, Pinkney papers, Princeton University Library; Brant, IV, 387–93.

25. AG memo, Oct. 1807, *Writings of TJ*, IX, 145; Adams, ed., *Memoirs of John Quincy Adams*, December 1807, I, 475–6.

26. Adams, *Hist.*, IV, 158–66.

27. AG to TJ, December 18, 1807, *Writings of AG*, I, 368.

28. Canning to Rose, October 24, 1807, Mayo, ed., *Instructions*, pp. 235–42; JM notes on conversations with Rose, February 1–24, 1808, to Monroe, March 18, 1808, Cong. ed., II, 411–22; Brant, IV, 404–18; Adams, *Hist.*, IV, 182.

29. Perkins, *Prologue*, p. 161.

30. To Armstrong, February 8 and May 2, 1808, official letters to Pinkney, February 19, March 8, April 4 and 30, 1808, Hunt, VII, 12–13, 17–31.

31. To Pinkney (private), April 4 and 8, May 1, 1808, Princeton University Library.

32. To TJ, May 11 and 15, 1808, DPM to Anna Cutts, May 5 and June 3, 1808, and to Anna Thornton, May 18, 1808, all quoted in Brant, IV, 438–9; DPM to Anna Cutts, August 28, 1808, Cutts, *Memoirs*, pp. 65–6.

33. To Pinkney (private), July 3 and 15, 1808, Princeton University Library.

34. To Pinkney (private), July 21, 1808, *Ibid.*; DPM to Anna Cutts, August 28, 1808, Cutts, *Memoirs*, 65–6.

35. AG to TJ, July 29 and August 9, 1808, to AG, August 19 and 31, 1808, *Writings of AG*, I, 396–9, 402–12; Brant, IV, 439; from AG, September 9, 1808, Rives-MPLC, quoted in Raymond Walters, Jr., *Albert Gallatin, Jeffersonian Financier and Diplomat* (New York, 1957), pp. 202–3; to Pinkney (private), September 9, 1808, Princeton University Library.

36. Perkins, *Prologue*, pp. 160–64.

37. *Ibid.*, pp. 166–9; from Armstrong, August 30, 1808, MPLC.

38. Canning to Pinkney, September 23, 1808, quoted in Perkins, *Prologue*, p. 176; to Pinkney, November 9, 1808, Hunt, VII, 425–6; Champagny to Armstrong, January 15, 1808, quoted in Brant, IV, 446–7.

39. From Pinkney, September 21, 1808, in Henry Wheaton, *Some Account of the Life, Writings, and Speeches of William Pinkney* (New York, 1826), pp. 402–6.

40. To Pinkney, November 9, 1808, Cong. ed., II, 425–6; JM draft for eighth annual message, November 8, 1808, *Writings of TJ*, XI, 56–65; to Pinkney (private), November 10, 1808, Princeton University Library.

41. TJ to Abraham Bishop, and to Levi Lincoln, November 13, 1808, *Writings of TJ*, IX, 72–5; AG to TJ, November 15, 1808, *Writings of AG*, I, 428.

42. Report, November 1808, *Writings of AG*, I, 446; Adams, *Hist.*, IV, 370–72; Brant, IV, 470–72; to Pinkney (private), November 25, 1808, Princeton University Library.

43. To Pinkney (private), December 5, 1808, Cong. ed., II, 427–8; Erskine to Canning, December 3, 1808, quoted in Adams, *Hist.*, IV, 386–7.

44. New England resolves quoted in Adams, *Hist.*, IV, 411–16; to Pinkney (private), January 3, 1809, Princeton University Library.

45. Erskine to Canning, February 10 and 13, 1809, quoted in Adams, *Hist.*, IV, 444–6; Brant, IV, 477–81; to Pinkney (private), February 11, 1809, Cong. ed., II, 429–31; TJ to Dupont de Nemours, March 2, 1809, *Fed. ed. Writings*, XII, 259–60.

46. Harry Ammon, "Monroe and the Election of 1808," *WMQ*, XX (1963), 31–45; Brant, IV, 243–4, 433–4; Norman K. Risjord, *The Old Republicans: Southern Conservatism in the Age of Jefferson* (New York, 1965), pp. 72–95.

47. Noble E. Cunningham, Jr., *Jeffersonian-Republicans in Power, 1801–1809* (Chapel Hill, 1963), pp. 111–116.

48. *National Intelligencer*, January 25, 1808, Richmond *Enquirer*, March 29, 1808, New York *American Citizen*, June 9 and 25, 1808, Philadelphia *Aurora*, November 26, 1808, quoted in Brant, IV, 427–8, 441–2, 448, 466.

49. Brant, IV, 441–68.

50. Cunningham, *Jeffersonian-Republicans in Power*, pp. 108–24.

51. Adams, ed., *Memoirs of John Quincy Adams*, October 24 and 28, 1803, June 8, 1808, I, 265, 267, 536; JQA to H. G. Otis, March 31, 1808, W. C. Ford, ed., *The Writings of John Quincy Adams* (7 vols., N.Y., 1914), III, 209–10; Samuel F. Bemis, *John Quincy Adams and the Foundations of American Foreign Policy* (New York, 1949), p. 131.

52. Brown, ed., *Plumer's Memorandum*, April 8, 1806, p. 478; Wm. Plumer's biographical notes, January 9, 1821, ms. at New Hampshire State Library, Concord, New Hampshire.

53. Hugh B. Grigsby, *The Virginia Convention of 1776* (Richmond, 1855), p. 182.

54. AG to Joseph Nicholson, December 26, 1808, AG papers, New York Historical Society.

Chapter 19

1. M. B. Smith to S. B. Smith, February 26, March 4 and 5, 1809, in Gaillard Hunt, ed., *The First Forty Years of Washington Society* (New York, 1906), pp. 54–64; JM inaugural address, March 4, 1809, *Messages*, II, 451–3; C. F. Adams, ed., *The Memoirs of John Quincy Adams* (12 vols., Philadelphia, 1874–1877), March 4, 1809, I, 544; Brant, V, 12–15.

2. Diary of Frances Few, March 3, 1809, Georgia Department of Archives and History.

3. Katharine Anthony, *Dolly Madison, Her Life and Times* (Garden City, New York, 1949), pp. 198–201.

4. Brant, V, 31–2.

5. Journal of Mr. Dick, June 7, 1809, quoted in Brant, V, 33; Thomas Cruse to James Hamilton, January 2, 1810, University of Virginia Library.

6. Brant, V, 69–70.

7. Journal of M. B. Smith, August 4, 1809, in Hunt, ed., *First Forty Years*, pp. 81–3.

8. Richard Cutts to T. Cutts, March 9 and July 10, 1809, H. S. Burrage, ed., "Cutts Letters," *Maine Historical Society Collection*, IX (1898), 33–5; to TJ, August 3, 16, and 23, 1809, Cong. ed., II, 449–53; JM to DPM, August 7, 1809, Cutts, *Memoirs*, pp. 66–7; TJ to William Thornton, August 24, 1809, Thornton papers, LC; Smith journal, August 1, 1809, in Hunt, ed., *First Forty Years*, pp. 65–76.

9. Randolph to Monroe, January 1, 1809, Brant, V, 22–7; Raymond Walters, Jr., *Albert Gallatin, Jeffersonian Financier and Diplomat* (New York, 1957), pp. 221–6.

10. TJ to AG, October 11, 1809, *Writings of TJ*, IX, 264–5; AG to TJ, November 8, 1809, *Writings of AG*, I, 464–6, discussing the August conversations.

11. Philadelphia *Aurora*, February 11 and September 3, 1811, and Alexandria,

Virginia, *Gazette*, January 20, 1810, cited in Walters, *Gallatin*, pp. 243, 232, 241.

12. Brant, V, 52–4, 113, 129, 161–3; Randolph to Nicholson, March 1811, quoted in Adams, *Hist.*, V, 360.

13. Monroe to John Taylor, September 10, 1810, *Writings of Monroe*, V, 138; Monroe speech in Charlottesville, Virginia, printed in the Richmond *Enquirer*, April 10, 1810, quoted in Chap. 15 of a forthcoming *Monroe biography* by Harry Ammon, Randolph to J. M. Garnett, September 28, 1810, and Randolph diary, January 12, 1811, quoted in Brant, V, 166, 271.

14. From AG, *ca.* March 4, 1811, *Writings of AG*, I, 495–6.

15. Monroe to L. W. Tazewell, February 25, 1811, to Monroe, March 20 and 26, 1811, and from Monroe, March 23 and 29, 1811, *Writings of Monroe*, V, 177, 181–4; Brant, V, 270–87; Ammon, *Monroe*, Chap. 15.

16. Brant, V, 273–5.

17. Conversation in this and following two paragraphs reconstructed from JM, "Memorandum as to R. Smith, April 1811," written "whilst the circumstances are fresh in remembrance," but not printed until 1865, Cong. ed., II, 495–503, and from *Robert Smith's Address to the People of the United States*, printed in Philadelphia *Aurora*, June 26, 1811, in other newspapers, and as a separate pamphlet.

18. Robert to Samuel Smith, March 22, 23, 25, and 26, 1811, Samuel Smith papers, LC, quoted in Brant, V, 288–9; JM "Memorandum," to TJ, April 1, 1811, Cong. ed., II, 492, 503–6.

19. To TJ, July 8, 1811, Cong. ed., II, 513–14; Tucker to James Garnett, July 1811, from Hawkins, October 13, 1811, and from Rodney, August 24, 1811, all quoted in Brant, V, 302–6.

20. To Pinkney, March 17, 1809, Princeton University Library.

21. TJ to Walter Jones, March 5, 1810, *Writings of TJ*, IX, 274; Smith (Madison) to Pinkney and to Armstrong, March 15, 1809, *American State Papers, Foreign*, III, 250.

22. Canning to Erskine, January 23, 1809, in Bernard Mayo, ed., "Instructions to the British Ministers to the United States, 1791–1812," pp. 264–7.

23. AG to Erskine August 13, 1809, to AG, July 30, 1809, *Writings of AG*, I, 459, 456; Brant, V, 34–47; Bradford Perkins, *Prologue to War: England and the United States, 1805–1812* (Berkeley and Los Angeles, 1961), pp. 211–13.

24. *National Intelligencer*, April 24, 1809, Philadelphia *Gazette*, April 1809, *Annals of Congress*, May 26, 1809, all cited in Brant, V, 48–9; Rush to Granville Sharp, June 20, 1809, "The Correspondence of Rush and Sharp,' J. A. Woods, ed., *Journal of American Studies*, London, I (April 1967), 37.

25. King to Trumbull, April 24, 1809, cited in Perkins, *Prologue*, pp. 218–19; JM message, May 23, 1809, *Messages*, II, 453–6.

26. To TJ, April 24, May 5 and 30, June 12 and 20, 1809, Cong. ed., II, 439–44; Erskine to Smith, June 15, 1809, *American State Papers, Foreign*, III, 297.

27. To AG, July 28, 1809, *Writings of AG*, I, 454–5; to TJ, August 3 and 16, 1809, Cong. ed., II, 449–52; JM proclamation, August 9, 1809, *Messages*, II, 458.

28. From George Joy, May 24, 1809, MPLC, cited in Brant, V, 72; Canning to F. J. Jackson, Mayo, ed., "Instructions," p. 284; Perkins, *Prologue*, pp. 212–18.

29. AG to John Montgomery, July 27, 1809, quoted in Perkins, *Prologue*, p. 219.
30. Jackson to his mother, October 7, 1809, Lady Jackson to George Jackson, November 21, 1809, Jackson to George Jackson, October 24, 1809, in Lady Jackson, ed., *The Bath Archives: A Further Selection from the Diaries and Letters of Sir George Jackson* (2 vols., London, 1873), I, 17, 20, 26, 57.
31. Smith (Madison) to Jackson, October 19, November 1 and 8, 1809, quoted in Adams, *Hist.*, V, 127–32; Jackson to G. Jackson, October 26, 1809, Lady Jackson to G. Jackson, November 21, 1809, and Jackson to Canning, October 24, 1809, *Bath Archives*, I, 28, 57–9.
32. To Pinkney, October 23, 1809, Princeton University Library.
33. To Pinkney, January 1, 1810, Cong. ed., II, 468; annual message, November 29, 1809, *Messages*, II, 458–60; Adams, *Hist.*, V, 163–75; AG to TJ, November 8, 1809, *Writings of AG*, I, 465–6.
34. JM message, January 3, 1810, *Messages*, II, 463–4; *Annals of Congress*, January 23, 1810, to Pinkney, January 20, 1810, and "Smith Memo," April 1811, Cong. ed., II, 468–9, 498; Jackson to George Jackson, January 10, 1810, and Jackson diary, May 5, 1810, *Bath Archives*, I, 116–17, 78–9.
35. New York *Evening Post*, April 11, 1810, quoted in Brant, V, 137; to TJ, April 23, 1810, and to Pinkney, May 23, 1810, Cong. ed., II, 473–6; London *Sun*, October 9, 1810, and James Hamilton to Jackson, May 21, 1810, quoted in Perkins, *Prologue*, pp. 243–4.
36. Perkins, *Prologue*, pp. 237–8, 244–5; to TJ, May 25, 1810, Cong. ed., II, 478; John Randolph ("Mucius"), in Richmond *Spirit of '76*, January 12, 1810, Brant, V, 131, 148–50.
37. To TJ, May 7, 1810, Cong. ed., II, 474; to TJ to Walter Jones, March 5, 1810, *Writings of TJ*, IX, 274; Brant, V, 142 and 157, quoting *National Intelligencer*, July 6, 1810.
38. To TJ, June 22, 1810, Hunt, VIII, 103; Brant, V, 173–6.
39. To TJ, October 19, 1810, and to H. Toulmin, September 10, 1810, Cong. ed., II, 485, 483; to AG, August 22, 1810, *Writings of AG*, I, 485; Thomas P. Abernethy, *The South in the New Nation, 1789–1819* (Baton Rouge, 1961), pp. 332–3.
40. To TJ, October 19, 1810, Cong. ed., II, 485; John Rhea to D. Holmes, September 26, 1810, quoted in Brant, V, 184, 239–43; JM proclamation, October 27, 1810 and message, January 3, 1811, *Messages*, II, 465–7, 473.
41. To Pinkney, October 30, 1810, Hunt, VIII, 121–2.
42. Cadore to Armstrong, August 5, 1810, *American State Papers, Foreign*, III, 386; to TJ, October 19, 1810, Hunt, VIII, 109.
43. Wellesley to Pinkney, August 31, 1810, cited in Brant, V, 194–9; Pinkney to JM, September 13, 1810, Henry Wheaton, *Some Account of the Life, Writings, and Speeches of William Pinkney* (New York, 1826), pp. 444–8.
44. To Armstrong, October 29, 1810, and to Pinkney, October 30, 1810, Hunt, VIII, 114–20; from TJ, October 15, 1810, *Writings of TJ*, IX, 282; William Lee and Joel Barlow, "Review of Robert Smith's Address," *National Intelligencer*, July 1811, quoted in Adams, *Hist.*, V, 301–2; JM proclamation, November 2, 1810, *Messages*, II, 466–7.
45. To C. A. Rodney, September 30, 1810, Rodney mss., LC, quoted in Perkins, *Prologue*, p. 251; TJ to William Duane, November 13, 1810, *Writings of TJ*, IX, 287; J. P. Morier to Wellesley, October 26, 1810,

quoted in Brant, V, 200–201; L.-M. Turreau to Cadore, November 1, 1810, quoted in Adams, *Hist.*, V, 302–3.

46. Napoleon to Montalivet, June 25, 1810, and to Cadore, August 2, 1810, quoted in Adams, *Hist.*, V, 244–5, 253; Cadore to Turreau, August 23, 1810, quoted in Perkins, *Prologue*, pp. 246–7; Short to TJ, June 19, 1810, *Massachusetts Historical Society Collections*, I (1900), 141.

47. Cadore to Napoleon, August 1810, quoted in Adams, *Hist.*, V, 260; Brant, V, 209–21.

48. Baltimore *Federal Republican*, December 8, 1810, and February 7, 1811, quoted in Brant, V, 227, 254; Adams, *Hist.*, V, 338–57; to C. J. Ingersoll, June 29, 1831, Cong. ed., IV, 186; Walters, *Gallatin*, pp. 237–40.

49. Adams, *Hist.*, V, 357–8; Irving to W. P. Van Ness, February 20, 1811, Parke-Bernet (New York) *Catalogue*, No. 1943, January 19–20, 1960, item 283.

50. To TJ, June 7, 1811, Cong. ed., II, 509–13; Sérurier to Cadore, May 25, 1811, *National Intelligencer*, May 28 and 30, 1811, and June 6, 1811, quoted in Brant, V, 320; Adams, *Hist.*, VI, 25–7; Perkins, *Prologue*, pp. 271–3.

51. Sérurier to Cadore, March–April 1811, Brant, V, 311, 328–36.

52. Sérurier to Bassano (Cadore's new title), July 20, 1811, quoted in Adams, *Hist.*, VI, 61–2 and Brant, V, 336; DPM to the Barlows, November 15, 1811, Cutts, *Memoirs*, p. 81.

53. Roger Brown, *1812: The Republic in Peril* (New York, 1964), pp. 30–31; Clay to C. A. Rodney, August 17, 1811, Hopkins *PC*, I, 574; from H. Lee, August 19, 1811, MPLC, quoted in Perkins, *Prologue*, p. 295, 261–7; Norman K. Risjord, "1812: Conservatives, War Hawks, and the Nation's Honor," *WMQ*, XVIII (1961), 196–210; John A. Harper to W. Plumer, December 2, 1811, quoted in Bernard Mayo, *Henry Clay, Spokesman for the West* (Boston, 1937), p. 424.

54. AG, memo on message of November 5, 1811, quoted in Brant, V, 361–3; JM message, November 5, 1811, *Messages*, II, 476–81.

55. W. Plumer to I. Hill, November 13, 1811, B. Rush to Monroe, November 8, 1811, TJ to A. Stuart, November 14, 1811, A. Jackson, divisional orders, November 28, 1811, Baltimore *Federal Republican*, November 7, 1811, Sérurier to Bassano, November 5 and 11, 1811, all quoted in Brant, V, 359–61; Foster to Wellesley, November 21 and 25, 1811, Adams, *Hist.*, VI, 130–31.

56. To Barlow, November 17, 1811, Hunt, VIII, 168–70.

57. DPM to the Barlows, November 15, 1811, Cutts, *Memoirs*, pp. 81–3; Jonathan Roberts, to M. Roberts, November 17 and 25, 1811, HSP.

58. Cutts, *Memoirs*, pp. 72–3; M. C. Yarborough, ed., *The Reminiscences of William C. Preston* (Chapel Hill, 1933), pp. 7–8; from Clay, November 1811, Hopkins *PC*, I, 594.

59. Anthony, *Dolly Madison*, pp. 204–7.

60. *Annals of Congress*, November 29, 1811.

61. *Ibid.*, December 10–19, 1811; Adams, Hist., VI, 136–47; Mayo, *Clay*, pp. 411–16; Norman K. Risjord, *The Old Republicans: Southern Conservatism in the Age of Jefferson* (New York, 1965), pp. 129–33; Charles M. Wiltse, *John C. Calhoun, Nationalist* (Indianapolis, 1944), pp. 56–9; DPM to Anna Cutts, December 20, 1811, Cutts, *Memoirs*, pp. 73–4; Foster to Wellesley, November 21 and 23, 1811, and February 2, 1812, quoted in Ammon, *Monroe*, Chap. XVI.

62. JM message, December 23, 1811, *Messages*, II, 482; Foster to Wellesley,

December 21, 1811, quoted in Brant, II, 383; W. A. Christian, *Richmond, Her Past and Present* (Richmond, 1912), pp. 76–9.

63. Sérurier to Bassano, January 2, 1812, quoted in Brant, V, 398–9; Monroe to John Taylor, June 13, 1812, *Writings of Monroe*, V, 206–9.

64. Paul Hamilton to L. Cheves, December 3, 1811, quoted in Brant, V, 517; Samuel Taggart to J. Taylor, January 22, 1812, *Proceedings of the American Antiquarian Society*, XXXIII, 379; *Annals of Congress*, January 16, 22, and 27, 1812.

65. To TJ, February 7, 1812, Hunt, VIII, 175–6; from TJ, February 19, 1812, *Writings of TJ*, IX, 337.

66. London *Courier*, December 5, 1811, quoted in Philadelphia *Aurora*, May 12, 1812, and elsewhere, Mayo, *Clay*, pp. 422, 468; to TJ, February 7, 1812, Hunt, VIII, 176–7; R. Rush to John Binns, February 1812, and to C. J. Ingersoll, February 26 and March 15, 1812, HSP.

67. AG to E. Bacon, January 10, 1812, and AG to TJ, March 10, 1812, *Writings of AG*, I, 501–17; Walters, *Gallatin*, pp. 245–7; Adams, *Hist.*, VI, 165–8; Mayo, *Clay*, pp. 450–54; *Annals of Congress*, March 2, 1812; to TJ, March 6, 1812, Hunt, VIII, 182.

68. To R. Cutts, February 25, 1812, Cutts, *Memoirs*, p. 75; Brant, V, 412–20; Adams, *Hist.*, VI, 176–86; JM message, March 9, 1812, *Messages*, II, 483.

69. *National Intelligencer*, March 10, 1812, quoted in Brant, V, 414; Rush to Ingersoll, March 12, 1812, HSP; Sérurier to Maret, March 23, 1812, quoted in Adams, *Hist.*, VI, 194; to TJ, March 9, 1812, Cong. ed., II, 530.

70. R. B. Davis, ed., *Jeffersonian America, Notes on the United States of America Collected in the Years 1805-6-7 and 11-12 by Sir Augustus John Foster, Bart.* (San Marino, California, 1954), pp. 60–88.

71. *Ibid.*, pp. 72–3; Foster diary, January 30, 1812, quoted in Brant, V, 412; DPM to Anna Cutts, March 20 and 27, 1812, Cutts, *Memoirs*, pp. 76–7.

72. *Ibid.*, Phoebe Morris to A. Morris, March 22, 1812, quoted in Anthony, *Dolly Madison*, pp. 207–8; DPM to Ruth Barlow, April 19, 1812, Huntington Library.

73. Lucy Todd to DPM, April 18 and May 29, 1812, papers of Mr. and Mrs. George B. Cutts, Brookline, Massachusetts.

74. Davis, ed., *Notes by Foster*, pp. 94–6, 183; Adams, ed., *Memoirs of John Quincy Adams*, January 15, 1806, I, 385.

75. DPM to Anna Cutts, March 27, April, and May 12, 1812, Cutts, *Memoirs*, pp. 77–9; Crawford to J. Milledge, May 12, 1812, quoted in Brant, V, 437–8.

76. Leonard D. White, *The Jeffersonians* (New York, 1951), p. 215; to R. Cutts, February 25, 1812, Cutts, *Memoirs*, pp. 76–7; Mayo, *Clay*, p. 447; Crawford to Monroe, September 27, 1812, quoted in Adams, *Hist.*, VI, 395; Glenn Tucker, *Poltroons and Patriots, a Popular Account of the War of 1812* (2 vols., Indianapolis, 1954), I, 145–8.

77. Macon to J. Nicholson, March 25, 1812, quoted in Adams, *Hist.*, VI, 290; White, *Jeffersonians*, pp. 269–70.

78. AG to J. H. Nicholson, May 21, 1812, *Writings of AG*, I, 518; DPM to the Barlows, *ca.* May 19, 1812, Cutts, *Memoirs*, p. 87; Brant, V, 452–8; Mayo, *Clay*, pp. 484–6; Risjord, *Old Republicans*, pp. 148–9; Adams, *Hist.*, VI, 209–10.

79. Wellesley to Foster, January 28, 1812, quoted in Adams, *Hist.*, VI, 191–2; to TJ, April 3, 1812, Cong. ed., II, 531.

80. Sérurier to Bassano, March 23, 1812, Macon to Nicholson, March 25,

1812, quoted in Adams, *Hist.*, VI, 194–6; *National Intelligencer*, March 24, 1812, quoted in Brant, V, 425; DPM to Anna Cutts, March 27, 1812, Cutts, *Memoirs*, p. 77.

81. Brant, V, 416, 426–36; to TJ, April 24, 1812, Cong. ed., II, 532–4; Rush to Ingersoll, April 29, 1812, HSP; *National Intelligencer*, April 14, 1812; DPM to the Barlows, *ca.* April 19, 1812, Cutts, *Memoirs*, pp. 86–7.

82. Foster diary, April 17, 1812, John Sevier to G. W. Sevier, April 26, 1812, quoted in Mayo, *Clay*, pp. 505–6; Adams, *Hist.*, VI, 211; Brant, V, 462–3; Hansard, XXII, 413, and Boston *Independent Chronicle*, May 25, 1812, quoted in Perkins, *Prologue*, p. 318; DPM to Anna Cutts, May 12, 1812, and to Ruth Barlow, *ca.* April 19, 1812, Cutts, *Memoirs*, pp. 79, 88.

83. Sérurier to Bassano, May 27, 1812, and Castlereagh to Foster, April 10, 1812, quoted in Adams, *Hist.*, VI, 215–21; Rush to Ingersoll, May 24, 1812, HSP.

84. To TJ, May 25, 1812, Cong. ed., II, 535.

85. Clay to W. Worsley, May 24, to ——, May 27, and to J. J. Crittenden, May 28, 1812, Hopkins *PC*, I, 657–60; Brant, V, 469.

86. DPM to Anna Cutts, May 29, 1812, Cutts, *Memoirs*, p. 79; *Annals of Congress*, May 29, 1812; Philadelphia *Democratic Press*, June 2, 1812, quoted in Mayo, *Clay*, p. 519n.

87. Adams, *Hist.*, VI, 221; JM message, June 1, 1812, *Messages*, II, 484–90; Macon to J. H. Nicholson, June 2, 1812, quoted in Perkins, *Prologue*, p. 406; Wiltse, *Calhoun, Nationalist*, p. 64; Mayo, *Clay*, p. 520; Brant, V, 472–3, presents plausible evidence that Monroe helped draft the committee report.

88. Foster diary, June 3, 1812, quoted in Brant, V, 474–5; C. C. Moore to Mrs. Moore, June 4, 1812, Museum of the City of New York; Brant, VI, 73.

89. Jonathan Roberts to M. Roberts, June 17, 1812, HSP; Foster diary, June 17, 1812, quoted in Perkins, *Prologue*, pp. 410–15 and Brant, V, 474–8; Rush to Ingersoll, June 9 and 15, 1812, HSP; JM proclamation, June 19, 1812, *Messages*, II, 497–8.

90. To Henry Wheaton, February 26, 1827, Cong. ed., III, 554; Monroe to Taylor, June 13, 1812, *Writings of Monroe*, V, 205–6.

91. Coles to W. C. Rives, January 21, 1856, *WMQ*, 2nd series, VII, 163; Brant, V, 479–81.

92. Rush to Ingersoll, April 12 and 29, 1812, HSP.

93. To H. Wheaton, February 26, 1827, Cong. ed., III, 555.

94. *Ibid.*, 556–7.

95. To Henry Lee, February 1827, Cong. ed., III, 561–3; Calhoun to James McBride, April 4 and December 25, 1812, R. L. Meriwether and others, eds., *The Papers of John C. Calhoun* (Vol. I, Columbia, South Carolina, 1959), pp. 99–100, 146.

96. Connecticut *Courant*, June 30, 1812, London *Independent Chronicle*, July 16, 1812, quoted in Perkins, *Prologue*, pp. 420, 436–7; Roberts memoirs, HSP.

97. JM annual message, November 4, 1812, *Messages*, II, 505.

Chapter 20

1. Rush to C. J. Ingersoll, June 18 and July 17, 1812, HSP; and to B. Rush, August 1812, quoted in John H. Powell, *Richard Rush, Republican Diplomat* (Philadelphia, 1942), p. 38; Monroe to AG, June 1, 1812, from

AG, June 21, 1812, *Writings of AG*, I, 520–21; Brant, VI, 36–52; Glenn Tucker, *Poltroons and Patriots, a Popular Account of the War of 1812* (2 vols., Indianapolis, 1954), I, 151–7.

2. Foster notes, June 23, 1812, Monroe to J. Russell, June 26, 1812, quoted in Brant, VI, 33–4.

3. Editorial identified and quoted in Brant, VI, 60; to Barlow, August 11, 1812, Cong. ed., II, 541.

4. To TJ, June 22, 1812, Cong. ed., II, 536; Rush to Ingersoll, July 23, 1812, HSP; M. Chittenden to J. Hubbard, June 23, 1812, quoted in Roger Brown, *1812: The Republic in Peril* (New York, 1964), pp. 171–2.

5. "Address of the Minority," *Annals of Congress*, July 1, 1812; proclamation of Strong, June 26, 1812, sermons of David Osgood of Medford, Massachusetts, and of the rector of Trinity Church, Boston, John Lowell, *Mr. Madison's War*, serialized in Boston *Evening Post*, July 31–August 10, 1812, all quoted in Brant, VI, 24–31; Pickering to E. Pennington, July 12, 1812, Henry Adams, ed., *Documents Relating to New England Federalism* (Boston, 1877), p. 389.

6. Adams, *Hist.*, VI, 400–401; to TJ, August 17, 1812, Cong. ed., II, 542.

7. To Spring, September 6, 1812, Cong. ed., II, 544–5.

8. Adams, *Hist.*, VI, 304–11; to Dearborn, August 9, 1812, Cong. ed., II, 540–42.

9. Dearborn to Eustis, August 7, 9, and 15, 1812, from Dearborn, August 15, 1812, Eustis to Dearborn, August 15, 1812, cited in Adams, *Hist.*, VI, 321–4, 337–41.

10. To Dearborn, August 9, 1812, and to TJ, August 17, 1812, Cong. ed., II, 540–44; Nelly C. Willis to DPM, July 14, 1812, Argosy Book Store *Catalogue*, 1958, p. 24; Rush to Ingersoll, August 19, 1812, HSP; DPM to Phoebe Morris, August 12, 1812, DPM papers, LC; *National Intelligencer*, August 8, 1812, quoted in Brant, VI, 68–70.

11. Monroe to Russell, August 21, 1812, Baker to Castlereagh, August 20, 1812, quoted in Brant, VI, 70–72; Rush to Ingersoll, August 19, 1812, HSP.

12. Adams, *Hist.*, VI, 312–41; James G. Forbes, *Report of the Trial of Brigadier General William Hull* (New York, 1814), pp. 36–108.

13. To Dearborn, October 7, 1812, Cong. ed., II, 547; Rush to Adams, June 6, 1813, *PMHB*, LX (1936), 437, Adams to M. Carey, July 7, 1813, quoted in Brant, VI, 72–5, 88.

14. Rush to Ingersoll, August 29, 1812, HSP; from TJ, November 6, 1812, *Writings of TJ*, IX, 370.

15. Harrison to Clay, August 29, 1812, Clay to Monroe, August 25 and September 21, 1812, Hopkins *PC*, I, 720, 723, 729; Monroe to Clay, September 17, 1812, *Writings of Monroe*, V, 222–3; Rush to Ingersoll, September 4, 1812, HSP.

16. To Monroe, September 5, 1812, from Rush, September 4, 1812, and Monroe to Clay, September 17, 1812, all quoted in Brant, VI, 82–5.

17. Van Rensselaer to Daniel Tompkins, August 31, 1812, Dearborn to Van Rensselaer, September 2 and 26, 1812, quoted in Adams, *Hist.*, VI, 342–5.

18. To Henry Lee, February 1827, Cong. ed., III, 562; London *Times*, January 12, 1813, from Dearborn, December 13, 1812, in Adams, *Hist.*, VI, 336–61; Tucker, *Poltroons and Patriots*, I, 179–205; Brant, VI, 84–95.

19. To TJ, October 14, 1812, Cong. ed., II, 549; Harrison to Eustis, October 22, 1812, and Harrison to Monroe, December 12, 1812, quoted in Adams, *Hist.*, VI, 78–83.

20. To TJ, October 14, 1812, Cong. ed., II, 549–50; Adams, *Hist.*, VI, 410;

Brant, VI, 99–113; Robert Ernst, *Rufus King, American Federalist*
(Chapel Hill, 1968), pp. 314–20.

21. AG to TJ, December 18, 1812, AG memo to JM, October 1812, from
AG, October 11, 1812, *Writings of AG*, I, 526–31; from AG, January 4
and 7, 1812, quoted in Brant, VI, 127; Raymond Walters, Jr., *Albert
Gallatin, Jeffersonian Financier and Diplomat* (New York, 1957), pp.
252–3; JM, review of statement attributed to General John Armstrong,
February 1824, Cong. ed., III, 384.

22. Sérurier to Bassano, January 8, 1813, quoted in Brant, VI, 126; to Henry
Lee, February 1827, Cong. ed., III, 563; Rush to Ingersoll, January 13,
1813, HSP.

23. Lowndes to T. Pinckney, December 13, 1812, Josiah Quincy in House of
Representatives, November 20, 1812, quoted in Brant, VI, 130; Rush to
Ingersoll, October 18 and November 17, 1812, HSP; JM annual message, November 4, 1812, *Messages*, II, 499–506; JM's amended draft is
owned by Mr. Ralph W. Earle of Philadelphia, and AG's statement is
in *Writings of AG*, I, 528–9.

24. Brant, VI, 130–37, 148; Adams, *Hist.*, 435–49; Ammon, *Monroe* ms., chap.
VII.

25. Brant, VI, 165–7.

26. From AG, March 5, 1813, *Writings of AG*, I, 532.

27. Adams, *Hist.*, VI, 379–87; JM message, February 22, 1813, *Messages*, II,
507; Rush to Ingersoll, February 20, 1813, HSP.

28. Adams, *Hist.*, VII, 1–11.

29. J. Q. Adams to John Adams, August 16, 1812, quoted in Samuel F. Bemis,
John Quincy Adams and the Foundations of American Foreign Policy
(New York, 1956), p. 177; to TJ, January 27 and March 10, 1813, to
Henry Wheaton, February 26, 1827, Cong. ed., II, 557–9, III, 555.

30. Rush to Ingersoll, March 17, 1813, HSP; Brant, VI, 155–6; to John Nicholas, April 2, 1813, and to TJ, March 10, 1813, Cong. ed., II, 558–63.

31. James S. Young, *The Washington Community, 1800–1829* (New York,
1966), pp. 30–31; Ralph Ketcham, "The Dictates of Conscience: Edward Coles and Slavery," *The Virginia Quarterly Review*, XXXVI
(1960), 47–52, quoting Cole's autobiographical letter of April 1844 in
HSP.

32. Brant, VI, 161–2; Walters, *Gallatin*, pp. 258–61.

33. Ralph Ketcham, "Uncle James Madison and Dickinson College," in C. C.
Sellers, ed., *Early Dickinsoniana* (Carlisle, Pennsylvania, 1961), pp. 169–
89.

34. *National Intelligencer*, November 28, 1812, December 10, 1812, and Jan-
uary 18, 1813, quoted in Brant, VI, 122–5; Katharine Anthony, *Dolly
Madison, Her Life and Times* (Garden City, New York, 1949), p. 239;
Preston, *Reminiscences*, p. 8; M. B. Smith to Mrs. Kirkpatrick, March
13, 1814, in Gaillard Hunt, ed., *The First Forty Years of Washington
Society* (New York, 1906), p. 97; memoir by Mary Cutts, owned by
George B. Cutts, Brookline, Massachusetts.

35. Hunt, ed., *First Forty Years*, pp. 96–7.

36. Clay speech, January 8 and 9, 1813, Hopkins *PC*, I, 754–74; Rush to Ingersoll, December 1, 1812, HSP; John Harper to W. Plumer, January 8,
1813, quoted in Brant, VI, 134.

37. JM address, March 4, 1813, *Messages*, II, 509–11; Sérurier to Bassano,
March 9, 1813, *National Intelligencer*, March 6, 1813, *U.S. Gazette*
(Philadelphia), March 10, 1813, quoted in Brant, III, 149–51.

38. From AG, March 5 and April 17, 1813, and Treasury Department letter, April 17, 1813, *Writings of AG*, I, 532–38; Walters, *Gallatin*, pp. 256–8.
39. Rush to John Adams, June 6, 1813, *PMHB*, LX (1936), 437; Brant, VI, 158–63; Walters, *Gallatin*, pp. 258–61.
40. Harry L. Coles, *The War of 1812* (Chicago, 1965), pp. 107–44; Brant, VI, 104–77.
41. Coles, *War of 1812*, pp. 88–92.
42. DPM to Edward Coles, May 12, 1813, Cutts, *Memoirs*, pp. 90–91.
43. Brant, VI, 178–80; Adams, *Hist.*, VII, 48–53.
44. JM message, May 25, 1813, *Messages*, II, 511–15; Adams, *Hist.*, VII, 53–5; Brant, VI, 196–7.
45. Adams, *Hist.*, VII, 55–60; Brant, VI, 182–4.
46. Webster to E. Cutts, May 25, 1813, and to C. March, June 19, 24, and 29, 1813, Webster and March papers, New Hampshire Historical Society. Concord, New Hampshire.
47. Monroe to TJ, June 28, 1813, *Writings of Monroe*, V, 271–3.
48. Sérurier to Bassano, June 21, 1813, quoted in Brant, VI, 184; *Annals of Congress*, June 21, 1813; Adams to R. Rush, September 6, 1813, *PMHB*, LX (1936), 449.
49. New York *Evening Post*, June 22, 1813, Georgetown *Federal Republican*, June 30, 1813, quoted in Brant, VI, 184–8; *Maryland Gazette*, July 16, 1813, quoted in Charles R. King, *The Life and Correspondence of Rufus King* (6 vols., Boston, 1894–1900), V, 321; John Lovett to Solomon Van Rensselaer, June 22, 1813, quoted in Robert Ernst, *Rufus King, American Federalist* (Chapel Hill, 1968), p. 323; Monroe to TJ, June 28, 1813, *Writings of Monroe*, V, 272–3.
50. DPM to E. Coles, July 2, 1813, Cutts, *Memoirs*, p. 93; E. Gerry, Jr., diary, July 13, 1813, and John Adams to W. Cranch, July 8, 1813, quoted in Brant, VI, 188; DPM to Hannah Gallatin, July 29, 1813, New York Historical Society; Rush to Adams, August 2, 1813, and Adams to Rush, August 11, 1813, *PMHB*, LX (1936), 442–5; to AG, August 2, 1813, Cong. ed., II, 569.
51. From Jones, July 15, 1813, MPLC; Jones to A. J. Dallas, July 19, 1813, quoted in Brant, VI, 206–7; M. B. Smith to Mrs. Kirkpatrick, July 20, 1813, in Hunt, ed., *First Forty Years*, pp. 89–91.
52. JM note to Senate, July 6, 1813, Hunt, VIII, 250–51; Adams, *Hist.*, VII, 59–60; Rush to Ingersoll, September 18, 1812, HSP.
53. DPM to Hannah Gallatin, July 29, 1813, New York Historical Society; to AG, August 2, 1813, Hunt, VIII, 252–6; Walters, *Gallatin*, pp. 269–72.
54. Monroe to TJ, June 7, 1813, *Writings of Monroe*, V, 266–7; Coles, *War of 1812*, pp. 84–6.
55. DPM to H. Gallatin, August 30, 1813, New York Historical Society; Brant, VI, 214–19; Coles, *War of 1812*, pp. 130–35.
56. Rush to Ingersoll, October 20, 1813, HSP; Adams to Rush, October 8, 1813, *PMHB*, LX (1936), 453–4.
57. Brant, VI, 221–6; Coles, *War of 1812*, pp. 143–8.
58. To D. Tompkins, January 25, 1814, Cong. ed., II, 580; Rush to Adams, December 31, 1813, Adams to Rush, January 7, 1814, *PMHB*, LXI (1937), 33–6; Powell, *Rush*, p. 44.
59. JM message, December 7, 1813, *Messages*, II, 519–25.
60. Morris to King, December 27, 1813, King, ed., *Life and Correspondence*, V, 357–61; Calhoun speech, January 15, 1814, in R. L. Meriwether and

others, eds., *The Papers of John C. Calhoun* (Vol. I, Columbia, South Carolina, 1959), p. 196.

61. Brant, VI, 228–37; Adams, *Hist.*, VII, 367–90.
62. A. Baring to AG, July 22, 1813, *Writings of AG*, I, 546–8; Brant, VI, 238–9.
63. Castlereagh to Monroe, November 4, 1813, Monroe to Castlereagh, January 5, 1814, quoted in Brant, VI, 239; Clay toast, January 28, 1814, Hopkins *PC*, I, 855.
64. Powell, *Rush*, pp. 46–9; Adams, *Hist.*, VII, 396–9.
65. H. Gallatin to DPM, January 14, 1814, University of Virginia Library; DPM to H. Gallatin, January 21, 1814, New York Historical Society; TJ to Granger, March 9, 1814, and from TJ, March 10, 1814, *Writings of TJ*, IX, 454–60.
66. Macon to Nicholson, February 17, 1814, in Adams, *Hist.*, VII, 399; King notes on conversation with Armstrong, February 25, 1814, King, ed., *Life and Correspondence*, V, 371; from Monroe, December 1813, *Writings of Monroe*, V, 276–7; Brant, VI, 243–5.
67. Brant, VI, 252–61.
68. To G. W. Campbell, May 7 and 25, 1814, Hunt, VIII, 276–9; to TJ, May 10, 1814, Cong. ed., II, 582–3; DPM to H. Gallatin, May 22, 1814, New York Historical Society; AG to Clay, April 22, 1814, and to W. H. Crawford, April 21, 1814, *Writings of AG*, I, 602–7.
69. JM cabinet memo, June 7, 1814, Hunt, VIII, 279–80; Adams, *Hist.*, VIII, 24–61.
70. To James Barbour, June 16, 1814, Cong. ed., II, 583–4.
71. AG and J. Bayard to Monroe, May 6, 1814, *Writings of AG*, I, 611–13; JM cabinet memos, June 23, 24, and 27, 1814, Hunt, VIII, 280–81; Sérurier to LeForest, June 27, 1814, quoted in Brant, VI, 268–9.

Chapter 21

1. DPM to H. Gallatin, July 28, 1814, New York Historical Society; Brant, VI, 275–89.
2. To Armstrong, August 13, 1814, in JM, "Review of a Statement Attributed to Gen. John Armstrong," 1824, Cong. ed., III, 373–419; Brant, VI, 260–61, 280–83; Ammon, *Monroe* ms., Chap. XVIII.
3. To Armstrong, May 20, 1814 (italics added), JM cabinet memo, July 1, 1814, Cong. ed., III, 399, 409; Brant, VI, 270–72.
4. Sérurier to Talleyrand, August 9, 1814, and from J. S. Skinner, August 13, 1814, quoted in Brant, VI, 284–9; Harry L. Coles, *The War of 1812* (Chicago, 1965), pp. 171–4.
5. DPM to H. Gallatin, August 17, 1814, New York Historical Society; Brant VI, 290–93; to Monroe, August 21, 1814, Hunt, VIII, 291.
6. DPM to Lucy Todd, August 23, 1814, Cutts, *Memoirs*, pp. 108–9; to DPM, August 23, 1814, Hunt, VIII, 293–4; Brant, VI, 293–7; Coles, *War of 1812*, pp. 175–6.
7. JM memo, August 24, 1814, Hunt, VIII, 294–7; Adams, *Hist.*, VIII, 137–44; Brant, VI, 298–302.
8. DPM to Lucy Todd, August 24, 1814, Cutts, *Memoirs*, pp. 109–11; DPM to Mrs. Latrobe, December 3, 1814, and Elbridge Gerry, Jr., diary, July 1, 1813, quoted in Katharine Anthony, *Dolly Madison, Her Life and Times* (Garden City, New York, 1949), pp. 215, 230; M. B. Smith to Mrs. Kirkpatrick, August 30, 1814, Gaillard Hunt, ed., *The First*

Forty Years of Washington Society (New York, 1906), pp. 111–12; Sérurier to Talleyrand, August 27, 1814, in Brant, VI, 302–6; Rush to J. S. Williams, July 10, 1855, in J. S. Williams, *History of the Invasion and Capture of Washington* (New York, 1857), pp. 274–5; J. W. Taylor to Mrs. Taylor, October 8, 1814, New York Historical Society, quoted in George Dangerfield, *The Awakening of American Nationalism, 1815–1828* (New York, 1965), p. 5n.

9. To Monroe, August 26, 1814, and to DPM, August 27, 1814, Hunt, VIII, 298–300; M. B. Smith to Mrs. Kirkpatrick, August 1814, Hunt, ed., *First Forty Years*, p. 107; to Jones, August 27 (HSP), and Jones memo of events of August 24, 1814 (HSP), Anne Thornton diary, August 28, 1814 (LC), Mordecai Booth report, September 10, 1814 (University of Indiana Library), all cited in Brant, VI, 304–10, which gives an accurate account of the Madisons' travels after leaving Washington, as does Charles G. Muller, *The Darkest Day: 1814* (Philadelphia, 1963).

10. Hunt, ed., *First Forty Years*, pp. 111, 113; to DPM, August 28, 1814, quoted in Anthony, *Dolley Madison*, p. 228.

11. Hunt, ed., *First Forty Years*, p. 110; Anne Thornton diary, August 28 and 29, 1814 (LC), Monroe memo on destruction of Washington (LC), J. Barnes to TJ, August 29, 1814 (University of Virginia Library), all cited in Brant, VI, 310–12.

12. JM memo, August 29, 1814, Hunt, VIII, 300–304.

13. Adams, *Hist.*, VIII, 153, 151; from Monroe, December 1813, *Writings of Monroe*, V, 276; Leonard D. White, *The Jeffersonians* (New York, 1951), pp. 220–23.

14. TJ to Monroe, January 1, 1815, *Writings of TJ*, IX, 498.

15. Brant, VI, 330–32, details instances of Monroe's "doctoring" of his papers, while Ammon, *Monroe*, Chap. XVIII, denies any dishonorable tampering.

16. King memo on "The Administration," 1814, Charles R. King, ed., *The Life and Correspondence of Rufus King* (6 vols., Boston, 1894–1900), V, 449; Monroe to TJ, December 21, 1814, *Writings of Monroe*, V, 303; Jones to A. J. Dallas, September 15, 1814 (HSP), quoted in Brant, VI, 329.

17. Rush to Ingersoll, March 28, 1812, HSP.

18. JM proclamation, September 1, 1814, *Messages*, II, 530–31; Brant, VI, 323; King to J. Mason, September 2, and to G. Morris, October 14, 1814, King, ed., *Life and Correspondence*, V, 414–15, 422.

19. Brant, VI, 324–6; Glenn Tucker, *Poltroons and Patriots, a Popular Account of the War of 1812* (2 vols., Indianapolis, 1954), II, 635–9.

20. JM message, September 20, 1814, *Messages*, II, 532–6.

21. Jones to A. J. Dallas, September 25, 1814 (HSP), quoted in Brant, VI, 327; King to G. Morris, October 13, 1814, King, ed., *Life and Correspondence*, V, 417–19.

22. Morris to King, November 1, 1814, King, ed., *Life and Correspondence*, V, 433; A. J. Dallas to House Committee on Ways and Means, October 17, 1814, G. M. Dallas, ed., *Life and Writings of Alexander James Dallas* (Philadelphia, 1871), pp. 234–5; to TJ, October 23, 1814, Cong. ed., II, 590–91; Adams, *Hist.*, VIII, 240–43.

23. Brant, VI, 329–33, 346; to Henry Lee, February 1827, Cong. ed., III, 563–4.

24. London *Courier*, January 27, 1814, and *Times*, May 24, 1814, quoted in Adams, *Hist.*, IX, 4–5; AG to Monroe, June 13 and 20, 1814, *Writings of AG*, I, 627–33.

25. Monroe to commissioners, October 4, 1814, in Brant, VI, 333–4; American commissioners to British commissioners, August 25, 1814, in Raymond Walters, Jr., *Albert Gallatin, Jeffersonian Financier and Diplomat* (New York, 1957), pp. 278–9; Samuel F. Bemis, *John Quincy Adams and the Foundations of American Foreign Policy* (New York, 1949), 208–10; AG to Monroe, August 20, 1814, *Writings of AG*, I, 637–9.

26. Rush to J. Adams, October 23, 1814, *PMHB*, LXI (1937), 41–3; to TJ, October 10 and 23, 1814, Cong. ed., II, 588–91.

27. King memo of October 1814 meeting, Morris to King, October 18, 1814, and November 1, 1814, King, ed., *Life and Correspondence*, V, 422–33; Robert Ernst, *Rufus King, American Federalist* (Chapel Hill, 1968), pp. 337–8.

28. Adams, *Hist.*, VIII, 287–92; Wirt to Mrs. Wirt, October 14, 1814, Maryland Historical Society; Sérurier to Talleyrand, November 5, 1814, Monroe to Jesup, November 26, 1814, quoted in Brant, VI, 346–7, 359.

29. Brown and Ives to John Wheaton, November 29, 1814, J. C. Brown Library; Winchester, Virginia, *Gazette*, December 1814, and *Annals of Congress*, December 2–9, 1814, quoted in Brant, VI, 346–9.

30. To W. C. Nicholas, November 25, 1814, Cong. ed., II, 593–4.

31. Coles, *War of 1812*, pp. 187–218.

32. DPM to H. Gallatin, December 26 and 29, 1814, New York Historical Society; from Payne Todd, October 9, 1814, New York Public Library; AG to Todd, July 21, 1814, and AG to Crawford, July 26, 1814, cited in Brant, VI, 351–2; C. F. Adams, ed., *The Memoirs of John Quincy Adams* (12 vols., Philadelphia, 1874–1877), September 18, 1814, III, 32.

33. Monroe to Dearborn, December 19, 1814, "Refederator" letters in Boston *Repertory*, November 15–24, 1814, from Monroe, January 10, 1815, Hartford Convention report, January 4, 1815, quoted in Brant, VI, 358–61; Marshall Smelser, *The Democratic Republic, 1801–1815* (New York, 1968), pp. 296–9.

34. *National Intelligencer*, January 8, 1815, *Federal Republican*, January 12–February 1, 1815, cited in Brant, VI, 363–6; DPM to H. Gallatin, January 14, 1815, New York Historical Society; *Life, Letters, and Journals of George Ticknor* (2 vols., Boston, 1876), I, 29; R. King to Charles King, February 11, 1815, King, ed., *Life and Correspondence*, V, 466, JM veto, January 30, 1815, *Messages*, II, 540–42.

35. Coles, *War of 1812*, pp. 218–30; Jackson to Monroe, January 13, 1815, J. W. Bassett, ed., *Correspondence of Andrew Jackson* (6 vols., Washington, D.C., 1927), II, 142–3; Smelser, *Democratic Republic*, p. 280.

36. Brant, VI, 367–9.

37. DPM to H. Gallatin, March 5, 1815, New York Historical Society; W. T. Barry to Mrs. Barry, February 24, 1815, quoted in Brant, VI, 370; Otis to Mrs. Otis, February 22, 1815, Massachusetts Historical Society; TJ to B. Waterhouse, October 13, 1815, *Writings of TJ*, IX, 532–3; Sérurier to Talleyrand, February 21, 1815, quoted in Brant, VI, 378; Adams to T. McKean, July 6, 1815, and from Adams, April 22, 1817, C. F. Adams, ed., *The Works of John Adams* (10 vols., Boston, 1856), X, 167–8, 258.

38. JM message, February 18, 1815, *Messages*, II, 54–5; Adams, ed., *The Memoirs of John Quincy Adams*, December 24, 1814, and January 5, 1815, III, 126, 139; to C. J. Ingersoll, January 4, 1818, Cong. ed., III, 58; *National Intelligencer*, February 20, 1815.

39. To TJ, March 12, 1815, Cong. ed., II, 602; DPM to H. Gallatin, March 5, 1815, New York Historical Society.

40. Brant, VI, 381–5; Adams, *Hist.*, IX, 80–89.
41. To Dallas, April 25, 1815, May 4 and 22, 1815, other letters between April 13 and June 1, 1815, Dallas, ed., *Life and Writings*, pp. 398–432; to Monroe, May 1815, Cong. ed., II, 609–12; James Maury to TJ, April 29, 1815, and from W. Eustis, August 10 and 18, 1815, quoted in Brant, VI, 392.
42. To B. W. Crowninshield, June 12, 1815, Cong. ed., II, 603–6; from Dallas, August 3, 1815, and to Dallas, September 15, 1815, Dallas, ed., *Life and Writings*, pp. 436, 445; TJ to T. Leiper, June 12, 1815, *Writings of TJ*, IX, 520; Brant, VI, 387–91.
43. Brant, VI, 390–97; Anthony, *Dolly Madison*, pp. 251–5; Walters, *Gallatin*, p. 294; Clay to Todd, January 5, 1815, Hopkins *PC*, II, 3.
44. TJ to T. Leiper, June 12, 1815, *Writings of TJ*, IX, 519; AG to TJ, September 6, 1815, and TJ to AG, October 16, 1815, *Writings of AG*, I, 651–2.
45. JM message, December 5, 1815, *Messages*, II, 547–54.
46. Randolph speech, *Annals of Congress*, January 31, 1816; Adams, *Hist.*, IX, 105; Macon to W. Jones, December 17, 1815, HSP.
47. Adams, *Hist.*, IX, 104–25; Isaac Briggs to Mrs. Briggs, January 7, 1816 (quoting from his diary for December 21, 1815), Maryland Historical Society.
48. To Eustis, May 12, 1816, Cong. ed., III, 2–4; Chargé Roth to Duc de Richelieu, April 5 and May 5, 1816, quoted in Brant, VI, 404–5.
49. To Dallas, June 8 and September 16, 1816, Dallas, ed., *Life and Writings*, pp. 452, 475; TJ to AG, September 8, 1816, *Writings of TJ*, X, 64.
50. DPM to A. Cutts, July 5, 1816, original owned by George B. Cutts, Brookline, Massachusetts (misdated July 5, 1820, in Cutts, *Memoirs*, pp. 173–4); Hyde de Neuville to Richelieu, July 12, 1816, in Brant, VI, 407–8; JM to Dey of Algiers, August 1816, Cong. ed., III, 15–17.
51. Baron de Montlezun, *Voyage de New-Yorck, à la Nouvelle-Orléans et de l'Orenoque au Mississippi* (Paris, 1818), p. 52, quoted in Brant, VI, 410–11; TJ to F. W. Gilmer, June 7, 1816, *Writings of TJ*, X, 33; Rush to Ingersoll, October 9, 1816, HSP.
52. Adams, *Hist.*, IX, 126–40.
53. JM message, December 3, 1816, *Messages*, II, 558–65.
54. To TJ, February 15, 1817, Cong. ed., III, 35; Norman K. Risjord, *The Old Republicans: Southern Conservatism in the Age of Jefferson* (New York, 1965), pp. 168–73; from Clay, March 3, 1817, Hopkins *PC*, II, 322.
55. JM veto message, March 3, 1817, *Messages*, II, 569–70; TJ to George Ticknor, May 1817, *Writings of TJ*, X, 81.
56. To Eustis, March 1817, and to TJ, February 15, 1817, Cong. ed., III, 39, 34; B. W. Crowninshield to Mrs. Crowninshield, December 20, 1816, Essex Institute, Salem, Massachusetts; Elijah Mills to Mrs. Mills, December 30, 1815, January 13 and December 25, 1816, and February 28, 1817, *Massachusetts Historical Society Proceedings*, XIX (1881–1882), 15–22.
57. Eliza Lee to DPM, March 1817, *MP*, I, xiii; Adams to TJ, February 2, 1817, Lester Cappon, ed., *The Adams-Jefferson Letters* (2 vols., Chapel Hill, 1959), II, 508.
58. Monroe address, March 4, 1817, *Writings of Monroe*, VI, 14; *National Intelligencer*, March 4 and 5, 1817, address of citizens of Washington, March 6, 1817, from TJ, April 15, 1817, quoted in Brant, VI, 418–19; JM to citizens of Washington, March 1817, Cong. ed., III, 36; from

AG, July 17, 1817, Rives-Madison papers, LC; Rush to Ingersoll, August 9, 1817, HSP.

59. Brant, VI, 420; "An Unpublished Sketch of James Madison by James K. Paulding," *VMHB*, LXVII (1959), 435.

Chapter 22

1. "Memoir of Montpelier," Mary E. E. Cutts, *ca.* 1854, owned by George B. Cutts, Brookline, Massachusetts; Katharine Anthony, *Dolly Madison, Her Life and Times* (Garden City, New York, 1949), pp. 260–63; Gailland Hunt, ed., *The First Forty Years of Washington Society* (New York, 1906), pp. 233–7.

2. DPM to Todd, December 1824, to Todd, November 13, 1825, DPM papers, LC; Anthony Morris to Anna Cutts, May 19, 1830, and DPM to Todd, July 20, 1834, in Anthony, *Dolly Madison*, pp. 273–7; Brant, VI, 447–8, 501, 503, 511; J. P. Todd "Memoranda Book," LC; J. C. Payne to J. M. Cutts, September 1, 1849, owned by Mrs. J. M. Cutts, III, Washington, D.C.; James H. Causten to J. C. Payne, February 16, 1852, DPM Memorial Association, Greensboro, North Carolina; Edward Coles to W. C. Rives, 1857, Rives papers, LC.

3. Family information gathered from descendants, notices in the Richmond *Enquirer* and other newspapers, family Bible and gravestone records, and references in letters.

4. To R. D. Cutts, *ca.* 1827 or 1828, and January 4, 1829, originals owned by George B. Cutts, Brookline, Massachusetts; information on DPM's relatives drawn from family sources, especially papers owned by G. B. Cutts, and by Charles M. Storey, Boston, Massachusetts.

5. "An Unpublished Sketch of James Madison by James K. Paulding," *VMHB*, LXVII (1959), 435–6.

6. M. B. Smith to Mrs. Boyd, August 17, 1828, in Hunt, ed., *First Forty Years*, pp. 232–7; H. D. Gilpin to his father, September 16, 1827, *VMHB*, LXXVI (October 1968), 469–70; Elizabeth Cometti and Valeria Gennaro-Lerda, "The Presidential Tour of Carlo Vidua with Letters on Virginia," *VMHB*, LXXVII (October 1969), 396, 400, 404; B. Miller to E. Lee, March 16, 1819, Lee mss., University of Virginia Library; D. N. Logan to S. Walker, November 22, 1824, HSP.

7. C. F. Adams, ed., *The Memoirs of John Quincy Adams* (12 vols., Philadelphia, 1874–1877), November 3, 1807, I, 473.

8. JM address, May 12, 1818, Cong. ed., III, 63–95.

9. Clement Eaton, *The Growth of Southern Civilization, 1790–1860* (New York, 1961), pp. 14–17.

10. Brant, VI, 446–9, 501–2; to TJ, February 24, 1826, Hunt, IX, 244.

11. To E. Everett, November 26, 1823, and to N. P. Trist, April 1827, Cong. ed., III, 348–50, 575–8.

12. To R. Walsh, March 2, 1819, and to R. Evans, May 15, 1819, Cong. ed., III, 121–2, 133–8.

13. Ralph Ketcham, "The Dictates of Conscience: Edward Coles and Slavery," *Virginia Quarterly Review*, XXXVI (1960), 56–7; to Coles, September 3, 1819, Hunt, VIII, 455.

14. To Monroe, February 10 and 23, 1820, Cong. ed., III, 164–9.

15. To Lafayette, November 25, 1829, Cong. ed., III, 188–90; A. Levasseur, *Lafayette et Amérique en 1824 et 1825* (2 vols., Paris, 1829), I, 477–501;

to F. Wright, September 1, 1825, and to Lafayette, November 1826, Hunt, IX, 224–9, 261–6.

16. To R. R. Gurley, December 28, 1831, and to T. R. Dew, February 23, 1833, Hunt, IX, 468–70, 498–502.

17. Harriet Martineau, *Retrospect of Western Travel* (3 vols., Saunders and Otley, London, 1838), II, 48.

18. From Coles, January 8, 1832, and to Coles, October 3, 1834, cited in Brant, VI, 510–11; JM will, April 19, 1835, Hunt, IX, 548–52.

19. Whitcomb journal, June 1, 1824, *WMQ*, VI (1949), 635–6.

20. To Monroe, October 2, 1818, November 28, 1818, February 13 and 18, 1819, October 30, 1823, and August 5, 1824, to Rush, November 13, 1823, and to Lafayette, November 25, 1820, Hunt, VIII, 414–23, IX, 157–66, 197–8, 35–6; to TJ, November 1, 1823, *Writings of Monroe*, VI, 395–6; Adams, ed., *The Memoirs of John Quincy Adams*, November 7, 1823, VI, 179.

21. JM notes, interleaved in third filling of Federal Convention debates of 1787, LC, but bearing watermark FELLOWS 1817, indicating JM made the notes during his retirement, while reflecting on issues raised in the 1787 debates; to J. Q. Adams, December 23, 1817, Hunt, VIII, 399–401.

22. To Roane, September 2, 1819, May 6, 1821, and June 29, 1821, to TJ, June 27, 1823, Hunt, VIII, 447–53, IX, 56–68, 137–44; to ——, 1834, Cong. ed., IV, 349; from Roane, April 27, 1821, and June 20, 1821, quoted in Brant, VI, 433; TJ to Roane, March 9, 1821, and June 27, 1821, *Writings of TJ*, X, 188–90.

23. TJ to Morse, March 6, 1822, from TJ, February 25, 1822, *Writings of TJ*, X, 203–8; JM to Morse, February 16, 1822, to TJ, March 5, 1822, to T. L. McKenney, May 2 and 14, 1825, February 10, 1826, and March 27, 1826, Cong. ed., III, 259–61, 487, 490, 515–16, 522.

24. To T. Cooper, March 23, 1824, and to Clay, April 1824, Hunt, IX, 177–87.

25. To J. C. Cabell, September 18, 1828, and October 30, 1828, Hunt, IX, 316–40.

26. *Niles' Register*, XXXV, cited in Brant, VI, 473–4; to Clay, March 22, 1832, and to Trist, May 29, 1832, Hunt, IX, 477–82.

27. George Tucker, memoir of JM, LC; Anne Royall, *Southern Tour* (Washington, D.C., 1830), quoted in Anthony, *Dolly Madison*, pp. 315–16; diary of Robert Scott, October 26, 1829, owned by Mrs. S. I. M. Majors, Versailles, Kentucky.

28. JM speech, December 2, 1829, Hunt, IX, 358–64; H. B. Grigsby diary, November–December 1829, Richmond *Enquirer*, October–December 1829, cited in Brant, VI, 463–6.

29. Brant, VI, 466–7; "James Madison's Autobiography," *WMQ*, II (1945), 208; DPM to Dolley Cutts, March 10, 1830, Cutts, *Memoirs*, pp. 177–8.

30. Richmond *Enquirer*, September 1829; to Cabell, September 7, 1829, and "Outline," September 1829, Hunt, IX, 346–57.

31. Brant, VI, 476–8; from Trist, February 6, 1830, Virginia Historical Society; to R. Y. Hayne, April 4, 1830, Hunt, IX, 383–94n.

32. Richmond *Whig*, May 21, 1830, Columbia, South Carolina, *Courier*, June 9, 1830, Richmond *Enquirer*, June 18, 1830, quoted in Brant, VI, 481–3; to M. L. Hurlbut, May 1830, Hunt, IX, 370–75.

33. To Everett, August 28, 1830, Hunt, IX, 383–403.

34. From Cabell, October 28, 1830, and from Coles, November 4, 1830, quoted in Brant, VI, 484; Marshall to Story, October 15, 1830, *Massachusetts Historical Society Proceedings*, XIV (1900–1901), 342–3.

35. Brant, VI, 484–7.
36. To A. Stevenson, November 27, 1830, to R. Chapman, January 6, 1831, to Trist, December 1831, May 1832, and December 23, 1832, Hunt, IX, 411–37, 471–91.
37. Brant, VI, 493–8; to Rives, March 12, 1833, Hunt, IX, 511–14; to Webster, March 15, 1833, original owned by Mr. and Mrs. Philip Sang, River Forest, Illinois.
38. Clay speech, March 1, 1833; to Clay, April 2, 1833, Cong. ed., IV, 567; to Clay, June 1833, Hunt, IX, 517–18.
39. Minutes of the Board of Visitors of Central College, May 5, July 28, and October 28, 1817, *Early History of the University of Virginia as Contained in the Letters of Thomas Jefferson and Joseph C. Cabell* (Richmond, 1856), pp. 393–9; Richmond *Enquirer*, October 10, 1817.
40. Central College subscription list, public education bill of February 21, 1818, TJ, JM, and others to Speaker, Virginia House of Delegates, January 6, 1818, Cabell to TJ, December 29, 1817, and January 22, 1818, TJ to Cabell, February 26, 1818, all in *Jefferson-Cabell Letters*, pp. 89–129, 400–432.
41. To DPM, *ca.* July 30, 1818, Chicago Historical Society; TJ to A. Stuart, May 28, 1818, *Writings of TJ*, X, 109–10; Herbert B. Adams, *Thomas Jefferson and the University of Virginia* (Washington, D.C., 1888), pp. 86–7.
42. "Report of Commissioners," signed by TJ, JM, and others, August 4, 1818, *Jefferson-Cabell Letters*, pp. 432–47.
43. *Jefferson-Cabell Letters*, pp. 432–3, 445–7; Cabell to TJ, March 15, 1818, *Jefferson-Cabell Letters*, pp. 130–32; Adams, *Jefferson and the University of Virginia*, pp. 86–8; TJ to Martha J. Randolph, August 4, 1818, in E. M. Betts and J. A. Bear, eds., *The Family Letters of Thomas Jefferson* (Columbia, Missouri, 1966), pp. 423–4.
44. Cabell to TJ, February 22, 1819, March 2 and 8, 1819, and April 17, 1819, minutes of Central College Board, February 26, 1819, and of Board of Visitors University of Virginia, March 29, 1819, all in *Jefferson-Cabell Letters*, pp. 165–76, 451–5; to F. Beasley, December 22, 1824, Hunt, IX, 212.
45. To TJ, March 6, 1819, Cong. ed., III, 126; TJ to Cabell, March 1, 1819, and minutes of Board of Visitors, October 4, 1819, and October 3, 1820, *Jefferson-Cabell Letters*, pp. 169, 456–61; TJ to R. Taylor, May 16, 1820, Adams, *Jefferson and University of Virginia*, pp. 108–9.
46. Minutes and TJ report, October 7, 1822, *Jefferson-Cabell Letters*, pp. 470–75; TJ to Cooper, November 2, 1822, Adams, *Jefferson and University of Virginia*, p. 91; to E. Everett, March 19, 1823, Cong. ed., III, 306–7.
47. To TJ, September 1824, Hunt, IX, 202–7.
48. Minutes and TJ report, October 5, 1824, Cabell to TJ, May 25, 1825, *Jefferson-Cabell Letters*, pp. 354, 480–83; TJ to Rush, April 26, 1824, Adams, *Jefferson and University of Virginia*, pp. 111–13; TJ to W. B. Giles, December 26, 1825, *Writings of TJ*, X, 357; to TJ, November 20, 1824, cited in Brant, VI, 453.
49. Adams, *Jefferson and University of Virginia*, pp. 158–9; to TJ, January 15, 1825, MPLC; Brant, VI, 453.
50. TJ to Cabell, February 3, 1825, *Jefferson-Cabell Letters*, p. 339; from TJ, February 1, 1825, MPLC; to TJ, February 8, 1825, Hunt, IX, 218–21; Gordon E. Baker, "Thomas Jefferson on Academic Freedom," *AAUP Bulletin*, XXXIX (1953), 381–2.

51. TJ to E. R. Coolidge, November 14, 1825, in Betts and Bear, eds., *Family Letters*, p. 460; Cabell to TJ, March 16, 1825, TJ to Cabell, April 15, 1825, and rector's report, October 7, 1825, *Jefferson-Cabell Letters*, pp. 343, 350, 484–5; Philip A. Bruce, *History of the University of Virginia* (6 vols., New York, 1920), II, 298–301; M. B. Smith to Mrs. Boyd, August 12, 1828, in Hunt, ed., *First Forty Years*, pp. 229–30; Brant, VI, 455.

52. TJ to E. R. Coolidge, November 14, 1825, and to T. J. Randolph, February 8 and 11, 1826, in Betts and Bear, eds., *Family Letters*, pp. 460, 469–70; from TJ, February 17, 1826, *Writings of TJ*, X, 377–8; to TJ, February 24, 1826, Hunt, IX, 244–5; Bruce, *U. of Va.*, II, 241.

53. Brant, VI, 457–60; Bruce, *University of Virginia*, II, 240–70; "Martin's Gazetteer," 1835, reprinting university catalogue of 1833–4, in P. B. Barringer and J. M. Garnett, eds., *University of Virginia* (4 vols., New York, 1904), I, 99–103; ms. minutes of Board of Visitors, University of Virginia Library.

54. To W. T. Barry, August 4, 1822, Hunt, IX, 105, 107–8.

55. To E. Coles, August 29, 1834, Hunt, IX, 536, 542.

56. To Monroe, December 18, 1827, and April 21, 1831, to Cabell, September 18, 1828, and October 15, 1828, and to T. Ringgold, July 12, 1831, Cong. ed., III, 603, 636–7, 647–8, and Hunt, IX, 457–9, 462.

57. DPM to Mary Cutts, September 18, 1831, and December 1831, and to Anna Cutts, August 2, 1832, Cutts, *Memoirs*, pp. 181–5; to N. P. Trist, May 29, 1832, and to A. Stevenson, November 20, 1832, Hunt, IX, 480–81, 488; Clay to R. S. Rose, September 10, 1832, University of Virginia Library; Brant, VI, 489–90.

58. DPM to Mary and Dolley Cutts, August 1, 1833, September 9, 1833, December 2, 1834, and May 11, 1835, and to Payne Todd, July 20, 1833, Cutts, *Memoirs*, pp. 186–93; DPM to Ann Maury, July 8, 1833, University of Virginia Library.

59. To Jacob Gideon, January 28, February 20, and August 20, 1818, to Jared Sparks, October 5, 1830, to J. K. Paulding, April 1831, to J. Q. Adams, November 2, 1818, June 7, 1819, and June 19, 1820, to Joseph Gales, August 26, 1821, and to E. Everett, March 19, 1823, Hunt, VIII, 408–11, 416–17, 438–9, IX, 28–9, 68–71, 128–9; from Everett, June 9, 1835, Everett papers, Massachusetts Historical Society.

60. To J. Elliot, February 14, 1827, and November 1827, Hunt, IX, 270–71, 291–2.

61. To Paulding, April 1831, Hunt, IX, 451–4.

62. "CC" Proctor, ed., "After-Dinner Anecdotes of James Madison: Excerpt from Jared Sparks' Journal for 1829–1831," *VMHB*, LX (1952), 255–65.

63. *MP*, I, xv–xxiv.

64. To DPM, November 5, 1824, and to Frances Wright, September 1, 1825, Hunt, IX, 201, 229; Levasseur, *Lafayette et Amérique*, I, 477, II, 553–5; TJ to F. Wright, August 7, 1825, *Writings of TJ*, X, 344; Brant, VI, 442–3.

65. From TJ, February 17, 1826, *Writings of TJ*, X, 377–8; to TJ, February 24, 1826, and to Trist, July 6, 1826, Hunt, IX, 245–8; from Dunglison, July 1, 1826, MPLC; Brant, VI, 456.

66. Hunt, ed., *First Forty Years*, pp. 236–7; Brant, VI, 460–61; DPM to R. Cutts, August 5, 1832, Cutts, *Memoirs*, p. 186.

67. From Monroe, April 11, 1831, *Writings of Monroe*, VII, 231–4; to Monroe, April 21, 1831, to T. Ringgold, July 12, 1831, and to J. Sparks, June 1, 1831, Hunt, IX, 457–61.

68. To J. G. Jackson, December 27, 1821, and to F. Beasley, November 20, 1825, Hunt, IX, 77, 229–31.

69. Paul Jennings, *A Colored Man's Reminiscences of James Madison* (Brooklyn, 1865), pp. 18–20; Martineau, *Retrospect*, II, 3; DPM to Dolley Cutts, May 11, 1835, Cutts, *Memoirs*, pp. 192–9; C. J. Ingersoll, letter in Washington *Globe*, August 12, 1836; to G. Tucker, June 27, 1836, MPLC; will, April 19, 1835, Hunt, IX, 548–52; Brant, VI, 516–20; George Tucker, "Memoir of James Madison," LC.

70. Brant, VI, 521–2.

71. Adams, ed., *Memoirs of John Quincy Adams*, August 29, 1836, IX, 305–6; John Q. Adams, *The Lives of James Madison and James Monroe* (Boston, 1850), pp. 11, 46–8, 101–4.

72. M. B. Smith to J. B. H. Smith, March 12, 1829, in Hunt, ed., *First Forty Years*, pp. 299–300.

73. JM, "Advice to My Country," 1834, MPLC; facsimile in JM's hand in Brant, VI, 530.

Index

Personal History